Lecture Notes in Computer Science 14583

The series Lecture Notes in Computer Science (LNCS), including its subseries Lecture Notes in Artificial Intelligence (LNAI) and Lecture Notes in Bioinformatics (LNBI), has established itself as a medium for the publication of new developments in computer science and information technology research, teaching, and education.

LNCS enjoys close cooperation with the computer science R & D community, the series counts many renowned academics among its volume editors and paper authors, and collaborates with prestigious societies. Its mission is to serve this international community by providing an invaluable service, mainly focused on the publication of conference and workshop proceedings and postproceedings. LNCS commenced publication in 1973.

Christina Pöpper · Lejla Batina
Editors

Applied Cryptography and Network Security

22nd International Conference, ACNS 2024
Abu Dhabi, United Arab Emirates, March 5–8, 2024
Proceedings, Part I

Editors
Christina Pöpper
New York University Abu Dhabi
Abu Dhabi, United Arab Emirates

Lejla Batina
Radboud University Nijmegen
Nijmegen, The Netherlands

ISSN 0302-9743 ISSN 1611-3349 (electronic)
Lecture Notes in Computer Science
ISBN 978-3-031-54769-0 ISBN 978-3-031-54770-6 (eBook)
https://doi.org/10.1007/978-3-031-54770-6

This Springer imprint is published by the registered company Springer Nature Switzerland AG
The registered company address is: Gewerbestrasse 11, 6330 Cham, Switzerland

Paper in this product is recyclable.

Preface

ACNS 2024, the 22nd International Conference on Applied Cryptography and Network Security, was held in Abu Dhabi, United Arab Emirates, on March 5–8, 2024. The conference covered all technical aspects of applied cryptography, network and computer security and privacy, representing both academic research work as well as developments in industrial and technical frontiers.

The conference had two submission deadlines, in July and October 2023. We received a total of 238 submissions over the two cycles (230 unique submissions incl. eight major revisions from the first submission cycle that were resubmitted as revisions in the second submission cycle). From all submissions, the Program Committee (PC) selected 54 papers for publication in the proceedings of the conference, some after minor or major revisions. This led to an acceptance rate of 23.5%.

The two program chairs were supported by a PC consisting of 76 leading experts in all aspects of applied cryptography and security whose expertise and work were crucial for the paper selection process. Each submission received around 4 reviews from the committee. Strong conflict of interest rules ensured that papers were not handled by PC members with a close personal or professional relationship with the authors. The program chairs were not allowed to submit papers and did not handle any submissions they were in conflict with. There were an additional 55 external reviewers, whose expertise the PC relied upon in the selection of papers. The review process was conducted as a double-blind peer review. The authors of 10 submissions rejected from the July deadline, but considered promising, were encouraged to resubmit to the October deadline after major revisions of their paper. From these 10 papers invited for a major revision, 8 papers got resubmitted to the second cycle, 5 of which were finally accepted.

Alongside the presentations of the accepted papers, the program of ACNS 2024 featured three invited talks given by Elisa Bertino, Nadia Heninger, and Gene Tsudik. The three volumes of the conference proceedings contain the revised versions of the 54 papers that were selected, together with the abstracts of the invited talks.

Following a long tradition, ACNS gives a best student paper award to encourage promising students to publish their best results at the conference. The award recipients share a monetary prize of 2,000 EUR generously sponsored by Springer.

Many people contributed to the success of ACNS 2024. We would like to thank the authors for submitting their research results to the conference. We are very grateful to the PC members and external reviewers for contributing their knowledge and expertise and for the tremendous amount of work and time involved in reviewing papers, contributing to the discussions, and shepherding the revisions. We are greatly indebted to Mihalis Maniatakos and Ozgur Sinanoglu, the ACNS'24 General Chairs, for their efforts and overall guidance as well as all the members of the organization committee. We thank the steering committee, Moti Yung and Jianying Zhou, for their direction and valuable advice throughout the preparation of the conference. We also thank the team at Springer for handling the publication of these conference proceedings, as well as Shujaat Mirza for working on the preparation of the proceedings volumes.

March 2024

Lejla Batina
Christina Pöpper

Organization

General Co-chairs

Michail Maniatakos	New York University Abu Dhabi, UAE
Ozgur Sinanoglu	New York University Abu Dhabi, UAE

Program Committee Co-chairs

Christina Pöpper	New York University Abu Dhabi, UAE
Lejla Batina	Radboud University, The Netherlands

Steering Committee

Jianying Zhou	SUTD, Singapore
Moti Yung	Google, USA

Local Arrangements Chair

Borja García de Soto	New York University Abu Dhabi, UAE

Publicity Chair

Elias Athanasopoulos	University of Cyprus, Cyprus

Web Chair

Christoforos Vasilatos	New York University Abu Dhabi, UAE

Poster Chair

Charalambos Konstantinou	KAUST, KSA

Registration Chair

Rafael Song — New York University Abu Dhabi, UAE

Workshop Chair

Martin Andreoni — Technology Innovation Institute, UAE

Publication Chair

Shujaat Mirza — New York University, USA

Student Travel Grants Chair

Lilas Alrahis — New York University Abu Dhabi, UAE

Program Committee

Adwait Nadkarni	William & Mary, USA
Alexander Koch	CNRS and IRIF, Université Paris Cité, France
Alexandra Dmitrienko	University of Wuerzburg, Germany
Amr Youssef	Concordia University, Canada
An Braeken	Vrije Universiteit Brussel, Belgium
Anna Lisa Ferrara	University of Molise, Italy
Archita Agarwal	MongoDB, USA
Atefeh Mohseni Ejiyeh	UCSB, USA
Benjamin Dowling	University of Sheffield, UK
Chao Sun	Osaka University, Japan
Chiara Marcolla	Technology Innovation Institute, UAE
Chitchanok Chuengsatiansup	The University of Melbourne, Australia
Christine Utz	CISPA Helmholtz Center for Information Security, Germany
Christoph Egger	Université Paris Cité and CNRS and IRIF, France
Claudio Soriente	NEC Laboratories Europe, Spain
Colin Boyd	NTNU-Norwegian University of Science and Technology, Norway
Daniel Dinu	Intel
Daniel Gardham	University of Surrey, UK

Daniel Slamanig	Universität der Bundeswehr München, Germany
Dave Singelee	KU Leuven, Belgium
Devashish Gosain	MPI-INF, Germany
Diego F. Aranha	Aarhus University, Denmark
Dimitrios Vasilopoulos	IMDEA Software Institute, Spain
Dominique Schröder	Friedrich-Alexander Universität Erlangen-Nürnberg, Germany
Eleftheria Makri	Leiden University, The Netherlands
Elena Dubrova	Royal Institute of Technology, Sweden
Elena Kirshanova	Technology Innovation Institute, UAE
Elif Bilge Kavun	University of Passau, Germany
Fatemeh Ganji	Worcester Polytechnic Institute, USA
Florian Hahn	University of Twente, The Netherlands
Francisco Rodríguez-Henríquez	Technology Innovation Institute, UAE
Ghassan Karame	Ruhr University Bochum, Germany
Gustavo Banegas	Qualcomm, France
Hyungsub Kim	Purdue University, USA
Jean Paul Degabriele	Technology Innovation Institute, UAE
Jianying Zhou	Singapore University of Technology and Design, Singapore
João S. Resende	University of Porto, Portugal
Karim Eldefrawy	SRI International, USA
Katerina Mitrokotsa	University of St. Gallen, Switzerland
Katharina Krombholz	CISPA Helmholtz Center for Information Security, Germany
Kazuo Sakiyama	UEC, Tokyo, Japan
Kehuan Zhang	The Chinese University of Hong Kong, China
Khurram Bhatti	Information Technology University (ITU), Pakistan
Lukasz Chmielewski	Masaryk University, Czech Republic
Mainack Mondal	Indian Institute of Technology, Kharagpur, India
Marc Manzano	SandboxAQ, USA
Matthias J. Kannwischer	QSMC, Taiwan
Melissa Azouaoui	NXP Semiconductors, Germany
Monika Trimoska	Eindhoven University of Technology, The Netherlands
Monowar Hasan	Washington State University, USA
Mridula Singh	CISPA Helmholtz Center for Information Security, Germany
Murtuza Jadliwala	University of Texas at San Antonio, USA
Nabil Alkeilani Alkadri	CISPA Helmholtz Center for Information Security, Germany

Additional Reviewers

Lorenz Panny
Marcus Brinkmann
Nada El Kassem
Nan Cheng
Nusa Zidaric
Octavio Pérez Kempner
Okan Seker
Patrick Harasser
Paul Huynh
Paul Gerhart
Pradeep Mishra
Quan Yuan
Raghav Bhaskar
Ritam Bhaumik
Robert Merget
Sacha Servan-Schreiber
Sebastian Faller
Sebastian Ramacher
Semyon Novoselov
Shahram Rasoolzadeh
Sylvain Chatel
Tianyu Li
Valerio Cini
Victor Miller
Viktoria Ronge
Vir Pathak
Vojtech Suchanek
Vukašin Karadžić
Yangguang Tian

Abstracts of Keynote Talks

Applying Machine Learning to Securing Cellular Networks

Elisa Bertino

Purdue University, Indiana, USA

Abstract. Cellular network security is more critical than ever, given the increased complexity of these networks and the numbers of applications that depend on them, including telehealth, remote education, ubiquitous robotics and autonomous vehicles, smart cities, and Industry 4.0. In order to devise more effective defenses, a recent trend is to leverage machine learning (ML) techniques, which have become applicable because of today's advanced capabilities for collecting data as well as high-performance computing systems for training ML models. Recent large language models (LLMs) are also opening new interesting directions for security applications. In this talk, I will first present a comprehensive threat analysis in the context of 5G cellular networks to give a concrete example of the magnitude of the problem of cellular network security. Then, I will present two specific applications of ML techniques for the security of cellular networks. The first application focuses on the use of natural language processing techniques to the problem of detecting inconsistencies in the "natural specifications" of cellular network protocols. The second application addresses the design of an anomaly detection system able to detect the presence of malicious base stations and determine the type of attack. Then I'll conclude with a discussion on research directions.

Real-World Cryptanalysis

Nadia Heninger

University of California, San Diego, USA

Abstract. Cryptography has traditionally been considered to be one of the strong points of computer security. However, a number of the public-key cryptographic algorithms that we use are fragile in the face of implementation mistakes or misunderstandings. In this talk, I will survey "weapons of math destruction" that have been surprisingly effective in finding broken cryptographic implementations in the wild, and some adventures in active and passive network measurement of cryptographic protocols.

CAPTCHAs: What Are They Good For?

Gene Tsudik

University of California, Irvine, USA

Abstract. Since about 2003, CAPTCHAs have been widely used as a barrier against bots, while simultaneously annoying great multitudes of users worldwide. As their use grew, techniques to defeat or bypass CAPTCHAs kept improving, while CAPTCHAs themselves evolved in terms of sophistication and diversity, becoming increasingly difficult to solve for both bots and humans. Given this long-standing and still-ongoing arms race, it is important to investigate usability, solving performance, and user perceptions of modern CAPTCHAs. This talk will discuss two such efforts:

In the first part, we explore CAPTCHAs in the wild by evaluating users' solving performance and perceptions of unmodified currently-deployed CAPTCHAs. We obtain this data through manual inspection of popular websites and user studies in which 1,400 participants collectively solved 14,000 CAPTCHAs. Results show significant differences between the most popular types of CAPTCHAs: surprisingly, solving time and user perception are not always correlated. We performed a comparative study to investigate the effect of experimental context – specifically the difference between solving CAPTCHAs directly versus solving them as part of a more natural task, such as account creation. Whilst there were several potential confounding factors, our results show that experimental context could have an impact on this task, and must be taken into account in future CAPTCHA studies. Finally, we investigate CAPTCHA-induced user task abandonment by analyzing participants who start and do not complete the task.

In the second part of this work, we conduct a large-scale (over 3,600 distinct users) 13-month real-world user study and post-study survey. The study, performed at a large public university, was based on a live account creation and password recovery service with currently prevalent captcha type: reCAPTCHAv2. Results show that, with more attempts, users improve in solving checkbox challenges. For website developers and user study designers, results indicate that the website context directly influences (with statistically significant differences) solving time between password recovery and account creation. We consider the impact of participants' major and education level, showing that certain majors exhibit better performance, while, in general, education level has a direct impact on solving time. Unsurprisingly, we discover that participants find image challenges to be annoying, while checkbox challenges are perceived as easy. We also show that, rated via System Usability Scale (SUS), image tasks are viewed as “OK”, while checkbox tasks are viewed as “good”. We explore the cost and security of reCAPTCHAv2 and conclude that it has an immense cost and no security. Overall, we believe that this study’s results prompt a natural conclusion: reCAPTCHAv2 and similar reCAPTCHA technology should be deprecated.

Contents – Part I

Cryptographic Protocols

CryptoZoo: A Viewer for Reduction Proofs 3
Chris Brzuska, Christoph Egger, and Kirthivaasan Puniamurthy

Element Distinctness and Bounded Input Size in Private Set Intersection and Related Protocols 26
Xavier Carpent, Seoyeon Hwang, and Gene Tsudik

A New Approach to Efficient and Secure Fixed-Point Computation 58
Tore Kasper Frederiksen, Jonas Lindstrøm, Mikkel Wienberg Madsen, and Anne Dorte Spangsberg

Auditable Attribute-Based Credentials Scheme and Its Application in Contact Tracing 88
Pengfei Wang, Xiangyu Su, Mario Larangeira, and Keisuke Tanaka

Verification Protocol for Stable Matching from Conditional Disclosure of Secrets 119
Kittiphop Phalakarn and Toru Nakamura

Non-malleable Fuzzy Extractors 135
Danilo Francati and Daniele Venturi

Upgrading Fuzzy Extractors 156
Chloe Cachet, Ariel Hamlin, Maryam Rezapour, and Benjamin Fuller

X-Lock: A Secure XOR-Based Fuzzy Extractor for Resource Constrained Devices 183
Edoardo Liberati, Alessandro Visintin, Riccardo Lazzeretti, Mauro Conti, and Selcuk Uluagac

Encrypted Data

Efficient Clustering on Encrypted Data 213
Mengyu Zhang, Long Wang, Xiaoping Zhang, Zhuotao Liu, Yisong Wang, and Han Bao

Generic Construction of Forward Secure Public Key Authenticated Encryption with Keyword Search 237
Keita Emura

Encryption Mechanisms for Receipt-Free and Perfectly Private Verifiable Elections 257
Thi Van Thao Doan, Olivier Pereira, and Thomas Peters

Two-Party Decision Tree Training from Updatable Order-Revealing Encryption 288
Robin Berger, Felix Dörre, and Alexander Koch

KIVR: Committing Authenticated Encryption Using Redundancy and Application to GCM, CCM, and More 318
Yusuke Naito, Yu Sasaki, and Takeshi Sugawara

Signatures

Subversion-Resilient Signatures Without Random Oracles 351
Pascal Bemmann, Sebastian Berndt, and Rongmao Chen

Practical Lattice-Based Distributed Signatures for a Small Number of Signers 376
Nabil Alkeilani Alkadri, Nico Döttling, and Sihang Pu

Building MPCitH-Based Signatures from MQ, MinRank, and Rank SD 403
Thibauld Feneuil

Exploring SIDH-Based Signature Parameters 432
Andrea Basso, Mingjie Chen, Tako Boris Fouotsa, Péter Kutas, Abel Laval, Laurane Marco, and Gustave Tchoffo Saah

Biscuit: New MPCitH Signature Scheme from Structured Multivariate Polynomials 457
Luk Bettale, Delaram Kahrobaei, Ludovic Perret, and Javier Verbel

Author Index 487

Contents – Part II

Post-quantum

Automated Issuance of Post-Quantum Certificates: A New Challenge 3
Alexandre Augusto Giron, Frederico Schardong, Lucas Pandolfo Perin, Ricardo Custódio, Victor Valle, and Victor Mateu

Algorithmic Views of Vectorized Polynomial Multipliers – NTRU Prime 24
Vincent Hwang, Chi-Ting Liu, and Bo-Yin Yang

Efficient Quantum-Safe Distributed PRF and Applications: Playing DiSE in a Quantum World 47
Sayani Sinha, Sikhar Patranabis, and Debdeep Mukhopadhyay

On the Untapped Potential of the Quantum FLT-Based Inversion 79
Ren Taguchi and Atsushi Takayasu

Breaking DPA-Protected Kyber via the Pair-Pointwise Multiplication 101
Estuardo Alpirez Bock, Gustavo Banegas, Chris Brzuska, Łukasz Chmielewski, Kirthivaasan Puniamurthy, and Milan Šorf

Cryptographic Protocols II

The Key Lattice Framework for Concurrent Group Messaging 133
Kelong Cong, Karim Eldefrawy, Nigel P. Smart, and Ben Terner

Identity-Based Matchmaking Encryption from Standard Lattice Assumptions 163
Roberta Cimorelli Belfiore, Andrea De Cosmo, and Anna Lisa Ferrara

Decentralized Private Stream Aggregation from Lattices 189
Uddipana Dowerah and Aikaterini Mitrokotsa

Wireless and Networks

A Security Analysis of WPA3-PK: Implementation and Precomputation Attacks 217
Mathy Vanhoef and Jeroen Robben

When and How to Aggregate Message Authentication Codes on Lossy Channels? 241
Eric Wagner, Martin Serror, Klaus Wehrle, and Martin Henze

DoSat: A DDoS Attack on the Vulnerable Time-Varying Topology of LEO Satellite Networks 265
Tianbo Lu, Xia Ding, Jiaze Shang, Pengfei Zhao, and Han Zhang

DDoSMiner: An Automated Framework for DDoS Attack Characterization and Vulnerability Mining 283
Xi Ling, Jiongchi Yu, Ziming Zhao, Zhihao Zhou, Haitao Xu, Binbin Chen, and Fan Zhang

Privacy and Homomorphic Encryption

Memory Efficient Privacy-Preserving Machine Learning Based on Homomorphic Encryption 313
Robert Podschwadt, Parsa Ghazvinian, Mohammad GhasemiGol, and Daniel Takabi

SNARKProbe: An Automated Security Analysis Framework for zkSNARK Implementations 340
Yongming Fan, Yuquan Xu, and Christina Garman

Privacy-Preserving Verifiable CNNs 373
Nuttapong Attrapadung, Goichiro Hanaoaka, Ryo Hiromasa, Yoshihiro Koseki, Takahiro Matsuda, Yutaro Nishida, Yusuke Sakai, Jacob C. N. Schuldt, and Satoshi Yasuda

A General Framework of Homomorphic Encryption for Multiple Parties with Non-interactive Key-Aggregation 403
Hyesun Kwak, Dongwon Lee, Yongsoo Song, and Sameer Wagh

Symmetric Crypto

Masked Iterate-Fork-Iterate: A New Design Paradigm for Tweakable Expanding Pseudorandom Function 433
Elena Andreeva, Benoît Cogliati, Virginie Lallemand, Marine Minier, Antoon Purnal, and Arnab Roy

Generalized Initialization of the Duplex Construction 460
Christoph Dobraunig and Bart Mennink

Alternative Key Schedules for the AES 485
Christina Boura, Patrick Derbez, and Margot Funk

Author Index 507

Contents – Part III

Blockchain

Mirrored Commitment: Fixing "Randomized Partial Checking" and Applications ... 3
Paweł Lorek, Moti Yung, and Filip Zagórski

Bitcoin Clique: Channel-Free Off-Chain Payments Using Two-Shot Adaptor Signatures ... 28
Siavash Riahi and Orfeas Stefanos Thyfronitis Litos

Programmable Payment Channels ... 51
Ranjit Kumaresan, Duc V. Le, Mohsen Minaei, Srinivasan Raghuraman, Yibin Yang, and Mahdi Zamani

Fair Private Set Intersection Using Smart Contracts ... 74
Sepideh Avizheh and Reihaneh Safavi-Naini

Powers-of-Tau to the People: Decentralizing Setup Ceremonies ... 105
Valeria Nikolaenko, Sam Ragsdale, Joseph Bonneau, and Dan Boneh

Smart Infrastructures, Systems and Software

Self-sovereign Identity for Electric Vehicle Charging ... 137
Adrian Kailus, Dustin Kern, and Christoph Krauß

"Hello? Is There Anybody in There?" Leakage Assessment of Differential Privacy Mechanisms in Smart Metering Infrastructure ... 163
Soumyadyuti Ghosh, Manaar Alam, Soumyajit Dey, and Debdeep Mukhopadhyay

Security Analysis of BigBlueButton and eduMEET ... 190
Nico Heitmann, Hendrik Siewert, Sven Moog, and Juraj Somorovsky

An In-Depth Analysis of the Code-Reuse Gadgets Introduced by Software Obfuscation ... 217
Naiqian Zhang, Zheyun Feng, and Dongpeng Xu

ProvIoT : Detecting Stealthy Attacks in IoT through Federated Edge-Cloud Security 241
Kunal Mukherjee, Joshua Wiedemeier, Qi Wang, Junpei Kamimura, John Junghwan Rhee, James Wei, Zhichun Li, Xiao Yu, Lu-An Tang, Jiaping Gui, and Kangkook Jee

Attacks

A Practical Key-Recovery Attack on LWE-Based Key-Encapsulation Mechanism Schemes Using Rowhammer 271
Puja Mondal, Suparna Kundu, Sarani Bhattacharya, Angshuman Karmakar, and Ingrid Verbauwhede

A Side-Channel Attack on a Higher-Order Masked CRYSTALS-Kyber Implementation 301
Ruize Wang, Martin Brisfors, and Elena Dubrova

Time Is Money, Friend! Timing Side-Channel Attack Against Garbled Circuit Constructions 325
Mohammad Hashemi, Domenic Forte, and Fatemeh Ganji

Related-Tweak and Related-Key Differential Attacks on HALFLOOP-48 355
Yunxue Lin and Ling Sun

Users and Usability

How Users Investigate Phishing Emails that Lack Traditional Phishing Cues ... 381
Daniel Köhler, Wenzel Pünter, and Christoph Meinel

Usable Authentication in Virtual Reality: Exploring the Usability of PINs and Gestures 412
H. T. M. A. Riyadh, Divyanshu Bhardwaj, Adrian Dabrowski, and Katharina Krombholz

Living a Lie: Security Analysis of Facial Liveness Detection Systems in Mobile Apps 432
Xianbo Wang, Kaixuan Luo, and Wing Cheong Lau

Author Index 461

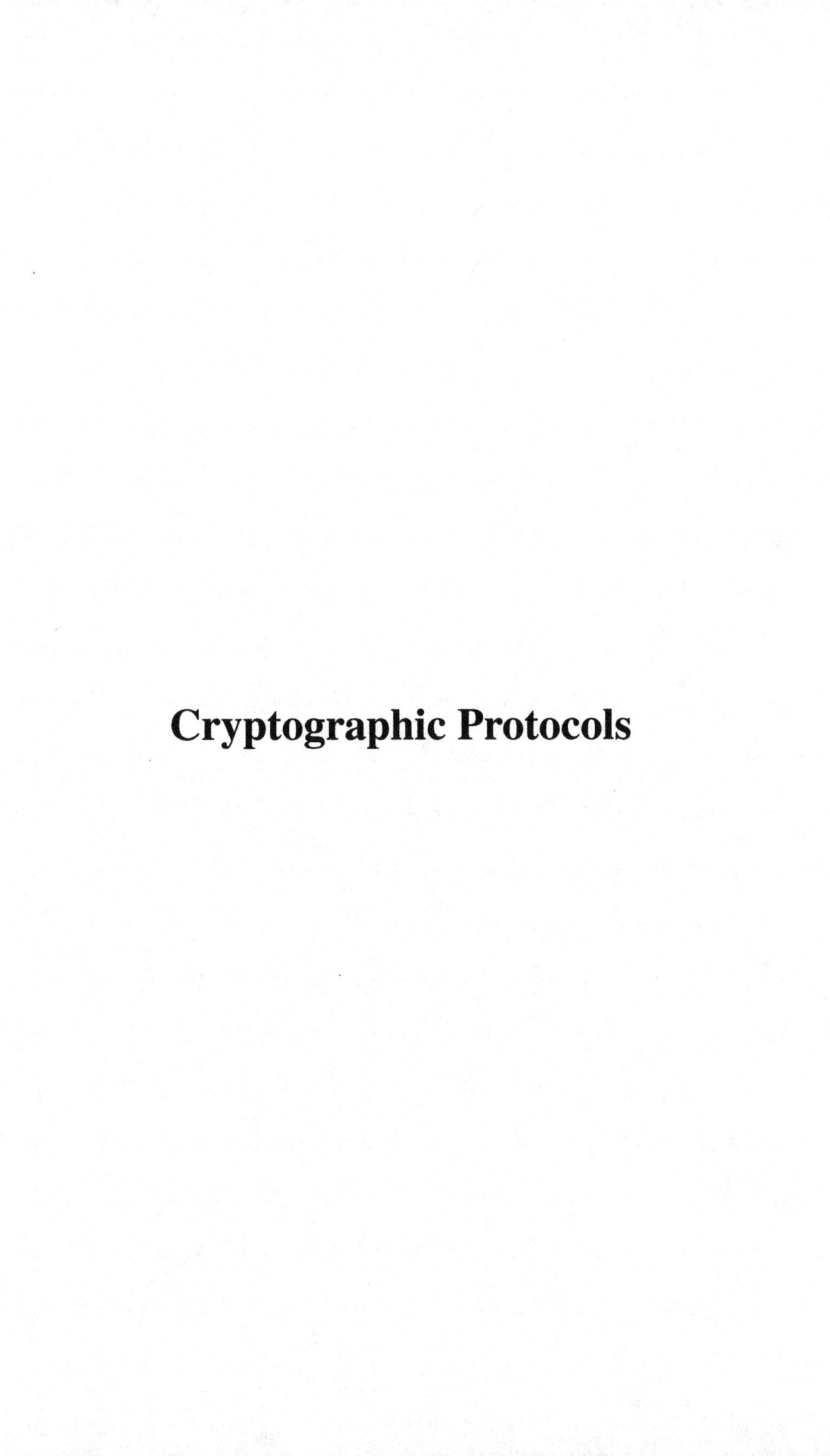

Cryptographic Protocols

CryptoZoo: A Viewer for Reduction Proofs

Chris Brzuska[1], Christoph Egger[2], and Kirthivaasan Puniamurthy[1](✉)

[1] Aalto University, Espoo, Finland
kirthivaasan.puniamurthy@aalto.fi
[2] Université Paris Cité, CNRS, IRIF, Paris, France

Abstract. Cryptographers rely on visualization to effectively communicate cryptographic constructions with one another. Visual frameworks such as constructive cryptography (TOSCA 2011), the joy of cryptography (online book) and state-separating proofs (SSPs, Asiacrypt 2018) are useful to communicate not only the construction, but also their *proof* visually by representing a cryptographic system as graphs.

One SSP core feature is the *re-use* of code, e.g., a package of code might be used in a game and be part of the description of a reduction as well. Thus, in a proof, the linear structure of a paper either requires the reader to turn pages to find definitions or writers to re-state them, thereby interrupting the visual flow of the game hops that are defined by a sequence of graphs.

We present an interactive proof viewer for state-separating proofs (SSPs) which addresses the limitations and perform three case studies: The equivalence between simulation-based and game-based notions for symmetric encryption, the security proof of the Goldreich-Goldwasser-Micali construction of a pseudorandom function from a pseudorandom generator, and Brzuska's and Oechsner's SSP formalization of the proof for Yao's garbling scheme.

Keywords: state-separation · proof viewer · reduction proofs · tooling

1 Introduction

Reduction proofs are a means to convince oneself and others of the security properties of a cryptographic design. In addition to communication and verification, (reduction) proofs help us gain understanding of the properties that are conducive to security and properties that are harmful. In order to improve verification, communication and understanding of proofs of complex systems, the cryptographic community has different techniques and styles which we briefly review below.

Black-box Primitives. Black-box primitives are abstractions which support modular proofs and information-hiding. For example, the concept of a symmetric encryption scheme (SE) with indistinguishability under chosen plaintext attacks (IND-CPA) allows one to build a system which uses SE without delving (or even knowing about) the details of the AES cipher and suitable ciphermodes.

C. Pöpper and L. Batina (Eds.): ACNS 2024, LNCS 14583, pp. 3–25, 2024.
https://doi.org/10.1007/978-3-031-54770-6_1

Cryptographic proofs of a complex system typically use multiple such black-box primitives. Additionally, a modular proof tends to first abstract away a sub-system, prove its security and then reduce the security of the bigger system to the sub-system in a black-box way. These neat black-box interfaces are a rich resource for structuring and understanding constructions and proofs, and they capture the *typical use* of primitives so that studying black-box proofs has become an established method also to understand the limitations of typical construction approaches [RTV04,BBF13].

Universal Composability. Useful security definitions for *primitives* which compose well tend to consider *adversarially chosen* inputs, and Canetti's universal composition framework (UC [Can01]) applies this insight to *protocols* as well, thereby providing the basis to also prove *protocol* security by means of useful intermediate notions. Since UC specifies how the adversary and the (adversarial) environment can interact with the protocol, defining security in UC boils down to specifying an ideal functionality, without the need to re-invent (and possibly mis-construct) the adversarial model and enabling information-hiding since the UC-savvy reader can focus on reading the ideal functionality alone. Several further frameworks implement a similar approach, notably including Maurer's abstract cryptography framework [Mau11] and Rosulek's *Joy of Cryptography* [Ros21], which both encourage the use of visual components to follow proofs.

Game-Hopping. Another important cryptographic technique that serves modular proofs are *game-hops*, explained by Shoup in [Sho04]. Game-hopping splits a large proof of indistinguishability between two games that formalize the security of a system into a sequence of smaller indistinguishability steps, each of which can be proven in isolation and the sequence of lemmas establishing the indistinguishability of each pairs of subsequent games then implies the indistinguishability of the two games in question.

Code-Based Game-Hopping. Bellare and Rogaway [BR06] introduced the use of code into game-hopping proofs, where pseudo-code allows to put two subsequent games next to each other and inspect how exactly the code changes between them. Code-based game-playing has a strong visual component which draws the attention to the changes in a game-hop while at the same time keeping all the relevant code at hand for the reader (since it is written above and below the code which changes). In turn, game-hopping which is not code-based tends to describe only the changes from one game to another, requiring the reader to remember or recover the entire context from different parts of the paper (game definition, construction definition, previous game-hops).

Modular Code-Writing. In the realm of real-world protocols, code-based games are frequently used (see, e.g., [DDGJ22,DGGP21] for recent works) and/or code-based game-hopping is widely used (see, e.g., [DHRR22,DHK+23] for recent works). Interestingly, *reductions* are often specified in text or omitted—although some works diligently provide reductions in pseudo-code, e.g., the proof of Yao's garbling scheme by Bellare, Hoang and Rogaway (BHR [BHR12]). BHR employ careful packaging of code into sub-routines in order to make the large amount of code in Yao's garbling scheme manageable and be able to argue that the reduction is sound. Concretely, reduction $\mathcal{R}$ that interacts with a smaller game $\text{Game}^b_{\text{small}}$ is sound if for the larger game $\text{Game}^b_{\text{big}}$ that the adversary $\mathcal{A}$ interacts with, it holds that for both $b \in \{0, 1\}$,

$$\mathcal{R} \rightarrow \text{Game}^b_{\text{small}} \equiv \text{Game}^b_{\text{big}}, \tag{1}$$

i.e., the behaviour of the reduction $\mathcal{R}$ composed with $\text{Game}^b_{\text{small}}$ is equivalent to the input-output behaviour of $\text{Game}^b_{\text{big}}$.

State-Separating Proofs. Modular code-writing with reductions in mind was systematically developed further by Brzuska, Delignat-Lavaud, Fournet, Kohbrok and Kohlweiss (BDFKK [BDF+18]) who structure the pseudo-code of a game into *stateful* pieces of code which can call one another, but else not access each others state whence the term *state-separation.* If $\text{Game}^b_{\text{big}}$ is defined by a call-graph of code packages and if the reduction $\mathcal{R}$ and the game $\text{Game}^b_{\text{small}}$ are defined via call-graphs of code packages as well, then we can compare the graph $\mathcal{R} \rightarrow \text{Game}^b_{\text{small}}$ obtained by "gluing" to the graph of $\text{Game}^b_{\text{big}}$. If the two call graphs are equal (i.e. they preserve the same edge relation), then Equation (1) holds trivially. Additionally, the reductions $\mathcal{R}$ can simply be defined by drawing a cut in the graph of $\text{Game}^b_{\text{big}}$, foregoing not only the need to prove the soundness of the reduction, but also the need to write the code of the reduction.

This *code re-use* approach is a core feature of SSPs which makes proofs concise and precise at the same time. On the other hand, code re-use also means that code packages are used many times across an article, while the package code is specified at a single place—or repeated redundantly at the cost of cluttering the paper and interrupting its flow. See [Koh23] for a gentle and thorough introduction to SSPs as well as a conceptual overview of recent works using and formalizing SSPs.

An SSP Viewer. We address the limitations of paper-based presentation by designing the proof viewer *CryptoZoo*[1] for SSPs. CryptoZoo presents the claims and call-graphs of games in the left pane, and the code-based definitions in the right pane, the latter of which is available at all times, enabling code-linkage without code repetition, without breaking the flow and without the need to scroll away from a proof step in the current context. Additionally, clicking on individual packages highlights the relevant code in the code pane.

In addition to addressing these SSP-specific challenges, CryptoZoo also addresses presentational obstacles present for proofs in mathematics and information about systems in general and in cryptography specifically. We now briefly review three key areas where improvement of presentation is necessary and useful and then describe how CryptoZoo addresses these.

[1] Available at https://proofviewer.cryptozoo.eu.

Information linkage Beyond code, proof steps reference different aspects, including previous lemmas and definitions. It is important to make this relationship functional and allow easy retrieval of all related facts.

Information hiding Since human memory is bounded, readers concentrate on facts and information immediately useful to the current task at hand. It is useful to *hide* information that does not contribute to understanding in a particular moment.

Soundness and structure Proofs are structured into claims and lemmas which form a proof tree (or DAG). The reader needs to verify that a set of claims indeed implies the statement of the parent node—and in the end, the reader can inspect the proofs of the claims at the leaves of the tree. In addition to the tree structure, the author of an article usually suggests a meaningful traversal which eases comprehension. A good medium for proofs should both provide the high-level tree structure and a recommended reading order while giving the reader freedom to deviate.

To address the latter point, CryptoZoo makes the proof tree visible and explicit at each point in the proof. In order to address retrieval speed challenges, CryptoZoo links cryptographic definitions and claims so that they can be retrieved quickly without losing the current context. Finally, to support user memory management and focus, CryptoZoo allows the user to hide text, definitions, lemmas, claims and their proofs, e.g., in order to focus on one particular subtree. The aforementioned approaches can be employed also generically when working with (cryptographic) proofs. It is, however, especially useful for the SSP method which inherently relies on a modular and visual approach. Additionally, SSPs have a quite well-defined set of proof steps which CryptoZoo supports while proofs in general (or even in cryptography) can be expressed in quite diverse ways which conflicts with the need of a proof viewing tool which supports more than the basic tree structure present in all mathematical proofs. For this reason, the SSP methodology is a useful scope for our proof-viewing tool.

Case Studies. We provide three case studies for the SSP proof viewer. As a simple example, we show that the standard game-based notion of indistinguishability under chosen plaintext attacks (IND-CPA) and simulation-based security for symmetric encryption are equivalent (Sect. 5). A more advanced example is a state-separating proof of a (constant-depth) version of the Goldreich-Goldwasser-Micali (GGM) theorem which transforms pseudo-random generators (PRGs) into pseudorandom functions (PRFs) by using the PRG in a tree-structured construction. This proof is interesting, since it involves a two-dimensional hybrid argument, i.e., a hybrid argument both over the depth and width of the tree (Sect. 6). Finally, as an advanced example, we present a proof of Yao's garbling scheme in the version by Brzuska and Oechsner [BO23] (Sect. 7) which covers circuits which are structured in layers. This proof also involves a two-dimensional hybrid argument, both over the width and depth of the garbled circuit. In both proofs, SSPs allow to make the reductions explicit and visually accessible. The (constant-depth) GGM proof becomes visually straightforward using the proof viewer, although it is known as a rather complex proof in the foundations of cryptography. The rather involved proof of Yao's garbling scheme does not become straightforward, but its structure is significantly simplified—moreover, the proof viewing tools is useful due to the amount of code which needs to be managed.

Our case study on (constant-depth) GGM is the first formalization of the GGM proof in SSPs and useful to understand GGM—but it is also useful to understand SSPs, since it is the first intermediate-size SSP example. While BDFKK gave several simple examples, most follow-up work (e.g. [BCK22, BDE+22]) study complex protocols which are too complex to learn the SSP methodology based on them. The GGM proof is a nice middle-ground between simple and complex case studies.

Outline. We cover related work on visual tools in Sect. 2. Subsequently, Sect. 3 introduces SSPs and elaborate on the interrelation between useful aspects of SSPs and proof viewer design. We then discuss the proof viewer design and further considerations in the implementation (Sect. 4) and then turn to the three case studies.

2 Related Work

Visual aids are a natural match for teaching and can be found in teaching not only cryptography, but also computer science at large. For example, Vamonos [CR15] combines visual and (pseudo-)code aspects to communicate algorithmic correctness, while e.g. ProtoViz [Elm04] and GRACE [CDSP08] focus on the message flow in protocols. Crucial in these tools is the combination of exploration by the user together with a visual representation of the results. One can see editors for proof assistants like Coq [The17] and Lean [dMKA+15] in a similar spirit. The user provides a further proof step and is presented with the statements which still require a proof. Similarly, Tamarin [SMCB12]—a prover for protocol security—can display a graph of its internal reasoning and update it step-by-step.

While exploring a theorem statement in e.g. Coq can give insights and help students learn to formally reason, once proofs become complex this access becomes insufficient, in particular if proof search features are used. While exploring intermediate states of the proof remains helpful, the high level structure of a complex proof is not easily accessible from the linear proof file. Here tools like the prooftree [Tew] plugin for Coq can help to visually explore the dependencies between intermediate claims in a structured manner.

Alectryon [Pit20] adds a different dimension by allowing to freely switch between a textual proof description and the formally verified proof script (which can also be used to deduce the intermediate proof state). To this end it combines text formatting tools with the Coq prover (and has been extended to LEAN [Bül22]) to provide an interactive HTML document detailing the complete proof in a manner optimized to be digested by a human reader—while still guaranteed to be in sync with the mechanically verified version.

Visual Cryptographic Proofs: The present work is inspired by the rational underlying SSPs, which bring the necessary rigor needed for formal verification while exposing similarities with teaching tools in cryptography which existed before, importantly, Rosulek's *Joy of Cryptography* [Ros21]. Rosulek groups blocks of code into libraries or packages and argues on the call-graph in a similar (although less formal) way. This, in particular, allows students to draw from experience e.g. in object oriented programming where internal state of objects remain hidden and cannot be accessed. Maurer's dot-calculus in constructive cryptography [Mau11] facilitates proof communication by giving a visual outline on the relationship between objects.

3 State-Separating Proofs

The state-separating proofs (SSP) methodology by Brzuska, Delignat-Lavaud, Fournet, Kohbrok and Kohlweiss (BDFKK [BDF+18]) specifies not only a proof style for game-hopping proofs, but also a definitional style. Similar to the UC framework, SSP-style definitions specify security as indistinguishability between two games, typically a real and an ideal game. Indistinguishability is useful for composability, because even for (strong) unforgeability under chosen message attacks (UNF-CMA)—conceptually a search problem—a game-hop typically replaces real signature verification by log-based ideal signature verification, so that reductions between indistinguishability games tend to be more straightforward.

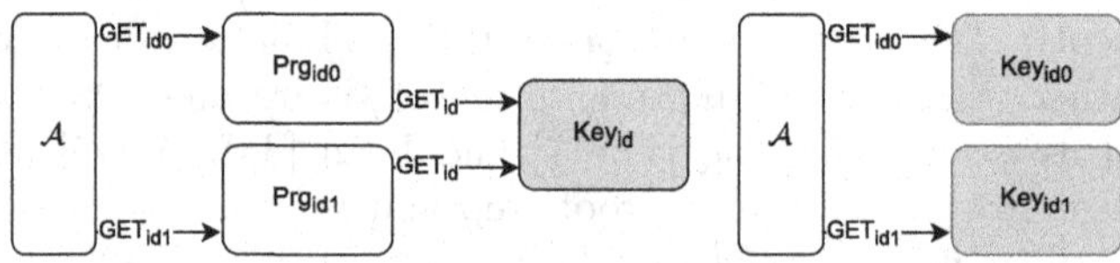

Fig. 1. Games Gprg_{id}^{0} and Gprg_{id}^{1}

Both in SSPs and UC, the adversary is the *main* algorithm which starts the system by activating other parts—in UC, the adversary activates the environment, the simulator or protocol parties (by sending messages to them), while in SSP-style games, the adversary activates the game by making oracle queries to it. For a game Game, we write $\Pr\left[1 = \mathcal{A} \overset{\mathsf{O}_1,\mathsf{O}_2}{\rightarrow} \text{Game}\right]$ for the probability that adversary $\mathcal{A}$ returns 1 when interacting with the oracles O_1 and O_2 of Game, where the oracles O_1 and O_2 are defined via pseudo-code that operates on the state of the Game. An SSP-style game typically splits its code into multiple packages with separate state—a package, like a game, consists of a set of oracles operating on its state, but in the case of a package, oracles can make queries to the oracles of other packages as well, giving rise to a call-graph. As an example, consider a length-doubling pseudorandom generator (PRG) $g : \{0,1\}^\lambda \rightarrow \{0,1\}^{2\lambda}$ such that

$g(x)$ (for x sampled uniformly at random) is indistinguishable from a uniformly random string y of length 2λ. We formalize security of PRGs as a game with two GET oracles, a GET_0 oracle which gives the adversary access to the left half of y and a GET_1 oracle which gives the adversary access to the right half of y. In the real game, the oracles return the left and right half of $y = g(x)$, respectively. In the ideal game, the oracles both return a uniformly random string of length n. Modeling a PRG to return the chunks separately is equivalent to returning them at once, but will be useful in the security proof of the pseudorandom function (PRF) construction by Goldreich Goldwasser and Micali (GGM [GGM86]), where each half is post-processed separately.

We now define the ideal game as a *composition* of two smaller games Key_0 and Key_1 which we compose in parallel (cf. Fig. 1 (right)). The GET_0 and GET_1 oracle of Key_0 and Key_1, respectively, each sample a uniformly random string and return it to the adversary. For the real game, we define two packages Prg_0 and Prg_1 whose oracles GET_0 and GET_1 each retrieve a key from the Key package via a GET oracle, then apply the PRG g to the value x they receive and return the left and right half of x, respectively.

Key_{id}	Prg_{id0}	Prg_{id1}
Parameters	Parameters	Parameters
λ : sec. param	λ : sec. param g : PRG	λ : sec. param g : PRG
State	State	State
x : string	no state	no state
GET_{id}	GET_{id0}	GET_{id1}
if $x = \bot$: $\quad x \leftarrow_{\$} \{0,1\}^{\lambda}$ **return** x	$x \leftarrow \mathsf{GET}_{id}()$ $z \leftarrow g(x)$ $y \leftarrow z_{1..\frac{\lambda}{2}}$ **return** y	$x \leftarrow \mathsf{GET}_{id}()$ $z \leftarrow g(x)$ $y \leftarrow z_{(\frac{\lambda}{2}+1)..\lambda}$ **return** y

Fig. 2. Code of Key_{id}, Prg_{id0} and Prg_{id1}

Definition 1 (Pseudorandom Generator). *A polynomial-time computable, deterministic function $g : \{0,1\}^* \to \{0,1\}^*$ with $\forall x \in \{0,1\}^*$, $|g(x)| = 2\,|x|$ is a PRG if for all indices $id \in \{0,1\}^*$ and all probabilistic polynomial-time (PPT) adversaries $\mathcal{A}$, the following advantage is a negligible function in λ (Fig. 2):*

$$\mathsf{Adv}(\mathcal{A}, \text{Gprg}^0_{id}, \text{Gprg}^1_{id}) := \left|\Pr\left[1 = \mathcal{A} \to \text{Gprg}^0_{id}\right] - \Pr\left[1 = \mathcal{A} \to \text{Gprg}^1_{id}\right]\right|.$$

Packages and adversaries receive the security parameter implicitly, i.e., advantage $\mathsf{Adv}(\mathcal{A}, \text{Gprg}^0_{id}, \text{Gprg}^1_{id})$ maps a value $\lambda \in \mathbb{N}$ to a number in the interval $[0,1]$.

Indices. Instead of defining the Key package in three variants, we simply allow it to carry a bitstring $id \in \{0,1\}^*$ as index and modifies oracle and package names for disambiguation, leading to Key, Key_0 and Key_1.

PRFs. As a 2nd example, we define a pseudorandom function. Here, we use the useful convention of defining the game *in terms of the construction*, i.e., we define a pseudorandom function as a *stateless package* Prf. I.e., a pseudorandom function Prf is a package which (a) does not remember state between invocations, (b) makes use of a key from a Key package and (c) is indistinguishable from a random oracle, see Fig. 4.

Definition 2 (Pseudorandom Function). *A pseudorandom function is a stateless package* Prf *which provides oracles* $[\rightarrow \text{Prf}] = \mathsf{EVAL}$ *and calls oracle* $[\text{Prf} \rightarrow] = \mathsf{GET}$ *such that for all PPT adversaries* $\mathcal{A}$*, the advantage*

$$\mathsf{Adv}(\mathcal{A}, \text{Prf} \rightarrow \text{Key}, \text{RO}) \quad := |\Pr[1 = \mathcal{A} \rightarrow \text{Prf} \rightarrow \text{Key}] - \Pr[1 = \mathcal{A} \rightarrow \text{RO}]|$$

is negligible in λ*.* Prf *and* RO *are assumed to use the same input length* in*.*

4 A Proof Viewer for SSPs

In Sect. 4.1, we discuss how we realize the proof viewing concepts outlined in Sect. 1 in the SSP proof viewer, and in Sect. 4.2, we consider further implementation considerations.

Prf Package	RO Package
Parameters	**Parameters**
λ : sec. param	λ : sec. param
in : input length	in : input length
State	**State**
no state	T : table
Oracle	**$\mathsf{EVAL}(x)$**
$[\rightarrow \text{Prf}]$: EVAL	**assert** $x \in \{0,1\}^{in}$
$[\text{Prf} \rightarrow]$: GET	**if** $T[x] = \bot$:
	$\quad y \leftarrow\!\!\$\ \{0,1\}^n$
	$y \leftarrow T[x]$
	return y

Fig. 3. Code of Prf and RO

4.1 Proof Viewing Concepts

Linking and Simultaneous Visibility. CryptoZoo displays code of packages in a separate pane from games and lemmas, so that the reader can reach the code without losing the context of the games and lemmas they are currently studying. Additionally, clicking on a package will highlight the relevant code in the right pane (and scroll to it if needed). Additionally, CryptoZoo has clickable security definitions which open in a separate window.

It is possible to emulate those features partially in static PDF also via clickable packages, and opening several instances of the same PDF, which contain code and definitions, but achieving linking (showing and highlighting code when clicking) at the same time as simultaneous visibility would require non-standard links across several PDFs.

Proof Structure and Information Hiding. When security definitions of a state separating proof are presented as suitable SSP graphs, a state-separating proof that involves many reductions can sometimes be not only more precise, but also shorter than a similar traditional proof since defining a reduction and proving its soundness consists only of drawing two graphs, cf. [BCK22]. In turn, when

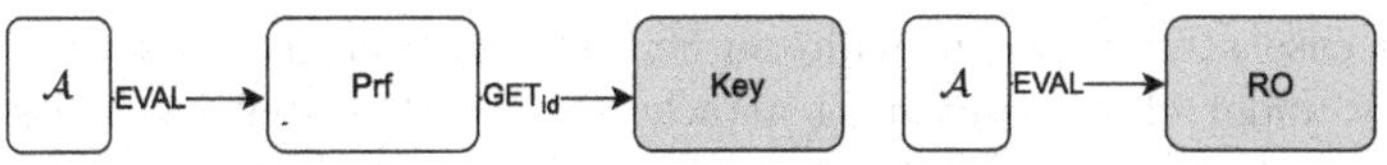

Fig. 4. The games Prf → Key and RO

proving equivalence with standard security definitions in addition, an SSP proof usually grows by at least two graphs and two inlining proofs for the high-level security definitions as well as at least two graphs and two inlining proofs for each of the underlying assumptions, cf. the proof of Yao's garbling scheme by Brzuska and Oechsner (BO [BO23]).

The proof viewer allows to hide sub-trees of a proof graph and, per default, hides code equivalence steps, but allows to display them next to the actual claim and relevant graphs and, again, with the code pane on the right. Again, one can emulate this feature partially by opening several instances of the same PDF, but the interactive hiding of arbitrary proof subtrees does not seem to be emulatable in PDF. An interesting and useful approach in static PDF has been taken in the thesis by Egger [Egg23] which presents security reductions for TLS 1.3 and first shows an overview proof tree and repeats sub-trees later in the relevant sections, recalling relevant context. Since CryptoZoo is not bound to linear structure, the user can fold and un-fold subtrees interactively. Additionally, the user can toggle between showing explanatory text or not, allowing to include comprehensive explanatory text while at the same allowing for compact representation.

4.2 Implementation Considerations

CryptoZoo is implemented as a web application, to allow user to access it without a dedicated application. To this end we believe assuming the availability of a web browser to be generally justified. The viewer is also designed to function offline, with minimal dependencies. Proofs/definitions are stored in a JSON format, which is loaded by the viewer when requested by the user.

5 Case Study: IND-CPA Vs. Simulation-Based Security

Simulation-based security notions for symmetric encryption state that the adversary should not learn more than some ideal leakage and that everything the adversary can do when given a ciphertext can also be done when only given the ideal leakage, but not the ciphertext. While different views on ideal leakage are possible, the minimal approach is to leak the *length* of the message that is encrypted, since an adversary can infer the length of the message from the length of the ciphertext[2]. Simulation-based notions which leak the length of the message are typically equivalent to their game-based counterparts, see, e.g., [DF18].

[2] Length-hiding encryption can mitigate this issue to some extent, but due to information-theory and correctness of decryption, the length of the ciphertext is always an upper bound on the length of the message.

In this case study[3], we provide an SSP-style proof showing that indistinguishability under chosen plaintext attacks (IND-CPA) security in its Real-or-Zeroes formulation is equivalent to a simulation-based formulation where the simulator receives only the length of the message m, encoded in unary as $0^{|m|}$. For completeness, let us state the correctness and security properties before turning to a discussion of the equivalence proof.

Definition 3 (Symmetric Encryption Syntax). *A* symmetric encryption scheme se *consists of two probabilistic polynomial-time (PPT) algorithms* $\mathsf{se.Enc}$ *and* $\mathsf{se.Dec}$

$$c \leftarrow\!\!\$\ \mathsf{se.Enc}(k, m)$$
$$m \leftarrow \mathsf{se.Dec}(k, c)$$

which satisfy that for all security parameters $n \in \mathbb{N}$, encryption is correct, i.e.,

$$\forall m \in \{0,1\}^* \ \Pr_{k \leftarrow\$ \{0,1\}^n} [\mathsf{se.Dec}(k, \mathsf{se.Enc}(k, m)) = m] = 1.$$

Definition 4 (IND-CPA security). *A symmetric-encryption scheme* se *is* indistinguishable under chosen plaintext attacks *if for all PPT adversaries $\mathcal{A}$, the advantage*

$$\mathsf{Adv}(\mathcal{A}, \mathrm{Genc}^0, \mathrm{Genc}^1) := \left|\Pr\left[1 = \mathcal{A} \rightarrow \mathrm{Genc}^0\right] - \Pr\left[1 = \mathcal{A} \rightarrow \mathrm{Genc}^1\right]\right|$$

is a negligible function in the security parameter, where $\mathrm{Genc}^0 := \mathrm{Enc} \rightarrow \mathrm{Key}$ *and* $\mathrm{Genc}^1 := \mathrm{Zeroer} \rightarrow \mathrm{Enc} \rightarrow \mathrm{Key}$, Key *is defined in Figure 2, and* Zeroer *and* Enc *are defined in Figure 7.*

Definition 5 (Simulation-based security). *A symmetric-encryption scheme* se *satisfies* simulation-based security *if there exists a PPT simulator* Sim *such that for all PPT adversaries $\mathcal{A}$, the advantage*

$$\mathsf{Adv}(\mathcal{A}, \mathrm{Genc}^0, \mathrm{Genc}(\mathsf{Sim}) := \left|\Pr\left[1 = \mathcal{A} \rightarrow \mathrm{Genc}^0\right] - \Pr[1 = \mathcal{A} \rightarrow \mathrm{Genc}(\mathsf{Sim})]\right|$$

is a negligible function in the security parameter, where $\mathrm{Genc}^0 := \mathrm{Enc} \rightarrow \mathrm{Key}$ *and* $\mathrm{Genc}(\mathsf{Sim}) := \mathrm{Zeroer} \rightarrow \mathrm{Sim}$ *are defined in Figure 7.*

[3] https://proofviewer.cryptozoo.eu/sim-ind-cpa-landing.html.

Claim 1: Equivalence

$$\text{Genc}^1 \overset{code}{\equiv} \text{Genc}(\text{Sim}_{Lemma2})$$

Proof of Claim 1

Below, in $\text{Genc}(\text{Sim}_{\text{Lemma2}})$, we replace Sim_{Lemma2} by its definition and thereby obtain Hybrid-Claim-1. We mark the definition of $\text{Genc}(\text{Sim}_{\text{Lemma2}})$ by a dashed line, Removing the dashed line yields Genc^1.

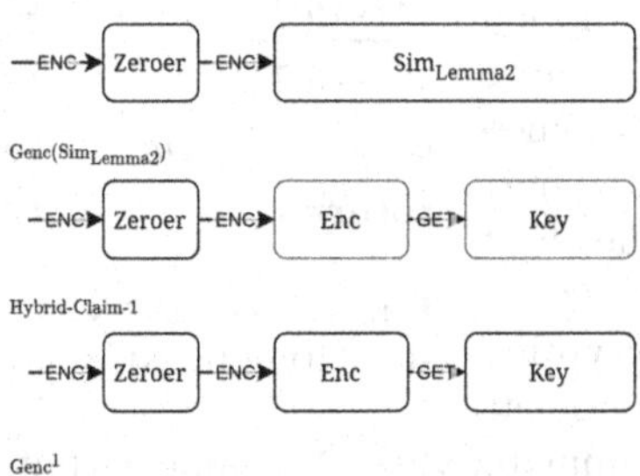

Fig. 5. Using the real game as a simulator.

Proof of Lemma 1

Let $\mathcal{A}$ be a PPT adversary. We prove Lemma 1 via three game-hops and bound the advantage of $\mathcal{A}$ via the triangle inequality.

$$\begin{aligned}\mathsf{Adv}(\mathcal{A}, \text{Genc}^1, \text{Genc}^0) \leq\ & \mathsf{Adv}(\mathcal{A}, \text{Genc}^1, \text{Hybrid-Lemma1}) \\ & + \mathsf{Adv}(\mathcal{A}, \text{Hybrid-Lemma1}, \text{Genc}(\mathsf{Sim})) \\ & + \mathsf{Adv}(\mathcal{A}, \text{Genc}(\text{Sim}), \text{Genc}^0)\end{aligned}$$

Where the first and last advantage are obtained by reduction to simulation security while the middle term follows from code equivalence and thus is 0. The proof is visualized by the following sequence of games:

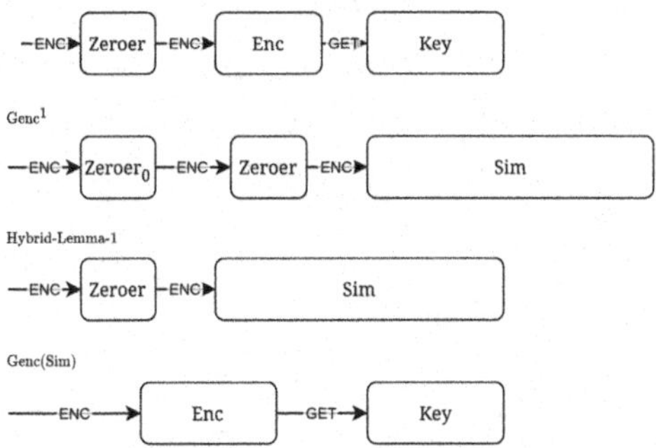

Fig. 6. Using the real game as a simulator.

We will see that the ideal encryption game can act as a simulator, since all the simulator needs to do is to encrypt zeroes. In this way, we obtain a straightforward proof that IND-CPA security implies the simulation-based security notion for symmetric encryption (See Fig. 5). In the converse direction, we need to use the simulation-based security notion twice in the proof—once to move away from encrypting real messages to encrypting simulated messages, and once to argue that encrypting simulated messages is indistinguishable from encrypting zeroes—since the ideal functionality which gives $0^{|m|}$ to the simulator yields the same output, regardless of whether m is an all-zeroes string or not. These arguments become visible in the proof structure (see Fig. 6) and its associated proof graphs. The game hop from Genc^1 to Hybrid-Lemma-1 is a reduction step which can be visualized as a cut in a graph, depicted in Fig. 8 which hatches the reduction in red. The last game hop is directly implied by the indistinguishability of the real game Genc^0 and the simulated game Genc(Sim), and the middle game hop follows by observing that two Zeroer packages are equivalent to a single one.

Enc^0 Package	Zeroer Package
Parameters	**Parameters**
λ : sec. param	no parameters
se : sym. enc. sch.	
State	**State**
no state	no state
$\mathsf{ENC}(m)$	$\mathsf{ENC}(m)$
$k \leftarrow \mathsf{GET}()$	$m' \leftarrow 0^{\lvert m \rvert}$
$c \leftarrow\$ \mathsf{se.enc}(k, m)$	$c \leftarrow \mathsf{ENC}(m')$
return c	**return** c

Fig. 7. Package definitions for IND-CPA and simulation-based security of se.

Claim 2: Indistinguishability between **Genc** and **Hybrid-Lemma-1**

For all simulators Sim and all adversary $\mathcal{A}$,

$$\mathsf{Adv}(\mathcal{A}, \mathrm{Genc}^1, \mathrm{Hybrid\text{-}Lemma1}) = \mathsf{Adv}(\mathcal{A} \to \mathrm{Zeroer}, \mathrm{Genc}^0, \mathrm{Genc}(\mathrm{Sim}))$$

Proof of Claim 2

Using Zeroer as a reduction, we observe that the remaining part of the graph constitute exactly Genc^0 and Genc(Sim), respectively, and Claim 2 follows.

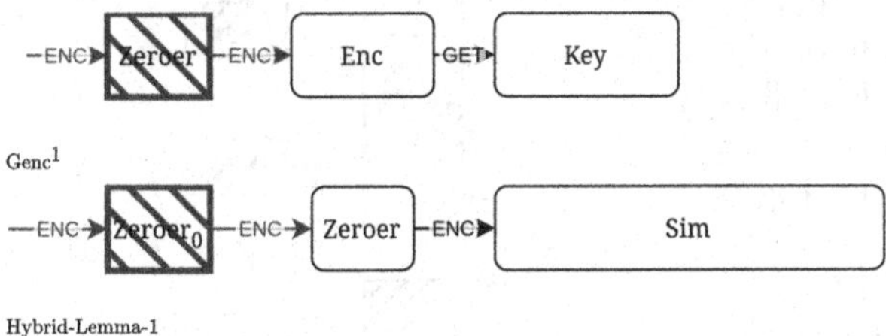

Fig. 8. Reduction hatched in red. (Color figure online)

6 Case Study: Constant-Depth GGM Tree

Goldreich, Goldwasser and Micali (GGM [GGM86]) introduced the notion of pseudorandom functions and provided a construction of a pseudorandom function based on a length-doubling pseudorandom generator (see Definition 1). The proof is commonly include in courses on the foundations of cryptography and contained, e.g., in Chap. 3.6.2 (Theorem 3.6.6) of the *Foundations of Cryptography I* textbook by Goldreich [Gol04]. The construction is naturally amenable to visualization: It structures PRG instances into a binary tree and the left halves and right halves of a PRG output become the input to the PRG instances on the next tree layer, until reaching the leaf layer.

The construction[4] is indeed often visualized as a tree. See, e.g., Fig. 3.5 in Chap. 3.6.2 of [Gol04]. As we will see, not only the construction, but also the proof can be visualized. We will see how the security of each of the PRG instances is applied and how the reduction looks like. The proof is a hybrid argument over all of the PRG instances. For illustration, consider the two hybrid games in Fig. 9. Their difference can be reduced to the PRG security by using the boxed hatched in red as a reduction (Fig. 10).

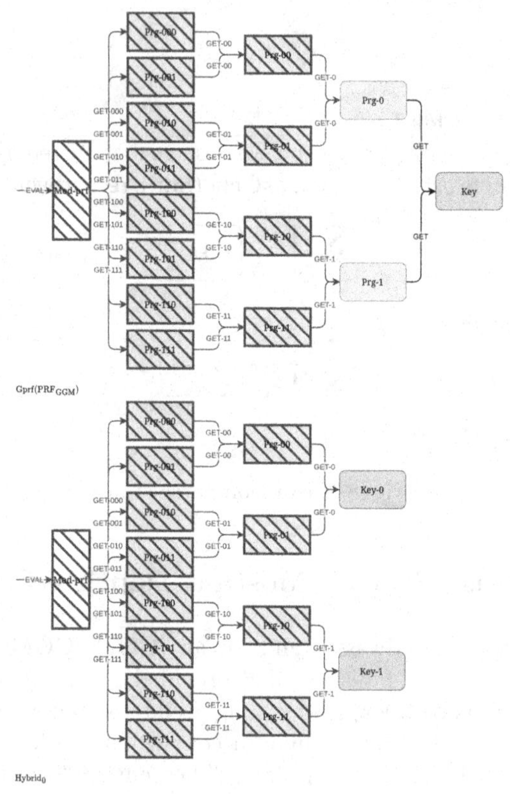

Fig. 9. Hybrid step in the GGM proof

The proof which we have chosen to implement into the proof viewer is a variant of the GGM proof where the tree is of constant depth. This is analogous to how the GGM construction is often depicted in books, namely restricted to a constant level, since the full GGM construction is an n-level tree with 2^n leaves which is harder to represent than a finite tree.

We depict the hybrid argument for tree depth 3 which requires $2^3-1=7$ PRG instances and thus also 7 game-hops. Each of the hybrid games is represented via a binary tree. The format of the proof viewer is convenient here since we avoid page boundaries and can depict the hybrids simply as a long sequence of 8 games. Note that the full GGM proof does not proceed via a hybrid over the entire tree, but only visits polynomially many of the PRG instances in the tree. Our constant-depth representation does not capture this subtlety of the proof, and the SSP version of the full GGM proof that we are aware of, is visually not as appealing (see Sect. 7 for a compelling hybrid argument over polynomially many hybrids). Therefore, we prefer to present a constant-depth version of GGM which captures the main essence of the construction and, importantly, its security proof.

[4] https://proofviewer.cryptozoo.eu/ggm-landing.html.

Claim0

Let R_0 be the reduction defined by the packages hatched in red in the graphs below and $\mathcal{A}$ be a PPT adversary, then

$$\mathsf{Adv}(\mathcal{A}, \mathrm{Hybrid}_0, \mathrm{Hybrid}_1) = \mathsf{Adv}(\mathcal{A} \to \mathrm{R}_0, \mathrm{Gprg}_0^0, \mathrm{Gprg}_0^1)$$

.

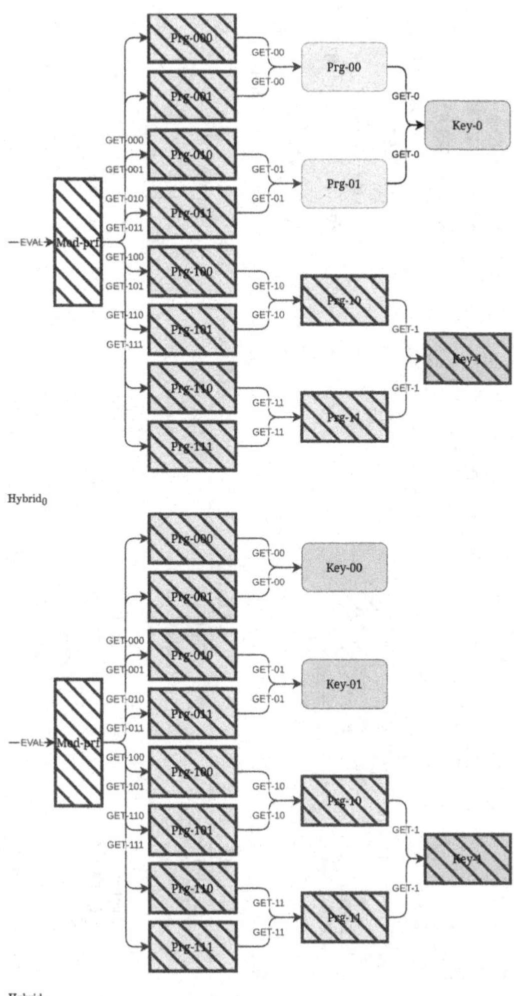

Fig. 10. Reduction step in the GGM proof

7 Case Study: Yao's Garbling Scheme

Secure multi-party computation constructs protocols where several parties *together* compute a function on the participants' input but without revealing their inputs to other protocol participants (beyond what the output of the

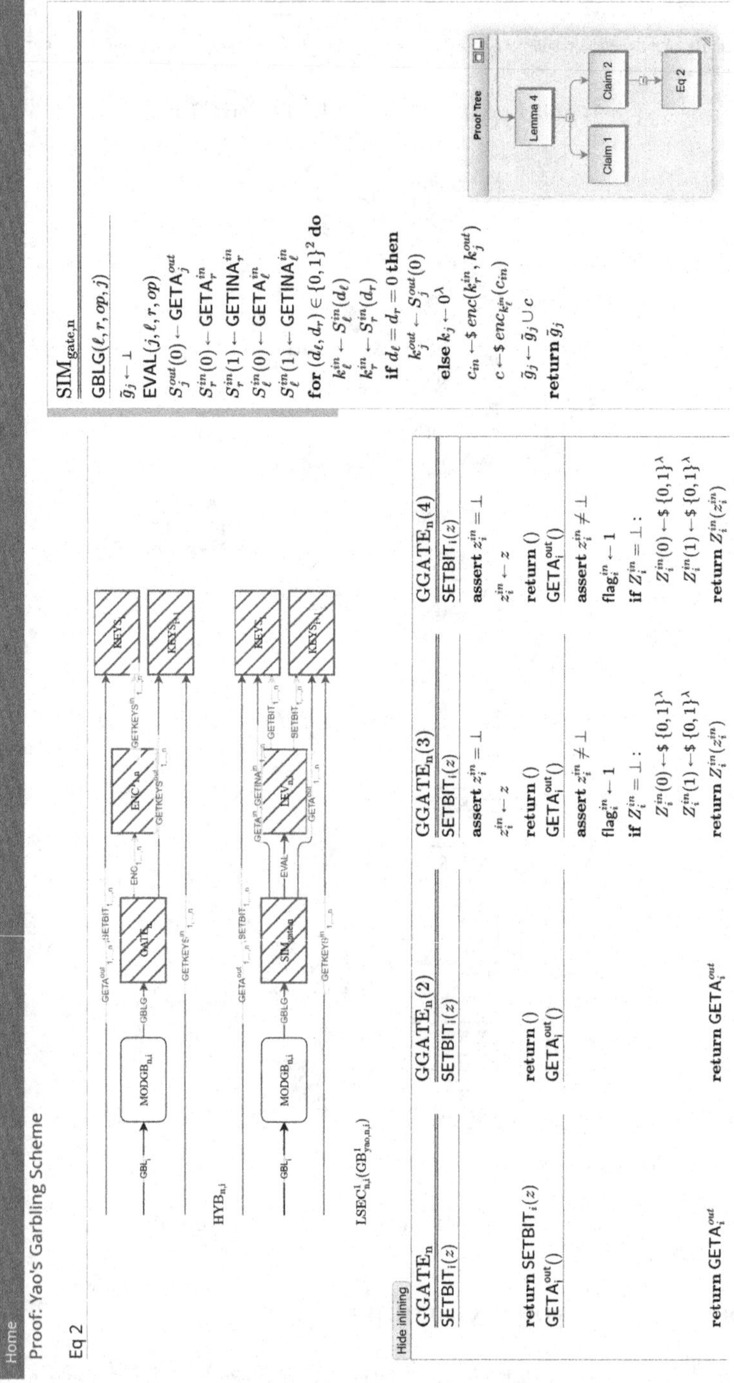

Fig. 11. Semantic switch step in the proof viewer (Eq. 2 of Yao, proof via inlining).

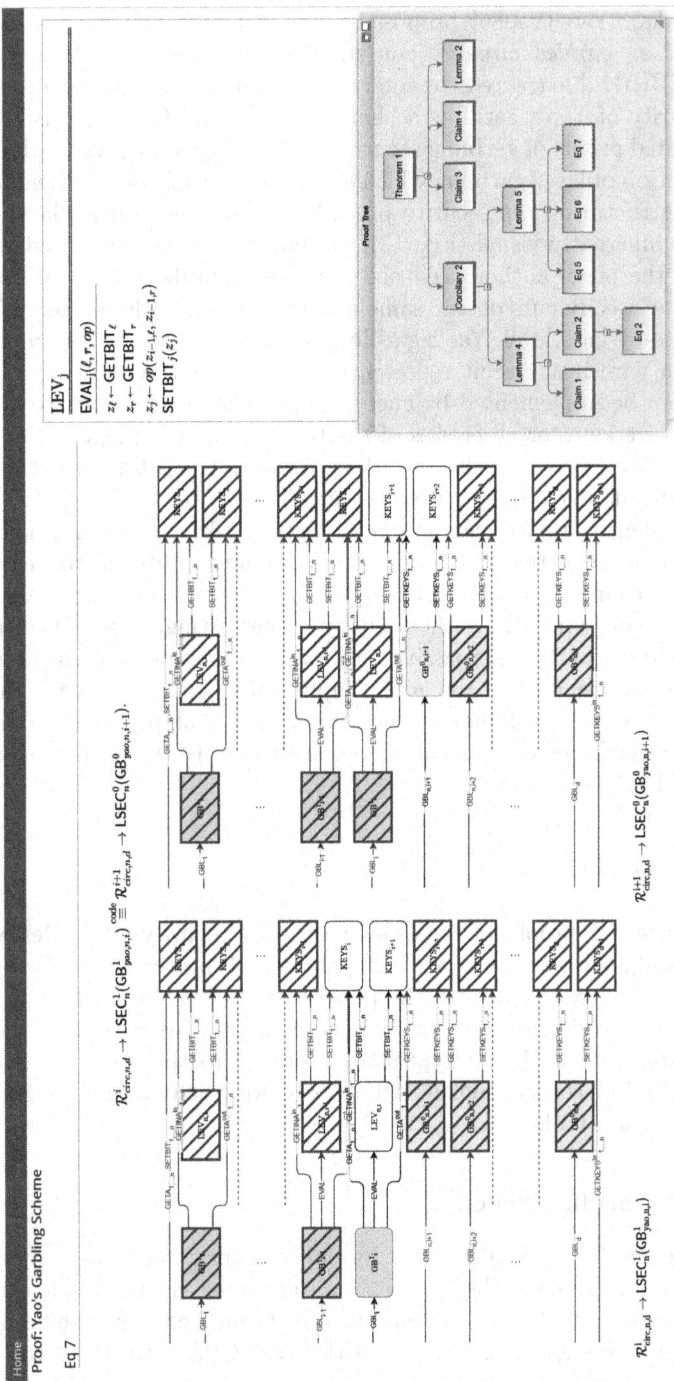

Fig. 12. Hybrids code equivalence in the proof viewer (Eq. 7 of Yao, proof via graph equality).

function leaks). Yao [Yao86] proposed a protocol for this purpose which we know today as *garbled circuits*. For analyzing the security of this construction, BHR [BHR12] extracted the intermediate notion of a garbling scheme and proved security of Yao's garbling scheme. Brzuska and Oechsner [BO23] give a state-separated proof[5] of garbling security for *layered* circuits where they further extract a notion of layer garbling which allows sequential composition and therefore allows structuring the security proof by composing security layer-by-layer. This step is inherently visual (Fig. 12). Moreover, to define these reductions for the viewer, the proof author need not produce separate graphs and code, but only needs to specify cuts on the same graph, enabling code re-use.

On a gate-by-gate level, Yao's garbling scheme operates by assigning two SE keys to each wire in a circuit representing the values 0 and 1. A binary logic gate can then be implemented by encrypting the key on the output wire under both input wire keys for all entries of the truth table: for a logic AND gate the output 1-key is encrypted under the 1-keys for both the left and right input wire while the output 0-key is encrypted under all other combinations of the input keys. Consequently, a party can access the output 1-key exactly if it knows both 1-keys for the input wires whereas the 0-key remains hidden in this case.

A central element of the security proof is a semantic switch – instead of considering 0-keys and 1-keys the security game distinguishes between "active" keys known to the party and "passive" keys which remain secret which makes the party's state independent of the actual input *value* when evaluating the circuit (Fig. 11). The formal code equivalence proof of this step is quite tedious, but the proof viewer keeps components necessary to verify this step close together, which should help the reader.

8 Comparison

We now review SSP proofs for the Transport Layer Security (TLS [Res18]) protocol, the Messaging Layer Security (MLS [BMO+23]) protocol and Yao's garbling scheme. In each case, we discuss the presentation of the respective papers and how CryptoZoo could further contribute to communication, and, in the case of Yao's garbling scheme, how CryptoZoo compares to the original presentation by Brzuska and Oechsner [BO23]. Afterwards, we briefly discuss SSP proofs in formal verification tools.

8.1 Yao's Garbling Scheme

Brzuska and Oechsner (BO [BO23]) formalize security and correctness of garbling schemes in SSPs and then revisit Yao's garbling scheme. While correctness can also be proven in SSPs, BO focus on security only and provide an SSP-style reduction for Yao's garbling scheme to the IND-CPA security of the underlying garbling scheme. The BO paper introduces games for IND-CPA security

[5] https://proofviewer.cryptozoo.eu/yao-landing.html.

and garbling security in a natural flow, slowly increasing complexity in order to familiarize the reader with the novel SSP encoding and, as a first proof, show an equivalence for different encodings for IND-CPA security. Our CryptoZoo implementation follows this outline by BO. Concretely, the CryptoZoo landing page for Yao's garbling scheme explains the purpose of the different pages and then recommends to the reader to first visit the IND-CPA security page which explains the SSP encoding of IND-CPA security and the equivalence proof with the encoding of IND-CPA security which is useful for the security proof of Yao's garbling scheme. Subsequently, BO discuss the SSP encoding of garbling scheme security and Yao's garbling scheme construction. Our CryptoZoo implementation follows this approach and provides a page introducing the garbling scheme security notion in SSP-style and also explains Yao's garbling scheme construction. Thus, up to the main theorem statement, the BO paper and our CryptoZoo implementation proceed analogously.

The main difference between CryptoZoo and the BO presentation is the proof of the main theorem which reduces security of Yao's garbling scheme to IND-CPA security. BO proceed in a bottom-up fashion, slowly building and explaining sub-packages needed in the proof and showing equivalence with the top-level security notion in the end.

In turn, CryptoZoo natively presents the proof in a top-down fashion and explains the code of the modular packages previously in the context of the Yao construction. Below the statement of the main theorem, CryptoZoo recommends to the reader, however, to first read the proof bottom-up and then, once more, top-down. CryptoZoo allows the reader to proceed through the proof in both directions, since clicking on a lemma hides all the remaining proof steps, focusing solely on the lemma and its sub-tree. The reason that we first recommend a bottom-up reading of the proof is analogous to the presentation rationale of BO: The reader's familiarity with all packages grows successively with each proof step until reaching a statement for the entire garbling construction. In turn, reading the proof top-down in the first reading iteration either requires reading and understanding all code at once or treating some of the packages as black-boxes (since most of the proof steps are purely syntactical). However, after a first bottom-up read that helps familiarizing with all code and steps, making a top-down pass through the proof seems useful to gain a conceptual understanding of how the proof connects the high-level garbling security notion to the low-level IND-CPA definition. CryptoZoo supports both, the bottom-up and the top-down reading flow, and the user can, of course, also read the proof in an arbitrary order based on their preference. The CryptoZoo proof tree and information-hiding helps the user to engage with the proof conveniently in an order of their choice while having all information conveniently at hand. In turn, the BO proof has a fixed order where code has a fixed place in the paper and needs to be manually connected. As mentioned previously, opening multiple PDFs of BO (and adding a proof tree to their paper) will reach a similar effect, but at a lower level of convenience than in CryptoZoo.

8.2 SSP Proofs of TLS 1.3

Brzuska, Delignat-Lavaud, Egger, Fournet, Kohbrok and Kohlweiss (BDEFKK [BDE+22]) analyze the TLS 1.3 key schedule and Egger [Egg23] further connects the TLS 1.3 key schedule security with the TLS 1.3 handshake security. BDEFKK and Egger both introduce different code, assumptions and games in a natural flow, starting from a conceptually simple game (collision-resistance of hash-functions in BDEFKK and PRF security in Egger).

A remarkable property of the TLS 1.3 security analysis is the strongly layered approach: Each layer comes with a main theorem which builds upon the result of the previous layer as well as additional lemmata specific to the current layer. As such each layer in isolation can be an insightful read, e.g. to learn how to relate key schedule hand handshake security. Highlighting such additional adhoc structure of the proof tree is easy to do in a PDF presentation, and Egger's thesis follows this approach with a proof tree with clickable lemma statements and chapters zooming in (both visually and content wise) into each layer of the tree. While currently not implemented, adding this layer structure to CryptoZoo would be a reasonable task if it turns out to be applicable to many projects. Finally, both, for BDEFKK and Egger (as well as in a possible future CryptoZoo implementation), the proof trees are also useful to compute final advantage statements, see [Egg23, p.48, p.56].

8.3 SSP Proofs of the MLS Key Schedule

Brzuska, Cornelissen and Kohbrok (BCK [BCK22]) analyze the MLS key schedule and its composition with TreeKEM [BBR18]. Again, BCK slowly build up complexity in their article and a CryptoZoo implementation would proceed analogously. Again, the main advantage of CryptoZoo lies in the availability and easy accessibility of code, and in this case, also in an additional proof tree—but a proof tree could also be added to BCK. Again, a proof tree would be useful to compute final advantage statements, cf. [BCK22, p.18–19].

8.4 Formal Verification Tools for SSPs

SSProve is a Coq-based formal verification tool for SSPs by Abate, Haselwarter, Rivas, Van Muylder, Winterhalter, Hritcu, Maillard and Spitters [AHR+21], and Dupressoir, Kohbrok and Oechsner [DKO22] formalized SSPs in EasyCrypt [BDG+14,BGHZ11]. Representation of SSPs in both, SSProve and EasyCrypt, is code-based and thus, CryptoZoo could help present the obtained proof visually. Potentially, CryptoZoo code could be generated automatically and thus not only help in proof communication but perhaps also in proof development, allowing the proof developer faster visual navigation of the proof draft.

9 Conclusion and Future Work

One useful feature of visual(izable) frameworks such as UC, abstract cryptography, the Joy of Cryptography and SSPs is the visualization of *proofs*. In this article, we explored the presentation of SSP proofs in the *interactive* proof viewer CryptoZoo which we developed. We would like to claim that CryptoZoo improves the *quality* of verification by providing improved navigation of proofs and by allowing users to conveniently and quickly retrieve relevant information. However, readers of PDFs can compensate by retrieving information in different (slower) ways (cf. Sect. 4.1). Therefore, it seems more accurate that CryptoZoo improves the *speed* of verification or the quality of verification given a fixed, limited amount of time.

Future Work. It would be interesting to conduct a user study to compare the verification of (well-written) PDF proofs with the verification of (well-written) CryptoZoo proofs. Furthermore, it would be interesting to see whether CryptoZoo is useful for helping a proof developer maintain state in a visual form while writing an SSP proof. Last, but not least, CryptoZoo might be connected with formal verification tools for SSPs, such as SSProve [AHR+21] and or a formalization of SSPs in EasyCrypt [BDG+14,BGHZ11]. In this case, reduction steps and, more importantly, code-equivalence steps could be verified by in the underlying tool (rather than by the user/reader), turning CryptoZoo into an interface which helps a user/reader gain understanding of proof conducted in a formal verification tool and thus serve to ease a notoriously hard communication task.

Acknowledgment. This project was supported by the Research Council of Finland and the European Commission under the Horizon2020 research and innovation programme, Marie Sklodowska-Curie grant agreement No 101034255.

References

[AHR+21] Abate, C., et al.: SSProve: a foundational framework for modular cryptographic proofs in coq. In: Küsters, R., Naumann, D., (eds.) CSF 2021 Computer Security Foundations Symposium, pp. 1–15. IEEE Computer Society Press (2021)

[BBF13] Baecher, P., Brzuska, C., Fischlin, M.: Notions of black-box reductions, revisited. In: Sako, K., Sarkar, P. (eds.) ASIACRYPT 2013. Part I, volume 8269 of LNCS, pp. 296–315. Springer, Heidelberg (2013)

[BBR18] Bhargavan, K., Barnes, R., Rescorla, E.: TreeKEM: Asynchronous Decentralized Key Management for Large Dynamic Groups A protocol proposal for Messaging Layer Security (MLS). Research report, Inria Paris (2018)

[BCK22] Brzuska, C., Cornelissen, E., Kohbrok, K.: Security analysis of the MLS key derivation. In: 2022 IEEE Symposium on Security and Privacy, pp. 2535–2553. IEEE Computer Society Press (2022)

[BDE+22] Brzuska, C., Delignat-Lavaud, A., Egger, C., Fournet, C., Kohbrok, K., Kohlweiss, M.: Key-schedule security for the TLS 1.3 standard. In: Agrawal, S., Lin, D. (eds.) ASIACRYPT 2022. Part I, volume 13791 of LNCS, pp. 621–650. Springer, Heidelberg (2022). https://doi.org/10.1007/978-3-031-22963-3_21

[BDF+18] Brzuska, C., Delignat-Lavaud, A., Fournet, C., Kohbrok, K., Kohlweiss, M.: State separation for code-based game-playing proofs. In: Peyrin, T.,

Galbraith, S. (eds.) ASIACRYPT 2018. Part III, volume 11274 of LNCS, pp. 222–249. Springer, Heidelberg (2018). https://doi.org/10.1007/978-3-030-03332-3_9

[BDG+14] Barthe, G., Dupressoir, F., Grégoire, B., Kunz, C., Schmidt, B., Strub, P.-Y.: EasyCrypt: a tutorial. In: Aldini, A., Lopez, J., Martinelli, F. (eds.) FOSAD 2012-2013. LNCS, vol. 8604, pp. 146–166. Springer, Cham (2014). https://doi.org/10.1007/978-3-319-10082-1_6

[BGHZ11] Barthe, G., Grégoire, B., Heraud, S., Béguelin, S.Z.: Computer-aided security proofs for the working cryptographer. In: Rogaway, P. (ed.) CRYPTO 2011. LNCS, vol. 6841, pp. 71–90. Springer, Heidelberg (2011). https://doi.org/10.1007/978-3-642-22792-9_5

[BHR12] Bellare, M., Hoang, V.T., Rogaway, P.: Foundations of garbled circuits. In: Yu, T., Danezis, G., Gligor, V.D., (eds.) ACM CCS 2012, pp. 784–796. ACM Press (2012)

[BMO+23] Barnes, R., Millican, J., Omara, E., Cohn-Gordon, K., Robert, R.: The Messaging Layer Security (MLS) Protocol. RFC 9420 (2023)

[BO23] Brzuska, C., Oechsner, S.: A state-separating proof for yao's garbling scheme. In: 2023 IEEE 36th Computer Security Foundations Symposium (CSF) (CSF), pp. 127–142. IEEE Computer Society, Los Alamitos, CA, USA (2023)

[BR06] Bellare, M., Rogaway, P.: The security of triple encryption and a framework for code-based game-playing proofs. In: Vaudenay, S. (ed.) EUROCRYPT 2006. LNCS, vol. 4004, pp. 409–426. Springer, Heidelberg (2006). https://doi.org/10.1007/11761679_25

[Bül22] Bülow, N.: Proof visualization for the lean 4 theorem prover (2022)

[Can01] Canetti, R.: Universally composable security: a new paradigm for cryptographic protocols. In: 42nd FOCS, pp. 136–145. IEEE Computer Society Press (2001)

[CDSP08] Cattaneo, G., De Santis, A., Petrillo, U.F.: Visualization of cryptographic protocols with grace. J. Vis. Lang. Comput. **19**(2), 258–290 (2008)

[CR15] Carmer, B., Rosulek, M.: Vamonos: embeddable visualizations of advanced algorithms. In: 2015 IEEE Frontiers in Education Conference (FIE), pp. 1–8 (2015)

[DDGJ22] Davis, H., Diemert, D., Günther, F., Jager, T.: On the concrete security of TLS 1.3 PSK mode. In: Dunkelman, O., Dziembowski, S. (eds.) Advances in Cryptology – EUROCRYPT 2022. EUROCRYPT 2022. Lecture Notes in Computer Science, vol. 13276, pp. 876–906. Springer, Heidelberg (2022). https://doi.org/10.1007/978-3-031-07085-3_30

[DF18] Degabriele, J.P., Fischlin, M.: Simulatable Channels: extended security that is universally composable and easier to prove. In: Peyrin, T., Galbraith, S. (eds.) ASIACRYPT 2018. LNCS, vol. 11274, pp. 519–550. Springer, Cham (2018). https://doi.org/10.1007/978-3-030-03332-3_19

[DGGP21] Degabriele, J.P., Govinden, J., Günther, F., Paterson, K.G.: The security of ChaCha20-Poly1305 in the multi-user setting. In: Vigna, G., Shi, E., (eds.) ACM CCS 2021, pp. 1981–2003. ACM Press (2021)

[DHK+23] Duman, J., Hövelmanns, K., Kiltz, E., Lyubashevsky, V., Seiler, G., Unruh, D.: A thorough treatment of highly-efficient NTRU instantiations. In: Boldyreva, A., Kolesnikov, V. (eds.) PKC 2023. Part I, volume 13940 of LNCS, pp. 65–94. Springer, Heidelberg (2023). https://doi.org/10.1007/978-3-031-31368-4_3

[DHRR22] Dowling, B., Hauck, E., Riepel, D., Rösler, P.: Strongly anonymous ratcheted key exchange. In: Agrawal, S., Lin, D. (eds.) ASIACRYPT 2022. Part III, volume 13793 of LNCS, pp. 119–150. Springer, Heidelberg (2022). https://doi.org/10.1007/978-3-031-22969-5_5

[DKO22] Dupressoir, F., Kohbrok, K., Oechsner, S.: Bringing state-separating proofs to EasyCrypt a security proof for cryptobox. In: CSF 2022 Computer Security Foundations Symposium, pp. 227–242. IEEE Computer Society Press (2022)

[dMKA+15] de Moura, L., Kong, S., Avigad, J., van Doorn, F., von Raumer, J.: the lean theorem prover (system description). In: Felty, A.P., Middeldorp, A. (eds.) CADE 2015. LNCS (LNAI), vol. 9195, pp. 378–388. Springer, Cham (2015). https://doi.org/10.1007/978-3-319-21401-6_26

[Egg23] Egger, C.: On abstraction and modularization in protocol analysis, Doctoral thesis, Friedrich-Alexander-Universität Erlangen-Nürnberg (FAU) (2023)

[Elm04] Elmqvist, N.: Protoviz: .a simple security protocol visualization, Tech. Rep., University of Gothenburg (2004)

[GGM86] Goldreich, O., Goldwasser, S., Micali, S.: How to construct random functions. J. ACM **33**(4), 792–807 (1986)

[Gol04] Goldreich, O.: Foundations of Cryptography: Basic Applications, vol. 2. Cambridge University Press, Cambridge, UK (2004)

[Koh23] Kohbrok, K.: State-separating proofs and their applications, Doctoral thesis, Aalto University School of Science (2023)

[Mau11] Maurer, U.: Constructive cryptography – a new paradigm for security definitions and proofs. In: Mödersheim, S., Palamidessi, C. (eds.) TOSCA 2011. LNCS, vol. 6993, pp. 33–56. Springer, Heidelberg (2012). https://doi.org/10.1007/978-3-642-27375-9_3

[Pit20] Pit-Claudel, C.: Untangling mechanized proofs. In: Lämmel, R., Tratt, L., de Lara, J., (eds.) Proceedings of the 13th ACM SIGPLAN International Conference on Software Language Engineering, SLE 2020, Virtual Event, USA, November 16–17, 2020, pp. 155–174. ACM (2020)

[Res18] Rescorla, E.: The Transport Layer Security (TLS) Protocol Version 1.3. RFC 8446 (2018)

[Ros21] Rosulek, M.: The joy of cryptography. Oregon State University (2021)

[RTV04] Reingold, O., Trevisan, L., Vadhan, S.: Notions of reducibility between cryptographic primitives. In: Naor, M. (ed.) TCC 2004. LNCS, vol. 2951, pp. 1–20. Springer, Heidelberg (2004). https://doi.org/10.1007/978-3-540-24638-1_1

[Sho04] Shoup, V.: Sequences of games: a tool for taming complexity in security proofs. Cryptology ePrint Archive, Report 2004/332 (2004). https://eprint.iacr.org/2004/332

[SMCB12] Schmidt, B., Meier, S., Cremers, C.J.F., Basin, D.A.: Automated analysis of diffie-hellman protocols and advanced security properties. In: Zdancewic, S., Cortier, V., (eds.) CSF 2012 Computer Security Foundations Symposium, pp. 78–94. IEEE Computer Society Press (2012)

[Tew] Tews, H.: Prooftrees (2023)

[The17] The Coq Development Team: The coq proof assistant, version 8.7.0 (2017)

[Yao86] Yao, A.C.C.: How to generate and exchange secrets (extended abstract). In: 27th FOCS, pp. 162–167. IEEE Computer Society Press (1986)

Element Distinctness and Bounded Input Size in Private Set Intersection and Related Protocols

Xavier Carpent[1(✉)], Seoyeon Hwang[2], and Gene Tsudik[2]

[1] University of Nottingham, Nottingham, UK
xavier.carpent@nottingham.ac.uk
[2] University of California, Irvine, Irvine, USA

Abstract. This paper considers Private Set Intersection (PSI) protocols where one party (server) imposes a minimum input size (lower bound) on the other party (client), and the latter wants to keep its input size private. This entails tackling two types of possible client misbehavior: (1) using fake/frivolous elements, and (2) duplicating genuine elements. The former can be addressed by pre-authorizing all client elements by a mutually trusted party, which translates into so-called Authorized PSI (APSI). However, the latter is more challenging. To this end, we construct a protocol for *Proof of Element-Distinctness (PoED)*, wherein one party convinces the other that all of its input elements are distinct, without revealing any information about them. Using this as a building block, we then construct a PSI variant, called *All-Distinct Private Set Intersection (AD-PSI)*, that outputs the intersection only when client input contains all distinct elements. We also present some AD-PSI variants where using duplicates can cause unexpected information leakage. Combining the AD-PSI with previous work for upper-bounded-input PSI, we construct a *Bounded-Size-Hiding-PSI (B-SH-PSI)* that outputs the intersection only if client's input size satisfies server's requirement on *both* lower and upper bounds, while keeping that size private. Finally, we present a protocol that prevents both types of misbehavior, called *All-Distinct Authorized PSI (AD-APSI)*.

Keywords: Private Set Intersection · Input Correctness · Element Distinctness · Bounded Input · Size-Hiding

1 Introduction

Private Set Intersection (PSI) is a cryptographic primitive that allows two parties to compute the intersection of their private input sets, without revealing any information about the set elements outside the intersection to each other. It attracted a lot of attention from various privacy-preserving applications, such as contact tracing [25,75], online targeted advertising [45], genomic testing [51], botnet detection [59], TV program history matching [47], private contact discovery [23,38], and private matchmaking [79].

C. Pöpper and L. Batina (Eds.): ACNS 2024, LNCS 14583, pp. 26–57, 2024.
https://doi.org/10.1007/978-3-031-54770-6_2

Due to its functionalities applicable to numerous real-world applications, there has been a long line of work in PSI and its variants (details in Sect. 2), starting from the earliest forms in 1980s [56,73]. While most PSI protocols reveal set (input) sizes as part of the protocol, [3] constructed the first PSI variant – *Size-Hiding PSI (SH-PSI)* – that allows one party (*Client*) to learn the intersection while keeping its input set size private against the other party (*Server*). Building upon this size-hiding property, Bradley et. al. [6] and Cerulli et. al. [9] suggested upper-bounding *Client*'s input set size to prevent it from learning too much information about *Server*'s input set.

This paper focuses on a related question: lower-bounding *Client*'s input set size while keeping it private. That is, suppose that *Server* requires *Client* to have at least l elements in its input set to run the PSI protocol with *Server*'s set. This requirement might be useful in social network settings, such as Facebook and LinkedIn, where a popular/prominent user would agree to connect to another user only if the latter has at least l genuine friends/followers to e.g., block the stalkers who keep creating bogus accounts and requesting to connect.

If we relax the size-hiding property, lower-bounding *Client* input size is straightforward: *Server* simply checks whether the *Client* set size (revealed as part of the PSI interaction) is $\geq l$, and if not, aborts the protocol. However, this only works if *Client* is honest. A dishonest *Client* can bypass this requirement by (1) generating and using fake set elements, and/or (2) duplicating its genuine set elements. Then, since PSI protocols typically obfuscate (often by blinding) *Client* set elements, *Server* cannot distinguish between the genuine and fake input elements.

One intuitive way to mitigate this misbehavior is via auditing: a trusted third party (TTP) regularly verifies the *Client* input by examining the transcripts of PSI protocol and looking for duplicate or spurious elements. However, this would be too late since the dishonest *Client* already obtained the intersection.

To deal with the type-(1) misbehavior, so-called *Authorized PSI* (APSI) techniques [19,20,77] have been proposed. This is achieved by having an offline TTP that pre-authorizes *Client* input by signing each element. Later, during PSI interaction, *Server* (implicitly or explicitly) verifies these signatures without learning *Client* input. This way, *Client* cannot obtain signatures of spurious elements, and thus, cannot learn the intersection using fake elements. However, APSI protocols cannot cope with the type-(2) misbehavior, i.e., *Client* can still bypass the requirement by using duplicated (TTP-authorized) signed elements. This prompts a natural question:

Can Client prove that each of its private input elements is not duplicated, i.e., all input elements are distinct while keeping them private?

To answer this question, we first investigate if current PSI protocols can detect duplicates (see Sect. 2.4). A few prior results [5,49] proposed protocols for *Private Multiset*[1] *Intersection (PMI)* which allows *multiset* inputs. However, we note that their goal is different because it outputs the intersection *multiset*, not the

[1] Recall that, a multiset allows duplicate elements, while a set does not.

intersection *set*, which yields more information than PSI, e.g., the number of occurrences (i.e., multiplicities) of common elements.

Next, we show how to prove *element distinctness* in two-party settings, whereby one party convinces the other that its input elements are all distinct, without revealing any information about them. We use the term *element distinctness* (a.k.a. *element uniqueness*) problem from the computational complexity theory: given n numbers $x_1, ..., x_n$, return "Yes" if all x_i's are distinct, and "No" otherwise. To the best of our knowledge, there is no prior work in the two-party settings where one party *proves element distinctness of its private input* to the other party. We call this ***P****roofs* ***o****f* ***E****lement-****D****istinctness (****PoED****)*.

We propose a concrete PoED construction by generalizing the two billiard balls problem, which can be an independent interest. Using this PoED construction as a building block, we propose a new PSI variant, called *All-Distinct Private Set Intersection (AD-PSI)*, and its construction. Informally speaking, AD-PSI allows *Client* to learn the intersection only if all of its input elements are distinct. It additionally guarantees that *Client* learns no information, not even *Server* input size, if it uses any duplicates as input.

Then, we extend AD-PSI to three PSI variants where using duplicates can be more problematic: (1) *AD-PSI-Cardinality (AD-PSI-CA)* that outputs the cardinality of the intersection; (2) *Existential AD-PSI (AD-PSI-X)* that outputs whether the intersection is non-empty; and (3) *AD-PSI with Data Transfer (AD-PSI-DT)* that transfers associated data along with the intersection; only when *Client* inputs all distinct elements. We also show a *Bounded-Size-Hiding-PSI (B-SH-PSI)* construction with both upper and lower bound on *Client* input, combining our AD-PSI with prior work on upper-bounded size-hiding PSI (U-SH-PSI) [6,9], which shows the applicability of PoED and AD-PSI.

Note that the protocols above work in the case where *Client* cannot generate fake elements, and to expand *Client*'s capabilities to both type-(1) and type-(2) misbehavior, including a TTP is unavoidable. To fill this gap, we finally present an *All-Distinct Authorized PSI (AD-APSI)* protocol that prevents both duplicate and spurious elements by ensuring the validity of *Client* input. We specify desired security properties for AD-APSI and prove that the proposed protocol satisfies them.

To summarize, the contributions of this work are:

- A PoED protocol with security analysis;
- Definition of AD-PSI and concrete construction with security proofs;
- Three AD-PSI variants: AD-PSI-CA, AD-PSI-X, AD-PSI-DT;
- Extension of U-SH-PSI to B-SH-PSI with both upper and lower bounds on *Client* input set size; and
- Definition of AD-APSI and concrete construction with security proofs;

Organization: After overviewing related work and preliminaries in Sect. 2, Sect. 3 presents a PoED construction and its analysis. Then, Sect. 4 defines AD-PSI and proposes a concrete protocol, followed by some variants in Sect. 5. Section 6 constructs a B-SH-PSI protocol atop U-SH-PSI, and Sect. 7 demonstrates an AD-APSI protocol and its security proofs.

2 Related Work and Background

2.1 Private Set Intersection (PSI)

Private Set Intersection (PSI) in two-party computation is an interaction between *Client* and *Server* that computes the intersection of their private input sets. A long line of work on PSI can be classified according to the underlying cryptographic techniques: (1) Diffie-Hellman key agreement [6,19,44,56,73]; (2) RSA [18,20,21]; (3) cryptographic accumulators [3,20]; (4) oblivious transfer (or oblivious pseudorandom function) [10,40,42,46,50,60,63,65–70]; (5) Bloom filter [22,24,64,69]; (6) oblivious polynomial evaluation [16,30,32,41,49]; and (7) generic multiparty computation [13,24,43,55,69]. This paper considers the *one-sided* PSI where *Client* learns the result. Most efficient protocols incur $O(n)$ computation/communication costs, where n is the input set size.

2.2 PSI Variants

Some PSI variants reveal less information than the actual intersection. For example, PSI-CA [18,22,25,72,76] outputs only the cardinality of the intersection, and PSI-X [8] outputs a one-bit value reflecting whether the intersection is non-empty. On the other hand, some reveal more information, such as associated data for each intersecting element [20,78] or additional private computation results (e.g., sum or average) along with the intersection [45,52,55,57]. The latter is more interesting because of their realistic applications, such as statistical analysis for, e.g., advertisement conversion rate [45], of intersecting data.

2.3 PSI with Restrictions

Certain PSI variants place conditions for *Client* to obtain the result. For example, *threshold PSI* (t-PSI) reveals the intersection only if the cardinality of the intersection meets a *Server*-set threshold value [32,33,39,68,78,79], and its variants, such as t-PSI-CA or t-PSI-DT (also called, *threshold secret transfer)* [78], reveals the intersection or additional data only when the threshold restriction is met or reveals only the cardinality, otherwise. Zhao and Chow [78] extend this to PSI with a generic access structure so that *Client* can learn the result only when the intersection satisfies a certain structure. Also, they build the below/over t-PSI [79] such that *Client* can reconstruct the secret key used by *Server* only when the threshold condition is met, which inspires some steps in our protocols.

On the other hand, Bradley et. al. [6] first suggest the *Bounded-Size-Hiding-PSI* which restricts the *Client input*, i.e., *Client* learns the intersection only if the size of its *input* does not exceed a *Server*-set upper bound in the random oracle model, and later Cerulli et. al. [9] improve it to be secure in the standard model. Compared to the other PSI literature which naturally reveals the input set sizes during the computation, [6] and [9] additionally hide that cardinality information from each other. We note that there has been no PSI variant that places a lower bound (or both lower and upper bounds) on *Client* input.

2.4 PSI with Multiset Input

We now consider how current PSI protocols handle multisets. Note that adversary models in PSI literature do include malicious *input*. Loosely speaking, Honest-but-Curious (HbC) (a.k.a. semi-honest) adversaries try to learn as much as possible while honestly following the protocol, while malicious adversaries arbitrarily deviate from the protocol. However, according to Lindell and Pinkas [54], such adversaries can not be prevented from refusing to participate in a protocol, supplying arbitrary input, or prematurely aborting a protocol instance. Since PSI security is generally based on *sets*, *multisets* can be viewed as malicious inputs. PSI protocols do not offer security against multiset inputs. i.e., Security against malicious adversaries does not mean that multiset inputs are "automatically" handled.

It turns out that some PSI protocols are incompatible with multiset inputs because they assume set input, i.e., distinctness of all elements. For example, [5] and [43] obliviously sort elements and compare the adjacent elements to compute the intersection by checking for equality [43] or erasing each element once [5]. Thus, these protocols output incorrect results with multiset inputs. Furthermore, PSI protocols based on Cuckoo hashing [30,65,68,69] can encounter unexpected errors with multiset inputs. Cuckoo hashing maps each input element into a hash table using some hash functions such that each bin contains at most one element. Since the hash of the same input value is always the same, duplicates can cause an infinite loop (to find an available bin) or result in a waste of resources, e.g., repeating steps until a certain threshold and increasing the stash size.

There exist some PSI protocols that either enforce input element distinctness or are compatible with multiset inputs. For example, the party creates a polynomial that has roots on its input values in [16,32,49] to perform oblivious polynomial evaluation, which by nature filters the duplicates. [64] also guarantees the set input by a new data structure, called PaXoS, which disables encoding any non-distinct elements. On the other hand, security of [40,46] is unaffected by duplicates because it uses an oblivious pseudo-random function to obtain some (random-looking) numbers for its private elements, and then compare the received messages.

Our work focuses on PSI protocols that are incompatible with multiset inputs and suggests adding some simple steps to ensure element distinctness of private input so that they can work properly.

2.5 Zero-Knowledge Proofs

The notion of Zero-Knowledge Proof (ZKP) is first introduced by [35] which is the zero-knowledge interactive proof system. Informally, an *interactive proof system* for a language L is defined between a prover (Prv) and a verifier (Vrf) with a common input string x and unbiased coins, where Prv tries to convince Vrf that x is indeed in L while keeping their coin tosses private. It must be *complete*, i.e., for any $x \in L$, Vrf accepts, and *sound*, i.e., for any $x \notin L$,

Vrf rejects no matter what Prv does. The interactive proof is *zero-knowledge* if given only x, Vrf could simulate the entire protocol transcript by itself without interacting with Prv. A *proof-of-knowledge* [4,29] is an interactive proof where Prv tries to convince Vrf that it has "knowledge" tying the common input x, which requires the *completeness* and *knowledge extractibility* (stronger notion of *soundness*) properties. *Knowledge extractibility* (a.k.a.*validity*) is that for any Prv who can make Vrf accept its claim with non-negligible probability, there exists an efficient program K called *knowledge extractor*, such that K can interact with Prv and output a witness w of the statement $x \in L$. *Zero-Knowledge Proof of Knowledge (ZKPoK)* adds the *zero-knowledge* property on top of them. Compared to ZKP, ZKPoK keeps the one-bit information (whether $x \in L$ or not) private from Vrf, thus realizing "zero"-knowledge.

2.6 Homomorphic Encryption

Homomorphic encryption (HE) is a special type of encryption that allows users to perform certain arithmetic operations on encrypted data such that results are meaningfully reflected in the plaintext. It is called *Fully Homomorphic Encryption (FHE)* when a HE supports *both* unlimited addition and multiplication of ciphertexts. Whereas, a scheme that supports a limited number of operations of either type is called *Somewhat Homomorphic Encryption (SWHE)* and a scheme that supports only one operation type is called *Partially Homomorphic Encryption (PHE)*. There are many PHE schemes such as [14,15,17,26,36,48,58,61,62,71]. For example, ElGamal encryption scheme [26] is a well-known PHE supporting multiplication, and a variant of ElGamal [15] having g^m instead of m and Paillier [62] are well-known PHE schemes supporting addition.

3 Proving Element Distinctness

We first define ***P**roofs of **E**lement-**D**istinctness (PoED)* in the two-party settings where Prv proves element distinctness of its private input elements to Vrf. i.e., PoED is an interactive proof system, where Prv tries to convince Vrf that its input $\mathcal{C} := [c_1, ..., c_n]$ consists of distinct elements, without revealing any other information about each c_i. As a result, Vrf *accepts* or *rejects* the Prv's claim. Following the notation for ZKPoK introduced by [7], PoED is denoted as:

$$PK\{\mathcal{C} \mid e_i = f(c_i) \text{ for each } c_i \in \mathcal{C}, \text{ and } c_i \neq c_j \text{ for } \forall c_i, c_j \in \mathcal{C} \text{ such that } i \neq j\},$$

where f is a function that "hides" c_i so that Vrf does not learn any information about c_i from e_i, while it "binds" c_i to e_i so that Prv cannot change c_i once e_i is computed, e.g., via randomized encryption or cryptographic commitments.

Proving Element Distinctness with λ Puzzles

Public: $G = \langle g \rangle$, a group with operator $\cdot$, and λ: a sec. param.
pk : the public key of Prv, while correlated sk kept private

Prv $(\mathcal{C} = [c_1, ..., c_n])$		Vrf $(\perp)$
for $i = 1, ..., n$:		
$e_i := Enc_{pk}(c_i)$	$\xrightarrow{(e_1, ..., e_n)}$	**for** $k = 1, ..., \lambda$:
		$\pi_k \in_R \mathcal{P}_n$
		for $i = 1, ..., n$:
		$e_{i,k} := e_i \cdot Enc_{pk}(u)$
		$E_k := \pi_k(e_{1,k}, ..., e_{n,k})$
for $k = 1, ..., \lambda$:	$\xleftarrow{E_1, ..., E_\lambda}$	$key \leftarrow H(\pi_1, ..., \pi_\lambda)$
Determine π'_k s.t.		
$Dec_{sk}(E_k) = \pi'_k(\mathcal{C})$		
$key' \leftarrow H(\pi'_1, ..., \pi'_\lambda)$	$\xrightarrow{key'}$	**return** $Accept$, if $key = key'$
		return $Reject$, otherwise

Fig. 1. The PoED-puzzle Protocol. (Enc, Dec) can be any PHE over G. $\mathcal{P}_n$ is a set of random permutations for n elements. H is a cryptographic hash function that maps the arbitrary-length messages to κ-bit values. u is the unit element of the message space.

3.1 Puzzle-Based PoED Construction

The main idea starts from the well-known *two billiard balls* problem where Prv has two billiard balls and (honest) Vrf is color-blind. To convince Vrf that two balls have different colors, the following "*puzzle*" is repeated k times:

1. Prv puts a ball in each hand of Vrf
2. Vrf puts both hands behind its back and decides (at random) whether to switch the balls
3. Vrf shows the balls to Prv
4. Prv declares whether a switch occurred
5. If Prv answers incorrectly, Vrf concludes that Prv cheated

If Prv answers correctly k times, Vrf concludes that, with probability 2^{-k}, the balls have different colors.

Extending this problem to many balls, we construct a PoED protocol and call it *PoED-puzzle* protocol. Instead of the color-blind Vrf, Prv encrypts each element with its public key under an encryption scheme satisfying the ciphertext indistinguishability (IND) property. Since all IND-secure encryption schemes are non-deterministic, Prv can hide the information about the input elements.

To form the puzzles such that Vrf can generate while Prv can solve only when all input elements are distinct, PoED-puzzle needs a PHE scheme over a cyclic group G[2] of prime order with a generator g. i.e., Assume that each of Prv

[2] We sometimes denote G as a subgroup of $\mathbb{Z}_p^*$ whose prime order is known, which will be explicitly indicated in such case.

input values is a group element in G, or we can assume a deterministic map that maps each input value c_i to a group element in G. Since any PHE allows Vrf to re-randomize received ciphertexts by multiplying the encryption of the unit element u (under *Prv*'s public key), this computation gives a new ciphertext of the same plaintext without learning/requiring anything about the plaintext.

Finally, Vrf chooses a random permutation π from $\mathcal{P}_n$, the set of all permutations of length n, and shuffles the re-randomized ciphertexts with π, as if it "switches or not" in the two billiard balls problem. Once it receives a puzzle, *Prv* decrypts each ciphertext with its private key, determines the permutation π' that shuffles original elements to received elements, and forwards π' to Vrf. Vrf accepts if $\pi' = \pi$.

There is a probability that *Prv* can solve the puzzle without having all distinct elements. In the worst case when *Prv* uses only one duplicate, *Prv* can correctly solve the puzzle with 50% probability. To make the cheating probability low, the puzzle should be repeated λ times, such that $1/2^\lambda$ becomes negligible.

Since each puzzle is independent, Vrf can hash the puzzles (using a suitable cryptographic hash function H) and check this hash value, instead of repeating this three-message exchange multiple times for each puzzle. This reduces the number of communication rounds and associated delays. Figure 1 presents the PoED-puzzle protocol described above.

3.2 Analysis of PoED-Puzzle Protocol

Theorem 1. *Assuming an IND-secure PHE scheme (Enc, Dec) over a cyclic group G, a secure cryptographic hash function $H : \{0,1\}^* \rightarrow \{0,1\}^\kappa$, and the statistical security parameter λ, the PoED-puzzle protocol described in Sect. 3.1 is a secure PoED protocol.*

(*Sketch Proof*) *Completeness* is straightforward because only one correct permutation π exists for distinct elements, and honest *Prv* can easily determine π after decrypting the ciphertexts. For the *knowledge extractability*, the private key of the underlying encryption scheme can be seen as the witness. Suppose *Prv* does not know the private key. Then, by the IND and homomorphic property, re-randomized and shuffled ciphertexts from Vrf are indistinguishable from random strings in the ciphertext space. Furthermore, after decryption, the probability of having duplicates and solving the puzzle correctly is *at most* $2^{-\lambda}$ which is set to be negligible by the security parameter λ. Lastly, *zero-knowledgeness* naturally follows from the IND property, since all Vrf can observe are the ciphertexts encrypted by an IND secure PHE. □

Table 1 summarizes the computation and communication complexities of the PoED-puzzle protocol with λ puzzles. C is denoted by the ciphertext space of *Enc* and H generates a κ-bit hash result. Overall, both complexities are $O(\lambda n)$, where n is the *Prv* input size.

Table 1. Cost Analysis of the PoED-puzzle Protocol

Computation Cost			
Operation \ Entity	*Prv*		*Vrf*
	Offline	Online	Online
Encryption	n	0	λn
Decryption	0	λn	0
Modular multiplication	0	0	λn
Random permutations (of length n)	0	0	λ
Cryptographic hash (input length)	0	λn	λn
Equality check	0	0	1

Group	**Communication Cost**
C	$(\lambda + 1)n$
$\{0,1\}^\kappa$	1

4 PSI with Element Distinctness Check

Using the PoED as a building block, now we propose a new variant of PSI that requires all the input elements to be distinct, which we call *All-Distinct Private Set Intersection (AD-PSI).*

4.1 Adversary Model

Among the two parties participating in the computation, *Client* and *Server*, we consider *Server* to be HbC while *Client* can be malicious. This assumption is reasonable in real-life scenarios because *Server* is the one who provides the service to *Client* and multiple barriers (e.g., law/regulation, security systems for their data, and loss of trust deriving loss of customers) exist for them to be malicious. However, *Client* typically maintains less secure systems and much less data than *Server* so they may be eager to learn more from *Server*'s large dataset. Note that we consider a stronger guarantee than normal malicious security in PSI literature, as now we aim to enforce the input correctness for *Client*.

4.2 Definition of AD-PSI

We define AD-PSI directly, instead of defining PSI and adding features. We follow the definitions of client and server privacy in related work [31,32,34, 40]. Let $View^{\Pi}_{\mathcal{A}^*}(\mathcal{C}, \mathcal{S}, \lambda)$ denotes a random variable representing the view of adversary $\mathcal{A}^*$ (acting as either *Client* or *Server*) during an execution of Π on inputs $\mathcal{C}$ and $\mathcal{S}$ and the security parameter λ.

Definition 1 (All-Distinct Private Set Intersection (AD-PSI)). *consists of two algorithms:* {*Setup, Interaction*}, *where:*

- *Setup: an algorithm selecting global/public parameters;*
- *Interaction: a protocol between Client and Server on respective inputs: a multiset* $\mathcal{C} = [c_1, ..., c_n]$ *and a set* $\mathcal{S} = \{s_1, ..., s_m\}$*, resulting in Client obtaining the intersection of the two inputs;*

An AD-PSI scheme satisfies the following properties:

- *Correctness: At the end of Interaction, Client outputs the exact intersection of two inputs, only when the elements in* $\mathcal{C}$ *are all distinct. It outputs* $\perp$*, o.w.*
- *Server Privacy: For every PPT adversary* $\mathcal{A}^*$ *acting as Client, we say that a AD-PSI scheme* Π *guarantees the server privacy if there exists a PPT algorithm* P_C *such that*

$$\{P_C(\mathcal{C}, \mathcal{C} \cap \mathcal{S}, \lambda)\}_{(\mathcal{C},\mathcal{S},\lambda)} \stackrel{c}{\approx} \{View^{\Pi}_{\mathcal{A}^*}(\mathcal{C}, \mathcal{S}, \lambda)\}_{(\mathcal{C},\mathcal{S},\lambda)}$$

  i.e., on each possible pair of inputs $(\mathcal{C}, \mathcal{S}, \lambda)$*, Client's view can be efficiently simulated by* P_C *on input* $(\mathcal{C}, \mathcal{C} \cap \mathcal{S}, \lambda)$*.*
- *Client Privacy: For every PPT adversary* $\mathcal{A}^*$ *acting as Server, we say that a AD-PSI scheme* Π *guarantees the client privacy if there exists a PPT algorithm* P_S *such that*

$$\{P_S(\mathcal{S}, \lambda)\}_{(\mathcal{C},\mathcal{S},\lambda)} \stackrel{c}{\approx} \{View^{\Pi}_{\mathcal{A}^*}(\mathcal{C}, \mathcal{S}, \lambda)\}_{(\mathcal{C},\mathcal{S},\lambda)}$$

  i.e., on each possible pair of inputs $(\mathcal{C}, \mathcal{S}, \lambda)$*, Server's view can be efficiently simulated by* P_S *on input* $(\mathcal{S}, \lambda)$*.*

We note that the security definition above is equivalent to the generic "real-vs-ideal" world simulation definition in the semi-honest model, as shown in [34], with the ideal functionality $\mathcal{F}$ below (Fig. 2):

1. Wait for an input multiset $\mathcal{C} = [c_1, .., c_n]$ from *Client*.
2. Wait for an input set $\mathcal{S} = \{s_1, ..., s_m\}$ from *Server*.
3. Give output $(|\mathcal{S}|, \mathcal{C} \cap \mathcal{S})$ to *Client* if $\mathcal{C}$ includes all distinct elements, or output $(|\mathcal{S}|)$, otherwise.
4. Give output $(|\mathcal{C}|)$ to *Server*.

Fig. 2. Ideal Functionality $\mathcal{F}$ for AD-PSI

According to the definition above, we propose a construction using PoED-puzzle protocol, so-called *AD-PSI-puzzle*, in the following section.

4.3 A Construction for AD-PSI Based on PoED-puzzle

AD-PSI-puzzle protocol starts with the PoED-puzzle protocol, i.e., *Client* encrypts each input element in G (or the mapped values for each input element to G with a public map) under a PHE and sends the ciphertexts to *Server*, and *Server* generates a secret key *key*, derived from multiple puzzles that shuffle re-randomized ciphertexts with random permutations. Note that now the underlying PHE scheme needs to be multiplicatively homomorphic (instead of any PHE) for the correct computation below.

AD-PSI based on PoED-puzzle (AD-PSI-puzzle)

Public: (p, g, h, G) where $G = \langle g \rangle$, a subgroup of $\mathbb{Z}_p^*$ of prime order q,

λ : statistical security parameter, pk : Prv's public key,

Private: sk : Prv's secret key correlated to pk

Client $(\mathcal{C} = [c_1, ..., c_n])$		Server $(\mathcal{S} = \{s_1, ..., s_m\})$
for $i = 1, ..., n$:		
$e_i := Enc_{pk}(c_i)$	$\xrightarrow{(e_1, ..., e_n)}$	**for** $k = 1, ..., \lambda$:
		$\pi_k \in_R \mathcal{P}_n$
		for $i = 1, ..., n$:
		$e_{i,k} := e_i \cdot Enc_{pk}(1)$
		$E_k := \pi_k(e_{1,k}, ..., e_{n,k})$
		$key \leftarrow H(\pi_1, ..., \pi_\lambda)$
		$R \in_R \mathbb{Z}_p^*$
		for $i = 1, ..., n$:
		$\hat{e_i} := e_i^R (= e_i \cdot ... \cdot e_i)$
		for $j = 1, ..., m$:
for $k = 1, ..., \lambda$:	$\xleftarrow[(t_1, ..., t_m)]{E_1, ..., E_\lambda, (\hat{e_1}, ..., \hat{e_n}),}$	$t_j := SEnc(key, H'(s_j^R))$
Determine π'_k s.t.		
$Dec_{sk}(E_k) = \pi'_k(\mathcal{C})$		
$key' \leftarrow H(\pi'_1, ..., \pi'_\lambda)$		
for $j = 1, ..., m$: $t'_j := SDec(key', t_j)$		
for $i = 1, ..., n$: $d_i := H'(\ Dec_{sk}(\hat{e_i}))$		
return $\{c_i \in \mathcal{C} \mid d_i \in \{t'_1, ..., t'_m\}\}$		

Fig. 3. AD-PSI-puzzle Protocol. (Enc, Dec) is a multiplicative PHE over G and $(SEnc, SDec)$ can be any symmetric encryption scheme over a key space $\{0,1\}^\kappa$. $\mathcal{P}_n$ and H are same as Fig. 1

For computing the intersection without revealing the other elements, *Server* hides *Client*'s ciphertexts and its own input values with the same random element $R \in \mathbb{Z}_p^*$. i.e., *Server* first homomorphically exponentiates *Client* elements with R by e_i^R, which is defined by R homomorphic operations, for each $e_i = Enc(c_i), \forall i$ (by multiplying e_i R times or directly exponentiating R[3]). For its own input values, *Server* computes s_j^R for each $s_j \in \mathcal{S}$ so that if some c_i and

[3] Usually, exponentiation of the underlying plaintext can be done more efficiently than multiplying the ciphertext R times. For example, in ElGamal, encryption of x is $Enc(x) = (g^r, xh^r)$ for some random r, and exponentiating to c can be done either $Enc(x) \cdot ... \cdot Enc(x) = (g^R, x^c h^R) = Enc(x^c)$ or $Enc(x)^c = (g^{cr}, x^c h^{cr}) = Enc(x^c)$.

s_j match, then the randomized c_i^R and s_j^R can also be matched. Then, it hashes each s_j^R using a cryptographic hash function H' and encrypts them under a symmetric encryption scheme with a key key, i.e., $t_j := SEnc(key, H'(s_j^R))$. Thus, unless $Client$ can derive the right key, it cannot decrypt/learn any information about $Server$ elements.

When receiving the messages from $Server$, $Client$ first derives the symmetric key key' by solving all the puzzles, as in PoED-puzzle. Then using the derived key, $Client$ decrypt t_j's, obtains $\{t'_j := H'(s_j^R)\}_j$, and compares them with $d'_i s$, the hash values of the decryption of re-randomized ciphertexts, i.e., $d_i := H'(c_i^R)$ for all i. Finally, $Client$ outputs all c_i's such that d_i matches for some t_j.

The protocol described above is depicted in Fig. 3. Due to the space limit, we show the full security proofs of the following theorem in Appendix A.

Theorem 2. *Assuming the hardness of the decisional Diffie-Hellman problem, the protocol described in Fig. 3 is a secure AD-PSI scheme, satisfying the Definition 1 in ROM.*

Though we define AD-PSI such that it does not reveal whether $\mathcal{C}$ satisfies the element distinctness or not to $Server$, this one-bit information may be favored by $Server$ to save its computing resources. We discuss this alternative definition and an idea of modifying the AD-PSI-puzzle protocol in the following section.

4.4 Alternative AD-PSI and Modified Construction

Checking the distinctness of $\mathcal{C}$ before proceeding to the next steps may be preferable by $Server$ with a large set $\mathcal{S}$ because the rest computation cost is linear to $|\mathcal{S}|$. Whereas, $Client$ may be reluctant as it reveals whether $Client$ used all distinct elements to $Server$, i.e., a trade-off between client privacy and server efficiency. For this alternative design, AD-PSI *Correctness* can be defined with $Server$ outputs $(|\mathcal{C}|, b)$ in Definition 1 instead, where b is a boolean result of whether $\mathcal{C}$ satisfies the element distinctness. Likewise, $\mathcal{F}$ is modified as below (Fig. 4):

1. Wait for an input multiset $\mathcal{C} = [c_1, .., c_n]$ from *Client*.
   Abort if $\mathcal{C}$ includes any duplicates.
2. Wait for an input set $\mathcal{S} = \{s_1, ..., s_m\}$ from $Server$.
3. Give output $(|\mathcal{S}|, \mathcal{C} \cap \mathcal{S})$ to *Client*.
4. Give output $(|\mathcal{C}|)$ to $Server$.

Fig. 4. Ideal Functionality $\mathcal{F}$ for Alternative AD-PSI

To meet this definition, the AD-PSI-puzzle protocol (in Fig. 3) can be modified as in Fig. 5. i.e., Before the intersection computation phase, $Server$ first sends all the puzzles to *Client* and proceeds to the next phase only if *Client* corrects all puzzles. Although this modification increases the number of communication rounds, *Server* can save its computation resources for the clients who do not cheat and have enough elements (by size checking) and use this one-bit information in another application (See Sect. 6).

AD-PSI-puzzle Alternative

Client ($\mathcal{C} = [c_1, ..., c_n]$)		*Server* ($\mathcal{S} = \{s_1, ..., s_m\}$)
for $i = 1, ..., n$:		
$e_i := Enc_{pk}(c_i)$	$\xrightarrow{(e_1, ..., e_n)}$	**for** $k = 1, ..., \lambda$:
		$\pi_k \in_R \mathcal{P}_n$
		for $i = 1, ..., n$:
		$e_{i,k} := e_i \cdot Enc_{pk}(1)$
for $k = 1, ..., \lambda$:	$\xleftarrow{E_1, ..., E_\lambda}$	$E_k := \pi_k(e_{1,k}, ..., e_{n,k})$
π'_k s.t. $Dec_{sk}(E_k) = \pi'_k(\mathcal{C})$		$key \leftarrow H(\pi_1, ..., \pi_\lambda)$
$key' \leftarrow H(\pi'_1, ..., \pi'_\lambda)$	$\xrightarrow{key'}$	**Abort** if $key' \neq key$
		$R \in_R \mathbb{Z}_p^*$
		$\hat{e_i} := e_i^R, \forall i \in [1, n]$
for $i = 1, ..., n$:	$\xleftarrow{\{\hat{e_i}\}_i, \{t_j\}_j,}$	$t_j := H'(s_j^R), \forall j \in [1, m]$
$d_i := H'(Dec(\hat{e_i}))$		
return $\{c_i \in \mathcal{C} \mid d_i \in \{t_1, ..., t_m\}\}$		

Fig. 5. Alternative AD-PSI Protocol

Table 2 summarizes the computation and communication complexities of the AD-PSI-puzzle protocols with λ puzzles. We denote the cost of the alternative protocol in parentheses only when it has a different cost from the original one. HE denotes the partial homomorphic encryption scheme and SE denotes the symmetric encryption scheme used in the protocol(s). C_Π represents the ciphertext space of a scheme Π and cryptographic hash functions H and H' generate a κ-bit and κ'-bit hash result, respectively. Overall, both complexities are $O(\lambda n + m)$, where n is the *Client* input size (including duplicates, if any) and m is the *Server* input size.

5 AD-PSI Variants

As mentioned earlier in Sects. 1 and 2.4, duplication can be more problematic in PSI variants that give additional/restricted information. In this section, we further discuss how duplication can leak more information, and propose a solution for each variant using AD-PSI. Although the solutions are simple, we provide the figures for each protocol in Appendix B for better presentation.

Table 2. Cost Analysis of AD-PSI-puzzle Protocols. We present the cost of the alternative protocol in $(\cdot)$ only when it is different from the original cost.

Computation Cost of AD-PSI-puzzle (and its alternative)				
Operation Entity		*Client*		*Server*
		Offline	Online	Online
HE.Encryption		n	0	λn
HE.Decryption		0	$(\lambda+1)n$	0
Modular Multiplication		0	0	$(\lambda+R)n$
Random number generation (in $\mathbb{Z}_p^*$)		0	0	1
Random permutations (of length n)		0	0	λ
Cryptographic hash	of input length λn	0	1	1
	of input length $\|\mathcal{M}\|$	0	n	m
Equality check		0	0	0 (1)
Involvement check (i.e., if $a \in A$)		0	n	0
SE.Encryption		0	0	m (0)
SE.Decryption		0	m (0)	0

Group	Communication Cost
$C_{\mathtt{HE}}$	$(\lambda+2)n$
$C_{\mathtt{SE}}$	m
$\{0,1\}^{\kappa}$	0 (1)
$\{0,1\}^{\kappa'}$	0 (m)
#(rounds)	1 (2)

Note that we follow the convention in PSI literature and do not consider the information leakage after multiple executions which will naturally reveal more than the one they are supposed to reveal in a single execution. For example, when *Client* deliberately adjusts its input elements to PSI-X and the protocol outputs 'No' in the previous rounds and 'Yes' in the next round, then *Client* learns that the exact element added in the last round is in the *Server* set. Though this is interesting, we consider it as a future work.

5.1 PSI-CA with Element Distinctness (AD-PSI-CA)

Recall that PSI-CA outputs only the cardinality of the intersection set. Suppose *Client* uses a single element as input to PSI-CA. In that case, although it is not malicious behavior, *Client* can learn if that exact element is in $\mathcal{S}$, which is more information than it is supposed to learn. Furthermore, by repeating PSI-CA with different single elements, it can eventually learn the intersection set, or the entire $\mathcal{S}$ if the message space is small enough. To prevent this, *Server* may want to restrict the minimum input set size as l and check if $|\mathcal{C}| > l$ during the computation phase.

However, *Client* still can bypass this simple check by duplicating a single element n times where n is greater than l. Although *Server* does not abort as the *Client* set size n is larger than l, the PSI-CA result with this input will be either '0' or '1' which reveals if the single element is in $\mathcal{S}$ or not. Thus, the simple size check is not enough, and *Server* needs a way to check the element distinctness of $\mathcal{C}$, which we call *AD-PSI-Cardinality (AD-PSI-CA)*.

The definition of AD-PSI-CA is similar to the one of AD-PSI, except that $(|\mathcal{S}|, |\mathcal{S} \cap \mathcal{C}|)$ is the *Client* output for correctness, and what the ideal functionality gives to *Client* as output. Adding this feature can be simply done by modifying the AD-PSI-puzzle protocol: *Server* additionally chooses a random permutation π and sends the permuted ciphertexts $\hat{e_i} := e^R_{\pi(i)}$ instead of $\hat{e_i} := e^R_i$. Since the ciphertexts are randomized with R by *Server*, and *Client* does not know π, now *Client* cannot match the d_i's to the original c_i's. Furthermore, AD-PSI-puzzle guarantees that *Client* cannot solve the puzzle correctly with overwhelming probability when using duplicated inputs. Therefore, *Client* learns $|\mathcal{C} \cap \mathcal{S}|$, only when it uses all distinct input elements.

5.2 PSI-X with Element Distinctness (AD-PSI-X)

PSI-X outputs very limited information, only the boolean result of whether the intersection of two private input sets is non-empty. Likewise, although *Server* decides on a lower-bound restriction on the size of $\mathcal{C}$, *Client* can obtain more information than the boolean result by using a small input set, because if the result is '1' (i.e., intersection exists), each element is in $\mathcal{S}$ with the probability of $1/|\mathcal{C}|$. *Server*, thus, may have more motivation to restrict the size of $\mathcal{C}$ to reduce this probability.

One way to construct a AD-PSI-Existence (AD-PSI-X) protocol is to add our PoED phase to the FHE-based PSI-X protocol. The basic idea of the FHE-based PSI-X protocol is to encrypt each element under an FHE, compute the subtraction of every pair of $\mathcal{C}$ and $\mathcal{S}$, and multiply all subtractions (with a random number) so that the decryption result can be zero if any of the pairs match. i.e., It computes the encryption of $R \cdot \Pi_{i,j}(c_i - s_j)$ for a random R, which becomes the encryption of zero if any pair of c_i and s_j matches. The recent benchmark [37] on FHE libraries shows that the addition can be done within 100 ms while multiplication requires about 1 s over the integer encoding in many libraries, such as Lattigo [2], PALISADE [1], SEAL [53], and TFHE [12]. The PoED phase can be easily added: *Server* can add the shuffling phase before the PSI-X steps, and just encrypt the final message with the key derived from the puzzles as in the PoED-puzzle protocol.

5.3 PSI-DT with Element Distinctness (AD-PSI-DT)

PSI-DT transfers additional data associated with the intersecting elements. Since this gives more data other than the intersection, when *Server* restricts the *Client* input size, *Client* without enough elements may have more motivation to cheat and bypass the restriction to obtain them. AD-PSI with data transfer (AD-PSI-DT) is defined similarly to AD-PSI, except it outputs $(|\mathcal{S}|, I := \mathcal{S} \cap \mathcal{C}, \{D_j\}_{s_j \in I})$ for *Client*.

An AD-PSI-DT protocol can be constructed as follows: It is the same as AD-PSI-puzzle protocol until randomizing *Client* ciphertexts. Then, for *Server* input elements, *Server* computes one more hash (or a one-way function) H'' and encrypts them under the key derived from the puzzles, i.e., $t_j := SEnc(key, H''(s'_j))$, where $s'_j := H'(s_j^R)$. For the associated data to transfer, *Server* encrypts each D_j using the pre-image of H'', i.e., $D'_j := SEnc(s'_j, D_j)$, and sends them along with the other messages. This prevents *Client* from trying all decryption results as key to decrypt the associated data.

Receiving the messages from *Server*, *Client* performs the same steps to learn the intersection as AD-PSI. To obtain the associated data, *Client* uses the matching d_i's for its own (randomized) values to decrypt and get the data. Security for the non-intersecting elements follows the security of AD-PSI, and the one-way property of H'' and the security of the underlying symmetric encryption scheme guarantee the security of the associated data.

6 Completing Bounded-Size-Hiding-PSI

As mentioned in Sect. 2.3, *Bounded-Size-Hiding-PSI* was introduced in [6], extending the concept of *Size-Hiding-PSI (SH-PSI)* from [3] by adding an upper bound on the size of *Client* input set $\mathcal{C}$, $|\mathcal{C}|$. For clarification, we denote this primitive by *Upper-bounded-SH-PSI (U-SH-PSI)*. Now we propose a *Bounded-Size-Hiding-PSI (B-SH-PSI) protocol* with **complete, both lower and upper, bounds on** $|\mathcal{C}|$.

In B-SH-PSI, *Server* publishes its restriction rules, L for lower bound and U for upper bound, for $|\mathcal{C}|$. i.e., *Server* wants *Client* to obtain the intersection only when $L \leq |\mathcal{C}| \leq U$. On the other hand, *Client* wants to hide its input size as well as any information about its elements from *Server*. Figure 6 shows the ideal functionality $\mathcal{F}_B$ for B-SH-PSI described above.

1. Wait for input $\mathcal{C} = [c_1, ..., c_n]$ from *Client*.
2. Wait for input $\mathcal{S} = \{s_1, ..., s_m\}$ from *Server*.
3. Abort if $\mathcal{C}$ does not contain at least L distinct elements, or $|\mathcal{C}| > U$. Give the output $(|\mathcal{S}|, \mathcal{C} \cap \mathcal{S})$ to *Client* only if $L \leq |\mathcal{C}| \leq U$.
4. Give output b to *Server*, where b is the boolean value of whether $|\mathcal{C}| \geq L$.

Fig. 6. Ideal Functionality $\mathcal{F}_B$ for B-SH-PSI

We construct a B-SH-PSI protocol using U-SH-PSI and the AD-PSI-puzzle protocols as building blocks, and briefly present it in Fig. 7. To enforce that *Client* cannot learn any information about the intersection without satisfying both upper- and lower-bound requirements, we need the alternative AD-PSI-puzzle protocol (in Sect. 4.4) that reveals the one-bit information if $\mathcal{C}$ satisfies the lower-bound or not.

Recall that *Client* cannot obtain the next message from *Server* with overwhelming probability if $\mathcal{C}_L$ includes any duplicates. Also, since *Server* can see the size of $\mathcal{C}_L$ during the AD-PSI phase, it can just abort (or send an error message to *Client*) if $\mathcal{C}_L$ does not satisfy the lower bound L. Otherwise, *Server* stores this size $|\mathcal{C}_L|$ and sends some puzzles for AD-PSI to *Client*. The honest *Client* can enclose the first message (the accumulator for the rest of the elements in $\mathcal{C}$, i.e., $\mathcal{C}^* := \mathcal{C} \setminus \mathcal{C}_L$), $\mathtt{msg}_1$, along with the *key'* derived from the given puzzles. If *key'* is correct, *Server* proceeds to the steps for U-SH-PSI using $\mathtt{msg}_1$ and the upper bound, $U' := (U - |\mathcal{C}_L|)$, or aborts, otherwise. *Client* obtains $I_1 := \mathcal{C}_L \cap \mathcal{S}$ from the response for AD-PSI (denoted by $\mathtt{msg}_2$ in Fig. 7), and $I_2 := \mathcal{C}^* \cap \mathcal{S}$ from the one for U-SH-PSI (denoted by $\mathtt{msg}_3$ in Fig. 7), which are combined to the final result, $I := I_1 \cup I_2$.

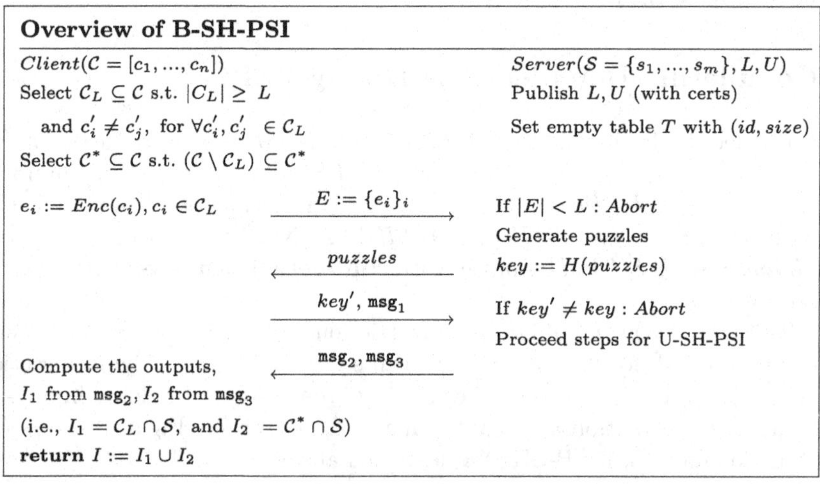

Fig. 7. Idea of B-SH-PSI with input bound $[L, U]$. $\mathtt{msg}_1$ and $\mathtt{msg}_3$ denote the first and responding messages for the U-SH-PSI protocol, whereas the others denote the messages for the alternative AD-PSI-puzzle protocol in Fig. 5

The security and efficiency of the idea above rely on the ones of underlying AD-PSI and U-SH-PSI protocols. The AD-PSI phase guarantees that $\mathcal{C}$ satisfies the lower bound L. Although there is no duplicate check in the U-SH-PSI phase, *Client* does not have the motivation for duplicating the elements because *Client* can learn the result only when $|\mathcal{C}^*| \leq U'$ (i.e., duplicates limit *Client* more, especially when $|\mathcal{C}|$ is close to U).

7 Authorized PSI with Element Distinctness

So far, we have seen multiple PSI and its variant protocols that check the duplicity of input values. However, as noted in Sect. 1, malicious *Client* can still bypass these duplicity checks by generating random inputs instead of duplicating valid inputs. And what is the meaning of "valid" inputs? To examine if *Client* uses valid inputs, including a trusted third party (TTP) who signs on valid inputs and later audits and punishes any invalid inputs is inevitable. i.e., Authorized PSI (APSI) that not only checks the element distinctness but also the validity of the input values. This section presents two versions of APSI: (v1) *stateful APSI*, where TTP tracks *Client* input values, and (v2) *stateless APSI*, where TTP does not save/track any information about *Client* input values.

7.1 AD-APSI Definition

Adopting the definitions of APSI from the related work [19,20,74,77] and referring to the definitions of general two-party computation from [28,34], secure AD-APSI can be defined as below. Let $REAL^{\Pi}_{\mathcal{A}(z),P}(C,S,\lambda)$ be the output of honest party and the adversary $\mathcal{A}$ corrupting P (either *Client* or *Server*) after a real execution of an AD-APSI protocol Π, where *Client* has input (potentially multi)set $\mathcal{C}$, *Server* has input set $\mathcal{S}$, $\mathcal{A}$ has auxiliary input z, and the security parameter is λ. Let $IDEAL^{\mathcal{F}}_{Sim(z),P}(\mathcal{C},\mathcal{S},\lambda)$ be the analogous distribution in an ideal execution with a trusted party who computes the ideal functionality $\mathcal{F}$ defined below.

Definition 2 (All-Distinct Authorized PSI (AD-APSI)). *is a tuple of three algorithms: {Setup, Authorize, Interaction}, where*

- *Setup: an algorithm selecting global/public parameters;*
- *Authorize: a protocol between Client and TTP resulting in Client committing to its input,* $\mathcal{C} = [c_1, ..., c_n]$*, and TTP issuing authorizations, one for each element of* $\mathcal{C}$*; and*
- *Interaction: a protocol between Client and Server on respective inputs: a (multi)set* $\mathcal{C}$ *and a set* $\mathcal{S}$*, resulting in Client obtaining the intersection of two inputs;*

An AD-APSI scheme satisfies the following properties:

- *Correctness: At the end of Interaction, Client outputs the exact intersection of two inputs, only when the elements in* $\mathcal{C}$ *are all distinct and authorized by TTP. Otherwise, Client outputs* $\perp$*;*
- *Server Privacy: Client learns no information about the subset of* $\mathcal{S}$ *that is not in the intersection, except its size. More formally, an AD-APSI scheme securely realizes the server privacy in the presence of malicious adversaries corrupting Client if for every real-world adversary* $\mathcal{A}$*, there exists a simulator Sim such that, for every* $\mathcal{C}$*,* $\mathcal{S}$*, and auxiliary input* z*,*

$$\{REAL^{\Pi}_{\mathcal{A}(z),Client}(\mathcal{C},\mathcal{S},\lambda)\}_{\lambda} \overset{c}{\approx} \{IDEAL^{\mathcal{F}}_{Sim(z),Client}(\mathcal{C},\mathcal{S},\lambda)\}_{\lambda}$$

– *Client Privacy: Server learns no information about Client input elements, except its size, authorization status, and element distinctness. More formally, an AD-APSI scheme securely realizes the client privacy in the presence of malicious adversaries corrupting Server if for every real-world adversary $\mathcal{A}$, there exists a simulator Sim such that, for every $\mathcal{C}$, $\mathcal{S}$, and z,*

$$\{REAL^{\Pi}_{\mathcal{A}(z),Server}(\mathcal{C},\mathcal{S},\lambda)\}_\lambda \overset{c}{\approx} \{IDEAL^{\mathcal{F}}_{Sim(z),Server}(\mathcal{C},\mathcal{S},\lambda)\}_\lambda$$

where the ideal functionality $\mathcal{F}$ is defined as follows:

– `Authorize` *: ($\mathcal{F}$ forwards the messages between Client and TTP and remembers the authorized elements for Client)*
  1. *Wait for an authorization request from Client, requesting TTP to authorize an element c*
  2. *Forward the request to TTP who either accepts or rejects it*
  3. *If TTP accepts, it forwards the messages from TTP to Client and remembers that TTP has authorized c for Client. Otherwise, it replies* `abort` *to Client*

– `Interaction` *: ($\mathcal{F}$ receives input elements from Client and Server and outputs the intersection to Client, only when Client inputs are all distinct and authorized, while giving Client input size and verification result (for authorization and duplication) to Server)*
  1. *Wait for an input (multi)set $\mathcal{C} = [c_1, .., c_n]$ from Client*
  2. *Wait for an input set $\mathcal{S} = \{s_1, ..., s_m\}$ from Server*
  3. *While sending $|\mathcal{C}|$ to Server, send* `abort` *to Client if $\mathcal{C}$ includes (1) any unauthorized element, or (2) duplicated elements. Otherwise, compute the intersection of $\mathcal{C}$ and $\mathcal{S}$ and send $(|\mathcal{S}|, \mathcal{C} \cap \mathcal{S})$ to Client. It also sends b to Server, where b is the result(s) for verifying the existence of (1) (and (2) in stateless version) above with their cardinality(ies).*

For clear notation, we denote the functionalities above as $\mathcal{F}_{\texttt{Auth}}$ and $\mathcal{F}_\cap$.

7.2 AD-APSI Construction

The main idea is from the double spending detection in [11]. i.e., TTP first divides each input value into two factors, where these factors are not revealed to anyone except *Client*. For the stateful TTP, the factors can be computed by choosing a random value in $\mathbb{Z}_p^*$ as the first factor and calculating the rest. For the stateless TTP, the first factor is computed so that it is unique per element value, e.g., with a pseudo-random function (under TTP's secret key) for each element in $\mathcal{C}$, and the second factor is calculated by dividing the element with the first factor. Then, the TTP signs a message such that it can be easily re-computed by a third party while not revealing each factor so that anyone with the message can verify the signature with the TTP's public key.

In the online phase, *Client* sends $G_\mathcal{C}$, the pre-computed values that effectively hide two factors for each input value, and Σ, all the signatures given by TTP. Then, *Server* first verifies each signature with a newly-computed message with

$G_{\mathcal{C}}$ and aborts if any signature verification fails. In the stateless TTP version, *Server* additionally checks if there are any same elements in $G_{\mathcal{C}}$ and aborts if so. If all passed, *Server* now proceeds to the intersection computation phase, similar to the other PSI protocols. i.e., It first chooses a random number R to hide its elements, and computes t_j, which can be also pre-computed. Then, *Server* exponentiates each $g^{e_{i,1}}$ to the same R so that *Client* can compute the same form, compare, and obtain the intersection result. Figure 8 shows the aforementioned offline and online phases with stateful and stateless TTP options, with an example form of message, $m_i := H(g^{e_{i,1}}, g^{e_{i,2}})$ for each $c_i = e_{i,1} * e_{i,2} \pmod p$ in $\mathcal{C}$. In the offline phase, *Client* can pre-compute $G_{\mathcal{C}}$ once it receives all the factors from TTP, or TTP can also send $G_{\mathcal{C}}$ along with the others, which is the trade-off between communication cost and *Client*'s computation cost.

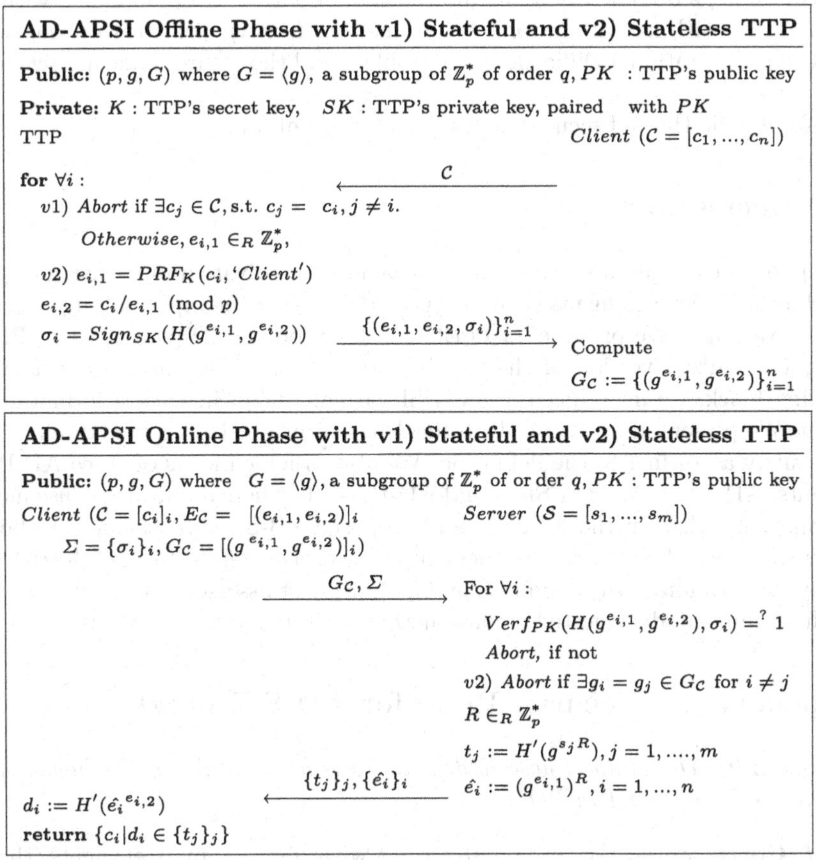

AD-APSI Offline Phase with v1) Stateful and v2) Stateless TTP

Public: (p, g, G) where $G = \langle g \rangle$, a subgroup of $\mathbb{Z}_p^*$ of order q, PK : TTP's public key

Private: K : TTP's secret key, SK : TTP's private key, paired with PK

TTP — *Client* $(\mathcal{C} = [c_1, ..., c_n])$

$\xleftarrow{\quad \mathcal{C} \quad}$

for $\forall i$:

v1) *Abort* if $\exists c_j \in \mathcal{C}$, s.t. $c_j = c_i, j \neq i$.

Otherwise, $e_{i,1} \in_R \mathbb{Z}_p^*$,

v2) $e_{i,1} = PRF_K(c_i, \text{'Client'})$

$e_{i,2} = c_i / e_{i,1} \pmod p$

$\sigma_i = Sign_{SK}(H(g^{e_{i,1}}, g^{e_{i,2}}))$ $\xrightarrow{\{(e_{i,1}, e_{i,2}, \sigma_i)\}_{i=1}^n}$ Compute

$G_{\mathcal{C}} := \{(g^{e_{i,1}}, g^{e_{i,2}})\}_{i=1}^n$

AD-APSI Online Phase with v1) Stateful and v2) Stateless TTP

Public: (p, g, G) where $G = \langle g \rangle$, a subgroup of $\mathbb{Z}_p^*$ of order q, PK : TTP's public key

Client $(\mathcal{C} = [c_i]_i, E_{\mathcal{C}} = [(e_{i,1}, e_{i,2})]_i$ — *Server* $(\mathcal{S} = [s_1, ..., s_m])$

$\Sigma = \{\sigma_i\}_i, G_{\mathcal{C}} = [(g^{e_{i,1}}, g^{e_{i,2}})]_i)$

$\xrightarrow{\quad G_{\mathcal{C}}, \Sigma \quad}$

For $\forall i$:

$Verf_{PK}(H(g^{e_{i,1}}, g^{e_{i,2}}), \sigma_i) \stackrel{?}{=} 1$

Abort, if not

v2) *Abort* if $\exists g_i = g_j \in G_{\mathcal{C}}$ for $i \neq j$

$R \in_R \mathbb{Z}_p^*$

$t_j := H'(g^{s_j R}), j = 1, ..., m$

$\xleftarrow{\quad \{t_j\}_j, \{\hat{e_i}\}_i \quad}$ $\hat{e_i} := (g^{e_{i,1}})^R, i = 1, ..., n$

$d_i := H'(\hat{e_i}^{e_{i,2}})$

return $\{c_i | d_i \in \{t_j\}_j\}$

Fig. 8. All-Distinct Authorized PSI (AD-APSI) scheme. PRF is a pseudo-random function, $(Sign, Verf)$ is a digital signature scheme over $\{0,1\}^\kappa$, and H, H' are cryptographic hash functions.

7.3 Security Analysis

Theorem 3. *The protocol described in Sect. 7.2 is a secure AD-APSI scheme, satisfying Definition 2 in ROM.*

(*Sketch proof*) Duplicated elements get caught by either the stateful TTP or *Server* (when TTP is stateless) because the $G_{\mathcal{C}}$ element is always the same for an input value. Also, *Server* detects if any unauthorized elements are used via signature verification. For the honest $\mathcal{C}$ (i.e., with all authorized and distinct elements), *Client* outputs the exact intersection of $\mathcal{C}$ and $\mathcal{S}$ because, for $c_i = s_j$,

$$d_i := H(\hat{e}_i^{e_{i,2}}) = H((g^{e_{i,1}R})^{e_{i,2}}) = H(g^{c_i R}) = H(g^{s_j R}) = t_j$$

Server responds only when all signature verification and duplication checks are passed, and t_j's do not reveal any information about s_j by randomizing with R and hashing with a cryptographic hash function. Lastly, client privacy depends on both computational Diffie-Hellman problem and the secure signature scheme. □

We provide the full security analysis of Theorem 3 in Appendix C.

8 Conclusion

This paper investigated two malicious behaviors for private input – using duplicated and spurious elements – and suggested checking the input validity in PSI and its variants. We proposed a PoED construction, PoED-puzzle, using PHE and a generalized version of the two billiard balls problem, and using it as a building block, we introduced a new PSI variant, AD-PSI, with a formal definition. We presented an AD-PSI protocol based on PoED-puzzle and analyzed its security according to the definition. We also provided ideas of three AD-PSI variants, AD-PSI-CA, AD-PSI-X, and AD-PSI-DT, where duplicates cause more information leakage without PoED, and proposed a B-SH-PSI scheme with both upper and lower bounds on the client input size, using AD-PSI and U-SH-PSI. Lastly, we formalized the definition of AD-APSI that assesses both misbehaviors on client input and suggested a construction with its security analysis.

Appendix A Security Proof for AD-PSI-puzzle

Theorem 2. *The protocol described in Fig. 3 is a secure AD-PSI scheme, satisfying the Definition 1 in ROM.*

Proof. **Correctness:** For an honest *Client* with distinct input elements, there exists only one permutation π_k such that $\pi_k(\mathcal{C}) = Dec(E_k)$. This is because the decryption results remain the same after the re-randomization due to the homomorphic property of the ElGamal scheme on multiplication. Thus, honest *Client* derives the same permutations as the ones *Server* used and the derived *key'*, the hash of these permutations, is equal to *key*. *Client* gets the

Server's tags, $\{t'_j = H'(s_j^R)\}_j$ by symmetric-decrypting each of them. Since $d_i = H'(Dec(\hat{e}_i)) = H'(Dec(e_i^R)) = H'(c_i^R)$, with overwhelming probability (due to the collision resistance of the cryptographic hash functions), we have $t'_j = d_i \Leftrightarrow s_j^R = c_i^R \Leftrightarrow s_j = c_i$. Therefore, *Client* obtains correct intersection $\{c_i\}_{i\in I}$, with $I := \{i \mid d_i \in \{t'_1, ..., t'_w\}\}$ with distinct input elements.

On the other hand, we show that any clients with duplicated elements in their input cannot obtain the intersection with overwhelming probability. Let's look at the case where a corrupted *Client* has the highest probability of successfully cheating, i.e., with $\mathcal{C} = [c_1, ..., c_n]$ with $(n-1)$ distinct items and one duplicate. Without loss of generality, let's say $c_1 = c_2$, and the others are all distinct. In this case, the probability that *Client* obtains the intersection is the same as the probability that *Client* guesses λ correct permutations, so $2^{-\lambda}$, which is negligible with a sufficiently large λ.

Client Privacy: Assume that *Server* is corrupted. Showing the client privacy is relatively easy: it only sends to *Server* the encryption of the element in its set. Assuming two input sets with the same sizes, if the adversary corrupting *Server* can distinguish whether *Client* used which set as an input, then it can be used for IND-CPA of the ElGamal encryption system. Since it is well-known that the ElGamal encryption system is semantically secure [27] assuming the hardness of the decisional Diffie-Hellman problem which is reduced to DLP, the adversary cannot distinguish which set is used as well as learn anything about the *Client*'s set elements.

Server Privacy: Assume that *Client* is corrupted, denoted by *Client**. To claim server privacy, we need to show that the *Client*'s view can be efficiently simulated by a PPT algorithm $\mathtt{Sim}_\mathcal{C}$. The simulator $\mathtt{Sim}_\mathcal{C}$ can be constructed as follows:

1. $\mathtt{Sim}_\mathcal{C}$ builds two tables $T = ((\pi_1, ..., \pi_\lambda), k)$ and $T' = (m, h')$ to answer the H and H' queries, respectively.
2. After getting the message $(\mathbb{G}, p, g, h)$ and $\{e_i\}_{i=1}^n$ of a corrupted real-world client *Client**, $\mathtt{Sim}_\mathcal{C}$ picks λ random permutations from $\mathcal{P}_n$ and n random numbers $r_{i,j}$ from $\mathbb{Z}$ where $i = 1, ..., n$ for each $j = 1, ..., \lambda$. Then, $\mathtt{Sim}_\mathcal{C}$ re-randomizes and shuffles $\{e_i\}_{i=1}^n$ by multiplying $(g^{r_{i,j}}, h^{r_{i,j}})$ to each e_i's for $i = 1, ..., n$, say $e_{i,j}$, and applying the permutation π_j to $\{e_{i,j}\}_{i=1}^n$, for each j, say $E_j := \pi_j(e_{1,j}, ..., e_{n,j})$.
3. Also, $\mathtt{Sim}_\mathcal{C}$ picks random $R \in \mathbb{Z}$, and exponentiates each component of e_i's, i.e., $\hat{e}_i := e_i^R = (e_{i,1}^R, e_{i,2}^R)$ for $i = 1, ..., n$. $\mathtt{Sim}_\mathcal{C}$ also picks m random elements from $\mathcal{M}$, say $u_1, ..., u_m$.
4. $\mathtt{Sim}_\mathcal{C}$ encrypts each u_j using *SymE* with the key, $key := H(\pi_1, ..., \pi_\lambda)$, i.e., $t_j := SymE(key, u_j)$, and replies $\{E_k\}_{k=1}^\lambda$, $\{\hat{e}_i\}_{i=1}^n$, $\{t_j\}_{j=1}^m$ to *Client**.
5. Then, $\mathtt{Sim}_\mathcal{C}$ answers the H, H' queries as follows:
   - For each query $(\pi_1, ..., \pi_\lambda)$ to H, $\mathtt{Sim}_\mathcal{C}$ checks if $\exists\ ((\pi_1, ..., \pi_\lambda), key) \in T$ and returns *key* if so. Otherwise, $\mathtt{Sim}_\mathcal{C}$ picks a random $key \in_R \mathcal{K}$ and checks if $\exists((\pi'_1, ..., \pi'_\lambda), key') \in T$ such that $key' = key$. If so, output

$\mathtt{fail}_1$ and aborts. Otherwise, it adds $((\pi_1, ..., \pi_\lambda), key)$ to T and returns key to $Client^*$ as $H(\pi_1, ..., \pi_\lambda)$.
- For each query m to H', $\mathtt{Sim}_\mathcal{C}$ checks if $(m, h') \in T'$. If so, $\mathtt{Sim}_\mathcal{C}$ returns h'. Otherwise, $\mathtt{Sim}_\mathcal{C}$ picks a random $h' \in_R \mathcal{M}$, and checks if $\exists(m'', h'')$ in T' where $h'' = h'$ and $m'' \neq m$. If so, $\mathtt{Sim}_\mathcal{C}$ outputs $\mathtt{fail}_2$ and aborts. Otherwise, $\mathtt{Sim}_\mathcal{C}$ adds (m, h') to T' and returns h' to $Client^*$ as $H'(m)$.

This finishes the construction $\mathtt{Sim}_\mathcal{C}$. The ideal-world server $\overline{Server}$ that interacts with the ideal function f, which answers the queries from $\mathtt{Sim}_\mathcal{C}$ as the ideal-world client $\overline{Client}$, gets $\perp$ from f, and the real-world server $Server$ which interacts with $Client^*$ in the real protocol also outputs $\perp$. We now argue that $Client^*$'s view in the interaction with $Server$ and with $\mathtt{Sim}_\mathcal{C}$ constructed as above are indistinguishable. The $Client^*$'s view is different only if one of the following happens:

- $\mathtt{fail}_1$ **occurs:** This happens if $\exists(Q' := (\pi'_1, ..., \pi'_\lambda), key')$ such that $key' = key$ but $Q' \neq Q$ existing in T, for a randomly chosen key from $\mathcal{K}$ for the query $Q = (\pi_1, ..., \pi_\lambda)$ to H. This means a collision of H is found, i.e., $H(Q) = H(Q')$ where $Q \neq Q'$. This occurs with negligible probability by the collision resistance of H.
- $\mathtt{fail}_2$ **occurs:** This happens if there exists the entry (m'', h'') such that $h'' = h'$ but $m'' \neq m$ existing in T', for a randomly chosen h' from $\mathcal{M}$ for the query m to H'. This means a collision of H' is found, i.e., $H'(m'') = H'(m)$ where $m'' \neq m$. This happens with negligible probability due to the collision resistance of H'.

Since all events above happen with negligible probability, $Client^*$'s views in the real protocol with the real-world server $Server$ can be efficiently simulated by $\mathtt{Sim}_\mathcal{C}$ in the ideal world. □

Appendix B AD-PSI Variants

This section presents the figures of the protocols described in Sect. 5, AD-PSI-CA in Fig. 9, AD-PSI-X in Fig. 10, and AD-PSI-DT in Fig. 11, respectively.

AD-PSI-CA

Public: (p, g, h, G) where $G = \langle g \rangle$, a subgroup of $\mathbb{Z}_p^*$ of order q,

λ : statistical security parameter, pk : Prv's public key,

Private: sk : Prv's secret key correlated to pk

Client $(\mathcal{C} = [c_1, ..., c_n])$ — *Server* $(\mathcal{S} = \{s_1, ..., s_m\})$

Client: **for** $i = 1, ..., n$:

$e_i := Enc_{pk}(c_i)$

Client → Server: $(e_1, ..., e_n)$

Server: **for** $k = 1, ..., \lambda$:

$\pi_k \in_R \mathcal{P}_n$

for $i = 1, ..., n$:

$e_{i,k} := e_i \cdot Enc_{pk}(u)$

$E_k := \pi_k(e_{1,k}, ..., e_{n,k})$

$key \leftarrow H(\pi_1, ..., \pi_\lambda)$

$R \in_R \mathbb{Z}_p^*, \pi \in_R \mathcal{P}_n$

for $i = 1, ..., n$:

$\hat{e_i} := e_{\pi(i)}^R$

for $j = 1, ..., m$:

$t_j := SEnc(key, H'(s_j^R))$

Server → Client: $E_1, ..., E_\lambda, (\hat{e_1}, ..., \hat{e_n}), (t_1, ..., t_m)$

Client: **for** $k = 1, ..., \lambda$:

Determine π_k' s.t.

$Dec_{sk}(E_k) = \pi_k'(\mathcal{C})$

$key' \leftarrow H(\pi_1', ..., \pi_\lambda')$

for $j = 1, ..., m$: $t_j' := SDec(key', t_j)$

for $i = 1, ..., n$: $d_i := H'(Dec_{sk}(\hat{e_i}))$

return $|d_i \mid d_i \in \{t_1', \cdots, t_m'\}|$

Fig. 9. AD-PSI-Cardinality (AD-PSI-CA) Protocol with same notation as Fig. 3

Appendix C Security Proof for AD-APSI

Theorem 3. *The protocol described in Sect. 7.2 is a secure AD-APSI scheme, satisfying Definition 2 in ROM.*

Proof. **Correctness:** For an honest *Client* with all authorized and distinct elements, the stateful TTP generates authentic signatures for each element so that *Server* can verify the signatures correctly. For the stateless TTP, instead of tracking all the input values of *Client*, TTP generates unique and deterministic factors of the input. Thus, *Server* can tell when *Client* uses duplicated elements as the corresponding elements in $G_\mathcal{C}$ are the same. When *Server* replies, *Client* outputs the exact intersection of $\mathcal{C}$ and $\mathcal{S}$ because, for $c_i = s_j$, $d_i := H'(\hat{e}_i^{e_{i,2}}) = H'((g^{e_{i,1}R})^{e_{i,2}}) = H'(g^{c_i R}) = H'(g^{s_j R}) = t_j$. Therefore, duplicated elements in $\mathcal{C}$ are caught by either the stateful TTP or *Server* (when TTP is stateless), unauthorized (i.e., not signed by TTP) elements are caught by *Server*, and honest *Client* obtains the exact intersection of the two input sets.

AD-PSI-X

Public: (p, g, h, G) whe re $G = \langle g \rangle$, a subgroup of $\mathbb{Z}_p^*$ of order q,

λ : statistical sec urity parameter, pk : Prv's public key,

Private: sk : Prv's secret key correlated to pk

Client $(\mathcal{C} = [c_1, ..., c_n]$)		Server $(\mathcal{S} = \{s_1, ..., s_m\})$
for $i = 1, ..., n$:		**for** $j = 1, ..., m$:
$ec_i := Enc_{pk}(c_i)$	$(ec_1, ..., ec_n)$ $\longrightarrow$	$es_j := Enc_{pk}(s_j)$
		for $k = 1, ..., \lambda$:
		$\pi_k \in_R \mathcal{P}_n$
		for $i = 1, ..., n$:
		$e_{i,k} := ec_i \cdot Enc_{pk}(1)$
		$E_k := \pi_k(e_{1,k}, ..., e_{n,k})$
		$key \leftarrow H(\pi_1, ..., \pi_\lambda)$
		$\hat{e} := 1$
		for $\forall i, j$:
		$\hat{e_{i,j}} := Add(ec_i, (es_j)^{-1})$
		$\hat{e} = Mult(\hat{e}, e_{i,j})$
for $k = 1, ..., \lambda$:	$E_1, ..., E_\lambda, \hat{t}$ $\longleftarrow$	$\hat{t} := SEnc(key, \hat{e}^R), R \in \mathbb{Z}_p^*$
Determine π_k' s.t.		
$Dec(E_k) = \pi_k'(\mathcal{C})$		
$key' \leftarrow H(\pi_1', ..., \pi_\lambda')$		
$t := SDec(key', \hat{t})$		
return YES, if $Dec(t) = 0$, *or* NO, otherwise		

Fig. 10. AD-PSI-Existence (AD-PSI-X) Protocol with same notation as Fig. 3 except that (Enc, Dec) should be a FHE over G satisfying $Add(Enc(a), Enc(b)) = Enc(a+b)$ and $Mult(Enc(a), Enc(b)) = Enc(a * b)$.

For server and client privacy, we show that the distribution of protocol execution in the real world is computationally indistinguishable from the output from interaction with $\mathcal{F}$ in the ideal world, assuming the same corrupted party (either *Client* or *Server*). Since the interaction between *Server* and *Client* is during the online phase for `Interaction`, it is compared with $\mathcal{F}_\cap$ (recall Definition 2), assuming $\mathcal{C}$ is authorized with $\mathcal{F}_{\texttt{Auth}}$.

Server Privacy: Assume that *Client* is corrupted, denoted by *Client**. We show that the distribution of *Client** outputs in the real world can be efficiently simulated by a PPT $\texttt{Sim}_\mathcal{C}$ constructed as below.

1. $\texttt{Sim}_\mathcal{C}$ builds two tables $T_1 = ((m_1, m_2), h)$ and $T_2 = (m, h')$ to answer the H and H' queries, respectively.
2. After getting the messages $G_\mathcal{C} := \{g_{i,1}, g_{i,2}\}_i$ and Σ of a corrupted real-world client, *Client**, $\texttt{Sim}_\mathcal{C}$ verifies the received signatures with respect to each $H(g_{i,1}, g_{i,2})$ via *Verf* and TTP's public key. If any of those fails, it aborts.

AD-PSI-DT

Public: (p, g, h, G) where $G = \langle g \rangle$, a subgroup of $\mathbb{Z}_p^*$ of order q,
λ : statistical security parameter, pk : Prv's public key,
Private: sk : Prv's secret key correlated to pk,
$\mathcal{C} = (c_1, ..., c_n)$, $\mathcal{S} = \{(s_1, D_1), ..., (s_m, D_m)\}$

Client ($\mathcal{C}$)		*Server* ($\mathcal{S}$)
for $i = 1, ..., n$:		
$e_i := Enc_{pk}(c_i)$	$\xrightarrow{(e_1, ..., e_n)}$	**for** $k = 1, ..., \lambda$:
		$\pi_k \in_R \mathcal{P}_n$
		for $i = 1, ..., n$:
		$e_{i,k} := e_i \cdot Enc_{pk}(1)$
		$E_k := \pi_k(e_{1,k}, ..., e_{n,k})$
		$key \leftarrow H(\pi_1, ..., \pi_\lambda)$
		$R \in_R \mathbb{Z}_p^*$
		for $i = 1, ..., n$:
		$\hat{e_i} := e_i^R$
		for $j = 1, ..., m$:
		$s'_j := H'(s_j^R)$
		$t_j := SEnc(key, H''(s'_j))$
for $k = 1, ..., \lambda$:	$\xleftarrow[(t_1, ..., t_m), (D'_1, ..., D'_m)]{E_1, ..., E_\lambda, (\hat{e_1}, ..., \hat{e_n}),}$	$D'_j := SEnc(s'_j, D_j)$
Determine π'_k s.t.		
$Dec_{sk}(E_k) = \pi'_k(\mathcal{C})$		
$key' \leftarrow H(\pi'_1, ..., \pi'_\lambda)$		
for $j = 1, ..., m$: $t'_j := SDec(key', t_j)$		
for $i = 1, ..., n$: $d_i := H'(Dec_{sk}(\hat{e_i}))$		

return $\{(c_i, D_j) \mid c_i \in \mathcal{C}$ such that $H''(d_i) = t'_j$ for some $j \in \{1, ..., m\}$ and $D_j := SDec(d_i, D'_j)$ for such $j\}$

Fig. 11. AD-PSI-Data Transfer (AD-PSI-DT) Protocol with same notation as Fig. 3. Additionally, H'' is a one-way function that maps k-bit messages to k-bit messages.

(Likewise, for the stateless version, $\texttt{Sim}_{\mathcal{C}}$ also checks the duplicates in $G_{\mathcal{C}}$ and aborts if any.

3. Otherwise, $\texttt{Sim}_{\mathcal{C}}$ picks m random elements, $u_1, ..., u_m$, in G and computes $t_j := H'(u_j)$ for $j = 1, ..., m$. It also picks a random R, computes $\{\hat{e_i} = g_{i,1}^R\}_i$, and replies $\{\hat{e_i}\}_i$ and $\{t_j\}_m$ to $Client^*$.
4. For each query to H and H', $\texttt{Sim}_{\mathcal{C}}$ answers as follows:
   - For each query (m_1, m_2) to H, $\texttt{Sim}_{\mathcal{C}}$ checks if $exists((m_1, m_2), h) \in T_1$ and returns h if so. Otherwise, $\texttt{Sim}_{\mathcal{C}}$ picks a random h (from the same space as other values) and checks if $exists((\tilde{m_1}, \tilde{m_2}), \tilde{h}) \in T_1$ such that $h = \tilde{h}$. If so, output $\texttt{fail}_1$ and abort. Otherwise, it adds $((m_1, m_2), h)$ to T_1 and returns h to $Client^*$ as $H((m_1, m_2))$.
   - For each query m to H', $\texttt{Sim}_{\mathcal{C}}$ checks if $exists(m, h') \in T_2$ and returns h' if so. Otherwise, $\texttt{Sim}_{\mathcal{C}}$ picks a random h' (from the same space as

other values) and checks if $exists(\tilde{m}, \tilde{h}) \in T_2$ such that $h' = \tilde{h}$. If so, output $\texttt{fail}_2$ and abort. Otherwise, it adds (m, h') to T_2 and returns h' to $Client^*$ as $H'(m)$.

This finishes the $\texttt{Sim}_\mathcal{C}$ construction. The $Client^*$'s view in the interaction with $\texttt{Sim}_\mathcal{C}$ above is different from the view in the real-world interaction with the real server, $Server$, only if $\texttt{fail}_1$ or $\texttt{fail}_2$ happen. However, due to the collision resistance property of cryptographic hash functions H, H', they occur with negligible probability. Thus, $Client^*$'s view when interacting with $Server$ can be efficiently simulated by $\texttt{Sim}_\mathcal{C}$ in the ideal world. For the outputs, the ideal-world server $\overline{Server}$ that interacts with $\mathcal{F}_\cap$, which answers the queries from $\texttt{Sim}_\mathcal{C}$ as the ideal-world $Client$, $\overline{Client}$, receives $(|\mathcal{C}, b)$ from $\mathcal{F}_\cap$. On the other hand, the real-world (honest) server $Server$ that interacts with $Client^*$ in the real protocol also outputs (learns) $(|\mathcal{C}, b)$. i.e., $\overline{Server}$ interacting with $\texttt{Sim}_\mathcal{C}$ and $Server$ interacting with $Client^*$ yield the identical outputs.

Client Privacy: Similarly, now we assume a corrupted server, $Server^*$, and show that $Server^*$'s view in the real world can be efficiently simulated by a PPT simulator, $\texttt{Sim}_\mathcal{S}$, constructed as below. Intuitively, $\texttt{Sim}_\mathcal{S}$ sits between $\mathcal{F}_\cap$ and $Server^*$, and interacts with both in such a way that $Server^*$ is unable to distinguish protocol runs with $\texttt{Sim}_\mathcal{S}$ from real-world protocol runs with $Client$. First, $\texttt{Sim}_\mathcal{S}$ builds tables T_1 and T_2, and answers similarly to $\texttt{Sim}_\mathcal{C}$ above for H and H' queries. Then for inputs, since $Client$ and TTP communicate in the offline phase before the online phase, the authorized elements for $Client$ are made available to $\texttt{Sim}_\mathcal{S}$. $\texttt{Sim}_\mathcal{S}$ uses a subset of authorized elements during the simulation to emulate $Client$'s behavior. If $Server^*$ does not abort and reply $(\{t_j\}_j, \{\hat{e_i}\}_i)$, $\texttt{Sim}_\mathcal{S}$ checks if $\hat{e_i}^{e_{i,2}} \in \{t_j\}_j$. If so, $\texttt{Sim}_\mathcal{S}$ adds $s_i := e_{i,1}e_{i,2} \pmod p$ in $\mathcal{S}$, and otherwise, adds a dummy element in $\mathbb{Z}_p^*$ in $\mathcal{S}$. Then, $\texttt{Sim}_\mathcal{S}$ plays the role of the ideal-world server, $\overline{Server}$, using $\mathcal{S}$ to respond to the queries from the ideal client ($\overline{Client}$). Since $\texttt{Sim}_\mathcal{S}$ uses the authorized inputs, $Server^*$'s view in the interaction with $\texttt{Sim}_\mathcal{S}$ is identical to the view in the interaction with honest $Client$ in the real world. Also, the output of the ideal-world client $\overline{Client}$ that interacts with $\mathcal{F}_\cap$, which answers the queries from $\texttt{Sim}_\mathcal{S}$ as the ideal-world $Server$, $\overline{Server}$, is identical to the output of the real-world $Client$ interacting with $Server^*$ as $(|\mathcal{S}, \mathcal{C} \cap \mathcal{S})$, only when all inputs in $\mathcal{C}$ are authorized and distinct. □

References

1. Palisade homomorphic encryption software library (2017). https://palisade-crypto.org/
2. Lattigo v4. https://github.com/tuneinsight/lattigo. August 2022, ePFL-LDS, Tune Insight SA
3. Ateniese, G., De Cristofaro, E., Tsudik, G.: (If) size matters: size-hiding private set intersection. In: Catalano, D., Fazio, N., Gennaro, R., Nicolosi, A. (eds.) PKC 2011. LNCS, vol. 6571, pp. 156–173. Springer, Heidelberg (2011). https://doi.org/10.1007/978-3-642-19379-8_10

4. Bellare, M., Goldreich, O.: On defining proofs of knowledge. In: Brickell, E.F. (ed.) CRYPTO 1992. LNCS, vol. 740, pp. 390–420. Springer, Heidelberg (1993). https://doi.org/10.1007/3-540-48071-4_28
5. Blanton, M., Aguiar, E.: Private and oblivious set and multiset operations. In: Proceedings of the 7th ACM Symposium on Information, Computer and Communications Security (ASIACCS) (2012)
6. Bradley, T., Faber, S., Tsudik, G.: Bounded size-hiding private set intersection. In: Zikas, V., De Prisco, R. (eds.) SCN 2016. LNCS, vol. 9841, pp. 449–467. Springer, Cham (2016). https://doi.org/10.1007/978-3-319-44618-9_24
7. Camenisch, J., Stadler, M.: Efficient group signature schemes for large groups. In: Kaliski, B.S. (ed.) CRYPTO 1997. LNCS, vol. 1294, pp. 410–424. Springer, Heidelberg (1997). https://doi.org/10.1007/BFb0052252
8. Carpent, X., Faber, S., Sander, T., Tsudik, G.: Private set projections & variants. In: Proceedings of the 2017 on Workshop on Privacy in the Electronic Society (WPES 2017). Association for Computing Machinery (2017)
9. Cerulli, A., De Cristofaro, E., Soriente, C.: Nothing refreshes like a REPSI: reactive private set intersection. In: Applied Cryptography and Network Security, pp. 280–300 (2018)
10. Chase, M., Miao, P.: Private set intersection in the internet setting from lightweight oblivious PRF. In: Micciancio, D., Ristenpart, T. (eds.) CRYPTO 2020. LNCS, vol. 12172, pp. 34–63. Springer, Cham (2020). https://doi.org/10.1007/978-3-030-56877-1_2
11. Chaum, D., Fiat, A., Naor, M.: Untraceable electronic cash. In: Goldwasser, S. (ed.) CRYPTO 1988. LNCS, vol. 403, pp. 319–327. Springer, New York (1990). https://doi.org/10.1007/0-387-34799-2_25
12. Chillotti, I., Gama, N., Georgieva, M., Izabachène, M.: Tfhe: fast fully homomorphic encryption library over the torus (2017). https://github.com/tfhe/tfhe. Accessed 31 Jan 2022
13. Ciampi, M., Orlandi, C.: Combining private set-intersection with secure two-party computation. In: Security and Cryptography for Networks (2018)
14. Clarkson, J.B.: Dense probabilistic encryption. In: Proceedings of the Workshop on Selected Areas of Cryptography, pp. 120–128 (1994)
15. Cramer, R., Gennaro, R., Schoenmakers, B.: A secure and optimally efficient multi-authority election scheme. In: Fumy, W. (ed.) EUROCRYPT 1997. LNCS, vol. 1233, pp. 103–118. Springer, Heidelberg (1997). https://doi.org/10.1007/3-540-69053-0_9
16. Dachman-Soled, D., Malkin, T., Raykova, M., Yung, M.: Efficient robust private set intersection. In: Abdalla, M., Pointcheval, D., Fouque, P.-A., Vergnaud, D. (eds.) ACNS 2009. LNCS, vol. 5536, pp. 125–142. Springer, Heidelberg (2009). https://doi.org/10.1007/978-3-642-01957-9_8
17. Damgård, I., Jurik, M.: A generalisation, a simplification and some applications of paillier's probabilistic public-key system. In: Kim, K. (ed.) PKC 2001. LNCS, vol. 1992, pp. 119–136. Springer, Heidelberg (2001). https://doi.org/10.1007/3-540-44586-2_9
18. De Cristofaro, E., Gasti, P., Tsudik, G.: Fast and private computation of cardinality of set intersection and union. In: Pieprzyk, J., Sadeghi, A.-R., Manulis, M. (eds.) CANS 2012. LNCS, vol. 7712, pp. 218–231. Springer, Heidelberg (2012). https://doi.org/10.1007/978-3-642-35404-5_17
19. De Cristofaro, E., Kim, J., Tsudik, G.: Linear-complexity private set intersection protocols secure in malicious model. In: Abe, M. (ed.) ASIACRYPT 2010. LNCS,

vol. 6477, pp. 213–231. Springer, Heidelberg (2010). https://doi.org/10.1007/978-3-642-17373-8_13
20. De Cristofaro, E., Tsudik, G.: Practical private set intersection protocols with linear complexity. In: Sion, R. (ed.) FC 2010. LNCS, vol. 6052, pp. 143–159. Springer, Heidelberg (2010). https://doi.org/10.1007/978-3-642-14577-3_13
21. De Cristofaro, E., Tsudik, G.: Experimenting with fast private set intersection. In: Katzenbeisser, S., Weippl, E., Camp, L.J., Volkamer, M., Reiter, M., Zhang, X. (eds.) Trust 2012. LNCS, vol. 7344, pp. 55–73. Springer, Heidelberg (2012). https://doi.org/10.1007/978-3-642-30921-2_4
22. Debnath, S.K., Dutta, R.: Secure and efficient private set intersection cardinality using bloom filter. In: Lopez, J., Mitchell, C.J. (eds.) ISC 2015. LNCS, vol. 9290, pp. 209–226. Springer, Cham (2015). https://doi.org/10.1007/978-3-319-23318-5_12
23. Demmler, D., Rindal, P., Rosulek, M., Trieu, N.: PIR-PSI: scaling private contact discovery. In: Proceedings on Privacy Enhancing Technologies, pp. 159–178 (2018)
24. Dong, C., Chen, L., Wen, Z.: When private set intersection meets big data: an efficient and scalable protocol. In: CCS (2013)
25. Duong, T., Phan, D.H., Trieu, N.: Catalic: delegated PSI cardinality with applications to contact tracing. In: Moriai, S., Wang, H. (eds.) ASIACRYPT 2020. LNCS, vol. 12493, pp. 870–899. Springer, Cham (2020). https://doi.org/10.1007/978-3-030-64840-4_29
26. ElGamal, T.: A public key cryptosystem and a signature scheme based on discrete logarithms. IEEE Trans. Inf. Theory **31**(4), 469–472 (1985)
27. ElGamal, T.: A public key cryptosystem and a signature scheme based on discrete logarithms. In: Blakley, G.R., Chaum, D. (eds.) CRYPTO 1984. LNCS, vol. 196, pp. 10–18. Springer, Heidelberg (1985). https://doi.org/10.1007/3-540-39568-7_2
28. Evans, D., Kolesnikov, V., Rosulek, M.: A Pragmatic Introduction to Secure Multi-Party Computation (2018)
29. Fiege, U., Fiat, A., Shamir, A.: Zero knowledge proofs of identity. In: Proceedings of the Nineteenth Annual ACM Symposium on Theory of Computing. STOC 1987, pp. 210–217. Association for Computing Machinery (1987)
30. Freedman, M.J., Hazay, C., Nissim, K., Pinkas, B.: Efficient set intersection with simulation-based security. J. Cryptol. **29**(1), 115–155 (2016)
31. Freedman, M.J., Ishai, Y., Pinkas, B., Reingold, O.: Keyword search and oblivious pseudorandom functions. In: Kilian, J. (ed.) TCC 2005. LNCS, vol. 3378, pp. 303–324. Springer, Heidelberg (2005). https://doi.org/10.1007/978-3-540-30576-7_17
32. Freedman, M.J., Nissim, K., Pinkas, B.: Efficient private matching and set intersection. In: Cachin, C., Camenisch, J.L. (eds.) EUROCRYPT 2004. LNCS, vol. 3027, pp. 1–19. Springer, Heidelberg (2004). https://doi.org/10.1007/978-3-540-24676-3_1
33. Ghosh, S., Nilges, T.: An algebraic approach to maliciously secure private set intersection. In: Ishai, Y., Rijmen, V. (eds.) EUROCRYPT 2019. LNCS, vol. 11478, pp. 154–185. Springer, Cham (2019). https://doi.org/10.1007/978-3-030-17659-4_6
34. Goldreich, O.: Foundations of Cryptography: Basic Applications, vol. 2. Cambridge University Press, Cambridge (2004)
35. Goldwasser, S., Micali, S., Rackoff, C.: The knowledge complexity of interactive proof-systems. In: Proceedings of the Seventeenth Annual ACM Symposium on Theory of Computing. STOC 1985, pp. 291–304 (1985)
36. Goldwasser, S., Micali, S.: Probabilistic encryption & how to play mental poker keeping secret all partial information. In: Proceedings of the Fourteenth Annual ACM Symposium on Theory of Computing. STOC 1982, pp. 365–377 (1982)

37. Gouert, C., Mouris, D., Tsoutsos, N.G.: SOK: new insights into fully homomorphic encryption libraries via standardized benchmarks. Proc. Priv. Enhancing Technol. **2023**(3), 154–172 (2023)
38. Hagen, C., Weinert, C., Sendner, C., Dmitrienko, A., Schneider, T.: All the numbers are us: large-scale abuse of contact discovery in mobile messengers. IACR Cryptology ePrint Archive, p. 1119 (2020)
39. Hallgren, P., Orlandi, C., Sabelfeld, A.: Privatepool: privacy-preserving ridesharing. In: IEEE 30th Computer Security Foundations Symposium (CSF) (2017)
40. Hazay, C., Lindell, Y.: Efficient protocols for set intersection and pattern matching with security against malicious and covert adversaries. In: Canetti, R. (ed.) TCC 2008. LNCS, vol. 4948, pp. 155–175. Springer, Heidelberg (2008). https://doi.org/10.1007/978-3-540-78524-8_10
41. Hazay, C., Nissim, K.: Efficient set operations in the presence of malicious adversaries. In: Nguyen, P.Q., Pointcheval, D. (eds.) PKC 2010. LNCS, vol. 6056, pp. 312–331. Springer, Heidelberg (2010). https://doi.org/10.1007/978-3-642-13013-7_19
42. Hemenway Falk, B., Noble, D., Ostrovsky, R.: Private set intersection with linear communication from general assumptions. In: Proceedings of the 18th ACM Workshop on Privacy in the Electronic Society, pp. 14–25. WPES 2019. Association for Computing Machinery (2019)
43. Huang, Y., Evans, D., Katz, J.: Private set intersection: are garbled circuits better than custom protocols? In: NDSS. ISOC (2012)
44. Huberman, B., Franklin, M., Hogg, T.: Enhancing privacy and trust in electronic communities. In: ACM Conference on Electronic Commerce (1999)
45. Ion, M., et al.: On deploying secure computing: Private intersection-sum-with-cardinality. In: 2020 IEEE European Symposium on Security and Privacy (EuroS&P), pp. 370–389 (2020)
46. Jarecki, S., Liu, X.: Efficient oblivious pseudorandom function with applications to adaptive OT and secure computation of set intersection. In: Reingold, O. (ed.) TCC 2009. LNCS, vol. 5444, pp. 577–594. Springer, Heidelberg (2009). https://doi.org/10.1007/978-3-642-00457-5_34
47. Kajita, K., Ohtake, G.: Private set intersection for viewing history with efficient data matching. In: Stephanidis, C., Antona, M., Ntoa, S. (eds.) HCI International 2022 Posters, pp. 498–505. Springer, Cham (2022). https://doi.org/10.1007/978-3-031-06394-7_63
48. Kawachi, A., Tanaka, K., Xagawa, K.: Multi-bit cryptosystems based on lattice problems. In: Okamoto, T., Wang, X. (eds.) PKC 2007. LNCS, vol. 4450, pp. 315–329. Springer, Heidelberg (2007). https://doi.org/10.1007/978-3-540-71677-8_21
49. Kissner, L., Song, D.: Privacy-preserving set operations. In: Shoup, V. (ed.) CRYPTO 2005. LNCS, vol. 3621, pp. 241–257. Springer, Heidelberg (2005). https://doi.org/10.1007/11535218_15
50. Kolesnikov, V., Kumaresan, R., Rosulek, M., Trieu, N.: Efficient batched oblivious PRF with applications to private set intersection. In: Proceedings of the 2016 ACM SIGSAC Conference on Computer and Communications Security, pp. 818–829. CCS, Association for Computing Machinery (2016)
51. Kolesnikov, V., Rosulek, M., Trieu, N.: SWiM: secure wildcard pattern matching from OT extension. In: Meiklejohn, S., Sako, K. (eds.) FC 2018. LNCS, vol. 10957, pp. 222–240. Springer, Heidelberg (2018). https://doi.org/10.1007/978-3-662-58387-6_12

52. Kulshrestha, A., Mayer, J.: Estimating incidental collection in foreign intelligence surveillance: Large-Scale multiparty private set intersection with union and sum. In: 31st USENIX Security Symposium, pp. 1705–1722. USENIX Association (2022)
53. Laine, K., Chen, H., Player, R.: Simple encrypted arithmetic library (seal) (2017). https://github.com/microsoft/SEAL. Accessed 31 Jan 2022
54. Lindell, Y., Pinkas, B.: An efficient protocol for secure two-party computation in the presence of malicious adversaries. J. Cryptol. **28**(2), 312–350 (2015)
55. Ma, J.P.K., Chow, S.S.M.: Secure-computation-friendly private set intersection from oblivious compact graph evaluation. In: ASIA CCS 2022 (2022)
56. Meadows, C.A.: A more efficient cryptographic matchmaking protocol for use in the absence of a continuously available third party. In: 1986 IEEE Symposium on Security and Privacy, pp. 134–134 (1986)
57. Miao, P., Patel, S., Raykova, M., Seth, K., Yung, M.: Two-sided malicious security for private intersection-sum with cardinality. In: Micciancio, D., Ristenpart, T. (eds.) CRYPTO 2020. LNCS, vol. 12172, pp. 3–33. Springer, Cham (2020). https://doi.org/10.1007/978-3-030-56877-1_1
58. Naccache, D., Stern, J.: A new public key cryptosystem based on higher residues. In: Proceedings of the 5th ACM Conference on Computer and Communications Security. CCS 1998, pp. 59–66 (1998)
59. Nagaraja, S., Mittal, P., Hong, C., Caesar, M., Borisov, N.: BotGrep: finding bots with structured graph analysis. In: Usenix Security (2010)
60. Nevo, O., Trieu, N., Yanai, A.: Simple, fast malicious multiparty private set intersection. In: CCS '21: ACM SIGSAC Conference on Computer and Communications Security, pp. 1151–1165 (2021)
61. Okamoto, T., Uchiyama, S.: A new public-key cryptosystem as secure as factoring. In: Nyberg, K. (ed.) EUROCRYPT 1998. LNCS, vol. 1403, pp. 308–318. Springer, Heidelberg (1998). https://doi.org/10.1007/BFb0054135
62. Paillier, P.: Public-key cryptosystems based on composite degree residuosity classes. In: Stern, J. (ed.) EUROCRYPT 1999. LNCS, vol. 1592, pp. 223–238. Springer, Heidelberg (1999). https://doi.org/10.1007/3-540-48910-X_16
63. Pinkas, B., Rosulek, M., Trieu, N., Yanai, A.: SpOT-light: lightweight private set intersection from sparse OT extension. In: Boldyreva, A., Micciancio, D. (eds.) CRYPTO 2019. LNCS, vol. 11694, pp. 401–431. Springer, Cham (2019). https://doi.org/10.1007/978-3-030-26954-8_13
64. Pinkas, B., Rosulek, M., Trieu, N., Yanai, A.: PSI from PaXoS: fast, malicious private set intersection. In: Canteaut, A., Ishai, Y. (eds.) EUROCRYPT 2020. LNCS, vol. 12106, pp. 739–767. Springer, Cham (2020). https://doi.org/10.1007/978-3-030-45724-2_25
65. Pinkas, B., Schneider, T., Zohner, M.: Scalable private set intersection based on OT extension. ACM Trans. Privacy Secur. (TOPS) **21**, 1–35 (2016)
66. Pinkas, B., Schneider, T., Segev, G., Zohner, M.: Phasing: Private set intersection using permutation-based hashing. In: Proceedings of the 24th USENIX Conference on Security Symposium, pp. 515–530. SEC 2015, USENIX Association (2015)
67. Pinkas, B., Schneider, T., Tkachenko, O., Yanai, A.: Efficient circuit-based PSI with Linear communication. In: Ishai, Y., Rijmen, V. (eds.) EUROCRYPT 2019. LNCS, vol. 11478, pp. 122–153. Springer, Cham (2019). https://doi.org/10.1007/978-3-030-17659-4_5
68. Pinkas, B., Schneider, T., Weinert, C., Wieder, U.: Efficient circuit-based PSI via cuckoo hashing. In: Nielsen, J.B., Rijmen, V. (eds.) EUROCRYPT 2018. LNCS, vol. 10822, pp. 125–157. Springer, Cham (2018). https://doi.org/10.1007/978-3-319-78372-7_5

69. Pinkas, B., Schneider, T., Zohner, M.: Faster private set intersection based on OT extension. In: 23rd USENIX Security Symposium (USENIX Security 14), pp. 797–812. USENIX Association (2014)
70. Rindal, P., Schoppmann, P.: VOLE-PSI: fast OPRF and circuit-PSI from vector-OLE. In: Canteaut, A., Standaert, F.-X. (eds.) EUROCRYPT 2021. LNCS, vol. 12697, pp. 901–930. Springer, Cham (2021). https://doi.org/10.1007/978-3-030-77886-6_31
71. Rivest, R.L., Shamir, A., Adleman, L.: A method for obtaining digital signatures and public-key cryptosystems. Commun. ACM **21**(2), 120–126 (1978)
72. Sathya Narayanan, G., Aishwarya, T., Agrawal, A., Patra, A., Choudhary, A., Pandu Rangan, C.: Multi party distributed private matching, set disjointness and cardinality of set intersection with information theoretic security. In: Garay, J.A., Miyaji, A., Otsuka, A. (eds.) CANS 2009. LNCS, vol. 5888, pp. 21–40. Springer, Heidelberg (2009). https://doi.org/10.1007/978-3-642-10433-6_2
73. Shamir, A.: On the power of commutativity in cryptography. In: de Bakker, J., van Leeuwen, J. (eds.) ICALP 1980. LNCS, vol. 85, pp. 582–595. Springer, Heidelberg (1980). https://doi.org/10.1007/3-540-10003-2_100
74. Stefanov, E., Shi, E., Song, D.: Policy-enhanced private set intersection: sharing information while enforcing privacy policies. In: Fischlin, M., Buchmann, J., Manulis, M. (eds.) PKC 2012. LNCS, vol. 7293, pp. 413–430. Springer, Heidelberg (2012). https://doi.org/10.1007/978-3-642-30057-8_25
75. Takeshita, J., Karl, R., Mohammed, A., Striegel, A., Jung, T.: Provably secure contact tracing with conditional private set intersection. In: Garcia-Alfaro, J., Li, S., Poovendran, R., Debar, H., Yung, M. (eds.) SecureComm 2021. LNICST, vol. 398, pp. 352–373. Springer, Cham (2021). https://doi.org/10.1007/978-3-030-90019-9_18
76. Vaidya, J., Clifton, C.: Secure set intersection cardinality with application to association rule mining. J. Comput. Secur. **13**(4), 593–622 (2005)
77. Wen, Y., Gong, Z., Huang, Z., Qiu, W.: A new efficient authorized private set intersection protocol from Schnorr signature and its applications. Clust. Comput. **21**(1), 287–297 (2018)
78. Zhao, Y., Chow, S.: Are you the one to share? secret transfer with access structure. In: Proceedings on Privacy Enhancing Technologies - PETS 2017 (2017)
79. Zhao, Y., Chow, S.S.: Can you find the one for me? In: Proceedings of the 2018 Workshop on Privacy in the Electronic Society. WPES 2018, pp. 54–65. Association for Computing Machinery (2018)

A New Approach to Efficient and Secure Fixed-Point Computation

Tore Kasper Frederiksen[1], Jonas Lindstrøm[2], Mikkel Wienberg Madsen[3](✉), and Anne Dorte Spangsberg[3]

[1] Zama, Paris, France
tore.frederiksen@zama.ai
[2] Mysten Labs, Paris, France
jonas@mystenlabs.com
[3] The Alexandra Institute, Aarhus, Denmark
{mikkel.wienberg,a.d.spangsberg}@alexandra.dk

Abstract. Secure Multi-Party Computation (MPC) constructions typically allow computation over a finite field or ring. While useful for many applications, certain real-world applications require the usage of decimal numbers. While it is possible to emulate floating-point operations in MPC, fixed-point computation has gained more traction in the practical space due to its simplicity and efficient realizations. Even so, current protocols for fixed-point MPC still require computing a *secure* truncation after *each* multiplication gate. In this paper, we show a new paradigm for realizing fixed-point MPC. Starting from an existing MPC protocol over arbitrary, large, finite fields or rings, we show how to realize MPC over a *residue number system* (RNS). This allows us to leverage certain mathematical structures to construct a secure algorithm for efficient approximate truncation by a static and public value. We then show how this can be used to realize highly efficient secure fixed-point computation. In contrast to previous approaches, our protocol does not require any multiplications of secret values in the underlying MPC scheme to realize truncation but instead relies on preprocessed pairs of correlated random values, which we show can be constructed very efficiently, when accepting a small amount of leakage and robustness in the strong, covert model. We proceed to implement our protocol, with SPDZ [28] as the underlying MPC protocol, and achieve significantly faster fixed-point multiplication.

Keywords: MPC · fixed-point · malicious security · covert security · UC · residue number systems

1 Introduction

Secure multi-party computation (MPC) is the area of cryptography concerned with the computation of arbitrary functions over private data held by mutually

This work has received funding from the Alexandra Institute's performance contracts for 2021-24 with the Danish Ministry of Higher Education and Science and by Innovation Fund Denmark in Grand Solution CRUCIAL 1063-00001B. Tore and Jonas performed part of their work while at the Alexandra Institute.

C. Pöpper and L. Batina (Eds.): ACNS 2024, LNCS 14583, pp. 58–87, 2024.
https://doi.org/10.1007/978-3-031-54770-6_3

distrusting parties. Since its inception by Andrew Yao [63], it has received a large amount of research interest [28,42,46,50,56]. Computation is usually represented as a Directed Acyclic Graph (DAG) of 2-input, 1-output gates where each gate operates on the inputs, most commonly over bits [50,56] (*boolean MPC*), large fields [28] or rings [22] (*arithmetic MPC*). Even though operations in an arithmetic MPC scheme over a large field are typically less efficient than operations in an MPC scheme over bits, they are significantly more efficient than a corresponding emulation by an MPC scheme over bits. Furthermore, arithmetic MPC computations are required in a plethora of different applications, for example in auctions [13], benchmarks [25], machine learning [26], private smart contracts [10,11], threshold signatures [24] and RSA key modulus generation with unknown factorization [20,40]. However, in certain applications, such as statistics [25,33] and machine learning [18,52,62,64] it is not sufficient to work over the integers, but instead require decimal numbers. While there are multiple ways of efficiently emulating decimal arithmetic using integers, doing so in MPC, without impacting efficiency significantly has proven elusive as we will discuss in the related works section below. Looking ahead, research in the area has pointed in the direction of fixed-point arithmetic, where integers are interpreted as decimal numbers with a static amount of digits after the decimal point, being the most efficient way of realizing secure decimal computation. This has the advantage that addition is exactly the same as for integer arithmetic, and multiplication is *almost* the same; in the sense that the multiplication operation is the same, but the result needs to be truncated with a constant. Such a truncation has proven expensive in MPC [17] and most researchers in that area [30,34,59] have gone in the direction of trying to combine MPC over bits and integers to realize bit operations, such as truncation, efficiently. In this paper, we take a different direction and ask if it is 1) possible to efficiently realize fixed-point arithmetic in MPC without emulating bit operations and 2) if it is doable only assuming black-box access to an *arithmetic* MPC protocol. By representing integers in a *residue number system (RNS)* and accepting small additive errors in the truncation we answer both of these in the affirmative.

An RNS is a method for representing integers by their residues modulo a fixed set of coprime integers. This allows the representation of large integers using smaller integers, and it has received some attention in recent years because multiplication and addition may be done in parallel by the smaller integers, allowing large computations to be parallelized. This again can lead to advantages in high-performance computation [31,61]. While our proposed scheme enjoys these advantages when preprocessing multiplication triples, it is the mathematical structure of an RNS we take advantage of to realize efficient truncation, and hence, efficient fixed-point computation.

Contributions. In this paper we show how to realize secure computation over a 2-component RNS, resulting in secure computation over a biprime ring. We build this from two separate MPC instances, using any MPC scheme supporting computation over arbitrary prime fields. An example of such a scheme is SPDZ [28], which relies on additive secret sharing of values, along with additively shared information-theoretic MACs for its underlying security against a statically and maliciously corrupted dishonest majority.

First, this provides us with an MPC system with more efficient preprocessing over very large domains, compared with the underlying MPC scheme used. This is advantageous in certain applications such as distributed generation of an RSA modulus [20,40]. However, the main motivating factor behind our scheme is a highly efficient realization of secure *approximate truncation*, with a few bits of leakage of the least significant bits. Concretely we introduce an algorithm working over a maliciously UC-secure MPC functionality over arbitrary fields and show how this can be used to realize approximate truncation in a preprocessing model. Both our main online protocol and the offline preprocessing it relies on, only require a constant number of rounds of communication and *no* secure multiplications or other heavy cryptographic machinery. We prove both information-theoretically UC-secure based on black-box access to a functionality for maliciously secure MPC over a large ring. We show the *robustness* of this construction secure in the *strong covert* model [9], while retaining maliciously *privacy*, against an adversary corrupting a majority of parties. We highlight that we are not the first authors considering such a compromise between efficiency and security for MPC protocols [27]. The cost of this efficient preprocessing is a small amount of leakage during the online protocol. Either $\log_2(n)$ bits or a single bit (if one can accept the addition of $O(n^2)$ extra multiplications during the online phase, where n is the number of parties). Furthermore, we note that due to an artifact of our simulation proof, we require the simulator to be allowed to perform $O(2^n)$ computations with low, but non-negligible probability. Hence, $O(2^n)$ will be polynomially bounded by any computational security parameter required to realize the underlying maliciously secure MPC functionality. Still, we highlight this has *no* influence on the actual efficiency of our protocols.

Based on this efficient preprocessing protocol and online phase we show how to construct an efficient fixed-point MPC scheme. Finally, we benchmark our scheme, based on SPDZ, through micro-benchmarks along with the versatile application of the Fast Fourier Transform. Depending on the size of the computation domain and network latency, our results show that the small reduction in security for approximate truncation allows us to get a 3.2-42x faster online phase. Suppose preprocessing is included (based on MASCOT [47]) then our protocol is 36-1,400x faster than the protocol of Catrina and Saxena [17] for fixed-point computation, which also exclusively requires access to a black box MPC scheme. We furthermore find our protocol competitive for large domain computation, when counting the preprocessing time.

1.1 Related Work

Our work is far from the first usage of RNS in cryptography, although, to the best of our knowledge, this is the first time it is used to achieve efficient MPC for fixed-point arithmetic.

On the other hand, RNS has been used as a tool for optimizing the implementation of large field arithmetic, which is highly relevant in many public-key systems such as RSA [57] or schemes based on general elliptic curves [7] and isogenies [45]. It has also been shown that such RNS-based implementations can help in thwarting certain types of fault-injection attacks [36]. The fact that RNS is an application of the Chinese Remainder Theorem (CRT) has in itself been used to optimize distributed RSA key generation [19,21,29].

As previously mentioned, working with decimal numbers is crucial in many MPC applications, such as statistics [25,33] and machine learning [18,52,62,64]. Many early works that require decimal numbers do not consider a formal treatment of how to represent decimal number systems in MPC but are instead rather pragmatic in how to achieve their specific computation goals. Examples include MPC computation of the natural logarithm through Taylor series expansion [52], or approximating $1/p$ through the use of Newton iteration [4]. Du and Atallah [33] presented a custom two-party protocol for general secure division to implement linear regression in the two-party setting. However, Kiltz *et al.* [49] showed that the protocol of Du and Atallah leaks some information, and demonstrated a leakage-free protocol for division in the two-party setting. Atallah *et al.* [8], presented yet further protocols for realizing floating point division for use in secure linear regression, this time working with more than two parties. Fouque *et al.* [35] showed how to do general computation over rationals, through the use of Paillier encryption. Although their scheme supports more than two parties, it only allows a limited number of consecutive operations. Another approach to floating point representation of values for two-party computation, based on Paillier encryption and oblivious PRFs (OPRFs), was given by Franz *et al.* [37], who thoroughly formalized a system closely related to the IEEE 754 standard [1] used by regular CPUs for floating point arithmetic. Later a full implementation of secure evaluation of IEEE 754 was done by Franz and Katzenbeisser based on garbled circuits [38]. Boyle *et al.* [14] showed how to achieve efficient fixed-point computation based on function secret sharing in the two-party model. Catrina and Saxena [17] showed how to realize secure fixed-point computation using *any* secret sharing-based MPC scheme for an arbitrary number of parties. Their approach is to do an efficient *approximate* truncation after each multiplication to move the decimal point back down. This approach, however, requires the computation of a bit-decomposed random number, which again requires $O(k)$ multiplications in MPC, when working over a field of at most 2^k elements. Besides the advantage of working over a generic MPC scheme with general inputs, the work by Catrina and Saxena also has the advantage of working over both positive and negative numbers and does not lose accuracy regardless of the number of computations. Later Catrina and de Hoogh [16] showed how to realize this without the need for probabilistic computation in the truncation. Their idea is to compute a bit-comparison circuit in MPC using the bit decomposition of the random pad, which leads to a constant penalty in complexity. Unfortunately, all the approaches referenced above for secure computation with decimal numbers only work in the semi-honest security model. In many real-world situations, passive security is not sufficient. However, it turns out, that due to the black-box construction of the solution by Catrina and Saxena, using an MPC scheme that is maliciously secure is enough to realize their algorithms maliciously securely, as shown by Damgård *et al.* [26]. Damgård *et al.* also showed that with only minor modifications, their probabilistic truncation algorithm could be used when the underlying MPC scheme performs computation over a ring.

Motivated by the need for bit-decomposition for truncation (and more general computation over bits) a series of works have been focused on efficiently combining MPC schemes over bits and fields/rings [30,53,54], Being able to perform a mix of arithmetic and bit operations can prove essential in certain applications, e.g. when computing the digest of a hash function in MPC. Dedicated schemes with a preprocessing phase generating raw material that works in both the binary and arithmetic domains have also been constructed [34,59], yielding significantly more efficient protocols in practice than the approach of Catrina and Saxena.

Even without the recent protocols for efficient bit-decomposition, researchers have found secure fixed-point computations to generally be more efficient than secure floating-point computation [5,48]. This is due to the complex computations needed for floating-point multiplications, which would be required to be carried out in MPC, compared to a single truncation in the fixed-point approach.

Finally, it should be mentioned that recently a lot of other authors have investigated MPC over rings [2,22,23], although their focus has generally been on arbitrary rings, or rings of the type $\mathbb{Z}_{2^k}$, as these afford a computation domain closer to traditional CPUs, when $k = 32$ or $k = 64$.

1.2 Construction Blueprint

The overall idea we present is to use two independent black-box realized MPC schemes, over $\mathbb{Z}_p$ and $\mathbb{Z}_q$, to realize an MPC scheme over $\mathbb{Z}_m$ with $m = p \cdot q$ by interpreting the elements in $\mathbb{Z}_p$ and $\mathbb{Z}_q$ as elements in an RNS over m, through the Chinese Remainder Theorem. Based on this we show that one can efficiently truncate elements in $\mathbb{Z}_m$ by p with an additive error of at most 1 without requiring any MPC multiplications, but only using sharings of correlated and uncorrelated randomness in both the MPC scheme over $\mathbb{Z}_p$ and $\mathbb{Z}_q$. Specifically, we need a random value $r \in \mathbb{Z}_p$ to be stored in an MPC scheme both over $\mathbb{Z}_p$ and $\mathbb{Z}_q$. We call a pair of such correlated random values a *noise pair* and show how to efficiently construct such pairs in the semi-honest and strong covert model but with an additive error in the sharing over $\mathbb{Z}_q$. We then use the RNS MPC scheme over $\mathbb{Z}_m$ to realize fixed-point computation in MPC with base p. By picking base p we can use our efficient truncation algorithm to perform the needed truncation after a fixed-point multiplication. We furthermore show that in this setting, the error in the noise pairs does not cause problems. Hence we circumvent the need for a general truncation of a 2-power, requiring a non-constant amount of multiplications, as is generally seen in fixed-point MPC computations [17,34].

2 Preliminaries

In all our protocols we assume n mutually distrusting parties participate. We denote the set of all parties by $\mathcal{P}$ and use Adv to denote the adversary corrupting a subset of $\mathcal{P}$ of size at most $n-1$. We let s denote a statistical security parameter. Hence, the statistical distance between the real execution and simulation will be at most 2^{-s} for any fixed s. Furthermore, we define $\tilde{s} = s+1$, which is an artifact used in the proofs to ensure 2^{-s} for the *entire* simulation. We let p and q be positive integers with $q > p \geq 2^s$ s.t. $\gcd(p, q) = 1$ and $m = p \cdot q$. We use $\sim$ in conjunction with standard distributions to denote "approximately distributed by" for certain variables. E.g. $x \sim \textbf{IrwinHall}(n)$.

Table 1. The parameters and variables in play in this paper.

s	Statistical security parameter
$\tilde{s}$	$\tilde{s} = s + 1$
γ	The covert deterrence factor
p q	Primes of at least $\tilde{s}$ bits. $p < q$.
m	The RNS domain $= p \cdot q$
n	The number of parties
U	The maximum error
Q	The maximum usable space modulo q

We let $a \leftarrow_R \mathbb{Z}_p$ mean that a is uniformly sampled from the ring $\mathbb{Z}_p$. Furthermore, in general, we use $a \leftarrow P$ to mean that the value a is computed by the procedure P. For integers y and $z > 0$, we let $y \bmod z$ denote the unique integer x for which $0 \leq x < z$ and $x \equiv y \pmod z$. Furthermore, throughout the paper, we use $[a]$ to denote the set of integers $\{1, \ldots a\}$.

We highlight that while most of our protocols are secure against a static adversary corrupting a dishonest majority of parties, our protocols for generating correlated randomness only achieve robustness in the *strong covert* [9] model. We recall that in this model the adversary may cheat but will get caught with a certain, non-negligible probability γ. Furthermore, if caught, the adversary gets no influence on the computation, nor learns anything about the honest parties' input, and all honest parties learn that cheating has occurred, along with the identification of one of the corrupt parties who cheated. If the adversary does *not* get discovered when cheating, then they learn the honest parties' input and get to influence the result of the computation. However, we emphasize, that our concrete protocols achieve even stronger security since the adversary does *not* learn the honest party's input, even if they cheat and don't get caught.

We use U to denote the *maximum* additive error that can occur in our protocol. The error that can occur in our specific noise pair preprocessing will be at most $U - 1$, and our main algorithm, Algorithm 5, adds 1 to any error of the preprocessed material.

We outline the different variables and their meaning in Table 1.

2.1 UC Functionalities

We prove our construction secure in the UC framework [15] and hence no rewinding is used in our proofs and our protocol is secure under arbitrary composition.

We require standard functionalities for coin-tossing and *maliciously* secure MPC with *abort* (modeled as an arithmetic black box) working over a *field or ring*, secure against a *dishonest majority*. We assume the computation in MPC over a domain of size at least 2^s for a statistical security parameter s.

$\mathcal{F}_{\mathsf{CT}}(n, m)$

This functionality is parametrized by the number of parties participating, n, and a modulo describing the range of sampling.

Sample: Upon receiving $(\texttt{sample}, \texttt{ssid})$ from all parties, if ssid has not been seen before, then sample $x \leftarrow_R \mathbb{Z}_m$ and send $(\texttt{sample}, \texttt{ssid}, x)$ to all parties as adversarially delayed output. If ssid has been seen before, then return $(\texttt{sample}, \texttt{ssid}, x)$ as adversarially delayed output.

Fig. 1. Ideal functionality for coin-tossing

Coin-Tossing. In Fig. 1 we introduce the standard coin-tossing functionality, which allows maliciously secure sampling of uniformly random integers modulo some m.

$\mathcal{F}_{\mathsf{ABB}}(n, m)$

This functionality is parametrized by the number of parties participating, n, and the modulo which the computation is over, $\mathbb{Z}_m$.

Rand: Upon receiving $(\texttt{random}, \texttt{ssid})$ from all parties for a fresh ssid, the box samples $x \leftarrow_R \mathbb{Z}_m$ and stores $(\texttt{ssid}, x)$.

Input: Upon receiving $(\texttt{input}, i, \texttt{ssid}, x)$ for a fresh ssid from some party $i \in [n]$ and $(\texttt{input}, i, \texttt{ssid}, ?)$ from all other parties $j \in [n] \setminus \{i\}$, then store $(\texttt{ssid}, x \mod m)$.

Linear: Upon receiving $(\texttt{linear}, \alpha, \beta, \texttt{ssid}_1, \texttt{ssid}_2)$ for $\alpha, \beta \in \mathbb{Z}_m$ and a fresh $\texttt{ssid}_2$ and existing $\texttt{ssid}_1$ from all parties $i \in [n]$, retrieve $(\texttt{ssid}_1, x)$ and store $(\texttt{ssid}_2, \alpha \cdot x + \beta)$.

Add: Upon receiving $(\texttt{add}, \texttt{ssid}_1, \texttt{ssid}_2, \texttt{ssid}_3)$ for a fresh $\texttt{ssid}_3$ and existing $\texttt{ssid}_1$ and $\texttt{ssid}_2$ from all parties $i \in [n]$, retrieve $(\texttt{ssid}_1, x)$, $(\texttt{ssid}_2, y)$ and store $(\texttt{ssid}_3, x + y)$.

Mult: Upon receiving $(\texttt{mult}, \texttt{ssid}_1, \texttt{ssid}_2, \texttt{ssid}_3)$ for a fresh $\texttt{ssid}_3$ and existing $\texttt{ssid}_1$ and $\texttt{ssid}_2$ from all parties $i \in [n]$, retrieve $(\texttt{ssid}_1, x)$, $(\texttt{ssid}_2, y)$ and store $(\texttt{ssid}_3, x \cdot y)$.

Output: Upon receiving $(\texttt{output}, \texttt{ssid}, \mathcal{P})$ for an existing ssid with $\mathcal{P} \subseteq [n]$ from all parties $i \in [n]$, retrieve $(\texttt{ssid}, x)$ and send x to the adversary Adv. Wait for Adv to return either deliver or abort. If the adversary returns deliver, output x to all parties in $\mathcal{P}$, otherwise output abort.

Abort: Adv may at any point input abort at which point the functionality returns abort to all parties and aborts by not accepting any more calls for the current sid.

Fig. 2. Ideal functionality for a maliciously secure arithmetic black box with abort.

We observe the model fits well with many modern schemes such as SPDZ [28] and SPD$\mathbb{Z}_{2^k}$ [22] for any number of parties or OLE schemes [32,43] in the two-party setting. We describe the ideal functionality in Fig. 2.

As a convenience, we denote a value x within the ABB box working on integers modulo m as $[x]_m$ and assume that $(\texttt{add}, \dots)$, $(\texttt{linear}, \dots)$ and $(\texttt{mult}, \dots)$ reflect the natural commands on $[\cdot]_m$. I.e. $[w]_m = (\alpha \cdot [x]_m + [y]_m) \cdot [z]_m$ implicitly defines a call to $(\texttt{linear}, \dots)$, $(\texttt{add}, \dots)$ and $(\texttt{mult}, \dots)$ in the natural way s.t. $w = (\alpha \cdot x + y) \cdot z \mod m$.

We furthermore assume that $[x]_m$ in practice consists of an additive sharing between the parties. That is, we assume party i for $i \in [n]$ hold x_i s.t. $x = \sum_{i \in [n]} x_i \mod m$. We note, that this does *not* require white-box usage of the underlying MPC scheme, as the command $\mathcal{F}_{\mathsf{ABB}}(n, m).(\texttt{random}, \dots)$ can be used to define $[x_i]_m$ for $i \in [n-1]$. Then $\mathcal{F}_{\mathsf{ABB}}(n, m).(\texttt{add}, \dots)$ can be used to define x_n and $\mathcal{F}_{\mathsf{ABB}}(n, m).(\texttt{random}, \dots)$ to sample a random additive sharing of $[x_n]_m = \sum_{i \in [n-1]} [x_i]_m$.

Similarly, we will use $\text{SHARE}_m(x) \rightarrow [x]_m$ from party i to denote the call $\mathcal{F}_{\mathsf{ABB}}(n, m).(\texttt{input}, i, \texttt{ssid}_x, x)$ by party i and the call $\mathcal{F}_{\mathsf{ABB}}(n, m).(\texttt{input}, j, \texttt{ssid}_x, ?)$ by all other parties $i \neq j \in [n]$ for a fresh subsession ID $\texttt{ssid}_x$ associated with x. That is, we use ? to denote a value defined by another party. Similarly, we will use $\text{OPEN}_m([x]_m) \rightarrow x$ from each party $i \in [n]$ to denote the call $\mathcal{F}_{\mathsf{ABB}}(n, m).(\texttt{output}, \texttt{ssid}_x, [n])$ where $\texttt{ssid}_x$ denotes the subsession ID of $[x]_m$. That is, to open a value towards all parties. We use a similar shorthand for opening values towards a subset of parties or a specific part i.e., we let $\text{OPEN}_m([x]_m, \mathcal{P}) \rightarrow x$ from each party $i \in [n]$ denote the call $\mathcal{F}_{\mathsf{ABB}}(n, m).(\texttt{output}, \texttt{ssid}_x, \mathcal{P})$ where $\texttt{ssid}_x$ denotes the subsession ID of $[x]_m$, and thus where party $j \in \mathcal{P}$ learns x and all other parties, learn nothing besides the fact that parties in $\mathcal{P}$ have learned the value associated with $\texttt{ssid}_x$. We will also assume this convenience when sampling random values, by letting $[r]_m \leftarrow_R \mathbb{Z}_m$ denote $\mathcal{F}_{\mathsf{ABB}}(n, m).(\texttt{random}, \texttt{ssid}_r)$ for a subsession ID $\texttt{ssid}_r$ associated with r.

Finally, we highlight that the command $\mathcal{F}_{\mathsf{ABB}}(n, m).(\texttt{random}, \dots)$ can be used to trivially realize $\mathcal{F}_{\mathsf{CT}}$.

3 Truncation

Below we present Theorem 1 which gives an efficient algorithm for truncation with the smaller moduli in an RNS with two moduli. Then we show how to work with an RNS in MPC in Sect. 3.1.

Consider an RNS of two components as follows: Let $p, q \in \mathbb{N}$ be distinct positive integers with $\gcd(p, q) = 1$ and let $m = p \cdot q$. The Chinese Remainder Theorem yields the existence of a ring isomorphism $\mathbb{Z}_m \cong \mathbb{Z}_p \times \mathbb{Z}_q$ which we will denote by $\phi : \mathbb{Z}_m \rightarrow \mathbb{Z}_p \times \mathbb{Z}_q$ defined by $\phi(x) = (x \bmod p, x \bmod q)$. To ease the notation later, we let $x^{(p)}$ denote $x \in \mathbb{Z}_p$ and $x^{(q)}$ denote $x \in \mathbb{Z}_q$. The inverse of $\phi(x)$ is

$$\phi^{-1}(x^{(p)}, x^{(q)}) = (bqx^{(p)} + apx^{(q)}) \bmod m$$

where $a, b \in \mathbb{N}$ are chosen such that

$$ap + bq = 1.$$

Note that this implies that $ap = 1 \mod q$ and $bq = 1 \mod p$, so $a = p^{-1} \mod q$ and $b = q^{-1} \mod p$. Representing integers in $\mathbb{Z}_m$ as their images under ϕ is an example of an RNS with ϕ being a ring isomorphism that implies addition and multiplication may simply be done coordinate-wise. An RNS representation may also be used to efficiently compute truncation by one of the components as shown in the following theorem:

Theorem 1. *Let* $\gcd(p, q) = 1$ *and* $x \in \mathbb{Z}$ *with* $0 \leq x < pq = m$ *and let* $(x^{(p)}, x^{(q)}) = \phi(x)$. *Then*

$$\lfloor x/p \rfloor = a(x^{(q)} - x^{(p)}) \bmod q$$

where $a = p^{-1} \bmod q$.

Proof. Let $a = p^{-1} \bmod q$ and $b = q^{-1} \bmod p$. Write $x = kp + r$ with $k \in \mathbb{Z}$ and $0 \leq r < p$. Then $r = x^{(p)}$ and $\lfloor x/p \rfloor = k$ and since $x < m$ we have $0 \leq k < q$, so we just need to prove that $k \equiv a(x^{(q)} - x^{(p)}) \pmod q$. Now

$$kp + x^{(p)} = x \equiv bqx^{(p)} + apx^{(q)} \pmod m$$

since $(x^{(p)}, x^{(q)}) = \phi(x)$. This implies

$$kp \equiv (bq - 1)x^{(p)} + apx^{(q)} \pmod m.$$

Since $q \mid m$, we may consider this congruence modulo q, and noting that $ap \equiv 1 \pmod q$ we get

$$k \equiv a((bq - 1)x^{(p)} + x^{(q)}) \equiv a(x^{(q)} - x^{(p)}) \pmod q$$

as desired. □

3.1 RNS in MPC

Consider an MPC scheme working over $\mathbb{Z}_m$. A value in such a scheme is defined using two MPC instances, one over $\mathbb{Z}_p$ and one over $\mathbb{Z}_q$ such that $\gcd(p, q) = 1$. We do so using ϕ as defined above to represent a value in $\mathbb{Z}_m$ for $m = pq$ by a pair of values in $\mathbb{Z}_p \times \mathbb{Z}_q$.

Concretely, we use two MPC instances, $\mathcal{F}_{\mathsf{ABB}}(n, p)$ and $\mathcal{F}_{\mathsf{ABB}}(n, q)$, which together with the linear function ϕ induces another MPC instance $\mathcal{F}_{\mathsf{ABB}}(n, m)$. We will abuse notation to use $[x]_m$ to denote an RNS realized through shares $[x^{(p)}]_p$ in $\mathcal{F}_{\mathsf{ABB}}(n, p)$ and $[x^{(q)}]_q$ in $\mathcal{F}_{\mathsf{ABB}}(n, q)$ where $m = p \cdot q$ and hence

$$x = (q \cdot (q^{-1}x^{(p)} \mod p) + p \cdot (p^{-1} \cdot x^{(q)} \mod q)) \mod pq\ .$$

That is, where $\phi(x) \rightarrow (x \mod p, x \mod q) = (x^{(p)}, x^{(q)})$. Concretely this means that $[x]_m = ([x \bmod p]_p, [x \bmod q]_q) = ([x^{(p)}]_p, [x^{(q)}]_q)$.

These values can be defined from the MPC commands:

$$\text{SHARE}_m(x) = (\text{SHARE}_p(x \bmod p), \text{SHARE}_q(x \bmod q))$$

and

$$\text{OPEN}_m([x^{(p)}]_p, [x^{(q)}]_q, \mathcal{P}) = \phi^{-1}(\text{OPEN}_p([x^{(p)}]_p, \mathcal{P}), \text{OPEN}_q([x^{(q)}]_q, \mathcal{P})).$$

3.2 Fixed-Point Arithmetic

Observe that fixed-point representation of a real number is given as follows: If we let $b \in \mathbb{N}$ with $b \geq 2$ be the *base*, we may represent a real number $x \in \mathbb{R}$ by its *fixed-point representation with base* b given by the integer $f_b(x) = \lfloor b \cdot x \rfloor$. The fixed-point representation allows us to approximate arithmetic (see [60] for an analysis of the error terms) on real numbers by integer arithmetic since $f_b(x) + f_b(y) \approx f_b(x + y)$ and $\lfloor \frac{1}{b} f_b(x) f_b(y) \rfloor \approx f_b(x \cdot y)$. The base b is usually a power of two since this allows the division by b after each multiplication to be done by bit shifts, but any integer $b \geq 2$ will work.

With this in mind, we can do fixed-point computation in MPC over a domain $\mathbb{Z}_m$ with base p when $m = p \cdot q$ for numbers p, q with $\gcd(p, q) = 1$, given a generic MPC construction that works over $\mathbb{Z}_p$ and $\mathbb{Z}_q$ through the RNS mapping in Sect. 3.1. That is, given $[x]_m$ with an RNS decomposition $\phi([x]_m) = ([x^{(p)}]_p, [x^{(q)}]_q)$, let $[y]_q = (p^{-1} \mod q) \cdot [x^{(q)}]_q - [x^{(p)}]_p$. Then compute $\lfloor [x]_m / p \rfloor = ([y \mod p]_q, [y]_q)$ by applying Theorem 1.

However, one problem remains; How do we move a value $[y]_q$ to $[y]_p$ and vice versa as these values live in two distinct MPC instances?

4 The Construction

To facilitate the transfer of values between two different MPC instances we present two algorithms $\text{LIFT}_{p \to q}$ (Algorithm 3) and $\text{LIFT}_{q \to p}$ (Algorithm 4) which allow exactly this. Although the first of these has the side effect of a small additive error. Both of these algorithms, however, require secret correlated randomness in $\mathcal{F}_{\mathsf{ABB}}(n, p)$ and $\mathcal{F}_{\mathsf{ABB}}(n, q)$. Assume $q > p$, we preprocess a pair of values $([r]_p, [r + \epsilon \cdot p]_q)$ for a uniformly random $r \in \mathbb{Z}_p$ and some small non-negative integer $\epsilon < U$. We denote such a correlated randomness pair a *noise pair*.

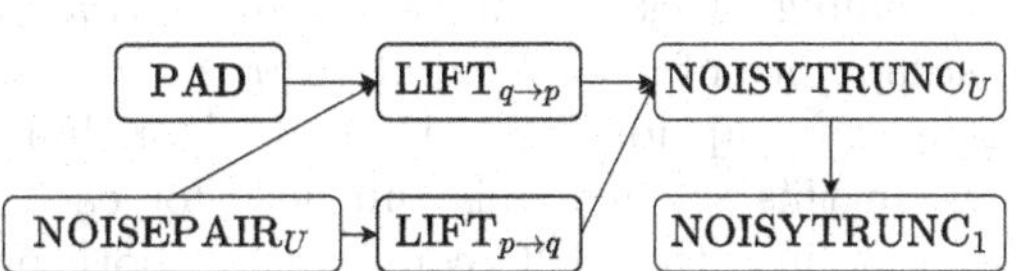

Fig. 3. Illustration of the dependencies between the different sub algorithms.

We present a concrete algorithm for generating such noise pairs NOISEPAIR_U (1) for $U = n$, which is used as a black-box in $\mathcal{F}_{\mathsf{ABB}}(n, \cdot)$. Using a noise pair it is possible to compute and publicly open $[x^{(p)}]_p + [r]_p$ in $\mathcal{F}_{\mathsf{ABB}}(n,p)$, and input this into $\mathcal{F}_{\mathsf{ABB}}(n,q)$ since r will hide the secret value $x^{(p)}$. However, to go from $\mathcal{F}_{\mathsf{ABB}}(n,p)$ and $\mathcal{F}_{\mathsf{ABB}}(n,q)$ is not as easy, since $r \in \mathbb{Z}_p$ it cannot statistically hide a value $[x^{(q)}]_q$ when $q > p$. Thus to realize $\text{LIFT}_{q\to p}$ we require another random value, denoted by ρ, which is larger than 2^s, and hence can statistically hide the part of the value $x^{(q)}$ which is larger than p. This is a standard technique known as *noise-drowning*. We specify the concrete randomness sampling procedure in algorithm PAD (Algorithm 2). Using a pad and another noise pair, $([r']_p, [r' + \epsilon \cdot p]_q)$, it is possible to compute and open $[x^{(q)}]_q + [r' + \epsilon \cdot p]_q + p \cdot [\rho]_q$ and input this into $\mathcal{F}_{\mathsf{ABB}}(n,p)$ followed by the subtraction of $[r']_q$ in order to transfer a value from $\mathcal{F}_{\mathsf{ABB}}(n,q)$ to $\mathcal{F}_{\mathsf{ABB}}(n,p)$.

The approach might cause over and underflows. However, we show that to a large extent, by carefully picking parameters, this can be avoided. Specifically, we show how to combine $\text{LIFT}_{p\to q}$ and $\text{LIFT}_{q\to p}$, based on the idea of Theorem 1, in NOISYTRUNC_U, which computes the $\lfloor [x]_m / p \rfloor$ with an additive error of at most U. Furthermore, we show how to reduce this error to at most 1, with algorithm NOISYTRUNC_1, which we present in Sect. 4.4.

In the sequel we formalize these algorithms, but defer the formal UC specification and UC proof to the full version [41].

4.1 Preprocessing

Noise Pairs. A *noise pair* consists of correlated randomness $([r]_p, [\bar{r}]_q)$, where $r \leftarrow_R \mathbb{Z}_p$ is uniformly random and $\bar{r} = r + \epsilon p$ for an integer ϵ in the range $0 \leq \epsilon < U$ with a constant $U > 0$. Constructing correlated randomness over multiple MPC schemes is not a problem unique to us [58]. Still, a small additive error typically only has minimal impact on fixed-point computations, and our truncation algorithm might introduce a small error *even* if $\bar{r} = r$. Hence instead of relying on previous results, we have tried to design a preprocessing protocol to facilitate transfer between two distinct MPC domains as lightweight as possible, *only* assuming black-box access to an *arithmetic* MPC scheme $\mathcal{F}_{\mathsf{ABB}}(n,\cdot)$, *but* with acceptance of a small additive error.

As a warm-up for our noise pair algorithm, first consider the semi-honest setting. In this setting, it is sufficient for each party to input random values $r^{(i)} \leftarrow_R \mathbb{Z}_p$ into the MPC computation both over $\mathbb{Z}_p$ and $\mathbb{Z}_q$. MPC can then be used to compute the values $[r]_p = \sum_{i\in[n]}[r^{(i)}]_p$ and $[\hat{r}]_q = [r + \epsilon \cdot p]_q = \sum_{i\in[n]}[r^{(i)}]_q$ where $\epsilon < n$ depended on the values of $r^{(i)}$. This approach is clearly correct, but only semi-honestly secure as a malicious party could simply input inconsistent values in $\mathbb{Z}_p$ and $\mathbb{Z}_q$.

Since the random value r is independent of any secret input, it is straightforward to make this covertly secure, through the standard covert paradigm of committing to multiple candidates, validating all but one, and then keeping the last one [9]. That is, each party i selects λ random values $r_1^{(i)}, \ldots, r_\lambda^{(i)} \leftarrow_R \mathbb{Z}_p$ for $\lambda = \lceil 1/(1-\gamma) \rceil$ with γ being the deterrence factor. Then input this into $\mathcal{F}_{\mathsf{ABB}}(n,p)$ and $\mathcal{F}_{\mathsf{ABB}}(n,q)$ through $\text{SHARE}_p(r_j^{(i)})$ and $\text{SHARE}_q(r_j^{(i)})$ for $i \in [n]$

and $j \in [\lambda]$. Using a coin-tossing protocol, the parties collaboratively select an index $c \leftarrow_R \mathbb{Z}_\lambda$ to keep and check $\text{OPEN}_p([r_j^{(i)}]_p = \text{OPEN}_q([r_j^{(i)}]_q)$ for $i \in [n]$ and $j \in [\lambda] \setminus \{c\}$. Finally the pair to keep is computed $[r]_p = \sum_{i \in [n]} [r_c^{(i)}]_p \mod p$ and $[\hat{r}]_q = [r + \epsilon \cdot p]_q = \sum_{i \in [n]} [r_c^{(i)}]_q$. However, one subtlety that occurs with this approach is that an adversary corrupting $n-1$ parties can now decide on a value $\tilde{\epsilon} < n-1$ and cause an error of $\epsilon = \tilde{\epsilon}$ or $\epsilon = \tilde{\epsilon} + 1$ (depending on the random choice of the honest party). This is because the adversary can choose not to pick the values $r_j^{(i)}$ randomly and hence control the amount of overflows modulo p that occurs when adding together the values modulo q.

Fortunately, this is easy to handle by having each party contribute part of each of the other party's random share modulo p. This ensures that as long as there is a single honest party, then all shares will be randomly distributed and thus the overflow cannot be controllable by the adversary, and is hence guaranteed to be Bernoulli distributed. We formally describe this in Algorithm 1.

Furthermore, observe that since we don't assume an underlying MPC scheme with identifiable abort, the adversary could cheat in one of the covertly generated pairs, and abort in case that pair gets selected for verification. To handle this problem we can use the folklore approach of *commit-and-open* wherein parties commit to the randomness they need to execute Algorithm 1 and are required to open this for validation by everyone else, in case of an abort in the underlying MPC scheme. Hence allowing everyone to find out who behaved maliciously.

Algorithm 1. Covert $\text{NOISEPAIR}_n() = ([r]_p, [\bar{r}]_q)$ with deterrence factor γ

Require: $\perp$
Ensure: $([r]_p, [\bar{r}]_q = [r + \epsilon \cdot p]_q)$ for $0 \le \epsilon < n$ with $\epsilon \sim$ **IrwinHall**(n)
Let $\lambda = \lceil 1/(1-\gamma) \rceil$
for $k \in [\lambda]$ **do**
  Each party j samples $(r_{1,j,k}, \cdots, r_{n,j,k}) \leftarrow \mathbb{Z}_p^n$
  $\text{SHARE}_p(r_{i,j,k}) \rightarrow [r_{i,j,k}]_p$ for each $i, j \in [n]$.
  $[r_{i,k}]_p = \sum_{j \in [n]} [r_{i,j,k}]_p$ for $i \in [n]$.
  $\text{OPEN}_p([r_{i,k}]_p, \{i\})$, so party i learns $r_{i,k}$, for $i \in [n]$.
  $\text{SHARE}_q(r_{i,k}) \rightarrow [r_{i,k}]_q$, for $i \in [n]$
end for
$\mathcal{F}_{\text{CT}}.\texttt{sample}(\texttt{ssid}, \lambda) \rightarrow c$ ▷ From Fig. 1
for For each party $i \in [n]$ and noise pair $k \in [\lambda] \setminus \{c\}$ **do**
  $r_{i,k}^{(p)} \leftarrow \text{OPEN}([r_{i,k}]_p)$ and $r_{i,k}^{(q)} \leftarrow \text{OPEN}([r_{i,k}]_q)$
end for
if $\exists r_{i,k}^{(p)} \neq r_{i,k}^{(q)}$ for any $i \in [n]$ and $k \in [\lambda] \setminus \{c\}$ **then**
  Output $(\texttt{cheat}, i)$ and terminate the algorithm.
end if
$[r_c]_p = \sum_{i \in [n]} [r_{i,c}]_p \mod p$ for $i \in [n]$
$[r_c + \epsilon \cdot p]_q = [\bar{r}_c]_q = \sum_{i \in [n]} [r_{i,c}]_q \mod q$, for $i \in [n]$
return $([r_c]_p, [\bar{r}_c]_q)$

Observe that we can somewhat accurately estimate the error ϵ as follows:

Remark 1. The variable ϵ in the output of Algorithm 1 is approximately Irwin-Hall[1] distributed when executed with at least one honest party,

$$\epsilon \sim \mathbf{IrwinHall}(n).$$

The proof of this remark can be found in the full version [41].

Padding. Our protocol also requires bounded randomness, used to hide overflow modulo p when trying to noise-drown a value from $\mathbb{Z}_p$ in $\mathbb{Z}_q$, without causing an overflow modulo q. In the semi-honest setting, this is easy to achieve by having each party sample uniform randomness of sufficient size and summing the contribution of each party. That is if the bound is A then each party i samples $\rho_i \leftarrow_R \mathbb{Z}_A$ and the parties compute $\rho = \sum_{i \in [n]} \rho_i$. Clearly $\rho \mod A$ is uniformly random if just a single party has been honest. Furthermore, if all parties follow the protocol then it will hold that $\rho < An$.

Because the input of each party (ρ_i) is independent of the underlying function we wish to evaluate in MPC, it becomes clear that we can perform this sampling with covert security following the same paradigm we used for noise pairs above.

As in the case for the noise pairs we use a standard commit-and-open approach to ensure that the adversary cannot abort to avoid detection.

We formalize this in Algorithm 2 in the $\mathcal{F}_{\mathsf{CT}}$, $\mathcal{F}_{\mathsf{ABB}}$-hybrid model.

Algorithm 2. Covert $\text{PAD}(A) \rightarrow [\rho]_q$ with deterrence factor γ.

Require: $An < q$
Ensure: $[\rho]_q$ with $\rho \mod A \leftarrow_R \mathbb{Z}_A$ and $\rho < An$
Let $\lambda = \lceil 1/(1-\gamma) \rceil$
Each party i samples $\rho_{i,k} \leftarrow \mathbb{Z}_A$ for $k \in [\lambda]$.
Each party i does $\text{SHARE}_q(\rho_{i,k}) \rightarrow [\rho_{i,k}]_q$.
$\mathcal{F}_{\mathsf{CT}}.\texttt{sample}(\texttt{ssid}, \lambda) \rightarrow c$ ▷ From Fig. 1
$\rho_{i,k} \leftarrow \text{OPEN}_q([\rho_{i,k}]_q)$ for $i \in [n]$ and $k \in [\lambda] \setminus \{c\}$.
if $\exists i, k : \rho_{i,k} \geq A$ **then**
    Output $(\texttt{cheat}, i)$ and abort
end if
return $[\rho]_q = \sum_{i \in [n]} [\rho_{i,c}]_q$.

4.2 Lifting

Based on noise pairs and pads we now introduce the lifting algorithms $\text{LIFT}_{p \rightarrow q}$ and $\text{LIFT}_{q \rightarrow p}$ in Algorithm 3 and Algorithm 4 respectively, which we use to move values from $\mathcal{F}_{\mathsf{ABB}}(n,p)$ to $\mathcal{F}_{\mathsf{ABB}}(n,q)$ and vice versa.

[1] Recall that the Irwin-Hall distribution is the distribution of a sum of n independent random variables each of which are uniformly distributed on $[0,1)$ and that the $\mathbf{Irwin\text{-}Hall}(n) \rightarrow \mathbf{N}(n/2, n/12)$ as $n \rightarrow \infty$.

Algorithm 3. Compute $\text{LIFT}_{p\to q}([x]_p) = [y]_q$

Require: $[x]_p$
Ensure: $[y]_q = [x - \epsilon p]_q$ with $0 \le \epsilon \le U$
Sample a pair $([r]_p, [\bar{r}]_q) \leftarrow \text{NOISEPAIR}_U()$ ▷ Using Algorithm 1
$\bar{x} \leftarrow \text{OPEN}([x]_p + [r]_p)$
$[y]_q \leftarrow \bar{x} - [\bar{r}]_q$
return $[y]_q$

Lemma 1. *Algorithm 3 computes $[y]_q = [x - \epsilon \cdot p]_q$ where ϵ is an integer with $0 \le \epsilon \le U$ when $\bar{r} = r + \tilde{\epsilon} \cdot p$ for $0 \le \tilde{\epsilon} < U$.*

Proof. Note that $\bar{x} = x + r - b \cdot p$ where $b \in \{0, 1\}$ and $b = 1$ if and only if $x + r \ge p$. Now, since $\bar{r} = r + \tilde{\epsilon} \cdot p$ for $0 \le \tilde{\epsilon} < U$ we have

$$\bar{x} - \bar{r} = x - b \cdot p - \tilde{\epsilon} \cdot p.$$

Setting $\epsilon = b + \tilde{\epsilon}$ finishes the proof as this implies $\epsilon \le U$. □

Algorithm 4. Compute $\text{LIFT}_{q\to p}([x]_q) = [y]_p$

Require: $[x]_q$ with $x < Q \le \frac{q-(U+1)p}{n(U+1)(2^{\tilde{s}}+1)}$
Ensure: $[y]_p = [x \mod p]_p$
$([r]_p, [\bar{r}]_q) \leftarrow \text{NOISEPAIR}_U()$
$[\rho]_q \leftarrow \text{PAD}((U+1)2^{\tilde{s}}Q/p)$ ▷ Using Algorithm 2
$\bar{x} \leftarrow \text{OPEN}_q([x]_q + [\bar{r}]_q + [\rho]_q \cdot p)$
$[y]_p \leftarrow (\bar{x} \bmod p) - [r]_p$
return $[y]_p$

Lemma 2. *Algorithm 4 computes $[x \bmod p]_p$ when $\rho < n(U+1)2^{\tilde{s}}Q/p$ for $p \le Q \le \frac{q-(U+1)p}{n(U+1)(2^{\tilde{s}}+1)}$.*

Proof. Since $x < Q \le \frac{q-(U+1)p}{n(U+1)(2^{\tilde{s}}+1)}$ we have

$$\begin{aligned} x + \bar{r} + \rho p &< x + Up + p + (n(U+1)2^{\tilde{s}}Q/p)p \\ &= Q + (U+1)p + n(U+1)2^{\tilde{s}}Q \\ &< (U+1)p + n((U+1)2^{\tilde{s}} + 1)Q \\ &\le (U+1)p + n((U+1)2^{\tilde{s}} + 1)\frac{q-(U+1)p}{n(U+1)(2^{\tilde{s}}+1)} \\ &= (U+1)p + q - (U+1)p = q \end{aligned}$$

Hence no overflow modulo q will happen. Thus we can define $\bar{x} = x + \bar{r} + \rho p$ as integers which implies that $\bar{x} \bmod p = x + r \bmod p$, so $y = x \bmod p$ as desired. □

For security, we require $\rho > 2^s$ to ensure statistically hiding noise-drowning.

4.3 Probabilistic Truncation

Algorithm 5. Compute $\text{NOISYTRUNC}_U([x]_m) = [y]_m$

Require: $[x]_m = ([x_1]_p, [x_2]_q)$ with $0 \le x < pQ - Up$
Ensure: $[y]_m = [\lfloor x/p \rfloor + \epsilon]_m$ with $0 \le \epsilon \le U$ for $[y]_m = ([y_1]_p, [y_2]_q)$
  $[\bar{x}_1]_q \leftarrow \text{LIFT}_{p \to q}([x_1]_p)$
  $[y_2]_q \leftarrow (p^{-1} \bmod q)([x_2]_q - [\bar{x}_1]_q)$
  $[y_1]_p \leftarrow \text{LIFT}_{q \to p}([y_2]_q)$
  return $([y_1]_p, [y_2]_q)$

Lemma 3. *Algorithm 5 computes* $[\lfloor x/p \rfloor + \epsilon]_m$ *with* $0 \le \epsilon \le U$.

Proof. From Algorithm 3 we get that $\bar{x}_1 = x_1 - \epsilon p$ for some integer ϵ with $0 \le \epsilon \le U$. Next, from Theorem 1 we get that $(p^{-1} \bmod q)(x_2 - x_1) = \lfloor x/p \rfloor$, so

$$[y_2]_q = (p^{-1} \bmod q)([x_2]_q - [\bar{x}_1]_q) = (p^{-1} \bmod q)([x_2]_q - [x_1 - \epsilon p]_q) = [\lfloor x/p \rfloor + \epsilon]_q.$$

Now,

$$y_2 = \lfloor x/p \rfloor + \epsilon < \lfloor \frac{pQ - Up}{p} \rfloor + \epsilon = Q - U + \epsilon \le Q,$$

hence the input size requirement of Algorithm 4 is fulfilled and will thus yield the correct result. This concludes the proof. □

Error. Observe that the Algorithm 3 may inherently cause a 1-bit additive error, *even* if there is no error in the NOISEPAIR used. Specifically, this occurs if $x + r > p$ as a modulo wrap-around will occur. This error is carried over to Algorithm 5, hence always resulting in the potential of a 1-bit additive error in the truncation result. This is unfortunately inevitable with our algorithms. However, we argue that when our scheme is used for fixed-point computation, this will rarely cause any issues. The reason is that any error will only be present in the least significant digits of the result of a multiplication. Fixed-point computation is already an approximation of true values, hence any usage of such algorithms must already take into account the potential of a rounding error. Thus, on an intuitive level, we expect any algorithm using fixed-point to not be highly sensitive to a slight error in the least significant digits, as a half-bit error can *always* be expected implicitly as part of inevitable rounding. The sensitivity can of course be reduced by increasing the precision. Even so, a small error *may* still accumulate through repeated multiplications. This would for example be the case if computing exponentiation through repeated multiplications. Hence, one should take into account how the multiplicative depth of a given computation can cause an increase in error, and increase the fixed-point precision (i.e. the choice of p) accordingly.

This has also been confirmed (for a 1-bit additive error) by Mohassel and Zhang [55] in the setting of machine learning regression training on standard datasets such as MNIST. In Sect. 5.1 we confirm that this is indeed also the case for the Fast Fourier Transform when using our protocol (even when allowing for an error up to n).

Reduction in computation space. Besides the potential of adding a small error, Algorithm 5 also requires a reduction of the available computation space. This is because noise-drowning is required to prevent any leakage when moving a secret shared value from $\mathcal{F}_{\mathsf{ABB}}(n, q)$ to $\mathcal{F}_{\mathsf{ABB}}(n, p)$. While an RNS over $\mathbb{Z}_q$ and $\mathbb{Z}_p$ should give a ring $\mathbb{Z}_m$ with $m = p \cdot q$, Algorithm 5 requires the value $x \in \mathbb{Z}_m$ to be less than $pQ - Up$ for $Q \leq \frac{q-(U+1)p}{n(U+1)(2^{\tilde{s}}+1)}$. Assuming we use Algorithm 1 for preprocessing and hence that $U = n$, then the amount of usable bits in $\mathbb{Z}_q$ is approximately $\log(q) - 2\log(n) - \tilde{s}$. Hence the largest value we can represent will have to consist of less than approximately $\log(p) + \log(q) - 2\log(n) - \tilde{s}$ bits. That is, we lose approximately $2\log(n) + \tilde{s}$ bits of $\mathbb{Z}_m$. Since we require $Q > p$ (otherwise we could not fully represent values from $\mathbb{Z}_p$ in $\mathbb{Z}_q$ when lifting in Algorithm 3), we can conclude that $q > n^2 p 2^{\tilde{s}}$. Such a domain size is significantly larger than 2^s which is typically the *minimally* required size by standard MPC schemes such as SPDZ [28]. However, requiring a gap in computation space when computing truncation is common. Several previous works [17,34] require at least the s most significant bits to be 0 to be able to do truncation correctly. It is also worth stressing that both in our and previous works, the limit in computation space is *only* relevant for the value being truncated. Hence general computation can use the full domain in both cases.

Input Constraints. Reduction in computation space is not the only constraint we encounter on the magnitude of *secret* values. Specifically corrupt parties are always allowed to choose their own input in MPC, and since the underlying scheme $\mathcal{F}_{\mathsf{ABB}}(n, q)$ supports the full domain $\mathbb{Z}_q$, we cannot simply hope that their input fulfills the constraints required by Lemma 2. However, this can be enforced by using a comparison operation [16]. Still, depending on the computation, such a check might be superfluous in the security model. Since the correctness of most computations will not be fulfilled if corrupt parties give malformed input. This is inherently something that cannot be prevented in MPC unless the input can be anchored in some manner. Hence, causing a computation to fail by giving bad input that yields a bad result, or giving bad input that yields an error in one of the underlying algorithms, might amount to the same thing.

Negative Numbers. One final problem that occurs when constraining the computation domain is that representing negative numbers using two's complement is no longer possible. This is because a negative number with a small absolute value, will not fulfill the input constraint of Algorithm 4. However, it fortunately turns out to be easy to still facilitate computation over signed values when q is odd and $p \mid (q-1)/2$ by applying the following approach: Given unsigned input

$x \in \mathbb{Z}_m$, let $x > m/2$ represent the negative integer $x - m$, similarly to two's complement.

However, before any truncation is computed we increase the unsigned input $x \in \mathbb{Z}_m$ by $p(q-1)/2 \approx m/2$. Note that this does not affect $x^{(p)}$ of $\phi(x) \rightarrow (x^{(p)}, x^{(q)})$ and since $p \mid (q-1)/2$, we have $\phi(x + p(q-1)/2) = (x^{(p)}, x^{(q)} + p(q-1)/2)$. Formally, we define a new operator $\textsc{NoisyTrunc}'_U$ by

$$\textsc{NoisyTrunc}'_U(x) = \textsc{NoisyTrunc}_U(x + ap) - a$$

where $a = \lfloor q/2 \rfloor \approx m/2$. Recall that $\textsc{NoisyTrunc}_U(x') = \lfloor x'/p \rfloor + \varepsilon$ for $0 \leq \varepsilon \leq U$ if x' satisfied the upper bound in Algorithm 5, hence the following holds:

$$\begin{aligned}
\textsc{NoisyTrunc}'_U(x) &= \textsc{NoisyTrunc}_U(x + ap) - a \\
&= \textsc{NoisyTrunc}_U(x + \lfloor q/2 \rfloor p) - \lfloor q/2 \rfloor \\
&= \lfloor x/p \rfloor + \varepsilon + (q-1)/2 - (q-1)/2 = \lfloor x/p \rfloor + \varepsilon.
\end{aligned}$$

4.4 Error Reduction

Below we show an approach for reducing the error that can occur in the approximate truncation Algorithm 5 above. In the full version [41] we show how to remove this error this, however, requires evaluating a very large polynomial of degree $\approx pU^2$ in MPC, after computing Algorithm 5. Which would completely remove any advantage of our algorithm. Instead, we propose an algorithm that reduces the error down to a single additive bit, and involves evaluating Algorithm 5 twice, along with evaluating a polynomial of degree $\approx U^2$ in MPC; something that requires the online computation of $O(U^2)$ secure multiplications. We describe this in Algorithm 6, which we prove in the full version.

Intuitively by first doing the truncation with an error up to U, it is possible to multiply the result with p to isolate the noise and then apply the truncation again. Hence, the result can be adjusted to have noise that is at most 1.

While a lower error is objectively desirable we believe this algorithm is more of theoretical interest than practical interest, as it requires running Algorithm 5 twice *along* with $O(n^2)$ multiplications. This is a very significant overhead, while the payoff is minimal when running with a small number of parties such as 2 or 3.

Algorithm 6. Compute $\textsc{NoisyTrunc}_1([x]_m) = [\lfloor x/p \rfloor + \varepsilon']_m$ with $0 \leq \varepsilon' \leq 1$. Let P be a polynomial of degree $U^2 + 3U - 1$ such that $P(x) = \lfloor x/(U+1) \rfloor$.

Require: $0 \leq x < m - (U+1)(2^{\tilde{s}} + 1)p^2 - Up$, $[x]_m = ([x_1]_p, [x_2]_q)$

$[y]_m \leftarrow \textsc{NoisyTrunc}_U([x]_m)$ $\quad \triangleright\ y = \lfloor \frac{x}{p} \rfloor + \epsilon$

$[x']_m = (U+1)([x]_m - p[y]_m + pU)$ $\quad \triangleright\ x' = (U+1)(p(U-\epsilon) + (x \bmod p))$

$[w]_m \leftarrow \textsc{NoisyTrunc}_U([x']_m)$ $\quad \triangleright\ w = \lfloor \frac{(U+1)(x \bmod p)}{p} \rfloor + (U+1)(U-\epsilon) + \varepsilon'$

$[y']_m = [y]_m - U - P([w]_m)$ $\quad \triangleright\ y' = \lfloor x/p \rfloor + \varepsilon'$. See the full version [41] for details.

return $[y']_m$

Remark 2. The variable ε' in the output of Algorithm 6 is distributed as follows when executing with at least one honest party:

$$\varepsilon' \sim \mathbf{Bernoulli}((x \bmod p)/p) + \mathbf{N}\left(\frac{1}{2}, \frac{1}{12U}\right)$$

Still, one more detail to consider is that the input to the second application of truncation has to satisfy the upper bound constraint of Algorithm 5. More concretely:

Remark 3. Assume $U^2+2U \leq 2^s$ and $Q > p > 2^s$ then when $x' = (U+1)([x]_m - p[y]_m + pU)$ as per Algorithm 6 then $x' < pQ - Up$.

We leave the proofs of Remark 2 and 3 and the full specification of polynomial P to the full version [41].

5 Efficiency

5.1 Implementation

We developed a proof-of-concept implementation[2] of our RNS based MPC scheme and NoisyTrunc$_U$ of Algorithm 5 and compare it against SPDZ [28] for fixed-point computation when using the algorithm of Catrina and Saxena [17] for probabilistic truncation. We specifically chose to compare with the probabilistic truncation of Catrina and Saxena because, to the best of our knowledge, it is the most efficient scheme that only requires black-box access to $\mathbb{F}_{\mathsf{ABB}}(n, \cdot)$, with a sufficiently large prime modulo, *and* which is also secure in the dishonest majority setting. Furthermore, this scheme is already implemented in our framework of choice, FRESCO, and hence makes it to make a more fair, apples-to-apples comparison. Concretely their scheme realizes *probabilistic approximate* truncation using a random value, bounded by a certain 2-power, with a known bit-decomposition, which is used to pad the value to truncate. This value is then opened and truncated in plain. The public, truncated value is then input to MPC again and the padding is subtracted and the decomposed random bits are used to account for any overflow that might happen from the random padding. We highlight that both their and our construction can be executed in constant rounds both during the online and preprocessing phases and that both constructions do not require any secure multiplications during the online phase. However, we also forgo the need for secure multiplications in the preprocessing phase.

Our benchmarks consist of micro-benchmarks in multiple network settings and with different-sized computation domains, but also through the real-world application of Fast Fourier Transform (FFT) using the Cooley-Tukey algorithm. All phases of the Catrina and Saxena protocol we benchmark are *maliciously* secure. While our online and triple preprocessing phases are also maliciously secure (see Damgård *et al.* [26]), our generation of correlated randomness

[2] Our FRESCO fork is freely available at https://github.com/jonas-lj/fresco and our benchmark setup can be found at https://github.com/jonas-lj/FFTDemo.

(NoisePairs and Pads) is only secure in the *strong covert* security model for robustness.

We chose to benchmark our protocol with the larger error $\epsilon \leq n$, instead of $\varepsilon' \leq 1$ as practically *efficient* MPC computations are generally only desirable for a small number of parties, such as 2 or 3. Thus, the improvement in error by running Algorithm 5 over Algorithm 6 is minimal. Furthermore, for our chosen real-world application of FFT, we empirically validated that the error in the accuracy of the result when using NoisyTrunc$_U$ was at most $5.81 \cdot 10^{-15}$ for any of our benchmarked setups.

Table 2. Domain sizes used in the benchmarks, assuming 3 parties and at least 39 bits of statistical security. Column "Usable" expresses the usable amount of bits.

$\log(m)$	Ours			[17]
	$\log(p)$	$\log(q)$	Usable	Usable
136	40	96	91	95
192	56	136	147	151
256	88	168	211	215
512	216	296	467	471
1536	728	808	1491	1495

Since our protocol offers security based on a malicious arithmetic secure MPC protocol and supports security for a dishonest majority, we found SPDZ [22,28] to be the most natural competitor and MPC scheme which we can base our underlying $\mathcal{F}_{\mathsf{ABB}}$ on. For this reason, we chose to implement our scheme in the FRESCO [3] framework, which is an open-source Java framework for MPC that natively has support for SPDZ. It is designed to allow developers to implement their own MPC back-end and then take advantage of an extensive library of functions such as sorting, searching, and statistics, which can be used to design real-world MPC applications. Furthermore, FRESCO has been used extensively in other academic works [6,12,25,26].

Code Design. We wrote our code as a new MPC back-end for FRESCO, aggregating two SPDZ instances, of appropriate moduli and using these to implement the basic arithmetic operations required by an MPC scheme (input, output, addition, linear operations, and multiplications). We then wrote our efficient, approximate truncation function and integrated this with the existing FRESCO code for performing fixed-point arithmetic. Our code uses no multi-threading on top of what is implicitly done in FRESCO, and we observe that FRESCO only takes advantage of multi-threading insofar as to allow asynchronous networking and in certain select locations implicitly through the Java class `ParallelStream`.

Experimental Setup. We ran all our experiments on AWS EC2 t2.xlarge servers located in Paris, Frankfurt, and London and observed that the average latency between any two servers is between 10–15 ms and an average of 0.43 ms when in the same data center. We observe that each of these machines has 4 virtual cores on Intel Xeon CPUs and 16 GiB of RAM. All machines were running Amazon Linux Coretto and OpenJDL 17. Network communication (even on same-machine tests) is done using a standard TCP/IP socket, *without* adding TLS or securing layers on top. Numbers are based on the average of *at least*

10 iterations and errors are the standard deviation. The only exception is triple preprocessing for SPDZ for a domain of 1536 bits, which is only done once.

In all the benchmarks, we have used the same overall choice of domain size, m. However, some slack in the computation space is needed to be able to carry out the probabilistic truncation correctly, both in our scheme and the one by Catrina and Saxena. For Catrina and Saxena this reduction is $n + s$ bits, and for our scheme, it is approximately $2n + \tilde{s}$ as discussed in Sect. 4.3. We show the concrete effect of this for our benchmarks in Table 2. Finally, observe that for all benchmarks we have ensured that $s \geq 39$.

Table 3. Timing in seconds for **1024** *regular* multiplications and triple preprocessing for both our scheme and SPDZ for 2 parties with domains with various *bits* available for computation. $s \geq 39$. The best numbers are marked in bold.

	Triple preprocessing		Integer multiplication	
log(m)	Ours (RNS SPDZ)	SPDZ	Ours (RNS SPDZ)	SPDZ
LAN, latency 0.43 ms				
136	11.6 ± 0.21	$\mathbf{10.7 \pm 0.18}$	0.197 ± 0.014	$\mathbf{0.190 \pm 0.029}$
192	$\mathbf{14.8 \pm 0.29}$	16.6 ± 0.48	0.205 ± 0.012	$\mathbf{0.180 \pm 0.008}$
256	$\mathbf{19.1 \pm 0.32}$	20.7 ± 0.18	0.206 ± 0.006	$\mathbf{0.184 \pm 0.004}$
512	$\mathbf{42.3 \pm 0.70}$	54.9 ± 1.3	0.275 ± 0.015	$\mathbf{0.214 \pm 0.008}$
1536	$\mathbf{233 \pm 1.8}$	462	0.467 ± 0.017	$\mathbf{0.337 \pm 0.003}$
WAN, latency 10 ms				
136	12.8 ± 1.1	$\mathbf{11.2 \pm 0.36}$	0.392 ± 0.136	$\mathbf{0.247 \pm 0.046}$
192	$\mathbf{15.8 \pm 0.37}$	17.3 ± 0.43	0.311 ± 0.079	$\mathbf{0.248 \pm 0.012}$
256	$\mathbf{21.2 \pm 1.3}$	$\mathbf{21.2 \pm 0.28}$	0.262 ± 0.028	$\mathbf{0.246 \pm 0.015}$
512	$\mathbf{44.5 \pm 1.4}$	56.1 ± 1.2	0.326 ± 0.010	$\mathbf{0.286 \pm 0.012}$
1536	$\mathbf{243 \pm 3.7}$	494	0.535 ± 0.012	$\mathbf{0.420 \pm 0.008}$

Micro Benchmarks. We took a micro-benchmark approach to our implementation, letting it consist of several interchangeable components for different levels of preprocessing. Concretely we obtain the following micro-benchmarks

Triple preprocessing. Preprocessing of multiplication triples for both Catrina and Saxena's and our scheme. This can be done before the input or function to compute is known. We based it on MASCOT [46], as this is currently the only multiplication triple preprocessing supported by FRESCO. However, more efficient approaches have been presented since MASCOT [47], so these numbers should be considered an upper bound.

Correlated randomness. For our scheme this involves preprocessing of NoisePairs and Pads; the process of Algorithm 1 and Algorithm 2. For Catrina and Saxena this involves bit-decomposition of a random number

Table 4. Timing in seconds for **1024** *fixed-point* multiplications and preparation of the *correlated randomness* required for this (NoisePair and Pad for our scheme with $\gamma = 2$ and random bit decomposition for SPDZ) for 2 parties with domains with various *bits* available for computation. Column #Triples express how many preprocessed multiplication triples are required for **1024** fixed-point multiplications. $s \geq 39$ The best numbers are marked in bold.

	#Triples		Correlated randomness		Fixed-point multiplication	
log(m)	Ours	[17]	Ours	[17]	Ours	[17]
LAN, latency 0.43 ms						
136	**1024**	41,984	0.355 ± 0.018	$\mathbf{0.263 \pm 0.006}$	$\mathbf{0.363 \pm 0.010}$	1.17 ± 0.015
192	**1024**	58,368	0.368 ± 0.011	$\mathbf{0.264 \pm 0.005}$	$\mathbf{0.365 \pm 0.007}$	1.42 ± 0.029
256	**1024**	91,136	0.365 ± 0.014	$\mathbf{0.312 \pm 0.007}$	$\mathbf{0.395 \pm 0.007}$	1.68 ± 0.027
512	**1024**	222,208	$\mathbf{0.401 \pm 0.062}$	0.669 ± 0.004	$\mathbf{0.438 \pm 0.016}$	2.82 ± 0.044
1536	**1024**	746,496	$\mathbf{0.505 \pm 0.023}$	8.86 ± 0.077	$\mathbf{0.787 \pm 0.010}$	11.0 ± 0.042
WAN, latency 10 ms						
136	**1024**	41,984	0.438 ± 0.008	$\mathbf{0.307 \pm 0.005}$	$\mathbf{0.402 \pm 0.014}$	4.99 ± 0.32
192	**1024**	58,368	0.453 ± 0.014	$\mathbf{0.314 \pm 0.006}$	$\mathbf{0.413 \pm 0.014}$	6.37 ± 0.10
256	**1024**	91,136	0.455 ± 0.014	$\mathbf{0.369 \pm 0.016}$	$\mathbf{0.441 \pm 0.013}$	8.15 ± 0.12
512	**1024**	222,208	$\mathbf{0.476 \pm 0.020}$	0.766 ± 0.008	$\mathbf{0.487 \pm 0.013}$	15.1 ± 0.35
1536	**1024**	746,496	$\mathbf{0.608 \pm 0.024}$	8.84 ± 0.042	$\mathbf{0.849 \pm 0.021}$	35.6 ± 0.42

of $\lceil \log_2(p) \rceil$ bits, (*excluding* the preprocessing of $\lceil \log_2(p) \rceil$ triples which is needed for the sampling of random bits) needed for the approximate truncation [17]. This phase can be done offline at the same time as triple preprocessing.

Fixed-point multiplication. Online time of fixed-point multiplication with base p and hence $\log(p)$ bits precision. Thus $\log(p) + 1$ preprocessed multiplication triples are required for Catrina and Saxena's protocol and 1 for our protocol (along with a correlated randomness element). Both protocols only require 1 multiplication to be executed during the online phase.

Integer multiplication. Online time of pure *integer* multiplications in MPC. This requires a preprocessed multiplication triple for both protocols.

We express these micro-benchmarks in Tables 3 and 4. From Table 3, we can conclude that triple preprocessing becomes cheaper for our RNS scheme compared to SPDZ, the larger m gets. Whereas for the online time for multiplications, our RNS scheme is slightly worse than SPDZ. While the first observation is expected, the second is surprising as we intuitively would expect our scheme to perform comparatively better for larger domains. This is because computation over Z_p and $\mathbb{Z}_q$ and generally more efficient than computation over $\mathbb{Z}_{pq}$, assuming pq does not fit within a word. This has been the motivation for several previous usages of RNSs [7,45,57]. From Table 4, when it comes to the correlated randomness, we again observe that our scheme is more efficient for larger m, whereas Catrina and Saxena's scheme is more efficient for smaller m. Concerning the online *fixed-point* multiplication time we see that our scheme is significantly faster than the one by Catrina and Saxena, *and* that it scales more gracefully for larger m. It is not unexpected that our scheme performs better for fixed-point computation (even excluding triple preprocessing) first; for the reason of more efficient computation over the smaller $\mathbb{Z}_p$ and $\mathbb{Z}_q$ domains, but also since our online truncation computation does not need to perform $O(\log(p))$ bit-fiddling operations, like Catrina and Saxena's scheme. Concerning the generation of correlated randomness, it is hard to predict how our scheme would fare against the other scheme since the approaches are so different. Although for similar reasons as above, we did expect it to scale better relatively, compared to Catrina and Saxena's scheme, which the benchmarks confirm. We give more detail about the time it takes to preprocess our correlated randomness in Fig. 4. This figure shows how the generation of correlated randomness scales with different choices of deterrence factors, both on LAN and WAN. More specifically it shows that network latency has a minimal effect on the time, as expected due to the protocol being constant round. As expected this loosely mimics a cost function $\lambda(\gamma) = \lceil 1/(1-\gamma) \rceil$, which reflects the number of times the heaviest parts of the preprocessing must be carried out as γ increases. More surprisingly it also shows that there is barely any performance penalty for larger computational domains, up to $\log(m) = 512$.

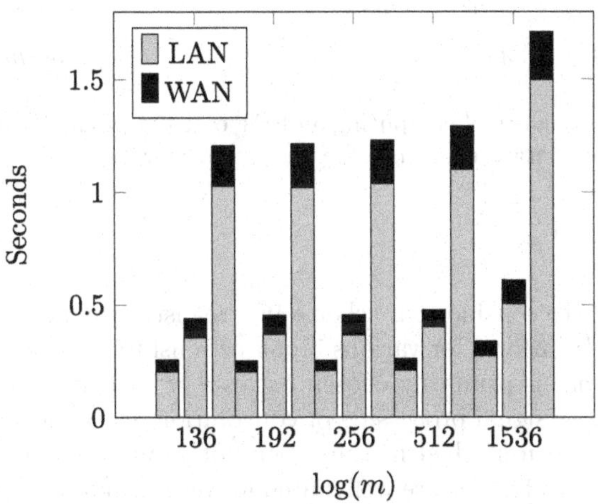

Fig. 4. Computation time in seconds for noise pair and padding preprocessing needed for **1024** truncations for 2 parties. $s \geq 39$. Left-side bars represent a semi-honest preprocessing ($\gamma = 0$), middle bars represent $\gamma = 0.5$ and right-side bars represent $\gamma = 0.875$.

Concerning the choice of domain, we picked the smallest possible (with reasonable statistical security, i.e. $s \geq 39$) that is supported by our scheme, along with certain larger sizes and the *largest* supported by FRESCO (domain size 1536 bits).

We observe that online time for fixed-point multiplications is between 3.2-42x faster using our scheme depending on the computation domain (as seen in the two right-most columns of Table 4). However, if we include the preprocessing time, our scheme is between 36-1,400x faster[3]. The reason for such a significant difference is that our scheme only requires 1 triple per fixed-point multiplication and Catrina and Saxena's protocol requires $1 + \ell$ triples where 2^{ℓ} is the domain size of the fractional digits, where $\ell = \lceil \log_2(p) \rceil$ in our benchmarks to allow a direct comparison (Fig. 5).

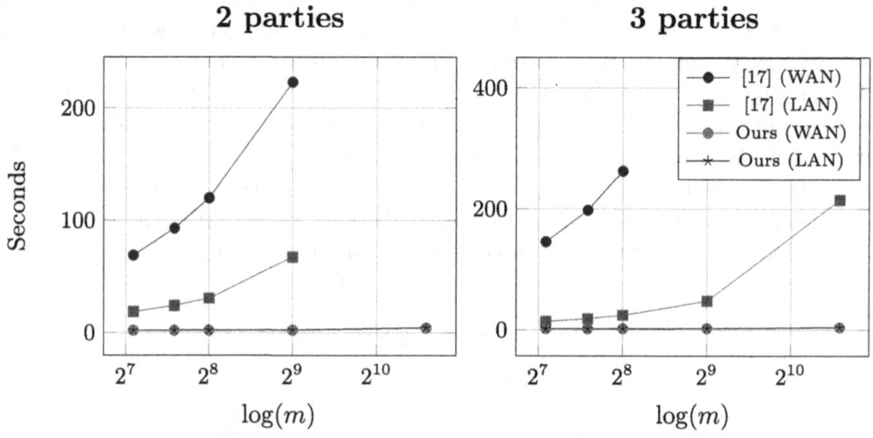

Fig. 5. Online performance of computing an FFT of **1024** inputs for different amount of parties in different network settings. $s \geq 39$. Latency for 2 servers is 10 ms and 10–14 ms for 3 servers.

FFT Benchmark. To consider our scheme in a realistic setting, we benchmarked the Fast Fourier Transform for various input sizes using the Cooley-Tukey Algorithm. This use-case is primarily chosen because of its pervasive appearance in computation such as signal processing or convolution neural networks, the latter of which has also been studied in the setting of secure computation [51]. Furthermore, FFT computations are well-suited for residue number systems because they only use multiplication and addition. The input to the computation is a vector of complex numbers, each of which is in our implementation represented by two fixed-point numbers, one for the real part and one for the imaginary part. We show the online time for evaluating Cooley-Tukey on 1024 inputs using our scheme in Fig. 5. More specifically the figure shows the increase in time as the computation domain increases, for 2 and 3 parties. The base for the fixed-point

[3] The factors are for $\gamma = 0.5$ and depend on the size of the domain and whether execution is over WAN/LAN. Concretely the factors are computed by taking the number of triples required for truncation from Table 4 and multiplying with the preprocessing time from Table 3 and adding the online time (again from Table 4).

computation is p and hence depends on the domain m, as defined in Table 2. The computation requires $O(|\text{input}| \log(|\text{input}|))$ multiplications executed over $O(\log(|\text{input}|))$ rounds. We here observe that while each of these multiplications consists of a secret value and public value, we still require a truncation after each multiplication since the input is a fixed-point number. Thus, our scheme does not require multiplication triples whereas the one by Catrina and Saxena does. From the figure we observe that our scheme is significantly faster for FFT than the one by Catrina and Saxena as we would expect because of the reasons and findings from the "Micro benchmark" section, but exacerbated by the fact that our scheme does not need to multiply two secret numbers in MPC.

5.2 Comparison with Related Techniques

Several schemes for efficient probabilistic truncation exist that perform better than the work of Catrina and Saxena [17], but also require access to a functionality $\mathbb{F}_{\mathsf{ABB}}(n, 2)$. While it is possible to emulate operations modulo 2 in large fields, addition (XOR) requires a multiplication. The same is true for sampling of a random bit. Furthermore, schemes working over modulo 2 are typically significantly more efficient than schemes working over a large modulo p [39,44,50]. Hence the possibility of sampling random bits using $\mathbb{F}_{\mathsf{ABB}}(n, 2)$ and moving these to $\mathbb{F}_{\mathsf{ABB}}(n, p)$ could lead to a more efficient version of the Catrina and Saxena protocol. The line of work trying to achieve this starts with the ABY protocol [30] which is a semi-honestly secure two-party protocol allowing mixed computation over bits and large domains when garbled circuits are used for bit computation. Later Rotaru and Wood [59] showed an efficient protocol for generating and computing over bits in an MPC scheme working modulo a large p with the help of garbled circuits. Their protocol works for an arbitrary amount of parties, in the dishonest majority setting against a malicious adversary. They coined the term *daBits* for a pair $([b]_2, [b]_p)$ where p is large. Several works improve upon this construction, culminating in the work by Escudero *et al.* [34]. They show a more efficient protocol for daBits which is maliciously secure against a dishonest majority that only requires black-box access to $\mathbb{F}_{\mathsf{ABB}}(n, 2)$ and $\mathbb{F}_{\mathsf{ABB}}(n, p)$. However, they also show how to extend the daBit notion to extended daBits (*edaBits*), which is a representation of $(\{[b_i]_2\}_i, [r]_p)$ s.t. $\sum_i 2^i \cdot [b_i]_2 = [r]_p$. That is, a full bit-decomposition of a random number modulo p, represented by its binary parts. This allows a more efficient execution of the probabilistic truncation protocol of Catrina and Saxena. For completeness, we mention that certain other computations that require bit-decomposition can be realized even faster using edaBits, than by adapting the existing protocols of Catrina, Saxena and de Hoogh. This is specifically the case for comparison when using the Rabbit protocol [53].

It is hard to make an apples-to-apples efficiency comparison between these schemes and ours (and the one by Catrina and Saxena) due to their need for $\mathcal{F}_{\mathsf{ABB}}(n, 2)$. This is because $\mathcal{F}_{\mathsf{ABB}}(n, 2)$ can typically not be realized using the same techniques as for $\mathcal{F}_{\mathsf{ABB}}(n, p)$ with $p > 2^s$. However, in Table 5 we try to

Table 5. Complexity comparison between our scheme and other approaches for a single probabilistic truncation in the amortized setting when truncating k bits of values over $\mathbb{Z}_m$. Row *Trip.* expresses the amount of preprocessed triples needed, whereas *Offline rounds* expresses the rounds of communication needed which is independent of the private inputs, and finally *Online* $\mathbb{F}_2/\mathbb{Z}_m$ expresses the multiplications required to compute truncation.

		[17]	daBits [34]	edaBits [34]	Ours
Trip.	$\mathbb{F}_2$	0	$O(\log(n) \cdot (k+s)$	$O(\log(n)^2 + \log(n) \cdot (n+k)$	0
	$\mathbb{Z}_m$	k	0	0	0
Offline rounds		1	$O(\log(k))$	$O(k)$	5
Online	$\mathbb{F}_2$	0	0	0	0
	$\mathbb{Z}_m$	0	0	0	0
	Rounds	1	1	1	2

compare the different schemes asymptotically, based on the heavy computations (multiplications in $\mathbb{F}_{\mathsf{ABB}}$ for $\mathbb{Z}_m$ and $\mathbb{F}_2$)[4].

Furthermore, we observe that the edaBits authors find a 5-9x improvement in computing the "comparison" operation, compared to the arithmetic approach of Catrina and de Hoogh [16] when *including* preprocessing. While comparison is not the same as probabilistic truncation, the main bottleneck of both protocols is the bit-decomposition of a random element in $\mathbb{F}_m$. Hence we believe a similar improvement would be found for probabilistic truncation. Thus we expect that our results will still be about a factor 4-280x more efficient than the edaBit approach when including preprocessing and using the "comparison" improvement factor verbatim.

It is worth emphasizing that both the online and preprocessing approach by Catrina and Saxena, daBits, and edaBits are maliciously secure against a dishonest majority. Our online phase is also maliciously secure, but our concrete suggestion for realizing the preprocessing phase is done in a strong covert security model for robustness. Furthermore, the possible error in the truncation of Catrina and Saxena is at most 1, whereas our error is at most $1 \leq U$. Finally, we require working in a domain of $o(p^3)$ bits (spread on two different MPC schemes working modulo p and modulo $q > p^2$), which gives us $o(p^2)$ usable bits in the secret shared value that gets truncated. Catrina and Saxena, daBits, and edaBits also require a gap in the usable bits of 2^s, hence they need a domain of $o(p^2)$ bits when $p \approx 2^s$.

[4] Observe that edaBits require many different components to achieve their efficient result. This includes *faulty multiplications* in MPC which are about $O(B)$ times more efficient than a "normal" multiplication in MPC. Here $B \in \{3, 4, 5\}$ depending on an amortization parameter. In the table, we have for simplicity only counted real multiplications and assumed $O(B)$ faulty multiplications are equivalent to a real one.

We leave as future work the possibility of incorporating daBit and edaBit techniques to sample random and correlated values in different domains in a manner that works with our protocols.

References

1. Ieee standard for floating-point arithmetic. IEEE Std 754–2019 (Revision of IEEE 754–2008), pp. 1–84 (2019). https://doi.org/10.1109/IEEESTD.2019.8766229
2. Abspoel, M., Dalskov, A.P.K., Escudero, D., Nof, A.: An efficient passive-to-active compiler for honest-majority MPC over rings. In: Sako, K., Tippenhauer, N.O. (eds.) ACNS 21, Part II. LNCS, vol. 12727, pp. 122–152. Springer, Heidelberg (2021). https://doi.org/10.1007/978-3-030-78375-4_6
3. Alexandra Institute: FRESCO - a FRamework for Efficient Secure COmputation. https://github.com/aicis/fresco
4. Algesheimer, J., Camenisch, J., Shoup, V.: Efficient computation modulo a shared secret with application to the generation of shared safe-prime products. In: Yung, M. (ed.) CRYPTO 2002. LNCS, vol. 2442, pp. 417–432. Springer, Heidelberg (2002). https://doi.org/10.1007/3-540-45708-9_27
5. Aliasgari, M., Blanton, M., Zhang, Y., Steele, A.: Secure computation on floating point numbers. In: NDSS 2013. The Internet Society, February 2013
6. Almeida, J.B., et al.: A fast and verified software stack for secure function evaluation. In: Thuraisingham, B.M., Evans, D., Malkin, T., Xu, D. (eds.) ACM CCS 2017, pp. 1989–2006. ACM Press, October/November 2017. https://doi.org/10.1145/3133956.3134017
7. Asif, S., Hossain, M.S., Kong, Y.: High-throughput multi-key elliptic curve cryptosystem based on residue number system. IET Comput. Digit. Tech. **11**(5), 165–172 (2017). https://doi.org/10.1049/iet-cdt.2016.0141
8. Atallah, M.J., Bykova, M., Li, J., Frikken, K.B., Topkara, M.: Private collaborative forecasting and benchmarking. In: Atluri, V., Syverson, P.F., di Vimercati, S.D.C. (eds.) Proceedings of the 2004 ACM Workshop on Privacy in the Electronic Society, WPES 2004, Washington, DC, USA, October 28, 2004, pp. 103–114. ACM (2004). https://doi.org/10.1145/1029179.1029204
9. Aumann, Y., Lindell, Y.: Security against covert adversaries: efficient protocols for realistic adversaries. J. Cryptol. **23**(2), 281–343 (2010). https://doi.org/10.1007/s00145-009-9040-7
10. Banerjee, A., Clear, M., Tewari, H.: zkHawk: practical private smart contracts from MPC-based hawk. Cryptology ePrint Archive, Report 2021/501 (2021). https://eprint.iacr.org/2021/501
11. Baum, C., Chiang, J.H., David, B., Frederiksen, T.K.: Eagle: Efficient privacy preserving smart contracts. IACR Cryptol. ePrint Arch., p. 1435 (2022). https://eprint.iacr.org/2022/1435
12. Baum, C., David, B., Frederiksen, T.K.: P2DEX: privacy-preserving decentralized cryptocurrency exchange. In: Sako, K., Tippenhauer, N.O. (eds.) ACNS 2021. LNCS, vol. 12726, pp. 163–194. Springer, Cham (2021). https://doi.org/10.1007/978-3-030-78372-3_7
13. Bogetoft, P., et al.: Secure multiparty computation goes live. In: Dingledine, R., Golle, P. (eds.) FC 2009. LNCS, vol. 5628, pp. 325–343. Springer, Heidelberg (2009). https://doi.org/10.1007/978-3-642-03549-4_20

14. Boyle, E., et al.: Function secret sharing for mixed-mode and fixed-point secure computation. In: Canteaut, A., Standaert, F.-X. (eds.) EUROCRYPT 2021. LNCS, vol. 12697, pp. 871–900. Springer, Cham (2021). https://doi.org/10.1007/978-3-030-77886-6_30
15. Canetti, R.: Universally composable security: a new paradigm for cryptographic protocols. In: 42nd Annual Symposium on Foundations of Computer Science, FOCS 2001, 14–17 October 2001, Las Vegas, Nevada, USA, pp. 136–145. IEEE Computer Society (2001). https://doi.org/10.1109/SFCS.2001.959888
16. Catrina, O., de Hoogh, S.: Improved primitives for secure multiparty integer computation. In: Garay, J.A., De Prisco, R. (eds.) SCN 2010. LNCS, vol. 6280, pp. 182–199. Springer, Heidelberg (2010). https://doi.org/10.1007/978-3-642-15317-4_13
17. Catrina, O., Saxena, A.: Secure computation with fixed-point numbers. In: Sion, R. (ed.) FC 2010. LNCS, vol. 6052, pp. 35–50. Springer, Heidelberg (2010). https://doi.org/10.1007/978-3-642-14577-3_6
18. Chandran, N., Gupta, D., Obbattu, S.L.B., Shah, A.: SIMC: ML inference secure against malicious clients at semi-honest cost. Cryptology ePrint Archive, Report 2021/1538 (2021). https://eprint.iacr.org/2021/1538
19. Chen, M., et al.: Multiparty generation of an RSA modulus. In: Micciancio, D., Ristenpart, T. (eds.) CRYPTO 2020. LNCS, vol. 12172, pp. 64–93. Springer, Cham (2020). https://doi.org/10.1007/978-3-030-56877-1_3
20. Chen, M., et al.: Multiparty generation of an RSA modulus. J. Cryptol. **35**(2), 12 (2022). https://doi.org/10.1007/s00145-021-09395-y
21. Chen, M., et al.: Diogenes: lightweight scalable RSA modulus generation with a dishonest majority. In: 2021 IEEE Symposium on Security and Privacy, pp. 590–607. IEEE Computer Society Press, May 2021. https://doi.org/10.1109/SP40001.2021.00025
22. Cramer, R., Damgård, I., Escudero, D., Scholl, P., Xing, C.: SPD$\mathbb{Z}_{2^k}$: efficient MPC mod 2^k for dishonest majority. In: Shacham, H., Boldyreva, A. (eds.) CRYPTO 2018. LNCS, vol. 10992, pp. 769–798. Springer, Cham (2018). https://doi.org/10.1007/978-3-319-96881-0_26
23. Dalskov, A.P.K., Escudero, D., Nof, A.: Fast fully secure multi-party computation over any ring with two-thirds honest majority. In: Yin, H., Stavrou, A., Cremers, C., Shi, E. (eds.) ACM CCS 2022, pp. 653–666. ACM Press, November 2022. https://doi.org/10.1145/3548606.3559389
24. Dalskov, A., Orlandi, C., Keller, M., Shrishak, K., Shulman, H.: Securing DNSSEC keys via threshold ECDSA from generic MPC. In: Chen, L., Li, N., Liang, K., Schneider, S. (eds.) ESORICS 2020. LNCS, vol. 12309, pp. 654–673. Springer, Cham (2020). https://doi.org/10.1007/978-3-030-59013-0_32
25. Damgård, I., Damgård, K., Nielsen, K., Nordholt, P.S., Toft, T.: Confidential benchmarking based on multiparty computation. In: Grossklags, J., Preneel, B. (eds.) FC 2016. LNCS, vol. 9603, pp. 169–187. Springer, Heidelberg (2017). https://doi.org/10.1007/978-3-662-54970-4_10
26. Damgård, I., Escudero, D., Frederiksen, T.K., Keller, M., Scholl, P., Volgushev, N.: New primitives for actively-secure MPC over rings with applications to private machine learning. In: 2019 IEEE Symposium on Security and Privacy, pp. 1102–1120. IEEE Computer Society Press, May 2019. https://doi.org/10.1109/SP.2019.00078

27. Damgård, I., Keller, M., Larraia, E., Pastro, V., Scholl, P., Smart, N.P.: Practical covertly secure MPC for dishonest majority – or: breaking the SPDZ limits. In: Crampton, J., Jajodia, S., Mayes, K. (eds.) ESORICS 2013. LNCS, vol. 8134, pp. 1–18. Springer, Heidelberg (2013). https://doi.org/10.1007/978-3-642-40203-6_1
28. Damgård, I., Pastro, V., Smart, N., Zakarias, S.: Multiparty computation from somewhat homomorphic encryption. In: Safavi-Naini, R., Canetti, R. (eds.) CRYPTO 2012. LNCS, vol. 7417, pp. 643–662. Springer, Heidelberg (2012). https://doi.org/10.1007/978-3-642-32009-5_38
29. Delpech de Saint Guilhem, C., Makri, E., Rotaru, D., Tanguy, T.: The return of eratosthenes: secure generation of RSA moduli using distributed sieving. In: Vigna, G., Shi, E. (eds.) ACM CCS 2021, pp. 594–609. ACM Press, November 2021. https://doi.org/10.1145/3460120.3484754
30. Demmler, D., Schneider, T., Zohner, M.: ABY - a framework for efficient mixed-protocol secure two-party computation. In: NDSS 2015. The Internet Society, February 2015
31. Deryabin, M., Chervyakov, N., Tchernykh, A., Babenko, M., Shabalina, M.: High performance parallel computing in residue number system. Int. J. Comb. Optim. Problems Inform. **9**(1), 62–67 (2018). https://ijcopi.org/ojs/article/view/80
32. Döttling, N., Ghosh, S., Nielsen, J.B., Nilges, T., Trifiletti, R.: TinyOLE: Efficient actively secure two-party computation from oblivious linear function evaluation. In: Thuraisingham, B.M., Evans, D., Malkin, T., Xu, D. (eds.) ACM CCS 2017, pp. 2263–2276. ACM Press, October/November 2017. https://doi.org/10.1145/3133956.3134024
33. Du, W., Atallah, M.J.: Privacy-preserving cooperative statistical analysis. In: 17th Annual Computer Security Applications Conference (ACSAC 2001), 11–14 December 2001, New Orleans, Louisiana, USA, pp. 102–110. IEEE Computer Society (2001). https://doi.org/10.1109/ACSAC.2001.991526
34. Escudero, D., Ghosh, S., Keller, M., Rachuri, R., Scholl, P.: Improved primitives for MPC over mixed arithmetic-binary circuits. In: Micciancio, D., Ristenpart, T. (eds.) CRYPTO 2020. LNCS, vol. 12171, pp. 823–852. Springer, Cham (2020). https://doi.org/10.1007/978-3-030-56880-1_29
35. Fouque, P.-A., Stern, J., Wackers, G.-J.: CryptoComputing with rationals. In: Blaze, M. (ed.) FC 2002. LNCS, vol. 2357, pp. 136–146. Springer, Heidelberg (2003). https://doi.org/10.1007/3-540-36504-4_10
36. Fournaris, A.P., Papachristodoulou, L., Batina, L., Sklavos, N.: Residue number system as a side channel and fault injection attack countermeasure in elliptic curve cryptography. In: 2016 International Conference on Design and Technology of Integrated Systems in Nanoscale Era, DTIS 2016, Istanbul, Turkey, April 12–14, 2016, pp. 1–4. IEEE (2016). https://doi.org/10.1109/DTIS.2016.7483807
37. Franz, M., Deiseroth, B., Hamacher, K., Jha, S., Katzenbeisser, S., Schröder, H.: Secure computations on non-integer values. In: 2010 IEEE International Workshop on Information Forensics and Security, WIFS 2010, Seattle, WA, USA, December 12–15, 2010, pp. 1–6. IEEE (2010). https://doi.org/10.1109/WIFS.2010.5711458
38. Franz, M., Katzenbeisser, S.: Processing encrypted floating point signals. In: Heitzenrater, C., Craver, S., Dittmann, J. (eds.) Proceedings of the thirteenth ACM multimedia workshop on Multimedia and security, MM&Sec '11, Buffalo, New York, USA, September 29–30, 2011, pp. 103–108. ACM (2011). https://doi.org/10.1145/2037252.2037271

39. Frederiksen, T.K., Keller, M., Orsini, E., Scholl, P.: A unified approach to MPC with preprocessing using OT. In: Iwata, T., Cheon, J.H. (eds.) ASIACRYPT 2015. LNCS, vol. 9452, pp. 711–735. Springer, Heidelberg (2015). https://doi.org/10.1007/978-3-662-48797-6_29
40. Frederiksen, T.K., Lindell, Y., Osheter, V., Pinkas, B.: Fast distributed RSA key generation for semi-honest and malicious adversaries. In: Shacham, H., Boldyreva, A. (eds.) CRYPTO 2018. LNCS, vol. 10992, pp. 331–361. Springer, Cham (2018). https://doi.org/10.1007/978-3-319-96881-0_12
41. Frederiksen, T.K., Lindstrøm, J., Madsen, M.W., Spangsberg, A.D.: A new approach to efficient and secure fixed-point computation. IACR Cryptol. ePrint Arch., p. 035 (2024). https://eprint.iacr.org/2024/035
42. Goldreich, O., Micali, S., Wigderson, A.: How to play any mental game or A completeness theorem for protocols with honest majority. In: Aho, A. (ed.) 19th ACM STOC, pp. 218–229. ACM Press, May 1987. https://doi.org/10.1145/28395.28420
43. Hazay, C., Ishai, Y., Marcedone, A., Venkitasubramaniam, M.: LevioSA: Lightweight secure arithmetic computation. In: Cavallaro, L., Kinder, J., Wang, X., Katz, J. (eds.) ACM CCS 2019. pp. 327–344. ACM Press, November 2019. https://doi.org/10.1145/3319535.3354258
44. Hazay, C., Scholl, P., Soria-Vazquez, E.: Low cost constant round MPC combining BMR and oblivious transfer. In: Takagi, T., Peyrin, T. (eds.) ASIACRYPT 2017. LNCS, vol. 10624, pp. 598–628. Springer, Cham (2017). https://doi.org/10.1007/978-3-319-70694-8_21
45. Jacquemin, D., Mert, A.C., Roy, S.S.: Exploring RNS for isogeny-based cryptography. IACR Cryptol. ePrint Arch., p. 1289 (2022). https://eprint.iacr.org/2022/1289
46. Keller, M., Orsini, E., Scholl, P.: MASCOT: Faster malicious arithmetic secure computation with oblivious transfer. In: Weippl, E.R., Katzenbeisser, S., Kruegel, C., Myers, A.C., Halevi, S. (eds.) ACM CCS 2016, pp. 830–842. ACM Press, October 2016. https://doi.org/10.1145/2976749.2978357
47. Keller, M., Pastro, V., Rotaru, D.: Overdrive: making SPDZ great again. In: Nielsen, J.B., Rijmen, V. (eds.) EUROCRYPT 2018. LNCS, vol. 10822, pp. 158–189. Springer, Cham (2018). https://doi.org/10.1007/978-3-319-78372-7_6
48. Kerik, L., Laud, P., Randmets, J.: Optimizing MPC for robust and scalable integer and floating-point arithmetic. In: Clark, J., Meiklejohn, S., Ryan, P.Y.A., Wallach, D., Brenner, M., Rohloff, K. (eds.) FC 2016. LNCS, vol. 9604, pp. 271–287. Springer, Heidelberg (2016). https://doi.org/10.1007/978-3-662-53357-4_18
49. Kiltz, E., Leander, G., Malone-Lee, J.: Secure computation of the mean and related statistics. In: Kilian, J. (ed.) TCC 2005. LNCS, vol. 3378, pp. 283–302. Springer, Heidelberg (2005). https://doi.org/10.1007/978-3-540-30576-7_16
50. Larraia, E., Orsini, E., Smart, N.P.: Dishonest majority multi-party computation for binary circuits. In: Garay, J.A., Gennaro, R. (eds.) CRYPTO 2014. LNCS, vol. 8617, pp. 495–512. Springer, Heidelberg (2014). https://doi.org/10.1007/978-3-662-44381-1_28

51. Li, S., Xue, K., Zhu, B., Ding, C., Gao, X., Wei, D.S.L., Wan, T.: FALCON: A fourier transform based approach for fast and secure convolutional neural network predictions. In: 2020 IEEE/CVF Conference on Computer Vision and Pattern Recognition, CVPR 2020, Seattle, WA, USA, June 13–19, 2020. pp. 8702–8711. Computer Vision Foundation / IEEE (2020). https://doi.org/10.1109/CVPR42600.2020.00873. https://openaccess.thecvf.com/content_CVPR_2020/html/Li_FALCON_A_Fourier_Transform_Based_Approach_for_Fast_and_Secure_CVPR_2020_paper.html
52. Lindell, Y., Pinkas, B.: Privacy preserving data mining. In: Bellare, M. (ed.) CRYPTO 2000. LNCS, vol. 1880, pp. 36–54. Springer, Heidelberg (2000). https://doi.org/10.1007/3-540-44598-6_3
53. Makri, E., Rotaru, D., Vercauteren, F., Wagh, S.: Rabbit: efficient comparison for secure multi-party computation. In: Borisov, N., Diaz, C. (eds.) FC 2021. LNCS, Part I, vol. 12674, pp. 249–270. Springer, Heidelberg (2021). https://doi.org/10.1007/978-3-662-64322-8_12
54. Mohassel, P., Rindal, P.: ABY^3: a mixed protocol framework for machine learning. In: Lie, D., Mannan, M., Backes, M., Wang, X. (eds.) ACM CCS 2018, pp. 35–52. ACM Press, October 2018. https://doi.org/10.1145/3243734.3243760
55. Mohassel, P., Zhang, Y.: SecureML: a system for scalable privacy-preserving machine learning. In: 2017 IEEE Symposium on Security and Privacy, pp. 19–38. IEEE Computer Society Press, May 2017. https://doi.org/10.1109/SP.2017.12
56. Nielsen, J.B., Orlandi, C.: LEGO for two-party secure computation. In: Reingold, O. (ed.) TCC 2009. LNCS, vol. 5444, pp. 368–386. Springer, Heidelberg (2009). https://doi.org/10.1007/978-3-642-00457-5_22
57. Quisquater, J.J.: Fast decipherment algorithm for rsa public-key cryptosystem. Electron. Lett. **18**, 905–907(2) (1982). https://digital-library.theiet.org/content/journals/10.1049/el_19820617
58. Rotaru, D., Smart, N.P., Tanguy, T., Vercauteren, F., Wood, T.: Actively secure setup for SPDZ. J. Cryptol. **35**(1), 5 (2022). https://doi.org/10.1007/s00145-021-09416-w
59. Rotaru, D., Wood, T.: MArBled circuits: mixing arithmetic and boolean circuits with active security. In: Hao, F., Ruj, S., Sen Gupta, S. (eds.) INDOCRYPT 2019. LNCS, vol. 11898, pp. 227–249. Springer, Cham (2019). https://doi.org/10.1007/978-3-030-35423-7_12
60. Simić, S., Bemporad, A., Inverso, O., Tribastone, M.: Tight error analysis in fixed-point arithmetic. Form. Asp. Comput. **34**(1) (2022). https://doi.org/10.1145/3524051
61. Szabo, N.S., Tanaka, R.I.: Residue arithmetic and its applications to computer technology / Nicholas S. Szabo, Richard I. Tanaka. McGraw-Hill series in information processing and computers, McGraw-Hill, New York (1967)
62. Wagh, S., Gupta, D., Chandran, N.: SecureNN: 3-party secure computation for neural network training. PoPETs **2019**(3), 26–49 (2019). https://doi.org/10.2478/popets-2019-0035
63. Yao, A.C.C.: Protocols for secure computations (extended abstract). In: 23rd FOCS, pp. 160–164. IEEE Computer Society Press, November 1982. https://doi.org/10.1109/SFCS.1982.38
64. Yuan, S., Shen, M., Mironov, I., Nascimento, A.C.A.: Practical, label private deep learning training based on secure multiparty computation and differential privacy. Cryptology ePrint Archive, Report 2021/835 (2021). https://eprint.iacr.org/2021/835

Auditable Attribute-Based Credentials Scheme and Its Application in Contact Tracing

Pengfei Wang[1(✉)], Xiangyu Su[1(✉)], Mario Larangeira[1,2], and Keisuke Tanaka[1]

[1] Department of Mathematical and Computing Science, School of Computing, Tokyo Institute of Technology, W8-55, 2-12-1 Ookayama, Meguro-ku, Tokyo-to, Japan
pengfei.w@outlook.com, su.x.ab@m.titech.ac.jp, mario@c.titech.ac.jp, keisuke@is.titech.ac.jp

[2] Input Output, Global, Singapore, Singapore
mario.larangeira@iohk.io

Abstract. During the pandemic, the limited functionality of existing privacy-preserving contact tracing systems highlights the need for new designs. Wang et al. proposed an environmental-adaptive framework (CSS '21) but failed to formalize the security. The similarity between their framework and attribute-based credentials (ABC) inspires us to reconsider contact tracing from the perspective of ABC schemes. In such schemes, users can obtain credentials on attributes from issuers and prove the credentials anonymously (i.e., hiding sensitive information of both user and issuer). This work first extends ABC schemes with auditability, which enables designated auditing authorities to revoke the anonymity of particular *issuers*. For this purpose, we propose an "auditable public key (APK)" mechanism that extends the updatable public key by Fauzi et al. (AsiaCrypt '19). We provide formal security definitions regarding auditability and build our auditable ABC scheme by adding a DDH-based APK to Connolly et al.'s ABC construction (PKC '22). Note that the APK mechanism can be used as a plug-in for other cryptographic primitives and may be of independent interest. Finally, regarding contact tracing, we refine Wang et al.'s framework and present a formal treatment that includes security definitions and protocol construction. An implementation is provided to showcase the practicality of our design.

Keywords: Attribute-Based Credentials · Auditable Public Keys · Contact Tracing

1 Introduction

Contact tracing, a method that prevents diseases from spreading, faces new challenges considering new findings in epidemiology research. Proposed in [37], the environmental-adaptive contact tracing (EACT) framework took different transmission modes (*i.e.*, droplet and airborne) and virus distribution (*e.g.*, lifespan

C. Pöpper and L. Batina (Eds.): ACNS 2024, LNCS 14583, pp. 88–118, 2024.
https://doi.org/10.1007/978-3-031-54770-6_4

and region size, which depends on environmental factors) into consideration (Appendix A recalls the rationale behind embedding environmental factors in contact tracing systems). However, their framework are based on an informal threat model and failed to unify the system syntax for different transmission modes, hence, leaving a gap between theoretical proofs and implementations.

The similarity between their framework and a self-issuing decentralized credentials scheme [27] inspires us to turn our eyes to credentials schemes, typically the *attribute-based* ones (ABC). Note that we consider ABC schemes, *e.g.*, [17,25], instead of more general anonymous credentials, *e.g.*, [10–12]. This is because the capability of embedding attributes in credentials empowers contact tracing systems to manage environmental factors as attributes. To the best of our knowledge, this approach has seen limited exploration or association with contact tracing in previous works despite its inherent viability[1]. We explain the reason as follows. Recall that an ABC scheme involves issuers, users, and verifiers. In the issuance phase, an issuer grants a credential to a user on the user's attributes. The user can then prove possession (showing) of the credential on their attributes without revealing identities, but they *cannot* prove attributes that are not embedded in their credentials. Hence, by building contact tracing systems atop ABC schemes: (1) users can take environmental factors and local information as attributes; (2) users can issue others credentials on these attributes as contact records; (3) users can anonymously prove their records to potentially malicious verifiers (in contact tracing, medical agencies). It is also convenient to bring the broad spectrum of functionalities in ABC to contact tracing, *e.g.*, selective showing [25], proof of disjoint attributes [17], issuer-hiding [5,17], delegation [3], *traceability* [31], etc.

Moreover, the security of ABC, *i.e.*, anonymity and unforgeability, can also be adapted to contact tracing (as we will show in Sect. 4.2)[2]. Intuitively, given any honest user's showing of contact records, anonymity prevents other users and medical agencies (even if they collude) from identifying the user or learning anything except what is intentionally revealed by the user. Whereas, unforgeability guarantees that no user can perform a valid showing if she does not possess a corresponding contact record (*i.e.*, a credential issued by another user according to some committed attributes, *e.g.*, environmental factors). The two properties resemble the "(pseudonym and trace) unlinkability" and "integrity" of contact tracing systems proposed in [18] (more discussion in Sect. 4.2).

However, existing ABC schemes cannot be utilized directly to build contact tracing systems due to the lack of tracing capability. Note that the traceability in [31] is similar to group signatures, *i.e.*, to revoke the anonymity of *regular users*. In contrast, the traceability of contact systems should enable the issuer of a contact record to be notified whenever the record is being shown. For example,

[1] Silde and Strand [36] proposed a contact tracing system based on anonymous tokens, *i.e.*, an anonymous credential variant that does not support attributes.

[2] Notably, game-based and simulation-based security definitions of contact tracing systems have been proposed in [4,18], respectively. This work will focus on the game-based ones because we proceed from the perspective of ABC schemes with game-based definitions.

when two users (A and B) have contact, they first exchange contact records by issuing each other a credential based on the contact. Then, when one user (say, user A) is diagnosed and presents her credential issued by her counterparty (user B) to medical agencies, user B should be able to check if the presented credential is issued by herself. If so, user B can confirm that she had close contact with user A. We formalize this functionality as auditability of issuers in the underlying credentials scheme, which we call an auditable ABC.

Our Approach and Contributions. We show a brief image of our approach. In order to build an auditable ABC scheme, we first propose a cryptographic tool called the "auditable public keys (APK)" mechanism, which extends the updatable public key given in [22]. The APK embeds extra structure in the secret and public key pair with a new auditing key. The structure will be preserved even after updating the public key and can be verified (we call it audit) by the auditing key. That is, a participant who holds the auditing key corresponding to some key pair can audit if a given public key is updated from the corresponding public key without knowing the secret randomness in the update algorithm. Like the updatable public key, our APK can be used as a plug-in for many different cryptographic primitives, hence, not being limited to credentials schemes (we show a concrete example in Appendix C).

Next, we adapt APK to the existing ABC scheme [25] and define the formal syntax of our auditable ABC. We show a concrete construction for the APK mechanism based on the matrix Diffie-Hellman problem over matrix distributions [21,34]. We prove that our APK construction can be inserted into the structure-preserving signatures on equivalence classes (SPS-EQ) scheme [17] without breaking the security of the original SPS-EQ (though incurring a slight reduction loss). By employing our modified SPS-EQ, a set-commitment scheme from [25], and a zero-knowledge proofs of knowledge protocol [23], we present a construction for the auditable ABC scheme.

Finally, we refine the EACT framework [37] and provide a construction based on our auditable ABC scheme. Hence, we can unify the tracing process of the conventional Bluetooth Low Energy (BLE)-based setting for droplet mode and their discrete-location-tracing setting (DLT) for airborne mode. Then, we argue that the security of the refined EACT can be derived from our auditable ABC scheme but requires sufficient adaptions, *e.g.*, in contact tracing, the verifier of credentials may be malicious and approve falsely shown credentials. We explain these adaptions and finally show an implementation (in Sect. 4.3) of our construction on real-life Android devices to demonstrate practicality.

Our Contributions. Our contributions are threefold: (1) we propose an APK mechanism that can be used as a plug-in tool for many cryptographic primitives; (2) we propose an auditable ABC scheme that inherits auditability from APK. Then, we show concrete constructions for APK and the auditable ABC scheme; (3) we refine and construct the EACT framework [37] based on credentials schemes. We also provide formal security definitions and implement the construction. Additionally, we add algorithms to jPBC library [14] to support matrix-based bilinear pairing operations during implementation.

Related Works. Despite the broad functionalities of ABC schemes, no existing work considers the same traceability (revoking issuer's anonymity) as in contact tracing systems. Regarding auditability of ABC schemes, existing works [6,16] focused on auditing the credentials back to their holders, *i.e.*, regular users. Instead, our auditability intends to identify issuers. This is because, as shown in Sect. 3.2, modifications are made into ABC syntax so that verifiers cannot identify *the issuer* of shown credentials even if they collude with the original issuer. However, such a property opens the gate of fabricating issuers. Hence, it is crucial to let issuers (or designated third parties chosen by the issuer, called auditors) check if a shown credential originates from the issuer herself.

To compare with existing contact tracing systems, we consider three aspects: (1) security (*i.e.*, anonymity/unlinkability and tracing-soundness/integrity); (2) extensibility (*e.g.*, the capability of handling different transmission modes and environmental factors); (3) efficiency (*e.g.*, requiring BLE handshakes during the recording phase or not). We notice that these requirements may contradict each other (in fact, unlinkability and integrity may also have contradictions [18]). For example, as mentioned above, revealing more data (extensibility) inevitably incurs breaches in anonymity (security). Then, to fix such breaches, we have to rely on heavy mechanisms that burden the system's efficiency. In the following, we evaluate several cryptographic contact tracing systems to prove our observation.

A simple paradigm of contact tracing utilizes symmetric primitives (*e.g.*, pseudo-random permutations/functions/generators (PRP/PRF/PRG) [1] and hash functions [13]) to generate period-specific keys and pseudonyms (here, the period can be several hours or days). As shown in [18], these systems can achieve *unlinkability* (*i.e.*, period-specific pseudonyms are unlinkable) due to the pseudo-randomness of the underlying building blocks; and *integrity* (*i.e.*, no adversary can forge recorded pseudonyms to trigger users' tracing) due to the pre-image resistance of these primitives; but suffer from *the relay (and replay) attacks* (*i.e.*, the adversary can relay or replay previous records to break integrity) [16] because users cannot tell if a pseudonym has been presented or not (without checking timestamps). The simplicity of this paradigm allows us to construct highly efficient systems. However, the simplicity also prevents us from recording anything but pseudonyms, hence, limiting the extension capability.

One method to enhance the aforementioned systems is to use re-randomizable primitives (*e.g.*, signature schemes) as in [33,37] and in our work. Concretely, a user obtains a piece of authorized information (in most cases, a signature) from her counterparty (in [37], the counterparty can be regarded as the user herself) during a close contact, and then presents an updated (re-randomized) signature to medical agencies when she is diagnosed. This approach achieves *unlinkability* from the re-randomizability of the building blocks; and *integrity* from unforgeability. Previous works [33,37] consider semi-honest verifiers (medical agencies) who only approve valid signatures to extend the bulletin board, hence, preventing *the relay and replay attacks* by requiring additionally the freshness of signatures.

Moreover, Wang et al. [37] demonstrate with the environmental-adaptive framework that contact tracing systems can handle more useful information to enhance tracing precision (as explained in Appendix A). Their drawback is that users must reveal all attributes to verifiers during the tracing phase. We push forward their idea of utilizing credential schemes and add selective showing capability to our system. Hence, users in our system only reveal what is necessary for deciding close contacts without leaking any other information. However, extensions come with associated costs: our system requires handshakes during BLE scanning (same to [33]) and is built atop pairing-based primitives (same to [37] and the third construction given in [13]).

Inherently shown in [1,13], where authors present various constructions of contact tracing systems with varying levels of security and efficiency, the trade-off among these requirements (security, extensibility, and efficiency) prevents us from finding the ultimate solution for contact tracing. We argue that our system is *secure* despite handling more sensitive data; is *extensible* to tackle new epidemiology findings; and is *efficient enough* to be implemented in real life.

Organization. We organize the content as follows. First, we present the necessary general building blocks and assumptions in Sect. 2. Section 3 formally introduces our first contribution, *i.e.*, an APK mechanism and an auditable ABC scheme. We show constructions and give security proofs to these schemes. Section 4 shows a construction for our refined EACT framework based on auditable ABC, argues its security, and provides implementation results. Finally, Sect. 5 concludes this work.

2 Preliminaries

Notation. Throughout this paper, we use λ for the security parameter and $\mathsf{negl}(\cdot)$ for the negligible function. PPT is short for probabilistic polynomial time. For an integer q, $[q]$ denotes the set $\{1,\ldots,q\}$. Given a set A, $x \xleftarrow{\$} A$ denotes that x is randomly and uniformly sampled from A; whereas, for an algorithm Alg, $x \leftarrow \mathsf{Alg}$ denotes that x is assigned the output of an algorithm Alg on fresh randomness. Let $\mathsf{Alg}_1, \mathsf{Alg}_2$ be two algorithms, $\langle \mathsf{Alg}_1, \mathsf{Alg}_2 \rangle$ denotes a potentially interactive protocol between the two algorithms. Let H denote a collision-free hash function. For an additive group $\mathbb{G}$, $\mathbb{G}^*$ denotes $\mathbb{G} \setminus \{0_{\mathbb{G}}\}$. For a set $A \subseteq \mathbb{Z}_p$, we refer to a monic polynomial of order $|A|$ defined over $\mathbb{Z}_p[X]$, $\mathsf{Ch}_A(X) \triangleq \Pi_{x \in A}(X - x) = \sum_{i=0}^{|A|} c_i \cdot X^i$ as A's characteristic polynomial.

We denote the asymmetric bilinear group generator as $\mathsf{BG} \leftarrow \mathsf{BGGen}(1^\lambda)$ where $\mathsf{BG} \triangleq (p, \mathbb{G}_1, \mathbb{G}_2, \mathbb{G}_T, P_1, P_2, e)$. Here, $\mathbb{G}_1, \mathbb{G}_2, \mathbb{G}_T$ are additive cyclic groups of prime order p with $\lceil \log_2 p \rceil = \lambda$, P_1, P_2 are generators of $\mathbb{G}_1, \mathbb{G}_2$, and $e : \mathbb{G}_1 \times \mathbb{G}_2 \rightarrow \mathbb{G}_T$ is a type-3, *i.e.*, efficiently computable non-degenerate bilinear map with no efficiently computable isomorphism between $\mathbb{G}_1$ and $\mathbb{G}_2$.

For an element $a \in \mathbb{Z}_p$ and $i \in \{1, 2\}$, $[a]_i$ denotes $aP_i \in \mathbb{G}_i$ as the representation of a in group $\mathbb{G}_i$. As mentioned in [17], for vectors or matrices $\mathbf{A}, \mathbf{B}$, the bilinear map e computes $e([\mathbf{A}]_1, [\mathbf{B}]_2) = [\mathbf{AB}]_T \in \mathbb{G}_T$.

General Building Blocks and Assumptions. This work takes the black-box use of three cryptographic primitives: (1) a digital signature scheme $\mathsf{SIG} \triangleq (\mathsf{KGen}, \mathsf{Sign}, \mathsf{Verify})$ that satisfies correctness and existentially unforgeability under adaptive chosen-message attacks (EUF-CMA) [28]; (2) a set-commitment scheme $\mathsf{SC} \triangleq (\mathsf{Setup}, \mathsf{Commit}, \mathsf{Open}, \mathsf{OpenSubset}, \mathsf{VerifySubset})$ that satisfies correctness, binding, subset-soundness, and hiding [25]; (3) a zero-knowledge proofs of knowledge (ZKPoK) protocol Π that satisfies completeness, perfect zero-knowledge, and knowledge-soundness [23]. Due to page limitations, the formal definitions of these primitives can be found in the corresponding reference.

Moreover, we assume the following assumptions hold over matrix distribution: the matrix decisional Diffie-Hellman (MDDH) assumption [21] and the kernel matrix Diffie-Hellman (KerMDH) assumption [34]. We also assume the Diffie-Hellman (DDH) assumption and the q-co-discrete-logarithm (q-co-DL) assumption holds over bilinear groups.

Definition 1 (Matrix Distribution). *Let $l, k \in \mathbb{N}$ with $l > k$. $\mathcal{D}_{l,k}$ is a matrix distribution that outputs matrices in $\mathbb{Z}_p^{l \times k}$ of full rank k in polynomial time. We further denote $\mathcal{D}_k \triangleq \mathcal{D}_{k+1,k}$.*

Let BGGen be the bilinear group generator that outputs $\mathsf{BG} = (p, \mathbb{G}_1, \mathbb{G}_2, \mathbb{G}_T, P_1, P_2, e)$ and $\mathcal{D}_{l,k}$ be a matrix distribution.

Definition 2 ($\mathcal{D}_{l,k}$-MDDH Assumption). *The $\mathcal{D}_{l,k}$-MDDH assumption holds in group $\mathbb{G}_i \in \mathsf{BG}$ where $i \in \{1, 2, T\}$ relative to BGGen, if for all $\mathsf{BG} \leftarrow \mathsf{BGGen}(1^\lambda), \mathbf{A} \xleftarrow{\$} \mathcal{D}_{l,k}, \mathbf{w} \xleftarrow{\$} \mathbb{Z}_p^k, \mathbf{u} \xleftarrow{\$} \mathbb{Z}_p^l$ and all PPT adversary $\mathcal{A}$, the following advantage is negligible of λ:*

$$\mathsf{Adv}_{\mathcal{D}_{l,k},\mathbb{G}_i}^{MDDH} = |\Pr[\mathcal{A}(\mathsf{BG}, [\mathbf{A}]_i, [\mathbf{Aw}]_i) = 1] - \Pr[\mathcal{A}(\mathsf{BG}, [\mathbf{A}]_i, [\mathbf{u}]_i) = 1]|.$$

Definition 3 ($\mathcal{D}_{l,k}$-KerMDH Assumption). *The $\mathcal{D}_{l,k}$-KerMDH assumption holds in group $\mathbb{G}_i \in \mathsf{BG}$ where $i \in \{1, 2\}$ relative to BGGen, if for all $\mathsf{BG} \leftarrow \mathsf{BGGen}(1^\lambda), \mathbf{A} \xleftarrow{\$} \mathcal{D}_{l,k}$ and all PPT adversary $\mathcal{A}$, the following advantage is negligible of λ:*

$$\Pr[[\mathbf{x}]_{3-i} \leftarrow \mathcal{A}(\mathsf{BG}, [\mathbf{A}]_i]) : e([\mathbf{x}^\top]_{3-i}, [\mathbf{A}]_i) = [\mathbf{0}]_T \wedge \mathbf{x} \neq \mathbf{0})].$$

Definition 4 (DDH Assumption). *The DDH assumption holds in $\mathbb{G}_i \in \mathsf{BG}$ where $i \in \{1, 2\}$ for BGGen, if for all $\mathsf{BG} \leftarrow \mathsf{BGGen}(1^\lambda), x, y, z \xleftarrow{\$} \mathbb{Z}_p$ and all PPT adversary $\mathcal{A}$, the following advantage is negligible of λ:*

$$|\Pr[\mathcal{A}(\mathsf{BG}, xP_i, yP_i, xyP_i) = 1] - \Pr[\mathcal{A}(\mathsf{BG}, xP_i, yP_i, zP_i) = 1]|.$$

Definition 5 (q-co-DL Assumption). *The q-co-DL assumption holds for* BGGen, *if for all* $\mathsf{BG} \leftarrow \mathsf{BGGen}(1^\lambda), a \xleftarrow{\$} \mathbb{Z}_p$ *and all PPT adversary* $\mathcal{A}$, *the following advantage is negligible of* λ*:*

$$\Pr[a' \leftarrow \mathcal{A}(\mathsf{BG}, ([a^j]_1, [a^j]_2)_{j\in[q]} : a' = a].$$

3 Auditable Attribute-Based Credentials Scheme

This section first presents an auditable public key (APK) mechanism, then an APK-aided ABC scheme, which will be the main building block of our refined environmental-adaptive contact tracing framework.

Conventionally, an attribute-based credentials (ABC) scheme involves three types of participants: Issuer (also called organization), user, and verifier. An issuer grants credentials to a user on the user's attributes. The user can then prove possession of credentials with respect to her attributes to verifiers. The basic requirements of a secure ABC include correctness, anonymity, and unforgeability [25]. On a high level, correctness guarantees that verifiers always accept the showing of a credential if the credential is issued honestly; Anonymity prevents verifiers and (malicious) issuers (even by colluding) from identifying the user or exposing information during a showing against the user's will; Unforgeability requires that users (even by colluding) cannot perform a valid showing of attributes if the users do not possess credentials for the attributes.

The recent specifications of decentralized identifiers and verifiable credentials [32,35] refueled the interest of the community in researching ABC schemes. New functionalities, as shown in Sect. 1, have been proposed to broaden the application of ABC schemes. Abstracted from the demands of contact tracing systems, we propose yet another functionality, *i.e.*, the auditability, that enables designated users to verify the particular *issuer* of a shown credential. In order to present our scheme, we first introduce the notion of the auditable public key (APK) mechanism that extends the updatable public key [22]. Then, we employ APK and present our auditable ABC scheme.

3.1 Auditable Public Keys

Proposed in [22], the updatable public key mechanism is a generic tool that can be integrated into many cryptographic primitives, *e.g.*, digital signature and public key encryption schemes. The mechanism enables public keys to be updated in a public fashion, and updated public keys are indistinguishable from freshly generated ones. The verification of public keys either requires the corresponding secret key (verifying the key pair) or the randomness used in the updating algorithm. However, these approaches are insufficient in multi-user cases, *e.g.*, in credentials schemes and contact tracing systems. The reasons are: (1) secret keys should only be known to their holders; (2) asking the user who runs the updating algorithm to store its random value or keep the value secret may require impractical assumptions (*e.g.*, assuming *every* user to be honest).

Therefore, we propose an APK mechanism to extend the updatable public key by embedding a structure represented by an auditing key into public keys. The structure enables designated third parties who hold the auditing key, the auditors, to decide whether a public key is updated from the corresponding public key of the auditing key. Moreover, we require that no auditor can learn the corresponding *secret* key of its auditing key. Hence, we separate the role of users, *i.e.*, a user can delegate her capability of auditing to an auditor without revealing the secret key, and a user who performs the updating algorithm can discard her randomness without the concern of being asked to provide it.

The formal syntax and security definitions of APK are given in the following. We recall and extend the definitions from [22].

Definition 6 (Auditable Public Key Mechanism). *An auditable public key (APK) mechanism involves a tuple of algorithms* $\mathsf{APK} \triangleq (\mathsf{Setup}, \mathsf{KGen}, \mathsf{Update}, \mathsf{VerifyKP}, \mathsf{VerifyAK}, \mathsf{Audit})$ *that are performed as follows.*

- $\mathsf{Setup}(1^\lambda)$ *takes as input the security parameter* λ *and outputs the public parameter* pp *that includes secret, public and auditing key space* $\mathcal{SK}, \mathcal{PK}, \mathcal{AK}$. *These are given implicitly as input to all other algorithms;*
- $\mathsf{KGen}(\mathsf{pp})$ *takes as input the public parameter* pp *and outputs a secret and public key pair* $(\mathsf{sk}, \mathsf{pk}) \in \mathcal{SK}{\times}\mathcal{PK}$, *and an auditing key* $\mathsf{ak} \in \mathcal{AK}$. *Later, we omit* pp *in algorithm inputs;*
- $\mathsf{Update}(\mathsf{pk}; r)$ *takes as input a public key* pk *and a randomness* r. *It outputs a new public key* $\mathsf{pk}' \in \mathcal{PK}$;
- $\mathsf{VerifyKP}(\mathsf{sk}, \mathsf{pk}', r)$ *is deterministic, and takes as input a secret key* $\mathsf{sk} \in \mathcal{SK}$, *a value* r *and a public key* $\mathsf{pk}' \in \mathcal{PK}$. *It outputs* 1 *if* $\mathsf{pk}' \leftarrow \mathsf{Update}(\mathsf{pk}; r)$ *given* $(\mathsf{sk}, \mathsf{pk}, \cdot) \leftarrow \mathsf{KGen}(\mathsf{pp})$, *or* 0 *otherwise;*
- $\mathsf{VerifyAK}(\mathsf{sk}, \mathsf{ak})$ *is deterministic, and takes as input a secret key* $\mathsf{sk} \in \mathcal{SK}$ *and an auditing key* $\mathsf{ak} \in \mathcal{AK}$. *It outputs* 1 *if* $(\mathsf{sk}, \cdot, \mathsf{ak}) \leftarrow \mathsf{KGen}(\mathsf{pp})$, *or* 0 *otherwise;*
- $\mathsf{Audit}(\mathsf{ak}, \mathsf{pk}', \mathsf{pk})$ *is deterministic and is performed by a designated auditor who holds the auditing key* $\mathsf{ak} \in \mathcal{AK}$ *of a secret and public key pair* $(\mathsf{sk}, \mathsf{pk}) \in \mathcal{SK}{\times}\mathcal{PK}$. Audit *takes as input a public key* $\mathsf{pk}' \in \mathcal{PK}$, *the auditing key* ak *and the public key* pk. *It outputs* 1 *if* pk' *is updated from* pk, *i.e., there exists* r *such that* $\mathsf{pk}' \leftarrow \mathsf{Update}(\mathsf{pk}; r)$, *or* 0 *otherwise.*

APK mechanism satisfies correctness, indistinguishability, and unforgeability.

Definition 7 (Correctness). *An APK mechanism satisfies perfect correctness if the following properties hold for any* $\lambda > 0, \mathsf{pp} \leftarrow \mathsf{Setup}(1^\lambda)$, *and* $(\mathsf{sk}, \mathsf{pk}, \mathsf{ak}) \leftarrow \mathsf{KGen}(\mathsf{pp})$: *(1) the update process verifies, i.e.,* $\mathsf{VerifyKP}(\mathsf{sk}, \mathsf{Update}(\mathsf{pk}; r), r) = 1$; *(2) the auditing key verifies, i.e.,* $\mathsf{VerifyAK}(\mathsf{sk}, \mathsf{ak}) = 1$; *(3) the auditing process verifies, i.e.,* $\mathsf{Audit}(\mathsf{ak}, \mathsf{pk}', \mathsf{pk}) = 1$ *for any* $\mathsf{pk}' \leftarrow \mathsf{Update}(\mathsf{pk})$.

The indistinguishability of APK follows [22], *i.e.*, no adversary can distinguish between an updated known public key and a freshly generated one. Note that (also applies in unforgeability) the adversary can query to KGen and Update since these algorithms are publicly available.

Definition 8 (Indistinguishability). *An APK mechanism satisfies indistinguishability if for any PPT adversary $\mathcal{A}$, the following probability holds for any $\lambda > 0, \mathsf{pp} \leftarrow \mathsf{Setup}(1^\lambda)$, and $(\mathsf{sk}^*, \mathsf{pk}^*, \mathsf{ak}^*) \leftarrow \mathsf{KGen}(\mathsf{pp})$*

$$\left| \Pr\left[\begin{array}{l} b \xleftarrow{\$} \{0,1\}; \mathsf{pk}_0 \leftarrow \mathsf{Update}(\mathsf{pk}^*); \\ (\mathsf{sk}_1, \mathsf{pk}_1, \mathsf{ak}_1) \leftarrow \mathsf{KGen}(\mathsf{pp}); \\ b^* \leftarrow \mathcal{A}(\mathsf{pk}^*, \mathsf{pk}_b) \end{array} : b^* = b \right] - \frac{1}{2} \right| \leq \mathsf{negl}(\lambda).$$

We formalize two types of unforgeability, *i.e.*, for secret key and auditing key. Concretely, the former requires that given an auditing key with its corresponding public key, the adversary cannot produce a secret and public key pair, and a randomness, such that: (1) the output public key is updated from the secret key's corresponding public key with respect to the randomness; (2) the output secret key and the given auditing key pass the verification given by $\mathsf{VerifyAK}$; (3) the auditing key, the output public key and the given public key pass the auditing given by Audit. This property captures adversarial auditors who hold an auditing key and intend to recover the corresponding secret key. Hence, it covers the one given in [22], in which the adversary is only given a public key.

Next, the auditing key unforgeability requires that given a public key, the adversary cannot produce an auditing key such that the corresponding secret key of the public key verifies the auditing key. This property captures adversarial participants who intend to trigger the auditing algorithm to output 1 for arbitrary public keys. The formal definitions are as follows.

Definition 9 (Secret Key Unforgeability). *An APK mechanism satisfies secret key unforgeability if for any PPT adversary $\mathcal{A}$, the following probability holds for any $\lambda > 0, \mathsf{pp} \leftarrow \mathsf{Setup}(1^\lambda)$, and $(\mathsf{sk}, \mathsf{pk}, \mathsf{ak}) \leftarrow \mathsf{KGen}(\mathsf{pp})$*

$$\Pr\left[(\mathsf{sk}', \mathsf{pk}', r) \leftarrow \mathcal{A}(\mathsf{ak}, \mathsf{pk}) \; : \begin{array}{r} \mathsf{VerifyKP}(\mathsf{sk}', \mathsf{pk}', r) = 1 \wedge \\ \mathsf{VerifyAK}(\mathsf{sk}', \mathsf{ak}) = 1 \wedge \\ \mathsf{Audit}(\mathsf{ak}, \mathsf{pk}', \mathsf{pk}) = 1 \end{array} \right] \leq \mathsf{negl}(\lambda).$$

Definition 10 (Auditing Key Unforgeability). *An APK mechanism satisfies auditing key unforgeability if for any PPT adversary $\mathcal{A}$, the following probability holds for any $\lambda > 0, \mathsf{pp} \leftarrow \mathsf{Setup}(1^\lambda)$, and $(\mathsf{sk}, \mathsf{pk}, \mathsf{ak}) \leftarrow \mathsf{KGen}(\mathsf{pp})$*

$$\Pr\left[\mathsf{ak}' \leftarrow \mathcal{A}(\mathsf{pk}) : \mathsf{VerifyAK}(\mathsf{sk}, \mathsf{ak}') = 1 \right] \leq \mathsf{negl}(\lambda).$$

For constructions, similar to the updatable public key [22], our APK can be constructed from the DDH problem and its variants. Section 3.3 will show a concrete construction based on the MDDH problem, which will further serve as a building block for our auditable ABC scheme[3].

---

[3] We will also give a DDH-based construction in Appendix C. There, we show an example that utilizes the DDH-based APK to extend the famous B(G)LS signature scheme [7,8].

3.2 Formal Definitions of Auditable ABC

The starting point of our auditable ABC is [25] which supports selective showing on subsets of attributes. Then, we integrate APK by modifying the key generation algorithm of issuers and adding the auditing algorithm. Given a credential showing, the auditing algorithm with an auditing key outputs 1 or 0 to indicate whether the shown credential is issued by a secret key corresponding to the auditing key. We show the formal syntax of auditable ABC in the following.

Definition 11 (Auditable ABC Scheme). *An auditable ABC scheme* AABC *consists of PPT algorithms* $(\mathsf{Setup}, \mathsf{OrgKGen}, \mathsf{UsrKGen})$, *two potentially interactive protocols* $\langle \mathsf{Obtain}, \mathsf{Issue} \rangle$ *and* $\langle \mathsf{Show}, \mathsf{Verify} \rangle$, *and a deterministic algorithm* Audit. *The participants in* AABC *perform as follows.*

- $\mathsf{Setup}(1^\lambda, q)$ *takes as input the security parameter* λ *and the size upper bound* q *of attribute sets. It outputs the public parameter* pp;
- $\mathsf{OrgKGen}(\mathsf{pp})$ *is executed by issuers.* $\mathsf{OrgKGen}$ *takes as input the public parameter* pp. *It outputs an issuer-secret and issuer-public key pair* $(\mathsf{osk}, \mathsf{opk})$ *with an auditing key* ak. *The issuer delegates* ak *to users (auditors) selected by herself (if there is none, the issuer is the auditor);*
- $\mathsf{UsrKGen}(\mathsf{pp})$ *is executed by users.* $\mathsf{UsrKGen}$ *takes as input the public parameter* pp. *It outputs a user-secret and user-public key pair* $(\mathsf{usk}, \mathsf{upk})$. *Later, we omit* pp *in algorithm inputs;*
- $\langle \mathsf{Obtain}(\mathsf{usk}, \mathsf{opk}, A), \mathsf{Issue}(\mathsf{upk}, \mathsf{osk}, A) \rangle$ *are PPT algorithms executed between a user and an issuer, respectively.* Obtain *takes as input the user-secret key* usk, *the issuer-public key* opk *and an attribute set* A *of size* $|A| \leq q$; Issue *takes as input the user-public key* upk, *the issuer-secret key* osk *and the attribute set* A. Obtain *returns* cred *on* A *to the user, and* $\mathsf{cred} = \perp$ *if protocol execution fails. The protocol outputs* (cred, I) *where* I *denotes the issuer's transcript;*
- $\langle \mathsf{Show}(\mathsf{opk}, A, D, \mathsf{cred}), \mathsf{Verify}(D) \rangle$ *are executed between a user and a verifier, respectively, where* Show *is a PPT algorithm, and* Verify *is deterministic.* Show *takes as input an issuer-public key* opk, *an attribute set* A *of size* $|A| \leq q$, *a non-empty set* $D \subseteq A$ *representing the attributes to be shown, and a credential* cred; Verify *takes as input the set of shown attributes* D. Verify *returns* 1 *if the credential showing is accepted, or* 0 *otherwise. The protocol outputs* (S, b) *where* S *denotes the showing (user's transcript), and* $b \in \{0, 1\}$. *For convenience, we also write* $b \leftarrow \langle \mathsf{Show}, \mathsf{Verify} \rangle (S)$;
- $\mathsf{Audit}(\mathsf{ak}, S, \mathsf{opk})$ *is executed by a designated auditor with an auditing key* ak *such that corresponding issuer-key pair is* $(\mathsf{osk}, \mathsf{opk})$. Audit *also takes as input a showing of credential* $(S, \cdot) \leftarrow \langle \mathsf{Show}, \mathsf{Verify} \rangle$ *and the issuer-public key* opk. *It outputs* 1 *if the shown credential is issued with* osk, *or* 0 *otherwise.*

In addition to the auditing process, we make two modifications to the ABC scheme from [25]. First, we write protocol transcriptions of $\langle \mathsf{Obtain}, \mathsf{Issue} \rangle$ and $\langle \mathsf{Show}, \mathsf{Verify} \rangle$ explicitly in our syntax concerning that the application in contact tracing may involve non-interactive proofs and require some transcripts to be publicly accessible (Sect. 4.1). In contrast, the previous works [17,25] only mentioned them in security definitions.

Second, our Verify algorithm of $\langle\mathsf{Show}, \mathsf{Verify}\rangle$ takes as input only the attribute sets to be shown. In contrast, the original scheme also takes the issuer-public key opk of the Show algorithm. Their purpose is to prevent credentials from being issued by unidentified issuers. However, as shown in [17], the exposure of the issuer identity affects the users' anonymity. Although some previous works [5,17] proposed the issuer-hiding property so that users can hide their credential issuers' identities within a list of identified issuers, achieving such security incurs heavy mechanisms. Here, we rely on the Audit algorithm to provide an extra verification layer. That is, given an updated issuer-public key in a credential showing, the auditor who holds an auditing key *corresponding to an identified public key* must prove whether the shown credential is issued by the corresponding secret key.

Security Properties. We formally define correctness, anonymity, and unforgeability (two types) for our auditable ABC scheme. Concretely, correctness requires auditors to output 1 on any valid showing of credentials if the credential was issued by the corresponding secret key of the auditing key. The unforgeability game grants its adversary access to auditing keys. In the following, we omit pp if the algorithm takes as input other variables.

Definition 12 (Correctness). *An* AABC *scheme satisfies perfect correctness, if the following properties hold for any* $\lambda > 0, q > 0$, *any non-empty sets* A, D *such that* $|A| \leq q$ *and* $D \subseteq A$, *and* $\mathsf{pp} \leftarrow \mathsf{Setup}(1^\lambda, q), (\mathsf{osk}, \mathsf{opk}, \mathsf{ak}) \leftarrow \mathsf{OrgKGen}(\mathsf{pp}), (\mathsf{usk}, \mathsf{upk}) \leftarrow \mathsf{UsrKGen}(\mathsf{pp}), (\mathsf{cred}, \cdot) \leftarrow \langle\mathsf{Obtain}(\mathsf{usk}, \mathsf{opk}, A), \mathsf{Issue}(\mathsf{upk}, \mathsf{osk}, A)\rangle$: *(1) the credential showing verifies, i.e.,* $(\cdot, 1) \leftarrow \langle\mathsf{Show}(\mathsf{opk}, A, D, \mathsf{cred}), \mathsf{Verify}(D)\rangle$; *(2) if the credential showing is accepted, the auditing verifies, i.e.,* $\mathsf{Audit}(\mathsf{ak}, S, \mathsf{opk}) = 1$ *for any* $(S, 1) \leftarrow \langle\mathsf{Show}, \mathsf{Verify}\rangle$.

For anonymity and unforgeability, we follow the approach given by [25], in which adversaries can corrupt some participants. We first introduce the following lists and oracles to model the adversary.

Lists and Oracles. At the beginning of each experiment, either the experiment generates the key tuple $(\mathsf{osk}, \mathsf{opk}, \mathsf{ak})$, or the adversary outputs opk. The sets HU, CU track all honest and corrupt users. We use the lists $\mathsf{USK}, \mathsf{UPK}, \mathsf{CRED}, \mathsf{ATTR}, \mathsf{OWNER}$ to track user-secret keys, user-public keys, issued credentials with the corresponding attribute sets, and the users who obtain the credentials. In the anonymity games, we use $J_{\mathsf{LoR}}, I_{\mathsf{LoR}}$ to store the issuance indices and the corresponding users that have been set during the first query to the left-or-right oracle. The adversary is required to guess a bit b.

Considering a PPT adversary $\mathcal{A}$, the oracles are listed in the following. Note that we add the $\mathcal{O}_{\mathsf{Audit}}$ oracle for the unforgeability experiment.

- $\mathcal{O}_{\mathsf{HU}}(i)$ takes as input a user index i. If $i \in \mathsf{HU} \cup \mathsf{CU}$, the oracle returns $\perp$; Otherwise, it creates a new honest user i with $(\mathsf{USK}[i], \mathsf{UPK}[i]) \leftarrow \mathsf{UsrKGen}(\mathsf{pp})$ and adds the user to the honest user list HU. It returns $\mathsf{UPK}[i]$ to the adversary.

- $\mathcal{O}_{\mathsf{CU}}(i, \mathsf{upk})$ takes as input i and (optionally) a user public key upk. If $i \in \mathsf{CU}$ or $i \in I_{\mathsf{LoR}}$, the oracle returns $\perp$; If $i \in \mathsf{HU}$, it moves i from HU to CU and returns $\mathsf{USK}[i]$ and $\mathsf{CRED}[j]$ for all j such that $\mathsf{OWNER}[j] = i$; If $i \notin \mathsf{HU} \cup \mathsf{CU}$, it adds i to CU and sets $\mathsf{UPK}[i] = \mathsf{upk}$.
- $\mathcal{O}_{\mathsf{ObtIss}}(i, A)$ takes as input i and a set of attributes A. If $i \notin \mathsf{HU}$, the oracle returns $\perp$; Otherwise, it generates a credential with $(\mathsf{cred}, \top) \leftarrow \langle \mathsf{Obtain}(\mathsf{USK}[i], \mathsf{opk}, A), \mathsf{Issue}(\mathsf{UPK}[i], \mathsf{osk}, A)\rangle$. If $\mathsf{cred} = \perp$, the oracle returns $\perp$; Otherwise, it adds (i, cred, A) to $(\mathsf{OWNER}, \mathsf{CRED}, \mathsf{ATTR})$ and returns $\top$.
- $\mathcal{O}_{\mathsf{Obtain}}(i, A)$ takes as input i and A. If $i \notin \mathsf{HU}$, the oracle returns $\perp$; Otherwise, it runs $(\mathsf{cred}, \cdot) \leftarrow \langle \mathsf{Obtain}(\mathsf{USK}[i], \mathsf{opk}, A), \cdot\rangle$ by interacting with the adversary $\mathcal{A}$ running Issue. If $\mathsf{cred} = \perp$, the oracle returns $\perp$; Otherwise, it adds (i, cred, A) to $(\mathsf{OWNER}, \mathsf{CRED}, \mathsf{ATTR})$ and returns $\top$.
- $\mathcal{O}_{\mathsf{Issue}}(i, A)$ takes as input i and A. If $i \notin \mathsf{CU}$, the oracle returns $\perp$; Otherwise, it runs $(\cdot, I) \leftarrow \langle \mathsf{Obtain}(\mathsf{USK}[i], \mathsf{opk}, A), \cdot\rangle$ by interacting with the adversary $\mathcal{A}$ running Obtain. If $I = \perp$, the oracle returns $\perp$; Otherwise, it adds $(i, \perp, A)$ to $(\mathsf{OWNER}, \mathsf{CRED}, \mathsf{ATTR})$ and returns $\top$.
- $\mathcal{O}_{\mathsf{Show}}(j, D)$ takes in the index j and a set of attributes D. Let $i = \mathsf{OWNER}[j]$, if $i \notin \mathsf{HU}$, the oracle returns $\perp$; Otherwise, it runs $(S, \cdot) \leftarrow \langle \mathsf{Show}(\mathsf{opk}, \mathsf{ATTR}[j], D, \mathsf{CRED}[j]), \cdot\rangle$ by interacting with the adversary $\mathcal{A}$ running Verify.
- $\mathcal{O}_{\mathsf{Audit}}(S)$ is an oracle that holds public and auditing keys for all identified *issuers*. Given a showing transcript of a credential S, it runs $b \leftarrow \langle \mathsf{Show}, \mathsf{Verify}\rangle(S)$. If there exists opk and ak pair such that $\mathsf{Audit}(\mathsf{ak}, S, \mathsf{opk}){=}1$, the oracle returns $(\mathsf{opk}, b, 1)$ to the adversary; Otherwise, it returns $\perp$.
- $\mathcal{O}_{\mathsf{LoR}}(j_0, j_1, D; b)$ takes as input two issuance indices j_0, j_1, a set of attributes D and a challenge bit $b \xleftarrow{\$} \{0,1\}$. If $J_{\mathsf{LoR}} \neq \emptyset$ and $J_{\mathsf{LoR}} \neq \{j_0, j_1\}$, the oracle returns $\perp$. Let $i_0 = \mathsf{OWNER}[j_0], i_1 = \mathsf{OWNER}[j_1]$. If $J_{\mathsf{LoR}} = \emptyset$, it sets $J_{\mathsf{LoR}} = \{j_0, j_1\}, I_{\mathsf{LoR}} = \{i_0, i_1\}$. If $i_0, i_1 \notin \mathsf{HU}$ or $D \not\subseteq (\mathsf{ATTR}[j_0] \cap \mathsf{ATTR}[j_1])$, the oracle returns $\perp$; Otherwise, it runs $(S_b, \cdot) \leftarrow \langle \mathsf{Show}(\mathsf{opk}_b, \mathsf{ATTR}[j_b], D, \mathsf{CRED}[j_b]), \cdot\rangle$ by interacting with the adversary $\mathcal{A}$ running Verify.

Then, the formal definitions are as follows.

Definition 13 (Anonymity). *An* AABC *scheme satisfies anonymity if for any PPT adversary $\mathcal{A}$ that has access to oracles $\mathcal{O} = \{\mathcal{O}_{\mathsf{HU}}, \mathcal{O}_{\mathsf{CU}}, \mathcal{O}_{\mathsf{ObtIss}}, \mathcal{O}_{\mathsf{Issue}}, \mathcal{O}_{\mathsf{Show}}, \mathcal{O}_{\mathsf{LoR}}\}$, the following probability holds for any $\lambda, q > 0, \mathsf{pp} \leftarrow \mathsf{Setup}(1^\lambda, q)$:*

$$\left| \Pr \begin{bmatrix} (\mathsf{opk}_0, \mathsf{opk}_1, \mathsf{st}) \leftarrow \mathcal{A}(\mathsf{pp}); & \\ b \xleftarrow{\$} \{0,1\}; & : b^* = b \\ b^* \leftarrow \mathcal{A}^{\mathcal{O}}(\mathsf{st}) & \end{bmatrix} - \frac{1}{2} \right| \leq \mathsf{negl}(\lambda).$$

Note that we modify the Verify in $\langle \mathsf{Show}, \mathsf{Verify}\rangle$ so that it does not take as input issuer-public keys. Hence, our anonymity also captures the indistinguishability of these keys. The definition above is arguably more close to the unlinkability from [5] because the $\mathcal{O}_{\mathsf{LoR}}$ oracle runs the Show algorithm with opk_b according to the challenge bit $b \xleftarrow{\$} \{0,1\}$.

Definition 14 (Unforgeability). *An* AABC *scheme satisfies unforgeability, if for any PPT adversary $\mathcal{A}$ that has access to oracles* $\mathcal{O} = \{\mathcal{O}_{\mathsf{HU}}, \mathcal{O}_{\mathsf{CU}}, \mathcal{O}_{\mathsf{ObtIss}}, \mathcal{O}_{\mathsf{Issue}}, \mathcal{O}_{\mathsf{Show}}, \mathcal{O}_{\mathsf{Audit}}\}$*, the following probability holds for any* $\lambda > 0, q > 0$, $\mathsf{pp} \leftarrow \mathsf{Setup}(1^\lambda, q)$*, and* $(\mathsf{osk}, \mathsf{opk}, \mathsf{ak}) \leftarrow \mathsf{OrgKGen}(\mathsf{pp})$

$$\Pr\left[\begin{array}{ll}(D, \mathsf{st}) \leftarrow \mathcal{A}^{\mathcal{O}}(\mathsf{opk}, \mathsf{ak}); & : b = 1 \wedge \textit{If } \mathsf{OWNER}[j] \in \mathsf{CU}, \\ (S, b) \leftarrow \langle \mathcal{A}(\mathsf{st}), \mathsf{Verify}(D) \rangle & D \notin \mathsf{ATTR}[j]\end{array}\right] \leq \mathsf{negl}(\lambda).$$

Like APK, unforgeability regarding to auditing keys is needed. A user should not recover the auditing key of a given public key even after querying the auditing oracles on other key tuples for polynomial times. Since the adversary can run key generation on its own in APK, the auditing unforgeability of auditable ABC is equivalent to the auditing key unforgeability in Definition 10.

3.3 Our Constructions and Analysis

Our auditable ABC construction has the same approach of [17], relying on a structure-preserving signatures on equivalence classes (SPS-EQ) and a set-commit schemes. We extend their ABC construction with our APK mechanism.

An MDDH-Based APK Construction. In order to work with the ABC scheme (precisely, the SPS-EQ) given in [17], the setup algorithm Setup runs $\mathsf{BG} \leftarrow \mathsf{BGGen}(1^\lambda)$ and samples a matrix $\mathbf{A} \xleftarrow{\$} \mathcal{D}_1$. It outputs $\mathsf{pp} \triangleq (\mathsf{BG}, [\mathbf{A}]_2, \ell)$ where $\mathsf{BG} = (p, \mathbb{G}_1, \mathbb{G}_2, \mathbb{G}_T, P_1, P_2, e)$, and ℓ is a parameter for message size in the SPS-EQ. We present a construction of APK based on group $(\mathbb{G}_2, P_2, p)$ where the MDDH and KerMDH assumptions are believed to hold.

Construction 1 (MDDH-Based APK APK**).** *The rest of the algorithms are:*

- $\mathsf{KGen}(\mathsf{pp})$*: Sample matrices* $\mathbf{K}_0 \xleftarrow{\$} \mathcal{D}_{\ell,2}$ *and* $\mathbf{K}_1 \xleftarrow{\$} \mathbb{Z}_p^{2\times 2}$ *of full rank* 2*. Set* $\mathbf{K} = \mathbf{K}_0\mathbf{K}_1$*. Then, compute* $[\mathbf{B}]_2 = [\mathbf{K}_1\mathbf{A}]_2$ *and* $[\mathbf{C}]_2 = [\mathbf{K}\mathbf{A}]_2$*. Finally, set* $\mathsf{sk} = (\mathbf{K}_1, \mathbf{K}), \mathsf{pk} = ([\mathbf{B}]_2, [\mathbf{C}]_2), \mathsf{ak} = \mathbf{K}_0$ *and output* $(\mathsf{sk}, \mathsf{pk}, \mathsf{ak})$*;*
- $\mathsf{Update}(\mathsf{pk}; r)$*: Sample* $r \xleftarrow{\$} \mathbb{Z}_p$ *and compute* $[\mathbf{B}']_2 = r \cdot [\mathbf{B}]_2, [\mathbf{C}']_2 = r \cdot [\mathbf{C}]_2$*. Output* $\mathsf{pk}' = ([\mathbf{B}']_2, [\mathbf{C}']_2)$*;*
- $\mathsf{VerifyKP}(\mathsf{sk}, \mathsf{pk}', r)$*: Parse* $\mathsf{sk} = (\mathsf{sk}_0, \mathsf{sk}_1)$ *and* $\mathsf{pk}' = (\mathsf{pk}'_0, \mathsf{pk}'_1)$*. Output* 1 *if* $\mathsf{pk}'_0 = r \cdot \mathsf{sk}_0 \cdot [\mathbf{A}]_2 \wedge \mathsf{pk}'_1 = r \cdot \mathsf{sk}_1 \cdot [\mathbf{A}]_2$*, or* 0 *otherwise;*
- $\mathsf{VerifyAK}(\mathsf{sk}, \mathsf{ak})$*: Parse* $\mathsf{sk} = (\mathsf{sk}_0, \mathsf{sk}_1)$*. Output* 1 *if* $\mathsf{sk}_1 = \mathsf{ak} \cdot \mathsf{sk}_0$*, or* 0 *otherwise;*
- $\mathsf{Audit}(\mathsf{ak}, \mathsf{pk}', \mathsf{pk})$*: Parse* $\mathsf{pk}' = (\mathsf{pk}'_0, \mathsf{pk}'_1), \mathsf{pk} = (\mathsf{pk}_0, \mathsf{pk}_1)$*. Output* 1 *if* $\mathsf{pk}_1 = \mathsf{ak} \cdot \mathsf{pk}_0 \wedge \mathsf{pk}'_1 = \mathsf{ak} \cdot \mathsf{pk}'_0$*, or* 0 *otherwise.*

Hence, we have the following theorem.

Theorem 1. *The APK mechanism* APK *given by Construction 1 satisfies the following properties.*

- *Correctness (Definition 7);*
- *Indistinguishability (Definition 8) if the $\mathcal{D}_{l,1}$-MDDH assumption where $l \in \{2, \ell\}$ holds on $\mathbb{G}_2$;*
- *Secret key and auditing key unforgeability (Definition 9 and 10) if the $\mathcal{D}_1$-KerMDH holds on $\mathbb{G}_2$.*

Proof. On the additive cyclic group $\mathbb{G}_2$, APK *correctness* can be yielded directly from our construction. To prove *indistinguishability*, let $\mathsf{pp} \leftarrow \mathsf{Setup}(1^\lambda)$ where $\mathsf{pp} = (\mathsf{BG}, [\mathbf{A}]_2, \ell)$ are given as above. The reduction receives an MDDH challenge over $\mathbb{G}_2$, $\mathsf{chl} = (P_2, [\mathbf{X}]_2, [\mathbf{z}]_2)$ where $\mathbf{X} \xleftarrow{\$} \mathcal{D}_{l,1}$. According the challenge bit $b \in \{0, 1\}$, $\mathbf{z}$ is set to $\mathbf{X}y$ with $y \xleftarrow{\$} \mathbb{Z}_p$ (when $b = 0$) or $\mathbf{z} \xleftarrow{\$} \mathbb{Z}_p^l$ (when $b = 1$). l takes its value from $\{2, \ell\}$ because the two components in a public key, $[\mathbf{B}]_2$ and $[\mathbf{C}]_2$, are matrices of size 2×1 and $\ell\times1$, respectively. Note that the reduction needs to prepare both components of the public key. That is, it samples a full-ranked $\mathbf{X}' \xleftarrow{\$} \mathbb{Z}_p^{l'\times l}$ such that $l' \in \{2, \ell\} \wedge l' \neq l$, and embeds the MDDH challenge chl by setting $\mathsf{pk}^* \triangleq ([\mathbf{X}]_2, \mathbf{X}'[\mathbf{X}]_2)$ and $\mathsf{pk}' \triangleq ([\mathbf{z}]_2, \mathbf{X}'[\mathbf{z}]_2)$. The indistinguishability adversary $\mathcal{A}$ takes as input $(\mathsf{pk}^*, \mathsf{pk}')$. If the challenge tuple satisfies $[\mathbf{z}]_2 = [\mathbf{X}y]_2$ (when $b = 0$), then pk' is distributed identically to pk_0 ($\mathsf{pk}_0 \leftarrow \mathsf{Update}(\mathsf{pk}^*)$, the adversary will output $b^* = 0$). Otherwise (when $b = 1$), pk' is distributed identically to pk_1 (a freshly generated public key, the adversary outputs $b^* = 1$). Therefore, the reduction has the same advantage in the $\mathcal{D}_{l,1}$-MDDH ($l \in \{2, \ell\}$) game as the adversary in the indistinguishability game of Definition 8.

The proofs of two types of unforgeability are similar. For *secret key unforgeability,* the reduction receives a KerMDH challenge over $\mathbb{G}_2$, $\mathsf{chl} = (P_2, [\mathbf{A}]_2)$ where $\mathbf{A} \xleftarrow{\$} \mathcal{D}_1$. The reduction prepares the inputs for the unforgeability adversary $\mathcal{A}$. That is, it samples $\mathbf{K}_0 \xleftarrow{\$} \mathcal{D}_{\ell,2}$ and $\mathbf{K}_1 \xleftarrow{\$} \mathbb{Z}_p^{2\times2}$ of full rank 2. Then, let $[\mathbf{X}]_2 = [\mathbf{K}_1\mathbf{A}]_2$, the reduction embeds the challenge chl by setting $\mathsf{ak} \triangleq \mathbf{K}_0$ and $\mathsf{pk} \triangleq ([\mathbf{X}]_2, [\mathbf{K}_0\mathbf{X}]_2)$. Hence, the input to the adversary in the reduction is distributed identically as in the definition of unforgeability. Suppose the adversary $\mathcal{A}$ breaks secret key unforgeability, which means that $\mathsf{VerifyKP}, \mathsf{VerifyAK}, \mathsf{Audit}$ verify the output tuple $(\mathsf{sk}', \mathsf{pk}', r)$. More precisely, parse $\mathsf{sk}' = (\mathsf{sk}'_0, \mathsf{sk}'_1)$, it holds that $\mathsf{sk}'_0[\mathbf{A}]_2 = [\mathbf{X}]_2 = [\mathbf{K}_1\mathbf{A}]_2$ and $\mathsf{sk}'_1[\mathbf{A}]_2 = [\mathbf{K}_0\mathbf{X}]_2$. If the adversary can find a non-zero vector $\mathsf{sk}'_0 - \mathbf{K}_1$ in the kernel of $\mathbf{A}$, it can break the secret key unforgeability. However, finding sk'_0 is equivalent to solving a $\mathcal{D}_1$-KerMDH problem (with sk'_0, the reduction outputs $[\mathsf{sk}'_0 - \mathbf{K}_1]_1$ to the KerMDH challenge and $e([\mathsf{sk}'_0 - \mathbf{K}_1]_1, [\mathbf{A}]_2) = [0]_T$). Thus, the reduction advantage in the $\mathcal{D}_1$-KerMDH game is the same as the adversary in the secret key unforgeability game.

Similarly, the *auditing key unforgeability* reduction receives a KerMDH challenge over $\mathbb{G}_2$, $\mathsf{chl} = (P_2, [\mathbf{X}]_2)$ where $\mathbf{X} \in \mathcal{D}_1$. The reduction samples $\mathbf{K}_0 \in \mathbb{Z}_p^{\ell\times2}$ of full rank 2 and relays $(P_2, [\mathbf{X}]_2, [\mathbf{K}_0\mathbf{X}]_2)$ to the adversary. Hence, the input of the adversary, *i.e.*, $\mathsf{pk} = ([\mathbf{X}]_2, [\mathbf{K}_0\mathbf{X}]_2)$, distributes identically to the definition. Suppose the adversary $\mathcal{A}$ breaks auditing key unforgeability, which means it finds ak' such that $\mathsf{VerifyAK}(\mathsf{sk}, \mathsf{ak}') = 1$. Note that although the reduction cannot prepare the corresponding secret key, the structure preserves in the public key, *i.e.*, the adversary must output a non-zero $\mathsf{ak}' - \mathbf{K}_0$ in the kernel of $\mathbf{X}$. As explained before, the reduction cannot gain advantages in the $\mathcal{D}_1$-KerMDH game by invoking the auditing key unforgeability adversary.

An Auditable ABC Construction. Before we present the full construction of our auditable ABC scheme, we first recall briefly the SPS-EQ scheme from [17] (the construction and security definitions can be found in Appendix B). We will note that the key generation in their construction differs from our APK.KGen. Hence, by further proving that the change only incurs slightly more advantage to the adversary in the original scheme, we show that our modification preserves the security definitions of the SPS-EQ. Moreover, as proven before, our modification also satisfies the security of the APK mechanism.

Extending the SPS-EQ [17]. We show the original key generation of the SPS-EQ in the following. Recall that the Setup algorithm outputs $\mathsf{pp} = (\mathsf{BG}, [\mathbf{A}]_2, \ell)$.

- SPSEQ.KGen(pp): Sample matrices $\mathbf{K}_1 \xleftarrow{\$} \mathbb{Z}_p^{2\times 2}$ and $\mathbf{K} \xleftarrow{\$} \mathcal{D}_{\ell,2}$ of full rank 2. Then, compute $[\mathbf{B}]_2 = [\mathbf{K}_1\mathbf{A}]_2$ and $[\mathbf{C}]_2 = [\mathbf{K}\mathbf{A}]_2$. Finally, set $\mathsf{sk} = (\mathbf{K}_1, \mathbf{K}), \mathsf{pk} = ([\mathbf{B}]_2, [\mathbf{C}]_2)$ and output $(\mathsf{sk}, \mathsf{pk})$.

The only difference here is that we further sample $\mathbf{K}_0 \xleftarrow{\$} \mathcal{D}_{\ell,2}$ of full rank 2 and compute $\mathbf{K}$ by the multiplication of $\mathbf{K}_0$ and $\mathbf{K}_1$. In the following lemma, we show that this change only increases the SPS-EQ adversary's advantage by at most the advantage of solving a $\mathcal{D}_{\ell,2}$-MDDH problem over $\mathbb{G}_2$.

Lemma 1. *Replacing* SPSEQ.KGen *with* APK.KGen *in the* SPSEQ *scheme given in Construction 4 (Appendix B) preserves the correctness, EUF-CMA and perfect adaption of signatures with respect to message space of the original scheme.*

Proof. Correctness is straightforward as proven in Theorem 1. We unify the proofs of EUF-CMA and perfect adaption of signatures with respect to message space by considering a sequence of two games: Game_1 is the EUF-CMA and perfect adaption of signatures with respect to message space games for the original SPS-EQ scheme with SPSEQ.KGen given in Definition 18 and 19 (in Appendix B); and Game_0 substitutes SPSEQ.KGen with our APK mechanism's APK.KGen. Hence, Game_0 is the game for our modified scheme. We further denote the adversary $\mathcal{A}$'s advantage with Adv_i for each game Game_i where $\in \{0, 1\}$. In the transition of $\mathsf{Game}_0 \rightarrow \mathsf{Game}_1$, $\mathsf{pk}_{\mathsf{Game}_1} = ([\mathbf{K}_1\mathbf{A}]_2, [\mathbf{K}_{\mathsf{Game}_1}\mathbf{A}]_2)$ replaces $\mathsf{pk}_{\mathsf{Game}_0} = ([\mathbf{K}_1\mathbf{A}]_2, [\mathbf{K}_0\mathbf{K}_1\mathbf{A}]_2)$. Note that all matrices are of full rank 2, hence, distinguishing $\mathsf{pk}_{\mathsf{Game}_1}$ and $\mathsf{pk}_{\mathsf{Game}_0}$ is equivalent to solve a challenge of $\mathcal{D}_{\ell,2}$-MDDH problem (because $\mathbf{K}_{\mathsf{Game}_1}$ is an $\ell \times 2$ matrix of full rank 2). That is, $|\mathsf{Adv}_0 - \mathsf{Adv}_1| \leq \mathsf{Adv}^{\mathrm{MDDH}}_{\mathcal{D}_{\ell,2},\mathbb{G}_2}$. Moreover, as shown in [17], the original SPS-EQ scheme satisfies EUF-CMA and perfect adaption of signatures with respect to message space. We conclude Lemma 1.

Constructing the Auditable ABC. Let BGGen be the bilinear group generation, $\mathsf{SC} = (\mathsf{Setup}, \mathsf{Commit}, \mathsf{Open}, \mathsf{OpenSubset}, \mathsf{VerifySubset})$ be the set-commitment [25] that satisfies correctness, binding, subset-soundness and hiding, and Π be a general ZKPoK protocol that satisfies completeness, perfect zero-knowledge and knowledge-soundness. With the necessary algorithms from our APK mechanism and the SPS-EQ [17], *i.e.*, $(\mathsf{KGen}, \mathsf{Update}, \mathsf{Audit}) \in \mathsf{APK}$ and $(\mathsf{Setup}, \mathsf{Sign}, \mathsf{ChgRep}, \mathsf{Verify}) \in \mathsf{SPSEQ}$, we show an auditable ABC AABC in the following. Note that the SPS-EQ scheme [17] utilizes a non-interactive zero-knowledge argument (which we take as a black-box) under the common reference string (CRS) model.

Construction 2 (Auditable ABC AABC**).** *The algorithms are as follows.*

- $\mathsf{Setup}(1^\lambda, q)$: *Run* $\mathsf{BG} \leftarrow \mathsf{BGGen}(1^\lambda)$ *where* $\mathsf{BG} = (p, \mathbb{G}_1, \mathbb{G}_2, \mathbb{G}_T, P_1, P_2, e)$. *Sample* $a \overset{\$}{\leftarrow} \mathbb{Z}_p^*$ *and compute* $([a^i]_1, [a^i]_2)_{i \in [q]}$. *Sample matrices* $[\mathbf{A}]_2, [\mathbf{A}_0]_1, [\mathbf{A}_1]_1 \overset{\$}{\leftarrow} \mathcal{D}_1$, *and a common reference string* crs *for* SPSEQ. *Output* $\mathsf{pp} = (\mathsf{BG}, ([a^i]_1, [a^i]_2)_{i \in [q]}, ([\mathbf{A}]_2, [\mathbf{A}_0]_1, [\mathbf{A}_1]_1), \mathsf{crs}, \ell = 3)$;
- $\mathsf{OrgKGen}(\mathsf{pp})$: *Output* $(\mathsf{osk}, \mathsf{opk}, \mathsf{ak}) \leftarrow \mathsf{APK.KGen}(\mathsf{BG}, [\mathbf{A}]_2, \ell)$ *and delegate* ak *to auditors selected by the issuer;*
- $\mathsf{UsrKGen}(\mathsf{pp})$: *Sample* $\mathsf{usk} \overset{\$}{\leftarrow} \mathbb{Z}_p^*$ *and output* $(\mathsf{usk}, \mathsf{upk} = \mathsf{usk} P_1)$;
- $\langle \mathsf{Obtain}, \mathsf{Issue} \rangle$ *and* $\langle \mathsf{Show}, \mathsf{Verify} \rangle$: *See Fig. 1. In* $\langle \mathsf{Obtain}, \mathsf{Issue} \rangle$, *following the arguments in [17], we consider malicious issuer-keys and user-keys. Hence, both the issuer and the user should run a ZKPoK protocol to prove their public keys to each other, i.e.,* $\Pi^{\mathsf{osk}}(\mathsf{opk})$ *and* $\Pi^{\mathsf{usk}}(\mathsf{upk})$ *in Fig. 1; Whereas, in* $\langle \mathsf{Show}, \mathsf{Verify} \rangle$, *the ZKPoK protocol, i.e.,* $(\pi_1, \pi_2, \pi_3) \leftarrow \Pi^{(C, rC, P_1)}(C_1, C_2, C_3)$, *proves freshness to prevent transcripts of valid showings from being replayed by someone not in possession of the credential [25];*
- $\mathsf{Audit}(\mathsf{ak}, S, \mathsf{opk})$: *Parse* $S = (\mathsf{opk}', \mathsf{cred}', W; D)$. *Return* $\mathsf{APK.Audit}(\mathsf{ak}, \mathsf{opk}', \mathsf{opk})$.

$\mathsf{Obtain}(\mathsf{pp}, \mathsf{usk}, \mathsf{opk}, A)$		$\mathsf{Issue}(\mathsf{pp}, \mathsf{upk}, \mathsf{osk}, A)$
	$\xleftrightarrow{\pi \leftarrow \Pi^{\mathsf{usk}}(\mathsf{upk})}$	If Π fails, return $\perp$
If Π fails, return $\perp$ $(C, O) \leftarrow \mathsf{SC.Commit}(A; \mathsf{usk})$; $r \xleftarrow{\$} \mathbb{Z}_p^*; R \triangleq rC$;	$\xleftrightarrow{\pi \leftarrow \Pi^{\mathsf{osk}}(\mathsf{opk})}$ $\xrightarrow{(C,R)}$	If $e(C, P_2) \neq e(\mathsf{upk}, \mathsf{Ch}_A(a)P_2$ and $\forall a' \in A{:}[a']_1 = [a]_1$: return $\perp$. Else return: $(\sigma, \tau) \leftarrow \mathsf{SPSEQ.Sign}(\mathsf{osk}, (C, R, P_1))$
Check $\mathsf{SPSEQ.Verify}(\mathsf{opk}, (C, R, P_1), (\sigma, \tau))$; Return $\mathsf{cred} \triangleq (C, (\sigma, \tau), r, O)$	$\xleftarrow{(\sigma,\tau)}$	

$\mathsf{AABC.Show}(\mathsf{opk}, A, D, \mathsf{cred})$		$\mathsf{AABC.Verify}(D)$
Parse $\mathsf{cred} = (C, \sigma, r, O)$; $\mu, \rho \xleftarrow{\$} \mathbb{Z}_p^*$; $((C_1, C_2, C_3), \sigma') \leftarrow \mathsf{SPSEQ.ChgRep}($ $(C, rC, P_1), (\sigma, \tau), \mu, \rho, \mathsf{opk})$; $(C_1, C_2, C_3) \triangleq \mu \cdot (C, rC, P_1)$; $\mathsf{cred}' \triangleq (C_1, C_2, C_3, \sigma')$; $\mathsf{opk}' \leftarrow \mathsf{APK.Update}(\mathsf{opk}, \rho)$; $O' \triangleq (b, \mu \cdot O)$ where $b \in \{0, 1\}$; $W \leftarrow \mathsf{SC.OpenSubset}(\mathsf{SC.pp}, \mu C, A, O', D)$ $S \triangleq (\mathsf{opk}', \mathsf{cred}', W)$; $(\pi_1, \pi_2, \pi_3) \leftarrow \Pi^{(C, rC, P_1)}(C_1, C_2, C_3)$		
	$\xleftrightarrow{(S, \pi_1, \pi_2, \pi_3)}$	If Π fails, return 0; Else return: $\mathsf{SPSEQ.Verify}(\mathsf{opk}', \mathsf{cred}') \wedge$ $\mathsf{SC.VerifySubset}(C_1, D, W)$

Fig. 1. $\langle \mathsf{Obtain}, \mathsf{Issue} \rangle$, $\langle \mathsf{Show}, \mathsf{Verify} \rangle$ in AABC.

Therefore, we have the following result.

Theorem 2. *The auditable ABC scheme* AABC *given by Construction 2 satisfies the following properties.*

- *Correctness (Definition 12);*
- *Anonymity (Definition 13) if the DDH assumption holds, the ZKPoK protocol has perfect zero-knowledge, the underlying APK satisfies indistinguishability and auditing key unforgeability, and the SPS-EQ scheme perfectly adapts signatures with respect to message space;*
- *Unforgeability (Definition 14) if the q-co-DL assumption holds, the ZKPoK protocol has perfect zero-knowledge, the set-commitment scheme* SC *satisfies subset-soundness, the APK satisfies secret key unforgeability, and SPS-EQ satisfies EUF-CMA;*

– *Auditing unforgeability (Definition 10) if the $\mathcal{D}_1$-KerMDH holds on $\mathbb{G}_2$.*

Proof. We show a brief proof here. *Correctness* follows directly from the correctness of building blocks. From now, we describe the proof rationale for anonymity, unforgeability, and auditing unforgeability properties, respectively. In general, we rely on [17] (Theorem 6 and 7) for properties of the ABC scheme and Theorem 1 for the APK part of our construction.

The proof for anonymity (Definition 13) is an adaptation of the one given in Theorem 7 of [17]. Note there are two slight modifications to the anonymity definition in our work: (1) the adversary in the anonymity game generates two issuer-public keys $(\mathsf{opk}_0, \mathsf{opk}_1)$; (2) the challenge oracle $\mathcal{O}_{\mathsf{LoR}}$ requires the adversary also to distinguish under which issuer-public key is the credential issued. To adjust the previous proof for these modifications, we first consider the two issuer-public keys $(\mathsf{opk}_0, \mathsf{opk}_1)$ and the updated issuer-public key in the credential showing, *i.e.*, $\mathsf{opk}'_b \leftarrow \mathsf{APK.Update}(\mathsf{opk}_b)$ where $b \in \{0, 1\}$ is the challenge bit in $\mathcal{O}_{\mathsf{LoR}}$. The adversary can win our introduced anonymity game if: (1) it can distinguish opk'_0 from opk'_1, then, the adversary can also win the *indistinguishability* game of the APK mechanism given in Definition 8; (2) it can recover the corresponding auditing keys $(\mathsf{ak}_0, \mathsf{ak}_1)$ from the issuer-public keys (hence, winning the anonymity game trivially by running $\mathsf{APK.Audit}(\mathsf{ak}^*_b, \mathsf{opk}'_b, \mathsf{opk}_b)$), which means the adversary wins the *auditing key unforgeability* game of the APK mechanism given in Definition 10. However, since the aforementioned APK properties have been proven in Theorem 1, our defined anonymity adversary gains no advantage over the anonymity adversary of [17].

Next, by the proof in [17], the anonymity of ABC requires that the DDH assumption holds, the ZKPoK protocol has perfect zero-knowledge (which is taken as a black-box in this work), and the SPS-EQ perfectly adapts signatures with respect to message space (which has been proven in Lemma 1), thus we conclude the anonymity part for our auditable ABC scheme.

Similarly, our proof of unforgeability (Definition 14) adapts the one given in Theorem 6 of [17]. The only modification we make is that the unforgeability game provides its adversary with auditing keys. With additional auditing keys, the adversary can win the unforgeability game if it can recover the secret key of the underlying APK mechanism, which violates the *secret key unforgeability* of APK as proven in Theorem 1. Then, by the proof in [17], the unforgeability of ABC requires that the q-co-DL assumption holds, the ZKPoK protocol has perfect zero-knowledge, the set-commitment scheme SC satisfies subset-soundness (which is also taken as a black-box in this work), and SPS-EQ satisfies EUF-CMA (which has been proven in Lemma 1), thus we conclude unforgeability for our auditable ABC scheme.

Finally, for the auditing unforgeability property, the adversary in the auditing unforgeability game aims to recover the issuer-public key's corresponding auditing key. Hence, the definition is equivalent to the auditing key unforgeability of APK (we use the same definition), which has been proven in Theorem 1.

4 Application: Contact Tracing

From the perspective of credentials, we review the environmental-adaptive contact tracing (EACT) framework proposed in [37]. We provide a construction based on our auditable ABC scheme and argue that the game-based security definitions of auditable ABC suffice the requirements in contact tracing systems. Finally, we implement our construction to showcase its practicality.

Overview. We start by recalling the EACT framework [37]. It utilizes a bulletin board to store contact records, which can be instantiated by a blockchain protocol satisfying the robust ledger properties [26], *i.e.*, the capability of achieving immutable consensus atomically. Concerning different virus transmission modes (droplet and airborne), EACT considered tracing approaches via Bluetooth Low Energy (BLE) and self-reported discrete location (DLT). However, the framework cannot unify the tracing approach in both settings because the recorded data are of different structures. As we will show later, ABC schemes enable us to circumvent this problem by regarding environmental and location data as *attributes*. Here, for completeness, we define a comparison algorithm to decide close contacts for BLE and DLT, *i.e.*, $\mathsf{Compare}_{\{\mathrm{BLE},\mathrm{DLT}\}}(\mathsf{envpp}, D, A)$ takes as input the environmental parameters envpp, an opened attributed set D (from other users, potentially downloaded from the bulletin board) and an attribute set A (of the user who runs the algorithm). We say the algorithm is "*well-defined*" if it outputs 1 when attributes in D and A are regarded as close contact concerning the tracing setting in $\{\mathrm{BLE}, \mathrm{DLT}\}$, and 0 otherwise.

The EACT framework involves three phases: key management, recording, and tracing, with two types of participants: user $\mathcal{U}$ and medical agency $\mathcal{M}$. We refine the algorithms with respect to our auditable ABC scheme. Intuitively, in the key management phase, users generate key pairs for participating as both issuers and regular users. The medical agency generates its key pair from a signature scheme. Users need to register their *issuer-public keys*, and medical agencies need to register their public keys. Then, in the recording phase, when users contact (two users in BLE or one user in DLT), we consider a pairwise executed $\langle \mathsf{Obtain}, \mathsf{Issue} \rangle$, *i.e.*, each user performs as an ABC issuer to grant its counterparty (itself in DLT) a credential on the attributes of current environmental data (or location data). This approach in the DLT setting can be easily adapted to the case in which the user can communicate to BLE beacons, providing additional evidence for the user's location data. Finally, in the tracing phase, whenever a user searches for medical treatment, she shows her records while the agency performs verification. The medical agency uploads records to the bulletin board (as we will show in tracing-soundness (Definition 16), we assume a malicious agency who can upload invalid records). Hence, users can refer to the bulletin board and audit if any shown credential is issued by themselves. Then, by comparing the environmental factors, they can detect close contact. The following section presents the full construction, including our modifications to the original framework.

4.1 An Auditable ABC-Based Construction

Let $\mathsf{SIG} = (\mathsf{KGen}, \mathsf{Sign}, \mathsf{Verify})$ be a signature scheme that satisfies correctness and EUF-CMA, and let AABC be our auditable ABC construction given in Construction 2.

Construction 3 (Refined EACT REACT**).** *Our refined EACT framework involves three phases, i.e., Key management:* $(\mathsf{Setup}, \mathsf{OrgKGen}, \mathsf{UsrKGen}, \mathsf{MedKGen}, \mathsf{KReg})$*; Recording:* $\mathsf{Exchange}$*; Tracing:* $(\langle \mathsf{Show}, \mathsf{Verify}\rangle, \mathsf{Merge}, \mathsf{Trace})$*. The algorithms are performed as follows.*

- $\mathsf{Setup}(1^\lambda, q, \mathsf{envpp})$ *is run by the system where* envpp *denotes the environmental parameters. It runs* $\mathsf{AABC.pp} \leftarrow \mathsf{AABC.Setup}(1^\lambda, q)$ *and outputs* $\mathsf{pp} = (\mathsf{AABC.pp}, \mathsf{envpp})$.
- $\mathsf{OrgKGen}(\mathsf{pp})$ *is run by a user and outputs* $(\mathsf{osk}, \mathsf{opk}, \mathsf{ak}) \leftarrow \mathsf{AABC.OrgKGen}(\mathsf{pp})$*. Note that in contact tracing, we consider the user auditing for herself;*
- $\mathsf{UsrKGen}(\mathsf{pp})$ *is run by a user and outputs* $(\mathsf{usk}, \mathsf{upk}) \leftarrow \mathsf{AABC.UsrKGen}(\mathsf{pp})$*;*
- $\mathsf{MedKGen}(\mathsf{pp})$ *is run by a medical agency. It outputs a medical agent key pair with* $(\mathsf{msk}, \mathsf{mpk}) \leftarrow \mathsf{SIG.KGen}(1^\lambda)$*. Later, we omit* pp *in algorithm inputs;*
- $\mathsf{KReg}(\mathsf{pk}, \mathsf{misc}, \mathbb{B})$ *is a DID [35] black-box, which takes as input a public key* $\mathsf{pk} \in \{\mathsf{opk}, \mathsf{mpk}\}$*, auxiliary information* misc*, and a bulletin board* $\mathbb{B}$*.* KReg *registers* pk *with the corresponding* misc *on* $\mathbb{B}$*.*
- $\mathsf{Exchange}(\{(\mathsf{osk}_i, \mathsf{opk}_i), (\mathsf{usk}_i, \mathsf{upk}_i), A_i\}_{i\in\{0,1\}})$ *is an interactive protocol executed between two users* $\mathcal{U}_0, \mathcal{U}_1$*, who may be identical, e.g., in the DLT setting. For* $i \in \{0,1\}$*, both users perform* $(\mathsf{cred}_i, \cdot) \leftarrow \langle \mathsf{Obtain}(\mathsf{usk}_i, \mathsf{opk}_{1-i}, A_i), \mathsf{Issue}(\mathsf{upk}_i, \mathsf{osk}_{1-i}, A_i)\rangle$ *to grant each other a credential. The protocol outputs* cred_0 *and* cred_1 *for each user, respectively.*
- $\langle \mathsf{Show}, \mathsf{Verify}\rangle$ *is the showing and verification protocol in our auditable ABC, which here, is executed between a user* $\mathcal{U}$ *and a medical agency* $\mathcal{M}$*. The protocol outputs* $(S, b) \leftarrow \mathsf{AABC}.\langle \mathsf{Show}, \mathsf{Verify}\rangle$ *where* S *is a showing of the credential and* $b \in \{0,1\}$*. Note that we explicitly add revealed attributes to* S*, i.e.,* $S \triangleq (\mathsf{opk}', \mathsf{cred}', W, D)$*. Moreover, we enable this protocol to process in batches, i.e., it can take a list of* n *credentials and verifies for each entry;*
- $\mathsf{Merge}(\mathsf{msk}, (S, b), \mathbb{B})$ *is run by a medical agency* $\mathcal{M}$*. If* $b = 1$*,* Merge *runs* $\sigma \leftarrow \mathsf{SIG.Sign}(\mathsf{msk}, S)$ *and outputs* $\mathbb{B}||(\mathsf{mpk}, S, \sigma)$*, or aborts otherwise;*
- $\mathsf{Trace}(\mathsf{ak}, A, \mathbb{B})$ *is run by a user* $\mathcal{U}$ *with issuer-public and auditing keys* $\mathsf{opk}, \mathsf{ak}$*. It parses* $\mathbb{B} = \{(\mathsf{mpk}_j, S_j, \sigma_j)\}_{j\in[|\mathbb{B}|]}$*, and for each entry, parses* $S_j = (\mathsf{opk}'_j, \mathsf{cred}'_j, W_j, D_j)$*. Then, for each entry, it runs* $b \leftarrow \mathsf{SIG.Verify}(\mathsf{mpk}_j, S_j, \sigma_j)$*, and* $b' \leftarrow \mathsf{AABC.Audit}(\mathsf{ak}, S_j, \mathsf{opk})$ *(which is* $\mathsf{APK.Audit}(\mathsf{ak}, \mathsf{opk}'_j, \mathsf{opk})$*). For all* $j\in[|\mathbb{B}|]$ *such that* $b = 1 \wedge b' = 1$*, it compares according to environmental parameters and tracing settings, i.e.,* $b_j \leftarrow \mathsf{Compare}_{\{BLE,DLT\}}(\mathsf{envpp}, D_j, A)$*. If there exists any* j *that satisfies* $b_j = 1$*,* Trace *outputs* 1*; Otherwise, it outputs* 0*.*

4.2 Security and Analysis

We directly employ the cryptographic game-based security definitions from our auditable ABC scheme given in Sect. 3.2, including correctness, anonymity, and unforgeability. Moreover, we consider two separate properties for tracing, *i.e.*, traceability and tracing-soundness. At the end of this section, we will compare our ABC-based security definitions to the ones in [18].

The refined EACT requires signatures from medical agencies in Merge and on the bulletin board $\mathbb{B}$ (satisfying robust ledger properties [26]). Hence, we first formalize the tracing process correctness to capture these new requirements.

Definition 15 (Traceability). *Given the bulletin board* $\mathbb{B}$*, a* REACT *system satisfies traceability, if for any* $\lambda > 0, q > 0$*, any non-empty sets* A *with* $|A| \leq q$*, and for any honest user* $\mathcal{U}$ *with a key tuple* $(\mathsf{osk}, \mathsf{opk}, \mathsf{ak}) \xleftarrow{\$} \mathsf{OrgKGen}(\mathsf{pp})$ *where* $\mathsf{pp} \leftarrow \mathsf{Setup}(1^\lambda, 1^q)$*, if there exists* $(\mathsf{mpk}, S, \sigma) \in \mathbb{B}$ *such that* $\langle \mathsf{Show}, \mathsf{Verify} \rangle(S) = 1$*,* $\mathsf{SIG.Verify}(\mathsf{mpk}, S, \sigma) = 1$*,* $D \in S$ *such that* $\mathsf{Compare}_{\{BLE,DLT\}}(\mathsf{envpp}, D, A) = 1$*, then* $\Pr[\mathsf{Trace}(\mathsf{ak}, A, \mathbb{B}) = 1] = 1$ *where* A *is the attribute set of* $\mathcal{U}$ *when she issues the credential being shown in* S*.*

Then, we have the following lemma.

Lemma 2. *Let the bulletin board satisfy the robust ledger properties [26]. The refined EACT* REACT *given by Construction 3 satisfies traceability if* AABC *and* SIG *satisfy correctness, and the* Compare *algorithm is well-defined.*

The proof follows directly from the correctness of AABC and SIG, and the well-defined comparing algorithm $\mathsf{Compare}_{\{\mathrm{BLE,DLT}\}}(\mathsf{envpp}, \cdot, \cdot)$. Moreover, we require the bulletin board to satisfy the robust ledger properties [26] so that any entry on it cannot be erased or modified after a period of time.

Next, we consider the soundness of tracing, *i.e.*, the situation in which an honest user's Trace outputs 1 falsely. The PPT adversary $\mathcal{A}$ either: (1) forges a valid credential on behalf of honest users; or (2) colludes with a malicious medical agency so that arbitrary showings can be uploaded to the bulletin board. The first case has been captured by our unforgeability game in the auditable ABC scheme (Definition 14) with additional assumptions for the bulletin board, signature scheme, and comparing algorithm (like in Lemma 2).

However, the second one is dedicated to contact tracing. The reason lies in the different use cases, *i.e.*, in auditable ABC, auditors audit credential showings on behalf of the original issuer, hence, triggering the auditing algorithm of another auditor gains the adversary no benefits; whereas, in contact tracing, it will cause false positive errors to the original issuer. In order to prevent such an attack, we require the proof in $\mathsf{AABC}.\langle \mathsf{Show}, \mathsf{Verify} \rangle$ to be non-interactive. Concretely, since our bulletin board is instantiated by a blockchain, users can apply the Fiat-Shamir transformation on the head block of the blockchain, *i.e.*, embedding the hash of the blockchain's head block into their proof. Note that this approach also guarantees the freshness of the proof that prevents the relay and replay attacks [16]. This is because the adversary cannot guess the head of the blockchain priorly due to the security of blockchain protocols.

As shown in Theorem 2, the anonymity and unforgeability of AABC (also for REACT in Theorem 3) requires perfect zero-knowledge of Π. Hence, we must rely on heavy mechanisms, *e.g.*, [29], to make such a protocol non-interactive. An alternative way is to prove these theorems with computational zero-knowledge with a looser security reduction. The transformation to a non-interactive protocol with computational zero-knowledge can be achieved with the Fiat-Shamir heuristic [24] to trade security tightness for efficiency. Then, the showing of a credential becomes publicly verifiable so that even if a malicious medical agency falsely uploads credential showings to the bulletin board, every user (including the one who runs Trace) can verify the showing.

Compared to the unforgeability of auditable ABC in Definition 14, due to the malicious $\mathcal{A}_{\mathcal{M}}$ setting, tracing-soundness removes the requirement of $b = 1$ (the credential showing can be invalid) but embeds the proof of freshness (the showing must be presented at most once). We formally define tracing-soundness (with respect to malicious $\mathcal{A}_{\mathcal{M}}$).

Definition 16 (Tracing-Soundness). *Given the bulletin board* $\mathbb{B}$, *a* REACT *system satisfies tracing-soundness (with respect to malicious* $\mathcal{A}_{\mathcal{M}}$*), if for any PPT adversary* $\mathcal{A}$ *that has access to oracles* $\mathcal{O} = \{\mathcal{O}_{\mathsf{HU}}, \mathcal{O}_{\mathsf{CU}}, \mathcal{O}_{\mathsf{ObtIss}}, \mathcal{O}_{\mathsf{Issue}}, \mathcal{O}_{\mathsf{Show}}, \mathcal{O}_{\mathsf{Audit}}\}$, *the following probability holds for any* $\lambda > 0, q > 0, \mathsf{pp} \leftarrow \mathsf{Setup}(1^\lambda, q, \mathsf{envpp})$, *and* $(\mathsf{osk}, \mathsf{opk}, \mathsf{ak}) \leftarrow \mathsf{OrgKGen}(\mathsf{pp})$*:*

$$\Pr\left[\begin{matrix}(D, \mathsf{st}) \leftarrow \mathcal{A}^{\mathcal{O}}(\mathsf{opk}, \mathsf{ak}); & \mathsf{Trace}(\mathsf{ak}, \cdot, (S, \pi)) = 1 \wedge \\ ((S, \pi), b) \leftarrow \langle \mathcal{A}(\mathsf{st}), \mathsf{Verify}(D)\rangle : & \textit{If } \mathsf{OWNER}[j] \in \mathsf{CU}, D \notin \mathsf{ATTR}[j]\end{matrix}\right] \leq \mathsf{negl}(\lambda),$$

where $\pi = (\pi_1, \pi_2, \pi_3) \leftarrow \Pi^{(C, rC, P_1)}(C_1, C_2, C_3)$, *and the variables are given in Fig. 1 of auditable ABC construction.*

Finally, we have the following theorem.

Theorem 3. *Our refined EACT* REACT *satisfies correctness, anonymity, unforgeability, traceability, and tracing-soundness (with respect to malicious* $\mathcal{A}_{\mathcal{M}}$*).*

Proof. The proofs of correctness, anonymity, and unforgeability follow directly from the underlying auditable ABC scheme, which has been given in Theorem 2. Traceability has been captured by Lemma 2. Hence, we only show the proof of tracing-soundness with respect to malicious $\mathcal{A}_{\mathcal{M}}$.

Let $(\mathsf{mpk}, (S, \pi)\sigma) \in \mathbb{B}$ be an entry stored on the bulletin board that triggers an honest user's tracing algorithm, *i.e.*, $\mathsf{Trace}(\mathsf{ak}, A, (\mathsf{mpk}, (S, \pi), \sigma)) = 1$. Here, ak and A are the user's auditing key and attribute set when issuing the shown credential; whereas, mpk and σ are the public key and signature of the malicious $\mathcal{A}_{\mathcal{M}}$. Now, we consider the adversary's outputs, $((S, \pi), b) \leftarrow \langle \mathcal{A}(\mathsf{st}), \mathsf{Verify}(D)\rangle$. By traceability (Lemma 2), if $b = 1$, then the Trace algorithm will output 1. However, by the unforgeability of the underlying auditable ABC, the probability of the adversary outputting $b = 1$ is negligible of λ. In contrast, since we assume the medical agency $\mathcal{A}_{\mathcal{M}}$ to be malicious, it may approve invalid showing transcripts, *i.e.*, $b = 0$, to be uploaded to the bulletin board. However, as discussed above, the non-interactive proof π enhanced the showing transcript S to be publicly verifiable (freshness and validity). Hence, the user who runs Trace can reproduce $b' \leftarrow \langle \mathsf{Show}, \mathsf{Verify} \rangle (S, \pi)$ on herself. Considering the situation where $b = 0$, we should have $b' = 0$. Therefore, Trace will also output 0, *i.e.*, the adversary fails to break tracing-soundness even if it colludes with a malicious medical agency.

Comparison with Existing Game-Based Security Definitions in [18]. The authors consider unlinkability and integrity. The former requires the adversary to distinguish two given pseudonyms, and the latter focuses on the false positive attack, *i.e.*, the adversary tries to trigger an honest user's tracing algorithm to output 1. Given the differences in syntax (their model [18] only considers pseudonyms; whereas, our system considers showing of credentials), we compare our definitions with theirs as follows.

Concretely, the unlinkability in [18] is further separated into pseudonym unlinkability (during the recording phase in which other users' pseudonyms are stored locally) and trace unlinkability (during the tracing phase in which recorded pseudonyms become publicly available). In comparison, the anonymity of our auditable ABC schemes (Definition 13) guarantees that no adversary can distinguish any two credential showings (similar to the revealed pseudonyms in trace unlinkability), even when the adversary has full control over issuing the challenge credentials. Note that the adversary can control issuer-public keys but not the corresponding auditing keys (this is guaranteed by the auditing key unforgeability of the underlying APK mechanism). Otherwise, it can trivially win the anonymity game by auditing the updated public keys in credential showings (as we explained in the proof of Theorem 2). Moreover, user-public keys (similar to the pseudonyms in [18]) are generated with $\mathsf{AABC.UsrKGen}$, which are distributed uniformly on $\mathbb{G}_1$ (since usk is sampled uniformly at random from $\mathbb{Z}_p^*$). Hence, no adversary, as in the pseudonym unlinkability game, can distinguish any two distinct user-public keys in our system. Therefore, our anonymity captures both of the unlinkability definitions.

Next, the integrity in [18] provides its adversary with oracles to: (1) create new users; (2) generate, record, and send pseudonyms (during the recording phase, similar to credentials in our system); (3) generate and upload pseudonyms for tracing (during tracing phase, similar to our credential showings); (4) set time periods. In comparison, our tracing-soundness (Definition 16) provides similar oracle accessibility to the adversary, *i.e.*, (1) create new users; (2) issue and obtain credentials (contact records); (3) show credentials and upload the showing. Hence, it resembles the integrity in [18] except for the oracle that sets time for the adversary (this is because our system model is not period-specific like the one in [18]).

4.3 Implementation

We provide a proof-of-concept implementation for the refined EACT construction to prove its practicality on mobile devices with comparatively limited performance. The implementation uses Java/Kotlin for the raw Android environment.

However, we also implement necessary functions since the Java Pairing-Based Cryptography (jPBC) library [14] cannot fully support matrix-based bilinear pairing operations. The library-level implementation, together with extended parts for jPBC [14] library, can also be found in our anonymous repository (https://anonymous.4open.science/r/EAHT_MODULE_TEST).

Overall, we implement the following algorithms $(\mathsf{Setup}, \mathsf{OrgKGen}, \mathsf{UsrKGen}, \mathsf{Exchange}) \in \mathsf{REACT}$. Moreover, in Exchange, we need to measure the performance of algorithms and transmission (which is written in the form of $\mathsf{Transmit}(\cdot)$ for simplicity), separately. Hence, we further divide Exchange into (Obtain-1, $\mathsf{Transmit}_1$, AABC.Issue, $\mathsf{Transmit}_2$, Obtain-2). The results are shown in Table 1.

Table 1. Experiment Results (Time in milliseconds)

Algorithms	Time	Algorithms	Time	Algorithms	Time
Setup	168.99	Obtain-1	40.08	$\mathsf{Transmit}(\sigma, \tau)$	75.16
OrgKGen	54.18	$\mathsf{Transmit}(\pi, C, R)$	38.32	Obtain-2	164.81
UsrKGen	9.05	AABC.Issue	257.50	GenProof	0.26

Experiment device: Samsung SM-S9080 Android 12, Bluetooth 5.0 (Bluetooth Low Energy); Time consumption is presented in milliseconds and calculated with the average of 100 attempts.

Setup and OrgKGen are performance-insensitive because they only need to be executed once. We implement them merely to support other algorithms. Although we do not require user key pairs to be renewed once per contact, UsrKGen should be run periodically (*e.g.*, once per hour) to prevent a user's complete track under its public key from being exposed. We leave the setting of the renewal interval for real-life users to decide. Finally, for Exchange, we consider the performance of AABC.Obtain = (Obtain-1, Obtain-2), AABC.Issue and the time cost of data transmission, *i.e.*, $\mathsf{Transmit}(\pi, C, R)$ and $\mathsf{Transmit}(\sigma, \tau)$. A one-sided round trip, *e.g.*, $\mathcal{U}_0$ issuing a credential to $\mathcal{U}_1$ is performed with ($\mathcal{U}_0$.Obtain-1 $\longrightarrow$ $\mathcal{U}_0.\mathsf{Transmit}(\pi, C, R) \longrightarrow \mathcal{U}_1.\mathsf{Issue} \longrightarrow \mathcal{U}_1.\mathsf{Transmit}(\sigma, \tau) \longrightarrow \mathcal{U}_0$.Obtain-2) takes approximately 575.87 milliseconds in total. Consider the worst case, *e.g.*, when a crowded train is filled with 101 users. Each of them needs to Exchange with the other 100, hence, taking approximately 57.6 s to finish the execution and transmission. We consider this result to be reasonable and plausible.

5 Conclusion

Motivated by the contact tracing new requirements, we adopt a novel approach from ABC schemes due to their similarity. By abstracting "traceability" in contact tracing systems, we propose an auditable public key (APK) mechanism that, like its predecessor, the updatable public keys can be applied in many cryptographic primitives, making it of independent interest.

Next, we extend the ABC schemes in [17,25] with our APK mechanism to port the auditability to the world of ABC. Such property enables auditors, delegated by an issuer, to audit if a shown credential is issued by the issuer. We argue that it adds an additional layer of accountability to the schemes in which credential showings can hide issuer identities. The capability of hiding issuer identities is usually considered an overpowerful anonymity property in real- life. The auditability for identifying issuers may also help credential revocation, which has been another long-worried problem of credentials schemes.

Finally, our refined EACT framework fixes the problems in the original work [37], *i.e.*, (1) distinct tracing approaches for different settings; (2) weak security guarantee from informal threat models. We achieve so by constructing it from our auditable ABC and adapting security properties accordingly. Moreover, we clarify that EACT is only one example application for our auditable primitives (public keys and ABC).

A The Necessity of Enhancing Contact Tracing Systems

This work considers the enhancement of contact tracing systems due to the following two epidemiology findings: (1) modes of transmission (droplet and airborne); (2) environmental factors (temperature, humidity, air velocity, etc.).

Droplet transmission refers to the infections caused by viruses ejected with droplets by sneezes or coughs; whereas, airborne transmission means that infections are caused by floating liquid drops carrying viruses suspended in the air [20]. Hence, "close contact" should be defined differently in the two transmission modes, *i.e.*, droplet transmissible viruses require face-to-face contact; whereas, airborne transmissible viruses only require people to come into the region of the floating virus during their lifespan. Conventional contact tracing systems utilize Bluetooth Low Energy (BLE) technology to trace face-to-face contact. In contrast, to the best of our knowledge, only Wang et al. [37] considered the airborne transmission with their discrete-location-tracing setting (DLT). Intuitively, the DLT setting records users' relative and absolute positions to decide close contact. However, due to the inherent decentralization of their system (*i.e.*, users are designed to issue their own contact records), they failed to achieve meaningful integrity guarantees for the DLT setting.

As mentioned above, virus distribution, *e.g.*, lifespan and region size, affects the infectiousness of viruses. Epidemiology research [15,19,30] concludes that virus distribution depends on environmental factors, including temperature, humidity, air velocity, etc. However, in conventional contact tracing systems, BLE usually scans according to predetermined parameters, *e.g.*, interval and radius. The mismatch between virus distribution and scan parameters may cause overwhelmingly false-positive records, burdening the medical system in real-life. Therefore, we consider that it is necessary to filter records according to environmental factors for practical contact tracing systems.

A problem caused by including more data (*i.e.*, position and environmental factors) is that revealing these data may result in the identification of users.

Therefore, this work embeds them into the attributes of an attribute-based credentials (ABC) scheme. Anonymity and selective showing capability of ABC schemes (from [17,25] and our Construction 2) empower users to reveal only necessary attributes to verifiers while keeping other attributes secret, *i.e.*, medical agencies and other users (including the issuer) cannot learn more than what is revealed during *the showing of credentials*[4]. Potentially, we can further tweak the set-commitment scheme [25] (mentioned in Sect. 2) to enable the proof of knowledge of the commitment content, hence, achieving blind issuance as shown in [9]. The blind issuance capability can prevent issuers from learning users' attributes during *the issuance of credentials.*

B The SPS-EQ Scheme from [17]

We show the SPS-EQ scheme given by [17] with respect to a fully adaptive NIZK argument $\mathsf{NIZK} \triangleq (\mathsf{PGen}, \mathsf{PPro}, \mathsf{PSim}, \mathsf{PRVer}, \mathsf{PVer}, \mathsf{ZKEval})$. It satisfies correctness, the EUF-CMA, and the property of Perfect Adaption of Signatures with respect to Message Space.

Construction 4 (SPS-EQ Scheme SPSEQ). *The algorithms are as follows.*

- $\mathsf{Setup}(1^\lambda)$. *Run* $\mathsf{BG} \leftarrow \mathsf{BGGen}(1^\lambda)$ *and sample matrices* $\mathbf{A}, \mathbf{A}_0, \mathbf{A}_1 \xleftarrow{\$} \mathcal{D}_1$ *from matrix distribution. Generate a common reference string and trapdoor for the malleable NIZK argument with* $(\mathsf{crs}, \mathsf{td}) \leftarrow \mathsf{NIZK.PGen}(1^\lambda, \mathsf{BG})$. *Return* $\mathsf{pp} = (\mathsf{BG}, [\mathbf{A}]_2, [\mathbf{A}_0]_1, [\mathbf{A}_1]_1, \mathsf{crs}, \ell)$;
- $\mathsf{KGen}(\mathsf{pp})$. *Sample* $\mathbf{K}_0 \xleftarrow{\$} \mathbb{Z}_p^{2\times 2}, \mathbf{K} \xleftarrow{\$} \mathbb{Z}_p^{\ell\times 2}$. *Compute* $[\mathbf{B}]_2 = [\mathbf{K}_0]_2[\mathbf{A}]_2$ *and* $[\mathbf{C}]_2 = [\mathbf{K}]_2[\mathbf{A}]_2$. *Set* $\mathsf{sk} = (\mathbf{K}_0, \mathbf{K})$ *and* $\mathsf{pk} = ([\mathbf{B}]_2, [\mathbf{C}]_2)$. *Return* $(\mathsf{sk}, \mathsf{pk})$;
- $\mathsf{Sign}(\mathsf{pp}, \mathsf{sk}, [\mathbf{m}]_1)$. *Sample* $r_1, r_2 \xleftarrow{\$} \mathbb{Z}_p$. *Compute* $[\mathbf{t}]_1 = [\mathbf{A}_0]_1 r_1$ *and* $[\mathbf{w}]_1 = [\mathbf{A}_0]_1 r_2$. *Compute* $\mathbf{u}_1 = \mathbf{K}_0^\top [\mathbf{t}]_1 + \mathbf{K}^\top [\mathbf{m}]_1$ *and* $\mathbf{u}_2 = \mathbf{K}_0^\top [\mathbf{w}]_1$. *Generate proof with* $(\Omega_1, \Omega_2, [z_0]_2, [z_1]_2, Z_1) \leftarrow \mathsf{NIZK.PPro}(\mathsf{crs}, [\mathbf{t}]_1, r_1, [\mathbf{w}]_1, r_2)$. *Set* $\sigma = ([\mathbf{u}_1]_1, [\mathbf{t}]_1, \Omega_1, [z_0]_2, [z_1]_2, Z_1)$ *and* $\tau = ([\mathbf{u}_2]_1, [\mathbf{u}_2]_1, [\mathbf{w}]_1, \Omega_2)$. *Return* (σ, τ);
- $\mathsf{ChgRep}(\mathsf{pp}, [\mathbf{m}]_1, (\sigma, \tau), \mu, \rho, \mathsf{pk})$. *Parse* $\sigma = ([\mathbf{u}_1]_1, [\mathbf{t}]_1, \Omega_1, [z_0]_2, [z_1]_2, Z_1)$ *and* $\tau \in \{([\mathbf{u}_2]_1, [\mathbf{w}]_1, \Omega_2), \perp\}$. *Let* $\Omega = (\Omega_1, \Omega_2, [z_0]_2, [z_1]_2, Z_1)$. *Check proof with* $\mathsf{NIZK.PVer}(\mathsf{crs}, [\mathbf{t}]_1, [\mathbf{w}]_1, \Omega)$. *Check if* $e([\mathbf{u}_2]_1^\top, \mathbf{A}]_2) = e([\mathbf{w}]_1^\top, \mathbf{B}]_2)$ *and* $e([\mathbf{u}_1]_1^\top, \mathbf{A}]_2) = e([\mathbf{t}]_1^\top, \mathbf{B}]_2) + e([\mathbf{m}]_1^\top, \mathbf{C}]_2)$. *Sample* $\alpha, \beta \xleftarrow{\$} \mathbb{Z}_p^*$. *Compute* $[\mathbf{u'}_1]_1 = \rho(\mu[\mathbf{u}_1]_1 + \beta[\mathbf{u}_2]_1)$ *and* $[\mathbf{t}']_1 = \mu[\mathbf{t}]_1 + \beta[\mathbf{w}]_1 = [\mathbf{A}_0]_1(\mu r_1 + \beta r_2)$. *And for* $i \in \{0,1\}$, *compute* $[z_i']_2 = \alpha[z_i]_2, [\mathbf{a'}_i]_1 = \alpha\mu[\mathbf{a}_i^1]_1 + \alpha\beta[\mathbf{a}_i^2]_1, [d_i']_2 = \alpha\mu[d_i^1]_2 + \alpha\beta[d_i^2]_2$. *Set* $\Omega' = (([\mathbf{a'}_i]_1, [d_i']_2, [z_i']_2)_{i\in\{0,1\}}, \alpha Z_1)$. *Set* $\sigma' = ([\mathbf{u'}_1]_1, [\mathbf{t}']_1, \Omega')$. *Return* $(\mu[\mathbf{m}]_1, \sigma')$;

---

[4] Users are required to report necessary data to decide if they are closed enough to be considered involved in a contact. The reveal of such data may also have privacy impacts. However, we found it hard to quantify such impacts and left this problem for further consideration.

- $\mathsf{Verify}(\mathsf{pp}, (\rho, \mathsf{pk}), [\mathbf{m}]_1, (\sigma, \tau))$. *Parse* $\sigma = ([\mathbf{u}_1]_1, [\mathbf{t}]_1, \Omega_1, [z_0]_2, [z_1]_2, Z_1)$ *and* $\tau \in \{([\mathbf{u}_2]_1, [\mathbf{w}]_1, \Omega_2), \perp\}$. *Check proof* Ω_1 *with* $\mathsf{NIZK.PRVer}(\mathsf{crs}, [\mathbf{t}]_1, \Omega_1, [z_0]_2, [z_1]_2, Z_1)$ *and check if* $e([\mathbf{u}_1]_1^\top, \mathbf{A}]_2) = e([\mathbf{t}]_1^\top, \mathbf{B}]_2) + e([\mathbf{m}]_1^\top, \mathbf{C}]_2)$. *If* $\tau \neq \perp$, *then check proof* Ω_2 *with* $\mathsf{NIZK.PRVer}(\mathsf{crs}, [\mathbf{w}]_1, \Omega_2, [z_0]_2, [z_1]_2, Z_1)$ *and check if* $e([\mathbf{u}_2]_1^\top, \mathbf{A}]_2) = e([\mathbf{w}]_1^\top, \mathbf{B}]_2)$.

Definition 17 (Correctness). *An SPS-EQ scheme satisfies correctness, if for any* $\lambda > 0, \ell > 1$, $\mathsf{pp} \leftarrow \mathsf{Setup}(1^\lambda)$, *and* $(\mathsf{sk}, \mathsf{pk}) \leftarrow \mathsf{KGen}(\mathsf{pp})$*:*

$$\begin{aligned}&\Pr[\mathsf{Verify}(\mathsf{pk}, \mathsf{Sign}(\mathsf{sk}, [\mathbf{m}]_1)] = 1 \wedge \\ &\Pr[\mathsf{Verify}(\rho \cdot \mathsf{pk}, \mathsf{ChgRep}([\mathbf{m}]_1, \mathsf{Sign}(\mathsf{sk}, [\mathbf{m}]_1), \mu, \rho, \mathsf{pk}))] = 1.\end{aligned}$$

Definition 18 (EUF-CMA). *An SPS-EQ scheme satisfies EUF-CMA, if for any adversary that has access to a signing oracle* $\mathcal{O}_{\mathsf{Sign}}(\mathsf{sk}, \cdot)$ *with queries* $[\mathbf{m}]_i \in \mathsf{Q}$*, the following probability is negligible of* λ *for any* $\lambda > 0, \ell > 1$ *and* $\mathsf{pp} \leftarrow \mathsf{Setup}(1^\lambda)$*:*

$$\Pr\left[\begin{array}{ll}(\mathsf{sk}, \mathsf{pk}) \leftarrow \mathsf{KGen}(\mathsf{pp});: & \forall [\mathbf{m}]_i \in \mathsf{Q}, [\mathbf{m}^*]_{\mathcal{R}} \neq [\mathbf{m}]_{\mathcal{R}} \wedge \\ ([\mathbf{m}]_i^*, \sigma^*) \leftarrow \mathcal{A}^{\mathcal{O}_{\mathsf{Sign}}}(\mathsf{pk}) & \mathsf{Verify}([\mathbf{m}]_i^*, \sigma^*, \mathsf{pk}) = 1\end{array}\right].$$

Definition 19 (Perfect Adaption of Signatures with respect to Message Space (under Malicious Keys in the Honest Parameters Model)). *An SPS-EQ scheme over a message space* $\mathcal{S}_{\mathbf{m}} \subseteq (\mathbb{G}_i^*)^\ell$ *perfectly adapts signatures with respect to the message space, if for all tuples* $(\mathsf{pp}, [\mathsf{pk}]_j, [\mathbf{m}]_i, (\sigma, \tau), \mu, \rho)$ *such that* $\mathsf{pp} \leftarrow \mathsf{Setup}(1^\lambda)$, $[\mathbf{m}]_i \in \mathcal{S}_{\mathbf{m}}$, $\mu, \rho \in \mathbb{Z}_p^*$, *and* $\mathsf{Verify}(\mathsf{pk}, [\mathbf{m}]_i, (\sigma, \tau)) = 1$, *we have the output* $([\mu \cdot \mathbf{m}]_i, \sigma^*) \leftarrow \mathsf{ChgRep}([\mathbf{m}]_i, (\sigma, \tau), \mu, \rho, [\mathsf{pk}]_j)$ *where* σ^* *is a* random *element in the signature space such that* $\mathsf{Verify}([\rho \cdot \mathsf{pk}, \mu \cdot \mathbf{m}]_i, \sigma^*) = 1$.

C Extending the BLS Signature [8] with APK

This section shows an example that utilizes a DDH-based APK construction as a plug-in pool in the BLS signature scheme [8]. Let $\mathsf{BGGen}(1^\lambda)$ be the bilinear group generator that outputs $\mathsf{BG} = (p, \mathbb{G}_1, \mathbb{G}_2, \mathbb{G}_T, P_1, P_2, e)$ as shown in Sect. 2. The DDH problem (in group $\mathbb{G}_2$)-based APK construction is as follows.

Construction 5 (DDH-Based APK $\mathsf{APK}_{\mathrm{DDH}}$). *Let* $\mathsf{BG} = (p, \mathbb{G}_1, \mathbb{G}_2, \mathbb{G}_T, P_1, P_2, e)$ *be the output of the bilinear group generator* $\mathsf{BGGen}(1^\lambda)$*. The algorithms of APK are as follows.*

- $\mathsf{KGen}(\mathsf{BG})$*: Sample* $\mathsf{ak}, \mathsf{sk}_0 \xleftarrow{\$} \mathbb{Z}_p$. *Set* $\mathsf{sk}_1 = \mathsf{ak} \cdot \mathsf{sk}_0$. *Then, compute* $\mathsf{pk}_0 = \mathsf{sk}_0 \cdot P_2$ *and* $\mathsf{pk}_1 = \mathsf{sk}_1 \cdot P_2$. *Finally, set* $\mathsf{sk} = (\mathsf{sk}_0, \mathsf{sk}_1), \mathsf{pk} = (\mathsf{pk}_0, \mathsf{pk}_1)$ *and output* $(\mathsf{sk}, \mathsf{ak}, \mathsf{pk})$*;*
- $\mathsf{Update}(\mathsf{pk}; r)$*: Parse* $\mathsf{pk} = (\mathsf{pk}_0, \mathsf{pk}_1)$. *Sample* $r \xleftarrow{\$} \mathbb{Z}_p$ *and compute* $\mathsf{pk}_0' = r \cdot \mathsf{pk}_0, \mathsf{pk}_1' = r \cdot \mathsf{pk}_1$. *Output* $\mathsf{pk}' = (\mathsf{pk}_0', \mathsf{pk}_1')$*;*
- $\mathsf{VerifyKP}(\mathsf{sk}, \mathsf{pk}', r)$*: Parse* $\mathsf{sk} = (\mathsf{sk}_0, \mathsf{sk}_1)$ *and* $\mathsf{pk}' = (\mathsf{pk}_0', \mathsf{pk}_1')$. *Output* 1 *if* $\mathsf{pk}_0' = r \cdot \mathsf{sk}_0 \cdot P_2 \wedge \mathsf{pk}_1' = r \cdot \mathsf{sk}_1 \cdot P_2$, *or* 0 *otherwise;*

- $\mathsf{VerifyAK}(\mathsf{sk}, \mathsf{ak})$: *Parse* $\mathsf{sk} = (\mathsf{sk}_0, \mathsf{sk}_1)$. *Output* 1 *if* $\mathsf{sk}_1 = \mathsf{ak} \cdot \mathsf{sk}_0$, *or* 0 *otherwise;*
- $\mathsf{Audit}(\mathsf{ak}, \mathsf{pk}', \mathsf{pk})$: *Parse* $\mathsf{pk}' = (\mathsf{pk}'_0, \mathsf{pk}'_1), \mathsf{pk} = (\mathsf{pk}_0, \mathsf{pk}_1)$. *Output* 1 *if* $\mathsf{pk}_1 = \mathsf{ak} \cdot \mathsf{pk}_0 \wedge \mathsf{pk}'_1 = \mathsf{ak} \cdot \mathsf{pk}'_0$, *or* 0 *otherwise.*

Recall the BLS signatures [8], let $\mathsf{H} : \mathcal{S}_{\mathbf{m}} \to \mathbb{G}_1$ be a cryptographic hash function where $\mathcal{S}_{\mathbf{m}}$ denotes the message space. For simplicity, we omit the algorithms for aggregation to focus on auditability. The integration works as follows.

Construction 6 (BLS with APK). *Let* $\mathsf{BG} = (p, \mathbb{G}_1, \mathbb{G}_2, \mathbb{G}_T, P_1, P_2, e)$ *be the output of the bilinear group generator* $\mathsf{BGGen}(1^\lambda)$. *Let* $\mathsf{H} : \mathcal{S}_{\mathbf{m}} \to \mathbb{G}_1$ *be a cryptographic hash function where* $\mathcal{S}_{\mathbf{m}}$ *denotes the message space. Let* $\mathsf{APK}_{\mathsf{DDH}} = (\mathsf{KGen}, \mathsf{Update}, \mathsf{VerifyKP}, \mathsf{VerifyAK}, \mathsf{Audit})$ *be a DDH-based APK mechanism. The algorithms of BLS with APK are as follows.*

- $\mathsf{KGen}, \mathsf{VerifyKP}, \mathsf{VerifyAK}, \mathsf{Audit}$ *are the same as in* $\mathsf{APK}_{\mathsf{DDH}}$*;*
- $\mathsf{Sign}(\mathsf{sk}, m)$: *Parse* $\mathsf{sk} = (\mathsf{sk}_0, \mathsf{sk}_1)$ *and output* $\sigma = \mathsf{sk}_1 \cdot \mathsf{H}(m) \in \mathbb{G}_1$*;*
- $\mathsf{Verify}(\mathsf{pk}, m, \sigma)$: *Parse* $\mathsf{pk} = (\mathsf{pk}_0, \mathsf{pk}_1)$ *and output* 1 *if* $e(\sigma, P_2) = e(\mathsf{H}(m), \mathsf{pk}_1)$, *or* 0 *otherwise;*
- $\mathsf{Update}(\mathsf{pk}, \sigma; r)$: *Output* $(\mathsf{pk}', \sigma') \triangleq (\mathsf{APK}_{\mathsf{DDH}}.\mathsf{Update}(\mathsf{pk}; r), r \cdot \sigma)$.

Since the EUF-CMA security of the (type-3) BLS signature is proven under the co-CDH assumption [7], and the APK given in Construction 5 considers the DDH problem in $\mathbb{G}_2$, it is convenient to assume the SXDH assumption [2] to hold for BGGen to prove the EUF-CMA security of our extended BLS construction (Construction 6).

References

1. AISEC, F.: Pandemic contact tracing apps: Dp-3t, PEPP-PT ntk, and ROBERT from a privacy perspective. IACR Cryptology ePrint Archive, p. 489 (2020). https://eprint.iacr.org/2020/489
2. Ateniese, G., Camenisch, J., Hohenberger, S., de Medeiros, B.: Practical group signatures without random oracles. IACR Cryptology ePrint Archive, p. 385 (2005). http://eprint.iacr.org/2005/385
3. Belenkiy, M., Camenisch, J., Chase, M., Kohlweiss, M., Lysyanskaya, A., Shacham, H.: Randomizable proofs and delegatable anonymous credentials. In: Halevi, S. (ed.) CRYPTO 2009. LNCS, vol. 5677, pp. 108–125. Springer, Heidelberg (2009). https://doi.org/10.1007/978-3-642-03356-8_7
4. Beskorovajnov, W., Dörre, F., Hartung, G., Koch, A., Müller-Quade, J., Strufe, T.: *ConTra Corona*: contact tracing against the coronavirus by bridging the centralized–decentralized divide for stronger privacy. In: Tibouchi, M., Wang, H. (eds.) ASIACRYPT 2021, Part II. LNCS, vol. 13091, pp. 665–695. Springer, Cham (2021). https://doi.org/10.1007/978-3-030-92075-3_23
5. Bobolz, J., Eidens, F., Krenn, S., Ramacher, S., Samelin, K.: Issuer-hiding attribute-based credentials. In: Conti, M., Stevens, M., Krenn, S. (eds.) CANS 2021. LNCS, vol. 13099, pp. 158–178. Springer, Cham (2021). https://doi.org/10.1007/978-3-030-92548-2_9

6. Bogatov, D., De Caro, A., Elkhiyaoui, K., Tackmann, B.: Anonymous transactions with revocation and auditing in hyperledger fabric. In: Conti, M., Stevens, M., Krenn, S. (eds.) CANS 2021. LNCS, vol. 13099, pp. 435–459. Springer, Cham (2021). https://doi.org/10.1007/978-3-030-92548-2_23
7. Boneh, D., Gentry, C., Lynn, B., Shacham, H.: Aggregate and verifiably encrypted signatures from bilinear maps. In: Biham, E. (ed.) EUROCRYPT 2003. LNCS, vol. 2656, pp. 416–432. Springer, Heidelberg (2003). https://doi.org/10.1007/3-540-39200-9_26
8. Boneh, D., Lynn, B., Shacham, H.: Short signatures from the Weil pairing. In: Boyd, C. (ed.) ASIACRYPT 2001. LNCS, vol. 2248, pp. 514–532. Springer, Heidelberg (2001). https://doi.org/10.1007/3-540-45682-1_30
9. Camenisch, J., Krenn, S., Lehmann, A., Mikkelsen, G.L., Neven, G., Pedersen, M.Ø.: Formal treatment of privacy-enhancing credential systems. In: Dunkelman, O., Keliher, L. (eds.) SAC 2015. LNCS, vol. 9566, pp. 3–24. Springer, Cham (2016). https://doi.org/10.1007/978-3-319-31301-6_1
10. Camenisch, J., Lysyanskaya, A.: An efficient system for non-transferable anonymous credentials with optional anonymity revocation. In: Pfitzmann, B. (ed.) EUROCRYPT 2001. LNCS, vol. 2045, pp. 93–118. Springer, Heidelberg (2001). https://doi.org/10.1007/3-540-44987-6_7
11. Camenisch, J., Lysyanskaya, A.: A signature scheme with efficient protocols. In: Cimato, S., Persiano, G., Galdi, C. (eds.) SCN 2002. LNCS, vol. 2576, pp. 268–289. Springer, Heidelberg (2003). https://doi.org/10.1007/3-540-36413-7_20
12. Camenisch, J., Lysyanskaya, A.: Signature schemes and anonymous credentials from bilinear maps. In: Franklin, M. (ed.) CRYPTO 2004. LNCS, vol. 3152, pp. 56–72. Springer, Heidelberg (2004). https://doi.org/10.1007/978-3-540-28628-8_4
13. Canetti, R., et al.: Privacy-preserving automated exposure notification. IACR Cryptology ePrint Archive, p. 863 (2020). https://eprint.iacr.org/2020/863
14. Caro, A.D., Iovino, V.: JPBC: Java pairing based cryptography. In: Proceedings of the 16th IEEE Symposium on Computers and Communications. ISCC 2011, Kerkyra, Corfu, Greece, 28 June–1 July 2011, pp. 850–855. IEEE Computer Society (2011). https://doi.org/10.1109/ISCC.2011.5983948
15. Chen, L.D.: Effects of ambient temperature and humidity on droplet lifetime – a perspective of exhalation sneeze droplets with COVID-19 virus transmission. Int. J. Hyg. Environ. Health (2020). https://doi.org/10.1016/j.ijheh.2020.113568
16. Connolly, A., Deschamps, J., Lafourcade, P., Perez-Kempner, O.: Protego: efficient, revocable and auditable anonymous credentials with applications to hyperledger fabric. In: Isobe, T., Sarkar, S. (eds.) INDOCRYPT 2022. LNCS, vol. 13774, pp. 249–271. Springer, Cham (2022). https://doi.org/10.1007/978-3-031-22912-1_11
17. Connolly, A., Lafourcade, P., Perez-Kempner, O.: Improved constructions of anonymous credentials from structure-preserving signatures on equivalence classes. In: Hanaoka, G., Shikata, J., Watanabe, Y. (eds.) PKC 2022, Part I. LNCS, vol. 13177, pp. 409–438. Springer, Cham (2022). https://doi.org/10.1007/978-3-030-97121-2_15
18. Danz, N., Derwisch, O., Lehmann, A., Pünter, W., Stolle, M., Ziemann, J.: Security and privacy of decentralized cryptographic contact tracing. IACR Cryptology ePrint Archive, p. 1309 (2020). https://eprint.iacr.org/2020/1309
19. Das, S.K., Alam, J.E., Plumari, S., Greco, V.: Transmission of airborne virus through sneezed and coughed droplets, September 2020. https://www.ncbi.nlm.nih.gov/pmc/articles/PMC7513825/

20. for Disease Control, C.: Prevention: transmission-based precautions (2016). https://www.cdc.gov/infectioncontrol/basics/transmission-based-precautions.html#anchor_1564058235
21. Escala, A., Herold, G., Kiltz, E., Ràfols, C., Villar, J.: An algebraic framework for diffie-hellman assumptions. In: Canetti, R., Garay, J.A. (eds.) CRYPTO 2013. LNCS, vol. 8043, pp. 129–147. Springer, Heidelberg (2013). https://doi.org/10.1007/978-3-642-40084-1_8
22. Fauzi, P., Meiklejohn, S., Mercer, R., Orlandi, C.: Quisquis: a new design for anonymous cryptocurrencies. In: Galbraith, S.D., Moriai, S. (eds.) ASIACRYPT 2019, Part I. LNCS, vol. 11921, pp. 649–678. Springer, Cham (2019). https://doi.org/10.1007/978-3-030-34578-5_23
23. Feige, U., Shamir, A.: Zero knowledge proofs of knowledge in two rounds. In: Brassard, G. (ed.) CRYPTO 1989. LNCS, vol. 435, pp. 526–544. Springer, New York (1990). https://doi.org/10.1007/0-387-34805-0_46
24. Fiat, A., Shamir, A.: How to prove yourself: practical solutions to identification and signature problems. In: Odlyzko, A.M. (ed.) CRYPTO 1986. LNCS, vol. 263, pp. 186–194. Springer, Heidelberg (1987). https://doi.org/10.1007/3-540-47721-7_12
25. Fuchsbauer, G., Hanser, C., Slamanig, D.: Structure-preserving signatures on equivalence classes and constant-size anonymous credentials. J. Cryptol. **32**(2), 498–546 (2019). https://doi.org/10.1007/s00145-018-9281-4
26. Garay, J., Kiayias, A., Leonardos, N.: The bitcoin backbone protocol: analysis and applications. In: Oswald, E., Fischlin, M. (eds.) EUROCRYPT 2015, Part II. LNCS, vol. 9057, pp. 281–310. Springer, Heidelberg (2015). https://doi.org/10.1007/978-3-662-46803-6_10
27. Garman, C., Green, M., Miers, I.: Decentralized anonymous credentials. In: 21st Annual Network and Distributed System Security Symposium, NDSS 2014, San Diego, California, USA, 23–26 February 2014. The Internet Society (2014). https://www.ndss-symposium.org/ndss2014/decentralized-anonymous-credentials
28. Goldwasser, S., Micali, S., Rivest, R.L.: A digital signature scheme secure against adaptive chosen-message attacks. SIAM J. Comput. **17**(2), 281–308 (1988). https://doi.org/10.1137/0217017
29. Groth, J., Ostrovsky, R., Sahai, A.: Perfect non-interactive zero knowledge for NP. In: Vaudenay, S. (ed.) EUROCRYPT 2006. LNCS, vol. 4004, pp. 339–358. Springer, Heidelberg (2006). https://doi.org/10.1007/11761679_21
30. Han, Z., Weng, W., Huang, Q.: Characterizations of particle size distribution of the droplets exhaled by sneeze. J. Roy. Soc. Interface/Roy. Soc. **10**, 20130560 (2013). https://doi.org/10.1098/rsif.2013.0560
31. Hébant, C., Pointcheval, D.: Traceable constant-size multi-authority credentials. In: Galdi, C., Jarecki, S. (eds.) SCN 2022. LNCS, vol. 13409, pp. 411–434. Springer, Cham (2022). https://doi.org/10.1007/978-3-031-14791-3_18
32. Jones, M., Sporny, M., Terbu, O., Cohen, G., Steele, O.: Verifiable credentials data model v2.0. W3C working draft, W3C, July 2023. https://www.w3.org/TR/2023/WD-vc-data-model-2.0-20230718/
33. Liu, J.K., et al.: Privacy-preserving COVID-19 contact tracing app: A zero-knowledge proof approach. IACR Cryptology ePrint Archive, p. 528 (2020). https://eprint.iacr.org/2020/528
34. Morillo, P., Ràfols, C., Villar, J.L.: The kernel matrix Diffie-Hellman assumption. In: Cheon, J.H., Takagi, T. (eds.) ASIACRYPT 2016. LNCS, vol. 10031, pp. 729–758. Springer, Heidelberg (2016). https://doi.org/10.1007/978-3-662-53887-6_27

35. Reed, D., Sporny, M., Sabadello, M., Guy, A.: Decentralized identifiers (DIDs) v1.0. W3C recommendation, W3C, July 2022. https://www.w3.org/TR/2022/REC-did-core-20220719/
36. Silde, T., Strand, M.: Anonymous tokens with public metadata and applications to private contact tracing. In: Eyal, I., Garay, J.A. (eds.) FC 2022. LNCS, vol. 13411, pp. 179–199. Springer, Cham (2022). https://doi.org/10.1007/978-3-031-18283-9_9
37. Xiao, F., Yang, F., Chen, S., Yang, J.: Encrypted malicious traffic detection based on ensemble learning. In: Meng, W., Conti, M. (eds.) CSS 2021. LNCS, vol. 13172, pp. 1–15. Springer, Cham (2022). https://doi.org/10.1007/978-3-030-94029-4_1

Verification Protocol for Stable Matching from Conditional Disclosure of Secrets

Kittiphop Phalakarn(✉) and Toru Nakamura

KDDI Research, Inc., Saitama, Japan
{xki-phalakarn,tr-nakamura}@kddi.com

Abstract. Stable matching is an important problem that receives attention from researchers in several fields. In the problem setting, there are two sets with the same number of members. Each member has its matching preference. The goal is to find a one-to-one matching between each member of the two sets such that no pairs want to change the matching result. Since an instance of the stable matching problem may have more than one possible stable matching, Nakamura et al. proposed a multi-stakeholder environment with selectability property, and applied it to the stable matching problem as an example use case. In their setting, the computing server could freely choose to return any stable matching depending on the benefits of the clients and the computing server. Their protocol also offered verifiability, but only against a semi-honest verifying server. To address this issue, we propose a verification protocol for stable matching against a malicious server. Our verification protocol is constructed from CDS schemes for stable matching, which do not require any asymmetric-key cryptographic primitives. From the implementation result, our proposed protocol is 4 to 5 orders of magnitude faster than the previous work.

Keywords: Verification protocol · Stable matching · Conditional disclosure of secrets

1 Introduction

Stable matching is one of the important problems in mathematics, economics, and computer science. We consider a setting with two sets $A = \{a_1, \ldots, a_n\}$ and $B = \{b_1, \ldots, b_n\}$ with the same number of members (e.g., a set of n men and a set of n women). Each member in each set has a matching preference for the members in the other set (e.g., the man a_1 prefers to match with the woman b_3 as his first choice, and then the woman b_2 as his second choice, and so on). The goal of the stable matching problem is to find a one-to-one matching between the members in the sets A and B such that no pairs want to change the matching result (e.g., no man and woman agree to leave their assigned partner).

Gale and Shapley [11] were the first to propose an algorithm to solve the stable matching problem. The matching result from their algorithm always provided the best possible matching for the members in the set A and the worst

C. Pöpper and L. Batina (Eds.): ACNS 2024, LNCS 14583, pp. 119–134, 2024.
https://doi.org/10.1007/978-3-031-54770-6_5

possible matching for the members in the set B, or vice versa. However, other matchings that are also stable may exist.

To address this issue, Nakamura et al. [21] proposed a multi-stakeholder environment, and applied it to the stable matching problem as an example use case. In their setting, the clients (the members in the sets A and B) sent their matching preferences to the computing server. The computing server then performed the computation and returned the matching result back to the clients. This multi-stakeholder environment offered selectability; the computing server could freely choose to return any stable matching depending on the benefits of the clients and the computing server.

If the computing server is dishonest, it may return an unstable matching in order to maximize its benefit. The multi-stakeholder environment in [21] then included a verification protocol to address this issue. However, their verification protocol assumed that the verifying server is semi-honest (the verifying server is expected to follow the protocol properly). This assumption may be too weak for real-life applications. If the verifying server is malicious (the verifying server may deviate from the protocol arbitrarily), it may output a counterfeit verification result, and the clients will never know the truth. Moreover, [21] used fully homomorphic encryption as a building block, which could make their protocol less efficient.

1.1 Our Contribution

In this paper, we improve the verification protocol for stable matching from [21] to a setting with a malicious server. To achieve this, we propose conditional disclosure of secrets (CDS) schemes for stable matching, and then use them to construct a verification protocol. This follows the framework from [5,22] that used two CDS schemes with opposite conditions to construct a verification protocol. However, the technical details of our two proposed CDS schemes are novel, including the algorithms and the proofs.

Since our CDS schemes and verification protocol are information theoretically secure, we do not need any asymmetric-key cryptographic primitives. This is different from all the existing works. Our proposed CDS schemes and verification protocol can also be considered as constant-round and non-interactive. From the implementation result, our proposed verification protocol is 4 to 5 orders of magnitude faster than the protocol from [21].

1.2 Applications

There are several applications for stable matching, for example, matching men and women (and also other genders), students and colleges, doctors and hospitals, and more. Men and women (and also other genders) provide their matching preferences to a computing server and receive the matching result. In the same way, students and colleges provide their admission preferences, and doctors and hospitals provide their assignment preferences.

As in [21], the computing server can freely choose to return any stable matching depending on the benefits of all stakeholders, including the computing server itself. However, the computing server may have motivations to output an unstable matching, for example, to save time and computation cost. This is obviously a problem to the clients. To address this problem, we need a verifying server to verify that the matching result is really stable.

With similar motivations, the verifying server in [21] may output an incorrect verification result. As the contribution of this paper, we propose a new verification protocol that fixes this issue. The verifying server in our proposed protocol can successfully output an incorrect verification result with only negligible probability.

1.3 Organization

We first review related works in Sect. 2. Then background knowledge and definitions are given in Sect. 3. CDS schemes for stable matching are proposed in Sect. 4, which are then used as building blocks in the verification protocol for stable matching in Sect. 5. We present the implementation result in Sect. 6. Finally, Sect. 7 concludes the paper.

2 Related Works

In this section, we review related works on stable matching, conditional disclosure of secrets, and multi-client verifiable computation.

2.1 Stable Matching

An algorithm for solving the stable matching problem was firstly proposed by Gale and Shapley [11]. Their algorithm output the stable matching result that is the best possible matching for the members in the set A and the worst possible matching for the members in the set B, or vice versa. The paper also showed that a stable matching always exists, and there may be several possible stable matchings for a problem instance. In addition to one-to-one matching (e.g., two sets with the same numbers of men and women), there are also stable matching problems for more general settings, such as many-to-one matching (e.g., assigning doctors to hospitals or assigning students to colleges).

From that time, many researchers have been working on this problem. New settings and conditions were continuously proposed. For example, [9,12] studied the properties of stable matching regarding optimality, falsification of matching preferences, and more. Several works [8,10,16,23] proposed secure stable matching computation, using techniques of additively homomorphic encryption and oblivious RAM (ORAM). However, they all stuck to the algorithm provided by [11].

Recently, Nakamura et al. [21] proposed a multi-stakeholder environment with selectability property, and applied it to the stable matching problem as an example use case. Their setting consisted of several clients, a computing server, and a verifying server. Firstly, The clients sent their matching preferences in the clear to the computing server. The computing server then performed the computation and returned the matching result back to the clients. Since the computing server could freely choose to return any stable matching depending on the benefits of the clients and the computing server, this multi-stakeholder environment provided selectability.

To make sure that the matching result is stable, the clients sent their matching preferences and the matching result as ciphertexts to the verifying server. Therefore, privacy is preserved against the verifying server (but not against the computing server). The verifying server then used fully homomorphic encryption operations to obliviously verify the matching result and returned the verification result back to the clients. Similar to the previous works [8,10,16,23], the protocol in [21] assumed that the verifying server is semi-honest, which may be too weak for some applications. Moreover, the use of fully homomorphic encryption could make their protocol less efficient.

In this work, we consider only the verification part of the protocol. Comparing our work to the setting of [21], we may let the computing server perform the verification part as well. Thus, an additional verifying server is not needed. (We then combine the "computing server" and the "verifying server", and call it as the "server" in our protocol.) This means there is no difference in the aspect of privacy. In other words, we assume that the matching preference and the matching result of each client can be known to the server but not to the other clients. This is acceptable in some men-women matchmaking, students-colleges admission, and doctors-hospitals assignment applications. For the aspect of security, our work is proposed against a malicious adversary, which is stronger than the setting against a semi-honest adversary in [21]. To sum up, we assume that the server can act dishonestly, but do not assume privacy against the server.

2.2 Conditional Disclosure of Secrets

Conditional disclosure of secrets (CDS) was firstly proposed by Gertner et al. [15]. At that time, the CDS scheme was used as a building block in symmetrically private information retrieval (SPIR) system. The CDS scheme was also used as a building block in priced oblivious transfer (i.e., SPIR with cost for each item) in [1]. Gay et al. [13] related the CDS scheme to attribute-based encryption (ABE). Recently, the CDS scheme was used to improve the complexity of secret sharing schemes [2–4,18,20]. Functionalities of the existing CDS schemes are summarized in Table 1.

2.3 Multi-client Verifiable Computation

A verifiable computation protocol was firstly defined by Gennaro et al. [14]. The protocol was only for two parties and was based on Yao's garbled circuit [25]. Choi et al. [7] then generalized the definition to a multi-client setting. Their work

Table 1. Functionalities of existing CDS schemes

CDS Schemes	Functionalities
Gertner et al. [15]	Monotone Boolean function, Sum
Gay et al. [13]	Equality, Inner product, Index, Prefix, Set disjointness
Liu et al. [19]	Index, Polynomial
Bhadauria and Hazay [5]	Equality, Inequality, Set intersection cardinality
Phalakarn et al. [22]	Deterministic finite automata
Ours (Sect. 4)	Stable matching

based on non-interactive key exchange (NIKE) protocol was secure against semi-honest clients and a malicious server. The security guarantee was then improved by Gordon et al. [17] to the setting with malicious clients by using homomorphic encryption and attribute-based encryption.

Recently, two-client verifiable computation protocols were proposed by Bhadauria and Hazay [5] based on CDS schemes. Their verifiable computation protocols were quite simple thanks to the property of the CDS schemes. Later, Phalakarn et al. [22] followed this framework and proposed two-client verifiable computation protocol for deterministic finite automata.

3 Preliminaries

In this section, we review background knowledge on stable matching, conditional disclosure of secrets, multi-client verifiable computation, and secret sharing.

3.1 Stable Matching

Let $A = \{a_1, \dots, a_n\}$ and $B = \{b_1, \dots, b_n\}$ be sets of n members. Each member a_i in the set A has a matching preference $(b_{i_1}, \dots, b_{i_n})$ which can be considered as a permutation of the members in the set B. Each member b_j in the set B also has a matching preference $(a_{j_1}, \dots, a_{j_n})$ which can be considered as a permutation of the members in the set A. A member that appears first in the matching preference is more preferred to members that come later.

A matching M is a subset of pairs from $A \times B$ such that each member in the sets A and B appears exactly once. In other words, a matching M is a bijection between the sets A and B. We denote $M(a_i) = b_j$ and $M(b_j) = a_i$ if $(a_i, b_j) \in M$. The definitions of a blocking pair and a stable matching are stated as follows.

Definition 1 (blocking pair). *Given sets A and B, a matching preference of each member in the sets A and B, and a matching M, a pair $(a_i, b_j) \in A \times B$ is a blocking pair if both conditions are met.*

1. *a_i prefers b_j to $M(a_i)$.*
2. *b_j prefers a_i to $M(b_j)$.*

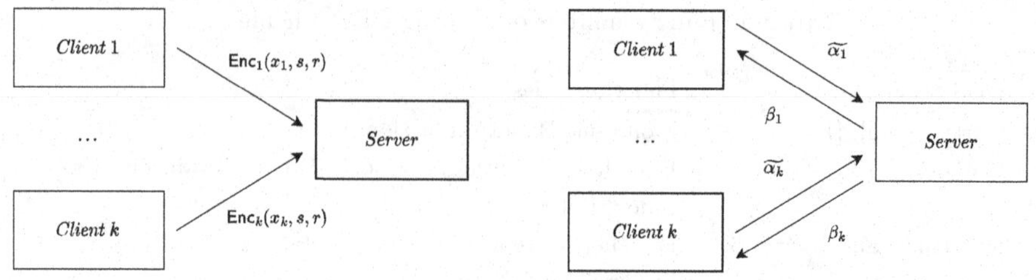

Fig. 1. Communication flows of the CDS scheme (left) and the MVC (right).

Definition 2 (stable matching). *Given sets A and B, and a matching preference of each member in the sets A and B, a matching M is a stable matching if there is no blocking pair.*

3.2 Conditional Disclosure of Secrets

We consider a setting with k clients and a server. Each i-th client has an input x_i from a domain X_i. This input x_i is also known to the server, but not the other clients. In addition, all the clients have a common secret s from a domain S and a common randomness r from a domain R. The values s and r are not known to the server. In a conditional disclosure of secrets (CDS) scheme, each i-th client sends only one message m_i to the server. The goal of the CDS scheme is to let the server learn the secret s if and only if the inputs $x_1, \ldots, x_k$ satisfy a condition f. The definition of the CDS scheme is stated as Definition 3, and the communication flow of the scheme is shown in Fig. 1 (left).

Definition 3 (CDS). *Let $f : X_1 \times \cdots \times X_k \to \{0, 1\}$ be a condition, $s \in S$ be a secret, and $r \in R$ be a randomness chosen randomly with uniform distribution. Let Enc_i be a probabilistic polynomial time encoding algorithm for all $1 \leq i \leq k$, and Dec be a deterministic decoding algorithm. The correctness and secrecy of a CDS scheme are as follows.*

Correctness: For all inputs $(x_1, \ldots, x_k) \in X_1 \times \cdots \times X_k$ where $f(x_1, \ldots, x_k) = 1$,

$$\mathsf{Dec}(x_1, \ldots, x_k, \mathsf{Enc}_1(x_1, s, r), \ldots, \mathsf{Enc}_k(x_k, s, r)) = s.$$

Secrecy: There exists a polynomial time algorithm (simulator) Sim such that for every input $(x_1, \ldots, x_k) \in X_1 \times \cdots \times X_k$ where $f(x_1, \ldots, x_k) = 0$, a secret $s \in S$, and a randomness $r \in R$, the following distributions are indistinguishable.

$$\{\mathsf{Sim}(x_1, \ldots, x_k)\} = \{\mathsf{Enc}_1(x_1, s, r), \ldots, \mathsf{Enc}_k(x_k, s, r)\}.$$

3.3 Multi-client Verifiable Computation

We consider a multi-client verifiable computation (MVC) where clients outsource a computation to a (potentially malicious) server. We focus on a non-interactive protocol where the clients do not need to interact with each other after the setup phase. For security, we assume a setting with semi-honest clients and a malicious server with no collusion. The definition of MVC from [5,7] is stated as follows.

Definition 4 (MVC). *Consider a setting with k clients where each i-th client has an input α_i, and the goal is to compute $f(\alpha_1, \ldots, \alpha_k)$ in a verifiable way. The MVC consists of the following four algorithms.*

- $\delta \leftarrow \mathsf{Setup}$: *The algorithm* Setup *generates a common randomness δ for all clients.*
- $(\widetilde{\alpha_i}, \tau_i) \leftarrow \mathsf{Input}(\alpha_i, \delta, 1^\lambda)$: *Using the input α_i, the common randomness δ, and the security parameter 1^λ, the algorithm* Input *generates an encoded input $\widetilde{\alpha_i}$ and a decoding secret τ_i.*
- $(\beta_1, \ldots, \beta_k) \leftarrow \mathsf{Compute}(f, \widetilde{\alpha_1}, \ldots, \widetilde{\alpha_k})$: *Using the description of the function f and the encoded inputs $\widetilde{\alpha_1}, \ldots, \widetilde{\alpha_k}$, the algorithm* Compute *generates encoded outputs $\beta_1, \ldots, \beta_k$.*
- $y \leftarrow \mathsf{Verify}(\beta_i, \tau_i)$: *Using the encoded output β_i and the decoding secret τ_i, the algorithm* Verify *generates the result y, which can be $\perp$ in the case that the protocol is aborted.*

The soundness of the protocol is defined as follows.

Soundness: For all inputs $(\alpha_1, \ldots, \alpha_k)$ and a malicious server $\mathcal{A}$, let $\delta \leftarrow \mathsf{Setup}$, $(\widetilde{\alpha_i}, \tau_i) \leftarrow \mathsf{Input}(\alpha_i, \delta, 1^\lambda)$, $(\beta_1, \ldots, \beta_k) \leftarrow \mathsf{Compute}(f, \widetilde{\alpha_1}, \ldots, \widetilde{\alpha_k})$, and $y \leftarrow \mathsf{Verify}(\beta_i, \tau_i)$ for all $1 \leq i \leq k$. It must hold that

$$Pr[y \neq f(\alpha_1, \ldots, \alpha_k) \wedge y \neq \perp] \leq \mathsf{negl}(\lambda)$$

where negl *is a negligible function.*

To perform the verifiable computation, all of the clients first execute the algorithm Setup to get the common randomness δ. Next, each i-th client generates $(\widetilde{\alpha_i}, \tau_i)$ from $\mathsf{Input}(\alpha_i, \delta, 1^\lambda)$, sends the encoded input $\widetilde{\alpha_i}$ to the server, and keeps the decoding secret τ_i to itself. After the server receives all the encoded inputs from the clients, it generates $(\beta_1, \ldots, \beta_k)$ from $\mathsf{Compute}(f, \widetilde{\alpha_1}, \ldots, \widetilde{\alpha_k})$, and sends each encoded output β_i to the i-th client. Finally, each i-th client generates the result y from $\mathsf{Verify}(\beta_i, \tau_i)$. According to the soundness of the protocol, y should be equal to $f(\alpha_1, \ldots, \alpha_k)$ with high probability. Communication flow of the protocol is shown in Fig. 1 (right).

3.4 Secret Sharing

Secret sharing is a technique to split a secret value into several parts called "shares". Only specific subsets of shares can reveal the secret value, while the other subsets of shares give no information. In this work, we use two secret sharing techniques: additive secret sharing and Shamir secret sharing [24].

In additive secret sharing, a secret s is divided into k shares as $\{s_i\}_{1 \leq i \leq k}$ where $s = \sum_{i=1}^{k} s_i$ in a specified group. All the k shares are needed for a reconstruction of the secret value.

In Shamir secret sharing, we need to specify a threshold t. To generate shares, we first randomly generate a degree t polynomial $p(x)$ in a specified field with a secret s as the constant term. For each $1 \leq i \leq k$, the i-th share can be generated as $p(i)$. Since the reconstruction process is performed as an interpolation of the degree t polynomial, $t+1$ shares are required.

4 Proposed CDS Schemes

Before considering our CDS schemes, we recall the setting of the protocol for stable matching in [21]. There are $2n$ clients, each represents a member in the sets A or B, a computing server, and a verifying server. The clients send their matching preferences in the clear to the computing server. After that, the computing server computes a stable matching, according to its selectability, and then returns the matching result to each client. To verify the matching result, the clients send their matching preferences and the matching result as ciphertexts to the verifying server. The verifying server then obliviously verifies the matching result and returns the verification result back to the clients.

In this work, we consider the same setting as above: $2n$ clients with matching preferences, but we combine the computing server and the verifying server into one server. We then propose two CDS schemes in this section: one for unstable matching and the other for stable matching. These CDS schemes are the main building blocks of our verification protocol in the next section.

4.1 CDS Scheme for Unstable Matching

We propose the CDS scheme for unstable matching first since it is easier to understand. To formally describe the setting of the CDS, each client representing the member a_i has the matching preference $(a_{i_1}, \ldots, a_{i_n})$ and the matching result $M(a_i)$ as inputs. Each client representing the member b_j has the matching preference $(b_{j_1}, \ldots, b_{j_n})$ and the matching result $M(b_j)$ as inputs. (Note that the clients know neither the matching preferences nor the matching results of the other clients.) All the clients have a common secret s and a common randomness r. The server knows all the matching preferences and the complete matching result M, but knows neither the secret s nor the randomness r. The goal of this CDS scheme is to let the server learn the secret s if and only if the matching result M is not a stable matching, i.e., there is a blocking pair.

The idea of our CDS scheme for unstable matching is that each client associates each of its potential blocking pair with an additive secret share. When the potential blocking pairs from two clients match, the secret s is disclosed to the server. The CDS scheme for unstable matching is proposed in Fig. 2. We then propose Theorem 1 together with the proof.

CDS scheme for unstable matching

Input:

- Each client has a matching preference $(a_{i_1}, \ldots, a_{i_n})$ or $(b_{j_1}, \ldots, b_{j_n})$, a matching result $M(a_i)$ or $M(b_j)$, a common secret s, and a common randomness $r = (r_{i,j})_{1 \leq i,j \leq n}$.
- The server has the matching preferences of all clients and the complete matching result M.

Algorithm:

1. For each client representing a member a_i, and for each member b_{i_k} that are more preferred to $M(a_i)$, the client generates a tuple $(a_i, b_{i_k}, s - r_{i,i_k})$. All the tuples together are considered as the output from $\mathsf{Enc}_{\mathsf{a_i}}$ and are sent to the server.
2. For each client representing a member b_j, and for each member a_{j_k} that are more preferred to $M(b_j)$, the client generates a tuple $(a_{j_k}, b_j, r_{j_k,j})$. All the tuples together are considered as the output from $\mathsf{Enc}_{\mathsf{b_j}}$ and are sent to the server.
3. If there is a blocking pair $(a_i, b_j, s - r_{i,j})$ from $\mathsf{Enc}_{\mathsf{a_i}}$ and $(a_i, b_j, r_{i,j})$ from $\mathsf{Enc}_{\mathsf{b_j}}$, the server outputs $(s - r_{i,j}) + (r_{i,j}) = s$. Otherwise, it outputs a random value.

Fig. 2. CDS scheme for unstable matching

Theorem 1. *The CDS scheme for unstable matching in Fig. 2 provides correctness and secrecy according to Definition 3.*

Proof. To show the correctness of the CDS scheme for unstable matching in Fig. 2, assume that the matching result M is not a stable matching. According to Definition 1, there is a blocking pair (a_i, b_j) for some i and j. Following our CDS scheme in Fig. 2, the client representing the member a_i sends a tuple $(a_i, b_j, s - r_{i,j})$ to the server, while the client representing the member b_j sends a tuple $(a_i, b_j, r_{i,j})$. It is now obvious that the secret s is disclosed to the server.

To show the secrecy of the CDS scheme in Fig. 2, assume that the matching result M is a stable matching. This means there is no blocking pair, and the values $s - r_{i,j}$ and $r_{i,j}$ cannot be both sent to the server. According to additive secret sharing, the server cannot learn any information about the secret s. The simulator Sim can be constructed by following steps 1 and 2 in Fig. 2 with random s and r. It is not difficult to see that the output from the simulator Sim and the real CDS execution have the same distribution. □

4.2 CDS Scheme for Stable Matching

We now propose the CDS scheme for stable matching. The setting is the same as in the previous subsection, except that the goal of the CDS scheme in this subsection is to let the server learn the secret s if and only if the matching result M is a stable matching, i.e., there is no blocking pair.

For the idea of our CDS scheme for stable matching, we first generate a degree $2n^2 - 1$ polynomial, according to Shamir secret sharing scheme, from a common randomness. Each client then generates n shares from its matching preference. If there is no blocking pair, the server learns $2n^2$ different shares, and the secret s can be disclosed. In the case that the matching result is not stable, shares generated from the blocking pair then provide the same value. This means the server fails to perform the interpolation. The CDS scheme for stable matching is proposed in Fig. 3. We then propose Theorem 2 together with the proof.

CDS scheme for stable matching

Input:

- Each client has a matching preference $(a_{i_1}, \ldots, a_{i_n})$ or $(b_{j_1}, \ldots, b_{j_n})$, a matching result $M(a_i)$ or $M(b_j)$, a common secret s, and a common randomness $r = (r_k)_{1 \leq k \leq 2n^2-1}$.
- The server has the matching preferences of all clients and the complete matching result M.

Algorithm:

1. All clients generate a degree $2n^2 - 1$ polynomial $p(x) = r_{(2n^2-1)}x^{(2n^2-1)} + \ldots + r_1 x + s$.
2. For each client representing a member a_i, and for each member b_{i_k} that are more preferred to $M(a_i)$, the client generates a tuple $(i(n+1)^2 + i_k(n+1), p(i(n+1)^2 + i_k(n+1)))$. For each member b_{i_ℓ} that are preferred less than or equal to $M(a_i)$, the client generates a tuple $(i(n+1)^2 + i_\ell(n+1) + 1, p(i(n+1)^2 + i_\ell(n+1) + 1))$. All the tuples together are considered as the output from $\mathsf{Enc}_{\mathsf{a}_i}$ and are sent to the server.
3. For each client representing a member b_j, and for each member a_{j_k} that are more preferred to $M(b_j)$, the client generates a tuple $(j_k(n+1)^2 + j(n+1), p(j_k(n+1)^2 + j(n+1)))$. For each member a_{j_ℓ} that are preferred less than or equal to $M(b_j)$, the client generates a tuple $(j_\ell(n+1)^2 + j(n+1) + 2, p(j_\ell(n+1)^2 + j(n+1) + 2))$. All the tuples together are considered as the output from $\mathsf{Enc}_{\mathsf{b}_j}$ and are sent to the server.
4. If there is no blocking pair, the server can collect $2n^2$ different tuples $(x, p(x))$. The server then reconstructs the polynomial $p(x)$ from interpolation, and outputs the secret s. In the case that there is at least one blocking pair, the server outputs a random value.

Fig. 3. CDS scheme for stable matching

Theorem 2. *The CDS scheme for stable matching in Fig. 3 provides correctness and secrecy according to Definition 3.*

Proof. To show the correctness of the CDS scheme for stable matching in Fig. 3, assume that the matching result M is a stable matching. This means there is no blocking pair, and all the tuples in the form $(i(n+1)^2 + j(n+1), p(i(n+1)^2 + j(n+1)))$ are unique. The tuples in the form $(i(n+1)^2 + j(n+1) + 1, p(i(n+1)^2 + j(n+1) + 1))$ and $(i(n+1)^2 + j(n+1) + 2, p(i(n+1)^2 + j(n+1) + 2))$ are already unique. Since the server learns n tuples from each of the $2n$ clients and all tuples are unique, this results in $2n^2$ unique tuples. It is sufficient for the server to perform interpolation, and learn the degree $2n^2 - 1$ polynomial $p(x)$ with the secret s.

To show the secrecy of the CDS scheme in Fig. 3, assume that the matching result M is not a stable matching. According to Definition 1, there is a blocking pair (a_i, b_j) for some i and j. Following our CDS scheme in Fig. 3, the server then receives the same tuple $(i(n+1)^2+j(n+1), p(i(n+1)^2+j(n+1)))$ from the clients representing the members a_i and b_j. Since the server receives $2n^2$ tuples in total, but some tuples are duplicated, the server cannot perform an interpolation to learn the degree $2n^2 - 1$ polynomial $p(x)$. According to Shamir secret sharing, the server cannot learn any information about the secret s. The simulator Sim can be constructed by following steps 2 and 3 in Fig. 3 with random s and r. It is not difficult to see that the output from the simulator Sim and the real CDS execution have the same distribution. □

4.3 Possible Improvements

In this subsection, we suggest some possible improvements on CDS schemes for unstable and stable matching.

- According to our CDS schemes, the server does not need to know the inputs in advance. All necessary information is already sent as the CDS messages. This can be applied to practical use, even though it is different from Definition 3.
- It is not difficult to revise and apply the idea in this section to more general settings of stable matching problem (e.g., many-to-one matching).

5 Verification Protocol for Stable Matching

In this section, we propose a verification protocol for stable matching from our CDS schemes for unstable and stable matching. We consider the same setting as in the CDS schemes, where each of the $2n$ clients has its matching preference and its matching result, and the server has the matching preferences of all clients and the complete matching result. The goal is to let each client learn whether the matching result is stable or not.

The verification protocol for stable matching is proposed in Fig. 4. Firstly, the clients get common secrets and common randomnesses. This can be done by a multi-party protocol or a common source of randomness. Note that these values are not known to the server. Next, the clients and the server execute the CDS schemes for unstable and stable matching. The two CDS schemes can be executed in parallel. After the clients receive the output values of the CDS schemes from the server, the clients compare with the common secrets. Finally, the clients output "not a stable matching" or "stable matching" according to the comparison. In the case that the server attempts to cheat, the clients output $\perp$.

For our proposed verification protocol for stable matching, it is important to execute two CDS schemes. Assume that the matching result is a stable matching and we only execute one CDS scheme for stable matching. Even though the secret of the CDS scheme is disclosed to the server, the malicious server may choose to output a random value instead. To make sure that the server cannot change the verification result, two CDS schemes are needed and the server must output a correct secret from one of the two CDS schemes. In this way, our scheme guarantees a correct verification result even in the setting with a malicious server. We then propose Theorem 3 together with the proof.

Verification protocol for stable matching

Input:

- Each client has a matching preference $(a_{i_1}, \ldots, a_{i_n})$ or $(b_{j_1}, \ldots, b_{j_n})$ and a matching result $M(a_i)$ or $M(b_j)$.
- The server has the matching preferences of all clients and the complete matching result M.

Algorithm:

1. $\delta = (s_1, s_2, r_1, r_2) \leftarrow \mathsf{Setup}$: The clients get common secrets (s_1, s_2) and common randomnesses (r_1, r_2) from a multi-party protocol or a common source of randomness. These values are not known to the server.
2. $(\widetilde{\alpha_i}, \tau_i) \leftarrow \mathsf{Input}(\alpha_i, \delta, 1^\lambda)$: The clients execute the CDS scheme for unstable matching (Figure 2) using the secret s_1 and the randomness r_1. They also execute the CDS scheme for stable matching (Figure 3) using the secret s_2 and the randomness r_2. For each $i \in A \cup B$, α_i includes all the inputs of i, $\widetilde{\alpha_i}$ includes all the CDS messages of i, and $\tau_i = (s_1, s_2)$.
3. $(\beta_i)_{i \in A \cup B} \leftarrow \mathsf{Compute}(f, \{\widetilde{\alpha_i}\}_{i \in A \cup B})$: The server computes the output values s_1' and s_2' according to both CDS schemes. Here, $\beta_i = (s_1', s_2')$ for each $i \in A \cup B$.
4. $y \leftarrow \mathsf{Verify}(\beta_i, \tau_i)$: If $s_1' = s_1$, each client outputs "not a stable matching". If $s_2' = s_2$, each client outputs "stable matching". Otherwise, each client outputs $\perp$.

Fig. 4. Verification protocol for stable matching

Theorem 3. *The verification protocol for stable matching in Fig. 4 provides soundness according to Definition 4.*

Proof. Consider the case that the server is honest and follows the protocol properly. The server should be able to return the correct secret s_1 or s_2 depending on the matching result M. If $s'_1 = s_1$, the matching result M is not a stable matching according to the correctness of our CDS scheme for unstable matching (Theorem 1). In the same way, if $s'_2 = s_2$, the matching result M is a stable matching according to the correctness of our CDS scheme for stable matching (Theorem 2).

Consider the case that the server is malicious and tries to change the verification result. According to the secrecy of our CDS scheme for unstable matching (Theorem 1), the server learns nothing if M is a stable matching. In the same way, according to the secrecy of our CDS scheme for stable matching (Theorem 2), the server learns nothing if M is not a stable matching. The server may try to output an incorrect result by trying to guess the secret. Assume that the size of the secrets s_1 and s_2 is λ bits, the probability that the server successfully outputs an incorrect result without being caught is $2^{-\lambda}$, which is negligible in λ. □

According to Sect. 4.3, the possible improvements can also be applied to our verification protocol as well. Note that when applying our proposed verification protocol for stable matching to the protocol in [21], since the computing server is expected to return a stable matching, the CDS scheme for unstable matching may not be required in this case.

6 Implementation

In this section, we implement our proposed verification protocol for stable matching and compare its performance to the protocol from [21]. Since the protocol in [21] is based on homomorphic encryption, the execution time for any input is similar. However, the execution time of our protocol is different between the case of unstable and stable matching. To have a fair comparison, we run the experiment with the inputs that give our protocol the worst case execution time.

For the environment setting, we implement the server side of both protocols in C++ using the NTL library, and implement BGV homomorphic encryption [6] using the HElib library. The security parameter λ is set to 190 for both protocols. The codes are run on Ubuntu 20.04.6 LTS with Intel Core i7-11700K CPU and 64 GB RAM. The results are shown in Table 2. For each n, we run the protocols 3 times and calculate the average execution time. Our protocol using secret sharing techniques is 4 to 5 orders of magnitude faster than the protocol from [21] using homomorphic encryption.

7 Concluding Remarks

In this paper, we propose the CDS schemes for unstable and stable matching, which are then used as building blocks to construct the verification protocol for stable matching. Since the proposed CDS schemes do not require any

Table 2. Execution time of our verification protocol and the protocol from [21]

n	Ours (sec)	[21] (sec)
3	0.000116	62.1937
4	0.000341	178.674
5	0.000828	279.338
6	0.001726	402.443
7	0.003164	549.403
8	0.005478	1103.80
9	0.008760	1399.70
10	0.012937	1747.26
15	0.065898	4061.04
20	0.204971	8770.92

asymmetric-key cryptographic primitives, our verification protocol is more efficient than the previous work. This claim is proved by the implementation result. Our proposed CDS schemes and verification protocol can also be considered as constant-round and non-interactive. Finally, we suggest some research directions as possible future studies.

- Although the proposed CDS schemes and verification protocol for stable matching in this work preserve privacy of the inputs against other clients, the privacy is not preserved against the server. This is the same as [21] for the case of the computing server. We may try to follow [5,22], and propose private or oblivious CDS schemes which preserve privacy of inputs and outputs against the server.
- The other interesting direction is to propose CDS schemes and verification protocols for other functionalities. Proposing CDS schemes and verification protocols that can be used for any functionality is also challenging.

References

1. Aiello, B., Ishai, Y., Reingold, O.: Priced Oblivious Transfer: How to Sell Digital Goods. In: Pfitzmann, B. (ed.) EUROCRYPT 2001. LNCS, vol. 2045, pp. 119–135. Springer, Heidelberg (2001). https://doi.org/10.1007/3-540-44987-6_8
2. Applebaum, B., Beimel, A., Farràs, O., Nir, O., Peter, N.: Secret-Sharing Schemes for General and Uniform Access Structures. In: Ishai, Y., Rijmen, V. (eds.) EUROCRYPT 2019. LNCS, vol. 11478, pp. 441–471. Springer, Cham (2019). https://doi.org/10.1007/978-3-030-17659-4_15
3. Applebaum, B., Beimel, A., Nir, O., Peter, N.: Better secret sharing via robust conditional disclosure of secrets. In: Proceedings of the 52nd Annual ACM SIGACT Symposium on Theory of Computing, pp. 280–293 (2020)

4. Beimel, A., Peter, N.: Optimal Linear Multiparty Conditional Disclosure of Secrets Protocols. In: Peyrin, T., Galbraith, S. (eds.) ASIACRYPT 2018. LNCS, vol. 11274, pp. 332–362. Springer, Cham (2018). https://doi.org/10.1007/978-3-030-03332-3_13
5. Bhadauria, R., Hazay, C.: Multi-clients Verifiable Computation via Conditional Disclosure of Secrets. In: Galdi, C., Kolesnikov, V. (eds.) SCN 2020. LNCS, vol. 12238, pp. 150–171. Springer, Cham (2020). https://doi.org/10.1007/978-3-030-57990-6_8
6. Brakerski, Z., Gentry, C., Vaikuntanathan, V.: (leveled) Fully homomorphic encryption without bootstrapping. ACM Trans. Comput. Theory (TOCT) **6**(3), 1–36 (2014)
7. Sahai, A. (ed.): TCC 2013. LNCS, vol. 7785. Springer, Heidelberg (2013). https://doi.org/10.1007/978-3-642-36594-2
8. Doerner, J., Evans, D., Shelat, A.: Secure stable matching at scale. In: Proceedings of the 2016 ACM SIGSAC Conference on Computer and Communications Security, pp. 1602–1613 (2016)
9. Dubins, L.E., Freedman, D.A.: Machiavelli and the gale-shapley algorithm. Am. Math. Mon. **88**(7), 485–494 (1981)
10. Franklin, M., Gondree, M., Mohassel, P.: Improved Efficiency for Private Stable Matching. In: Abe, M. (ed.) CT-RSA 2007. LNCS, vol. 4377, pp. 163–177. Springer, Heidelberg (2006). https://doi.org/10.1007/11967668_11
11. Gale, D., Shapley, L.S.: College admissions and the stability of marriage. Am. Math. Mon. **69**(1), 9–15 (1962)
12. Gale, D., Sotomayor, M.: Some remarks on the stable matching problem. Discret. Appl. Math. **11**(3), 223–232 (1985)
13. Gay, R., Kerenidis, I., Wee, H.: Communication Complexity of Conditional Disclosure of Secrets and Attribute-Based Encryption. In: Gennaro, R., Robshaw, M. (eds.) CRYPTO 2015. LNCS, vol. 9216, pp. 485–502. Springer, Heidelberg (2015). https://doi.org/10.1007/978-3-662-48000-7_24
14. Gennaro, R., Gentry, C., Parno, B.: Non-interactive Verifiable Computing: Outsourcing Computation to Untrusted Workers. In: Rabin, T. (ed.) CRYPTO 2010. LNCS, vol. 6223, pp. 465–482. Springer, Heidelberg (2010). https://doi.org/10.1007/978-3-642-14623-7_25
15. Gertner, Y., Ishai, Y., Kushilevitz, E., Malkin, T.: Protecting data privacy in private information retrieval schemes. In: Proceedings of the thirtieth annual ACM symposium on Theory of computing, pp. 151–160 (1998)
16. Golle, P.: A private stable matching algorithm. In: Di Crescenzo, G., Rubin, A. (eds.) FC 2006. LNCS, vol. 4107, pp. 65–80. Springer, Heidelberg (2006). https://doi.org/10.1007/11889663_5
17. Gordon, S.D., Katz, J., Liu, F.H., Shi, E., Zhou, H.S.: Multi-client verifiable computation with stronger security guarantees. In: Dodis, Y., Nielsen, J.B. (eds.) TCC 2015. LNCS, vol. 9015, pp. 144–168. Springer, Heidelberg (2015). https://doi.org/10.1007/978-3-662-46497-7_6
18. Liu, T., Vaikuntanathan, V.: Breaking the circuit-size barrier in secret sharing. In: Proceedings of the 50th Annual ACM SIGACT Symposium on Theory of Computing, pp. 699–708 (2018)
19. Liu, T., Vaikuntanathan, V., Wee, H.: Conditional disclosure of secrets via non-linear reconstruction. In: Katz, J., Shacham, H. (eds.) CRYPTO 2017. LNCS, vol. 10401, pp. 758–790. Springer, Cham (2017). https://doi.org/10.1007/978-3-319-63688-7_25

20. Liu, T., Vaikuntanathan, V., Wee, H.: Towards breaking the exponential barrier for general secret sharing. In: Nielsen, J.B., Rijmen, V. (eds.) EUROCRYPT 2018. LNCS, vol. 10820, pp. 567–596. Springer, Cham (2018). https://doi.org/10.1007/978-3-319-78381-9_21
21. Nakamura., T., Okada., H., Fukushima., K., Isohara., T.: Achieving private verification in multi-stakeholder environment and application to stable matching. In: Proceedings of the 25th International Conference on Enterprise Information Systems - Volume 1: ICEIS, pp. 768–775. INSTICC, SciTePress (2023). https://doi.org/10.5220/0011995800003467
22. Phalakarn, K., Attrapadung, N., Matsuura, K.: Efficient oblivious evaluation protocol and conditional disclosure of secrets for DFA. In: Applied Cryptography and Network Security: 20th International Conference, ACNS 2022, Rome, Italy, June 20–23, 2022, Proceedings, pp. 605–625. Springer (2022)
23. Riazi, M.S., Songhori, E.M., Sadeghi, A.R., Schneider, T., Koushanfar, F.: Toward practical secure stable matching. Proc. Priv. Enhancing Technol. **2017**(1), 62–78 (2017)
24. Shamir, A.: How to share a secret. Commun. ACM **22**(11), 612–613 (1979)
25. Yao, A.C.C.: How to generate and exchange secrets. In: 27th Annual Symposium on Foundations of Computer Science, pp. 162–167. IEEE (1986)

Non-malleable Fuzzy Extractors

Danilo Francati[1(✉)] and Daniele Venturi[2]

[1] Aarhus University, Aarhus, Denmark
danilofrancati@gmail.com
[2] Sapienza University of Rome, Rome, Italy

Abstract. Fuzzy extractors (Dodis *et al.* EUROCRYPT'04) allow to generate close to uniform randomness using correlated distributions outputting samples that are close over some metric space. The latter requires to produce a helper value (along with the extracted key) that can be used to recover the key using close samples. Robust fuzzy extractors (Dodis *et al.*, CRYPTO'06) further protect the helper string from arbitrary active manipulations, by requiring that the reconstructed key using a modified helper string cannot yield a different extractor output.

It is well known that statistical robustness inherently requires large min-entropy (in fact, $m > n/2$ where n is the bit length of the samples) from the underlying correlated distributions, even assuming trusted setup. Motivated by this limitation, we start the investigation of security properties weaker than robustness, but that can be achieved in the plain model assuming only minimal min-entropy (in fact, $m = \omega(\log n)$), while still being useful for applications. We identify one such property and put forward the notion of *non-malleable* fuzzy extractors. Intuitively, non-malleability relaxes the robustness property by allowing the reconstructed key using a modified helper string to be different from the original extractor output, as long as it is a completely unrelated value.

We give a black-box construction of non-malleable fuzzy extractors in the plain model for min-entropy $m = \omega(\log n)$, against interesting families of manipulations including split-state tampering, small-depth circuits tampering, and space-bounded tampering (in the information-theoretic setting), as well as tampering via partial functions (assuming one-way functions). We leave it as an open problem to establish whether non-malleability is possible for arbitrary manipulations of the helper string. Finally, we show an application of non-malleable fuzzy extractors to protect stateless cryptographic primitives whose secret keys are derived using fuzzy correlated distributions.

Keywords: fuzzy extractors · non-malleability · tampering attacks

1 Introduction

Cryptography inherently requires uniform randomness in order to generate secret keys. A (seeded) randomness extractor [50] allows to obtain a (statistically-close to) uniform random string y using a sample x from a *weak* random source which is only unpredictable—typically measured in terms of min-entropy—along

C. Pöpper and L. Batina (Eds.): ACNS 2024, LNCS 14583, pp. 135–155, 2024.
https://doi.org/10.1007/978-3-031-54770-6_6

with a short *truly random* seed s. Of course, the length k of the seed must be much smaller than the number ℓ of extracted bits, and we would also like to require the weak random source to only have a minimum amount of min-entropy $m = \omega(\log n)$, where n is the number of bits from the source.

Fuzzy Extractors. Fuzzy extractors [29,30] cover the setting in which the extractor has access to a weak random source that outputs samples x that are "close" with respect to a given distance metric (over the space where x is defined). In particular, given x, we can now produce the output y along with an helper string α, with the guarantee that the same key y can be recovered given α along with a sample x' which is sufficiently close to x. This settings models faithfully the scenario in which the samples x and x' are, say, correlated readings of a user's biometric trait such as a fingerprint or an iris scan.

Several constructions of fuzzy extractors exist, for different distance metrics including Hamming distance, set difference and edit distance [30]. These constructions achieve information-theoretic security, and only require $m = \omega(\log n)$ bits of min-entropy. However, differently from classical randomness extraction, there is no crisp characterization of when fuzzy extraction is possible. On the positive side, Fuller, Reyzin, and Smith [41,42], as well as Woodage *et al.* [59], show an *inefficient* algorithm that derives a key from each distribution with so-called *fuzzy* min-entropy. On the negative side, Fuller, Reyzin, and Smith [41,42], and Fuller and Peng [40], show families of distributions where no fuzzy extractor can simultaneously work for the whole family, despite the fact that a fuzzy extractor exists for each element of the family. Motivated by these negative results, a line of work explores constructions of fuzzy extractors with *computational* (rather than statistical) security, for distributions for which no information-theoretic fuzzy extractor is known [16,17,39,60].

Robust Fuzzy Extractors. Fuzzy extractors provide no guarantee in the presence of an adversary that can tamper with the helper string α. *Robust* fuzzy extractors [28] tackle this shortcoming by requiring that, for every possible tampering function $f(\cdot)$ yielding a mauled helper string $\tilde{\alpha} = f(\alpha)$, the reconstructed key is either equal to the original key y, or yields an error message. In case the helper string can be modified after (resp. without) seeing the final key y we speak of *post-application* (resp. *pre-application*) robustness.

Dodis *et al.* [28], as well as Kanukurthi and Reyzin [46] show how to obtain a post-application robust fuzzy extractor with information-theoretic security in the plain model, by requiring weak sources with large min-entropy $m > n/2$ where n is the bit-length of x. The lower bound $m > n/2$ is known to be optimal for statistical post-application robustness in the plain model [31], as well as for statistical pre-application robustness in the common reference string (CRS) model[1] in the case of CRS-dependent sources [38]. On the other hand, the lower bound can be circumvented either in the information-theoretic setting in the random oracle

[1] The latter means that the construction requires a trusted third party to sample a public string, according to some distribution.

model [14] and in the CRS model with CRS-independent sources [25], or in the computational setting in the CRS model (both with CRS-independent [56–58] and with CRS-dependent sources [38]), as well as in the plain model [6] (albeit under a non-standard group-theoretic hardness assumption recently introduced by Bartusek, Ma, and Zhandry [12]). See Table 1 for an overview of these results.

Given the above state of affairs, the following question arises naturally:

Is there a weaker robustness property that can be achieved in the plain model for $m = \omega(\log n)$, while still being interesting for applications?

We remark that the above question makes sense both for the information-theoretic and for the computational settings.

1.1 Our Results

In this paper, we make further progress towards answering the above question. In particular, for a family of manipulations $\mathcal{F}$, we introduce the notion of $\mathcal{F}$-non-malleable fuzzy extractors, which guarantees that the reconstructed key $\tilde{y}$ using a tampered helper string $\tilde{\alpha} = f(\alpha)$, for any tampering function $f \in \mathcal{F}$, is either equal to the original untampered key y, or completely independent of it. More precisely, an $\mathcal{F}$-non-malleable fuzzy extractor should satisfy two properties:

- **Pseudorandomness.** For every sample x from a weak random source with m bits of min-entropy, the key y generated using x is (computationally or statistically) close to uniform even given the helper string α.
- **Non-malleability.** For every tampering function $f \in \mathcal{F}$, there exists an efficient simulator $\mathsf{S}(f)$ that outputs a value $\tilde{y}$ that is (computationally or statistically) close[2] to that of the following experiment: (i) Generate (α, y) using a sample x from a weak random source with m bits of min-entropy; (ii) Reconstruct the key $\tilde{y}$ using a close sample x' along with the tampered helper string $\tilde{\alpha} = f(\alpha)$. Similar to robustness, one can consider both pre-application and post-application non-malleability.

Black-Box Construction. Next, we give a black-box construction of an $\mathcal{F}$-non-malleable fuzzy extractor by combining a fuzzy extractor with an $\mathcal{F}$-non-malleable code [33]. The latter allows to encode a message into a codeword, in such a way that decoding a tampered codeword via any tampering function $f \in \mathcal{F}$, either yields the original message or a completely unrelated value.

Our construction simply runs the underlying fuzzy extractor using a sample x from a weak random source, thus obtaining an extracted key y and helper string α'; hence, it encodes α' using the non-malleable code and outputs y along with the encoded helper string α. The reconstruction procedure first decodes α, and then uses it along with a close sample x' in order to derive the key y.

2 The actual definition is slightly more complex, as one needs to account for the possibility that the tampering function does not modify the helper string.

Theorem 1 (Main Theorem, informal). *There is a construction of pre-application $\mathcal{F}$-non-malleable fuzzy extractors for any metric space and weak random source admitting a fuzzy extractor, and for any tampering family $\mathcal{F}$ admitting an $\mathcal{F}$-non-malleable code.*

Importantly, the construction inherits the same security and setup requirements of the underlying building blocks. Thus, plugging known non-malleable codes constructions, we obtain non-malleable fuzzy extractors in the plain model for weak random sources with min-entropy $m = \omega(\log n)$, and for interesting tampering families $\mathcal{F}$ including: bit-wise tampering and permutations [4], split-state tampering [1–3,19,21,23,24,32,47,49,52], NC0 and AC0 tampering [9,20,43], space-bounded tampering [7,10,34], and decision tree tampering [11] in the information-theoretic setting, as well as arbitrary polynomial-size circuits with bounded polynomial depth [8,26] and tampering via partial[3] functions [48] in the computational setting.[4]

We remark that the aforementioned lower bounds for robust fuzzy extractors do not seem to hold for non-malleable fuzzy extractor. Thus, there is hope that fuzzy non-malleability could be achieved in the plain model for $m = \omega(\log n)$ and for arbitrary manipulations. We leave settling this question as an open problem.

Table 1 provides a comparison between our construction and the state of the art. In particular, our main construction is in the plain model while supporting low min-entropy sources (i.e., $\omega(\log n)$). In contrast, [14,25,28,38,46,56–58] either require larger min-entropy sources or are not in the plain model (e.g., CRS and RO model). On the other hand, [6] is secure in the computational setting whereas our construction achieves information-theoretic security.

Fuzzy Tamper Simulatability. Finally, we investigate applications of non-malleable fuzzy extractors to secure cryptographic primitives whose secret keys are derived using a shared weak random source outputting close samples. Practical examples of such a source include sampling behavioral data [44] and reading physical sources such as sunspots [18] and physically unclonable functions [27,53].

More in details, let G be a cryptographic primitive implemented, say, using a smartcard. Instead of storing the secret key y on the smartcard, we use a sample x from the weak random source to generate the key y along with helper value α via an $\mathcal{F}$-non-malleable fuzzy extractor, and store α on the smartcard. This allows to recover the key y, and run the underlying primitive $\mathsf{G}(y, \cdot)$ on additional inputs, given any close sample x'. Furthermore, (pre-application) non-malleability guarantees that, for any tampering function $f \in \mathcal{F}$, the key $\tilde{y}$ that is obtained by combining x' with the tampered helper string $\tilde{\alpha} = f(\alpha)$, is independent of y, which in turn implies a way to protect the smartcard against memory tampering

[3] These are functions that read/write on an arbitrary subset of bits with specific cardinality.

[4] The result of [26] requires keyless hash functions and time-lock puzzles (along other standard computational assumptions), whereas the result of [48] only requires one-way functions.

Table 1. Comparing our results with state-of-the-art constructions for robust fuzzy extractors. † The result in [38] works even for CRS-dependent sources. ‡ Non-malleability holds for all tampering families for which there is a non-malleable code (with either statistical or computational security).

Reference	Model	Security	IT	Min-entropy
[14]	RO	Robustness	✓	$\omega(\log n)$
[28,46]	Plain	Robustness	✓	$n/2$
[25]	CRS	Robustness	✓	$\omega(\log n)$
[38,56–58]†	CRS	Robustness	✗	$\omega(\log n)$
[6]	Plain	Robustness	✗	$\omega(\log n)$
Section 4	Plain	Non-malleability‡	✓	$\omega(\log n)$
Section 4	Plain	Non-malleability‡	✗	$\omega(\log n)$

attacks. The above application can be extended to deal with multiple tampering attacks against the memory; however, the latter requires to re-generate both α and y using a fresh sample x after each invocation.

Dziembowsky, Pietrzak, and Wichs [33] considered a similar application using non-malleable codes, where the smartcard in their case stores an encoding of the secret key. Thus, the above can be considered as a generalization of their application to the fuzzy setting, in which the secret key for the underlying primitive G is derived using a shared weak random source.

1.2 Related Work

Fuzzy extractors further exist also for weak random sources modeled as continuous distributions [15,40,51,54]. To the best of our knowledge, none of these constructions achieve robustness. In contrast, our construction can be instantiated starting with any fuzzy extractor, yielding a non-malleable fuzzy extractor for continuous sources.

There exist also constructions of non-malleable codes in the CRS model (e.g., [10,37,45]); however, using those in our construction does not improve the state of the art for robust fuzzy extractors.

Dodis and Wichs [31] build a two-round (interactive) key agreement protocol in the fuzzy setting, using a so-called non-malleable extractor. The latter is a seeded extractor with the following non-malleability property: the adversary gets the seed and comes up with an arbitrarily related seed; then, it learns the value extracted from a weak random source under the modified seed. The extracted value should still look uniformly random even when given the modified seed.

2 Preliminaries

Notation. Capital bold-face letters (such as $\mathbf{X}$) are used to denote probability distributions, small letters (such as x) to denote concrete values, calligraphic letters (such as $\mathcal{X}$) to denote sets, sans serif letters (such as A) to denote algorithms. We denote with $\mathbf{U}_\ell$ the uniform distribution over $\{0,1\}^\ell$. For a string $x \in \{0,1\}^*$, we let $|x|$ be its length; if $\mathcal{X}$ is a set, $|\mathcal{X}|$ represents the cardinality of $\mathcal{X}$. When x is chosen uniformly from a set $\mathcal{X}$, we write $x \leftarrow\$ \mathcal{X}$. Similarly, if $\mathbf{X}$ is a distribution, we denote with $x \leftarrow\$ \mathbf{X}$ the sample x chosen according to $\mathbf{X}$. All of our algorithms are modeled as Turing machines; if A is a deterministic algorithm, we write $y = \mathsf{A}(x)$ to denote a run of A on input x and output y; if A is randomized, we write $y \leftarrow\$ \mathsf{A}(x)$ (or $y = \mathsf{A}(x;r)$) to denote a run of A on input x and (uniform) randomness r, and output y. If $\mathbf{X}$ is a distribution, we write $\mathsf{A}(\mathbf{X})$ for the probability distribution obtained by sampling $x \leftarrow\$ \mathbf{X}$ and executing $\mathsf{A}(x)$. An algorithm A is *probabilistic polynomial-time* (PPT) if A is randomized and for any input $x, r \in \{0,1\}^*$ the computation of $\mathsf{A}(x;r)$ terminates in a polynomial number of steps (in the input size).

Statistical Distance and Min-Entropy. Let $\mathbf{X}_1$ and $\mathbf{X}_2$ be two probability distributions over a set $\mathcal{S}$. The *statistical distance* between $\mathbf{X}_1$ and $\mathbf{X}_2$ is defined as follows: $\Delta(\mathbf{X}_1, \mathbf{X}_2) \stackrel{\text{def}}{=} \frac{1}{2}\sum_{x \in \mathcal{S}} \left| \mathbb{P}[\mathbf{X}_1 = x] - \mathbb{P}[\mathbf{X}_2 = x] \right|$, where $\mathbb{P}[\mathbf{X} = x]$ denotes the probability that the distribution $\mathbf{X}$ takes at value x. We say that two distributions are ϵ-close, denoted by $\mathbf{X}_1 \approx_\epsilon \mathbf{X}_2$, if their statistically distance is at most ϵ, i.e., $\Delta(\mathbf{X}_1, \mathbf{X}_2) \leq \epsilon$.

The *min-entropy* of a probability distribution $\mathbf{X}$ is defined as $\mathbb{H}_\infty(\mathbf{X}) \stackrel{\text{def}}{=} -\log(\max_x \mathbb{P}[\mathbf{X} = x])$. The *(average) conditional min-entropy* of distribution $\mathbf{X}$ given distribution $\mathbf{Y}$ is defined as: $\widetilde{\mathbb{H}}_\infty(\mathbf{X}|\mathbf{Y}) \stackrel{\text{def}}{=} -\log\left(\mathbf{E}_{y \leftarrow\$ \mathbf{Y}}\left(2^{-\mathbb{H}_\infty(\mathbf{X}|\mathbf{Y}=y)}\right)\right)$.

2.1 (Keyless) Fuzzy Extractors

In this section, we recall different notions of extractors.

Strong Extractors. Let $\mathbf{X}$ be a distribution. A strong extractor is an algorithm Ext that, on input $x \leftarrow\$ \mathbf{X}$ and a random seed $s \leftarrow\$ \mathbf{U}_k$ (where $\mathbf{U}_k$ is the uniform distribution over $\{0,1\}^k$), it outputs a string y. For any $\mathbf{X}$ with sufficiently high min-entropy, a strong extractor guarantees that y is close to a uniformly random string, even if the output is conditioned to the random seed. The formal definition follows.

Definition 1. (Strong $(\mathcal{X}, m, k, \ell, \epsilon)$-extractors). *Let $\mathbf{U}_k$ be the uniform distribution over the set $\{0,1\}^k$. An algorithm $\mathsf{Ext} : \mathcal{X} \times \{0,1\}^k \to \{0,1\}^\ell$ is a strong $(\mathcal{X}, m, k, \ell, \epsilon)$-extractor if for every distribution $\mathbf{X}$ over $\mathcal{X}$ such that $\mathbb{H}_\infty(\mathbf{X}) \geq m$, we have $\Delta\left((\mathsf{Ext}(\mathbf{X}, s), s), (\mathbf{U}_\ell, \mathbf{U}_k)\right) \leq \epsilon$ where $s \leftarrow\$ \mathbf{U}_k$.*

Fuzzy Extractors. Let $\mathsf{dist}(\cdot,\cdot)$ be a distance metric over a set $\mathcal{X}$. We say that $x_1, x_2 \in \mathcal{X}$ are t-close (according to $\mathsf{dist}(\cdot,\cdot)$) if $\mathsf{dist}(x_1, x_2) \leq t$. A stronger notion of extractors are *fuzzy extractors.* Informally, a fuzzy extractor allows to (i) generate an extracted string y from a sample $x_1 \leftarrow\$ \mathbf{X}_1$ and (ii) reconstruct y from any sample x_2 that is t-close (w.r.t. to a distance metric $\mathsf{dist}(\cdot,\cdot)$ and threshold t) to the original sample x_1, i.e., $\mathsf{dist}(x_1, x_2) \leq t$. In order to make the reconstruction possible, an helper string α is generated along with y. The former will be then combined with x_2 to regenerate y. Similarly to (standard) strong extractors (Definition 1), we require that y is close to an uniformly random string even if conditioned to the helper string α, when $\mathbf{X}_1$ has high enough min-entropy.

Definition 2. (($\mathcal{X}, m, k, \ell, t, \epsilon$)-fuzzy extractors). *Let* $\mathsf{dist}(\cdot,\cdot)$ *be a distance metric. A scheme* $\Pi = (\mathsf{Gen}, \mathsf{Rec})$ *is an* $(\mathcal{X}, m, k, \ell, t, \epsilon)$*-fuzzy extractor (for metric* $\mathsf{dist}(\cdot,\cdot)$*) with input space* $\mathcal{X}$ *and output space* $\{0,1\}^\ell$ *if* Π *satisfies the following properties:*

- Syntax: *The algorithms* Gen *and* Rec *have the following syntax:*
  $\mathsf{Gen}(x_1)$**:** *The deterministic generation algorithm takes as input a sample* $x_1 \in \mathcal{X}$ *and outputs a string* $y \in \{0,1\}^\ell$ *and a helper string* $\alpha \in \{0,1\}^*$.
  $\mathsf{Rec}(x_2, \alpha)$ *The deterministic reconstruction algorithm takes as input a sample* $x_2 \in \mathcal{X}$ *and a string* $\alpha \in \{0,1\}^*$*, and outputs a string* $y \in \{0,1\}^\ell$.
- Correctness: *For every* $x_1, x_2 \in \mathcal{X}$ *such that* $\mathsf{dist}(x_1, x_2) \leq t$*, we have that* $\mathbb{P}[y = \mathsf{Rec}(x_2, \alpha) | (y, \alpha) = \mathsf{Gen}(x_1)] = 1$.
- Security: *For every distribution* $\mathbf{X}_1$ *over the set* $\mathcal{X}$ *such that* $\mathbb{H}_\infty(\mathbf{X}_1) \geq m$*, we have* $\Delta((y, \alpha), (\mathbf{U}_\ell, \alpha)) \leq \epsilon$ *where* $(y, \alpha) = \mathsf{Gen}(\mathbf{X}_1)$.

Robust Fuzzy Extractors. As discussed in [28], fuzzy extractors (Definition 2) offer security only in the case of *passive* attackers: Given α, an adversary cannot infer any information about the extracted string y (corresponding to α). For this reason, the notion of *robust fuzzy extractors* [14,28] has been proposed. In a nutshell, a robust fuzzy extractor is able to detect any manipulation of the helper string α. This is achieved by allowing the reconstruction algorithm Rec to output either an extracted string y or a special value $\perp$. Intuitively, with reasonably high probability, we want Rec to output $\perp$ for any value $\widetilde{\alpha} \neq \alpha$ produced by an adversary after seeing the original helper string α.

Following Dodis *et al.* [28], we consider two manipulation scenarios:

1. *Pre-application:* An adversary A produces the manipulated helper string $\widetilde{\alpha}$ given the original helper string α, i.e., $\widetilde{\alpha} \leftarrow\$ \mathsf{A}(\alpha)$. Observe that the extracted string y is kept secret from the adversary.
2. *Post-application:* This notion is a strengthening of the pre-application case. Here, the adversary produces the manipulated helper string $\widetilde{\alpha}$ given both the helper string α and the corresponding extracted string y, i.e., $\widetilde{\alpha} \leftarrow\$ \mathsf{A}(y, \alpha)$.

Definition 3. ((t, m)-pair of distributions). *Let two (possibly correlated) distributions* $\mathbf{X}_1, \mathbf{X}_2$ *over a set* $\mathcal{X}$*. We say* $(\mathbf{X}_1, \mathbf{X}_2)$ *is a* (t, m)*-pair of distributions for a distance metric* $\mathsf{dist}(\cdot,\cdot)$ *if* $\mathbb{P}[\mathsf{dist}(\mathbf{X}_1, \mathbf{X}_2) \leq t] = 1$ *and* $\mathbb{H}_\infty(\mathbf{X}_1) \geq m$.

Definition 4. (Pre-application and post-application δ-robustness of ($\mathcal{X}, m, k, \ell, t, \epsilon$)-fuzzy extractors). *Let* $\mathsf{dist}(\cdot,\cdot)$ *be distance metric. An* $(\mathcal{X}, m, k, \ell, t, \epsilon)$*-fuzzy extractor* $\Pi = (\mathsf{Gen}, \mathsf{Rec})$ *(for metric* $\mathsf{dist}(\cdot,\cdot)$*) with input space* $\mathcal{X}$ *and output space* $\{0,1\}^\ell$ *satisfies pre-application (resp. post-application)* δ*-robustness if for every* (t, m)*-pair of distributions* $(\mathbf{X}_1, \mathbf{X}_2)$ *for the distance metric* $\mathsf{dist}(\cdot,\cdot)$*, and for every adversary* A*, we have:*

$\mathbf{Tamper}_{\Pi,f}(x)$	$\mathbf{SimTamper}_{\Pi,f,\mathsf{S}}(x)$
$c = \mathsf{Enc}(x)$	$\widetilde{x} \leftarrow\!\$\ \mathsf{S}(f)$
$\widetilde{c} = f(c)$	**If** $\widetilde{x} = \mathsf{same}$: **return** x
$\widetilde{x} = \mathsf{Dec}(\widetilde{c})$	**return** $\widetilde{x}$
return $\widetilde{x}$	

Fig. 1. Experiments defining $(\mathcal{F}, \epsilon)$-NM coding schemes.

- Pre-application δ-robustness:

$$\left[\widetilde{\alpha} \neq \alpha \wedge \mathsf{Rec}(x_2, \widetilde{\alpha}) \neq \bot \middle| \begin{array}{l}(x_1, x_2) \leftarrow\!\$\ (\mathbf{X}_1, \mathbf{X}_2),\\ (y, \alpha) = \mathsf{Gen}(x_1), \widetilde{\alpha} \leftarrow\!\$\ \mathsf{A}(\alpha)\end{array}\right] \leq \delta.$$

- Post-application δ-robustness:

$$\left[\widetilde{\alpha} \neq \alpha \wedge \mathsf{Rec}(x_2, \widetilde{\alpha}) \neq \bot \middle| \begin{array}{l}(x_1, x_2) \leftarrow\!\$\ (\mathbf{X}_1, \mathbf{X}_2),\\ (y, \alpha) = \mathsf{Gen}(x_1), \widetilde{\alpha} \leftarrow\!\$\ \mathsf{A}(y, \alpha)\end{array}\right] \leq \delta.$$

2.2 Non-malleable Codes

Non-malleable codes [33] are a relaxation of error-correction and error-detection codes. Instead of correcting/detecting modified codewords, non-malleable codes guarantee that the message contained in a modified codeword is either the original message or a completely unrelated value. The main advantage of non-malleable codes (w.r.t. error-correcting and error-detecting codes) is that non-malleability can be obtained for richer classes of tampering/modification functions. We recall the definition of coding schemes below.

Definition 5 (Coding scheme). *A scheme* $\Pi = (\mathsf{Enc}, \mathsf{Dec})$ *is a coding scheme with message space* $\mathcal{X}$ *and codeword space* $\mathcal{C}$ *if* Π *satisfies the following properties:*

- Syntax: *The algorithms* Enc *and* Dec *have the following syntax.*
  $\mathsf{Enc}(x)$: *The randomized encoding algorithm takes as input a message* $x \in \mathcal{X}$ *and outputs a codeword* $c \in \mathcal{C}$.
  $\mathsf{Dec}(c)$: *The deterministic decoding algorithm takes as input a codeword* $c \in \mathcal{C}$ *and outputs either a message* x *or* $\bot$.
- Correctness: *For every* $x \in \mathcal{X}$, *we have* $\mathbb{P}[x = \mathsf{Dec}(\mathsf{Enc}(x))] = 1$.

Regarding non-malleability, it guarantees that for every tampering function $f \in \mathcal{F}$ (where $\mathcal{F}$ is the tapering family considered) the decoded message $\widetilde{x} = \mathsf{Dec}(\widetilde{c})$ of the modified codeword $\widetilde{c} = f(c)$ (where $c = \mathsf{Enc}(x)$ for some x) is either $\widetilde{x} = x$ or completely unrelated from the original message x. The formal definition follows.

Definition 6. ($(\mathcal{F}, \epsilon)$-non-malleability of coding schemes). *A coding scheme* $\Pi = (\mathsf{Enc}, \mathsf{Dec})$ *(Definition 5) with message space* $\mathcal{X}$ *and codeword space* $\mathcal{C}$ *is*

$\mathbf{Tamper}_{\Pi,f}(\mathbf{X}_1, \mathbf{X}_2)$	$\mathbf{SimTamper}_{\Pi,f,\mathsf{S}}(\mathbf{X}_1, \mathbf{X}_2)$
$(x_1, x_2) \leftarrow\$ (\mathbf{X}_1, \mathbf{X}_2)$	$(x_1, x_2) \leftarrow\$ (\mathbf{X}_1, \mathbf{X}_2)$
$(y, \alpha) = \mathsf{Gen}(x_1)$	$(y, \alpha) = \mathsf{Gen}(x_1)$
$\widetilde{\alpha} = f(\alpha)$	$\widetilde{y} \leftarrow\$ \mathsf{S}(f)$
$\widetilde{y} = \mathsf{Rec}(x_2, \widetilde{\alpha})$	**If** $\widetilde{y} = \mathsf{same}$: **return** y
return $\widetilde{y}$	**return** $\widetilde{y}$

Fig. 2. Experiments defining $(\mathcal{F}, \delta)$-pre-NM of fuzzy extractors.

$(\mathcal{F}, \epsilon)$-non-malleable ($(\mathcal{F}, \epsilon)$-NM) if there exists a simulator S *such that for every $f \in \mathcal{F}$, and for every $x \in \mathcal{X}$, we have* $\mathbf{Tamper}_{\Pi,f}(x) \approx_\epsilon \mathbf{SimTamper}_{\Pi,f,\mathsf{S}}(x)$ *where the experiments* $\mathbf{Tamper}_{\Pi,f}(x)$ *and* $\mathbf{SimTamper}_{\Pi,f,\mathsf{S}}(x)$ *are defined in Fig. 1.*

While the above definition is information-theoretic, we note that the same definition can be adapted to the computational setting where now ϵ is a bound on the distinguishing advantage between the two experiments (for every PPT machine). The reason for considering computational non-malleability is that there are families of tampering functions for which we do not know coding schemes satisfying statistical non-malleability (e.g., the family of all tampering circuits of arbitrary polynomial size and bounded polynomial depth [8,26] and the family of partial tampering functions [48]).

We also recall that non-malleability is impossible to achieve (even computationally) against the family of all possible manipulations (because the encoding and decoding algorithms are keyless and public).

3 Non-malleable Fuzzy Extractors

We introduce the notion of *non-malleable* fuzzy extractors which guarantees that the tampered $\widetilde{\alpha}$ corresponding to helper string α (and extracted value y) is such that the value $\widetilde{y}$ reconstructed using $\widetilde{\alpha}$ is either equal to y or independent of it.

Definition 7. (Pre-application $(\mathcal{F}, \delta)$-non-malleability of $(\mathcal{X}, m, k, \ell, t, \epsilon)$-fuzzy extractors). *Let* $\mathsf{dist}(\cdot,\cdot)$ *be a distance metric. An $(\mathcal{X}, m, k, \ell, t, \epsilon)$-fuzzy extractor Π =* $(\mathsf{Gen}, \mathsf{Rec})$ *(for metric* $\mathsf{dist}(\cdot,\cdot)$*) with input space $\mathcal{X}$ and output space $\{0,1\}^\ell$ satisfies pre-application $(\mathcal{F}, \delta)$-non-malleability ($(\mathcal{F}, \delta)$-pre-NM) if for every (t, m)-pair of distributions* $(\mathbf{X}_1, \mathbf{X}_2)$ *for the distance metric* $\mathsf{dist}(\cdot,\cdot)$ *there exists a simulator* S *such that for every $f \in \mathcal{F}$, we have* $\mathbf{Tamper}_{\Pi,f}(\mathbf{X}_1, \mathbf{X}_2) \approx_\delta \mathbf{SimTamper}_{\Pi,f,\mathsf{S}}(\mathbf{X}_1, \mathbf{X}_2)$ *where* $\mathbf{Tamper}_{\Pi,f}(\mathbf{X}_1, \mathbf{X}_2)$ *and* $\mathbf{SimTamper}_{\Pi,f,\mathsf{S}}(\mathbf{X}_1, \mathbf{X}_2)$ *are depicted in Fig. 2.*

The above definition covers the pre-application setting which is sufficient for our application of fuzzy tamper simulatability (Sect. 5). For completeness, we highlight that the post-application version of Definition 7 is identical except that the tampering function $f \in \mathcal{F}$ additionally takes as input the extracted string y, i.e., the tampered helper string $\widetilde{\alpha}$ of $\mathbf{Tamper}_{\Pi,f}(\mathbf{X}_1, \mathbf{X}_2)$ (Fig. 2) is computed as $\widetilde{\alpha} = f(\alpha, y)$. This is reminiscent of the definition of post-application robustness of fuzzy extractors (see Definition 4).

4 Construction

Next, we give our construction of non-malleable fuzzy extractors combining standard fuzzy extractors with non-malleable codes.

Construction 1. *Consider the following ingredients:*

1. *A $(\mathcal{X}, m, k, \ell, t, \epsilon)$-fuzzy extractor $\Pi_{\mathsf{fuzzyExt}} = (\mathsf{Gen}_{\mathsf{fuzzyExt}}, \mathsf{Rec}_{\mathsf{fuzzyExt}})$ (Definition 2) with input space $\mathcal{X}$ and output space $\{0,1\}^\ell$ for a distance metric $\mathsf{dist}(\cdot,\cdot)$. Without loss of generality, let $\mathcal{H}$ be the helper string space of Π_{fuzzyExt}.*
2. *A coding scheme $\Pi_{\mathsf{coding}} = (\mathsf{Enc}_{\mathsf{coding}}, \mathsf{Dec}_{\mathsf{coding}})$ (Definition 5) with message space $\mathcal{H}$ and codeword space $\mathcal{C}$.*

We build a non-malleable $(\mathcal{X}, m, k, \ell, t, \epsilon)$-fuzzy extractor $\Pi = (\mathsf{Gen}, \mathsf{Rec})$ (for $\mathsf{dist}(\cdot,\cdot)$) with input space $\mathcal{X}$ and output space $\{0,1\}^\ell$ in the following way:

$\mathsf{Gen}(x_1)$: *Upon input a sample $x_1 \in \mathcal{X}$, the deterministic generation algorithm outputs $(y, \alpha) = (y', c)$ where $(y', \alpha') = \mathsf{Gen}_{\mathsf{fuzzyExt}}(x_1)$, and $c = \mathsf{Enc}_{\mathsf{coding}}(\alpha')$.*

$\mathsf{Rec}(x_2, \alpha)$: *Upon input a sample $x_2 \in \mathcal{X}$ and an helper string $\alpha = c$, the deterministic reconstruction algorithm first runs $\alpha' = \mathsf{Dec}_{\mathsf{coding}}(c)$; then, if $\alpha' = \bot$ it returns $\bot$ and otherwise it outputs $y = \mathsf{Rec}_{\mathsf{fuzzyExt}}(x_2, \alpha')$.*

The proof of security of the above construction Π (Theorem 2) is divided into two parts. First, we show that Π is a fuzzy extractor (Lemma 1). Then, we show that Π satisfies non-malleability (Lemma 2).

Lemma 1. *Let Π_{fuzzyExt} as defined in Construction 1. If Π_{fuzzyExt} is an $(\mathcal{X}, m, k, \ell, t, \epsilon)$-fuzzy extractor (Definition 2) for the distance metric $\mathsf{dist}(\cdot,\cdot)$, then Π from Construction 1 is an $(\mathcal{X}, m, k, \ell, t, \epsilon)$-fuzzy extractor (Definition 2) for the same metric $\mathsf{dist}(\cdot,\cdot)$.*

Proof. Suppose there exists a distribution $\mathbf{X}_1$ over $\mathcal{X}$ with min-entropy $\mathbb{H}_\infty(\mathbf{X}_1) \geq m$ such that $\Delta((y, \alpha), (\mathbf{U}_\ell, \alpha)) > \epsilon$ where $(y, \alpha) = \mathsf{Gen}(\mathbf{X}_1)$, i.e., there exists an algorithm D with advantage ϵ in distinguishing between the distributions (y, α) and $(\mathbf{U}_\ell, \alpha)$. We build a distinguisher D' that breaks the security of the $(\mathcal{X}, m, k, \ell, t, \epsilon)$-fuzzy extractor Π_{fuzzyExt} (w.r.t. the distribution $\mathbf{X}_1$). D' is defined as follows:

1. Receive (y', α') from the challenger.
2. Return the output of $\mathsf{D}(y', \mathsf{Enc}_{\mathsf{coding}}(\alpha'))$.

$\overline{\mathbf{Tamper}}_{\Pi,f}(\mathbf{X}_1,\mathbf{X}_2)$	Simulator $\mathsf{S}(f)$
$(x_1,x_2) \leftarrow\$ (\mathbf{X}_1,\mathbf{X}_2)$	$\widetilde{\alpha}' \leftarrow\$ \mathsf{S}_{\mathsf{coding}}(f)$
$(y,\alpha') = \mathsf{Gen}_{\mathsf{fuzzyExt}}(x_1)$	**If** $\widetilde{\alpha}' = \mathsf{same}$: **return** same
$\widetilde{\alpha}' \leftarrow\$ \mathsf{S}_{\mathsf{coding}}(f)$	$(x_1',x_2') \leftarrow\$ (\mathbf{X}_1,\mathbf{X}_2)$
If $\widetilde{\alpha}' = \mathsf{same}$: **return** y	$\widetilde{y} = \mathsf{Rec}_{\mathsf{fuzzyExt}}(x_2',\widetilde{\alpha}')$
$\widetilde{y} = \mathsf{Rec}_{\mathsf{fuzzyExt}}(x_2,\widetilde{\alpha}')$	**return** $\widetilde{y}$
return $\widetilde{y}$	

Fig. 3. The intermediate distribution $\overline{\mathbf{Tamper}}_{\Pi,f}(\mathbf{X}_1,\mathbf{X}_2)$ and the final simulator S of Π. The algorithm $\mathsf{S}_{\mathsf{coding}}$ is the simulator of the non-malleable coding scheme Π_{coding}.

We can observe that if $(y',\alpha') = \mathsf{Gen}_{\mathsf{fuzzyExt}}(\mathbf{X}_1)$, then D is executed over the input distribution $(y,\alpha) = \mathsf{Gen}(\mathbf{X}_1)$. On the other hand, if (y',α') is sampled as $y' \leftarrow\$ \mathbf{U}_\ell$ and α' is the helper string output by $\mathsf{Gen}_{\mathsf{fuzzyExt}}(\mathbf{X}_1)$, then D is executed over the input distribution $(\mathbf{U}_\ell,\alpha)$ where α is the helper string output by $\mathsf{Gen}(\mathbf{X}_1)$. Hence, D' correctly simulates the view of D. This implies that D' retains the same advantage of D. This concludes the proof. □

Lemma 2. *Let Π_{coding} as defined in Construction 1. If Π_{coding} is $(\mathcal{F},\delta)$-NM (Definition 6), then Π from Construction 1 is $(\mathcal{F},\delta)$-pre-NM (Definition 7).*

Proof. Fix $(\mathbf{X}_1,\mathbf{X}_2)$ to be any (t,m)-pair of distributions, and consider the simulator S depicted in Fig. 3. First, we prove that $\mathbf{Tamper}_{\Pi,f}(\mathbf{X}_1,\mathbf{X}_2)$ is δ-close to the intermediate distribution $\overline{\mathbf{Tamper}}_{\Pi,f}(\mathbf{X}_1,\mathbf{X}_2)$ depicted in Fig. 3. Second, we prove that $\overline{\mathbf{Tamper}}_{\Pi,f}(\mathbf{X}_1,\mathbf{X}_2)$ and $\mathbf{SimTamper}_{\Pi,f,\mathsf{S}}(\mathbf{X}_1,\mathbf{X}_2)$ are identically distributed where S is the simulator depicted in Fig. 3.

Claim. For every (t,m)-pair of distributions $(\mathbf{X}_1,\mathbf{X}_2)$, for every $f \in \mathcal{F}$, then: $\mathbf{Tamper}_{\Pi,f}(\mathbf{X}_1,\mathbf{X}_2) \approx_\delta \overline{\mathbf{Tamper}}_{\Pi,f}(\mathbf{X}_1,\mathbf{X}_2)$.

Proof. Suppose there exists an $f \in \mathcal{F}$ such that the distributions $\mathbf{Tamper}_{\Pi,f}(\mathbf{X}_1,\mathbf{X}_2)$ and $\overline{\mathbf{Tamper}}_{\Pi,f}(\mathbf{X}_1,\mathbf{X}_2)$ are not δ-close, i.e., there exists an algorithm D with advantage δ in distinguishing between the distributions $\mathbf{Tamper}_{\Pi,f}(\mathbf{X}_1,\mathbf{X}_2)$ and $\overline{\mathbf{Tamper}}_{\Pi,f}(\mathbf{X}_1,\mathbf{X}_2)$. We build a distinguisher D' that breaks the $(\mathcal{F},\delta)$-NM of Π_{coding}. D' is defined as follows:

1. Sample $(x_1,x_2) \leftarrow\$ (\mathbf{X}_1,\mathbf{X}_2)$ and compute $(y,\alpha') = \mathsf{Gen}_{\mathsf{fuzzyExt}}(x_1)$.
2. Send α' to the challenger as the message of the $(\mathcal{F},\delta)$-NM experiment of Π_{coding}.
3. Receive $\widetilde{\alpha}'$ and return the output of $\mathsf{D}(\mathsf{Rec}_{\mathsf{fuzzyExt}}(x_2,\widetilde{\alpha}'))$.

It is easy to see that, if $\widetilde{\alpha}'$ is computed as described in $\mathbf{Tamper}_{\Pi_{\mathsf{coding}},f}(\alpha')$, then D' simulates $\mathbf{Tamper}_{\Pi,f}(\mathbf{X}_1,\mathbf{X}_2)$. On the other hand, if $\widetilde{\alpha}'$ is computed as described in $\mathbf{SimTamper}_{\Pi_{\mathsf{coding}},f,\mathsf{S}_{\mathsf{coding}}}(\alpha')$, then D' simulates $\overline{\mathbf{Tamper}}_{\Pi,f}(\mathbf{X}_1,\mathbf{X}_2)$. This concludes the proof of the claim. □

Claim. Let $(\mathbf{X}_1, \mathbf{X}_2)$ and S be, respectively, a (t, m)-pair of distributions $(\mathbf{X}_1, \mathbf{X}_2)$ and the simulator depicted in Fig. 3. For every $f \in \mathcal{F}$, we have $\mathbf{Tamper}_{\Pi,f}(\mathbf{X}_1, \mathbf{X}_2) \equiv \mathbf{SimTamper}_{\Pi,f,\mathsf{S}}(\mathbf{X}_1, \mathbf{X}_2)$.

Proof. The claim follows by leveraging the following two observations:

1. If $\mathsf{S}_{\mathsf{coding}}$ outputs $\widetilde{\alpha}' = \mathsf{same}$ and Π_{fuzzyExt} is correct, then the final output y of both $\mathbf{Tamper}_{\Pi,f}(\mathbf{X}_1, \mathbf{X}_2)$ and $\mathbf{SimTamper}_{\Pi,f,\mathsf{S}}(\mathbf{X}_1, \mathbf{X}_2)$ is computed in the same way.
2. If $\mathsf{S}_{\mathsf{coding}}$ outputs $\widetilde{\alpha}' \neq \mathsf{same}$, then $\mathbf{SimTamper}_{\Pi,f,\mathsf{S}}(\mathbf{X}_1, \mathbf{X}_2)$ outputs $\widetilde{y} = \mathsf{Rec}_{\mathsf{fuzzyExt}}(x_2', \widetilde{\alpha}')$ where x_2' is sampled (by the simulator S) as $(x_1', x_2') \leftarrow\$ (\mathbf{X}_1, \mathbf{X}_2)$. On the other hand, $\mathbf{Tamper}_{\Pi,f}(\mathbf{X}_1, \mathbf{X}_2)$ outputs $\widetilde{y} = \mathsf{Rec}_{\mathsf{fuzzyExt}}(x_2, \widetilde{\alpha}')$ where x_2 is the original sample. Still, these distributions are identically distributed since $\widetilde{\alpha}'$ is computed as $\mathsf{S}_{\mathsf{coding}}(f)$ and it does not depend on the original sampled pair $(x_1, x_2) \leftarrow\$ (\mathbf{X}_1, \mathbf{X}_2)$ (note that (x_1, x_2) and (x_1', x_2') comes from the same distribution $(\mathbf{X}_1, \mathbf{X}_2)$). □

Lemma 2 follows by combining the above two claims. □

The following theorem states the security of Construction 1.

Theorem 2. *Let Π_{fuzzyExt} and Π_{coding} be as above.*

1. *If Π_{fuzzyExt} is an $(\mathcal{X}, m, k, \ell, t, \epsilon)$-fuzzy extractor (Definition 2) for the distance metric $\mathsf{dist}(\cdot,\cdot)$, then Π from Construction 1 is an $(\mathcal{X}, m, k, \ell, t, \epsilon)$-fuzzy extractor (Definition 2) for the same metric $\mathsf{dist}(\cdot,\cdot)$.*
2. *If Π_{coding} is $(\mathcal{F}, \delta)$-NM (Definition 6), then Π from Construction 1 is $(\mathcal{F}, \delta)$-pre-NM (Definition 7).*

Proof. Theorem 2 follows by simply combining Lemmas 1 and 2. □

Remark 1 (Statistical vs computational security). We note that the above proof also works in the computational setting, assuming the underlying non-malleable code is only computationally secure. This allows to get non-malleable fuzzy extractors (in the plain model and with sources with minimal min-entropy) against tampering families for which non-malleable codes are known only in the computational setting.

5 Fuzzy Tamper-Resilient Security

Dziembowski *et al.* [33] showed that non-malleable codes are sufficient to compile a (possibly stateful) system into one that implements the same functionality, while being resilient to tampering attacks (against its internal state). This is achieved by simply encoding the internal state using a non-malleable code.

In this section, we show that non-malleable fuzzy extractors can be used to achieve an analogous result in the fuzzy setting. In more details, starting from a stateless system G that relies on a random key from $\{0,1\}^\ell$ (stored by the system itself),[5] we can compile G into an hardened stateless system G^Π (through a non-malleable fuzzy extractor Π) in order to obtain the following properties:

[5] The term "stateless system" refers to a system which does not store any additional state (e.g., data structure) except from a uniform secret key required for security.

1. *(Fuzzyness).* The hardened system G^{Π} achieves the same functionality of G but in the fuzzy setting. In particular, G^{Π} computes its random key y by letting $(y, \alpha) = \mathsf{Gen}(x_1)$ where $\Pi = (\mathsf{Gen}, \mathsf{Rec})$ is a fuzzy extractor and x_1 is sampled from a distribution $\mathbf{X}_1$ (with sufficiently high min-entropy). Then, instead of storing y, the system G^{Π} stores the helper string α. We denote the functionality of G^{Π} w.r.t. α as $\mathsf{G}^{\Pi}_{\alpha}$. Users can issue commands on an input v to the hardened fuzzy system $\mathsf{G}^{\Pi}_{\alpha}$, by sending an execute command together with an input v and a sample x_2. Then, the system $\mathsf{G}^{\Pi}_{\alpha}$ will use x_2 and its internal helper string α to reconstruct y and execute $\mathsf{G}_y(v)$ where G_y is the original stateless system with key y. It is easy to see that whenever $\mathsf{dist}(x_1, x_2) \leq t$ (where $\mathsf{dist}(\cdot,\cdot)$ and t are the distance metric and its corresponding threshold of the underlying non-malleable fuzzy extractor) then the fuzzy system G^{Π}_{α} implements the same functionality of the original system $G_{\mathbf{U}_\ell}$ (where $\mathbf{U}_\ell$ denotes the uniform distribution over the key space $\{0,1\}^\ell$). This is because $\mathsf{Rec}(x_2, \alpha) = y' = y$ where $(y, \alpha) \leftarrow_{\$} \mathsf{Gen}(x_1)$ for $\mathsf{dist}(x_1, x_2) \leq t$ and $x_1 \leftarrow_{\$} \mathbf{X}_1$, and y is indistinguishable from a random string from $\mathbf{U}_\ell$ whenever $\mathbb{H}_\infty(\mathbf{X}_1) \geq m$.
2. *(Tamper resiliency).* The system $\mathsf{G}^{\Pi}_{\alpha}$ described above is also tamper resilient, i.e., tampering attacks are useless. In other words, a malicious user (i.e., adversary) that tampers with the stored helper string α cannot leak any sensitive information regarding the random key y (output by the extractor). This intuitively follows from the non-malleability property of the fuzzy extractor.

We now formalize the notions of stateless (fuzzy) systems with random keys.

Definition 8 (Interactive stateless system with random keys). *For $y \leftarrow_{\$} \{0,1\}^\ell$, an interactive system G_y with input space $\mathcal{V}$ and output space $\mathcal{W}$ is a system which accepts the following mode of interaction:*

$\mathsf{Execute}(v)$: *A user can issue to the system a command $\mathsf{Execute}(v)$, for $v \in \mathcal{V}$. As a result, the system outputs $w \in \mathcal{W}$ where $w = \mathsf{G}_y(v)$.*

The above definition assumes that G_y is untamperable, i.e., a malicious user cannot tamper with the system's random key y. We now define the hardened fuzzy version G^{Π} of G as described at the beginning of this section. Contrarily to G, the hardened system G^{Π} allows for tampering attacks, i.e., its interface provides a command $\mathsf{Tamper}(f)$ where f is a tampering function that modifies its internal helper string α.

Definition 9 (Hardened fuzzy interactive stateless system G^{Π} of G). *Let $\Pi = (\mathsf{Gen}, \mathsf{Rec})$ be an $(\mathcal{X}, m, k, \ell, t, \epsilon)$-fuzzy extractor (Definition 2) with input space $\mathcal{X}$ and distance metric $\mathsf{dist}(\cdot,\cdot)$, and $(\mathbf{X}_1, \mathbf{X}_2)$ be a (t, m)-pair of distributions over $\mathcal{X}$. Let G be an interactive stateless system with key space $\{0,1\}^\ell$, input space $\mathcal{V}$, and output space $\mathcal{W}$ (Definition 8). For $(y, \alpha) = \mathsf{Gen}(x_1)$ where $(x_1, x_2) \leftarrow_{\$} (\mathbf{X}_1, \mathbf{X}_2)$, the hardened fuzzy interactive stateless system $\mathsf{G}^{\Pi}_{\alpha}$ of G_y is a fuzzy system which accepts the following mode of interaction:*

$\mathsf{Execute}(v)$: *A user can issue to the system a command $\mathsf{Execute}(v)$ to $\mathsf{G}^{\Pi}_{\alpha}$, for $v \in \mathcal{V}$. As a result, the hardened fuzzy system $\mathsf{G}^{\Pi}_{\alpha}$ outputs $w = \mathsf{G}_{\mathsf{Rec}(x_2, \alpha)}(v)$.*

$\mathsf{Tamper}(f)$: *A malicious user can issue a tampering query $f \in \mathcal{F}$, where $\mathcal{F}$ is a class of allowed modifications. As a result, the local helper string α of G_α^Π is set to $\alpha = f(\alpha)$.*

Intuitively, the above system is the fuzzy version of the original stateless system. However, Definition 9 allows for tampering queries that may affect the security of the system. As an example, a malicious users can tamper with α in order to leak information about the key y (output by the extractor). Our objective is to demonstrate that any non-malleable fuzzy extractor is *tamper simulatable*. Here, tamper simulatability means that, independently from the original interactive system G_y, the hardened fuzzy system G_α^Π (where $(y, \alpha) \leftarrow\!\!\$\, \mathsf{Gen}(\mathbf{X})$) is tamper-resilient, meaning that tampering attacks are useless and they do not allow an attacker to gain any information about the random key y. Following [33], in the fuzzy setting tamper simulatability is formalized by requiring that the hardened system G_α^Π can be simulated by a simulator having only oracle access to the functionality $\mathsf{G}_{(\cdot)}(\cdot)$ of the original non-hardened system. Here, the oracle $\mathsf{G}_{(\cdot)}(\cdot)$ allows the simulator to choose both the key y (yielding $\mathsf{G}_y(\cdot)$) and the input v (execute command $\mathsf{Execute}(v)$). The formal definition follows.

Definition 10 (($\mathcal{F}, q, \delta$)-Tamper simulatability of ($\mathcal{X}, m, k, \ell, t, \epsilon$)-fuzzy extractors). *Let* $\mathsf{dist}(\cdot,\cdot)$ *be a distance metric. We say an $(\mathcal{X}, m, k, \ell, t, \epsilon)$-fuzzy extractor $\Pi = (\mathsf{Gen}, \mathsf{Rec})$ (for metric $\mathsf{dist}(\cdot,\cdot)$) with input space $\mathcal{X}$ and output space $\{0,1\}^\ell$ is $(\mathcal{F}, q, \delta)$-tamper-simulatable, if for every (t, m)-pair of distributions $(\mathbf{X}_1, \mathbf{X}_2)$, and for every interactive stateless system G with key space $\{0,1\}^\ell$, input space $\mathcal{V}$, and output space $\mathcal{W}$ (Definition 8), there exists a simulator S such that for every* valid *adversary A, we have that* $\mathbf{TamperInteract}_{\mathsf{A},\Pi,\mathsf{G}}(\mathbf{X}_1, \mathbf{X}_2, q) \approx_\delta \mathbf{SimTamperInteract}_{\mathsf{A},\mathsf{S},\mathsf{G}}(q)$ *where* $\mathbf{TamperInteract}_{\mathsf{A},\Pi,\mathsf{G}}(\mathbf{X}_1, \mathbf{X}_2, q)$ *and* $\mathbf{SimTamperInteract}_{\mathsf{A},\mathsf{S},\mathsf{G}}(q)$ *are defined as follows:*

$\mathbf{TamperInteract}_{\mathsf{A},\Pi,\mathsf{G}}(\mathbf{X}_1, \mathbf{X}_2, q)$: *The hardened fuzzy system $\mathsf{G}_{\alpha^1}^\Pi$ is initialized by computing $(y^1, \alpha^1) = \mathsf{Gen}(x_1^1)$ where $(x_1^1, x_2^1) \leftarrow\!\!\$\, (\mathbf{X}_1, \mathbf{X}_2)$. The adversary A executes q rounds of interaction with the hardened fuzzy system. In particular, for $i \in [q]$, the i-th round of interaction between A and $\mathsf{G}_{\alpha^i}^\Pi$ is defined as follows:*

1. *A submits the command $\mathsf{Tamper}(f_i)$ to $\mathsf{G}_{\alpha^i}^\Pi$, for $f_i \in \mathcal{F}$, as defined in Definition 9. As a result, α^i is updated to $\alpha^i = \widetilde{\alpha}^i = f_i(\alpha^i)$.*
2. *A submits the command $\mathsf{Execute}(v_i)$ to $\mathsf{G}_{\alpha^i}^\Pi$, for $v_i \in \mathcal{V}$, as defined in Definition 9. As a result, A receives the output $w_i = \mathsf{G}_{\mathsf{Rec}(x_2^i, \alpha^i)}(v_i)$.*
3. *The fuzzy hardened system is refreshed (to handle more tampering queries) by computing $\mathsf{G}_{\alpha^{i+1}}^\Pi$ where $(y^{i+1}, \alpha^{i+1}) = \mathsf{Gen}(x_1^{i+1})$ for $(x_1^{i+1}, x_2^{i+1}) \leftarrow\!\!\$\, (\mathbf{X}_1, \mathbf{X}_2)$, i.e., in the next round the adversary A will interact with the system $\mathsf{G}_{\alpha^{i+1}}^\Pi$.*

The output of the experiment is composed of the output of the adversary A at the end of the interaction, together with all the inputs $v_1, \ldots, v_q$ of the execute queries.

SimTamperInteract$_{\mathsf{A},\mathsf{S},\mathsf{G}}(q)$: *The simulator* S*, with black-box oracle access to* $\mathsf{A}(\cdot)$ *and the functionality of the non-hardened stateless system* $\mathsf{G}_{(\cdot)}(\cdot)$*, executes* q *rounds of interaction with the system* $\mathsf{G}_{(\cdot)}(\cdot)$*. In particular, for* $i \in [q]$*, the* i*-th round of interaction between* S *and* $\mathsf{G}_{(\cdot)}(\cdot)$ *is defined as follows:*

1. S *chooses a key* y^i *and send it to the oracle* $\mathsf{G}_{(\cdot)}(\cdot)$*. In turn, the oracle for this round will be set to* $\mathsf{G}_{y^i}(\cdot)$*.*
2. S *submits the command* $\mathsf{Execute}(v_i)$ *to the oracle* $\mathsf{G}_{y^i}(\cdot)$*, for* $v_i \in \mathcal{V}$*, as defined in Definition 8. As a result,* A *receives the output* $w_i = \mathsf{G}_{y^i}(v_i)$*.*

The output of the experiment is composed of the output of the adversary S *at the end of the interaction, together with all the inputs* $v_1, \ldots, v_q$ *of the execute queries.*

An adversary is called valid if for every tamper query f_i *to the system* $\mathsf{G}^{\Pi}_{\alpha^i}$ *we have* $f_i \in \mathcal{F}$*.*

Remark 2 (On refreshing the helper string). Note that the above definition requires to refresh the helper string after each execute command by using a new sample from the weak random source. This is required because non-malleable fuzzy extractors are only secure against a single tampering query.

The above limitation is also present in the non-fuzzy setting, and in fact the transformation of Dziembowski *et al.* [33] yields a stateful hardened system even in case the original non-hardened system is stateless. In the fuzzy setting, however, changing the helper string additionally results in an updated secret key for the underlying system. Hence, our transformation is mainly thought to be applied to secret-key primitives, as in the public-key setting the latter would require to update the public key as well (which is not practical).

We establish the following result.

Theorem 3. *Let* $\mathsf{dist}(\cdot,\cdot)$ *be a distance metric. If* Π *is is an* $(\mathcal{X}, m, k, \ell, t, \epsilon)$*-fuzzy extractor (Definition 2), for the distance metric* $\mathsf{dist}(\cdot,\cdot)$*, and* Π *is* $(\mathcal{F}, \delta)$*-pre-NM (Definition 7) then* Π *is* $(\mathcal{F}, q, q \cdot (\delta + \epsilon))$*-tamper-simulatable (Definition 10).*

Proof. Fix any (t, m)-pair of distributions $(\mathbf{X}_1, \mathbf{X}_2)$, and any interactive stateless system G. Consider the following simulator S:

Simulator S: For every $i \in [q]$, the simulator S, with black box access to $\mathsf{A}(\cdot)$ and the functionality of the non-hardened stateless system $\mathsf{G}_{(\cdot)}(\cdot)$, simulates the i-th round of interaction as follows:

1. On input the command $\mathsf{Tamper}(f_i)$ from A, S executes $\widetilde{y^i} \leftarrow\$ \mathsf{S}_{\mathsf{fuzzyExt}}(f_i)$ where $\mathsf{S}_{\mathsf{fuzzyExt}}$ is the simulator of the (m, ϵ)-fuzzy extractor with respect to the (t, m)-pair of distributions $(\mathbf{X}_1, \mathbf{X}_2)$.
2. If $\widetilde{y^i} = \mathsf{same}$, S samples $y^i \leftarrow\$ \mathbf{U}_\ell$ and sends y^i to the oracle $\mathsf{G}_{(\cdot)}(\cdot)$. Otherwise, if $\widetilde{y^i} \neq \mathsf{same}$, S sets $y^i = \widetilde{y^i}$ and sends y^i to the oracle $\mathsf{G}_{(\cdot)}(\cdot)$. (At the end of this step, in this round, the oracle of the non-hardened stateless system will be set to $\mathsf{G}_{y^i}(\cdot)$.)

3. On input the command $\mathsf{Execute}(v_i)$, S executes $\mathsf{Execute}(v_i)$ by sending v_i to the oracle $\mathsf{G}_{y^i}(\cdot)$. After receiving $w_i = \mathsf{G}_{y^i}(v_i)$ from the oracle, S returns w_i to the adversary A.

After completing the q rounds of interactions, S returns the output of A.

We now demonstrate that the distributions $\mathbf{TamperInteract}_{\mathsf{A},\Pi,\mathsf{G}}(\mathbf{X}_1, \mathbf{X}_2, q)$ and $\mathbf{SimTamperInteract}_{\mathsf{A},\mathsf{S},\mathsf{G}}(q)$ are $(q \cdot (\delta + \epsilon))$-close.

First, let us consider the i-th round of interaction such that $\widetilde{y}^i \neq \mathsf{same}$. In such a case, S simulates the subsequent execute command $\mathsf{Execute}(v_i)$ (submitted by A) by returning $w_i = \mathsf{G}_{\widetilde{y}^i}(v_i)$. It is easy to see that the adversary A cannot distinguish between a real $w_i = \mathsf{G}^{\Pi}_{\mathsf{Rec}(x_2, f_i(\alpha^i))}(v_i)$ (i.e., computed as defined in the real experiment $\mathbf{TamperInteract}_{\mathsf{A},\Pi,\mathsf{G}}(\mathbf{X}_1, \mathbf{X}_2, q)$) and a w_i simulated by S, except with probability at most δ. Otherwise, A would contradict the $(\mathcal{F}, \delta)$-pre-NM property (Definition 7) of the $(\mathcal{X}, m, k, \ell, t, \epsilon)$-fuzzy extractor Π.[6]

Second, let us consider the i-th round of interaction such that $\widetilde{y}^i = \mathsf{same}$. In such a case, S simulates the subsequent execute command $\mathsf{Execute}(v_i)$ (submitted by the adversary) by returning $w_i = \mathsf{G}_{y^i}(v_i)$ where $y^i \leftarrow\!\!\$\ \mathbf{U}_\ell$. We observe that the adversary cannot distinguish between a real $w_i = \mathsf{G}^{\Pi}_{\mathsf{Rec}(x_2, \alpha^i)}(v_i)$ (as defined in the real experiment $\mathbf{TamperInteract}_{\mathsf{A},\Pi,\mathsf{G}}(\mathbf{X}_1, \mathbf{X}_2, q)$) and $w_i = \mathsf{G}_{y^i}(v_i)$ (simulated by the simulator S), except with probability at most $(\delta + \epsilon)$. This can be demonstrated by leveraging two hybrid arguments:

In the first hybrid, we can show that the real $w_i = \mathsf{G}^{\Pi}_{\mathsf{Rec}(x_2, \alpha^i)}(v_i)$ (as defined in the real experiment $\mathbf{TamperInteract}_{\mathsf{A},\Pi,\mathsf{G}}(\mathbf{X}_1, \mathbf{X}_2, q)$) cannot be distinguished, with probability greater than δ, from an intermediate simulated $w_i = \mathsf{G}_{y^i}(v_i)$ where $(y^i, \alpha^i) = \mathsf{Gen}(x^i)$ for $(x_1^i, x_2^i) \leftarrow\!\!\$\ (\mathbf{X}_1, \mathbf{X}_2)$. This follows from the $(\mathcal{F}, \delta)$-pre-NM of the $(\mathcal{X}, m, k, \ell, t, \epsilon)$-fuzzy extractor, i.e., if $\mathsf{S}_{\mathsf{fuzzyExt}}(f_i)$ correctly returns same (which happens with probability at least $1 - \delta$), then these two scenarios are identically distributed. (see footnote 6)

In the second hybrid, we can show that, the intermediate simulated $w_i = \mathsf{G}_{y^i}(v_i)$ (for $(y^i, \alpha^i) = \mathsf{Gen}(x^i)$ and $(x_1^i, x_2^i) \leftarrow\!\!\$\ (\mathbf{X}_1, \mathbf{X}_2)$) cannot be distinguished, with probability greater than ϵ, from $w_i = \mathsf{G}_{y^i}(v_i)$ simulated by S (for $y^i \leftarrow\!\!\$\ \mathbf{U}_\ell$). This follows from the security of the $(\mathcal{X}, m, k, \ell, t, \epsilon)$-fuzzy extractor. Note that this second hybrid argument holds since $\mathbb{H}_\infty(\mathbf{X}_1) \geq m$ (by definition of (t, m)-pair of distributions) and the fact that x_2 (correlated to x_1) is not revealed to A.

Let $q_1 \leq q$ be the number of rounds in which $\mathsf{S}_{\mathsf{fuzzyExt}}$ (executed by S) outputs same, for some input $f_i \in \mathcal{F}$. By leveraging q hybrid arguments, the fact that S invokes the functionality $\mathsf{G}_{(\cdot)}(\cdot)$ on the same inputs $v_1, \ldots, v_q$ issued by the adversary A (trough execute commands), and the two hybrids described above, we have that $\mathbf{TamperInteract}_{\mathsf{A},\Pi,\mathsf{G}}(\mathbf{X}_1, \mathbf{X}_2, q)$ and $\mathbf{SimTamperInteract}_{\mathsf{A},\mathsf{S},\mathsf{G}}(q)$ are $(q_1 \cdot (\delta + \epsilon) + (q - q_1) \cdot \delta)$-close. This implies that $\mathbf{TamperInteract}_{\mathsf{A},\Pi,\mathsf{G}}(\mathbf{X}_1, \mathbf{X}_2, q)$ and $\mathbf{SimTamperInteract}_{\mathsf{A},\mathsf{S},\mathsf{G}}(q)$ are also $(q \cdot (\delta + \epsilon))$-close since $q_1 \leq q$ and, in turn, $(q_1 \cdot (\delta + \epsilon) + (q - q_1) \cdot \delta) \leq q \cdot (\delta + \epsilon)$. This concludes the proof. □

[6] Note that A is a valid adversary for the $(\mathcal{F}, \delta)$-pre-NM experiment since A is valid w.r.t. tamper-simulatability, i.e., $f_i \in \mathcal{F}$.

6 Conclusions

We have introduced a flavor of non-malleability for fuzzy extractors, which provides security guarantees even in case the helper string is subject to manipulations. Being weaker than robustness, there is hope that non-malleable fuzzy extractors exist in the plain model (even with information-theoretic security) for weak random sources with min-entropy $m = \omega(\log n)$. Our construction confirms this hope to be true for many interesting families of manipulations.

The main open problem left by our paper is to establish whether non-malleable fuzzy extractors exist against *arbitrary* manipulations in the plain model for weak random sources with min-entropy $m = \omega(\log n)$. Our construction fails in this setting as non-malleable codes are impossible against tampering attacks against all polynomial-time computable functions.[7] Such an impossibility may not apply to non-malleable extractors since the latter additionally take as input an unpredictable min-entropy source.

Another interesting direction for future research is that of combining non-malleability with additional properties of fuzzy extractors, such as reusability [5,13,16,17,22,55]. The latter means that a fuzzy extractor should remain secure even when the generation algorithm is run on multiple samples that are correlated in an adversarial manner. Yet another extension would be to consider *continuous* non-malleability [35,36], where the attacker can manipulate the same helper string multiple times. The latter would allow to improve our application by removing the need to re-generate the secret key after each invocation; however, even assuming a continuously non-malleable code, it is unclear how to extend the security proof of our construction.

Acknowledgements. The first author was supported by the Carlsberg Foundation under the Semper Ardens Research Project CF18-112 (BCM). The second author was supported by project SERICS (PE00000014) and by project PARTHENON (B53D23013000006), under the MUR National Recovery and Resilience Plan funded by the European Union - NextGenerationEU.

References

1. Aggarwal, D., Dodis, Y., Kazana, T., Obremski, M.: Non-malleable reductions and applications. In: Servedio, R.A., Rubinfeld, R. (eds.) 47th ACM STOC, pp. 459–468. ACM Press (2015)
2. Aggarwal, D., Dodis, Y., Lovett, S.: Non-malleable codes from additive combinatorics. In: Shmoys, D.B. (ed.) 46th ACM STOC, pp. 774–783. ACM Press
3. Aggarwal, D., Obremski, M.: A constant rate non-malleable code in the split-state model. In: 61st FOCS, pp. 1285–1294. IEEE Computer Society Press (2020)
4. Agrawal, S., Gupta, D., Maji, H.K., Pandey, O., Prabhakaran, M.: Explicit non-malleable codes against bit-wise tampering and permutations. In: Gennaro, R., Robshaw, M. (eds.) CRYPTO 2015. LNCS, vol. 9215, pp. 538–557. Springer, Heidelberg (2015). https://doi.org/10.1007/978-3-662-47989-6_26

[7] The reason is that an attacker in this setting can always decode the message, and re-encode a related value.

5. Alamélou, Q., et al.: Pseudoentropic isometries: a new framework for fuzzy extractor reusability. In: Kim, J., Ahn, G.J., Kim, S., Kim, Y., López, J., Kim, T. (eds.) ASIACCS 18, pp. 673–684. ACM Press (2018)
6. Apon, D., Cachet, C., Fuller, B., Hall, P., Liu, FH.: Nonmalleable digital lockers and robust fuzzy extractors in the plain model. In: Agrawal, S., Lin, D. (eds.) Advances in Cryptology – ASIACRYPT 2022. ASIACRYPT 2022. LNCS, vol. 13794. Springer, Cham (2022). https://doi.org/10.1007/978-3-031-22972-5_13
7. Ball, M., Dachman-Soled, D., Guo, S., Malkin, T., Tan, L.Y.: Non-malleable codes for small-depth circuits. In: Thorup, M. (ed.) 59th FOCS, pp. 826–837. IEEE Computer Society Press (2018)
8. Ball, M., Dachman-Soled, D., Kulkarni, M., Lin, H., Malkin, T.: Non-malleable codes against bounded polynomial time tampering. In: Ishai, Y., Rijmen, V. (eds.) EUROCRYPT 2019. LNCS, vol. 11476, pp. 501–530. Springer, Cham (2019). https://doi.org/10.1007/978-3-030-17653-2_17
9. Ball, M., Dachman-Soled, D., Kulkarni, M., Malkin, T.: Non-malleable codes for bounded depth, bounded fan-in circuits. In: Fischlin, M., Coron, J.-S. (eds.) EUROCRYPT 2016. LNCS, vol. 9666, pp. 881–908. Springer, Heidelberg (2016). https://doi.org/10.1007/978-3-662-49896-5_31
10. Ball, M., Dachman-Soled, D., Kulkarni, M., Malkin, T.: Non-malleable codes from average-case hardness: AC^0, decision trees, and streaming space-bounded tampering. In: Nielsen, J.B., Rijmen, V. (eds.) EUROCRYPT 2018. LNCS, vol. 10822, pp. 618–650. Springer, Cham (2018). https://doi.org/10.1007/978-3-319-78372-7_20
11. Ball, M., Guo, S., Wichs, D.: Non-malleable codes for decision trees. In: Boldyreva, A., Micciancio, D. (eds.) CRYPTO 2019. LNCS, vol. 11692, pp. 413–434. Springer, Cham (2019). https://doi.org/10.1007/978-3-030-26948-7_15
12. Bartusek, J., Ma, F., Zhandry, M.: The distinction between fixed and random generators in group-based assumptions. In: Boldyreva, A., Micciancio, D. (eds.) CRYPTO 2019. LNCS, vol. 11693, pp. 801–830. Springer, Cham (2019). https://doi.org/10.1007/978-3-030-26951-7_27
13. Boyen, X.: Reusable cryptographic fuzzy extractors. In: Atluri, V., Pfitzmann, B., McDaniel, P. (eds.) ACM CCS 2004, pp. 82–91. ACM Press (2004)
14. Boyen, X., Dodis, Y., Katz, J., Ostrovsky, R., Smith, A.: Secure remote authentication using biometric data. In: Cramer, R. (ed.) EUROCRYPT 2005. LNCS, vol. 3494, pp. 147–163. Springer, Heidelberg (2005). https://doi.org/10.1007/11426639_9
15. Buhan, I., Doumen, J., Hartel, P.H., Veldhuis, R.N.J.: Fuzzy extractors for continuous distributions. In: Bao, F., Miller, S. (eds.) ASIACCS 07, pp. 353–355. ACM Press (2007)
16. Canetti, R., Fuller, B., Paneth, O., Reyzin, L., Smith, A.: Reusable fuzzy extractors for low-entropy distributions. In: Fischlin, M., Coron, J.-S. (eds.) EUROCRYPT 2016. LNCS, vol. 9665, pp. 117–146. Springer, Heidelberg (2016). https://doi.org/10.1007/978-3-662-49890-3_5
17. Canetti, R., Fuller, B., Paneth, O., Reyzin, L., Smith, A.D.: Reusable fuzzy extractors for low-entropy distributions. J. Cryptol. **34**(1), 2 (2021)
18. Canetti, R., Pass, R., shelat, A.: Cryptography from sunspots: how to use an imperfect reference string. In: 48th FOCS, pp. 249–259. IEEE Computer Society Press
19. Chattopadhyay, E., Goyal, V., Li, X.: Non-malleable extractors and codes, with their many tampered extensions. In: Wichs, D., Mansour, Y. (eds.) 48th ACM STOC, pp. 285–298. ACM Press (2016)

20. Chattopadhyay, E., Li, X.: Non-malleable codes and extractors for small-depth circuits, and affine functions. In: Hatami, H., McKenzie, P., King, V. (eds.) 49th ACM STOC, pp. 1171–1184. ACM Press (2017)
21. Chattopadhyay, E., Zuckerman, D.: Non-malleable codes against constant split-state tampering. In: 55th FOCS, pp. 306–315. IEEE Computer Society Press
22. Cheon, J.H., Jeong, J., Kim, D., Lee, J.: A reusable fuzzy extractor with practical storage size: modifying Canetti *et al.*'s construction. In: Susilo, W., Yang, G. (eds.) ACISP 2018. LNCS, vol. 10946, pp. 28–44. Springer, Cham (2018). https://doi.org/10.1007/978-3-319-93638-3_3
23. Cheraghchi, M., Guruswami, V.: Capacity of non-malleable codes. In: Naor, M. (ed.) ITCS 2014, pp. 155–168. ACM (2014)
24. Cheraghchi, M., Guruswami, V.: Non-malleable coding against bit-wise and split-state tampering. In: Lindell, Y. (ed.) TCC 2014. LNCS, vol. 8349, pp. 440–464. Springer, Heidelberg (2014). https://doi.org/10.1007/978-3-642-54242-8_19
25. Cramer, R., Dodis, Y., Fehr, S., Padró, C., Wichs, D.: Detection of algebraic manipulation with applications to robust secret sharing and fuzzy extractors. In: Smart, N. (ed.) EUROCRYPT 2008. LNCS, vol. 4965, pp. 471–488. Springer, Heidelberg (2008). https://doi.org/10.1007/978-3-540-78967-3_27
26. Dachman-Soled, D., Komargodski, I., Pass, R.: Non-malleable codes for bounded parallel-time tampering. In: Malkin, T., Peikert, C. (eds.) CRYPTO 2021. LNCS, vol. 12827, pp. 535–565. Springer, Cham (2021). https://doi.org/10.1007/978-3-030-84252-9_18
27. Delvaux, J., Gu, D., Verbauwhede, I., Hiller, M., Yu, M.-D.M.: Efficient fuzzy extraction of PUF-induced secrets: theory and applications. In: Gierlichs, B., Poschmann, A.Y. (eds.) CHES 2016. LNCS, vol. 9813, pp. 412–431. Springer, Heidelberg (2016). https://doi.org/10.1007/978-3-662-53140-2_20
28. Dodis, Y., Katz, J., Reyzin, L., Smith, A.: Robust fuzzy extractors and authenticated key agreement from close secrets. In: Dwork, C. (ed.) CRYPTO 2006. LNCS, vol. 4117, pp. 232–250. Springer, Heidelberg (2006). https://doi.org/10.1007/11818175_14
29. Dodis, Y., Ostrovsky, R., Reyzin, L., Smith, A.D.: Fuzzy extractors: How to generate strong keys from biometrics and other noisy data. SIAM J. Comput. **38**(1), 97–139 (2008)
30. Dodis, Y., Reyzin, L., Smith, A.: Fuzzy extractors: how to generate strong keys from biometrics and other noisy data. In: Cachin, C., Camenisch, J.L. (eds.) EUROCRYPT 2004. LNCS, vol. 3027, pp. 523–540. Springer, Heidelberg (2004). https://doi.org/10.1007/978-3-540-24676-3_31
31. Dodis, Y., Wichs, D.: Non-malleable extractors and symmetric key cryptography from weak secrets. In: Mitzenmacher, M. (ed.) 41st ACM STOC, pp. 601–610. ACM Press (2009)
32. Dziembowski, S., Kazana, T., Obremski, M.: Non-malleable Codes from two-source extractors. In: Canetti, R., Garay, J.A. (eds.) CRYPTO 2013. LNCS, vol. 8043, pp. 239–257. Springer, Heidelberg (2013). https://doi.org/10.1007/978-3-642-40084-1_14
33. Dziembowski, S., Pietrzak, K., Wichs, D.: Non-Malleable Codes. In: Yao, A.C.C. (ed.) ICS 2010, pp. 434–452. Tsinghua University Press (2010)
34. Faust, S., Hostáková, K., Mukherjee, P., Venturi, D.: Non-malleable codes for space-bounded tampering. In: Katz, J., Shacham, H. (eds.) CRYPTO 2017. LNCS, vol. 10402, pp. 95–126. Springer, Cham (2017). https://doi.org/10.1007/978-3-319-63715-0_4

35. Faust, S., Mukherjee, P., Nielsen, J.B., Venturi, D.: Continuous non-malleable codes. In: Lindell, Y. (ed.) TCC 2014. LNCS, vol. 8349, pp. 465–488. Springer, Heidelberg (2014). https://doi.org/10.1007/978-3-642-54242-8_20
36. Faust, S., Mukherjee, P., Nielsen, J.B., Venturi, D.: Continuously non-malleable codes in the split-state model. J. Cryptol. **33**(4), 2034–2077 (2020)
37. Faust, S., Mukherjee, P., Venturi, D., Wichs, D.: Efficient non-malleable codes and key-derivation for poly-size tampering circuits. In: Nguyen, P.Q., Oswald, E. (eds.) EUROCRYPT 2014. LNCS, vol. 8441, pp. 111–128. Springer, Heidelberg (2014). https://doi.org/10.1007/978-3-642-55220-5_7
38. Feng, H., Tang, Q.: Computational robust (Fuzzy) extractors for CRS-dependent sources with minimal min-entropy. In: Nissim, K., Waters, B. (eds.) TCC 2021. LNCS, vol. 13043, pp. 689–717. Springer, Cham (2021). https://doi.org/10.1007/978-3-030-90453-1_24
39. Fuller, B., Meng, X., Reyzin, L.: Computational fuzzy extractors. In: Sako, K., Sarkar, P. (eds.) ASIACRYPT 2013. LNCS, vol. 8269, pp. 174–193. Springer, Heidelberg (2013). https://doi.org/10.1007/978-3-642-42033-7_10
40. Fuller, B., Peng, L.: Continuous-source fuzzy extractors: source uncertainty and insecurity. In: IEEE International Symposium on Information Theory, ISIT 2019, Paris, France, July 7-12, 2019, pp. 2952–2956. IEEE (2019)
41. Fuller, B., Reyzin, L., Smith, A.: When are fuzzy extractors possible? In: Cheon, J.H., Takagi, T. (eds.) ASIACRYPT 2016. LNCS, vol. 10031, pp. 277–306. Springer, Heidelberg (2016). https://doi.org/10.1007/978-3-662-53887-6_10
42. Fuller, B., Reyzin, L., Smith, A.D.: When are fuzzy extractors possible? IEEE Trans. Inf. Theory **66**(8), 5282–5298 (2020)
43. Gupta, D., Maji, H.K., Wang, M.: Explicit rate-1 non-malleable codes for local tampering. In: Boldyreva, A., Micciancio, D. (eds.) CRYPTO 2019. LNCS, vol. 11692, pp. 435–466. Springer, Cham (2019). https://doi.org/10.1007/978-3-030-26948-7_16
44. Islam, M.M., Safavi-Naini, R., Kneppers, M.: Scalable behavioral authentication. IEEE Access **9**, 43458–43473 (2021)
45. Jafargholi, Z., Wichs, D.: Tamper detection and continuous non-malleable codes. In: Dodis, Y., Nielsen, J.B. (eds.) TCC 2015. LNCS, vol. 9014, pp. 451–480. Springer, Heidelberg (2015). https://doi.org/10.1007/978-3-662-46494-6_19
46. Kanukurthi, B., Reyzin, L.: An improved robust fuzzy extractor. In: Ostrovsky, R., De Prisco, R., Visconti, I. (eds.) SCN 2008. LNCS, vol. 5229, pp. 156–171. Springer, Heidelberg (2008). https://doi.org/10.1007/978-3-540-85855-3_11
47. Kiayias, A., Liu, F.H., Tselekounis, Y.: Practical non-malleable codes from l-more extractable hash functions. In: Weippl, E.R., Katzenbeisser, S., Kruegel, C., Myers, A.C., Halevi, S. (eds.) ACM CCS 2016, pp. 1317–1328. ACM Press (2016)
48. Kiayias, A., Liu, F.-H., Tselekounis, Y.: Non-malleable codes for partial functions with manipulation detection. In: Shacham, H., Boldyreva, A. (eds.) CRYPTO 2018. LNCS, vol. 10993, pp. 577–607. Springer, Cham (2018). https://doi.org/10.1007/978-3-319-96878-0_20
49. Li, X.: Improved non-malleable extractors, non-malleable codes and independent source extractors. In: Hatami, H., McKenzie, P., King, V. (eds.) 49th ACM STOC, pp. 1144–1156. ACM Press (2017)
50. Nisan, N., Zuckerman, D.: Randomness is linear in space. J. Comput. Syst. Sci. **52**(1), 43–52 (1996)
51. Parente, V.P., van de Graaf, J.: A practical fuzzy extractor for continuous features. In: Nascimento, A.C.A., Barreto, P. (eds.) ICITS 2016. LNCS, vol. 10015, pp. 241–258. Springer, Cham (2016). https://doi.org/10.1007/978-3-319-49175-2_12

52. Rasmussen, P.M.R., Sahai, A.: Expander graphs are non-malleable codes. In: Kalai, Y.T., Smith, A.D., Wichs, D. (eds.) ITC 2020, pp. 6:1–6:10. Schloss Dagstuhl (Jun.)
53. Suh, G.E., Devadas, S.: Physical unclonable functions for device authentication and secret key generation. In: Proceedings of the 44th Design Automation Conference, DAC 2007, San Diego, CA, USA, June 4–8, 2007, pp. 9–14. IEEE (2007)
54. Verbitskiy, E.A., Tuyls, P., Obi, C., Schoenmakers, B., Skoric, B.: Key extraction from general non discrete signals. IEEE Trans. Inf. Forensics Secur. **5**(2), 269–279
55. Wen, Y., Liu, S.: Reusable fuzzy extractor from LWE. In: Susilo, W., Yang, G. (eds.) ACISP 2018. LNCS, vol. 10946, pp. 13–27. Springer, Cham (2018). https://doi.org/10.1007/978-3-319-93638-3_2
56. Wen, Y., Liu, S.: Robustly reusable fuzzy extractor from standard assumptions. In: Peyrin, T., Galbraith, S. (eds.) ASIACRYPT 2018. LNCS, vol. 11274, pp. 459–489. Springer, Cham (2018). https://doi.org/10.1007/978-3-030-03332-3_17
57. Wen, Y., Liu, S., Gu, D.: Generic constructions of robustly reusable fuzzy extractor. In: Lin, D., Sako, K. (eds.) PKC 2019. LNCS, vol. 11443, pp. 349–378. Springer, Cham (2019). https://doi.org/10.1007/978-3-030-17259-6_12
58. Wen, Y., Liu, S., Hu, Z., Han, S.: Computational robust fuzzy extractor. Comput. J. **61**(12), 1794–1805 (2018)
59. Woodage, J., Chatterjee, R., Dodis, Y., Juels, A., Ristenpart, T.: A new distribution-sensitive secure sketch and popularity-proportional hashing. In: Katz, J., Shacham, H. (eds.) CRYPTO 2017. LNCS, vol. 10403, pp. 682–710. Springer, Cham (2017). https://doi.org/10.1007/978-3-319-63697-9_23
60. Zhou, Y., Liu, S., Cui, N.: Computational fuzzy extractor from LWE. Theor. Comput. Sci. **945**, 113681 (2023)

Upgrading Fuzzy Extractors

Chloe Cachet[1(✉)], Ariel Hamlin[2], Maryam Rezapour[3], and Benjamin Fuller[3]

[1] Digital Technologies Research Center, National Research Council Canada, Montreal, QC, Canada
chloe.cachet@nrc-cnrc.gc.ca

[2] Khoury College of Computer Sciences, Northeastern University, Boston, MA, USA
a.hamlin@northeastern.edu

[3] University of Connecticut, Storrs, CT, USA
{maryam.rezapour,benjamin.fuller}@uconn.edu

Abstract. Fuzzy extractors derive stable keys from noisy sources non-interactively (Dodis et al., SIAM Journal of Computing 2008). Since their introduction, research has focused on two tasks: 1) showing security for as many distributions as possible and 2) providing stronger security guarantees including allowing one to enroll the same value multiple times (reusability), security against an active attacker (robustness), and preventing leakage about the enrolled value (privacy).

Given the need for progress on the basic fuzzy extractor primitive, it is prudent to seek generic mechanisms to transform a fuzzy extractor into one that is robust, private, and reusable so that it can inherit further improvements.

This work asks if one can generically upgrade fuzzy extractors to achieve robustness, privacy, and reusability. We show positive and negative results: we show upgrades for robustness and privacy, but we provide a negative result on reuse.

1. We upgrade (private) fuzzy extractors to be robust under weaker assumptions than previously known in the common reference string model.
2. We show a generic upgrade for a private fuzzy extractor using multi-bit compute and compare (MBCC) obfuscation (Wichs and Zirdelis, FOCS 2017) that requires less entropy than prior work.
3. We show one cannot arbitrarily compose private fuzzy extractors. In particular, we show that assuming MBCC obfuscation and collision-resistant hash functions, there does not exist a private fuzzy extractor secure against unpredictable auxiliary inputs, strengthening a negative result of Brzuska et al. (Crypto 2014).

Keywords: Fuzzy extractors · obfuscation · biometrics · key derivation

1 Introduction

Fuzzy extractors [1–3,7,16,19,23–25,30,31,33–35,40,43,44,46] derive stable keys from noisy sources. They are used on devices to derive keys from

C. Cachet—Most work done while at the University of Connecticut.

C. Pöpper and L. Batina (Eds.): ACNS 2024, LNCS 14583, pp. 156–182, 2024.
https://doi.org/10.1007/978-3-031-54770-6_7

biometrics, physical unclonable functions and quantum information. They also are used in interactive protocols such as distributed key agreement and password-authenticated key exchange. [6,10,11,14,20,22,23,27,28]. A fuzzy extractor is a pair of algorithms called generate (Gen) and reproduce (Rep) with two properties:

Correctness For all $w, w' \in \mathcal{M}$ such that $\mathsf{dist}(w, w') \leq t$, let $(\mathsf{key}, \mathsf{pub}) \leftarrow \mathsf{Gen}(w)$ where pub is a public *helper* value used to provide correctness. Then it should be the case that $\mathsf{key} \leftarrow \mathsf{Rep}(w', \mathsf{pub})$.

Security Let W be a probability distribution of noisy values. For $(\mathsf{key}, \mathsf{pub}) \leftarrow \mathsf{Gen}(W)$ it should be the case that key is indistinguishable from uniform even knowing pub.

Security is defined relative to the statistics of the probability distribution. The most common and useful of which is fuzzy min-entropy [34,35,48] which measures the adversary's success when provided with the functionality of reproduce. For security to be possible, it must be the case that a negligible fraction of the weight of W lies within any ball of radius t. Fuzzy min-entropy measures the adversary's success when providing the fixed "best" point w^* to the reproduce functionality. Even after 25 years of research, the design of fuzzy extractors for distributions with fuzzy min-entropy is an unsettled problem with advancements yet to be made.

There are constructions for distributions with high entropy, where bits are independent, or display additional statistical properties (see [19] for an overview of considered properties). There are two known methods to build a fuzzy extractor for all such distributions, using virtual grey box obfuscation for NC1 evasive circuits [9][1] or with a new subset-product assumption [36]. Both of these assumptions require additional study before deployment.

Fuzzy extractor security is also insufficient for many applications. There are three primary augmentations to the definition that exist in the literature:

Reusability [12] One can enroll the noisy source multiple times with different devices. Crucially, the multiple enrollments are subject to noise. In prior work [12,16], this noise is controlled by an adversary.

Robustness [13] If an attacker modifies pub to a related value pub′, this behavior is detectable. That is, $\mathsf{Rep}(w', \mathsf{pub}')$ should only output the original key or $\perp$.

Privacy [26] Privacy ensures no information is leaked about the enrolled value. More specifically, it ensures that no predicate of the enrollment value can be guessed better after seeing pub.

Table 1 summarizes prior constructions of fuzzy extractors with at least one of these additional properties. No previous construction that is reusable or robust supports all distributions with fuzzy min-entropy. The prior gray-box obfuscation [9] and subset product constructions [36] are obfuscations of the

[1] Virtual gray box obfuscation of all evasive programs implies virtual gray box obfuscation for all programs [4]. Virtual gray box and virtual black box obfuscation are equivalent in the distributional setting for evasive circuit families [9].

Table 1. Previous constructions of fuzzy extractors that are reusable, robust, or private. See Demarest, Fuller, and Russell [19] for descriptions of distributional properties. "High entropy" is used when the construction relies on an information-theoretic error correction component. Such constructions usually require the input source W to have entropy of at least $h_2(t/n)$, see [16, Proposition 1]. For Boyen's [12] work, the RO model is only required for insider security, when keys are seen from other enrollments.

Scheme	Model	Distribution	Reuse	Robust	Private
[12]	RO*	High entropy	Shift	✓	✗
[26]	Plain	High entropy	✗	✗	✓
[16]		Avg. Subsets Entropy	Correlation	✗	✗
[3]		Independent	Shift	✗	✗
[9]	Plain	All	✗	✗	✓
[46]	CRS	High entropy	Shift	✗	✗
[44]	CRS	High entropy	Shift	✓	✗
[45]	CRS	High entropy	Shift	✓	✗
[36]		All	✗	✗	✓
[19]		MIPURS	Correlation	✗	✗

fuzzy extractor functionality; they are by definition private. Given the unsettled nature of constructing fuzzy extractors for distributions with fuzzy min-entropy, it is prudent to seek generic mechanisms to transform a fuzzy extractor into a reusable, robust, and private one.

1.1 Our Contribution

We present three contributions, 1) an upgrade for privacy 2) an upgrade for robustness that preserves privacy, and 3) a negative result for reusability.

Privacy. We show how to construct a private fuzzy extractor from either a secure sketch or a non-private fuzzy extractor. Our contribution is a strengthening of the previous upgrade from a secure sketch to a private secure sketch using multi-bit compute and compare obfuscation (MBCC) [47]. We support a wider family of distributions with lower entropy than prior work [47]. We first introduce Wichs and Zirdelis' [47] construction and then the advantages of our construction.

Both our work and prior work is based on the notion of a secure sketch. A secure sketch recovers the original value w rather than deriving a random key. It is a pair of algorithms $(\mathsf{Sketch}, \mathsf{Rec})$ such that

Correctness For all $w, w' \in \mathcal{M}$ such that $\mathsf{dist}(w, w') \leq t$, then $\mathsf{Rec}(w', \mathsf{Sketch}(w)) = w$.

Security Let W be a probability distribution of noisy values. Given $\mathsf{Sketch}(W)$, W has high min-entropy. (One can also use computational notions of security using pseudoentropy or unpredictability [32].)

Wichs and Zirdelis use MBCC program obfuscation at the core of their scheme. MBCC program has three values f, y, z. On input x it computes $f(x)$, if $f(x) = y$ then it outputs z otherwise it outputs $\perp$. In their prior construction they showed how to obfuscate a family of such programs where y has pseudoentropy [41] conditioned on f and z. They show how to upgrade a secure sketch into a private one by obfuscating $h(\mathsf{Rec}(\cdot, ss))$ where h is a pairwise independent hash function. They have to choose the output length of the hash function based on the entropy of the input, which keeps the construction from working for all distributions with sufficient entropy for the MBCC obfuscation to be secure.

In our work, we use a secure sketch to construct a private fuzzy extractor to directly analyze the construction without h, making the same construction work for any distribution where the secure sketch retains (a super-logarithmic amount of) min-entropy. By removing the hash function, we also reduce the amount of entropy required as one doesn't "leak" the hash value in the security analysis. We also show a similar upgrade from fuzzy extractors to private fuzzy extractors. There are stronger negative results on constructing secure sketches [24,30,34], so direct constructions from fuzzy extractors may yield better parameters.

The privacy definition of Wichs and Zirdelis [47] considers predicting predicates of the source w in contrast to Dodis and Smith [26] who consider functions. We call this weak-privacy to distinguish from Dodis and Smith's definition. Restriction to predicates is standard in the obfuscation literature as an obfuscation itself is a function that a simulator cannot hope to reproduce.

Robustness. We provide a simpler construction of robust fuzzy extractors than prior work. Our result only requires the existence of true simulation extractable NIZKs [21]. Prior work of Feng and Tang [29] also required the existence of extremely lossy functions or ELFs [49].[2] Additionally, our result shows that this transform preserves privacy, which was not considered by any prior robustness upgrade.

Reuse. One cannot expect reuse of arbitrary fuzzy extractors. Each value of pub can leak a constant fraction of the entropy in the source w while remaining secure. However, a (weakly) private fuzzy extractor cannot "leak" on input w. There are multiple private fuzzy extractors (see Table 1) that are not known to be reusable. The most natural approach for a reusable private fuzzy extractor is to construct a fuzzy extractor for all sources W that are unpredictable in the presence of auxiliary input available to the adversary. The security analysis would follow by including other enrollments of the same source in the auxiliary input.

We show this proof technique is not possible. Namely, we show that the existence of MBCC obfuscation and collision-resistant hash functions imply that one cannot construct private fuzzy extractors for all W that are unpredictable conditioned on auxiliary input. We do this by showing that auxiliary-input secure

[2] Feng and Tang's primary goal was to construct robust extractors, not robust fuzzy extractors. Unlike Feng and Tang we work in the standard CRS model, they allow the source W to depend on the CRS.

Table 2. Previous upgrades of fuzzy extractors. If there is an ✗ in the Any FE. column the construction requires the use of the syndrome secure sketch. As mentioned in Table 1 this places a lower bound on entropy of the distribution W. CRS* is the CRS model where the distribution W being enrolled can depend on the CRS. Err. column describes how many errors the underlying primitive is required to correct. Multiple robust constructions require a secure sketch or fuzzy extractor that corrects $2t$ errors to be able to extract a value from the adversary.

Upgrade	Scheme	Model	Any FE	Tools	Err
Reusability	[1]	Plain	✓	composable DL [8]	t
Robustness	[13]	RO	✗	RO	t
	[18]	CRS	✗	IT	2t
	[22]	Plain	✗	IT	t
	[29]	CRS*	✓	ELFS [49] + true sim. extract NIZK [21]	2t
	[2]	Plain	✗	comp.* DL [5, Assumption 3]+ true sim. extract NIZK [21]	2t
	This work	CRS	✓	true sim. extract NIZK [21]	2t
Private	[47]	Plain	✓	LWE + ELFS [49]	t
	This work	Plain	✓	LWE + ELFS [49]	t

digital lockers cannot be secure in the presence of MBCC obfuscation. We then show that a variant of private fuzzy extractors imply digital lockers. Brzuska et al. [15] proved an analogous result where auxiliary-input secure digital lockers were incompatible with indistinguishability obfuscation [37,38].[3] Since MBCC obfuscation implies auxiliary-input secure digital lockers, this shows MBCC obfuscation cannot be safely composed either.

1.2 Related Work

Reusability. Alamelou et al. [1] show how to create reuse for the Hamming and set difference metrics when the source has symbols that are super polynomial size. However, most natural sources consider small, often binary, alphabets. Alamelou et al.'s technique cannot work in this setting.[4] We note this technique is applied before the source is input to the fuzzy extractor.

[3] Their actual result showed the impossibility of auxiliary input universal computational extractors. This object implies auxiliary-input secure digital lockers.

[4] Alamelou et al. use a *pseudoentropic isometry* that maps points to a new metric space while 1) preserving distance and 2) the value in the new metric space doesn't reveal the value on the original metric space. For the Hamming metric, the only such transforms are equivalent to a per-symbol permutation and a permutation of symbol order. Such a transform can only be one-way if symbols are super-polynomial size. No pseudoentropic isometric exists for the Hamming metric with polynomial size symbols.

Robustness. In the random oracle model, for a fuzzy extractor with output $\mathsf{key}, \mathsf{pub}$ and random oracle h one can split $\mathsf{key} = (\mathsf{key}_1, \mathsf{key}_2)$ and include $h(\mathsf{key}_2 || \mathsf{pub})$ as part of pub. As needed the random oracle can expand the amount of available keying material.[5] Without resorting to random oracles, one can use algebraic manipulation detection codes [18] and pairwise independent hashes as one-time MACs. In the CRS model, Feng and Tang [29] codify the security required from the MAC, and show how to generically lift a secure sketch into a robust fuzzy extractor using a primitive they call a κ-MAC that is secure for low-entropy keys that can be manipulated by an adversary. This upgrade is agnostic in the underlying secure sketch. Apon et al. [2] propose a standard model upgrade that requires the syndrome secure sketch.

Privacy. For privacy, if one has a secure sketch that retains superlogarithmic entropy, one can upgrade it to a private secure sketch using multi-bit compute and compare (MBCC) obfuscation [47]. Roughly, MBCC allows one to compute a function on some input and compare the result with a target value. If the output of the function matches the target, the MBCC circuit returns a fixed value.

1.3 Discussion and Future Work

The privacy upgrade is this work is not yet of practical efficiency. MBCC obfuscation has nearly as much overhead as indistinguishability obfuscation. A natural question is whether an upgrade that preserves privacy must use a type of obfuscation and if so, can one use a obfuscation of a weaker class of obfuscation?

Our negative result for reuse does leave open the possibility of upgrading fuzzy extractors to be reusable. It does not rule out techniques that transform w to a new metric space [1]. Furthermore, one may able to use a more fine grained argument for reuse. As a reminder, our negative result only rules out private fuzzy extractors secure in the presence of unpredictable auxiliary input. One may be able to sidestep the result by only showing security when the auxiliary input is a fuzzy extractor enrollment. We tried to extend our negative result to this setting but were not successful.

Organization. The rest of this work is organized as follows: Sect. 2 covers mathematical preliminaries, Sect. 3 shows our privacy upgrade, Sect. 4 covers robustness, and Sect. 5 covers reuse. Appendix A shows that weak-privacy does not imply fuzzy extractor security and Appendix B shows that a composable MBCC obfuscation would yield a reusable upgrade (but is ruled out by our negative result).

2 Preliminaries

Let λ be the security parameter throughout this paper. A function $\mathsf{ngl}(\lambda)$ is negligible in λ if for all $a \in \mathbb{Z}^+$ we have $\mathsf{ngl}(\lambda) = o(\frac{1}{\lambda^a})$. A function $\mathsf{poly}(\lambda)$ is

[5] Boyen [13] considers a secure sketch, the same idea works for a fuzzy extractor.

polynomial in λ if there exists some constant $a \in \mathbb{Z}^+$ such that $\mathsf{poly}(\lambda) = O(\lambda^a)$. We use $\mathsf{poly}(\lambda)$ and $\mathsf{ngl}(\lambda)$ to denote unspecified functions that are polynomial and negligible in λ, respectively. The notation id is used to denote the identity function: $\forall x, \mathsf{id}(x) = x$. For some $n \in \mathbb{N}$, $[n]$ denotes the set $\{1, \cdots, n\}$. Let $x \xleftarrow{\$} S$ denote sampling x uniformly at random from the finite set S. We say that distributions X and Y are computationally indistinguishable if for all PPT (in λ) adversaries $\mathcal{A}$, $|\Pr[\mathcal{A}(X) = 1] - \Pr[\mathcal{A}(Y) = 1]| \leq \mathsf{ngl}(\lambda)$.

2.1 Entropy Definitions

Definition 1 (Min-entropy). *For a discrete random variable X, the* min-entropy *of X is*

$$\mathrm{H}_\infty(X) = -\log\left(\max_x \Pr[X = x]\right)$$

Definition 2 (Average conditional min-entropy [24]). *For a pair of discrete random variables X, Y, the average min-entropy of $X|Y$ is*

$$\tilde{\mathrm{H}}_\infty(X \mid Y) = -\log\left(\mathit{Exp}_{y \in Y}\left(2^{-\mathrm{H}_\infty(X|Y)}\right)\right).$$

Definition 3 (Conditional HILL entropy [41,42]). *Let X, Y be ensembles of jointly distributed random variables. The conditional pseudo-entropy of X conditioned on Y, denoted as $H_{\mathsf{HILL}}(X \mid Y)$, is greater or equal to $\ell(\lambda)$ if there exists some ensemble X' such that (X, Y) and (X', Y) are computationally indistinguishable and $\mathrm{H}_\infty(X' \mid Y) \geq \ell(\lambda)$.*

2.2 Obfuscation Definitions

Definition 4 (Distributional Virtual Black Box (dist-VBB) obfuscation). *Let $\mathcal{P}$ be a family of programs and Obf be a PPT algorithm that takes as input a program $P \in \mathcal{P}$, a security parameter $\lambda \in \mathbb{N}$ and outputs a program $\tilde{P} \leftarrow \mathsf{Obf}(1^\lambda, P)$. Let $\mathcal{D}$ be a class of distribution ensembles $D = \{D_\lambda\}_{\lambda \in \mathbb{N}}$ which samples $(P, \mathsf{aux}) \leftarrow D_\lambda$ with $P \in \mathcal{P}$. Then Obf is an obfuscator for the distribution class $\mathcal{D}$ over the program family $\mathcal{P}$ if it satisfies the following:*

- ***Functionality preserving:*** *For all $P \in \mathcal{P}$ and for all inputs $x \in \{0,1\}^n$, we have*
$$\Pr[P(x) = \tilde{P}(x)] \geq 1 - \mathsf{ngl}(\lambda)$$
- ***Polynomial slowdown:*** *For all sufficiently large $\lambda \in \mathbb{N}$ and for all $P \in \mathcal{P}_\lambda$,*
$$|\tilde{P}| \leq \mathsf{poly}(|P|)$$
- ***Distributional Virtual Black-Box:*** *For every PPT adversary $\mathcal{A}$ there exists a non-uniform polynomial size simulator Sim, such that for every distribution ensemble $D = \{D_\lambda\} \in \mathcal{D}$, and every predicate $\phi : \mathcal{P} \to \{0,1\}$, we have*

$$\left| \Pr_{(P,\mathsf{aux})\leftarrow D_\lambda}[\mathcal{A}(\mathsf{Obf}(1^\lambda, P), \mathsf{aux}) = \phi(P)] - \Pr_{(P,\mathsf{aux})\leftarrow D_\lambda}[\mathsf{Sim}^P(1^\lambda, 1^{|P|}, \mathsf{aux}) = \phi(P)] \right| \leq \mathsf{ngl}(\lambda)$$

where Sim^P *has black-box access to the program* P.

Wichs and Zirdelis [47] build a dist-VBB obfuscator for α-pseudo entropy distributions (see Definition 6) over multi-bit-compute-and-compare circuits.[6]

Definition 5 (Multi-bit compute-and-compare circuit). *Let* $n, \ell, \kappa \in \mathbb{N}$ *and consider a function* $f : \{0,1\}^n \to \{0,1\}^\ell$, *a target value* $y \in \{0,1\}^\ell$ *and some value* $z \in \{0,1\}^\kappa$. *A multi-bit compute-and-compare circuit is defined for all inputs* $x \in \{0,1\}^n$ *as*

$$\mathsf{MBCC}_{f,y,z}(x) = \begin{cases} z & \text{if } f(x) = y \\ \bot & \text{otherwise.} \end{cases}$$

Wichs and Zirdelis [47] also define α-pseudo entropy, a specific case of HILL entropy:

Definition 6 (α-pseudo entropy). *For function* $\alpha(\lambda)$, *the class of* α-*pseudo-entropy distributions consists of ensembles* $D = \{D_\lambda\}$ *such that* $(\mathsf{MBCC}[f, y, z], \mathsf{aux}) \leftarrow D_\lambda$ *satisfies* $H_{\mathsf{HILL}}(y \mid f, z, \mathsf{aux}) \geq \alpha(\lambda)$.

2.3 Fuzzy Extractors

Fuzzy extractors allow to generate stable cryptographic keys from noisy sources. We focus on computational fuzzy extractors.

Definition 7 (Computational Fuzzy Extractor [31,32]**).** *An* $(\mathcal{M}, \mathcal{W}, \ell, t, \epsilon)$-*fuzzy extractor with error* δ *is a pair of PPT algorithms* $(\mathsf{Gen}, \mathsf{Rep})$ *where for all* $w, w' \in \mathcal{M}$,

- $(\mathsf{key}, \mathsf{pub}) \leftarrow \mathsf{Gen}(w)$, *where* $\mathsf{key} \in \{0,1\}^\ell$ *and* $\mathsf{pub} \in \{0,1\}^*$
- $\mathsf{key}' \leftarrow \mathsf{Rep}(\mathsf{pub}, w')$

the following properties are true:

1. ***Correctness*** *: For all* $w, w' \in \mathcal{M}$ *such that* $\mathsf{dist}(w, w') \leq t$,

$$\Pr\left[\mathsf{key}' = \mathsf{key} \;\middle|\; (\mathsf{key}, \mathsf{pub}) \leftarrow \mathsf{Gen}(w), \mathsf{key}' \leftarrow \mathsf{Rep}(\mathsf{pub}, w')\right] \geq 1 - \delta$$

2. ***Security*** *: For any PPT distinguisher* $\mathcal{A}$ *and distribution* $W \in \mathcal{W}$,

$$|\Pr[\mathcal{A}(\mathsf{key}, \mathsf{pub}) = 1] - \Pr[\mathcal{A}(U_\ell, \mathsf{pub}) = 1]| \leq \epsilon$$

where $(\mathsf{key}, \mathsf{pub}) \leftarrow \mathsf{Gen}(W)$ *and* U_ℓ *is a uniformly distributed random variable over* $\{0,1\}^\ell$.

[6] In an independent and concurrent work, Goyal et al. [39] proposed a similar object they called *lockable obfuscation*.

3 Weakly-Private Fuzzy Extractors

Fuzzy extractor security does not prevent leaking information about the value w, called a *template*. For example, consider a fuzzy extractor where the public value leaks a random bit of the template. This can be problematic, especially if the biometric source is used in different contexts. Preventing such leakage, although not mandatory to achieve fuzzy extractor security, is thus desirable. Constructions that prevent such leakage are said to be *private* [26]. We adapt Wichs and Zirdelis [47] privacy definition for secure sketches to fuzzy extractors, we call this weak privacy. This definition differs from Dodis and Smith's [26] in that the adversary is restricted to predicting predicates about the value W (in place of general functions). We start by introducing the definition of a weakly private fuzzy extractor.

Definition 8 (Weakly Private Fuzzy Extractor). *Let* $\mathsf{FE} = (\mathsf{Gen}, \mathsf{Rep})$ *satisfy the correctness condition of Definition 7 for parameters* t *and* δ*. We say that* FE *is* η*-weakly-private if for all adversary* $\mathcal{A}$*, there exists a simulator* Sim *such that for every source* W *over* $\mathcal{W}$ *and every predicate* $\phi : \{0,1\}^* \to \{0,1\}$*, we have*

$$\Big| \Pr[\mathcal{A}(\mathsf{pub}, \mathsf{key}) = \phi(W) \mid (\mathsf{key}, \mathsf{pub}) \leftarrow \mathsf{FE.Gen}(W)] - \Pr[\mathsf{Sim}(1^\lambda, 1^{|\mathsf{pub}|}, 1^{|\mathsf{key}|}) = \phi(W)] \Big| \leq \eta$$

Fuzzy extractors were originally built following a *sketch-then-extract* approach. First, a secure sketch [25] is used to recover the enrolled w from a close value w', then a randomness extractor is used to derive the secret key. We add the definition for secure sketches:

Definition 9 (Secure sketch). *Let* λ *be a security parameter. Let* $\mathcal{W} = \mathcal{W}_\lambda$ *be a family of random variables over the metric space* $(\mathcal{M}, \mathsf{dist}) = (\mathcal{M}_\lambda, \mathsf{dist}_\lambda)$*. Then* $(\mathsf{Sketch}, \mathsf{Rec})$ *is a* $(\mathcal{M}, \mathcal{W}, \ell, t, \delta)$*-secure sketch if the following hold:*

- ***Correctness:*** *For all* $w, w' \in \mathcal{M}$ *such that* $\mathsf{dist}(w, w') \leq t$*,*

$$\Pr[\mathsf{Rec}(w', \mathsf{Sketch}(w)) = w] \geq 1 - \delta.$$

- ***Security:*** *For all distributions* $W \in \mathcal{W}$ *it is true that*

$$H_\infty(W \mid \mathsf{Sketch}(W)) \geq \ell.$$

We propose two weakly private fuzzy extractors constructions using dist-VBB obfuscation for multi-bit-compute-and-compare (MBCC) circuits. The first construction builds on a non-private fuzzy extractor whereas the second builds on a non-private secure sketch.

Intuitively, we can build weakly private fuzzy extractors as follows: we first build an MBCC circuit for function $f_{w,y,t}$ that outputs target value y on input w'

only when $\mathsf{dist}(w, w') \leq t$ and we set the output value z to be sampled uniformly at random. We then set pub to be the obfuscated MBCC program and key to be z. Note that in this case, since z is sampled independently from all other values, the entropy requirement for the MBCC circuit to be obfuscable can be simplified to

$$H_{\mathsf{HILL}}(y \mid f, \mathsf{aux}) \geq \alpha.$$

3.1 Weakly Private FE from FE and MBCC Obfuscation

Our first construction builds weakly-private fuzzy extractors from non-private fuzzy extractors and MBCC obfuscation.

Construction 1 (Weakly Private FE from MBCC obfuscation and FE). *Let* FE *be an* $(\mathcal{M}, \mathcal{W}, \ell, t, s, \epsilon)$*-fuzzy extractor and* Obf *be an obfuscator for* ℓ*-pseudo-entropy distributions over multi-bit compute-and-compare circuits. We can build an* $(\mathcal{M}, \mathcal{W}, \kappa, t, s, \epsilon)$*-fuzzy extractor* PFE *as follows:*

- $(\mathsf{key}', \mathsf{pub}') \leftarrow \mathsf{PFE.Gen}(w)$*:*
  1. *Compute* $(\mathsf{key}, \mathsf{pub}) \leftarrow \mathsf{FE.Gen}(w)$.
  2. *Sample* $\mathsf{key}' \xleftarrow{\$} \{0, 1\}^\kappa$.
  3. *Define the circuit* $f_{\mathsf{pub}}(\cdot) := \mathsf{FE.Rep}(\cdot, \mathsf{pub})$.
  4. *Compute* $\mathsf{pub}' \leftarrow \mathsf{Obf}(1^\lambda, \mathsf{MBCC}_{f_{\mathsf{pub}}, \mathsf{key}, \mathsf{key}'})$.
  5. *Output* $(\mathsf{key}', \mathsf{pub}')$.
- $\mathsf{key}' \leftarrow \mathsf{PFE.Rep}(\mathsf{pub}', w')$*: Interpret* pub' *as an obfuscated program and return* $\mathsf{key}' \leftarrow \mathsf{pub}'(w')$.

Theorem 1. *Construction 1 is a secure and weakly-private* $(\mathcal{M}, \mathcal{W}, \kappa, t, s, \epsilon)$*-fuzzy extractor.*

Proof (Theorem 1).

Correctness: Recall that pub' is an obfuscated MBCC circuit such that

$$\begin{aligned}
\mathsf{pub}'(w') &= \mathsf{Obf}(1^\lambda, \mathsf{MBCC}_{f_{\mathsf{pub}}, \mathsf{key}, \mathsf{key}'})(w') \\
&= \mathsf{MBCC}_{f_{\mathsf{pub}}, \mathsf{key}, \mathsf{key}'}(w') \\
&= \begin{cases} \mathsf{key}' & \text{if } f_{\mathsf{pub}}(w') = \mathsf{key} \\ \perp & \text{otherwise.} \end{cases} \\
&= \begin{cases} \mathsf{key}' & \text{if } \mathsf{FE.Rep}(w', \mathsf{pub}) = \mathsf{key} \\ \perp & \text{otherwise.} \end{cases}
\end{aligned}$$

Then since FE is a fuzzy extractor, it is true that

$$\begin{aligned}
&\Pr\left[\mathsf{PFE.Rep}(\mathsf{pub}', w') = \mathsf{key}' \;\middle|\; (\mathsf{pub}', \mathsf{key}') \leftarrow \mathsf{PFE.Gen}(w) \text{ and } \mathsf{dist}(w, w') \leq t\right] \\
&= \Pr\left[\mathsf{FE.Rep}(\mathsf{pub}, w') = \mathsf{key} \mid (\mathsf{pub}, \mathsf{key}) \leftarrow \mathsf{FE.Gen}(w) \text{ and } \mathsf{dist}(w, w') \leq t\right] \\
&\geq 1 - \delta
\end{aligned}$$

and PFE is thus correct.

Security: We proceed by contradiction. Suppose PFE is not a secure fuzzy extractor, then there exists some PPT adversary $\mathcal{A}$ and polynomial $p(\lambda)$ such that

$$\left|\Pr[\mathcal{A}(\mathsf{key}', \mathsf{pub}') = 1] - \Pr[\mathcal{A}(U_\kappa, \mathsf{pub}') = 1]\right| > 1/p(\lambda)$$

where $(\mathsf{key}', \mathsf{pub}') \leftarrow \mathsf{PFE.Gen}(W)$ and $U_\kappa \xleftarrow{\$} \{0,1\}^\kappa$. Now note that $\mathsf{pub}' = \mathsf{Obf}(1^\lambda, \mathsf{MBCC}_{f_{\mathsf{pub}}, \mathsf{key}, \mathsf{key}'})$ is distributional VBB secure. Define $r(\lambda) = 3p(\lambda)$ and let Sim be the simulator of $\mathcal{A}$ for polynomial $r(\lambda)$. Then we have

$$\left|\Pr[\mathcal{A}(\mathsf{pub}', \mathsf{key}) = 1] - \Pr[\mathsf{Sim}^{\mathsf{pub}'}(1^\lambda, 1^{|\mathsf{pub}'|}, \mathsf{key}) = 1]\right| \leq \frac{1}{3p(\lambda)}. \tag{1}$$

Note that the above is also true if key is replaced by U_κ, a uniform random variable over $\{0,1\}^\kappa$. In other words, we have

$$\left|\Pr[\mathcal{A}(\mathsf{pub}', U_\kappa) = 1] - \Pr[\mathsf{Sim}^{\mathsf{pub}'}(1^\lambda, 1^{|\mathsf{pub}'|}, U_\kappa) = 1]\right| \leq \frac{1}{3p(\lambda)}. \tag{2}$$

We adapt Canetti et al.'s lemma [16, Lemma 2]:

Lemma 1. *Let U_κ denote the uniform distribution over $\{0,1\}^\kappa$, then*

$$\begin{aligned}&\Big|\Pr[\mathsf{Sim}^{\mathsf{MBCC}[\mathsf{Rep}_{\mathsf{pub}}, \mathsf{key}, \mathsf{key}']}(1^\lambda, \left|\mathsf{MBCC}[\mathsf{Rep}_{\mathsf{pub}}, \mathsf{key}, \mathsf{key}']\right|, \mathsf{key}') = 1]\\ &- \Pr[\mathsf{Sim}^{\mathsf{MBCC}[\mathsf{Rep}_{\mathsf{pub}}, \mathsf{key}, \mathsf{key}']}(1^\lambda, \left|\mathsf{MBCC}[\mathsf{Rep}_{\mathsf{pub}}, \mathsf{key}, \mathsf{key}']\right|, U_\kappa) = 1]\Big|\\ &\leq \frac{1}{3p(\lambda)}\end{aligned}$$

Proof (Lemma 1). Fix any $u \in \{0,1\}^\kappa$, the lemma will follow by averaging over all u. The information about whether the key value, denoted V, is key or u can only be obtained by Sim through the query responses. First, we modify Sim to quit immediately when it gets a response not equal to $\perp$. Such Sim is equally successful at distinguishing between key and u since the first non-$\perp$ response tells Sim if its input is equal to key. Subsequent responses add nothing to this knowledge. Since Sim can make at most q queries, there are $q+1$ possible values for the view of Sim on a given input. Of those, q views consist of some number of non-$\perp$ responses followed by a $\perp$ response, and one view consists of all q responses equal to $\perp$. Then by [25, Lemma 2.2b],

$$\begin{aligned}\tilde{H}_\infty(V|View(\mathsf{Sim}), \mathsf{aux}) &\geq \tilde{H}_\infty(V) - \log(q+1)\\ &\geq \alpha - \log(q+1).\end{aligned}$$

where $\mathsf{aux} = \left(|\mathsf{MBCC}[\mathsf{Rep}_{\mathsf{pub}}, \mathsf{key}, \mathsf{key}']|\right)$.

Thus, at each query, the probability that Sim gets a non-$\perp$ response and guesses V is at most $(q+1)/2^\alpha$. Since there are q queries of Sim, the overall probability is at most $q(q+1)/2^\alpha$. Then since 2^α is negligible in λ, there exists some λ_0 such that for all $\lambda \geq \lambda_0$, $q(q+1)/2^\alpha \leq 1/(3p(\lambda))$.

We know continue the proof of Theorem 1, from Lemma 1, we have

$$\big| \Pr[\mathsf{Sim}^{\mathsf{pub}'}(1^\lambda, 1^{|\mathsf{pub}'|}, \mathsf{key}') = 1] - \Pr[\mathsf{Sim}^{\mathsf{pub}'}(1^\lambda, 1^{|\mathsf{pub}'|}, U_\kappa) = 1]\big| \leq \frac{1}{3p(\lambda)}$$

Using the triangle inequality on Eqs. 1, 2 and 3 we obtain

$$\big|\ \Pr[\mathcal{A}(\mathsf{pub}', \mathsf{key}') = 1] - \Pr[\mathcal{A}(\mathsf{pub}', U_\kappa) = 1]\ \big| \leq \frac{1}{p(\lambda)}$$

which is a contradiction and ends the proof of security.

Weak Privacy: Let FE be an $(\mathcal{M}, \mathcal{W}, \ell, t, \epsilon)$-computational fuzzy extractor. Consider random variables W, aux, and U_ℓ, the uniform distribution over ℓ bit strings, and $(\mathsf{key}, \mathsf{pub}) \leftarrow \mathsf{FE.Gen}(W)$. Then by definition, for any PPT adversary $\mathcal{A}$, we have

$$|\Pr[\mathcal{A}(\mathsf{key}, \mathsf{pub}) = 1] - \Pr[\mathcal{A}(U_\ell, \mathsf{pub}) = 1]| \leq \epsilon$$

which implies

$$H_{\mathsf{HILL}}(\mathsf{key} \mid \mathsf{pub}) = \ell.$$

Since key' is sampled independently from key,

$$\begin{aligned} H_{\mathsf{HILL}}\big(\mathsf{key} \mid (\mathsf{FE.Rep}(\cdot, \mathsf{pub}), \mathsf{key}', \mathsf{aux})\big) &= H_{\mathsf{HILL}}\big(\mathsf{key} \mid (\mathsf{FE.Rep}(\cdot, \mathsf{pub}), \mathsf{aux})\big) \\ &= H_{\mathsf{HILL}}\big(\mathsf{key} \mid \mathsf{pub}\big) \\ &\geq \ell \end{aligned}$$

Let Obf be a distributional VBB secure obfuscator for ℓ-pseudo-entropy distributions. Then

$$\mathsf{pub}' = \mathsf{Obf}\big(1^\lambda, \mathsf{MBCC}_{\mathsf{FE.Rep}(\cdot, \mathsf{pub}), \mathsf{key}, \mathsf{key}'}\big)$$

can be simulated and for every $\mathcal{A}$, there exists a simulator Sim such that for every predicate ϕ we have:

$$\Big|\Pr[\mathcal{A}(\mathsf{pub}', \mathsf{aux}) = \phi(\mathsf{pub}')] - \Pr[\mathsf{Sim}^{\mathsf{MBCC}_{\mathsf{FE.Rep}(\cdot, \mathsf{pub}), \mathsf{key}, \mathsf{key}'}}(1^\lambda, \mathsf{param}, \mathsf{aux}) = \phi(\mathsf{pub}')]\Big| \\ \leq \mathsf{ngl}(\lambda).$$

Note that if we set $\mathsf{aux} = \mathsf{key}'$ and since key' is drawn randomly and independently, it is true that

$$\begin{aligned} &\big|\Pr[\mathcal{A}(\mathsf{pub}', \mathsf{key}') = \phi(\mathsf{pub}')] - \Pr[\mathsf{Sim}(1^\lambda, \mathsf{param}, \mathsf{key}') = \phi(\mathsf{pub}')]\big| \\ &= \big|\Pr[\mathcal{A}(\mathsf{pub}', \mathsf{key}') = \phi(W)] - \Pr[\mathsf{Sim}(1^\lambda, \mathsf{param}) = \phi(W)]\big| \\ &\leq \mathsf{ngl}(\lambda) \end{aligned}$$

which concludes the proof that PFE is a weakly private fuzzy extractor.

3.2 Weakly Private FE from Secure Sketch and MBCC Obfuscation

Our second construction builds weakly-private fuzzy extractors from non-private secure sketches and MBCC obfuscation. Although this construction relies on a secure sketch, like Wichs and Zirdelis's private secure sketch scheme, we show that the pairwise independent hash function they use isn't necessary. This reduces the amount of entropy required and allows support of a wider family of distributions. However, we build a fuzzy extractor not a secure sketch, some constructions may rely on the functionality of a secure sketch.

Construction 2 (Weakly Private Fuzzy Extractor from SS and MBCC). *Let* $(\mathsf{Sketch}, \mathsf{Rec})$ *be an* $(\mathcal{M}, \mathcal{W}, \ell, t, \delta)$*-secure sketch and* Obf *be an obfuscator for* ℓ*-pseudo-entropy distributions over multi-bit compute-and-compare circuits. Then we can build an* $(\mathcal{M}, \mathcal{W}, \kappa, t, s, \epsilon)$*-fuzzy extractor* PFE *as follows:*

- $(\mathsf{key}, \mathsf{pub}) \leftarrow \mathsf{PFE.Gen}(w)$*:*
  1. *Compute* $\mathsf{SS} \leftarrow \mathsf{Sketch}(w)$.
  2. *Sample* $\mathsf{key} \xleftarrow{\$} \{0,1\}^{\kappa}$.
  3. *Define the circuit* $f_{\mathsf{SS}}(\cdot) := \mathsf{Rec}(\cdot, \mathsf{SS})$.
  4. *Compute* $\mathsf{pub} \leftarrow \mathsf{Obf}\left(1^{\lambda}, \mathsf{MBCC}_{f_{\mathsf{SS}}, w, \mathsf{key}}\right)$.
  5. *Output* $(\mathsf{key}, \mathsf{pub})$.
- $\mathsf{key} \leftarrow \mathsf{PFE.Rep}(\mathsf{pub}, w')$*: Interpret* pub *as an obfuscated program and return* $\mathsf{key} \leftarrow \mathsf{pub}(w')$.

Theorem 2. *Construction 2 is a secure and weakly private* $(\mathcal{M}, \mathcal{W}, \kappa, t, s, \epsilon)$*-fuzzy extractor.*

Proof (Theorem 2).

Correctness: Recall that pub' is an obfuscated MBCC circuit such that

$$\begin{aligned}
\mathsf{pub}(w') &= \mathsf{Obf}\left(1^{\lambda}, \mathsf{MBCC}_{f_{\mathsf{SS}}, w, \mathsf{key}}\right)(w') \\
&= \mathsf{MBCC}_{f_{\mathsf{SS}}, w, \mathsf{key}}(w') \\
&= \begin{cases} \mathsf{key} & \text{if } f_{\mathsf{SS}}(w') = w \\ \perp & \text{otherwise.} \end{cases} \\
&= \begin{cases} \mathsf{key} & \text{if } \mathsf{Rec}(w', \mathsf{SS}) = w \\ \perp & \text{otherwise.} \end{cases}
\end{aligned}$$

Then since $(\mathsf{Sketch}, \mathsf{Rec})$ is a secure sketch, it is true that

$$\begin{aligned}
&\Pr\left[\mathsf{PFE.Rep}(\mathsf{pub}, w') = \mathsf{key} \mid (\mathsf{pub}, \mathsf{key}) \leftarrow \mathsf{PFE.Gen}(w) \text{ and } \mathsf{dist}(w, w') \leq t\right] \\
&= \Pr\left[\mathsf{Rec}(w', \mathsf{SS}) = w \mid \mathsf{SS} \leftarrow \mathsf{Sketch}(w) \text{ and } \mathsf{dist}(w, w') \leq t\right] \\
&\geq 1 - \delta
\end{aligned}$$

and PFE is thus correct.

Security: This proof is the same as the security proof of Theorem 1.

Weak Privacy: Let $(\mathsf{Sketch}, \mathsf{Rec})$ be an $(\mathcal{M}, \mathcal{W}, \ell, t, \delta)$-secure sketch. Then for random variables W, aux, and $\mathsf{SS} \leftarrow \mathsf{Sketch}(W)$ we have

$$H_{\mathsf{HILL}}(W \mid \mathsf{SS}) \geq \ell$$

Since key is sampled independently from all other values,

$$\begin{aligned} H_{\mathsf{HILL}}(w \mid \mathsf{Rec}(\cdot, \mathsf{SS}), \mathsf{key}, \mathsf{aux})) &= H_{\mathsf{HILL}}(w \mid \mathsf{Rec}(\cdot, \mathsf{SS})) \\ &= H_{\mathsf{HILL}}(w \mid \mathsf{SS}) \geq \ell \end{aligned}$$

Let Obf be a distributional VBB secure obfuscator for ℓ-pseudo-entropy distributions. Then

$$\mathsf{pub}' = \mathsf{Obf}(1^\lambda, \mathsf{MBCC}_{\mathsf{Rec}(\cdot,\mathsf{SS}),w,\mathsf{key}})$$

can be simulated and for every $\mathcal{A}$, there exists a simulator Sim such that for every predicate ϕ we have:

$$\left|\Pr[\mathcal{A}(\mathsf{pub}, \mathsf{aux}) = \phi(\mathsf{pub})] - \Pr[\mathsf{Sim}^{\mathsf{MBCC}_{\mathsf{Rec}(\cdot,\mathsf{SS}),w,\mathsf{key}}}(1^\lambda, \mathsf{param}, \mathsf{aux}) = \phi(\mathsf{pub})]\right| \leq \mathsf{ngl}(\lambda)$$

Note that if we set $\mathsf{aux} = \mathsf{key}$ and since key is drawn randomly and independently, it is true that

$$\begin{aligned} &\left|\Pr[\mathcal{A}(\mathsf{pub}, \mathsf{key}) = \phi(\mathsf{pub})] - \Pr[\mathsf{Sim}(1^\lambda, \mathsf{param}, \mathsf{key}) = \phi(\mathsf{pub})]\right| \\ &= \left|\Pr[\mathcal{A}(\mathsf{pub}, \mathsf{key}') = \phi(W)] - \Pr[\mathsf{Sim}(1^\lambda, \mathsf{param}) = \phi(W)]\right| \leq \mathsf{ngl}(\lambda) \end{aligned}$$

which concludes the proof that PFE is a weakly private fuzzy extractor.

4 Robustness

We first define robustness of a fuzzy extractor.

Definition 10 (Robust Fuzzy extractor). *Let* FE *be an* $(\mathcal{M}, \mathcal{W}, \ell, t, s, \epsilon)$*-fuzzy extractor with error* δ *as defined above.* FE *is a robust fuzzy extractor if for all* $W, W' \in \mathcal{W}$*, such that*

$$\Pr_{(w,w') \leftarrow (W,W')}[\mathsf{dist}(w, w') \leq t] = 1,$$

and for all adversaries $\mathcal{A}$*, the advantage of* $\mathcal{A}$ *in the following experiment is at most* $\mathsf{ngl}(\lambda)$*:*

1. *Sample* $(w, w') \leftarrow (W, W')$.
2. *Compute* $(\mathsf{key}, \mathsf{pub}) \leftarrow \mathsf{FE.Gen}(w)$ *and send it to* $\mathcal{A}$.
3. $\mathcal{A}$ *outputs* pub' *and wins if* $\mathsf{pub}' \neq \mathsf{pub}$ *and* $\mathsf{FE.Rep}(\mathsf{pub}', w') \notin \{\perp, \mathsf{key}\}$.

We propose a generic technique to upgrade a fuzzy extractor and achieve robustness. This method relies on non-interactive zero-knowledge (NIZK) [21]. We also show that this technique preserves privacy of the underlying fuzzy extractor. This yields a robust, weakly-private fuzzy extractor construction in the common reference string (CRS) model.

Definition 11 (True simulation extractable NIZK). *Let R be an NP relation on pairs (x, w) with corresponding language $L_R = \{x : \exists w \text{ such that } (x, w) \in R\}$. A true-simulation extractable non-interactive zero-knowledge (NIZK) argument for a relation R consists of three algorithms* $(\mathsf{Setup}, \mathsf{Prove}, \mathsf{Verify})$ *with the following syntax:*

- $(\mathtt{crs}, \mathsf{TK}, \mathsf{EK}) \leftarrow \mathsf{Setup}(1^\lambda)$*: creates a common reference string* $\mathtt{crs}$*, a trapdoor* TK*, and an extraction key* EK.
- $\pi \leftarrow \mathsf{Prove}(\mathtt{crs}, x, w)$*: creates an argument π that $R(x, w) = 1$.*
- $0/1 \leftarrow \mathsf{Verify}(\mathtt{crs}, x, \pi)$*: verifies whether or not the argument π is correct.*

For presentation simplicity, we omit $\mathtt{crs}$ *in the* Prove *and* Verify. *We require that the following three properties hold:*

- ***Completeness.*** *For any $(x, w) \in R$, if* $(\mathtt{crs}, \mathsf{TK}, \mathsf{EK}) \leftarrow \mathsf{Setup}(1^\lambda)$, $\pi \leftarrow \mathsf{Prove}(x, w)$, *then* $\mathsf{Verify}(x, \pi) = 1$.
- ***Soundness.*** *For any PPT adversary $\mathcal{A}$, the following probability is negligible: for* $(\mathtt{crs}, \mathsf{TK}, \mathsf{EK}) \leftarrow \mathsf{Setup}(1^\lambda)$, $(x^*, \pi^*) \leftarrow \mathcal{A}(\mathtt{crs})$ *such that $x^* \notin L_R$ but* $\mathsf{Verify}(x^*, \pi^*) = 1$.
- ***Composable Zero-knowledge.*** *There exists a PPT simulator* Sim *such that for any PPT $\mathcal{A}$, the advantage (the probability $\mathcal{A}$ wins minus one half) is negligible in the following game.*
  - *The challenger samples* $(\mathtt{crs}, \mathsf{TK}, \mathsf{EK}) \leftarrow \mathsf{Setup}(1^\lambda)$ *and sends* $(\mathtt{crs}, \mathsf{TK})$ *to $\mathcal{A}$*
  - *$\mathcal{A}$ chooses $(x, w) \in R$ and sends to the challenger.*
  - *The challenger generates* $\pi_0 \leftarrow \mathsf{Prove}(x, w)$, $\pi_1 \leftarrow \mathsf{Sim}(x, \mathsf{TK})$, *and then samples a random bit $b \leftarrow \{0, 1\}$. Then he sends π_b to $\mathcal{A}$.*
  - *$\mathcal{A}$ outputs a guess bit b', and wins if $b' = b$.*
- ***Extractibility.*** *Additionally, true simulation extractability requires that there exists a PPT extractor* Ext *such that for any PPT adversary $\mathcal{A}$, the probability $\mathcal{A}$ wins is negligible in the following game:*
  - *The challenger picks* $(\mathtt{crs}, \mathsf{TK}, \mathsf{EK}) \leftarrow \mathsf{Setup}(1^\lambda)$ *and sends* $\mathtt{crs}$ *to $\mathcal{A}$.*
  - *$\mathcal{A}$ is allowed to make oracle queries to the simulation algorithm* $\mathsf{Sim}'((x, w), \mathsf{TK})$ *adaptively.* Sim' *first checks if $(x, w) \in R$ and returns* $\mathsf{Sim}(x, TK)$ *if that is the case.*
  - *$\mathcal{A}$ outputs a tuple x^*, L^*, π^*.*
  - *The challenger runs the extractor* $w^* \leftarrow \mathsf{Ext}(L^*, (x^*, \pi^*), \mathsf{EK})$.
  - *$\mathcal{A}$ wins if 1) the pair (x^*, L^*) was not part of the simulator query, 2) the proof π^* verifies, and (3) $R(x^*, w^*) = 0$.*

Construction 3 (Robust, weakly-private fuzzy extractor). *Let* FE *be a weakly-private fuzzy extractor and* (Setup, Prove, Verify) *be a NIZK system for language* $\mathcal{L} = \{\mathsf{pub} \mid \mathsf{FE.Gen}(w; r) = (\mathsf{pub}, \mathsf{key})\}$*. Here, the statement is* $\mathsf{pub} = \mathsf{FE.Gen}(w; r)$ *and the witness is the pair of values* (w, r)*, where* w *is the original reading and* r *the internal randomness of* Gen.

- $(\mathsf{key}, \mathsf{pub}^*) \leftarrow \mathsf{FE}'.\mathsf{Gen}(w)$:
  1. *Sample* $(\mathtt{crs}, \mathsf{TK}, \mathsf{EK}) \leftarrow \mathsf{Setup}(1^\lambda)$.
  2. *Compute* $(\mathsf{key}, \mathsf{pub}) \leftarrow \mathsf{FE.Gen}(w; r)$.
  3. *Compute* $\pi \leftarrow \mathsf{Prove}(\mathtt{crs}, \mathsf{pub}, w, r)$ *and set* $\mathsf{pub}^* = (\mathsf{pub}, \pi)$.
  4. *Output* $(\mathsf{key}, \mathsf{pub}^*)$.
- $\mathsf{key}' \leftarrow \mathsf{FE}'.\mathsf{Rep}(\mathsf{pub}^*, w')$:
  1. *Run* $b \leftarrow \mathsf{Verify}(\mathtt{crs}, \mathsf{pub}, \pi)$ *and output* $\perp$ *if* $b = 0$.
  2. *Output* $\mathsf{key}' \leftarrow \mathsf{FE.Rep}(\mathsf{pub}, w')$.

Theorem 3. *Let* FE *be an weakly-private,* $(\mathcal{M}, \mathcal{W}, \ell, 2t, s, \epsilon)$*-fuzzy extractor and* (Setup, Prove, Verify) *be a NIZK system. Then* FE′ *as described in Construction 3 is a weakly-private, robust,* $(\mathcal{M}, \mathcal{W}, \ell, t, s, \epsilon)$*-fuzzy extractor.*

Note that in this theorem the underlying fuzzy extractor FE corrects **2t** errors while the resulting fuzzy extractor FE′ corrects only **t** errors. This is important for the corresponding proof to work. This requirement was present in some prior robustness upgrades for fuzzy extractors, see Table 2.

Proof (Theorem 3).

Correctness: Correctness is straightforward from the correctness of the underlying fuzzy extractor and the completeness of the NIZK system.

Security: Security is straightforward from the security of the underlying fuzzy extractor and the zero-knowledge property of the NIZK system.

Privacy: Privacy is straightforward from the privacy of the underlying fuzzy extractor and the zero-knowledge property of the NIZK system. We provide a short sketch below.

Let Sim denote a simulator for the underlying weakly private FE. Suppose FE′ is not weakly private, then there exists an adversary $\mathcal{A}'$, such that for any simulators $\mathsf{Sim}'(|\mathsf{pub}|, |\pi|, |\mathsf{key}|)$, we have

$$\left|\Pr[\mathcal{A}'(\mathsf{pub}, \pi, \mathsf{key}) = 1] - \Pr[\mathsf{Sim}'(|\mathsf{pub}|, |\pi|, |\mathsf{key}|) = 1]\right| > \mathsf{ngl}(\lambda)$$

We note that $\mathsf{Sim}'(|\mathsf{pub}|, |\pi|, |\mathsf{key}|) = \mathsf{Sim}(|\mathsf{pub}|, |\mathsf{key}|)$ is one such valid simulator.

Then we can build an adversary $\mathcal{A}$ for FE,

1. Receive inputs pub and key.
2. Run NIZK setup $(\mathsf{TK}, \mathsf{EK}) \leftarrow \mathsf{Setup}(1^\lambda)$.
3. Run the NIZK simulator $\pi \leftarrow \mathsf{Sim}_{\mathrm{NIZK}}(\mathsf{pub}, \mathsf{TK})$.

4. Run the FE' adversary $b \leftarrow \mathcal{A}'(\mathsf{pub}, \pi, \mathsf{key})$.
5. Return b.

Then

$$|\Pr[\mathcal{A}(\mathsf{pub}, \mathsf{key}) = 1] - \Pr[\mathsf{Sim}(|\mathsf{pub}|, |\mathsf{key}|) = 1]| > \mathsf{ngl}(\lambda)$$

which is a contradiction of FE's weak privacy.

Robustness: We proceed by contradiction. Suppose FE' is not a robust fuzzy extractor, that is, for distributions W, W' such that $\mathsf{dist}(W, W') \leq t$, there exists a PPT adversary $\mathcal{A}'_{\mathsf{FE}}$ such that

$$\Pr_{(w,w') \leftarrow (W,W')}\left[\begin{array}{r|r} \mathsf{Verify}(\mathtt{crs}, \mathsf{pub}', \pi') = 1 & (\mathsf{key}, \mathsf{pub}) \leftarrow \mathsf{FE.Gen}(w) \\ \wedge\ \mathsf{FE.Rep}(\mathsf{pub}', w') \neq \{\mathsf{key}, \perp\} & \pi \leftarrow \mathsf{Prove}(\mathtt{crs}, \mathsf{pub}, \mathsf{key}, w) \\ \wedge\ (\mathsf{pub}' \neq \mathsf{pub} \vee \pi' \neq \pi) & (\mathsf{pub}', \pi') \leftarrow \mathcal{A}_{\mathsf{PFE}}(\mathsf{key}, \mathsf{pub}, \pi) \end{array}\right] > \mathsf{ngl}(\lambda).$$

We can then build a PPT distinguisher $\mathcal{A}$ for the fuzzy extractor security game as follows:

1. Receive $(\mathsf{pub}, \mathsf{key}_b)$ from the challenger, where for $w \leftarrow W$, $(\mathsf{pub}, \mathsf{key}) \leftarrow \mathsf{FE.Gen}(w; r)$ and for $b \in \{0, 1\}$, $\mathsf{key}_1 = \mathsf{key}$ and $\mathsf{key}_0 = U_\ell$.
2. Sample $(\mathtt{crs}, \mathsf{TK}, \mathsf{EK}) \leftarrow \mathsf{Setup}(1^\lambda)$ from the NIZK proof system.
3. Run the NIZK simulator $\pi \leftarrow \mathsf{Sim}(\mathsf{pub}, \mathsf{TK})$.
4. Send $(\mathsf{key}_b, \mathsf{pub}, \pi)$ to $\mathcal{A}'_{\mathsf{FE}}$ and receives back (pub', π').
5. Run the NIZK extractor $(w^*, r^*) \leftarrow \mathsf{Ext}(\mathsf{pub}', \pi', \mathsf{EK})$.
6. Run $\mathsf{key}' \leftarrow \mathsf{FE.Rep}(\mathsf{pub}, w^*)$.
7. If $\mathsf{key}' = \mathsf{key}_b$ return 1, otherwise return 0.

Recall that a break in robustness requires $(\mathsf{pub}', \pi') \neq (\mathsf{pub}, \pi)$ and π' to be a valid proof. Suppose $\mathsf{pub}' = \mathsf{pub}$, then $\mathsf{dist}(w, w^*) \leq t$ and $\mathsf{FE.Rep}(\mathsf{pub}, w^*) = \mathsf{key}$. So $\mathsf{FE}'.\mathsf{Rep}(\mathsf{pub}'||\pi', w^*) = \mathsf{key}$, which does not count as a break of the robustness property.

So it must be true that $\mathsf{pub}' \neq \mathsf{pub}$. In this situation, $\mathcal{A}'_{\mathsf{FE}}$ outputs the pair (pub', π') such that for some w', with $\mathsf{dist}(w, w') \leq t$, $\mathsf{FE}'.\mathsf{Rep}(\mathsf{pub}'||\pi', w') = \mathsf{key}^* \neq \mathsf{key}$. Then the NIZK extractor outputs point w^* such that $\mathsf{FE.Gen}(w^*; r^*) = (\mathsf{key}^*, \mathsf{pub}'||\pi')$. So $\mathsf{dist}(w, w') \leq t$ and $\mathsf{dist}(w^*, w') \leq t$, which means that $\mathsf{dist}(w, w^*) \leq 2t$. Finally, since FE corrects $2t$ errors, when $b = 1$, $\mathsf{key}' = \mathsf{FE.Rep}(\mathsf{pub}, w^*) = \mathsf{key} = \mathsf{key}_1$ and

$$|\Pr[\mathcal{A}(\mathsf{pub}, \mathsf{key}) = 1] - \Pr[\mathcal{A}(\mathsf{pub}, U_\ell) = 1]| > \mathsf{ngl}(\lambda)$$

which concludes our proof.

5 Reuse

In this section, we show that one cannot hope to compose MBCC obfuscation with an auxiliary input secure digital locker. We then show this implies a impossibility of a variant of private fuzzy extractors that can be constructed from MBCC obfuscation. This variant never outputs a value outside of the ball of the enrolled value.

Definition 12. *Let* (Gen, Rep) *be an* $(\mathcal{M}, \mathcal{W}, \ell, t, \epsilon)$*-fuzzy extractor with error* δ *(Definition 7). The pair is perfectly correct if for all* $w, w' \in \mathcal{M}$ *such that* $\mathsf{dist}(w, w') > t$*:*

$$\Pr\left[\perp \leftarrow \mathsf{Rep}(\mathsf{pub}, w') \mid (\mathsf{key}, \mathsf{pub}) \leftarrow \mathsf{Gen}(w)\right] \geq 1 - \mathsf{ngl}(\lambda).$$

We assume that any randomness for Rep *is included in the string* pub *so this probability statement is only over the randomness of* Gen.

We now define digital lockers, which have the same functionality as perfectly correct fuzzy extractors for $t = 0$. Digital lockers [17] are also a specific case of MBCC obfuscation where the function is the identity function, $f(x) = \mathsf{id}(x) = x$.

Definition 13 (Digital Locker). *An* $(\mathcal{W}, n)$*-digital locker is a pair of PPT algorithms* (lock, unlock) *where for all* $\mathsf{val} \in D^\lambda$ *and* $\mathsf{key} \in \{0,1\}^n$,

- $\mathsf{unlock} \leftarrow \mathsf{lock}(\mathsf{val}, \mathsf{key})$
- $\mathsf{key}' \leftarrow \mathsf{unlock}(\mathsf{val}')$

such that the following properties are true:

1. ***Completeness:*** *For all* $\mathsf{val} \in \mathsf{D}^\lambda, \mathsf{key} \in \{0,1\}^n$ *it holds that*

$$\Pr[\mathsf{unlock}(\cdot) \equiv I_{\mathsf{val},\mathsf{key}}(\cdot) \mid \mathsf{unlock} \leftarrow \mathsf{lock}(\mathsf{val}, \mathsf{key})] \geq 1 - \mathsf{ngl}(\lambda),$$

where the probability is over the randomness of lock*. Here* $I_{\mathsf{val},\mathsf{key}}$ *is a function that returns* key *when provided input* val*, otherwise* $I_{\mathsf{val},\mathsf{key}}$ *returns* $\perp$.

2. ***Virtual Black Box Security:*** *For all PPT* $\mathcal{A}$ *and* $p = \mathsf{poly}(\lambda)$, $\exists \mathsf{Sim}$ *and* $q(\lambda) = \mathsf{poly}(\lambda)$ *such that for all large enough* $\lambda \in \mathbb{N}$, $\forall \mathsf{val} \in \mathsf{D}_\lambda, \mathsf{key} \in \{0,1\}^n, \mathcal{P} : \mathsf{D}_\lambda \times \{0,1\}^n \mapsto \{0,1\}$,

$$\left|\Pr[\mathcal{A}(\mathsf{lock}(\mathsf{val}, \mathsf{key})) = \mathcal{P}(\mathsf{val}, \mathsf{key})] - \Pr[\mathsf{Sim}^{I_{\mathsf{val},\mathsf{key}}}(1^\lambda) = \mathcal{P}(\mathsf{val}, \mathsf{key})]\right| \leq \frac{1}{p(\lambda)},$$

where Sim *is allowed* $q(\lambda)$ *oracle queries to* $I_{\mathsf{val},\mathsf{key}}$ *and the probabilities are over the internal randomness of* $\mathcal{A}$ *and* lock*, and of* Sim*, respectively.*

Construction. One can construct a perfectly correct private fuzzy extractor by applying Construction 2 on a well-formed secure sketch [13, Definition 4]. A well-formed secure sketch on input w' never outputs a value with distance $\geq t$ from w'. One can always construct a well-formed secure sketch with no loss in parameters by adding a distance check before output.

Since the circuit being obfuscated in Construction 2 only has an output when the output of the secure sketch is equal to w, these two modifications suffice to form a (private) perfectly correct fuzzy extractor.

Proposition 1. *Perfectly correct private fuzzy extractors with auxiliary input imply digital lockers with auxiliary inputs.*

Proof. This proposition easily follows by setting the required distance t equal to 0.

Definition 14 (Collision-resistant Hash function). *Consider function* $h : \{0,1\}^n \to \{0,1\}^m$, *$h$ is a collision-resistant hash function if the following are true:*

1. ***Compression:*** $m < n$.
2. ***Collision-resistance:*** *For any PPT adversary* $\mathcal{A}$,

$$\Pr\left[(x_0, x_1) \leftarrow \mathcal{A}(1^n, h) \mid x_0 \neq x_1 \wedge h(x_0) = h(x_1)\right] \leq \mathsf{ngl}(n).$$

Theorem 4 (Private FE with auxiliary input impossibility). *If dist-VBB obfuscation for MBCC programs with α-pseudo entropy and collision-resistant hash functions exist, no perfectly-correct private fuzzy extractor can be secure in the presence of unpredictability auxiliary inputs.*

Proof (Theorem 4). This proof is built from a main lemma (see Lemma 2) which is then combined with Proposition 1. Lemma 2 shows that digital lockers with auxiliary input for unpredictable sources cannot exist if dist-VBB obfuscation for MBCC programs with α-pseudo entropy exists.

Lemma 2 (Digital locker with auxiliary input impossibility). *If dist-VBB obfuscation for MBCC programs with α-pseudo entropy and collision-resistant hash functions exist, then security for digital lockers with auxiliary inputs for unpredictable sources cannot be achieved.*

Proof (Lemma 2). Let U_x denote the universal circuit that takes as input circuit C and computes $U_x(C) = C(x)$. Define the following MBCC program

$$\mathsf{MBCC}[U_x, \mathsf{key}, x](C) = \begin{cases} x & \text{if } C \text{ is a well-formed } \mathsf{unlock} \text{ program and } C(x) = \mathsf{key}. \\ \perp & \text{otherwise.} \end{cases}$$

Let $h : \{0,1\}^{|x|} \to \{0,1\}^m$, with $m < |x|$, be a collision-resistant hash function. Suppose x and key are independent and let $\mathsf{aux} = h(x)$, then we have

$$H^{\mathsf{HILL}}(\mathsf{key} \mid U_x, x, \mathsf{aux}) \geq \alpha(\lambda)$$

which implies that there exists a dist-VBB obfuscator Obf for this MBCC circuit. We now need to show that X remains unpredictable given $\mathsf{Obf}(\mathsf{MBCC}[U_X, \mathsf{key}, x])$, that is

$$H^{\mathsf{unp}}(X \mid \mathsf{Obf}(\mathsf{MBCC}[U_X, \mathsf{key}, x]) \geq \omega(\log \lambda)$$

In other words, we want to show that if $\mathsf{Obf}(\mathsf{MBCC}[U_x, \mathsf{key}, x])$ is dist-VBB secure, then for all PPT $\mathcal{A}$, we have

$$\Pr\left[\mathcal{A}\left(\mathsf{Obf}(\mathsf{MBCC}[U_x, \mathsf{key}, x])\right) = x\right] \leq \mathsf{ngl}(\lambda).$$

We proceed by contradiction. Suppose the above is not true and there exists a PPT $\mathcal{A}$ that can predict x from $\mathsf{Obf}(\mathsf{MBCC}[U_x, \mathsf{key}, x])$ with non-negligible probability. Then we can build a distinguisher for the MBCC obfuscation that breaks dist-IND security (which is equivalent to dist-VBB for evasive functions such as MBCC [8]). The distinguisher works as follows:

1. Receive P^* and $\mathsf{aux} = h(x)$ as inputs.
2. Run $x^* \leftarrow \mathcal{A}(P^*)$.
3. If $h(x^*) = h(x)$, return 1, otherwise return 0.

If $P^* = \mathsf{Obf}(1^\lambda, P)$, then $\mathcal{A}$ should be able to extract $x^* = x$ and $h(x^*) = h(x)$. However, if $P^* \leftarrow \mathsf{Sim}(1^\lambda, P.\mathsf{params})$, $\mathcal{A}$ should not be able to extract correct x^*. Then the probability that $x^* = x$ is $\frac{1}{2^n}$ and when $x^* \neq x$, $h(x^*) = h(x)$ with negligible probability. This is a contradiction of dist-IND security of the MBCC obfuscator so we conclude that X remains unpredictable.

We now need to show that that this construction breaks digital locker security. Recall that digital locker security is VBB, that is for any PPT adversary $\mathcal{A}$ and any polynomial p, there exists a simulator Sim such that

$$\Pr\left[\mathcal{A}(\mathsf{unlock}, \mathsf{aux}) = 1\right] - \Pr\left[\mathsf{Sim}^{\mathsf{unlock}(\cdot)}(1^\lambda, \mathsf{aux}) = 1\right] \leq \frac{1}{p(\lambda)}$$

where $\mathsf{unlock} \leftarrow \mathsf{lock}(\mathsf{val}, \mathsf{key})$.

It is obvious that this does not hold when we set $\mathsf{aux} = \mathsf{MBCC}[U_{\mathsf{val}}, \mathsf{key}, \mathsf{val}]$. Indeed, $\mathcal{A}$ can then run $\mathsf{aux}(\mathsf{unlock})$ and retrieve the correct val (and then key by running $\mathsf{unlock}(\mathsf{val})$), whereas Sim cannot.

By chaining Lemma 2 and the contrapositive of Proposition 1, we obtain that if dist-VBB MBCC obfuscation exists then private fuzzy extractors with auxiliary inputs cannot be achieved, which conclude this Theorem's proof.

Acknowledgements. The authors are grateful to anonymous reviewers for their help improving the manuscript. The authors thank Giorgos Zirdelis for helpful discussions. C.C. was supported by NSF grant #2141033. B.F. and M.R. were supported by NSF grants #2141033 and #2232813.

A Privacy vs FE Security

Showing that fuzzy extractor security does not imply privacy is straightforward. Let FE' be a fuzzy extractor for which $\mathsf{pub}' = w_1||\mathsf{pub}$, where $w_1 \in \{0,1\}$ denotes the first bit of w and pub is a valid public value such that $\mathsf{key} \leftarrow \mathsf{FE.Rep}(\mathsf{pub}, w^*)$ when $\mathsf{dist}(w, w^*) \leq t$. Then it is obvious that even though FE' is a secure fuzzy extractor, it is not private.

We will now show that the reverse is also not true.

Theorem 5. *Privacy (Definition 8) does not imply fuzzy extractor security (Definition 7).*

Proof (Proof of Theorem 5). We will prove this by presenting a counter example. Consider the following construction:

- $(\mathsf{pub}, \mathsf{key}) \leftarrow \mathsf{Gen}(w)$: key is sampled uniformly at random and pub is an obfuscation of the program p such that, for inputs $x \in \{0,1\}^*$ and $b \in \{0,1\}$,

$$p(b,x) = \begin{cases} \mathsf{key} & \text{if } b = 1 \text{ and } \mathsf{dist}(w,x) \leq t \\ \top & \text{if } b = 0 \text{ and } x = \mathsf{key} \\ \bot & \text{otherwise.} \end{cases}$$

- $\mathsf{key} \leftarrow \mathsf{Rep}(\mathsf{pub}, b, w')$: run $\mathsf{pub}(1, w')$ and return its output.

Notice that for $w, w' \in \mathcal{W}$ such that $\mathsf{dist}(w, w') \leq t$, we have

$$\Pr\left[\mathsf{key} \leftarrow \mathsf{Rep}(\mathsf{pub}, w') \mid (\mathsf{pub}, \mathsf{key}) \leftarrow \mathsf{Gen}(w)\right] \geq 1 - \mathsf{ngl}(\lambda)$$

which is the expected behavior of a fuzzy extractor. Furthermore, note that this construction is private since by the obfuscation definition, for any PPT adversary $\mathcal{A}$, there exists simulator Sim such that for any predicate ϕ

$$\left|\Pr[\mathcal{A}(\mathsf{pub}, \mathsf{key}) = \phi(W)] - \Pr[\mathsf{Sim}(1^\lambda, 1^{|\mathsf{pub}|}, 1^{|\mathsf{key}|}) = \phi(W)]\right| \leq \mathsf{ngl}(\lambda)$$

Now let's check fuzzy extractor security. Consider the following experiment:

1. Run $(\mathsf{key}, \mathsf{pub}) \leftarrow \mathsf{Gen}(w)$.
2. Draw $b \leftarrow \{0,1\}$.
3. If $b = 0$, sample $U_\ell \xleftarrow{\$} \{0,1\}^\ell$ and send (U_ℓ, pub) to $\mathcal{A}$. Otherwise, send $(\mathsf{key}, \mathsf{pub})$ to $\mathcal{A}$.
4. $\mathcal{A}$ outputs $b' \in \{0,1\}$ and wins if $b' = b$.

$\mathcal{A}$ has a straightforward way of winning this experiment by running $\mathsf{pub}(0, x)$, where $x = \mathsf{key}$ or $x = U_\ell$ depending on drawn b. Then $\mathcal{A}$ outputs $b' = 1$ if $\mathsf{pub}(0, x) = \top$ and $b' = 0$ if $\mathsf{pub}(0, x) = \bot$. Thus we have

$$|\Pr[\mathcal{A}(\mathsf{key}, \mathsf{pub}) = 1] - \Pr[\mathcal{A}(U_\ell, \mathsf{pub}) = 1]| > \mathsf{ngl}$$

and we can conclude that this construction, although private, is not a secure fuzzy extractor.

B Reusability from Composable MBCC Obfuscation

Reusability for Constructions 1 and 2 is achievable when the MBCC obfuscator is composable. We start by defining reuse.

Definition 15 (Reusable Fuzzy extractor [16]). *Let* FE *be an* $(\mathcal{M}, \mathcal{W}, \ell, t, s, \epsilon)$*-fuzzy extractor with error* δ *as defined above. Let* $(W_1, \cdots, W_\rho)$ *be* $\rho \in \mathbb{N}$ *correlated variables such that* $W_i \in \mathcal{W}$*. Let adversary* $\mathcal{A}$ *be a PPT adversary, then for all* $j \in [1, \rho]$*:*

1. *The challenger samples* $w_j \leftarrow W_j$ *and computes* $(\mathsf{key}_j, \mathsf{pub}_j) \leftarrow \mathsf{FE.Gen}(w)$.
2. *The challenger samples a uniform* $u \xleftarrow{\$} \{0,1\}^\ell$ *and sets* $K_0 = \mathsf{key}_i$ *and* $K_1 = u$.
3. *The challenger draws* $b \xleftarrow{\$} \{0,1\}$ *and sends to* $\mathcal{A}$

$$(\mathsf{key}_1, \cdots, \mathsf{key}_{i-1}, K_b, \mathsf{key}_{i+1}, \cdots, \mathsf{key}_\rho, \mathsf{pub}_1, \cdots, \mathsf{pub}_\rho)$$

4. $\mathcal{A}$ *outputs* $b' \in \{0,1\}$ *and wins if* $b' = b$.

We denote the above experiment as $\mathsf{Exp}^{\mathsf{reusable}}_{\mathcal{A},b}$*, the advantage of* $\mathcal{A}$ *is*

$$\mathsf{Adv}(\mathcal{A}) = \left|\Pr[\mathsf{Exp}^{\mathsf{reusable}}_{\mathcal{A},0} = 1] - \Pr[\mathsf{Exp}^{\mathsf{reusable}}_{\mathcal{A},1} = 1]\right|.$$

FE *is a* (ρ, ϵ)*-reusable fuzzy extractor if for all* $\mathcal{A}$*, for all* $i \in [1, \rho]$ *the advantage of* $\mathcal{A}$ *is at most* ϵ.

However, as we show in Sect. 5 this is not possible without restricting the class of circuits being obfuscated.

Definition 16 (ℓ-Composable Obfuscation with auxiliary input). Obf *is a* ℓ*-composable obfuscator for distribution class* $\mathcal{D}$ *over the family of circuits* $\mathcal{P}_\lambda$ *if for any PPT adversary* $\mathcal{A}$ *and polynomial* p*, there exists a simulator* Sim *such that for every distribution ensemble* $D = \{D_\lambda\} \in \mathcal{D}$ *and* $(P_1, \cdots, P_\ell, \mathsf{aux}) \leftarrow D_\lambda$*, with* $\ell = \mathsf{poly}(\lambda)$,

$$\Big|\Pr[\mathcal{A}(\mathsf{Obf}(P_1), \cdots, \mathsf{Obf}(P_\ell), \mathsf{aux}) = 1] - \Pr[\mathsf{Sim}^{P_1, \cdots, P_\ell}(1^{|P_1|}, \cdots, 1^{|P_\ell|}, \mathsf{aux}) = 1]\Big| \leq \frac{1}{p(\lambda)}$$

Theorem 6. *Let* Obf *be a composable dist-VBB obfuscator for MBCC circuits, then Constructions 1 and 2 are reusable.*

Proof (Proof of Theorem 6). Suppose PFE is not a reusable fuzzy extractor, that is, there exists a PPT adversary $\mathcal{A}$ and a polynomial $p(\lambda)$ such that for all $1 \leq j \leq \rho$:

$$\Big| \Pr[\mathcal{A}(\mathsf{key}_1, \cdots, \mathsf{key}_\rho, \mathsf{pub}_1, \cdots, \mathsf{pub}_\rho) = 1] - \Pr[\mathcal{A}(\mathsf{key}_1, \cdots, \mathsf{key}_{i-1}, U_\ell, \mathsf{key}_{i+1}, \cdots, \mathsf{key}_\rho, \mathsf{pub}_1, \cdots, \mathsf{pub}_\rho) = 1] \Big| > \frac{1}{p(\lambda)}$$

where U_ℓ is a uniform random string in $\{0,1\}^\ell$.
Remember that Obf is a composable obfuscator for $\mathsf{MBCC}[\mathsf{Rep}_{\mathsf{pub}}, k, \mathsf{key}]$. Let $r(\lambda) = 3p(\lambda)$ and suppose Sim is the simulator for $\mathcal{A}$ for $r(\lambda)$, then we have

$$\Big| \Pr[\mathcal{A}(\{\mathsf{Obf}(1^\lambda, \mathsf{MBCC}[\mathsf{Rep}_{\mathsf{pub}}, k, \mathsf{key}_i])\}_{i=1}^{\rho}, \mathsf{aux}) = 1] - \Pr[\mathsf{Sim}^{\{\mathsf{MBCC}[\mathsf{Rep}_{\mathsf{pub}}, k, \mathsf{key}_i]\}_{i=1}^{\rho}}(1^\lambda, \{|\mathsf{MBCC}[\mathsf{Rep}_{\mathsf{pub}}, k, \mathsf{key}_i]|\}_{i=1}^{\rho}, \mathsf{aux}) = 1]\Big| \leq \frac{1}{3p(\lambda)}$$

Note that in Construction 1, $\mathsf{pub}_i = \mathsf{Obf}(1^\lambda, \mathsf{MBCC}[\mathsf{Rep}_{\mathsf{pub}'}, k, \mathsf{key}_i])$ and set $\mathsf{aux} = \mathsf{key}_1, \cdots, \mathsf{key}_\rho$ so we have

$$\begin{aligned} &\big|\Pr[\mathcal{A}(\{\mathsf{pub}_i\}_{i=1}^{\rho}, \{\mathsf{key}_i\}_{i=1}^{\rho}) = 1] \\ &- \Pr[\mathsf{Sim}^{\{\mathsf{pub}_i\}_{i=1}^{\rho}}(1^\lambda, \{|\mathsf{pub}_i|\}_{i=1}^{\rho}, \{\mathsf{key}_i\}_{i=1}^{\rho}) = 1]\big| \le \frac{1}{3p(\lambda)} \end{aligned} \tag{3}$$

Notice that this also holds if we replace key_j by an independent uniform random variable U_ℓ over $\{0,1\}^\ell$. Then for any $j \in \{1, \rho\}$ we have:

$$\begin{aligned} &\big|\Pr[\mathcal{A}(\{\mathsf{pub}_i\}_{i=1}^{\rho}, \mathsf{key}_1, \cdots, \mathsf{key}_{j-1}, U_\ell, \mathsf{key}_{j+1}, \cdots, \mathsf{key}_\rho) = 1] \\ &- \Pr[\mathsf{Sim}^{\{\mathsf{pub}_i\}_{i=1}^{\rho}}(1^\lambda, \{|\mathsf{pub}_i|\}_{i=1}^{\rho}, \mathsf{key}_1, \cdots, \mathsf{key}_{j-1}, U_\ell, \mathsf{key}_{j+1}, \cdots, \mathsf{key}_\rho) = 1]\big| \le \frac{1}{3p(\lambda)} \end{aligned} \tag{4}$$

Again we adapt Canetti et al.'s lemma [16, Lemma 2]:

Lemma 3. *Let U_ℓ denote the uniform distribution over $\{0,1\}^\ell$, then for $1 \le j \le \rho$,*

$$\begin{aligned} &\Big|\Pr[\mathsf{Sim}^{\{\mathsf{MBCC}[\mathsf{Rep}_{\mathsf{pub}}, k, \mathsf{key}_i]\}_{i=1}^{\rho}}\left(1^\lambda, \{|\mathsf{MBCC}[\mathsf{Rep}_{\mathsf{pub}}, k, \mathsf{key}_i]|\}_{i=1}^{\rho}, \{\mathsf{key}\}_{i=1}^{\rho}\right) = 1] \\ &- \Pr[\mathsf{Sim}^{\{\mathsf{MBCC}[\mathsf{Rep}_{\mathsf{pub}}, k, \mathsf{key}_i]\}_{i=1}^{\rho}}\left(1^\lambda, \{|\mathsf{MBCC}[\mathsf{Rep}_{\mathsf{pub}}, k, \mathsf{key}_i]|\}_{i=1}^{\rho}, \{\mathsf{key}_i\}_{i=1}^{j-1}, U_\ell, \{\mathsf{key}_i\}_{i=j+1}^{\rho}\right) = 1]\Big| \\ &\le \frac{1}{3p(\lambda)} \end{aligned}$$

Proof. Fix any $u \in \{0,1\}^\ell$, the lemma will follow by averaging over all u. The information about whether the jth key value, denoted V_j, is key_j or u can only be obtain by Sim through the query responses. First, we modify Sim to quit immediately when it gets a response not equal to $\perp$. Such Sim is equally successful at distinguishing between key_j and u since the first non-$\perp$ response tells Sim if its input is equal to key_j. Subsequent responses add nothing to this knowledge. Since Sim can make at most q queries, there are $q+1$ possible values for the view of Sim on a given input. Of those, q views consist of some number of non-$\perp$ responses followed by a $\perp$ response, and one view consists of all q responses equal to $\perp$.
Then by [25, Lemma 2.2b],

$$\begin{aligned} \tilde{H}_\infty(V_j|View(\mathsf{Sim}), \mathsf{aux}) &\ge \tilde{H}_\infty(V_j) - \log(q+1) \\ &\ge \alpha - \log(q+1). \end{aligned}$$

where $\mathsf{aux} = \left(\{|\mathsf{MBCC}[\mathsf{Rep}_{\mathsf{pub}}, k, \mathsf{key}_i]|\}_{i=1}^{\rho}, \mathsf{key}_1, \cdots, \mathsf{key}_{j-1}, \mathsf{key}_{j+1}, \cdots, \mathsf{key}_\rho\right)$.

Thus, at each query, the probability that Sim gets a non-$\perp$ response and guesses V_j is at most $(q+1)/2^\alpha$. Since there are q queries of Sim, the overall probability is at most $q(q+1)/2^\alpha$. Then since 2^α is negligible in λ, there exists some λ_0 such that for all $\lambda \ge \lambda_0$, $q(q+1)/2^\alpha \le 1/(3p(\lambda))$.

Then from Lemma 3, we have

$$\begin{aligned}&\Big|\Pr[\mathsf{Sim}^{\{\mathsf{pub}_i\}_{i=1}^{\rho}}(1^\lambda, \{|\mathsf{pub}_i|\}_{i=1}^{\rho}, \{\mathsf{key}_i\}_{i=1}^{\rho}) = 1]\\&- \Pr[\mathsf{Sim}^{\{\mathsf{pub}_i\}_{i=1}^{\rho}}(1^\lambda, \{|\mathsf{pub}_i|\}_{i=1}^{\rho}, \mathsf{key}_1, \cdots, \mathsf{key}_{j-1}, U_\ell, \mathsf{key}_{j+1}, \cdots, \mathsf{key}_\rho) = 1]\Big| \le \frac{1}{3p(\lambda)}\end{aligned} \quad (5)$$

Using the triangle inequality on Eqs. 3, 4 and 5 we obtain

$$\begin{aligned}&\Big|\ \Pr[\mathcal{A}(\mathsf{key}_1, \cdots, \mathsf{key}_\rho, \mathsf{pub}_1, \cdots, \mathsf{pub}_\rho) = 1]\\&- \Pr[\mathcal{A}(\mathsf{key}_1, \cdots, \mathsf{key}_{i-1}, U_\ell, \mathsf{key}_{i+1}, \cdots, \mathsf{key}_\rho, \mathsf{pub}_1, \cdots, \mathsf{pub}_\rho) = 1]\ \Big| \le \frac{1}{p(\lambda)}\end{aligned}$$

which is a contradiction and completes this proof.

Composable MBCC Obfuscation. Wichs and Zirdelis [47] build obfuscation for *multi-bit* compute-and-compare circuits from single bit compute-and-compare by composing the function f with a strongly injective PRG. By doing so they ensure that the target values $(y_1, \cdots, y_\ell)$ are indistinguishable from uniform, even when given f, z and aux. Their proof then relies on the security of the obfuscator for the ith circuit by passing all remaining circuits as auxiliary information.

Unfortunately this technique cannot be directly applied to build *composable* MBCC obfuscation since it requires keeping track of which parts of the PRG output have already been used. This is reasonable for their MBCC obfuscation scheme, where all obfuscated compute-and-compare circuits will be generated at the same time. However this is not practical in the case of composable obfuscation, where the obfuscator will typically be run at different times and without a shared state. One could use a PRG with exponential stretch and select a random part of its output, then the probability of reuse should be low. Another issue is that in Wichs and Zirdelis's scheme, the function and the input to the PRG are always the same. For composability, especially with the goal of building reusable FE, it would need to handle distinct but possibly correlated functions and values. It then is unclear what the auxiliary information (i.e. the other obfuscated programs) may leak on the current obfuscated circuit.

References

1. Alamélou, Q., et al.: Pseudoentropic isometries: a new framework for fuzzy extractor reusability. In: AsiaCCS (2018)
2. Apon, D., Cachet, C., Fuller, B., Hall, P., Liu, F.H.: Nonmalleable digital lockers and robust fuzzy extractors in the plain model. In: Agrawal, S., Lin, D. (eds.) Advances in Cryptology - ASIACRYPT 2022, pp. 353–383. Springer Nature Switzerland, Cham (2022)
3. Apon, D., Cho, C., Eldefrawy, K., Katz, J.: Efficient, reusable fuzzy extractors from LWE. In: Dolev, S., Lodha, S. (eds.) CSCML 2017. LNCS, vol. 10332, pp. 1–18. Springer, Cham (2017). https://doi.org/10.1007/978-3-319-60080-2_1

4. Barak, B., Bitansky, N., Canetti, R., Kalai, Y.T., Paneth, O., Sahai, A.: Obfuscation for evasive functions. In: Lindell, Y. (ed.) TCC 2014. LNCS, vol. 8349, pp. 26–51. Springer, Heidelberg (2014). https://doi.org/10.1007/978-3-642-54242-8_2
5. Bartusek, J., Lepoint, T., Ma, F., Zhandry, M.: New techniques for obfuscating conjunctions. In: Ishai, Y., Rijmen, V. (eds.) EUROCRYPT 2019. LNCS, vol. 11478, pp. 636–666. Springer, Cham (2019). https://doi.org/10.1007/978-3-030-17659-4_22
6. Bennett, C.H., Brassard, G., Crépeau, C., Skubiszewska, M.-H.: Practical quantum oblivious transfer. In: Feigenbaum, J. (ed.) CRYPTO 1991. LNCS, vol. 576, pp. 351–366. Springer, Heidelberg (1992). https://doi.org/10.1007/3-540-46766-1_29
7. Bennett, C.H., Brassard, G., Robert, J.M.: Privacy amplification by public discussion. SIAM J. Comput. **17**(2), 210–229 (1988)
8. Bitansky, N., Canetti, R.: On strong simulation and composable point obfuscation. In: Rabin, T. (ed.) CRYPTO 2010. LNCS, vol. 6223, pp. 520–537. Springer, Heidelberg (2010). https://doi.org/10.1007/978-3-642-14623-7_28
9. Bitansky, N., Canetti, R., Kalai, Y.T., Paneth, O.: On virtual grey box obfuscation for general circuits. Algorithmica **79**(4), 1014–1051 (2017)
10. Blanton, M., Gasti, P.: Secure and efficient protocols for iris and fingerprint identification. In: Atluri, V., Diaz, C. (eds.) ESORICS 2011. LNCS, vol. 6879, pp. 190–209. Springer, Heidelberg (2011). https://doi.org/10.1007/978-3-642-23822-2_11
11. Blundo, C., De Cristofaro, E., Gasti, P.: EsPRESSo: efficient privacy-preserving evaluation of sample set similarity. In: Di Pietro, R., Herranz, J., Damiani, E., State, R. (eds.) DPM/SETOP -2012. LNCS, vol. 7731, pp. 89–103. Springer, Heidelberg (2013). https://doi.org/10.1007/978-3-642-35890-6_7
12. Boyen, X.: Reusable cryptographic fuzzy extractors. In: Proceedings of the 11th ACM Conference on Computer and Communications Security, pp. 82–91 (2004)
13. Boyen, X., Dodis, Y., Katz, J., Ostrovsky, R., Smith, A.: Secure remote authentication using biometric data. In: Cramer, R. (ed.) EUROCRYPT 2005. LNCS, vol. 3494, pp. 147–163. Springer, Heidelberg (2005). https://doi.org/10.1007/11426639_9
14. Bringer, J., Chabanne, H., Patey, A.: SHADE: secure HAmming DistancE computation from oblivious transfer. In: Adams, A.A., Brenner, M., Smith, M. (eds.) FC 2013. LNCS, vol. 7862, pp. 164–176. Springer, Heidelberg (2013). https://doi.org/10.1007/978-3-642-41320-9_11
15. Brzuska, C., Farshim, P., Mittelbach, A.: Indistinguishability obfuscation and UCEs: the case of computationally unpredictable sources. In: Garay, J.A., Gennaro, R. (eds.) CRYPTO 2014. LNCS, vol. 8616, pp. 188–205. Springer, Heidelberg (2014). https://doi.org/10.1007/978-3-662-44371-2_11
16. Canetti, R., Fuller, B., Paneth, O., Reyzin, L., Smith, A.: Reusable fuzzy extractors for low-entropy distributions. J. Cryptol. **34**(1), 1–33 (2020). https://doi.org/10.1007/s00145-020-09367-8
17. Canetti, R., Tauman Kalai, Y., Varia, M., Wichs, D.: On symmetric encryption and point obfuscation. In: Micciancio, D. (ed.) Theory Crypt., pp. 52–71. Springer, Berlin, Heidelberg (2010). https://doi.org/10.1007/978-3-642-11799-2_4
18. Cramer, R., Dodis, Y., Fehr, S., Padró, C., Wichs, D.: Detection of algebraic manipulation with applications to robust secret sharing and fuzzy extractors. In: Smart, N. (ed.) EUROCRYPT 2008. LNCS, vol. 4965, pp. 471–488. Springer, Heidelberg (2008). https://doi.org/10.1007/978-3-540-78967-3_27
19. Demarest, L., Fuller, B., Russell, A.: Code offset in the exponent. In: 2nd Conference on Information-Theoretic Cryptography (ITC 2021) (2021)

20. Deshmukh, S., Carter, H., Hernandez, G., Traynor, P., Butler, K.: Efficient and secure template blinding for biometric authentication. In: Communications and Network Security (CNS), 2016 IEEE Conference on, pp. 480–488. IEEE (2016)
21. Dodis, Y., Haralambiev, K., López-Alt, A., Wichs, D.: Efficient public-key cryptography in the presence of key leakage. In: Abe, M. (ed.) ASIACRYPT 2010. LNCS, vol. 6477, pp. 613–631. Springer, Heidelberg (2010). https://doi.org/10.1007/978-3-642-17373-8_35
22. Dodis, Y., Kanukurthi, B., Katz, J., Reyzin, L., Smith, A.: Robust fuzzy extractors and authenticated key agreement from close secrets. IEEE Trans. Inf. Theory **58**(9), 6207–6222 (2012). https://doi.org/10.1109/TIT.2012.2200290
23. Dodis, Y., Katz, J., Reyzin, L., Smith, A.: Robust fuzzy extractors and authenticated key agreement from close secrets. In: Dwork, C. (ed.) CRYPTO 2006. LNCS, vol. 4117, pp. 232–250. Springer, Heidelberg (2006). https://doi.org/10.1007/11818175_14
24. Dodis, Y., Ostrovsky, R., Reyzin, L., Smith, A.: Fuzzy extractors: How to generate strong keys from biometrics and other noisy data. SIAM J. Comput. **38**(1), 97–139 (2008)
25. Dodis, Y., Reyzin, L., Smith, A.: Fuzzy extractors: How to generate strong keys from biometrics and other noisy data. In: Cachin, C., Camenisch, J.L. (eds.) Advances in Cryptology - EUROCRYPT 2004, pp. 523–540. Springer, Berlin Heidelberg, Berlin, Heidelberg (2004)
26. Dodis, Y., Smith, A.: Correcting errors without leaking partial information. In: Proceedings of the Thirty-Seventh Annual ACM Symposium on Theory of Computing, pp. 654–663 (2005)
27. Dupont, P.-A., Hesse, J., Pointcheval, D., Reyzin, L., Yakoubov, S.: Fuzzy password-authenticated key exchange. In: Nielsen, J.B., Rijmen, V. (eds.) EUROCRYPT 2018. LNCS, vol. 10822, pp. 393–424. Springer, Cham (2018). https://doi.org/10.1007/978-3-319-78372-7_13
28. Evans, D., Huang, Y., Katz, J., Malka, L.: Efficient privacy-preserving biometric identification. In: Proceedings of the 17th Conference Network and Distributed System Security Symposium, NDSS (2011)
29. Feng, H., Tang, Q.: Computational robust (Fuzzy) extractors for CRS-dependent sources with minimal min-entropy. In: Nissim, K., Waters, B. (eds.) TCC 2021. LNCS, vol. 13043, pp. 689–717. Springer, Cham (2021). https://doi.org/10.1007/978-3-030-90453-1_24
30. Fuller, B.: Impossibility of efficient information-theoretic fuzzy extraction. Cryptology ePrint Archive, Paper 2023/172 (2023). https://eprint.iacr.org/2023/172
31. Fuller, B., Meng, X., Reyzin, L.: Computational fuzzy extractors. In: Sako, K., Sarkar, P. (eds.) ASIACRYPT 2013. LNCS, vol. 8269, pp. 174–193. Springer, Heidelberg (2013). https://doi.org/10.1007/978-3-642-42033-7_10
32. Fuller, B., Meng, X., Reyzin, L.: Computational fuzzy extractors. Inf. Comput., 104602 (2020)
33. Fuller, B., Peng, L.: Continuous-source fuzzy extractors: source uncertainty and insecurity. In: 2019 IEEE International Symposium on Information Theory (ISIT), pp. 2952–2956. IEEE (2019)
34. Fuller, B., Reyzin, L., Smith, A.: When are fuzzy extractors possible? In: International Conference on the Theory and Application of Cryptology and Information Security, pp. 277–306. Springer (2016). https://doi.org/10.1007/978-3-662-53887-6_10
35. Fuller, B., Reyzin, L., Smith, A.: When are fuzzy extractors possible? IEEE Trans. Inf. Theory **66**(8), 5282–5298 (2020)

36. Galbraith, S.D., Zobernig, L.: Obfuscated fuzzy hamming distance and conjunctions from subset product problems. In: Theory of Cryptography (2019). https://eprint.iacr.org/2019/620
37. Garg, S., Gentry, C., Halevi, S.: Candidate multilinear maps from ideal lattices. In: Johansson, T., Nguyen, P.Q. (eds.) EUROCRYPT 2013. LNCS, vol. 7881, pp. 1–17. Springer, Heidelberg (2013). https://doi.org/10.1007/978-3-642-38348-9_1
38. Garg, S., Gentry, C., Halevi, S., Raykova, M., Sahai, A., Waters, B.: Candidate indistinguishability obfuscation and functional encryption for all circuits. In: Proceedings of FOCS (2013)
39. Goyal, R., Koppula, V., Waters, B.: Lockable obfuscation. In: 2017 IEEE 58th Annual Symposium on Foundations of Computer Science (FOCS), pp. 612–621. IEEE Computer Society, Los Alamitos, CA, USA (2017). https://doi.org/10.1109/FOCS.2017.62, https://doi.ieeecomputersociety.org/10.1109/FOCS.2017.62
40. Hao, F., Anderson, R., Daugman, J.: Combining crypto with biometrics effectively. Comput. IEEE Trans. **55**(9), 1081–1088 (2006)
41. HÅstad, J., Impagliazzo, R., Levin, L.A., Luby, M.: A pseudorandom generator from any one-way function. SIAM J. Comput. **28**(4), 1364–1396 (1999). https://doi.org/10.1137/S0097539793244708
42. Hsiao, C.Y., Lu, C.J., Reyzin, L.: Conditional computational entropy, or toward separating pseudoentropy from compressibility. In: Naor, M. (ed.) Advances in Cryptology - EUROCRYPT 2007, pp. 169–186. Springer, Berlin Heidelberg, Berlin, Heidelberg (2007)
43. Škorić, B., Tuyls, P., Ophey, W.: Robust key extraction from physical uncloneable functions. In: Applied Cryptography and Network Security: Third International Conference, ACNS 2005, New York, NY, USA, June 7–10, 2005. Proceedings 3. pp. 407–422. Springer (2005)
44. Wen, Y., Liu, S.: Robustly reusable fuzzy extractor from standard assumptions. In: International Conference on the Theory and Application of Cryptology and Information Security. pp. 459–489. Springer (2018)
45. Wen, Y., Liu, S., Gu, D.: Generic constructions of robustly reusable fuzzy extractor. In: IACR International Workshop on Public Key Cryptography. pp. 349–378. Springer (2019)
46. Wen, Y., Liu, S., Han, S.: Reusable fuzzy extractor from the decisional Diffie-Hellman assumption. Designs, Codes and Cryptography (Jan 2018). https://doi.org/10.1007/s10623-018-0459-4, https://doi.org/10.1007/s10623-018-0459-4
47. Wichs, D., Zirdelis, G.: Obfuscating compute-and-compare programs under LWE. In: 2017 IEEE 58th Annual Symposium on Foundations of Computer Science (FOCS). pp. 600–611 (2017). https://doi.org/10.1109/FOCS.2017.61
48. Woodage, J., Chatterjee, R., Dodis, Y., Juels, A., Ristenpart, T.: A new distribution-sensitive secure sketch and popularity-proportional hashing. In: Annual International Cryptology Conference. pp. 682–710. Springer (2017)
49. Zhandry, M.: The magic of ELFs. J. Cryptol. **32**, 825–866 (2019)

X-Lock: A Secure XOR-Based Fuzzy Extractor for Resource Constrained Devices

Edoardo Liberati[1(✉)], Alessandro Visintin[2], Riccardo Lazzeretti[1], Mauro Conti[2,3], and Selcuk Uluagac[4]

[1] Sapienza University of Rome, Rome, Italy
e.liberati@diag.uniroma1.it
[2] University of Padua, Padua, Italy
[3] Delft University of Technology, Delft, Netherlands
[4] Florida International University, Miami, FL, USA

Abstract. The Internet of Things rapid growth poses privacy and security challenges for the traditional key storage methods. Physical Unclonable Functions offer a potential solution but require secure fuzzy extractors to ensure reliable replication. This paper introduces X-Lock, a novel and secure computational fuzzy extractor that addresses the limitations faced by traditional solutions in resource-constrained IoT devices. X-Lock offers a reusable and robust solution, effectively mitigating the impacts of bias and correlation through its design. Leveraging the preferred state of a noisy source, X-Lock encrypts a random string of bits that can be later used as seed to generate multiple secret keys. To prove our claims, we provide a comprehensive theoretical analysis, addressing security considerations, and implement the proposed model. To evaluate the effectiveness and superiority of our proposal, we also provide practical experiments and compare the results with existing approaches. The experimental findings demonstrate the efficacy of our algorithm, showing comparable memory cost ($\approx$ 2.4 KB for storing 5 keys of 128 bits) while being 3 orders of magnitude faster with respect to the state-of-the-art solution (0.086 ms against 15.51 s).

Keywords: Fuzzy extractor · Physical Unclonable Functions · Error tolerant cryptography

1 Introduction

Within the domain of Internet of Things (IoT), the presence of resource-constrained devices poses significant obstacles in ensuring the development of robust privacy and security mechanisms. While numerous cryptographic algorithms can be customized to address these challenges, their effectiveness hinges on the availability of securely maintained keys. Presently, prevalent practices involve the storage of digital keys in a Non-Volatile Memory (NVM), typically

C. Pöpper and L. Batina (Eds.): ACNS 2024, LNCS 14583, pp. 183–210, 2024.
https://doi.org/10.1007/978-3-031-54770-6_8

situated externally to the computing platform. However, the practical realization of secure digital key storage has emerged as a formidable endeavor, primarily attributed to technical limitations or cost-related considerations [14].

In this context, Physical Unclonable Functions (PUFs) [20] arise as a promising alternative solution. PUFs represent a viable replacement for NVM-based keys and offer several notable advantages, including cost-effectiveness, inherent uniqueness, and heightened resistance against various attacks [18]. PUFs derive confidential information from inherent process variations, similar to distinctive device fingerprints [7]. The replication of identical PUF instances becomes then practically unattainable, even when originating from the same manufacturer. Nevertheless, PUFs rely on physical circuit properties for generating responses, making them susceptible to factors such as thermal noise and environmental conditions. Consequently, achieving reliable replication of PUF responses poses a significant challenge [14].

The notion of fuzzy extractor [10] emerged as a highly regarded approach for addressing key management issues associated with error-prone data. A fuzzy extractor offers the ability to extract an identical random string from a noisy source without the need to store the string itself, therefore allowing the usage of noisy sources such as PUFs as cryptographic primitives. The general construction comprises two algorithms. The generation algorithm *Gen* takes an initial string S_{read} of the noisy source as input and produces a string K along with a helper data H. Subsequently, the reproduction algorithm *Rep* leverages the helper data H to reproduce the string K from a second string S'_{read} of the same source, given that the distance between S_{read} and S'_{read} is sufficiently small. The correctness property of a fuzzy extractor ensures that the reproduction process yields the same string K when the fuzzy data is generated from the same source. Additionally, the security aspect of a fuzzy extractor guarantees that the helper data H does not divulge any information about the original fuzzy data.

Previous works employed secure sketches and randomness extractors as core components for their constructions [2,25,26]. A secure sketch is an information reconciliation protocol that enables the recovery of the original S_{read} from a received S'_{read} when they are sufficiently close. Subsequently, a random string is extracted from S_{read} using a randomness extractor. However, it has been observed that secure sketches leak information through the helper data, leading to a loss of security [13]. Consequently, the construction of a fuzzy extractor based on secure sketches necessitates the utilization of high entropy source data.

Recently, a novel class of solutions introduced an innovative approach to construct fuzzy extractors [5,6,13,28]. These solutions employ S_{read} to encrypt a random string in a manner that allows for decryption with knowledge of a closely related string S'_{read}. Fuller et al. [13] presented a computational fuzzy extractor based on the Learning With Errors (LWE) problem. Their approach effectively mitigates information leakage from the helper data by concealing secret randomness within it. However, this construction exhibits notable inefficiency and only tolerates sub-linear errors. Additionally, it lacks guarantees of reusability (see Definition 2) and robustness (see Definition 3). Canetti et al. [5,6] employed digital lockers as their cryptographic primitive. Their solution is applicable even with low-entropy sources and ensures reusability. However, their sample-then-lock technique necessitates excessive storage space for the helper values. Woo et al. [28] proposed a solution based on non-linear LWE, which offers memory efficiency while simultaneously guaranteeing both reusability and robustness. Nevertheless, their solution is computationally demanding and may not be suitable for restricted environments.

This paper presents X-Lock, a novel design for a secure and cost-effective computational fuzzy extractor. Similar to [5,6,13,28], X-Lock utilizes the noisy strings obtained from a fuzzy source to protect a random string of bits. X-Lock encrypts each bit of the random string by XOR-ing it multiple times with a subset of bits from the noisy string. Through this approach, X-Lock offers reusability and robustness while inherently addressing bias and correlation issues within the fuzzy source. Bias quantifies the equilibrium between 0 s and 1 s within the fuzzy response, whereas correlation evaluates the degree of independence among distinct bits within the same fuzzy response. To substantiate these assertions, we conducted a comprehensive theoretical analysis encompassing both the security and the implementation aspects of our model. Furthermore, we conducted practical experiments and comparisons with existing state-of-the-art approaches to demonstrate the superiority of our proposal.

The empirical results demonstrate the optimal performance of our proposed model. With a key size of 128 bits, our algorithm uses ≈ 2.4 KB to store 5 keys. Furthermore, the execution time for the *Rep* procedure amounts to 0.086 ms. In contrast, Canetti et al. [5,6] necessitates 216.20 MB and ≈ 1 min computational time, while Woo et al. [28] utilizes ≈ 2.8 KB and operates at a speed of 15.51 s (see Sect. 6). Overall, our model achieves comparable memory cost with the state-of-the-art solutions while outperforming them by being 3 orders of magnitude faster.

Contributions. In summary, this paper offers the following contributions:

- We present X-Lock, a novel design for a secure and cost-effective fuzzy extractor based on XOR operations;
- We introduce the XOR iteration (XOR-ation) as our cryptographic primitive that efficiently mitigates source bias and correlation;
- We provision our model with robustness, reusability and insider security through straightforward and effective strategies;
- We provide a thorough theoretical analysis of our model including storage, computational and security aspects;
- We implement X-Lock in C language and conduct practical experiments to compare our results to the current state-of-the-art solutions.

Organization. The rest of the paper is organized as follows. In Sect. 2 we introduce previous works and the state-of-the-art in reusable and robust fuzzy extractors. In Sect. 3 we provide background information on PUFs, fuzzy extractors, bias and correlation. In Sect. 4 we describe the algorithm of X-Lock in details. In Sect. 5 we explain the rationale and conduct a security analysis over our methodology. In Sect. 6 we describe our implementation of the algorithm and show the results of the comparison with both Canetti et al. [5,6] and Woo et al. [28]. Finally, Sect. 7 closes the paper with some final remarks.

2 Related Works

Since the pioneering work of Dodis et al. [10], the concept of fuzzy extractor has emerged as a prominent solution for managing keys derived from noisy sources. Most fuzzy extractors adopt the sketch-then-extract paradigm, employing secure sketches and randomness extractors as fundamental components [2,25,26]. However, secure sketches entail a minor data leakage from the helper data, leading to compromised security [13]. Consequently, the utilization of a secure sketch-based fuzzy extractor necessitates high-entropy source data.

The notion of reusability, as formalized by Boyen [2], pertains to the security of multiple pairs of extracted strings and associated helper data, even when such helper data is exposed to an adversary. The work showcases that achieving information-theoretic reusability requires a significant reduction in security, thereby implying an inherent trade-off. Related again to fuzzy extractors security, Boyen et al. [3] introduce the notion of a robust fuzzy extractor to safeguard the helper data against malicious modifications, ensuring the detection of any such alterations. Both these security criteria must be satisfied to ensure the viability of fuzzy extractors as secure authentication methods in real-life scenarios.

In a departure from secure sketch-based approaches, Fuller et al. [13] propose a computational fuzzy extractor based on the LWE problem. Their methodology employs noisy strings to encrypt a random string in such a way that it can be decrypted with the knowledge of another closely related string. By concealing secret randomness within the helper data instead of extracting it from the noisy string, their approach mitigates data leakage concerns. Nonetheless, their construction exhibits significant inefficiency in terms of memory requirements and computational time and can only tolerate sub-linear errors, while lacking reusability. Apon et al. [1] improve upon Fuller's construction to fulfill the reusability requirement by utilizing either a random oracle or a lattice-based symmetric encryption technique. However, their solution remains unable to overcome the limitations of the construction by Fuller et al. [13], allowing only a logarithmic fraction of error tolerance. Another proposal by Wen et al. [25] presents a reusable fuzzy extractor based on the LWE problem, resilient to linear fractions of errors. Nevertheless, their scheme relies on a secure sketch and consequently results in the leakage of sensitive data.

Addressing the limitations of prior works, Canetti et al. [5,6] introduce a fuzzy extractor construction employing inputs from low-entropy distributions, leveraging the concept of digital lockers [4,16] as a symmetric key cryptographic primitive. Their strategy involves sampling multiple partial strings from a noisy input string, hashing them independently, and then locking individual secret keys with each hashed partial string. Correctness ensues if there is a high likelihood of successfully recovering at least one hashed subset of data upon a second measurement. To achieve this, the scheme necessitates a large helper data size for storing the hashed values and employs an inefficient reproduction algorithm. To address this concern, Cheon et al. [8] made adjustments to the first scheme proposed by Canetti et al. [5], reducing the size of the helper data. However, this modification results in an increased computational cost for the reproduction algorithm due to the introduction of a significant amount of hashing operations.

A recent contribution by Woo et al. [28] presents a novel computational fuzzy extractor that does not rely on a secure sketch or digital lockers. Their construction offers security under the non-linear LWE problem and encodes the extracted key using two cryptographic primitives: error correcting codes (ECCs) and the EMBLEM encoding method [21]. This innovative approach achieves both robustness and reusability while tolerating linear errors. However, it assumes that the source data is drawn from a uniform distribution and, although more efficient than previous works, it still entails a non-negligible computational effort that may limit its adoption on low-end devices.

In contrast with previous works, X-Lock efficiently satisfies all the security properties required from a secure fuzzy extractor. The protocol only uses XOR operations in its procedure, thus cutting the computational complexity. Additionally, the XOR primitive inherently introduces a mitigation for both source bias and correlation issues (see Sect. 3). It is noteworthy that none of the previous works adequately addresses such bias and correlation issues. In real-world setups, fuzzy sources rarely produce perfectly random outputs and may exhibit biases towards a specific value, as well as correlations among bits. While the construction by Canetti et al. [5,6] implicitly addresses the correlation problem, the bias issue remains unaddressed in the existing literature. Security guarantees of proposals in the existing literature are summarized in Table 1.

Table 1. Properties comparison.

Construction	Correctness	Leak Prevention	Reusability	Robustness	Correlation	Bias
Canetti et al. [5,6]	•	•	•	•	•	
Fuller et al. [13]	•	•				
Apon et al. [1]	•	•				
Wen et al. [25]	•		•			
Cheon et al. [9]	•	•	•	•	•	
Woo et al. [28]	•	•	•	•		
Our work	•	•	•	•	•	•

3 Background

General Notation. We use lowercase letters to denote single values. We use capital letters to denote groups of values that are either organized in sets or strings. With $\{\cdot\}^x$ we denote a group of cardinality x that contains values from those described inside the braces. We denote with $|X|$ the cardinality of the group X. We define $||X||$ as the Hamming weight of X, i.e. the number of its non-zero values. The notation $Pr[\cdot]$ expresses the probability of the event described inside the square brackets. We denote the XOR logical operation with $\oplus$. When applied to sequences of bits, $\oplus$ is intended to perform a bit-wise XOR. We introduce the XOR-ation operator $\bigoplus_{i=0}^{I}$, performing the XOR operation iteratively over a sequence of bits denoted by the indexes $0 \leq i \leq I$. Note that the order of the indexes does not change the final result. We provide a summary of the notation used throughout the paper in Table 2. As a final remark, notice that we adapted definitions coming from the literature according to our notation, for sake of clarity and coherence.

Table 2. Notation summary.

Symbol	Meaning
$\|X\|$	Cardinality of group X
$\|\|X\|\|$	Hamming weight of group X
$\bigoplus_{y \in Y}$	XOR-ation over the set of indexes Y
F	Fuzzy source
S_{read}, S_{pref}	Random string and preferred string of a fuzzy source
e_{rel}, e_{abs}	Relative error and absolute error
Gen, *Rep*	Procedures involved in a fuzzy extractor
K, H	Secret key and helper data generated by *Gen*
p_{bias}	Number of 1s in a string over its total number of bits
ϕ	Correlation factor of a fuzzy source
B	Poll of random bits
C	Bits involved in the XOR-ation
L	Bit-locker, group of locks relative to the same bit
K_{pre}	Final values before obtaining K
V	Vault
n	nonce
R	Set of random indices of original bits constituting a key
T	Authentication token
$\perp$	None value

PUFs Characterization. PUFs leverage the inherent random variations introduced during the silicon manufacturing process to generate secret keys on the fly [20]. These variations, akin to unique fingerprints, serve as a cost-effective source of randomness. Conceptually, a PUF can be viewed as a function where a specific binary input (*i.e.*, a challenge) elicits distinct binary outputs (*i.e.*, responses) specific to each individual PUF instance. However, outputs obtained from the same PUF circuit may exhibit variations due to factors such as thermal noise and environmental conditions.

Consequently, we conceptualize a PUF circuit as a fuzzy source F that provides a string of bits S_{read} upon request. When comparing two such sequences from F they can exhibit different values in certain positions. We formalize this aspect with the relative error $e_{rel} = \frac{||S_{read} \oplus S'_{read}||}{|S_{read}|}$, that is the ratio of bits in S_{read} that differ from S'_{read}. Together with S_{read}, we introduce the concept of preferred string S_{pref}, which is obtained by identifying the value appearing most frequently (*i.e.*, more than 50% of the times) for each bit within the string. We calculate it by using a statistically significant number of S_{read} (*e.g.*, more than 100 strings). Figure 1 reports the estimation of the number of bits we expect to be incorrectly identified with respect to the number of strings read to craft S_{pref}. The plot shows both the trend of the expected number of errors, which exponentially decreases as the number of strings increases, and the threshold on the number of strings that brings such expectation below 1. Similarly to e_{rel}, we define the absolute error e_{abs} as the ratio of bits in S_{read} that differ from S_{pref}. Notably, the two errors are linked by the inequality $0 \leq e_{rel} \leq 2 \cdot e_{abs}$. Indeed, consider two strings S_{read} and S'_{read} that have wrong bits in the same positions, if any. Then their relative error is $e_{rel} = 0$. On the other hand, consider two strings S_{read} and S'_{read} that exhibit the maximum possible error e_{abs} with respect to S_{pref} but have no wrong shared bit. Then their relative error is $e_{rel} = 2 \cdot e_{abs}$.

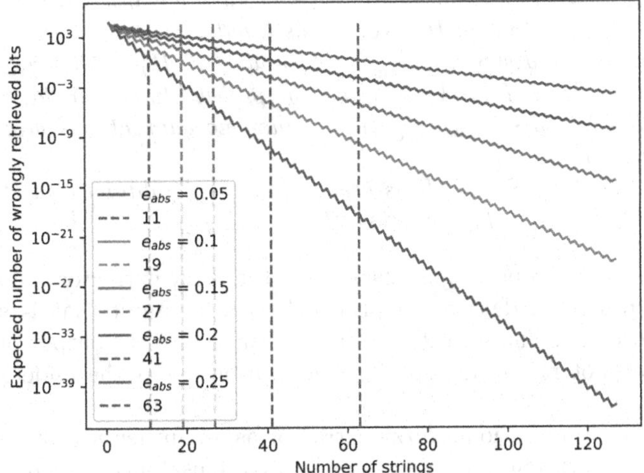

Fig. 1. Expected number of wrong bits (logarithmic scale) over number of strings. (Color figure online)

It is crucial to underscore that when setting up the fuzzy extractor using the raw S_{read} instead of S_{pref}, it is likely to introduce additional errors into the process, ultimately increasing the likelihood of recovering an incorrect key. Hence, in the context of this paper, we employ S_{pref} as our reference string and, consequently, we consider e_{abs} to be the error rate associated with F.

Fuzzy Extractors. Fuzzy extractors [10] are cryptographic constructions designed to derive reliable and uniformly distributed cryptographic keys from sources prone to noise or errors. This process involves two probabilistic procedures. The *Gen* procedure takes a string S_{read} and produces a random string K along with a public helper string H. If another string S'_{read} is sufficiently close to S_{read} (*i.e.*, $||S_{read} \oplus S'_{read}|| \leq t$ for a small t), the *Rep* procedure can utilize the helper string H to correctly reproduce the original random string K from S'_{read}.

In this work, we focus on computational fuzzy extractors that consider the scenario where potential attackers possess knowledge about the noise distribution and have control over the errors. To formalize this concept, we define a metric space as a finite set $\mathcal{M}$ equipped with a distance function $dis : \mathcal{M} \times \mathcal{M} \rightarrow R^+ = [0, \infty)$ that satisfies the identity property ($dis(x, y) = 0$ if and only if $x = y$), the symmetry property ($dis(x, y) = dis(y, x)$), and the triangle inequality ($dis(x, z) \leq dis(x, y) + dis(y, z)$). The statistical distance [5,6] $SD(X, Y)$ is defined as $\frac{1}{2}\sum_x(Pr[X = x] - Pr[Y = x])$.

Definition 1 (Computational fuzzy extractor, [12] **Definition** 4**).** *Given a metric space* $(\mathcal{M}, dis)$*, let* $\mathcal{F}$ *be a family of probability distributions over* $\mathcal{M}$*. A pair of randomized procedures (Gen,Rep) is an* $(\mathcal{M}, \mathcal{F}, k, t, \epsilon)$*-computational fuzzy extractor with error* δ *if Gen and Rep satisfy the following properties:*

- *Gen on input* $S_{read} \in \mathcal{M}$ *outputs* $K \in \{0,1\}^k$ *and a helper string* $H \in \{0,1\}^*$*.*
- *Rep takes* $S'_{read} \in \mathcal{M}$ *and* $H \in \{0,1\}^*$ *as inputs.*
- ***Correctness.*** *If* $dis(S_{read}, S'_{read}) \leq t$ *and* $(K, H) \leftarrow Gen(S_{read})$*, then* $Pr[Rep(S'_{read}, H) = K] \geq 1 - \delta$*, where the probability is over the randomness of* (Gen, Rep)*. If* $dis(S_{read}, S'_{read}) > t$*, then no guarantee is provided about the output of Rep.*
- ***Security.*** *For any* $F \in \mathcal{F}$*,* K *is pseudo-random conditioned on* H*, that is if* $(K, H) \leftarrow Gen(S_{read})$ *then* $SD((K, H), (U_k, H)) \leq \epsilon$*.*

The correctness property guarantees that the fuzzy extractor can accurately retrieve the protected data when provided with an input that is sufficiently close to the original. The security property ensures that the output of the fuzzy extractor does not reveal any specific information about the underlying noisy distribution.

To utilize a computational fuzzy extractor as an authentication mechanism, it must possess both reusability and robustness. Reusability [2] is related to the case where the helper data associated to several extracted strings is revealed to an adversary.

Definition 2 (Reusability, [6] **Definition** 6**).** *Let* $\mathcal{F}$ *be a family of distributions over* $\mathcal{M}$*. Let* $(F^1, F^2, \ldots, F^\rho)$ *be* ρ *correlated random variables such that* $\forall i = 1, \ldots, \rho : F^i \in \mathcal{F}$*. Let* (Gen, Rep) *be a* $(\mathcal{M}, \mathcal{F}, k, t, \epsilon)$*-computational fuzzy extractor with error* δ*. Let* D *be a distinguisher that outputs* 0 *when it believes that the input was randomly produced and* 1 *when it believes it was produced by* (Gen, Rep)*. Define the following game* $\forall j = 1, \ldots, \rho$*:*

- ***Sampling.*** *The challenger samples* $S^j_{read} \leftarrow F^j$ *and* $u \leftarrow \{0,1\}^k$.
- ***Generation.*** *The challenger computes* $(K^j, H^j) \leftarrow Gen(S^j_{read})$.
- ***Distinguishing.*** *The advantage of* D *is quantifiable as* $Adv(D) = Pr[D(K^1, \ldots, K^{j-1}, K^j, K^{j+1}, \ldots, K^\rho, H^1, \ldots, H^\rho) = 1] - Pr[D(K^1, ..., K^{j-1}, u, K^{j+1}, ..., K^\rho, H^1, ..., H^\rho) = 1]$.

(Gen, Rep) is (ρ, σ)*-reusable if* $\forall D \in \mathcal{D}$ *and* $\forall j = 1, \ldots, \rho$*, the advantage is at most* σ.

In an intuitive sense, if a fuzzy extractor is reusable, it implies that a specific key K remains secure even when the adversary possesses knowledge of all associated helper data. This includes both the helper data linked to the key K and the helper data related to all other keys. In other words, this property ensures the security of keys generated by the fuzzy extractor even when the generation process is repeated multiple times across different strings, consequently permitting the reuse of the same secret noisy source (*e.g.,* the same iris, the same fingerprint, the same PUF, etc.) in multiple contexts.

As underlined in Canetti et al. [5,6], the key aspect is that the family of distributions $\mathcal{F}$ is arbitrarily correlated, meaning no assumption is made on the correlation between the distributions.

Robustness [3] addresses the scenario where an adversary modifies the helper data H before it is given to the user. A robust fuzzy extractor ensures that any changes made by an adversary to H will be detected.

Definition 3 (Robustness, [3] **Definition** 6). *Let* $\mathcal{F}$ *be a family of distributions over* $\mathcal{M}$. *Let* $\perp$ *denote that Rep detected a tampered output. Let (Gen, Rep) be a* $(\mathcal{M}, \mathcal{F}, k, t, \epsilon)$*-computational fuzzy extractor with error* δ. *Let* $(K, H) \leftarrow Gen(S_{read})$*, with* S_{read} *output of* F. *Let* A *be an adversary, and* $H' \leftarrow A(K, H)$ *with* $H \neq H'$. *Then (Gen, Rep) is a* τ*-robust fuzzy extractor if* $Pr[Rep(S'_{read}, H') \neq \perp] \leq \tau$.

Bias and Correlation in Fuzzy Sources. In real-world scenarios, fuzzy sources often exhibit non-uniform distributions in their output bit strings. These deviations from uniformity can arise from two main factors: bias and correlation among the physical components of the source. When bias is present [17], it means that either 0-bits or 1-bits occur more frequently than the other. We quantify bias by the parameter p_{bias}, with $p_{bias} \cdot l$ being the expected number of 1-bits in a l-bit response. An unbiased source would have $p_{bias} = 0.5$, indicating an equal probability for 0-bits and 1-bits. A biased (non-uniform) source, instead, exhibits unbalanced quantities of 1-bits and 0-bits, offering the adversary an advantage when trying to compromise the source itself. Correlation, on the other hand [27], refers to the lack of independence among the values of the bits generated by the noisy source. This lack of independence arises due to physical dependencies, such as cross-talk noise among Static Random Access Memory (SRAM) cells [19], where the value of one bit can be influenced by neighboring bits in the physical medium. Such relationship among bits significantly decreases the security guarantees of the system since disclosing a bit may compromise several other bits, reducing the overall search space size. To precisely define the concept of correlation, we introduce the notion of correlation classes of bits.

Definition 4 (Correlation class of a bit). *Let $F \in \mathcal{F}$ be a fuzzy source drawn from a family of noisy sources $\mathcal{F}$. Let $\sim$ denote the equivalence relation such that, given two bits b and b', the value of a bit can be inferred by knowing the value of the other one if $b \sim b'$. The equivalence relation exhibits the commutative property, i.e., $b \sim b'$ if and only if $b' \sim b$. Let S_{pref} be the preferred string of F. Then, the correlation class $[b]$ of bit b is the set $\{b' \in S_{pref} : b' \sim b\}$ of elements that are equivalent to b.*

It is important to note that the correlation classes are disjoint, meaning that a bit can only belong to a single class. The total number of correlation classes corresponds to the maximum number of independent values that can be extracted from a particular source. In this work, we assume that the correlation classes have approximately the same size, meaning that each independent value has an equal probability of being selected in a random draw. To quantify the level of correlation, we introduce the correlation factor ϕ.

Definition 5 (Correlation factor). *Let $F \in \mathcal{F}$ be a fuzzy source drawn from a family of noisy sources $\mathcal{F}$. Let S_{pref} be the preferred string of F. Let $[S_{pref}]$ denote the set of all correlation classes in S_{pref} and $||[S_{pref}]||$ the total number of correlation classes in S_{pref}. Then, the correlation factor is defined as $\phi = 1 - \frac{||[S_{pref}]||}{|S_{pref}|}$.*

The correlation factor provides an immediate measure of dependency between the source bits.

For example, a correlation factor of $\phi = 0.75$ indicates that we expect three dependant values for every four bits in the source.

Threat Model. The model involves two parties, a legit user and an attacker. The user leverages the PUF to extract multiple secure keys out of the noisy source. The user may be either a human owning a device or the device itself. Instead, the attacker aims at compromising the extracted keys. In this scenario, we consider an adversary who has complete control over the communication channels [11]. The adversary has access to the appliance that executes the algorithm and stores its data. However, we explicitly exclude the possibility of extensive physical attacks or invasive side-channel attacks by the adversary. These types of attacks would require unrestricted access to the device for extended periods of time, which would raise suspicion and allow for their detection. Furthermore, we assume that the adversary can read data from standard non-volatile memory and modify it. However, the PUF in the system possesses a tamper-evidence property. If the adversary attempts to learn the secret stored in it, the behavior of the PUF will change significantly or be destroyed, thereby indicating the tampering. Lastly, we assume that all algorithms related to our protocol are public, but implemented in a way that prevents modification. This assumption ensures that the adversary cannot tamper with or modify the algorithms to their advantage. Overall, our focus is to design a theoretically secure protocol which ensures reliable replication of a key out of a PUF. Other potential vulnerabilities are then out of the scope of this work.

4 X-Lock: Construction Details

We consider a noisy source F that outputs a bit-string S_{read} of length $|S_{read}|$ upon request. We denote S_{pref} as the preferred state of F and e_{rel}, e_{abs} to be respectively its relative and absolute errors. Section 3 provides a thorough description of these quantities.

Similarly to existing works [5,6,13,28], our algorithm shares a common thread in leveraging the outputs generated by F to encrypt a random string of bits B. However, we significantly differentiate from the previous proposals as we employ S_{pref} to encrypt a large pool of bits B by means of the XOR-ation operator. We then decrypt and combine random subsets of B to generate multiple secret keys. The core element of the algorithm is the vault V resulting from the encryption of B. We provide a reference of the structure of V in Fig. 2. It consists of a sequence of bit-lockers, which individually guard the encryption of a single bit $b \in B$. Each bit-locker is a collection of locks L, where each lock is the XOR of a distinct b with the XOR-ation of a random subset of bits from S_{pref}. To restore the bit value b is then sufficient to retrieve a S_{read} from F and perform the XOR-ation on the lock value with same subset of bits. In Sect. 5 we show that this construction indeed forms a valid computational fuzzy extractor.

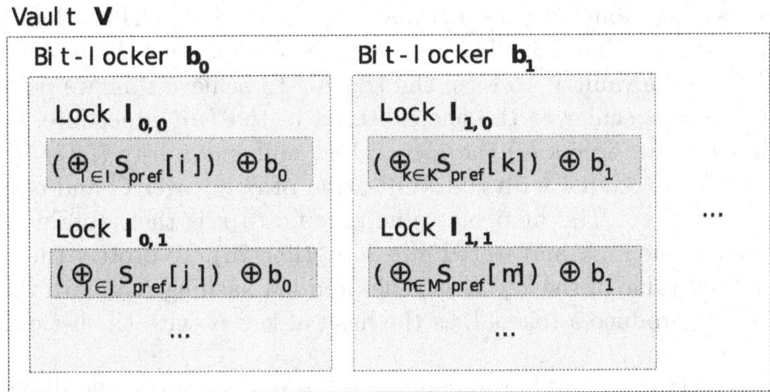

Fig. 2. Composition of the vault V. It is a collection of bit-lockers, each referring to a specific bit $b \in B$. A bit-locker contains multiple locks that XOR the bit of reference with the XOR-ation of a random subset of bits from the source F.

To perform the initial encryption of B into V, our algorithm introduces an $Init$ procedure that needs to be executed only once.

Subsequently, our approach involves the two standard probabilistic procedures *Gen* and *Rep*. In the following, we provide a thorough description of the three procedures, integrated by the pseudo-code of the design presented in Algorithm 1.

Init. The *Init* procedure (line 1) is responsible for generating the initial vault V.

The procedure receives in input the preferred string S_{pref}, the random pool of bits B, the number of locks $|L|$ per bit-locker, and the number of bits $|C|$ to use in each XOR-ation. We provide details on the generation of S_{pref} in Sect. 3. We first iterate over all the bits $b \in B$ (line 3), and for each b we generate $|L|$ locks (line 5). For each lock l, we select $|C|$ random indexes (line 6) and use them to select the bits in S_{pref} for the XOR-ation (line 7). The procedure eventually returns V (line 10).

The function $drawVaultIndexes$ (line 6) selects $|C|$ indexes spanning from 1 to $|S_{pref}|$ without replacement, *i.e.*, with no index selected more than once. We provide details of its implementation in Sect. 5.3.

The use of multiple locks adds correctness to our construction. We demonstrate this aspect in Sect. 5.1. Additionally, the XOR-ation mitigates the effects of bias and correlation in F. We provide an explanation in Sect. 5.2.

Gen. The *Gen* procedure (line 11) generates a novel key K, the nonce n, the set of indexes R and its authentication token T. Notice that $H' = (n, R, T)$ constitutes part of the helper data $H = (V, H')$. In particular, H' is the portion of helper data specifically related to each key, whilst V is common and shared among all keys.

The procedure takes in input the string S_{read}, the vault V, the number of bits $|B|$ of the random pool B, and the number of bits $|K|$ of the key K. We first generate a random nonce n (line 12) and a sequence R of $|K|$ random indexes in the range $[1, |B|]$ (line 13). The indexes $r \in R$ represent the subset of bits decrypted from the vault V to form the key K. To achieve this, we perform an operation that is specular to the one executed in the *Init* procedure. For each $r \in R$ (line 15), we access all the lock values and index lists (l, C) (line 17). For each (l, C), we XOR l with the XOR-ation of S_{read} over C and collect the resulting bit b' in X. The final bit value specific to r is then obtained as the most common value in X and stored into K_{pre} (line 20). To protect the restored values, the final value of the key K is generated via hashing $K_{pre}$with the nonce n (line 21). We produce a token T as the hash of key K with the list of indexes R.

The generation of T adds robustness to the methodology. We discuss it in further detail in Sect. 5.1. The procedure returns the key K, the nonce n, the list of indexes R, and the token T.

The function $drawKeyIndexes$ (line 13) selects $|K|$ indexes spanning from 1 to $|B|$ without replacement. We provide more details in Section 5.3. Notice that $drawVaultIndexes$ and $drawKeyIndexes$ could be implemented with the same procedure since both draw a certain number of indexes spanning in a certain range without replacement.

Rep. The *Rep* procedure (line 24) restores the key K from the vault V.

The procedure receives in input the string S'_{read} and the helper data $H = (V, H') = (V, (n, R, T))$, where V is the vault, n is the nonce, R is the list of indexes, and T is the authentication token. The procedure first iterates over $r \in R$ and restores the majority values similarly to the *Gen* procedure (lines 26 - 31). It then generates the key K' (line 32) and the token T' (line 33). In case T' does not coincide with T, the procedure returns a null value (line 35). Otherwise, it outputs the restored key K' as valid (line 36).

5 X-Lock: Algorithm Analysis

5.1 Security Analysis

We first introduce two definitions that are propaedeutic to the security analysis.

Definition 6 (Common elements between combinations). *Let X be a group of elements with cardinality $|X|$. Consider the process of drawing a random combination of y elements without replacement out of X. Then the probability p_{share} for two combinations to share at most z elements is quantifiable as*

$$p_{share} = \sum_{i=0}^{z} \frac{\binom{y}{i}\binom{|X|-y}{y-i}}{\binom{|X|}{y}}.$$

The numerator computes the number of combinations that share exactly i elements. It selects i elements out of the y available, followed by choosing the remaining $y - i$ elements out of the remaining $|X| - y$ values. Dividing by the total number of available combinations yields the partial percentage. The summation then sums all the contributions up to z common elements.

Definition 7 (Odd binomial distribution). *Let consider a Bernoulli trial with probability p of success and y independent trials. Then the odd binomial distribution considers the contributions of odd indexes in the summation of trial probabilities. In formula,*

$$p_{odd} = \sum_{i=0}^{\frac{y}{2}} \binom{y}{2i+1} \cdot p^{2i+1} \cdot (1-p)^{y-2i-1}.$$

The formula employs Bernoulli trials to assess the probability of having exactly $2i + 1$ successes in the elements. The summation from 0 to $y/2$ and the index $2i + 1$ permit to consider all the odd numbers between 0 and y.

We then introduce the Roucé-Capelli theorem that stands at the core of our security demonstration.

Theorem 1 (Rouché-Capelli). *A system of linear equations with n variables has a solution if and only if the rank of its coefficient matrix A is equal to the rank of its augmented matrix $A|b$. If there are solutions, they form an affine subspace $\mathbb{R}^n$ of dimension $n - rank(A)$. In particular:*

Algorithm 1. X-Lock algorithm. [] denotes an empty array. X[y] denotes the value at index y in array X. [x,y] denotes the interval of numbers from x to y.

```
procedure Init(S_pref, B, |L|, |C|)
    V ← []
    for b ∈ B do
        L ← []
        for _ in [1, |L|] do
            C ← drawVaultIndexes([1, |S_pref|], |C|)
            l ← (⊕_{c∈C} S_pref[c]) ⊕ b
            L.append(l, C)
        V.append(L)
    return V
procedure Gen(S_read, V, |B|, |K|)
    n ← getNonce()
    R ← drawKeyIndexes([1, |B|], |K|)
    K_pre ← []
    for r ∈ R do
        X ← []
        for (l, C) ∈ V[r] do
            b' ← (⊕_{c∈C} S_read[c]) ⊕ l
            X.append(b')
        K_pre.append(getMajorityValue(X))
    K ← hash(K_pre, n)
    T ← hash(K, R)
    return K, n, R, T
procedure Rep(S'_read, V, n, R, T)
    K'_pre ← []
    for r ∈ R do
        X ← []
        for (l, C) ∈ V[r] do
            b' ← (⊕_{c∈C} S'_read[c]) ⊕ l
            X.append(b')
        K'_pre.append(getMajorityValue(X))
    K' ← hash(K'_pre, n)
    T' ← hash(K', R)
    if T ≠ T' then
        return ⊥
    return K'
```

- *if* $n = rank(A)$*, then the solution is unique;*
- *otherwise there are infinitely many solutions.*

Proof. See introductory level book on linear algebra and geometry [22]. □

The Rouché-Capelli theorem states that a system of linear equations possesses a unique solution only if the number of independent equations equals the number of total variables. If there are more equations than variables, the system may become inconsistent, leading to the absence of a solution. Conversely, if there are fewer equations, the system becomes under-determined, providing an infinite number of potential solutions.

We are now ready to provide the proof of the security of the vault V.

Theorem 2 (Solution space of the vault). *Let S_{pref} be the preferred string of F. Let V be a vault with $|L|$ locks per bit-locker and $|C|$ bits per XOR-ation. Let ϕ be the correlation factor related to F. Then the solution space of V has at least dimension $(1-\phi)\cdot|S_{pref}|+(1-|L|)\cdot|B|$.*

Proof. The pool vault V is a collection of bit-lockers, each composed of $|L|$ locks that guard an individual bit from B (see Fig. 2). Each lock XORs a distinct bit from B with a XOR-ation of $|C|$ bits from S_{pref}. It is easy to see that a lock is a linear equation, thus making the vault V a system of $|B|\cdot|L|$ equations. Given the correlation factor ϕ, the independent variables provided by F to the system are $|S_{pref}|-\phi\cdot|S_{pref}|=(1-\phi)\cdot|S_{pref}|$. B provides exactly $|B|$ variables as its bits are independent by definition. Thus the number of variables in the system is $(1-\phi)\cdot|S_{pref}|+|B|$. We then recall from Theorem 1 that the dimension of the solution space is calculated as $n-rank(A)$, with n the total number of involved variables. In our case, $rank(V)\leq|B|\cdot|L|$ as some of the equations may not be independent. Hence we end up with the inequality $n-rank(V)\geq((1-\phi)\cdot|S_{pref}|+|B|)-(|B|\cdot|L|)$, thus proving the statement. □

The solution space of the vault is directly related to the security of the protocol, as it determines the number of parameters a potential attacker needs to provide to solve the linear system. A closer look to Theorem 2 suggests that, for increasing the security of the vault V, we want high $|S_{pref}|, |B|$ and low $\phi, |L|$.

Definition 8 (Security of the vault). *A vault V is (α,β)-secure if the number of total locks equals α and the probability for two locks to share at most half of the elements is less than β.*

By imposing that at most half of the elements are dependent, we make sure that combining two equations results in an equation with more variables than the initial ones. We provide experimental evidence of this in Sect. 6. The definition permits to manage the security of the vault V. Notice that the dimension of the random pool B is determined by the two parameters α,β. As per Theorem 2, $\phi, |S_{pref}|, |L|, |B|$ determine the solution space. $\phi, |S_{pref}|$ are determined by the physical parameters of the fuzzy source F. We can then set $|L|$ and require the vault V to provide a certain probability that mixing locks does not provide information to the attacker. By doing this, we set the desired solution space and thus the dimension of $|B|$.

We can now show that Algorithm 1, described in Sect. 4, satisfies the interpretation of computational fuzzy extractor given in Definition 1.

Theorem 3. *X-Lock is a $(\mathcal{M},\mathcal{F},k,t,\epsilon)$-computational fuzzy extractor with error δ.*

Proof. We first notice that the helper data for a particular key in our construction is $H = (V, (n, R, T))$. The vault V is generated once and shared by all keys, while $H' = (n, R, T)$ is specific for each key. Following Definition 1, we first show that (Gen, Rep) are valid functions for a computational fuzzy extractor. Procedure Gen takes in input $S_{read}, V, |B|, |K|$ and outputs K, n, R, T. This aligns with the definition $(K, H) \leftarrow Gen(S_{read})$, where $V, |B|, |K|$ are supporting input parameters and $H = H' = (n, R, T)$ for the output. Procedure Rep takes in input S'_{read}, V, n, R, T and outputs either K' or $\perp$. This again conforms to the general definition $K \leftarrow Rep(S'_{read}, H)$, with $H = (V, (n, R, T))$ in the input and $K = K'$ for the output.

We now proceed in demonstrating the correctness of the algorithm. Specifically, we show that the procedure correctly retrieves the keys with distance t between strings measured through e_{abs} and retrieval error δ proportional to $e_{bitlock}$. We focus on a single bit-locker, as the generalization is trivial. Recalling from Sect. 4, a bit-locker is a collection of locks that XOR a bit $b \in B$ with a XOR-ation of bits from S_{pref}. By using multiple incorrect bits the probability of having an error augments. Considering the absolute error e_{abs}, we can calculate the probability e_{lock} for a lock to return the wrong value by using the odd binomial distribution in Definition 7. In particular, we set the probability of success $p = e_{abs}$ and the number of trials $y = |C|$. This formulation captures the idea that a XOR-ation returns an incorrect value whenever there is an odd number of errors in its elements. Using e_{lock}, we can now estimate the probability $e_{bitlock}$ for a bit-locker to reconstruct an incorrect bit:

$$e_{bitlock} = \sum_{i=\frac{|L|}{2}}^{|L|} \binom{|L|}{i} \cdot {e_{lock}}^{i} \cdot (1 - e_{lock})^{|L|-i} \tag{1}$$

The final bit is calculated by majority voting. Therefore, the procedure restores the wrong bit value whenever the number of errors is greater than half of the total elements $|L|$. We use a Bernoulli trial to calculate probability of having exactly i errors, and use a summation to aggregate all the results from $\frac{|L|}{2}$ to $|L|$. To achieve the desired level of correctness we can tune the number of locks $|L|$ to meet a given error. The same procedure is valid for all bit-lockers, thus the final error is proportional to $e_{bitlock}$, hence satisfying the initial claim.

We eventually provide proof of security of the construction. To satisfy Definition 1, we need to show that the key K appears random even if a potential attacker possesses knowledge of the helper data $(V, (n, R, T))$. It is important to note that both K and T are derived using a cryptographic hash function, where $K \leftarrow hash(K_{pre}, n)$ and $T \leftarrow hash(K, R)$. We assume that the hash function exhibits the typical secure properties (*i.e.*, pre-image resistance, second pre-image resistance, and collision resistance). Considering all these properties together, the hash function generates outputs that appear to be random. Therefore, the pseudo-randomness of the resulting key K is conditioned solely on the amount of information leaked by the helper data $(V, (n, R, T))$. $H' = (n, R, T)$ does not leak any information on the underlying vault V: n is a random nonce,

R is a random collection of indexes, and T is computed through a hash function. Regarding the vault V, we previously showed that it is (α, β)-secure under Definition 8. The parameters (α, β) can be used to tune ϵ, thus satisfying the requirements in Definition 1. □

We now provide proof that X-Lock is reusable under Definition 2. Reusability means that the fuzzy extractor can support multiple independent enrollments of the same value, allowing users to reuse the same source in different contexts.

Theorem 4. *X-Lock is (ρ, σ)-reusable.*

Proof. The procedure *Gen* can be run multiple times on correlated strings of the same source, $S^1_{read}, \ldots, S^{\rho}_{read}$. Each time, *Gen* produces a different pair of values $(K_1, H_1), \ldots, (K_\rho, H_\rho)$. The security for each extracted string K_i should hold even in the presence of all the helper strings $H_1, \ldots, H_\rho$. In our specific case, $H = (V, (n, R, T))$. Having all H values does not compromise the security of the respective keys, as n, R are randomly determined and T is generated through hashing, making it pseudo-random by definition. Additionally, the vault V remains the same for each key, meaning that the overall reusability is only conditioned on the security of the vault V. We provide definition of the security of the pool vault in Definition 8. □

Notably, our model also provides insider security [5,6]. This means that the algorithm provides reusability even in the case where the attacker is given all the K_j for $j \neq i$. Each key K_j is the output of a hash function and provides no information about the input. Hence, a specific key cannot be used to infer information about another one, even in the presence of correlation in the input data between the two keys.

According to Definition 3, a fuzzy extractor is deemed robust if a user is able to detect any tampering with the public data H. We provide proof that X-Lock is indeed a robust algorithm.

Theorem 5. *X-Lock is a τ-robust fuzzy extractor with error δ.*

Proof. The attacker may attempt to change one or more in the helper data $H = (V, (n, R, T))$. Nevertheless, any alteration would be detected by the authentication token $T \leftarrow hash(K, R) = hash(hash(K_{pre}, n), R)$. Tampering with the vault V would lead to changes in the recovered values of K_{pre}, inevitably affecting the resulting hash. Furthermore, modifying the nonce n or the indexes R directly impacts the resulting hash. Additionally, changing token T to T' would require to find suitable values n', R', K'_{pre} such that $T' \leftarrow hash(hash(K'_{pre}, n'), R')$. This is infeasible, given the properties of cryptographic hash functions. Consequently, the pair (*Gen*, *Rep*) strictly adheres to the requirements specified in Definition 3, as any alterations introduced by an attacker can be effectively detected through the validation token T. □

5.2 Bias and Correlation Analysis

The scheme proposed in Algorithm 1 offers perfect secrecy when utilizing a perfectly random source F and employing uncorrelated bits to XOR with the bits from B. However, obtaining a perfectly random source using physical mediums poses considerable challenges due to issues related to bias and correlation between bits. Nevertheless, Algorithm 1 helps in mitigating these concerns. Notice that both bias and correlation are intrinsic properties of fuzzy sources. Some works in literature [23, 24] propose methodologies to reduce or even remove dependencies between bits, but they either require high computational processing or extensive analysis of the physical medium. For instance, removing correlated bits requires a perfect identification of such relationships, which is a costly and partial procedure. Missing even one correlation could be significantly harmful. Instead, our protocol implicitly mitigates bias and correlation without making assumptions about their structure. The XOR-ation adopted in the locks inherently diminishes the final bias (see Sect. 3). The probability p_{cbias} of an XOR-ation outputting value 1 can be represented by the equation:

$$p_{cbias} = \sum_{i=0}^{\frac{|C|}{2}} \binom{|C|}{2i+1} \cdot p_{bias}^{2i+1}(1 - p_{bias})^{|C|-2i-1} \tag{2}$$

The XOR-ation outputs 1 whenever there is an odd number of 1s in C. Thus, the summation between 0 and $|C|$ and the indexes $2i + 1$ consider only the odd numbers. For instance, with $p_{bias} = 0.77$ and $|C| = 3$, $p_{cbias} \approx 0.579$. Consequently, an almost random source is derived from a skewed one. However, it is crucial to note that the same mechanism that reduces bias also amplifies errors. In Sect. 5.3, we provide an analysis of the cost in memory related to a particular error tolerance.

The XOR-ation also aids in mitigating the effects of correlations among bits in the source F. The correlation factor ϕ (see Sect. 3) only requires an estimate of the level of correlated bits without any specific assumption on its type. By employing it, we can evaluate how the correlation impacts the overall security of the linear system. Figure 3 illustrates the impact of correlation on bit security with varying numbers of elements in the XOR-ation, considering $|S_{pref}| = 2^{16}$, $|B| = 2^9$, $|L| = 33$, $|C| = 4$, and $\phi = 0.75$. We randomly drew the XOR-ation bits from the source F and measured the number of exposed bits from the random pool while bits from F were defined. The graph clearly illustrates the significant improvement achieved with an increasing number of elements in the XOR-ation. Starting with just a single element in the XOR-ation, the system fails to provide adequate security, as all the 2^9 pool bits become exposed after defining only a couple of bits. This is attributable to the relationships among locks in different bit-lockers. The setting allows one bit-locker to be entirely solved by merely defining a single bit from F, which, in turn, sets a value for all other variables in the bit-locker. This creates a cascading effect that subsequently unlocks multiple other bit-lockers, thus leading to the compromised security. However, by augmenting the number of elements in the XOR-ation to three, the

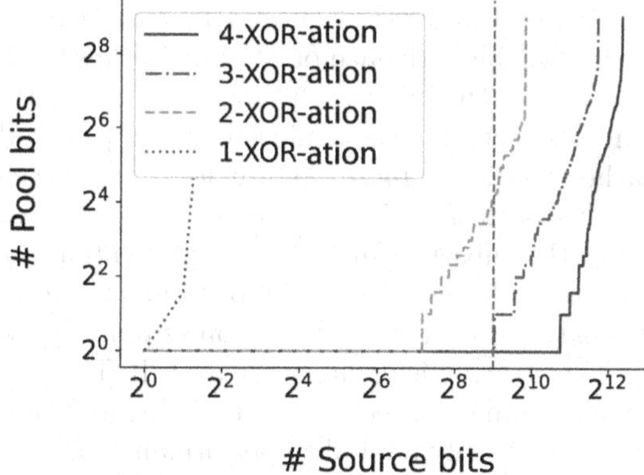

Fig. 3. Impact of correlation on bit security with varying number of elements in the XOR cascade. The x-axis considers the number of defined bits from the source. The y-axis shows the corresponding number of exposed bits from the random pool. Using a single element provides virtually no security. From three elements onwards the number of defined bits is greater than those in the protected pool (vertical, dashed line). (Color figure online)

number of required source bits becomes closely aligned with the actual number of protected bits from the pool (as denoted by the vertical dashed line). This indicates that a potential attacker would not gain any additional advantage by exploiting the correlation among variables, as the number of variables to be defined is equivalent to the number of bits in the random pool they are attempting to set. Furthermore, when employing four elements in the XOR-ation, the system significantly surpasses the reference line, demonstrating that the impact of correlation becomes negligible in this context. The higher the bias, the correlation and the security requirements to achieve adversarial non-advantageous contexts, the higher the number of bits in the XOR-ation. However, the higher $|C|$, the higher the resulting error rate in reconstructing the keys. We can estimate such value taking into account the absolute error rate e_{abs} of F.

5.3 Costs Analysis

Memory Cost. Procedure *Init* creates the supporting pool vault. The vault V contains $|B|$ bit-lockers, one for each bit in the random pool B. Each bit-locker hosts $|L|$ locks, with each lock being a single bit. To generate the locks, the algorithm has to choose a subset of bits from S_{pref}. If randomly chosen, the subset of indexes must be stored in order to permit subsequent recovery. However, this strategy would consume a lot more memory than V itself. The same applies to the storage of the set of indexes R related to each key. A more effective solution would be to design an index routine that can generate the corresponding bits on the fly. We deployed an example of a custom dynamic strategy that works as follows. To generate the requisite set of indices, we utilize a Pseudo Random

Number Generator (PRNG) and define a seed to ensure reproducibility. The PRNG generates a dependable sequence of random numbers with a given seed, though collisions may occur. To address collisions, we increase the colliding number until a fresh and distinct index is achieved. We apply modular arithmetic when the value reaches the upper limit. As previously discussed in Sect. 4, this routine is applicable to both $drawVaultIndexes$ and $drawKeyIndexes$. The dynamic generation of the subset of indexes does not entail any security implications when compared to the naive strategy of random generation and subsequent storage. In the latter case, the subset becomes publicly available, whereas in the former case, the algorithm is open-source as well. The system's security is not contingent on maintaining the secrecy of the indexes. The tradeoff between these two approaches is primarily related to performance. Dynamic index generation reduces memory costs, albeit with a manageable increase in computational overhead. Conversely, the naive strategy involves a straightforward lookup but necessitates storing each index, leading to higher memory expenses. In particular, to store all the indexes leveraging the static approach requires storing an index spanning between 1 and $|S_{pref}|$ for $|B|$ bit-lockers, each constituted by $|L|$ locks implementing a XOR-ation of $|C|$ bits for the vault and an index spanning between 1 and $|B|$ for $|K|$ bits for each key. Considering the dynamic approach, the cost for storing the pool vault indexes is rather nothing more than the bits required to represent the seed for the PRNG. The same holds for the set of indexes for each key. Let us denote the PRNG seed as *seed* and its size in bits as $|seed|$. Hence, the cost for storing the vault boils down to $|B| \cdot |L| + |seed|$ bits using the dynamic approach from $|B| \cdot |L| \cdot (1 + |C| \cdot log_2(|S_{pref}|))$ bits obtained with the static approach. Procedure *Gen* generates a novel key K. It requires storing a nonce n, an authentication token T and the set of indexes R used to generate the key. The static approach requires $|n| + |T| + |K| \cdot log_2(|B|)$ bits, whilst the dynamic approach just necessitates of $|n| + |T| + |seed|$ bits. Procedure *Rep* does not require additional elements to be stored. Therefore, let us denote with $\mathcal{K}$ the total number of keys generated. Then, the total cost for the static strategy is $\mathcal{O}(|B| \cdot |L| \cdot (1 + |C| \cdot log_2(|S_{pref}|)) + \mathcal{K} \cdot (|n| + |T| + |K| \cdot log_2(|B|)))$ bits. Rather, leveraging the dynamic strategy decreases the total cost to $\mathcal{O}(|B| \cdot |L| + |seed| + \mathcal{K} \cdot (|n| + |T| + |seed|))$ bits.

Computational Cost. Procedure $Init$ necessitates the preferred state S_{pref} to generate the vault V. To determine the correct value, multiple strings from F are required to obtain a statistically relevant sample, often comprising hundreds of samples. The time to gather this sample may vary depending on the physical support used. For instance, SRAMs require a non-negligible amount of time (in the order of milliseconds) for the chip to discharge after shutdown [15]. As a result, collecting a sufficient sample might take several seconds. Once the preferred state is obtained, the procedure employs a series of XOR operations to compute the locks. Each lock utilizes $|C| - 1$ XORs for the XOR-ation and an additional XOR for the final bit. Assuming each XOR operation is $\mathcal{O}(1)$, the overall cost of computing all locks is $\mathcal{O}(|C| \cdot |B| \cdot |L|)$. Notably, procedure $Init$ is only computed once, and if energy is a limited resource, it can be performed before deploying

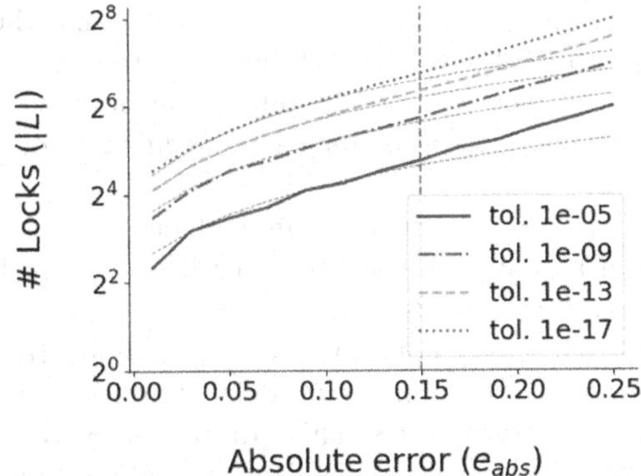

Fig. 4. Number of locks required to achieve a given error tolerance for varying absolute errors. The x-axis considers the absolute error. The y-axis uses logarithmic scale and considers the number of lockers. The gray dashed lines provide a linear reference for the four curves. The curves show an initial linear trend that slowly diverges to exponential at around value 0.85 for the error. (Color figure online)

the appliance, as the vault V can be made public. Procedure *Gen* utilizes the normal state S_{read} to recover the bits from the vault and generate a new key. It then draws a random nonce n and $|K|$ random values. Considering these operations to be $\mathcal{O}(1)$, the cost becomes $\mathcal{O}(|K|+1)$. Subsequently, it proceeds to recover the protected bit from each lock, requiring $|C|$ XORs for each unlocking operation. This process must be performed $|K| \cdot |L|$ times, resulting in a cost of $\mathcal{O}(|K| \cdot |C| \cdot |L|)$. Finally, it computes two hashes, denoted as $\mathcal{O}(2 \cdot t_{hash})$. Thus, the overall cost is $\mathcal{O}(|K| \cdot (1+|C| \cdot |L|) + 1 + 2 \cdot t_{hash})$. Procedure *Rep* follows a similar pattern to *Gen*. For each lock, it unlocks the protected bit, incurring a cost of $\mathcal{O}(|K| \cdot |C| \cdot |L|)$. Additionally, it computes two hashes, yielding a total cost of $\mathcal{O}(|K| \cdot (1 + |C| + |L|) + 1 + 2 \cdot t_{hash})$. The dynamic index generation strategy adds extra computational cost to the algorithm. In particular, let us denote with t_{PRNG} the time required to query the PRNG and with *collisions* the number of collisions. Generating and reproducing the indexes for the vault takes $\mathcal{O}(t_{PRNG} \cdot |B| \cdot |L| \cdot |C| + collisions)$, whereas the same routine for the set of indexes for each key takes $\mathcal{O}(t_{PRNG} \cdot |K| + collisions)$. The decision to utilize dynamic index generation or static index storage depends on the specific scenario. Dynamic index generation proves advantageous in contexts characterized by limited memory resources and available energy supply. On the other hand, static index storage is a more viable option when energy is scarce but memory resources are more readily available.

Impact of Error Tolerance. In Sect. 5.1, we demonstrated that by adjusting the number of locks $|L|$ within a bit-locker, it is possible to manage the error tolerance e_{lock} of the system. In this analysis, we examine the impact of e_{lock} on $|L|$ and set four different levels of tolerance as reference points. Utilizing the formula provided in Sect. 5.1, we computed the number of expected locks required to achieve a given tolerance for each specified error rate. The results are plot in Fig. 4.

The four lines in the graph represent distinct error tolerances. We observe that the trend is approximately linear for lower rates of absolute errors. However, at around an error rate of 0.85, the trends start to diverge and become exponential. Notably, the curve corresponding to $e_{lock} = 1e - 05$ presents an interesting exception. Here, the number of locks exhibits an under-linear trend that extends until an error rate of 0.8. This graph effectively demonstrates that our solution experiences linear growth for low to medium error rates, resulting in linear memory and computational costs within that range.

6 Implementation and Comparison

In order to further validate the correctness and efficiency of our approach, we implemented the algorithm on a physical test-bed using a 2.3 GHz Intel Core i5 quad-core processor with 8 GB of 2133 MHz LPDDR3 memory. We employed a SRAM as our PUF, which was easily accessible using a Keystudio MEGA 2560 R3 microcontroller board with an 8 KB SRAM. The selection of an SRAM PUF was motivated by several factors, including its user-friendly nature, ease of development, cost-effectiveness, and its widespread availability as a piece of hardware. To determine the preferred state S_{pref} of the SRAM, we collected 200 strings and computed the majority value for each bit. We found that 88% of the bits presented a stable value, with the remaining 12% showing an average absolute error of 0.0223 and a maximum error of 0.0455.

The algorithm was implemented in C language and compared against both Woo et al. [28], which is the best-performing algorithm in terms of both memory and computational complexity, and Canetti et al. [5,6], which is the algorithm providing the highest security guarantees. We evaluated three sets of parameters based on security levels: 80-bit, 128-bit, and 256-bit. For each level, we performed two experiments with different setups. Table 3 presents the parameters used for each security level.

The values for $|C|$ were carefully chosen in order to mitigate the effect of correlation as shown in Sect. 5.2. We did not consider the bias in this simulation because also the comparison works did not consider it. We decided to experiment with two specific values for the correlation factor: $\phi = 0.75$ represents a realistic correlation factor for SRAMs [19], and $\phi = 0.00$ corresponds to a limit case where all the PUF bits are independent. In such scenario, no correlation relationship affects the bits of the PUF meaning that no XOR-ation is mandatory, net of the bias phenomenon. The correlation factor directly impacts the error tolerance by determining the number of available equations for the linear system (see Sect. 5.1). The sixth column (*i.e.*, Exp. key error rate) reports the expected error rates in recovering the key for each configuration. We kept it at around 1 error

Table 3. Parameters for the three security levels.

Chosen params			PUF params		Resulting params		
$\|K\|$	$\|L\|$	$\|C\|$	ϕ	e_{abs}	e_{lock}	$e_{bitlock}$	Exp. key error rate
80	64	2	0.75	0.15	0.255	$2.243 \cdot 10^{-5}$	0.0018
80	256	2	0.00	0.25	0.375	$3.089 \cdot 10^{-5}$	0.0025
128	64	2	0.75	0.15	0.255	$2.243 \cdot 10^{-5}$	0.0029
128	256	2	0.00	0.245	0.370	$1.483 \cdot 10^{-5}$	0.0019
256	64	3	0.75	0.10	0.244	$8.519 \cdot 10^{-6}$	0.0022
256	256	3	0.00	0.175	0.363	$4.891 \cdot 10^{-6}$	0.0013

every 500. We set $|S_{read}| = 2^{16}$ based on the size of our SRAM and $|B| = 2^8$ for the random pool size. Expected key error rate parameter is resulting from the choice of the other parameters. In particular, recall Eq. 1 which is the probability that a bit-locker is wrongly unlocked. Then, the probability that all bit-lockers of a given key are successfully unlocked is $(1 - e_{lock})^{|K|}$. Finally, the expected key error rate is the probability that at least one bit-locker of a given key is wrongly unlocked and it is given by $1 - (1 - e_{lock})^{|K|}$.

We measured the time needed to perform the *Rep* procedure. We performed 100000 experiments. To perform a fair comparison with the state-of-the-art, we downloaded the code of Woo et al. [28] from the public repository[1], we implemented by ourselves the algorithm proposed by Canetti et al. [5,6], and run them on the same appliance in order to obtain results originating from the same evaluation environment. In fact, differences affecting computational power among distinct machines could compromise the reliability of our experiments.

Table 4 summarizes the results and compares our work with [28] and [5,6]. Different e_{abs} values are arising from other parameters, such as key length $|K|$, correlation factor ϕ and expected key error rate. In particular, we set each e_{abs} value as the maximum we could afford in each configuration before performance degradation and security flaws significantly increased.

We considered two state-of-the-art constructions for the comparison with our work. Our choice was driven by the guarantees they offer and the performances, in terms of memory requirements and computational time, they achieve. In particular we chose the proposal of Canetti et al. [5,6] and the proposal of Woo et al. [28]. The former one provides optimal security guarantees, offering reusability, insider security and robustness, while also addressing source correlation. The latter one offers reusability and robustness with an easily manageable memory overhead and linear error tolerance.

The other works either do not provide a sufficient level of security, exhibiting data leakage or not supplying reusability and/or robustness, or are completely unfeasible. In particular:

- Secure sketch-based constructions [2,25,26] suffer from data leakage;

[1] https://github.com/KU-Cryptographic-Protocol-Lab/Fuzzy_Extractor.

Table 4. Performance comparisons. The time value includes both the generation and the reproduction procedure.

Solution	$\|K\|$	e_{abs}	Memory	Time
Canetti et al. [5,6] ($\phi = 0.00$)	80	0.25	$\mathcal{K} \cdot 143.95$ MB	43.50 s
	128	0.245	$\mathcal{K} \cdot 216.20$ MB	57.71 s
	256	0.175	$\mathcal{K} \cdot 431.02$ MB	104.99 s
Woo et al. [28] ($\phi = 0.00$)	80	0.30	$\mathcal{K} \cdot 297$ B	4.62 s
	128	0.20	$\mathcal{K} \cdot 559$ B	15.51 s
	256	0.11	$\mathcal{K} \cdot 1087$ B	52.209 s
Our work ($\phi = 0.75$)	80	0.15	2064 B + $\mathcal{K} \cdot 64$ B	0.054 ms
	128	0.15	2064 B + $\mathcal{K} \cdot 64$ B	0.086 ms
	256	0.10	2064 B + $\mathcal{K} \cdot 64$ B	0.222 ms
Our work ($\phi = 0.00$)	80	0.25	8208 B + $\mathcal{K} \cdot 64$ B	0.205 ms
	128	0.245	8208 B + $\mathcal{K} \cdot 64$ B	0.305 ms
	256	0.175	8208 B + $\mathcal{K} \cdot 64$ B	0.845 ms

- The construction proposed by Cheon et al. [9] improves the proposal of Canetti et al. [5,6] by reducing the memory requirements. Nevertheless, the price to pay for such improvement is the introduction of a significant amount of hashing operations, which are costly, determining an increase of the already expensive computational cost;
- Fuller et al. [13] and Apon et al. [1] constructions lack of reusability.

The memory cost of Woo et al. [28] algorithms is comparable with our implementation incurring an initial overhead for storing the vault V. However, our memory consumption grows slower with the number of generated keys $\mathcal{K}$. For instance, the memory cost for a security class of 128-bit and $\phi = 0.75$ would become equivalent to [28] after generating 5 keys. In terms of computation time, our algorithm outperforms [28] by at least three orders of magnitude. The significant difference is due to the use of more efficient operations, mainly XORs and a limited number of hashes, in our work. On the other hand, [28] employs more resource-intensive LWE-based cryptography and error correction codes.

As for the error tolerance, our implementation with $\phi = 0.75$ handles smaller amounts of error, which is a side effect of the XOR-ation mechanism (see Sect. 5.1). The correlation factor ϕ and the resulting number of available bits in the SRAM PUF significantly affect the overall performances. In fact, by setting $\phi = 0.00$ the error tolerance of our solution becomes superior to [28] in two security levels, while being almost comparable in the third level. This setting is equivalent of having a source F with 2^{17} bits and a correlation factor $\phi = 0.75$.

To validate the result from Sect. 5.1, we also measured the number of errors committed in each security class. We measured 163 errors for class 80-bits, 259 for class 128-bits, and 129 for class 256-bits. These are in line with the expected errors calculated in Table 3 (respectively 180, 280, and 220) We then checked the claim made in Sect. 5.1 by assessing the capability of an adversary to combine different locks for gaining additional knowledge. We performed 100000 cycles, with every cycle randomly shuffling the locks and adding them together. We monitored the total number of elements forming the XOR-ation. Figure 5 plots the minimum number of elements observed in a XOR-ation by combining multiple locks. The graph clearly shows a growing trend that finds its upper bound at a value that is half of the total dimension of the source. This result validates the claim made in Sect. 5.1 on the security of the pool vault. The vast majority of locks shares no common elements, hence combining them greatly increase the XOR-ation dimension. The presence of locks with more than half common elements has little to no impact on the overall security.

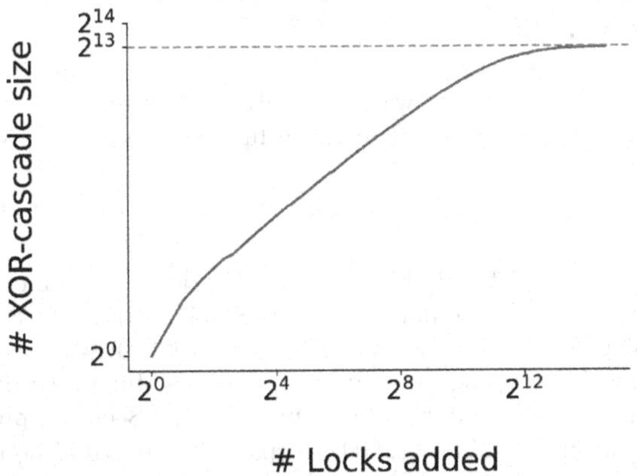

Fig. 5. XOR-ation size while combining multiple locks. The x-axis considers the number of locks added. The y-axis considers the number of elements forming the XOR-ation. Both axes are logarithmic. The graph considers the worst case, that is the minimum number of elements in the resulting cascade. (Color figure online)

7 Conclusion

The proliferation of resource-constrained devices within the IoT domain has caused considerable challenges concerning privacy and security. Traditional methods of storing digital keys in non-volatile memory have proven intricate and costly, prompting the need for alternative solutions. This paper introduces X-Lock, a novel computational fuzzy extractor specifically designed to address the limitations faced by traditional solutions in resource-constrained IoT devices. X-Lock employs a unique approach, utilizing the preferred state of a noisy source to encrypt a random string of bits, which subsequently serves as a seed to generate multiple secret keys. This design not only ensures both reusability (even insider security), and robustness, but also effectively mitigates bias and correlation, enhancing overall security. To substantiate the claims of X-Lock, a comprehensive theoretical analysis is presented, encompassing security considerations and detailed implementation insights. The rigorous analysis validates the effectiveness and security of the proposed model. To evaluate the superiority of X-Lock, an extensive set of practical experiments is also conducted, and the results are compared against existing approaches. The experimental findings demonstrate the efficacy of our proposed model, showcasing its comparable memory cost (approximately 2.4 KB for storing 5 keys of 128 bits) and remarkable speed gains, which outperform the state-of-the-art solution by three orders of magnitude (0.086 ms compared to 15.51 s). By offering reusability, insider security, and robustness, X-Lock presents a compelling solution to the challenges posed by traditional key storage methods. The comprehensive theoretical analysis and practical experiments affirm the superior performance of X-Lock, making it a promising advancement for enhancing privacy and security in the rapidly evolving IoT landscape.

Acknowledgments. This work was partially supported by project SERICS (PE00000014) under the NRRP MUR program funded by the EU - NGEU.

References

1. Apon, D., Cho, C., Eldefrawy, K., Katz, J.: Efficient, Reusable fuzzy extractors from LWE. In: Dolev, S., Lodha, S. (eds.) CSCML 2017. LNCS, vol. 10332, pp. 1–18. Springer, Cham (2017). https://doi.org/10.1007/978-3-319-60080-2_1
2. Boyen, X.: Reusable cryptographic fuzzy extractors. In: Proceedings of the 11th ACM Conference on Computer and Communications Security, pp. 82–91. Association for Computing Machinery (2004). https://doi.org/10.1145/1030083.1030096
3. Boyen, X., Dodis, Y., Katz, J., Ostrovsky, R., Smith, A.: Secure remote authentication using biometric data. In: 24th Annual International Conference on the Theory and Applications of Cryptographic Techniques, Aarhus, Denmark, May 22–26, 2005. Proceedings 24, pp. 147–163 (2005)
4. Canetti, R., Dakdouk, R.R.: Obfuscating point functions with multibit output. In: Smart, N. (ed.) EUROCRYPT 2008. LNCS, vol. 4965, pp. 489–508. Springer, Heidelberg (2008). https://doi.org/10.1007/978-3-540-78967-3_28
5. Canetti, R., Fuller, B., Paneth, O., Reyzin, L., Smith, A.: Reusable fuzzy extractors for low-entropy distributions. In: Fischlin, M., Coron, J.S. (eds.) Advances in Cryptology - EUROCRYPT 2016, pp. 117–146. Springer, Berlin Heidelberg, Berlin, Heidelberg (2016)
6. Canetti, R., Fuller, B., Paneth, O., Reyzin, L., Smith, A.: Reusable fuzzy extractors for low-entropy distributions. J. Cryptol. **34**, 1–33 (2021)
7. Chang, C.H., Zheng, Y., Zhang, L.: A retrospective and a look forward: fifteen years of physical unclonable function advancement. IEEE Circuits Syst. Mag. **17**(3), 32–62 (2017)
8. Chen, B., Ignatenko, T., Willems, F., Maes, R., van der Sluis, E., Selimis, G.: High-rate error correction schemes for sram-pufs based on polar codes. arXiv preprint arXiv:1701.07320 (2017)
9. Cheon, J.H., Jeong, J., Kim, D., Lee, J.: A reusable fuzzy extractor with practical storage size: Modifying canetti et al'.s construction. In: Information Security and Privacy: 23rd Australasian Conference, ACISP 2018, Wollongong, NSW, Australia, July 11–13, 2018, Proceedings 23, pp. 28–44 (2018)

10. Dodis, Y., Ostrovsky, R., Reyzin, L., Smith, A.: Fuzzy extractors: how to generate strong keys from biometrics and other noisy data. SIAM J. Comput. **38**(1), 97–139 (2008). https://doi.org/10.1137/060651380
11. Dolev, D., Yao, A.: On the security of public key protocols. IEEE Trans. Inf. Theory **29**(2), 198–208 (1983)
12. Fuller, B., Meng, X., Reyzin, L.: Computational fuzzy extractors. In: Advances in Cryptology-ASIACRYPT 2013: 19th International Conference on the Theory and Application of Cryptology and Information Security, Bengaluru, India, December 1–5, 2013, Proceedings, Part I 19. pp. 174–193. Springer (2013)
13. Fuller, B., Meng, X., Reyzin, L.: Computational fuzzy extractors. Inf. Comput. **275**, 104602 (2020)
14. Hiller, M.: Key derivation with physical unclonable functions. Ph.D. thesis, Technische Universität München (2016)
15. Liu, M., Zhou, C., Tang, Q., Parhi, K.K., Kim, C.H.: A data remanence based approach to generate 100% stable keys from an sram physical unclonable function. In: 2017 IEEE/ACM International Symposium on Low Power Electronics and Design (ISLPED), pp. 1–6 (2017)
16. Lynn, B., Prabhakaran, M., Sahai, A.: Positive results and techniques for obfuscation. In: Cachin, C., Camenisch, J.L. (eds.) EUROCRYPT 2004. LNCS, vol. 3027, pp. 20–39. Springer, Heidelberg (2004). https://doi.org/10.1007/978-3-540-24676-3_2
17. Maes, R., van der Leest, V., van der Sluis, E., Willems, F.: Secure key generation from biased PUFs. In: Güneysu, T., Handschuh, H. (eds.) CHES 2015. LNCS, vol. 9293, pp. 517–534. Springer, Heidelberg (2015). https://doi.org/10.1007/978-3-662-48324-4_26
18. Obermaier, J., Immler, V., Hiller, M., Sigl, G.: A measurement system for capacitive puf-based security enclosures. In: Proceedings of the 55th Annual Design Automation Conference, pp. 1–6 (2018)
19. Rahman, M.T., Hosey, A., Guo, Z., Carroll, J., Forte, D., Tehranipoor, M.: Systematic correlation and cell neighborhood analysis of sram puf for robust and unique key generation. J. Hardw. Syst. Secur. **1**, 137–155 (2017)
20. Roel, M.: Physically unclonable functions: Constructions, properties and applications, pp. 148–160. Katholieke Universiteit Leuven, Belgium pp (2012)
21. Seo, M., Kim, S., Lee, D.H., Park, J.H.: Emblem:(r) lwe-based key encapsulation with a new multi-bit encoding method. Int. J. Inf. Secur. **19**, 383–399 (2020)
22. Shafarevich, I.R., Remizov, A.O.: Linear algebra and geometry. Springer Science & Business Media (2012)
23. Suzuki, M., Ueno, R., Homma, N., Aoki, T.: Efficient fuzzy extractors based on ternary debiasing method for biased physically unclonable functions. IEEE Trans. Circuits Syst. I Regul. Pap. **66**(2), 616–629 (2018)
24. Ueno, R., Suzuki, M., Homma, N.: Tackling biased pufs through biased masking: A debiasing method for efficient fuzzy extractor. IEEE Trans. Comput. **68**(7), 1091–1104 (2019)
25. Wen, Y., Liu, S.: Reusable fuzzy extractor from lwe. In: Information Security and Privacy: 23rd Australasian Conference, ACISP 2018, Wollongong, NSW, Australia, July 11–13, 2018, Proceedings, pp. 13–27 (2018)
26. Wen, Y., Liu, S.: Robustly reusable fuzzy extractor from standard assumptions. In: Peyrin, T., Galbraith, S. (eds.) ASIACRYPT 2018. LNCS, vol. 11274, pp. 459–489. Springer, Cham (2018). https://doi.org/10.1007/978-3-030-03332-3_17

27. Wilde, F., Gammel, B.M., Pehl, M.: Spatial correlation analysis on physical unclonable functions. IEEE Trans. Inf. Forensics Secur. **13**(6), 1468–1480 (2018). https://doi.org/10.1109/TIFS.2018.2791341
28. Woo, J., Kim, J., Park, J.H.: Robust and reusable fuzzy extractors from non-uniform learning with errors problem. Comput. Mater. Continua **74**(1) (2023)

Encrypted Data

Efficient Clustering on Encrypted Data

Mengyu Zhang[1], Long Wang[1,2], Xiaoping Zhang[3](✉), Zhuotao Liu[1,2], Yisong Wang[3], and Han Bao[3]

[1] Institute for Network Sciences and Cyberspace, Tsinghua University, Beijing, China
mengyu-z23@mails.tsinghua.edu.cn, {longwang,zhuotaoliu}@tsinghua.edu.cn
[2] Zhongguancun Laboratory, Beijing, China
[3] Department of Computer Science and Technology, Tsinghua University, Beijing, China
zhxp@tsinghua.edu.cn, {wys19,baoh17}@mails.tsinghua.edu.cn

Abstract. Clustering is a significant unsupervised machine learning task widely used for data mining and analysis. Fully homomorphic encryption allows data owners to outsource privacy-preserving computations without interaction. In this paper, we propose a fully privacy-preserving, effective, and efficient clustering scheme based on CKKS, in which we construct two iterative formulas to solve the challenging ciphertext comparison and division problems, respectively. Although our scheme already outperforms existing work, executing it on datasets MNIST and CIFAR-10 still results in unacceptable run time and memory consumption. To further address the above issues, we propose a block privacy-preserving clustering algorithm that splits records into subvectors and clusters these subvectors. Experimental results show that the clustering accuracy of our original algorithm is almost equivalent to the classical k-means algorithm. Compared to a state-of-the-art FHE-based scheme, our original algorithm not only outperforms theirs in accuracy but is also 4 orders of magnitude faster than theirs. In experiments testing our block algorithm, we conclude that the run time and memory consumption of this algorithm are greatly reduced.

Keywords: Fully Homomorphic Encryption · clustering · privacy-preserving

1 Introduction

Clustering is a significant tool for data mining and data analysis. It reveals intrinsic patterns in many real-world problems and is widely used in many fields [4,23]. In many scenarios, different dimensions of the same records are held by two parties respectively, that is, the dataset is split vertically. For example, a bank wants to perform cluster analysis on customers, but the customer clustering based on the customer information held by the bank is not accurate enough. The

This research is partially supported by Zhongguancun Laboratory.

C. Pöpper and L. Batina (Eds.): ACNS 2024, LNCS 14583, pp. 213–236, 2024.
https://doi.org/10.1007/978-3-031-54770-6_9

government holds private information such as the income status of citizens, which can help banks obtain more accurate clustering results. Note that government data is generally stored on specific servers and cannot be transmitted to any organization or individual in any form. Additionally, these two organizations typically communicate over a WAN, with no guarantees of latency or bandwidth. Therefore, to obtain more accurate results, the bank (the data owner) needs to send the data to the government (the server), and the government (the server) performs clustering on the joint dataset and returns the result. However, sending customer information to the government in plaintexts can lead to the disclosure of private information. Thence, it is necessary to propose a privacy-preserving and efficient clustering scheme.

Fully Homomorphic Encryption (FHE) is a cryptographic primitive that protects private information contained in data by performing homomorphic operations on encrypted data. FHE is more suitable for scenarios with high latency as the FHE-based algorithms allow non-interactive setting. However, the previous FHE-based privacy-preserving clustering works [3,11,18] leak partial private information to servers during the calculation. To avoid the disclosure of private information during the calculation, Jäschke and Armknecht [13] propose a fully privacy-preserving clustering scheme based on FHE. However, their approximate ciphertext division introduces errors, and their expensive bitwise ciphertext comparison leads to impractical run times (about 6 days for 400 records).

To solve the above problems, in this paper, we propose a fully privacy-preserving, effective, and efficient clustering scheme based on FHE. We choose the approximate homomorphic encryption scheme CKKS [7] as our encryption algorithm, which performs approximate arithmetic and is able to encode floating point numbers. It is a challenge that CKKS does not directly support ciphertext comparison and division used in the clustering algorithm. To achieve ciphertext comparison, we construct an iterative formula with two fixed points of opposite signs to approximate the sign function. For ciphertext division, we construct a function whose root is the reciprocal of the divisor, and apply Newton's method to approximate the root of this function. After making minor changes to k-means clustering algorithm, we propose a fully privacy-preserving and efficient clustering algorithm that prevents the server from inferring private information.

Although, our fully privacy-preserving clustering algorithm has outperformed existing schemes, executing it on some well-known large datasets (e.g. MNIST, CIFAR-10, etc.) leads to unacceptable run time and memory consumption (about 3500 minutes and 1303GB memory on MNIST). Through theoretical analysis, the number of clusters k is an important factor affecting the run time and memory consumption, therefore, reducing k can greatly increase the practicability of our algorithm. To reduce k, we split the input vectors into disjoint subvectors and cluster these subvectors. We refer to this optimized clustering algorithm as the block privacy-preserving clustering algorithm. In addition, this optimized scheme also reduces the number of consecutive multiplications, which is limited by a predetermined parameter since CKKS is a leveled homomorphic encryption.

We first test our fully privacy-preserving clustering scheme on several popular small datasets to assess clustering accuracy and efficiency. In terms of accuracy, the results show that our method performs as well as the original k-means clustering algorithm and significantly outperforms the state-of-the-art privacy-preserving clustering work [13]. As for efficiency, we adopt two implementation optimization techniques, one batching, and the other multithreading. The results show that these two optimizations reduce the run time by three orders of magnitude in total, making our scheme more efficient. Then, we compare the efficiency of our scheme with state-of-the-art [13]. We use our fully privacy-preserving clustering algorithm with batching, which achieves nearly identical accuracy as the original (plaintext) k-means clustering algorithm. Compared with the FHE-based scheme [13], our method is about 19573x faster. In summary, our fully privacy-preserving clustering scheme is efficient and effective compared to existing works.

Afterwards, we test our block privacy-preserving clustering algorithm on two large datasets (MNIST, CIFAR-10) on which our vanilla fully privacy-preserving clustering algorithm fails to run using our server due to the long run time and excessive memory consumption. As can be seen from the results, our block clustering solution can be performed on these datasets with acceptable run time and memory consumption. In addition, this block clustering algorithm is also suitable for users who would like to trade a little accuracy for high efficiency.

- We construct two iterative formulas to solve the ciphertext comparison and division problems respectively, and propose a fully privacy-preserving clustering scheme based on FHE, which can ensure that no private information is revealed during the calculation.
- To further reduce the run time and memory consumption of our algorithm, we propose the block privacy-preserving clustering algorithm. This algorithm divides the input vectors into disjoint subvectors and performs clustering on these subvectors.
- We conduct a series of experiments on various widely used datasets to evaluate our scheme. From the results, it can be concluded that our block clustering solution performs well in terms of both efficiency and memory consumption.

2 Related Works

In recent years, privacy-preserving clustering has been widely discussed in the literature. Some literature [27,29,30,36] leverage Partially Homomorphic Encryption (PHE) and two non-colluding clouds and design an interactive protocol between them. However, these schemes are not suitable for large data scenarios due to the high communication cost. Some previous works [5,12,26,31,32] apply differential privacy to protect the private information of individuals. However, the accuracy drops significantly due to the noise introduced in the clustering algorithm. Multiparty Computation (MPC) is proposed to implement privacy-preserving clustering in [24,35], which requires interaction between data owners.

Focusing on FHE, Liu et al. [18] propose an outsourced clustering scheme. Almutairi et al. [3] create an updatable distance matrix (UDM) and apply it to improve the efficiency of their clustering algorithm. Gheid et al. [11] present a clustering protocol that does not use any cryptographic scheme. However, these works leak intermediate values which contain private information, such as the sizes of clusters or the distances between records and cluster centers. Wu et al. [37] propose an efficient and privacy-preserving outsourced k-means clustering scheme based on Yet Another Somewhat Homomorphic Encryption (YASHE). There are two non-colluding cloud servers in their model, one of which is used for addition and multiplication in ciphertexts, and the other is responsible for comparison in plaintexts. Therefore, the server that computes in plaintexts can infer partially private information from the data. Different from these works, our clustering scheme is fully privacy-preserving, which allows data owners to outsource clustering without revealing any private information.

Jäschke and Armknecht present a completely privacy-preserving clustering scheme based on FHE in [13]. Due to the impractical run time of their algorithm, they trade accuracy for efficiency. In other words, they create an approximate comparison scheme by truncating the few least significant bits in ciphertexts. However, the run time of the dataset with 400 records is still 25.79 days, which is far from practical for large datasets. Different from their bitwise approximate comparison scheme, our ciphertext comparison is more efficient through an iterative approach. Also, their ciphertext division is approximate and introduces errors into their clustering algorithm, whereas our ciphertext division is exact.

3 Background

3.1 Approximate Homomorphic Encryption CKKS

To achieve privacy-preserving clustering, we choose the approximate homomorphic encryption algorithm CKKS [7] as our cryptographic scheme. We use CKKS instead of other RLWE-based schemes for two main reasons, one is its ability to encode floating point numbers, and the other is its high efficiency.

Cheon et al. propose the formal definitions of CKKS in [7]. We define that N is a power of two and $R = \mathbb{Z}[X]/(X^N + 1)$ is a ring of integers, where $\mathbb{Z}[X]$ is a polynomial ring with integer coefficients. A message $\mathbf{m} \in \mathbb{C}^{N/2}$ is firstly encoded into a polynomial $m \in R$ called plaintext. Let L be a level parameter and $q_l = 2^l$ for $1 \leq l \leq L$. We denote $R_q = \mathbb{Z}_q[X]/(X^N + 1)$ as a modulo-q quotient ring of R. The modulo q operation on each element of R_q is denoted as $[\cdot]_q$. The distribution $X_{\text{s}} = HWT(h)$ outputs a polynomial with coefficients $\{-1, 0, 1\}$, whose Hamming weight is h. The distributions X_{enc} and X_{e} are the discrete Gaussian distribution.

Set the secret key to be $sk \leftarrow (1, s)$ and the public key to be $pk \leftarrow ([-a \cdot s + e]_{q_L}, a)$, where $s \leftarrow X_{\text{s}}$, $a \leftarrow U(R_{q_L})$, and $e \leftarrow X_{\text{e}}$. To encrypt the plaintext m, we can compute $c = [v \cdot pk + (m + e_0, e_1)]_{q_L}$, where $v \leftarrow X_{\text{enc}}$ and $e_0, e_1 \leftarrow X_{\text{e}}$. The ciphertext $c = (c_0, c_1)$ is decrypted by calculating $m' = [c_0 + c_1 \cdot s]_{q_l}$.

CKKS is a leveled homomorphic encryption, which means that this homomorphic encryption scheme limits the number of consecutive multiplications by a pre-determined parameter. Cheon et al. [6] extend CKKS to a fully homomorphic encryption scheme by proposing a bootstrapping algorithm that can refresh low-level ciphertexts. The input of the bootstrapping algorithm is a ciphertext with the lowest modulus $c \in R^2_{q_1}$ and the output is a ciphertext with a refreshed modulus $c' \in R^2_{q_{L'}}$, where $L' < L$. And the results of decrypting c and c' are almost equal.

3.2 Newton's Method

Newton's method is an approximate root-finding algorithm. This method can solve equations of the form $f(x) = 0$, where f is a real-valued function and the derivative of f is denoted by f'.

Suppose $x_0 \in [a, b]$ is an initial guess for a root of f, denoted as r. We find the line tangent to $f(x)$ at $x = x_0$ and compute the intersection of the x-axis with this tangent, denoted by $(x_1, 0)$. $x_1 = x_0 - \frac{f(x_0)}{f'(x_0)}$, where x_1 is a better approximation of r than x_0. Repeat the above steps to continuously refine the approximation, and x_{n+1} can be computed as follows [10]:

$$x_{n+1} = x_n - \frac{f(x_n)}{f'(x_n)} \tag{1}$$

If Newton's method converges on $[a, b]$, a sufficiently accurate value can be reached when the number of iterations is large enough [25]. That is $\lim_{n \to +\infty} x_n = r$.

4 System Architecture and Threat Model

4.1 System Architecture

In our system architecture, there are two actors (server and data owner). The dataset is split vertically, with the server and the data owner holding different dimensions of the same records. The joint dataset, denoted D, has n records of m dimensions. We assume that the dataset D_1 held by the data owner contains n records of m_1 dimensions, and the dataset D_2 owned by the server contains the same n records of m_2 dimensions, where $m = m_1 + m_2$. Since the private set intersection technique has been proposed in previous work, we can suppose that D_1 and D_2 are already aligned. Therefore, $D = D_1 || D_2$.

In the scenario we describe, to get better clustering results, the data owner has to send D_1 to the server, which executes the clustering algorithm on the joint dataset D. The server is untrusted, which means it tries to infer private information from the data, thus the data owner needs to outsource the clustering to the server in ciphertexts (Fig. 1).

Before exploiting the outsourced clustering service, the data owner needs to generate the secret key sk kept private by itself as well as the public key pk and the evaluation key evk both shared with the server. Then, the data owner encodes n records into plaintexts and encrypts these plaintexts into ciphertexts.

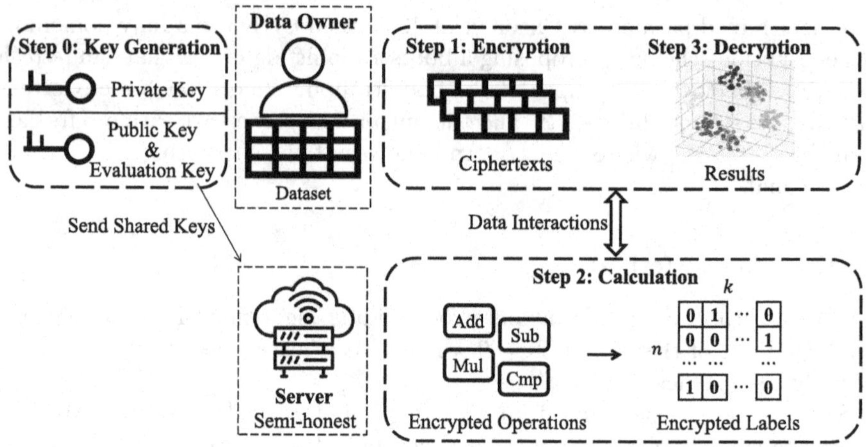

Fig. 1. Our System Architecture

After that, the data owner sends these ciphertexts and some parameters to the server. Among them, the parameters include m_1, the number of clusters denoted by k, and the number of iterations for clustering denoted by T. After receiving these ciphertexts and parameters, the server executes k-means clustering in ciphertexts and returns the ciphertext results to the data owner. Finally, the data owner decrypts the results and obtains the labels of all records through a simple calculation.

4.2 Threat Model

In this paper, we consider a semi-honest security model, which means that the server and the user strictly follow the protocol, but they may try to infer private information about the datasets D_1 and D_2. We assume that m_1, k, T are the public system parameters known by both parties: m_1 only represents the dimensions of the records owned by the data owner, and k, and T are the parameters for clustering. Furthermore, we consider the communication channel to be insecure, which means that eavesdropping attacks are possible.

In our protocol, D_1 is homomorphically encrypted locally and transmitted to the server as ciphertexts for clustering. Therefore, an adversary eavesdropping the communication channel or the server cannot deduce private information from the encrypted D_1. In addition, all records in D_2 are not sent to the user in any form, so the user cannot infer any private information from D_2.

Baiyu and Micciancio [16] point out that CKKS does not satisfy indistinguishability under chosen plaintext attacks with decryption oracles (IND-CPA^{D}) security. However, chosen plaintext attacks with decryption oracles cannot occur in our system, since (1) only the data owner can choose the plaintexts to be encrypted; (2) no ciphertext and the corresponding plaintext are sent to the server simultaneously; (3) the data owner never sends the decryption results to the server.

4.3 Security

In this paper, our goal is to achieve a simulation-based security definition.

Definition. *A protocol Π between a data owner having as input a dataset D_1 and a server having as input a dataset D_2 is a cryptographic clustering protocol if it satisfies the following guarantees:*

- ***Correctness.*** *On each input dataset D_1 of the data owner and each dataset D_2 held by the server, the output of the data owner at the end of the protocol is the correct clustering result on the joint dataset.*
- ***Security:***
  - *We require that a corrupted, semi-honest data owner does not learn anything about the input D_2 of the server. Formally, we require the existence of an efficient simulator $\texttt{Sim}_C$ such that $\texttt{View}_C^\Pi \approx_c \texttt{Sim}_C(D_1, \texttt{out})$, where $\texttt{View}_C^\Pi$ denotes the view of the data owner in the execution of Π and $\texttt{out}$ denotes the output of the clustering.*
  - *We also require that a corrupted, semi-honest server does not learn anything about the input D_1 of the data owner. Formally, we require the existence of an efficient simulator $\texttt{Sim}_S$ such that $\texttt{View}_S^\Pi \approx_c \texttt{Sim}_S(D_2)$, where $\texttt{View}_S^\Pi$ denotes the view of the server in the execution of Π.*

5 Fully Privacy-Preserving Clustering Scheme Based on FHE

In this section, we propose a fully privacy-preserving clustering scheme based on FHE algorithm CKKS. We choose Lloyd's algorithm to solve the k-means clustering problem. The reasons for choosing Lloyd's algorithm are (1) it is simple to implement; (2) it has effective local fine-tuning capability [9]. However, CKKS cannot directly support division and comparison in ciphertexts, which are used in Lloyd's algorithm. Therefore, we adopt iterative method and Newton's method to solve ciphertext comparison and division respectively. After making minor changes to Lloyd's algorithm, we implement a fully privacy-preserving clustering algorithm.

5.1 Preliminaries

The goal of k-means clustering is to partition the dataset into k sets [21]. Lloyd's algorithm [19] can solve the k-means clustering problem and is one of the most extensively used clustering algorithms for statistical data analysis.

The dataset D held by the data owner contains n records denoted $t_1, \ldots, t_n$. Each record t_i is an m-dimensional real vector, denoted as $t_i = (t_{i1}, \ldots, t_{im}) \in$

Algorithm 1: The Lloyd's algorithm

1 **Input** n, m, k, T, $D = \{t_1, \dots, t_n\}$
2 Initialize centroids $c_1, \dots, c_k$ randomly
repeat T **times**
3 Calculate distance of each record to each centroid
  $\text{diff}_{ij} \leftarrow \sum_q (t_{iq} - c_{jq})^2$
  $(i = 1, \dots, n,\ j = 1, \dots, k,\ q = 1, \dots, m)$
4 Find the closest centroid to each record
  $\text{label}_i \leftarrow j$ with minimal diff_{ij}
  $(i = 1, \dots, n,\ j = 1, \dots, k)$
5 Count the number of records in each cluster
  $\text{cnt}_j \leftarrow$ the number of i-s where $\text{label}_i = j$
  $(i = 1, \dots, n,\ j = 1, \dots, k)$
6 Update centroids
  $c_j \leftarrow \frac{\sum_i t_i}{\text{cnt}_j}$ where $\text{label}_i = j$
  $(i = 1, \dots, n,\ j = 1, \dots, k)$
7 **Output** label and $c_1, \dots, c_k$

$\mathbb{R}^m$. Lloyd's algorithm divides the dataset into k clusters $u_1, \dots, u_k$, whose centroids are denoted by $c_1, \dots, c_k$, where $c_i = (c_{i1}, \dots, c_{im}) \in \mathbb{R}^m$. The complete Lloyd's algorithm is shown in Algorithm 1.

Since we are concerned with the vertical partition scenario, for each record t_i, the data owner holds $t_{i1}, \dots, t_{im_1}$ and the server holds $t_{i(m_1+1)}, \dots, t_{im}$. According to our threat model (described in Sect. 4.2), the data owner only provides encrypted $t_{i1}, \dots, t_{im_1}$ to the server, so the operation between ciphertext and plaintext is involved in Step 3 because $t_{i(m_1+1)}, \dots, t_{im}$ is in plaintexts. Since CKKS supports addition, subtraction, and multiplication between ciphertext and plaintext, and the results of these operations are in ciphertexts, the distance array diff is in ciphertexts.

In addition, in Step 3, since CKKS cannot directly support square root and absolute value operations, we calculate the square of the Euclidean distance between each record t_i and each cluster center c_j as diff_{ij}. Each element diff_{ij} in diff array is only used to compare with some other elements, so squaring all elements in diff does not affect the result. Step 4 to 6 must be calculated in ciphertexts, and the ciphertext comparison in Step 4 and the ciphertext division in Step 6 are challenging for CKKS.

5.2 Ciphertext Comparison

In Step 4, we compare the distance between each record and each centroid to find the closest centroid for each record. Since CKKS does not support comparison in ciphertexts directly, the label array cannot be simply calculated, and we need to transform it into some HE-friendly representation.

Considering that the result of Step 4 is used to count the number of records in each cluster and update centroids (Step 5 and 6), it is natural to construct a one-hot encoding vector for each record. The one-hot encoding vector of record t_i is denoted as minIndex_i $(i = 1, \ldots, n)$:

$$\text{minIndex}_i = (0, \ldots, 0, 1, 0, \ldots, 0)$$
$$\text{minIndex}_{ij} = \begin{cases} 1, & j = \text{label}_i \\ & (\min\{\text{diff}_{i1}, \ldots, \text{diff}_{ik}\} = \text{diff}_{ij}) \\ 0, & j \neq \text{label}_i \\ & (\text{diff}_{ij} \text{ is not the minimum}) \end{cases} \tag{2}$$

where only the label_i-th dimension of minIndex_i is set to 1 and all other dimensions are 0. In other words, minIndex_{ij} equals one only when c_j is the closest centroid to t_i. After this transformation, Steps 5 and 6 can be immediately rewritten as follows:

$$\text{Step 5:} \quad \text{cnt}_j = \sum_{i=1}^{n} \text{minIndex}_{ij} \tag{3}$$

$$\text{Step 6:} \quad c_j = \frac{\sum_{i=1}^{n} t_i \cdot \text{minIndex}_{ij}}{\text{cnt}_j} \tag{4}$$

Now the challenge is to calculate the minIndex array in ciphertexts. And we introduce the sign function sgn(x) to facilitate comparison, where sgn(x) = 1 if $x > 0$, sgn(x) = 0 if $x = 0$, and sgn(x) = −1 if $x < 0$.

During the ciphertext calculation process, the server will not obtain any intermediate results and related information. Therefore, in order to find the cluster center closest to the record t_i and mark the corresponding dimension of minIndex_i as 1, the server needs to compare the k numbers pairwise. Obviously, if diff_{ij} is the minimum value, then for any $q \in [1, k]$ and $q \neq j$, $\frac{\text{sgn}(\text{diff}_{iq} - \text{diff}_{ij}) + 1}{2}$ always equals 1. If diff_{ij} is not the minimum, then there exists $q \in [1, k]$ and $q \neq j$ such that $\frac{\text{sgn}(\text{diff}_{iq} - \text{diff}_{ij}) + 1}{2} = 0$. Therefore, to compute minIndex_{ij}, we compare diff_{ij} with the other $k - 1$ distance differences and multiply all the results:

$$\text{minIndex}_{ij} = \prod_{q=1,\ q \neq j}^{k} \frac{\text{sgn}(\text{diff}_{iq} - \text{diff}_{ij}) + 1}{2} \tag{5}$$

According to Eq. 5, if diff_{ij} is the minimum value over $\{\text{diff}_{i1}, \ldots, \text{diff}_{ik}\}$, then all $k - 1$ factors of minIndex_{ij} equal to 1, i.e., $\text{minIndex}_{ij} = 1$; otherwise, minIndex_{ij} has at least one 0 in its multiplication factors, thus $\text{minIndex}_{ij} = 0$. Therefore, minIndex_{ij} in Eq. 5 satisfies the definition in Eq. 2.

However, $\text{sgn}(x)$ cannot be computed in CKKS directly since it is not a polynomial function. Therefore, the goal is to approximate $\text{sgn}(x)$ using HE-friendly operations. We use the iterative method to solve the above problem. We construct an iterative formula containing two fixed points, requiring that the signs of these two fixed points be different:

$$a_{i+1} = \varphi_c(a_i) = -\frac{3}{2} a_i (a_i - 1)(a_i + 1) \quad (i \in \mathbb{N}) \tag{6}$$

We can determine the convergence of Eq. 6 with $a_0 \in (-1, 1)$:

$$\lim_{n \to +\infty} \sqrt{3} a_n = \begin{cases} 1, & a_0 \in (0, 1) \\ -1, & a_0 \in (-1, 0) \\ 0, & a_0 = 0 \end{cases} \tag{7}$$

Therefore, the domain of Eq. 6 is defined as $(-1, 1)$, and the initial value a_0 is chosen as the input to the sign function denoted as x_{in}, where $x_{in} \in (-1, 1)$.

Algorithm 2: The sign function in ciphertexts

```
Input: x_in, R_c
Output: the approximate value of sgn(x_in)
a_0 = x_in
for i ← 0 to R_c − 1 do
    a_{i+1} = −(3/2) a_i (a_i − 1)(a_i + 1)
return √3 a_{R_c}
```

We can also handle the case where x_{in} are not in the range $(-1, 1)$. Suppose x'_{in} is in $(-M, M)$ for some constant M. In this case, the initial value a_0 is assigned as x'_{in}/M. Since the above ciphertext sign function only contains HE-friendly operations, CKKS can directly compute it.

5.3 Ciphertext Division

In Step 6, we need to divide the sum $\sum_{i=1}^{n} t_i \cdot \text{minIndex}_{ij}$ by the count cnt_j to get the centroid c_j. We apply Newton's method (described in Sect. 3.2) to solve the ciphertext division. We define the output of the function $\text{div}(a)$ as the reciprocal of a, where a is in $(0, M)$ for some constant M. Construct a function f(x), whose root is $\frac{1}{a}$, such as: $f(x) = \frac{1}{x} - a$. And we utilize Newton's method to approximate the root of this function. According to Eq. 1, we can obtain the iterative formula:

$$x_{i+1} = \varphi_d(x_i) = x_i - \frac{f(x_i)}{f'(x_i)} = x_i(2 - a \cdot x_i) \tag{8}$$

We need to determine the domain (a neighborhood of $\frac{1}{a}$) where the above iteration converges, and choose an appropriate initial value x_0 in the domain. Equation 8 converges if $x_0 = \frac{1}{a}$ or $\exists \delta > 0, \forall x \in (\frac{1}{a} - \delta, \frac{1}{a} + \delta) \setminus \{\frac{1}{a}\}$ satisfy

$$\left| \varphi_d(x) - \frac{1}{a} \right| < \left| x - \frac{1}{a} \right| \tag{9}$$

According to the above criteria, we can calculate that the domain is $(0, \frac{2}{a})$. Since $0 < a < M$, we choose $x_0 = \frac{2}{M} \in (0, \frac{2}{a})$ as the initial value. Therefore, we utilize this iteration to construct our ciphertext division algorithm (Algorithm 3).

Algorithm 3: The ciphertext division algorithm

Input: a, M, R_d

Output: the approximate value of $\frac{1}{a}$

```
x_0 = 2/M
for i ← 0 to R_d − 1 do
    x_{i+1} = x_i(2 − a · x_i)
return x_{R_d}
```

The above complete division algorithm uses only subtractions and multiplications in ciphertexts, which are directly supported by the CKKS homomorphic encryption. Hence $c_j = \sum_{i=1}^{n} t_i \cdot \text{minIndex}_{ij} \cdot \text{div}(\text{cnt}_j)$, where $\text{cnt}_j \in (0, n]$.

5.4 Converting the One-Hot Vectors to Label in Plaintexts

To achieve Step 5 and 6, we convert the label array into the one-hot encoding array minIndex. After receiving and decrypting the minIndex array, the data owner needs to extract the label from the minIndex. The data owner finds the index of the element which equals one in minIndex_{ij} for each record i as label_i:

$$\text{label}_i = j \ s.t. \ \text{minIndex}_{ij} = 1 \tag{10}$$

5.5 The Complete Algorithm for Privacy-Preserving Clustering

We summarize the above steps and describe the complete algorithm for fully privacy-preserving clustering. Our scheme contains only HE-friendly operations and is completely secure which means that no private information is revealed to the server during calculation. In Step 2, the data owner randomly generates k cluster centers $c_1, \ldots, c_k$ and encrypts them.

In Step 3, the server calculates the distance between each record t_i and each cluster center c_j, denoted as diff_{ij}. According to our problem setting, the records in D_1 are in ciphertexts, the records in D_2 are in plaintexts, and the centroids are in ciphertexts. CKKS directly supports addition, subtraction, and multiplication between ciphertext and plaintext, and the results of these operations are in ciphertexts. Therefore, all terms of sum are in ciphertexts, and diff_{ij} is also in ciphertexts. In Step 4, the server compares diff_{ij} with diff_{iq} by computing $\text{sgn}(\text{diff}_{iq} - \text{diff}_{ij})$ (Algorithm 2), where $1 \leq q \leq k, q \neq j$. Then, the server multiplies the $k-1$ results to get minIndex_{ij}, where $\text{minIndex}_{ij} = 1$ when diff_{ij} is the minimum value, and $\text{minIndex}_{ij} = 0$ otherwise.

In Step 5, the server counts the number of records belonging to each cluster. In Step 6, the server recalculates each cluster center c_j. Afterwards, the server repeats Step 3 to 6 for T iterations. In Step 7, the server sends the encrypted minIndex array to the data owner. After decrypting minIndex, the data owner extracts the label array according to Eq. 10.

Algorithm 4: The fully privacy-preserving clustering algorithm

Input n, $m = m_1 + m_2$, k, T
  $D_1 = \{t_{11}, \dots, t_{1m_1}, \dots, t_{n1}, \dots, t_{nm_1}\}$ (in ciphertexts)
  $D_2 = \{t_{1(m_1+1)}, \dots, t_{1m}, \dots, t_{n(m_1+1)}, \dots, t_{nm}\}$ (in plaintexts)
Data owner generates centroids $c_1, \dots, c_k$ in $[0,1]^m$ randomly and sends them to the server in ciphertexts
repeat T **times**
  Calculate distance of each record to each centroid
  for (i, j) **in** $\{1, \dots, n\} \times \{1, \dots, k\}$ **do**
    $\text{diff}_{ij} \leftarrow \sum_{q=1}^{m} (t_{iq} - c_{jq})^2$
  Calculate the minIndex array
  for (i, j) **in** $\{1, \dots, n\} \times \{1, \dots, k\}$ **do**
    $\text{minIndex}_{ij} \leftarrow \prod_{q=1, q \neq j}^{k} \frac{\text{sgn}(\text{diff}_{iq} - \text{diff}_{ij}) + 1}{2}$
  Count the number of records in each cluster
  for $j \leftarrow 1$ ***to*** k **do**
    $\text{cnt}_j \leftarrow \sum_{i=1}^{n} \text{minIndex}_{ij}$
  Update centroids
  for $j \leftarrow 1$ ***to*** k **do**
    $c_j \leftarrow \sum_{i=1}^{n} (t_i \cdot \text{minIndex}_{ij} \cdot \text{div}(\text{cnt}_j))$
Output minIndex (in ciphertexts)
Data owner extracts label from minIndex

5.6 Security Proof

The view of the server includes the ciphertext dataset from data owner, the dimension of the input dataset, the number of clusters, and the number of iterations for clustering. When the data owner is corrupted, `Sim` receives the plaintext parameters m_1, k, T, the public key and the ciphertext $\texttt{HE.Enc}(pk, D_1)$ from the data owner. In return, it sends $\texttt{HE.Enc}(pk, \texttt{res})$ for a randomly chosen `res` from $\mathbb{R}^n$, and the data owner cannot distinguish between real-world distributions and simulated distributions.

The view of the data owner includes the input dataset of the data owner, the dimension of the input dataset, the number of clusters, and the number of iterations for clustering. When the server is corrupted, `Sim` sends the plaintext parameters m_1, k, T, a randomly chosen `inp` from $\mathbb{R}^n$ and the public key $\texttt{HE.Enc}(pk, \texttt{inp})$ to the server. The server cannot distinguish between real-world distributions and simulated distributions.

6 An Optimized Algorithm

In this section, to further reduce the run time and memory consumption, we propose an optimized clustering algorithm called block privacy-preserving clustering algorithm. We have described a fully privacy-preserving clustering scheme in Sect. 5.5, however, when we test this algorithm on the popular MNIST dataset [15], the results show that the run time and memory consumption are unacceptable (about 3500 min and 1303 GB memory).

In terms of run time, since ciphertext multiplication is a time-consuming operation, multiple multiplications dramatically affect the efficiency of our clustering algorithm. On the other hand, CKKS is a leveled homomorphic encryption and limits the multiplication level by a pre-determined parameter. Multiple consecutive multiplications are also unfriendly to CKKS. In our algorithm, computing the minIndex array (Step 4 in Algorithm 4) requires multiple multiplications in ciphertexts. This step contains two parts: evaluating the sign function using the difference of two distances and multiplying the evaluation results. And there are $\Theta(nk^2)$ ciphertext multiplications in the second part of this step, where $\Theta(k)$ consecutive multiplications are required to calculate each element in the minIndex array. That is, reducing k can reduce run time.

In terms of memory consumption, in order to calculate the minIndex array with multithreading enabled, $\Theta(nk^2)$ memory is required. That is, when k is large, calculating the minIndex requires a large amount of memory.

However, with the advent of the big data era, the scale of the dataset to be clustered is gradually increasing, and the number of clusters k of the dataset becomes larger. Therefore, it is necessary to propose a new clustering algorithm that reduces run time and memory consumption by reducing k.

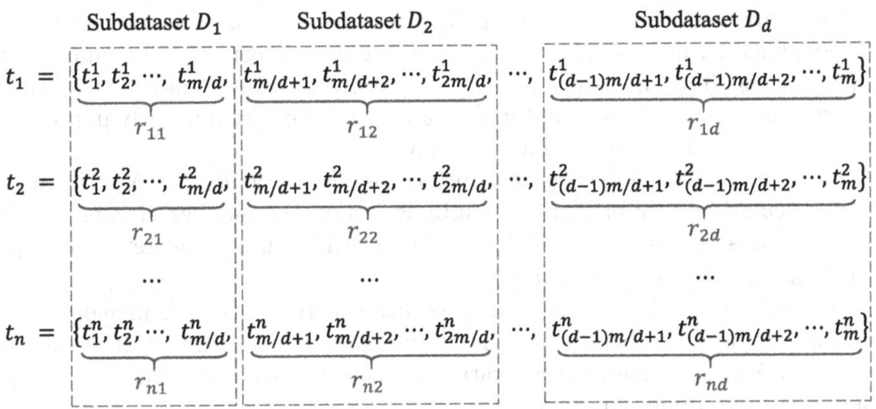

Fig. 2. Schematic Diagram of Splitting the Dataset

6.1 Block Clustering Scheme

To reduce k, we split the input vectors into disjoint subvectors and cluster these subvectors. As shown in Fig. 2, each record t_i in the dataset D is divided into d subvectors denoted $r_{i1}, \ldots, r_{id}$. Each subvector r_{iq} is of m/d dimensions, where m is a multiple of d and q is in $[1, d]$. We denote the set of subvectors $r_{1q}, \ldots, r_{nq}$ as the subdataset D_q.

We perform our privacy-preserving clustering scheme on each subdataset D_q independently, and each subvector r_{iq} is identified by a label L_{iq}. The label L_i of the record t_i is defined as the Cartesian product of the labels of its corresponding subvectors:

$$L_i = L_{i1} \times L_{i2} \times \ldots \times L_{id} \tag{11}$$

Since all subdatasets are equally important, they have the same number of subclusters. In that case, each subdataset is divided into k' subclusters, where

$$k' = \sqrt[d]{k} \tag{12}$$

We assume that k' is always a positive integer. The centroid c_j is the concatenation of the centroids of its corresponding subclusters.

We now summarize our complete scheme for block privacy-preserving clustering. Before delivering the ciphertexts and the parameters to the server, the data owner needs to preprocess the dataset D, including dividing t_i to generate r_{iq} and calculating k'. Then, the fully privacy-preserving block clustering algorithm can be described as Algorithm 5.

In Step 7, the data owner needs to extract the label of each subvector from minIndex$'$ according to the method described in Sect. 5.4. Afterward, the data owner obtains the label of each record by calculating the Cartesian product of its corresponding subvector labels according to Eq. 11.

The above algorithm only contains HE-friendly operations and does not break our threat model in Sect. 4.2. As shown in Table 1, we compare the number of multiplications in each calculation step between Algorithm 4 and Algorithm 5. The efficiency of the block clustering algorithm has been significantly improved, especially when calculating the minIndex array.

The number of consecutive multiplications also decreases in Algorithm 5. When calculating each element in minIndex array, the number of consecutive multiplications decreases from $\Theta(k)$ to $\Theta(\sqrt[d]{k})$. Additionally, memory consumption drops from $\Theta(nk^2)$ to $\Theta(nk^{\frac{2}{d}})$.

Although Algorithm 5 can greatly reduce the run time and memory consumption, it loses the clustering accuracy compared to Algorithm 4. In addition, Algorithm 5 is more suitable for datasets whose records are relatively evenly distributed in m-dimensional space.

6.2 Block Clustering Scheme with Cluster Selection

The fully privacy-preserving block clustering scheme described in Sect. 6.1 is efficient. However, Algorithm 5 only works on datasets with a certain k. When

Algorithm 5: The block privacy-preserving clustering algorithm

Input n, m, k', T, d
$r_{11}, \ldots, r_{1d}, r_{21}, \ldots, r_{2d}, \ldots, r_{n1}, \ldots, r_{nd}$ (Figure 2)
for $q \leftarrow 1$ *to* d **do**
  Data owner generates centroids $c'_1, \ldots, c'_{k'}$ in $[0,1]^{m/d}$ randomly and sends them to the server in ciphertexts
  repeat T **times**
    Calculate distance of each record to each centroid
    for (i, j) **in** $\{1, \ldots, n\} \times \{1, \ldots, k'\}$ **do**
      $\text{diff}'_{ij} \leftarrow \sum_{l=1}^{m/d} (r_{iql} - c'_{jl})^2$
    Calculate the minIndex′ array
    for (i, j) **in** $\{1, \ldots, n\} \times \{1, \ldots, k'\}$ **do**
      $\text{minIndex}'_{ij} \leftarrow \prod_{l=1, l \neq j}^{k'} \frac{\text{sgn}(\text{diff}'_{il} - \text{diff}'_{ij}) + 1}{2}$
    Count the number of records in each cluster
    for $j \leftarrow 1$ *to* k' **do**
      $\text{cnt}'_j \leftarrow \sum_{i=1}^{n} \text{minIndex}'_{ij}$
    Update centroids
    for $j \leftarrow 1$ *to* k' **do**
      $c'_j \leftarrow \sum_{i=1}^{n} (r_{iq} \cdot \text{minIndex}'_{ij} \cdot \text{div}(\text{cnt}'_j))$
  Send minIndex′ (in ciphertexts), and the data owner extracts label′ from minIndex′

for any d, there is no positive integer k' such that $k = {k'}^d$, this algorithm fails. Therefore, to make our block clustering algorithm applicable to datasets with arbitrary k, we add a function called cluster selection to it.

We still split each input vector into d disjoint subvectors, where each subvector is of m/d dimensions. Then we cluster each subdataset (defined in Sect. 6.1) separately and compute the Cartesian product of corresponding subvectors' labels to obtain the label for each vector according to the Eq. 11. Since $\sqrt[d]{k}$ is not a positive integer, we require each subdataset to be divided into k_s subclusters, where $k_s > \sqrt[d]{k}$ and $k_s \in \mathbb{N}^*$, and the specific value of k_s is determined by the data owner. Thus, the dataset D is partitioned into ${k_s}^d$ clusters, where ${k_s}^d > k$.

Since the goal of the data owner is to divide D into k clusters, we now propose the cluster selection algorithm to remove ${k_s}^d - k$ redundant clusters. We sort all ${k_s}^d$ clusters according to the number of records in each cluster from most to least, then keep the top k clusters and record their centroids. The records that do not belong to these top k clusters are called remaining records and need to be reassigned to these clusters. We separately calculate the distance between each remaining record and each centroid, then assign each remaining record to

Table 1. The number of multiplications involved in each step of Algorithm 4 and Algorithm 5 in each step. Note that no multiplication is needed in Step 5.

	Step 3 (distances)	Step 4 (minIndex)	Step 6 (centroids)
Algorithm 4	$\Theta(nmk)$	$\Theta(nk^2)$	$\Theta(nk)$
Algorithm 5	$\Theta(nmk^{\frac{1}{d}})$	$\Theta(dnk^{\frac{2}{d}})$	$\Theta(dnk^{\frac{1}{d}})$

the nearest centroid. Afterward, the centroids of these k clusters need to be recalculated.

We recommend that the data owner implement the cluster selection algorithm. The reason is that this algorithm is time-consuming in ciphertexts, but requires a small amount of computation resource in plaintexts. In addition, the communication costs remain almost unchanged.

The data owner needs to own all dimensions of the records and centroids to guarantee correct clustering of the remaining records. Therefore, our block clustering scheme with plaintext cluster selection only works if the data owner possesses the complete dataset. At this time, the data owner outsources clustering in order to utilize the computation resource of the server. Only Algorithm 4 and Algorithm 5 support the user to simultaneously utilize the server's dataset and computation resource.

7 Experiment Results

7.1 Experiment Setup

Server Configuration. We use the Lattigo library [1] (version 4.1.0) to implement our fully privacy-preserving clustering algorithm. We choose a Ubuntu-20.04 server with an Intel(R) Xeon(R) CPU E5-2620 v4 (2.1 GHz, 32 threads) and 100GB RAM to perform all experiments. Our approach is written in Go.

Datasets. We select several datasets from different sources to evaluate our algorithm. G2 [9] is a series of synthetic datasets, each of which contains 2048 points divided into two Gaussian clusters of equal size. We choose G2-1-20, G2-2-20, G2-4-20, G2-8-20, and G2-16-20 for experiments, where 1,2,4,8,16 represent the dimensions of the dataset.

The fundamental clustering problems suite (FCPS) [33] contains nine different datasets, and we choose seven of them which are widely used in [8,17,20,28,34]. As shown in Table 2, these datasets with known labels are low-dimensional and simple, and each of them solves a certain problem in clustering.

To demonstrate the effectiveness of the scheme described in Sect. 6, we select two large datasets to test our block clustering scheme. The MNIST dataset [15] of handwritten digits contains 60000 training images and 10000 testing images, where $m = 784$. We run our algorithm on the testing images with 10 clusters. The CIFAR-10 dataset [14] consists of 60000 images divided into 10 clusters. We choose 10000 test images to perform our approach.

Table 2. The datasets chosen from FCPS [33].

Dataset	n	m	k	Main Problems
Chainlink	1000	3	2	Not linearly separable
EngyTime	4096	2	2	Gaussian mixture
Hepta	212	3	7	None
Lsun	400	2	3	Different variances and shapes
Tetra	400	3	4	Almost touching
TwoDiamonds	800	2	2	Touching clusters
WingNut	1016	2	2	Non-uniform density

Parameter Selection. We choose the following parameters for our experiments:

- Parameters of CKKS: We use a default parameter set in the Lattigo library called PN16QP1761CI. $logN$ is 16, which means that at most 65536 values can be batched simultaneously. The multiplication level is 34, indicating that the number of consecutive multiplications cannot exceed 34.
- Number of iterations: 5, 10, 20.

In all experiments, the initial k centroids are uniformly and independently randomly sampled from $[0, 1]^m$. We run each experiment with five different random seeds and average the results.

Since we focus on the vertical partition scenario, the input to Algorithm 4 consists of encrypted dataset D_1 and unencrypted dataset D_2. The operation between plaintext and ciphertext is faster than that between ciphertext, therefore, in order to make the result more convincing, we encrypt all dimensions of the records in all experiments.

7.2 Clustering Accuracy

In this section, we conduct experiments on datasets G2 and FCPS to test the clustering accuracy of the algorithm described in Sect. 5. We then compare the accuracy of our approach with the state-of-the-art privacy-preserving clustering algorithm proposed in [13].

We separately run our algorithm and vanilla Lloyd's algorithm on the datasets and count the number of records that are correctly clustered. Then we calculate the clustering accuracy by dividing the number of correctly clustered records by n. In this part, we choose $T = 5$ for G2 and $T = 10$ for FCPS. Since the order of clusters in the experiments may be different from that in the ground truths, we enumerate full permutations of $\{1, \ldots, k\}$ as the mapping of labels from the algorithm outputs to the ground truth, and find the one with most correctly clustered records.

As shown in Table 3, for all datasets, the clustering accuracy of our approach is almost identical to that of Lloyd's algorithm. On most datasets, our algorithm

Table 3. Clustering accuracy of our algorithm and Lloyd's algorithm on G2 and FCPS.

Dataset	Our Algorithm	Lloyd's Algorithm	Difference
G2-1-20	99.3%	99.4%	0.1%
G2-2-20	100%	100%	0.0%
G2-4-20	100%	100%	0.0%
G2-8-20	100%	100%	0.0%
G2-16-20	100%	100%	0.0%
Chainlink	66.5%	65.9%	−0.6%
EngyTime	94.9%	95.1%	0.2%
Hepta	85.8%	85.4%	−0.4%
Lsun	77.5%	76.8%	−0.7%
Tetra	100%	100%	0.0%
TwoDiamonds	100%	100%	0.0%
WingNut	96.3%	96.4%	0.1%

correctly clusters the same number of records as Lloyd's algorithm. Therefore, we conclude that adding privacy protection to the clustering scheme does not affect accuracy.

We compare the clustering accuracy of our approach with that of the approximate algorithm proposed in [13] and record the results in Table 4. Since the bitwise ciphertext comparison used in their algorithm would lead to unacceptable run time, they propose an approximate version that improves efficiency by truncating several least significant bits. They compute the difference in clustering accuracy between the exact clustering and their approximate algorithm to demonstrate the accuracy (exact – approximate). In addition, we calculate the difference in clustering accuracy between Lloyd's algorithm and ours, and compare our results to theirs on the four datasets, as shown in Table 4. There are two negative numbers in the second line, indicating that the accuracy of our scheme is higher than that of Lloyd's algorithm. For these four datasets, our algorithm obviously outperforms theirs in clustering accuracy.

Table 4. Accuracy difference between exact algorithm and privacy-preserving version

	Lsun	Hepta	Tetra	WingNut
Approximate Version in [13]	3.5%	4%	13%	1.25%
This Work	−0.8%	−0.5%	0%	0.1%

7.3 Run Time

In this section, we test the run time of our fully privacy-preserving clustering algorithm described in Sect. 5. Then, we compare the efficiency of our algorithm with that of the state-of-the-art FHE-based clustering scheme [13].

Due to the inefficiency of direct implementation based on CKKS, we optimize our method for efficiency by parallelizing ciphertext computation (a.k.a. batching) and multithreading. First, we leverage the SIMD capability of CKKS to parallelize operations. Denote N as the ring dimension, which defines the number of coefficients of the plaintext/ciphertext polynomials. Since we choose the conjugate-invariant variant of CKKS for the ring type, at most N real values of the plaintext can be packed into one ciphertext. In Algorithm 4, the calculation of the diff array and the minIndex array can be parallelized $\min(n, N)$ times by simply packing $\min(n, N)$ coordinates into a single ciphertext. When counting the number of records in each cluster, we sum the n values (w.l.o.g. assuming $n \leq N$) in the packed minIndex array, which can be solved by rotations and additions.

Second, we can further improve the efficiency of our algorithm by multithreading. All operations in our algorithm are independent of each cluster. When computing the distances and the minIndex array, the operations are independent of each record. Therefore, we can achieve multithreading across different batches and different clusters.

We execute the unoptimized algorithm and the algorithm with batching and multithreading on G2 and FCPS respectively, then record the results in Table 5. In this part, we choose $T = 5$ for G2 and $T = 10$ for FCPS. As shown in Table 5, batching and multithreading can significantly reduce the run time of our scheme, and the total speedup of these two optimizations reaches a maximum value of about 6426x on G2-16-20. As shown in Table 6, our optimized algorithm is 4~5 orders of magnitude slower than vanilla Lloyd's algorithm. It is known that FHE-based algorithms are generally 9 orders of magnitude slower than corresponding plaintext algorithms [22]. We conclude that our privacy-preserving clustering scheme is efficient.

Table 5. Run time of G2 and FCPS with and without batching

Dataset	Without Optimization[4]	With Optimizations	Speedup
G2-1-20	271.0 h	222.41 s	4386 x
G2-2-20	305.5 h	221.11 s	4974 x
G2-4-20	374.6 h	250.20 s	5390 x
G2-8-20	512.6 h	311.55 s	5923 x
G2-16-20	788.8 h	441.89 s	6426 x
Chainlink	106.3 h	421.09 s	909 x
EngyTime	488.5 h	394.87 s	4454 x
Hepta	440.2 h	1213.90 s	1305 x
Lsun	129.7 h	442.65 s	1055 x
Tetra	239.6 h	620.42 s	1390 x
TwoDiamonds	95.5 h	397.73 s	864 x
WingNut	121.2 h	395.45 s	1103 x

To avoid the long run time, we run several synthetic datasets with small sizes and fit the run time in the table using least squares.

Table 6. Plaintext run time of vanilla Lloyd's algorithm on G2 and FCPS

G2-1-20	G2-2-20	G2-4-20	G2-8-20	G2-16-20	Chainlink
0.042 s	0.048 s	0.060 s	0.084 s	0.130 s	0.050 s
EngyTime	Hepta	Lsun	Tetra	TwoDiamonds	WingNut
0.177 s	0.025 s	0.023 s	0.031 s	0.036 s	0.045 s

We then compare the efficiency of our algorithm with that of [13] on the Lsun dataset. The run time reported in [13] is single-threaded. Thus, to achieve a fair comparison, we test the run time of our algorithm with a single thread. Since our method does not lose clustering accuracy, we choose the exact version of their work for comparison. As shown in Table 7, our approach spends 1606.36 s on the Lsun dataset, which is 19573x faster than [13]. Furthermore, our approach is still 1258x faster than their approximate algorithm (the fastest version in [13]), which trades accuracy for efficiency. To sum up, our fully privacy-preserving clustering scheme significantly outperforms [13] in terms of efficiency.

Table 7. Efficiency comparison with [13] on Lsun.

Work	Version	Threads	Run Time ($T = 10$)
Jäschke et al. [13]	exact	one	363.90 days
Jäschke et al. [13]	approximate	one	154.70 h
This work	exact	one	1606.36 s

7.4 Performance of Block Clustering Scheme with Cluster Selection

In this section, we evaluate the efficiency, memory consumption, and accuracy of our block clustering scheme described in Sect. 6. To demonstrate the superior performance of our block clustering algorithm, we select two large-scale, widely used datasets (MNIST, CIFAR-10) to test the run time and memory consumption. For CIFAR-10, we use the resnet20 model [2] to extract the feature vectors with $m = 64$. We choose $T = 20$ for all experiments in this section. Since $k = 10$ for MNIST and CIFAR-10, there is no d greater than 1, making $\sqrt[d]{k}$ a positive integer. Therefore, we execute our block clustering scheme with cluster selection described in Sect. 6.2 on them, where $d = 4, k_s = 2$ for MNIST, and $d = 2, k_s = 4$ for CIFAR-10.

As shown in Table 8, we first measure the run time and memory consumption of our block clustering algorithm, where $\text{time}_{\text{block}}$ and $\text{memory}_{\text{block}}$ represent the run time and memory consumption of the block clustering algorithm respectively, and $\text{time}_{\text{original}}$ and $\text{memory}_{\text{original}}$ represent these two indicators of our vanilla privacy-preserving clustering algorithm. Since our server configuration does not support our original algorithm to perform on such large datasets, $\text{time}_{\text{original}}$

and $\text{memory}_{\text{original}}$ in Table 8 are estimated. Notably, our block clustering solution can be executed on these datasets with acceptable run time. Among them, only 127 min and 47GB memory are required on CIFAR-10. That is, our block clustering scheme makes it possible to outsource privacy-preserving clustering on large datasets.

Table 8. Efficiency of block clustering scheme on MNIST and CIFAR-10

	MNIST($d = 4, k_s = 2$)	CIFAR-10($d = 2, k_s = 4$)
$\text{time}_{\text{original}}$[2]	about 3500 min	about 350 min
$\text{time}_{\text{block}}$	850 min	127 min
$\text{memory}_{\text{original}}$[2]	about 1303 GB	about 226 GB
$\text{memory}_{\text{block}}$	75 GB	47 GB

Due to insufficient memory, we run our original algorithm on several small datasets and fit the memory consumption and run time in the table by least squares.

We then test the clustering accuracy of our method on MNIST and CIFAR-10. We count the number of correctly clustered records and divide them by n to calculate the accuracy. The experimental results show that the accuracy loss is 10.35% on MNIST and 8.55% on CIFAR-10, which can be acceptable. In summary, our block privacy-preserving clustering algorithm is suitable for data owners who would like to trade a little accuracy for high efficiency. Furthermore, this solution enables outsourced clustering of large-scale datasets while preserving privacy.

8 Conclusions

We achieve ciphertext comparison by constructing an iterative formula with two fixed points of opposite signs to approximate the sign function. The solution of ciphertext division is to use Newton's method to approximate the reciprocal of the divisor. After solving the challenging ciphertext comparison and division, we propose a fully privacy-preserving, effective, and efficient clustering algorithm based on CKKS. However, executing our fully privacy-preserving clustering scheme on the large-scale datasets results in unacceptable run time and memory consumption. To further reduce the run time and memory consumption of our algorithm, we propose a block privacy-preserving clustering algorithm that splits records into subvectors and clusters these subvectors. Experiment results show that our original clustering algorithm has the same accuracy as Lloyd's algorithm and has a huge efficiency advantage over the baseline. In experiments testing our block clustering algorithm, it can be concluded that this algorithm performs well in terms of both efficiency and memory consumption.

References

1. Lattigo v4, August 2022. https://github.com/tuneinsight/lattigo, ePFL-LDS, Tune Insight SA
2. Pytorch cifar models, August 2022. https://github.com/chenyaofo/pytorch-cifar-models
3. Almutairi, N., Coenen, F., Dures, K.: K-means clustering using homomorphic encryption and an updatable distance matrix: secure third party data clustering with limited data owner interaction. In: Bellatreche, L., Chakravarthy, S. (eds.) DaWaK 2017. LNCS, vol. 10440, pp. 274–285. Springer, Cham (2017). https://doi.org/10.1007/978-3-319-64283-3_20
4. Ashari, I., Banjarnahor, R., Farida, D., Aisyah, S., Dewi, A., Humaya, N.: Application of data mining with the k-means clustering method and davies bouldin index for grouping imdb movies. J. Appl. Inform. Comput. **6**(1), 07–15 (2022). https://doi.org/10.30871/jaic.v6i1.3485. https://jurnal.polibatam.ac.id/index.php/JAIC/article/view/3485
5. Balcan, M.F., Dick, T., Liang, Y., Mou, W., Zhang, H.: Differentially private clustering in high-dimensional Euclidean spaces. In: Precup, D., Teh, Y.W. (eds.) Proceedings of the 34th International Conference on Machine Learning. Proceedings of Machine Learning Research, vol. 70, pp. 322–331. PMLR (06–11 Aug 2017). https://proceedings.mlr.press/v70/balcan17a.html
6. Cheon, J.H., Han, K., Kim, A., Kim, M., Song, Y.: Bootstrapping for approximate homomorphic encryption. In: Nielsen, J.B., Rijmen, V. (eds.) EUROCRYPT 2018. LNCS, vol. 10820, pp. 360–384. Springer, Cham (2018). https://doi.org/10.1007/978-3-319-78381-9_14
7. Cheon, J.H., Kim, A., Kim, M., Song, Y.: Homomorphic encryption for arithmetic of approximate numbers. In: Takagi, T., Peyrin, T. (eds.) ASIACRYPT 2017. LNCS, vol. 10624, pp. 409–437. Springer, Cham (2017). https://doi.org/10.1007/978-3-319-70694-8_15
8. Estévez, P.A., Figueroa, C.J.: Online data visualization using the neural gas network. Neural Netw. **19**(6), 923–934 (2006). https://doi.org/10.1016/j.neunet.2006.05.024. advances in Self Organising Maps - WSOM'05
9. Fränti, P., Sieranoja, S.: K-means properties on six clustering benchmark datasets. Appl. Intell. **48**(12), 4743–4759 (2018). https://doi.org/10.1007/s10489-018-1238-7
10. Galántai, A.: The theory of newton's method. Journal of Computational and Applied Mathematics **124**(1), 25–44 (2000). https://doi.org/10.1016/S0377-0427(00)00435-0. https://www.sciencedirect.com/science/article/pii/S0377042700004350, numerical Analysis 2000. Vol. IV: Optimization and Nonlinear Equations
11. Gheid, Z., Challal, Y.: Efficient and privacy-preserving k-means clustering for big data mining. In: 2016 IEEE Trustcom/BigDataSE/ISPA, pp. 791–798 (2016). https://doi.org/10.1109/TrustCom.2016.0140
12. Huang, Z., Liu, J.: Optimal differentially private algorithms for k-means clustering. In: Proceedings of the 37th ACM SIGMOD-SIGACT-SIGAI Symposium on Principles of Database Systems, PODS 2018, pp. 395–408. Association for Computing Machinery, New York (2018). https://doi.org/10.1145/3196959.3196977, https://doi.org/10.1145/3196959.3196977
13. Jäschke, A., Armknecht, F.: Unsupervised machine learning on encrypted data. In: Cid, C., Jacobson, M.J., Jr. (eds.) Selected Areas in Cryptography - SAC 2018, pp. 453–478. Springer, Cham (2018). https://doi.org/10.1007/978-3-030-10970-7_21

14. Krizhevsky, A.: Learning multiple layers of features from tiny images. Tech. rep. (2009)
15. LeCun, Y., Cortes, C., Burges, C.: Mnist handwritten digit database. ATT Labs [Online]. (2010). http://yann.lecun.com/exdb/mnist**2**
16. Li, B., Micciancio, D.: On the security of homomorphic encryption on approximate numbers. Springer-Verlag (2021). https://doi.org/10.1007/978-3-030-77870-5_23
17. Li, F., Qian, Y., Wang, J., Dang, C., Jing, L.: Clustering ensemble based on sample's stability. Artif. Intell. **273**, 37–55 (2019). https://doi.org/10.1016/j.artint.2018.12.007
18. Liu, D., Bertino, E., Yi, X.: Privacy of outsourced k-means clustering. In: Proceedings of the 9th ACM Symposium on Information, Computer and Communications Security, pp. 123–134. ASIA CCS '14, Association for Computing Machinery, New York (2014). https://doi.org/10.1145/2590296.2590332. https://doi.org/10.1145/2590296.2590332
19. Lloyd, S.: Least squares quantization in PCM. IEEE Trans. Inf. Theory **28**(2), 129–137 (1982). https://doi.org/10.1109/TIT.1982.1056489
20. Lopez, C., Tucker, S., Salameh, T., Tucker, C.: An unsupervised machine learning method for discovering patient clusters based on genetic signatures. J. Biomed. Inform. **85**, 30–39 (2018). https://doi.org/10.1016/j.jbi.2018.07.004
21. MacQueen, J.: Some methods for classification and analysis of multivariate observations. In: Proceedings of the Fifth Berkeley Symposium on Mathematical Statistics and Probability, vol. 1, pp. 281–297. University of California Press (1967)
22. Matsuoka, K., Banno, R., Matsumoto, N., Sato, T., Bian, S.: Virtual secure platform: A {Five-Stage} pipeline processor over {TFHE}. In: 30th USENIX security symposium (USENIX Security 21), pp. 4007–4024 (2021)
23. Minh, H.L., Sang-To, T., Abdel Wahab, M., Cuong-Le, T.: A new metaheuristic optimization based on k-means clustering algorithm and its application to structural damage identification. Knowl.-Based Syst. **251**, 109189 (2022). https://doi.org/10.1016/j.knosys.2022.109189. https://www.sciencedirect.com/science/article/pii/S0950705122005913
24. Mohassel, P., Rosulek, M., Trieu, N.: Practical privacy-preserving k-means clustering. Cryptology ePrint Archive, Paper 2019/1158 (2019), https://eprint.iacr.org/2019/1158. https://eprint.iacr.org/2019/1158
25. More, J.J., Sorensen, D.C.: Newton's method (2 1982). https://doi.org/10.2172/5326201. https://www.osti.gov/biblio/5326201
26. Ni, L., Li, C., Wang, X., Jiang, H., Yu, J.: Dp-mcdbscan: differential privacy preserving multi-core dbscan clustering for network user data. IEEE Access **6**, 21053–21063 (2018). https://doi.org/10.1109/ACCESS.2018.2824798
27. Rao, F.Y., Samanthula, B.K., Bertino, E., Yi, X., Liu, D.: Privacy-preserving and outsourced multi-user k-means clustering. In: 2015 IEEE Conference on Collaboration and Internet Computing (CIC), pp. 80–89 (2015). https://doi.org/10.1109/CIC.2015.20
28. Rodriguez, M.Z., Comin, C.H., Casanova, D., Bruno, O.M., Amancio, D.R., Costa, L.d.F., Rodrigues, F.A.: Clustering algorithms: A comparative approach. PLOS ONE **14**(1), 1–34 (01 2019). https://doi.org/10.1371/journal.pone.0210236. https://doi.org/10.1371/journal.pone.0210236
29. Rong, H., Wang, H.M., Liu, J., Xian, M.: Privacy-preserving k-nearest neighbor computation in multiple cloud environments. IEEE Access **4**, 9589–9603 (2016). https://doi.org/10.1109/ACCESS.2016.2633544

30. Samanthula, B.K., Elmehdwi, Y., Jiang, W.: k-nearest neighbor classification over semantically secure encrypted relational data. IEEE Trans. Knowl. Data Eng. **27**(5), 1261–1273 (2015). https://doi.org/10.1109/TKDE.2014.2364027
31. Stemmer, U.: Locally private k-means clustering. In: Proceedings of the Thirty-First Annual ACM-SIAM Symposium on Discrete Algorithms, SODA 2020, pp. 548–559. Society for Industrial and Applied Mathematics, USA (2020)
32. Su, D., Cao, J., Li, N., Bertino, E., Jin, H.: Differentially private k-means clustering. In: Proceedings of the Sixth ACM Conference on Data and Application Security and Privacy, CODASPY 2016, pp. 26–37. Association for Computing Machinery, New York (2016). https://doi.org/10.1145/2857705.2857708. https://doi.org/10.1145/2857705.2857708
33. Ultsch, A.: Clustering wih som: U* c. Proc. Workshop on Self-Organizing Maps (01 2005)
34. Ultsch, A.: Emergence in self organizing feature maps. In: The 6th International Workshop on Self-Organizing Maps (WSOM 2007) (2007). https://doi.org/10.2390/biecoll-wsom2007-114. https://doi.org/10.2390/biecoll-wsom2007-114
35. Wei, W., ming Tang, C., Chen, Y.: Efficient privacy-preserving k-means clustering from secret-sharing-based secure three-party computation. Entropy 24 (2022)
36. Wu, W., Liu, J., Rong, H., Wang, H., Xian, M.: Efficient k-nearest neighbor classification over semantically secure hybrid encrypted cloud database. IEEE Access **6**, 41771–41784 (2018). https://doi.org/10.1109/ACCESS.2018.2859758
37. Wu, W., Liu, J., Wang, H., Hao, J., Xian, M.: Secure and efficient outsourced k-means clustering using fully homomorphic encryption with ciphertext packing technique. IEEE Trans. Knowl. Data Eng. **33**(10), 3424–3437 (2021). https://doi.org/10.1109/TKDE.2020.2969633

Generic Construction of Forward Secure Public Key Authenticated Encryption with Keyword Search

Keita Emura[1,2(✉)]

[1] Kanazawa University, Kanazawa, Ishikawa, Japan
[2] National Institute of Information and Communications Technology (NICT), Koganei, Tokyo, Japan
k-emura@se.kanazawa-u.ac.jp

Abstract. In this paper, we propose a generic construction of forward secure public key authenticated encryption with keyword search (FS-PAEKS) from PAEKS. In addition to PAEKS, we employ 0/1 encodings proposed by Lin et al. (ACNS 2005). Here, forward security means that a newly generated ciphertext is not allowed to be searched by previously generated trapdoors. We also show that the Jiang et al. FS-PAEKS scheme (The Computer Journal 2023) does not provide forward security. Our generic construction is quite simple, and it can also be applied to construct forward secure public key encryption with keyword search (FS-PEKS). Our generic construction yields a comparably efficient FS-PEKS scheme compared to the previous scheme. Moreover, it eliminates the hierarchical structure (Abdalla et al. (JoC 2008)) or attribute-based feature (Zeng et al. (IEEE Transactions on Cloud Computing 2022)) of the previous generic constructions which is meaningful from a feasibility perspective.

1 Introduction

Searchable encryption is a fundamental tool to provide data confidentiality and data searchability simultaneously, and there are two types, searchable symmetric encryption (SSE) [53] and public key encryption with keyword search (PEKS) [8]. In the (dynamic) SSE context, forward security, which is also referred to as forward privacy, has been a default security notion since the seminal work by Stefanov et al. [54] where a newly generated ciphertext is not allowed to be searched by previously generated trapdoors. However, forward security is somewhat overlooked in the PEKS context [8]. Currently, six forward secure PEKS (FS-PEKS) schemes have been proposed [36,58–60], to the best of our knowledge. Kim et al. [36] constructed FS-PEKS from hierarchical identity-based encryption (HIBE). In their construction, a fixed message (ind_i in their paper) is encrypted by the underlying HIBE scheme. However, this construction does not provide consistency due to the observation of Abdalla et al. [1]. Zhang et al. [60], Yu et al. [58], and Islam et al. [28] proposed FS-PEKS schemes from lattices. Their constructions employ a secret key update algorithm, and an adversary is allowed to

C. Pöpper and L. Batina (Eds.): ACNS 2024, LNCS 14583, pp. 237–256, 2024.
https://doi.org/10.1007/978-3-031-54770-6_10

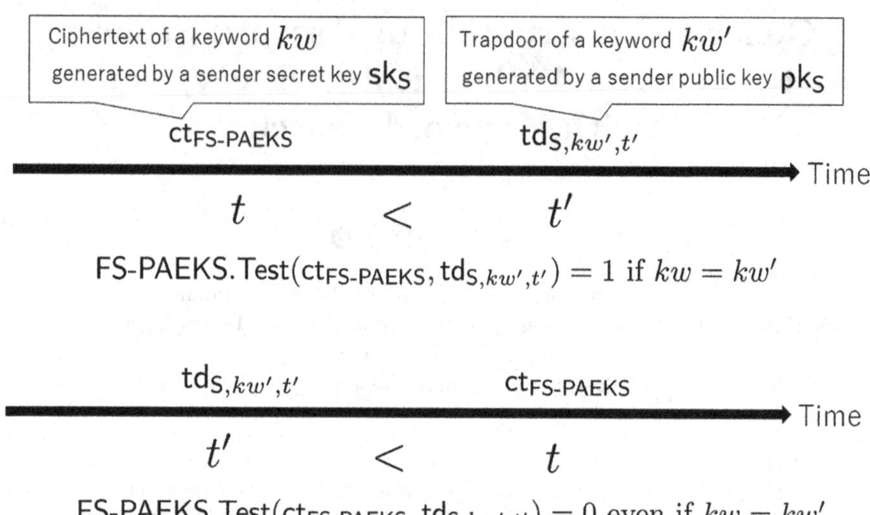

Fig. 1. FS-PAEKS

obtain secret keys under some restrictions, which is reminiscent of forward secure public key encryption [12] that considers other scenario to the trapdoor leakage. Tang [55] considered forward security properties for PEKS where forward-secure trapdoor unlinkability and forward-secure function privacy. In both notions, an adversary declares two distributions, and the challenge keyword is chosen according to one of the distributions. This considers other scenario to ours. Zeng et al. [59] proposed an FS-PEKS scheme in bilinear groups. They also mentioned that FS-PEKS can be constructed from attribute-based searchable encryption supporting OR gates, and FS-PEKS is essentially the same as public key encryption with temporary keyword search (PETKS) [1], which can be constructed generically from HIBE with level-1 anonymity.

In PEKS, a keyword is encrypted by a receiver public key. The receiver generates a trapdoor for a keyword using the receiver secret key. A server runs the test algorithm that takes a ciphertext and a trapdoor, and outputs 1 if the encrypted keyword and the keyword associated to the trapdoor is the same. That is, a trapdoor works as a distinguisher. Since anyone can generate a ciphertext of a keyword, if one obtains a trapdoor, then information about which keyword is associated with the trapdoor is leaked by running the test algorithm with self-made ciphertexts. To prevent this keyword guessing attack, public key authenticated encryption with keyword search (PAEKS) has been proposed [11,16–21,26,44–46,48,49] where a sender secret key is required for encryption. As in PEKS, forward secure PAEKS (FS-PAEKS) can be defined where the encryption algorithm takes a time period t and the trapdoor generation algorithm takes a time period t'. In addition to the search condition defined in PAEKS, a trapdoor works if $t < t'$, that is, a newly generated ciphertext is not allowed to be searched by previously generated trapdoors. See Fig. 1.

Our Contribution. In this paper, we propose a generic construction of FS-PAEKS from PAEKS. We employ 0/1 encodings, which were originally proposed for solving the Millionaires' problem by Lin et al. [41]. We focus on the fact that the encodings are effective way to translate an inequality condition $t < t'$ to an equality condition, and PAEKS originally supports keyword equality matching. Our generic construction yields FS-PAEKS schemes under several complexity assumptions. For example, a lattice-based FS-PAEKS scheme by employing the Cheng-Meng PAEKS scheme [17] and a pairing-based FS-PAEKS scheme by employing the Qin et al. PAEKS scheme [49]. These instantiations require random oracles because the underlying PAEKS schemes are secure in the random oracle model. Other FS-PAEKS schemes can be obtained by employing PAEKS schemes instantiated by a generic construction of PAEKS [21]. Especially, the generic construction of PAEKS [21] does not require random oracles, and thus our generic construction yields FS-PAEKS schemes without random oracles. To date, a concrete FS-PAEKS scheme has been proposed by Jiang et al. [30]. We remark that Jiang et al. [30] employed symmetric pairings which can be seen as a DDH solver (where DDH stands for decisional Diffie-Hellman), but they assumed that the DDH problem is hard. Actually, their FS-PAEKS scheme does not provide forward security. We give a concrete attack in Sect. 6. As an independent work, Xu et al. [56] proposed a generic construction of FS-PAEKS. They employed the Liu et al. generic construction of PAEKS [44] that requires random oracles as mentioned in [21].[1] Thus, our generic construction yields the first secure FS-PAEKS schemes without random oracles.

FS-PEKS: Our generic construction is quite simple, and it can also be applied to construct FS-PEKS. This eliminates the hierarchical structure or attribute-based feature of the previous generic constructions which is meaningful from a feasibility perspective. In addition, since PEKS can be constructed from anonymous IBE [1], efficient FS-PEKS constructions can be obtained easily. For example, if we employ the Boneh-Franklin (BF) IBE scheme [9] as the component of the underlying PEKS scheme, then an efficient pairing-based FS-PEKS scheme in the random oracle model can be constructed. If the Gentry-Peikert-Vaikuntanathan (GPV) IBE scheme [24] is employed, then an efficient lattice-based FS-PEKS scheme in the quantum random oracle model can be constructed.[2] Moreover, FS-PEKS schemes that are secure in the standard model also can be obtained from the Gentry IBE scheme [23], the Lewko IBE scheme [40], the Chen-Wei-Ling-Wang-Wee IBE (CLLWW) scheme [15], the Kurosawa-Phong IBE scheme [37], the Jutla-Roy (JR) IBE scheme [31], the Katsumata IBE scheme [34], the Yamada IBE scheme [57], and the Jager-Kurek-Niehues IBE scheme [29]. In the Zeng et al. FS-PEKS scheme [59], the ciphertext size and the trapdoor size depend on the bit length of the time period. Thus, our generic construction yields a comparably efficient FS-PEKS scheme, in terms of ciphertext/trapdoor size and search complexity. In Table 1, we give comparisons among the Zeng

[1] A flaw in the security proof of the generic construction [44] is identified in [21], and random oracles are introduced to fix the flaw in the ePrint version [43].

[2] The GPV-IBE scheme is secure in the quantum random oracle model [35].

Table 1. Comparison among the Zeng et al. FS-PEKS scheme, the Abdalla et al. PETKS scheme, and our two pairing-based instantiations. First we construct PEKS schemes from the BF-IBE scheme [9] (over symmetric bilinear groups $(\mathbb{G}, \mathbb{G}_T)$) and the CLLWW IBE scheme [15] (over asymmetric bilinear groups $(\mathbb{G}_1, \mathbb{G}_2, \mathbb{G}_T)$) via the Abdalla et al. transformation [1], and next we construct FS-PEKS schemes from these PEKS schemes. We denote "Ours + BF-IBE" or "Ours + CLLWW-IBE" as these FS-PEKS schemes. Let ℓ be the bit length of time period specified in the encryption and trapdoor generation algorithms, i.e., $\ell = O(\log t)$. We employ the security parameter λ to indicate the output size of the hash function (from $\mathbb{G}_T$ to $\{0,1\}^\lambda$) used in the BF-IBE scheme. ROM stands for random oracle model, STD stands for standard model, GGM stands for generic group model, BDH stands for bilinear Diffie-Hellman, and SXDH stands for symmetric external Diffie-Hellman.

FS-PEKS Scheme	Ciphertext Size	Trapdoor Size	Assump	STD /ROM
Zeng et al. [59]	$(4+\ell)\lvert\mathbb{G}\rvert$	$(3+\ell)\lvert\mathbb{G}\rvert$	GGM	ROM
Abdalla et al. [1] (PETKS)	$\ell\lvert\mathbb{G}\rvert + \lambda$	$\ell((\ell+1)\lvert\mathbb{G}\rvert + \lvert\mathbb{Z}_p\rvert)$	BDH	ROM
Ours + BF-IBE	$\ell(\lvert\mathbb{G}\rvert + 2\lambda)$	$\ell\lvert\mathbb{G}\rvert$	BDH	ROM
Ours + CLLWW-IBE	$\ell(2\lvert\mathbb{G}_T\rvert + 4\lvert\mathbb{G}_1\rvert)$	$4\ell\lvert\mathbb{G}_2\rvert$	SXDH	STD

et al. FS-PEKS scheme, the Abdalla et al. PETKS scheme instantiated by the Gentry-Silverberg HIBE scheme [25] with a slight modification to provide level-1 anonymity, and our two pairing-based instantiations from PEKS schemes which are instantiations of the Abdalla et al. transformation from the BF-IBE scheme [9] and the CLLWW IBE scheme [15]. We remark that other PETKS schemes can be obtained from other HIBE schemes via the Abdalla et al. generic construction, e.g., anonymous HIBE from pairings [7,38,39,50,51] or from lattices [2,3,10,14]. Especially, these pairing-based instantiations provide PETKS schemes secure in the standard model. Nevertheless, our construction is more efficient in terms of the trapdoor size.

2 Preliminaries

Notation. For a positive integer $n \in \mathbb{N}$, we write $[1,n] = \{1,2,\ldots,n\}$. $x \xleftarrow{\$} S$ denotes choosing an element x from a finite set S uniformly at random. For a security parameter λ, $\mathsf{negl}(\lambda)$ is a negligible function where for any $c > 0$, there exists an integer I such that $\mathsf{negl}(\lambda) < 1/\lambda^c$ for all $\lambda > I$. PPT stands for probabilistic polynomial-time.

2.1 PAEKS

Definition 1 (Syntax of PAEKS). *A PAEKS scheme* PAEKS *consists of the following six algorithms* (PAEKS.Setup, $\mathsf{PAEKS.KG_R}$, $\mathsf{PAEKS.KG_S}$, PAEKS.Enc, PAEKS.Trapdoor, PAEKS.Test) *defined as follows.*

PAEKS.Setup: *The setup algorithm takes a security parameter λ as input, and outputs a common parameter* pp. *We assume that* pp *implicitly contains the keyword space $\mathcal{KS}$.*

$\mathsf{PAEKS.KG_R}$: *The receiver key generation algorithm takes* pp *as input, and outputs a public key* $\mathsf{pk_R}$ *and secret key* $\mathsf{sk_R}$.

$\mathsf{PAEKS.KG_S}$: *The sender key generation algorithm takes* pp *as input, and outputs a public key* $\mathsf{pk_S}$ *and secret key* $\mathsf{sk_S}$.

$\mathsf{PAEKS.Enc}$: *The keyword encryption algorithm takes* $\mathsf{pk_R}$, $\mathsf{pk_S}$, $\mathsf{sk_S}$, *and a keyword* $kw \in \mathcal{KS}$ *as input, and outputs a ciphertext* $\mathsf{ct_{PAEKS}}$.

$\mathsf{PAEKS.Trapdoor}$: *The trapdoor algorithm takes* $\mathsf{pk_R}$, $\mathsf{pk_S}$, $\mathsf{sk_R}$, *and a keyword* $kw' \in \mathcal{KS}$ *as input, and outputs a trapdoor* $\mathsf{td}_{\mathsf{S},kw'}$.

$\mathsf{PAEKS.Test}$: *The test algorithm takes* $\mathsf{ct_{PAEKS}}$ *and* $\mathsf{td}_{\mathsf{S},kw'}$ *as input, and outputs 1 or 0.*

Definition 2 (Correctness). *For any security parameter* λ, *any common parameter* $\mathsf{pp} \leftarrow \mathsf{PAEKS.Setup}(1^\lambda)$, *any key pairs* $(\mathsf{pk_R}, \mathsf{sk_R}) \leftarrow \mathsf{PAEKS.KG_R}(\mathsf{pp})$ *and* $(\mathsf{pk_S}, \mathsf{sk_S}) \leftarrow \mathsf{PAEKS.KG_S}(\mathsf{pp})$, *and any keyword* $kw \in \mathcal{KS}$, *let* $\mathsf{ct_{PAEKS}} \leftarrow \mathsf{PAEKS.Enc}(\mathsf{pk_R}, \mathsf{pk_S}, \mathsf{sk_S}, kw)$ *and* $\mathsf{td}_{\mathsf{S},kw} \leftarrow \mathsf{PAEKS.Trapdoor}(\mathsf{pk_R}, \mathsf{pk_S}, \mathsf{sk_R}, kw)$. *Then* $\Pr[\mathsf{PAEKS.Test}(\mathsf{ct_{PAEKS}}, \mathsf{td}_{\mathsf{S},kw}) = 1] = 1 - \mathsf{negl}(\lambda)$ *holds.*

Next, we define consistency that defines the condition by which the $\mathsf{PAEKS.Test}$ algorithm outputs 0. As in PEKS, essentially, $0 \leftarrow \mathsf{PAEKS.Test}(\mathsf{ct_{PAEKS}}, \mathsf{td}_{\mathsf{S},kw})$ when $\mathsf{ct_{PAEKS}} \leftarrow \mathsf{PAEKS.Enc}(\mathsf{pk_R}, \mathsf{pk_S}, \mathsf{sk_S}, kw)$, $\mathsf{td}_{\mathsf{S},kw'} \leftarrow \mathsf{PAEKS.Trapdoor}(\mathsf{pk_R}, \mathsf{pk_S}, \mathsf{sk_R}, kw')$, and $kw \neq kw'$. However, due to its authenticity, a trapdoor associated with a sender should not work against ciphertexts generated by the secret key of another sender, even if the same keyword is associated. Thus, we introduce the definition given in [21] that considers consistency in a multi-sender setting.

Definition 3 (Computational Consistency). *For all PPT adversaries* $\mathcal{A}$, *we define the following experiment.*

$$
\begin{aligned}
&\mathsf{Exp}^{\mathsf{consist}}_{\mathsf{PAEKS},\mathcal{A}}(\lambda):\\
&\quad \mathsf{pp} \leftarrow \mathsf{PAEKS.Setup}(1^\lambda);\ (\mathsf{pk_R}, \mathsf{sk_R}) \leftarrow \mathsf{PAEKS.KG_R}(\mathsf{pp})\\
&\quad (\mathsf{pk_{S[0]}}, \mathsf{sk_{S[0]}}) \leftarrow \mathsf{PAEKS.KG_S}(\mathsf{pp});\ (\mathsf{pk_{S[1]}}, \mathsf{sk_{S[1]}}) \leftarrow \mathsf{PAEKS.KG_S}(\mathsf{pp})\\
&\quad (kw, kw', i, j) \leftarrow \mathcal{A}(\mathsf{pp}, \mathsf{pk_R}, \mathsf{pk_{S[0]}}, \mathsf{pk_{S[1]}})\\
&\qquad s.t.\ kw, kw' \in \mathcal{KS} \wedge i, j \in \{0,1\} \wedge (kw, i) \neq (kw', j)\\
&\quad \mathsf{ct_{PAEKS}} \leftarrow \mathsf{PAEKS.Enc}(\mathsf{pk_R}, \mathsf{pk_{S[\mathit{i}]}}, \mathsf{sk_{S[\mathit{i}]}}, kw)\\
&\quad \mathsf{td}_{\mathsf{S}[j],kw'} \leftarrow \mathsf{PAEKS.Trapdoor}(\mathsf{pk_R}, \mathsf{pk_{S[\mathit{j}]}}, \mathsf{sk_R}, kw')\\
&\quad \textit{If } \mathsf{PAEKS.Test}(\mathsf{ct_{PAEKS}}, \mathsf{td}_{\mathsf{S}[j],kw'}) = 1,\ \textit{then output } 1,\ \textit{and } 0\ \textit{otherwise.}
\end{aligned}
$$

We say that a PAEKS scheme PAEKS *is consistent if the advantage* $\mathsf{Adv}^{\mathsf{consist}}_{\mathsf{PAEKS},\mathcal{A}}(\lambda) := \Pr[\mathsf{Exp}^{\mathsf{consist}}_{\mathsf{PAEKS},\mathcal{A}}(\lambda) = 1]$ *is negligible in the security parameter* λ.

Next, we define indistinguishability against the chosen keyword attack (IND-CKA) which guarantees that no information about the keyword is leaked from ciphertexts.

Definition 4 (IND-CKA). *For all PPT adversaries $\mathcal{A}$, we define the following experiment.*

$$\begin{aligned}
&\mathsf{Exp}^{\mathsf{IND\text{-}CKA}}_{\mathsf{PAEKS},\mathcal{A}}(\lambda, n):\\
&\quad \mathsf{pp} \leftarrow \mathsf{PAEKS.Setup}(1^\lambda);\ (\mathsf{pk_R}, \mathsf{sk_R}) \leftarrow \mathsf{PAEKS.KG_R}(\mathsf{pp})\\
&\quad \textit{For } i \in [1,n],\ (\mathsf{pk_{S[\mathit{i}]}}, \mathsf{sk_{S[\mathit{i}]}}) \leftarrow \mathsf{PAEKS.KG_S}(\mathsf{pp})\\
&\quad (kw_0^*, kw_1^*, i^*, \mathsf{state}) \leftarrow \mathcal{A}^{\mathcal{O}}(\mathsf{pp}, \mathsf{pk_R}, \{\mathsf{pk_{S[\mathit{i}]}}\}_{i\in[1,n]})\\
&\qquad \textit{s.t. } kw_0^*, kw_1^* \in \mathcal{KS} \land\ kw_0^* \neq kw_1^* \land i^* \in [1,n]\\
&\quad b \xleftarrow{\$} \{0,1\};\ \mathsf{ct}^*_{\mathsf{PAEKS}} \leftarrow \mathsf{PAEKS.Enc}(\mathsf{pk_R}, \mathsf{pk_{S[\mathit{i}^*]}}, \mathsf{sk_{S[\mathit{i}^*]}}, kw_b^*)\\
&\quad b' \leftarrow \mathcal{A}^{\mathcal{O}}(\mathsf{state}, \mathsf{ct}^*_{\mathsf{PAEKS}})\\
&\quad \textit{If } b = b' \textit{ then output } 1, \textit{ and } 0 \textit{ otherwise.}
\end{aligned}$$

Here, $\mathcal{O} := \{\mathcal{O}_C(\mathsf{pk_R}, \cdot, \cdot), \mathcal{O}_T(\mathsf{pk_R}, \cdot, \mathsf{sk_R}, \cdot)\}$. $\mathcal{O}_C$ takes $kw \in \mathcal{KS}$ and $i \in [1,n]$ as input, and returns the result of $\mathsf{PAEKS.Enc}(\mathsf{pk_R}, \mathsf{pk_{S[\mathit{i}]}}, \mathsf{sk_{S[\mathit{i}]}}, kw)$. *Here, there is no restriction. $\mathcal{O}_T$ takes $kw' \in \mathcal{KS}$ and $i \in [1,n]$ as input, and returns the result of* $\mathsf{PAEKS.Trapdoor}(\mathsf{pk_R}, \mathsf{pk_{S[\mathit{i}]}}, \mathsf{sk_R}, kw')$. *Here $(kw', i) \notin \{(kw_0^*, i^*), (kw_1^*, i^*)\}$. We say that a PAEKS scheme* PAEKS *is IND-CKA secure if the advantage* $\mathsf{Adv}^{\mathsf{IND\text{-}CKA}}_{\mathsf{PAEKS},\mathcal{A}}(\lambda, n) := |\Pr[\mathsf{Exp}^{\mathsf{IND\text{-}CKA}}_{\mathsf{PAEKS},\mathcal{A}}(\lambda, n) = 1] - 1/2|$ *is negligible in the security parameter λ.*

Qin et al. [48] considered multi-ciphertext indistinguishability (MCI) where in the IND-CKA experiment $\mathcal{A}$ declares two keyword vectors $(kw_{0,1}^*, \ldots, kw_{0,N}^*)$ and $(kw_{1,1}^*, \ldots, kw_{1,N}^*)$ for some N, and the challenger returns the challenge ciphertexts of $kw_{b,i}^*$ for $i \in [1, N]$. The concept of MCI is to capture unlinkability of ciphertexts where it is difficult to distinguish whether two ciphertexts are encryptions of the same keyword or not. As mentioned in [49], if the encryption oracle $\mathcal{O}_C$ has no restriction (i.e., any input is allowed), then IND-CKA implies MCI. Thus, the above definition provides MCI security.

Next, we define indistinguishability against the inside keyword guessing attack (IND-IKGA) which guarantees that no information about the keyword is leaked from trapdoors.

Definition 5 (IND-IKGA). *For all PPT adversaries $\mathcal{A}$, we define the following experiment.*

$$\begin{aligned}
&\mathsf{Exp}^{\mathsf{IND\text{-}IKGA}}_{\mathsf{PAEKS},\mathcal{A}}(\lambda, n):\\
&\quad \mathsf{pp} \leftarrow \mathsf{PAEKS.Setup}(1^\lambda);\ (\mathsf{pk_R}, \mathsf{sk_R}) \leftarrow \mathsf{PAEKS.KG_R}(\mathsf{pp})\\
&\quad \textit{For } i \in [1,n],\ (\mathsf{pk_{S[\mathit{i}]}}, \mathsf{sk_{S[\mathit{i}]}}) \leftarrow \mathsf{PAEKS.KG_S}(\mathsf{pp})\\
&\quad (kw_0^*, kw_1^*, i^*, \mathsf{state}) \leftarrow \mathcal{A}^{\mathcal{O}}(\mathsf{pp}, \mathsf{pk_R}, \{\mathsf{pk_{S[\mathit{i}]}}\}_{i\in[1,n]})\\
&\qquad \textit{s.t. } kw_0^*, kw_1^* \in \mathcal{KS} \land\ kw_0^* \neq kw_1^* \land i^* \in [1,n]\\
&\quad b \xleftarrow{\$} \{0,1\};\ \mathsf{td}^*_{\mathsf{S}[i^*], kw_b^*} \leftarrow \mathsf{PAEKS.Trapdoor}(\mathsf{pk_R}, \mathsf{pk_{S[\mathit{i}^*]}}, \mathsf{sk_R}, kw_b^*)\\
&\quad b' \leftarrow \mathcal{A}^{\mathcal{O}}(\mathsf{state}, \mathsf{td}^*_{\mathsf{S}[i^*], kw_b^*})\\
&\quad \textit{If } b = b' \textit{ then output } 1, \textit{ and } 0 \textit{ otherwise.}
\end{aligned}$$

Here, $\mathcal{O} := \{\mathcal{O}_C(\mathsf{pk_R}, \cdot, \cdot), \mathcal{O}_T(\mathsf{pk_R}, \cdot, \mathsf{sk_R}, \cdot)\}$. $\mathcal{O}_C$ *takes* $kw \in \mathcal{KS}$ *and* $i \in [1, n]$ *as input, and returns the result of* $\mathsf{PAEKS.Enc}(\mathsf{pk_R}, \mathsf{pk_{S[i]}}, \mathsf{sk_{S[i]}}, kw)$. *Here,* $(kw, i) \notin \{(kw_0^*, i^*), (kw_1^*, i^*)\}$. $\mathcal{O}_T$ *takes* $kw' \in \mathcal{KS}$ *and* $i \in [1, n]$ *as input, and returns the result of* $\mathsf{PAEKS.Trapdoor}(\mathsf{pk_R}, \mathsf{pk_{S[i]}}, \mathsf{sk_R}, kw')$. *Here* $(kw', i) \notin \{(kw_0^*, i^*), (kw_1^*, i^*)\}$. *We say that a PAEKS scheme* PAEKS *is IND-IKGA secure if the advantage* $\mathsf{Adv}^{\mathsf{IND\text{-}IKGA}}_{\mathsf{PAEKS},\mathcal{A}}(\lambda, n) := |\Pr[\mathsf{Exp}^{\mathsf{IND\text{-}IKGA}}_{\mathsf{PAEKS},\mathcal{A}}(\lambda, n) = 1] - 1/2|$ *is negligible in the security parameter* λ.

Pan and Li [46] considered multi-trapdoor indistinguishability (MTI) where in the IND-IKGA experiment $\mathcal{A}$ declares two keyword vectors $(kw_{0,1}^*, \ldots, kw_{0,N}^*)$ and $(kw_{1,1}^*, \ldots, kw_{1,N}^*)$ for some N, and the challenger returns the challenge trapdoors of $kw_{b,i}^*$ for $i \in [1, N]$. The concept of MTI is to capture unlinkability of trapdoors where it is difficult to distinguish whether two trapdoors are generated for the same keyword or not. Although the above definition does not capture MTI, it can be modified to capture MTI if $\mathcal{A}$ is allowed to send either (kw_0^*, i^*) or (kw_1^*, i^*) to the trapdoor oracle $\mathcal{O}_T$.

2.2 0/1 Encodings

Here, we introduce 0/1 encodings [41]. Let $t \in \mathbb{N}$ be a ℓ-bit positive integer, and its binary representation is denoted $t = t_\ell t_{\ell-1} \cdots t_1$ where $t_i \in \{0, 1\}$ for all $i \in [1, \ell]$. The 0-encoding algorithm takes ℓ and t as input, and outputs a set of strings S_t^0 defined as follows.

$$S_t^0 = \{t_\ell t_{\ell-1} \cdots t_{i+1} 1 \mid t_i = 0, i \in [1, \ell]\}$$

We denote $S_t^0 = \{s_{t,1}^0, s_{t,2}^0, \ldots, s_{t,\ell_t^0}^0\}$ where ℓ_t^0 is the number of strings contained in S_t^0 and is at most $O(\log t) = O(\ell)$. Similarly, the 1-encoding algorithm takes ℓ and t' as input and outputs a set of strings $S_{t'}^1$ defined as follows.

$$S_{t'}^1 = \{t'_\ell t'_{\ell-1} \cdots t'_i \mid t'_i = 1, i \in [1, \ell]\}$$

We denote $S_{t'}^1 = \{s_{t',1}^1, s_{t',2}^1, \ldots, s_{t',\ell_{t'}^1}^1\}$ where $\ell_{t'}^1$ is the number of strings contained in $S_{t'}^1$ and is at most $O(\log t') = O(\ell)$. As an example, $\ell = 4$ and $t, t' \in \{7, 12\}$ define $S_7^0 = \{1\}$, $S_7^1 = \{01, 011, 0111\}$, $S_{12}^0 = \{111, 1101\}$, and $S_{12}^1 = \{1, 11\}$, since $7_{(10)} = (0111)_{(2)}$ and $12_{(10)} = (1100)_{(2)}$. We remark that "1" and "01" are different strings. The encodings are effective to compare two integer values, t and t', because the following holds as shown by Lin et al. [41].

$$S_t^0 \cap S_{t'}^1 \neq \emptyset \iff t < t'$$

In other word, the encodings are effective to translate an inequality condition $t < t'$ to an equality condition, i.e., for all $s_{t,i}^0 \in S_t^0$ and $s_{t',j}^1 \in S_{t'}^1$, check whether $s_{t,i}^0 = s_{t',j}^1$ or not where $i \in [1, \ell_t^0]$ and $j \in [1, \ell_{t'}^1]$. The number of equality checks is at most $\ell_t^0 \cdot \ell_{t'}^1 = O(\log t \cdot \log t') = O(\ell^2)$. Previous FS-PAEKS [30] and FS-PEKS [36,59] also employed the encodings. Moreover, group signatures with time-bound keys [42] also employed these encodings.

3 Definition of FS-PAEKS

In this section, we define FS-PAEKS. The encryption algorithm takes a time period t and the trapdoor generation algorithm takes a time period t' (in addition to other inputs required in the syntax of PAEKS). In addition to the search condition defined in PAEKS, a trapdoor works if $t < t'$, that is, a newly generated ciphertext is not allowed to be searched by previously generated trapdoors.

Definition 6 (Syntax of FS-PAEKS). *An FS-PAEKS scheme* $\mathsf{FS\text{-}PAEKS}$ *consists of the following six algorithms* ($\mathsf{FS\text{-}PAEKS.Setup}$, $\mathsf{FS\text{-}PAEKS.KG_R}$, $\mathsf{FS\text{-}PAEKS.KG_S}$, $\mathsf{FS\text{-}PAEKS.Enc}$, $\mathsf{FS\text{-}PAEKS.Trapdoor}$, $\mathsf{FS\text{-}PAEKS.Test}$) *defined as follows.*

$\mathsf{FS\text{-}PAEKS.Setup}$: *The setup algorithm takes a security parameter* λ *as input, and outputs a common parameter* pp. *We assume that* pp *implicitly contains the keyword space* $\mathcal{KS}$ *and the time space* $\mathcal{T}$.

$\mathsf{FS\text{-}PAEKS.KG_R}$: *The receiver key generation algorithm takes* pp *as input, and outputs a public key* $\mathsf{pk_R}$ *and a secret key* $\mathsf{sk_R}$.

$\mathsf{FS\text{-}PAEKS.KG_S}$: *The sender key generation algorithm takes* pp *as input, and outputs a public key* $\mathsf{pk_S}$ *and a secret key* $\mathsf{sk_S}$.

$\mathsf{FS\text{-}PAEKS.Enc}$: *The keyword encryption algorithm takes* $\mathsf{pk_R}$, $\mathsf{pk_S}$, $\mathsf{sk_S}$, *a keyword* $kw \in \mathcal{KS}$, *and a time period* $t \in \mathcal{T}$ *as input, and outputs a ciphertext* $\mathsf{FS\text{-}ct_{PAEKS}}$.

$\mathsf{FS\text{-}PAEKS.Trapdoor}$: *The trapdoor algorithm takes* $\mathsf{pk_R}$, $\mathsf{pk_S}$, $\mathsf{sk_R}$, *a keyword* $kw' \in \mathcal{KS}$, *and a time period* $t' \in \mathcal{T}$ *as input, and outputs a trapdoor* $\mathsf{td}_{\mathsf{S},kw',t'}$.

$\mathsf{FS\text{-}PAEKS.Test}$: *The test algorithm takes* $\mathsf{ct_{PAEKS}}$ *and* $\mathsf{td}_{\mathsf{S},kw',t'}$ *as input, and outputs 1 or 0.*

Definition 7 (Correctness). *For any security parameter* λ, *any common parameter* $\mathsf{pp} \leftarrow \mathsf{FS\text{-}PAEKS.Setup}(1^\lambda)$, *any key pairs* $(\mathsf{pk_R}, \mathsf{sk_R}) \leftarrow \mathsf{FS\text{-}PAEKS.KG_R}(\mathsf{pp})$ *and* $(\mathsf{pk_S}, \mathsf{sk_S}) \leftarrow \mathsf{FS\text{-}PAEKS.KG_S}(\mathsf{pp})$, *and any keyword* $kw \in \mathcal{KS}$ *and any time periods* $t', t \in \mathcal{T}$ *where* $t < t'$, *let* $\mathsf{FS\text{-}ct_{PAEKS}} \leftarrow \mathsf{FS\text{-}PAEKS.Enc}(\mathsf{pk_R}, \mathsf{pk_S}, \mathsf{sk_S}, kw, t)$ *and* $\mathsf{td}_{\mathsf{S},kw,t'} \leftarrow \mathsf{FS\text{-}PAEKS.Trapdoor}(\mathsf{pk_R}, \mathsf{pk_S}, \mathsf{sk_R}, kw, t')$. *Then* $\Pr[\mathsf{FS\text{-}PAEKS.Test}(\mathsf{FS\text{-}ct_{PAEKS}}, \mathsf{td}_{\mathsf{S},kw,t'}) = 1] = 1 - \mathsf{negl}(\lambda)$ *holds.*

Next, we define consistency. As in PAEKS, due to its authenticity, a trapdoor associated with a sender should not work against ciphertexts generated by the secret key of another sender, even if the same keyword is associated. In addition, due to the forward security, a newly generated ciphertext should not be searchable by previously generated trapdoors, even if the same keyword and legitimate sender public key are specified. Thus, we add the condition $(kw, i) = (kw', j) \wedge t > t'$ below.

Definition 8 (Computational Consistency). *For all PPT adversaries $\mathcal{A}$, we define the following experiment.*

$$
\begin{aligned}
&\mathsf{Exp}^{\mathsf{consist}}_{\mathit{FS\text{-}PAEKS},\mathcal{A}}(\lambda):\\
&\quad \mathsf{pp} \leftarrow \mathit{FS\text{-}PAEKS.Setup}(1^\lambda);\ (\mathsf{pk_R},\mathsf{sk_R}) \leftarrow \mathit{FS\text{-}PAEKS.KG_R}(\mathsf{pp})\\
&\quad (\mathsf{pk}_{\mathsf{S}[0]},\mathsf{sk}_{\mathsf{S}[0]}) \leftarrow \mathit{FS\text{-}PAEKS.KG_S}(\mathsf{pp});\ (\mathsf{pk}_{\mathsf{S}[1]},\mathsf{sk}_{\mathsf{S}[1]}) \leftarrow \mathit{FS\text{-}PAEKS.KG_S}(\mathsf{pp})\\
&\quad (kw, kw', t, t', i, j) \leftarrow \mathcal{A}(\mathsf{pp},\mathsf{pk_R},\mathsf{pk}_{\mathsf{S}[0]},\mathsf{pk}_{\mathsf{S}[1]})\\
&\qquad s.t.\ kw, kw' \in \mathcal{KS} \wedge i,j \in \{0,1\} \wedge t,t' \in \mathcal{T}\\
&\qquad \wedge \big((kw,i) \neq (kw',j) \vee \big((kw,i) = (kw',j) \wedge t > t'\big)\big)\\
&\quad \mathit{FS\text{-}ct_{PAEKS}} \leftarrow \mathit{FS\text{-}PAEKS.Enc}(\mathsf{pk_R},\mathsf{pk}_{\mathsf{S}[i]},\mathsf{sk}_{\mathsf{S}[i]}, kw, t)\\
&\quad \mathsf{td}_{\mathsf{S}[j],kw',t'} \leftarrow \mathit{FS\text{-}PAEKS.Trapdoor}(\mathsf{pk_R},\mathsf{pk}_{\mathsf{S}[j]},\mathsf{sk_R}, kw', t')\\
&\quad \textit{If } \mathit{FS\text{-}PAEKS.Test}(\mathit{FS\text{-}ct_{PAEKS}},\mathsf{td}_{\mathsf{S}[j],kw',t'}) = 1 \textit{ then output } 1, \textit{ and } 0 \textit{ otherwise.}
\end{aligned}
$$

We say that an FS-PAEKS scheme FS-PAEKS is consistent if the advantage $\mathsf{Adv}^{\mathsf{consist}}_{\mathsf{PAEKS},\mathcal{A}}(\lambda) := \Pr[\mathsf{Exp}^{\mathsf{consist}}_{\mathit{FS\text{-}PAEKS},\mathcal{A}}(\lambda) = 1]$ *is negligible in the security parameter* λ.

Next, we define indistinguishability against the chosen keyword attack with forward security (IND-FS-CKA) which guarantees that no information about the keyword is leaked from ciphertexts. Due to the forward security, an adversary $\mathcal{A}$ is allowed to obtain trapdoors for the challenge keyword and the challenge sender if the trapdoor is generated at $t' < t^*$ where the challenge ciphertext is generated at t^*. Thus, we add the condition $(kw', i) \in \{(kw_0^*, i^*), (kw_1^*, i^*)\} \wedge t' < t^*$ to the $\mathcal{O}_T$ oracle. We also remark that Jiang et al. [30] introduced selective forward security where an adversary declares t^* prior to the setup phase. We consider adaptive security where an adversary declares t^* in the challenge phase.[3]

Definition 9 (IND-FS-CKA). *For all PPT adversaries $\mathcal{A}$, we define the following experiment.*

$$
\begin{aligned}
&\mathsf{Exp}^{\mathsf{IND\text{-}FS\text{-}CKA}}_{\mathit{FS\text{-}PAEKS},\mathcal{A}}(\lambda, n):\\
&\quad \mathsf{pp} \leftarrow \mathit{FS\text{-}PAEKS.Setup}(1^\lambda);\ (\mathsf{pk_R},\mathsf{sk_R}) \leftarrow \mathit{FS\text{-}PAEKS.KG_R}(\mathsf{pp})\\
&\quad \textit{For } i \in [1,n],\ (\mathsf{pk}_{\mathsf{S}[i]},\mathsf{sk}_{\mathsf{S}[i]}) \leftarrow \mathit{FS\text{-}PAEKS.KG_S}(\mathsf{pp})\\
&\quad (kw_0^*, kw_1^*, i^*, t^*, \mathsf{state}) \leftarrow \mathcal{A}^{\mathcal{O}}(\mathsf{pp},\mathsf{pk_R},\{\mathsf{pk}_{\mathsf{S}[i]}\}_{i\in[1,n]})\\
&\qquad s.t.\ kw_0^*, kw_1^* \in \mathcal{KS} \wedge\ kw_0^* \neq kw_1^* \wedge i^* \in [1,n] \wedge t^* \in \mathcal{T}\\
&\quad b \xleftarrow{\$} \{0,1\};\ \mathsf{ct}^*_{\mathit{FS\text{-}PAEKS}} \leftarrow \mathit{FS\text{-}PAEKS.Enc}(\mathsf{pk_R},\mathsf{pk}_{\mathsf{S}[i^*]},\mathsf{sk}_{\mathsf{S}[i^*]}, kw_b^*, t^*)\\
&\quad b' \leftarrow \mathcal{A}^{\mathcal{O}}(\mathsf{state},\mathsf{ct}^*_{\mathit{FS\text{-}PAEKS}})\\
&\quad \textit{If } b = b' \textit{ then output } 1, \textit{ and } 0 \textit{ otherwise.}
\end{aligned}
$$

[3] They are equivalent to $|\mathcal{T}|$ reduction and selective forward security is sufficient if $|\mathcal{T}|$ is a polynomial of the security parameter.

Here, $\mathcal{O} := \{\mathcal{O}_C(\mathsf{pk_R},\cdot,\cdot,\cdot), \mathcal{O}_T(\mathsf{pk_R},\cdot,\mathsf{sk_R},\cdot,\cdot)\}$. $\mathcal{O}_C$ *takes* $kw \in \mathcal{KS}$, $t \in \mathcal{T}$, *and* $i \in [1,n]$ *as input, and returns the result of* $\mathsf{FS\text{-}PAEKS.Enc}(\mathsf{pk_R}, \mathsf{pk_{S[\mathit{i}]}}, \mathsf{sk_{S[\mathit{i}]}}, kw, t)$. *Here, there is no restriction.* $\mathcal{O}_T$ *takes* $kw' \in \mathcal{KS}$, $t' \in \mathcal{T}$, *and* $i \in [1,n]$ *as input, and returns the result of* $\mathsf{FS\text{-}PAEKS.Trapdoor}(\mathsf{pk_R}, \mathsf{pk_{S[\mathit{i}]}}, \mathsf{sk_R}, kw', t')$. *Here* $(kw', i) \notin \{(kw_0^*, i^*), (kw_1^*, i^*)\}$ *or* $(kw', i) \in \{(kw_0^*, i^*), (kw_1^*, i^*)\} \wedge t' < t^*$. *We say that an FS-PAEKS scheme* $\mathsf{FS\text{-}PAEKS}$ *is IND-FS-CKA secure if the advantage* $\mathsf{Adv}^{\mathsf{IND\text{-}FS\text{-}CKA}}_{\mathsf{FS\text{-}PAEKS},\mathcal{A}}(\lambda, n) := |\Pr[\mathsf{Exp}^{\mathsf{IND\text{-}FS\text{-}CKA}}_{\mathsf{FS\text{-}PAEKS},\mathcal{A}}(\lambda, n) = 1] - 1/2|$ *is negligible in the security parameter* λ.

Next, we define indistinguishability against the inside keyword guessing attack with forward security (IND-FS-IKGA) which guarantees that no information about the keyword is leaked from trapdoors. Due to the forward security, an adversary $\mathcal{A}$ is allowed to obtain ciphertexts for the challenge keyword and the challenge sender if the ciphertext is generated at $t > t^*$ where the challenge trapdoor is generated at t^*. Thus, we add the condition $(kw, i) \in \{(kw_0^*, i^*), (kw_1^*, i^*)\} \wedge t > t^*$ to the $\mathcal{O}_C$ oracle. As in IND-FS-CKA, we consider adaptive security where an adversary declares t^* in the challenge phase, although Jiang et al. [30] introduced selective forward security.

Definition 10 (IND-FS-IKGA). *For all PPT adversaries* $\mathcal{A}$, *we define the following experiment.*

$$
\begin{aligned}
&\mathsf{Exp}^{\mathsf{IND\text{-}FS\text{-}IKGA}}_{\mathsf{FS\text{-}PAEKS},\mathcal{A}}(\lambda, n):\\
&\quad \mathsf{pp} \leftarrow \mathsf{FS\text{-}PAEKS.Setup}(1^\lambda);\ (\mathsf{pk_R}, \mathsf{sk_R}) \leftarrow \mathsf{FS\text{-}PAEKS.KG_R}(\mathsf{pp})\\
&\quad \mathit{For}\ i \in [1,n],\ (\mathsf{pk_{S[\mathit{i}]}}, \mathsf{sk_{S[\mathit{i}]}}) \leftarrow \mathsf{FS\text{-}PAEKS.KG_S}(\mathsf{pp})\\
&\quad (kw_0^*, kw_1^*, i^*, t^*, \mathsf{state}) \leftarrow \mathcal{A}^{\mathcal{O}}(\mathsf{pp}, \mathsf{pk_R}, \{\mathsf{pk_{S[\mathit{i}]}}\}_{i \in [1,n]})\\
&\qquad s.t.\ kw_0^*, kw_1^* \in \mathcal{KS} \wedge\ kw_0^* \neq kw_1^* \wedge i^* \in [1,n] \wedge t^* \in \mathcal{T}\\
&\quad b \xleftarrow{\$} \{0,1\};\ \mathsf{td}^*_{\mathsf{S}[i^*], kw_b^*, t^*} \leftarrow \mathsf{FS\text{-}PAEKS.Trapdoor}(\mathsf{pk_R}, \mathsf{pk_{S[\mathit{i^*}]}}, \mathsf{sk_R}, kw_b^*, t^*)\\
&\quad b' \leftarrow \mathcal{A}^{\mathcal{O}}(\mathsf{state}, \mathsf{td}^*_{\mathsf{S}[i^*], kw_b^*, t^*})\\
&\quad \mathit{If}\ b = b'\ \mathit{then\ output}\ 1,\ \mathit{and}\ 0\ \mathit{otherwise}.
\end{aligned}
$$

Here, $\mathcal{O} := \{\mathcal{O}_C(\mathsf{pk_R},\cdot,\cdot,\cdot), \mathcal{O}_T(\mathsf{pk_R},\cdot,\mathsf{sk_R},\cdot,\cdot)\}$. $\mathcal{O}_C$ *takes* $kw \in \mathcal{KS}$, $t \in \mathcal{T}$, *and* $i \in [1,n]$ *as input, and returns the result of* $\mathsf{FS\text{-}PAEKS.Enc}(\mathsf{pk_R}, \mathsf{pk_{S[\mathit{i}]}}, \mathsf{sk_{S[\mathit{i}]}}, kw, t)$. *Here,* $(kw, i) \notin \{(kw_0^*, i^*), (kw_1^*, i^*)\}$ *or* $(kw, i) \in \{(kw_0^*, i^*), (kw_1^*, i^*)\} \wedge t > t^*$. $\mathcal{O}_T$ *takes* $kw' \in \mathcal{KS}$, $t' \in \mathcal{T}$, *and* $i \in [1,n]$ *as input, and returns the result of* $\mathsf{FS\text{-}PAEKS.Trapdoor}(\mathsf{pk_R}, \mathsf{pk_{S[\mathit{i}]}}, \mathsf{sk_R}, kw', t')$. *Here* $(kw', i) \notin \{(kw_0^*, i^*), (kw_1^*, i^*)\}$. *We say that an FS-PAEKS scheme* $\mathsf{FS\text{-}PAEKS}$ *is IND-FS-IKGA secure if the advantage* $\mathsf{Adv}^{\mathsf{IND\text{-}FS\text{-}IKGA}}_{\mathsf{FS\text{-}PAEKS},\mathcal{A}}(\lambda, n) := |\Pr[\mathsf{Exp}^{\mathsf{IND\text{-}FS\text{-}IKGA}}_{\mathsf{FS\text{-}PAEKS},\mathcal{A}}(\lambda, n) = 1] - 1/2|$ *is negligible in the security parameter* λ.

4 Our Generic Construction of FS-PAEKS

Trivial and Insecure Construction. One trivial construction of FS-PAEKS is to employ a double encryption method. That is, a PAEKS ciphertext is encrypted by a public key encryption scheme supporting time-related functionality, e.g., past time-specific encryption (PTSE) [32,33] which is a special case of time-specific encryption [47]. In PTSE, the encryption and key extraction algorithms take a time t and t' as input, respectively, and the decryption key works when $t < t'$. Thus, a PAEKS ciphertext of a keyword kw is encrypted by PTSE with a time period t, and a trapdoor is a PAEKS trapdoor of a keyword kw' and a PTSE decryption key associated with time period t'. If $t < t'$, then a PTSE ciphertext can be decrypted by the decryption key, and then the test algorithm of the underlying PAEKS scheme determines whether $kw = kw'$ or not using a PAEKS trapdoor. This construction provides correctness and appears to be secure because no information about the keyword is revealed from ciphertexts (owing to the IND-CPA security of PTSE) and trapdoors (owing to the IND-IKGA security of PAEKS). However, this construction does not provide the IND-FS-CKA security because the keyword-related and time-related parts of a trapdoor are generated separately. For example, an adversary obtains a trapdoor for the challenge keyword kw_0^* and a time period $t' < t^*$, and obtains a trapdoor for any keyword $kw \notin \{kw_0^*, kw_1^*\}$ and a time period t^*. Then, the adversary can generate a trapdoor for kw_0^* at t^* which works to distinguish whether the challenge ciphertext is an encryption of kw_0^* or kw_1^*. This insecure construction suggests that we connect the keyword-related and time-related parts in an inseparable manner, and this is the reason behind of our attack works against the Jiang et al. FS-PAEKS scheme.

High-Level Description. A naive way to connect the keyword-related and time-related parts in an inseparable manner is to consider $kw||t$ for encryption and $kw'||t'$ for trapdoor as keywords. However, this construction only provides the equality matching as in PAEKS, i.e., it checks whether $kw||t = kw'||t'$ or not, and does not check the inequality condition $t < t'$. Thus, we employ 0/1 encodings to translate the inequality condition $t < t'$ to an equality condition. Essentially, a ciphertext of FS-PAEKS for a keyword kw and a time period t is a set of PAEKS ciphertexts for the keyword $kw||s_{t,i}^0$ for all $s_{t,i}^0 \in S_t^0$. Similarly, a trapdoor of FS-PAEKS for a keyword kw' and a time period t' is a set of PAEKS trapdoors for the keyword $kw'||s_{t',j}^1$ for all $s_{t',j}^1 \in S_{t'}^1$. $t < t'$ holds if and only if there exists i and j such that $s_{t,i}^0 = s_{t',j}^1$ since $S_t^0 \cap S_{t'}^1 \neq \emptyset$. For such i and j, $kw||s_{t,i}^0 = kw'||s_{t',j}^1$ holds if $kw = kw'$. Thus, by using the test algorithm of the underlying PAEKS scheme, we can check both $t < t'$ and $kw = kw'$ simultaneously. Thus, obviously correctness holds. For consistency, let i and j be selected by the adversary $\mathcal{A}$ in $\mathsf{Exp}_{\mathsf{FS\text{-}PAEKS},\mathcal{A}}^{\mathsf{consist}}$. When $(kw, i) \neq (kw', j)$, our construction provides consistency since the underlying PAEKS scheme is consistent. When $(kw, i) = (kw', j) \wedge t > t'$, since $S_t^0 \cap S_{t'}^1 = \emptyset$, this case is reduced to the case $kw||s_{t,i}^0 \neq kw'||s_{t',j}^1 \wedge i = j$ but the test algorithm outputs 1. Since this contradicts the consistency of the underlying PAEKS scheme, our construction provides consistency. Moreover, intuitively, no information about the keyword is revealed from ciphertexts and trapdoors due to the IND-CKA security and IND-IKGA security of the underlying PAEKS scheme. The size of $\mathsf{FS\text{-}ct_{PAEKS}}$ (resp. $\mathsf{td_{S,}}_{kw',t'}$) is ℓ_t^0-times (resp. $\ell_{t'}^1$-times) greater than that of $\mathsf{ct_{PAEKS}}$ (resp. $\mathsf{td_{S,}}_{kw'}$). Since ℓ_t^0 and $\ell_{t'}^1$ are at most the bit length of time period, our construction is scalable. We remark that information of time period could be leaked unless information of keyword is not leaked. Thus, the FS-PAEKS.Test algorithm needs to run the PAEKS.Test algorithm only once by finding i and j such that $s_{t,i}^0 = s_{t',j}^1$. This technique is also employed in the FS-PEKS scheme proposed by Zeng et al. [59].

As a remaining issue, we must consider the following trapdoor/ciphertext re-use cases. For example, $S_7^1 = \{01, 011, 0111\}$ contains $S_6^1 = \{01, 011\}$. That is, $\mathcal{A}$ can obtain a trapdoor at $t' = 6$ when $\mathcal{A}$ obtains a trapdoor at $t' = 7$ because a trapdoor at $t' = 7$ contains a trapdoor at $t' = 6$. However, this trapdoor derivation for previous time period does not affect the IND-FS-CKA security because $\mathcal{A}$ is allowed to obtain trapdoors for a challenge keyword and sender $(kw', i) \in \{(kw_0^*, i^*), (kw_1^*, i^*)\}$ only when the trapdoors are associated with a previous time period $t' < t^*$. That is, if other trapdoor is derived from the trapdoors for a challenge keyword and sender, it does not work for distinguishing which keyword is selected for generating the challenge ciphertext. Towards this direct trapdoor derivation case, we need to guarantee that any combination of trapdoors obtained via the trapdoor oracle does not affect the IND-FS-CKA security. This can be shown by the fact that $t > t'$ if and only if $S_t^0 \cap S_{t'}^1 = \emptyset$. Similarly, $\mathcal{A}$ may obtain ciphertexts associated to a future time period. For example, $S_8^0 = \{11, 101, 1001\}$ contains $S_9^0 = \{11, 101\}$. That is, $\mathcal{A}$ can obtain a ciphertext at $t = 9$ when $\mathcal{A}$ obtains a ciphertext at $t = 8$ because a ciphertext at $t = 9$ contains a ciphertext at $t = 8$. However, this situation also does not affect the IND-FS-IKGA security because $\mathcal{A}$ is allowed to obtain ciphertexts for the challenge keyword and sender $(kw, i) \in \{(kw_0^*, i^*), (kw_1^*, i^*)\}$ only when the ciphertexts are associated with a future time period $t > t^*$. That is, if other ciphertext is derived from the ciphertexts for a challenge keyword and sender, it does not work for distinguishing which keyword is selected for generating the challenge trapdoor. Towards this direct ciphertext derivation case, we need to guarantee that any combination of ciphertexts obtained via the encryption oracle does not affect the IND-FS-IKGA security. This can be shown by the fact that $t > t'$ if and only if $S_t^0 \cap S_{t'}^1 = \emptyset$.[4]

We construct FS-PAEKS = (FS-PAEKS.Setup, FS-PAEKS.$\mathsf{KG_R}$, FS-PAEKS.$\mathsf{KG_S}$, FS-PAEKS.Enc, FS-PAEKS.Trapdoor, FS-PAEKS.Test) from PAEKS = (PAEKS.Setup, PAEKS.$\mathsf{KG_R}$, PAEKS.$\mathsf{KG_S}$, PAEKS.Enc, PAEKS.Trapdoor, PAEKS.Test) as follows. We assume that the underlying PAEKS scheme supports the

[4] Although the trapdoor/ciphertext derivation does not affect IND-FS-CKA/IND-FS-IKGA security, it violates unforgeability of the time period where a trapdoor (resp. ciphertext) associated with a time period is converted to a trapdoor (resp. ciphertext) associated to a previous (resp. future) time period. Because such unforgeability is not required as a security of FS-PAEKS, we do not consider the time delegatability anymore. We remark that, in the group signatures with time-bound keys context, such unforgeability is considered [22,52]. It might be interesting to consider such unforgeability in the FS-P(A)EKS context.

keyword space $\{0,1\}^{2\ell}$ where ℓ is a polynomial of λ. Then, our construction supports $\mathcal{KS} = \mathcal{T} = \{0,1\}^{\ell}$ because we consider $kw||s^0_{t,i}$ or $kw'||s^1_{t',j}$ as keyword.

Generic Construction of FS-PAEKS

$\mathsf{FS\text{-}PAEKS.Setup}(1^\lambda)$: Run $\mathsf{pp} \leftarrow \mathsf{PAEKS.Setup}(1^\lambda)$ and output pp that contains $\mathcal{KS} = \{0,1\}^{\ell}$ and $\mathcal{T} = \{0,1\}^{\ell}$ where ℓ is a polynomial of λ.

$\mathsf{FS\text{-}PAEKS.KG_R}(\mathsf{pp})$: Run $(\mathsf{pk_R}, \mathsf{sk_R}) \leftarrow \mathsf{PAEKS.KG_R}(\mathsf{pp})$ and output $(\mathsf{pk_R}, \mathsf{sk_R})$.

$\mathsf{FS\text{-}PAEKS.KG_S}(\mathsf{pp})$:] Run $(\mathsf{pk_S}, \mathsf{sk_S}) \leftarrow \mathsf{PAEKS.KG_S}(\mathsf{pp})$ and output $(\mathsf{pk_S}, \mathsf{sk_S})$.

$\mathsf{FS\text{-}PAEKS.Enc}(\mathsf{pk_R}, \mathsf{pk_S}, \mathsf{sk_S}, kw, t)$: Define $S^0_t = \{s^0_{t,1}, s^0_{t,2}, \dots, s^0_{t,\ell^0_t}\}$. For all $i \in [1, \ell^0_t]$, run $\mathsf{ct_{PAEKS}}{}_i \leftarrow \mathsf{PAEKS.Enc}(\mathsf{pk_R}, \mathsf{pk_S}, \mathsf{sk_S}, kw||s^0_{t,i})$. Output $\mathsf{FS\text{-}ct_{PAEKS}} = (t, \{\mathsf{ct_{PAEKS}}{}_i\}_{i \in [1,\ell^0_t]})$.

$\mathsf{FS\text{-}PAEKS.Trapdoor}(\mathsf{pk_R}, \mathsf{pk_S}, \mathsf{sk_R}, kw', t')$: Define $S^1_{t'} = \{s^1_{t',1}, s^1_{t',2}, \dots, s^1_{t',\ell^1_{t'}}\}$. For all $j \in [1, \ell^1_{t'}]$, run $\mathsf{td}_{\mathsf{S},kw'||s^1_{t',j}} \leftarrow \mathsf{PAEKS.Trapdoor}(\mathsf{pk_R}, \mathsf{pk_S}, \mathsf{sk_R}, kw'||s^1_{t',j})$. Output $\mathsf{td}_{\mathsf{S},kw',t'} = (t', \{\mathsf{td}_{\mathsf{S},kw'||s^1_{t',j}}\}_{j \in [1,\ell^1_{t'}]})$.

$\mathsf{FS\text{-}PAEKS.Test}(\mathsf{FS\text{-}ct_{PAEKS}}, \mathsf{td}_{\mathsf{S},kw',t'})$: Parse $\mathsf{FS\text{-}ct_{PAEKS}} = (t, \{\mathsf{ct_{PAEKS}}{}_i\}_{i \in [1,\ell^0_t]})$ and $\mathsf{td}_{\mathsf{S},kw,t'} = (t', \{\mathsf{td}_{\mathsf{S},kw'||s^1_{t',j}}\}_{j \in [1,\ell^1_{t'}]})$. If $t > t'$, then output 0. Otherwise, if $t < t'$, then find i and j such that $s^0_{t,i} = s^1_{t',j}$. If $1 = \mathsf{PAEKS.Test}(\mathsf{ct_{PAEKS}}{}_i, \mathsf{td}_{\mathsf{S},kw'||s^1_{t',j}})$, then output 1, and 0 otherwise.

As mentioned in the high-level description paragraph, our generic construction is correct if the underlying PAEKS scheme is correct, due to 0/1 encodings.

Generic Construction of FS-PEKS. Our technique can also be employed to construct FS-PEKS. The definition of FS-PEKS can be trivially derived from those of FS-PAEKS by eliminating sender key related parts. As in our generic construction of FS-PAEKS, a ciphertext at t is a set of PEKS ciphertexts generated by $kw||s^0_{t,i}$ for all $s^0_{t,i} \in S^0_t$ and a trapdoor at t' is a set of PEKS trapdoors generated by $kw'||s^1_{t',i}$ for all $s^1_{t',i} \in S^1_{t'}$. We remark that anyone can generate a ciphertext unlike to (FS-)PAEKS, and thus an encryptor may not follow to employ the 0 encoding and can encrypt any keyword. However, this situation does not affect the security (i.e., still no information about the keyword is revealed from ciphertexts due to the security of the underlying PEKS scheme).

5 Security Analysis

Theorem 1. *Our generic construction is consistent if the underlying PAEKS scheme is consistent.*

Proof. Let i and j be chosen by the adversary $\mathcal{A}$ in $\mathsf{Exp}^{\mathsf{consist}}_{\mathsf{FS\text{-}PAEKS},\mathcal{A}}$. If $(kw, i) \neq (kw', j)$, then obviously consistency holds due to the consistency of the underlying PAEKS scheme because the winning conditions of the both experiments are the same. Thus, we consider the case $(kw, i) =$

$(kw', j) \wedge t > t'$ as follows. Let $\mathcal{A}$ be the adversary of FS-PAEKS consistency and $\mathcal{C}$ be the challenger of PAEKS consistency. We construct an algorithm $\mathcal{B}$ that breaks the consistency of the PAEKS scheme as follows. First, $\mathcal{C}$ sends $(\mathsf{pp}, \mathsf{pk_R}, \mathsf{pk_{S[0]}}, \mathsf{pk_{S[1]}})$ to $\mathcal{B}$. $\mathcal{B}$ forwards $(\mathsf{pp}, \mathsf{pk_R}, \mathsf{pk_{S[0]}}, \mathsf{pk_{S[1]}})$ to $\mathcal{A}$. $\mathcal{A}$ declares (kw, kw', t, t', i, j) where $(kw, i) = (kw', j) \wedge t > t'$. $\mathcal{B}$ defines $S_t^0 = \{s_{t,1}^0, s_{t,2}^0, \ldots, s_{t,\ell_t^0}^0\}$ and $S_{t'}^1 = \{s_{t',1}^1, s_{t',2}^1, \ldots, s_{t',\ell_{t'}^1}^1\}$. Since $t > t'$, $S_t^0 \cap S_{t'}^1 = \emptyset$. Now, $\mathsf{FS\text{-}PAEKS.Test}(\mathsf{FS\text{-}ct_{PAEKS}}, \mathsf{td}_{\mathsf{S}[j],kw',t'}) = 1$ holds where $\mathsf{FS\text{-}ct_{PAEKS}} \leftarrow \mathsf{FS\text{-}PAEKS.Enc}(\mathsf{pk_R}, \mathsf{pk_{S[\mathit{i}]}}, \mathsf{sk_{S[\mathit{i}]}}, kw, t)$ and $\mathsf{td}_{\mathsf{S}[j],kw',t'} \leftarrow \mathsf{FS\text{-}PAEKS.Trapdoor}(\mathsf{pk_R}, \mathsf{pk_{S[\mathit{j}]}}, \mathsf{sk_R}, kw', t')$ since $\mathcal{A}$ breaks the consistency. Thus, there exist $i^* \in [1, \ell_t^0]$ and $j^* \in [1, \ell_{t'}^1]$ such that $1 = \mathsf{PAEKS.Test}(\mathsf{ct_{PAEKS}}_{i^*}, \mathsf{td}_{\mathsf{S}[j],kw'||s_{t',j^*}^1})$ and $kw||s_{t,i^*}^0 \neq kw'||s_{t',j^*}^1$ hold. $\mathcal{B}$ randomly guesses such i^* and j^* and sends $(kw||s_{t,i^*}^0, kw'||s_{t',j^*}^1, i, j)$ to $\mathcal{C}$. If the guess is correct (with probability of at least $1/(\ell_t^0 \ell_{t'}^1)$ which is non-negligible), $\mathcal{B}$ breaks the consistency of the underlying PAEKS scheme. This concludes the proof. □

Theorem 2. *Our generic construction is IND-FS-CKA secure if the underlying PAEKS scheme is IND-CKA secure.*

Proof. Let $\mathcal{A}$ be the adversary of IND-FS-CKA and $\mathcal{C}$ be the challenger of IND-CKA. We construct an algorithm $\mathcal{B}$ that breaks the IND-CKA security of the PAEKS scheme as follows. First, $\mathcal{C}$ sends $(\mathsf{pp}, \mathsf{pk_R}, \{\mathsf{pk_{S[\mathit{i}]}}\}_{i \in [1,n]})$ to $\mathcal{B}$. $\mathcal{B}$ forwards $(\mathsf{pp}, \mathsf{pk_R}, \{\mathsf{pk_{S[\mathit{i}]}}\}_{i \in [1,n]})$ to $\mathcal{A}$.

When $\mathcal{A}$ sends $kw \in \mathcal{KS}$, $t \in \mathcal{T}$, and $i \in [1, n]$ to $\mathcal{O}_C$, $\mathcal{B}$ defines $S_t^0 = \{s_{t,1}^0, s_{t,2}^0, \ldots, s_{t,\ell_t^0}^0\}$. Then, for all $k \in [1, \ell_t^0]$, $\mathcal{B}$ sends $kw||s_{t,k}^0$ and i to $\mathcal{C}$ and obtains $\mathsf{ct_{PAEKS}}_k$. $\mathcal{B}$ returns $\mathsf{FS\text{-}ct_{PAEKS}} = (t, \{\mathsf{ct_{PAEKS}}_i\}_{i \in [1,\ell_t^0]})$ to $\mathcal{A}$. Since there is no restriction, the simulation of $\mathcal{O}_C$ is perfect.

Similarly, when $\mathcal{A}$ sends $kw' \in \mathcal{KS}$, $t' \in \mathcal{T}$, and $i \in [1, n]$ to $\mathcal{O}_T$, $\mathcal{B}$ defines $S_{t'}^1 = \{s_{t',1}^1, s_{t',2}^1, \ldots, s_{t',\ell_{t'}^1}^1\}$. Then, for all $j \in [1, \ell_{t'}^1]$, $\mathcal{B}$ sends $kw'||s_{t',j}^1$ and i to $\mathcal{C}$ and obtains $\mathsf{td}_{\mathsf{S},kw'||s_{t',j}^1}$. $\mathcal{B}$ returns $\mathsf{td}_{\mathsf{S},kw',t'} = (t', \{\mathsf{td}_{\mathsf{S},kw'||s_{t',j}^1}\}_{j \in [1,\ell_{t'}^1]})$ to $\mathcal{A}$. Here, we need to guarantee that $\mathcal{B}$'s queries do not violate the condition of the $\mathcal{O}_T$ oracle in $\mathsf{Exp}_{\mathsf{PAEKS},\mathcal{A}}^{\mathsf{IND\text{-}CKA}}(\lambda, n)$. In the case of $(kw', i) \notin \{(kw_0^*, i^*), (kw_1^*, i^*)\}$, the simulation is perfect because it does not violate the condition of the $\mathcal{O}_T$ oracle in $\mathsf{Exp}_{\mathsf{PAEKS},\mathcal{A}}^{\mathsf{IND\text{-}CKA}}(\lambda, n)$. In the case of $(kw', i) \in \{(kw_0^*, i^*), (kw_1^*, i^*)\} \wedge t' < t^*$, $S_{t^*}^0 \cap S_{t'}^1 = \emptyset$. Thus, for all $i \in [1, \ell_{t^*}^0]$ and $j \in [1, \ell_{t'}^1]$, $kw'||s_{t',j}^1 \notin \{kw_0^*||s_{t^*,i}^0, kw_1^*||s_{t^*,i}^0\}$ holds. Thus, this case also does not violate the condition of the $\mathcal{O}_T$ oracle in $\mathsf{Exp}_{\mathsf{PAEKS},\mathcal{A}}^{\mathsf{IND\text{-}CKA}}(\lambda, n)$. To sum up, the simulation of $\mathcal{O}_T$ is perfect.

In the challenge phase, $\mathcal{A}$ declares $(kw_0^*, kw_1^*, i^*, t^*)$. $\mathcal{B}$ defines $S_{t^*}^0 = \{s_{t^*,1}^0, s_{t^*,2}^0, \ldots, s_{t,\ell_t^0}^0\}$. We define sequential of games $\mathsf{Game}_0, \ldots, \mathsf{Game}_{\ell_{t^*}^0}$ as follows. In Game_0, the challenge ciphertext is generated by $\mathsf{PAEKS.Enc}(\mathsf{pk_R}, \mathsf{pk_{S[\mathit{i}^*]}}, \mathsf{sk_{S[\mathit{i}^*]}}, kw_0^*||s_{t^*,i}^0)$ for all $i = 1, \ldots, \ell_{t^*}^0$. In $\mathsf{Game}_{\ell_{t^*}^0}$, the challenge ciphertext is generated by $\mathsf{PAEKS.Enc}(\mathsf{pk_R}, \mathsf{pk_{S[\mathit{i}^*]}}, \mathsf{sk_{S[\mathit{i}^*]}}, kw_1^*||s_{t^*,i}^0)$ for all $i = 1, \ldots, \ell_{t^*}^0$. In Game_i where $i \in [1, \ell_{t^*}^0 - 1]$, the j-th challenge ciphertext is generated by $\mathsf{PAEKS.Enc}(\mathsf{pk_R}, \mathsf{pk_{S[\mathit{i}^*]}}, \mathsf{sk_{S[\mathit{i}^*]}}, kw_0^*||s_{t^*,j}^0)$ for all $j = i + 1, \ldots,$

$\ell^0_{t^*}$ and the k-th challenge ciphertext is generated by $\mathsf{PAEKS.Enc}(\mathsf{pk_R}, \mathsf{pk_{S[i^*]}}, \mathsf{sk_{S[i^*]}}, kw_1^*||s^0_{t^*,k})$ for all $k = 1, \ldots, i$. Thus, the difference of the success probability between two neighbor games Game_i and Game_{i+1} are bound by $\mathsf{Adv}^{\mathsf{IND\text{-}CKA}}_{\mathsf{PAEKS},\mathcal{A}}(\lambda, n)$. That is, the ciphertext generated by (kw_0^*, i^*, t^*) and the ciphertext generated by (kw_1^*, i^*, t^*) are indistinguishable with the advantage $\ell^0_{t^*} \cdot \mathsf{Adv}^{\mathsf{IND\text{-}CKA}}_{\mathsf{PAEKS},\mathcal{A}}(\lambda, n)$. This concludes the proof. □

Theorem 3. *Our generic construction is IND-FS-IKGA secure if the underlying PAEKS scheme is IND-IKGA secure.*

The proof of Theorem 3 is very similar to that of Theorem 2. The main difference is: the challenge trapdoor is generated by the $\mathsf{PAEKS.Trapdoor}$ algorithm, and the trapdoor generated by (kw_0^*, i^*, t^*) and the trapdoor generated by (kw_1^*, i^*, t^*) are indistinguishable with the advantage $\ell^1_{t^*} \cdot \mathsf{Adv}^{\mathsf{IND\text{-}IKGA}}_{\mathsf{PAEKS},\mathcal{A}}(\lambda, n)$. Thus, we omit the proof.

Remark. Due to our security proofs above, our construction inherits the security of the underlying PAEKS scheme because the security is reduced to that of the underlying PAEKS. For example, several PAEKS schemes do not consider the case that a trapdoor associated with a sender does not work against ciphertexts generated by the secret key of another sender, even if the same keyword is associated. They just consider keywords, i.e., if $kw \neq kw'$ then the test algorithm outputs 0. Even this weaker notion is employed, our generic construction provides the same security level that the underlying PAEKS schemes provide. Similarly, if the underlying PAEKS scheme provides MCI/MTI security, then the FS-PAEKS scheme obtained via our generic construction also provides MCI/MTI security. In this sense, our generic construction can be instantiated by any previous PAEKS scheme.

6 Vulnerability of the Jiang Et Al. FS-PAEKS Scheme

In this section, we show that the Jiang et al. FS-PAEKS scheme [30] does not provide forward security. As mentioned in the introduction section, the main problem is their pairing selection where a symmetric pairing is employed but the DDH problem is assumed to be held (Theorem 4.2 in [30]). Let $e : \mathbb{G} \times \mathbb{G} \to \mathbb{G}_T$ be a pairing where $\mathbb{G}$ and $\mathbb{G}_T$ have the prime order p, and let $g \in \mathbb{G}$ be a generator. For a DDH tuple (g, g^a, g^b, g^c), one can check whether $c = ab$ or not by checking $e(g^a, g^b) = e(g^c, g)$ holds or not. Thus, e can be seen as a DDH solver.

Although the Jiang et al. FS-PAEKS scheme provides conjunctive keyword search, for the sake of simplicity, we consider the single keyword case as follows (but our attack works for conjunctive keyword search). In their scheme, $\mathsf{pk_R} = g^\alpha$, $\mathsf{sk_R} = \alpha$, $\mathsf{pk_S} = g^\beta$, and $\mathsf{sk_S} = \beta$ where $\alpha, \beta \in \mathbb{Z}_p$. Briefly, a ciphertext contains $X = g^{r_1}$ and $\mathsf{CT} = h^{r_1} f^{r_2}$ where $r_1, r_2 \in \mathbb{Z}_p$. Here, h and f are related to the keyword kw to be encrypted and are defined as $h = H(kw, \mathsf{pk_R}^{\mathsf{sk_S}})$ and $f = H'(kw, \mathsf{pk_R}^{\mathsf{sk_S}})$ for some hash functions H and H'. That is, a Diffie-Hellman key $\mathsf{pk_R}^{\mathsf{sk_S}} = \mathsf{pk_S}^{\mathsf{sk_R}} = g^{\alpha\beta}$ is regarded as a key for deriving h and

f. Moreover, the ciphertext contains $(R_0, \ldots, R_\ell)$ where $R_i = \mathsf{pk_R}^{a_i}$ and a_i is a coefficient of a Lagrange polynomial for all $i \in [0, \ell]$ (here ℓ is the bit-length of a time period t) which is defined by points $(H''(s^0_{t,k}, \mathsf{pk_R}^{\mathsf{sk_S}}), r_2)$ for some hash function H'' and $s^0_{t,k} \in S^0_t$. That is, $\prod_{0 \le i \le \ell} R_i^{\pi^i_{(k)}} = \mathsf{pk_R}^{r_2}$ holds where $\pi_{(k)} := H''(s^0_{t,k}, \mathsf{pk_R}^{\mathsf{sk_S}})$ for any $s^0_{t,k} \in S^0_t$. A trapdoor contains $\pi_1 = g^s$, $\pi_2 = h'^s$, and $\pi_3 = f'^{s/\alpha}$. Here, h' and f' are related to the keyword kw' to be searched and are defined as $h' = H(kw', \mathsf{pk_S}^{\mathsf{sk_R}})$ and $f' = H'(kw', \mathsf{pk_S}^{\mathsf{sk_R}})$. If $kw = kw'$, then $h = h'$ and $f = f'$. Let a ciphertext be generated at t and a trapdoor be generated at t', and assume $t < t'$. Since $S^0_t \cap S^1_{t'} \neq \emptyset$, there exist i and j such that $s^0_{t,i} = s^1_{t',j}$. Because the Lagrange polynomial is defined by points $(H''(s^0_{t,k}, \mathsf{pk_R}^{\mathsf{sk_S}}), r_2)$, $\mu := \prod_{0 \le i \le \ell} R_i^{\pi^i_{(j)}} = \mathsf{pk_R}^{r_2}$ holds where $\pi_{(j)} = H''(s^1_{t',j}, \mathsf{pk_R}^{\mathsf{sk_S}})$ since $(\pi_{(j)}, r_2)$ is a point on the polynomial. The trapdoor contains $\pi_{(j)}$.

Our attack is described as follows. We distinguish whether the challenge trapdoor generated at t^* is for kw^*_0 or kw^*_1. One observation here is that the value CT is related to a keyword, and is independent to a time period, and the values $(R_0, \ldots, R_\ell)$ are related to a time period, and are independent to a keyword. Thus, there is room for combining CT for the challenge keyword and $(R_0, \ldots, R_\ell)$ for the challenge time period, and our attack below instantiates this observation.

1. An adversary $\mathcal{A}$ issues an encryption query kw^*_0 and $t^* < t$ where kw^*_0 is a challenge keyword. Since a newly generated ciphertext is not allowed to be searched by previously generated trapdoors, this query is not prohibited in the security model. The ciphertext contains $X = g^{r_1}$, $\mathsf{CT} = h^{*r_1}_0 f^{*r_2}_0$, and $(R_0, \ldots, R_\ell)$ where $h^*_0 = H(kw^*_0, \mathsf{pk_R}^{\mathsf{sk_S}})$ and $f^*_0 = H'(kw^*_0, \mathsf{pk_R}^{\mathsf{sk_S}})$.
2. $\mathcal{A}$ issues a trapdoor query $kw' \notin \{kw^*_0, kw^*_1\}$ and t' where $t < t'$. Since $kw' \notin \{kw^*_0, kw^*_1\}$, this query is also not prohibited in the security model. Of course, the test algorithm with the ciphertext and the trapdoor outputs 0. However, the trapdoor contains π such that $\mu := \prod_{0 \le i \le \ell} R_i^{\pi^i} = \mathsf{pk_R}^{r_2}$ holds since $t < t'$.

Through the procedure, $\mathcal{A}$ can obtain X, CT, and μ which are used later.

When $\mathcal{A}$ declares kw^*_0 and kw^*_1, the challenger generates the challenge trapdoor at t^* for kw^*_b where $b \in \{0, 1\}$, and it contains $\pi^*_1 = g^s$, $\pi^*_2 = h^{*s}_b$, and $\pi^*_3 = f^{*s/\alpha}_b$ where $h^*_b = H(kw^*_b, \mathsf{pk_R}^{\mathsf{sk_S}})$ and $f^*_b = H'(kw^*_b, \mathsf{pk_R}^{\mathsf{sk_S}})$. Now

$$\begin{aligned}
e(\pi^*_1, \mathsf{CT}) &= e(g^s, h^{*r_1}_0 f^{*r_2}_0) \\
&= e(g^s, h^{*r_1}_0) e(g^s, f^{*r_2}_0) \\
&= e(g^{r_1}, h^{*s}_0) e(g^{r_2}, f^{*s}_0) \\
&= e(X, h^{*s}_0) e(g^{\alpha r_2}, f^{*s/\alpha}_0) \\
&= e(X, h^{*s}_0) e(\mathsf{pk_R}^{r_2}, f^{*s/\alpha}_0) \\
&= e(X, h^{*s}_0) e(\mu, f^{*s/\alpha}_0)
\end{aligned}$$

holds. Thus, if $b = 0$, then $e(\pi_1^*, \mathsf{CT}) = e(X, \pi_2^*)e(\mu, \pi_3^*)$ holds, and $b = 1$, otherwise. So $\mathcal{A}$ can distinguish b correctly. We remark that the equation $e(\pi_1, \mathsf{CT}) = e(X, \pi_2)e(\mu, \pi_3)$ is employed in their test algorithm. Thus, it seems not trivial to fix the vulnerability even if DDH-hard asymmetric pairings, such as [4,5], are employed.

7 Conclusion

In this paper, we proposed a generic construction of FS-PAEKS from PAEKS and 0/1 encodings. Our generic construction is quite simple, and it can be used to construct FS-PEKS. It would be interesting to investigate a generic construction of FS-P(A)EKS without $O(\log t)$-size ciphertext/trapdoor blowup. Considering frequency analysis attacks [18], which has recently been considered in the PAEKS context, is also an interesting future work.

Similar to forward security, leakage-abuse attacks (e.g., [6,13,27]) have been widely researched in the SSE context, and have been overlooked in the PEKS context, to the best of our knowledge. It would be interesting to investigate the attack in the P(A)EKS context.

Acknowledgment. The author would like to thank anonymous reviewers of ACNS 2024 for their invaluable comments and suggestions. This work was supported by JSPS KAKENHI Grant Number JP21K11897. The main part of study was done when the author was with the National Institute of Information and Communications Technology (NICT), Japan.

References

1. Abdalla, M., et al.: Searchable encryption revisited: consistency properties, relation to anonymous IBE, and extensions. J. Cryptol. **21**(3), 350–391 (2008)
2. Agrawal, S., Boneh, D., Boyen, X.: Efficient lattice (H)IBE in the standard model. In: EUROCRYPT, pp. 553–572 (2010)
3. Agrawal, S., Boneh, D., Boyen, X.: Lattice basis delegation in fixed dimension and shorter-ciphertext hierarchical IBE. In: CRYPTO, pp. 98–115 (2010)
4. P.S.L.M., Barreto, Lynn, B., Scott, M.: Constructing elliptic curves with prescribed embedding degrees. In: SCN, pp. 257–267 (2002). https://doi.org/10.1007/3-540-36413-7_19
5. Barreto, P.S.L.M., Naehrig, M.: Pairing-friendly elliptic curves of prime order. In: Selected Areas in Cryptography, pp. 319–331 (2005). https://doi.org/10.1007/11693383_2
6. Blackstone, L., Kamara, S., Moataz, T.: Revisiting leakage abuse attacks. The Internet Society, in NDSS (2020)
7. Blazy, O., Kiltz, E., Pan, J.: (hierarchical) identity-based encryption from affine message authentication. In: CRYPTO, pp. 408–425 (2014)
8. Boneh, D., Di Crescenzo, G., Ostrovsky, R., Persiano, G.: Public key encryption with keyword search. In: EUROCRYPT, pp. 506–522 (2004)
9. Boneh, D., Franklin, M.K.: Identity-based encryption from the weil pairing. In: CRYPTO, pp. 213–229 (2001)

10. Boyen, X., Li, Q.: Towards tightly secure lattice short signature and id-based encryption. In: ASIACRYPT, pp. 404–434 (2016)
11. Calderini, M., Longo, R., Sala, M., Villa, I.: Searchable encryption with randomized ciphertext and randomized keyword search. IACR Cryptol. ePrint Arch., 945 (2022)
12. Canetti, R., Halevi, S., Katz, J.: A forward-secure public-key encryption scheme. J. Cryptol. **20**(3), 265–294 (2007)
13. Cash, D., Grubbs, P., Perry, J., Ristenpart, T.: Leakage-abuse attacks against searchable encryption. In: Ray, I., Li, N., Kruegel, C., editors, ACM CCS, pp. 668–679 (2015)
14. Cash, D., Hofheinz, D., Kiltz, E., Peikert, C.: Bonsai trees, or how to delegate a lattice basis. J. Cryptol. **25**(4), 601–639 (2012)
15. Chen, J., Lim, H.W., Ling, S., Wang, H., Wee, H.: Shorter IBE and signatures via asymmetric pairings. Pairing-Based Crypt. 122–140 (2012)
16. Cheng, L., Meng, F.: Security analysis of Pan et al'.s public-key authenticated encryption with keyword search achieving both multi-ciphertext and multi-trapdoor indistinguishability. J. Syst. Archit. **119**, 102248 (2021)
17. Cheng, L., Meng, F.: Public key authenticated encryption with keyword search from LWE. In: ESORICS, pp. 303–324 (2022)
18. Cheng, L., Meng, F.: Public key authenticated searchable encryption against frequency analysis attacks. Inf. Sci. **640**, 119060 (2023)
19. Cheng, L., Qin, J., Feng, F., Meng, F.: Security-enhanced public-key authenticated searchable encryption. Inf. Sci. **647**, 119454 (2023)
20. Chi, T., Qin, B., Zheng, D.: An efficient searchable public-key authenticated encryption for cloud-assisted medical internet of things. Wireless Commun. Mobile Comput. **2020**, 8816172:1–8816172:11 (2020)
21. Emura, K.: Generic construction of public-key authenticated encryption with keyword search revisited: stronger security and efficient construction. In: ACM APKC, pp. 39–49 (2022)
22. Emura, K., Hayashi, T., Ishida, A.: Group signatures with time-bound keys revisited: a new model, an efficient construction, and its implementation. IEEE Trans. Dependable Secure Comput. **17**(2), 292–305 (2020)
23. Gentry, C.: Practical identity-based encryption without random oracles. In: EUROCRYPT, pp. 445–464 (2006)
24. Gentry, C., Peikert, C., Vaikuntanathan, V.: Trapdoors for hard lattices and new cryptographic constructions. In: ACM STOC, pp. 197–206 (2008)
25. Gentry, C., Silverberg, A.: Hierarchical id-based cryptography. In: Zheng, Y., editor, ASIACRYPT, pp. 548–566 (2002)
26. Huang, Q., Li, H.: An efficient public-key searchable encryption scheme secure against inside keyword guessing attacks. Inf. Sci. **403**, 1–14 (2017)
27. Saiful Islam, M., Kuzu, M., Kantarcioglu, M.: Ramification, attack and mitigation. In: NDSS. The Internet Society, Access Pattern Disclosure on Searchable Encryption (2012)
28. Hafizul Islam, S.K., Mishra, N., Biswas, S., Keswani, B., Zeadally, S.: An efficient and forward-secure lattice-based searchable encryption scheme for the big-data era. Comput. Electr. Eng. **96**, 107533 (2021)
29. Jager, T., Kurek, R., Niehues, D.: Efficient adaptively-secure IB-KEMs and VRFs via near-collision resistance. In: Public-Key Cryptography, pp. 596–626 (2021)
30. Jiang, Z., Zhang, K., Wang, L., Ning, J.: Forward secure public-key authenticated encryption with conjunctive keyword search. Comput. J. **66**(9), 2265–2278 (2023)

31. Jutla, C.S., Roy, A.: Shorter quasi-adaptive NIZK proofs for linear subspaces. In: ASIACRYPT, pp. 1–20 (2013)
32. Kasamatsu, K., Matsuda, T., Emura, K., Attrapadung, N., Hanaoka, G., Imai, H.: Time-specific encryption from forward-secure encryption. In: SCN, pp. 184–204 (2012)
33. Kasamatsu, K., Matsuda, T., Emura, K., Attrapadung, N., Hanaoka, G., Imai, H.: Time-specific encryption from forward-secure encryption: generic and direct constructions. Int. J. Inf. Secur. **15**(5), 549–571 (2016)
34. Katsumata, S.: On the untapped potential of encoding predicates by arithmetic circuits and their applications. In: ASIACRYPT, pp. 95–125 (2017)
35. Katsumata, S., Yamada, S., Yamakawa, T.: Tighter security proofs for GPV-IBE in the quantum random oracle model. J. Cryptol. **34**(1), 5 (2021)
36. Kim, H., Hahn, C., Hur, J.: Forward secure public key encryption with keyword search for cloud-assisted IoT. In: IEEE CLOUD, pp. 549–556 (2020)
37. Kurosawa, K., Phong, L.T.: Anonymous and leakage resilient IBE and IPE. Des. Codes Crypt. **85**(2), 273–298 (2017)
38. Langrehr, R., Pan, J.: Hierarchical identity-based encryption with tight multi-challenge security. In: Public-Key Cryptography, pp.153–183 (2020)
39. Lee, K., Park, J.H., Lee, D.H.: Anonymous HIBE with short ciphertexts: full security in prime order groups. Designs, Codes Crypt. **74**(2), 395–425 (2015)
40. Lewko, A.B.: Tools for simulating features of composite order bilinear groups in the prime order setting. In: EUROCRYPT, pp. 318–335 (2012)
41. Lin, H.-Y., Tzeng, W.-G.: An efficient solution to the millionaires' problem based on homomorphic encryption. In: ACNS, pp. 456–466 (2005)
42. Liu, J.K., Chu, C.-K., Chow, S.S.M., Huang, X., Ho Au, M., Zhou, J.: Time-bound anonymous authentication for roaming networks. IEEE Trans. Inf. Forensics Secur. **10**(1), 178–189 (2015)
43. Liu, Z.-Y., Tseng, Y.-F., Tso, R., Mambo, M., Chen, y.-C.: Public-key authenticated encryption with keyword search: cryptanalysis, enhanced security, and quantum-resistant instantiation. In: IACR Cryptology ePrint Archive, p. 1008 (2021)
44. Liu, Z.-Y., Tseng, Y.-F., Tso, R., Mambo, M., Chen, Y.-C.: Public-key authenticated encryption with keyword search: cryptanalysis, enhanced security, and quantum-resistant instantiation. In: ACM ASIACCS, pp. 423–436 (2022)
45. Noroozi, M., Eslami, Z.: Public key authenticated encryption with keyword search: revisited. IET Inf. Secur. **13**(4), 336–342 (2019)
46. Pan, X., Li, F.: Public-key authenticated encryption with keyword search achieving both multi-ciphertext and multi-trapdoor indistinguishability. J. Syst. Architect. **115**, 102075 (2021)
47. Paterson, K.G., Quaglia, E.A.: Time-specific encryption. In: SCN, pp. 1–16 (2010)
48. Baodong Qin, Yu., Chen, Q.H., Liu, X., Zheng, D.: Public-key authenticated encryption with keyword search revisited: security model and constructions. Inf. Sci. **516**, 515–528 (2020)
49. Qin, B., Cui, H., Zheng, X., Zheng, D.: Improved security model for public-key authenticated encryption with keyword search. In: ProvSec, pp. 19–38 (2021)
50. Ramanna, S.C., Sarkar, P.: Anonymous constant-size ciphertext HIBE from asymmetric pairings. In: IMACC, pp. 344–363 (2013)
51. Ramanna, S.C., Sarkar, P.: Efficient (anonymous) compact HIBE from standard assumptions. In: ProvSec, pp. 243–258 (2014)
52. Sanders, O.: Improving revocation for group signature with redactable signature. In: Public-Key Cryptography, pp. 301–330 (2021)

53. Xiaodong Song, D., Wagner, D.A., Perrig, A.: Practical techniques for searches on encrypted data. In: IEEE Symposium on Security and Privacy, pp. 44–55 (2000)
54. Stefanov, E., Papamanthou, C., Shi, E.: Practical dynamic searchable encryption with small leakage. In: NDSS (2014)
55. Tang, Q.: Towards forward security properties for PEKS and IBE. In: ACISP, pp. 127–144 (2015)
56. Xu, S., Cao, Y., Chen, X., Yiu, S.-M., Zhao, Y.: Post-quantum public-key authenticated searchable encryption with forward security: general construction, implementation, and applications. In: IACR Cryptology ePrint Archive, p. 591 (2023)
57. Yamada, S.: Asymptotically compact adaptively secure lattice IBEs and verifiable random functions via generalized partitioning techniques. In: CRYPTO, pp. 161–193 (2017)
58. Yu, X., Xu, L., Huang, X., Xu, C.: An efficient lattice-based encrypted search scheme with forward security. In: Network and System Security, pp. 712–726 (2022)
59. Zeng, M., Qian, H., Chen, J., Zhang, K.: Forward secure public key encryption with keyword search for outsourced cloud storage. IEEE Trans. Cloud Comput. **10**(1), 426–438 (2022)
60. Zhang, X., Chunxiang, X., Wang, H., Zhang, Y., Wang, S.: FS-PEKS: lattice-based forward secure public-key encryption with keyword search for cloud-assisted industrial internet of things. IEEE Trans. Dependable Secure Comput. **18**(3), 1019–1032 (2021)

Encryption Mechanisms for Receipt-Free and Perfectly Private Verifiable Elections

Thi Van Thao Doan[1(✉)], Olivier Pereira[1,2], and Thomas Peters[1]

[1] Université catholique de Louvain ICTEAM - Crypto Group, B-1348, Louvain-la-Neuve, Belgium
{thi.doan,olivier.pereira,thomas.peters}@uclouvain.be
[2] Microsoft Research, Redmond, WA, USA

Abstract. We design new encryption mechanisms that enable the design of the first universally verifiable voting schemes, supporting both receipt-freeness and everlasting privacy without assuming the existence of an anonymous channel.

Our schemes support the two most traditional election tallying methods: One is additively homomorphic, supporting elections in which votes simply need to be added, but decryption is only efficient for a message space of polylogarithmic size. The other is randomizable, is compatible with traditional mixnet-based tallying methods, and supports efficient message encoding, which makes it compatible with virtually any election type.

Our approach builds on the recently proposed traceable receipt-free encryption (TREnc) primitive to support the design of a perfectly private audit trail. In particular, we propose two TREnc that are secure under SXDH and rely on a public coin CRS (or on the random oracle model). This improves on previous TREnc mechanisms that required a structured CRS and is of independent interest. A prototype implementation of our mechanisms is proposed, which shows that ballot preparation and verification can be executed in less than a second.

Keywords: Traceable receipt-free encryption · Everlasting privacy · Perfectly private audit trail · Pairing-based cryptography

1 Introduction

Verifiable elections enable internal players and external observers to verify the validity of individual votes and the final election outcome, even in situations where potentially all participants have malicious intent. Verifiability is typically obtained through the use of a public bulletin board [1,13,14,18,34].

While being central to support public verifiability at scale, this bulletin board raises central issues in secret ballot elections. In order to guarantee the secrecy of the vote, a bulletin board will typically have ballots and/or voter names hidden by some form of encryption. This is a good solution to guarantee the computational privacy of the votes [6], but it does not address two other central concerns:

C. Pöpper and L. Batina (Eds.): ACNS 2024, LNCS 14583, pp. 257–287, 2024.
https://doi.org/10.1007/978-3-031-54770-6_11

1. The bulletin board may support vote selling or voter coercion. For instance, a voter who keeps track of all the random coins he used to prepare a ballot may be able to demonstrate how he voted to a third party, who would be able to recompute the encrypted ballot using the coins and claimed vote intent and confirm its presence on the bulletin board.
2. The bulletin board may raise long-term privacy concerns: when privacy is computational, encrypted votes (or encrypted voter identities) will eventually become public, either through cryptanalytic advances, or through the advent of new hardware, including quantum computers. This may have a chilling effect on voters who may not feel that they can vote freely.

As discussed in a recent review by Haines et al. [24], the design of secure and efficient voting protocols that offer both receipt-freeness (RF) and a perfectly private audit trail (PPAT) is a long-standing open problem. In particular, the few existing proposals that support these properties are either designed for in-person voting [32], or rely on the existence of an anonymous ballot submission channel [22,30], which seems hardly realistic in a large-scale election context (see further discussions in the related works section below).

An alternative approach to obtain receipt-freeness relies on the help of a ballot-box manager, who is trusted for receipt-freeness, but not for verifiability or for privacy, following a general approach pioneered by Hirt and Sako [25]. This approach led to the recent development of a new Traceable Receipt-Free Encryption (TREnc) primitive by Devillez et al. [20], which enables receipt-free ballot submission following the Hirt and Sako paradigm. In a nutshell, using a TREnc, voters can encrypt their vote intent, which will provide them with a trace and a ciphertext that can be submitted to the ballot-box manager. The trace can be kept by the voter for verifiability purpose and is actually independent of the vote itself, supporting receipt-freeness. The ballot-box manager then re-randomizes the TREnc ciphertext and posts the result on a public bulletin board. The security of the TREnc guarantees that the resulting ciphertext is distributed just like a fresh encryption of a vote with an identical trace (this is the strong randomization property) and that, if the trace did not change, then it must be the same vote that is still encrypted (this is the traceability). The voter can then verify on the bulletin board that a ciphertext with the correct trace is published, but is unable to explain the vote that is encrypted there to any third party. Finally, a TREnc guarantees that, even when ballots are computed with adversarially chosen randomness, no adversary can turn a re-randomized ballot into a related ballot that would have a different trace and contain a related vote (this is implied by the TCCA security). The existing TREnc mechanisms however do not support a PPAT and, as a side constraint, require a structured common reference string (CRS), which may be an obstacle in any practical deployment.

1.1 Our Contributions

We propose two new encryption mechanisms that make it possible to obtain both receipt-freeness (RF) and a perfectly private audit trail (PPAT) in a natural way, following the general structure of a single-pass voting system [7] for instance.

Our first encryption mechanism is additively homomorphic and suitable for elections with a homomorphic tally, that is, where the vote for each candidate can be encrypted as a 0 or a 1 counter, proven correct in zero-knowledge proof (ZK), and where the tally for each candidate is obtained by verifiably decrypting the homomorphic sum of all the ciphertexts provided for that candidate – this is the mechanism used by default in systems like Helios [2], Belenios [15] or ElectionGuard [4]. However, this encryption mechanism only supports a message space of polylogarithmic size, just as the exponential ElGamal encryption mechanism used in the previously cited systems, which makes it unsuitable to encrypt complex choice expressions in a single ciphertext.

Our second encryption mechanism addresses this limitation by supporting the encryption of arbitrary group elements and supporting efficient bijective mappings between bit strings and group elements, at the cost of losing the additive homomorphism. Still, this encryption mechanism is randomizable and compatible with traditional mixnets like Verificatum [36] that operate on arrays of group elements. Such mixnets have been used in national elections of various countries, including Norway, Estonia, and Switzerland.

From a technical point of view, our new encryption mechanisms are secure under symmetric external Diffie-Hellman assumption (SXDH) and provide new TREnc mechanisms that rely on a public-coin CRS. This is an advance over previous proposals, that is of independent interest, since the previously known mechanisms relied on a structured CRS, which may be complicated to generate in practice and introduces new trust assumptions. Here, a simple way of producing the CRS in practice would be to sample the outputs of a hash function modeled as a random oracle, which is already of common use in practical voting systems when implementing the Fiat-Shamir transform on sigma protocols.

Finally, we evaluate the efficiency of our new mechanisms. Our additively homomorphic mechanism produces ciphertexts in the two source groups of our pairing-friendly setting: they lie in $\mathbb{G}^{50} \times \hat{\mathbb{G}}^{46}$. Our mixnet-compatible mechanism produces slightly smaller ciphertexts in $\mathbb{G}^{47} \times \hat{\mathbb{G}}^{45}$. The gains essentially come from the inclusion, in the first case, of ZK proofs that a bit is encrypted, which is not needed for a mixnet-based tallying process. We also implemented our two mechanisms, relying on the MIRACL library for the group operations, and observed that both encryption operations require less than 0.3 s, and that the verification of the validity of a ciphertext takes less than a second.

1.2 Our Techniques

Commitment-Consistent Encryption. Our starting point for obtaining a PPAT is the use of a commitment-consistent encryption (CCE) scheme [19]. The CCE encryption of a message m provides two components: a perfectly hiding commitment com that comes out of a commitment scheme $(\mathsf{com}, \mathsf{open}) \leftarrow \mathsf{Com}(m)$, and an encryption enc of m and open that is provided together with a proof π_{cc} ensuring that $\mathsf{VerC}(\mathsf{com}, m, \mathsf{open}) = 1$, where VerC is the verification algorithm associated to Com. The proof π_{cc} is provided in order to guarantee that the CCE ciphertext is valid and that the tally will be computable. It can be augmented with a proof π_{pub} that demonstrates that a valid opening of com (e.g., as a bit) is known.

When a CCE encryption scheme is used in a voting application, the value $D = (\mathsf{com}, \pi_{pub})$ is posted on a public bulletin board PB. If π_{pub} is perfect ZK, then this is perfectly hiding, as desired. Additionally, $CT = (\mathsf{enc}, \pi_{cc})$ is posted on a secret bulletin board SB, for use by the talliers. The election tally can then be computed using various techniques, as outlined in [19] for instance, preserving the PPAT. This approach however does not offer receipt-freeness, since the voter could use open as a receipt for his vote, for instance.

A TREnc on Top of CCE Encryption. In order to obtain the RF property, we then explore how to build a TREnc, whose ciphertexts contain a commitment-consistent encryption instead of an ElGamal encryption as in existing designs.

To satisfy all the TREnc properties that are needed need to achieve receipt-freeness in our voting scheme, all the components of $C = (D, CT)$ must be rerandomizable up to a trace which will allow voters to check the presence of their rerandomized commitments and proofs $D' = (\mathsf{com}', \pi'_{pub})$ on PB. Therefore, the traceability property must be supported by D and its randomization. For that purpose, we adapt the linearly homomorphic structure-preserving (LHSP) signature [28] techniques of [20] used during the computation of the encryption algorithm of their ad-hoc construction to our "commitment case". More precisely, the trace of a TREnc ciphertext C is the one-time LHSP verification key opk generated by the encryption algorithm. In a nutshell, the corresponding one-time LHSP secret key osk is used to sign a basis of a sub-vector space, where the vectors of this basis are derived from an internal CPA-encryption of the plaintext and its public key. The LHSP properties allow us to derive a signature on any rerandomization of this CPA part, and all its rerandomizations actually consist of the sub-vector space that is authenticated. Traceability comes from the fact that signing a CPA encryption of another plaintext requires authenticating a vector outside the linear spanned sub-space, which is unfeasible thanks to the unforgeability of the one-time LHSP signature scheme. Unfortunately, the unforgeability of the LHSP signatures cannot directly be used in our case to ensure that the rerandomized commitment com' still contains the same committed message. After all, there is just no meaning of which message is really contained in the perfectly hiding com' since it could be equally opened on *any* message. To restore this property and to contradict the security of the LHSP signatures when the committed message has been successfully modified, we use a dual-commitment compatible with $(\mathsf{Com}, \mathsf{VerC})$. To show traceability, we only have to turn the commitment public key into an extractable and perfectly binding mode at the start of the proof. We will thus have LHSP signatures and opk contained in D.

Finding the Right Tools. Finding most of the compatible building blocks is not straightforward, but only requires making careful choices and adapting techniques except for the TCCA property, and the simulation soundness in particular. Since we need rerandomizable proofs, we naturally focus on the SXDH-based

Groth-Sahai (GS) proof system that is also known to be malleable. Randomizing our TREnc ciphertexts C also requires adapting the statement under the GS proofs. Indeed, the witness underlying the commitment-consistent and validity proofs are subject to adaptation when com and Enc are rerandomized: the random coins are refreshed and the witness of the GS proofs may depend on these coins. In the perfect non-interactive witness indistinguishable (NIWI) setting to prove pairing-product equations, the common reference string (CRS) consists of random group elements of the two source groups and is thus public coin. However, NIWI proofs are not enough for our constructions as we need them to be zero-knowledge when we have to include an SXDH challenge in enc during the randomization in the challenge phase of the TCCA game, and for which the reduction is of course not given the random coin. There exist generic solutions to turn NIWI GS-proofs into ZK proofs but they are expensive. In spirit, we follow [29] which still partially relies on a generic OR-proof technique that makes it possible to prove another statement in the security proof than the one in the real execution of the scheme. The idea is that no adversary can use the second branch of the OR-proof for a TREnc ciphertext containing a different trace than the one of the challenge phase. In order to trigger the possibility of proving the second branch, we rely on the unforgeability of (yet another) one-time LHSP signature whose public key is generated in the key generation of the TREnc. Fortunately, this public key is a single uniformly distributed pair of group elements and is then public coin as well, while no one knows the corresponding signing key. The branch that is being proved is encoded as a vector of group elements with the following property: if the real statement is being proved, the vector only contains neutral elements (i.e., it is the null-vector, but we will use multiplicative notation); to simulate, we prove the second statement and the vector is non-trivial and lies in a one-dimensional subspace determined by the trace. Since, on the one hand, it is easy to compute a degenerated LHSP signature on the neutral vector from the public key, and, on the other hand, it is hard to compute an LHSP signature on a different one-dimensional subspace for another trace, simulation soundness holds for any proof with another trace than the one of the challenge. This vector as well as the (degenerated) LHSP signature are only given in a committed form with a GS-proof (with the same CRS) that the LHSP verification equation holds. Another difficulty in the TCCA proof is to switch the kind of encoded vector by simulating the randomization of one of the ciphertexts given in the challenge phase, but surprisingly this task can be handled only thanks to the perfect WI property of the GS-proof.

Following [20], we also need to commit-and-prove to the one-time LHSP signature generated during encryption (for the traceability) for technical reasons. Otherwise, even if it looks hard to embed subliminal information into the LHSP signatures related to com, we have no ground to prove the TCCA security. This additional layer of GS-proof solves the issue thanks to the perfect WI property. However, even when we should extract the witness of the proof of validity and consistency to figure out which branch the adversary tried to prove in a given ciphertext in a decryption query, this part of the proof related to the LHSP signature for traceability must remain in the perfect WI mode. that is because we have to avoid leaking the internal bit of the game (i.e., which ciphertext between C_0 and C_1 have been rerandomized in the challenge phase) in an information-theoretic sense to conclude. To circumvent this opposing requirement, we use another GS CRS for the traceable part that can remain in the perfect WI mode.

1.3 Related Work

Receipt-Free Voting. The study of receipt-free elections was initiated by Benaloh and Tuinstra [5], who presented the first verifiable secret-ballot election protocols in which voters cannot prove to others how they voted. In order to achieve receipt-freeness, they required a physical voting booth to establish completely untappable channels between the voting authority and the voter. A year later, Sako and Kilian [35] argued that a one-way untappable channel is sufficient for this purpose. Additionally, they explained how to implement a receipt-free and universally verifiable voting system using the first verifiable mixnet. Thereafter, there has been a flurry of activity in the design and analysis of receipt-free voting protocols relying on the use of an untappable channel proposed by different authors. A prominent approach, that we outlined above and follow here, was proposed by Hirt and Sako [25], then simplified by Blazy et al. [9], refined by Chaidos et al. [12] and formalized by Devillez et al. [20]. Of course, many other approaches have been proposed in parallel and are out of scope of this work [21, 26, 34].

Voting with a PPAT. A recent and detailed account of the efforts towards voting with perfectly private ballots is provided by Haines et al. [24]. They identify the approach of commitment-consistent encryption, which we are using here, as one of the two strongest proposals, the other one being based on ballots that are secret-shared between a set of trustees [16]. We did not adopt the secret sharing approach here as it is more demanding to the voters, requiring a computational effort that grows linearly with the number of trustees that receive vote shares, and only offers privacy benefits over CCE if we assume that the voters have direct communication channels with every trustee, which may be quite demanding.

Voting with RF and PPAT. There are very few proposals that offer both RF and a PPAT, and they rely on the existence of anonymous channels for ballot submission, an assumption that we are avoiding here and that is hardly practical at a large scale.

The first is based on blind signatures [22, 33], where voters obtain a blindly signed voting token from an authority, which is then used to submit a ballot through an anonymous communication channel. Verifiability is hard to obtain in such a setting: a malicious authority can for instance produce tokens on behalf of abstaining voters and cast ballots in their stead.

A second approach was proposed by Locher and Haenni [30] and addresses the problem of eligibility verifiability by having voters registering a public key and submitting their ballot together with a proof that they know the secret key matching one of these public keys, using a mechanism similar to list signatures [11]. Again, ballots are submitted using an anonymous communication channel.

Our work aims at developing solutions that offer a PPAT in the sense of Cuvelier et al. [19], together with receipt-freeness, following the definitional approach of Chaidos et al. [12].

1.4 Overview of Paper

We structure our paper as follows. Standard building blocks and the computational assumptions are introduced in Sect. 2. In Sect. 3, we present the intuition and the full description of our first construction to verifiably encrypt bits, followed by its theorem statements. The second construction is postponed to Appendix A due to space limit. Then, Sect. 4 shows the voting application implied by our combined primitive and describes an election based on homomorphic aggregation for the simple ballot case and an election with mixnet for the complex ballot case. To conclude, Sect. 5 makes some important remarks. The security analysis is deferred to Appendix B. This choice is compensated by the thorough overview of our techniques given above.

2 Background

We review some standard building blocks and introduce the corresponding notations.

2.1 Assumptions and Primitives

We will work in asymmetric bilinear groups and assume the existence of a bilinear-group generator $\mathcal{G}$ which takes the security parameter λ as input and outputs $\mathsf{pp} = (\mathbb{G}, \hat{\mathbb{G}}, \mathbb{G}_T, e, g, h, \hat{g}, p)$, where $\mathbb{G}, \hat{\mathbb{G}}, \mathbb{G}_T$ are groups of prime order $p > 2^{\mathsf{poly}(\lambda)}$, $g, h \xleftarrow{\$} \mathbb{G}$, $\hat{g} \xleftarrow{\$} \hat{\mathbb{G}}$ are random generators, and $e : \mathbb{G} \times \hat{\mathbb{G}}$ is a non-degenerate bilinear map. Our setting relies on the SXDH (symmetric external Diffie-Hellman) assumption, which states that the decisional Diffie-Hellman problem (DDH) [10] must be intractable in both $\mathbb{G}$ and $\hat{\mathbb{G}}$.

Assumption 1 (DDH). *Let λ be a security parameter and g be a generator of a group $\mathbb{G}$ of prime order $p > 2^{\mathsf{poly}(\lambda)}$. It is computationally hard to distinguish the tuple (g^a, g^b, g^{ab}) from the tuple (g^a, g^b, g^c) where $a, b, c \xleftarrow{\$} \mathbb{Z}_p$.*

Groth-Sahai Proofs. Groth-Shai (GS) proofs [23] offer an efficient approach to proving the satisfiability of quadratic equations in bilinear settings. On input pp, common reference strings (CRS) $\mathbf{u} \in \mathbb{G}^4$ and $\mathbf{v} \in \hat{\mathbb{G}}^4$ are generated to commit to groups elements of $\mathbb{G}$ and $\hat{\mathbb{G}}$. For instance, the commitments to $X \in \mathbb{G}$ and $\hat{Y} \in \hat{\mathbb{G}}$ are denoted by $\mathbf{C}_X$ and $\mathbf{C}_{\hat{Y}}$ respectively. In accordance with the GS standard notation, we also define the linear maps: $\iota_1 : \mathbb{G} \rightarrow \mathbb{G}^2$ with $\iota_1 : X \mapsto (1, X)$ and $\iota_2 : \hat{\mathbb{G}} \rightarrow \hat{\mathbb{G}}^2$ with $\iota_2 : \hat{Y} \mapsto (1, \hat{Y})$.

Linearly Homomorphic Structure-Preserving Signatures (LHSP Signature). LHSP signature was introduced by Libert et al. [28] to perform linear computations on encrypted data. Structure-preserving property allows signing messages that are vectors of group elements, whereas the linearly homomorphic feature makes it possible to derive a signature on any linear combination of already signed vectors. In our context, we rely on a one-time LHSP signature scheme of [28] in the SXDH setting as in [27], where each voter signs only one linear subspace using his secret signing key.

$\mathsf{Gen}(\mathsf{pp}, \lambda, n)$: given the public parameter pp and the dimension $n \in \mathbb{N}$ of the subspace to be signed, pick $\chi_i, \gamma_i \stackrel{\$}{\leftarrow} \mathbb{Z}_p$ and compute $f_i = g^{\chi_i} h^{\gamma_i}$, for $i = 1$ to n. The private key is $\mathsf{sk} = \{(\chi_i, \gamma_i)\}_{i=1}^n$ and the public key is $\mathsf{pk} = \{f_i\}_{i=1}^n \in \mathbb{G}^n$.

$\mathsf{Sign}(\mathsf{sk}, (M_1, \ldots, M_n))$: to sign a vector $(M_1, \ldots, M_n) \in \hat{\mathbb{G}}^n$, using sk, output $\sigma = (\hat{Z}, \hat{R}) = (\prod_{i=1}^n M_i^{\chi_i}, \prod_{i=1}^n M_i^{\gamma_i})$.

$\mathsf{Ver}(\mathsf{pk}, \sigma, (M_1, \ldots, M_n))$: given a signature $\sigma = (\hat{Z}, \hat{R}) \in \hat{\mathbb{G}}^2$ and a vector $(M_1, \ldots, M_n)$, return 1 if and only if $(M_1, \ldots, M_n) \neq (1_{\hat{\mathbb{G}}}, \ldots, 1_{\hat{\mathbb{G}}})$ and $(\hat{Z}, \hat{R})$ satisfies

$$e(g, \hat{Z}) \cdot e(h, \hat{R}) = \prod_{i=1}^{n} e(f_i, M_i). \tag{1}$$

In our case, the LHSP signature has three key advantages. Firstly, it allows ciphertexts to be re-randomized and the adaptation of their signatures, while guaranteeing the non-malleability of the plaintext. Secondly, it notably ensures that it is infeasible to publicly compute a signature on a vector outside the linear span of originally signed vectors, which is essential for our system security. Thirdly, the verification Eq. (1), which is a pairing product equation, still holds for $(M_1, \ldots, M_n) = (1_{\hat{\mathbb{G}}}, \ldots, 1_{\hat{\mathbb{G}}})$ with a degenerated signature $(\hat{Z}, \hat{R}) = (1, 1)$. This feature allows hiding whether we trivially satisfy the equation or if we have a valid signature thanks to the Groth-Sahai proof system. We use it to implement an OR-technique useful to simulation soundness.

2.2 Traceable Receipt-Free Encryption (TREnc)

TREnc [20] is a public key encryption scheme (Gen, Enc, Dec), augmented with a 5-tuple of algorithms: LGen, on input a security parameter λ and a public encryption key PK, outputs a link key lk; LEnc encrypts a message m using (PK, lk) and outputs a ciphertext c. Trace outputs the trace t of c. Rand randomizes c to output a randomized ciphertext c'. Ver checks if a ciphertext is valid and outputs 1 if true, and 0 otherwise.

Verifiability. A TREnc is *verifiable* if no PPT adversary can produce, with non-negligible probability, a ciphertext that satisfies Ver but is not in the range of Enc. In other words, Ver guarantees that a valid ciphertext is necessarily in the range of the honestly generated encryptions. More formally, for any efficient $\mathcal{A}$, $\Pr[c \notin \mathsf{Enc}(\mathsf{PK}, \cdot) \wedge \mathsf{Ver}(\mathsf{PK}, c) = 1 \mid (\mathsf{PK}, \mathsf{SK}) \leftarrow \mathsf{Gen}(1^\lambda), c \leftarrow\$ \mathcal{A}(\mathsf{PK}, \mathsf{SK})]$ is negligible. We denote the event of $\mathcal{A}$ winning this game as $\mathsf{Exp}^{\mathrm{ver}}_{\mathcal{A}}(\lambda) = 1$.

Strong Randomization. To achieve receipt-freeness, a ballot from a voter must be re-randomized before being placed on the PB. Strong randomization requires that the output of the Rand algorithm be indistinguishable from any encryption of the same message with the same link key. More precisely, A TREnc is *strongly randomizable* if for every $c \in \mathsf{LEnc}(\mathsf{PK}, \mathsf{lk}, m)$ with PK in the range of Gen and lk in the range of $\mathsf{LGen}(\mathsf{PK})$, the following computational indistinguishability relation holds: $\mathsf{Rand}(\mathsf{PK}, c) \approx_c \mathsf{LEnc}(\mathsf{PK}, \mathsf{lk}, m)$.

TCCA Security. Security against traceable chosen ciphertexts attacks, also called TCCA security, is a TREnc's central security requirement. An adversary $\mathcal{A}$, who has a public key and is allowed to access a decryption oracle, submits a pair of valid ciphertexts of its choice that have identical traces. One of the ciphertexts is randomized and returned to $\mathcal{A}$, who must decide which one it is. After receiving this challenge ciphertext, $\mathcal{A}$ can still query the decryption oracle, but only on ciphertexts that have a trace different from his challenge ciphertext. TREnc is said to be *TCCA secure* if no PPT adversary can decide which ciphertext was randomized. Achieving TCCA security implies a form of non-malleability of the trace of ciphertexts. This essentially guarantees the absence of a vote receipt and is formalized in the $\mathsf{Exp}^{\mathrm{tcca}}_{\mathcal{A}}(\lambda)$ game in Fig. 1.

Traceability. A TREnc is *traceable* if no efficient adversary $\mathcal{A}$ can produce another ciphertext that traces to the same trace and decrypts to a different message. The traceability property of the TREnc then guarantees that nobody (including the rerandomizing server and decryption-key holders) could have forged another valid ciphertext of another vote linked to the given ballot with non-negligible probability. This property is fundamental for the verifiability of an election and is defined in $\mathsf{Exp}^{\mathrm{trace}}_{\mathcal{A}}(\lambda)$ game of Fig. 1.

Link Traceability. TREnc allows the encryption of any message using a single link key and all resulting ciphertexts have the same trace. Thanks to this property, LEnc makes the TCCA game possible by encrypting different messages that trace to each other. This non-binding feature is essential for receipt-free voting.

Receipt-Freeness. To be receipt-free, TREnc relies on a semi-trusted entity called a ballot box manager. This entity checks the validity of the encrypted vote sent by the voter without requiring a secret key and then re-randomizes every valid ciphertext before posting it on the PB. Since the randomness contained in the published ballot is no longer under the control of the voter, he cannot prove how he voted. On the one hand, link traceability allows voters to vote for different messages with a single link key, preventing them from proving their vote. On the other hand, traceability ensures that no corrupted authority should be able to modify the encrypted vote while keeping the trace unchanged.

In a model where the voting client may be corrupted, strong randomization and TCCA security guarantees that the encryption hides the message. In contrast, the traceability property plays an important role when the voting client is honest, and the re-randomization server might be corrupted.

Definition 2.1 (TREnc correctness). *A TREnc scheme is required to satisfy the following correctness requirements.*

Encryption compatibility. *For every* PK *in the range of* Gen *and message* m, *the distributions of* Enc(PK, m) *and* LEnc(PK, LGen(PK), m) *are identical.*

Link traceability. *For every* PK *in the range of* Gen, *every* lk *in the range of* LGen(PK), *the encryptions of every pair of messages* (m_0, m_1) *trace to the same trace, that is, it always holds that* $\mathsf{Trace}(\mathsf{PK}, \mathsf{LEnc}(\mathsf{PK}, \mathsf{lk}, m_0)) = \mathsf{Trace}(\mathsf{PK}, \mathsf{LEnc}(\mathsf{PK}, \mathsf{lk}, m_1))$.

Publicly Traceable Randomization. *For every* PK *in the range of* Gen, *every message* m *and every* c *in the range of* Enc(PK, m), *we have that* $\mathsf{Dec}(\mathsf{SK}, c) = \mathsf{Dec}(\mathsf{SK}, \mathsf{Rand}(\mathsf{PK}, c))$ *and* $\mathsf{Trace}(\mathsf{PK}, c) = \mathsf{Trace}(\mathsf{PK}, \mathsf{Rand}(\mathsf{PK}, c))$.

Honest verifiability. *For every* PK *in the range of* Gen *and every message* m, *it holds that* $\mathsf{Ver}(\mathsf{PK}, \mathsf{Enc}(\mathsf{PK}, m)) = 1$.

$\mathsf{Exp}^{\mathsf{tcca}}_{\mathcal{A}}(\lambda)$

$(\mathsf{PK}, \mathsf{SK}) \leftarrow\$ \mathsf{Gen}(1^\lambda)$
$(c_0, c_1, \mathsf{st}) \leftarrow\$ \mathcal{A}_1^{\mathsf{Dec}(.)}(\mathsf{PK})$
$b \leftarrow\$ \{0,1\}$
if $\mathsf{Trace}(\mathsf{PK}, c_0) \neq \mathsf{Trace}(\mathsf{PK}, c_1)$ **or**
$\mathsf{Ver}(\mathsf{PK}, c_0) = 0$ **or** $\mathsf{Ver}(\mathsf{PK}, c_1) = 0$
then return b
$c^* \leftarrow\$ \mathsf{Rand}(\mathsf{PK}, c_b)$
$b' \leftarrow\$ \mathcal{A}_2^{\mathsf{Dec}^*(.)}(c^*, \mathsf{st})$
return $b' = b$

$\mathsf{Exp}^{\mathsf{trace}}_{\mathcal{A}}(\lambda)$

$(\mathsf{PK}, \mathsf{SK}) \leftarrow\$ \mathsf{Gen}(1^\lambda)$
$(m, \mathsf{st}) \leftarrow\$ \mathcal{A}_1(\mathsf{PK}, \mathsf{SK})$
$c \leftarrow\$ \mathsf{Enc}(\mathsf{PK}, m)$
$c^* \leftarrow\$ \mathcal{A}_2(c, \mathsf{st})$
if $\mathsf{Trace}(\mathsf{PK}, c) = \mathsf{Trace}(\mathsf{PK}, c^*)$ **and**
$\mathsf{Ver}(\mathsf{PK}, c^*) = 1$ **and** $\mathsf{Dec}(\mathsf{SK}, c^*) \neq m$
then return 1
else return 0

Fig. 1. The experiments of TCCA security, and traceability. In the TCCA game, $\mathcal{A}_2$ has access to a decryption oracle $\mathsf{Dec}^*(.)$ which, on input c, returns $\mathsf{Dec}(c)$ if $\mathsf{Trace}(\mathsf{PK}, c) \neq \mathsf{Trace}(\mathsf{PK}, c^*)$ and test otherwise.

2.3 Commitment Consistent Encryption (CCE)

CCE [19] is a cryptographic mechanism providing audit data for public verification that will never leak any information about the vote, even if the private keys are compromised or the cryptographic assumptions are broken.

To cast a ballot, voters are expected to encrypt their vote and produce a perfectly hiding commitment to the vote. The committed vote and an auxiliary value used to compute the commitment are called the openings for that commitment. The encryption is computed so that from any encrypted vote, it is possible to extract a commitment and an encryption of openings for that commitment. To verify the validity of the ballots, voters also have to provide a non-interactive zero-knowledge proof demonstrating the consistency between these components. The commitment is then cast on PB, whereas the encryption of the openings and the consistency proof are sent to SB. Since the election audit data in PB is perfectly hiding, we can ensure the confidentiality of the votes.

However, it is easy to observe that if a voter is willing to sell his vote, he can store the openings of the commitment and communicate it to an adversary. Thus, although CCE makes an e-voting system everlastingly private, it is not designed to protect against the vote-selling/buying threat. In other words, such a CCE protocol is not receipt-free.

3 The Construction of Our Scheme

Sections 3.1 and 3.2 describe our first construction of a commitment-consistent TREnc tailored to simple ballot. That is, the message space is bits encoded as scalars (in the exponents), and ciphertexts contain publicly verifiable proof of so. Our second construction tailored for complex ballot is deferred to Appendix A, where the message is a group element. In Sect. 3.3, we give the correctness and the security theorem statements of the construction. Finally, we provide a performance evaluation of our encryption algorithm in Sects. 3.4.

3.1 Description

Gen(1^λ): Choose bilinear groups $(\mathbb{G}, \hat{\mathbb{G}}, \mathbb{G}_T)$ of prime order $p > 2^{\mathsf{poly}(\lambda)}$, pick $g, g_1, h_1 \xleftarrow{\$} \mathbb{G}$ and $\hat{g}, \hat{h}, \hat{g}_1, \hat{h}_1, \hat{g}_2, \hat{h}_2 \xleftarrow{\$} \hat{\mathbb{G}}$.

1. Pick random $\{(\alpha_i, \beta_i)\}_{i=1}^3 \xleftarrow{\$} \mathbb{Z}_p$ and set $\{f_i\}_{i=1}^3 = g_1^{\alpha_i} h_1^{\beta_i}$.
2. To commit to groups elements of $\mathbb{G}$ and $\hat{\mathbb{G}}$ respectively, we generate one Groth-Sahai CRS $\mathbf{u} = (\vec{u}_1, \vec{u}_2)$ in $\mathbb{G}^4$ and two others $\mathbf{v} = (\vec{v}_1, \vec{v}_2)$ and $\mathbf{v}' = (\vec{v}'_1, \vec{v}'_2)$ in $\hat{\mathbb{G}}^4$ such that $\vec{u}_1 = (u_{11}, u_{12})$, $\vec{u}_2 = (u_{21}, u_{22})$, $\vec{v}_1 = (v_{11}, v_{12})$, $\vec{v}_2 = (v_{21}, v_{22})$, $\vec{v}'_1 = (v'_{11}, v'_{12})$, and $\vec{v}'_2 = (v'_{21}, v'_{22})$ are generated in the perfect NIWI mode.
3. Pick random $\hat{f}_1, \hat{f}_2 \leftarrow \hat{\mathbb{G}}$ that will be used as a verification key for the LHSP signature but for which no one knows the corresponding secret key.

The private and public keys respectively are $\mathsf{SK} = \{(\alpha_i, \beta_i)\}_{i=1}^3$ and $\mathsf{PK} = (g, g_1, h_1, \hat{g}, \hat{h}, \hat{g}_1, \hat{h}_1, \hat{g}_2, \hat{h}_2, \{f_i\}_{i=1}^3, \hat{f}_1, \hat{f}_2, \mathbf{u}, \mathbf{v}, \mathbf{v}')$.

Enc(PK, m): To encrypt $m \in \mathbb{Z}_p$, first run $\mathsf{LGen}(\mathsf{PK})$: Generate a key pair $(\mathsf{osk}, \mathsf{opk})$ for the one-time linearly homomorphic signature from the public generators g_1, h_1 to sign vectors of dimension 3. Let the signing key $\mathsf{lk} = \mathsf{osk} = \{(\eta_i, \zeta_i)\}_{i=1}^3$, the corresponding public key is $\mathsf{opk} = \{k_i\}_{i=1}^3 = \{g_1^{\eta_i} h_1^{\zeta_i}\}_{i=1}^3$. Then, conduct the following steps of $\mathsf{LEnc}(\mathsf{PK}, \mathsf{lk}, m)$:

1. In the ciphertext CT:
   (a) Compute $M = g^m \in \mathbb{G}$. For random $r, q \xleftarrow{\$} \mathbb{Z}_p$, compute the commitments $\hat{d}_1 = \hat{g}^m \hat{g}_1^r \hat{h}_1^q \in \hat{\mathbb{G}}$, $\hat{d}_2 = \hat{g}_2^r \hat{h}_2^q \in \hat{\mathbb{G}}$ and the openings $R = g^r \in \mathbb{G}, Q = g^q \in \mathbb{G}$. Choose $\theta \xleftarrow{\$} \mathbb{Z}_p$, compute the ciphertexts of M, R, and Q respectively as $\mathbf{c}_m = (c_0, c_1, c_2) = (Mf_1^\theta, g_1^\theta, h_1^\theta)$, $c_r = Rf_2^\theta$, and $c_q = Qf_3^\theta$.
   (b) Commit to the openings using the Groth-Sahai CRS by computing $\mathbf{C}_M = \iota_1(M)\vec{u}_1^{z_1}\vec{u}_2^{z_2} \in \mathbb{G}^2$, $\mathbf{C}_R = \iota_1(R)\vec{u}_1^{r_1}\vec{u}_2^{r_2} \in \mathbb{G}^2$, and $\mathbf{C}_Q = \iota_1(Q)\vec{u}_1^{t_1}\vec{u}_2^{t_2} \in \mathbb{G}^2$ for random $z_1, z_2, r_1, r_2, t_1, t_2 \xleftarrow{\$} \mathbb{Z}_p$, then derive the commitment $\mathbf{C}_{f_1} = \iota(c_0)/\mathbf{C}_M$, $\mathbf{C}_{f_2} = \iota(c_r)/\mathbf{C}_R$, and $\mathbf{C}_{f_3} = \iota(c_q)/\mathbf{C}_Q$.
   (c) To allow simulating the proof, set the bit $\bar{b} = 1$ and compute $G = g^{\bar{b}} \in \mathbb{G}$ and $\hat{H} = \hat{h}^{\bar{b}} \in \hat{\mathbb{G}}$. Commit to G, $\hat{H}$, and $\hat{H}^\theta$ respectively to have $\mathbf{C}_G = \iota_1(G)\vec{u_1}^{w_1}\vec{u_2}^{w_2} \in \mathbb{G}^2$, $\mathbf{C}_{\hat{H}} = \iota_2(\hat{H})\vec{v_1}^{x_1}\vec{v_2}^{x_2} \in \hat{\mathbb{G}}$, and $\mathbf{C}_\theta = \iota_2(\hat{H}^\theta)\vec{v_1}^{x_3}\vec{v_2}^{x_4} \in \hat{\mathbb{G}}$ for $w_1, w_2, x_1, x_2, x_3, x_4 \xleftarrow{\$} \mathbb{Z}_p$. To make sure G and $\hat{H}$ are well-formed, compute GS proof π_b such that

$$e(g, \boxed{\hat{H}}) = e(\boxed{G}, \hat{h}) \tag{2}$$

   For the sake of simplicity, we signify that the group element represented in the box is the one that is committed in the corresponding commitment. For example, in Eq. 2, $\hat{H}$ and G are committed in $\mathbf{C}_{\hat{H}}$ and $\mathbf{C}_G$ respectively.
   (d) To make sure CT is well-formed, compute the GS proof π_θ to ensure that $(c_1, c_2, c_0/M, c_r/R, c_q/Q)$ are in the form of $(g_1, h_1, f_1, f_2, f_3)^\theta$. In other words, these equations below must be satisfied with $\boxed{\hat{H}^\theta}$, $\boxed{f_1^\theta}$, $\boxed{f_2^\theta}$, and $\boxed{f_3^\theta}$ respectively being committed in $\mathbf{C}_\theta, \mathbf{C}_{f_1}, \mathbf{C}_{f_2}$, and $\mathbf{C}_{f_3}$.

$$\begin{aligned}
e(c_1, \boxed{\hat{H}}) &= e(g_1, \boxed{\hat{H}^\theta}) && \text{(a)}\\
e(c_2, \boxed{\hat{H}}) &= e(h_1, \boxed{\hat{H}^\theta}) && \text{(b)}\\
e(\boxed{f_1^\theta}, \boxed{\hat{H}}) &= e(f_1, \boxed{\hat{H}^\theta}) && \text{(c)}\\
e(\boxed{f_2^\theta}, \boxed{\hat{H}}) &= e(f_2, \boxed{\hat{H}^\theta}) && \text{(d)}\\
e(\boxed{f_3^\theta}, \boxed{\hat{H}}) &= e(f_3, \boxed{\hat{H}^\theta}) && \text{(e)}
\end{aligned} \tag{3}$$

   (e) Return $CT = (\mathbf{c}_m, c_r, c_q, \mathbf{C}_{\hat{H}}, \mathbf{C}_\theta, \pi_b, \pi_\theta) \in \mathbb{G}^{25} \times \hat{\mathbb{G}}^{20}$.
2. In the commitment D:
   (a) For the proof of the openings for commitments:
      - The GS proof of openings π_{open} needs to make sure that the values committed in $\mathbf{C}_M, \mathbf{C}_R, \mathbf{C}_Q, \mathbf{C}_G$ in CT are the openings of the commitments $\hat{d}_1, \hat{d}_2$ in D. To put it differently, π_{open} must satisfy that

$$\begin{aligned}
e(\boxed{M}, \hat{g}) \cdot e(\boxed{R}, \hat{g}_1) \cdot e(\boxed{Q}, \hat{h}_1) &= e(\boxed{G}, \hat{d}_1) && \text{(a)}\\
e(\boxed{R}, \hat{g}_2) \cdot e(\boxed{Q}, \hat{h}_2) &= e(\boxed{G}, \hat{d}_2) && \text{(b)}
\end{aligned} \tag{4}$$

where $\boxed{M}$, $\boxed{R}$, $\boxed{Q}$ are values committed in $\mathbf{C}_M, \mathbf{C}_R, \mathbf{C}_Q$ in their respective order.
Thus, the proofs π_θ computed in the CT and π_{open} in D constitute the *proof of consistency* between $\hat{d}_1, \hat{d}_2$ and $\mathbf{c}_m, c_r, c_q$, i.e., the commitments can be opened by encrypted values in the ciphertexts.

(b) For traceability property:
   - Sign each row of the matrix T using $\mathsf{lk} = \mathsf{osk}$, resulting in signatures $\hat{\sigma}_1, \hat{\sigma}_2, \hat{\sigma}_3$, where $\hat{\sigma}_i = (\hat{Z}_i, \hat{R}_i) \in \hat{\mathbb{G}}^2$ for $i = 1, 2, 3$.

$$T = \begin{pmatrix} \hat{g} & \hat{d}_1 & \hat{d}_2 \\ 1 & \hat{g}_1 & \hat{g}_2 \\ 1 & \hat{h}_1 & \hat{h}_2 \end{pmatrix} \quad (5)$$

   - To allow strong randomizability, commit to $\hat{\sigma}_1$ using the GS CRS $\mathbf{v}'$ by computing $C_{\hat{Z}} = \iota_2(\hat{Z}_1)\vec{v}_1'^{l_1}\vec{v}_2'^{l_2}$ and $C_{\hat{R}} = \iota_2(\hat{R}_1)\vec{v}_1'^{l_3}\vec{v}_2' l_4$ for random scalars $l_1, l_2, l_3, l_4 \xleftarrow{\$} \mathbb{Z}_p$.
   - To ensure that $\hat{\sigma}_1$ is a valid one-time LHSP signature on $(\hat{g}, \hat{d}_1, \hat{d}_2)$, compute the proof π_{sig} such that

$$e(g_1, \boxed{\hat{Z}_1}) \cdot e(h_1, \boxed{\hat{R}_1}) = e(k_1, \hat{g}) \cdot e(k_2, \hat{d}_1) \cdot e(k_3, \hat{d}_2) \quad (6)$$

   where $\boxed{\hat{Z}_1}$ and $\boxed{\hat{R}_1}$ are committed in $C_{\hat{Z}}, C_{\hat{R}}$ respectively.

(c) For TCCA security:
   - Set $(A, B) = (1_{\mathbb{G}}, 1_{\mathbb{G}})$ as a degenerated LHSP signature, and $X = g/G = g^{1-\bar{b}} \in \mathbb{G}$. Since $\bar{b} = 1$, $X = 1_{\mathbb{G}}$. The commitment of X is computed by $\mathbf{C}_X = \iota_1(g)/\mathbf{C}_G \in \mathbb{G}^2$. Commit to A and B to have $\mathbf{C}_A = \iota_1(A)\vec{u}_1^{a_1}\vec{u}_2^{a_2}$ and $\mathbf{C}_B = \iota_1(B)\vec{u}_1^{b_1}\vec{u}_2^{b_2}$ for $a_1, a_2, b_1, b_2 \xleftarrow{\$} \mathbb{Z}_p$.
   - The randomizable simulation-sound proof π_{ss} must ensure that

$$e(\boxed{A}, \hat{g}) \cdot e(\boxed{B}, \hat{h}) = e(g/\boxed{G}, \hat{f}_1 \hat{f}_2^{\tau}) \quad (7)$$

   where $\tau = \mathsf{Hash}(\mathsf{opk})$. In the honest case, 7 is trivially fulfilled. In the simulated case, $\bar{b} \neq 1$ and (A, B) must be a valid LHSP signature on $(X, X^{\tau}) \neq (1, 1)$ with verification keys being public elements $(\hat{f}_1, \hat{f}_2)$.

(d) For well-formedness proof of a vote:
The vote m must be 0 or 1. To this end, we commit to $\hat{M} = \hat{g}^m$ to have $\mathbf{C}_{\hat{M}} = \iota_2(\hat{M})\vec{v}_1^{s_1}\vec{v}_2^{s_2}$ for random scalars $s_1, s_2 \xleftarrow{\$} \mathbb{Z}_p$. The proof π_{01} is computed such that

$$\begin{aligned} e(\boxed{M}, \hat{g}) &= e(g, \boxed{\hat{M}}) && \text{(a)} \\ e(\boxed{M}, \hat{g}/\boxed{\hat{M}}) &= 1 && \text{(b)} \end{aligned} \quad (8)$$

(e) Return the commitment part $D = (\hat{d}_1, \hat{d}_2, \mathbf{C}_{\hat{M}}, \mathbf{C}_M, \mathbf{C}_R, \mathbf{C}_Q, \mathbf{C}_G, \mathbf{C}_{\hat{Z}}, \mathbf{C}_{\hat{R}}, \mathbf{C}_A, \mathbf{C}_B, \pi_{open}, \hat{\sigma}_2, \hat{\sigma}_3, \pi_{sig}, \pi_{ss}, \pi_{01}, \mathsf{opk}) \in \mathbb{G}^{25} \times \hat{\mathbb{G}}^{26}$.

At the end of the encryption, output $C = (CT, D) \in \mathbb{G}^{50} \times \hat{\mathbb{G}}^{46}$.

Trace(PK, C)**:** Parse PK and C as above, and output opk in the obvious way.
Rand(PK, C)**:** If PK and $C = (CT, D)$ do not parse as the outputs of Gen and Enc, abort. Otherwise, conduct the steps as follows:

1. <u>Randomizing CT</u>:
   (a) Parse the CPA encryption part $\mathbf{c}_m, c_r, c_q$, pick $\theta', r', q' \xleftarrow{\$} \mathbb{Z}_p$, set $R' = g^{r'}, Q' = g^{q'}$, and compute $\mathbf{c}'_m = (c'_0, c'_1, c'_2) = \mathbf{c}_m \cdot (f_1, g_1, h_1)^{\theta'} = (M f_1^{\theta+\theta'}, g_1^{\theta+\theta'}, h_1^{\theta+\theta'}), c'_r = c_r \cdot R' f_2^{\theta'}$, and $c'_q = c_q \cdot Q' f_3^{\theta'}$.
   (b) Adapt the commitments $\mathbf{C}'_G = \mathbf{C}_G \cdot \vec{u_1}^{w'_1} \vec{u_2}^{w'_2}$, and $\mathbf{C}'_{\hat{H}} = \mathbf{C}_{\hat{H}} \cdot \vec{v_1}^{x'_1} \vec{v_2}^{x'_2}$ for $w'_1, w'_2, x'_1, x'_2 \xleftarrow{\$} \mathbb{Z}_p$. Likewise, randomize the commitments $C'_{\hat{H}} = \mathbf{C}_{\hat{H}} \cdot \vec{v_1}^{x'_1} \vec{v_2}^{x'_2}$, $\mathbf{C}'_\theta = \mathbf{C}_\theta \cdot \iota_2(1) \cdot \iota_2(\hat{H}^{\theta'}) \vec{v_1}^{x'_3} \vec{v_2}^{x'_4}$, $\mathbf{C}'_M = \mathbf{C}_M \cdot \vec{u_1}^{z'_1} \vec{u_2}^{z'_2}$, $\mathbf{C}'_R = \mathbf{C}_R \cdot \iota_1(R') \vec{u_1}^{r'_1} \vec{u_2}^{r'_2}$, $\mathbf{C}'_Q = \mathbf{C}_Q \cdot \iota_1(Q') \vec{u_1}^{t'_1} \vec{u_2}^{t'_2}$ for $x'_1, x'_2, x'_3, x'_4, z'_1, z'_2, r'_1, r'_2, t'_1, t'_2 \xleftarrow{\$} \mathbb{Z}_p$. The derived commitments are then $\mathbf{C}'_{f_1} = \iota(c'_0)/\mathbf{C}'_M$, $\mathbf{C}'_{f_2} = \iota(c'_r)/\mathbf{C}'_R$; $\mathbf{C}'_{f_3} = \iota(c'_q)/\mathbf{C}'_Q$.
   (c) Adapt the proof π'_θ and π'_b accordingly.
   (d) Return $CT' = (\mathbf{c}'_m, c'_r, c'_q, \mathbf{C}'_{\hat{H}}, \mathbf{C}'_\theta, \pi'_b, \pi'_\theta)$.
2. <u>Randomizing D</u>:
   (a) For proof of openings π_{open}:
      i. Randomize the commitments $\hat{d}'_1 = \hat{d}_1 \cdot \hat{g}_1^{r'} \hat{h}_1^{q'} = \hat{g}^m \hat{g}_1^{r+r'} \hat{h}_1^{q+q'}$, $\hat{d}'_2 = \hat{d}_2 \cdot \hat{g}_2^{r'} \hat{h}_2^{q'} = \hat{g}_2^{r+r'} \hat{h}_2^{q+q'}$ for the same r', q' in CT.
      ii. Update the corresponding proof π'_{open}.
   (b) For the proof of signature π_{sig}:
      i. Implicitly adapt the committed signature $\hat{\sigma}_1$ of the tracing part by computing $\tilde{\sigma}_1 = (\tilde{Z}_1, \tilde{R}_1) = (\hat{Z}_2^{r'} \hat{Z}_3^{q'}, \hat{R}_2^{r'} \hat{R}_3^{q'})$ which consists of a one-time LHSP signature on $(1, \hat{g}_1, \hat{g}_2)^{r'} \cdot (1, \hat{h}_1, \hat{h}_2)^{q'}$ for opk.
      ii. Adapt the commitment $\mathbf{C}'_{\hat{Z}} = \mathbf{C}_{\hat{Z}} \cdot \iota_2(\tilde{Z}_1) \vec{v_1}^{l'_1} \vec{v_2}^{l'_2}$ and $\mathbf{C}'_{\hat{R}} = \mathbf{C}_{\hat{R}} \cdot \iota_2(\tilde{R}_1) \vec{v_1}^{l'_3} \vec{v_2}^{l'_4}$ for some random $l'_1, l'_2, l'_3, l'_4 \xleftarrow{\$} \mathbb{Z}_p$, which should commit to the valid one-time LHSP signature $\hat{\sigma}'_1 = \hat{\sigma}_1 \hat{\sigma}_2^{r'} \hat{\sigma}_3^{q'}$ on $(g, \hat{d}'_1, \hat{d}'_2)$ for opk. Then, randomize the proof π'_{sig}.
   (c) For the proof of simulation soundness π_{ss}:
      i. Adapt the commitment $\mathbf{C}_X$ corresponding to $\mathbf{C}'_G$ by computing $\mathbf{C}'_X = \iota_1(g)/\mathbf{C}'_G$. Similarly, computing $\mathbf{C}'_A = \mathbf{C}_A \cdot \vec{u_1}^{a'_1} \vec{u_2}^{a'_2}$ and $\mathbf{C}'_B = \mathbf{C}_B \cdot \vec{u_1}^{b'_1} \vec{u_2}^{b'_2}$ for some $a'_1, a'_2, b'_1, b'_2 \xleftarrow{\$} \mathbb{Z}_p$.
      ii. Adapt the proof π_{ss} to have π'_{ss}.
   (d) For well-formedness proof of a vote:
   Adapt the commitment $\mathbf{C}'_{\hat{M}} = \mathbf{C}_{\hat{M}} \cdot \vec{v_1}^{s'_1} \vec{v_2}^{s'_2}$ for $s'_1, s'_2 \xleftarrow{\$} \mathbb{Z}_p$. Similarly, adapt the proof π_{01} to have π'_{01}.
   (e) Return $D' = (\hat{d}'_1, \hat{d}'_2, \mathbf{C}'_{\hat{M}}, \mathbf{C}'_M, \mathbf{C}'_R, \mathbf{C}'_Q, \mathbf{C}'_G, \mathbf{C}'_A, \mathbf{C}'_B, \mathbf{C}'_{\hat{Z}}, \mathbf{C}'_{\hat{R}}, \hat{\sigma}_2, \hat{\sigma}_3, \pi'_{sig}, \pi'_{open}, \pi'_{ss}, \pi'_{01}, \mathsf{opk})$.

At the end of the randomization, output $C = (CT', D')$.

Ver (PK, C)**:** Abort and output 0 if either PK or C fails to parse correctly. Else, check the validity of the LHSP signatures $\hat{\sigma}_2, \hat{\sigma}_3$ respectively on $(1, \hat{g}_1, \hat{g}_2)$ and $(1, \hat{h}_1, \hat{h}_2)$ with respect to opk, as well as all the Groth-Sahai proofs with $\tau = \mathsf{Hash}(\mathsf{opk})$ and output 0 if at least one of them fails; otherwise, output 1. (All the verification equations are given in Sect. 3.2.)

Dec(SK, C)**:** If Ver$(\mathsf{PK}, C) = 0$, output $\perp$. Otherwise, given $\mathsf{SK}= \{(\alpha_i, \beta_i)\}_{i=1}^3$ and $(\mathbf{c}_m = (c_0, c_1, c_2), c_r, c_q)$ included in CT, output $M = c_0 \cdot c_1^{-\alpha_1} \cdot c_2^{-\beta_1}$, $R = c_r \cdot c_1^{-\alpha_2} \cdot c_2^{-\beta_2}$, and $Q = c_q \cdot c_1^{-\alpha_3} \cdot c_2^{-\beta_3}$.

3.2 Verification Equations

We now turn to the specification of the verification equations of the Groth-Sahai proofs that must be satisfied by valid ciphertexts produced using this first construction. While they are not necessary to follow the security proofs, we expand them here in order to have a clear view about the cost of publicly verifying ciphertexts, which will be evaluated through a prototype implementation below.

Ver (PK, C)**:** Abort and output 0 if either PK or C fails to parse correctly. Then, privately verify the first verification, which concerns the CPA encryption part, while the remaining four will be checked publicly on PB.

1. The CPA encryption part is well-formed, i.e., $(c_1, c_2, c_0/M, c_r/R, c_q/Q)$ are all in the form of the same exponent; and $(G, \hat{H})$ are also raised to the same exponent. To hold, the proofs π_θ, π_b in CT (of Eq. 3, Eq. 2) and commitments $\mathbf{C}_{f_1}, \mathbf{C}_{f_2}, \mathbf{C}_{f_3}, \mathbf{C}_{\hat{H}}, \mathbf{C}_\theta, \mathbf{C}_G$ must satisfy:
$$E(c_1, \mathbf{C}_{\hat{H}}) = E(g_1, \mathbf{C}_\theta) \cdot E(\pi_{\theta,a}[0], \vec{v}_1) \cdot E(\pi_{\theta,a}[1], \vec{v}_2)$$
$$E(c_2, \mathbf{C}_{\hat{H}}) = E(h_1, \mathbf{C}_\theta) \cdot E(\pi_{\theta,b}[0], \vec{v}_1) \cdot E(\pi_{\theta,b}[1], \vec{v}_2)$$
and
$$\begin{aligned} E(\mathbf{C}_{f_i}, \mathbf{C}_{\hat{H}}) =& E(\iota_1(f_i), \mathbf{C}_\theta) \cdot E(\vec{u}_1, \pi_{\theta,j}[0]) \cdot E(\vec{u}_2, \pi_{\theta,j}[1]) \\ & \cdot E(\pi_{\theta,j}[2], \vec{v}_1) \cdot E(\pi_{\theta,j}[3], \vec{v}_2) \end{aligned}$$
for $(i, j) \in \{(1, c), (2, d), (3, e)\}$ and
$$\begin{aligned} E(\iota_1(g), \mathbf{C}_{\hat{H}}) =& E(\mathbf{C}_G, \iota_2(\hat{h})) \cdot E(\vec{u}_1, \pi_b[0]) \cdot E(\vec{u}_2, \pi_b[1]) \cdot \\ & E(\pi_b[2], \vec{v}_1) \cdot E(\pi_b[3], \vec{v}_2) \end{aligned}$$
2. The values committed in $\mathbf{C}_M, \mathbf{C}_R, \mathbf{C}_Q, \mathbf{C}_G$ are the openings of the commitments in Eq. 4. That means
$$E(\mathbf{C}_M, \hat{g}) \cdot E(\mathbf{C}_R, \hat{g}_1) \cdot E(\mathbf{C}_Q, \hat{h}_1) = E(\mathbf{C}_G, \hat{d}_1) \cdot E(\mathbf{u}, \pi_{open,a})$$
$$E(\mathbf{C}_R, \hat{g}_2) \cdot E(\mathbf{C}_Q, \hat{h}_2) = E(\mathbf{C}_G, \hat{d}_2) \cdot E(\mathbf{u}, \pi_{open,b})$$
where $E(\mathbf{u}, \pi_{open,i}) = E(\vec{u}_1, \pi_{open,i}[0]) \cdot E(\vec{u}_2, \pi_{open,i}[1])$ with $i \in \{a, b\}$. The verifications 1. and 2. constitute a consistency between $\hat{d}_1, \hat{d}_2$ in D and $\mathbf{c}_m, c_r, c_q$ in CT, i.e., the commitments can be opened by encrypted values in the ciphertexts.

3. The committed signature of the tracing part is valid, i.e., $\hat{\sigma}_1 = (\hat{Z}_1, \hat{R}_1)$ is a valid one-time LHSP signature on the vector $(\hat{g}, \hat{d}_1, \hat{d}_2)$. To this end, the commitments $\mathbf{C}_{\hat{Z}}, C_{\hat{R}}$ and the proof π_{sig} must ensure that

$$\begin{aligned} E(g_1, \mathbf{C}_{\hat{Z}}) \cdot E(h_1, \mathbf{C}_{\hat{R}}) =& E(k_1, \iota_2(\hat{g})) \cdot E(k_2, \iota_2(\hat{d}_1)) \cdot E(k_3, \iota_2(\hat{d}_2)) \cdot \\ & E(\pi_{sig}[0], \vec{v}_1') \cdot E(\pi_{sig}[1], \vec{v}_2') \end{aligned}$$

4. The committed values of the simulation part are valid, i.e., (A, B) must be a valid LHSP signature on (X, X^τ) by verifying

$$E(\mathbf{C}_A, \hat{g}) \cdot E(\mathbf{C}_B, \hat{h}) = E(\iota_1(g)/\mathbf{C}_G, \hat{f}_1 \hat{f}_2^\tau) \cdot E(\vec{u}_1, \pi_{ss}[0]) \cdot E(\vec{u}_2, \pi_{ss}[1])$$

5. The vote m is 0 or 1 using the proof π_{01} from Eq. 8

$$\begin{aligned} E(\mathbf{C}_M, \iota_2(\hat{g})) =& E(\iota_1(g), \mathbf{C}_{\hat{M}}) \cdot E(\vec{u}_1, \pi_{01,a}[0]) \cdot E(\vec{u}_2, \pi_{01,a}[1]) \cdot \\ & E(\pi_{01,a}[2], \vec{v}_1) \cdot E(\pi_{01,a}[3], \vec{v}_2) \\ E(\mathbf{C}_M, \iota_2(\hat{g})/\mathbf{C}_{\hat{M}}) =& E(\vec{u}_1, \pi_{01,b}[0]) \cdot E(\vec{u}_2, \pi_{01,b}[1]) \cdot \\ & E(\pi_{01,b}[2], \vec{v}_1) \cdot E(\pi_{01,b}[3], \vec{v}_2) \end{aligned}$$

If at least one of these checks fails, output 0; otherwise, output 1.

3.3 Security Analysis

The above scheme enjoys (perfect) correctness. Moreover, its security solely relies on the SXDH assumption as claimed below. All the proofs are given in Appendix B.

Theorem 3.1. *The above scheme is perfectly strongly randomizable.*

Theorem 3.2. *The above scheme is TCCA-secure under the SXDH assumption and the collision resistance of the hash function. We have the advantage* $|\Pr[\mathsf{Exp}_{\mathcal{A}}^{\mathsf{tcca}}(\lambda) = 1] - \frac{1}{2}| \leq \epsilon_{cr} + 6\epsilon_{sxdh} + \frac{4}{p}$.

Theorem 3.3. *The above scheme is traceable under the SXDH assumption. More precisely, we have* $\Pr[\mathsf{Exp}_{\mathcal{A}}^{\mathsf{trace}}(\lambda) = 1] \leq 5\epsilon_{sxdh} + \frac{1}{p}$.

Theorem 3.4. *The above scheme is verifiable under the SXDH assumption. More precisely, for any adversary $\mathcal{A}$, we have* $\Pr[\mathsf{Exp}_{\mathcal{A}}^{\mathsf{ver}}(\lambda) = 1] \leq 3\epsilon_{sxdh} + \frac{1}{p}$.

3.4 Efficiency

Up to constant factors, the encryption scheme we just described and the one we describe in Appendix A are optimal in the sense of Cramer, Gennaro and Schoenmakers [17]: the ballot size and the voter computational load do not depend on the number of voters nor on the number of authorities, the computational workload of the tallying authorities grows linearly with the number of voters and candidates.

In order to evaluate the constants, we built a C implementation of the ballot preparation (key generation, encryption) and verification algorithms using the MIRACL Core Cryptographic Library [31]. The implementation, which can be found on https://github.com/uclcrypto/TREnc-PPAT, is carried out on an average commodity laptop equipped with an Intel i5-1245U processor running Ubuntu 22.04. The time unit is seconds and all our results are averaged over 100 runs. The running time of verification includes all verification equations in Sect. 3.1 for both individual and universal verification. Likewise, the encryption process timing also includes signature and proof computation. To provide at least 128-bit security, we use a BN curve [3] on a 462-bit prime field, so-called BN462. As seen in Table 1, it appears that the cost of computing ballots for

Table 1. Time for key generation, encryption, and verification of one ballot.

Tally type	Gen	Enc	Ver
Homomorphic	0.023	0.228	0.802
Mixnet	0.019	0.214	0.782

both instances is almost similar and largely under a second. However, there is a slight difference in the verification timing of the two methods. This is because a mixnet-based tally does not require a well-formedness proof of the vote, whereas a homomorphic tally does. We note that the computation of multiple ciphertexts could also largely benefit of fixed-base exponentiation methods: these costs can then grow much more slowly than linearly with the number of ciphertexts to be computed.

4 Application to E-Voting

One important application of our scheme is the construction of single-pass voting systems [8], where voters interact with the system only by submitting their ballots. The described protocol involves four entities as introduced in TREnc, consisting of: *voters*, who have the right to vote; *election administrator (EA)*, who is in charge of setting up the election and generating PK and SK. A *ballot box manager* is responsible for randomizing the ballots of the voters. A *tallier* is in charge of correctly tallying the ballot box and providing the correctness proof of the tally. Also, it provides tallying results on a public view PB for verifiability.

Our proposed voting protocol is defined as a tuple of probabilistic polynomial-time algorithms based on the two most crucial tallying techniques: homomorphic aggregation, tailored for elections with a small number of candidates, and mixnet that is suitable for elections with complex ballots.

$\mathsf{SetUp}(1^\lambda)$: On input security parameter 1^λ, generates the public and secret keys $(\mathsf{PK}, \mathsf{SK})$ of the election.

Vote(id, v): Upon receiving a voter id and a vote v, outputs a ballot b $= (CT, D)$.

Valid(b): On input ballot b, outputs 0 or 1. The algorithm outputs 1 if and only if the ballot satisfies all verification equations.

ProcessBallot(b): On the input ballot b, outputs an updated ballot b′, a re-randomization of b where b′ $= (CT', D')$.

TraceBallot(b): On input a commitment D, outputs a trace t. The trace is the information that a voter can use to track his ballot, using VerifyBallot.

Append(PB, SB, b) : On input PB, SB, and ballot b, appends D to PB and CT to SBif Valid(b) = 1.

VerifyBallot(PB, t): On input the public board PB and a trace t, outputs 0 or 1. This algorithm is used by voters to check if their ballot has been processed and recorded properly.

Tally(PB, SB, SK): On input PB, SB, and private key SK, outputs the tally result and a proof of correctness. Depending on the tallying technique, runs HomoTally or MixnetTally correspondingly.

VerifyResult(PB): On input PB, result of the tally and proof of the tally, outputs 0 or 1. Depending on the tallying technique, runs either HomoVerify or MixnetVerify.

It is implicit that PK is given to all these algorithms except SetUp.

Following [20], we describe our voting scheme based on a TREnc with the difference that only the perfectly private parts of our ballots are published on PB. More precisely, EAs first generate the election public and secret keys with SetUp by running Gen of our TREnc. The public key PK is published and stored on the PB, and shares of SK are only known by the tallier (SK can be securely generated in a distributed way in our prime-order groups using standard techniques). Each voter can then prepare a ballot b and submit it to the ballot box manager using the Vote algorithm that runs the encryption of the vote using our TREnc. The validity of the ballot is defined as the validity of our D and CT output by Vote(id, v). Although the ballot will be randomized, a voter can store TraceBallot(b) that is defined as the trace of the TREnc ciphertext and confirm if it has been correctly recorded on PB by utilizing VerifyBallot(PB, t). After receiving a ballot, the ballot box manager checks its validity and that no ballot with the same trace was recorded before. Invalid ballots are dropped and valid ones will go through Append(PB, SB, b) after being re-randomized by ProcessBallot(b) thanks to Rand. As said, Append(PB, SB, b) simply computes PB ← PB$||D$ and SB ← PB$||CT$ from (previously rerandomized) b $= (CT, D)$. Once every voter has cast a vote, the tallier checks the validity of each ballot using Valid(b). A tallying protocol is then carried out based on the ballot type and the election outcome is published. To verify the election result, anyone can utilize VerifyResult(PB) by referring to the content of PB, and which can be based on common techniques.

4.1 Voting Scheme with a Homomorphic Tally

One of the two main approaches for tallying an election is homomorphic aggregation. The homomorphic property makes it possible to homomorphically combine a number of ballots to compute the encrypted sum of the votes. Then only the sum is decrypted instead of individual votes so that the secrecy of an individual's ballot is preserved. Since the vote can be only 0 or 1, it can be encoded as a group element and subsequently decoded by an exhaustive search of the plaintext. Thus, the voter needs to add a non-interactive randomizable proof of vote well-formedness to the public commitment part (see Eq. 8). The tallier computes tally by HomoTally algorithm as follows.

1. *Aggregation*: For all l valid CT in SB, the tallier performs element-wise multiplication of the encryption $(\mathbf{c}_m, c_r, c_q)$, obtaining a result vector $\mathbf{v} = (\prod_i \mathbf{c}_m, \prod_i c_r, \prod_i c_q)$ for $i = 1, \ldots l$.
2. *Decryption*: The tallier decrypts $\mathbf{v}$ in order to obtain the openings $(M, R, Q) = \mathsf{Dec}(\mathsf{SK}, \mathbf{v})$, then finds m and appends (m, R, Q) to PB.

Since both the commitment and the encryption schemes are additively homomorphic, the votes are homomorphically combined into a single ciphertext containing the final result, which is then decrypted by the tallier. To check that the tally matches the posted votes, anyone can run HomoVerify algorithm as follows.

1. Multiply all the commitments $(\hat{d}_1, \hat{d}_2)$ element-wise for l valid entries on PB to obtain a commitment on the election outcome $(\mathsf{com}_1, \mathsf{com}_2)$.
2. Verify that (m, R, Q) provided by the tallier are openings of the outcome commitment by checking if the given equations are satisfied

$$e(g^m, \hat{g}) \cdot e(R, \hat{g}_1) \cdot e(Q, \hat{h}_1) = e(g, \mathsf{com}_1)$$
$$e(R, \hat{g}_2) \cdot e(Q, \hat{h}_2) = e(g, \mathsf{com}_2)$$

Given that the commitment scheme is binding, it makes sure that the only openings that the authorities are able to provide come from an honest tallying process. Moreover, its perfectly hiding property can guarantee the perfect ballot privacy of the whole audit trail.

4.2 Voting Scheme with a Mixnet Tally

Unlike homomorphic tallying, verifiable mixnet-based systems decrypt individual ballots after anonymization, which disassociates encrypted ballots from their corresponding voters. This anonymization procedure will be performed by shuffling the votes through several shuffling centers (so-called mixers). Since each shuffled ballot is decrypted individually, its validity is verified by the fact that the decrypted vote and auxiliary values are the openings of the corresponding commitment. As a result, the voter is not required to compute the well-formedness proof of the vote. Due to page limitations, our adapted encryption scheme of mixnet tallying is presented in the Appendix A, which is not additively homomorphic anymore, but still randomizable. Thus, there are no specific concerns regarding the necessary randomization properties for mixing. We sketch the MixnetTally algorithm in the following.

1. *Stripping*: On each input of $C = (CT, D)$, the authorities only keep the encryption $(\mathbf{c}_m, \mathbf{c}_r, c_s)$ in CT and the commitments (d_1, d_2) in D, obtaining an encryption vector $\mathbf{v} = \{(\mathbf{c}_m^i, \mathbf{c}_r^i, c_s^i)\}_{i=1}^l$ and corresponding commitment vector $\mathbf{d} = \{(d_1^i, d_2^i)\}_{i=1}^l$ of l valid ballots.
2. *Permutation Selection*: A random permutation π is chosen and a validity proof P_π for π is computed.
3. *Shuffle*: The mixers shuffle $(\mathbf{v}, \mathbf{d})$, resulting in $(\mathbf{v}', \mathbf{d}')$. While $\mathbf{v}'$ is kept private on SB, $\mathbf{d}'$ is posted on PB. Additionally, two commitment consistent proofs are provided with respect to the permutation π: $P_\mathbf{v}$ shows that $\mathbf{v}'$ is a shuffle on $\mathbf{v}$ and $P_\mathbf{d}$ shows that $\mathbf{d}'$ is a shuffle on $\mathbf{d}$. $P_\mathbf{v}$ and $P_\mathbf{d}$ are then posted on SB and PB respectively.
4. *Decryption*: After verifying the proofs, the encryption in $\mathbf{v}'$ is decrypted to have the message M and auxiliary values $\hat{R}$ and $\hat{S}$. The results are published on PB.

Since the published proofs do not disclose the permutation used in the mixing process or the decryption key, it would not violate any anonymity. Thus, everyone can verify if the election outcome is the correct decryption of the shuffled valid votes using the MixnetVerify algorithm below.

1. *Verification of the permutation*: One can verify the proof P_π of the chosen permutation π and abort if it fails.
2. *Verification of the proof of shuffle*: One can verify the validity of the proof $P_\mathbf{d}$ and abort if it fails.
3. *Verification of the openings*: One can verify if decrypted values of $\mathbf{v}'$ provided on PB are valid openings for the shuffled commitments in $\mathbf{d}'$ and abort otherwise.

5 Conclusion

Our paper proposes two encryption mechanisms for verifiable elections that supports both receipt-freeness and a perfectly private audit trail. To the best of our knowledge, this is the first proposal that can achieve these properties without relying on the presence of an anonymous channel for submitting the ballots.

On our way, we develop new traceable receipt-free encryption (TREnc) mechanisms that are secure under SXDH, assuming a public coin CRS. This last assumption brings a noticeable benefit over the existing mechanisms, which required a structured CRS, bringing the question of the practical generation of this CRS, and of the underlying trust assumptions.

We demonstrate the efficiency of our mechanism through a prototype implementation. While demanding, they still support encryption and ciphertext verification under a second of time. It would be appealing to explore solutions that could reduce the complexity of this encryption process, both in time and in space.

Acknowledgments. Thomas Peters is a research associate of the Belgian Fund for Scientific Research (F.R.S.-FNRS). This work has been funded in part by the Walloon Region through the project CyberExcellence (convention number 2110186).

A Scheme Description for Complex Ballots

Gen(1^λ): Choose bilinear groups $(\mathbb{G}, \hat{\mathbb{G}}, \mathbb{G}_T)$ of prime order $p > 2^{\mathsf{poly}(\lambda)}$ together with $g, h, g_1, h_1 \xleftarrow{\$} \mathbb{G}$ and $\hat{g}, \hat{h} \xleftarrow{\$} \hat{\mathbb{G}}$.

1. Pick random $\{(\alpha_i, \beta_i)\}_{i=1}^2 \xleftarrow{\$} \mathbb{Z}_p$ and set $\{\hat{f}_i\}_{i=1}^2 = \hat{g}^{\alpha_i}\hat{h}^{\beta_i}$. Pick random $\alpha, \beta \xleftarrow{\$} \mathbb{Z}_p$ and set $f = g^\alpha h^\beta$.
2. Generate Groth-Sahai CRS $\mathbf{u} = (\vec{u}_1, \vec{u}_2) \in \mathbb{G}^4$, $\mathbf{u}' = (\vec{u}'_1, \vec{u}'_2) \in \mathbb{G}^4$ and $\mathbf{v} = (\vec{v}_1, \vec{v}_2) \in \hat{\mathbb{G}}^4$ to commit to groups elements of $\mathbb{G}$ and $\hat{\mathbb{G}}$, where $\vec{u}'_1 = (u'_{11}, u'_{12}) = (g, h)$, $\vec{u}'_2 = (u'_{21}, u'_{22}) = (g_1, h_1)$, $\vec{v}_1 = (v_{11}, v_{12})$, and $\vec{v}_2 = (v_{21}, v_{22})$ are generated in the perfect NIWI mode.
3. Pick random $k_1, k_2 \leftarrow \mathbb{G}$ that will be used as a verification key for the LHSP signature.

The private key is $\mathsf{SK} = (\alpha_1, \beta_1, \alpha_2, \beta_2, \alpha, \beta)$ and the public key $\mathsf{PK} = (g, h, g_1, h_1, \hat{g}, \hat{h}, f, \hat{f}_1, \hat{f}_2, k_1, k_2, \mathbf{u}, \mathbf{v}, \mathbf{u}')$.

Enc(PK, M): To encrypt a message $M \in \mathbb{G}$, first run $\mathsf{LGen}(\mathsf{PK})$: Generate a key pair $(\mathsf{osk}, \mathsf{opk})$ for the one-time linearly homomorphic signature from the public generators $\hat{g}, \hat{h}$ in order to sign vectors of dimension 3. Let the signing key $\mathsf{lk} = \mathsf{osk} = \{(\eta_i, \zeta_i)\}_{i=1}^3$, the corresponding public key is $\mathsf{opk} = \{\hat{y}_i\}_{i=1}^3$. Then, conduct the following steps of $\mathsf{LEnc}(\mathsf{PK}, \mathsf{lk}, M)$:

1. <u>In the ciphertext CT:</u>
   (a) For random $r, s \xleftarrow{\$} \mathbb{Z}_p$, compute the commitments $d_1 = Mg^r h^s \in \mathbb{G}, d_2 = g_1^r h_1^s \in \mathbb{G}$ and the openings $\hat{R} = \hat{g}^r \in \hat{\mathbb{G}}, \hat{S} = \hat{g}^s \in \hat{\mathbb{G}}$. Randomly choose $\theta, \gamma \xleftarrow{\$} \mathbb{Z}_p$, compute the ciphertexts of M, $\hat{R}$, and $\hat{S}$ respectively as $\mathbf{c}_m = (c_m^0, c_m^1, c_m^2) = (Mf^\theta, g^\theta, h^\theta)$, $\mathbf{c}_r = (c_r^0, c_r^1, c_r^2) = (\hat{R}\hat{f}_1^\gamma, \hat{g}^\gamma, \hat{h}^\gamma)$, and $c_s = \hat{S}\hat{f}_2^\gamma$.
   (b) Commit to the openings using the Groth-Sahai CRS by computing $\mathbf{C}_M = \iota_1(M)\vec{u}_1^{z_1}\vec{u}_2^{z_2}$, $\mathbf{C}_{\hat{R}} = \iota_1(\hat{R})\vec{v}_1^{r_1}\vec{v}_2^{r_2}$, and $\mathbf{C}_{\hat{S}} = \iota_1(\hat{S})\vec{v}_1^{t_1}\vec{v}_2^{t_2}$ for random $z_1, z_2, r_1, r_2, t_1, t_2 \xleftarrow{\$} \mathbb{Z}_p$. For the sake of simplicity, from now we denote the GS commitments as $\mathbf{C}_M = \mathsf{Com}(\mathbf{u}, M), \mathbf{C}_{\hat{R}} = \mathsf{Com}(\mathbf{v}, \hat{R})$, and $\mathbf{C}_{\hat{S}} = \mathsf{Com}(\mathbf{v}, \hat{S})$. Next, derive the commitments $\mathbf{C}_f = \iota_1(c_m^0)/\mathbf{C}_M$, $\mathbf{C}_{\hat{f}_1} = \iota_2(c_r^0)/\mathbf{C}_{\hat{R}}$, and $\mathbf{C}_{\hat{f}_2} = \iota_2(c_s)/\mathbf{C}_{\hat{S}}$.
   (c) To allow simulating the proof, set the bit $\bar{b} = 1$ and compute $G = g^{\bar{b}} \in \mathbb{G}$ and $\hat{G} = \hat{g}^{\bar{b}} \in \hat{\mathbb{G}}$. Commit to $G, \hat{G}$ to have $\mathbf{C}_G = \mathsf{Com}(\mathbf{u}, G)$, $\mathbf{C}_{\hat{G}} = \mathsf{Com}(\mathbf{v}, \hat{G})$. Compute GS proof π_b such that $e(g, \hat{G}) = e(G, \hat{g})$.
   (d) To ensure CT is well-formed, the proof π_θ is computed to make sure that $(c_m^1, c_m^2, c_m^0/M)$ and $(c_r^1, c_r^2, c_r^0/\hat{R}, c_s/\hat{S})$ are in the form of $(g, h, f)^\theta$ and $(\hat{g}, \hat{h}, \hat{f}_1, \hat{f}_2)^\gamma$ respectively. To do that, commit also to $\hat{G}^\theta$ and G^γ such that $\mathbf{C}_\theta = \mathsf{Com}(\mathbf{v}, \hat{G}^\theta)$ and $\mathbf{C}_\gamma = \mathsf{Com}(\mathbf{u}, G^\gamma)$, and compute a GS proof π_θ that

$$e(c_m^1, \hat{G}) = e(g, \hat{G}^\theta), e(c_m^2, \hat{G}) = e(h, \hat{G}^\theta), \quad e(G, c_r^1) = e(G^\gamma, \hat{g}),$$
$$e(G, c_r^2) = e(G^\gamma, \hat{h}), e(f^\theta, \hat{G}) = e(f, \hat{G}^\theta), \quad e(G, \hat{f}_1^\gamma) = e(G^\gamma, \hat{f}_1),$$
$$e(G, \hat{f}_2^\gamma) = e(G^\gamma, \hat{f}_2).$$

(e) Return $CT = (\mathbf{c}_m, \mathbf{c}_r, c_s, \mathbf{C}_G, \mathbf{C}_\theta, \mathbf{C}_\gamma, \pi_b, \pi_\theta) \in \mathbb{G}^{27} \times \hat{\mathbb{G}}^{26}$.

2. <u>In the commitment D</u>:
   (a) *The proof of the openings for commitments*: The proof of openings π_{open} needs to make sure that the values committed in $\mathbf{C}_M, \mathbf{C}_{\hat{R}}, \mathbf{C}_{\hat{S}}, \mathbf{C}_{\hat{G}}$ in CT are the openings of the commitments. In other words, $\mathbf{C}_M, \mathbf{C}_{\hat{R}}, \mathbf{C}_{\hat{S}}$, and $\mathbf{C}_{\hat{G}}$ must ensure that $e(M, \hat{g}) \cdot e(g, \hat{R}) \cdot e(h, \hat{S}) = e(d_1, \hat{G})$ and $e(g_1, \hat{R}) \cdot e(h_1, \hat{S}) = e(d_2, \hat{G})$.
   (b) *Traceability property*: Sign each row of the matrix T using $\mathsf{lk} = \mathsf{osk}$ to have signatures $\sigma_1, \sigma_2, \sigma_3$, where $\sigma_i = (Z_i, R_i) \in \mathbb{G}^2$ for $i = 1, 2, 3$.

$$T = \begin{pmatrix} g & d_1 & d_2 \\ 1 & g & g_1 \\ 1 & h & h_1 \end{pmatrix}$$

   Next, commit to σ_1 using $\mathbf{u}'$ with $\mathbf{C}_Z = \mathsf{Com}(\mathbf{u}', Z_1)$ and $\mathbf{C}_R = \mathsf{Com}(\mathbf{u}', R_1)$. To ensure that σ_1 is a valid one-time LHSP signature on (g, d_1, d_2), compute the proof $\pi_{sig} \in \hat{\mathbb{G}}^2$ such that $e(Z_1, \hat{g}) \cdot e(R_1, \hat{h}) = e(g, \hat{y}_1) \cdot e(d_1, \hat{y}_2) \cdot e(d_2, \hat{y}_3)$.
   (c) *TCCA security*: Set $\hat{A} = 1_{\hat{\mathbb{G}}}, \hat{B} = 1_{\hat{\mathbb{G}}}$, $\hat{X} = \hat{g}/\hat{G} = \hat{g}^{1-\bar{b}}$, and $\tau = \mathsf{Hash}(\mathsf{opk})$. Commit to $\hat{A}$ and $\hat{B}$ using CRS $\mathbf{v}$. Compute the proof π_{ss} that $e(g, \hat{A}) \cdot e(h, \hat{B}) = e(k_1 k_2^\tau, \hat{g}/\hat{G})$.
   (d) Return $D = (d_1, d_2, \mathbf{C}_M, \mathbf{C}_{\hat{R}}, \mathbf{C}_{\hat{S}}, \mathbf{C}_{\hat{G}}, \mathbf{C}_Z, \mathbf{C}_R, \mathbf{C}_{\hat{A}}, \mathbf{C}_{\hat{B}}, \pi_{open}, \sigma_2, \sigma_3, \pi_{sig}, \pi_{ss}, \mathsf{opk}) \in \mathbb{G}^{20} \times \hat{\mathbb{G}}^{19}$.

At the end of the encryption, output $C = (CT, D) \in \mathbb{G}^{47} \times \hat{\mathbb{G}}^{45}$.

Trace(PK, C): Parse PK and C as above, and output opk in the obvious way.

Rand(PK, C): If PK and $C = (CT, D)$ do not parse as the outputs of Gen and Enc, abort. Otherwise, conduct the similar steps as presented in $\mathsf{Rand}(\mathsf{PK}, C)$ (Sect. 3.1). At the end of the randomization, output the ciphertext $C' = (CT', D')$.

Ver (PK, C): First, abort and output 0 if either PK or C fails to parse correctly. Second, verify the validity of the signatures σ_2 and σ_3 on the 2 last rows of the matrix T, and output 0 if it does not hold. Third, verify all the provided GS proofs $\pi_b, \pi_\theta, \pi_{open}, \pi_{sig}$, and π_{ss} regarding their the corresponding equations. The first two proofs will be privately verified, which concerns the CPA encryption part, while the others will be checked publicly on PB. If at least one of these checks fails, output 0; otherwise, output 1.

Dec(SK, C): If $\mathsf{Ver}(\mathsf{PK}, C) = 0$, output $\perp$. Otherwise, given $\mathsf{SK} = (\alpha_1, \beta_1, \alpha_2, \beta_2, \alpha, \beta)$ and $(\mathbf{c}_m = (c_m^0, c_m^1, c_m^2), \mathbf{c}_r = (c_r^0, c_r^1, c_r^2), c_s)$ included in CT, output $M = c_m^0 \cdot {c_m^1}^{-\alpha} \cdot {c_m^2}^{-\beta}$, $\hat{R} = c_r^0 \cdot {c_r^1}^{-\alpha_1} \cdot {c_r^2}^{-\beta_1}$, and $\hat{S} = c_s \cdot {c_r^1}^{-\alpha_2} \cdot {c_r^2}^{-\beta_2}$.

The security analysis of this second scheme directly follows that of our first construction.

B Deferred Proofs

B.1 Correctness

The construction satisfies TREnc's correctness as defined in Definition 2.1.

Correctness of encryption compatibility By construction, we define Enc such that the distributions of $\mathsf{Enc}(\mathsf{PK}, m)$ and $\mathsf{LEnc}(\mathsf{PK}, \mathsf{LGen}(\mathsf{PK}), m)$ are identical.

Correctness of link traceability For every PK in the range of Gen, the scheme runs $\mathsf{LGen}(\mathsf{PK})$ to output a key pair $(\mathsf{osk}, \mathsf{opk})$ for the one-time linearly homomorphic signature, where $\mathsf{opk} = f(\mathsf{osk})$ for a deterministic function f. Then, for every $\mathsf{lk} = \mathsf{osk}$ in the range of $\mathsf{LGen}(\mathsf{PK})$, $\mathsf{LEnc}(\mathsf{PK}, \mathsf{lk}, m)$ produces a ciphertext C, where $\mathsf{Trace}(\mathsf{PK}, C) = f(\mathsf{osk}) = \mathsf{opk}$. That is, $\mathsf{Trace}(\mathsf{PK}, \mathsf{LEnc}(\mathsf{PK}, \mathsf{lk}, \cdot))$ is the constant function $f(\mathsf{osk}) = \mathsf{opk}$.

Correctness of publicly traceable randomization As described in 3.1, the trace opk is kept unchanged in randomization step. Thus, we have $\mathsf{Trace}(\mathsf{PK}, C)$ $= \mathsf{Trace}(\mathsf{PK}, \mathsf{Rand}(\mathsf{PK}, C))$ by definition. Additionally, in Rand algorithm, we honestly randomize the CPA part of the ciphertext, where $\mathbf{c}'_m = \mathbf{c}_m \cdot (f_1, g_1, h_1)^{\theta'} = (M f_1^{\theta+\theta'}, g_1^{\theta+\theta'}, h_1^{\theta+\theta'})$ with $\theta' \xleftarrow{\$} \mathbb{Z}_p$. Obviously, $\mathbf{c}'_m$ is distributed exactly as a fresh CPA encryption of m since $\theta + \theta'$ is random over $\mathbb{Z}_p$. There exists no random θ' that can modify the message, even the coin might not have been taken from a uniform distribution. Hence, $\mathsf{Dec}(\mathsf{SK}, C) = \mathsf{Dec}(\mathsf{SK}, \mathsf{Rand}(\mathsf{PK}, C))$.

Correctness of honest verifiability Given a ciphertext C in an honest range of $\mathsf{Enc}(\mathsf{PK}, m)$, there exists random coins that explain how to compute the ciphertext. This always leads to valid GS proofs and valid LHSP signatures. Based on that, we have verifiability since all the verification equations are satisfied. In other words, thanks to the perfect correctness of GS proofs and LHSP signatures, if C is honestly generated, for all the coins, we have validity or $\mathsf{Ver}(\mathsf{PK}, \mathsf{Enc}(\mathsf{PK}, m)) = 1$.

B.2 Strong Randomizability

Theorem 3.1. *The TREnc is perfectly strongly randomizable. More precisely, for every* $c \in \mathsf{LEnc}(\mathsf{PK}, \mathsf{lk}, m)$ *with* pk *in the range of* Gen *and* lk *in the range of* $\mathsf{LGen}(\mathsf{PK})$, *the distributions* $\{\mathsf{Rand}(\mathsf{PK}, c)\}$ and $\{\mathsf{LEnc}(\mathsf{PK}, \mathsf{lk}, m)\}$ *are identical.*

Proof. Given a ciphertext $C = (CT, D)$ in the range of $\mathsf{Enc}(\mathsf{PK}, m)$, for some message m and internal link key $\mathsf{lk} = \mathsf{osk}$, the perfect correctness of honest verifiability of our TREnc implies that C is valid. It is easy to see that the opening values R, Q are fully redistributed as uniform group elements during rerandomization. The CPA part is then also fully rerandomized and distributed as a fresh CPA part. In the WI mode, valid GS-proofs can also be perfectly rerandomized and fully redistributed after adaptation. Finally, the LHSP signatures on the last two rows of the T-matrix are deterministic. The indistinguishability is actually perfect.

B.3 TCCA Security

Theorem 3.2. *The above scheme is TCCA-secure under the SXDH assumption and the collision resistance of the hash function. More precisely, we have* $\left|\Pr[\mathsf{Exp}^{\mathsf{tcca}}_{\mathcal{A}}(\lambda) = 1] - \frac{1}{2}\right| \leq \epsilon_{cr} + 6\epsilon_{sxdh} + \frac{4}{p}$.

Proof. We consider a sequence of games. In Game i, we denote by S_i the event that an adversary $\mathcal{A}$ wins by correctly guessing the internal random bit b of the game, which makes the game output 1.

$\mathsf{Game}_1(\lambda)$: This is the real game as described in the experiment Fig. 1. By definition, $\Pr[S_1] = \Pr[\mathsf{Exp}^{\mathsf{tcca}}_{\mathcal{A}}(\lambda) = 1]$.

$\mathsf{Game}_2(\lambda)$: In this game, we introduce a failure event F_2 which causes this game to abort and output a random bit if the adversary produces two valid ciphertexts C and C' as output of Enc such that $\mathsf{Hash}(\mathsf{opk}) = \mathsf{Hash}(\mathsf{opk}')$ but $\mathsf{opk} \neq \mathsf{opk}'$. This even prevents the situation when $\mathcal{A}$ can successfully use the same tag with different signatures in decryption queries after the challenge phase. F_2 implies a collision on the hash function, so $\Pr[F_2] = \epsilon_{cr}$. We thus have, $|\Pr[S_2] - \Pr[S_1]| \leq \Pr[F_2] = \epsilon_{cr}$.

$\mathsf{Game}_3(\lambda)$: This game is as Game 2 except that we introduce a failure event which occurs during the challenge phase if $\mathcal{A}$ can produce the valid ciphertexts C_0, C_1 but $(\hat{\sigma}_2^{(0)}, \hat{\sigma}_3^{(0)}) \neq (\hat{\sigma}_2^{(1)}, \hat{\sigma}_3^{(1)})$. The event should be aborted since the challenge ciphertext C^* has the same values of $(\hat{\sigma}_2^*, \hat{\sigma}_3^*)$ as the ones in C_0 or C_1. This causes a distinguishability between them. Obviously, $|\Pr[S_0] - \Pr[S_1]|$ is bounded by the probability that $(\hat{\sigma}_2^{(0)}, \hat{\sigma}_3^{(0)})$ and $(\hat{\sigma}_2^{(1)}, \hat{\sigma}_3^{(1)})$ are 2 distinct signatures on the same vector. Thus, $|\Pr[S_3] - \Pr[S_2]| \leq \epsilon_{sxdh}$.

$\mathsf{Game}_4(\lambda)$: This game is the same as Game 3 except in the way we generate the challenge ciphertext C^* from C_b in the randomization step. When we generate PK, we compute $\hat{f}_1, \hat{f}_2$ in such a way that they are corresponding verification keys for a signing key $\mathsf{sk_{lhsp}}$ of a one-time linearly homomorphic signature in order to sign vectors of dimension $n = 2$, given the common public parameters $\hat{g}, \hat{h}$. We keep in memory $\mathsf{sk_{lhsp}}$ and output $\mathsf{pk_{lhsp}} = \{\hat{f}_1, \hat{f}_2\}$. Since the distribution of the output is not changed, it is indistinguishable from $\mathcal{A}$'s view. The simulated randomization is as follows:

1. Randomizing D^*
   (a) For the proof of openings π^*_{open}
   - Randomize the commitments $\hat{d}_1^* = \hat{d}_1^{(b)} \cdot \hat{g}_1^{r^*} \hat{h}_1^{q^*}$, $\hat{d}_2^* = \hat{d}_2^{(b)} \cdot \hat{g}_2^{r^*} \hat{h}_2^{q^*}$ for $r^*, q^* \xleftarrow{\$} \mathbb{Z}_p$.
   - Switch $\bar{b} = 0$, then we have $G^* = g^{\bar{b}} = 1_{\mathbb{G}} \in \mathbb{G}$. Re-compute the commitment of G^* by $\mathbf{C}^*_G = \mathsf{Com}(\mathbf{u}, 1_{\mathbb{G}})$. Since CRS $\mathbf{u}$ is generated in the perfect NIWI mode, the resulting commitments

and proofs are distributed among all the possible group elements that satisfy the verification equation. That means, it is not able to distinguish between $\mathbf{C}_G = \mathsf{Com}(\mathbf{u}, g)$ and $\mathbf{C}_G^* = \mathsf{Com}(\mathbf{u}, 1_{\mathbb{G}})$.

 - Similarly, update randomized commitments $\mathbf{C}_M^* = \mathsf{Com}(\mathbf{u}, 1_{\mathbb{G}})$, $\mathbf{C}_R^* = \mathsf{Com}(\mathbf{u}, 1_{\mathbb{G}})$, and $\mathbf{C}_Q^* = \mathsf{Com}(\mathbf{u}, 1_{\mathbb{G}})$. The Eqs. 4.a and 4.b are verified as valid since both sides of the equations are equal to 1. Then, update the simulated proof $\pi_{open}^* = (\pi_{4.a}^*, \pi_{4.b}^*)$ with corresponding randomness. Since GS proof is WI, the simulated proof cannot be distinguished from a real one.

(b) For the proof of signature π_{sig}^*, it is done as usual as Rand would do.

(c) For the proof of simulation soundness π_{ss}^*

 - Since $\bar{b}$ is switched to 0, $X^* = g^{1-\bar{b}} = g \in \mathbb{G}$. Adapt the commitment of X^* to be $\mathbf{C}_X^* = \iota_1(g)/\mathbf{C}_G^* = \mathsf{Com}(\mathbf{u}, g)$.
 - We simulate the proof π_{ss}^* by resigning the message $(X^*, X^{*\tau^*})$ from scratch using the secret key $\mathsf{sk_{lhsp}}$ at step 2c. That is, when we randomize $\mathbf{C}_A^{(b)}, \mathbf{C}_B^{(b)}$ from an adversary, first computing the LHSP signature (A^*, B^*) on $(X^*, X^{*\tau^*})$. In other words, $(A^*, B^*) = \mathtt{Sign}(\mathsf{sk_{lhsp}}, (X^*, X^{*\tau^*}))$, where $\tau^* = \mathsf{Hash}(\mathsf{opk}_0) = \mathsf{Hash}(\mathsf{opk}_1) = \tau^b$. The Eq. 7 is still valid since $\hat{f}_1, \hat{f}_2$ was generated as the public verification keys corresponding to $\mathsf{sk_{lhsp}}$. Indeed, since $\mathbf{C}_A', \mathbf{C}_B'$ computed in Rand and $\mathbf{C}_A^*, \mathbf{C}_B^*$ are indistinguishable under NIWI CRS, their distributions are exactly the same in the adversary's view.
 - Commit to (A^*, B^*) by computing $\mathbf{C}_A^* = \mathsf{Com}(\mathbf{u}, A^*)$, $\mathbf{C}_B^* = \mathsf{Com}(\mathbf{u}, B^*)$, then adapt the correspondingly simulated proof π_{ss}^*. As a side effect, π_{ss}^* is a valid proof of a false statement, where X is no longer equal to $1_{\mathbb{G}}$ as in Enc.

(d) For the proof π_{01}^*, since $\mathbf{C}_M^* = \mathsf{Com}(\mathbf{u}, 1_{\mathbb{G}})$, we update $\mathbf{C}_{\hat{M}^*} = \mathsf{Com}(\mathbf{v}, 1_{\hat{\mathbb{G}}})$. The Eq. 8 is valid as both sides of the equations are equal to 1. Then, compute the simulated proof π_{01}^* accordingly.

2. Randomizing CT^*
 - Parse the CPA encryption part and randomize it as Rand at step 1a.
 - Since $\bar{b} = 0$, recompute $\hat{H} = \hat{h}^{\bar{b}} = 1$ and $\hat{H}^\theta = 1$. Compute the corresponding commitments $\mathbf{C}_{\hat{H}}^* = \mathsf{Com}(\mathbf{v}, 1_{\hat{\mathbb{G}}})$ and $\mathbf{C}_\theta^* = \mathsf{Com}(\mathbf{v}, 1_{\hat{\mathbb{G}}})$. The verification Eqs. 2 and 3 are all valid since both sides are equal to 1. As a consequence, the encryption part is no more in the range of the honest CPA encryptions of $\mathsf{Dec}(\mathsf{SK}, C_b)$ except with probability $1/p$. Next, compute the proof π_b^* and π_θ^* as in Enc.

Game 3 and Game 4 abort in the same cases. When both games do not abort, their views are exactly the same thanks to the perfect witness indistinguishability of GS proofs. Particularly, the distributions of π_{ss}^* and randomized π_{ss}' are indistinguishable. We thus have $\Pr[S_4] = \Pr[S_3]$.

$\mathsf{Game}_5(\lambda)$**:** This game is as the previous game except that the Groth Sahai CRS $\mathbf{u}$ and $\mathbf{v}$ of the public key are now generated in the extractable mode. Namely, we pick $\vec{u}_1 \stackrel{\$}{\leftarrow} \mathbb{G}^2$, $\gamma \stackrel{\$}{\leftarrow} \mathbb{Z}_p$, and compute $\vec{u}_2 = \vec{u}_1^{\gamma}$. The CRS forms a random DH tuple over $\mathbb{G}$. Thus, $|\Pr[S_5] - \Pr[S_4]| \leq 2\epsilon_{sxdh}$.

$\mathsf{Game}_6(\lambda)$: We bring the following modification to the previous game. When sampling CRS $\mathbf{u} = (\vec{u}_1, \vec{u}_1^{\gamma})$, we compute $\vec{u}_1 = (u_{11}, u_{12})$, where $u_{12} = u_{11}^{\mu}$ with $\mu \stackrel{\$}{\leftarrow} \mathbb{Z}_p$. As per [23], the distribution of the public key is unchanged, but we keep μ as an ElGamal secret key to extract the committed group elements of the Groth-Sahai commitments. Moreover, when receiving $\mathbf{C}_A^{(b)}, \mathbf{C}_B^{(b)}, \mathbf{C}_G^{(b)}$ from the adversary, we extract some $A^{(b)}, B^{(b)}, G^{(b)} \in \mathbb{G}$. Here, we introduce a failure event F_6 when $\mathcal{A}$ can produce a valid signature satisfying Eq. 7 when $G^{(b)} \neq g$ (and then $\hat{H}^{(b)} \neq \hat{h}$) in at least one of the following situations: in any pre-challenge decryption query, in the challenge phase with C_0 or C_1. In other words, we reject all the valid ciphertexts in the sense of Game 5 for which $\pi_{ss}^{(b)}$ is a valid proof for a false statement. As a result, we abort and output 0 if the adversary can successfully create a valid but dishonest signature $(A^{(b)}, B^{(b)})$ on a message different from (1, 1). We have $|\Pr[S_6] - \Pr[S_5]| \leq \Pr[F_6]$.
To compute $\Pr[F_6]$, let $(A^{\dagger}, B^{\dagger})$ the honest signature on $g/G^{(b)}$, $(A^{\dagger}, B^{\dagger}) = \mathtt{Sign}(\mathsf{sk}_{\mathsf{lhsp}}, (g/G^{(b)}, g/G^{(b)^{\tau}})$. There are 2 cases that F_6 can occur: (1) The adversary $\mathcal{A}$ can correctly guess $(A^{(b)}, B^{(b)}) = (A^{\dagger}, B^{\dagger})$ with a probability of $1/p$ or (2) $(A^{(b)}, B^{(b)}) \neq (A^{\dagger}, B^{\dagger})$ is a valid but dishonest signature on $(g/G^{(b)}, (g/G^{(b)})^{\tau})$. Considering the second case, we have both $(A^{\dagger}, B^{\dagger})$ and $(A^{(b)}, B^{(b)})$ satisfying Eq. 7 with the same right-hand side member. This implies an SXDH distinguisher. We thus have $\Pr[F_6] \leq 1/p + (1-1/p)\epsilon_{sxdh} \leq 1/p + \epsilon_{sxdh}$, therefore $|\Pr[S_6] - \Pr[S_5]| \leq 1/p + \epsilon_{sxdh}$.

$\mathsf{Game}_7(\lambda)$: This game is the same as Game 6 except that we introduce a failure event when $\mathcal{A}$ can produce a valid signature when $G^{(i)} \neq g$ in post-challenge decryption query with $\mathrm{Trace}(\mathsf{PK}, C^{(i)}) \neq \mathsf{opk}^*$. Similarly to the previous game, when receiving $\mathbf{C}_A^{(i)}, \mathbf{C}_B^{(i)}, \mathbf{C}_G^{(i)}$ from the adversary for a decryption query, we extract some $A^{(i)}, B^{(i)}, G^{(i)} \in \mathbb{G}$. Since $\mathcal{A}$ has to use a different tag $\tau \neq \tau^*$ for post-challenge decryption queries, the message $(X^{(i)}, X^{(i)^{\tau}}) = (g/G^{(i)}, g/G^{(i)^{\tau}})$ is not in $\mathrm{span}\langle(X^*, X^{*\tau^*})\rangle$. Thanks to the unforgeability of the LHSP signature, the validity of Eq. 7 implies trivial, when $X^{(i)} = 1$ and $G^{(i)} = g$. Hence, after observing a simulated proof π_{ss}^* for a false statement in Game 6, the adversary is not able to validate another falsely simulated proof for a false statement. Thus, $|\Pr[S_7] - \Pr[S_6]| \leq 1/p + \epsilon_{sxdh}$.

$\mathsf{Game}_8(\lambda)$: Up to this point, if the game does not abort, all the ciphertexts from an adversary can not contain a valid signature of a message different to $(1_{\mathbb{G}}, 1_{\mathbb{G}})$. That means all the ciphertexts that will be decrypted are honest and do not reveal any information of SK, except those provided in the challenge phase. In this game, we bring another modification in the way we generate the CPA encryption part. To make sure the challenge ciphertext C^* does not contain any information of which C_b is used in randomization, let us call $G_1 = g_1^{\theta^*} \in \mathbb{G}$, $H_1 = h_1^{\theta^*} \in \mathbb{G}$, since $f_1 = g_1^{\alpha_1} h_1^{\beta_1}$ we compute $F_1 = G_1^{\alpha_1} H_1^{\beta_1}$ using the secret key $\mathsf{SK} = (\alpha_1, \beta_1)$. (g_1, h_1, G_1, H_1) forms a random DDH tuple over $\mathbb{G}$. The challenge ciphertext in Game 4 is then $\mathbf{c}_m^* = (c_0^*, c_1^*, c_2^*) =$

$\mathbf{c}_m^{(b)} \cdot (f_1, g_1, h_1)^{\theta^*} = \mathbf{c}_m \cdot (F_1, G_1, H_1)$. Now, instead of choosing G_1, H_1 like this, we pick random $G_1, H_1 \xleftarrow{\$} \mathbb{G}$ and compute $F_1 = G_1^{\alpha_1} H_1^{\beta_1}$, the tuple (g_1, h_1, G_1, H_1) is a random quadruple in $\mathbb{G}$. As a result, $\mathbf{c}_m^* = (c_0^*, c_1^*, c_2^*) = \mathbf{c}_m \cdot (F_1, G_1, H_1)$ is no more in the range of the honest CPA encryptions of $\mathsf{Dec}(\mathsf{SK},\ C_b)$ except with probability $1/p$. Consequently, π_θ^* is a proof of a false statement but valid since $\hat{H} = \hat{H}^{\theta^*} = 1$ as set in Game 4. Obviously, $\mid \Pr[S_8] - \Pr[S_7] \mid \leq \epsilon_{sxdh}$ since the distinction between them is the distinction between a random DDH tuple and a random quadruple in $\mathbb{G}$.

In fact, after observing the simulated proof π_θ^*, the adversary is not able to do the same, i.e., setting $\hat{H} = \hat{H}^{\theta^*} = 1$. Since π_b^* has to be valid, the soundness of GS proof shows that $(G, \hat{H})$ is in the form of $(g^{\bar{b}}, \hat{h}^{\bar{b}})$. However, $G^{(b)} = g$ because $G^{(b)} \neq g$ is aborted from Game 7. Therefore, $\bar{b} = 1$ and $\hat{H} = \hat{h} \neq 1$.

To conclude, we need to compute the $\Pr[S_8]$. Firstly, we argue that A's view in Game 8 is statistically independent of the hidden bit b. If the game aborts and outputs a random bit, the probability of returning 1 is 1/2. If there is no abort, that is, all the ciphertexts C for decryption queries are honest and $\mathsf{Dec}(\mathsf{SK},\ C)= (c_0 \cdot c_1^{-\alpha_1} \cdot c_2^{-\beta_1})$ does not reveal any additional information about the secret key SK, except what can be inferred from $f_1 = g_1^{\alpha_1} h_1^{\beta_1}$ and $F_1 = G_1^{\alpha_1} H_1^{\beta_1}$, where G_1, H_1 are kept secret during the computation of the challenge ciphertext. Suppose that $G_1 = g_1^y$ and $H_1 = h_1^y f_1^z$ for random $y, z \xleftarrow{\$} \mathbb{Z}_p$, we have $F_1 = f_1^{y+z\beta}$. As a consequence, the computation of $\mathbf{c}_m^* = \mathbf{c}_m^{(b)} \cdot (F_1, G_1, H_1) = (c_0^{(b)} \cdot f_1^{y+z\beta}, c_1^{(b)} \cdot g_1^y, c_2^{(b)} \cdot h_1^y f_1^z)$. If at least one of the two values (y, z) is 0, the probability that $\mathcal{A}$ wins is $P_1 \leq 2/p + 1/p^2$. If both $y, z \neq 0$, $\mathbf{c}_m^*$ is a random triple over $\mathbb{G}^3$, $\mathcal{A}$ wins with the probability of $P_2 = 1/2(1 - 2/p - 1/p^2)$. Finally, the probability that $\mathcal{A}$ wins in this game is $\Pr[S_8] \leq P_1 + P_2 \leq 1/2 + 2/p$.

In summary, we have $\left| \Pr[\mathsf{Exp}_{\mathcal{A}}^{\mathsf{tcca}}(\lambda) = 1] - \frac{1}{2} \right| \leq \epsilon_{cr} + 6\epsilon_{sxdh} + \frac{4}{p}$.

B.4 Traceability

Theorem 3.3. *The above scheme is traceable (Fig. 1) under the SXDH assumption. More precisely, for any adversary $\mathcal{A}$, we have* $\Pr[\mathsf{Exp}_{\mathcal{A}}^{\mathsf{trace}}(\lambda) = 1] \leq 5\epsilon_{sxdh} + \frac{1}{p}$.

Proof. Let $\mathcal{A}$ be an efficient adversary against the traceability of our scheme. We consider a sequence of games. In Game i, we denote by S_i the event that $\mathcal{A}$ wins by correctly guessing the internal random bit b of the game, which makes the game output 1.

$\mathsf{Game}_1(\lambda)$: This is the real game as described in the experiment Fig. 1, where $(\mathsf{PK}, \mathsf{SK}) \leftarrow \mathsf{Gen}(1^\lambda)$. Then, $(m, \mathsf{st}) \leftarrow \mathcal{A}_1(\mathsf{PK}, \mathsf{SK})$, $C = (CT, D) \leftarrow \mathrm{Enc}(\mathsf{PK}, m)$, and $C^* = (CT^*, D^*) \leftarrow \mathcal{A}_2(\mathsf{st}, C)$. By definition, S_1 occurs if $\mathrm{Ver}(\mathsf{PK},\ C^*) = 1$, $\mathrm{Dec}(\mathsf{SK},\ C^*) \neq m$, and $\mathsf{opk}^* = \mathrm{Trace}(\mathsf{PK},\ C^*) = \mathrm{Trace}(\mathsf{PK},\ C) = \mathsf{opk}$. Thus, $\Pr[S_1] = \Pr[\mathsf{Exp}_{\mathcal{A}}^{\mathsf{trace}}(\lambda) = 1]$.

$\mathsf{Game}_2(\lambda)$: This game is as the real game except that the Groth Sahai CRSes $\mathbf{u} = (\vec{u}_1, \vec{u}_2) \in \mathbb{G}^4$ and $\mathbf{v} = (\vec{v}_1, \vec{v}_2), \mathbf{v}' = (\vec{v}'_1, \vec{v}'_2) \in \hat{\mathbb{G}}^4$ of the public key are now generated in the extractable mode. In particular, instead of picking them uniformly at random, we pick them as random Diffie-Hellman tuples over the appropriate groups. Under the DDH assumptions in $\mathbb{G}$ and $\hat{\mathbb{G}}$, the adversary does not notice the difference. Thus, any adversary's behavior to distinguish between Game 1 and Game 2 leads to a SXDH distinguisher. That means $|\Pr[S_1] - \Pr[S_2]| \leq 3\epsilon_{sxdh}$.

$\mathsf{Game}_3(\lambda)$: We introduce one more modification to Game 2 in the way to generate the commitment key $\hat{g}_1, \hat{h}_1, \hat{g}_2, \hat{h}_2$ of PK. Instead of picking them all uniformly over $\hat{\mathbb{G}}$, we pick a random scalar $x \overset{\$}{\leftarrow} \mathbb{Z}_p$ and set $(\hat{g}_2, \hat{h}_2) = (\hat{g}_1, \hat{h}_1)^x$. This modification turns the perfectly hiding commitment $(\hat{d}_1, \hat{d}_2) = (\hat{g}^m, 1) \cdot (\hat{g}_1, \hat{g}_2)^r \cdot (\hat{h}_1, \hat{h}_2)^q$ into an extractable commitment $(\hat{g}^m \hat{g}_1^r \hat{h}_1^q, (\hat{g}_1^r \hat{h}_1^q)^x)$. Moreover, the last two lines of the matrix T in Eq. (5) are now linearly dependent, so that the row space of T is now a 2-dimensional sub-space over $\hat{\mathbb{G}}^3$. By the SXDH assumption, we have $|\Pr[S_2] - \Pr[S_3]| \leq \epsilon_{sxdh}$.

$\mathsf{Game}_4(\lambda)$: This game is the same as the previous game except that we introduce a failure event, which causes the game to be aborted and output 0. When we generate $C \leftarrow \mathsf{Enc}(\mathsf{PK}, m)$ given m from $\mathcal{A}_1$, we first compute $(\mathsf{opk}, \mathsf{osk}) \leftarrow \mathsf{LGen}(\mathsf{PK})$ and then $C \leftarrow \mathsf{LEnc}(\mathsf{PK}, \mathsf{osk}, m)$ as before, but we keep osk. Then, as soon as we get C^* from $\mathcal{A}_2$ with the commitment $(\hat{d}_1^*, \hat{d}_2^*)$, we extract the necessarily valid $\hat{\sigma}_1^* = (\hat{Z}^*, \hat{R}^*)$ LHSP signature from the (now perfectly sound) GS proof and compare it to $\hat{\sigma}_1^\dagger = \mathsf{Sign}(\mathsf{osk}, (\hat{g}, \hat{d}_1^*, \hat{d}_2^*))$. The failure event happens if $\hat{\sigma}_1^* \neq \hat{\sigma}_1^\dagger$. Due to the property of the LHSP signature [28], if we have two distinct signatures on a same vector we can solve the DDH problem. We thus have $|\Pr[S_3] - \Pr[S_4]| \leq \epsilon_{sxdh}$.

We conclude by showing that $\Pr[S_4] = 1/p$. Indeed, S_4 is an event when $\mathcal{A}$ wins by correctly guessing $\hat{\sigma}_1^* = \mathsf{Sign}(\mathsf{osk}, (\hat{g}, \hat{d}_1^*, \hat{d}_2^*))$, but $m \neq \mathsf{Dec}(\mathsf{SK}, C^*)$. That is, $(\hat{g}, \hat{d}_1^*, \hat{d}_2^*)$ is not in the 2-dimensional linear span of the row vectors of T signed in C. Since osk contains enough entropy after C was given to the adversary, $Z^\dagger$ is still unknown and uniform over $\mathbb{G}$. Therefore the probability to have $\hat{Z}^* = \hat{Z}$ is $1/p$.

In summary, we have $\Pr[\mathsf{Exp}_{\mathcal{A}}^{\mathsf{trace}}(\lambda) = 1] \leq 5\epsilon_{sxdh} + \frac{1}{p}$.

B.5 Verifiability

Theorem 3.4. *The above TREnc is verifiable under the SXDH assumption. More precisely, for any adversary* $\mathcal{A}$, *we have* $\Pr[\mathsf{Exp}_{\mathcal{A}}^{\mathsf{ver}}(\lambda) = 1] \leq 3\epsilon_{sxdh} + \frac{1}{p}$.

Proof. Given $(\mathsf{PK}, \mathsf{SK}) \leftarrow \mathsf{Gen}(1^\lambda)$, we have to show that any ciphertext from $\mathcal{A}$ which passes the verification equations is necessarily in the range of the honestly generated encryptions with overwhelming probability. In other words, $\Pr[\mathsf{Exp}_{\mathcal{A}}^{\mathsf{ver}}(\lambda) = 1]$ is defined that if $C \leftarrow \mathcal{A}(\mathsf{PK}, \mathsf{SK})$ is not in the honest encryption range, the probability that it is considered as valid is negligible.

Let $C = (CT, D) \leftarrow \mathcal{A}(\mathsf{PK}, \mathsf{SK})$ satisfying $\mathsf{Ver}(\mathsf{PK}, C) = 1$, where $CT = (\mathbf{c}_m, c_r, c_q, \mathbf{C}_{\hat{H}}, \mathbf{C}_\theta, \pi_b, \pi_\theta)$ and $D = (\hat{d}_1, \hat{d}_2, \mathbf{C}_{\hat{M}}, \mathbf{C}_M, \mathbf{C}_R, \mathbf{C}_Q, \mathbf{C}_G, \mathbf{C}_{\hat{Z}}, \mathbf{C}_{\hat{R}}, \mathbf{C}_A, \mathbf{C}_B, \pi_{open}, \hat{\sigma}_2, \hat{\sigma}_3, \pi_{sig}, \pi_{ss}, \pi_{01}, \mathsf{opk})$.

To show that the CPA part of CT is well formed, we rely on the soundness of the proof related to the CRS $\mathbf{u}, \mathbf{v}$. As in the TCCA proof, we switch these CRSes to the extractable mode, which leads to a security loss of $2\epsilon_{sxdh}$. Next, we extract a witness from the valid proofs associated with $\mathbf{u}, \mathbf{v}$. If $(A, B, X) \neq (1, 1, 1)$, we abort. That is, the adversary manages to produce a valid LHSP signature for the public key $(\hat{f}_1, \hat{f}_2)$. By generating this pair in the key generation so that we know a corresponding secret key, we can show that this happens with negligible probability $\epsilon_{sxdh} + 1/p$ from the LHSP unforgeability. From now on, we can thus assume that the extracted $G = g$, $\hat{H} = \hat{h}$. Therefore, the soundness of GS proofs allows extracting non-trivial witness from the satisfiability of Eq. (3), which shows that $\mathbf{c}_m = (c_0, c_1, c_2)$, c_r and c_q have the expected honest structure.

The LHSP signatures and the GS proof associated with the CRS $\mathbf{v}'$ can always be explained honestly, even if it is not efficient to compute their discrete log representation. The same happens for the perfectly hiding commitment $(\hat{d}_1, \hat{d}_2)$ since we can extract the opening in Eq. (4) with respect to $\mathbf{u}, \mathbf{v}$, which must be consistent with decryption of (M, R, Q). Moreover, $M = g^m$ must be a bit thanks to Eq. (8).

To conclude, we have $\Pr[\mathsf{Exp}^{\mathsf{ver}}_{\mathcal{A}}(\lambda) = 1] \leq 3\epsilon_{sxdh} + \frac{1}{p}$.

References

1. Adida, B.: Helios: web-based open-audit voting. In: Proceedings of the 17th USENIX Security Symposium, pp. 335–348. USENIX Association (2008)
2. Adida, B., de Marneffe, O., Pereira, O., Quisquater, J.: Electing a university president using open-audit voting: analysis of real-world use of Helios. In: 2009 Electronic Voting Technology Workshop/Workshop on Trustworthy Elections, EVT/WOTE '09. USENIX Association (2009)
3. Barreto, P.S.L.M., Naehrig, M.: Pairing-friendly elliptic curves of prime order. In: Preneel, B., Tavares, S. (eds.) SAC 2005. LNCS, vol. 3897, pp. 319–331. Springer, Heidelberg (2006). https://doi.org/10.1007/11693383_22
4. Benaloh, J., Naehrig, M.: Electionguard design specification version 2.0.0. https://www.electionguard.vote/spec/. Accessed Aug 2023
5. Benaloh, J., Tuinstra, D.: Receipt-free secret-ballot elections. In: Proceedings of the Twenty-Sixth Annual ACM Symposium on Theory of Computing, pp. 544–553 (1994)
6. Bernhard, D., Cortier, V., Galindo, D., Pereira, O., Warinschi, B.: SoK: a comprehensive analysis of game-based ballot privacy definitions. In: 2015 IEEE Symposium on Security and Privacy, SP 2015, San Jose, CA, USA, 17–21 May 2015, pp. 499–516. IEEE Computer Society (2015). https://doi.org/10.1109/SP.2015.37
7. Bernhard, D., Cortier, V., Pereira, O., Smyth, B., Warinschi, B.: Adapting Helios for provable ballot privacy. In: Atluri, V., Diaz, C. (eds.) ESORICS 2011. LNCS, vol. 6879, pp. 335–354. Springer, Heidelberg (2011). https://doi.org/10.1007/978-3-642-23822-2_19

8. Bernhard, D., Pereira, O., Warinschi, B.: On necessary and sufficient conditions for private ballot submission. Cryptology ePrint Archive (2012)
9. Blazy, O., Fuchsbauer, G., Pointcheval, D., Vergnaud, D.: Signatures on randomizable ciphertexts. In: Catalano, D., Fazio, N., Gennaro, R., Nicolosi, A. (eds.) PKC 2011. LNCS, vol. 6571, pp. 403–422. Springer, Heidelberg (2011). https://doi.org/10.1007/978-3-642-19379-8_25
10. Boneh, D.: The decision Diffie-Hellman problem. In: Buhler, J.P. (ed.) ANTS 1998. LNCS, vol. 1423, pp. 48–63. Springer, Heidelberg (1998). https://doi.org/10.1007/BFb0054851
11. Canard, S., Schoenmakers, B., Stam, M., Traoré, J.: List signature schemes. Discret. Appl. Math. **154**(2), 189–201 (2006)
12. Chaidos, P., Cortier, V., Fuchsbauer, G., Galindo, D.: Beleniosrf: a non-interactive receipt-free electronic voting scheme. In: Proceedings of the 2016 ACM SIGSAC Conference on Computer and Communications Security, pp. 1614–1625 (2016)
13. Chaum, D., et al.: Scantegrity II: end-to-end verifiability by voters of optical scan elections through confirmation codes. IEEE Trans. Inf. Forensics Secur. **4**(4), 611–627 (2009)
14. Chaum, D., Ryan, P.Y.A., Schneider, S.: A practical voter-verifiable election scheme. In: di Vimercati, S.C., Syverson, P., Gollmann, D. (eds.) ESORICS 2005. LNCS, vol. 3679, pp. 118–139. Springer, Heidelberg (2005). https://doi.org/10.1007/11555827_8
15. Cortier, V., Gaudry, P., Glondu, S.: Belenios: a simple private and verifiable electronic voting system. In: Guttman, J.D., Landwehr, C.E., Meseguer, J., Pavlovic, D. (eds.) Foundations of Security, Protocols, and Equational Reasoning. LNCS, vol. 11565, pp. 214–238. Springer, Cham (2019). https://doi.org/10.1007/978-3-030-19052-1_14
16. Cramer, R., Franklin, M., Schoenmakers, B., Yung, M.: Multi-authority secret-ballot elections with linear work. In: Maurer, U. (ed.) EUROCRYPT 1996. LNCS, vol. 1070, pp. 72–83. Springer, Heidelberg (1996). https://doi.org/10.1007/3-540-68339-9_7
17. Cramer, R., Gennaro, R., Schoenmakers, B.: A secure and optimally efficient multi-authority election scheme. Eur. Trans. Telecommun. **8**(5), 481–490 (1997)
18. Culnane, C., Ryan, P.Y.A., Schneider, S.A., Teague, V.: vvote: A verifiable voting system. ACM Trans. Inf. Syst. Secur. **18**(1), 3:1–3:30 (2015)
19. Cuvelier, É., Pereira, O., Peters, T.: Election verifiability or ballot privacy: do we need to choose? In: Crampton, J., Jajodia, S., Mayes, K. (eds.) ESORICS 2013. LNCS, vol. 8134, pp. 481–498. Springer, Heidelberg (2013). https://doi.org/10.1007/978-3-642-40203-6_27
20. Devillez, H., Pereira, O., Peters, T.: Traceable receipt-free encryption. In: Agrawal, S., Lin, D. (eds.) ASIACRYPT 2022, Part III. LNCS, vol. 13793, pp. 273–303. Springer, Cham (2023). https://doi.org/10.1007/978-3-031-22969-5_10
21. Grewal, G.S., Ryan, M.D., Bursuc, S., Ryan, P.Y.A.: Caveat coercitor: coercion-evidence in electronic voting. In: 2013 IEEE Symposium on Security and Privacy, SP 2013, pp. 367–381. IEEE Computer Society (2013)
22. Grontas, P., Pagourtzis, A., Zacharakis, A., Zhang, B.: Towards everlasting privacy and efficient coercion resistance in remote electronic voting. In: Zohar, A., et al. (eds.) FC 2018. LNCS, vol. 10958, pp. 210–231. Springer, Heidelberg (2019). https://doi.org/10.1007/978-3-662-58820-8_15
23. Groth, J., Sahai, A.: Efficient non-interactive proof systems for bilinear groups. In: Smart, N. (ed.) EUROCRYPT 2008. LNCS, vol. 4965, pp. 415–432. Springer, Heidelberg (2008). https://doi.org/10.1007/978-3-540-78967-3_24

24. Haines, T., Mueller, J., Mosaheb, R., Pryvalov, I.: SoK: secure e-voting with everlasting privacy. In: Proceedings on Privacy Enhancing Technologies (PoPETs) (2023)
25. Hirt, M., Sako, K.: Efficient receipt-free voting based on homomorphic encryption. In: Preneel, B. (ed.) EUROCRYPT 2000. LNCS, vol. 1807, pp. 539–556. Springer, Heidelberg (2000). https://doi.org/10.1007/3-540-45539-6_38
26. Juels, A., Catalano, D., Jakobsson, M.: Coercion-resistant electronic elections. In: Proceedings of the 2005 ACM Workshop on Privacy in the Electronic Society, pp. 61–70 (2005)
27. Kiltz, E., Wee, H.: Quasi-adaptive NIZK for linear subspaces revisited. In: Oswald, E., Fischlin, M. (eds.) EUROCRYPT 2015. LNCS, vol. 9057, pp. 101–128. Springer, Heidelberg (2015). https://doi.org/10.1007/978-3-662-46803-6_4
28. Libert, B., Peters, T., Joye, M., Yung, M.: Linearly homomorphic structure-preserving signatures and their applications. Des. Codes Crypt. **77**, 441–477 (2015)
29. Libert, B., Peters, T., Qian, C.: Structure-preserving chosen-ciphertext security with shorter verifiable ciphertexts. In: Fehr, S. (ed.) PKC 2017. LNCS, vol. 10174, pp. 247–276. Springer, Heidelberg (2017). https://doi.org/10.1007/978-3-662-54365-8_11
30. Locher, P., Haenni, R.: Receipt-free remote electronic elections with everlasting privacy. Ann. Telecommun. **71**, 323–336 (2016)
31. The miraCL core cryptographic library. https://github.com/miracl/core
32. Moran, T., Naor, M.: Receipt-free universally-verifiable voting with everlasting privacy. In: Dwork, C. (ed.) CRYPTO 2006. LNCS, vol. 4117, pp. 373–392. Springer, Heidelberg (2006). https://doi.org/10.1007/11818175_22
33. Okamoto, T.: Receipt-free electronic voting schemes for large scale elections. In: Christianson, B., Crispo, B., Lomas, M., Roe, M. (eds.) Security Protocols 1997. LNCS, vol. 1361, pp. 25–35. Springer, Heidelberg (1998). https://doi.org/10.1007/BFb0028157
34. Ryan, P.Y.A., Rønne, P.B., Iovino, V.: Selene: voting with transparent verifiability and coercion-mitigation. In: Clark, J., Meiklejohn, S., Ryan, P.Y.A., Wallach, D., Brenner, M., Rohloff, K. (eds.) FC 2016. LNCS, vol. 9604, pp. 176–192. Springer, Heidelberg (2016). https://doi.org/10.1007/978-3-662-53357-4_12
35. Sako, K., Kilian, J.: Receipt-free mix-type voting scheme: a practical solution to the implementation of a voting booth. In: Guillou, L.C., Quisquater, J.-J. (eds.) EUROCRYPT 1995. LNCS, vol. 921, pp. 393–403. Springer, Heidelberg (1995). https://doi.org/10.1007/3-540-49264-X_32
36. Wikström, D.: Verificatum. https://www.verificatum.org/. Accessed May 2022

Two-Party Decision Tree Training from Updatable Order-Revealing Encryption

Robin Berger[1(✉)], Felix Dörre[1], and Alexander Koch[2]

[1] KASTEL Security Research Labs, Karlsruhe Institute of Technology, Karlsruhe, Germany
{robin.berger,felix.doerre}@kit.edu
[2] CNRS and IRIF, Université Paris Cité, Paris, France
alexander.koch@irif.fr

Abstract. Running machine learning algorithms on encrypted data is a way forward to marry functionality needs common in industry with the important concerns for privacy when working with potentially sensitive data. While there is already a variety of protocols in this setting based on fully homomorphic encryption or secure multiparty computation (MPC), we are the first to propose a protocol that makes use of a specialized Order-Revealing Encryption scheme. This scheme allows to do secure comparisons on ciphertexts and update these ciphertexts to be encryptions of the same plaintexts but under a new key. We call this notion Updatable Order-Revealing Encryption (uORE) and provide a secure construction using a key-homomorphic pseudorandom function.

In a second step, we use this scheme to construct an efficient three-round protocol between two parties to compute a decision tree (or forest) on labeled data provided by both parties. The protocol is in the passively-secure setting and has some leakage on the data that arises from the comparison function on the ciphertexts. We motivate how our protocol can be compiled into an actively-secure protocol with less leakage using secure enclaves, in a graceful degradation manner, e.g. falling back to the uORE leakage, if the enclave becomes fully transparent. We also analyze the leakage of this approach, giving an upper bound on the leaked information. Analyzing the performance of our protocol shows that this approach allows us to be much more efficient (especially w.r.t. the number of rounds) than current MPC-based approaches, hence allowing for an interesting trade-off between security and performance.

Keywords: Secure Computation · Order-Revealing Encryption · Decision Tree Learning · Enclaves · Privacy-Preserving Machine Learning

1 Introduction

Privacy-preserving machine learning has gained a lot of traction in recent years, due to the tremendous benefits of having automated data-driven decision making,

C. Pöpper and L. Batina (Eds.): ACNS 2024, LNCS 14583, pp. 288–317, 2024.
https://doi.org/10.1007/978-3-031-54770-6_12

while caring for the legitimate privacy interests of the user, especially in a multi-party setting. More importantly, due to legal requirements, many uses of machine learning (ML) algorithms would not even be possible in a setting where access to sensitive information (such as medical data) is required.

One ML algorithm that is relatively popular, due to its simplicity and interpretability, is decision tree learning. It is usually employed in the more general decision forest version. Here, we use a training data set of entries with many attributes and a label, to build a decision tree. This tree branches based on thresholds w.r.t. the attribute values, and has labels annotated to its leaf nodes. To classify a new entry, one follows the tree from the root to a leaf node by comparing the attributes against the thresholds. The classification result is the label annotated to the reached leaf node.

Training such trees via secure multiparty computation has already been proposed by [2,16]. Because this is in a strong privacy model, these protocols are relatively expensive regarding computation and round complexity. The overall round complexity of [16] is $\mathcal{O}(h(\log m + \log n))$, where h is the a priori fixed depth of the tree, m is the number of attributes and n is the number of data entries. Hence, in the setting where they add a realistic 50 ms delay to each message on the network, the overall running time of the protocols increases by several orders of magnitude.

This motivates the following research question: Can we greatly improve the performance and round complexity of the protocol by allowing for some leakage. (This leakage can later be partly avoided again, with the help of secure enclaves.) Ideally, we would want a small constant number of rounds.

As comparisons or sorting are the main ingredients to Decision Tree training algorithms, we propose to use an extended version of Order-Revealing Encryption (ORE). In ORE schemes, the values are encrypted using a secret key, but given two ciphertexts, one can evaluate the order of the messages they encrypt without knowing this key. We extend this by a way to update the ciphertexts to a new key, in a setting where the key space is a multiplicative group. Hence, given a ciphertext $c = \mathsf{Enc}(k, m)$ and second key k', one can run $\mathsf{Upd}(k', c)$ to obtain a new ciphertext c' that is equal to $\mathsf{Enc}(k \cdot k', m)$, making use of key-homomorphic pseudorandom functions (PRFs).

Using this new primitive, which we believe to be of independent interest, we construct a conceptually simple protocol, using only three rounds, that allows two parties to jointly compute a decision tree on their data. Here, the two parties A and B both have a horizontal partition of the data set and B does the main tree computation. In a nutshell this works as follows:

- To have all data points ORE-encrypted under the same keys (using one key per attribute), the parties proceed in a Diffie-Helman key exchange-like manner: B encrypts his data under his keys k_j. A updates these ciphertexts with her keys k'_j, obtaining ciphertexts under $k_j \cdot k'_j$. B then updates these ciphertexts using k_j^{-1}, obtaining ciphertexts under keys k'_j.
- A also sends her own data points encrypted under k'_j to B, together with the used labels (outcome attributes).

- Now, B has all the data points under the same keys k'_j, and can use the comparison function and the labels to compute a decision tree that uses the encrypted values as thresholds.
- B sends this encrypted tree to A, who can now decrypt it using her keys k'_j.

This is a three-round protocol in the honest-but-curious setting, and hence much faster than the MPC protocols of Hamada et al. [16] and Abspoel, Escudero, and Volgushev [2], if one assumes plausible latency. However, this also comes at the cost of considerable overall leakage due to what can be inferred from the comparisons (and the leakage of the ORE scheme), if the scheme is used in the bare (non-enclave) version. We give a more general analysis on the leakage, as well as an information-theoretic upper bound thereof in Sect. 5.

1.1 Related Work

Order-Revealing Encryption. Order-Revealing Encryption (ORE) was introduced by Boneh et al. [5] as a more flexible and more secure notion of Order-Preserving Encryption (OPE). In contrast to OPE, where the natural ordering of ciphertexts must be identical to the natural ordering of the messages they encrypt, Order-Revealing Encryption allows to define a dedicated comparison function on the ciphertexts for evaluating the natural order of the elements contained within the ciphertexts. The main motivation for this was to enable efficient search operations in encrypted databases. Following the introduction of ORE, Chenette et al. [10] formalized security of ORE schemes, as well as giving a construction of such a scheme. This construction inspired a new scheme by Lewi and Wu [23], which is in a slightly different setting, namely the left–right framework, where there are "left" ciphertexts and "right" ciphertexts and a left ciphertext can be compared only with a right ciphertext. To allow for ORE schemes to be used in a multi-user setting, Li, Wang, and Zhao [24] introduced the notion of delegatable ORE schemes, where it is possible to issue comparison tokens, which allows one to compare ciphertexts of different users. In a similar way, Lv et al. [27] extend ORE schemes to a multi-user setting. One problem with this approach, however, is that if one party has a comparison token allowing another party's ciphertexts to be compared to her own, it can decrypt the other party's ciphertexts again.

As ORE schemes allow comparisons of elements, they inherently leak information about the messages encrypted in ciphertexts, as soon as more than one message is encrypted under the same key. This has led to several investigations on how severely this leakage affects the data privacy. Grubbs et al. [15] and Durak, DuBuisson, and Cash [13] have shown that under some circumstances, ORE schemes provide no meaningful security. Jurado, Palamidessi, and Smith [18] however show that ORE schemes still provide some security if the message space is significantly larger than the amount of messages encrypted.

Privacy-Preserving Machine Learning. Since machine learning models have become more widespread, there has been work towards being able to perform the training process thereof in a privacy-preserving manner. Several machine learning models have been considered in this setting, ranging from simple regression tasks [8,19] to neural networks. Approaches for the latter include Fully-Homomorphic Encryption (FHE) [22], and MPC protocols [20]. Multiparty computation has also been used for training decision trees, where it is the most prevalent approach since the work by Lindell and Pinkas [25]. In their work, they discuss how MPC protocols can use the ID3 algorithm for training a decision tree. Since then, there have been several improvements over this work [12,17].

Since the ID3 algorithm only supports discrete attributes, these approaches are not applicable to a setting with with continuous attributes. To overcome this issue, [2] use a variation of the C4.5 algorithm, which also supports continuous attributes. Their protocol works by computing the training process for each possible node in the resulting decision tree. However, this results in the runtime of their protocol being linear in the maximum number of possible nodes in a decision tree, and therefore exponential in the depth of the tree. Hamada et al. [16] improve over this with a protocol, which is linear in the depth of the tree, by partitioning the dataset in an oblivious way and performing the training once for each layer, considering this partitioning. This comes at the cost of requiring many network rounds. While these two state-of-the-art-approaches perform well under ideal circumstances, due to their runtime [2] is not applicable in a setting, where a high-depth decision tree is to be trained and [16] is not applicable in a high-latency environment.

Privacy-Preserving protocols based on fully-homomorphic encryption (FHE) are mostly restricted to decision tree evaluation (e.g. [11,14]) and do not consider the secure training of decision trees. Most of those papers considering training a decision tree, consider a different setting. For example [3] consider the setting, where their goal is to outsource the training to a server, while some of the computationally intensive steps (for FHE) are still done by the client. Hence, it is not directly comparable to our work. Vaidya et al. [32] consider a setting, where the training data is partitioned vertically and FHE is only used to evaluate a heuristic in the training process, but the remaining computation is done in plain text. So far, there are no efficient decision tree training protocols, that perform the entire training using FHE. This is due to the fact that comparisons are computationally expensive in FHE. Indeed, Liu et al. [26] aim to provide a FHE-bsed protocol allowing comparisons in a multi-user setting, however a single plaintext to ciphertext comparison in their case takes a computation time of 100 ms and 1 s for a ciphertext-ciphertext comparison, rendering this approach infeasable in our setting.

1.2 Our Contribution

Our main contributions are as follows:

- We extend the notion of Order-Revealing Encryption (ORE) to Updatable ORE and give an instantiation thereof.

- Using this Updatable ORE scheme, we construct a three-round two-party protocol to compute a decision tree on a horizontal partitioning of a dataset with both parties providing training data. With this approach, we can apply the same training algorithms as used in plaintext training.
- We describe how this protocol can be combined with enclaves providing different security guarantees, in order to eliminate or reduce the introduced ORE leakage and to make the protocol actively secure. We also use an information-theoretic approach to quantify and give an upper bound for the ORE leakage.
- We implemented and experimentally verified the efficiency of our protocol, showing that it is faster than current state-of-the-art protocols, while achieving this speedup at the cost of some information leakage.

1.3 Outline

We introduce necessary preliminaries including the universal composability (UC) model, ORE and decision tree learning in Sect. 2. We propose our notion of Updatable Order-Revealing encryption and also present a construction and a security proof in Sect. 3. Section 4 contains the decision tree learning protocol, together with its security proof, and a remark on how to translate it into an actively-secure version using secure enclaves in a graceful-degradation manner. In Sect. 5, we discuss the implications of the ORE leakage on the protocol. Finally in Sect. 6, we evaluate our constructions based on a practical implementation.

2 Preliminaries

In the remainder of this work, PPT refers to a probabilistic Turing Machine with a polynomial runtime bound. Furthermore, $(\mathbb{G}, p, [1])$ is an additive group of prime order $p > 3$. We use the additive implicit notation for group operations with the group generator $[1]$. In implicit notation, $x \cdot [y] = [x \cdot y]$. In this notation, the DDH assumption means that $([1], [x], [y], [x \cdot y])$ and $([1], [x], [y], [z])$ are computationally indistinguishable for $x, y, z \leftarrow \mathbb{Z}_p^\times$. A function $\mathsf{PRF}\colon \mathbb{Z}_p \times \{0,1\}^* \to \mathbb{G}$ is a pseudorandom function (PRF), if oracle access to PRF with a random key $k \leftarrow \mathbb{Z}_p$ is computationally indistinguishable to oracle access to a random function. A PRF is key-homomorphic, if for all messages $m \in \{0,1\}^*$ and keys $k, k' \in \mathbb{Z}_p$

$$\mathsf{PRF}(k, m) + \mathsf{PRF}(k', m) = \mathsf{PRF}(k + k', m)$$

and therefore also

$$a \cdot \mathsf{PRF}(k, m) = \mathsf{PRF}(a \cdot k, m)$$

for all $a \in \mathbb{Z}_p$.

Naor, Pinkas, and Reingold [28] have constructed a key-homomorphic PRF under the DDH assumption in the random oracle model for $\mathsf{RO}\colon \{0,1\}^* \to \mathbb{G} \setminus \{[0]\}$:

$$\mathsf{PRF}(k, m) := k \cdot \mathsf{RO}(m) \tag{1}$$

2.1 The Universal Composability Model

The universal composability (UC) model introduced by Canetti [7] is a well established security model for cryptographic protocols. It extends from the real-ideal paradigm, meaning that the security of a protocol is captured by an ideal functionality, that is secure by definition. If a protocol is then shown to be secure, relative to an ideal functionality (in which case we say that the *protocol realizes the ideal functionality*), all security guarantees present in the ideal functionality carry over to the protocol. Protocols secure in the universal composition theorem remain secure under universal composition.

For a more in-depth introduction to the UC framework, see Appendix A or [7].

2.2 Order-Revealing Encryption

We follow the definition in [10]. An *ORE scheme* is defined as a 3-tuple of PPT algorithms $\mathsf{ORE} = (\mathsf{Gen}, \mathsf{Enc}, \mathsf{Cmp})$ over message space $\mathcal{M}$, key space $\mathcal{K}$ and ciphertext space $\mathcal{C}$, where

- $\mathsf{Gen}(1^\kappa)$ returns a secret key $k \in \mathcal{K}$
- $\mathsf{Enc}(k, m)$ takes a key $k \in \mathcal{K}$ and a message $m \in \mathcal{M}$ as input and returns a ciphertext $c \in \mathcal{C}$
- $\mathsf{Cmp}(c_0, c_1)$ is a deterministic, takes two ciphertexts $ct_0, ct_1 \in \mathcal{C}$ and returns a bit b or $\perp$.

We require correctness for the scheme:

$$\forall m_0, m_1 \in \mathcal{M}, k \leftarrow \mathsf{Gen}(1^\kappa): \\ \Pr\left[\mathsf{Cmp}(\mathsf{Enc}(k, m_0), \mathsf{Enc}(k, m_1)) = 1 \Leftrightarrow m_0 < m_1\right] \geq 1 - \mathrm{negl}(\kappa).$$

In addition, ORE schemes have an implicit $\mathsf{Dec}(k, c)$ algorithm, which takes a secret key $k \in \mathcal{K}$ and a ciphertext $c \in \mathcal{C}$ and outputs a message $m \in \mathcal{M}$. Dec is implicitly defined using Enc and Cmp to perform a binary search on the message space and return the result or $\perp$ if the ciphertext is invalid under key k.

Security of ORE Schemes. For the security definition of an ORE schemes w.r.t. some leakage function $\mathcal{L}(m_1, \ldots, m_n)$, we use the security notion defined in [10]. Let $\mathsf{ORE} = (\mathsf{Gen}, \mathsf{Enc}, \mathsf{Cmp})$ be an ORE scheme. For some $q = \mathrm{poly}(\kappa)$, let $\mathcal{A}$ be a stateful adversary and let $\mathcal{S}^{\mathsf{ORE}}$ be a stateful simulator. Then, the experiments $\mathsf{REAL}_{\mathcal{A}}^{\mathsf{ORE}}$ and $\mathsf{SIM}_{\mathcal{A},\mathcal{S},\mathcal{L}}^{\mathsf{ORE}}$ are defined as in Fig. 1. We say an ORE scheme ORE is *secure w.r.t. the leakage function* $\mathcal{L}$, if there exists a PPT simulator $\mathcal{S}^{\mathsf{ORE}}$, such that for all PPT adversaries $\mathcal{A}$, the games $\mathsf{REAL}_{\mathcal{A}}^{\mathsf{ORE}}$ and $\mathsf{SIM}_{\mathcal{A},\mathcal{S},\mathcal{L}}^{\mathsf{ORE}}$ are computationally indistinguishable.

$\mathsf{REAL}^{\mathsf{ORE}}_{\mathcal{A}}(\kappa)$:

$k \leftarrow \mathsf{Gen}(1^\kappa)$
$m \leftarrow \mathcal{A}(1^\kappa)$
$ct_1 \leftarrow \mathsf{Enc}(k, m_1)$
for $i = 2, \ldots, q$ **do**
  $m \leftarrow \mathcal{A}(ct_1, \ldots, ct_{i-1})$
  $ct_i = \mathsf{Enc}(k, m)$
end for
output $(ct_1, \ldots, ct_q)$ and the state of $\mathcal{A}$

$\mathsf{SIM}^{\mathsf{ORE}}_{\mathcal{A},\mathcal{S},\mathcal{L}}(\kappa)$:

$M = \emptyset$
$m \leftarrow \mathcal{A}(1^\kappa)$
M.append(m)
$ct_1 \leftarrow \mathcal{S}^{\mathsf{ORE}}(\mathcal{L}(M))$
for $i = 2, \ldots, q$ **do**
  $m \leftarrow \mathcal{A}(ct_1, \ldots, ct_{i-1})$
  M.append(m)
  $ct_i \leftarrow \mathcal{S}^{\mathsf{ORE}}(1^\kappa, \mathcal{L}(M))$
end for
output $(ct_1, \ldots, ct_q)$ and the state of $\mathcal{A}$

Fig. 1. Definition of experiments $\mathsf{REAL}^{\mathsf{ORE}}_{\mathcal{A}}$ and $\mathsf{SIM}^{\mathsf{ORE}}_{\mathcal{A},\mathcal{S},\mathcal{L}}$ for ORE scheme ORE and stateful TMs $\mathcal{A}$ and $\mathcal{S}^{\mathsf{ORE}}$, cf. [10].

Best-Possible Leakage for ORE Schemes. Naturally, one is interested in an ORE scheme with the least amount of leakage. Given t ORE ciphertexts $c_1, \ldots, c_t \in \mathcal{C}$ of messages $m_1, \ldots, m_t \in \mathcal{M}$ under the same key, then for each pair (c_i, c_j), one can inevitably learn whether $m_i \leq m_j$ by using the comparison algorithm. We call a leakage function $\mathcal{L}_{\text{ideal}}$ *best-possible* or *ideal*, if one learns nothing else, i.e., if the leakage is given by

$$\mathcal{L}_{\text{ideal}}(m_1, \ldots, m_t) = \{(i, j) \mid m_i \leq m_j\}.$$

Note that unfortunately there is no known ORE scheme for superpolynomial message space with this ideal leakage, except for one that uses very strong assumptions, such as multilinear maps [5], rendering this scheme unsuitable in practice.

Assumptions on the Leakage Functions. In the remainder of this work, we make a few assumptions about the leakage function.

Assumption 1. $\forall m : \mathcal{L}(m) = \emptyset$.

While one could think of ORE schemes, for which this assumption does not hold, the assumption holds for established schemes like the ones in [10,23], as well as our ORE scheme.

Assumption 2. For t messages $m_1, \ldots, m_t$ and index $0 \leq i \leq t$, it holds that $L^{\leq i} := \mathcal{L}(m_1, \ldots, m_i)$ can be efficiently computed from $L = \mathcal{L}(m_1, \ldots, m_t)$.

While this assumption does not have to hold for all ORE leakage functions, it does hold for leakage functions that tightly capture the leakage of the respective ORE scheme. Again, this assumption holds for the ORE schemes in [10,23], as well as for our ORE scheme.

2.3 Decision Tree Training

We consider a domain with data points x with X continuous attributes x_j and a label $\ell(x)$ from a small discrete set of labels. In this context, a decision tree is a binary tree, where each leaf node contains a label and each inner node contains a tuple (j, t), where j is an index of an attribute and t is a value of the j-th attribute. When performing a classification on a data point x at an inner node (j, t), we recurse to the left child node, if $x_j \leq t$, and to the right child node, otherwise. This is repeated until reaching a leaf node, where the label of the node is returned.

Decision tree training is the task of building a decision tree given a set of labeled training data. Established decision tree frameworks like [1,6] use variations of the recursive C4.5 algorithm by Quinlan [30]. An adaption of this algorithm can be seen in Algorithm 1. One source of variation in this algorithm is the heuristic H used in Line 11. A common example used here is the *Information Gain heuristic.* Following the definition in [21], it is defined as

$$H'(S) = -\sum_{l \in \mathbb{L}} \frac{|\{x \in S\colon \ell(x) = l\}| \log(|\{x \in S\colon \ell(x) = l\}|)}{|S|},$$

$$H(S, L, R) = H'(S) - \frac{|L|}{|S|} H'(L) - \frac{|R|}{|S|} H'(R),$$

where $\mathbb{L}$ is the set of labels. This heuristic describes the information-theoretic gain when separating the set S into sets L and R. Another common heuristic is the GINI Index, which performs nearly identically as the information gain

Algorithm 1. Decision tree training with a heuristic H.

1: **function** TRAINDECISIONTREE(*data*)
2: **assert** $\forall x, y \in data : \exists j : x_j \neq y_j$
3: **if** $\forall x \in data\colon \ell(x) = \ell(data_0)$ **then**
4: **return** LeafNode($\ell(data_0)$)
5: **end if**
6: $j^* := thresh^* := \bot, h^* := -\infty$
7: **for** $1 \leq j \leq X$ **do**
8: $L := \emptyset$
9: **for** $thresh \in \{x_j \mid x \in data\}$ in ascending order **do**
10: $L := L \cup \{x \in data \mid x_j = thresh\}$
11: $h := H(data, L, data \setminus L)$
12: **if** $h > h^*$ **then**
13: $j^* := j, thresh^* := thresh, h^* := h$
14: **end if**
15: **end for**
16: **end for**
17: $L := \{x \in data \mid x_{j^*} \leq thresh^*\}$, $R := data \setminus L$
18: **return** InnerNode(j^*, $thresh^*$, trainDecisionTree(L), trainDecisionTree(R))
19: **end function**

heuristic [31]. The other common variation is the threshold value used in Line 13, where most frameworks use an intermediate value between the threshold and the next larger occurring attribute value. While in a classical setting both the labels as well as the attribute values, are numeric values, we note that the training algorithm itself only needs to evaluate the order of attribute values. This is required in Lines 9, 10 and 17. While one could think of a heuristic H which requires additional operations on the attributes, established heuristics like Information Gain do not consider the attribute values, but only take the labels into consideration.

It is possible to use different training algorithms and variations of trees, such as XBoost [9], which trains gradient-boosted trees. In this approach, the training process requires performing arithmetic operations on the attributes. Another variation is the use of decision forests consisting of multiple decision trees. A classification of a data point in such a decision forest is done by classifying it with each tree and performing a majority vote on the resulting labels. Bentéjac, Csörgő, and Martínez-Muñoz [4] have empirically shown that in a real-world scenario, gradient boosted trees, although requiring arithmetic operations on the training data, do not perform significantly better than decision forest that can be trained with Algorithm 1 only comparing elements and performing equality checks on the labels.

3 Updatable Order-Revealing Encryption

We now augment the definition of ORE to allow for updating a ciphertext from one key to another, while retaining the messages contained in the ciphertexts.

Definition 1 (Updatable ORE). *A 4-tuple of PPT algorithms* $\mathsf{ORE} = (\mathsf{Gen}, \mathsf{Enc}, \mathsf{Cmp}, \mathsf{Upd})$ *is an* Updatable ORE (uORE) scheme *over key space* $\mathcal{K} = \mathbb{Z}_p^\times$*, message space* $\mathcal{M}$ *and ciphertext space* $\mathcal{C}$*, if*

- $(\mathsf{Gen}, \mathsf{Enc}, \mathsf{Cmp})$ *is an ORE scheme over key space* $\mathcal{K}$*, message space* $\mathcal{M}$*, and ciphertext space* $\mathcal{C}$*.*
- $\mathsf{Upd}(k, c)$ *takes a key* $k \in \mathcal{K}$ *and a ciphertext* $c \in \mathcal{C}$ *as input and outputs a new ciphertext* $c' \in \mathcal{C}$*.*
- Enc *and* Upd *are deterministic.*

ORE *is correct, if* $(\mathsf{Gen}, \mathsf{Enc}, \mathsf{Cmp})$ *is a correct ORE scheme and satisfies the updatability property:*

$$\forall k, k' \in \mathcal{K} \colon \mathsf{Upd}(k', \mathsf{Enc}(k, m)) = \mathsf{Enc}(k \cdot k', m)$$

Moreover, ORE *is a* secure uORE scheme w.r.t. a leakage function $\mathcal{L}$ *iff* $(\mathsf{Gen}, \mathsf{Enc}, \mathsf{Cmp})$ *is a secure ORE scheme w.r.t.* $\mathcal{L}$*.*

Note that in our definition, we require that the key space $\mathcal{K} := \mathbb{Z}_p^\times$. This means that any key k is invertible modulo p.

For our construction of an uORE scheme, we adapt the scheme from [10]:

Construction 1. *Let $(\mathbb{G}, p, [1])$ be an additive group with prime order $p > 3$ and let* $\mathsf{PRF}\colon \mathbb{Z}_p \times \{0,1\}^* \to \mathbb{G}$ *be a key-homomorphic PRF with key space $\mathbb{Z}_p$ and message space $\{0,1\}^*$. Then, we define the uORE scheme* $\mathsf{ORE} = (\mathsf{Gen}, \mathsf{Enc}, \mathsf{Cmp}, \mathsf{Upd})$ *with message space $\mathcal{M} = \{0,1\}^n$ for a parameter n, and ciphertext space $\mathcal{C} = \mathbb{G}^n$, as follows:*

- $\mathsf{Gen}(1^\kappa)$: *Return a uniformly random $k \leftarrow \mathbb{Z}_p^\times$*
- $\mathsf{Enc}(k, m = (m_1, \dots, m_n))$: *For $i = 1, \dots, n$, set*

$$u_i = (1 + m_i) \cdot \mathsf{PRF}(k, (m_1, \dots, m_{i-1})).$$

  Return $ct = (u_1, \dots, u_n)$.
- $\mathsf{Cmp}(ct = (u_1, \dots, u_n), ct' = (u'_1, \dots u'_n))$: *Find the smallest i, such that $u_i \neq u'_i$. If such an i exists and $u'_i = 2 \cdot u_i$, return 1. Otherwise, return 0.*
- $\mathsf{Upd}(k', ct = (u_1, \dots, u_n))$: *Set $u'_i = k' \cdot u_i$. Return $ct' = (u'_1, \dots, u'_n)$.*

Our construction is similar to the one by Chenette et al. [10]. In both cases, the key generation algorithm $\mathsf{Gen}(1^\kappa)$ samples a random element from the PRF key space, and $\mathsf{Enc}(k, (m_1, \dots, m_n))$ is done bit by bit, by first computing $u'_i = \mathsf{PRF}(k, (m_1, \dots, m_{i-1}))$ and then returning $u_i = u'_i$ if $m_i = 0$. If $m_i = 1$, both schemes return $u_i = \pi(u'_i)$ for an efficiently invertible permutation π. In both schemes, $\mathsf{Cmp}((u_1, \dots, u_n), (u'_1, \dots, u'_n))$ works by identifying the smallest i, for which $u_i \neq u'_i$ and checking if $u'_i = \pi(u_i)$ with the same permutation.

Comparing these two schemes, the only two differences are the PRF and the permutation π being used. In our scheme, we require the PRF to be key-homomorphic, which does not need to be the case in their scheme. This allows them to use $\mathbb{Z}_3$ as output space of the PRF and $\mathbb{Z}_3^n$ as the ciphertext space, whereas our used ciphertext space is $\mathbb{G}^n$. Moreover, we use $\pi(x) = 2 \cdot x$ as a permutation, whereas in their scheme, $\pi(x) = x + 1 \mod 3$ is used.

Because of this similarity, their security proof and ORE simulator also applies to our construction, when adjusting the permutation. Hence, both schemes are secure under the same leakage function:

Theorem 1. *Construction 1 is secure with the leakage function*

$$\mathcal{L}(m_1, \dots, m_t) = \{(i, j, \mathsf{hsb}(m_i \oplus m_j)) \mid 1 \leq i, j \leq t\},$$

where $\mathsf{hsb}(x)$ returns the position of the highest set bit of x.

Because of the similarity to the proof of [10], we will only give a proof intuition: For (u)ORE security to hold, there needs to be a simulator $\mathcal{S}^{\mathsf{ORE}}$ that, given only the leakage of messages, needs to be able to generate ciphertexts that are indistinguishable from encryptions of the messages with a random but (during the games) fixed key. In a first step, one replaces the PRF with a random function via lazy sampling. When asked to generate the first ciphertext, $\mathcal{S}^{\mathsf{ORE}}$ samples n elements from the output space of the PRF uniformly at random and outputs them as the first ciphertext. When asked to generate ciphertexts for any subsequent messages, it learns the position of the leftmost differing bit between this message and previous messages, as well as the message bit at these positions. This allows it to answer with consistent parts of ciphertexts, where message prefixes are equal, and with $\pi(x)$ or $\pi^{-1}(x)$ where the most significant difference is. Finally, for all other positions, for which no common prefix with another message exists, it proceeds as in the case for the first message, sampling and outputting elements from the output space of the PRF.

Since this proof only requires the security of PRF and the efficient computation/inversion of π, the proof from [10] directly translates to our setting.

Remark 1. The leakage $\mathcal{L}$ of our scheme is actually sufficient to use faster sorting algorithms than plain comparison-based algorithms. For example MSD radix sort uses exactly the information provided by $\mathcal{L}$ to allow sorting in linear time. Sorting all ciphertexts by the first bit is easy, as there are only two comparable group elements for the first bit. After that, sorting the two partitions after the second bit is possible with the same approach. This reduces the amount of group operations required for sorting from $\mathcal{O}(n \log n)$ to $\mathcal{O}(n)$. This is especially interesting, as a main use-case for ORE are encrypted databases, where sorting is a major concern. Large databases often use advanced sorting algorithms that are not comparison-based, so the additional leakage of $\mathcal{L}$ over $\mathcal{L}_{\text{ideal}}$ can be used to speed up sorting.

Theorem 2. *Construction 1 is a correct ORE scheme.*

Proof. Fix two messages $m, m' \in \{0,1\}^n$ with $m = (m_1, \ldots, m_n)$ and $m' = (m'_1, \ldots, m'_n)$. Then, we show that the correctness property holds for any $k \leftarrow \mathsf{Gen}(1^\kappa)$, $(u_1, \ldots, u_n) \leftarrow \mathsf{Enc}(k, m)$ and $(u'_1, \ldots, u'_n) \leftarrow \mathsf{Enc}(k, m')$. We consider each case separately.

- $m < m'$**:** In this case, there exists an i, such that $m_j = m'_j$ for $j < i$ and $m_j = 0$ and $m'_j = 1$. In this case, it holds that $u_j = u'_j$ for $j < i$. For PRF output $o = \mathsf{PRF}(k, (m_1, \ldots, m_{i-1}))$, and by definition of Enc, it holds that $u_i = o$ and $u'_i = 2 \cdot o$. If $o \neq 0_{\mathbb{G}}$, u_i and u'_i are different and Cmp returns 1 in this case. The probability for the event that $o = 0_{\mathbb{G}}$ is negligible (which follows from the fact that this probability is $1/p$ for a random function and because PRF is a PRF). Therefore, Cmp will output 1 with overwhelming probability.
- $m = m'$**:** In this case $u_i = u'_i$ for all i, as Enc is deterministic and Cmp will output 0.
- $m > m'$**:** Similarly to the first case, there exists an i, such that $m_j = m'_j$ for $j < i$ and $m_j = 1$ and $m'_j = 0$. With the same argument as in the case for $m < m'$, we know that $u_j = u'_j$ for $j < i$ and $u_i = 2 \cdot u'_i$. Since $\mathbb{G}$ is of prime order with $p > 3$, it also holds that $u'_i \neq 2 \cdot u_i = 2 \cdot 2 \cdot u'_i$ and therefore Cmp returns 0 with overwhelming probability. □

Theorem 3. *Construction 1 satisfies the updatability property.*

Proof. The updatability follows from the key-homomorphism of PRF. For all $k, k' \in \mathcal{K}$ and $m \in \{0,1\}^n$, it holds that

$$\begin{aligned}\mathsf{Upd}(k', \mathsf{Enc}(k, m)) &= \mathsf{Upd}(k', ((1 + m_i) \cdot \mathsf{PRF}(k, m_{1..i-1}))_{i=1,\dots,n}) \\ &= (k' \cdot (1 + m_i) \cdot \mathsf{PRF}(k, m_{1..i-1}))_{i=1,\dots,n} \\ &= ((1 + m_i) \cdot \mathsf{PRF}(k' \cdot k, m_{1..i-1}))_{i=1,\dots,n} \\ &= \mathsf{Enc}(k' \cdot k, m),\end{aligned}$$

where $m_{1..i-1} := (m_1, \dots, m_{i-1})$. □

4 Secure Decision Tree Training

In our protocol, we want to train a decision tree without revealing the training data, using the previously constructed Updatable ORE scheme. The core idea is to have training data from one party uORE encrypted under a key which the party itself does not know. To accomplish this, we make use of the updatability of the created ciphertexts. In the second step, we apply the decision tree training algorithm in Algorithm 1 to the ORE ciphertexts from the previous step. Here, we make use of the fact that Algorithm 1 only requires the comparability of attributes, and is deterministic.

In principle, any decision tree training algorithm with these properties can be used. While the determinism of the training algorithm is required, de-randomization can be done by prepending the protocol with a secure coin-toss and using these coins as input for the decision tree training. If randomness in the training algorithm does not have a security impact, an alternative and more performant way of de-randomization is to use a non-cryptographic PRG with a fixed seed.

Let us first formalize an ideal functionality that captures the security of secure decision tree protocols.

Definition 2 (Ideal functionality $\mathcal{F}_{\mathsf{DTTrain}}$). *$\mathcal{F}_{\mathsf{DTTrain}}$ in Fig. 2 models the security of the decision tree training protocol. A graphical representation thereof is in Fig. 3. In this setting, there are two parties* A *and* B. *The training data has* X *attributes and discrete labels.*

- Upon receiving input $(\mathtt{Input}, n_{\mathsf{B}}, m^{\mathsf{B}}_{1,1}, \dots m^{\mathsf{B}}_{n_{\mathsf{B}},X})$ from B, send $(\mathtt{InputReceived}, n_{\mathsf{B}})$ to A
- Upon receiving $(\mathtt{Input}, n_{\mathsf{A}}, m^{\mathsf{A}}_{1,1}, \dots, m^{\mathsf{A}}_{n_{\mathsf{A}},X}, l^{\mathsf{A}}_1, \dots, l^{\mathsf{A}}_{n_{\mathsf{A}}})$ from A, compute $L_j := \mathcal{L}(m^{\mathsf{A}}_{1,j}, \dots, m^{\mathsf{A}}_{n_{\mathsf{A}},j}, m^{\mathsf{B}}_{1,j}, \dots, m^{\mathsf{B}}_{n_{\mathsf{B}},j})$ and send $(\mathtt{Leakage}, (L_1, \dots, L_X), (l^{\mathsf{A}}_1, \dots, l^{\mathsf{A}}_{n_{\mathsf{A}}}))$ to B.
- Upon receiving input $(\mathtt{Labels}, l^{\mathsf{B}}_1, \dots, l^{\mathsf{B}}_{n_{\mathsf{B}}})$ from B, compute the decision tree $tree = \mathsf{train}(m^{\mathsf{A}}_{1,1}, \dots, m^{\mathsf{A}}_{n_{\mathsf{A}},X}, m^{\mathsf{B}}_{1,1}, \dots, m^{\mathsf{B}}_{n_{\mathsf{B}},X}, l^{\mathsf{A}}_1, \dots, l^{\mathsf{A}}_{n_{\mathsf{A}}}, l^{\mathsf{B}}_1, \dots, l^{\mathsf{B}}_{n_{\mathsf{B}}})$ and output $(\mathtt{Trained}, tree)$ to A

Fig. 2. Ideal functionality $\mathcal{F}_{\mathsf{DTTrain}}$.

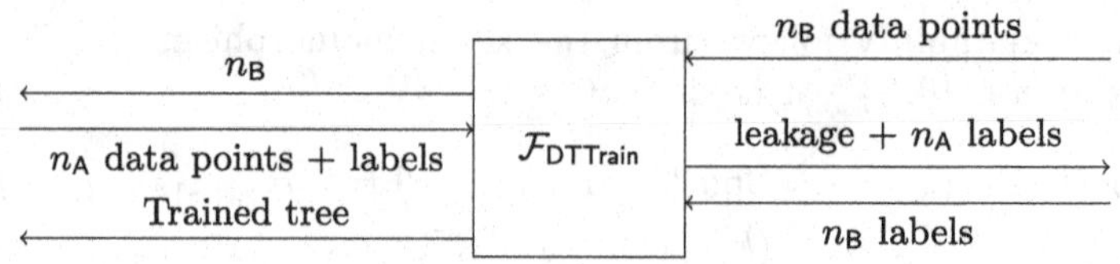

Fig. 3. Graphical representation of $\mathcal{F}_\mathsf{DTTrain}$. Some details about the concrete values being sent to/from the ideal functionality are omitted.

Construction 2 (Protocol π_DTTrain) *Here, we define the two-party protocol π_DTTrain between parties* A *and* B. *As before, let X be the number of attributes of the training data. Also, let $m^\mathsf{A}_{i,j}$ be the j-th attribute of the i-th training data of* A *with the labels l^A_i (respectively for the dataset of* B*), and let* (Gen, Enc, Cmp, Upd) *be an uORE scheme. Then we define the protocol π_DTTrain as follows:*

B:
- *Generate ORE keys $k^\mathsf{B}_{i,j}$ for $1 \le i \le n_\mathsf{B}, 1 \le j \le X$*
- *Send $c^\mathsf{B}_{i,j} = \mathsf{Enc}(k^\mathsf{B}_{i,j}, m^\mathsf{B}_{i,j})$ for $1 \le i \le n_\mathsf{B}, 1 \le j \le X$ to* A

A:
- *Generate ORE keys k^A_j for $1 \le j \le X$*
- *Send $C^\mathsf{A}_{i,j} = \mathsf{Enc}(k^\mathsf{A}_j, m^\mathsf{A}_{i,j})$ for $1 \le i \le n_\mathsf{A}, 1 \le j \le X$ to* B
- *Send labels l^A_i for $1 \le i \le n_\mathsf{A}$ to* B
- *Send $c'^\mathsf{B}_{i,j} = \mathsf{Upd}(k^\mathsf{A}_j, c^\mathsf{B}_{i,j})$ for $1 \le i \le n_\mathsf{B}, 1 \le j \le X$ to* B

B:
- *Compute $C^\mathsf{B}_{i,j} = \mathsf{Upd}(1/k^\mathsf{B}_{i,j}, c'^\mathsf{B}_{i,j})$ for $1 \le i \le n_\mathsf{B}, 1 \le j \le X$*
- *Train the decision tree on the data points $(C^\mathsf{A}_i, l^\mathsf{A}_i)_{i=1\ldots,n_\mathsf{A}}$ and $(C^\mathsf{B}_i, l^\mathsf{B}_i)_{i=1\ldots,n_\mathsf{B}}$, obtaining a trained decision tree.*
- *Send the tree to* A

A:
- *Decrypt and output the decision tree: For each inner node in the tree containing an attribute id j and an encrypted value v, replace v with $\mathsf{Dec}(k^\mathsf{A}_j, v)$.*

Note that this protocol has a constant number of rounds, as only three messages are exchanged. Here, A learns no additional information beyond what can be learned from her own training data and the trained decision tree. B receives only the leakage of the ORE scheme of both parties training data for each attribute separately and the respective label. Note that because A uses different keys to encrypt the values of different attributes, B only receives the leakage $\mathcal{L}(m^\mathsf{A}_{1,j}, \ldots m^\mathsf{A}_{n_\mathsf{A},j}, m^\mathsf{B}_{1,j}, \ldots m^\mathsf{B}_{n_\mathsf{B},j})$ for each j. This leakage is much smaller than the entire leakage $\mathcal{L}(m^\mathsf{A}_{1,1}, \ldots m^\mathsf{A}_{n_\mathsf{A},X}, m^\mathsf{B}_{1,1}, \ldots m^\mathsf{B}_{n_\mathsf{B},X})$, because attribute values of different attributes cannot be compared.

Theorem 4. *π_DTTrain securely realizes $\mathcal{F}_\mathsf{DTTrain}$ for static corruption and semi-honest adversaries if the uORE scheme is secure with leakage $\mathcal{L}$.*

To show this theorem, we follow the UC framework and construct a simulator, such that the real world running the protocol and ideal world with $\mathcal{F}_{\mathsf{DTTrain}}$ are indistinguishable. Concretely, for any PPT-environment controlling a corrupted party A or B, we show that the environment cannot distinguish between a real interaction of the corrupted party with the uncorrupted one and an interaction of the corrupted party with the ideal functionality through the simulator. Because we consider semi-honest adversaries, the environment chooses the inputs of the honest and corrupted parties and learns their output. It also learns sent and received messages, internal state and randomness of corrupted parties.

We give two different simulators, one for the case where A is corrupted and one for the case where B is corrupted. (If both parties are corrupted, no meaningful security guarantees are left.)

- When receiving $(\texttt{InputReceived}, n_{\mathsf{B}})$ from $\mathcal{F}_{\mathsf{DTTrain}}$, invoke the n_{B} instances of the ORE simulator with the leakage $\emptyset$ (possible by Assumption 1) and send the resulting ciphertexts to A.
- When receiving ciphertexts $C^{\mathsf{A}}_{i,j}$, updated ciphertexts $c'^{\mathsf{B}}_{i,j}$ and labels l^{A}_i from A, extract A's ORE keys k^{A}_j and messages $m^{\mathsf{A}}_{i,j}$. Send $(\texttt{Input}, n_{\mathsf{A}}, m^{\mathsf{A}}_{1,1}, \dots, m^{\mathsf{A}}_{n_{\mathsf{A}},x}, l^{\mathsf{A}}_1, \dots, l^{\mathsf{A}}_{n_{\mathsf{A}}})$ to $\mathcal{F}_{\mathsf{DTTrain}}$ in the name of A.
- When receiving $(\texttt{Trained}, \mathit{tree})$ from $\mathcal{F}_{\mathsf{DTTrain}}$ for A, encrypt each value v in a node branching by attribute j as $\mathsf{Enc}(k^{\mathsf{A}}_j, v)$ and send the resulted encrypted tree to A.
- When receiving a query for $\mathcal{F}_{\mathsf{RO}}$, answer consistently or draw a random $x \leftarrow \mathbb{Z}_p^{\times}$ and return $[x]$ if the message has not previously been queried.

Fig. 4. Simulator for a corrupted A.

For the case, where A is corrupted, we use the simulator $\mathcal{S}$ from Fig. 4. To show its validity, we define a number of games G_i, each having (implicitly defined) ideal functionalities $\mathcal{F}_i$ and simulators $\mathcal{S}_i$, and each being a modified version of the previous one. The first game is defined, s.t. the corrupted A interacts with the honest B through the protocol and the last game is the game where the corrupted A interacts with the ideal functionality through the simulator. We show that games G_i are indistinguishable from G_{i+1}.

- G_0: The execution of π_{DTTrain} with dummy adversary $\mathcal{D}$.
- G_1: The execution with a dummy ideal functionality $\mathcal{F}_1$ that lets the adversary determine all inputs and learn all outputs of the honest party. $\mathcal{S}_1$ is the simulator that executes the protocol π_{DTTrain} honestly on behalf of the honest party using the inputs from $\mathcal{F}_1$ and making outputs through $\mathcal{F}_1$.
- G_2: The same as G_1, except that when sending the encrypted decision tree to A, instead of sending the tree, $\mathcal{S}_2$ extracts the keys k_j from A, uses them to decrypt and reencrypt the tree and sends this reencrypted tree.
- G_3: The same as G_2, except that now $\mathcal{S}_3$ does not perform the training on the ciphertexts, it now performs the training on the plaintext training data, where it extracted A's training data and received B's training data from $\mathcal{F}_4$.

- G_4: The same as G_3, except that instead of sending the values $c_{i,j} = \mathsf{Enc}(k_{i,j}, m_{i,j})$ to A, $\mathcal{S}_4$ generates $c'_{i,j} = \mathcal{S}^{\mathsf{ORE}}(\emptyset)$ and sends these values to A instead.
- G_5: The execution of the ideal functionality $\mathcal{F}_{\mathsf{DTTrain}}$ with the simulator $\mathcal{S}$ as in Fig. 4.

As we can see, the game G_0 is the game, in which the corrupted party interacts with the honest one using the protocol, whereas G_5 is the game, where the corrupted party interacts with the ideal functionality through the simulator.

Claim 1 $\mathsf{G}_0 \overset{c}{\approx} \mathsf{G}_1$

Proof. These changes are only syntactic and therefore oblivious to the environment. The claim follows. □

Claim 2 $\mathsf{G}_1 \overset{c}{\approx} \mathsf{G}_2$

Proof. The simulator participates in the protocol as the honest party would. Therefore, each inner node of the tree contains elements (j, c), where c is either a ciphertext from A, in which case $c = \mathsf{Enc}(k_j^{\mathsf{A}}, m)$ for some m, or a ciphertext from the simulator, in which case

$$c = \mathsf{Upd}(k'^{-1}, \mathsf{Upd}(k_j^{\mathsf{A}}, \mathsf{Enc}(k', m))) = \mathsf{Enc}(k_j^{\mathsf{A}}, m)$$

for some k' and m. Therefore, decrypting c with k_j^{A} and deterministically reencrypting the result again with the same key results in the same ciphertext. Hence, the games are indistinguishable. □

Claim 3 $\mathsf{G}_2 \overset{c}{\approx} \mathsf{G}_3$

Proof. It follows from the uORE correctness that evaluating the order on the ciphertexts is equivalent to evaluating the order on the plaintexts (with overwhelming probability), if the ciphertexts to be compared are ciphertexts under the same key. The decision tree training algorithm only compares ciphertexts associated with the same attribute and ciphertexts for an attribute j are all ciphertexts under key k_j^{A} (either directly or by updating and reverse-updating). Therefore, it follows from the correctness of the ORE scheme that encrypting the messages, training the decision tree on the ciphertexts and decrypting the decision tree again (as done in G_2) results (with overwhelming probability) in the same tree as directly training the decision tree on the plaintexts (as done in G_3). □

Claim 4 $\mathsf{G}_3 \overset{c}{\approx} \mathsf{G}_4$

Proof. This change is only relevant for the ciphertexts the simulator sends to A. While it receives these ciphertexts back, updated with A's keys, they are no longer used by the simulator in any further computations. Because of Assumption 1 and the fact that the keys $k_{i,j}$ are only ever used for encryption once, it holds that for all messages m, including the messages the simulator encrypts in G, that $\mathcal{L}(m) = \emptyset$. Therefore, an adversary that can distinguish between G_3 and G_4 can be used to distinguish between $\mathsf{REAL}_{\mathcal{A}}^{\mathsf{ORE}}(\kappa)$ and $\mathsf{SIM}_{\mathcal{A},\mathcal{S},\mathcal{L}}^{\mathsf{ORE}}(\kappa)$ using a hybrid argument. □

Claim 5 $\mathsf{G}_4 \overset{c}{\approx} \mathsf{G}_5$

Proof. The only difference between these two games is who performs the training of the decision tree. In G_5, the simulator $\mathcal{S}_5$ performs the training of the decision tree, while in G_6, the ideal functionality $\mathcal{F}_6$ performs the training. In both cases, the training is performed on the same training data and as training is deterministic, it results in the same decision tree in both cases. □

- When receiving ciphertexts $c_{i,j}^{\mathsf{B}}$ from B, extract the messages $m_{i,j}^{\mathsf{B}}$ from B and send $(\texttt{Input}, n_{\mathsf{B}}, m_{1,1}^{\mathsf{B}}, \dots m_{n_{\mathsf{B}},X}^{\mathsf{B}})$ to $\mathcal{F}_{\mathsf{DTTrain}}$ in the name of B.
- Upon receiving $(\texttt{Leakage}, (L_1, \dots, L_X), (l_1^{\mathsf{A}}, \dots, l_{n_{\mathsf{A}}}^{\mathsf{A}}))$ from $\mathcal{F}_{\mathsf{DTTrain}}$ for B, proceed as follows for all j:
  - For each i, compute the sub-leakage $L_j^{\leq i}$ from L_j. This is possible using Assumption 2.
  - Generate ciphertexts $C_{i,j} = \mathcal{S}^{\mathsf{ORE}}(L_j^{\leq i})$ for $1 \leq i \leq n_{\mathsf{A}} + n_{\mathsf{B}}$
  - Set $c_{i,j}'^{\mathsf{B}} \leftarrow \mathsf{Upd}(k_{i,j}^{\mathsf{B}}, C_{i+n_{\mathsf{A}},j})$ for $1 \leq i \leq n_{\mathsf{B}}$

  Send the $C_{i,j}$, $c_{i,j}'^{\mathsf{B}}$ and l_j^{A} to B.
- Upon receiving *tree* from B, extract labels l_j^{B} from B and send $(\texttt{Labels}, l_1^{\mathsf{B}}, \dots, l_{n_{\mathsf{B}}}^{\mathsf{B}})$ to $\mathcal{F}_{\mathsf{DTTrain}}$ in the name of B.

Fig. 5. Simulator for corrupted B.

For the case, where B is corrupted, we use the simulator $\mathcal{S}$ from Fig. 5. Again, we define hybrid games to show its validity:

- G_0': The execution of π_{DTTrain} with dummy adversary $\mathcal{D}$.
- G_1': The execution with an ideal functionality $\mathcal{F}_1'$ that lets the adversary determine all inputs and learn all outputs. $\mathcal{S}_1'$ is the simulator that executes the protocol π_{DTTrain} honestly on behalf of the honest party using the inputs from $\mathcal{F}_1'$ and making outputs through $\mathcal{F}_1'$.
- G_2': The same as G_1', except that when $\mathcal{S}_2'$ would update a ciphertext, which B computed as $ct = \mathsf{Enc}(k', m)$ to $ct^* = \mathsf{Upd}(k, ct)$, instead it computes $ct^* = \mathsf{Upd}(k', \mathsf{Enc}(k, m))$ using the corresponding key k' and message m it extracts from B.
- G_3': The same as G_2', but instead of decrypting and outputting the tree received from B, the simulator extracts the training data from B. Then it uses both parties training data and labels to train the decision tree in plain text and outputs the tree to A through $\mathcal{F}_3'$.
- G_4': The same as G_3', except that whenever we would perform an encryption (both in the encrypt- or update-step) as $\mathsf{Enc}(k, m)$, we compute it with $\mathcal{S}^{\mathsf{ORE}}$ using the corresponding leakage, using one instance per k.

- G_5': The ideal functionality $\mathcal{F}_{\mathsf{DTTrain}}$ with the simulator $\mathcal{S}$.

Now we look at the case, where B is corrupted:

Claim 6 $\mathsf{G}_0' \overset{c}{\approx} \mathsf{G}_1'$

Proof. These changes are only syntactic and therefore oblivious to the environment. The claim follows. □

Claim 7 $\mathsf{G}_1' \overset{c}{\approx} \mathsf{G}_2'$

Proof. As the difference between these two games is the order in which Enc and Upd are applied, this claim follows directly from the updatability property. □

Claim 8 $\mathsf{G}_2' \overset{c}{\approx} \mathsf{G}_3'$

Proof. The only difference between these two games is the decision tree that is oututted to A. In G_3, the simulator knows A's training data, because it received them from $\mathcal{F}_3$ and it knows B's training data, because it can extract them from B. From the uORE correctness and the fact that the decision tree training is deterministic, it follows that the decision tree $\mathcal{S}_3'$ computes in plaintext is identical to the one B computes in G_3' and G_2' on the ciphertexts. □

Claim 9 $\mathsf{G}_3' \overset{c}{\approx} \mathsf{G}_4'$

Proof. In G_3', the ORE encryption is performed using real keys k_j, whereas in G_4', the ORE simulator is used to generate ciphertexts. To show this indistinguishability, we define additional hybrids H_j, where for the first j attributes, the ORE simulator is used to generate ciphertexts, and for all other attributes, a real encryption is performed. It holds that $\mathsf{G}_4' = \mathsf{H}_0$ and $\mathsf{G}_5' = \mathsf{H}_X$.

The indistinguishability of these games therefore follows from the ORE-security using a standard hybrid argument. □

Claim 10 $\mathsf{G}_4' \overset{c}{\approx} \mathsf{G}_5'$

Proof. The difference between these two games is that in G_5', the simulator performs the training and sends the trained decision tree to A through the ideal functionality, while in G_6' the ideal functionality performs the training and outputs it directly. As the decision tree training algorithm is deterministic and the same input to the training process is used by $\mathcal{S}_5'$ and $\mathcal{F}_6'$, the tree is identical and the games are indistinguishable. □

The security of the protocol π_{DTTrain} (Theorem 4) now follows from Claim 1–5 and Claim 6–10.

4.1 Variations of the Training Process

In the protocol from Construction 2, we only considered standard decision tree training. When using decision trees in practice, additional steps are usually taken like pruning, limiting the depth of the tree, gradient boosted training or training a decision forest for better classification accuracy.

Performing gradient boosted training is inherently not compatible with our approach, as it requires performing arithmetic operations on attribute values, which ORE schemes do not support.

Pruning and limiting the depth of the tree could be performed by B by adding a leaf node instead of an inner node to the tree, whenever the number of datapoints at the current position in the tree is small enough or if a certain depth of the tree is reached during the training process. Both of these techniques are compatible with our decision tree training protocol. Indeed any form of pruning that adheres to the limitation that attributes can only be compared, but no arithmetic can be performed on the attribute values, is compatible with our approach.

Additionally, our protocol can be used for training a decision forest. Training a T-tree decision forest can be done as follows:

1. Each party partitions their training data into T subsets.
2. The parties run π_{DTTrain} once for each subset in parallel to perform the training on each data.
3. After receiving the T decision trees from B, A outputs the decision forest containing these trees.

This realizes a forest-variant of the ideal functionality $\mathcal{F}_{\mathsf{DTTrain}}$. The security of the protocol follows from the universal composability theorem in the UC model.

Another variation is to consider training data that is split vertically between parties, i.e. A has one part of the attributes and B has a different set of the attributes of the same dataset (and they share some kind of id attribute to match up the data). In this setting, training is easily possible with the ORE-based approach by having A encrypt her attribute values using an ORE scheme with one key per attribute and sending the ciphertexts to B. B can then train a decision tree using A's encrypted attributes and his own attributes in plaintext, as no comparison between his and A's data is required. Indeed this does not even require the ORE scheme to be updatable.

4.2 Graceful Degradation Using Enclaves

Hardware enclaves allow other parties to verify the code running in them while ideally hiding all internal state. While hiding internal state is difficult due to side channels, either inherent in the enclave program (like timing or memory access patterns), or due to the used platform (like power consumption, cache timing or other microarchitecural state side channels), the minimal functionality of an enclave, namely to attest the correct program execution, is usually well hardened and implemented side-channel free. These side channels have motivated two major security models for the functionality provided by an enclave system: "regular" enclaves (hiding all internal state) and transparent enclaves (revealing all internal state, especially the used randomness, but not attestation keys). If additionally attestation keys are leaked, the enclave provides no meaningful security. In between transparent and regular, enclave models with varying amount of side channels can be useful, like explicitly modeling a memory access side channel, as done in [29].

In the minimal form of a transparent enclave, they can be seen as a generic passive-to-active compiler. Executing an arbitrary passively secure protocol inside an enclave allows other involved parties to verify the produced attestation evidence to ensure that the other parties executed their part of the protocol correctly.

When applied to the presented decision tree training protocol (Construction 2), we can go one step further: When the protocol for B is executed inside a non-transparent enclave, the leakage from the ORE scheme to B is hidden. To implement this, A needs to send her ciphertexts to the enclave of B confidentially, which can be done by performing a key exchange into the enclave. Additional care needs to be taken to ensure that the enclave program does not leak more information about the input than necessary. Also, the enclave needs to hold a significant amount of memory to store the ORE-encrypted training data. Requiring access to this amount of data will result in many memory-management operations by the enclave system and thus has an impact on the overall performance.

Table 1. Comparison of security under different enclave security assumptions with radix sort and comparison-based sorting.

	ours with radix	ours without radix	plaintext with radix	plaintext without radix
fully secure enclaves	✓	✓	✓	✓
with memory side channels	ORE leakage	ideal-ORE leakage	ORE-leakage	ideal-ORE leakage
transparent enclaves	ORE leakage	ORE leakage	full leakage	full leakage

An overview of the provided security in the different scenarios is given in Table 1. The algorithms that are compared are:

- the proposed algorithm with MSD radix sort inside an enclave
- the proposed algorithm with comparison-based sorting, where all comparisons are done memory-oblivious (e.g. using the primitives from [29])
- the plaintext decision tree training algorithm executed inside an enclave using MSD radix sort
- the plaintext decision tree training algorithm executed inside an enclave with comparison-based sorting using memory-oblivious comparisons

When using a fully secure enclave, all computation happens inside the enclave and cannot be eavesdropped or tampered with, so all algorithms are secure. When we assume memory side channels, radix sort exploits the concrete ORE leakage and thereby leaks it via the memory access patterns, both in the plaintext and encrypted variant. The other two algorithms only use the result of pairwise comparisons and thereby leak at most an ideal-ORE leakage (cf. Sect. 2.2). Using comparison-based sorting and memory-oblivious comparisons, memory access patterns can only leak at most the results of those comparisons. When the enclave becomes fully transparent, all information stored inside the enclave is potentially leaked, which are ORE ciphertexts for the first two algorithms and the plain training data for the last two.

As can be seen, our algorithm provides a more graceful degradation of security when the enclave fails to provide its security promise (e.g. due to expected or unexpected side channels in the implementation), at the cost of higher computational overhead. Therefore, if the trust model of the enclave is uncertain, combining our approach with secure enclaves allows decision tree training with less leakage than solely relying on either approach exclusively.

Note that the *plaintext* algorithm needs to employ similar techniques to the decision tree evaluation algorithm from [29] to avoid additional leakage. However as the authors only describe an evaluation but no training algorithm, no direct comparison can be made with the decision tree algorithm they provide.

5 Analysis of the Leakage

Grubbs et al. [15] have shown that in the context of encrypted databases, there are datasets, such that when encrypting them using ORE schemes, no meaningful security guarantees are left. They have shown that in one of their datasets containing first and last names, they could recover 98% of all first names and 75% of all last names in a database encrypted using the scheme from [10].

While these results also apply to our scheme and therefore also to our decision tree training protocol, we want to emphasize that these results are not universally applicable to all datasets. In their example, the dataset of first names had relatively low entropy with the most common first name appearing in 5% of all cases. Jurado, Palamidessi, and Smith [18] have shown for example that attacks recovering all ORE-encrypted data is possible when the amount of ciphertexts is large compared to the message space, whereas this is not possible if the amount of ciphertexts is significantly smaller than the message space.

To give meaningful security guarantees, we analyze the leakage from an information-theoretic point of view. We consider the uniform distribution of messages, because for this distribution, each bit of the message space contains one bit of information. In a first step, we analyze the leakage when both parties use uniformly random training data. In a second step, we give an upper bound for the leakage, when an adversary (B in the case of the decision tree training protocol) selects its training data maliciously. Finally, we argue why considering only the uniform distribution is sufficient.

5.1 Leakage for Random Message Selection

In the case where both parties use uniformly random messages as inputs, we can experimentally estimate the information leaked on different datasets. We consider a bit to be leaked, if the leakage function allows to infer the value of this bit. In our experiments, we sample n data samples uniformly at random from the bitstrings of length k and count the number of leaked bits. These results are available in Table 2. As we can see, the experiments show a significant leakage when the amount of data samples is large compared to the domain, leaking nearly all bits if there are more data samples than there are possible messages in the domain. If the message space is significantly larger than the amount of messages leaking information, the amount of bits leaked is less than 25% (for messages chosen uniformly at random). This matches the result of Jurado, Palamidessi, and Smith [18], namely that for ORE to provide a benefit over comparing the messages in plain text, the message space must be much larger than the amount of messages encrypted under the same key.

Table 2. Proportion of leaked bits to total bits, for leakage $\mathcal{L}$ on n uniformly random messages of length k bits.

	$k = 8, n = 8$	$k = 8, n = 256$	$k = 8, n = 512$	$k = 64, n = 1000$	$k = 64, n = 10000$	$k = 64, n = 50000$
Leaked Bits	39.1%	93.6%	97.7%	16.0%	21.3%	24.9%

This suggests that the leakage from our ORE approach is small enough to provide some security if the attributes of the training data have sufficiently large entropy, compared to the amount of training data. An example for attributes that have naturally high entropy are geopositions with latitude and longitude.

5.2 Additional Leakage for Malicious Message Selection

We also want to give an analytical upper bound of the additionally leaked information for independently uniformly distributed training data if one party selects their inputs maliciously. This is not a classical setting for ORE, but makes sense in our case, because here, the party receiving the leakage (B in the case of π_{DTTrain}) contributes data influencing the leakage.

Let $\mathcal{L}$ be the leakage function as in Theorem 1. Consider the following experiment with an attacker choosing $N = 2^k$ messages:

1. The adversary chooses N messages $m_i^* \in \mathcal{M} = \{0, 1\}^n$.
2. The experiment chooses a message $m \leftarrow \mathcal{M}$ uniformly at random.
3. The adversary learns $\mathcal{L}(m, m_1^*, \ldots, m_N^*)$.

Choosing the messages optimally to have the maximum (over the attacker-chosen $m_1^*, \ldots, m_N^*$) leaked information on average (over m), the adversary receives no more than $(k + 2)$bit of information.

Consider the first attacker-chosen message m_1^*. The leakage contains the information whether the first bit of m is equal to the first bit of m_1^* (the position of the most significant different bit is $\mathsf{hsb}(m \oplus m_1^*) > 1$) or if they are unequal ($\mathsf{hsb}(m \oplus m_1^*) = 1$). Therefore, the attacker learns the first bit of m containing 1bit of information. The same argument also holds for the second bit, but only if the first bit is the same in m and m_1^*.

Therefore, he obtains the second bit (and therefore one additional bit of information) with probability 1/2, as m's first bit was chosen uniformly at random. Generalizing this for more bits, he learns the i-th bit of m with probability $1/2^{i-1}$. For the expected information, we get the geometric series:

$$\sum_{i=1}^{n} \frac{1}{2^{i-1}} \cdot 1\text{bit} \leq 2\text{bit}.$$

To generalize the maximum leakage to $N = 2^k$ attacker-chosen messages, we consider the information stored in the first $k+1$ bits of m and the remaining bits separately. (Here, we assume $k+1 < n$, as otherwise, the attacker would choose every second message from $\mathcal{M} = \{0,1\}^n$ and learn the content of all ciphertexts.) The first $k+1$ bits of m contain $(k+1)$bit of information, so that is the maximum amount of information an attacker can infer. For the remaining message bits, the probability of m having the same $k+1$-bit prefix as any of the m_i^*, and therefore causing a bit to leak, is $1/2^{k+1}$. Ignoring possible overlap between messages gives us an upper bound of

$$2^k \cdot \frac{1}{2^{k+1}} \cdot 2\text{bit} = 1\text{bit},$$

where the 2bit is again an upper bound for the geometric series over the expected leaked information in the remaining bits.

Combining the two leakages, we get $(k+1)\text{bit} + 1\text{bit} = (k+2)\text{bit}$. This establishes an upper bound for the average leakage.

While we only considered a single message m selected by the experiment, it can naturally be extended to a setting, where the experiment chooses multiple messages $m_1, \ldots, m_{N'}$ and the adversary receives $\mathcal{L}(m_1, m_1^*, \ldots, m_N^*), \ldots, \mathcal{L}(m_{N'}, m_1^*, \ldots, m_N^*)$ instead. (We are only interested in the *additional leakage* by the attacker, the leakage $\mathcal{L}(m_1, \ldots, m_{N'})$ is already analyzed in the previous subsection.) As long as these messages are chosen independently from each other, the maximum leakage *per message* m_i remains the same. This multi-message scenario captures the leakage B receives about A's training data in π_{DTTrain} for each attribute when selecting his messages maliciously.

Note that this analysis extends to the use of multiple uncorrelated attributes, due to the use of separate ORE keys per attribute. If multiple attributes are correlated, this correlation can be interpreted as information known in advance by the adversary. Hence, the upper bound on the average leakage also holds for the information given what is known to the adversary, due to a union bound.

Overall, for any adversarially selected input data of B in π_{DTTrain} consisting of $N = 2^k$ training data, the expected leaked information consists of $(\log_2(N) + 2)$bit per A's training data per attribute.

5.3 Transformation for Non-uniform Distributions

While the distribution of input data is important because changing the encoding of messages (and therefore also the distribution over the message space) influences how much and what information is leaked, we want to emphasize that this is not a restriction, as any input data distribution can be encoded in such a way that the resulting distribution is uniform. We now sketch one way to do this.

Let μ be the probability measure of the distribution over the message space $\mathcal{M}$. Assume there exists a l, such that $\mu(m) \cdot 2^l \in \mathbb{N}$ holds for all $m \in \mathcal{M}$.[1] Then we encode the messages into $\{0,1\}^l$ as follows: The valid encodings of a message m are the $\mu(m) \cdot 2^l$ bitstrings starting from the bitstring of the binary representation of $\mu(\{m' \in \mathcal{M} \mid m' < m\}) \cdot 2^l$. To encode a message, one of its valid encodings is used uniformly at random. This encoding preserves the order, but the resulting distribution is uniform over $\{0,1\}^l$.

6 Implementation and Evaluation

We implemented the ORE scheme from [10], our updatable ORE scheme from Construction 1, as well as our decision tree training protocol from Construction 2 in Java/Kotlin[2] and used it to evaluate the practical efficiency of our protocol. For the group $\mathbb{G}$, we used the Ed25519 curve. We used the PRF from Eq. (1), implemented the random oracle using SHA-256 and mapped its output to points on the curve $\mathbb{G} \setminus \{[0]\}$. We ran our experiments on a machine with two AMD EPYC-Rome 7282 processors with 16 Cores/32 Threads and 90 GB of RAM.

6.1 Evaluation of the Updatable ORE Scheme

For completeness, we start by comparing our updatable ORE scheme with the non-updatable scheme from Chenette et al. [10]. The benchmark results can be seen in Table 3.

Table 3. Operations per second using ORE with a 32-bit message space. Sort refers sorting 1000 ciphertexts using Java's Arrays.sort() or our own implementation of MSD radix sort.

	Our scheme	Scheme from [10]
Encryption	$1.6 \cdot 10^2$	$7.2 \cdot 10^4$
Update	$2.0 \cdot 10^2$	–
Comparison	$7.0 \cdot 10^4$	$6.9 \cdot 10^7$
Sort	$8.0 \cdot 10^0$	$3.8 \cdot 10^5$
Radix sort	$6.9 \cdot 10^1$	$1.0 \cdot 10^3$

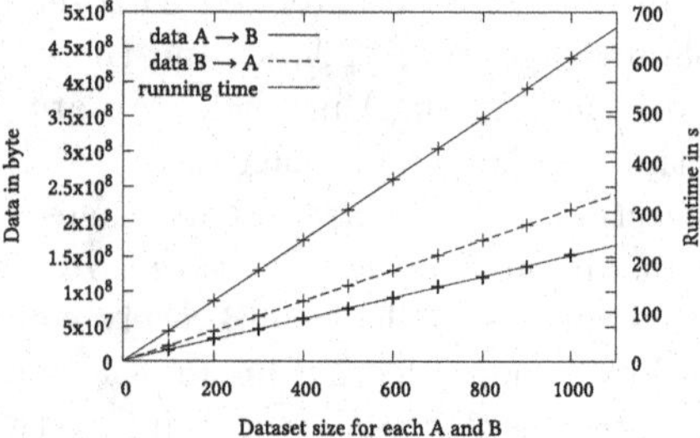

Fig. 6. Full results of the benchmarks from Table 4 where the datasets of A and B are of the same size.

[1] If the assumption does not hold, an approximation of μ with powers of 2^{-l} for some l results in a distribution, that is computationally indistinguishable from uniform.

[2] https://github.com/kastel-security/ORE-Decision-Tree.

For encryption, our scheme is two orders of magnitude slower, because they only need to evaluate a PRF, while evaluating the key-homomorphic PRF in our case requires a scalar multiplication in the group. Updating a ciphertext is roughly as fast as encryption with the running time of both operations being dominated by the scalar multiplication.

Comparisons using our updatable scheme are three orders of magnitude slower than with the non-updatable scheme because the non-updatable scheme requires no cryptographic operations, while we require one group operation per comparison. This translates over to comparison-based sorting. Radix sort offers a running time improvement of one order of magnitude, because – in contrast to comparison-based sorting, where one group operation is required per comparison per element – only one group operation is required per element in total. Radix sort does not offer a performance improvement with the non-updatable scheme, because the running time is not dominated by comparing the elements (or bits thereof), but by the sorting algorithm itself.

6.2 Evaluation of the Protocol

For our experiments of the training protocol, we used the unmodified MNIST dataset using all 784 attributes and datapoints of all 10 labels. We also ran experiments on the Boston Housing and Titanic dataset[3], which we modified to ignore entries with `null`-attributes, as well as discrete attributes. As required for decision tree training, we also discretized the labels. This leaves seven attributes in the Boston Housing dataset and five attributes in the Titanic dataset.

In the MNIST dataset, attribute values are 8 bit unsigned integers. In the other datasets, we converted all attributes to integers by taking their 32 bit IEEE 754 representation, reinterpreting it as a 32 bit unsigned integer and dropping

Table 4. Benchmark results of the protocol on the MNIST dataset and modified versions of the Boston Housing and Titanic datasets, and a custom dataset comparable to the one used by [16], with and without 50 ms of network latency.

Dataset	#Attributes	Compute Threads per party	Dataset Size		Computation time	Network traffic	
			A	B		A ← B	A → B
MNIST	784	1	100	100	243.9 s	21.7 MB	43.4 MB
		16	100	100	22.6 s	21.7 MB	43.4 MB
		16	500	500	106.3 s	108.6 MB	217.2 MB
		16	500	1000	180.6 s	217.2 MB	325.8 MB
		16	1000	500	135.1 s	108.6 MB	325.8 MB
		16	1000	1000	213.6 s	217.2 MB	434.3 MB
Boston Housing	7	1	253	253	23.2 s	1.9 MB	3.6 MB
		16	253	253	3.7 s	1.9 MB	3.6 MB
Titanic	5	1	357	357	23.8 s	2.1 MB	3.6 MB
		16	357	357	5.0 s	2.1 MB	3.6 MB
Custom	7	16	4096	4096	20.1 s	8.8 MB	15.9 MB
Custom (with latency)		16	4096	4096	20.2 s	8.8 MB	15.9 MB

[3] The datasets are available on https://www.kaggle.com/.

the last bit, therefore obtaining an unsigned 31-bit integer, which preserves the order of all positive floating point numbers, including "+0". We used the first n_{A} datapoints as training data for A and the last n_{B} datapoints as training data for B. We used the training algorithm in Algorithm 1 with the Information Gain heuristic. As the training algorithm used here is the same as for plaintext training, the accuracy of the trained model is identical to a model trained on the same data in plaintext. The results can be seen in Table 4 and Fig. 6.

As we can see, the protocol is viable, both computationally, as well as from a network traffic perspective. We can also see that the effects of the dataset size of A are less significant than the effects of the dataset size of B, as B's data needs to be processed three times – when encrypting, when updating, when reverse updating – whereas A's data only needs to be processed once during encryption. A similar argument holds for the network traffic. While we did run the experiments on the same machine, we expect the performance to only differ insignificantly from our test results when run on separate machines over a LAN or WAN. This is because we only have three rounds of interaction, so the effects of network latency are insignificant. Additionally, the total network traffic is well below the limits of a normal internet uplink.

Running Time Comparison with Hamada et al. [16]. To compare our results with the results of [16], the current state-of-the-art in MPC-based decision tree training, we generate a dataset consisting of 2^{13} samples with 11 attributes each, which results in a trained decision tree of depth 42. On this dataset, our protocol takes 20.1 s. In [16], they have performed a benchmark on a dataset of the same size and amount of attributes and a tree depth of 40 on a machine comparable to ours. In this scenario, their protocol takes 43.61 s, which is slower than our protocol by a factor of ≈ 2.

When adding 50 ms of artificial network latency, the running time of their protocol increases to 4821.56 s, which is caused by the many rounds of interaction in their protocol. In contrast to this, when adding the same artificial network latency to our protocol, the running time does not change noticeably, still only requiring 20.2 s, because our protocol only consists of three rounds. In this scenario, our protocol is faster by several orders of magnitude.

Running Time Comparison with Abspoel, Escudero, and Volgushev [2]. In [2], the authors did not measure the running time of the entire decision tree training algorithm, but only extrapolated its runtime based on benchmarks of its basic operations. To compare the runtime performance of their approach with ours, we use their extrapolation formula for their runtime to a setting, for which we have have benchmark results with our approach. They use

$$T(N, m, \Delta) \approx m \cdot (S(N) + (2^{\Delta} - 1)I(N) + 2^{\Delta}L(N))$$

to estimate their runtime, where N, m and Δ are the number of training data, the amount of attributes and the maximum depth of the decision tree and $S(N), I(N)$ and $L(N)$ are the time for sorting, and computing an inner or leaf node on N training data points.

We use this formula to estimate the runtime of their approach to the titanic dataset, where $N = 357, m = 5$ and the depth of the resulting decision tree is $\Delta = 25$. Using the optimistic values $S(256) = 0.392$ s, $I(256) = 0.127$ s and $L(256) = 0.004$ s, we obtain a runtime estimate of $\approx 2.2 \cdot 10^7$ s in the passively secure setting. This is several orders of magnitude slower than with our approach, which is mostly caused by their training algorithm having exponential runtime in the tree depth.

Limiting the depth of the decision tree to $\Delta = 10$ only affects the runtime of our approach insignificantly, as the majority of the runtime comes from encrypting and updating the training data. Their approach, however, is significantly sped up by this change, estimated to only have a runtime of ≈ 672 s, which is still significantly slower than our approach.

Applicability Comparison with [2,16]. While our protocol solely relies on Order-Revealing Encryption, both of the protocols from [2,16] are built on top of generic MPC primitives. Therefore, future advances in (u)ORE or general purpose MPC respectively, will lead to performance improvements of these protocols.

Due to the asymmetric nature of our protocol, it is fixed for the two-party setting with one passive corruption. In addition to this setting, Hamada et al. [16] and Abspoel, Escudero, and Volgushev [2] state that their protocols can fulfill different trust models, such as two-out-of-three corruptions, if the underlying protocol for these MPC primitives is chosen accordingly, however this may cause additional computational/network overhead.

While their protocol can only be applied to the training algorithms they consider, our protocol can generically use any decision tree training algorithm that adheres to the limitations of being deterministic and only requiring comparisons on the training data. Indeed this is even covered by our security proof.

7 Conclusion

We have constructed an Updatable Order-Revealing Encryption scheme, which allows to update ciphertexts from one key to another using a key-homomorphic PRF. This construction is secure under the same leakage function as established ORE schemes, leaking the order of the encrypted messages, as well as the position of the most significant bit in which they differ.

Using such an Updatable ORE scheme, we have constructed a passively secure protocol that allows for securely training a decision tree on two parties' inputs without revealing the inputs to the other party. This protocol can either be used by itself or can be used as a building block to train a decision forest.

We have experimentally verified this decision tree protocol and are able to compute a decision tree on the Titanic dataset, equally partitioned between both parties, within 5.0 s. The experiments have also shown that this approach is faster than the current state-of-the-art approaches [2,16] and orders of magnitude faster when considering network latency or training high-depth decision trees. However, this speedup comes at the cost of some information leakage.

Analyzing the leakage of the ORE scheme, we have found that while it is significant, it is also hides a large proportion of the training data. This provides us with an interesting trade-off between security and efficiency: We leak more information but are faster than relying entirely on MPC to train a decision tree, but we are more secure, but less efficient than performing training in plaintext. We have also found that the proportional information leaked is larger on low-entropy attributes than on high entropy attributes. Whether this leakage is acceptable needs to be decided for each usecase individually. To further reduce the leakage, we show how this approach can also be used in a secure enclave, reducing the leakage even more in a graceful degradation manner, even in the presence of low-entropy attributes.

This leaves us with a special-purpose protocol for decision tree learning that is more performant than generic solutions in a scenario that fits its limitations:

- The protocol has some information leakage and can only be used in a scenario, in which this is acceptable.
- The concrete algorithm for training needs to fulfill some constraints:
  - The training algorithm needs to be deterministic.
  - The split heuristic needs to be evaluated based on comparisons only.
  - As described the protocol allows training between exactly two parties.
  - For training forests: The partitioning of each party's data needs to be independent of the data of the other party.
- The protocol requires more computation compared to the number of communication rounds, so its strength shows better in a higher-latency setting.

While some leakage is inherent with this approach, this also leads us to two interesting open questions:

- How to construct an Updatable ORE scheme with a smaller leakage or in the left-right framework of [23]?
- How to devise an efficient actively-secure protocol based on Updatable ORE schemes?

Acknowledgements. We thank the anonymous reviewers for their helpful and constructive feedback. This work was supported by funding from the topic Engineering Secure Systems of the Helmholtz Association (HGF) and by KASTEL Security Research Labs. Robin Berger: This work was supported by funding from SAP Security Research. Felix Dörre: This work was supported by funding by the German Federal Ministry of Education and Research (BMBF) under the project "VE-ASCOT" (ID 16ME0275). Alexander Koch: This work was supported by the France 2030 ANR Project ANR-22-PECY-003 SecureCompute.

Appendix

A A Brief Introduction to the UC Framework

In the following, we give a brief introduction to into the Universal Composability framework by Canetti [7], tailored to our usecase. As the framework is quite complex, we omit any details that are not relevant for our work.

The UC model extends the notion of the real-ideal paradigm, where the security of a protocol is defined through some ideal functionality, that captures the computation to be done and is secure by definition.

All parties are modeled as an interactive PPT machines. In addition to parties existing in the protocol, UC execution is defined with two additional entities, namely the environment and the adversary, which are modeled in the same way.

The adversary can corrupt any subset of parties. Considering passive security, the adversary can see the view of parties it corrupts (including all internal state, randomness, incoming and outgoing messages), but it cannot make corrupted parties deviate from the protocol. If it accesses variables from the internal state of a corrupted party, we say it *extracts* this information.

The environment selects inputs for honest parties and receives their outputs. Additionally, it can freely interact with the adversary, sending and receiving arbitrary messages.

To prove the security of a protocol, UC uses the notion of protocol emulation. We say a protocol π in the real world securely realizes an ideal functionality $\mathcal{F}$ in the ideal world, if for all adversaries $\mathcal{A}$, there exists a simulator $\mathcal{S}$, such that no environment can distinguish between an interaction with π and $\mathcal{A}$ in the real world and an interaction with $\mathcal{F}$ and $\mathcal{S}$ in the ideal world. This can be done by constructing a simulator for each $\mathcal{A}$, which internally runs $\mathcal{A}$ and translates ideal messages from/to the ideal functionality and protocol messages from/to corrupted parties. Additionally, it is sufficient to only consider the dummy adversary, that sends all protocol messages it receives to the environment and sends any messages it receives from the environment as protocol messages. In the real world, the honest parties execute the protocol and the environment can interact with them using the real adversary. In the ideal world, the input of honest parties is directly sent to the ideal functionality and the output of the ideal functionality to the honest parties is directly outputted by them.

If a protocol π is proven to realize an ideal functionality $\mathcal{F}$, all security properties from $\mathcal{F}$ carry over to π, as this could otherwise be used to distinguish the real and ideal execution.

In UC, the universal composition theorem says that if a protocol is proven to realize an ideal functionality, it remains secure under universal composition. Therefore, it can for example be run in parallel, concurrently or as a subprotocol to other protocols without becoming insecure. If a protocol π' realizes a functionality $\mathcal{F}'$ using $\mathcal{F}$ as a building block, we say π' realizes $\mathcal{F}'$ in the $\mathcal{F}$-hybrid model. Due to the universal composition theorem, π' still realizes $\mathcal{F}'$, even after $\mathcal{F}$ is instantiated with a protocol that securely realizes $\mathcal{F}$.

References

1. Abadi, M., et al.: TensorFlow: Large-Scale Machine Learning on Heterogeneous Systems. Software available from tensorflow.org (2015). https://www.tensorflow.org/

2. Abspoel, M., Escudero, D., Volgushev, N.: Secure training of decision trees with continuous attributes. Proc. Privacy Enhanc. Technol. **2021**(1), 167–187 (2021). https://doi.org/10.2478/popets-2021-0010
3. Akavia, A., Leibovich, M., Resheff, Y.S., Ron, R., Shahar, M., Vald, M.: Privacy-preserving decision trees training and prediction. ACM Trans. Priv. Secur. **25**(3), 24:1–24:30 (2022). https://doi.org/10.1145/3517197
4. Bentéjac, C., Csörgő, A., Martínez-Muñoz, G.: A comparative analysis of gradient boosting algorithms. Artif. Intell. Rev. **54**(3), 1937–1967 (2021). https://doi.org/10.1007/s10462-020-09896-5
5. Boneh, D., Lewi, K., Raykova, M., Sahai, A., Zhandry, M., Zimmerman, J.: Semantically secure order-revealing encryption: multi-input functional encryption without obfuscation. In: Oswald, E., Fischlin, M. (eds.) EUROCRYPT 2015, LNCS, vol. 9057, pp. 563–594. Springer, Heidelberg (2015). https://doi.org/10.1007/978-3-662-46803-6_19
6. Buitinck, L., et al.: API design for machine learning software: experiences from the scikit-learn project. In: ECML PKDD Workshop: Languages for Data Mining and Machine Learning, pp. 108–122 (2013)
7. Canetti, R.: Universally Composable Security: A New Paradigm for Cryptographic Protocols. Cryptology ePrint Archive, Report 2000/067 (2000). https://eprint.iacr.org/2000/067
8. Chaudhuri, K., Monteleoni, C.: Privacy-preserving logistic regression. Adv. Neural Inf. Process. Syst. **21** (2008)
9. Chen, T., Guestrin, C.: Xgboost: a scalable tree boosting system. In: Proceedings of the 22nd ACM SIGKDD International Conference on Knowledge Discovery and Data Mining, pp. 785–794 (2016)
10. Chenette, N., Lewi, K., Weis, S.A., Wu, D.J.: Practical order-revealing encryption with limited leakage. In: Peyrin, T. (eds) FSE 2016. LNCS, vol. 9783. Springer, Heidelberg (2016). https://doi.org/10.1007/978-3-662-52993-5_24
11. Cong, K., Das, D., Park, J., Pereira, H.V.L.: SortingHat: Efficient Private Decision Tree Evaluation via Homomorphic Encryption and Transciphering, pp. 563–577 (2022). https://doi.org/10.1145/3548606.3560702
12. Du, W., Zhan, Z.: Building decision tree classifier on private data (2002)
13. Betül Durak, F., DuBuisson, T.M., Cash, D.: What Else is Revealed by Order-Revealing Encryption?, pp. 1155–1166 (2016). https://doi.org/10.1145/2976749.2978379
14. Frery, J., et al.: Privacy-Preserving Tree-Based Inference with Fully Homomorphic Encryption. Cryptology ePrint Archive, Report 2023/258 (2023). https://eprint.iacr.org/2023/258
15. Grubbs, P., Sekniqi, K., Bindschaedler, V., Naveed, M., Ristenpart, T.: Leakage-abuse attacks against order-revealing encryption. In: 2017 IEEE Symposium on Security and Privacy (SP), pp. 655–672 (2017). https://doi.org/10.1109/SP.2017.44
16. Hamada, K., Ikarashi, D., Kikuchi, R., Chida, K.: Efficient decision tree training with new data structure for secure multi-party computation. Proc. Privacy Enhanc. Technol. **2023**(1), 343–364 (2023). https://doi.org/10.56553/popets-2023-0021
17. de Hoogh, S., Schoenmakers, B., Chen, P., op den Akker, H.: Practical secure decision tree learning in a teletreatment application. In: Christin, N., Safavi-Naini, R. (eds.) FC 2014, LNCS, vol. 8437, pp. 179–194. Springer, Heidelberg (2014). https://doi.org/10.1007/978-3-662-45472-5_12

18. Jurado, M., Palamidessi, C., Smith, G.: A Formal Information-Theoretic Leakage Analysis of Order-Revealing Encryption, pp. 1–16 (2021). https://doi.org/10.1109/CSF51468.2021.00046
19. Keller, M.: MP-SPDZ: A Versatile Framework for Multi-Party Computation, pp. 1575–1590 (2020). https://doi.org/10.1145/3372297.3417872
20. Knott, B., Venkataraman, S., Hannun, A., Sengupta, S., Ibrahim, M., van der Maaten, L.: Crypten: secure multi-party computation meets machine learning. Adv. Neural. Inf. Process. Syst. **34**, 4961–4973 (2021)
21. Kubat, M.: An Introduction to Machine Learning. Springer, Cham (2017). https://doi.org/10.1007/978-3-319-63913-0
22. Lee, J.-W., et al.: Privacy-preserving machine learning with fully homomorphic encryption for deep neural network. IEEE Access **10**, 30039–30054 (2022)
23. Lewi, K., Wu, D.J.: Order-Revealing Encryption: New Constructions, Applications, and Lower Bounds, pp. 1167–1178 (2016). https://doi.org/10.1145/2976749.2978376
24. Li, Y., Wang, H., Zhao, Y.: Delegatable Order-Revealing Encryption, pp. 134–147 (2019). https://doi.org/10.1145/3321705.3329829
25. Lindell, Y., Pinkas, B.: Privacy preserving data mining. In: Bellare, M. (eds.) CRYPTO 2000. LNCS, vol. 1880. Springer, Heidelberg (2000). https://doi.org/10.1007/3-540-44598-6_3
26. Liu, X., Deng, R.H., Raymond, K.-K., Choo, J.: An efficient privacy-preserving outsourced calculation toolkit with multiple keys. IEEE Trans. Inf. Forens. Secur. **11**(11), 2401–2414 (2016). https://doi.org/10.1109/TIFS.2016.2573770
27. Lv, C., Wang, J., Sun, S.-F., Wang, Y., Qi, S., Chen, X.: Towards practical multi-client order-revealing encryption: improvement and application. In: IEEE Transactions on Dependable and Secure Computing (2023)
28. Naor, M., Pinkas, B., Reingold, O.: Distributed Pseudo-random Functions and KDCs, pp. 327–346 (1999). https://doi.org/10.1007/3-540-48910-X_23
29. Ohrimenko, O., et al.: Oblivious Multi-party Machine Learning on Trusted Processors, pp. 619–636 (2016)
30. Ross Quinlan, J. C4. 5: Programs for Machine Learning. Elsevier (2014)
31. Tangirala, S.: Evaluating the impact of GINI index and information gain on classification using decision tree classifier algorithm. Int. J. Adv. Comput. Sci. Appl. **11**(2), 612–619 (2020)
32. Vaidya, J., Clifton, C., Kantarcioglu, M., Scott Patterson, A.: Privacy-preserving decision trees over vertically partitioned data. ACM Trans. Knowl. Discov. Data **2**(3), 14:1–14:27 (2008). https://doi.org/10.1145/1409620.1409624

KIVR: Committing Authenticated Encryption Using Redundancy and Application to GCM, CCM, and More

Yusuke Naito[1(✉)], Yu Sasaki[2,3], and Takeshi Sugawara[4]

[1] Mitsubishi Electric Corporation, Kanagawa, Japan
Naito.Yusuke@ce.MitsubishiElectric.co.jp
[2] NTT Social Informatics Laboratories, Tokyo, Japan
yusk.sasaki@ntt.com
[3] Associate of National Institute of Standards and Technology, Gaithersburg, USA
[4] The University of Electro-Communications, Tokyo, Japan
sugawara@uec.ac.jp

Abstract. Constructing a committing authenticated encryption (AE) satisfying the **CMT**-4 security notion is an ongoing research challenge. We propose a new mode KIVR, a black-box conversion for adding the **CMT**-4 security to existing AEs. KIVR is a generalization of the Hash-then-Enc (HtE) [Bellare and Hoang, EUROCRYPT 2022] and uses a collision-resistant hash function to generate an initial value (or nonce) and a mask for redundant bits, in addition to a temporary key. We obtain a general bound $r/2 + \mathsf{tag\text{-}col}$ with r-bit redundancy for a large class of CTR-based AEs, where tag-col is the security against tag-collision attacks. Unlike HtE, the security of KIVR linearly increases with r, achieving beyond-birthday-bound security. With a t-bit tag, tag-col lies $0 \leq \mathsf{tag\text{-}col} \leq t/2$ depending on the target AE. We set $\mathsf{tag\text{-}col} = 0$ for GCM, GCM-SIV, and CCM, and the corresponding bound $r/2$ is tight for GCM and GCM-SIV. With CTR-HMAC, $\mathsf{tag\text{-}col} = t/2$, and the bound $(r + t)/2$ is tight.

Keywords: Key Commitment · Context Commitment · Authenticated Encryption · Security Proof · CTR · GCM · GCM-SIV · CCM · HMAC

1 Introduction

Authenticated encryption with associated data (AE) schemes that achieve confidentiality and authenticity are essential components in symmetric-key cryptography. The security of AE is well-studied, and the schemes usually come with security proofs based on a formal security notion. However, AE schemes are sometimes misused in a way beyond their promise, resulting in security problems. Committing security of AEs falls in this category and has been actively studied in the last few years [1,5,6,9,11,15,16,21,22].

Farshim et al. initiated the theoretical study of key commitment in 2017 [15], followed by the real-world attacks, including the multi-recipient integrity attack that delivers malicious content to a targeted user [1,11,16] and the

C. Pöpper and L. Batina (Eds.): ACNS 2024, LNCS 14583, pp. 318–347, 2024.
https://doi.org/10.1007/978-3-031-54770-6_13

partitioning oracle attack that achieves efficient password brute-force attacks [21]. The absence of the commitment to a secret key is the root cause of these problems. An AE encryption Π_{Enc} receives a secret key K, nonce N, associated data A, and plaintext M and generates a ciphertext $\Pi_{\mathsf{Enc}}(K, N, A, M)$. Without key-committing security, an adversary can efficiently find a ciphertext decrypted with multiple keys, i.e., $\Pi_{\mathsf{Enc}}(K, N, A, M) = \Pi_{\mathsf{Enc}}(K', N', A', M')$ with $K \neq K'$. Unfortunately, the previous AE security notions do not support key commitment, and there are $O(1)$ attacks on GCM [11,16], GCM-SIV [21], CCM [22], and ChaCha20-Poly1305 [16].

In the meantime, standardization bodies are starting to support committing security in AEs. For example, the recent RFC draft on usage limits on AEs considers key-committing security [19]. Similarly, the recent NIST workshop for updating the federal standard of block-cipher modes noted explicitly that key commitment is an additional security feature [25].

Context commitment is the generalization considering a stronger adversary. Bellare and Hoang [6] (and Chan and Rogaway independently [9]) proposed the security notions for context commitment. The security notions **CMT**-1, **CMT**-3, and **CMT**-4 consider $K \neq K'$, $(K, N, A) \neq (K', N', A')$, and $(K, N, A, M) \neq (K', N', A', M')$, respectively [6]. **CMT**-1 is the previous key-committing security. **CMT**-3 and **CMT**-4 are equivalent, and they are strictly more secure than **CMT**-1, covering a broader range of misuses.

As discussed above, ensuring and building AEs with committing security is an ongoing research challenge [1,11,16,21]. Before introducing the details about the concrete methods, we summarize the desired properties regarding this challenge, which are also our goals in this paper.

1. We want a conversion for adding the committing security to the standard AEs. In particular, we target a class of the AE schemes based on CTR [12], referred to as CTRAE, that includes GCM [14], GCM-SIV [17,18], and CCM [13]. We also target CTR-HMAC, the CTR combined with HMAC [24] comprising particular hash functions, such as SHA-256.
2. The schemes should satisfy the context-committing security, i.e., **CMT**-4.
3. A black-box conversion that respects the interface of the existing AEs is preferred for maintaining compatibility with the specifications of the standardized AE schemes and the hardware already deployed in the field.
4. The bit-security level for committing security is ideally the key size k, or at least greater than $\frac{k}{2}$, i.e., the beyond-birthday-bound (BBB) security regarding the key size. That is necessary to achieve an offline security level comparable with the standard AE-security, which is basically k bits.

1.1 Research Challenges

Here, we explain that the previous works [1,11,15,16,21] cannot achieve the above desired properties perfectly.

There is a line of works for designing a dedicated scheme with committing security [11,15], but they are not blackbox. In particular, Farshim et al. proposed to use a collision-resistant pseudo-random function (PRF) [15].

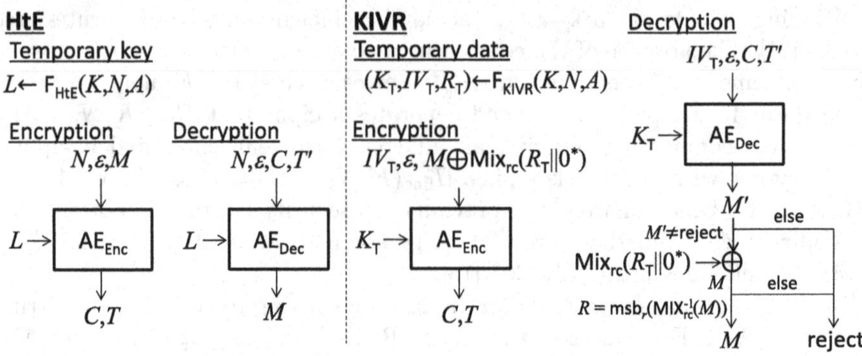

Fig. 1. HtE [6] (left) and KIVR (right). The function $\mathsf{F}_{\mathsf{KIVR}}$ generates a tuple of temporary key, IV, and redundant data. $\mathsf{Mix}_{\mathsf{rc}}$ is a function representing the positions of redundant bits.

The padding fix [1] prepends zero bits at the beginning of the message and enhances security by checking whether the prepended zero bits are successfully recovered in decryption. This method provides excellent compatibility because the changes to the original AE scheme are limited to messages. However, the security of the padding fix is proved for GCM only and is limited to CMT-1.

CTX [9] converts arbitrary AEs to **CMT**-4 secure ones. After computing a ciphertext C and tag T' using an underlying AE, it generates a new tag $T = H(K, N, A, T')$ by using a collision resistant (CR) hash function H. Unfortunately, CTX's compatibility with existing AEs is limited. In decryption, CTX should first regenerate T' and then $T = H(K, N, A, T')$ for comparison. Here, T' is an unverified tag within the original AE and is unavailable when the interface of the original AEAD is strict, e.g., in cryptographic APIs in a hardware security module or when there is a security policy regarding the release of unverified plaintexts [2]. NC4, a CTX-based scheme with reduced ciphertext expansion [7], has the same limitation.

HtE [6] shown in Fig. 1-(left) converts a **CMT**-1-secure AE to a **CMT**-4-secure one [6]. It generates a temporary key $L \leftarrow \mathsf{F}_{\mathsf{HtE}}(K, N, A)$ using a CR hash function $\mathsf{F}_{\mathsf{HtE}}$, and then L is used as the key of an underlying AE. Although HtE requires an additional CR hash function, it only changes the original AE's key values, thus maintaining high compatibility. The security of HtE combined with a non-**CMT**-1-secure AE, e.g., GCM, GCM-SIV, or CCM, is not guaranteed and is unknown. In particular, the security of HtE with GCM/CCM is limited by $\frac{k}{2}$, i.e., the birthday bound of the key. This is because the encryption results will also collide if two temporary keys collide. $\frac{k}{2}$ bits of security is too short for common cases, e.g., $k = n$ in AES-GCM, and can be even smaller considering concrete AEs.

In summary, designing a method to convert CTRAEs to achieve BBB security for **CMT**-4 in a black-box manner is a meaningful research challenge.[1]

1.2 Contributions

We propose a new black-box conversion KIVR that achieves BBB and **CMT**-4 security. The security bound is proved for CTRAE, including GCM, GCM-SIV, CCM, and CTR-HMAC.

The considerable difficulty is that the **CMT**-4 security of CTRAE is limited by $\frac{t}{2}$ bits due to a birthday attack on a tag, wherein the tag length t is often $t \leq k$. We approach the problem by adding redundancy to plaintexts, a natural extension of the padding fix [1]. Let M_{origin} be an original plaintext and R redundancy. We then define a plaintext with redundancy as $M = \mathsf{Mix}_{\mathsf{rc}}(R \| M_{\mathsf{origin}})$ wherein $\mathsf{Mix}_{\mathsf{rc}}$ is a function for defining the positions of each bit (or byte) of redundancy. The CMT security notion is naturally extended considering this plaintext with redundancy. We can increase the security by adding redundancy to messages. Besides adding extra redundancy, we can optionally exploit the redundancy already present in the message, such as constant strings or magic numbers found in popular file formats [20,28].[2]

The receiver who decrypts the message can check the decrypted message for redundancy, which potentially improves the context-committing security. However, such an improvement turns out to be non-trivial. The previous $O(1)$ attacks still break GCM, GCM-SIV, and CCM, even with redundancy (see Table 1). Similarly, the security of CTR-HMAC with redundancy is limited to $\frac{t}{2}$ due to a birthday attack on a tag. Combining HtE with redundancy is a viable option, but its security is upper-bounded by a simple attack using a collision either in redundancy or a key.

New Mode. KIVR shown in Fig. 1-(right) is a generalization of HtE. In HtE, a temporary key L is generated by $\mathsf{F}_{\mathsf{HtE}}(K, N, A)$. In contrast, KIVR generates a tuple of temporary values $(K_{\mathsf{T}}, IV_{\mathsf{T}}, R_{\mathsf{T}})$ using $\mathsf{F}_{\mathsf{KIVR}}(K, N, A)$, preventing the output size of the hash function $\mathsf{F}_{\mathsf{KIVR}}$ from becoming a security bottleneck. In encryption, we get a masked message $M \oplus \mathsf{Mix}_{\mathsf{rc}}(R_{\mathsf{T}} \| 0^*)$: a modified message wherein the redundant bits are masked with R_{T}. Finally, the original AE encrypts the masked message along with K_{T}, IV_{T}, and empty associated data. Decryption is naturally defined, but we additionally check if the redundancy R is correctly recovered.

We give a general bound for the **CMT**-4 security of KIVR with CTRAE that covers a large class of practical AEs, i.e., CTR combined with any MAC.

[1] An alternative approach for **CMT**-4 security is designing an indifferentiable AE scheme [4]. It can be used as an ideal AE scheme, where an adversary is allowed to select AE's keys, and is **CMT**-4-secure. An indifferentiable AE claims the security beyond the committing security notions, and thus its design is harder than that of a **CMT**-4-secure AE scheme.

[2] PNG and XML files have 64 and 192 bits of redundancy, respectively [20,28].

Table 1. AE schemes with black-box conversions for **CMT**-4 security using r-bit redundancy. k and t are the key and tag lengths, respectively.

Conversion	AE	CMT-4 Security	Ref.
Naive	GCM, GCM-SIV, CCM	0	[16,21,22]
Naive	CTR-HMAC	$\frac{t}{2}$	[15]
HtE [6]	GCM, GCM-SIV, CCM	$\min\{\frac{r}{2}, \frac{k}{2}\}$	—[†]
KIVR	GCM, GCM-SIV, CCM	$\frac{r}{2}$	Cor. 1
KIVR	CTR-HMAC	$\frac{r+t}{2}$	Cor. 2

[†]The security determined by a collision either in redundancy or a key.

Table 2. Attacks on KIVR-based AE schemes.

Conversion	AE	Complexity	Security	Ref.
KIVR	GCM, GCM-SIV	$\frac{r}{2}$	**CMT**-1	Theorem 2
KIVR	CCM	—	—	—
KIVR	CTR-HMAC	$\frac{r+t}{2}$	**CMT**-1	Theorem 3

The obtained **CMT**-4 security bound is $\frac{r}{2}$ + tag-col, where tag-col is the security against tag-collision attacks by changing any of (K, N, A).[3] In other words, KIVR's security linearly increases with r, unlike HtE upper-bounded by $\frac{k}{2}$. We ensure that KIVR causes no adverse side effects by proving that the conventional AE security after applying KIVR reduces to the multi-user (mu) security of the original AE.

Evaluation with Representative AEAD Instantiations. The term tag-col lies $0 \leq$ tag-col $\leq \frac{t}{2}$ depending on the target AE, as summarized in Table 1. We set tag-col $= 0$ for GCM and GCM-SIV and obtain $\frac{r}{2}$ as a corresponding bound. This bound is tight because the attacker achieves full control over GHASH, and tag-col of GMAC is 0. Analyzing tag-col with CCM is more complicated, and we conservatively set tag-col $= 0$ considering the worst case. The corresponding bound is $\frac{r}{2}$, and its tightness is unclear. In the case of CTR-HMAC, on the other hand, tag-col $= \frac{t}{2}$, and the bound is $\frac{r+t}{2}$. It achieves tag-col $= \frac{t}{2}$ because of the collision-resistant property of HMAC. This bound is proven tight. Table 2 summarizes the attacks. Since **CMT**-1 is weaker than **CMT**-4, a **CMT**-1-security bound can be better than a **CMT**-4-security bound. However, in the case of the KIVR-based AE schemes with GCM, GCM-SIV, and CTR-HMAC, the matching attacks break the **CMT**-1 security, and there is no room for further improving the **CMT**-1-security bounds. Meanwhile, finding an attack for KIVR with CCM remains open, and a better **CMT**-1-security bound is still possible.

[3] Specifically, the bound given in Theorem 1 is $O(\frac{\mu}{2^r})$ plus the advantage of finding μ-collisions for tags. By choosing the parameter μ so that these terms are balanced according to the structure of the tagging function, we have the security $\frac{r}{2}$ + tag-col.

With $r = 256$, KIVR combined with GCM, GCM-SIV, and CCM achieves 128-bit security. KIVR combined with CTR-HMAC, on the other hand, achieves $(\frac{r}{2} + 64)$-bit security with a 128-bit tag. In this case, KIVR achieves 128-bit **CMT**-4 security with $r = 128$.

Comparison with the Padding Fix. KIVR achieves higher security and supports a wider range of AEs compared with the padding fix. Specifically, KIVR enables **CMT**-4 with CTRAE, including GCM, GCM-SIV, CCM, and CTR-HMAC, in contrast with the padding fix that enables **CMT**-1 with GCM only. KIVR achieves those with a reasonable overhead and is still a one-pass scheme with a one-pass underling AE. The main overhead is processing K and N in the hash function $\mathsf{F}_{\mathsf{KIVR}}$, approximately two more blocks considering the lengths of K and N. There is no (or minor) overhead for processing AD in $\mathsf{F}_{\mathsf{KIVR}}$ because instead we can skip AD processing in the underlying AE.

1.3 Organization

We begin by giving basic definitions in Sect. 2. Then, we formally define a plaintext with redundancy and an extended CMT security considering redundancy in Sect. 3. We introduce the KIVR conversion in Sect. 4. Section 5 gives KIVR's general security bound with CTRAE, followed by the proof in Sect. 6. Section 7 discusses the security and its tightness of KIVR combined with GCM, GCM-SIV, and CCM. Similarly, Sect. 8 shows the tight security bound of KIVR with CTR-HMAC. Section 9 is a conclusion.

2 Preliminaries

Notation. For integers $0 \le i \le j$, let $[i,j] := \{i, i+1, \ldots, j\}$ and $[j] := [1,j]$. If $i > j$ then $[i,j] := \emptyset$. Let ε be an empty string, $\emptyset$ an empty set, and $\{0,1\}^*$ be the set of all bit strings. For an integer $n \ge 0$, let $\{0,1\}^n$ be the set of all n-bit strings, $\{0,1\}^0 := \{\varepsilon\}$, $\{0,1\}^{\le n} := \{X \in \{0,1\}^* \mid |X| \le n\}$, and $\{0,1\}^{n*} := \{X \in \{0,1\}^* \mid |X| \bmod n = 0\}$. Let 0^i be the bit string of i-bit zeros. For $X \in \{0,1\}^j$, let $|X| := j$. The concatenation of two bit strings X and Y is written as $X\|Y$ or XY when no confusion is possible. For integers $i \ge 0$ and $0 \le X \le 2^i - 1$, let $\mathsf{str}_i(X)$ be the i-bit representation of X. For integers $0 \le j \le i$ and $X \in \{0,1\}^i$, let $\mathsf{msb}_j(X)$ (resp. $\mathsf{lsb}_j(X)$) be the most (resp. least) significant j bits of X. For an integer $1 \le n$ and $X \in \{0,1\}^*$, let $\mathsf{zp}_n(X) := X\|0^{\lceil |X|/n \rceil \cdot n - |X|}$ be a zero-padding function such that the length of the padded value becomes a multiple of n. For a non-empty set $\mathcal{T}$, $T \xleftarrow{\$} \mathcal{T}$ means that an element is chosen uniformly at random from $\mathcal{T}$ and assigned to T. For two sets $\mathcal{T}$ and $\mathcal{T}'$, $\mathcal{T} \xleftarrow{\cup} \mathcal{T}'$ means $\mathcal{T} \leftarrow \mathcal{T} \cup \mathcal{T}'$. For an integer $l \ge 0$ and $X \in \{0,1\}^*$, $(X_1, \ldots, X_\ell) \xleftarrow{l} X$ means parsing of X into fixed-length l-bit strings, where if $X \ne \varepsilon$ then $X = X_1\|\cdots\|X_\ell$, $|X_i| = l$ for $i \in [\ell - 1]$, and $0 < |X_\ell| \le l$; if $X = \varepsilon$ then $\ell = 1$ and $X_1 = \varepsilon$.

For μ pairs with four values $\mathcal{S}[i] = \{(K_i', N_i', A_i', D_i'), (K_i'', N_i'', A_i'', D_i'')\}$ ($i \in [\mu]$), Boolean function $\mathsf{diff}_{\mathsf{KNA}}$ with the input $\mathcal{S} := (\mathcal{S}[1], \ldots, \mathcal{S}[\mu])$ is defined as

- $\mathsf{diff}_{\mathsf{KNA}}(\mathcal{S}) = 1$ if $\left(\forall i \in [\mu] : (K_i', N_i', A_i') \neq (K_i'', N_i'', A_i'')\right)$ and $\left(\forall i \in [\mu], j \in [i-1] : \{(K_i', N_i', A_i'), (K_i'', N_i'', A_i'')\} \neq \{(K_j', N_j', A_j'), (K_j'', N_j'', A_j'')\}\right)$;
- $\mathsf{diff}_{\mathsf{KNA}}(\mathcal{S}) = 0$ otherwise.

Block Cipher (BC). A BC is a set of permutations indexed by a key. For positive integers κ and n, let $E : \{0,1\}^k \times \{0,1\}^n \to \{0,1\}^n$ be an encryption of a BC with k-bit keys and n-bit blocks that is used in CTR and BC-based MACs such as GMAC, GMAC$^+$, and CBC. Let $E^{-1} : \{0,1\}^k \times \{0,1\}^n \to \{0,1\}^n$ be its decryption. For positive integers b and v, let $F : \{0,1\}^b \times \{0,1\}^v \to \{0,1\}^v$ be an encryption of a BC with b-bit keys and v-bit blocks that is used in Merkle-Damgård hash function.

Ideal Cipher (IC). Let $\mathcal{BC}(k,n)$ be a set of all encryptions of BCs with k-bit keys and n-bit blocks. An IC is an ideal BC and defined as $E \xleftarrow{\$} \mathcal{BC}$. An IC E can be implemented by lazy sampling. Let $\mathcal{T}_E$ be a table that is initially empty and keeps query-response tuples of E and E^{-1}. Let $\mathcal{T}_{E,2}[W] := \{Y \mid (W,X,Y) \in \mathcal{T}_E\}$ and $\mathcal{T}_{E,1}[W] := \{X \mid (W,X,Y) \in \mathcal{T}_E\}$ be tables that respectively keep ciphertext and plaintext blocks defined in $\mathcal{T}_E$ such that the key elements are W. For a new forward query (W,X) to E (resp. inverse query (W,Y) to E^{-1}), the response is defined as $Y \xleftarrow{\$} \{0,1\}^n \backslash \mathcal{T}_{E,2}[W]$ (resp. $X \xleftarrow{\$} \{0,1\}^n \backslash \mathcal{T}_{E,1}[W]$), and $\mathcal{T}_E \xleftarrow{\cup} \{(W,X,Y)\}$. For a query stored in the table $\mathcal{T}_E$, the same response is returned.

Hash Function. Let $\mathcal{M} \subseteq \{0,1\}^*$ and h be a positive integer. Let $H[\Psi] : \mathcal{M} \to \{0,1\}^h$ be a hash function with a primitive Ψ that on an input message in $\mathcal{M}$ returns an h-bit hash value. In this paper, we assume that Ψ is ideal, and use the following security notions for hash function.

μ-Collision Resistance. $H[\Psi]$ is μ-collision resistance if it is hard to find μ pairs of distinct messages such that for each pair the hash values are the same. The μ-collision-resistant advantage function of $\mathbf{A}$ with access to an ideal primitive Ψ against $H[\Psi]$ is defined as

$$\begin{aligned}\mathbf{Adv}^{\mathsf{colls}}_{H,\mu}(\mathbf{A}) := \Pr\Big[&((M^{(1)}, M'^{(1)}), \ldots, (M^{(\mu)}, M'^{(\mu)})) \leftarrow \mathbf{A}^{\Psi} \text{ s.t.} \\ &\left(\forall i \in [\mu] : H[\Psi](M^{(i)}) = H[\Psi](M'^{(i)}) \wedge M^{(i)} \neq M'^{(i)}\right) \wedge \\ &\left(\forall i,j \text{ s.t. } i \neq j : \{M^{(i)}, M'^{(i)}\} \neq \{M^{(j)}, M'^{(j)}\}\right)\Big] .\end{aligned}$$

The notion with $\mu = 1$ is the standard notion for collision resistance. Let $\mathbf{Adv}^{\mathsf{coll}}_{H}(\mathbf{A}) := \mathbf{Adv}^{\mathsf{colls}}_{H,1}(\mathbf{A})$ be a collision-resistant advantage function of $\mathbf{A}$.

Random Oracle (RO). An RO is an ideal hash function from $\mathcal{M}$ to $\{0,1\}^h$. An RO can be realized by lazy sampling. Let $\mathcal{T}_{\mathsf{RO}}$ be a table that is initially empty and keeps query-response pairs of RO. For a new query X to RO, the response is defined as $Y \xleftarrow{\$} \{0,1\}^h$, and the query-response pair (X, Y) is added to $\mathcal{T}_{\mathsf{RO}}$: $\mathcal{T}_{\mathsf{RO}} \xleftarrow{\cup} \{(X, Y)\}$. For a query stored in the table $\mathcal{T}_{\mathsf{RO}}$, the same response is returned.

Authenticated Encryption (AE). Let $\Pi[\Psi]$ be a (tag-based) AE scheme using a primitive (or set of primitives) Ψ. $\Pi[\Psi]$ is a pair of encryption and decryption algorithms $(\Pi_{\mathsf{Enc}}[\Psi], \Pi_{\mathsf{Dec}}[\Psi])$. $\mathcal{K}$, $\mathcal{N}$, $\mathcal{M}$, $\mathcal{C}$, $\mathcal{A}$, and $\mathcal{T}$ are the sets of keys, nonces, plaintexts, ciphertexts, associated data (AD), and tags, respectively. Let ν and t be respectively nonce and tag sizes, i.e., $\mathcal{N} = \{0,1\}^\nu$ and $\mathcal{T} = \{0,1\}^t$. The encryption algorithm $\Pi_{\mathsf{Enc}}[\Psi] : \mathcal{N} \times \mathcal{A} \times \mathcal{M} \to \mathcal{C} \times \mathcal{T}$ takes a tuple (N, A, M), and returns, deterministically, a pair (C, T). The decryption algorithm $\Pi_{\mathsf{Dec}}[\Psi] : \mathcal{N} \times \mathcal{A} \times \mathcal{C} \times \mathcal{T} \to \{\mathbf{reject}\} \cup \mathcal{M}$ takes a tuple (N, A, C, T') and returns, deterministically, either the distinguished invalid symbol **reject** $\notin \mathcal{M}$ or a plaintext $M \in \mathcal{M}$. We require that $\forall (K, N, A, M), (K', N', A', M') \in \mathcal{K} \times \mathcal{N} \times \mathcal{A} \times \mathcal{M}$ s.t. $|M| = |M'| : |\Pi_{\mathsf{Enc}}[\Psi](K, N, A, M)| = |\Pi_{\mathsf{Enc}}[\Psi](K', N', A', M')|$. We also require that $\forall K \in \mathcal{K}, N \in \mathcal{N}, A \in \mathcal{A}, M \in \mathcal{M} : \Pi_{\mathsf{Dec}}[\Psi](K, N, A, \Pi_{\mathsf{Enc}}[\Psi](K, N, A, M)) = M$.

3 Committing Security with Plaintext Redundancy

In this section, we define notions for committing security with plaintext redundancy. The notions are defined by extending the original notions [6] such that plaintext redundancy is incorporated.

3.1 Plaintext with Redundancy

We formalize a plaintext with redundancy that extends the idea of zero padding in the padding fix [1]. A plaintext consists of redundancy R and original message M_{origin}. Let r be the length of redundancy. A plaintext with redundancy is defined as $M = \mathsf{Mix}_{\mathsf{rc}}(R \| M_{\mathsf{origin}})$ wherein $\mathsf{Mix}_{\mathsf{rc}}$ is a function for defining the positions of each bit (or byte) of redundancy in a plaintext. If $R = 0^r$ and $\mathsf{Mix}_{\mathsf{rc}}$ is an identity function, then the plaintexts are equal to those of the padding fix. The generalization covers not only the padding fix but also other padding schemes and plaintexts with inherent redundancy discussed later.

In this paper, we assume that $\mathsf{Mix}_{\mathsf{rc}}$ is length-preserving (i.e., $|R \| M_{\mathsf{origin}}| = |\mathsf{Mix}_{\mathsf{rc}}(R \| M_{\mathsf{origin}})|$), linear, invertible, and bijective. Then, redundancy in a plaintext M can be obtained by $\mathsf{msb}_r \circ \mathsf{Mix}_{\mathsf{rc}}^{-1}(M)$. We call $\mathsf{Mix}_{\mathsf{rc}}$ "(ω, n)-mixing function" if the number of n-bit blocks with redundant bits is at most ω. Specifically, let $\mathsf{Mix}_{\mathsf{rc}}(R \| M_{\mathsf{origin}}) := M_1 \| M_2 \| \cdots \| M_m$ such that $|M_i| = n$ $(i \in [m-1])$ and $|M_m| \leq n$. Then, for any original message M_{origin}, and distinct r-bit redundant values R' and R^*, there exist ω distinct indexes $i_1, \ldots, i_\omega \in [m]$ such that $(M'_{i_1}, \ldots, M'_{i_\omega}) \neq (M^*_{i_1}, \ldots, M^*_{i_\omega})$ and $\forall j \in [m] \backslash \{i_1, \ldots, i_\omega\} : M'_j = M^*_j$. For example, if $\mathsf{Mix}_{\mathsf{rc}}(R \| M_{\mathsf{origin}}) = R \| M_{\mathsf{origin}}$, then $\omega = \lceil \frac{r}{n} \rceil$.

The above definition covers a case where the original message has inherent redundancy, such as constant strings in popular file formats. For example, PNG and XML files have 64 and 192 bits of magic numbers, respectively [20,28]. Such inherent redundancy that a receiver knows in advance can be counted as a part of the redundancy R, thus reducing the number of extra redundant bits.

3.2 Definitions for Committing Security with Redundancy

For $i \in \{1, 3, 4\}$, let WiC_i be a function that on input tuple (K, N, A, M) of a key, a nonce, AD, and a plaintext (with redundancy), returns the first i elements to which a ciphertext is committed: $\mathsf{WiC}_1(K, N, A, M) = K$, $\mathsf{WiC}_3(K, N, A, M) = (K, N, A)$, and $\mathsf{WiC}_4(K, N, A, M) = (K, N, A, M)$.

Let $\Pi[\Psi]$ be an AE scheme with an ideal primitive(s) Ψ. In the **CMT-**i-security game where $i \in \{1, 3, 4\}$, the goal of an adversary $\mathbf{A}$ with access to Ψ is to return two tuples of a key, a nonce, AD, and a plaintext on which the outputs of $\Pi_{\mathsf{Enc}}[\Psi]$ are the same. Since we consider plaintexts with redundancy, the game is defined so that the plaintexts in the $\mathbf{A}$'s output tuples contain redundancy. For $i \in \{1, 3, 4\}$, redundancy R, and a mixing function $\mathsf{Mix}_{\mathsf{rc}}$, the **CMT-**$i$-security advantage of an adversary $\mathbf{A}$ is defined as

$$\begin{aligned}\mathbf{Adv}^{\mathsf{cmt}\text{-}i}_{\Pi,\mathsf{Mix}_{\mathsf{rc}},R}(\mathbf{A}) := \Pr\Big[&(K^{\dagger}, N^{\dagger}, A^{\dagger}, M^{\dagger}), (K^{\ddagger}, N^{\ddagger}, A^{\ddagger}, M^{\ddagger}) \leftarrow \mathbf{A}^{\Psi} \text{ s.t.}\\ &\left(\mathsf{WiC}_i(K^{\dagger}, N^{\dagger}, A^{\dagger}, M^{\dagger}) \neq \mathsf{WiC}_i(K^{\ddagger}, N^{\ddagger}, A^{\ddagger}, M^{\ddagger})\right)\\ &\wedge \left(\Pi_{\mathsf{Enc}}[\Psi](K^{\dagger}, N^{\dagger}, A^{\dagger}, M^{\dagger}) = \Pi_{\mathsf{Enc}}[\Psi](K^{\ddagger}, N^{\ddagger}, A^{\ddagger}, M^{\ddagger})\right)\\ &\wedge \left(\mathsf{msb}_r \circ \mathsf{Mix}_{\mathsf{rc}}^{-1}(M^{\dagger}) = \mathsf{msb}_r \circ \mathsf{Mix}_{\mathsf{rc}}^{-1}(M^{\ddagger}) = R\right)\Big].\end{aligned}$$

$\Pi[\Psi]$ is **CMT-**i secure if for any R, $\mathsf{Mix}_{\mathsf{rc}}$, and $\mathbf{A}$, the advantage function is upper-bounded by a negligible probability. In other words, $\Pi[\Psi]$ is not **CMT-**i secure if there exist R, $\mathsf{Mix}_{\mathsf{rc}}$, and $\mathbf{A}$ such that the **CMT-**i security of $\Pi[\Psi]$ is lower-bounded by a non-negligible probability. Note that **CMT-3** and **CMT-4** security are equivalent [6]. In this paper, we consider computationally unbounded adversaries.

4 KIVR Transform

In this section, we present KIVR, a generalization of HtE that enhances the committing security by using plaintext redundancy.

4.1 Specification of KIVR

KIVR, on an input tuple of a key, a nonce, and AD, generates a temporary key, a temporary nonce, and a mask value that are defined by using a hash function $\mathsf{F}_{\mathsf{KIVR}}$. The mask value is applied to redundancy in a plaintext. $\mathsf{F}_{\mathsf{KIVR}}$ should be

Algorithm 1. KIVR Transform

Encryption $\mathsf{KIVR}[\Pi_{\mathsf{Enc}}][\mathsf{Mix}_{\mathsf{rc}}, R, \Psi, \Psi_{\mathsf{KIVR}}](K, N, A, M)$

$(K_{\mathsf{T}}, IV_{\mathsf{T}}, R_{\mathsf{T}}) \leftarrow \mathsf{F}_{\mathsf{KIVR}}[\Psi_{\mathsf{KIVR}}](K, N, A)$

$(C, T) \leftarrow \Pi_{\mathsf{Enc}}[\Psi](K_{\mathsf{T}}, IV_{\mathsf{T}}, \varepsilon, M \oplus \mathsf{Mix}_{\mathsf{rc}}(R_{\mathsf{T}} \| 0^{|M|-r_{\mathsf{T}}}))$; **return** (C, T)

Decryption $\mathsf{KIVR}[\Pi_{\mathsf{Dec}}][\mathsf{Mix}_{\mathsf{rc}}, R, \Psi, \Psi_{\mathsf{KIVR}}](K, N, A, C, T')$

$(K_{\mathsf{T}}, IV_{\mathsf{T}}, R_{\mathsf{T}}) \leftarrow \mathsf{F}_{\mathsf{KIVR}}[\Psi_{\mathsf{KIVR}}](K, N, A)$

$M' \leftarrow \Pi_{\mathsf{Dec}}[\Psi](K_{\mathsf{T}}, IV_{\mathsf{T}}, \varepsilon, C, T')$ **if** $M' =$ **reject then return reject end if**

$M \leftarrow M' \oplus \mathsf{Mix}_{\mathsf{rc}}(R_{\mathsf{T}} \| 0^{|M|-r_{\mathsf{T}}})$

if $R = \mathsf{msb}_r \circ \mathsf{Mix}_{\mathsf{rc}}^{-1}(M)$ **then return** M **else return reject end if**

collision resistant for **CMT**-4 security and be pseudorandom-function secure for **mu-AE** security.

The specification of $\mathsf{KIVR}[\Pi]$ (KIVR with an AE scheme Π) is given in Algorithm 1 and Fig. 1. Let Ψ (resp. Ψ_{KIVR}) be the underlying primitive(s) of Π (resp. $\mathsf{F}_{\mathsf{KIVR}}$). Let R be redundancy, $r = |R|$, and $\mathsf{Mix}_{\mathsf{rc}}$ a mixing function. Let r_{T} be the length of the mask value defined by $\mathsf{F}_{\mathsf{KIVR}}$ such that $r_{\mathsf{T}} \leq r$. Let $\mathsf{F}_{\mathsf{KIVR}} : \mathcal{K} \times \mathcal{N} \times \mathcal{A} \rightarrow \mathcal{K} \times \mathcal{N} \times \{0,1\}^{r_{\mathsf{T}}}$ be a function of KIVR that on an input tuple (K, N, A) of a key, a nonce, and AD, derives a tuple $(K_{\mathsf{T}}, IV_{\mathsf{T}}, R_{\mathsf{T}})$ of a temporary key, an IV, and a mask value.[4]

4.2 Security of KIVR

Regarding the **mu-AE** security of AE schemes $\mathsf{KIVR}[\Pi]$, assuming that $\mathsf{F}_{\mathsf{KIVR}}$ is a pseudorandom function secure in the mu-setting, for each tuple of a key, a nonce, and AD, the temporary key is chosen uniformly at random from $\mathcal{K}$. Hence, the **mu-AE** security of $\mathsf{KIVR}[\Pi]$ is reduced to the **mu-AE** security of the underlying AE scheme Π. The detail is given in Supplementary material C.

Regarding committing security, in Sects. 5, 7, and 8, we show that KIVR enhances the committing security of CTR-based AE schemes by the length of redundancy r. In Sect. 5, we define CTRAE, which is a CTR-based AE scheme with a general tagging function and covers GCM, GCM-SIV, CCM, and CTR-HMAC (CTR-based AE with HMAC). We show a general bound of the **CMT**-4 security of CTRAE. In Sect. 7, we derive **CMT**-4-bounds of KIVR[GCM], KIVR[GCM-SIV], and KIVR[CCM] by using the general bound of CTRAE. In Sect. 8, we similarly derive a **CMT**-4-bound of KIVR[CTR-HMAC].

5 Committing Security of KIVR with CTR-Based AE

In this section, we first define CTRAE, a CTR-based AE scheme with a generalized tagging function. We then show a **CMT**-4-security bound of KIVR[CTRAE].

[4] We exemplify the structure of the masked plaintext $M \oplus \mathsf{Mix}_{\mathsf{rc}}(R_{\mathsf{T}} \| 0^{|M|-r_{\mathsf{T}}})$ by using the padding fix. In the padding fix, $R_{\mathsf{T}} = 0^r$ and $\mathsf{Mix}_{\mathsf{rc}}$ is an identity function. Then, the masked plaintext is $(0^r \| M_{\mathsf{origin}}) \oplus (R_{\mathsf{T}} \| 0^{|M|-r_{\mathsf{T}}}) = (R_{\mathsf{T}} \| 0^{r-r_{\mathsf{T}}}) \| M_{\mathsf{origin}}$.

Algorithm 2. Counter Mode

Encryption/Decryption $\mathsf{CTR}[E](K_{\mathsf{bc}}, IV, D)$

for $i = 1, \ldots, \lceil |D|/n \rceil$ **do** $KS_i \leftarrow E(K_{\mathsf{bc}}, \mathsf{add}(IV, i))$ **end for**

$KS \leftarrow \mathsf{msb}_{|D|}(KS_1 \| \cdots \| KS_{\lceil |D|/n \rceil})$; $D' \leftarrow D \oplus KS$; **return** D'

Algorithm 3. CTR-based AE CTRAE

Encryption $\mathsf{CTRAE}_{\mathsf{Enc}}[E, \Psi_{\mathsf{tag}}]((K_{\mathsf{bc}}, K_{\mathsf{tag}}), N, A, M)$

$T \leftarrow \mathsf{TagGen}[\Psi_{\mathsf{tag}}](K_{\mathsf{tag}}, N, A, M)$; $C \leftarrow \mathsf{CTR}[E](K_{\mathsf{bc}}, \mathsf{GetIV}(N, T), M)$

return (C, T)

Decryption $\mathsf{CTRAE}_{\mathsf{Dec}}[E, \Psi_{\mathsf{tag}}]((K_{\mathsf{bc}}, K_{\mathsf{tag}}), N, A, C, T')$

$M \leftarrow \mathsf{CTR}[E](K_{\mathsf{bc}}, \mathsf{GetIV}(N, T'), C)$; $T \leftarrow \mathsf{TagGen}[\Psi_{\mathsf{tag}}](K_{\mathsf{tag}}, N, A, M)$

if $T = T'$ **then return** M; **else return reject end if**

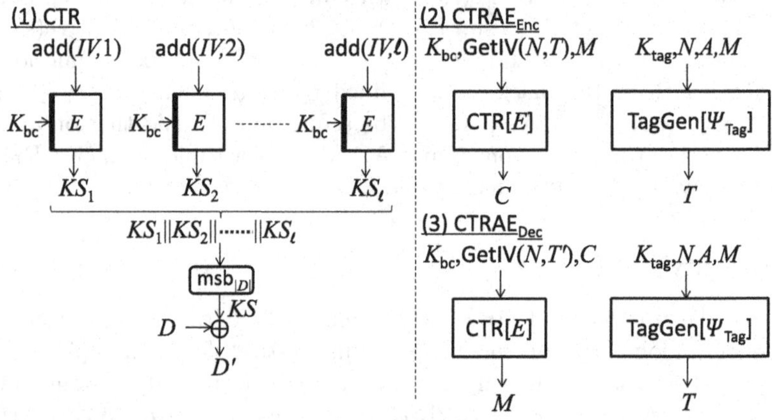

Fig. 2. (1) CTR Mode where $\ell = \lceil |D|/n \rceil$ and (D, D') is a pair of plaintext and ciphertext or of ciphertext and plaintext; (2) $\mathsf{CTRAE}_{\mathsf{Enc}}$; (3) $\mathsf{CTRAE}_{\mathsf{Dec}}$.

5.1 Specification of CTR-Based AE

Counter Mode. The specification of the counter mode CTR is given in Algorithm 2 and Fig. 2(1), where E is the underlying BC. Let c be the counter size such that $c \leq n$. Let $\mathcal{D} \subset \{0,1\}^*$ be the plaintext/ciphertext space. $\{0,1\}^k$ is the key space. $\mathsf{CTR}[E] : \{0,1\}^k \times \{0,1\}^n \times \mathcal{D} \rightarrow \mathcal{D}$ takes a tuple of a key K_{bc}, an initial value IV, and a plaintext/ciphertext D, and returns its ciphertext/plaintext D' such that $|D| = |D'|$. If D is a plaintext (resp. ciphertext), then D' is the ciphertext (resp. plaintext). KS is a key stream with which a ciphertext (resp. plaintext) is defined by XORing a plaintext (resp. ciphertext). $\mathsf{add} : \{0,1\}^n \times [0, 2^c - 1] \rightarrow \{0,1\}^n$ is a function that on an input pair of an IV and a counter, returns an input block of E. Regarding add, we consider the following two types of functions. The type-1 is used in the standard CTR (used in GCM, CCM, and CTR-HMAC) and the type-2 is used in GCM-SIV.

- The type-1 function is defined as $\mathsf{add}(IV, i) := (\mathsf{msb}_\nu(IV)) \| (\mathsf{lsb}_c(IV) + i + 1 \bmod 2^c)$, where $n = \nu + c$, for the counter addition $\mathsf{lsb}_c(IV)$ is considered as an integer, and the added value is regarded as a c-bit string.
- The type-2 function is defined as $\mathsf{add}(IV, i) := (1 \| (\mathsf{msb}_{n-c-1}(IV)) \| (\mathsf{lsb}_c(IV) + i \bmod 2^c))$, where $\mathsf{lsb}_c(IV)$ is considered as an integer and the added value is regarded as a c-bit string.

CTRAE. We define CTRAE, a CTR-based AE scheme with primitives E and Ψ_{tag}. CTRAE is a generalization of GCM, GCM-SIV, CCM, and CTR-HMAC. The specification of $\mathsf{CTRAE}[E, \Psi_{\mathsf{tag}}]$ is given in Algorithm 3 and Fig. 2. Let $\mathcal{K}_{\mathsf{tag}}$ be the key space of the tagging function. Hence, $\mathcal{K} := \{0,1\}^k \times \mathcal{K}_{\mathsf{tag}}$ is the key space of CTRAE. Let $\mathsf{TagGen}[\Psi_{\mathsf{tag}}]$ be the tagging function with the primitive Ψ_{tag} that on an input tuple of a key K_{tag}, a nonce N, and a plaintext M, returns a t-bit tag. Note that although the tagging functions of GCM, CCM, and CTR-HMAC take a ciphertext instead of a plaintext, $\mathsf{TagGen}[\Psi_{\mathsf{tag}}]$ covers these functions by incorporating the procedure of CTR into the tagging functions. Let GetIV be a function that on an input tuple of a nonce and a tag, returns an IV of CTR. The function of GCM, CCM, and CTR-HMAC is defined as $\mathsf{GetIV}(N, T) := \mathsf{zp}_n(N)$. The function of GCM-SIV is defined as $\mathsf{GetIV}(N, T) := T$.

Let $\mathsf{KIVR}[\mathsf{CTRAE}_{\mathsf{Enc}}]$ and $\mathsf{KIVR}[\mathsf{TagGen}]$ be the encryption and tagging functions of $\mathsf{KIVR}[\mathsf{CTRAE}]$, respectively. Let $\mathsf{F}_{\mathsf{K_{bc}}IVR}$ be a function that returns a tuple of a temporary key of CTR, an IV, and a mask value, i.e., $\mathsf{F}_{\mathsf{K_{bc}}IVR}[\Psi_{\mathsf{KIVR}}](K, N, A) := (K_{\mathsf{bcT}}, IV_{\mathsf{T}}, R_{\mathsf{T}})$.

5.2 CMT-4-Security of KIVR[CTRAE]

Let $\Pi^* := \mathsf{KIVR}[\mathsf{CTRAE}]$, $\Pi^*_{\mathsf{Enc}} := \mathsf{KIVR}[\mathsf{CTRAE}_{\mathsf{Enc}}]$ and $\Pi^*_{\mathsf{TGen}} := \mathsf{KIVR}[\mathsf{TagGen}]$. The following theorem shows an upper-bound of the **CMT**-4-security of Π^*.

Theorem 1. *For any redundancy R, (ω, n)-mixing function $\mathsf{Mix}_{\mathsf{rc}}$, and* **CMT**-4 *adversary* $\mathbf{A}$ *making p_{ic} queries to E or E^{-1}, p_{tag} queries to Ψ_{tag}, and p_{kivr} queries to Ψ_{KIVR}, there exist adversaries $\mathbf{A}_1$ and $\mathbf{A}_2$ such that $\mathbf{Adv}^{\mathsf{cmt}\text{-}4}_{\Pi^*, \mathsf{Mix}_{\mathsf{rc}}, R}(\mathbf{A}) \leq \frac{2^\omega \cdot (\mu - 1)}{2^r} + \mathbf{Adv}^{\mathsf{colls}}_{\Pi^*_{\mathsf{TGen}}, \mu}(\mathbf{A}_1) + \mathbf{Adv}^{\mathsf{coll}}_{\mathsf{F}_{\mathsf{K_{bc}}IVR}}(\mathbf{A}_2)$, for the $\mathbf{A}_1$'s output $\mathcal{S}_1$, $\mathsf{diff}_{\mathsf{KNA}}(\mathcal{S}_1) = 1$, and for each $i \in [2]$, $\mathbf{A}_i$ makes p_{ic} queries to E or E^{-1}, p_{tag} queries to Ψ_{tag}, and p_{kivr} queries to Ψ_{KIVR}.*

Note that $\mathbf{Adv}^{\mathsf{colls}}_{\Pi^*_{\mathsf{TGen}}, \mu}(\mathbf{A}_1)$ is the μ-collision advantage of Π^*_{TGen} with the condition of $\mathsf{diff}_{\mathsf{KNA}}$, i.e., for each pair of $\mathbf{A}_1$, the tuples of a key, a nonce, and AD are distinct. Although the parameter r_{T} does not appear in the bound, the last term depends on the parameter. The proof is given in Sect. 6.

6 Proof of Theorem 1

Since **CMT**-3-security and **CMT**-4-security are equivalent [6], we evaluate the **CMT**-3-security advantage of $\mathbf{A}$ for Π^*.

6.1 Tools

Full-Block Query. To ensure the randomnesses of the outputs of an IC E or E^{-1}, we use the technique given in [3].

- For a key element W of an IC, after $\mathbf{A}$ makes 2^{n-1} queries with W to E or E^{-1}, we permit an adversary $\mathbf{A}$ to obtain the remaining input-output tuples of E with W, i.e., $\mathbf{A}$ obtains all input-output tuples with W. We call the additional queries "full-block queries."

The full-block queries ensure that the outputs of E or E^{-1} are chosen uniformly at random from 2^{n-1} elements in $\{0,1\}^n$.[5] Specifically, fixing Y^*, for a full-block query (W,X), the probability that the output Y is equal to Y^* is $\frac{(2^{n-1}-1)!}{(2^{n-1})!} = \frac{1}{2^{n-1}}$. Without loss of generality, full-block queries are forward ones.

Property of CTR with Redundancy. The following lemma shows that a collision of CTR with redundancy implies that the sum of the key streams meets the sum of redundancy. The lemma is used in our proofs.

Lemma 1. *Let $\mathsf{Mix}_{\mathsf{rc}}$ be a (ω, n)-mixing linear function. Let R' and R'' be r-bit (masked) redundancy. Let (K', IV', M') and (K'', IV'', M'') be tuples of a key, an IV, and a plaintext with redundancy such that $(K', IV') \neq (K'', IV'')$, $|M'| = |M''|$, $\mathsf{msb}_r \circ \mathsf{Mix}_{\mathsf{rc}}^{-1}(M') = R'$, and $\mathsf{msb}_r \circ \mathsf{Mix}_{\mathsf{rc}}^{-1}(M'') = R''$. For $\square \in \{', ''\}$, let $C^\square := \mathsf{CTR}[E](K^\square, IV^\square, M^\square)$ and $KS^\square$ the key stream. Then, we have*

$$C' = C'' \Rightarrow \mathsf{msb}_r \circ \mathsf{Mix}_{\mathsf{rc}}^{-1}(KS' \oplus KS'') = R' \oplus R''.$$

Proof (Lemma 1). The relation in the lemma is obtained as follows.

$$\begin{aligned} C' = C'' &\Rightarrow KS' \oplus KS'' = M' \oplus M'' \\ &\Rightarrow \mathsf{msb}_r \circ \mathsf{Mix}_{\mathsf{rc}}^{-1}(KS' \oplus KS'') = \mathsf{msb}_r \circ \mathsf{Mix}_{\mathsf{rc}}^{-1}(M' \oplus M'') \\ &\Rightarrow \mathsf{msb}_r \circ \mathsf{Mix}_{\mathsf{rc}}^{-1}(KS' \oplus KS'') = R' \oplus R''. \end{aligned}$$

6.2 Symbol Definitions

Let $\mathcal{I}_{\mathsf{KIVR}}$ be the set of all possible input tuples of $\mathsf{F}_{\mathsf{KIVR}}[\Psi_{\mathsf{KIVR}}]$ derived from query-response tuples of Ψ_{KIVR}. Let $\mathcal{I}_{\mathsf{TGen}}$ be the set of all possible input tuples of Π^*_{TGen} derived from query-response tuples of Ψ_{tag} and Ψ_{KIVR}. Let $(K^\dagger, N^\dagger, A^\dagger, M^\dagger)$, $(K^\ddagger, N^\ddagger, A^\ddagger, M^\ddagger)$ be $\mathbf{A}$'s outputs. For an input tuple $(K^\square, N^\square, A^\square, M^\square)$ of a key, a nonce, AD and a plaintext with redundancy,

- $(C^\square, T^\square) := \Pi^*_{\mathsf{Enc}}[\mathsf{Mix}_{\mathsf{rc}}, R, E, \Psi_{\mathsf{tag}}, \Psi_{\mathsf{KIVR}}](K^\square, N^\square, A^\square, M^\square)$,
- $(K^\square_{\mathsf{bcT}}, IV^\square_{\mathsf{T}}, R^\square_{\mathsf{T}}) := \mathsf{F}_{\mathsf{K}_{\mathsf{bc}}IVR}(K^\square, N^\square, A^\square)$, and
- $KS^\square$ is the key stream of $\mathsf{CTR}[E](K^\square_{\mathsf{T}}, IV^\square_{\mathsf{T}}, M^\square)$.

In the following proof, the symbol $\square$ is replaced with $(i), ', '', \dagger$, and $\ddagger$ where i is an integer.

[5] In [3], the additional queries are called super queries.

6.3 Deriving the CMT-4-Security Bound

We derive the upper-bound of $\mathbf{Adv}^{\mathsf{cmt\text{-}3}}_{\Pi^*}(\mathbf{A}) = \Pr[(C^\dagger, T^\dagger) = (C^\ddagger, T^\ddagger)]$ by using the following collision event for $\mathsf{F}_{\mathsf{K}_{\mathsf{bc}}IVR}$.

- coll: $\exists X, X' \in \mathcal{I}_{\mathsf{KIVR}}$ s.t. $X \neq X' \wedge \mathsf{F}_{\mathsf{K}_{\mathsf{bc}}IVR}(X) = \mathsf{F}_{\mathsf{K}_{\mathsf{bc}}IVR}(X')$.

Using the events, we have

$$\mathbf{Adv}^{\mathsf{cmt\text{-}3}}_{\Pi^*,\mathsf{Mix}_{\mathsf{rc}},R}(\mathbf{A}) \leq \Pr[\mathsf{coll}] + \Pr[(C^\dagger, T^\dagger) = (C^\ddagger, T^\ddagger) \wedge \neg\mathsf{coll}] \ .$$

The event coll implies that there exists an adversary $\mathbf{A}_2$ finding a collision of $\mathsf{F}_{\mathsf{K}_{\mathsf{bc}}IVR}$, i.e., $\Pr[\mathsf{coll}] \leq \mathbf{Adv}^{\mathsf{coll}}_{\mathsf{F}_{\mathsf{K}_{\mathsf{bc}}IVR}}(\mathbf{A}_2)$. The bound of $\Pr[(C^\dagger, T^\dagger) = (C^\ddagger, T^\ddagger) \wedge \neg\mathsf{coll}]$ is given in Eq. (1). These bounds provide the bound in Theorem 1.

6.4 Bounding $\Pr[(C^\dagger, T^\dagger) = (C^\ddagger, T^\ddagger) \wedge \neg\mathsf{coll}]$

We define the following event that considers μ-collisions of Π^*_{TGen} such that for each of the μ-collision, the input tuples of a key, a nonce, and AD are distinct.

$$\begin{aligned}
&\mathsf{colls} \Leftrightarrow \\
&\exists \mathcal{S} := \left\{\left\{(K'^{(i)}, N'^{(i)}, A'^{(i)}, C'^{(i)}), (K''^{(i)}, N''^{(i)}, A''^{(i)}, C''^{(i)})\right\} \in (\mathcal{I}_{\mathsf{TGen}})^2 : i \in [\mu]\right\} \\
&\text{s.t.} \left(\forall i \in [\mu] : \Pi^*_{\mathsf{TGen}}(K'^{(i)}, N'^{(i)}, A'^{(i)}, C'^{(i)}) = \Pi^*_{\mathsf{TGen}}(K''^{(i)}, N''^{(i)}, A''^{(i)}, C''^{(i)})\right) \\
&\qquad \wedge (\mathsf{diff}_{\mathsf{KNA}}(\mathcal{S}) = 1).
\end{aligned}$$

Using the event, we have

$$\begin{aligned}
&\Pr[(C^\dagger, T^\dagger) = (C^\ddagger, T^\ddagger) \wedge \neg\mathsf{coll}] \\
&\leq \Pr[\mathsf{colls}] + \Pr[(C^\dagger, T^\dagger) = (C^\ddagger, T^\ddagger) \mid \neg(\mathsf{coll} \vee \mathsf{colls})].
\end{aligned}$$

These bounds are given below. Using the bounds, we have

$$\Pr[(C^\dagger, T^\dagger) = (C^\ddagger, T^\ddagger) \wedge \neg\mathsf{coll}] \leq 2^\omega \cdot \frac{\mu - 1}{2^r} + \mathbf{Adv}^{\mathsf{colls}}_{\Pi^*_{\mathsf{TGen}},\mu}(\mathbf{A}_1) \ . \tag{1}$$

Bounding $\Pr[\mathsf{colls}]$. The event colls implies that there exists an adversary $\mathbf{A}_1$ finding μ-collisions of Π^*_{TGen} with the condition of $\mathsf{diff}_{\mathsf{KNA}}$. We thus have

$$\Pr[\mathsf{colls}] \leq \mathbf{Adv}^{\mathsf{colls}}_{\Pi^*_{\mathsf{TGen}},\mu}(\mathbf{A}_1) \ .$$

Bounding $\Pr[(C^\dagger, T^\dagger) = (C^\ddagger, T^\ddagger) \mid \neg(\mathsf{coll} \vee \mathsf{colls})]$. Regarding the ciphertext collision, by Lemma 1, we have

$$\begin{aligned}
C^\dagger = C^\ddagger &\Rightarrow \mathsf{msb}_r \circ \mathsf{Mix}_{\mathsf{rc}}^{-1}\left(KS^\dagger \oplus KS^\ddagger\right) = (R \oplus \mathsf{zp}_r(R^\dagger_{\mathsf{T}})) \oplus (R \oplus \mathsf{zp}_r(R^\ddagger_{\mathsf{T}})) \\
&\Rightarrow \mathsf{msb}_r \circ \mathsf{Mix}_{\mathsf{rc}}^{-1}\left(KS^\dagger \oplus KS^\ddagger\right) = \mathsf{zp}_r(R^\dagger_{\mathsf{T}} \oplus R^\ddagger_{\mathsf{T}})
\end{aligned}$$

where $KS^\dagger$ and $KS^\ddagger$ are respectively determined from $(K^\dagger, N^\dagger, A^\dagger)$ and $(K^\ddagger, N^\ddagger, A^\ddagger)$. By $\neg\mathsf{colls}$, there are at most $\mu - 1$ pairs with a key, a nonce, and AD with which tag collision occurs. Fix distinct tuples $(K', N', A'), (K'', N'', A'') \in \mathcal{I}_{\mathsf{KIVR}}$ and assume that coll does not occur. We then consider the following two cases.

Algorithm 4. GHASH

GHASH $\mathsf{GHASH}(L, A, D)$

1: $X_1, \ldots, X_l \xleftarrow{n} \mathsf{zp}_n(A) \| \mathsf{zp}_n(D) \| \mathsf{str}_{n/2}(|A|) \| \mathsf{str}_{n/2}(|D|)$

2: $Y \leftarrow X_1 \bullet L^l \oplus X_2 \bullet L^{l-1} \oplus \cdots X_l \bullet L$; **return** Y

- If $(K'_{\mathsf{bcT}}, IV'_{\mathsf{T}}) = (K''_{\mathsf{bcT}}, IV''_{\mathsf{T}})$, then since $KS' = KS''$, we have $C^\dagger = C^\ddagger \Rightarrow R^\dagger_{\mathsf{T}} = R^\ddagger_{\mathsf{T}}$. Hence, a collision of $\mathsf{F}_{\mathsf{K}_{\mathsf{bc}}IVR}$ occurs, which contradicts the condition $\neg\mathsf{coll}$. We thus have $\Pr[C' = C''] = 0$.
- If $(K'_{\mathsf{bcT}}, IV'_{\mathsf{T}}) \neq (K''_{\mathsf{bcT}}, IV''_{\mathsf{T}})$, then in the processes of CTR, the IC's input-output tuples are defined by E or E^{-1}. Due to full-block queries, for $Z \in \{0,1\}^n$ and $j \in \{0,1\}^c$,

$$\Pr[E(K'_{\mathsf{bcT}}, \mathsf{add}(IV'_{\mathsf{T}}, j)) = Z] \leq \frac{2}{2^n}, \quad \Pr[E^{-1}(K'_{\mathsf{bcT}}, Z) = \mathsf{add}(IV'_{\mathsf{T}}, j)] \leq \frac{2}{2^n},$$
$$\Pr[E(K''_{\mathsf{bcT}}, \mathsf{add}(IV''_{\mathsf{T}}, j)) = Z] \leq \frac{2}{2^n}, \quad \Pr[E^{-1}(K''_{\mathsf{bcT}}, Z) = \mathsf{add}(IV''_{\mathsf{T}}, j)] \leq \frac{2}{2^n} .$$

As there are ω blocks that depend on redundant data, we have

$$\Pr[C' = C''] \leq 2^{\omega n - r} \cdot \left(\frac{2}{2^n}\right)^{\omega} = \frac{2^\omega}{2^r} .$$

By $\neg\mathsf{colls}$, the number of collisions of Π^*_{TGen} is at most $\mu - 1$. In order to have the collision $(C^\dagger, T^\dagger) = (C^\ddagger, T^\ddagger)$, one of the (at most) $\mu - 1$ pairs of key stream must satisfy the relation $\mathsf{msb}_r \circ \mathsf{Mix}^{-1}_{\mathsf{rc}} (KS^\dagger \oplus KS^\ddagger) = \mathsf{zp}_r(R^\dagger_{\mathsf{T}} \oplus R^\ddagger_{\mathsf{T}})$. The probability that the relation is satisfied is at most $(\mu - 1) \cdot \frac{2^\omega}{2^r}$, and we have

$$\Pr[(C^\dagger, T^\dagger) = (C^\ddagger, T^\ddagger) \mid \neg(\mathsf{coll} \vee \mathsf{colls})] \leq 2^\omega \cdot \frac{\mu - 1}{2^r} .$$

7 Committing Security of KIVR with GCM, GCM-SIV, and CCM

In this section, we derive the **CMT**-4-bounds of KIVR with the CTR-based AE schemes GCM, GCM-SIV, and CCM by using the bound in Theorem 1.

7.1 Specifications of GCM, GCM-SIV, and CCM

GHASH. GHASH used in GCM and GCM-SIV is a polynomial hash function defined in Algorithm 4. GHASH takes an n-bit hash key L, AD A, and a plaintext/ciphertext D, and returns an n-bit hash value Y. GHASH is the hash function used in GCM and GCM-SIV. Let $\mathbb{F}$ be a finite field of 2^n elements. We can interpret a string in $\{0,1\}^n$ as an element in $\mathbb{F}$, and the addition in $\mathbb{F}$ is the same as $\oplus$ in $\{0,1\}^n$. Let $\bullet$ be the finite-field multiplication in $\mathbb{F}$.

Algorithm 5. Tag Generation of GCM

Tag Generation $\mathsf{GMAC}[E]((K_{\mathsf{bc}}, L), N, A, C)$

1: $H \leftarrow \mathsf{GHASH}(L, A, C)$; $X \leftarrow N \| 0^{c-1}1$; $T \leftarrow \mathsf{msb}_t(H \oplus E(K_{\mathsf{bc}}, X))$; **return** T

Algorithm 6. Tag Generation GMAC^+

Tag Generation $\Pi_{\mathsf{TGen}}[E]((K_{\mathsf{bc}}, L), N, A, M)$

1: $H \leftarrow \mathsf{GHASH}(L, A, M)$; $X \leftarrow 0 \| \mathsf{lsb}_{n-1}(H) \oplus (0^c \| N)$; $T \leftarrow E(K_{\mathsf{bc}}, X)$; **return** T

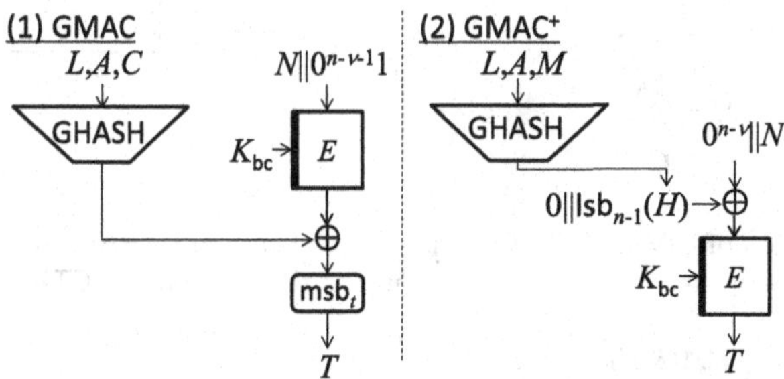

Fig. 3. Tagging functions GMAC (1) and of GMAC^+ (2).

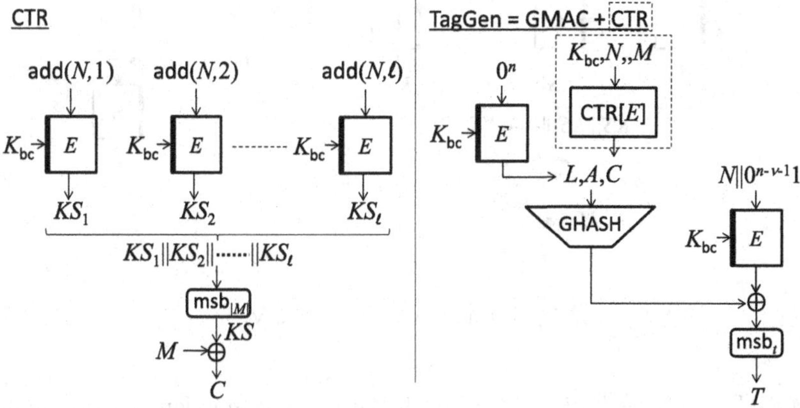

Fig. 4. Encryption of GCM. GCM is a special case of CTRAE: By introducing the redundant procedure in the dot line, GCM meets the interface of CTRAE.

GCM. GCM is a single-key CTRAE scheme with the tagging function GMAC. Hence, the key of the tag generation function is equal to that of CTR (i.e., $K_{\mathsf{tag}} = K_{\mathsf{bc}}$ and $\mathcal{K}_{\mathsf{tag}} = \{0,1\}^k$). The specification of GMAC is given in Algorithm 5 and Fig. 3(1). The hash key of GMAC is defined as $L \leftarrow E(K, 0^n)$. The encryptions of GCM and of KIVR[GCM] are respectively given in Figs. 4 and 5.

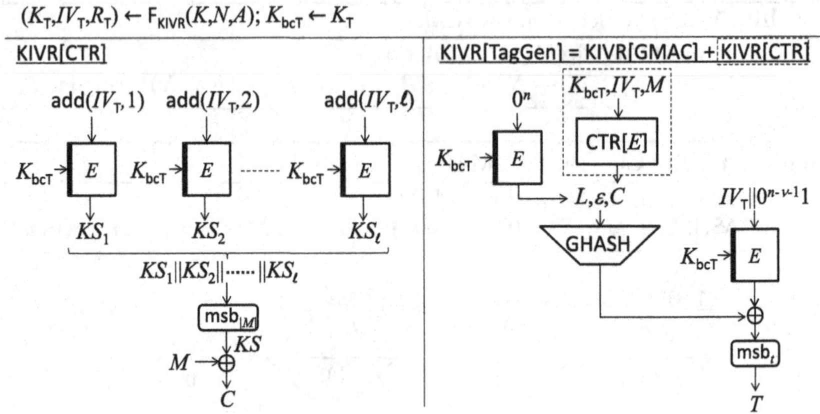

Fig. 5. Encryption of KIVR[GCM]. GCM is a special case of CTRAE: by introducing the redundant procedure in the dot line, GCM meets the interface of CTRAE.

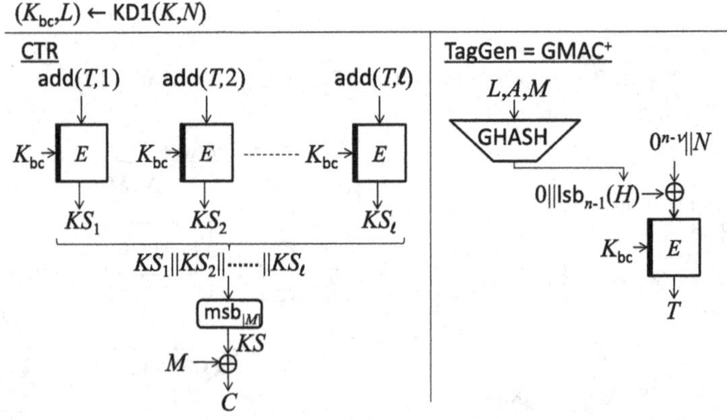

Fig. 6. Encryption of GCM-SIV.

GCM-SIV. GCM-SIV [8] is CTRAE with the tagging function GMAC^+ and the key derivation KD1. The specification of GMAC^+ is given in Algorithm 6 and Fig. 3(2). (K_{bc}, L) is a pair of (temporary) keys of $\mathsf{GMAC}^+[E]$, where K_{bc} is equal to the key of CTR. $\mathsf{GMAC}^+[E] : \{0,1\}^k \times \{0,1\}^n \times \mathcal{A} \times \mathcal{M} \rightarrow \{0,1\}^n$ takes an input tuple $(K_{\mathsf{bc}}, L, N, A, M)$ and returns an n-bit tag T. Note that (K_{bc}, L) is derived by using KD1. KD1 is a concatenation of truncated BCs where each BC call takes input tuple of a key, a nonce, and a counter. For the sake of simplifying the proof, when considering KIVR with GCM-SIV, KD1 is incorporated into $\mathsf{F}_{\mathsf{KIVR}}$. The encryptions of GCM-SIV and of KIVR[GCM-SIV] are respectively given in Figs. 6 and 7.

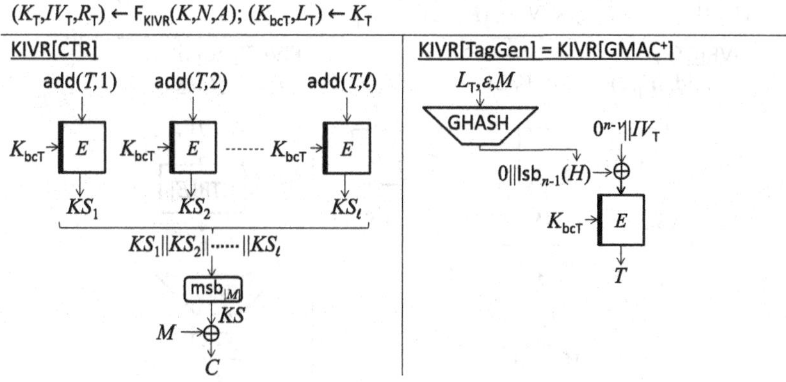

Fig. 7. Encryption of KIVR[GCM-SIV]. KD1 is incorporated into $\mathsf{F}_{\mathsf{KIVR}}$.

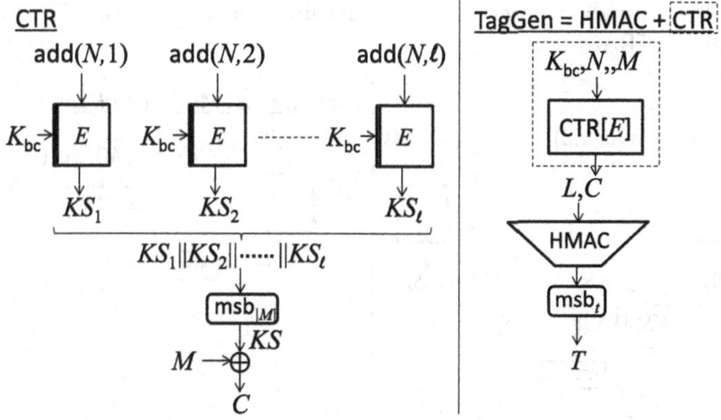

Fig. 8. Encryption of CTR-HMAC. CTR-HMAC is a special case of CTRAE: by introducing the redundant procedure in the dot line, the interface of CTR-HMAC meets the interface of CTRAE.

CCM. CCM is a single-key CTRAE with the CBC MAC as the tagging function. Hence, the key of the tagging function is equal to that of CTR (i.e., $K_{\mathsf{tag}} = K_{\mathsf{bc}}$ and $\mathcal{K}_{\mathsf{tag}} = \{0,1\}^k$). The encryption of CCM, the CBC MAC, and the encryption of KIVR[CCM] are respectively given in Figs. 10, 11, and 12.

7.2 CMT-4-Security of KIVR[GCM], KIVR[GCM-SIV], and KIVR[CCM]

We derive the **CMT**-4-security bounds of KIVR[GCM], KIVR[GCM-SIV], and KIVR[CCM] by using the bound in Theorem 1. For the sake of simplicity, we assume that $\mathsf{F}_{\mathsf{KIVR}}$ is a RO. Then, p_{kivr} is the number of queries to the RO, and we have $\mathbf{Adv}^{\mathsf{coll}}_{\mathsf{F}_{\mathsf{K}_{\mathsf{bc}}IVR}}(\mathbf{A}_2) \le \frac{0.5p_{\mathsf{kivr}}^2}{2^{k+\nu+r_T}}$ by the birthdaty analysis. We define the parameter as $\mu := 0.5p_{\mathsf{kivr}}^2 + 1$. Then, the size of S_1 which is $\mathbf{A}_1$'s output with

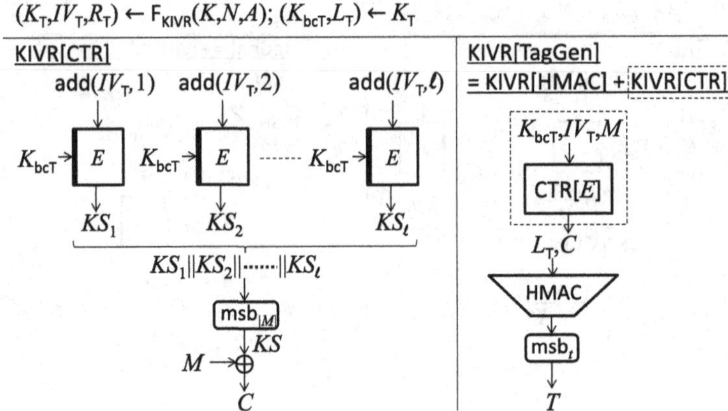

Fig. 9. Encryption of KIVR[CTR-HMAC]. CTR-HMAC is a special case of CTRAE: by introducing the redundant procedure in the dot line, the interface of CTR-HMAC meets the interface of CTRAE.

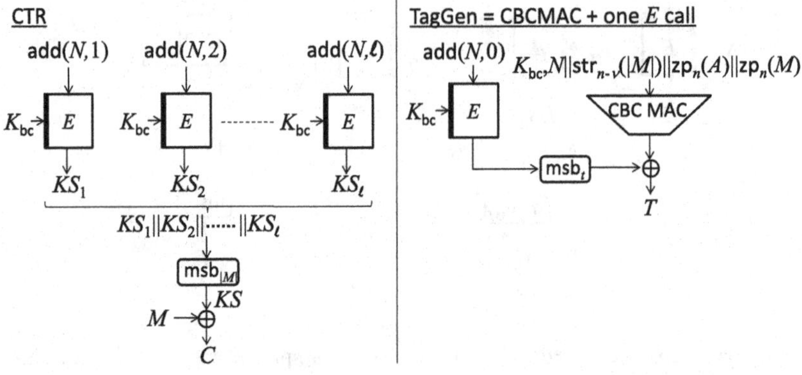

Fig. 10. Encryption of CCM.

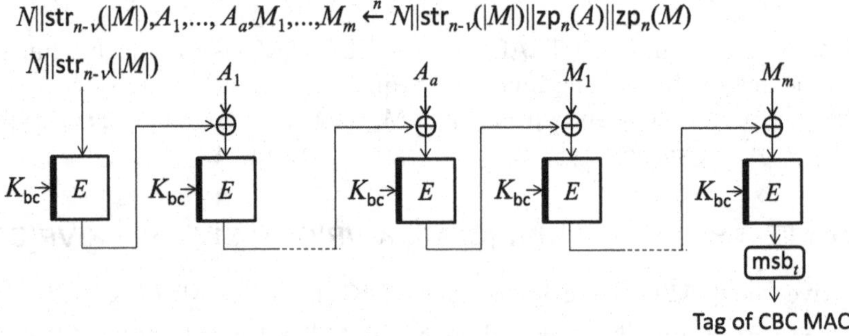

Fig. 11. CBC MAC.

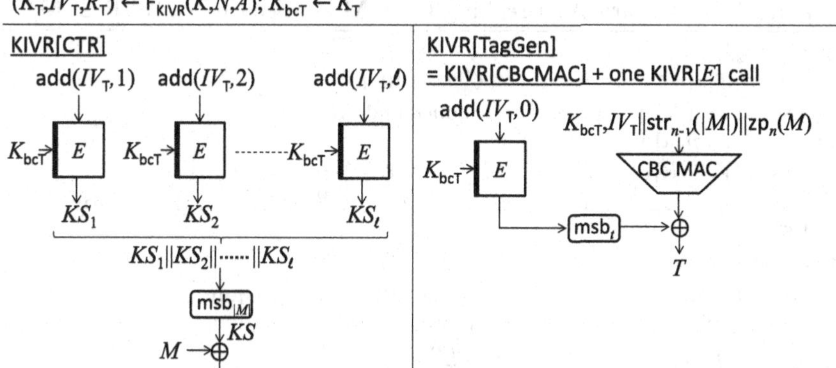

Fig. 12. Encryption of KIVR[CCM].

the condition $\mathsf{diff}_{\mathsf{KNA}}(\mathcal{S}_1) = 1$ is upper-bounded by $\binom{p_{\mathsf{kivr}}}{2} = 0.5p_{\mathsf{kivr}}(p_{\mathsf{kivr}} - 1)$, and we have $\mathbf{Adv}^{\mathsf{colls}}_{\Pi^*_{\mathsf{TGen}},\mu}(\mathbf{A}_1) = 0$. Hence, we obtain the following bounds.

Corollary 1. *Let $\Pi^* \in \{\mathsf{KIVR[GCM]}, \mathsf{KIVR[GCM\text{-}SIV]}, \mathsf{KIVR[CCM]}\}$. Assume that $\mathsf{F}_{\mathsf{KIVR}}$ is a RO. For any redundancy R, (ω, n)-mixing function $\mathsf{Mix}_{\mathsf{rc}}$, and* **CMT**-4 *adversary* $\mathbf{A}$ *making p_{ic} queries to an IC, and p_{kivr} queries to a RO, there exists an adversary $\mathbf{A}_2$ such that $\mathbf{Adv}^{\mathsf{cmt\text{-}4}}_{\Pi^*,\mathsf{Mix}_{\mathsf{rc}},R}(\mathbf{A}) \leq \frac{2^{\omega-1} \cdot p_{\mathsf{ic}}^2}{2^r} + \frac{0.5p_{\mathsf{kivr}}^2}{2^{k+\nu+r_{\mathsf{T}}}}$ and $\mathbf{A}_2$ makes p_{ic} queries to an IC and p_{kivr} queries to a RO.*

We assume that the term $\frac{0.5p_{\mathsf{kivr}}^2}{2^{k+\nu+r_{\mathsf{T}}}}$ is negligible, which can be ensured by choosing the parameter r_{T} such that $r \leq \kappa + \nu + r_{\mathsf{T}}$. Then, the above bound shows that KIVR[GCM], KIVR[GCM-SIV], and KIVR[CCM] achieve $\frac{r}{2}$-bit **CMT**-4-security.

7.3 Tightness of the CMT-4-Security of KIVR[GCM] and KIVR[GCM-SIV]

We show attacks whose probabilities are the same as Corollary 1, ensuring that the tightness of the bounds of KIVR[GCM] and of KIVR[GCM-SIV] in Corollary 1. The attacks are extensions of the **CMT**-1-attack given in [1] that makes use of the linearity of GHASH.

Theorem 2. *Let $\Pi^* \in \{\mathsf{KIVR[GCM]}, \mathsf{KIVR[GCM\text{-}SIV]}\}$. Assume that $\mathsf{F}_{\mathsf{KIVR}}$ is a RO. There exist redundancy R, a (ω, n)-mixing function $\mathsf{Mix}_{\mathsf{rc}}$, and an adversary $\mathbf{A}$ making p queries to an IC or a RO such that $\mathbf{Adv}^{\mathsf{cmt\text{-}1}}_{\Pi^*,\mathsf{Mix}_{\mathsf{rc}},R}(\mathbf{A}) = O\left(\max\left\{\frac{p^2}{2^r}, \frac{p^2}{2^{k+\nu+r_{\mathsf{T}}}}\right\}\right)$.*

Proof of Theorem 2 for KIVR[GCM]. Fix redundancy $R \in \{0,1\}^r$. We consider the following mixing function: $\mathsf{Mix}_{\mathsf{rc}}(R \| M_{\mathsf{origin}}) = R \| M_{\mathsf{origin}}$ for each core data M_{origin}. We then define two adversaries $\mathbf{A}_1$ and $\mathbf{A}_2$ that offer the first and second terms, respectively.

Algorithm 7. Adversary $\mathbf{A}_1$ Breaking the **CMT**-1-Security of $\mathsf{KIVR}[\mathsf{GCM}]$

1: $p_1 \leftarrow \lceil \frac{p}{\omega+2} \rceil - 4$
2: Choose p_1 distinct keys $K^{(1)}, \ldots, K^{(p_1)} \in \{0,1\}^k$
3: Choose a pair $(N, A) \in \mathcal{N} \times \mathcal{A}$ of a nonce and AD
4: **for** $i = 1, \ldots, p_1$ **do**
5: $\quad (K_\mathsf{T}^{(i)}, IV_\mathsf{T}^{(i)}, R_\mathsf{T}^{(i)}) \leftarrow \mathsf{F}_{\mathsf{KIVR}}(K^{(i)}, N, A)$; $KS^{(i)} \leftarrow \varepsilon$
6: $\quad$ **for** $j = 1, \ldots, \omega + 1$ **do** $KS^{(i)} \leftarrow KS^{(i)} \| E(K_\mathsf{T}^{(i)}, \mathsf{add}(IV_\mathsf{T}^{(i)}, j))$ **end for**
7: **end for**
8: **if** $\exists \alpha, \beta \in [p_1]$ s.t.
$\quad \alpha \neq \beta \wedge \mathsf{msb}_r(KS^{(\alpha)} \oplus KS^{(\beta)}) = \mathsf{zp}_r(R_\mathsf{T}^{(\alpha)} \oplus R_\mathsf{T}^{(\beta)})$ **then**
9: $\quad Z^{(\alpha)} \leftarrow E(K_\mathsf{T}^{(\alpha)}, IV_\mathsf{T}^{(\alpha)} \| 0^{n-\nu-1}1)$; $Z^{(\beta)} \leftarrow E(K_\mathsf{T}^{(\beta)}, IV_\mathsf{T}^{(\beta)} \| 0^{n-\nu-1}1)$
10: $\quad L^{(\alpha)} \leftarrow E(K_\mathsf{T}^{(\alpha)}, 0^n)$; $L^{(\beta)} \leftarrow E(K_\mathsf{T}^{(\beta)}, 0^n)$
11: $\quad$ Find C s.t. $|C| = n(\omega+1)$, $\mathsf{msb}_r(C) = R \oplus KS^{(\alpha)} \oplus \mathsf{zp}_r(R_\mathsf{T}^{(\alpha)})$,
$\quad\quad$ and $\mathsf{GHASH}(L^{(\alpha)}, \varepsilon, C) \oplus \mathsf{GHASH}(L^{(\beta)}, \varepsilon, C) = Z^{(\alpha)} \oplus Z^{(\beta)}$
12: $\quad M^{(\alpha)} \leftarrow C \oplus KS^{(\alpha)} \oplus \mathsf{zp}_{|C|}(R_\mathsf{T}^{(\alpha)})$; $M^{(\beta)} \leftarrow C \oplus KS^{(\beta)} \oplus \mathsf{zp}_{|C|}(R_\mathsf{T}^{(\beta)})$
13: $\quad$ **return** $((K^{(\alpha)}, N, A, M^{(\alpha)}), (K^{(\beta)}, N, A, M^{(\beta)}))$
14: **end if**
15: **return** $((K^{(1)}, N, A, KS^{(1)}), (K^{(2)}, N, A, KS^{(2)}))$

ADVERSARY $\mathbf{A}_1$. $\mathbf{A}_1$ breaking the **CMT**-1-security of $\mathsf{KIVR}[\mathsf{GCM}]$ is defined in Algorithm 7. $\mathbf{A}_1$ returns tuples $((K^{(\alpha)}, N^{(\alpha)}, A^{(\alpha)}, M^{(\alpha)}), (K^{(\beta)}, N^{(\beta)}, A^{(\beta)}, M^{(\beta)}))$ of a key, a nonce, AD, and a plaintext with redundancy such that $(N^{(\alpha)}, A^{(\alpha)}) = (N^{(\beta)}, A^{(\beta)})$, $K^{(\alpha)} \neq K^{(\beta)}$, and $M^{(\alpha)} \neq M^{(\beta)}$. We explain the algorithm below.

- Steps 2 and 3 define p_1 tuples of a key, a nonce, and AD, where the keys are all distinct. Using the tuples, Steps 4–7 calculate key streams.
- Step 8 searches a pair (α, β) with the relation $\mathsf{msb}_r \circ \mathsf{Mix}_{\mathsf{rc}}^{-1}$ $(KS^{(\alpha)} \oplus KS^{(\beta)}) = \mathsf{zp}_r\left(R_\mathsf{T}^{(\alpha)} \oplus R_\mathsf{T}^{(\beta)}\right)$ that is the sufficient condition to obtain a ciphertext collision from Lemma 1. For each pair (α, β), $KS^{(\alpha)}$ and $KS^{(\beta)}$ are (almost) r-bit random values, and thus the probability that the relation is satisfied is $O(\frac{1}{2^r})$. Summing the bound for each pair, we have the bound $O\left(\frac{p^2}{2^r}\right)$ of the probability that the relation is satisfied.
- If such a pair is found, then we can find the collision $(C^{(\alpha)}, T^{(\alpha)}) = (C^{(\beta)}, T^{(\alpha)})$ by using the freeness of plaintext blocks. In Step 11, by using the linearity of GHASH, a ciphertext C that yields a tag collision is found by solving the equation $\mathsf{GHASH}(L^{(\alpha)}, \varepsilon, C) \oplus \mathsf{GHASH}(L^{(\beta)}, \varepsilon, C) = Z^{(\alpha)} \oplus Z^{(\beta)}$. In Step 12, we have plaintexts $M^{(\alpha)}$ and $M^{(\beta)}$ with the redundancy R that yield the collision.

Hence, the probability that $\mathbf{A}_1$ breaks the **CMT**-1-security of $\mathsf{KIVR}[\mathsf{GCM}]$ is at least $O\left(\frac{p^2}{2^r}\right)$.

ADVERSARY $\mathbf{A}_2$. $\mathbf{A}_2$ breaks the **CMT**-1-security of $\mathsf{KIVR}[\mathsf{GCM}]$ by using a collision of $\mathsf{F}_{\mathsf{K_{bc}}IVR}$. If $\mathsf{F}_{\mathsf{K_{bc}}IVR}(K^{(\alpha)}, N^{(\alpha)}, A^{(\alpha)}) = \mathsf{F}_{\mathsf{K_{bc}}IVR}(K^{(\beta)}, N^{(\beta)}, A^{(\beta)})$ such

Algorithm 8. MD Hash Function with DM Compression Function

Hash Function $\mathsf{MD}^{\mathsf{DM}^F}(D)$

1: $D_1, \ldots, D_d \xleftarrow{b} \mathsf{sfpad}(D)$; $S \leftarrow IS$; **for** $i = 1, \ldots, d$ **do** $S \leftarrow \mathsf{DM}^F(S, D_i)$ **end for**
2: **return** S

Algorithm 9. Tag Generation HMAC

Tag Generation $\mathsf{HMAC}[\mathsf{MD}^{\mathsf{DM}^F}](L, D)$

1: $S \leftarrow \mathsf{MD}^{\mathsf{DM}^F}(\mathsf{ipad} \oplus \mathsf{ozp}_b(L) \| D)$; $T \leftarrow \mathsf{lsb}_t\left(\mathsf{MD}^{\mathsf{DM}^F}(\mathsf{opad} \oplus \mathsf{ozp}_b(L) \| S)\right)$
2: **return** T

that $K^{(\alpha)} \neq K^{(\beta)}$ and $(N^{(\alpha)}, A^{(\alpha)}) = (N^{(\beta)}, A^{(\beta)})$, then by choosing the same plaintexts $M^{(\alpha)} = M^{(\beta)}$ with the redundancy R, we obtain the output collision $(C^{(\alpha)}, T^{(\alpha)}) = (C^{(\beta)}, T^{(\beta)})$. By the birthday analysis, we have the bound of the collision probability $O\left(\frac{p^2}{2^{k+\nu+r_T}}\right)$. □

Outline of Proof for KIVR[GCM-SIV]. The proof is the same as that of Theorem 2. The first bound is obtained by an attack that finds a pair of input to CTR such that the key streams satisfy the condition in Lemma 1 (i.e., a ciphertext collision occurs). Note that the tag collision is found with the probability 1 by using the linearity of GHASH. The second bound is obtained by an attack that makes use of a collision of $\mathsf{F}_{\mathsf{K}_{\mathsf{bc}}IVR}$. □

7.4 On the Tightness of CMT-4-Security of KIVR[CCM]

Since the CBC MAC does not have the linearity as GMAC, the attack of the adversary $\mathbf{A}_1$ in the proof of Theorem 2 does not work, and there is a possibility that the bound $\frac{2^{\omega-1} \cdot p_{\mathsf{ic}}^2}{2^r}$ is improved. Proving the tightness for the **CMT**-4-Security of KIVR[CCM] is an open problem.

8 Committing Security of KIVR with CTR-HMAC

By using the bound in Theorem 1, we derive the **CMT**-4-bound of KIVR with the CTR-based AE scheme with HMAC with the Merkle-Damgård (MD) hash function. Since SHA-2 family has the MD structure, the bound supports the widely used MAC HMAC-SHA-256.

8.1 Specification of CTR-HMAC

CTR-HMAC is CTRAE that uses HMAC as the underlying MAC. HMAC is a hash-function-based MAC and we consider the Merkle-Damgård (MD) hash function with the Davies-Meyer (DM) compression function as the underlying hash function which is employed in the SHA-2 family.

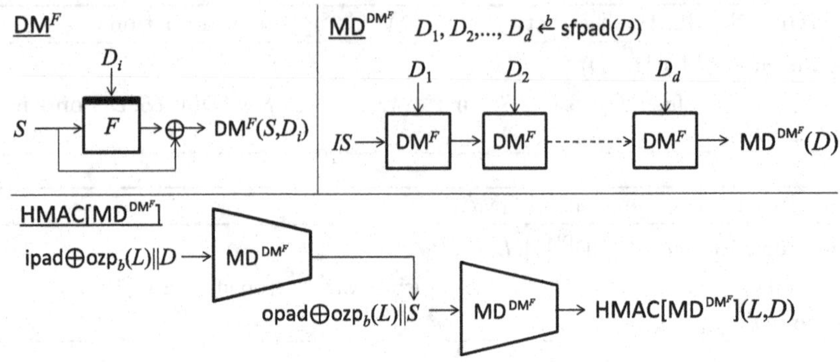

Fig. 13. DM, MD, and HMAC.

Let $F : \{0,1\}^v \times \{0,1\}^b \rightarrow \{0,1\}^v$ be the underlying primitive (or block cipher) of DM with v-bit blocks and b-bit key elements. Then, DM with F is defined as $\mathsf{DM}^F(S, D_i) = S \oplus F(S, D_i)$.

$\mathsf{MD}^{\mathsf{DM}^F}$ is a hash function that iterates DM^F. Let IS be a v-bit constant and initial value of $\mathsf{MD}^{\mathsf{DM}^F}$. Let $\mathsf{sfpad} : \{0,1\}^* \rightarrow \{0,1\}^{b*}$ be a suffix-free padding function such that for any distinct inputs D and D', $\mathsf{sfpad}(D)$ is not a prefix of $\mathsf{sfpad}(D')$.[6] MD with DM^F is defined in Algorithm 8.

Let L be the HMAC's key such that $|L| \leq b$. Let ipad and opad be distinct b-bit constants that are used to define the inner key $\mathsf{zp}_b(L) \oplus \mathsf{ipad}$ and the outer key $\mathsf{zp}_b(L) \oplus \mathsf{opad}$. HMAC processes the underlying hash function twice. The first hash call takes the inner key and the input D. The second hash call takes the outer key and the output of the first hash call. The output of the second hash call (with truncation) is a tag of HMAC. HMAC is defined in Algorithm 9.

DM, MD, and HMAC are given in Fig. 13, and the encryptions of CTR-HMAC and of KIVR[CTR-HMAC] are respectively given in Figs. 8 and 9. Note that CTR-HMAC with AES-128 and SHA-256 is a widely used AE scheme and does not support AD inputs. By using KIVR, one can convert the AE scheme so that the AD inputs are supported.

8.2 CMT-4-Security Bound of KIVR[CTR-HMAC]

Regarding the collision resistance of HMAC, Damgård [10] and Merkle [26] showed that an iterated structure of a compression function preserves its collision resistance of the underlying function. Hence, the collision resistance of HMAC is reduced to the collision resistance of $\mathsf{MD}^{\mathsf{DM}^F}$ that is further reduced to the collision resistance of DM^F. We use the collision bound in the IC model proven by Stam [27]: for any adversary $\mathbf{A}'$ making p_{tag} queries

[6] SHA-2 uses the following suffix-free padding function: for an input D, a one-zero value 10^i is appended to D, followed by the 64-bit encoding of $|D|$ so that the total length is a multiple of b and i is minimum.

to F or F^{-1}, $\mathbf{Adv}^{\mathsf{coll}}_{\mathsf{HMAC}}(\mathbf{A}') \leq \frac{p_{\mathsf{tag}}(p_{\mathsf{tag}}+1)}{2^t}$. By using Markov's inequality, $\mathbf{Adv}^{\mathsf{colls}}_{\mathsf{KIVR[HMAC]},\mu}(\mathbf{A}_1) \leq \frac{p_{\mathsf{tag}}(p_{\mathsf{tag}}+1)}{\mu 2^t}$. Then, we choose μ such that $\frac{2^\omega \cdot (\mu-1)}{2^r} \simeq \frac{p_{\mathsf{tag}}(p_{\mathsf{tag}}+1)}{\mu 2^t}$, i.e., $\mu = \frac{(p_{\mathsf{tag}}(p_{\mathsf{tag}}+1))^{1/2}}{2^{\frac{t-r+\omega}{2}}}$. Putting the bound into Theorem 1, we obtain the following corollary.

Corollary 2. *For any redundancy R, (ω, n)-mixing function $\mathsf{Mix}_{\mathsf{rc}}$, and* **CMT**-4 *adversary* $\mathbf{A}$ *making p_{ic} queries to E or E^{-1}, p_{tag} queries to F or F^{-1}, and p_{kivr} queries to Ψ_{KIVR}, there exists an adversary $\mathbf{A}_2$ such that* $\mathbf{Adv}^{\mathsf{cmt\text{-}4}}_{\mathsf{KIVR}[\mathsf{CTR\text{-}HMAC}],\mathsf{Mix}_{\mathsf{rc}},R}(\mathbf{A}) \leq \left(\frac{2^{\omega+2}\cdot p_{\mathsf{tag}}(p_{\mathsf{tag}}+1)}{2^{r+t}}\right)^{\frac{1}{2}} + \mathbf{Adv}^{\mathsf{coll}}_{\mathsf{F}_{\mathsf{K_{bc}}IVR}}(\mathbf{A}_2)$ *and* $\mathbf{A}_2$ *makes p_{ic} queries to E or E^{-1}, p_{tag} queries to F or F^{-1}, and p_{kivr} queries to Ψ_{KIVR}.*

We assume that the term $\mathbf{Adv}^{\mathsf{coll}}_{\mathsf{F}_{\mathsf{K_{bc}}IVR}}(\mathbf{A}_2)$ is negligible, which can be ensured by using a secure hash function. Then, the above bound shows that KIVR[CTR-HMAC] achieves $\frac{r+t}{2}$-bit **CMT**-4-security. $2^{\omega+2}$ is a small constant.

8.3 Tightness of the CMT-4-Security of KIVR[CTR-HMAC]

We show attacks on KIVR[CTR-HMAC] whose bound matches the one in Corollary 1, thereby ensuring the tightness of the bound. In this proof, we assume that HMAC is a random oracle that is an ideal hash function.

Theorem 3. *Let $\delta_{\mathsf{coll}}(p)$ be the lower-bound of the probability that a collision of $\mathsf{F}_{\mathsf{K_{bc}}IVR}$ is found with p queries to Ψ_{KIVR} such that the input keys are distinct and the other inputs are the same. Assume that* HMAC *is a random oracle* RO*. There exist redundancy R, a (ω, n)-mixing function $\mathsf{Mix}_{\mathsf{rc}}$, and an adversary breaking the* **CMT**-1*-security of Π^* making p queries to E, E^{-1},* RO*, or Ψ_{KIVR} such that* $\mathbf{Adv}^{\mathsf{cmt\text{-}1}}_{\mathsf{KIVR}[\mathsf{CTR\text{-}HMAC}],\mathsf{Mix}_{\mathsf{rc}},R}(\mathbf{A}) = O\left(\max\{\frac{p^2}{2^{r+t}}, \delta_{\mathsf{coll}}(p)\}\right)$.

Proof (Outline). The first bound is obtained by an attack that finds two input tuples of KIVR[CTR-HMAC] such that the key streams satisfy the condition in Lemma 1 (i.e., a ciphertext collision occurs) and a collision of the tags occurs. By the birthday analysis, we obtain the first bound. The second bound is obtained by an attack that makes use of a collision of $\mathsf{F}_{\mathsf{K_{bc}}IVR}$. The formal proof is given in Appendix E. □

9 Conclusion

We propose the KIVR conversion for enabling the BBB and CMT-4 security by exploiting redundancy. KIVR uses a collision-resistant hash function to convert a tuple of a key, a nonce, and associated data into a temporary key, an initial value (or nonce), and a masking value applied to redundant data used by an underlying AE. We give a general bound for the **CMT**-4 security of KIVR with CTRAE, CTR combined with any MAC, covering a large class of practical AEs.

The bound is $\frac{r}{2}$ + tag-col bits wherein r is the number of redundant bits and tag-col is the tag-collision security of the underlying AE. We set tag-col = 0 for GCM, GCM-SIV, and CCM, and the corresponding bound becomes $\frac{r}{2}$, which is tight for GCM and GCM-SIV. Meanwhile, KIVR with CTR-HMAC achieves a better tight bound, $\frac{r+t}{2}$ bits, with a t-bit tag. There are interesting open research questions. In particular, analyzing/salvaging the other popular AEs, including ChaCha20-Poly1305 [23], for committing security is open for future research.

Acknowledgement. We thank Dong Hoon Chang, an associate of National Institute of Standards and Technology, for helpful comments on the formalization of the redundant plaintext. We also thank anonymous reviewers for constructive feedback.

A Multi-user Security for AE

Multi-user-AE (**mu-AE**) security is the indistinguishability between the real and ideal worlds. Let $\Pi = (\Pi_{\mathsf{Enc}}, \Pi_{\mathsf{Dec}})$ be an AE scheme that has encryption and decryption algorithms. Let u be the number of users. In the **mu-AE**-security game, an adversary **A** has access to either real-world oracles $(\Pi_{K_1}, \ldots, \Pi_{K_u})$ or ideal-world ones $((\$_1, \bot), \ldots, (\$_u, \bot))$. $K_1, \ldots, K_u$ are user's keys defined as $K_i \xleftarrow{\$} \mathcal{K}$ where $i \in [u]$. $\$_\xi$ is a random-bit oracle of the ξ-th user that takes an input tuple (N, A, M) of nonce, AD, and plaintext, and returns a pair of random ciphertext and tag defined as $(C, T) \xleftarrow{\$} \{0,1\}^{|\Pi_{\mathsf{Enc}}[E](K,N,A,M)|}$. $\bot$ is a reject oracle that returns **reject** for each query. At the end of this game, **A** return a decision bit in $\{0, 1\}$. If the underlying primitive is ideal, then **A** has access to the ideal primitive. Let $\mathbf{A}^{\mathcal{O}} \in \{0,1\}$ be an output of **A** with access to a set of oracles $\mathcal{O}$. Then, the **mu-AE**-security advantage function of **A** is defined as $\mathbf{Adv}_{\Pi}^{\mathbf{mu\text{-}ae}}(\mathbf{A}) := \Pr\left[\mathbf{A}^{\Pi_{K_1}, \ldots, \Pi_{K_u}} = 1\right] - \Pr\left[\mathbf{A}^{(\$_1, \bot), \ldots, (\$_u, \bot)} = 1\right]$. We consider nonce-respecting adversaries where for each user, all nonces in queries to the encryption oracle are distinct. In this game, making a trivial query (ξ, N, A, C, T') to the decryption oracle is forbidden, which was received by some previous query to the encryption one.

B Multi-user PRF Security

The **mu-AE** security of KIVR-based schemes relies on multi-user pseudo-random-function (mu-PRF) security. Let $\mathsf{F}_K : \mathcal{M} \to \{0,1\}^s$ be a keyed function with a key $K \in \mathcal{K}_{\mathsf{F}}$ where $\mathcal{M} \subseteq \{0,1\}^*$ is the input space, s is the output length, and $\mathcal{K}_{\mathsf{F}}$ is the key space. Let u be the number of users. Let Func be the set of all functions from $\mathcal{M}$ to $\{0,1\}^s$. In the mu-PRF-security game, an adversary **A** has access to either real-world oracles $(\mathsf{F}_{K_1}, \ldots, \mathsf{F}_{K_u})$ or ideal-world ones $(\mathcal{R}_1, \ldots, \mathcal{R}_u)$, where K_i is the i-th user's key defined as $K_i \xleftarrow{\$} \{0,1\}^{\mathcal{K}}$ and $\mathcal{R}_i$ is a random function of the i-th user defined as $\mathcal{R}_i \xleftarrow{\$}$ Func. At the end of this game, **A** return a decision bit. Let $\mathbf{A}^{\mathcal{O}_1, \ldots, \mathcal{O}_u}$ be an output of **A** with access to oracles $(\mathcal{O}_1, \ldots, \mathcal{O}_u)$. Then, the mu-PRF-security advantage function of **A** is defined as $\mathbf{Adv}_{\mathsf{F}}^{\mathsf{mu\text{-}prf}}(\mathbf{A}) := \Pr\left[\mathbf{A}^{\mathsf{F}_{K_1}, \ldots, \mathsf{F}_{K_u}} = 1\right] - \Pr\left[\mathbf{A}^{\mathcal{R}_1, \ldots, \mathcal{R}_u} = 1\right]$.

C mu-AE Security of AE Schemes with KIVR

The following theorem shows that the **mu-AE** security of an AE scheme Π with KIVR is reduced to the **mu-AE**-security of the underlying AE scheme Π and the mu-PRF security of $\mathsf{F}_{\mathsf{KIVR}}$. Note that in the theorem, $\mathsf{F}_{\mathsf{KIVR}}$ is a keyed function.

Theorem 4. *Let Π be an AE scheme. Let R be redundancy and $\mathsf{Mix}_{\mathsf{rc}}$ a (ω, n)-mixing function. For any* **mu-AE** *adversary* $\mathbf{A}$ *against KIVR[Π] making at most q queries and running in time T, there exists an* **mu-AE** *adversary* $\mathbf{A}_1$ *against Π and a mu-PRF adversary $\mathbf{A}_2$ against $\mathsf{F}_{\mathsf{KIVR}}$ such that $\mathbf{Adv}^{\mathbf{mu\text{-}ae}}_{\mathsf{KIVR}[\Pi]}(\mathbf{A}) \leq \mathbf{Adv}^{\mathbf{mu\text{-}ae}}_{\Pi}(\mathbf{A}_1) + \mathbf{Adv}^{\mathsf{mu\text{-}prf}}_{\mathsf{F}_{\mathsf{KIVR}}}(\mathbf{A}_2)$, where $\mathbf{A}$ makes at most q construction queries and runs in time T, and $\mathbf{A}_1$ and $\mathbf{A}_2$ respectively make at most q construction queries and runs in time $T + O(q)$.*

Proof. Firstly, the keyed functions $\mathsf{F}_{\mathsf{KIVR}}(K_1, \cdot, \cdot), \ldots, \mathsf{F}_{\mathsf{KIVR}}(K_u, \cdot, \cdot)$ are replaced with random functions $\mathcal{R}_1, \ldots, \mathcal{R}_u$. Then, the mu-PRF-advantage function of $\mathbf{A}_2$ is introduced in the **mu-AE**-security bound.

We next consider the **mu-AE**-security of KIVR[Π] where $\mathsf{F}_{\mathsf{KIVR}}$ is a random function $\mathcal{R}_i$. By random functions, for each of tuples of a key, nonce, and AD, the temporary key is chosen uniformly at random from $\mathcal{K}$, the **mu-AE**-security of KIVR[Π] is reduced to the **mu-AE**-security of Π, i.e., for any adversary breaking the **mu-AE**-security of KIVR[Π], there exists an adversary $\mathbf{A}_1$ breaking the **mu-AE**-security of Π.

Hence, we have $\mathbf{Adv}^{\mathbf{mu\text{-}ae}}_{\mathsf{KIVR}[\Pi]}(\mathbf{A}) \leq \mathbf{Adv}^{\mathbf{mu\text{-}ae}}_{\Pi}(\mathbf{A}_1) + \mathbf{Adv}^{\mathsf{mu\text{-}prf}}_{\mathsf{F}_{\mathsf{KIVR}}}(\mathbf{A}_2)$. □

D Proof of Theorem 2 for KIVR[GCM-SIV]

Fix redundancy $R \in \{0,1\}^r$. We consider the mixing function: $\mathsf{Mix}_{\mathsf{rc}}(R \| M_{\mathsf{origin}}) = R \| M_{\mathsf{origin}}$ for each core data M_{origin}. We then define two adversaries $\mathbf{A}_1$ and $\mathbf{A}_2$ that offer the terms $\frac{p^2}{2^r}$ and $\frac{p^2}{2^{k+\nu+r_{\mathsf{T}}}}$, respectively.

Adversary $\mathbf{A}_1$. $\mathbf{A}_1$ breaking the **CMT**-1-security of KIVR[GCM-SIV] is given in Algorithm 10. $\mathbf{A}_1$ returns a pair $((K^{(\alpha)}, N, A, M^{(\alpha)}), (K^{(\beta)}, N, A, M^{(\beta)}))$ such that $K^{(\alpha)} \neq K^{(\beta)}$. We explain the algorithm below.

- Steps 2 and 3 define p_1 tuples of a key, a nonce, and AD, where the keys are all distinct. In Steps 4-7, $\mathbf{A}$ calculates key streams for the input tuples.
- Step 8 searches a pair (α, β) with the following conditions: $\mathsf{msb}_1(X^{(\alpha)}) = \mathsf{msb}_1(X^{(\beta)}) = 0$ and $\mathsf{msb}_r\left(KS^{(\alpha)} \oplus KS^{(\beta)}\right) = \mathsf{zp}_r(R_{\mathsf{T}}^{(\alpha)} \oplus R_{\mathsf{T}}^{(\beta)})$. The second condition is a sufficient one to obtain a ciphertext collision due to Lemma 1. For each pair (α, β), $KS^{(\alpha)}$ and $KS^{(\beta)}$ are (almost) r-bit random values, and thus the probability that the relation is satisfied is $O(\frac{1}{2^r})$. Summing the bound for each pair, we have the bound $O\left(\frac{p^2}{2^r}\right)$ of the probability that the relation is satisfied.

Algorithm 10. Adversary $\mathbf{A}$ Breaking the **CMT**-1-Security of $\mathsf{KIVR}[\mathsf{GCM\text{-}SIV}]$

1: $\omega \leftarrow \lceil \frac{r}{n} \rceil$; $p_1 \leftarrow \lceil \frac{p}{\omega+4} \rceil$
2: Choose p_1 distinct keys $K^{(1)}, \ldots, K^{(p_1)} \in \mathcal{K}$
3: Choose a pair $(N, A) \in \mathcal{N} \times \mathcal{A}$ of nonce and AD and a tag $T \in \{0,1\}^n$
4: **for** $i = 1, \ldots, p_1$ **do**
5: $((K_{\mathsf{bcT}}^{(i)}, L_{\mathsf{T}}^{(i)}), IV_{\mathsf{T}}^{(i)}, R_{\mathsf{T}}^{(i)}) \leftarrow \mathsf{F}_{\mathsf{KIVR}}(K^{(i)}, N, A)$; $X^{(i)} \leftarrow E^{-1}(K_{\mathsf{bcT}}^{(i)}, T)$
6: **for** $j = 1, \ldots, \omega + 2$ **do** $KS^{(i)} \leftarrow KS^{(i)} \| E(K_{\mathsf{bcT}}^{(i)}, \mathsf{add}(T, j))$ **end for**
7: **end for**
8: **if** $\exists \alpha, \beta \in [p_1]$ s.t. $\alpha \neq \beta \wedge \mathsf{msb}_1(X^{(\alpha)}) = \mathsf{msb}_1(X^{(\beta)}) = 0 \wedge$ $\mathsf{msb}_r\left(KS^{(\alpha)} \oplus KS^{(\beta)}\right) = \mathsf{zp}_r(R_{\mathsf{T}}^{(\alpha)} \oplus R_{\mathsf{T}}^{(\beta)})$ **then**
9: $H^{(\alpha)} \leftarrow X^{(\alpha)} \oplus 0^{n-\nu} \| IV_{\mathsf{T}}^{(\alpha)}$; $H^{(\beta)} \leftarrow X^{(\beta)} \oplus 0^{n-\nu} \| IV_{\mathsf{T}}^{(\beta)}$
10: Find $\omega + 2$ block plaintexts $M^{(\alpha)}, M^{(\beta)}$ s.t.
$\mathsf{msb}_r(M^{(\alpha)}) = \mathsf{msb}_r(M^{(\beta)}) = R$,
$C^{(\alpha)} = C^{(\beta)}$,
$\mathsf{lsb}_{n-1}(\mathsf{GHASH}(L_{\mathsf{T}}^{(\alpha)}, \varepsilon, M^{(\alpha)})) = \mathsf{lsb}_{n-1}(H^{(\alpha)})$, and
$\mathsf{lsb}_{n-1}(\mathsf{GHASH}(L_{\mathsf{T}}^{(\beta)}, \varepsilon, M^{(\beta)})) = \mathsf{lsb}_{n-1}(H^{(\beta)})$
11: **return** $((K^{(\alpha)}, N, A, M^{(\alpha)}), (K^{(\beta)}, N, A, M^{(\beta)}))$
12: **end if**
13: **return** $((K^{(1)}, N, A, 0), (K^{(2)}, N, A, 0))$

- If such pair is found, then $\mathbf{A}$ can find a pair $((K^{(\alpha)}, N, A, M^{(\alpha)}), (K^{(\beta)}, N, A, M^{(\beta)}))$ such that $(C^{(\alpha)}, T^{(\alpha)}) = (C^{(\beta)}, T^{(\beta)})$ by solving the equations: $\mathsf{msb}_r(M^{(\alpha)}) = \mathsf{msb}_r(M^{(\beta)}) = R$, $C^{(\alpha)} = C^{(\beta)}$ ($\Leftrightarrow M^{(\alpha)} \oplus M^{(\beta)} = KS^{(\alpha)} \oplus KS^{(\beta)}$), $\mathsf{GHASH}(L^{(\alpha)}, \varepsilon, M^{(\alpha)}) = H^{(\alpha)}$, and $\mathsf{GHASH}(L^{(\beta)}, \varepsilon, M^{(\beta)}) = H^{(\beta)}$. Since Step 8 ensures that the ciphertext collision occurs, this step searches the pair that yields the tag collision. In the equations, there are $2(\omega + 2)$ plaintext blocks and there are $\omega + 4$ equations for the blocks. Fixing the 2ω message blocks with redundancy such that $\mathsf{msb}_{\omega n}(C^{(\alpha)}) = \mathsf{msb}_{\omega n}(C^{(\beta)})$, the remaining 4 message blocks are uniquely determined from the equations $\mathsf{lsb}_{2n}(C^{(\alpha)}) = \mathsf{lsb}_{2n}(C^{(\beta)})$, $\mathsf{lsb}_{n-1}(\mathsf{GHASH}(L_{\mathsf{T}}^{(\alpha)}, A^{(\alpha)}, M^{(\alpha)})) = \mathsf{lsb}_{n-1}(H^{(\alpha)})$, and $\mathsf{lsb}_{n-1}(\mathsf{GHASH}(L_{\mathsf{T}}^{(\beta)}, A^{(\beta)}, M^{(\beta)})) = \mathsf{lsb}_{n-1}(H^{(\beta)})$. Then, we have a pair with the output collision.

Hence, the probability that $\mathbf{A}$ win the **CMT**-1 game is $O\left(\frac{p^2}{2^r}\right)$.

Adversary $\mathbf{A}_2$. The second adversary $\mathbf{A}_2$ that breaks the **CMT**-1-security of $\mathsf{KIVR}[\mathsf{GCM\text{-}SIV}]$ by using a collision of $\mathsf{F}_{\mathsf{K_{bc}}IVR}$. If $\mathsf{F}_{\mathsf{K_{bc}}IVR}(K^{(\alpha)}, N^{(\alpha)}, A^{(\alpha)}) = \mathsf{F}_{\mathsf{K_{bc}}IVR}(K^{(\beta)}, N^{(\beta)}, A^{(\beta)})$ such that $K^{(\alpha)} \neq K^{(\beta)}$ and $(N^{(\alpha)}, A^{(\alpha)}) = (N^{(\beta)}, A^{(\beta)})$, then by choosing the same plaintexts $M^{(\alpha)}$ and $M^{(\beta)}$ such that $\mathsf{msb}_r(M^{(\alpha)}) = \mathsf{msb}_r(M^{(\beta)}) = R$ and the tag collision occurs, we obtain the output collision $(C^{(\alpha)}, T^{(\alpha)}) = (C^{(\beta)}, T^{(\beta)})$. The collision probability is $O\left(\frac{p^2}{2^{k+\nu+r_{\mathsf{T}}}}\right)$. Note that the plaintexts with the tag collision can be found by the same procedure as $\mathbf{A}_1$ that finds ciphertexts with the tag collision by making use of the linearity of GHASH. □

Algorithm 11. Adversary $\mathbf{A}_1$ Breaking the **CMT**-1-Security of KIVR [CTR-HMAC]

1: $p_1 \leftarrow 0.5\lceil \frac{p}{\omega+1} \rceil$
2: Choose p_1 distinct keys $K^{(1)}, \ldots, K^{(p_1)} \in \{0,1\}^k$
3: Choose a pair $(N, A) \in \mathcal{N} \times \mathcal{A}$ of a nonce and AD
4: **for** $i = 1, \ldots, p_1$ **do**
5: $\quad (K_\mathsf{T}^{(i)}, IV_\mathsf{T}^{(i)}, R_\mathsf{T}^{(i)}) \leftarrow \mathsf{F}_\mathsf{KIVR}(K^{(i)}, N, A)$; $KS^{(i)} \leftarrow \varepsilon$
6: $\quad$ **for** $j = 1, \ldots, \omega + 1$ **do** $KS^{(i)} \leftarrow KS^{(i)} \| E(K_\mathsf{T}^{(i)}, \mathsf{add}(IV_\mathsf{T}^{(i)}, j))$ **end for**
7: **end for**
8: **for** each $(\alpha, \beta) \in [p_1]^2$ s.t. $\alpha \neq \beta \wedge \mathsf{msb}_r(KS^{(\alpha)} \oplus KS^{(\beta)}) = \mathsf{zp}_r(R_\mathsf{T}^{(\alpha)} \oplus R_\mathsf{T}^{(\beta)})$ **do**
9: $\quad M^{(\alpha)} \leftarrow R \| \mathsf{lsb}_{(\omega+1)n-r}(KS^{(\alpha)} \oplus \mathsf{zp}_{(\omega+1)n}(R_\mathsf{T}^{(\alpha)}))$
10: $\quad M^{(\beta)} \leftarrow R \| \mathsf{lsb}_{(\omega+1)n-r}(KS^{(\beta)} \oplus \mathsf{zp}_{(\omega+1)n}(R_\mathsf{T}^{(\beta)}))$
11: $\quad C \leftarrow M^{(\alpha)} \oplus (KS^{(\alpha)} \oplus \mathsf{zp}_{(\omega+1)n}(R_\mathsf{T}^{(\alpha)}))$
12: $\quad T^{(\alpha)} \leftarrow \mathsf{RO}(K_{\mathsf{tagT}}^{(\alpha)}, IV_\mathsf{T}^{(\alpha)}, C)$; $T^\beta \leftarrow \mathsf{RO}(K_{\mathsf{tagT}}^{(\beta)}, IV_\mathsf{T}^{(\beta)}, C)$
13: $\quad$ **if** $T^\alpha = T^\beta$ **then return** $((K^{(\alpha)}, N, A, M^{(\alpha)}), (K^{(\beta)}, N, A, M^{(\beta)}))$ **end if**
14: **end for**
15: **return** $((K^{(1)}, N, A, KS^{(1)}), (K^{(2)}, N, A, KS^{(2)}))$

E Proof of Theorem 3

In this proof, we assume that HMAC is a random oracle RO which is an ideal hash function. Let $R \in \{0,1\}^r$ be redundancy. We consider the following mixing function: $\mathsf{Mix}_\mathsf{rc}(R \| M_\mathsf{origin}) = R \| M_\mathsf{origin}$ for each core data M_origin. We then define two adversaries $\mathbf{A}_1$ and $\mathbf{A}_2$ that offer the terms $\frac{p^2}{2^{r+t}}$ and $\delta_\mathsf{coll}(p)$, respectively.

Adversary $\mathbf{A}_1$. The adversary $\mathbf{A}_1$ breaking the **CMT**-1-security of KIVR[CTR-HMAC] is defined in Algorithm 11. The adversary returns a pair $((K^{(\alpha)}, N^{(\alpha)}, A^{(\alpha)}, M^{(\alpha)})$ $(K^{(\beta)}, N^{(\beta)}, A^{(\beta)}, M^{(\beta)}))$ such that $(N^{(\alpha)}, A^{(\alpha)}) = (N^{(\beta)}, A^{(\beta)})$, $K^{(\alpha)} \neq K^{(\beta)}$, and $M^{(\alpha)} \neq M^{(\beta)}$. We explain the algorithm below.

- Steps 2 and 3 define p_1 tuples of a key, a nonce, and AD, where the keys are all distinct. Steps 4-7 calculates the key streams of these input tuples.
- Step 8 searches a pair (α, β) with the following relations: $\mathsf{msb}_1(X^{(\alpha)}) = \mathsf{msb}_1(X^{(\beta)}) = 0$ and $\mathsf{msb}_r\left(KS^{(\alpha)} \oplus KS^{(\beta)}\right) = \mathsf{zp}_r(R_\mathsf{T}^{(\alpha)} \oplus R_\mathsf{T}^{(\beta)})$, which is the sufficient condition to obtain a ciphertext collision from Lemma 1. For each pair (α, β), $KS^{(\alpha)}$ and $KS^{(\beta)}$ are (almost) r-bit random values, and thus the probability that the relation is satisfied is $O(\frac{1}{2^r})$.
- For such pair, Steps 10 and 11 calculate a pair of plaintexts $(M^{(\alpha)}, M^{(\beta)})$ that yield the same ciphertext C, and Step 12 calculates the tags. Step 13 checks the equality of the tags. If the tag collision occurs, $\mathbf{A}_1$ breaks the **CMT**-1-security of CTR-HMAC. The probability that the tag collision occurs is at most $\frac{1}{2^t}$.

– Summing the bound $\frac{1}{2^r} \cdot \frac{1}{2^t}$ for each pair (α, β), we have the bound $O\left(\frac{p^2}{2^{r+t}}\right)$.

Hence, the probability that $\mathbf{A}_1$ breaks the **CMT**-1-security of $\mathsf{KIVR}[\mathsf{GCM}]$ is at least $O\left(\frac{p^2}{2^{r+t}}\right)$.

ADVERSARY $\mathbf{A}_2$. The second adversary $\mathbf{A}_2$ that breaks the **CMT**-1-security of $\mathsf{KIVR}[\mathsf{CTR\text{-}HMAC}]$ by using a collision of $\mathsf{F}_{\mathsf{KIVR}}$. If the collision is found: $\mathsf{F}_{\mathsf{KIVR}}(K^{(\alpha)}, N^{(\alpha)}, A^{(\alpha)}) = \mathsf{F}_{\mathsf{KIVR}}(K^{(\beta)}, N^{(\beta)}, A^{(\beta)})$ such that $K^{(\alpha)} \neq K^{(\beta)}$ and $(N^{(\alpha)}, A^{(\alpha)}) = (N^{(\beta)}, A^{(\beta)})$, then by choosing the same plaintexts $M^{(\alpha)} = M^{(\beta)}$, we obtain the output collision $(C^{(\alpha)}, T^{(\alpha)}) = (C^{(\beta)}, T^{(\beta)})$. The collision probability is $\delta_{\mathsf{coll}}(p)$. □

References

1. Albertini, A., Duong, T., Gueron, S., Kölbl, S., Luykx, A., Schmieg, S.: How to abuse and fix authenticated encryption without key commitment. In: USENIX Security 2022, pp. 3291–3308 (2022)
2. Andreeva, E., Bogdanov, A., Luykx, A., Mennink, B., Mouha, N., Yasuda, K.: How to securely release unverified plaintext in authenticated encryption. In: Sarkar, P., Iwata, T. (eds.) ASIACRYPT 2014. LNCS, vol. 8873, pp. 105–125. Springer, Heidelberg (2014). https://doi.org/10.1007/978-3-662-45611-8_6
3. Armknecht, F., Fleischmann, E., Krause, M., Lee, J., Stam, M., Steinberger, J.: The preimage security of double-block-length compression functions. In: Lee, D.H., Wang, X. (eds.) ASIACRYPT 2011. LNCS, vol. 7073, pp. 233–251. Springer, Heidelberg (2011). https://doi.org/10.1007/978-3-642-25385-0_13
4. Barbosa, M., Farshim, P.: Indifferentiable authenticated encryption. In: Shacham, H., Boldyreva, A. (eds.) CRYPTO 2018. LNCS, vol. 10991, pp. 187–220. Springer, Cham (2018). https://doi.org/10.1007/978-3-319-96884-1_7
5. Bellare, M., et al.: Ask your cryptographer if context-committing AEAD is right for you. In: Real World Crypto Symposium (RWC), vol. 2023 (2023)
6. Bellare, M., Hoang, V.T.: Efficient schemes for committing authenticated encryption. In: EUROCRYPT 2022, vol. 13276, pp. 845–875 (2022). https://doi.org/10.1007/978-3-031-07085-3_29
7. Bellare, M., Hoang, V.T., Wu, C.: The landscape of committing authenticated encryption. https://csrc.nist.gov/Presentations/2023/landscape-of-committing-authenticated-encryption (2023), the Third NIST Workshop on Block Cipher Modes of Operation
8. Bose, P., Hoang, V.T., Tessaro, S.: Revisiting AES-GCM-SIV: multi-user security, faster key derivation, and better bounds. In: Nielsen, J.B., Rijmen, V. (eds.) EUROCRYPT 2018. LNCS, vol. 10820, pp. 468–499. Springer, Cham (2018). https://doi.org/10.1007/978-3-319-78381-9_18
9. Chan, J., Rogaway, P.: On committing authenticated-encryption. In: ESORICS 2022, vol. 13555, pp. 275–294 (2022)
10. Damgård, I.B.: A design principle for hash functions. In: Brassard, G. (ed.) CRYPTO 1989. LNCS, vol. 435, pp. 416–427. Springer, New York (1990). https://doi.org/10.1007/0-387-34805-0_39
11. Dodis, Y., Grubbs, P., Ristenpart, T., Woodage, J.: Fast message franking: from invisible salamanders to encryptment. In: Shacham, H., Boldyreva, A. (eds.) CRYPTO 2018. LNCS, vol. 10991, pp. 155–186. Springer, Cham (2018). https://doi.org/10.1007/978-3-319-96884-1_6

12. Dworkin, M.: NIST Special Publication 800–38A: Recommendation for block cipher modes of operation: Methods and techniques (2001). https://csrc.nist.gov/pubs/sp/800/38/a/final
13. Dworkin, M.: NIST Special Publication 800–38C: Recommendation for block cipher modes of operation: the CCM mode for authentication and confidentiality (2007). https://csrc.nist.gov/pubs/sp/800/38/c/upd1/final
14. Dworkin, M.: NIST Special Publication 800–38D: Recommendation for block cipher modes of operation: Galois/counter mode (GCM) and GMAC (2007). https://csrc.nist.gov/pubs/sp/800/38/d/final
15. Farshim, P., Orlandi, C., Rosie, R.: Security of symmetric primitives under incorrect usage of keys. IACR Trans. Symmetric Cryptol. **2017**(1), 449–473 (2017)
16. Grubbs, P., Lu, J., Ristenpart, T.: Message Franking via Committing Authenticated Encryption. In: Katz, J., Shacham, H. (eds.) CRYPTO 2017. LNCS, vol. 10403, pp. 66–97. Springer, Cham (2017). https://doi.org/10.1007/978-3-319-63697-9_3
17. Gueron, S., Langley, A., Lindell, Y.: AES-GCM-SIV: nonce misuse-resistant authenticated encryption. RFC **8452**, 1–42 (2019)
18. Gueron, S., Lindell, Y.: GCM-SIV: full nonce misuse-resistant authenticated encryption at under one cycle per byte. In: CCS 2015. pp. 109–119. ACM (2015)
19. Günther, F., Thomson, M., Wood, C.A.: Usage limits on AEAD algorithms (2023). https://www.ietf.org/archive/id/draft-irtf-cfrg-aead-limits-06.txt
20. Kessler, G.C.: GCK's file signatures table (2023). https://www.garykessler.net/library/file_sigs.html, (Accessed 19 Oct 2023)
21. Len, J., Grubbs, P., Ristenpart, T.: Partitioning oracle attacks. In: USENIX Security 2021, pp. 195–212 (2021)
22. Menda, S., Len, J., Grubbs, P., Ristenpart, T.: Context discovery and commitment attacks - how to break CCM, EAX, SIV, and more. In: EUROCRYPT 2023. LNCS, pp. 379–407 (2023). https://doi.org/10.1007/978-3-031-30634-1_13
23. Nir, Y., Langley, A.: ChaCha20 and Poly1305 for IETF protocols. RFC **8439**, 1–46 (2018)
24. NIST: FIPS 198–1: The keyed-hash message authentication code (HMAC) (2008). https://csrc.nist.gov/pubs/fips/198-1/final
25. NIST: The third NIST workshop on block cipher modes of operation 2023 (2023). https://csrc.nist.gov/Events/2023/third-workshop-on-block-cipher-modes-of-operation (Acessed 20 Oct 2023)
26. Merkle, R.C.: One way hash functions and DES. In: Brassard, G. (ed.) CRYPTO 1989. LNCS, vol. 435, pp. 428–446. Springer, New York (1990). https://doi.org/10.1007/0-387-34805-0_40
27. Stam, M.: Blockcipher-based hashing revisited. In: Dunkelman, O. (ed.) FSE 2009. LNCS, vol. 5665, pp. 67–83. Springer, Heidelberg (2009). https://doi.org/10.1007/978-3-642-03317-9_5
28. Wikipedia: List of file signatures (2023). https://en.wikipedia.org/wiki/List_of_file_signatures, (Accessed 19 Oct 2023)

Signatures

Subversion-Resilient Signatures Without Random Oracles

Pascal Bemmann[1(✉)], Sebastian Berndt[2], and Rongmao Chen[3]

[1] Bergische Universität Wuppertal, Wuppertal, Germany
bemmann@uni-wuppertal.de
[2] Universität zu Lübeck, Lübeck, Germany
s.berndt@uni-luebeck.de
[3] National University of Defense Technology, Changsha, China
chromao@nudt.edu.cn

Abstract. In the aftermath of the Snowden revelations in 2013, concerns about the integrity and security of cryptographic systems have grown significantly. As adversaries with substantial resources might attempt to subvert cryptographic algorithms and undermine their intended security guarantees, the need for subversion-resilient cryptography has become paramount. Security properties are preserved in subversion-resilient schemes, even if the adversary implements the scheme used in the security experiment. This paper addresses this pressing concern by introducing novel constructions of subversion-resilient signatures and hash functions while proving the subversion-resilience of existing cryptographic primitives. Our main contribution is the first construction of subversion-resilient signatures under *complete* subversion in the offline watchdog model (with trusted amalgamation) *without* relying on random oracles. We demonstrate that one-way permutations naturally yield subversion-resilient one-way functions, thereby enabling us to establish the subversion-resilience of Lamport signatures, assuming a trusted comparison is available. Additionally, we develop subversion-resilient target-collision-resistant hash functions using a trusted XOR. By leveraging this approach, we expand the arsenal of cryptographic tools that can withstand potential subversion attacks. Our research builds upon previous work in the offline watchdog model with trusted amalgamation (Russell et al. ASIACRYPT'16) and subversion-resilient pseudorandom functions (Bemmann et al. ACNS'23), culminating in the formal proof of subversion-resilience for the classical Naor-Yung signature construction.

Keywords: Subversion · Digital Signatures · Public-key Cryptography

1 Introduction

Subversion attacks have garnered increasing attention from the cryptography research community in recent years. In a subversion setting, attackers can tamper with or even take control of the implementation of cryptographic algorithms to leak secrets covertly, thereby weakening or breaking the security

C. Pöpper and L. Batina (Eds.): ACNS 2024, LNCS 14583, pp. 351–375, 2024.
https://doi.org/10.1007/978-3-031-54770-6_14

of the cryptosystems. For a long time, subversion attacks, dating back to the notion of kleptography by Young and Yung in the 1990s [31,32], were thought to be unrealistic and far-fetched by some cryptographers. However, the Snowden revelations in 2013 debunked this belief and exposed that subversion attacks were among the primary approaches certain law enforcement agencies employed to achieve mass surveillance. Particularly, it is reported that these agencies could intentionally "insert vulnerabilities into commercial encryption systems, IT systems, networks, and endpoint communications devices used by targets" [25]. As a result, numerous researchers have demonstrated the theoretical feasibility and potential dangers of subversion attacks against various cryptographic primitives [1,4,5,8,9,11,14], and as a specific case against digital signatures [2,3,17,20,30].

Consequently, the research community has devoted extensive efforts exploring effective countermeasures and designing subversion-resilient cryptographic primitives. In recent discussions on the standardization of post-quantum cryptography, specific treatments have been considered to prevent subversion attacks [26], highlighting the practical significance of this area of research. There is no hope for security when attackers can arbitrarily tamper with cryptographic implementations. For instance, a subverted encryption algorithm could always reveal the secret key, regardless of the input plaintext intended to be encrypted. Also, a subverted signature verification algorithm might always return `valid` when it takes as input a specific signature or message (e.g., a certain hard-coded string). Thus, as it turned out in the literature, achieving meaningful security in the subversion setting requires reliance on additional assumptions such as architectural requirements [6,7,13,27–29] or trusted components [2,10,12,15,16,22]. We remark that all these approaches for subversion resilience have their plausibility and thus are generally incomparable and may be useful in different application contexts. The details of these models, with associated commentary about their relevance to practice, will be provided in Sect. 1.4.

The Watchdog Model. In this work, we mainly consider the model introduced by Russell et al. [27] at ASIACRYPT 2016. Precisely, they formalized the so-called *watchdog model*, which has become one of the most prominent approaches for subversion-resilient cryptography in recent years. The rationale behind their consideration is that in the subversion setting, it is highly desirable for the attackers, often referred to as "big brother", to conceal their attacks. The watchdog model allows the adversary to supply potentially subverted implementations of cryptographic algorithms, while an efficient "watchdog" verifies these implementations against their corresponding specifications. Depending on how the watchdog performs testing of cryptographic algorithms, there are *offline watchdogs* which only perform a one-time check of the supplied implementations before deployment, and *online watchdogs* that could fully access the real-time transcripts of cryptographic algorithms. Note that achieving subversion resilience only using offline watchdogs is often preferable from a practical perspective, as only a "one-time" check is required instead of continuous monitoring.

Cryptographic designs in the watchdog model are often based on an architectural assumption called the *split-program* methodology and the *trusted amalgamation* assumption that is required to be as simple as possible. In such a setting, each algorithm is divided into several functional components, which the watchdog could separately test and then amalgamated into the complete algorithm via the trusted (not subverted) amalgamation function (e.g., trusting the computing base). A cryptographic scheme is said to be subversion-resilient in the watchdog model if *either* a watchdog exists that can effectively detect the subverted components *or* the security of the composed cryptographic scheme still holds even if the underlying components are subverted. By leveraging such a model, various subversion-resilient primitives have been proposed, including one-way-permutations [27], pseudorandom generators [27], randomness generators [7,27], public-key encryption schemes [7,28], authenticated encryption [6], random oracles [29], and signature schemes [13,27].

1.1 Subversion-Resilient Signatures with Watchdogs

Our work primarily focuses on digital signature schemes and aims to advance the construction of subversion-resilient signature schemes within the watchdog model. We provide an overview of the current state-of-the-art and present the question that motivates our work.

Online Watchdogs. Russell et al. proposed the first subversion-resilient signature scheme in the online watchdog model with random oracles [27]. In particular, they consider the *complete-subversion* setting where all cryptographic algorithms—including key generation and verification algorithms—are subject to subversion attacks. At the core of their design is a slight variant of a full domain hash scheme where the message is hashed together with the public key. Precisely, such a modification enables provable security by rendering any random oracle queries made before the implementations provided (by the adversary) useless, as the public key is generated freshly after the adversary commits to the implementations. More generally, they pointed out that in their definitional framework, it is impossible to construct a subversion-resistant signature scheme with just an offline watchdog, even if only the signing algorithm is subverted. Note that in the same work [27], Russell et al. also proposed subversion-resilient one-way permutations. They considered a stronger security setting, where the adversary can choose the function index (*pp* in our definition). This, in turn, makes the use of random oracles necessary. We will see that this stronger notion is not needed to construct subversion-resilient signatures, and we can thus remove the random oracle dependency.

Offline Watchdogs. In [13], Chow et al. improved Russell et al.'s construction by presenting two schemes with offline watchdogs. They bypassed Russell et al.'s impossibility [27] by using a more fine-grained split-program model adopted in [28] for a semantically secure encryption scheme. The first construction is without random oracles and only considers the partial-subversion model where key generation and signing are subverted while the verification algorithm is not. By adopting the domain-separation technique and the one-time random tag structure, they extended the idea by Russell et al. (originally for an encryption algorithm) to the context of a signature scheme. They also proposed another subversion-resilient signature scheme in the complete-subversion model but with random oracles. Their main idea is inspired by the correction of subverted random oracles due to Russell et al. [29].

Motivation. Despite significant progress made in constructing subversion-resilient signature schemes in the watchdog model, the state-of-the-art constructions (using offline watchdogs) require random oracles for achieving security in the complete-subversion model, and if without random oracles, only security in the partial-subversion model (where the verification algorithm is not subverted) is achieved. This motivates us to ask the following question.

Is it possible to design a subversion-resilient signature without random oracles in the complete-subversion model with an offline watchdog?

While being attractive for building security, the offline watchdog model has inherent limitations. For example, an offline watchdog can not defend against stateful subversions[1] such as time bomb attacks, which only become active when the underlying algorithm is at some specific state. Nevertheless, since it is up to a practitioner to trade off security and performance constraints, we hope our improvements in subversion-resilient signature schemes (using watchdogs) could help practitioners make well-informed decisions regarding their suitability for specific applications.

1.2 Technical Challenges

The difficulty of designing signature schemes secure against complete subversion mainly lies in the fact that it is challenging to restore the security of the subverted verification algorithm. The main reason is twofold. The first reason is the existence of *input trigger attacks*, where an adversary prepares a special signature $\tilde{\sigma}$, which the verification algorithm accepts for all messages. An attacker can randomly choose $\tilde{\sigma}$ and hard-code it into the subverted implementation. A black-box polynomial time watchdog now has only a negligible chance to detect this, while the attacker can trivially break security. Intuitively, this attack is possible as the attacker chooses the *input distribution* to the verification algorithm which is not publicly available to the watchdog (unless we assume some strategy by the adversary, see subversion under random messages attacks for comparison [2]). Thus, similar to previous works [6], more fine-grained access to the verification algorithm seems necessary. However, the situation in a setting with asymmetric keys is substantially more difficult than in the symmetric setting studied by Bemmann et al. [6], as the attacker sees the public verification

[1] Assuming universal watchdogs that do not depend on the adversary, which is the class of watchdogs we aim for in this work. For a deeper discussion on stateful subversion consider [27].

key and can thus use this knowledge. A common technique to develop signature schemes based on symmetric primitives [21] is the use of a collision-resistant hash function. But, due to the structure of the security experiment of collision-resistant hash functions, they are also highly vulnerable to input trigger attacks. Previous constructions thus needed heavy machinery such as the random oracle model [13,29], sophisticated online watchdogs [2,29], or a trusted initialization phase [16]. Approaches using a collision-resistant hash function in the standard model with an offline watchdog thus seem somewhat futile.

Both problems around input triggers described above rely on the fact that the adversary can prepare its implementation with input triggers as the challenge goes through the (possibly) subverted implementation. In our constructions, we will utilize primitives, where the adversary needs to commit to its implementation *before* a challenge is chosen. This way, the adversary can freely choose the inputs to the primitives, but since the implementation is set up before the challenge, it is hard for the adversary to adapt. As described above, Russell et al. [29] also used a similar idea but needed the random oracle model. We can circumvent the need for the random oracle model by choosing our primitives carefully and revisiting classical results in a subversion setting. As will be shown later, in this work we use a classic result that target-collision-resistant (TCR) hash functions are sufficient to build digital signatures. To break target-collision-resistance, the adversary first commits to an input, then the hash function is specified, and afterward, the adversary tries to find a collision. The task thus becomes to construct target-collision-resistant hash functions in a subversion-resilient manner.

1.3 Our Contributions

Our work provides an affirmative answer to the above question. The main contributions of this work can be summarized as follows:

- We show that one-way permutations (OWPs) are subversion-resilient one-way functions in the offline watchdog model, by taking advantage of the order of events in the security experiment. Russell et al. also showed how to construct subversion-resilient OWPs with random oracles [27]. Our construction of OWFs does not rely on random oracles; in our case, we only need the standard version of OWPs.
- Lamport one-time signatures (OTS) are subversion-resilient if built from subversion-resilient OWFs and a trusted comparison;
- We prove that a classical construction to obtain TCR hash functions from a rTCR hash function can be used to obtain subversion-resilient TCR hash function making use of a random blinding value, given the XOR in the construction is part of the trusted amalgamation;
- From subversion-resilient OTS, subversion-resilient target-collision resistant hash functions, and subversion-resilient PRFs, we build subversion-resilient signatures via the classical Naor-Yung [24] construction of digital signatures.

Thus, similar to the work of Chow et al. [13], we allow the watchdog more fine-grained access to the verification algorithm by breaking it down into smaller building blocks. This, in turn, allows for a similar approach as Bemmann et al. [6] for the case of authenticated encryption. We build signatures from symmetric primitives by revisiting classical results and show that we can construct the necessary building blocks in a subversion-resilient manner. This way, during the verification of the signatures, we recompute symmetric primitives, which allows the watchdog to do meaningful testing. A key insight of our work is that the security of some primitives can be guaranteed if we consider an adversary who has to commit to its implementation before a random challenge is computed. We then see that all the ingredients can be combined to prove the classical Naor-Yung construction for digital signatures to be subversion-resilient. However, while achieving subversion-resilience without random oracles, this comes with the price of decreased efficiency (both in signature size and computational costs) if compared to the state-of-the-art. Nevertheless, as mentioned above, we hope our work could help practitioners make well-informed decisions regarding the suitability of different signature schemes for specific applications. See Fig. 1b for an illustration of our overall approach.

1.4 Alternative Models

Several works in the field of cryptography have explored different angles of defense against subversion attacks, resulting in the proposal of various subversion-resilient signature schemes. Although these schemes may be generally incomparable due to the different models and assumptions they are built upon, understanding their differences can provide valuable insights into the landscape of subversion-resilient cryptography. Below we present an overview of current subversion-resilient signature schemes in other models.

Subversion-Resilient Signatures via Reverse Firewalls. In [2], Ateniese et al. showed that signature schemes with unique signatures are subversion-resilient against all subversion attacks that meet the so-called "verifiability condition". This condition essentially requires that signatures produced by the subverted signature algorithm should almost always verify correctly under the target verification key[2]. They adopted the cryptographic reverse firewall (RF) for constructing subversion-resilient signature schemes to relax such a strong requirement. Mironov and Stephens-Davidowitz originally introduced the notion of RF [22], which is assumed to be non-subverted and has access to a reliable source of randomness to re-randomize cryptographic transcripts. In the context of signature schemes, a RF is a (possibly stateful) algorithm that takes a message/signature pair as input and produces an updated signature. The main goal of a RF is to prevent potential covert leakage of sensitive information from subverted signatures. As a general result, Ateniese et al. showed that every re-randomizable signature scheme (including unique signatures as a special case) admits a RF that preserves unforgeability against arbitrary subversion attacks. Such a RF must have self-destruct capability, which means that the RF can publicly check the validity

[2] In [2], only subverted signing algorithms are considered while both key generation and verification algorithms are assumed to be trusted.

of each outgoing message/signature pair before updating the signature. If the RF encounters an invalid pair during this process, it stops processing further queries. The self-destruct capability is essential for the RF to maintain functionality and preserve the unforgeability of the signature scheme simultaneously. One could note that a RF could be viewed as an "active" online watchdog with the additional self-destruct capability. Thus, like the online watchdog model, a RF can defend against stateful subversion, which is inherently not captured by the offline watchdog model.

Subversion-Resilient Signatures via Self-guarding. In [16], Fischlin and Mazaheri proposed a novel defense mechanism called "self-guarding", which could counter stateless subversion of deterministic unforgeable signature schemes. The self-guarding signature scheme introduces a trusted initialization phase during which genuine message-signature pairs are generated for randomly chosen messages. More precisely, a random message denoted as $m_\$$ is signed in the initialization phase, resulting in a signature sample $\sigma_\$$. Later, when signing a message m, the (possibly) subverted signing algorithm is executed twice, once with $m_\$$ and once with the bitwise XOR of m and $[m_\$||\sigma_\$]$, where $||$ represents concatenation. The order of signing these two messages is chosen randomly. If the signing algorithm deviates for one of the two signatures, the subversion is detected with a probability of 1/2. This process can be repeated multiple times with independent key pairs to increase the detection probability to an overwhelming level. From the above, we know that unlike in the reverse firewall model, where a good source of randomness and the self-destruct capability are required, self-guarding schemes rely on a temporary trust phase during initialization. Also, one might think that the initialization phase of self-guarding schemes could be executed by a watchdog, where a specified program could immediately provide a detection solution. However, there is a notable difference: self-guarding schemes involve passing states between the initialization and later phases, whereas watchdogs typically do not forward data to individual users. Another significant distinction between self-guarding and the watchdog model is that self-guarding schemes do not require the subverted algorithm to be available from the start.

The diversity of subversion-resilient signature schemes reflects the complexity of defending against subversion attacks. The choice of models and assumptions is crucial in determining the scheme's effectiveness and practicality. Understanding the strengths and limitations of these subversion-resilient signature schemes is essential for designing secure cryptographic systems in the presence of potential subversion attacks.

2 Model and Preliminaries

In this section, we define the notion of subversion-resilience, and we will use the notations and definitions presented by Bemmann, Berndt, Diemert, Eisenbarth, and Jager [6] which in turn are based on the work of Russell, Tang, Yung, and Zhou [27].

2.1 Notation and Model

Notation. In order to distinguish between the *specification* of a primitive Π and the *implementation* of Π provided by the adversary, we will write $\widehat{\Pi}$ to denote the honest specification of the primitive and $\widetilde{\Pi}$ to denote the implementation of that primitive provided by the adversary. In this paper, we focus on game-based security. Hence, we define security for a cryptographic primitive Π with security objective GOAL by defining a *security experiment* Exp. In a usual experiment, a single party, called the *adversary* $\mathcal{A}$, tries to break the security objective against $\widehat{\Pi}$, and the game is managed by a *challenger*. When dealing with subverted implementation in the watchdog model, we consider a *subversion experiment* ExpSR consisting of three phases:

1. First, the adversary $\mathcal{A}$ provides a subverted implementation $\widetilde{\Pi}$.
2. Then, the *watchdog* WD is run and tries to detect the subversion.
3. Finally, the original security experiment Exp is performed by the adversary, but the subverted implementation is used therein.

To simplify notation, we always treat $\mathcal{A}$ as pair $(\mathcal{A}_0, \mathcal{A}_1)$, where $\mathcal{A}_0$ provides the subverted implementation $\widetilde{\Pi}$ and $\mathcal{A}_1$ takes part in the security experiment in the final phase. As usual, we denote the security parameter by λ.

Amalgamation. As discussed earlier, there is no black-box way to prevent subversion attacks in the watchdog model, as universal undetectable attacks are known, e.g., by Berndt and Liśkiewicz [8]. To still give security guarantees against subverted implementations, different non-black-box models were presented in the literature. In this work, we follow Russell, Tang, Yung, and Zhou [27] who introduced the *trusted amalgamation model*. Intuitively, this model splits all its components into *subroutines* with a more fine-granular resolution than the usual division into different algorithms. For example, a signature scheme consists of the three algorithms (KGen, Sign, Ver), but each might again consist of several subroutines (which might even be shared among the algorithms). We denote the list of subroutines by $\pi = (\pi_1, \ldots, \pi_n)$. The idea behind the trusted amalgamation model is each of these subroutines π_i might be subverted by the attacker, but the composition of them is performed by a *trusted amalgamation function* Am that is not subverted. Hence, Am is given the list π, producing all the needed algorithms for the primitive. The security experiment is then played on $\widetilde{\Pi} = \mathsf{Am}(\widetilde{\pi})$, where $\widetilde{\pi}$ denotes the list of subverted subroutines provided by the attacker. To provide meaningful security guarantees, one thus aims to make the amalgamation functions as simple as possible to allow automatic or manual verification. Typically, these amalgamation functions only consist of a few XOR operations and equality checks [6,7,28]. To formalize this scenario, we always represent the specification $\widehat{\Pi}$ of a primitive as $\widehat{\Pi} = (\mathsf{Am}, \pi)$. Sometimes, we consider the amalgamation function for a *single* algorithm Π_i of a primitive, denoted by Am_i.

Split-Program Model. In addition to trusted amalgamation, Russell, Tang, Yung, and Zhou [27] also used the *split-program* methodology. Like modern programming techniques, randomness generation is assumed to be split from a ran-

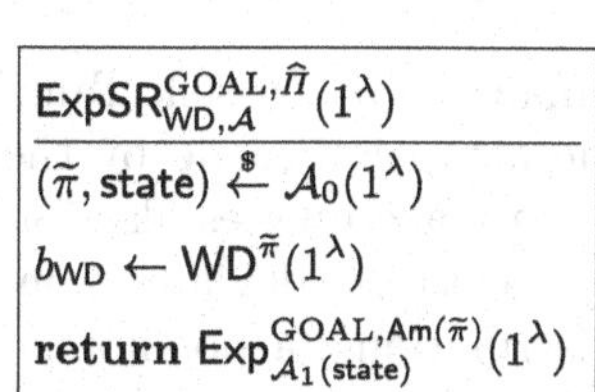

(a) The experiment for GOAL-security under subversion.

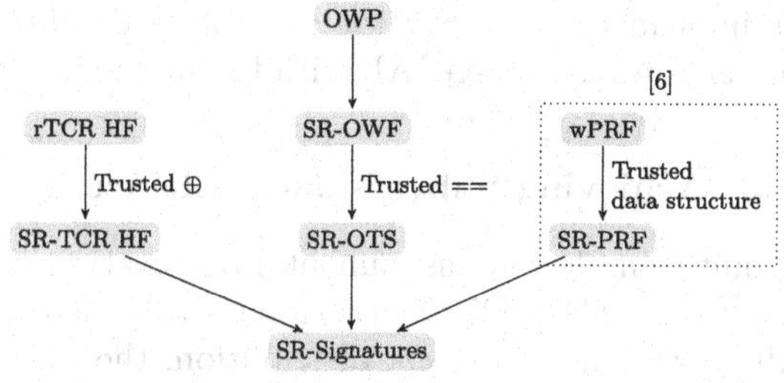

(b) Overview of our construction. Here, SR denotes subversion-resilience, HF denotes hash function, OWP/OWF denotes one-way permutation/-function, PRF denotes pseudo-random function, TCR denotes target collision-resistance, and OTS denotes one-time signature.

Fig. 1. Subversion experiment and construction overview

domized algorithm. The watchdog can then test the randomness generator and the deterministic algorithm individually. We also use this methodology.

2.2 Subversion-Resilience

Now, we describe the notion of a subversion-resilience experiment more formally. As described above, such an experiment consists of three phases, illustrated in Fig. 1a. In this paper, we will use both decision and search experiments and thus need to associate a naive win probability $\delta \in [0,1]$ to each experiment Exp, which will be 0 for search experiments (such as forgery experiments) and 1/2 for decision experiments (such as real-or-random experiments). First, $\mathcal{A}_0$ provides a subverted implementation $\widetilde{\pi}$. Then, the watchdog WD can run the implementation to detect the subversion. Finally, the usual security experiment Exp is run by the adversary $\mathcal{A}_1$ on the subverted implementation $\widetilde{\Pi} = \mathsf{Am}(\widetilde{\pi})$. The watchdog outputs 1 if it detects a subversion. To formalize subversion-resilience, consider the next definition and the corresponding security experiment shown in Fig. 1a.

Definition 1. *A specification of a primitive* $\widehat{\Pi} = (\mathsf{Am}, \pi)$ *is* GOAL-subversion-resilient in the offline watchdog model with trusted amalgamation *if one can efficiently construct a ppt watchdog algorithm* WD *such that for any ppt adversary* $\mathcal{A} = (\mathcal{A}_0, \mathcal{A}_1)$ *it holds that* $\mathsf{AdvSR}^{\mathrm{GOAL},\widehat{\Pi}}_{\mathcal{A}}(1^\lambda, \delta)$ *is negligible or* $\mathsf{Det}_{\mathsf{WD},\mathcal{A}}(1^\lambda)$ *is non-negligible where* $\mathsf{AdvSR}^{\mathrm{GOAL},\widehat{\Pi}}_{\mathcal{A}}(1^\lambda, \delta) = |\Pr[\mathsf{ExpSR}^{\mathrm{GOAL},\widehat{\Pi}}_{\mathsf{WD},\mathcal{A}}(1^\lambda) = 1] - \delta|$ *and* $\mathsf{Det}_{\mathsf{WD},\mathcal{A}}(1^\lambda) = |\Pr[\mathsf{WD}^{\widetilde{\pi}}(1^\lambda) = 1] - \Pr[\mathsf{WD}^{\pi}(1^\lambda) = 1]|$ *using the experiment shown in Fig. 1a, with* $\delta \in \{0, \frac{1}{2}\}$ *indicating whether a search or a decision problem is considered.*

Note that GOAL-subversion-resilience implies GOAL security as the above definition also has to hold for the adversary which outputs the specification as its implementation. For the sake of readability, we will call primitives simply *subversion-resilient*-GOAL with the understanding that they fulfill Definition 1.

2.3 Achieving Subversion-Resilience

A quite simple but instrumental observation was formalized by Russell, Tang, Yung, and Zhou [27]: If the inputs to a deterministic algorithm made by the adversary follow a *public* distribution, the watchdog can make queries also following this distribution. Hence, if the subverted implementation deviates from the specification with probability δ on such input distributions, a polynomial time watchdog can detect the presence of the subversion with probability at least δ. Hence, to have a negligible detection rate by the watchdog, the probability of deviating from the specification must also be very low.

Lemma 1. *Consider an implementation* $\widetilde{\Pi} := (\widetilde{\pi}_1, \ldots, \widetilde{\pi}_k)$ *of a specification* $\widehat{\Pi} = (\widehat{\pi}_1, \ldots, \widehat{\pi}_k)$*, where* $\pi_1, \ldots, \pi_k$ *are deterministic algorithms. Additionally, for each security parameter* λ*, public input distributions* $X^1_\lambda, \ldots, X^k_\lambda$ *are defined respectively. If there exists a* $j \in [k]$ *such that* $\Pr[\widetilde{\pi}_j(x) \neq \widehat{\pi}_j(x) : x \xleftarrow{\$} X^j_\lambda] = \delta$*, this can be detected by a ppt offline watchdog with probability at least* δ*.*

This lemma will be used to argue for the subversion-resilience of one-way functions (Sect. 3) and hash functions (Sect. 4).

2.4 Assumptions

We make several assumptions throughout this work which we shortly summarize here to enable a quick overview. First, we only consider stateless subversion to rule out the aforementioned time bomb attacks. Second, our results are in the split-program model with trusted amalgamation [27]. Third, since subversion-resilient randomness generators have been already shown to be achievable without using random oracles [6,7], we will simply assume uniform random coins are available in our constructions to simplify notation and point to the mentioned prior work for more details. In particular, in our constructions, all key generation algorithms are assumed to be subversion-resilient, as we could decouple them (in the split-program model) into a randomness generation algorithm and a deterministic algorithm that takes as input the random coins and outputs the key. Note that an offline watchdog could effectively detect the later component as its input is drawn from a public distribution. In addition to these architectural assumptions, our amalgamation will use a trusted XOR and a trusted comparison.

2.5 Pseudorandom Functions

For our signature scheme to be stateless, we also utilize PRFs. Bemmann et al. [6] showed how to construct subversion-resilient PRFs from weak PRFs based on the classical Naor-Reingold construction for PRFs [23]. We thus only state their definitions and results in a summarized form, point to their work for more details, and assume subversion-resilient PRFs can be constructed and used.

Intuitively, a PRF is a keyed function $F\colon \mathcal{K} \times \mathcal{D} \to \mathcal{R}$ associated with a key space $\mathcal{K}$, that is indistinguishable from a function sampled uniformly at random from the set of all functions $\mathcal{D} \to \mathcal{R}$. More formally, $\mathcal{K} = \bigcup_{\lambda \in \mathbb{N}} \mathcal{K}_\lambda$, $\mathcal{D} = \bigcup_{\lambda \in \mathbb{N}} \mathcal{D}_\lambda$, and $\mathcal{R} = \bigcup_{\lambda \in \mathbb{N}} \mathcal{R}_\lambda$. Additionally, we use $\mathsf{Func}(\mathcal{D}, \mathcal{R})$ to denote the set of all functions mapping elements from $\mathcal{D}$ to $\mathcal{R}$. Let us recall the standard definition of PRFs.

Definition 2 ([6]). *Let $\mathsf{Exp}^{PR}_{\mathcal{A},F}$ be defined as shown in Fig. 2. We define*

$$\mathsf{Adv}^{PR}_{\mathcal{A},F}(1^\lambda) := |\Pr[\mathsf{Exp}^{PR}_{\mathcal{A},F}(1^\lambda) = 1] - 1/2|.$$

We say that F is pseudorandom *if $\mathsf{Adv}^{\mathsf{PR}}_{\mathcal{A},F}(1^\lambda)$ is negligible for all ppt adversaries $\mathcal{A}$.*

$\mathsf{Exp}^{\mathsf{PR}}_{\mathcal{A},F}(1^\lambda)$

$b \xleftarrow{\$} \{0,1\};\ K \xleftarrow{\$} \mathcal{K}_\lambda$
if $b = 1$ **then** $b' \leftarrow \mathcal{A}^{F(K,\cdot)}(1^\lambda)$
else $g \xleftarrow{\$} \mathsf{Func}(\mathcal{D}_\lambda, \mathcal{R}_\lambda);\ b' \leftarrow \mathcal{A}^{g(\cdot)}(1^\lambda)$
return $b' == b$

Fig. 2. The security experiment for PRFs.

Theorem 1 ([6]). *Let F be a weak PRF. Then one can construct subversion-resilient PRFs in the trusted amalgamation model.*

Note that their construction does not need any trusted operation like an XOR, but rather that the trusted amalgamation parses the input as a bit string and then forwards one of two possible keys to a weak PRF.

3 Subversion-Resilient One-Way Functions

One of the major observations Bemmann et al. [6] make is that certain primitives are *inherently* subversion-resilient. One such primitive is weak PRFs, which do not allow the attacker to input any value during the security game. Thus, one could hope a similar result also holds for one-way functions. Unfortunately, it seems that solely relying on one-wayness is insufficient, as we will need the outputs of the considered function also to be (pseudo-) random and sufficiently large. By guaranteeing these properties, we can argue that an adversary has a low chance that a prepared trigger matches a random challenge and thus wins the security experiment. Therefore, instead of one-way functions, we consider one-way permutations, which we will later use to construct one-time signatures, particularly Lamport signatures [19]. This way, the challenge given to the adversary in the security game is a uniformly random element from the domain of the permutation. The critical point in our security proof will be that an adversary cannot access enough entropy to "hit" a *random* output of the one-way function/permutation while avoiding detection. In general, we can not assess the output distribution of a one-way function, even if the input is random. However, this is different for a one-way *permutation*, as the uniform input distribution implies a uniform output distribution. Thus, since the input distribution of the one-way permutation is public, Lemma 1 implies that there is only a negligible probability that the one-way permutation deviates from the specification. Then we can argue that the adversary cannot access enough entropy to develop an input that matches its challenge after being evaluated.

3.1 One-Way Permutations

We recall the standard definition of one-way functions and permutations.

Definition 3. *A (family of)* one-way functions Π *consists of two ppt algorithms* Gen *and* Eval. *On input* 1^λ, *the randomized algorithm* Gen *returns the* public parameters pp. *The deterministic algorithm* Eval *takes the public parameters* pp *and an element* $x \in \{0,1\}^\lambda$ *and returns an element* $y \in \{0,1\}^\lambda$. *If* $\mathsf{Eval}(pp, \cdot)$ *is a permutation on* $\{0,1\}^\lambda$, *we call* Π *a family of* one-way permutations.

Definition 4. *We say that* $\Pi = (\mathsf{KGen}, \mathsf{Eval})$ *is* secure, *if there is a negligible function* negl *such that for all ppt attackers* $\mathcal{A}$, *the probability* $\Pr[\mathsf{ExpInv}_\Pi^\mathcal{A}(1^\lambda) = 1] \leq \mathsf{negl}(\lambda)$ *with* $\mathsf{ExpInv}_\Pi^\mathcal{A}(1^\lambda)$ *displayed in Fig. 3.*

$\mathsf{ExpInv}_\Pi^\mathcal{A}(1^\lambda)$	$\mathsf{ExpSig}_\Sigma^\mathcal{A}(1^\lambda)$
$(pp) \leftarrow \mathsf{Gen}(1^\lambda)$	$(\mathsf{sk}, \mathsf{vk}) \leftarrow \mathsf{KGen}(1^\lambda)$
if Π is permutation : $y^* \xleftarrow{\$} \{0,1\}^\lambda$	$(m, \sigma) = \mathcal{A}^{\mathsf{Sign}(\mathsf{sk},\cdot)}(1^\lambda, \mathsf{vk})$
else : $x \xleftarrow{\$} \{0,1\}^\lambda, y^* = \mathsf{Eval}(pp, x)$	**if** $\mathsf{Vf}(pk, (m, \sigma)) = 1$ and $m \notin Q$:
$x^* = \mathcal{A}(pp, y^*)$	**return** 1
if $\mathsf{Eval}(pp, x^*) == y^*$: **return** 1	**return** 0
return 0	

Fig. 3. Left: One-way function/permutation security experiment. Right: Unforgeability experiment for digital signatures.

Note that other definitions exist in which x^* is chosen uniformly at random from the domain and $y^* = \mathsf{Eval}(pp, x^*)$ is given to the adversary. In the classical, i.e., non-subversion setting, both definitions are equivalent for permutations. In our case, there is also little difference in our results. Since all inputs to Eval are known, i.e., public, an adversary can guarantee that Eval follows the specification but with negligible probability. Thus, in our proof in the next section, we could introduce an additional game hop and replace $\widetilde{\mathsf{Eval}}$ with $\widehat{\mathsf{Eval}}$, but instead, we will use this more straightforward way of defining security.

3.2 Subversion-Resilient One-Way Functions

We will see that starting from an "ordinary" one-way permutation, we directly obtain a subversion-resilient one-way function *without* the need of any further amalgamation, assuming that we already have a subversion-resilient key generation algorithm as stated in Sect. 2.4. The idea is that by applying Lemma 1 and using a permutation, the challenge handed to the adversary is a random element. Then we can use that the adversary has to provide its implementation *before* the execution of the inverting experiment, i.e., the challenge is *independent* from the subverted implementation. Since the subversion can only utilize negligible many triggers to avoid detection by the watchdog, the probability that a trigger can be used to break security is also negligible. Thus, it needs to find an input that can then be used to break the one-wayness of the specification *without* making use of an input trigger, which contradicts the usual non-subversion security.

Note that it is impossible (with polynomial testing time) to ensure that the implementation provided by an adversary is still a permutation. Even changing the output under a single input leads to the function not being a permutation anymore, which can only be detected with negligible probability by a polynomial time watchdog. Fortunately, we will only utilize the permutation property of the specification to guarantee a uniform output distribution of honest evaluations. Thus, we lose the permutation property in exchange for subversion-resilience.

Theorem 2. *Let* $\Pi = (\mathsf{Gen}, \mathsf{Eval})$ *be a one-way permutation. Then the trivial specification* $\widehat{\Pi} = (\mathsf{Gen}, \mathsf{Eval})$ *is a subversion-resilient one-way function in the split-program model with trusted amalgamation.*

Proof. Let $\widehat{\Pi} = (\mathsf{Gen}, \mathsf{Eval})$ be the specification of a permutation, and $\widetilde{\Pi}$ be the implementation of $\widehat{\Pi}$ provided by $\mathcal{A}$. First, the watchdog simply runs KGen for pp, samples x and compares $\widetilde{\mathsf{Eval}}(pp, x)$ to $\widehat{\mathsf{Eval}}(pp, x)$. Whenever a mismatch between these values is found, the watchdog returns 1. To prove the subversion-resilience, let $\mathcal{T} \subseteq \mathcal{PP} \times \{0,1\}^\lambda$ denote the *trigger set* such that $(pp, x) \in \mathcal{T} \Leftrightarrow \widetilde{\mathsf{Eval}}(pp, x) \neq \widehat{\mathsf{Eval}}(pp, x)$ where $\mathcal{PP}$ denotes the public parameter space. Thus, $\mathcal{T}$ contains *all* inputs for which the implementation deviates from the specification. To avoid the detection by a watchdog, we know that the density of $\mathcal{T}$ needs to be negligible, i.e., we have $|\mathcal{T}| / (|\mathcal{PP}| \cdot 2^\lambda) \in \mathsf{negl}(\lambda)$. Due to the flow of the subversion experiment, the attacker needs to provide the implementation $\widetilde{\Pi}$ *before* the parameters pp and the challenge y^* are chosen in the security game. Hence, the set $\mathcal{T}$ is *independent* of pp and y^* and so is the image of $\mathcal{T}$, i.e., $\mathsf{img}(\mathcal{T})$. Now, whenever the attacker is successful (as in 'wins the security experiment') on input y^*, they will output a value x^* such that $\widetilde{\mathsf{Eval}}(pp, x^*) = y^*$. We now distinguish whether the adversary uses a trigger, i.e., whether $(pp, x^*) \in \mathcal{T}$ or $(pp, x^*) \notin \mathcal{T}$ holds. If $(pp, x^*) \notin \mathcal{T}$, we know that $y^* = \widetilde{\mathsf{Eval}}(pp, x^*) = \widehat{\mathsf{Eval}}(pp, x^*)$. Thus, the attacker on the subverted implementation can be transformed into an attacker on the non-subverted specification, breaking the one-wayness of Π. If $(pp, x^*) \in \mathcal{T}$, we can't predict $\widetilde{\mathsf{Eval}}(pp, x^*)$, however it can only redistribute weight within $\mathcal{T}$, as $\mathsf{Eval}(pp, \cdot)$ is a deterministic mapping on $\{0,1\}^\lambda \setminus \mathcal{T}$. Now, $\mathcal{T}$ is independent from y^* and y^* is uniformly drawn from $\{0,1\}^\lambda$. Together, this implies that the expected probability (upon the random choice of y^*) of a subversion attacker to win when submitting any trigger x^* (and setting up its implementation accordingly beforehand) is at most $|\mathcal{T}|/(|\mathcal{PP}| \cdot 2^\lambda)$, i.e., negligible. Hence, the probability that a trigger x^* with $\widetilde{\mathsf{Eval}}(pp, x^*) = y^*$ exists is negligible. □

4 Subversion-Resilient Hash Functions

Another crucial building block we will use is hash functions. Since we build one-time signatures from one-way functions, we need a way to hash two public keys (of the one-time signature) down to the size of one public key to make the signature construction of [24] work. Unfortunately, subversion-resilient collision-resistant hash functions seem impossible (without any further assumptions), as discussed in Sect. 6. On the positive side, just like in the case of ordinary signatures, subversion-resilient target collision-resistant hash functions are sufficient for our case, and we will see that they can be constructed by using a trusted XOR. So, let us begin by providing the necessary (security) definitions.

Definition 5. *A family of hash functions $\mathcal{H}$ is a pair of ppt algorithms* (Gen, H) *where* Gen *takes as input the security parameter* 1^λ *and outputs a (non-secret) key s and* H *takes as input a key s and a string $x \in \{0,1\}^*$ and outputs* $\mathsf{H}_s(x)$.

Note that we only consider keyed hash functions that take a fixed-length input. We will assume that inputs have length 2λ. Our approach can also handle inputs with lengths up to 2λ, but this would imply more encoding and notation overhead as inputs would need to be interpreted as 2λ long items with leading zeros.

In the following, we consider two different but very related security notions concerning hash functions.

Definition 6. *Let $\mathcal{H} =$* (Gen, H) *be a family of hash functions. Then we say that $\mathcal{H}$ is* target collision resistant (TCR) *iff* $\Pr[\mathsf{ExpTCR}^{\mathcal{H}}_{\mathcal{A}}(1^\lambda) = 1] \leq \mathsf{negl}(\lambda)$ *where* $\mathsf{ExpTCR}^{\mathcal{H}}_{\mathcal{A}}(1^\lambda)$ *is depicted in Fig. 4.*

Definition 7. *Let $\mathcal{H} =$* (Gen, H) *be a family of hash functions. Then we say that $\mathcal{H}$ is* random target collision resistant (rTCR) *iff* $\Pr[\mathsf{ExpRTCR}^{\mathcal{H}}_{\mathcal{A}}(1^\lambda) = 1] \leq \mathsf{negl}(\lambda)$ *where* $\mathsf{ExpRTCR}^{\mathcal{H}}_{\mathcal{A}}(1^\lambda)$ *is depicted in Fig. 4.*

$\mathsf{ExpTCR}^{\mathcal{H}}_{\mathcal{A}}(1^\lambda)$	$\mathsf{ExpRTCR}^{\mathcal{A}}_{\mathcal{H}}(1^\lambda)$
$(x, \mathsf{st}) = \mathcal{A}_1(1^\lambda)$	$x \stackrel{\$}{\leftarrow} \mathcal{D}$
$s \stackrel{\$}{\leftarrow} \mathsf{Gen}(1^\lambda)$	$s \leftarrow \mathsf{Gen}(1^\lambda)$
$y = \mathcal{A}_2(s, x, \mathsf{st})$	$y = \mathcal{A}(s, x)$
if $\mathsf{H}_s(x) == \mathsf{H}_s(y)$ and $x \neq y$:	**if** $\mathsf{H}_s(x) == \mathsf{H}_s(y)$ and $x \neq y$:
return 1	**return** 1
return 0	**return** 0

Fig. 4. (random) Target-collision resistance security experiment for hash functions. In the left experiment, we use that $\mathcal{A} = (\mathcal{A}_1, \mathcal{A}_2)$ and use st to denote the state passed between the subroutines of the adversary.

Big Domains. Before we present our construction, let us quickly illustrate a powerful subversion attack against hash function families with big domains, which is inspired by the attack on one-way permutations by Russel et al. in [27]. Let $\mathcal{H} = (\mathsf{Gen}, \mathsf{H})$ with $\mathsf{H}\colon \{0,1\}^{2\lambda} \to \{0,1\}^\lambda$ be a family of hash functions, which hashes inputs to outputs half the input size. Then an adversary could prepare its implementation such that $\tilde{\mathsf{H}}_s(\mathsf{k} \parallel y) := y$ for some randomly sampled (or simply chosen by the adversary) string k. With this construction, an input trigger exists for *every* element in the range of H, enabling the adversary to win the security experiment trivially. Additionally, detecting this attack is very hard for an offline watchdog without knowledge of k. Assuming the watchdog samples random inputs for the hash function, the probability for a random input to match y is $(\frac{1}{2})^\lambda$, which is negligible in λ. Since the watchdog only has a polynomial running time, it has a negligible probability of detecting this attack. Thus, we only use hash functions where the domain and range of the hash functions are of similar size to rule out this otherwise unpreventable attack. More concretely, we only consider hash functions where the output is one bit shorter than the input. Larger input sizes are then handled by constructing hash functions for different input sizes and hashing the input down through these different hash functions. To guarantee subversion-resilience, we need to run a watchdog for each input length individually. However, this seems unavoidable to prevent the above attack.

Construction. Similar to our construction of subversion-resilient one-way functions, we make use of the fact that rTCR hash functions have a *random* challenge. More formally, let $\mathcal{H} = (\mathsf{Gen}, \mathsf{H})$ be a family of rTCR hash functions. Then we construct a TCR hash function $\mathcal{H}' = (\mathsf{Gen}', \mathsf{H}')$ as follows: To sample a key s, the algorithm Gen' first executes Gen and then additionally samples a uniformly random element r from the domain of the hash function and finally outputs $s' = (s, r)$ as the key. Now, H' evaluates inputs as $\mathsf{H}'_{s'}(x) := \mathsf{H}_s(x \oplus r)$. Thus, this construction has an additional blinding value as part of its key, which is XORed to the input before evaluating the hash function. In order to sanitize key generation, our watchdog will test Gen for uniformly random coins. Thus, just as in [28] we can guarantee that either s is computed in accordance with the specification or the watchdog detects subversion. To compute the blinding value, we can use any construction from [28] or [7] to produce random coins in a subversion-resilient manner that does not use random oracles.

We note that the $\oplus$ operation will be part of the trusted amalgamation when we prove subversion-resilience. This is essential to the construction and prevents the attacker from feeding adversarially chosen inputs directly into subverted components, similar to Russell et al. [28]. Just like in the section about one-way functions, the order of events is critical for our analysis. Our security proof again uses that the hash function (and especially the random value provided along) is provided to the adversary *after* the adversary provides its implementation. Note that in a non-subverted setting, our construction is the folklore[3] construction to obtain a TCR hash function from a rTCR hash function.

In the proof, we will use that target collision resistant hash functions with small input domain need to distribute their inputs somewhat 'equally' into the range of the hash functions. Otherwise, this would contradict its target collision resistance property.

Lemma 2. *Let* $\mathcal{H} = (\mathsf{Gen}, \mathsf{H})$ *with* $\mathsf{H} : \{0,1\}^\lambda \to \{0,1\}^{\lambda-1}$ *be a* rTCR *family of hash functions. Then, the set* $\{x \in \{0,1\}^\lambda \mid \mathsf{H}_s(x) = z\}$ *is negligible in* λ *with probability* $1 - \mathsf{negl}(\lambda)$ *upon random choice of* z *and* s.

Theorem 3. *Let* $\mathcal{H} = (\mathsf{Gen}, \mathsf{H})$ *with* $\mathsf{H} : \{0,1\}^\lambda \to \{0,1\}^{\lambda-1}$ *be a* rTCR *family of hash functions. Then* $\mathcal{H}' = (\mathsf{Gen}', \mathsf{H}')$ *with* $\mathsf{H}' : \{0,1\}^\lambda \to \{0,1\}^{\lambda-1}$ *as described above is a subversion-resilient* TCR *family of hash functions in the split-program model with trusted amalgamation where the* $\oplus$ *is part of the amalgamation.*

Proof. Let $\mathcal{H}$ be a rTCR hash function family, and let $\mathcal{T}$ be the trigger set of H, i.e., $(s, x) \in \mathcal{T} \Leftrightarrow \widetilde{\mathsf{H}}_s(x) \neq \widehat{\mathsf{H}}_s(x)$. Just as in [28], we can use Lemma 1 to argue that either the keys s' output by Gen' are computed according to the specification or the watchdog detects subversion. Further, due to Lemma 1, we know that $|\mathcal{T}| \in \mathsf{negl}(\lambda)$. Hence, our watchdog for H will query Gen and H' on random inputs. Due to the trusted XOR used in H', Lemma 1 implies that with high probability the value $\mathsf{H}_s(x \oplus r)$ is a non-subverted output, as $s' = (s, r)$ is chosen *after* the adversary provides its implementation. Now, let $\mathcal{A}$ be an adversary against the subversion-resilience of H', i.e., $\mathcal{A}$ first outputs x, is then handed $s' = (s, r)$ and then outputs a value $y \neq x$ and succeeds if $\mathsf{H}_s(x \oplus r) = \mathsf{H}_s(y \oplus r)$. We now distinguish two cases. In the first case, we have $(s, y) \notin \mathcal{T}$. If $\mathcal{A}$ can output $y \neq x$ such that $\mathsf{H}'_{s'}(x) = \mathsf{H}'_{s'}(y)$ (where both inputs do *not* lead to input trigger), we can construct an adversary $\mathcal{B}$ which breaks the rTCR of $\mathcal{H}$ as follows. After $\mathcal{A}$ outputs some value x, the adversary $\mathcal{B}$ obtains (s, x') from its challenger. Now, $\mathcal{B}$ forwards $s' = (s, r)$ with $r = x \oplus x'$ to $\mathcal{A}$ which answers with some y. Finally, $\mathcal{B}$ forwards $y \oplus r$ to its challenger. We observe that in the case that $\mathcal{A}$ finds a collision such that $\mathsf{H}'_{s'}(x) = \mathsf{H}'_{s'}(y)$, it holds that $\mathsf{H}'_{s'}(x) = \mathsf{H}_s(x' \oplus x \oplus x) = \mathsf{H}_s(x')$ and $\mathsf{H}'_{s'}(y) = \mathsf{H}_s(y \oplus x \oplus x')$. Since $x \neq y$, it

[3] Unfortunately, we were not able to find an explicit reference for this construction.

also holds that $x' \neq y \oplus x' \oplus x$. Thus, if $\mathcal{A}$ finds a collision, so does $\mathcal{B}$, at least if H does not deviate from its specification with regard to (s, y)[4].

The other case is $(s, y) \in \mathcal{T}$. But, as we will now argue, this can only happen with negligible probability. Remember that H maps λ-bit string to $(\lambda - 1)$-bit strings. Now, let $\mathsf{H}_s^{-1}(z) \subseteq \{0,1\}^\lambda$ denote the set of preimages of an element $z \in \{0,1\}^{\lambda-1}$. By Lemma 2, the size of $\mathsf{H}_s^{-1}(z)$ must be negligible for all but negligible many pairs (s, z). Hence, the probability that there is some $y \in \mathsf{H}_s^{-1}(\mathsf{H}s(x))$ with $(s, y) \in \mathcal{T}$ is negligible, since $\mathcal{A}$ commits to its implementation before H and its associated blinding value is chosen and $\mathcal{A}$ has only negligible many input trigger. Thus, any adversary which breaks the subversion-resilience of $\mathcal{H}'$ can also be used to break the security of $\mathcal{H}$. □

As stated before, the above construction only reduces the input size by a single bit. Hence, to hash a string of length 2λ down to length λ, we will need a hash family $\mathcal{H}_\ell \colon \{0,1\}^\ell \rightarrow \{0,1\}^{\ell-1}$ for each $\ell = 2\lambda, 2\lambda - 1, \ldots, \lambda + 1$.

5 Subversion-Resilient Signatures

Finally, we have all the ingredients to prove the signature scheme based on the Naor-Yung construction [24] subversion-resilient. As a necessary stepping stone, we will see that the classical Lamport signatures are subversion-resilient if instantiated with a subversion-resilient one-way function. Then, all the previous sections' building blocks can be combined to obtain a subversion-resilient signature, where even the verification algorithm is subject to subversion.

5.1 Digital Signatures

We continue by recalling the standard definition of digital signatures.

Definition 8. *A digital signature scheme Σ consists of three ppt algorithms* $(\mathsf{KGen}, \mathsf{Sign}, \mathsf{Vf})$*. On input 1^λ the key generation algorithm* KGen *outputs a pair of keys* $(\mathsf{sk}, \mathsf{vk})$*. The signing algorithm* Sign *takes as input the secret signing key* sk *and a message m from the message space and outs a signature σ. The verification algorithm* Vf *takes as input the public verification key* vk*, a message m, and a signature σ. It outputs a bit b where $b = 1$ indicates a valid signature, while $b = 0$ means that the signature cannot be verified. We say a signature scheme is* correct *if for every key pair* $(\mathsf{sk}, \mathsf{vk})$ *generated by* $\mathsf{KGen}(1^\lambda)$ *and every message $m \in M$ it holds that* $\mathsf{Vf}(\mathsf{vk}, (m, \mathsf{Sign}(\mathsf{sk}, m))) = 1$ *but with negligible probability.*

Next, we recall the standard definition of existential unforgeability.

Definition 9. *We say that a signature scheme Σ is* existentially unforgeable *if for all ppt adversaries $\mathcal{A}$ there exists a negligible function* $\mathsf{negl}(1^\lambda)$ *such that* $\Pr[\mathsf{ExpSig}_\Sigma^\mathcal{A}(1^\lambda) = 1] \leq \mathsf{negl}(\lambda)$ *where* $\mathsf{ExpSig}_\Sigma^\mathcal{A}(1^\lambda)$ *is displayed in Fig. 3 and $\mathcal{A}$ has access to an oracle returning* $\sigma_i = \mathsf{Sign}(\mathsf{sk}, m_i)$ *on input m_i and where Q denotes the set of all queries that $\mathcal{A}$ issued to its signing oracle.*

[4] This resembles the 'classical' security proof of the construction.

Definition 10. *We say a signature is a* one-time *signature if the above holds and the attacker can only issue a single query to its signing oracle.*

5.2 Lamport Signatures

Using the results of Sect. 3, we have access to subversion-resilient one-way functions and can directly obtain Lamport signatures [19] given a trusted comparison. So let us quickly recall the definition of the aforementioned Lamport signatures for messages of length ℓ, which uses a family of one-way functions $(\mathsf{Gen}, \mathsf{Eval})$.

The key generation algorithm chooses ℓ many values $x_{i,0}, x_{i,1} \in \{0,1\}^\lambda$ uniformly at random as well as $pp = \mathsf{Gen}(1^\lambda)$. Then compute $y_{i,0} = \mathsf{Eval}(pp, x_{i,0})$ and $y_{i,1} = \mathsf{Eval}(pp, x_{i,1})$. The verification key vk consists of all y values and the signing key of all x values. On input a message $m \in \{0,1\}^\ell$ with $m = m_1 \dots m_\ell$, the signing algorithm simply outputs the signature $\sigma = (x_{1,m_1}, \dots, x_{\ell,m_\ell})$. On input a verification key vk, a message $m \in \{0,1\}^\ell$ with $m = (m_1 \dots m_\ell)$, and a signature $\sigma = (x_1, \dots, x_\ell)$, the verification algorithm outputs 1 iff $\mathsf{Eval}(pp, x_i) = y_{i,m_i}$ for all $1 \le i \le \ell$.

Then it is not hard to see that the security of the Lamport signatures scheme follows directly from the security of the used one-way function. Similarly, the Lamport signature's subversion-resilience follows from the subversion-resilience of the used one-way function. However, additionally, we need a trusted comparison for the above construction to be secure. As discussed in [6] for the context of MACs, a trusted comparison seems unavoidable. Otherwise, the subverted implementation could ignore the output of Eval and output 1 for a value chosen by the adversary and embedded into the implementation. Thus, the subversion-resilience of Lamport signatures directly boils down to the subversion-resilience of the one-way function.

Theorem 4. *Let Π be a subversion-resilient one-way function. Then Lamport Signatures using Π as the one-way function are subversion-resilient one-time signatures where the trusted amalgamation makes a trusted comparison.*

5.3 The Naor-Yung Construction

Before we dive into the classical Naor-Yung construction, let us provide some intuition on the approach. The main idea is to follow a tree-based approach and heavily use one-time signatures, which sign pairs of verification keys to form an authenticated path in a tree based on the message to be signed. Since the Lamport signature can not sign messages bigger than its public key, a hash function is used to allow the signing of two verification keys. Here a target-collision-resistant hash function is sufficient to guarantee security. While the original construction is stateful, it is known that it can be extended via PRFs and deterministically recomputing keys to make the construction stateless. Note that the PRFs are only needed to sign messages and not for signature verification. We continue with the construction and are given a one-time signature scheme $(\mathsf{KGen}_{\mathsf{OTS}}, \mathsf{Sign}_{\mathsf{OTS}}, \mathsf{Vf}_{\mathsf{OTS}})$, a target-collision resistant hash function family $\mathcal{H} =$

$(\mathsf{Gen}, \mathsf{H})$ with $\mathsf{H} = \{\mathsf{H}_s\colon \{0,1\}^{2\lambda} \to \{0,1\}^{\lambda}\}$, and a pseudorandom function $(\mathsf{KGen}_{\mathsf{PRF}}, F)$. Furthermore, for a string $w \in \{0,1\}^*$, we define $\mathsf{Pre}(w) \subseteq \{0,1\}^*$ as the set of prefixes of w, including the empty string ϵ and w itself. For technical reasons, we assume that for $w \in \{0,1\}^{\lambda}$, we have $\mathsf{Pre}(w) \subseteq \{0,1\}^{\lambda+\lceil\log(\lambda)\rceil}$ and $|\mathsf{Pre}(w)| = |w| + 1$ to guarantee that all prefixes have the same length and to differentiate them uniquely.[5] We also assume that the verification key vk corresponding to a secret key sk can easily be derived from sk. Now, we define our signature scheme $(\mathsf{KGen}, \mathsf{Sign}, \mathsf{Vf})$ as follows (Fig. 5):

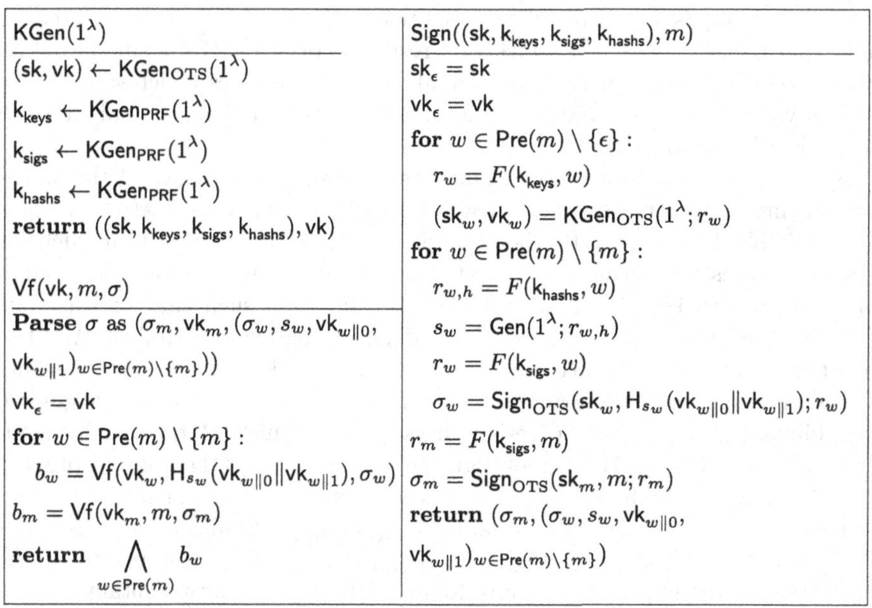

Fig. 5. Our proposed signature scheme.

Theorem 5. *Given subversion-resilient one-time signatures, subversion-resilient target-collision-resistant hash functions, and subversion-resilient PRFs, then the above construction is a stateless, subversion-resilient digital signature scheme in the split-program model with trusted amalgamation where all algorithms are subject to subversion.*

In the following proof, we follow the proof sketch by Naor and Yung [24], but need to adapt the proof somewhat. First, Naor and Yung only considered a stateful signature while our use of the PRF makes the complete construction stateless. Furthermore, we need to make sure that we reduce the security to the subversion-resilience of the building blocks rather than their original security

[5] This prevents complications and allows us to identify each prefix uniquely.

properties, as we only work with the (possibly) subverted implementation here and not with the specification.

Proof. As a first step, the watchdog for the signature scheme simply runs the watchdog of the one-time signature, the watchdog of the hash function, and the watchdog of the PRF. If none of these watchdogs detect a subversion, we follow an adaption of the proof by Naor and Yung [24].

Now, we replace the values generated by the PRF with completely random strings, i.e., all strings r_w, $r_{w,h}$, and r_m are now independent random strings that are stored by the system for reuse in case that the values are needed again. If this would be distinguishable from the setting where the PRF is used, we can easily build an attacker against the subversion-resilience of the PRF by simulating all other parts of the construction. We will also ignore the cases which some of the randomly chosen values (random strings or keys) collide, as this will only happen with negligible probability.

Now, let $\mathcal{A}_{\mathsf{sigs}}$ be an attacker against the subversion-resilience of the signature scheme that is successful with non-negligible probability $1/p(\lambda)$ for some non-negligible function p. In the following, we will now show that such an attacker implies the existence of an attacker $\mathcal{A}_{\mathrm{OTS}}$ against the one-time signature and an attacker $\mathcal{A}_{\mathsf{hashs}}$ against the hash function such that at least one of these attackers is also successful with non-negligible probability. As $\mathcal{A}_{\mathsf{SIG}}$ wins the subversion-resilience game with non-negligible probability, it outputs a valid message-signature pair (m^*, σ^*) with $m^* \notin Q_M$ with non-negligible probability. Here, Q_M is the set of messages for which $\mathcal{A}$ queried its signing oracle. Let Q_S be the set of signatures returned by the signing oracles. By definition, for each $m \in Q_M$ and each corresponding answer $\sigma \in Q_S$, we have $\sigma = (\sigma_m, (\sigma_w, s_w, \mathsf{vk}_{w\|0}, \mathsf{vk}_{w\|1})_{w \in \mathsf{Pre}(m) \setminus \{m\}})$. Similarly, we also have $\sigma^* = (\sigma^*_{m^*}, (\sigma^*_{w^*}, s_{w^*}, \mathsf{vk}_{w^*\|0}, \mathsf{vk}_{w^*\|1})_{w^* \in \mathsf{Pre}(m^*) \setminus \{m^*\}})$. By construction of the verification algorithm, a successfully forged signature σ^* must contain a tuple $(\sigma^*_{w^*}, s_{w^*}, \mathsf{vk}_{w^*\|0}, \mathsf{vk}_{w^*\|1})$ that is not contained in any signature in Q_S. Now, we need to distinguish two cases.

If $\mathsf{H}_{s_{w^*}}(\mathsf{vk}_{w^*\|0} \| \mathsf{vk}_{w^*\|1}) \neq \mathsf{H}_{s_{w^*}}(\mathsf{vk}_{w'\|0} \| \mathsf{vk}_{w'\|1})$ for all $\mathsf{vk}_{w'\|0}$ and $\mathsf{vk}_{w'\|1}$ contained in the signatures in Q_S, we can construct an attacker $\mathcal{A}_{\mathrm{OTS}}$ against the one-time signature. The attacker $\mathcal{A}_{\mathrm{OTS}}$ is given some verification key vk' from the one-time signature and simulates the complete security experiment, but instead of sampling the key pair $(\mathsf{sk}_{w^*}, \mathsf{vk}_{w^*})$, it sets $\mathsf{vk}_{w^*} = \mathsf{vk}'$. To sign a message with sk_{w^*}, it uses its oracle to the signing algorithm of the one-time signature. Finally, $\mathcal{A}_{\mathrm{OTS}}$ outputs the message-signature pair $(m', \sigma') = (\mathsf{H}_{s_{w^*}}(\mathsf{vk}_{w^*\|0} \| \mathsf{vk}_{w^*\|1}), \sigma^*_{w^*})$, which is a valid pair as (m^*, σ^*) was a valid pair for the signature scheme. Furthermore, as $\mathsf{H}_{s_{w^*}}(\mathsf{vk}_{w^*\|0} \| \mathsf{vk}_{w^*\|1}) \neq \mathsf{H}_{s_{w^*}}(\mathsf{vk}_{w'\|0} \| \mathsf{vk}_{w'\|1})$ holds for all verification keys $\mathsf{vk}_{w'\|0}$ and $\mathsf{vk}_{w'\|1}$ contained in Q_S, the one-time signing oracle was never queried on the value $\mathsf{H}_{s_{w^*}}(\mathsf{vk}_{w^*\|0} \| \mathsf{vk}_{w^*\|1})$. Hence, (m', σ') is a successful forgery of the one-time signature.

If some signature in Q_S contains a tuple $(\sigma^*_{w^*}, s_{w^*}, \mathsf{vk}_{w'\|0} \| \mathsf{vk}_{w'\|1})$ with

$$\mathsf{H}_{s_{w^*}}(\mathsf{vk}_{w^*\|0} \| \mathsf{vk}_{w^*\|1}) = \mathsf{H}_{s_{w^*}}(\mathsf{vk}_{w'\|0} \| \mathsf{vk}_{w'\|1}),$$

which was created by signing a message m', we can build the attacker $\mathcal{A}_{\mathsf{hashs}}$ against the hash function as follows: The attacker $\mathcal{A}_{\mathsf{hashs}}$ simulates the complete experiment but does not sample a hash function $\mathsf{H}_{s_{w^*}}$. Instead, before $\mathsf{H}_{s_{w^*}}$ is evaluated during a signing operation of m', the attacker returns the value $\mathsf{vk}_{w'\|0}\|\mathsf{vk}_{w'\|1}$ to the hash function challenge and then obtains a hash function h, which will be used as $\mathsf{H}_{s_{w^*}}$. Finally, the attacker $\mathcal{A}_{\mathsf{H}}$ outputs $\mathsf{vk}_{w^*\|0}\|\mathsf{vk}_{w^*\|1}$. As $\mathsf{H}_{s_{w^*}}(\mathsf{vk}_{w^*\|0}\|\mathsf{vk}_{w^*\|1}) = \mathsf{H}_{s_{w^*}}(\mathsf{vk}_{w'\|0}\|\mathsf{vk}_{w'\|1})$, this is a valid collision of the hash function keyed with s_{w^*}.

If $\mathcal{A}$ wins the security experiment with probability $p(\lambda)$ for some non-negligible function $p(\lambda)$, the attacker $\mathcal{A}_{\mathrm{OTS}}$ wins with probability $p_{\mathrm{OTS}}(\lambda)$, and the attacker $\mathcal{A}_{\mathsf{hashs}}$ wins with probability $p_{\mathsf{hashs}}(\lambda)$, we have $p(\lambda) \leq p_{\mathrm{OTS}}(\lambda) + p_{\mathsf{hashs}}(\lambda)$. Hence, either $\mathcal{A}_{\mathrm{OTS}}$ or $\mathcal{A}_{\mathsf{hashs}}$ is successful if $\mathcal{A}$ is successful. □

6 Discussion

Efficiency. To better assess our results, in Table 1 we provide an overview of the available constructions of subversion-resilient signatures found in the literature. The table shows that while our construction grants the strongest security in the watchdog model, i.e. no random oracle and complete subversion, it also has the biggest signature size. Note that for the reverse firewall (RF) model and the self-guarding (SG) model, additional/other assumptions are applied (verifiability, honest sample phase).

Table 1. Comparison of different approaches for subversion-resilient signature schemes. Here σ denotes the size of an underlying signature scheme, m denotes the length of the messages to be signed, and s is the size of the key of our hash function.

	Model	RO	Complete Subv	Signature size	Stateful subv
[2]	RF	✗	✗	σ	✓
[16]	SG	✗	✗	$\approx \lambda \cdot m + 2\lambda\sigma$	✗
[27]	online WD	✓	✓	m	✓
[13]	offline WD	✓	✗	m	✗
[13]	offline WD	✗	✗	$2(m+\sigma)$	✗
This work	offline WD	✗	✓	$m(\sigma + \lvert s\rvert + 2\lvert vk\rvert) + \sigma$	✗

It is well known that digital signatures can be constructed from one-way and collision-resistant hash functions. Thus, we now focus on constructing collision-resistant hash functions and explain why this seems impossible if the hash function is not idealized as a random oracle.

Subversion-Resilient Collision Resistance via Black-Box Testing. Similar to the case of weak PRFs [6] and one-way permutations (see Sect. 3), one may hope that simply taking any hash function and testing it sufficiently may already grant positive results. Unfortunately, this seems impossible. Consider an adversary which provides an implementation $\tilde{H}$ of H, which only differ for two values m_0, m_1 from H in the sense that $\tilde{H}(m_0) = 0 = \tilde{H}(m_1)$. Any watchdog that samples messages from the (finite) domain[6] of the hash function uniformly at random only has negligible probability in testing for m_0 or m_1. Conversely, the adversary can trivially output a collision by outputting m_0, m_1. While this observation is not very involved, to the best of our knowledge, it was not yet formally written down in previous works.

Implications for Signatures. In some textbooks for modern cryptography, such as [18], the construction of Naor-Yung is often displayed by utilizing collision-resistant hash functions instead of target-collision-resistant hash functions. This is useful from a teaching perspective, as collision resistance is introduced in courses, and there is little benefit in introducing target-collision resistance if only the Naor-Yung construction is considered. While the classical setting makes little difference in which notion is used, the distinction between these two notions is crucial in the subversion setting. As the stronger notion seems impossible to achieve, the weaker and sufficient property allows for the subversion-resilient construction.

Correctness. Note that both of our signature construction satisfies our correctness definition, even under subversion. This is because due to the testing of the watchdog Lemma 1 can be used to argue that only for negligible many inputs correctness is violated. Unfortunately, our approach cannot achieve perfect correctness (as achieved by the symmetric encryption construction in [6]). Note that no work achieves perfect correctness other than assuming verifiability in the reverse firewall model [2], thus assuming correctness.

Acknowledgements. The authors would like to thank all anonymous reviewers for their valuable comments. The work of Rongmao Chen is supported by the National Natural Science Foundation of China (Grant No. 62122092, No. 62032005).

References

1. Armour, M., Poettering, B.: Algorithm substitution attacks against receivers. Int. J. Inf. Secur. **21**(5), 1027–1050 (2022)
2. Ateniese, G., Magri, B., Venturi, D.: Subversion-resilient signature schemes. In: Ray, I., Li, N., Kruegel, C. (eds.) ACM CCS 2015: 22nd Conference on Computer and Communications Security, pp. 364–375. ACM Press, October 2015
3. Baek, J., Susilo, W., Kim, J., Chow, Y.W.: Subversion in practice: how to efficiently undermine signatures. Cryptology ePrint Archive, Report 2018/1201 (2018). https://eprint.iacr.org/2018/1201

[6] As is the case for tree-based signatures.

4. Bellare, M., Jaeger, J., Kane, D.: Mass-surveillance without the state: strongly undetectable algorithm-substitution attacks. In: Ray, I., Li, N., Kruegel, C. (eds.) ACM CCS 2015: 22nd Conference on Computer and Communications Security, pp. 1431–1440. ACM Press, October 2015
5. Bellare, M., Paterson, K.G., Rogaway, P.: Security of symmetric encryption against mass surveillance. In: Garay, J.A., Gennaro, R. (eds.) Advances in Cryptology - CRYPTO 2014, Part I. LNCS, vol. 8616, pp. 1–19. Springer, Heidelberg (2014). https://doi.org/10.1007/978-3-662-44371-2_1
6. Bemmann, P., Berndt, S., Diemert, D., Eisenbarth, T., Jager, T.: Subversion-resilient authenticated encryption without random oracles. In: Tibouchi, M., Wang, X. (eds.) ACNS. LNCS, vol. 13906, pp. 460–483. Springer, Cham (2023). https://doi.org/10.1007/978-3-031-33491-7_17
7. Bemmann, P., Chen, R., Jager, T.: Subversion-resilient public key encryption with practical watchdogs. In: Garay, J. (ed.) PKC 2021: 24th International Conference on Theory and Practice of Public Key Cryptography, Part I. LNCS, vol. 12710, pp. 627–658. Springer, Heidelberg (2021). https://doi.org/10.1007/978-3-030-75245-3_23
8. Berndt, S., Liskiewicz, M.: Algorithm substitution attacks from a steganographic perspective. In: Thuraisingham, B.M., Evans, D., Malkin, T., Xu, D. (eds.) ACM CCS 2017: 24th Conference on Computer and Communications Security, pp. 1649–1660. ACM Press, October/November 2017
9. Berndt, S., Wichelmann, J., Pott, C., Traving, T.H., Eisenbarth, T.: ASAP: algorithm substitution attacks on cryptographic protocols. In: Suga, Y., Sakurai, K., Ding, X., Sako, K. (eds.) ASIACCS 2022: 17th ACM Symposium on Information, Computer and Communications Security, pp. 712–726. ACM Press, May/June 2022
10. Chakraborty, S., Dziembowski, S., Nielsen, J.B.: Reverse firewalls for actively secure MPCs. In: Micciancio, D., Ristenpart, T. (eds.) Advances in Cryptology - CRYPTO 2020, Part II. LNCS, vol. 12171, pp. 732–762. Springer, Heidelberg (2020). https://doi.org/10.1007/978-3-030-56880-1_26
11. Chen, R., Huang, X., Yung, M.: Subvert KEM to break DEM: practical algorithm-substitution attacks on public-key encryption. In: Moriai, S., Wang, H. (eds.) Advances in Cryptology - ASIACRYPT 2020, Part II. LNCS, vol. 12492, pp. 98–128. Springer, Heidelberg (2020). https://doi.org/10.1007/978-3-030-64834-3_4
12. Chen, R., Mu, Y., Yang, G., Susilo, W., Guo, F., Zhang, M.: Cryptographic reverse firewall via malleable smooth projective hash functions. In: Cheon, J.H., Takagi, T. (eds.) Advances in Cryptology - ASIACRYPT 2016, Part I. LNCS, vol. 10031, pp. 844–876. Springer, Heidelberg (2016). https://doi.org/10.1007/978-3-662-53887-6_31
13. Chow, S.S.M., Russell, A., Tang, Q., Yung, M., Zhao, Y., Zhou, H.S.: Let a non-barking watchdog bite: cliptographic signatures with an offline watchdog. In: Lin, D., Sako, K. (eds.) PKC 2019: 22nd International Conference on Theory and Practice of Public Key Cryptography, Part I. LNCS, vol. 11442, pp. 221–251. Springer, Heidelberg (2019). https://doi.org/10.1007/978-3-030-17253-4_8
14. Degabriele, J.P., Farshim, P., Poettering, B.: A more cautious approach to security against mass surveillance. In: Leander, G. (ed.) Fast Software Encryption - FSE 2015. LNCS, vol. 9054, pp. 579–598. Springer, Heidelberg (2015). https://doi.org/10.1007/978-3-662-48116-5_28
15. Dodis, Y., Mironov, I., Stephens-Davidowitz, N.: Message transmission with reverse firewalls–secure communication on corrupted machines. In: Robshaw, M., Katz, J. (eds.) Advances in Cryptology - CRYPTO 2016, Part I. LNCS, vol. 9814, pp. 341–372. Springer, Heidelberg (2016). https://doi.org/10.1007/978-3-662-53018-4_13

16. Fischlin, M., Mazaheri, S.: Self-guarding cryptographic protocols against algorithm substitution attacks. In: Chong, S., Delaune, S. (eds.) CSF 2018: IEEE 31st Computer Security Foundations Symposium, pp. 76–90. IEEE Computer Society Press (2018)
17. Galteland, H., Gjøsteen, K.: Subliminal channels in post-quantum digital signature schemes. Cryptology ePrint Archive, Report 2019/574 (2019). https://eprint.iacr.org/2019/574
18. Katz, J., Lindell, Y.: Introduction to Modern Cryptography, 2nd edn. CRC Press, New York (2014)
19. Lamport, L.: Constructing digital signatures from a one-way function. Technical report SRI-CSL-98, SRI International Computer Science Laboratory, October 1979
20. Liu, C., Chen, R., Wang, Y., Wang, Y.: Asymmetric subversion attacks on signature schemes. In: Susilo, W., Yang, G. (eds.) ACISP 2018: 23rd Australasian Conference on Information Security and Privacy. LNCS, vol. 10946, pp. 376–395. Springer, Heidelberg (2018). https://doi.org/10.1007/978-3-319-93638-3_22
21. Merkle, R.C.: A certified digital signature. In: Brassard, G. (ed.) Advances in Cryptology - CRYPTO 1989. LNCS, vol. 435, pp. 218–238. Springer, Heidelberg (1990). https://doi.org/10.1007/0-387-34805-0_21
22. Mironov, I., Stephens-Davidowitz, N.: Cryptographic reverse firewalls. In: Oswald, E., Fischlin, M. (eds.) Advances in Cryptology - EUROCRYPT 2015, Part II. LNCS, vol. 9057, pp. 657–686. Springer, Heidelberg (2015). https://doi.org/10.1007/978-3-662-46803-6_22
23. Naor, M., Reingold, O.: Synthesizers and their application to the parallel construction of pseudo-random functions. J. Comput. Syst. Sci. **58**(2), 336–375 (1999)
24. Naor, M., Yung, M.: Universal one-way hash functions and their cryptographic applications. In: 21st Annual ACM Symposium on Theory of Computing, pp. 33–43. ACM Press, May 1989
25. Perlroth, N., Larson, J., Shane, S.: Secret documents reveal NSA campaign against encryption (2013). https://archive.nytimes.com/www.nytimes.com/interactive/2013/09/05/us/documents-reveal-nsa-campaign-against-encryption.html
26. Discussion about Kyber's tweaked FO transform (2023). https://groups.google.com/a/list.nist.gov/g/pqc-forum/c/WFRDl8DqYQ4, Discussion Thread on the PQC mailing list
27. Russell, A., Tang, Q., Yung, M., Zhou, H.S.: Cliptography: clipping the power of kleptographic attacks. In: Cheon, J.H., Takagi, T. (eds.) Advances in Cryptology - ASIACRYPT 2016, Part II. LNCS, vol. 10032, pp. 34–64. Springer, Heidelberg (2016). https://doi.org/10.1007/978-3-662-53890-6_2
28. Russell, A., Tang, Q., Yung, M., Zhou, H.S.: Generic semantic security against a kleptographic adversary. In: Thuraisingham, B.M., Evans, D., Malkin, T., Xu, D. (eds.) ACM CCS 2017: 24th Conference on Computer and Communications Security, pp. 907–922. ACM Press, October/November 2017
29. Russell, A., Tang, Q., Yung, M., Zhou, H.S.: Correcting subverted random oracles. In: Shacham, H., Boldyreva, A. (eds.) Advances in Cryptology - CRYPTO 2018, Part II. LNCS, vol. 10992, pp. 241–271. Springer, Heidelberg (2018). https://doi.org/10.1007/978-3-319-96881-0_9
30. Teseleanu, G.: Threshold kleptographic attacks on discrete logarithm based signatures. In: Lange, T., Dunkelman, O. (eds.) Progress in Cryptology - LATINCRYPT 2017: 5th International Conference on Cryptology and Information Security in Latin America. LNCS, vol. 11368, pp. 401–414. Springer, Heidelberg (2019). https://doi.org/10.1007/978-3-030-25283-0_21

31. Young, A., Yung, M.: The dark side of "black-box" cryptography, or: should we trust capstone? In: Koblitz, N. (ed.) Advances in Cryptology – CRYPTO 1996. LNCS, vol. 1109, pp. 89–103. Springer, Heidelberg (1996). https://doi.org/10.1007/3-540-68697-5_8
32. Young, A., Yung, M.: Kleptography: using cryptography against cryptography. In: Fumy, W. (ed.) Advances in Cryptology - EUROCRYPT 1997. LNCS, vol. 1233, pp. 62–74. Springer, Heidelberg (1997). https://doi.org/10.1007/3-540-69053-0_6

Practical Lattice-Based Distributed Signatures for a Small Number of Signers

Nabil Alkeilani Alkadri(✉), Nico Döttling, and Sihang Pu

CISPA Helmholtz Center for Information Security, Saarbrücken, Germany
{nabil.alkadri,doettling,sihang.pu}@cispa.de

Abstract. n-out-of-n distributed signatures are a special type of threshold t-out-of-n signatures. They are created by a group of n signers, each holding a share of the secret key, in a collaborative way. This kind of signatures has been studied intensively in recent years, motivated by different applications such as reducing the risk of compromising secret keys in cryptocurrencies. Towards maintaining security in the presence of quantum adversaries, Damgård et al. (J Cryptol 35(2), 2022) proposed lattice-based constructions of n-out-of-n distributed signatures and multi-signatures following the Fiat-Shamir with aborts paradigm (ASIACRYPT 2009). Due to the inherent issue of aborts, the protocols either require to increase their parameters by a factor of n, or they suffer from a large number of restarts that grows with n. This has a significant impact on their efficiency, even if n is small. Moreover, the protocols use trapdoor homomorphic commitments as a further cryptographic building block, making their deployment in practice not as easy as standard lattice-based Fiat-Shamir signatures. In this work, we present a new construction of n-out-of-n distributed signatures. It is designed specifically for applications with small number of signers. Our construction follows the Fiat-Shamir with aborts paradigm, but solves the problem of large number of restarts without increasing the parameters by a factor of n and utilizing any further cryptographic primitive. To demonstrate the practicality of our protocol, we provide a software implementation and concrete parameters aiming at 128 bits of security. Furthermore, we select concrete parameters for the construction by Damgård et al. and for the most recent lattice-based multi-signature scheme by Chen (CRYPTO 2023), and show that our approach provides a significant improvement in terms of all efficiency metrics. Our results also show that the multi-signature schemes by Damgård et al. and Chen as well as a multi-signature variant of our protocol produce signatures that are not smaller than a naive multi-signature derived from the concatenation of multiple standard signatures.

Keywords: n-out-of-n distributed signatures · threshold n-out-of-n signatures · Fiat-Shamir with aborts · lattice-based cryptography

1 Introduction

An n-out-of-n distributed signature is a signature on a single message that is jointly generated by a group of n signers. Before signing this message, the signers

C. Pöpper and L. Batina (Eds.): ACNS 2024, LNCS 14583, pp. 376–402, 2024.
https://doi.org/10.1007/978-3-031-54770-6_15

invoke a key generation protocol to create a pair of public and secret key, where each signer learns the public key and a share of the secret key only. The signature can be verified by the public key. An n-out-of-n distributed signature is a special type of threshold t-out-of-n signatures [18], hence also called a threshold n-out-of-n signature. The required security property of n-out-of-n distributed signatures is that it should be infeasible to generate a valid signature even if at most $n - 1$ signers are corrupted. Distributed signature protocols constitute a fundamental cryptographic primitive, most notably, in the blockchain domain when it comes to authorize transactions in the presence of multiple signers. This minimizes the risk of compromising the secret key. Distributed signatures can provide institutional and personal account key management by multiple people.

Currently, real-life applications employing distributed signatures rely on constructions whose security is based on the hardness of number-theoretic assumptions. However, when taking into account recent developments of quantum computers, it is meanwhile known that these assumptions cannot be used long-term. In an effort to develop new constructions that are conjectured to be secure in the presence of quantum computers, few works based on lattice assumptions considered threshold t-out-of-n signatures (see Appendix A). Recently, Damgård et al. [17] proposed a lattice-based construction of n-out-of-n distributed signatures following the Fiat-Shamir with aborts paradigm [25]. Hence, it relies on the so-called *rejection sampling* when generating signatures. In the context of Fiat-Shamir signatures based on lattices, rejection sampling is a crucial tool that is used as a security check. Using a so-called masking term, it allows to verify that a secret (or secret-related) term is concealed and distributed independently from a public term that is computed using both the masking and secret term. In particular, it makes sure that signatures are distributed independently from the secret key. If the check fails, i.e., if rejection sampling rejects, the signing protocol is restarted in order to sample a fresh masking term. This is because all computations carried out up to rejection sampling are related to a certain masking term. In interactive protocols with multiple rejection sampling procedures such as distributed signatures, this has a significant negative impact on the efficiency. To see this, suppose that n signers would like to generate a signature, and each one has to restart the protocol M times on average, where M is determined in accordance to other parameters of the protocol (the smaller M is, the larger the signature size). Then, the total average number of restarts in such a protocol is given by M^n, which is large even for a small n. One way to make this number reasonably small is to increase the parameters by a factor of n [17]. However, this induces larger sizes of keys and signatures, even if n is small. In addition to the large number of restarts, the construction by Damgård et al. [17] uses a trapdoor homomorphic commitment scheme as a further cryptographic building block, which affects its efficiency in a significant way.

Due to the above mentioned drawbacks, we conclude that the protocol of [17] is not suitable for deployment in practice, even when it comes to applications with small number of signers, which is our main focus in this work and is apparent in real-world applications as we argue in the following. Consider the well-known problem of fraud management (CEO fraud), where a fraudster pretends to be a senior manager – often the CEO – in order to persuade a staff member to make an urgent payment to a supplier or business partner. This kind of social engineering can be easily prevented by employing distributed signatures. By means of a defined policy, contracts are only authorized by various decision makers, typically 2 or 3. In cryptocurrencies, distributed signatures add a great level of security by requiring few devices to authenticate transactions. A so-called *distributed wallet* requires all signers involved in the generation of such a wallet to agree before any transaction can be created. For instance, wallets developed by *Armory* allow at most 7 signers to authorize a transaction, while those developed by *BitGo* and *Coinbase* provide up to 3 signers[1].

1.1 Contribution

We present a new construction of n-out-of-n distributed signatures based on lattices over modules. It is designed to support applications with a small number of signers only. Similar to the protocol by Damgård et al. [17], our construction follows the Fiat-Shamir with aborts approach, but solves its drawbacks that we mentioned above. More precisely, it solves the problem of the large number of restarts without increasing the parameters by a factor of n, and it does not rely on any additional primitives like trapdoor homomorphic commitments. It also supports the *offline-online* paradigm. This feature is desirable in practice, since it allows expensive operations of our signing protocol to be pre-processed. Using the *rewinding* technique [7], we prove the security of our construction in the random oracle model [8] assuming the hardness of the Module Learning With Errors (MLWE) problem and Module Small Integer Solution (MSIS) problem. We provide a proof-of-concept implementation of our protocol demonstrating its practicality, and propose concrete parameters targeting 128 bits of security. In order to give a fair comparison, we also select concrete parameters for the distributed signature and multi-signature protocols by Damgård et al. [17] and for the most recent multi-signature protocol by Chen [13]. The reason of considering multi-signatures is because a distributed signature protocol can be derived from [13], and conversely we can derive a multi-signature scheme from our construction (see Sect. 1.3 for more details). The comparison is summarized in Table 1, which shows that our approach provides a significant improvement regarding all efficiency metrics.

1.2 Technical Overview

Similar to [17], our construction follows the Fiat-Shamir with aborts approach and can be seen as a distributed variant of the standard signature scheme Dilithium-G [21]. Basically, the key generation protocol generates an instance of the MLWE problem in a distributed way. Therefore, we give in this overview a high-level explanation of our signing protocol only. For ease of exposition, we

[1] https://coinsutra.com/best-multi-signature-bitcoin-wallets/.

Table 1. Comparison between our construction, the constructions of distributed signatures and multi-signatures introduced by Damgård et al. [17], and the multi-signature scheme by Chen [13]. The corresponding parameters are given in Table 2 and consider 7 signers. Performance measures are only provided for our protocol, since no implementations are given in [13,17]. Parameter selection is described in Sect. 3.3. All numbers are rounded to the nearest integer. Sizes and communication costs are provided in kilobytes, while performance measures in milliseconds.

Protocol	Sizes			Communication per signer		Performance per signer		
	Public key	Distributed signature	Multi-signature	Key generation	Signature generation	Key generation	Signature generation	Signature verification
This work	7	12	12	7	25	2	41	2
[17]	21	2538	2594	21	2536	-	-	-
[13]	8	-	25	-	53	-	-	-

consider a group of just two signers. A generalization to $n \geq 2$ signers can be derived in a straightforward manner and is considered in Sect. 3. Our protocol operates over the rings $R = \mathbb{Z}[X]/\langle X^N + 1\rangle$ and $R_q = \mathbb{Z}_q[X]/\langle X^N + 1\rangle$. Let $\bar{\mathbf{A}} = [\mathbf{I}_k|\mathbf{A}]$ be a joint public matrix, where $\mathbf{I}_k$ is the identity matrix of dimension k and $\mathbf{A} \in R_q^{k\times\ell}$ is uniformly random. The public and secret key share of each signer are given by $(pk, sk_j) = ((\bar{\mathbf{A}}, \mathbf{b}), \mathbf{s}_j)$, where $\mathbf{b} = \bar{\mathbf{A}} \cdot \mathbf{s} \pmod q$, $\mathbf{s} = \mathbf{s}_1 + \mathbf{s}_2 \in R^{k+\ell}$, and $j \in \{1, 2\}$. Each share $\mathbf{s}_j$ is chosen uniformly random over a small subset of R. In Fig. 1, we present an informal overview of our signing protocol. We only present the behavior of signer S_1, as each signer plays the same role and performs the same steps. Note that all operations up to computing g_1 can be pre-processed without knowledge of the message. The remaining steps are carried out online. This reflects the support of offline-online paradigm. In the following we highlight the major techniques and differences to [17].

Removing Homomorphic Commitments. In lattice-based Fiat-Shamir signatures like Dilithium-G [21], a signer computes a *commitment* $\mathbf{v}$ to some randomness $\mathbf{y}$. In our case, $\mathbf{y}$ follows the Gaussian distribution $D_{\mathbb{Z}^N,\sigma}^{k+\ell}$ with standard deviation σ. Together with the message m, $\mathbf{v}$ is used to generate a *challenge* c via a cryptographic hash function Hash. Then, a *response* $\mathbf{z}$ is computed as $\mathbf{z} = \mathbf{y} + \mathbf{s}c$. After that, rejection sampling is carried out on $\mathbf{z}$ in order to make sure that $\mathbf{z}$ is distributed independently from $\mathbf{s}c$. The signing process is restarted if rejection sampling does not accept. Otherwise, the signature is given by $(\mathbf{z}, c)$. In n-out-of-n distributed signatures, the challenge is created via the sum of the commitments of all signers, and the final response is given by aggregating all individual responses. This means that each signer reveals its own commitment whether rejection sampling accepts or not. As indicated in [17], security cannot be proven if commitments of aborted executions are revealed. To circumvent this issue, [17] employ a lattice-based homomorphic commitment scheme whose statistical hiding property ensures that no information can be leaked from a commitment to $\mathbf{v}$, which is only revealed if rejection sampling is successful. Our approach is to use a specific regularity property [27]. It ensures that aborted executions do not leak any information so that security can be proven with-

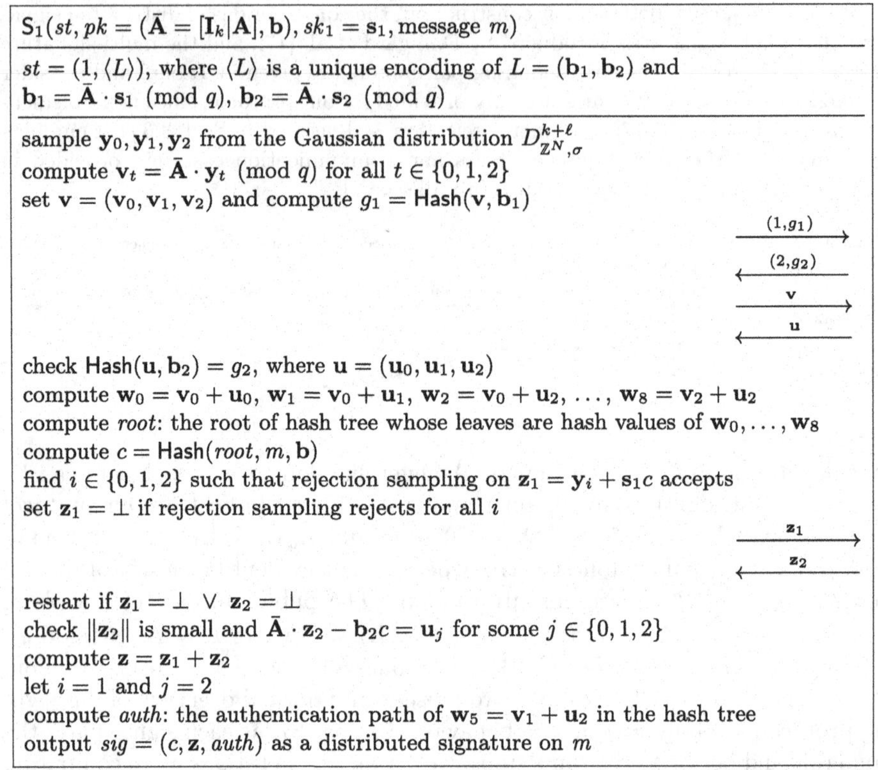

Fig. 1. Overview of our n-out-of-n distributed signature protocol. For simplicity, we consider in this overview a group of two signers only, where each signer computes and sends commitments to three Gaussian distributed masking vectors. The choice of three Gaussian masking vectors is only for presentation purposes.

out utilizing any additional primitive. More concretely, increasing the standard deviation σ of $\mathbf{y}$ according to the regularity property makes the distribution of $\mathbf{v}$ statistically close to uniform over R_q^k. As demonstrated in Table 1, this improves the performance and complexity of the protocol, and produces much shorter signatures. We remark that the same regularity property must be satisfied by the commitment scheme used in [17]. In other words, we directly endow $\mathbf{v}$ with the regularity property, without having to compute an additional homomorphic commitment to $\mathbf{v}$ that is statistically hiding by the regularity property.

Removing Restarts. [17] suggest to increase σ by a factor of n in order to reduce the large number of protocol restarts inherent in carrying out rejection sampling. We use the tree of commitments technique by Alkadri et al. [3], where each signer generates and sends a specified number of commitments to the remaining signers. For example, in Fig. 1 we let signer S_1 generate three commitments $\mathbf{v}_0, \mathbf{v}_1, \mathbf{v}_2$. Then, each one is added to $\mathbf{u}_0, \mathbf{u}_1, \mathbf{u}_2$ individually, where $\mathbf{u}_0, \mathbf{u}_1, \mathbf{u}_2$ are the commitments of signer S_2. After that, each signer computes a binary hash tree whose leaves are the hash values of the aggregated commitments $\mathbf{w}_0, \ldots, \mathbf{w}_8$. The root of this hash tree is used to generate the challenge c. Note that the input of the signing protocol includes a state information $st = (1, \langle L \rangle)$, where $\langle L \rangle$ is a unique encoding (e.g., lexicographical ordering) of the list of public key shares $L = (\mathbf{b}_1, \mathbf{b}_2)$. This state is obtained during executing the key generation protocol. Here, we assume, w.l.o.g., that $\mathbf{b}_1$ is the first entry of $\langle L \rangle$. The unique encoding of signers is crucial in our construction, since otherwise each signer may compute a different hash tree, and hence a different challenge. In order to obtain the same local ordering by each signer and allow to map them to the index of their public key shares in $\langle L \rangle$, each signer sends the entry of its public key share in the first round of the protocol. The correctness of the ordering is verified when checking the validity of the hash values (see Fig. 1). The commitments generated by each signer allow to carry out rejection sampling up to three times without the need to restart the signing protocol. The response for which rejection sampling accepts is sent out, and the signature is given by $(c, \mathbf{z}, auth)$, where $\mathbf{z}$ is the aggregated response, and $auth$ is the authentication path of the aggregated commitment corresponding to the used masking vectors. Using this technique not only reduces the number of restarts, or removes it at all, but also reduces the signature size. This is because an aggregated (homomorphic) commitment together with its opening, which are part of the signature in [17], are replaced with the root of the tree $root$ and an authentication path $auth$, where the pair $(root, auth)$ is just a short sequence of hash values. However, the number of commitment additions is given by ω^n, where ω is the number of commitments created by each of the n signers (in Fig. 1 we have $\omega = 3$ and $n = 2$). In other words, the computational complexity is $O(\omega^n)$. This is why our construction is only suitable for a limited number of signers, which is sufficient for several applications as demonstrated in the introduction. We note that in Fig. 1 we set $\omega = 3$ only for presentation purposes. In practice, ω is selected such that the protocol is restarted with a probability of choice. In our sample parameters, ω is selected such that each signer aborts with probability ≈ 0.

Round Complexity. Our signing protocol consists of three rounds (see Fig. 1). The first round, where the hash value of the commitments is sent, is a standard technique that is required to prove security. It allows the security reduction to simulate honest signer by extracting the commitments of corrupt signers from incoming queries to the hash function Hash (when modeled as random oracle). It also allows programming Hash accordingly before revealing the commitments. This standard first round is removed in [17] by adding a trapdoor feature to the homomorphic commitment scheme, while in [13] a straight-line simulation via a dual secret key is used. In order to reduce the complexity to two rounds, our construction can be instantiated with a trapdoor as in [12]. We choose to keep the first round instead in order to obtain an improved communication cost and smaller sizes of public keys and signatures.

1.3 Related Work

In Appendix A, we provide related work on lattice-based threshold signatures.

Multi-Signatures. A multi-signature scheme [23] resembles n-out-of-n distributed signature protocols. The differences are (1) each signer has its own key pair, i.e., it locally generates its public and secret key, where the public key is published before signing, (2) the group of signers is not required to be fixed, and each signer can initiate the signing protocol with a set of signers of its choice, and (3) unless a so-called *key aggregation* property is supported, verification does not use a single public key. Instead, it takes the set of public keys involved in signing the message. When it comes to the flexibility of choosing the group of signers, multi-signatures are more suitable than distributed signatures, but at the cost of more verification time and larger size of joint public key. The crucial property of a multi-signature is that it is *compact*, i.e., its size is not larger than the total size of signatures generated by each signer individually. If this property is not satisfied, then it is meaningful to use the *naive approach*, i.e., by simply concatenating the individual signatures created by each signer to produce a multi-signature. For instance, the signature scheme Dilithium [20] or Dilithium-G [21] can be used, which produces signatures of size less than 2.5 KB.

[17] observed that lattice-based multi-signature schemes prior their work have incomplete proof of security. In particular, their security proof does not consider simulating aborted executions of the signing protocol, which are inherent in the lattice setting due to carrying out rejection sampling. To solve this issue, [17] proposed a scheme that utilizes lattice-based trapdoor homomorphic commitments, while Boschini et al. [12] used trapdoors without homomorphic commitments. Chen [13] improved the schemes of [12,17] by introducing a so-called *dual signing simulation* technique, which allows to prove security without trapdoors.

Our construction can be easily turned into a multi-signature scheme. The difference is that each signer computes its own challenge and response using its own key pair. A multi-signature is given by the tuple $(root, \mathbf{z}, auth)$. In particular, the parameters are exactly the same, and the security proof is even simpler, since there is no dedicated key generation protocol. However, the compactness property is not satisfied for every small n. It seems that the regularity property of the commitments is the reason for this, even without using the tree of commitments technique. More concretely, commitments must be statistically hiding, while in standard signature schemes like Dilithium, they are only computationally hiding, since aborted executions are never revealed. Therefore, we choose not to present a multi-signature variant of our protocol. In fact, Table 1 shows that all current multi-signature schemes may be compact only for a large n.

Reducing Restarts. In order to solve the problem of the large number of restarts inherent in lattice-based interactive protocols following the Fiat-Shamir with aborts paradigm, Alkadri et al. [3] introduced a technique called *tree of commitments*. A tree of commitments is a binary hash tree whose leaves are constructed from many masking terms. This allows to reduce the number of restarts of lattice-based protocols by iteratively applying rejection sampling using different masking terms in one execution. By using a large enough number of masking terms, this even allows to completely eliminate restarts, i.e., with probability very close to one. However, this technique was used to construct efficient lattice-based blind signature schemes only [3,4], which involve just two parties (a signer and a user). The user blinds the signer's commitments via many random values, builds a hash tree from the blind commitments, and generates a blind signature from one of them without the need to abort and request a protocol restart from the signer. In this work, we use the technique in a multi-user setting, where each user generates multiple commitments and builds a hash tree to create a partial signature. Each leave of the tree corresponds to the sum of commitments, and each summand is created by one user. We show how to ensure that each signer computes the same hash tree, i.e., adding commitments in exactly the same way as the remaining signers. Otherwise, each signer would obtain a different root and signatures would not be verified.

2 Background

Notation. We denote by $\mathbb{N}, \mathbb{Z}$, and $\mathbb{R}$ the sets of natural numbers, integers, and real numbers, respectively. If $n \in \mathbb{N}$, we let $[n]$ denote the set $\{1, \ldots, n\}$. We denote the security parameter by $\lambda \in \mathbb{N}$, and abbreviate probabilistic polynomial-time by PPT and deterministic polynomial-time by DPT. We write $x \leftarrow\!\!\$\ D$ to denote that x is sampled randomly according to a distribution D. If S is a finite set, we also write $x \leftarrow\!\!\$\ S$ if x is chosen randomly from the uniform distribution over S. Let $q \in \mathbb{Z}_{>0}$. We write $\mathbb{Z}_q$ to denote the ring of integers modulo q with representatives in $[-\frac{q}{2}, \frac{q}{2}) \cap \mathbb{Z}$. Let N be a fixed power of two and consider the polynomial ring $\mathbb{Z}[X]$ in a variable X. We define the rings $R := \mathbb{Z}[X]/\langle X^N + 1\rangle$ and $R_q := \mathbb{Z}_q[X]/\langle X^N + 1\rangle$. Elements in R and R_q are denoted by regular font letters. Column vectors and matrices with coefficients in R or R_q are denoted by bold lower-case letters and bold upper-case letters, respectively. The identity matrix of dimension k is denoted by $\mathbf{I}_k$. The ℓ_p-norm of any $a \in R$ is defined by $\|a\|_p := (\sum_{i=0}^{N-1} |a_i|^p)^{1/p}$ if $p < \infty$ and by $\max\{|a_0|, \ldots, |a_{N-1}|\}$ if $p = \infty$. Similarly, the ℓ_p-norm of any $\mathbf{b} = (b_1, \ldots, b_k)^\top \in R^k$ is defined by $\|\mathbf{b}\|_p := (\sum_{i=1}^{k} \|b_i\|_p^p)^{1/p}$ if $p < \infty$ and by $\max\{\|b_1\|_p, \ldots, \|b_k\|_p\}$ if $p = \infty$. We write $\|\cdot\|$ instead of $\|\cdot\|_2$. We define the sets $S_\eta := \{f \in R_q \colon \|f\|_\infty \leq \eta\}$ and $\mathbb{T}_\kappa := \{f \in R_q \colon \|f\|_\infty = 1 \wedge \|f\|_1 = \kappa\}$. The discrete Gaussian distribution over $\mathbb{Z}^m$ with standard deviation $\sigma > 0$ and center $\mathbf{c} \in \mathbb{R}^m$ is the probability distribution $D_{\mathbb{Z}^m,\sigma,\mathbf{c}}$, which assigns to every $\mathbf{x} \in \mathbb{Z}^m$ the probability of occurrence given by $D_{\mathbb{Z}^m,\sigma,\mathbf{c}}(\mathbf{x}) := \rho_{\sigma,\mathbf{c}}(\mathbf{x})/\rho_{\sigma,\mathbf{c}}(\mathbb{Z}^m)$, where $\rho_{\sigma,\mathbf{c}}(\mathbf{x}) := \exp(-\frac{\|\mathbf{x}-\mathbf{c}\|^2}{2\sigma^2})$ and $\rho_{\sigma,\mathbf{c}}(\mathbb{Z}^m) := \sum_{\mathbf{x}\in\mathbb{Z}^m} \rho_{\sigma,\mathbf{c}}(\mathbf{x})$. The subscript $\mathbf{c}$ is omitted when $\mathbf{c} = \mathbf{0}$. Additional background is provided in Appendix B.

Hardness Assumptions. We define the lattice problems: Module Learning With Errors (MLWE) and Module Small Integer Solution (MSIS).

Definition 1. *Let $pp = (N, k, \ell, q, \eta)$, where N, k, ℓ, q, η are positive integers. We say that* MLWE *holds w.r.t. pp if for every PPT algorithm* A *the advantage*

$\mathrm{Adv}_{\mathsf{A}}^{\mathsf{MLWE}}(pp)$ *is negligible in* λ, *where* $\mathrm{Adv}_{\mathsf{A}}^{\mathsf{MLWE}}(pp) :=$

$$\left| \Pr\left[b = 1 : \begin{array}{c} \mathbf{A} \leftarrow\!\!\$\; R_q^{k\times\ell}; \mathbf{s} \leftarrow\!\!\$\; S_\eta^{k+\ell}; \\ \mathbf{t} := [\mathbf{I}_k|\mathbf{A}] \cdot \mathbf{s} \in R_q^k; \\ b \leftarrow\!\!\$\; \mathsf{A}(pp, \mathbf{A}, \mathbf{t}) \end{array} \right] - \Pr\left[b = 1 : \begin{array}{c} \mathbf{A} \leftarrow\!\!\$\; R_q^{k\times\ell}; \\ \mathbf{t} \leftarrow\!\!\$\; R_q^k; \\ b \leftarrow\!\!\$\; \mathsf{A}(pp, \mathbf{A}, \mathbf{t}) \end{array} \right] \right|.$$

Definition 2. *Let* $pp = (N, k, \ell, q, \beta)$, *where* N, k, ℓ, q *are positive integers and* β *is a positive real. We say that* MSIS *holds w.r.t. pp if for every algorithm* A *the advantage* $\mathrm{Adv}_{\mathsf{A}}^{\mathsf{MSIS}}(pp)$ *is negligible in* λ, *where* $\mathrm{Adv}_{\mathsf{A}}^{\mathsf{MSIS}}(pp) :=$

$$\Pr[0 < \|\mathbf{x}\| \leq \beta \wedge \mathbf{0} = [\mathbf{I}_k|\mathbf{A}] \cdot \mathbf{x} \pmod q) : \mathbf{A} \leftarrow\!\!\$\; R_q^{k\times\ell}; \mathbf{x} \in R^{k+\ell} \leftarrow\!\!\$\; \mathsf{A}(pp, \mathbf{A})].$$

Estimating the hardness of MLWE and MSIS is described in Appendix C.

Distributed Signatures. We follow [17] to recall the syntax and security of n-out-of-n distributed signatures. We assume that many sessions of the signing protocol can be invoked concurrently, while key generation can be executed only once. All signers participating in both key and signature generation play the same role. Hence, we only present n^{th} signer's behavior, who is the first one sending out a message in each round of interaction. Consequently, we assume that the adversary is *rushing*, i.e., based on the honest n^{th} signer's message, the adversary is allowed to choose messages of the remaining $n-1$ corrupted signers.

Definition 3. *An n-out-of-n distributed signature protocol is a tuple of algorithms* $\mathsf{DSig} = (\mathsf{PGen}, \mathsf{KGen}_j, \mathsf{Sign}_j, \mathsf{Verify})$, *where:*

PGen *is a PPT parameter generation algorithm that, on input* 1^λ, *returns public parameters pp, which implicitly contains* 1^λ. *We assume that pp is given as an implicit input to all algorithms.*

KGen_j, *for all* $j \in [n]$, *is a PPT interactive key generation algorithm that is run by each signer* S_j. *At the end of the protocol,* S_j *returns a state st and a pair* (pk, sk_j), *where pk is a public key and* sk_j *is a secret key share.*

Sign_j, *for all* $j \in [n]$, *is a PPT interactive signing algorithm that is run by each signer* S_j. *Each* S_j *runs* Sign_j *on input a session identifier sid, a state information st, a public key pk, a secret key share* sk_j, *and a message m. At the end of the protocol,* S_j *returns a signature sig.*

Verify *is a DPT verification algorithm that, on input a public key pk, a message m, and a signature sig, returns 1 if sig is valid and 0 otherwise.*

Definition 4. *We say that* DSig *is* UF-CMA *secure (distributed signature unforgeability against chosen message attacks) w.r.t.* $pp \in \mathsf{PGen}(1^\lambda)$ *if for every adversary* A *that makes* q_{Sign} *signing queries to an oracle* $\mathsf{O}_n^{\mathsf{DSig}}$, *the following advantage is negligible in* λ:

$$\mathrm{Adv}_{\mathsf{DSig},\mathsf{A}}^{\text{UF-CMA}}(pp) = \Pr[\mathrm{Exp}_{\mathsf{DSig},\mathsf{A}}^{\text{UF-CMA}}(pp) = 1],$$

where the oracle $\mathsf{O}_n^{\mathsf{DSig}}$ *and the experiment* $\mathrm{Exp}_{\mathsf{DSig},\mathsf{A}}^{\text{UF-CMA}}$ *are defined in Fig. 2.*

$\mathrm{Exp}^{\text{UF-CMA}}_{\mathsf{DSig},\mathsf{A}}(pp)$

$\mathrm{L}_m \leftarrow \varnothing$
$(m^*, sig^*) \leftarrow\!\!\$\ \mathsf{A}^{\mathsf{O}^{\mathsf{DSig}}_n}(pp)$
if $m^* \in \mathrm{L}_m$ **then**
  return 0
return $\mathsf{Verify}(pk, m^*, sig^*)$

$\mathsf{O}^{\mathsf{DSig}}_n(sid, m)$

$\mathit{flag} \leftarrow$ **false**
if $sid = 0$ **then**
  if $\mathit{flag} =$ **true then**
    return $\perp$
  $(st, (pk, sk_n)) \leftarrow\!\!\$\ \mathsf{KGen}_n()$
  $\mathit{flag} \leftarrow$ **true**
if $\mathit{flag} =$ **false then**
  return $\perp$
$\mathrm{L}_m \leftarrow \mathrm{L}_m \cup \{m\}$
$sig \leftarrow\!\!\$\ \mathsf{Sign}_n(sid, st, pk, sk_n, m)$
return sig

Fig. 2. Experiment $\mathrm{Exp}^{\text{UF-CMA}}_{\mathsf{DSig},\mathsf{A}}$. We define by L_m the set of all messages m such that (sid, m) was queried by A to its oracle as the first query with identifier $sid \neq 0$.

3 Distributed Signature Protocol

3.1 Protocol Description

Let $\mathsf{G}\colon \{0,1\}^* \to \{0,1\}^{\ell_\mathsf{G}}$, $\mathsf{F}\colon \{0,1\}^* \to \{0,1\}^{\ell_\mathsf{F}}$, and $\mathsf{H}\colon \{0,1\}^* \to \mathbb{T}_\kappa$ be cryptographic hash functions. Define by $\mathsf{Expand}\colon \{0,1\}^* \to R_q^{k\times\ell}$ an extendable output function (XOF), e.g., SHAKE. Let $\omega \in \mathbb{N}_{>1}$. Following [3,4], we define the algorithms that build a tree of commitments:

1. HashTree is a DPT algorithm whose input is ω commitments $\mathbf{v}_0, \ldots, \mathbf{v}_{\omega-1}$, where $\mathbf{A} \in R_q^{k\times\ell}$ and for all $j \in \{0\ldots,\omega-1\}$: $\mathbf{v}_j = [\mathbf{I}_k|\mathbf{A}]\cdot\mathbf{y}_j \pmod q$ and $\mathbf{y}_j \in R^{k+\ell}$. It returns a pair $(\mathit{root}, \mathit{tree})$, where root is the root of a binary hash tree of height $h = \lceil\log(\omega)\rceil$ whose leaves are the hash values $\mathsf{F}(\mathbf{v}_j)$, and tree is the sequence that consists of all leaves and inner nodes of the tree.

2. BuildAuth is a DPT algorithm whose input is an index t, a sequence of nodes tree, and a height h. It returns $\mathit{auth} = (t, \mathbf{a}_0, \ldots, \mathbf{a}_{h-1})$, where $\mathbf{a}_i \in \{0,1\}^{\ell_\mathsf{F}}$, $0 \le t < \omega$, and $0 \le i < h$. Let $\mathbf{z}'$ be some secret vector. The output auth represents the authentication path of a vector $\mathbf{z}_t = \mathbf{y}_t + \mathbf{z}'$, for which the rejection sampling procedure accepts, i.e., masking vector $\mathbf{y}_t$ ensures that $\mathbf{z}_t$ hides $\mathbf{z}'$.

3. RootCalc is a DPT algorithm whose input is a commitment $\mathbf{v}$ and its authentication path $\mathit{auth} = (t, \mathbf{a}_0, \ldots, \mathbf{a}_{h-1})$. It returns the root of the hash tree that includes the leaf $\mathsf{F}(\mathbf{v})$ at index t and the inner nodes $\mathbf{a}_0, \ldots, \mathbf{a}_{h-1}$.

We define the following bijective mapping:

$$\mathsf{IntIndex}_{\omega,n}\colon \{0,\ldots,\omega-1\}^n \to \{0,\ldots,\omega^n-1\};\ (i^{(1)},\ldots,i^{(n)}) \mapsto \sum_{j=0}^{n-1} i^{(n-j)}\cdot\omega^j.$$

$\mathsf{IntIndex}_{\omega,n}$ converts a tuple $(i^{(1)},\ldots,i^{(n)})$ into a unique positive integer. Let L be a finite set, we define by $\mathsf{Encode}(L)$ a unique encoding of L, e.g., lexicographical ordering. We also write $L[j]$ to denote the jth entry of L. We let Compress

$\mathsf{KGen}_n()$

$seed^{(n)} \leftarrow_{\$} \{0,1\}^{\ell_{seed}}$
$\bar{g}^{(n)} \leftarrow \mathsf{G}(seed^{(n)}, n)$
broadcast $\bar{g}^{(n)}$
receive $\bar{g}^{(j)}$ for all $j \in [n-1]$
broadcast $seed^{(n)}$
receive $seed^{(j)}$ for all $j \in [n-1]$
for $j = 1$ **to** $n-1$ **do**
    if $\bar{g}^{(j)} \neq \mathsf{G}(seed^{(j)}, j)$ **then**
        broadcast *abort*
        return $(\perp, \perp, \perp)$
$seed \leftarrow \bigoplus_{j=1}^{n} seed^{(j)}$
$\mathbf{A} \leftarrow \mathsf{Expand}(seed)$, $\bar{\mathbf{A}} \leftarrow [\mathbf{I}_k | \mathbf{A}]$
$\mathbf{s}^{(n)} \leftarrow_{\$} S_{\eta}^{k+\ell}$
$\mathbf{b}^{(n)} \leftarrow \bar{\mathbf{A}} \cdot \mathbf{s}^{(n)} \pmod q$
$\hat{g}^{(n)} \leftarrow \mathsf{G}(\mathbf{b}^{(n)}, n)$
broadcast $\hat{g}^{(n)}$
receive $\hat{g}^{(j)}$ for all $j \in [n-1]$
broadcast $\mathbf{b}^{(n)}$
receive $\mathbf{b}^{(j)}$ for all $j \in [n-1]$
for $j = 1$ **to** $n-1$ **do**
    if $\hat{g}^{(j)} \neq \mathsf{G}(\mathbf{b}^{(j)}, j)$ **then**
        broadcast *abort*
        return $(\perp, \perp, \perp)$
$\mathbf{b} \leftarrow \sum_{j=1}^{n} \mathbf{b}^{(j)} \pmod q$
$L \leftarrow \mathsf{Encode}(\mathbf{b}^{(1)}, \ldots, \mathbf{b}^{(n)})$
let $L[int] = \mathbf{b}^{(n)}$, $int \in [n]$
$st \leftarrow (int, L)$
$pk \leftarrow (seed, \mathbf{b})$
$sk^{(n)} \leftarrow \mathbf{s}^{(n)}$
return $(st, (pk, sk^{(n)}))$

Fig. 3. Key generation of our lattice-based n-out-of-n distributed signature protocol.

and Decompress define algorithms for representing Gaussian elements via Huffman encoding. The first algorithm is used in the signing process to reduce the signature size, while the latter is used in the verification algorithm to reconstruct the Gaussian vector computed during signature generation. In the following we give a detailed description of our n-out-of-n distributed signature protocol. Its respective algorithms are given in Fig. 3,4. Since all signers play the same role, we only present n^{th} signer's behavior.

Parameter and Key Generation. PGen generates public parameters as given in Table 3. We assume that PGen is invoked by a trusted party. KGen_n first generates a uniformly random $\mathbf{A} \in R_q^{k\times\ell}$ in a distributed way. That is, it samples $seed^{(n)} \leftarrow_{\$} \{0,1\}^{\ell_{seed}}$, computes $\bar{g}^{(n)} = \mathsf{G}(seed^{(n)}, n)$, and sends out $\bar{g}^{(n)}$. After receiving $\bar{g}^{(j)}$ for all $j \in [n-1]$, it sends out $seed^{(n)}$ and then receives $seed^{(j)}$. If $\bar{g}^{(j)} \neq \mathsf{G}(seed^{(j)}, j)$ for any $j \in [n-1]$, it aborts. Otherwise, it computes $seed = \bigoplus_{j=1}^{n} seed^{(j)}$, $\mathbf{A} = \mathsf{Expand}(seed)$, and sets $\bar{\mathbf{A}} = [\mathbf{I}_k|\mathbf{A}]$. KGen_n proceeds by sampling $\mathbf{s}^{(n)} \leftarrow_{\$} S_{\eta}^{k+\ell}$, computing a public key share $\mathbf{b}^{(n)} = \bar{\mathbf{A}}\cdot\mathbf{s}^{(n)} \pmod q$, and then sending out $\hat{g}^{(n)} = \mathsf{G}(\mathbf{b}^{(n)}, n)$. After receiving $\hat{g}^{(j)}$ for all $j \in [n-1]$, it sends out $\mathbf{b}^{(n)}$ and then receives $\mathbf{b}^{(j)}$. If $\hat{g}^{(j)} \neq \mathsf{G}(\mathbf{b}^{(j)}, j)$ for any $j \in [n-1]$, it aborts. Otherwise, it computes $\mathbf{b} = \sum_{j=1}^{n} \mathbf{b}^{(j)} \pmod q$, and encodes the list of public key shares $(\mathbf{b}^{(1)}, \ldots, \mathbf{b}^{(n)})$ via Encode to obtain an ordered list L. The state information is given by $st = (int, L)$, where int is the index of $\mathbf{b}^{(n)}$ in L, i.e., $L[int] = \mathbf{b}^{(n)}$. The public key and secret key share are given by $(pk, sk^{(n)}) = ((seed, \mathbf{b}), \mathbf{s}^{(n)})$. Note that based on the security of Expand and as long as at least one honest signer samples a seed correctly, the computed matrix

$\mathsf{Sign}_n(sid, st, pk, sk^{(n)}, m)$

1: **if** $sid \in \mathrm{L}_{sid}$ **then**
2:     **return** $\perp$
3: **parse** $st = (n, L = (L[1], \ldots, L[n]) = (\mathbf{b}^{(1)}, \ldots, \mathbf{b}^{(n)}))$
4: **parse** $(pk, sk^{(n)}) = ((seed, \mathbf{b}), \mathbf{s}^{(n)})$
5: $\mathbf{A} \leftarrow \mathsf{Expand}(seed)$, $\bar{\mathbf{A}} \leftarrow [\mathbf{I}_k|\mathbf{A}]$
6: **for** $i = 0$ **to** $\omega - 1$ **do**
7:     $\mathbf{y}_i \leftarrow\!\!\$\ D^{k+\ell}_{\mathbb{Z}^N,\sigma}$
8:     $\mathbf{v}_i^{(n)} \leftarrow \bar{\mathbf{A}} \cdot \mathbf{y}_i \pmod q$
9: $\mathbf{y} \leftarrow (\mathbf{y}_0, \ldots, \mathbf{y}_{\omega-1})$
10: $\mathbf{v}^{(n)} \leftarrow (\mathbf{v}_0^{(n)}, \ldots, \mathbf{v}_{\omega-1}^{(n)})$
11: $g^{(n)} \leftarrow \mathsf{G}(\mathbf{v}^{(n)}, \mathbf{b}^{(n)})$
12: **broadcast** $(n, g^{(n)})$
13: **receive** $(j, g^{(j)})$ for all $j \in [n-1]$
14: **broadcast** $\mathbf{v}^{(n)}$
15: **receive** $\mathbf{v}^{(j)} = (\mathbf{v}_0^{(j)}, \ldots, \mathbf{v}_{\omega-1}^{(j)})$, $j \in [n-1]$
16: **for** $j = 1$ **to** $n - 1$ **do**
17:     **if** $g^{(j)} \neq \mathsf{G}(\mathbf{v}^{(j)}, L[j])$ **then**
18:         **broadcast** *abort* and **return** $\perp$
19: **for** $t = 0$ **to** $\omega^n - 1$ **do**
20:     $(i^{(1)}, \ldots, i^{(n)}) \leftarrow \mathsf{IntIndex}^{-1}_{\omega,n}(t)$
21:     $\mathbf{w}_t \leftarrow \sum_{j=1}^{n} \mathbf{v}_{i^{(j)}}^{(j)}$
22: $(root, tree) \leftarrow \mathsf{HashTree}(\mathbf{w}_0, \ldots, \mathbf{w}_{\omega^n-1})$
23: $c \leftarrow \mathsf{H}(root, m, \mathbf{b})$
24: $\mathbf{z}' \leftarrow \mathbf{s}^{(n)} c$
25: $(\mathbf{z}^{(n)}, i^{(n)}) \leftarrow\!\!\$\ \mathsf{IterateRej}(\mathbf{y}, \mathbf{z}')$
26: **if** $(\mathbf{z}^{(n)}, i^{(n)}) = (\perp, \perp)$ **then**
27:     **broadcast** $\perp$ and goto 6
28: **broadcast** $\mathbf{z}^{(n)}$
29: **receive** $\mathbf{z}^{(j)}$ for all $j \in [n-1]$
30: **for** $j = 1$ **to** $n - 1$ **do**
31:     **if** $\mathbf{z}^{(j)} = \perp$ **then**
32:         goto 6
33:     $(b, i^{(j)}) \leftarrow \mathsf{Vrf}(\bar{\mathbf{A}}, \mathbf{b}^{(j)}, \mathbf{v}^{(j)}, c, \mathbf{z}^{(j)})$
34:     **if** $(b, i^{(j)}) = (0, -1)$ **then**
35:         **broadcast** *abort* and **return** $\perp$
36: $\mathbf{z} \leftarrow \sum_{j=1}^{n} \mathbf{z}^{(j)}$
37: $\mathbf{z} \leftarrow \mathsf{Compress}(\mathbf{z})$
38: $t \leftarrow \mathsf{IntIndex}_{\omega,n}(i^{(1)}, \ldots, i^{(n)})$
39: $auth \leftarrow \mathsf{BuildAuth}(t, tree, h)$
40: **return** $sig = (c, \mathbf{z}, auth)$

$\mathsf{IterateRej}(\mathbf{y}, \mathbf{z}')$

1: **parse** $\mathbf{y} = (\mathbf{y}_0, \ldots, \mathbf{y}_{\omega-1})$
2: $T \leftarrow \{0, \ldots, \omega - 1\}$
3: **while** $T \neq \varnothing$ **do**
4:     $i \leftarrow\!\!\$\ T$
5:     $T \leftarrow T \setminus \{i\}$
6:     $\mathbf{z} \leftarrow \mathbf{y}_i + \mathbf{z}'$
7:     **if** $\mathsf{RejSamp}(\mathbf{z}, \mathbf{z}') = 1$ **then**
8:         **return** $(\mathbf{z}, i)$
9: **return** $(\perp, \perp)$

$\mathsf{Vrf}(\bar{\mathbf{A}}, \mathbf{b}^{(j)}, \mathbf{v}^{(j)}, c, \mathbf{z}^{(j)})$

1: **if** $\|\mathbf{z}^{(j)}\| > B_z$ **then**
2:     **return** $(0, -1)$
3: **parse** $\mathbf{v}^{(j)} = (\mathbf{v}_0^{(j)}, \ldots, \mathbf{v}_{\omega-1}^{(j)})$
4: $\mathbf{w}^{(j)} \leftarrow \bar{\mathbf{A}} \cdot \mathbf{z}^{(j)} - \mathbf{b}^{(j)} c \pmod q$
5: **for** $i = 0$ **to** $\omega - 1$ **do**
6:     **if** $\mathbf{v}_i^{(j)} = \mathbf{w}^{(j)}$ **then**
7:         **return** $(1, i)$
8: **return** $(0, -1)$

$\mathsf{Verify}(pk, m, sig)$

1: **parse** $pk = (seed, \mathbf{b})$
2: $\mathbf{A} \leftarrow \mathsf{Expand}(seed)$, $\bar{\mathbf{A}} \leftarrow [\mathbf{I}_k|\mathbf{A}]$
3: **parse** $sig = (c, \mathbf{z}, auth)$
4: $\mathbf{z} \leftarrow \mathsf{Decompress}(\mathbf{z})$
5: **if** $\|\mathbf{z}\| > B$ **then**
6:     **return** 0
7: $\mathbf{w} \leftarrow \bar{\mathbf{A}} \cdot \mathbf{z} - \mathbf{b}c \pmod q$
8: $root \leftarrow \mathsf{RootCalc}(\mathbf{w}, auth)$
9: **if** $c \neq \mathsf{H}(root, m, \mathbf{b})$
10:     **return** 0
11: **return** 1

Fig. 4. Signing protocol of our lattice-based n-out-of-n distributed signature protocol.

$\mathbf{A}$ is guaranteed to be uniformly random. The same applies to the combined public key. As explained in [17], this prevents the so-called *rogue key attack* [28], i.e., to choose some malicious key share depending on the honest signer's share. For the sake of domain separation [6], we also follow [17] by setting the index of the signer as part of the value to be hashed via G. This prevents a rushing adversary from forwarding a hash value sent by the honest signer and claiming knowledge of its preimage after receiving it from the honest signer. To save space, $\mathbf{s}^{(n)}$ can also be generated by expanding a random seed via an XOF.

Signing. S_n first checks that *sid* has not been used before, i.e., S_n is not executed if $sid \in \mathrm{L}_{sid}$, where L_{sid} is the list of already used session identifiers. We assume, w.l.o.g., that after ordering the list of public key shares in KGen_n, the index of $\mathbf{b}^{(n)}$ in the encoded list L is given by $int = n$, i.e., $L[n] = \mathbf{b}^{(n)}$. Then, S_n reconstructs $\mathbf{A}$ using Expand and sets $\bar{\mathbf{A}} = [\mathbf{I}_k|\mathbf{A}]$. It proceeds by sampling ω vectors $\mathbf{y}_i$ from the Gaussian distribution $D^{k+\ell}_{\mathbb{Z}^N,\sigma}$ and computing commitments $\mathbf{v}_i^{(n)} = \bar{\mathbf{A}} \cdot \mathbf{y}_i \pmod q$, where $i \in \{0, \ldots, \omega - 1\}$. Note that σ is chosen according to Lemma 2 so that each vector $\mathbf{v}_i^{(n)}$ is distributed statistically close to uniform over R_q^k. This prevents learning any information from the commitments in case of aborts, and hence maintains the security of the secret key share. Afterwards, signer S_n sets $\mathbf{v}^{(n)} = (\mathbf{v}_0^{(n)}, \ldots, \mathbf{v}_{\omega-1}^{(n)})$, computes $g^{(n)} = \mathsf{G}(\mathbf{v}^{(n)}, \mathbf{b}^{(n)})$, and sends out $(n, g^{(n)})$ to the remaining signers $\mathsf{S}_1, \ldots, \mathsf{S}_{n-1}$ in order to receive $(j, g^{(j)})$ for all $j \in [n-1]$. Sending the index $j \in [n]$ together with $g^{(j)}$ allows to map each signer to the index of its public key share in L. This way, all signers use the same local ordering of $\mathsf{S}_1, \ldots, \mathsf{S}_n$, which corresponds to the indices of the public key shares in L. Then, S_n sends out $\mathbf{v}^{(n)}$ and receives a similar vector $\mathbf{v}^{(j)}$ from each S_j. After that, S_n verifies that $g^{(j)} = \mathsf{G}(\mathbf{v}^{(j)}, \mathbf{b}^{(j)})$ for all $j \in [n-1]$, and aborts if this is not the case. S_n proceeds by computing ω^n vectors $\mathbf{w}_t$, where $t \in \{0, \ldots, \omega^n - 1\}$. These vectors correspond to all possible sums of n different commitments $\mathbf{v}_{i(j)}^{(j)}$, i.e., each sum includes one commitment from each signer. The commitments $\mathbf{w}_t$ are then used to generate a tree of commitments of height $h = \lceil \log(\omega^n) \rceil$ via algorithm $\mathsf{HashTree}$, which outputs $(root, tree)$. Note that due to the unique encoding of L, the indices of the signers are the same by all signers. Thus, all signers compute the same hash tree. Then, H is called on input $(root, m, \mathbf{b})$ to obtain c. After that, S_n runs $\mathsf{IterateRej}$ on input $(\mathbf{y}, \mathbf{z}')$, where $\mathbf{y} = (\mathbf{y}_0, \ldots, \mathbf{y}_{\omega-1})$ and $\mathbf{z}' = \mathbf{s}^{(n)}c$. This algorithm repeatedly keeps applying the rejection sampling algorithm $\mathsf{RejSamp}$ on input $(\mathbf{z}, \mathbf{z}')$, where $\mathbf{z} = \mathbf{y}_i + \mathbf{z}'$, until it accepts for some randomly chosen masking vector $\mathbf{y}_i$, where $i \in \{0, \ldots, \omega - 1\}$. $\mathsf{IterateRej}$ outputs $(\mathbf{z}^{(n)}, i)$, where i corresponds to the masking vector for which $\mathsf{RejSamp}(\mathbf{z}^{(n)}, \mathbf{z}') = 1$. If $\mathsf{RejSamp}$ does not accept for all $\mathbf{y}_i$, then $\mathsf{IterateRej}$ returns $(\perp, \perp)$ and the protocol has to be restarted. In this case S_n broadcasts $\perp$ and restarts by generating ω fresh masking vectors $\mathbf{y}_i$, i.e., from line 6 of Sign_n. Otherwise, S_n broadcasts $\mathbf{z}^{(n)}$ and receives $\mathbf{z}^{(j)}$ from each S_j, where $j \in [n-1]$. If $\mathbf{z}^{(j)} = \perp$ for any $j \in [n-1]$, then S_n restarts from line 6. Otherwise, S_n verifies the correctness of each cosigner's signature by running Vrf on input $(\bar{\mathbf{A}}, \mathbf{b}^{(j)}, \mathbf{v}^{(j)}, c, \mathbf{z}^{(j)})$ for all $j \in [n-1]$. Vrf outputs a pair (b, i), where $b \in \{0, 1\}$

indicates accept or reject and i is the index of commitment $\mathbf{v}_i$ that corresponds to response $\mathbf{z}_i$. If one cosigner's signature is not valid, then Vrf returns $(0, -1)$, and S_n aborts. Otherwise, S_n proceeds by computing $\mathbf{z} = \sum_{j=1}^{n} \mathbf{z}^{(j)}$, compressing the sum $\mathbf{z}$ via $\mathsf{Compress}$, and running $\mathsf{BuildAuth}$ to generate the authentication path $auth$ associated to the index $t = \mathsf{IntIndex}_{\omega,n}(i^{(1)}, \ldots, i^{(n)})$ of commitment $\mathbf{w}_t$, where $\mathbf{w}_t$ is the sum of signer's commitments $\mathbf{v}_{i^{(j)}}^{(j)}$ that correspond to $\mathbf{z}$. Finally, S_n returns the signature $sig = (c, \mathbf{z}, auth)$.

Verification. Verify first computes $\mathbf{A}$ via Expand, sets $\bar{\mathbf{A}} = [\mathbf{I}_k|\mathbf{A}]$, and checks that $\|\mathbf{z}\| \leq B$ after reconstructing $\mathbf{z}$ using algorithm $\mathsf{Decompress}$. Then, it computes $\mathbf{w} = \bar{\mathbf{A}} \cdot \mathbf{z} - \mathbf{b}c \pmod q$, and runs $\mathsf{RootCalc}$ on input $(\mathbf{w}, auth)$ to compute the root $root'$ of the tree of commitments that includes the leaf $\mathsf{F}(\mathbf{w})$ and its authentication path $auth$. The signature is accepted if and only if $c = \mathsf{H}(root, m, \mathbf{b})$.

3.2 Security Analysis

In this section we prove the security of our distributed signature protocol.

Theorem 1. *Let* DSig *be the n-out-of-n distributed signature protocol depicted in Fig. 3,4. For any PPT adversary that initiates a single key generation protocol of* DSig *by querying* $\mathsf{O}_n^{\mathsf{DSig}}$ *with* $sid = 0$, *initiates* q_{Sign} *signature generation protocols of* DSig *by querying* $\mathsf{O}_n^{\mathsf{DSig}}$ *with* $sid \neq 0$, *and makes* $q_E, q_{\mathsf{G}}, q_{\mathsf{F}}, q_{\mathsf{H}}$ *queries to the random oracle* $\mathsf{Expand}, \mathsf{G}, \mathsf{F}, \mathsf{H}$, *respectively,* DSig *is* UF-CMA *secure w.r.t.* $pp \in \mathsf{PGen}(1^\lambda)$ *if* MLWE *is hard w.r.t.* $pp' = (N, k, \ell, q, \eta)$ *and* MSIS *is hard w.r.t.* $pp'' = (N, k, \ell + 1, q, 2\sqrt{B^2 + \kappa})$, *where*

$$\begin{aligned}\mathrm{Adv}_{\mathsf{DSig},\mathsf{A}}^{\mathrm{UF\text{-}CMA}}(pp) \leq & \frac{q_{\mathsf{F}}^2 + q_{\mathsf{F}}}{2^{\ell_{\mathsf{F}}}} + \frac{(q_{\mathsf{G}} + nq_{\mathsf{Sign}} + 1)^2}{2^{\ell_{\mathsf{G}}+1}} + \frac{q_E}{q^{k\ell N}} + \\ & q_{\mathsf{Sign}} \cdot \left(\frac{q_{\mathsf{G}} + nq_{\mathsf{Sign}}}{|\mathbb{T}_\kappa|} + \frac{q_{\mathsf{H}} + q_{\mathsf{Sign}}}{|\mathbb{T}_\kappa|} + \frac{n}{2^{\ell_{\mathsf{G}}}} + \frac{2^{-\Omega(N)-100+1}}{M} \right) + \\ & 2 \cdot \left(\frac{(q_{\mathsf{G}} + 1)^2}{2^{\ell_{\mathsf{G}}+1}} + \frac{n}{2^{\ell_{\mathsf{G}}}} \right) + \frac{q_{\mathsf{G}}}{2^{\ell_{seed}}} + \frac{q_{\mathsf{G}}}{q^{kN}} + \mathrm{Adv}_{\mathsf{D}}^{\mathsf{MLWE}}(pp') + \\ & \frac{(q_{\mathsf{H}} + q_{\mathsf{Sign}}) \cdot \omega^n}{|\mathbb{T}_\kappa|} + \sqrt{(q_{\mathsf{H}} + q_{\mathsf{Sign}}) \cdot \omega^n \cdot \mathrm{Adv}_{\mathsf{A}}^{\mathsf{MSIS}}(pp'')}.\end{aligned}$$

Proof. Let A be an adversary that wins the experiment $\mathrm{Exp}_{\mathsf{DSig},\mathsf{A}}^{\mathrm{UF\text{-}CMA}}(pp)$ given in Fig. 2 with advantage $\mathrm{Adv}_{\mathsf{DSig},\mathsf{A}}^{\mathrm{UF\text{-}CMA}}(pp)$. We assume, w.l.o.g., that S_n is an honest signer. We construct a reduction R that uses A in a black-box manner and simulates the behavior of S_n without using honestly generated key pairs. Then, we use the forking algorithm (see Appendix B.1) to solve MSIS w.r.t. pp''. The simulation of key and signature generation is presented in Fig. 5 and 6, respectively. They are derived via the following intermediate hybrids:

Hybrid H_0 :

Random oracle simulation. We assume that R is given $h_i \leftarrow\!\!\$\ \mathbb{T}_\kappa$ as input, for all $i \in [q_{\mathsf{Sign}} + q_{\mathsf{H}}]$. For each of oracles $\mathsf{O}_{\mathsf{Expand}}, \mathsf{O}_{\mathsf{G}}, \mathsf{O}_{\mathsf{F}}$, and O_{H}, reduction R maintains a list $\mathrm{L}_{\mathsf{Expand}}, \mathrm{L}_{\mathsf{G}}, \mathrm{L}_{\mathsf{F}}$, and L_{H}, respectively. These lists are initialized

$\mathsf{SimKGen}_n(\mathbf{A}, \mathbf{b})$

$seed \leftarrow\!\!\$\ \{0,1\}^{\ell_{seed}}$
$\mathsf{O}_{\mathsf{Expand}}(seed) \leftarrow \mathbf{A}$
$\bar{g}^{(n)} \leftarrow\!\!\$\ \{0,1\}^{\ell_{\mathsf{G}}}$
broadcast $\bar{g}^{(n)}$
receive $\bar{g}^{(j)}$ for all $j \in [n-1]$
$(bad_1', alert, (seed^{(1)}, 1), \ldots, (seed^{(n-1)}, n-1)) \leftarrow \mathsf{Search}(\bar{g}^{(1)}, \ldots, \bar{g}^{(n-1)})$
if $bad_1' =$ **true then**
  return $(\perp, \perp)$ {simulation fails}
if $alert =$ **true then**
  $seed^{(n)} \leftarrow\!\!\$\ \{0,1\}^{\ell_{seed}}$
$seed^{(n)} \leftarrow seed \bigoplus_{j=1}^{n-1} seed^{(j)}$
if $(seed^{(n)}, n)$ is set **then**
  $bad_2' \leftarrow$ **true**
  return $(\perp, \perp)$ {simulation fails}
$\mathsf{O}_{\mathsf{G}}(seed^{(n)}, n) \leftarrow \bar{g}^{(n)}$
broadcast $seed^{(n)}$
receive $seed^{(j)}$ for all $j \in [n-1]$
for $j = 1$ **to** $n-1$ **do**
  if $\bar{g}^{(j)} \neq \mathsf{O}_{\mathsf{G}}(seed^{(j)}, j)$ **then**
    broadcast *abort*
    return $(\perp, \perp)$
if $alert =$ **true then**
  $bad_3' \leftarrow$ **true**
  return $(\perp, \perp)$ {simulation fails}
$\hat{g}^{(n)} \leftarrow\!\!\$\ \{0,1\}^{\ell_{\mathsf{G}}}$
broadcast $\hat{g}^{(n)}$
receive $\hat{g}^{(j)}$ for all $j \in [n-1]$
$(bad_4', alert', (\mathbf{b}^{(1)}, 1), \ldots, (\mathbf{b}^{(n-1)}, n-1)) \leftarrow \mathsf{Search}(\hat{g}^{(1)}, \ldots, \hat{g}^{(n-1)})$
if $bad_4' =$ **true then**
  return $(\perp, \perp)$ {simulation fails}
if $alert' =$ **true then**
  $\mathbf{b}^{(n)} \leftarrow\!\!\$\ R_q^k$
$\mathbf{b}^{(n)} \leftarrow \mathbf{b} - \sum_{j=1}^{n-1} \mathbf{b}^{(j)}$
if $(\mathbf{b}^{(n)}, n)$ is set **then**
  $bad_5' \leftarrow$ **true**
  return $(\perp, \perp)$ {simulation fails}
$\mathsf{O}_{\mathsf{G}}(\mathbf{b}^{(n)}, n) \leftarrow \hat{g}^{(n)}$
broadcast $\mathbf{b}^{(n)}$
receive $\mathbf{b}^{(j)}$ for all $j \in [n-1]$
for $j = 1$ **to** $n-1$ **do**
  if $\hat{g}^{(j)} \neq \mathsf{O}_{\mathsf{G}}(\mathbf{b}^{(j)}, j)$ **then**
    broadcast *abort*
    return $(\perp, \perp)$
if $alert' =$ **true then**
  $bad_6' \leftarrow$ **true**
  return $(\perp, \perp)$ {simulation fails}
$L \leftarrow \mathsf{Encode}(\mathbf{b}^{(1)}, \ldots, \mathbf{b}^{(n)})$
let $L[int] = \mathbf{b}^{(n)}$, $int \in [n]$
$st \leftarrow (int, L)$
$pk \leftarrow (seed, \mathbf{b})$
return (st, pk)

$\mathsf{Search}(g^{(1)}, \ldots, g^{(n-1)})$

$bad \leftarrow$ **false**, $alert \leftarrow$ **false**
for $j = 1$ **to** $n-1$ **do**
  if $g^{(j)}$ is set **then**
    let $(str, \mathsf{O}_{\mathsf{G}}(str)) \in \mathrm{L}_{\mathsf{G}}$: $\mathsf{O}_{\mathsf{G}}(str) = g^{(j)}$
    if $\exists (str', \mathsf{O}_{\mathsf{G}}(str')) \in \mathrm{L}_{\mathsf{G}}$: $(str \neq str') \wedge (\mathsf{O}_{\mathsf{G}}(str') = g^{(j)})$ **then**
      $bad \leftarrow$ **true** {more than one preimage found}
    $str^{(j)} \leftarrow str$
  else
    $str^{(j)} \leftarrow \perp$, $alert \leftarrow$ **true** {no preimage found}
return $(bad, alert, str^{(1)}, \ldots, str^{(n-1)})$

Fig. 5. Simulation of key generation.

$\mathsf{SimSign}_n(sid, st, pk, m)$

if $sid \in \mathrm{L}_{sid}$ **then**
  return $\perp$
parse $st = (n, L = (L[1], .., L[n]))$
parse $pk = (seed, \mathbf{b})$
$\mathbf{A} \leftarrow \mathsf{O}_{\mathsf{Expand}}(seed)$
$\bar{\mathbf{A}} \leftarrow [\mathbf{I}_k|\mathbf{A}]$
$c \leftarrow\$ \mathbb{T}_\kappa$
With probability δ **do**
  $\mathbf{v}_0^{(n)}, \ldots, \mathbf{v}_{\omega-1}^{(n)} \leftarrow\$ R_q^k$
  $\mathbf{z}^{(n)} \leftarrow \perp$
With probability $1 - \delta$ **do**
  $i^{(n)} \leftarrow\$ \{0, \ldots, \omega - 1\}$
  $\mathbf{z}^{(n)} \leftarrow\$ D_{\mathbb{Z}^N,\sigma}^{k+\ell}$
  $\mathbf{v}_{i^{(n)}}^{(n)} \leftarrow \bar{\mathbf{A}} \cdot \mathbf{z}^{(n)} - \mathbf{b}^{(n)} c \pmod q$
  for $i = 0$ **to** $\omega - 1$ **do**
    if $i = i^{(n)}$ **then**
      continue
    $\mathbf{y}_i \leftarrow\$ D_{\mathbb{Z}^N,\sigma}^{k+\ell}$
    $\mathbf{v}_i^{(n)} \leftarrow \bar{\mathbf{A}} \cdot \mathbf{y}_i \pmod q$
$\mathbf{v}^{(n)} \leftarrow (\mathbf{v}_0^{(n)}, \ldots, \mathbf{v}_{\omega-1}^{(n)})$
$g^{(n)} \leftarrow \mathsf{O}_\mathsf{G}(\mathbf{v}^{(n)}, \mathbf{b}^{(n)})$
broadcast $(n, g^{(n)})$
receive $(j, g^{(j)})$ for all $j \in [n-1]$
$(bad_1, alert, (\mathbf{v}^{(1)}, \mathbf{b}^{(1)}), \ldots, (\mathbf{v}^{(n-1)}, \mathbf{b}^{(n-1)})) \leftarrow \mathsf{Search}(g^{(1)}, \ldots, g^{(n-1)})$
if $bad_1 =$ **true then**
  return $\perp$ {simulation fails}
if $alert =$ **true then**
  broadcast $\mathbf{v}^{(n)}$
else
  parse $\mathbf{v}^{(j)} = (\mathbf{v}_0^{(j)}, \ldots, \mathbf{v}_{\omega-1}^{(j)})$ for all $j \in [n-1]$
  for $t = 0$ **to** $\omega^n - 1$ **do**
    $(i^{(1)}, \ldots, i^{(n)}) \leftarrow \mathsf{IntIndex}_{\omega,n}^{-1}(t)$
    $\mathbf{w}_t \leftarrow \sum_{j=1}^n \mathbf{v}_{i^{(j)}}^{(j)}$
  $(root, tree) \leftarrow$
    $\leftarrow \mathsf{HashTree}(\mathbf{w}_0, \ldots, \mathbf{w}_{\omega^n-1})$
  if $\mathsf{O}_\mathsf{H}(root, m, \mathbf{b})$ is set **then**
    $bad_2 \leftarrow$ **true**
    return $\perp$ {simulation fails}
  $\mathsf{O}_\mathsf{H}(root, m, \mathbf{b}) \leftarrow c$
  broadcast $\mathbf{v}^{(n)}$
receive $\mathbf{v}^{(j)} = (\mathbf{v}_0^{(j)}, \ldots, \mathbf{v}_{\omega-1}^{(j)})$ for all $j \in [n-1]$
for $j = 1$ **to** $n - 1$ **do**
  if $g^{(j)} \neq \mathsf{O}_\mathsf{G}(\mathbf{v}^{(j)}, L[j])$ **then**
    broadcast *abort* **and return** $\perp$
if $alert =$ **true then**
  $bad_3 \leftarrow$ **true**
  return $\perp$ {simulation fails}
if $\mathbf{z}^{(n)} = \perp$ **then**
  broadcast $\perp$ and goto 8
broadcast $\mathbf{z}^{(n)}$
receive $\mathbf{z}^{(j)}$ for all $j \in [n-1]$
for $j = 1$ **to** $n - 1$ **do**
  if $\mathbf{z}^{(j)} = \perp$ **then** goto 8
  $(b, i^{(j)}) \leftarrow \mathsf{Vrf}(\bar{\mathbf{A}}, \mathbf{b}^{(j)}, \mathbf{v}^{(j)}, c, \mathbf{z}^{(j)})$
  if $(b, i^{(j)}) = (0, -1)$ **then**
    broadcast *abort* **and return** $\perp$
$\mathbf{z} \leftarrow \sum_{j=1}^n \mathbf{z}^{(j)}$, $\mathbf{z} \leftarrow \mathsf{Compress}(\mathbf{z})$
$t \leftarrow \mathsf{IntIndex}_{\omega,n}(i^{(1)}, \ldots, i^{(n)})$
$auth \leftarrow \mathsf{BuildAuth}(t, tree, h)$
return $sig = (c, \mathbf{z}, auth)$

Fig. 6. Simulation of signature generation. Simulator $\mathsf{SimSign}_n$ assumes that $\mathsf{SimKGen}_n$ has been previously invoked. Algorithm Search is given in Fig. 5, and Vrf in Fig. 4.

with the empty set, and store pairs consisting of queries to the respective oracle and their answers. Also, R maintains a counter *ctr* initialized by 0. If an oracle was previously queried on some input, then R looks up its entry in the respective list and returns its answer. Otherwise, for queries to $\mathsf{O}_{\mathsf{Expand}}, \mathsf{O}_\mathsf{G}, \mathsf{O}_\mathsf{F}$, reduction R selects a uniformly random answer from the respective range and updates the respective list. However, for each query to O_H, the counter *ctr* is incremented by one. Then, the answer $h_{ctr} \in \mathbb{T}_\kappa$ is returned and the list L_H is updated.

Honest Signer Simulation. R invokes Sign_n exactly as given in Fig. 4.

Forgery. When A returns a forgery $(sig^* = (c^*, \mathbf{z}^*, auth^*), m^*)$, R proceeds as follows: It returns $(0, 0, \perp)$ if $m^* \in \mathrm{L}_m$ or $\mathsf{Verify}(pk, m^*, sig^*) \neq 1$. Otherwise, R finds an index $i^* \in [q_{\mathsf{Sign}} + q_{\mathsf{H}}]$ such that $c^* = h_{i^*}$, and returns (i^*, t^*, out^*), where $t^* \in \{0, \ldots, \omega^n - 1\}$ is included in $auth^*$ and $out^* = (root^*, c^*, \mathbf{z}^*, auth^*, m^*)$. $root^*$ is obtained by running Verify. We let $\Pr[H_i]$ denote the probability that R does not return $(0, 0, \perp)$ at hybrid H_i. Then we have $\Pr[H_0] = \mathrm{Adv}^{\mathrm{UF\text{-}CMA}}_{\mathsf{DSig},\mathsf{A}}(pp)$.

Hybrid H_1 : In this hybrid we modify R from H_0 as follows:

Random Oracle Simulation. Oracle O_F is simulated as follows:

1. If $\mathsf{O}_\mathsf{F}(str)$ is set, then return $\mathsf{O}_\mathsf{F}(str)$.
2. Select $\mathsf{O}_\mathsf{F}(str) \leftarrow\!\!\$\ \{0,1\}^{\ell_\mathsf{F}}$.
3. If there exists a pair $(str', \mathsf{O}_\mathsf{F}(str')) \in \mathrm{L}_\mathsf{F}$: $(str \neq str') \wedge (\mathsf{O}_\mathsf{F}(str) = \mathsf{O}_\mathsf{F}(str'))$, then simulation fails.
4. If there exists $(str', \mathsf{O}_\mathsf{F}(str')) \in \mathrm{L}_\mathsf{F}$: $str' = \mathsf{O}_\mathsf{F}(str)$, then simulation fails.
5. Return $\mathsf{O}_\mathsf{F}(str)$ and update L_F.

Note that oracle O_F is simulated in a way that excludes collisions and chains. This ensures that each node output by algorithm HashTree has a unique preimage, and prevents spanning hash trees with cycles. This simulation is within statistical distance of at most $(q_\mathsf{F}^2 + q_\mathsf{F})/2^{\ell_\mathsf{F}}$ from an oracle that allows collisions and chains.

Honest Signer Simulation. R selects $c \leftarrow\!\!\$\ \mathbb{T}_\kappa$ and computes signature part $\mathbf{z}^{(n)}$ without interacting with A. After that, R proceeds as in previous hybrid by sending out $(n, g^{(n)})$. Upon receiving $(j, g^{(j)})$ for all $j \in [n-1]$, R finds corresponding preimages $(\mathbf{v}^{(j)}, \mathbf{b}^{(j)})$. Then, R proceeds by computing $root$ and programming O_H such that $c := \mathsf{O}_\mathsf{H}(root, m, \mathbf{b})$. Simulation fails if for any $g^{(j)}$ more that one preimage were found or no corresponding preimage exists in L_G. Note that H_1 is identical to H_0 from A's point of view, except at simulating O_F and the events bad_1, bad_2, bad_3 appeared in Fig. 6, where bad_1 is the event that at least one collision is found during at most $q_\mathsf{G} + nq_{\mathsf{Sign}}$ queries to O_G, bad_3 is the event that A predicted one of the $n-1$ outputs of O_G without querying it, and bad_2 is the event that programming O_H fails at least once out of q_{Sign} queries to O_H due to one of the following cases:

1. O_G has been queried by A on $(\mathbf{v}^{(n)}, \mathbf{b}^{(n)})$ during at most $q_\mathsf{G} + nq_{\mathsf{Sign}}$ queries. This means that A knows $(root, m, \mathbf{b})$ and could intentionally query O_H on $(root, m, \mathbf{b})$.
2. $\mathsf{O}_\mathsf{H}(root, m, \mathbf{b})$ has been set during at most $q_\mathsf{H} + q_{\mathsf{Sign}}$ prior queries to O_H.

Therefore $\left|\Pr[H_1] - \Pr[H_0]\right| \leq \frac{q_\mathsf{F}^2 + q_\mathsf{F}}{2^{\ell_\mathsf{F}}} + \Pr[bad_1] + \Pr[bad_2] + \Pr[bad_3]$, where

$$\Pr[bad_1] \leq \frac{(q_\mathsf{G} + nq_{\mathsf{Sign}})(q_\mathsf{G} + nq_{\mathsf{Sign}} + 1)/2}{2^{\ell_\mathsf{G}}} \leq \frac{(q_\mathsf{G} + nq_{\mathsf{Sign}} + 1)^2}{2^{\ell_\mathsf{G}+1}},$$

$$\Pr[bad_2] \leq q_{\mathsf{Sign}}\left(\frac{q_\mathsf{G} + nq_{\mathsf{Sign}}}{|\mathbb{T}_\kappa|} + \frac{q_\mathsf{H} + q_{\mathsf{Sign}}}{|\mathbb{T}_\kappa|}\right), \text{ and } \Pr[bad_3] \leq \frac{nq_{\mathsf{Sign}}}{2^{\ell_\mathsf{G}}}.$$

Hybrid H_2 : This hybrid is identical to H_1 except at the following points:

Honest Signer Simulation. R does not generate $\mathbf{z}^{(n)}$ honestly, and simulates rejection sampling as follows: With probability δ, sample $\mathbf{v}_0^{(n)}, \ldots, \mathbf{v}_{\omega-1}^{(n)} \leftarrow\!\!\$\ R_q^k$ and set $\mathbf{z}^{(n)} = \perp$. Otherwise, sample $i^{(n)} \leftarrow\!\!\$\ \{0, \ldots, \omega - 1\}$ and $\mathbf{z}^{(n)} \leftarrow\!\!\$\ D_{\mathbb{Z}^N,\sigma}^{k+\ell}$. Then, compute $\mathbf{v}_{i^{(n)}}^{(n)} = \bar{\mathbf{A}} \cdot \mathbf{z}^{(n)} - \mathbf{b}^{(n)}c \pmod q$. The remaining $\mathbf{v}_i^{(n)}$, for all $i \in \{0, \ldots, \omega - 1\} \backslash \{i^{(n)}\}$, are computed honestly (see Fig. 6). By Lemma 5 in Appendix D we obtain $\left|\Pr[H_2] - \Pr[H_1]\right| \leq q_{\mathsf{Sign}} \cdot \frac{2^{-\Omega(N)-100+1}}{M}$.

Hybrid H_3 : At this point, simulation does not rely on the actual secret key share $\mathbf{s}^{(n)}$ (see $\mathsf{SimSign}_n$, Fig. 6). In this hybrid, R samples $seed \leftarrow\!\!\$\ \{0,1\}^{\ell_{seed}}$ and programs $\mathsf{O}_{\mathsf{Expand}}$ such that $\mathbf{A} := \mathsf{O}_{\mathsf{Expand}}(seed)$. Then, it computes $seed^{(n)}$ a posteriori, after extracting A's committed shares $seed^{(1)}, \ldots, seed^{(n-1)}$ via algorithm Search, i.e., by searching the recorded queries to O_G (see $\mathsf{SimKGen}_n$, Fig. 5). Note that H_3 is identical to H_2 from A's point of view, except at programming $\mathsf{O}_{\mathsf{Expand}}$ and the events bad_1', bad_2', bad_3' appeared in $\mathsf{SimKGen}_n$. Therefore we have $\left|\Pr[H_3] - \Pr[H_2]\right| \leq \frac{q_E}{q^{k\ell N}} + \frac{(q_\mathsf{G}+1)^2}{2^{\ell_\mathsf{G}+1}} + \frac{q_\mathsf{G}}{2^{\ell_{seed}}} + \frac{n}{2^{\ell_\mathsf{G}}}$, where $\Pr[bad_1'] \leq ((q_\mathsf{G}+1)q_\mathsf{G}/2)/2^{\ell_\mathsf{G}}$ is the probability that at least one collision is found during at most q_G queries to O_G, $\Pr[bad_2']$ is the probability that programming O_G fails, which occurs if O_G has been previously queried by A on $(seed^{(n)}, n)$ during at most q_G queries, and the probability that guessing a uniformly random $seed^{(n)}$ is at most $1/2^{\ell_{seed}}$ for each query, and $\Pr[bad_3'] \leq n/2^{\ell_\mathsf{G}}$ is the probability that A predicted one of the $n-1$ outputs of O_G without querying it.

Hybrid H_4 : This hybrid is identical to H_3 except that R samples public key share $\mathbf{b}^{(n)} \leftarrow\!\!\$\ R_q^k$ instead of computing $\mathbf{b}^{(n)} = \bar{\mathbf{A}} \cdot \mathbf{s} \pmod q$, where $\mathbf{s}^{(n)} \leftarrow\!\!\$\ S_\eta^{k+\ell}$. If A can distinguish between H_3 and H_4, then A can be used to break the MLWE assumption w.r.t. pp'. Therefore we have $\left|\Pr[H_4] - \Pr[H_3]\right| \leq \mathrm{Adv}_\mathsf{D}^{\mathsf{MLWE}}(pp')$.

Hybrid H_5 : In this hybrid, R computes its public key share $\mathbf{b}^{(n)}$ a posteriori, after extracting A's committed shares $\mathbf{b}^{(1)}, \ldots, \mathbf{b}^{(n-1)}$ via Search, i.e., by searching the recorded queries to O_G (see $\mathsf{SimKGen}_n$, Fig. 5). Note that H_5 is identical to H_4 from A's point of view, except at the events bad_4', bad_5', bad_6' appeared in $\mathsf{SimKGen}_n$. Therefore we have $\left|\Pr[H_5] - \Pr[H_4]\right| \leq \frac{(q_\mathsf{G}+1)^2}{2^{\ell_\mathsf{G}+1}} + \frac{q_\mathsf{G}}{q^{kN}} + \frac{n}{2^{\ell_\mathsf{G}}}$, where $\Pr[bad_4'], \Pr[bad_5']$, and $\Pr[bad_6']$ are calculated as in H_3.

Forking: Given $\mathbf{A}' \in R_q^{k\times(\ell+1)}$ as input, the goal is to solve MSIS w.r.t. pp''. To this end, R writes $\mathbf{A}' = [\mathbf{A}|\mathbf{b}] \in R_q^{k\times\ell} \times R_q^k$ and generates the remaining parameters of DSig to obtain pp and run A on input pp. This does not change the view of A at all. In order to use the forking lemma (Appendix B.1), we define its instance generator algorithm IGen such that it outputs $(\mathbf{A}, \mathbf{b})$. Then, R runs forking algorithm $\mathsf{Frk}_{\mathbb{T}_\kappa,\mathsf{A}}$ on input $(\mathbf{A}, \mathbf{b})$. With probability frk, we obtain two forgeries out, out', where $out = (root, c, \mathbf{z}, auth, m)$ and $out' = (root', c', \mathbf{z}', auth', m')$. Thus we obtain $\Pr[H_5] = acc \leq \frac{(q_\mathsf{H}+q_{\mathsf{Sign}})\cdot\omega^n}{|\mathbb{T}_\kappa|} + \sqrt{(q_\mathsf{H}+q_{\mathsf{Sign}})\cdot\omega^n \cdot frk}$. Simulating O_F as given in hybrid H_1 ensures that both $auth = (t, str_0, \ldots, str_{h-1})$

and $auth' = (t', str'_0, \ldots, str'_{h-1})$ include the same sequence of hash values, i.e., $str_i = str'_i$ for all $i \in \{0, \ldots, h-1\}$ and $h = \lceil \log(\omega^n) \rceil$. By the forking lemma we have $root = root'$, $t = t'$, $m = m'$, and $c \neq c'$. Moreover, the view of A is identical in both executions until the forking index i^*. Since $auth = auth'$, we have $\mathbf{w} = \mathbf{w}'$, where $\mathbf{w} = \bar{\mathbf{A}} \cdot \mathbf{z} - \mathbf{b}c$ and $\mathbf{w}' = \bar{\mathbf{A}} \cdot \mathbf{z}' - \mathbf{b}c'$. Thus, we obtain

$$[\mathbf{I}_k|\mathbf{A}|\mathbf{b}] \cdot \begin{bmatrix} \mathbf{z} - \mathbf{z}' \\ c' - c \end{bmatrix} = \mathbf{0}.$$

Note that $0 < \|c' - c\| \leq 2\sqrt{\kappa}$, and since both forgeries are valid we have $\|\mathbf{z}\| \leq B$ and $\|\mathbf{z}'\| \leq B$. Therefore, $\|\mathbf{z} - \mathbf{z}'\| \leq 2B$ and the vector $[\mathbf{z} - \mathbf{z}' | c' - c]^{\mathsf{T}}$ constitutes a non-trivial solution to MSIS w.r.t. pp''. Hence, $frk \leq \mathrm{Adv}_{\mathsf{A}}^{\mathsf{MSIS}}(pp'')$.

3.3 Concrete Parameters

In this section we propose sample parameters for our distributed signature protocol and the protocols introduced by Damgård et al. [17] and Chen [13]. The parameters are presented in Table 2. The corresponding sizes of public keys and signatures as well as the communication cost of key and signature generation are given in Table 1. The hardness of the underlying instances of MLWE and MSIS are estimated as described in Appendix C. We provide a proof-of-concept implementation for our protocol in C++[2] and evaluate it on a regular laptop (Macbook Air M1) with 3.2 GHz CPU and 8 GB RAM. The performance results are shown in Table 1. In the following we highlight some key points regarding the parameter selection.

The parameters of our protocol are chosen according to the constraints given in Table 3. In particular, the modulus q together with the standard deviation σ are selected such that each commitment generated by a signer is distributed statistically close to uniform over R_q^k, and the underlying instances of MLWE and MSIS are sufficiently hard. We note that for all schemes we set $q > \beta$, where β is the bound of a solution to MSIS. This prevents the existence of trivial solutions like $(q, 0, \ldots, 0)$. The number of commitments ω is chosen such that with probability very close to 1, signers compute a response without the need to restart the signing protocol, i.e., the number of restarts per signer is $S = 1/(1 - 2^{-25}) \approx 1$. Therefore, the whole signing protocol does not abort at all with very high probability, i.e., $\bar{M} \approx 1$. Note that this value of S is reasonable in practice, and there is no need to increase ω to obtain a value of S more closer to 1, e.g., $S = 1/(1 - 2^{-50})$. Increasing ω would reduce the performance of the signing protocol in a significant way, which is not desired in practice. For a reasonably small $\bar{M}$, [17] suggests to set $\alpha = 11n$ to obtain $\bar{M} = 3$, while $\alpha = 8.5n$ is suggested in [13] so that $\bar{M} \approx 5$. We set $\alpha = 11n = 77$ to obtain $\bar{M} = 3$ for both schemes. The trapdoor homomorphic commitment scheme used in [17] commits to a single element from R_q. Therefore, a commitment to each coefficient of a vector from R_q is computed separately[3]. Concrete parameters of the commitment

[2] Source code: https://anonymous.4open.science/r/distSig-Lattice-2D48.

[3] As stated in [17], there is no efficiency gain from extending the construction to commit to vectors from R_q.

scheme are given by the tuple $(N, q, s) = (1024, \approx 2^{45}, \approx 2^{25})$. The remaining parameters can be easily derived form this tuple. They are selected to support homomorphic additions of 7 commitments, and such that all security properties are satisfied (see [17, Section 5.2] for details). The communication cost of each signing protocol is given by the total amount of data sent per signer, including the number of restarts, i.e., $\bar{M} \cdot (|R_1| + |R_2|) + |R_3|$, where for $i \in \{1, 2, 3\}$, the term $|R_i|$ denotes the length of the bit string sent by each signer in the ith round. Note that $|R_1| = 0$ in [13,17]. The size of any Gaussian element is computed according to Lemma 1, i.e., the values of t and γ are selected such that the bounds in Lemma 1 hold with probability at most 2^{-80}. Finally, we would like to note that the scheme by Chen [13] is the most suitable one for applications requiring a large number of signers.

Table 2. Concrete parameters for our distributed signature protocol and the protocols proposed in [13,17]. The parameters consider $n = 7$ signers and target 128 bits of security. We fix $N = 256$ and set $\kappa = 23$ for all schemes so that $|\mathbb{T}_\kappa| \geq 2^{128}$ and the challenge space $\mathbb{T}_\kappa$ provides at least 128 bits of entropy. In [13,17], the total number of restarts $\bar{M}$ is denoted by M_n. The output length of hash functions is set to 256 bits.

Parameter	Our protocol	Damgård et al. [17]	Chen [13]
k	5	5	6
ℓ	7	4	9
q	$\approx 2^{45}$	$\approx 2^{27}$	$\approx 2^{43}$
η	1	3	1
ω	2	-	-
α	72090	77	77
σ	91899568	255024	78293860
σ'	-	-	37127790
$\bar{M}$	1	3	3

Conclusion

In this paper we have presented a new lattice-based construction of n-out-of-n distributed signatures. Our protocol follows the Fiat-Shamir with aborts paradigm and supports applications with a small number of signers only. We proposed sample parameters and provided a comparison with similar works showing the significant improvement and practicality of our approach. An interesting extension to our work is to provide a security proof in the quantum random oracle model [10]. The possibility of both rewinding and programming the random oracle in the quantum setting have already been shown, e.g., in [19,24,31].

Acknowledgements. This work was funded by the European Union (ERC, LACONIC, 101041207). Views and opinions expressed are however those of the authors only and do not necessarily reflect those of the European Union or the European Research Council. Neither the European Union nor the granting authority can be held responsible for them.

A More Related Work

Threshold Signatures. Few works proposed lattice-based constructions of t-out-of-n threshold signatures [1,9,11,16]. The first one by Bendlin et al. [9] gives a threshold variant of standard hash-and-sign signatures by Gentry et al. [22]. The main downside of this protocol is that only a priori bounded number of online non-interactive signing operations can be performed before an offline interactive protocol must be performed. This offline protocol includes a threshold Gaussian sampling phase, which is carried out using generic multiparty computation (MPC). Cozzo and Smart [16] show that the lattice-based signature schemes that have been submitted to the NIST post-quantum standardization process have significant issues when converting them into threshold ones using relatively generic MPC techniques. The main issue is the need to carry out the rejection sampling procedure, which requires to keep intermediate values secret until after performing rejection sampling and comparing them with given constants. Moreover, they require several rounds of communication and a mixture of linear and non-linear operations that incur costly transformations between both representations. Boneh et al. [11] propose a generic framework that requires several other cryptographic primitives as building blocks, including deterministic signatures, threshold fully homomorphic encryption, and a homomorphic signature scheme. Due to the involvement of heavy cryptographic primitives, it is not clear if their construction can be adapted in practical applications. Agrawal et al. [1] improve the construction by Boneh et al. [11] bringing it closer to practice.

B Additional Background

The next lemma is for the tail bound of Gaussian vectors.

Lemma 1 **([26, Lemma 4.4]).** *Let $\sigma, t, \gamma \in \mathbb{R}_{>0}$ and $m \in \mathbb{N}_{>0}$. Then we have:*

1. $\Pr_{\mathbf{x} \leftarrow\!\$\, D_{\mathbb{Z}^m,\sigma}}[\|\mathbf{x}\|_\infty > t\sigma] \leq 2m \exp(-t^2/2)$.
2. $\Pr_{\mathbf{x} \leftarrow\!\$\, D_{\mathbb{Z}^m,\sigma}}[\|\mathbf{x}\| > \gamma\sigma\sqrt{m}] \leq \gamma^m \exp(\frac{m}{2}(1-\gamma^2))$.

We rely on the following lemma, which is a certain regularity theorem.

Lemma 2 **([27, Corollary 7.5]).** *Let $\mathbf{A} \leftarrow\!\$\, R_q^{k\times\ell}$ and $\bar{\mathbf{A}} = [\mathbf{I}_k|\mathbf{A}] \in R_q^{k\times(k+\ell)}$. Let $\sigma > \frac{2N\cdot q^{\frac{k}{k+\ell}+\frac{2}{N(k+\ell)}}}{\sqrt{2\pi}}$ and $\mathbf{x} \leftarrow\!\$\, D_{\mathbb{Z}^N,\sigma}^{k+\ell}$. Then, the distribution of $\bar{\mathbf{A}}\cdot\mathbf{x} \pmod q$ is within statistical distance $2^{-\Omega(N)}$ of the uniform distribution over R_q^k.*

The next lemma is a variant of the rejection sampling lemma specified for $D_{\mathbb{Z}^m,\sigma}$.

Lemma 3 (**[26, Theorem 4.6]**). *Define* $V := \{\mathbf{v} \in \mathbb{Z}^m : \|\mathbf{v}\| \leq T\}$, *where* $T > 0$. *Let* $\sigma = \alpha T$ *for some* $\alpha > 0$, *and* $h : V \to \mathbb{R}$ *be a probability distribution. Then, there exists a constant* $M > 0$ *such that* $\exp(\frac{12}{\alpha} + \frac{1}{2\alpha^2}) \leq M$, *and the following two algorithms are within statistical distance of at most* $2^{-100}/M$:

1. $\mathbf{v} \leftarrow\!\!\$\ h$; $\mathbf{z} \leftarrow\!\!\$\ D_{\mathbb{Z}^m,\sigma,\mathbf{v}}$; *output* $(\mathbf{z}, \mathbf{v})$ *with probability* $\frac{1-2^{-100}}{M}$.
2. $\mathbf{v} \leftarrow\!\!\$\ h$; $\mathbf{z} \leftarrow\!\!\$\ D_{\mathbb{Z}^m,\sigma}$; *output* $(\mathbf{z}, \mathbf{v})$ *with probability* $1/M$.

We let RejSamp denote an algorithm that carries out rejection sampling on $\mathbf{z}$, where $\mathbf{z} \leftarrow\!\!\$\ D_{\mathbb{Z}^m,\sigma,\mathbf{v}}$, $\|\mathbf{v}\| \leq T$, and $\sigma = \alpha T$. That is, on input $(\mathbf{z}, \mathbf{v})$, RejSamp returns 1 if $\mathbf{z}$ is accepted and 0 if rejected. By Lemma 3, the output 1 indicates that the distribution of $\mathbf{z}$ is within statistical distance of at most $2^{-100}/M$ from $D_{\mathbb{Z}^m,\sigma}$, where $\exp(\frac{12}{\alpha} + \frac{1}{2\alpha^2}) \leq M$. RejSamp returns 1 with probability $\approx 1/M$, and hence the expected number of restarts necessary to return 1 is given by M.

$\mathrm{Exp}^{\mathrm{Acc}}_{\mathsf{IGen},\mathcal{C},\mathsf{A}}$

- $x \leftarrow\!\!\$\ \mathsf{IGen}$
- $h_1, \ldots, h_q \leftarrow\!\!\$\ \mathcal{C}$
- $(idx_1, idx_2, out) \leftarrow\!\!\$\ \mathsf{A}(x, h_1, \ldots, h_q)$
- **if** $1 \leq idx_1 \leq q$ **then**
  - **return** 1
- **return** 0

$\mathrm{Exp}^{\mathrm{Frk}}_{\mathsf{IGen},\mathcal{C},\mathsf{A}}$

- $x \leftarrow\!\!\$\ \mathsf{IGen}$
- $(b, out, out') \leftarrow\!\!\$\ \mathsf{Frk}_{\mathcal{C},\mathsf{A}}(x)$
- **return** b

$\mathsf{Frk}_{\mathcal{C},\mathsf{A}}(x)$

- $r \leftarrow\!\!\$\ \mathcal{R}$
- $h_1, \ldots, h_q \leftarrow\!\!\$\ \mathcal{C}$
- $(idx_1, idx_2, out) \leftarrow \mathsf{A}(x, h_1, \ldots, h_q; r)$
- **if** $idx_1 = 0$ **then**
  - **return** $(0, \perp, \perp)$
- $h'_{idx_1}, \ldots, h'_q \leftarrow\!\!\$\ \mathcal{C}$
- $(idx'_1, idx'_2, out') \leftarrow$
  $\leftarrow \mathsf{A}(x, h_1, \ldots, h_{idx_1-1}, h'_{idx_1}, \ldots, h'_q; r)$
- **if** $(idx_1 = idx'_1) \wedge (idx_2 = idx'_2) \wedge$
  $(h_{idx_1} \neq h'_{idx_1})$ **then**
  - **return** $(1, out, out')$
- **return** $(0, \perp, \perp)$

Fig. 7. Definition of experiments $\mathrm{Exp}^{\mathrm{Acc}}_{\mathsf{IGen},\mathcal{C},\mathsf{A}}$, $\mathrm{Exp}^{\mathrm{Frk}}_{\mathsf{IGen},\mathcal{C},\mathsf{A}}$, and forking algorithm $\mathsf{Frk}_{\mathcal{C},\mathsf{A}}$.

B.1 Forking Lemma

Let $\mathcal{C}$ be some finite set and $\mathcal{R}$ be some randomness space. Let IGen be a PPT algorithm, and consider an algorithm A that, on input an instance $x \in \mathsf{IGen}$ and random values $h_1, \ldots, h_q \in \mathcal{C}$, returns a pair (idx, out), where $0 \leq idx \leq q$ and *out* is a side output related to h_{idx}. The index $idx = 0$ indicates that A has failed to compute a side output *out* related to any of the values $h_1, \ldots, h_q$. The general forking lemma [7] gives a lower bound on the probability of the forking experiment in which A, if run twice on the same instance x and randomness $r \in \mathcal{R}$, but partially different values from $\mathcal{C}$, will return the same index *idx* and two side outputs *out* and *out'*, which are related to the values h_{idx} and h'_{idx}, respectively. The experiment fails if both runs of A return two different indices, or if $h_{idx} = h'_{idx}$. For the security proof of our n-out-of-n distributed signature protocol we need a minor version of the general forking lemma. This version was given in [4]. It considers an algorithm A that further returns a second index as part of the output, i.e., A returns a tuple (idx_1, idx_2, out), where idx_1 and out are as before, and $0 \leq idx_2 < \omega$ for $\omega \in \mathbb{N}_{>0}$. The forking experiment succeeds only if both runs of A return the same pair of indices (idx_1, idx_2) and $h_{idx_1} \neq h'_{idx_1}$.

Lemma 4. *Let $q, \omega \in \mathbb{N}_{>0}$, $\mathcal{C}$ be a finite set of size $|\mathcal{C}| \geq \in$, and $\mathcal{R}$ be a randomness space. Let IGen be a PPT algorithm, and A be a PPT algorithm that, on input $x \in \mathsf{IGen}$ and $h_1, \ldots, h_q \in \mathcal{C}$, outputs a tuple (idx_1, idx_2, out), where $0 \leq idx_1 \leq q$ and $0 \leq idx_2 < \omega$. Define the accepting probability and the forking probability of A by*

$$acc := \Pr[\mathrm{Exp}^{\mathrm{Acc}}_{\mathsf{IGen},\mathcal{C},\mathsf{A}} = 1] \quad and \quad frk := \Pr[\mathrm{Exp}^{\mathrm{Frk}}_{\mathsf{IGen},\mathcal{C},\mathsf{A}} = 1],$$

where the experiments $\mathrm{Exp}^{\mathrm{Acc}}_{\mathsf{IGen},\mathcal{C},\mathsf{A}}$ and $\mathrm{Exp}^{\mathrm{Frk}}_{\mathsf{IGen},\mathcal{C},\mathsf{A}}$ are depicted in Fig. 7. Then, we have $frk \geq acc \cdot \left(\frac{acc}{q \cdot \omega} - \frac{1}{|\mathcal{C}|}\right)$. Alternatively, $acc \leq \frac{q \cdot \omega}{|\mathcal{C}|} + \sqrt{q \cdot \omega \cdot frk}$.

C Hardness Estimation of MLWE and MSIS

In this section, we explain the methodology that we follow in this work to estimate the hardness of MLWE and MSIS. First, we remark that all known algorithms solving MLWE and MSIS do not exploit their algebraic structure.

Estimating the hardness of MLWE w.r.t. $pp = (N, k, \ell, q, \eta)$ is carried out by using the LWE-*Estimator*[4] presented by Albrecht et al. [2].

Given $pp = (N, k, \ell, q, \beta)$ and $\mathbf{A} = [a_{i,j}]_{1 \leq i \leq k, 1 \leq j \leq \ell} \in R_q^{k \times \ell}$, the hardness of MSIS w.r.t. pp is equivalent to solving the Shortest Vector Problem (SVP), i.e., finding a non-trivial vector, whose ℓ_2-norm is bounded by β, in the lattice $\{\mathbf{x} \in \mathbb{Z}^m \colon \mathbf{0} = [\mathbf{I}_d|\mathbf{A}'] \cdot \mathbf{x} \pmod q\}$, where $d = kN$, $m = (k+\ell)N$, and $\mathbf{A}'$ is the matrix obtained by computing the *rotation matrix* of each entry of $\mathbf{A}$, i.e.,

$$\mathbf{A}' = \begin{bmatrix} \mathsf{Rot}(a_{1,1}) & \ldots & \mathsf{Rot}(a_{1,\ell}) \\ \vdots & \ddots & \vdots \\ \mathsf{Rot}(a_{k,1}) & \ldots & \mathsf{Rot}(a_{k,\ell}) \end{bmatrix} \in \mathbb{Z}_q^{kN \times \ell N}.$$

We recall that the rotation matrix of any $a = \sum_{i=0}^{N-1} a_i X^i \in R$ is defined by

$$\mathsf{Rot}(a) := (\mathbf{a}, \mathsf{rot}(a), \mathsf{rot}^2(a), \ldots, \mathsf{rot}^{N-1}(a)) \in \mathbb{Z}^{N \times N},$$

where $\mathbf{a} = (a_0, \ldots, a_{N-1})^\top$, $\mathsf{rot}(a) := (-a_{N-1}, a_0, \ldots, a_{N-2})^\top$, and for all other $k \in \{2, \ldots, N-1\}$: $\mathsf{rot}^k(a) := \mathsf{rot}(\mathsf{rot}^{k-1}(a))$.

The best known algorithm for finding short non-trivial vectors is due to Schnorr and Euchner [30]. It is called the Block-Korkine-Zolotarev algorithm (BKZ), and was improved in practice by Chen and Nguyen [15]. As a subroutine, BKZ uses an SVP solver in lattices of dimension b, where b is called the *block size*. The best known classical algorithm for SVP with no memory restrictions is

[4] https://github.com/malb/lattice-estimator.

due to Becker et al. [5], and it takes time $\approx 2^{0.292\,b}$. The time required by BKZ to run with block size b on an m-dimensional lattice $\mathcal{L}$ is given by (see, e.g. [5])

$$8m\, 2^{0.292\,b+16.4}. \tag{1}$$

The output of BKZ is a vector of length $\delta^m \det(\mathcal{L})^{1/m}$, where δ is called the *Hermite delta* and it is given by (see, e.g. [14,15])

$$\delta = \left(b\,(\pi b)^{\frac{1}{b}}/(2\pi e)\right)^{\frac{1}{2(b-1)}}, \tag{2}$$

and $\det(\mathcal{L})$ is the determinant of $\mathcal{L}$. Micciancio and Regev [29] showed that it is better to run algorithm BKZ with a maximum of $m = \sqrt{d\log(q)/\log(\delta)}$ columns of the matrix $[\mathbf{I}_d|\mathbf{A}']$. The coefficients of the solution output by BKZ and correspond to the dropped columns are then set to zero. This allows to find a non-zero vector of length $\min(q, 2^{2\sqrt{d\log(q)\log(\delta)}})$. In other words, when considering $\delta^m \det(\mathcal{L})^{1/m}$ as a function of m, Micciancio and Regev [29] showed that the minimum of this function is given by the value $2^{2\sqrt{d\log(q)\log(\delta)}}$, and it is obtained when $m = \sqrt{d\log(q)/\log(\delta)}$. Therefore, in order to compute the time required by BKZ to solve MSIS w.r.t. pp, we first determine δ by setting $\beta = 2^{2\sqrt{d\log(q)\log(\delta)}}$, where $d = kN$ and $m = (k+\ell)N$. After that, we compute the minimum block size b required to achieve δ by using (2). The resulted b is put in (1) to obtain the desired time.

$\mathsf{A}_0(\bar{\mathbf{A}}, \mathbf{b}, \mathbf{s})$	$\mathsf{A}_1(\bar{\mathbf{A}}, \mathbf{b})$
$c \leftarrow\!\!\$\; \mathbb{T}_\kappa$	$c \leftarrow\!\!\$\; \mathbb{T}_\kappa$
$T \leftarrow \{0,\ldots,\omega-1\}$	$T \leftarrow \{0,\ldots,\omega-1\}$
for $j = 0$ **to** $\omega - 1$ **do**	$i \leftarrow\!\!\$\; T$
$\mathbf{y}_j \leftarrow\!\!\$\; D^{k+\ell}_{\mathbb{Z}^N,\sigma}$	$\mathbf{z} \leftarrow\!\!\$\; D^{k+\ell}_{\mathbb{Z}^N,\sigma}$
$\mathbf{v}_j \leftarrow \bar{\mathbf{A}} \cdot \mathbf{y}_j \pmod q$	$\mathbf{v}_i \leftarrow \bar{\mathbf{A}} \cdot \mathbf{z} - \mathbf{b}c \pmod q$
$\mathbf{v} \leftarrow (\mathbf{v}_0, \ldots, \mathbf{v}_{\omega-1})$	**for** $j = 0$ **to** $\omega - 1$ **do**
$\mathbf{z}' \leftarrow \mathbf{s}c$	**if** $j = i$ **then**
while $T \neq \varnothing$ **do**	**continue**
$i \leftarrow\!\!\$\; T$	$\mathbf{y}_j \leftarrow\!\!\$\; D^{k+\ell}_{\mathbb{Z}^N,\sigma}$
$T \leftarrow T \setminus \{i\}$	$\mathbf{v}_j \leftarrow \bar{\mathbf{A}} \cdot \mathbf{y}_j \pmod q$
$\mathbf{z} \leftarrow \mathbf{y}_i + \mathbf{z}'$	$\mathbf{v} \leftarrow (\mathbf{v}_0, \ldots, \mathbf{v}_{\omega-1})$
$\rho \leftarrow\!\!\$\; [0,1)$	$\rho \leftarrow\!\!\$\; [0,1)$
if $\rho \leq \frac{1}{M} \cdot \exp\left(\frac{-2\langle \mathbf{z}, \mathbf{z}'\rangle + \|\mathbf{z}'\|^2}{2\sigma^2}\right)$ **then**	**if** $\rho \leq 1 - \delta$ **then**
	return $(\mathbf{A}, \mathbf{b}, \mathbf{v}, c, \mathbf{z}, i)$
return $(\mathbf{A}, \mathbf{b}, \mathbf{v}, c, \mathbf{z}, i)$	$(\mathbf{z}, i) \leftarrow (\perp, \perp)$
$(\mathbf{z}, i) \leftarrow (\perp, \perp)$	**return** $(\mathbf{A}, \mathbf{b}, \mathbf{v}, c, \mathbf{z}, i)$
return $(\mathbf{A}, \mathbf{b}, \mathbf{v}, c, \mathbf{z}, i)$	

Fig. 8. The algorithms that show the Indistinguishability of hybrids H_2 and H_1 defined in the proof of Theorem 1.

D Indistinguishability of Hybrids H_2 and H_1

The following lemma establishes the statistical distance between the hybrids H_2 and H_1 defined in the proof of Theorem 1.

Lemma 5. *Let σ be as in Lemma 2, M be as in Lemma 3, and $\delta > 0$ such that $(1 - \frac{1-2^{-100}}{M})^{\omega} \leq \delta$. Let $\mathbf{A} \leftarrow\$ R_q^{k\times\ell}$, $\bar{\mathbf{A}} = [\mathbf{I}_k|\mathbf{A}] \in R_q^{k\times(k+\ell)}$, $\mathbf{s} \leftarrow\$ S_\eta^{k+\ell}$, and $\mathbf{b} = \bar{\mathbf{A}} \cdot \mathbf{s} \pmod q$. Then, the output distributions of the algorithms A_0 and A_1 defined in Fig. 8 are within statistical distance of at most $2^{-\Omega(N)+1} \cdot 2^{-100}/M$.*

Proof. The proof is similar to the one of [12, Lemma B.8], which is performed via standard hybrid arguments. The only difference here is that in algorithm A_0 rejection sampling is carried out at most ω times, using Gaussian masking vectors $\mathbf{y}_0, \ldots, \mathbf{y}_{\omega-1}$. The goal is to make sure that the distribution of $\mathbf{z} = \mathbf{y}_i + \mathbf{s}c$ is independent of $\mathbf{s}c$. The random choice of $\rho \in [0, 1)$ and doing the test in line 13 is a standard implementation of the rejection sampling procedure. By Lemma 3, rejection sampling accepts with probability $(1 - 2^{-100})/M$, and $\mathbf{z}$ is within statistical distance of $2^{-100}/M$ from the Gaussian distribution $D_{\mathbb{Z}^N,\sigma}^{k+\ell}$. When using ω masking vectors $\mathbf{y}_0, \ldots, \mathbf{y}_{\omega-1}$, instead of only one, algorithm A_0 returns $(\mathbf{z}, i) \neq (\perp, \perp)$ with probability $1 - (1 - \frac{1-2^{-100}}{M})^{\omega} \leq 1 - \delta$. Lemma 2 is

Table 3. Parameters of our distributed signature protocol.

Parameter	Description	Bounds
n	No. signers	ω^n small
N	Defines the ring R	power of two
k, ℓ	Dimension of matrix $\mathbf{A}$	$k, \ell \in \mathbb{N}_{>0}$
q	Modulus	prime, $q = 1 \pmod{2N}$
η	Bound of $\lVert\mathbf{s}^{(n)}\rVert_\infty$	$\eta \in \mathbb{Z}_{>0}$
κ	Specifies the set $\mathbb{T}_\kappa$	$2^\kappa \binom{N}{\kappa} \geq 2^\lambda$
σ	Standard deviation of $\mathbf{z}^{(n)}$	$\sigma = \alpha\lVert\mathbf{s}c\rVert = \alpha\kappa\eta\sqrt{(k+\ell)N}$, $\alpha > 0$, $\sigma > \frac{2N \cdot q^{\frac{k}{k+\ell} + \frac{2}{N(k+\ell)}}}{\sqrt{2\pi}}$
ω	No. vectors $\mathbf{y}_i$	$\omega \in \mathbb{N}_{>1}$, $(1 - \frac{1-2^{-100}}{M})^{\omega} \leq \delta$, $M = \exp(\frac{12}{\alpha} + \frac{1}{2\alpha^2})$, $\delta > 0$
h	Tree height	$h = \lceil \log(\omega^n) \rceil$
S	No. restarts of Sign_n	$S = 1/(1-\delta)$
$\bar{M}$	Total No. restarts	$\bar{M} = S^n$
B_z	Bound of $\lVert\mathbf{z}^{(n)}\rVert$	$B_z = \gamma\sigma\sqrt{(k+\ell)N}$, $\gamma > 0$
B	Bound of $\lVert\mathbf{z}\rVert$	$B = \sqrt{n}B_z$
ℓ_{seed}	Input length of Expand	$\ell_{seed} \geq \lambda$
$\ell_{\mathsf{G}}, \ell_{\mathsf{F}}$	Output length of G, F	$\ell_{\mathsf{G}}, \ell_{\mathsf{F}} \geq 2\lambda$

applied twice in order to obtain a statistical distance of $2^{-\Omega(N)}$ between a vector $\bar{\mathbf{A}} \cdot \mathbf{y} \in R_q^k$, for $\mathbf{y} \leftarrow\!\!\$\ D_{\mathbb{Z}^N,\sigma}^{k+\ell}$, and a uniformly random vector from R_q^k. We refer to [12, Lemma B.8] for more details.

References

1. Agrawal, S., Stehlé, D., Yadav, A.: Round-optimal lattice-based threshold signatures, revisited. In: Bojanczyk, M., Merelli, E., Woodruff, D.P. (eds.) 49th International Colloquium on Automata, Languages, and Programming, ICALP 2022. LIPIcs, vol. 229, pp. 8:1–8:20. Schloss Dagstuhl - Leibniz-Zentrum für Informatik (2022)
2. Albrecht, M.R., Player, R., Scott, S.: On the concrete hardness of learning with errors. J. Math. Cryptol. **9**(3), 169–203 (2015)
3. Alkeilani Alkadri, N., El Bansarkhani, R., Buchmann, J.: On lattice-based interactive protocols: An approach with less or no aborts, pp. 41–61 (2020). https://doi.org/10.1007/978-3-030-55304-3_3
4. Alkeilani Alkadri, N., Harasser, P., Janson, C.: BlindOR: an efficient lattice-based blind signature scheme from OR-proofs, pp. 95–115 (2021). https://doi.org/10.1007/978-3-030-92548-2_6
5. Becker, A., Ducas, L., Gama, N., Laarhoven, T.: New directions in nearest neighbor searching with applications to lattice sieving, pp. 10–24 (2016). https://doi.org/10.1137/1.9781611974331.ch2
6. Bellare, M., Davis, H., Günther, F.: Separate your domains: NIST PQC KEMs, oracle cloning and read-only indifferentiability, pp. 3–32 (2020). https://doi.org/10.1007/978-3-030-45724-2_1
7. Bellare, M., Neven, G.: Multi-signatures in the plain public-key model and a general forking lemma, pp. 390–399 (2006). https://doi.org/10.1145/1180405.1180453
8. Bellare, M., Rogaway, P.: Random oracles are practical: a paradigm for designing efficient protocols, pp. 62–73 (1993). https://doi.org/10.1145/168588.168596
9. Bendlin, R., Krehbiel, S., Peikert, C.: How to share a lattice trapdoor: threshold protocols for signatures and (H)IBE, pp. 218–236 (2013). https://doi.org/10.1007/978-3-642-38980-1_14
10. Boneh, D., Dagdelen, Ö., Fischlin, M., Lehmann, A., Schaffner, C., Zhandry, M.: Random oracles in a quantum world, pp. 41–69 (2011). https://doi.org/10.1007/978-3-642-25385-0_3
11. Boneh, D., et al.: Threshold cryptosystems from threshold fully homomorphic encryption, pp. 565–596 (2018). https://doi.org/10.1007/978-3-319-96884-1_19
12. Boschini, C., Takahashi, A., Tibouchi, M.: MuSig-L: Lattice-based multi-signature with single-round online phase, pp. 276–305 (2022). https://doi.org/10.1007/978-3-031-15979-4_10
13. Chen, Y.: DualMS: Efficient lattice-based two-round multi-signature with trapdoor-free simulation. In: Advances in Cryptology - CRYPTO 2023, pp. 716–747 (2023). https://doi.org/10.1007/978-3-031-38554-4_23
14. Chen, Y.: Réduction de réseau et sécurité concrete du chiffrement completement homomorphe. Ph.D. thesis, ENS-Lyon, France (2013)
15. Chen, Y., Nguyen, P.Q.: BKZ 2.0: Better lattice security estimates, pp. 1–20 (2011). https://doi.org/10.1007/978-3-642-25385-0_1
16. Cozzo, D., Smart, N.P.: Sharing the LUOV: threshold post-quantum signatures, pp. 128–153 (2019). https://doi.org/10.1007/978-3-030-35199-1_7

17. Damgård, I., Orlandi, C., Takahashi, A., Tibouchi, M.: Two-round n-out-of-n and multi-signatures and trapdoor commitment from lattices **35**(2), 14 (2022). https://doi.org/10.1007/s00145-022-09425-3
18. Desmedt, Y., Frankel, Y.: Threshold cryptosystem, pp. 307–315 (1990). https://doi.org/10.1007/0-387-34805-0_28
19. Don, J., Fehr, S., Majenz, C., Schaffner, C.: Security of the Fiat-Shamir transformation in the quantum random-oracle model, pp. 356–383 (2019). https://doi.org/10.1007/978-3-030-26951-7_13
20. Ducas, L., et al.: CRYSTALS-Dilithium: a lattice-based digital signature scheme 2018(1), 238–268 (2018). https://doi.org/10.13154/tches.v2018.i1.238-268, https://tches.iacr.org/index.php/TCHES/article/view/839
21. Ducas, L., Lepoint, T., Lyubashevsky, V., Schwabe, P., Seiler, G., Stehle, D.: Crystals - dilithium: Digital signatures from module lattices. Cryptology ePrint Archive, Paper 2017/633 (2017), https://eprint.iacr.org/archive/2017/633/20170627:201152
22. Gentry, C., Peikert, C., Vaikuntanathan, V.: Trapdoors for hard lattices and new cryptographic constructions, pp. 197–206 (2008). https://doi.org/10.1145/1374376.1374407
23. Itakura, K., Nakamura, K.: A public-key cryptosystem suitable for digital multisignatures. NEC Res. Develop. **71**, 1–8 (1983)
24. Liu, Q., Zhandry, M.: Revisiting post-quantum Fiat-Shamir, pp. 326–355 (2019). https://doi.org/10.1007/978-3-030-26951-7_12
25. Lyubashevsky, V.: Fiat-shamir with aborts: applications to lattice and factoring-based signatures, pp. 598–616 (2009). https://doi.org/10.1007/978-3-642-10366-7_35
26. Lyubashevsky, V.: Lattice signatures without trapdoors, pp. 738–755 (2012). https://doi.org/10.1007/978-3-642-29011-4_43
27. Lyubashevsky, V., Peikert, C., Regev, O.: A toolkit for ring-LWE cryptography, pp. 35–54 (2013). https://doi.org/10.1007/978-3-642-38348-9_3
28. Micali, S., Ohta, K., Reyzin, L.: Accountable-subgroup multisignatures: extended abstract, pp. 245–254 (2001). https://doi.org/10.1145/501983.502017
29. Micciancio, D., Regev, O.: Lattice-based cryptography. In: Bernstein, D.J., Buchmann, J., Dahmen, E. (eds.) Post-Quantum Cryptography, pp. 147–191. Springer Berlin Heidelberg, Berlin, Heidelberg (2009). https://doi.org/10.1007/978-3-540-88702-7_5
30. Schnorr, C., Euchner, M.: Lattice basis reduction: improved practical algorithms and solving subset sum problems. Math. Program. **66**, 181–199 (1994). https://doi.org/10.1007/BF01581144
31. Zhandry, M.: How to record quantum queries, and applications to quantum indifferentiability, pp. 239–268 (2019). https://doi.org/10.1007/978-3-030-26951-7_9

Building MPCitH-Based Signatures from MQ, MinRank, and Rank SD

Thibauld Feneuil[1,2(✉)]

[1] CryptoExperts, Paris, France
thibauld.feneuil@cryptoexperts.com
[2] Sorbonne Université, CNRS, INRIA, Institut de Mathématiques, de Jussieu-Paris Rive Gauche, Ouragan, Paris, France

Abstract. The MPC-in-the-Head paradigm is a useful tool to build practical signature schemes. Many such schemes have been already proposed, relying on different assumptions. Some are relying on standard symmetric primitives like AES, some are relying on MPC-friendly primitives like LowMC or Rain, and some are relying on well-known hard problems like the syndrome decoding problem.

This work focuses on the third type of MPCitH-based signatures. Following the same methodology as the work of Feneuil, Joux and Rivain (CRYPTO'22), we apply the MPC-in-the-Head paradigm to several problems: the multivariate quadratic problem, the MinRank problem, and the rank syndrome decoding problem. Our goal is to study how this paradigm behaves for each of those problems.

For the multivariate quadratic problem, our scheme outperforms slightly the former schemes when considering large fields (as GF(256)). Even if the scheme does not always outperform the existing ones according to the communication cost, they are compatible with some MPC-in-the-Head techniques while the former proposals were not.

Moreover, we propose two efficient MPC protocols to check that the rank of a matrix over a field $\mathbb{F}_q$ is upper bounded by a public constant. The first one relies on the rank decomposition while the second one relies on q-polynomials. We then use them to build signature schemes relying on the MinRank problem and the rank syndrome decoding problem. Those schemes outperform the former schemes, achieving sizes below 6 KB (while using only 256 parties for the MPC protocol).

Keywords: zero-knowledge proofs · post-quantum signatures · MPC-in-the-head

1 Introduction

The MPC-in-the-Head paradigm [IKOS07] is a versatile framework to design zero-knowledge proofs of knowledge, by relying on secure multi-party computation (MPC) techniques. After sharing the secret witness, the prover emulates "in

C. Pöpper and L. Batina (Eds.): ACNS 2024, LNCS 14583, pp. 403–431, 2024.
https://doi.org/10.1007/978-3-031-54770-6_16

her head" an MPC protocol with N parties and commits each party's view independently. The verifier then challenges the prover to reveal the views of a random subset of parties. By the privacy of the MPC protocol, nothing is revealed about the witness, which implies the zero-knowledge property. On the other hand, a malicious prover needs to cheat for at least one party, which shall be discovered by the verifier with high probability, hence ensuring the soundness property.

Combined with the Fiat-Shamir transform [FS87], the MPCitH paradigm provides a useful tool for building practical signatures. The security of the resulting scheme only depends on the security of commitment/hash functions and the security of a one-way function. The choice of this one-way function is left to the signature designers. A first research track [ARS+15, DKR+21] consists in designing MPC-friendly primitives and in using them with the MPC-in-the-Head paradigm to get short signatures. This methodology has the disadvantage of requiring deep cryptanalysis of the introduced primitives. Another strategy would be to use standard symmetric primitives like AES as security assumptions for the MPCitH-based signatures, but it tends to produce larger signatures. As a last option, we can rely on a hard problem that exists for a long time and thus is well understood. For example, [FJR22] succeeds in designing an efficient signature scheme using the syndrome decoding problem (over the Hamming weight), which is one of the oldest problems of code-based cryptography. The case of the syndrome decoding problem has been covered, but a natural question would be

Which performances can we have when using
the MPC-in-the-Head paradigm with other hard problems?

Some articles [Wan22, FJR21, BG22, FMRV22] already apply this paradigm to hard problems (multivariate quadratic problem, MinRank problem, subset sum problem, ...). One of the drawbacks of almost all the schemes is that, when there is no structure to exploit, they need to rely on *protocols with helpers* [Beu20]. This technique introduced by [KKW18] and formalized by [Beu20] is quite powerful, but suffers from a high computational cost. As a consequence, the number of parties involved in the MPC protocol must stay low to have a practical scheme (in practice, many works take 32 as a limit for the number of parties), preventing achieving smaller sizes. Recently, [BG22] succeeds in leveraging the structure when considering structured hard problems (as the ideal rank syndrome decoding problem) and thus succeeds in achieving smaller sizes by removing the helper from [FJR21].

The present work aims to complete the state of the art of the MPC-in-the-Head applied to hard problems.

Our Contribution. In this article, we consider several hard problems for which we propose new zero-knowledge proofs using the MPC-in-the-Head paradigm.

First, we propose a new zero-knowledge proof of knowledge for the *multivariate quadratic* problem. The resulting signature scheme outperforms [Wan22] only when the base field is large enough (*e.g.* $\mathbb{F}_{256}$).

Secondly, we propose two efficient MPC protocols which take as input a matrix $M \in \mathbb{F}_q^{n\times m}$ and which check that the rank of M is upper bounded by r, where r is a public positive integer:

- the first one decomposes M as a product TR where $T \in \mathbb{F}_q^{n\times r}$ and $R \in \mathbb{F}_q^{r\times m}$, and uses an MPC protocol that checks the correctness of a matrix multiplication;
- the second one relies on the fact that the rows of M (represented as elements of $\mathbb{F}_{q^m}$) are roots of a q-polynomial of degree q^r and on the fact that computing a q-polynomial is efficient in MPC while exploiting the linearity of the Frobenius endomorphism $v \mapsto v^q$.

We then use those protocols to build efficient signatures relying on the *MinRank* problem or on the *rank syndrome decoding* problem. Our schemes outperform all the previous proposals, by achieving sizes below 7 KB. They also outperform the [BG22]'s proposals which use structured problems (as the ideal rank syndrome decoding problem) to achieve small sizes.

Related Works. Our work aims to propose efficient conservative signature schemes using the MPC-in-the-Head paradigm. Other approaches are possible to design signatures:

- the schemes built from the Fiat-Shamir transformation of an identification scheme relying on an equivalence problem such as LESS [BMPS20,BBPS21] and MEDS [CNP+23]. Those schemes tend to have large keys (a few tens of kilobytes), so the MPCitH-based schemes outperform them for the common "signature size + public key size" metric.
- the schemes built using the hash-and-sign paradigm such as UOV [KPG99] and Wave [DST19]. Those schemes have very competitive signature sizes (less than one kilobyte), but suffer large public keys. Some schemes have shorter public keys as MAYO [Beu22], but they rely on more recent security assumptions.

The MPCitH paradigm (applied to non-structured problems) provides interesting alternatives to SPHINCS$^+$ [BHK+19] by being conservative without the large signing times of SPHINCS$^+$. Other schemes can be considered as less conservative (either because relying on a recent assumption or on a structured one) or have large public keys.

In July 2023, the NIST released the first-round candidates of the new call for additional post-quantum signatures [NIS22]. Several of those schemes are related to our work. RYDE [ABB+23a] and MIRA [ABB+23b] are schemes based on our linearized-polynomial MPC protocols respectively for the rank syndrome decoding problem and the MinRank problem. MIRITH [ARZV+23] is a scheme combining ideas from [ARZV22] with our rank-decomposition MPC protocol for the MinRank problem. Finally, MQOM [FR23] succeeded in improving our scheme on the $\mathcal{MQ}$ problem, decreasing the obtained signature size by $500-800$ bytes.

Paper Organization. The paper is organized as follows: In Sect. 2, we introduce some background on the MPC-in-the-Head paradigm and present our methodology. Then we apply the latter to the *multivariate quadratic* problem in Sect. 3, to the *MinRank* problem and the *rank syndrome decoding* problem in Sect. 4. Finally, we discuss the computational cost of the obtained schemes in Sect. 5.

2 Preliminaries

Throughout the paper, $\mathbb{F}_q$ shall denote the finite field with q elements. For any $m \in \mathbb{N}^*$, the integer set $\{1, \ldots, m\}$ is denoted $[m]$. For a probability distribution D, the notation $s \leftarrow D$ means that s is sampled from D. For a finite set S, the notation $s \leftarrow S$ means that s is uniformly sampled at random from S.

In this paper, we shall use the standard cryptographic notions of (honest verifier) zero-knowledge proof of knowledge and secure multiparty computation protocols (in the semi-honest model). We refer to [FR22] for the formal definition of those notions.

2.1 The MPC-in-the-Head Paradigm

The MPC-in-the-Head (MPCitH) paradigm introduced in [IKOS07] offers a way to build zero-knowledge proofs from secure multi-party computation (MPC) protocols. Let us assume we have an MPC protocol in which N parties $\mathcal{P}_1, \ldots, \mathcal{P}_N$ securely and correctly evaluate a function f on a secret input x with the following properties:

- the secret x is encoded as a sharing $[\![x]\!]$ and each $\mathcal{P}_i$ takes a share $[\![x]\!]_i$ as input;
- the function f outputs ACCEPT or REJECT;
- the views of t parties leak no information about the secret x.

We can use this MPC protocol to build a zero-knowledge proof of knowledge of an x for which $f(x)$ evaluates to ACCEPT. The prover proceeds as follows:

- she builds a random sharing $[\![x]\!]$ of x;
- she simulates locally ("in her head") all the parties of the MPC protocol;
- she sends commitments to each party's view, *i.e.* party's input share, secret random tape and sent and received messages, to the verifier;
- she sends the output shares $[\![f(x)]\!]$ of the parties, which should correspond to ACCEPT.

Then the verifier randomly chooses t parties and asks the prover to reveal their views. After receiving them, the verifier checks that they are consistent with an honest execution of the MPC protocol and with the commitments. Since only t parties are opened, revealed views leak no information about the secret x, while the random choice of the opened parties makes[1] the cheating probability upper bounded by $(N-t)/N$, thus ensuring the soundness of the zero-knowledge proof.

[1] We implicitly assume here that the communication between parties is broadcast.

All MPC protocols described in this article fit the model described in [FR22], meaning that the parties take as input an additive sharing $[\![x]\!]$ of the secret x (one share per party) and that they compute one or several rounds in which they perform three types of actions:

Receiving randomness: the parties receive a random value ε from a randomness oracle $\mathcal{O}_R$. When calling this oracle, all the parties get the same random value ε.

Receiving hint: the parties can receive a sharing $[\![\beta]\!]$ (one share per party) from a hint oracle $\mathcal{O}_H$. The hint β can depend on the witness w and the previous random values sampled from $\mathcal{O}_R$.

Computing & broadcasting: the parties can locally compute $[\![\alpha]\!] := [\![\varphi(v)]\!]$ from a sharing $[\![v]\!]$ where φ is an $\mathbb{F}$-linear function, then broadcast all the shares $[\![\alpha]\!]_1, \ldots, [\![\alpha]\!]_N$ to publicly reconstruct $\alpha := \varphi(v)$. The function φ can depend on the previous random values $\{\varepsilon^i\}_i$ from $\mathcal{O}_R$ and on the previous broadcasted values.

We refer to [FR22] for the detailed transformation of such MPC protocols into zero-knowledge proofs of knowledge and for the resulting performance.

2.2 Methodology

In each of the following sections, we focus on a specific hard problem that is supposed quantum-resilient. For each of them, we will use the MPC-in-the-Head paradigm to build a new zero-knowledge protocol. To proceed, we first describe the MPC protocol we use, then we present the achieved performance when applying the paradigm. *We do not exhibit the obtained proof of knowledge since the transformation is standard. We refer the reader to* [FR22] *for a detailed explanation of how to concretely apply the MPC-in-the-Head paradigm.* Finally, we use the Fiat-Shamir transform [FS87] on the obtained protocol to get a signature scheme. Because of the space constraints, we put a more detailed description of our methodology in Appendix A.

2.3 Matrix Multiplication Checking Protocol

In our constructions, we need an MPC protocol that checks that three matrices X, Y, Z satisfy $Z = X \cdot Y$. We describe in Fig. 1 such a protocol Π^{η}_{MM} which has a positive parameter η. This protocol is a matrix variant of the multiplication checking protocol of [BN20] (optimized in [KZ22]).

Lemma 1. *If $Z = X \cdot Y$ and if C are genuinely computed, then Π^{η}_{MM} always outputs* Accept. *If $Z \neq X \cdot Y$, then Π^{η}_{MM} outputs* Accept *with probability at most $\frac{1}{q^{\eta}}$.*

Proof. We have

$$V = X(Y\Sigma + A) - C - Z\Sigma = (XY - Z)\Sigma - (C - XA).$$

Inputs: Each party takes a share of the following sharings as inputs: $[\![X]\!]$ where $X \in \mathbb{F}_q^{m\times p}$, $[\![Y]\!]$ where $Y \in \mathbb{F}_q^{p\times n}$, $[\![Z]\!]$ where $\mathbb{F}_q^{m\times n}$, $[\![A]\!]$ where A has been uniformly sampled from $\mathbb{F}_q^{p\times \eta}$, and $[\![C]\!]$ where $C \in \mathbb{F}_q^{m\times \eta}$ satisfies $C = XA$.

MPC Protocol:

1. The parties get a random $\Sigma \in \mathbb{F}_q^{n\times \eta}$.
2. The parties locally set $[\![D]\!] = [\![Y]\!]\Sigma + [\![A]\!]$.
3. The parties broadcast $[\![D]\!]$ to obtain $D \in \mathbb{F}_q^{p\times \eta}$.
4. The parties locally set $[\![V]\!] = [\![X]\!]D - [\![C]\!] - [\![Z]\!]\Sigma$.
5. The parties open $[\![V]\!]$ to obtain $V \in \mathbb{F}_q^{m\times \eta}$.
6. The parties outputs Accept if $V = 0$ and Reject otherwise.

Fig. 1. The MPC protocol Π_{MM}^{η} which checks that $Z = X \cdot Y$ (MM stands for Matrix Multiplication).

If $Z = XY$ and $C = XA$, V is equal to zero and thus the parties will always output Accept. In contrast, if $Z \neq XY$, then there exists $(i^*, j^*) \in [m] \times [n]$ such that $Z_{i^*,j^*} - (X \cdot Y)_{i^*,j^*} \neq 0$. Given $k \in \{1, \ldots, \eta\}$, $\Sigma_{j^*,k}$ is uniformly sampled in $\mathbb{F}_q$ and then $((Z - X \cdot Y)\Sigma)_{i^*,k}$ is uniformly random in $\mathbb{F}_q$ (because one term of the term is uniformly random). Thus, the probability that V is zero is at most the probability that $(Z - X \cdot Y)\Sigma$ is equal to $(C - XA)$ on the row i^* whereas the row i^* of $(Z - X \cdot Y)\Sigma$ is uniformly random in $\mathbb{F}_q^{\eta}$, *i.e.* the probability that V is zero (at row i^*) is at most $\frac{1}{q^{\eta}}$. □

3 Proof of Knowledge for $\mathcal{MQ}$

We want to build a zero-knowledge proof of knowledge for the *multivariate quadratic problem*:

Definition 1 (Multivariate Quadratic Problem - Matrix Form). *Let (q, m, n) be positive integers. The multivariate quadratic problem with parameters (q, m, n) is the following problem:*

Let $(A_i)_{i\in[m]}$, $(b_i)_{i\in[m]}$, x and y be such that:
1. *x is uniformly sampled from $\mathbb{F}_q^n$,*
2. *for all $i \in [m]$, A_i is uniformly sampled from $\mathbb{F}_q^{n\times n}$,*
3. *for all $i \in [m]$, b_i is uniformly sampled from $\mathbb{F}_q^n$,*
4. *for all $i \in [m]$, y_i is defined as $y_i := x^T A_i x + b_i^T x$.*

From $((A_i)_{i\in[m]}, (b_i)_{i\in[m]}, y)$, find x.

The prover wants to convince the verifier that she knows $x \in \mathbb{F}_q^n$ such that

$$\forall i \in [m],\ y_i = x^T A_i x + b_i^T x$$

To proceed, she will rely on the MPC-in-the-Head paradigm: she will first share the secret vector x and then use an MPC protocol which verifies that this vector satisfies the above relations.

MPC Protocol. Instead of checking the m relations separately, we batch them into a linear combination where coefficients $\gamma_1, \ldots, \gamma_m$ are uniformly sampled in the field extension $\mathbb{F}_{q^\eta}$. The MPC protocol will check that

$$\sum_{i=1}^{m} \gamma_i (y_i - x^T A_i x - b_i^T x) = 0. \tag{1}$$

If one of the relations was not satisfied, then Eq. (1) would be satisfied only with a probability $\frac{1}{q^\eta}$. By defining

$$z := \sum_{i=1}^{m} \gamma_i (y_i - b_i^T x) \quad \text{and} \quad w := \left(\sum_{i=1}^{m} \gamma_i A_i \right) x,$$

proving Eq. (1) is equivalent to proving that $z = \langle x, w \rangle$. And to prove this last equality, we can rely on the subprotocol Π_{MM} described in Sect. 2.3 (assuming that all the scalars live in $\mathbb{F}_{q^\eta}$). Thus, the MPC protocol proceeds as follows:

1. The parties get random $\gamma_1, \ldots, \gamma_m \in \mathbb{F}_{q^\eta}$.
2. The parties locally set $[\![z]\!] = \sum_{i=1}^{m} \gamma_i (y_i - b_i^T [\![x]\!])$.
3. The parties locally set $[\![w]\!] = (\sum_{i=1}^{m} \gamma_i A_i) [\![x]\!]$.
4. The parties execute the protocol Π_{MM} to check that $z = \langle w, x \rangle$.

Since this sub-protocol Π_{MM} produces false positive events with a rate of $\frac{1}{q^\eta}$, if x does not satisfy the m $\mathcal{MQ}$ relations, the complete MPC protocol outputs Accept only with a probability of at most

$$\frac{1}{q^\eta} + \left(1 - \frac{1}{q^\eta}\right) \frac{1}{q^\eta} = \frac{2}{q^\eta} - \frac{1}{q^{2\eta}}.$$

The complete MPC protocol is described in Fig. 2.

Proof of Knowledge. Using the MPC-in-the-Head paradigm (see Sect. 2.1), we transform the above MPC protocol into an interactive zero-knowledge proof of knowledge which enables us to convince a verifier that a prover knows the solution of a $\mathcal{MQ}$ problem. The soundness error of the resulting protocol is

$$\varepsilon := \frac{1}{N} + \left(1 - \frac{1}{N}\right) \left(\frac{2}{q^\eta} - \frac{1}{q^{2\eta}}\right).$$

By repeating the protocol τ times, we get a soundness error of ε^τ. To obtain a soundness error of λ bits, we can take $\tau = \left\lceil \frac{-\lambda}{\log_2 \varepsilon} \right\rceil$. We can transform the interactive protocol into a non-interactive argument/signature thanks to the Fiat-Shamir transform [FS87]. According to [KZ20], the security of the resulting scheme is

$$\text{cost}_{\text{forge}} := \min_{\tau_1, \tau_2 : \tau_1 + \tau_2 = \tau} \left\{ \frac{1}{\sum_{i=\tau_1}^{\tau} \binom{\tau}{i} p^i (1-p)^{\tau - i}} + N^{\tau_2} \right\}$$

where $p := \frac{2}{q^\eta} - \frac{1}{q^{2\eta}}$.

Public values: The matrices $A_1, \ldots, A_m \in \mathbb{F}_q^{n\times n}$, the vectors $b_1, \ldots, b_m \in \mathbb{F}_q^n$, and the outputs $y_1, \ldots, y_m \in \mathbb{F}_q$.

Inputs: Each party takes a share of the following sharings as inputs: $[\![x]\!]$ where $x \in \mathbb{F}_q^n$, $[\![a]\!]$ where a has been uniformly sampled from $\mathbb{F}_{q^\eta}^n$, and $[\![c]\!]$ where $c \in \mathbb{F}_{q^\eta}$ satisfies $c = -\langle a, x\rangle$.

MPC Protocol:

1. The parties get random $\gamma_1, \ldots, \gamma_m \in \mathbb{F}_{q^\eta}$ and a random $\varepsilon \in \mathbb{F}_{q^\eta}$.
2. The parties locally set $[\![z]\!] = \sum_{i=1}^m \gamma_i (y_i - b_i^T [\![x]\!])$.
3. The parties locally set $[\![w]\!] = \left(\sum_{i=1}^m \gamma_i A_i\right) [\![x]\!]$.
4. The parties locally set $[\![\alpha]\!] = \varepsilon \cdot [\![w]\!] + [\![a]\!]$.
5. The parties open $\alpha \in \mathbb{F}_{q^\eta}^n$.
6. The parties locally set $[\![v]\!] = \varepsilon \cdot [\![z]\!] - \langle \alpha, [\![x]\!]\rangle - [\![c]\!]$.
7. The parties open $v \in \mathbb{F}_{q^\eta}$.
8. The parties outputs ACCEPT if $v = 0$ and REJECT otherwise.

Fig. 2. An MPC protocol that verifies that the given input corresponds to a solution of an $\mathcal{MQ}$ problem.

The communication cost of the scheme (in bits) is

$$4\lambda + \tau \cdot \left(\underbrace{n \cdot \log_2(q)}_{x} + \underbrace{n \cdot \eta \cdot \log_2(q)}_{\alpha} + \underbrace{\eta \cdot \log_2(q)}_{c} + \underbrace{\lambda \cdot \log_2 N + 2\lambda}_{\text{MPCitH}} \right)$$

where λ is the security level, η is a scheme parameter and τ is computed such that the soundness error is of λ bits in the interactive case and such that $\text{cost}_{\text{forge}}$ is of λ bits in the non-interactive case. The public key corresponds to the coefficients of the $\mathcal{MQ}$ equations (namely $(A_i)_{i\in[m]}$ and $(b_i)_{i\in[m]}$) which can be represented by a λ-bit seed and the vector $y \in \mathbb{F}_q^m$. Its size is thus $\lambda + m \log_2 q$ bits.

Performance and Comparison. In what follows, we compare our scheme with the state of the art on two $\mathcal{MQ}$ instances:

Instance 1. Multivariate Quadratic equations over a small field:

$$(q, m, n) = (4, 88, 88),$$

Instance 2. Multivariate Quadratic equations over a larger field:

$$(q, m, n) = (256, 40, 40).$$

Both of these instances are believed to correspond to a security of 128 bits [BMSV22].

We provide in Table 1 a complete comparison of our scheme with the state of the art. In the comparison, we put MQ-DSS [CHR+16] which corresponds to the non-interactive version of the 5-round identification scheme of [SSH11]. For the sake of completeness, we also put how the 3-round identification scheme of [SSH11] would perform when applying the Fiat-Shamir transform on it.

Over a small field, the Mesquite [Wan22] scheme has the smallest communication cost, even if our scheme produces competitive signature sizes. Over a larger field, we can produce signature sizes close to 7 KB, and thus we outperform all the former schemes.

Remark 1. In contrast with the former state of the art, the communication cost of our scheme is independent of the number m of $\mathcal{MQ}$ relations.

Table 1. Sizes of the signatures relying on the $\mathcal{MQ}$ problem (restricting to the schemes using the FS heuristics). Numerical comparison. We refer the reader to Table 5 (Appendix B) for the formulae giving the signature sizes for all those schemes.

Instance	Protocol Name	Variant	Parameters				Signature Size	Public Key Size
			N	M	τ	η		
$q = 4$ $m = 88$ $n = 88$	[SSH11] (3 rounds)	-	-	219	-	-	28 502 B	38 B
	MQ-DSS [CHR+16]	-	-	316	-	-	41 444 B	
	MUDFISH [Beu20]	-	4	191	68	-	14 640 B	
	Mesquite [Wan22]	Fast	8	187	49	-	9 578 B	
		Short	32	389	28	-	**8 609 B**	
	Our scheme	Fast	32	-	40	6	10 764 B	
		Short	256	-	25	8	9 064 B	
$q = 256$ $m = 40$ $n = 40$	[SSH11] (3 rounds)	-	-	219	-	-	40 328 B	56 B
	MQ-DSS [CHR+16]	-	-	156	-	-	28 768 B	
	MUDFISH [Beu20]	Fast	8	176	51	-	15 958 B	
		Short	16	250	36	-	13 910 B	
	Mesquite [Wan22]	Fast	8	187	49	-	11 339 B	
		Short	32	389	28	-	9 615 B	
	Our scheme	Fast	32	-	36	2	8 488 B	
		Short	256	-	25	2	**7 114 B**	

4 Proofs of Knowledge for MinRank and Rank SD

In this section, we propose arguments of knowledge for the MinRank problem (Sect. 4.2) and the Rank SD problem (Sect. 4.3). But before that, in Sect. 4.1, we propose two efficient MPC protocols which check that a matrix M has a rank of at most r.

In what follows, we denote $\mathrm{wt}_R(M)$ the rank of a matrix M.

4.1 Matrix Rank Checking Protocols

We want to build MPC protocols which check that a matrix has rank at most r. Such MPC protocols will be used for arguments of knowledge with the MPC-in-the-Head paradigm. We propose two protocols:

- the first one relies on the rank decomposition of matrices. It has the advantage of being quite *simple*, but its false positive rate is *large*.
- the second one relies on linearized polynomials. It has the advantage of having a *very small* false positive rate, but it sometimes requires to handle field extensions of *large degrees*.

Using Rank Decomposition. Let us design an MPC protocol which checks that a matrix $M \in \mathbb{F}^{m \times n}$ has a rank of at most r, *i.e.* $\text{wt}_R(M) \leq r$. To proceed, we will rely on the *rank decomposition*:

$$\text{a matrix } M \in \mathbb{F}_q^{n \times m} \text{ has a rank of at most } r$$
$$\text{if and only if there exists } T \in \mathbb{F}_q^{n \times r} \text{ and } R \in \mathbb{F}_q^{r \times m} \text{ such that } M = TR.$$

In practice, our MPC protocol that we will denote $\Pi^{\eta}_{textRC-RD}$ takes as input such matrices T and R (in addition to M) and simply executes the matrix multiplication checking protocol Π^{η}_{MM} (see Sect. 2.3), for some positive integer η.

Theorem 1. *If* $\text{wt}_R(M) \leq r$ *and if* T, R *are genuinely computed, then* $\Pi^{\eta}_{textRC-RD}$ *always outputs* Accept. *If* $\text{wt}_R(M) > r$, *then* $\Pi_{textRC-RD}$ *outputs* Accept *with probability at most* $\frac{1}{q^{\eta}}$. *More precisely, if* $\text{wt}_R(M) = w + \delta$ *with* $\delta \geq 1$, *then* $\Pi^{\eta}_{textRC-RD}$ *outputs* Accept *with probability at most* $\frac{1}{q^{\delta \cdot \eta}}$.

Proof. The final broadcast matrix V in Π^{η}_{MM} satisfies

$$V = (TR - M)\Sigma - (C - TA)$$

where matrices A and C have been built before receiving the random Σ. We have

$$\begin{aligned} \text{wt}_R(M - TR) &\geq \text{wt}_R(M) - \text{wt}_R(TR) \\ &\geq (r + \delta) - r = \delta \end{aligned}$$

It means that $TR - M$ has at least δ non-zero coefficients $(i_1, j_1), \ldots, (i_\delta, j_\delta)$ which are over δ different rows and over δ different columns, *i.e.*

$$\forall k_1, k_2 \in [\delta],\ (i_{k_1} \neq i_{k_2}) \wedge (j_{k_1} \neq j_{k_2}).$$

Let us consider $k \in [\delta]$. The j_kth row of Σ is uniformly sampled in $\mathbb{F}_q^{\eta}$ and thus the i_kth row of $(M - TR)\Sigma$ is uniformly random in $\mathbb{F}_q^{\eta}$ (because one term of the sum is uniformly random). Thus, the probability that the i_kth row of V is zero is the probability that $(M - TR)\Sigma$ is equal to $(C - TA)$ on the row i_k whereas the row i_k of $(M - TR)\Sigma$ is uniformly random in $\mathbb{F}_q^{\eta}$, *i.e.* the probability that the i_kth row of V is zero is $\frac{1}{q^{\eta}}$. By taking a union bound over all k, we get that the probability that V is zero is at most $\frac{1}{q^{\delta \cdot \eta}}$. □

Using Linearized Polynomials. In what follows, we represent a matrix of $\mathbb{F}_q^{m\times n}$ as an element of $(\mathbb{F}_q^m)^n$. We want to design an MPC protocol which checks that a matrix $M = (x_1, \dots, x_n) \in (\mathbb{F}_{q^m})^n$ has a rank of at most r. Equivalently, it means that all x_i belongs to an $\mathbb{F}_q$-linear subspace U of $\mathbb{F}_{q^m}$ of dimension r. Let us define the polynomial $L_U(X)$ as

$$L_U(X) := \prod_{u\in U}(X-u) \in \mathbb{F}_{q^m}[X].$$

The degree of L_U is q^r since U has q^r elements. Showing that $\mathrm{wt}(M) \leq r$ can be done by showing that all x_i's are roots of L_U.

According to [LN96, Theorem 3.52], L_U is a q-polynomial over $\mathbb{F}_{q^m}$, meaning that it is of the form

$$L_U(X) = X^{q^r} + \sum_{i=0}^{r-1}\beta_i X^{q^i}.$$

Such polynomials are convenient for multi-party computation since the Frobenius endomorphism $X \mapsto X^q$ is a linear application in field extensions of $\mathbb{F}_q$ and thus it is communication-free to compute $[\![x^q]\!], [\![x^{q^2}]\!], \dots$ from $[\![x]\!]$.

The core idea of the rank checking protocol is to check that $L_U(x_1) = L_U(x_2) = \dots = L_U(x_n) = 0$. To proceed, the MPC protocol will batch these checkings by uniformly sampling $\gamma_1, \dots, \gamma_n \in \mathbb{F}_{q^m}$ and checking that

$$\sum_{j=1}^{n}\gamma_j \cdot L_U(x_j) = 0. \tag{2}$$

If one x_i is not a root of the polynomial L_U, then Eq. (2) is satisfied only with probability $\frac{1}{q^m}$. Let us rewrite the left term of (2):

$$\begin{aligned}\sum_{j=1}^{n}\gamma_j \cdot L_U(x_j) &= \sum_{j=1}^{n}\gamma_j \cdot \left(x_j^{q^r} + \sum_{i=0}^{r-1}\beta_i x_j^{q^i}\right)\\ &= \underbrace{\sum_{j=1}^{n}\gamma_j \cdot x_j^{q^r}}_{:=-z} + \sum_{i=0}^{r-1}\beta_i \cdot \underbrace{\sum_{j=1}^{n}\gamma_j x_j^{q^i}}_{:=w_i}\end{aligned}$$

By defining $z := -\sum_{j=1}^{n}\gamma_j \cdot x_j^{q^r}$ and $w_i := \sum_{j=1}^{n}\gamma_j x_j^{q^i}$ for $i \in \{0, \dots, r-1\}$, proving Eq. (2) is equivalent to proving

$$z = \langle \beta, w\rangle.$$

Our MPC protocol that we will denote $\Pi^{\eta}_{textRC-LP}$ takes as input $[\![x_1]\!], \dots, [\![x_n]\!]$ and $[\![L_U]\!] := X^{q^r} + \sum_{i=0}^{r-1}[\![\beta_i]\!]X^{q^i}$ proceeds as follows:

1. The parties get random $\gamma_1, \dots, \gamma_n \in \mathbb{F}_{q^{m\cdot\eta}}$.
2. The parties locally set $[\![z]\!] = -\sum_{j=1}^{n}\gamma_j[\![x_j]\!]^{q^r}$.

3. The parties locally set $[\![w_i]\!] = \sum_{j=1}^{n} \gamma_j [\![x_j]\!]^{q^i}$ for all $i \in \{0, \ldots, r-1\}$.
4. The parties execute the protocol Π_{MM} to check that $z = \langle \beta, w \rangle$ over $\mathbb{F}_{q^{m \cdot \eta}}$.

Theorem 2. *If* $\text{wt}_R(M) \leq r$ *and if* L_U *are genuinely computed, then* $\Pi^{\eta}_{textRC-LP}$ *always outputs* ACCEPT. *If* $\text{wt}_R(M) > r$*, then* $\Pi^{\eta}_{textRC-LP}$ *outputs* ACCEPT *with probability at most* $\frac{1}{q^{m \cdot \eta}} + \left(1 - \frac{1}{q^{m \cdot \eta}}\right) \frac{1}{q^{m \cdot \eta}}$.

Proof. $[\![L_U]\!]$ is a q-polynomial over $\mathbb{F}_{q^m}$ of degree exactly q^r. It means that its number of roots is at most q^r. According to [LN96, Theorem 3.50], the roots form a $\mathbb{F}_q$-linear subspace V of the field extension $\mathbb{F}_{q^s}$ of $\mathbb{F}_{q^m}$. Since $\mathbb{F}_{q^m}$ is also a linear subspace of $\mathbb{F}_{q^s}$, $V \cap \mathbb{F}_{q^m}$ is a linear subspace of $\mathbb{F}_{q^s}$ (and of $\mathbb{F}_{q^m}$). Its dimension is at most r (since it has at most q^r elements). If $\text{wt}_R(M) > r$, there exist i^* such that

$$L_U(x_{i^*}) \neq 0.$$

We then have two options resulting in $\Pi^{\eta}_{textRC-LP}$ outputing ACCEPT:

- Either $\sum_{j=1}^{n} \gamma_j \cdot L_U(x_j) = 0$, which occurs with probability $\frac{1}{q^{m \cdot \eta}}$;
- Or $\sum_{j=1}^{n} \gamma_j \cdot L_U(x_j) \neq 0$, *i.e.* $z \neq \langle \beta, w \rangle$ and Π_{MM} outputs ACCEPT, which occurs with probability $\frac{1}{q^{m \cdot \eta}}$ since Π_{MM} has a false positive rate of $\frac{1}{q^{m \cdot \eta}}$. □

4.2 Proof of Knowledge for MinRank

We want to build a zero-knowledge proof of knowledge for the *MinRank problem*:

Definition 2 (MinRank Problem). *Let* (q, m, n, k) *be positive integers. The MinRank problem with parameters* (q, m, n, k) *is the following problem:*

Let $M_0, M_1, \ldots, M_k$*,* E *and* x *such that:*
- x *is uniformly sampled from* $\mathbb{F}_q^k$*,*
- *for all* $i \in [k]$*,* M_i *is uniformly sampled from* $\mathbb{F}_q^{n \times m}$*,*
- E *is uniformly sampled from* $\{E \in \mathbb{F}_q^{n \times m} : \text{wt}_R(E) \leq w\}$*,*
- M_0 *is defined as* $M_0 = E - \sum_{i=1}^{k} x_i M_i$*.*

From $(M_0, M_1, \ldots, M_k)$*, find* x*.*

The prover wants to convince the verifier that she knows such an x. To proceed, the prover will first share the secret vector x and then use an MPC protocol which verifies that this vector satisfies the above property.

MPC Protocol. We want to build an MPC protocol which takes as input (a sharing of) x and which outputs

$$\begin{cases} \text{ACCEPT} & \text{if } \text{wt}_R(E) \leq r \\ \text{REJECT} & \text{otherwise.} \end{cases}$$

where $E := M_0 + \sum_{i=1}^{k} x_i M_i$.

Given $[\![x]\!]$, the parties can locally build $[\![E]\!]$ as $M_0 + \sum_{i=1}^{k} [\![x_i]\!] M_i$. It remains to check that $[\![E]\!]$ corresponds to the sharing of a matrix of rank at most r. It can be done using one of the two rank checking protocols described in Sect. 4.1: $\Pi^{\eta}_{textRC-RD}$ relying on the rank decomposition or $\Pi^{\eta}_{textRC-LP}$ relying on linearized polynomials, for some parameter η.

The complete MPC protocol is described in Fig. 3 when relying on the rank decomposition and in Fig. 4 when relying on linearized polynomials. In the second case, the rows of the matrix E are rewritten as elements of $\mathbb{F}_{q^m}$, but when $m \neq n$, it can be more convenient to work on the columns (depending of the values of m and n).

Public values: $M_0, M_1, \ldots, M_k \in \mathbb{F}_q^{n \times m}$.

Inputs: Each party takes a share of the following sharings as inputs: $[\![x]\!]$ where $x \in \mathbb{F}_q^k$, $[\![T]\!]$ where $T \in \mathbb{F}_q^{n \times r}$, $[\![R]\!]$ where $R \in \mathbb{F}_q^{r \times m}$, $[\![a]\!]$ where a has been uniformly sampled from $\mathbb{F}_q^{r \times \eta}$, and $[\![c]\!] \in \mathbb{F}_q^{n \times \eta}$, such that $M_0 + \sum_{i=1}^{k} x_i M_i = TR$ and $c = Ta$.

MPC Protocol:

1. The parties get a random $\Sigma \in \mathbb{F}_q^{m \times \eta}$.
2. The parties locally set $[\![E]\!] = M_0 + \sum_{i=1}^{k} [\![x_i]\!] M_i$.
3. The parties locally set $[\![\alpha]\!] = [\![R]\!]\Sigma + [\![a]\!]$.
4. The parties open $\alpha \in \mathbb{F}_q^{r \times \eta}$.
5. The parties locally set $[\![v]\!] = [\![T]\!]\alpha - [\![c]\!] - [\![E]\!]\Sigma$.
6. The parties open $v \in \mathbb{F}_q^{n \times \eta}$.
7. The parties outputs ACCEPT if $v = 0$ and REJECT otherwise.

Fig. 3. An MPC protocol based on the *rank decomposition* technique ($\Pi_{textRC-RD}$) which verifies that the given input corresponds to a solution of a MinRank problem.

Proof of Knowledge. Using the MPC-in-the-Head paradigm (see Sect. 2.1), we transform the above MPC protocol into an interactive zero-knowledge proof of knowledge which enables us to convince a verifier that a prover knows the solution of a MinRank problem. The soundness error of the resulting protocol is

$$\varepsilon := \frac{1}{N} + \left(1 - \frac{1}{N}\right) p_\eta$$

where $p_\eta := \frac{1}{q^\eta}$ when using $\Pi^{\eta}_{textRC-RD}$ and $p_\eta := \frac{2}{q^{m \cdot \eta}} - \frac{1}{q^{2 \cdot m \cdot \eta}}$ when using $\Pi^{\eta}_{textRC-LP}$. By repeating the protocol τ times, we get a soundness error of ε^τ. To obtain a soundness error of λ bits, we can take $\tau = \left\lceil \frac{-\lambda}{\log_2 \varepsilon} \right\rceil$. We can transform the interactive protocol into a non-interactive proof/signature thanks to the Fiat-Shamir transform [FS87]. According to [KZ20], the security of the resulting scheme is

$$\text{cost}_{\text{forge}} := \min_{\tau_1, \tau_2 : \tau_1 + \tau_2 = \tau} \left\{ \frac{1}{\sum_{i=\tau_1}^{\tau} \binom{\tau}{i} p_\eta^i (1 - p_\eta)^{\tau - i}} + N^{\tau_2} \right\}.$$

Public values: $M_0, M_1, \ldots, M_k \in \mathbb{F}_q^{n\times m}$.

Inputs: Each party takes a share of the following sharings as inputs: $[\![x]\!]$ where $x \in \mathbb{F}_q^k$, $[\![L_U]\!] := X^{q^r} + \sum_{i=0}^{r-1} [\![\beta_i]\!] X^{q^i}$ where $L_U(X) := \prod_{u\in U}(X-u) \in \mathbb{F}_{q^m}[X]$, $[\![a]\!]$ where a has been uniformly sampled from $\mathbb{F}_{q^{m\cdot\eta}}^r$, and $[\![c]\!] \in \mathbb{F}_{q^{m\cdot\eta}}$, such that $c = -\langle\beta, a\rangle$.

MPC Protocol:

1. The parties get random $\gamma_1, \ldots, \gamma_n \in \mathbb{F}_{q^{m\cdot\eta}}$.
2. The parties get a random $\varepsilon \in \mathbb{F}_{q^{m\cdot\eta}}$.
3. The parties locally set $[\![E]\!] = M_0 + \sum_{i=1}^k [\![x_i]\!] M_i$.
4. The parties locally write the rows of $[\![E]\!]$ as elements $(e_1, \ldots, e_m)$ of $\mathbb{F}_{q^m}$
5. The parties locally set $[\![z]\!] = -\sum_{j=1}^n \gamma_j [\![e_j]\!]^{q^r}$.
6. The parties locally set $[\![w_i]\!] = \sum_{j=1}^n \gamma_j [\![e_j]\!]^{q^i}$ for all $i \in \{0, \ldots, r-1\}$.
7. The parties locally set $[\![\alpha]\!] = \varepsilon \cdot [\![w]\!] + [\![a]\!]$.
8. The parties open $\alpha \in \mathbb{F}_{q^{m\cdot\eta}}^r$.
9. The parties locally set $[\![v]\!] = \varepsilon \cdot [\![z]\!] - \langle\alpha, [\![\beta]\!]\rangle - [\![c]\!]$.
10. The parties open $v \in \mathbb{F}_{q^{m\cdot\eta}}$.
11. The parties outputs Accept if $v = 0$ and Reject otherwise.

Fig. 4. An MPC protocol based on the technique using *linearized polynomials* ($\Pi_{textRC-LP}$) which verifies that the given input corresponds to a solution of a Min-Rank problem. U is a $\mathbb{F}_q$-linear subspace of $\mathbb{F}_{q^m}$ of dimension r which contains the rows $(e_1, \ldots, e_n)$ of $E := M_0 + \sum_{i=1}^k x_i M_i \in \mathbb{F}_q^{n\times m}$ represented as elements of $\mathbb{F}_{q^m}$.

When using $\Pi_{textRC-RD}$, the communication cost of the scheme (in bits) is

$$4\lambda + \tau \cdot \left((\underbrace{k}_{x} + \underbrace{r\times m}_{R} + \underbrace{r\times n}_{T} + \underbrace{r\times\eta}_{\alpha} + \underbrace{n\times\eta}_{c}) \cdot \log_2 q + \underbrace{\lambda \cdot \log_2 N + 2\lambda}_{\text{MPCitH}} \right)$$

where λ is the security level, r is a scheme parameter and τ is computed such that the soundness error is of λ bits in the interactive case and such that $\text{cost}_{\text{forge}}$ is of λ bits in the non-interactive case.

And when using $\Pi_{textRC-LP}$, the communication cost of the scheme (in bits) is

$$4\lambda + \tau \cdot \left((\underbrace{k}_{x} + \underbrace{r\times m}_{L_U} + \underbrace{r\times m\times\eta}_{\alpha} + \underbrace{m\times\eta}_{c}) \cdot \log_2 q + \underbrace{\lambda \cdot \log_2 N + 2\lambda}_{\text{MPCitH}} \right).$$

The public key corresponds to the $k+1$ matrices $M_0, \ldots, M_k$. The matrices $M_1, \ldots, M_k$ can be represented by a λ-bit seed and [BESV22] showed that we can generate M_0 such that it requires only $(mn-k)\log_2 q$ bits to send. The size of the public key is thus $\lambda + (mn-k)\log_2 q$ bits.

Performance and Comparison. In what follows, we compare our scheme with the state of the art on the MinRank instance [BESV22]:

$$(q, m, n, k, r) = (16, 16, 16, 142, 4),$$

which targets the security level that corresponds to the NIST category I. We provide in Table 2 a complete comparison of our scheme with the state of the art. To provide a fair comparison, we propose two variants for [Cou01, SINY22]: the first one corresponds to the scheme as described in the original article and the second one is a version optimized with several tricks to save communication (see Appendix B.2 for the description of those tricks). In the comparison, we put how [BG22, Section 2] would perform if we apply the same technique for MinRank problem ([BG22] does not consider the MinRank problem in their article).

First, let us remark that [SINY22] presents no advantage compared to [Cou01]. The soundness error of each iteration is 1/2 instead of 2/3, but each iteration is more expensive. The achieved communication cost is thus equivalent to [Cou01]. [BESV22] is a protocol with helper [Beu20]. The components in the proof transcript are the same as for [Cou01] (and [SINY22]), but it succeeds in achieving a bit smaller signature size just by sending a smaller number of seeds and digests. The MPC-in-the-Head paradigm enables to obtain much smaller sizes. Using techniques from [BG22], the resulting size is around 10 KB. In an independent work, [ARZV22] recently proposes a new scheme using techniques which are similar to our protocol with $\Pi_{textRC-RD}$: they are working on another matrix relation[2] but use a less efficient matrix multiplication checking protocol. They succeed in producing signatures with sizes below 8 KB. Our scheme with $\Pi_{textRC-RD}$ achieves similar sizes as [ARZV22], but our scheme with $\Pi_{textRC-LP}$ outperforms all the previous ones achieving sizes below 6 KB. For the sake of completeness, we put in the comparison tables how [ARZV22] would perform if we use Π_{MM} as a subroutine.

4.3 Proof of Knowledge for Rank SD

We want to build a zero-knowledge proof of knowledge for the *rank syndrome decoding problem*:

Definition 3 (Rank Syndrome Decoding Problem - Standard Form). *Let $\mathbb{F}_{q^m}$ be the finite field with q^m elements. Let (n, k, r) be positive integers such that $k \leq n$. The rank syndrome decoding problem with parameters (q, m, n, k, r) is the following problem:*

Let H, x and y be such that:
1. *H is uniformly sampled from $\{(H'|I_{n-k}), H' \in \mathbb{F}_{q^m}^{(n-k)\times n}\}$,*
2. *x is uniformly sampled from $\{x \in \mathbb{F}_{q^m}^n : \mathrm{wt}_R(x) \leq r\}$,*
3. *y is built as $y := Hx$.*

From (H, y), find x.

The prover wants to convince the verifier that she knows such an x, *i.e.* a vector $x \in \mathbb{F}_{q^m}^n$ such that $y = Hx$ and $\mathrm{wt}_R(x) \leq r$. Previous works propose proofs of knowledge where the constraint on the weight is an equality, but it is sometimes easier to just prove an inequality (see [FJR22] for the case of the

[2] They express the $m - r$ last columns *w.r.t.* the r first ones.

Table 2. Comparison of the signatures relying on the MinRank problem (restricting to the schemes using the FS heuristics). Numerical comparison. We refer the reader to Table 6 (Appendix B) for the formulae giving the signature sizes for all those schemes.

Instance	Protocol Name	Variant	Parameters				Signature Size	Public Key Size
			N	M	τ	η		
$q = 16$ $m = 16$ $n = 16$ $k = 142$ $r = 4$	[Cou01]	-	-	-	219	-	52 430 B	73 B
		Optimized	-	-	219	-	28 575 B	
	[SINY22]	-	-	-	128	-	50 640 B	
		Optimized	-	-	128	-	28 128 B	
	[BESV22]	-	-	256	128	-	26 405 B	
	[BG22]	Fast	8	187	49	-	13 644 B	
		Short	32	389	28	-	10 937 B	
	[ARZV22]	Fast	32	-	28	-	10 116 B	
		Short	256	-	18	-	7 422 B	
	[ARZV22]+Π_{MM}	Fast	32	-	33	9	8 155 B	
		Short	256	-	19	9	6 277 B	
	Our scheme (RD)	Fast	32	-	33	5	9 288 B	
		Short	256	-	19	9	7 122 B	
	Our scheme (LP)	Fast	32	-	28	1	7 204 B	
		Short	256	-	18	1	**5 518 B**	

Hamming weight). To proceed, the prover will first share the secret vector x and then use an MPC protocol that verifies that this vector satisfies the above property.

MPC Protocol. We want to build an MPC protocol which takes as input (a sharing of) x and which outputs

$$\begin{cases} \text{ACCEPT} & \text{if } y = Hx \text{ and } \mathrm{wt}_R(x) \leq r \\ \text{REJECT} & \text{otherwise.} \end{cases}$$

Since H is in standard form, the equality $y = Hx$ implies that x can be written as

$$x = \begin{pmatrix} x_A \\ y - H'x_A \end{pmatrix}$$

for some $x_A \in \mathbb{F}_q^k$. Therefore, we will build an MPC protocol which takes as input (a sharing of) x_A and which outputs

$$\begin{cases} \text{ACCEPT} & \text{if } \mathrm{wt}_R(x) \leq r \text{ where } x := \begin{pmatrix} x_A \\ y - H'x_A \end{pmatrix} \\ \text{REJECT} & \text{otherwise.} \end{cases}$$

Given $[\![x_A]\!]$, the parties can locally build $[\![x_B]\!]$ as $[\![x_B]\!] := y - H'[\![x_A]\!]$, and so they can deduce a sharing $[\![x]\!]$ of x (simply by concatenating the shares of $[\![x_A]\!]$

with the shares of $[\![x_B]\!]$). It remains to check that $[\![x]\!]$ corresponds to the sharing of a vector of $\mathbb{F}_{q^m}^n$ of rank at most r. The latter can be done using one of the two rank checking protocols described in Sect. 4.1: $\Pi^\eta_{textRC-RD}$ relying on the rank decomposition or $\Pi^\eta_{textRC-LP}$ relying on linearized polynomials, for some parameter η.

The complete MPC protocol is described in Fig. 5 when relying on the rank decomposition and in Fig. 6 when relying on linearized polynomials.

Public values: $H = (H'|I_{n-k}) \in \mathbb{F}_{q^m}^{(n-k)\times n}$ and $y \in \mathbb{F}_{q^m}^{n-k}$.

Inputs: Each party takes a share of the following sharings as inputs: $[\![x_A]\!]$ where $x_A \in \mathbb{F}_{q^m}^k$, $[\![T]\!]$ where $T \in \mathbb{F}_q^{n\times r}$, $[\![R]\!]$ where $R \in \mathbb{F}_q^{r\times m}$, $[\![a]\!]$ where a has been uniformly sampled from $\mathbb{F}_q^{r\times\eta}$, and $[\![c]\!]$ where $c \in \mathbb{F}_q^{n\times\eta}$, such that $c = Ta$ and $X = TR$ where X is the matrix form of x.

MPC Protocol:

1. The parties get a random $\Sigma \in \mathbb{F}_q^{m\times\eta}$.
2. The parties locally set $[\![x_B]\!] = y - H'[\![x_A]\!]$.
3. The parties locally write $[\![x]\!] := ([\![x_A]\!], [\![x_B]\!])$ as a matrix $[\![X]\!]$.
4. The parties locally set $[\![\alpha]\!] = [\![R]\!]\Sigma + [\![a]\!]$.
5. The parties open $\alpha \in \mathbb{F}_q^{r\times\eta}$.
6. The parties locally set $[\![v]\!] = [\![T]\!]\alpha - [\![c]\!] - [\![X]\!]\Sigma$.
7. The parties open $v \in \mathbb{F}_q^{m\times\eta}$.
8. The parties outputs Accept if $v = 0$ and Reject otherwise.

Fig. 5. An MPC protocol based on the *rank decomposition* technique ($\Pi_{textRC-RD}$) which verifies that the given input corresponds to a solution of a rank syndrome decoding problem.

Proof of Knowledge. Using the MPC-in-the-Head paradigm (see Sect. 2.1), we transform the above MPC protocol into an interactive zero-knowledge proof of knowledge which enables us to convince a verifier that a prover knows the solution of a rank syndrome decoding problem. The soundness error of the resulting protocol is

$$\varepsilon := \frac{1}{N} + \left(1 - \frac{1}{N}\right) p_\eta$$

where $p_\eta := \frac{1}{q^\eta}$ when using $\Pi^\eta_{textRC-RD}$ and $p_\eta := \frac{2}{q^{m\cdot\eta}} - \frac{1}{q^{2\cdot m\cdot\eta}}$ when using $\Pi^\eta_{textRC-LP}$. By repeating the protocol τ times, we get a soundness error of ε^τ. To obtain a soundness error of λ bits, we can take $\tau = \left\lceil \frac{-\lambda}{\log_2 \varepsilon} \right\rceil$. We can transform the interactive protocol into a non-interactive proof/signature thanks to the Fiat-Shamir transform [FS87]. According to [KZ20], the security of the resulting scheme is

$$\mathrm{cost}_{\mathrm{forge}} := \min_{\tau_1,\tau_2:\tau_1+\tau_2=\tau} \left\{ \frac{1}{\sum_{i=\tau_1}^{\tau} \binom{\tau}{i} p_\eta^i (1-p_\eta)^{\tau-i}} + N^{\tau_2} \right\}.$$

Public values: $H = (H'|I_{n-k}) \in \mathbb{F}_{q^m}^{(n-k)\times n}$ and $y \in \mathbb{F}_{q^m}^{n-k}$.

Inputs: Each party takes a share of the following sharings as inputs: $[\![x_A]\!]$ where $x \in \mathbb{F}_{q^m}^k$, $[\![L_U]\!] := X^{q^r} + \sum_{i=0}^{r-1} [\![\beta_i]\!] X^{q^i}$ where $L_U(X) := \prod_{u\in U}(X-u) \in \mathbb{F}_{q^m}[X]$, $[\![a]\!]$ where a has been uniformly sampled from $\mathbb{F}_{q^{m\cdot\eta}}^r$, and $[\![c]\!] \in \mathbb{F}_{q^{m\cdot\eta}}$, such that $c = -\langle\beta, a\rangle$.

MPC Protocol:

1. The parties get random $\gamma_1,\dots,\gamma_n \in \mathbb{F}_{q^{m\cdot\eta}}$.
2. The parties get a random $\varepsilon \in \mathbb{F}_{q^{m\cdot\eta}}$.
3. The parties locally set $[\![x_B]\!] = y - H'[\![x_A]\!]$.
4. The parties locally set $[\![z]\!] = -\sum_{j=1}^n \gamma_j [\![x_j]\!]^{q^r}$.
5. The parties locally set $[\![w_i]\!] = \sum_{j=1}^n \gamma_j [\![x_j]\!]^{q^i}$ for all $i \in \{0,\dots,r-1\}$.
6. The parties locally set $[\![\alpha]\!] = \varepsilon \cdot [\![w]\!] + [\![a]\!]$.
7. The parties open $\alpha \in \mathbb{F}_{q^{m\cdot\eta}}^r$.
8. The parties locally set $[\![v]\!] = \varepsilon \cdot [\![z]\!] - \langle\alpha, [\![\beta]\!]\rangle - [\![c]\!]$.
9. The parties open $v \in \mathbb{F}_{q^{m\cdot\eta}}$.
10. The parties outputs ACCEPT if $v = 0$ and REJECT otherwise.

Fig. 6. An MPC protocol based on the technique using *linearized polynomials* ($\Pi_{textRC-LP}$) which verifies that the given input corresponds to a solution of a rank syndrome decoding problem. U is a $\mathbb{F}_q$-linear subspace U of $\mathbb{F}_{q^m}$ of dimension r which contains $x_1,\dots,x_n$.

When using $\Pi_{textRC-RD}$, the communication cost of the scheme (in bits) is

$$4\lambda + \tau \cdot \left((\underbrace{k\cdot m}_{x_A} + \underbrace{r\times m}_{R} + \underbrace{r\times n}_{T} + \underbrace{r\times\eta}_{\alpha} + \underbrace{n\times\eta}_{c}) \cdot \log_2 q + \underbrace{\lambda\cdot\log_2 N + 2\lambda}_{\text{MPCitH}} \right)$$

where λ is the security level, η is a scheme parameter and τ is computed such that the soundness error is of λ bits in the interactive case and such that $\text{cost}_{\text{forge}}$ is of λ bits in the non-interactive case.

And when using $\Pi_{textRC-LP}$, the communication cost of the scheme (in bits) is

$$4\lambda + \tau \cdot \left((\underbrace{k\cdot m}_{x_A} + \underbrace{r\times m}_{L_U} + \underbrace{r\times m\times\eta}_{\alpha} + \underbrace{m\times\eta}_{c}) \cdot \log_2 q + \underbrace{\lambda\cdot\log_2 N + 2\lambda}_{\text{MPCitH}} \right).$$

The public key corresponds to the matrix H which can be represented by a λ-bit seed and the vector $y \in \mathbb{F}_{q^m}^{n-k}$. Its size is thus $\lambda + m(n-k)\log_2 q$ bits.

Performance and Comparison. In what follows, we compare our scheme with the state of the art on the Rank Syndrome Decoding instance [BG22]:

$$(q, m, n, k, r) = (2, 32, 30, 14, 9),$$

which targets a 128-bit security level. We provide in Table 3 a complete comparison of our scheme with the state of the art. To get a more complete comparison, we include the schemes [Ste94, Vér96, FJR21] which can be easily adapted for the rank metric (by replacing the permutations by rank isometries). Moreover, we put in Table 3 the achieved performance of [BG22] when relying on the structured rank syndrome decoding problem (the parameters of the structured problem come from the original article).

The first schemes [Ste94] and [Vér96] can achieve signature sizes of around 30 KB (let us remark that some optimization tricks have been used to achieve these sizes). Then, using the MPC-in-the-Head technique of the "shared permutation", [FJR21] and [BG22] divide this size by half, achieving communication cost around 15 KB (13–19 KB). Finally, our new schemes outperform all these schemes by achieving sizes around 6–11 KB. The scheme using a q-polynomial even outperforms the [BG22]'s proposals[3] which rely on structured rank syndrome decoding problems.

Table 3. Sizes of the signatures relying on the rank syndrome decoding problem (restricting to the schemes using the FS heuristics). Numerical comparison. We refer the reader to Table 7 (Appendix B) for the formulae giving the signature sizes for all those schemes.

Instance	Protocol Name	Variant	Parameters				Signature Size	Public Key Size
			N	M	τ	η		
$q=2$, $m=31$, $n=30$, $k=15$, $r=9$	Stern [Ste94]	-	-	-	219	-	31 358 B	75 B
	Véron [Vér96]	-	-	-	219	-	27 115 B	
	[FJR21]	Fast	8	187	49	-	19 328 B	
		Short	32	389	28	-	14 181 B	
	[BG22]	Fast	8	187	49	-	15 982 B	
		Short	32	389	28	-	12 274 B	
	Our scheme (RD)	Fast	32	-	33	19	11 000 B	
		Short	256	-	21	24	8 543 B	
	Our scheme (LP)	Fast	32	-	30	1	7 376 B	
		Short	256	-	20	1	**5 899 B**	
Ideal RSD	[BG22]	Fast	32	-	37	-	12 607 B	95 B
		Short	256	-	26	-	10 126 B	
Ideal RSL	[BG22]	Fast	32	-	27	-	9 392 B	410 B
		Short	256	-	17	-	6 754 B	

5 Running Times

To provide a fair comparison of our work with the state of the art, we need to give an estimation of the computational performances of our proposals. The best way

[3] Theses sizes are larger than the ones in [BG22] because they take $N = 1024$, but here to have a fair comparison with the other schemes, we take $N = 256$.

to proceed would be to have optimized implementations for them, but producing such implementations requires dedicated work for each of the proposed signature schemes. Since the code of those schemes would be similar except for the part about the MPC protocols, we decided to develop a unified MPC-in-the-Head library[4]. The idea is to factorize as much as possible the common code of the MPCitH-based signatures. As long as they respect the expected API, a user just needs to implement the code that generates an instance of the hard problem with its solution and the code that corresponds to the computation of a party in the MPC protocol. Then they can rely on the library to get the desired signature scheme. Thanks to this library, we were able to estimate the running times of the schemes proposed in this article.

Until recently, the only way to implement an MPCitH-based proof system was by emulating all the parties of the underlying MPC protocol, implying that we would need to emulate N times a party per repetition. The recent work [AGH+23] changes this drastically. The authors suggest generating the input shares of the parties in a correlated way using a hypercube approach. This optimization enables us to emulate only $1 + \log_2(N)$ parties per repetition. For example, in Sect. 3, we propose to take $\tau = 25$ and $N = 256$ for the "short" trade-off of our scheme. Without the optimization of [AGH+23], we would need to emulate $\tau \cdot N = 6400$ times a party per signing. With it, we just need to emulate $\tau \cdot (1 + \log_2 N) = 225$ times a party, reducing the computational cost of the MPC emulation by a factor of 28.

We included the [AGH+23] optimization in the library. The obtained signing times are given in Table 4. We put the running time of [AGH+23] for SDitH in the table, but to provide a fairer comparison with the other schemes, we reimplement it using our library and give the achieved performances. In our implementations, the pseudo-randomness is generated using AES in counter mode, the hash function is instantiated with SHA3, and the MPC challenge (*i.e.* the challenge provided by $\mathcal{O}_R$, see Sect. 2.1) is sampled using SHAKE. We benchmarked our schemes on a 3.8 GHz Intel Core i7-10700K CPU with the support of AVX2 and AES instructions (disabling Intel Turbo Boost).

In our benchmarks, we decompose the running time of our schemes in six parts: the expansion of the seed trees, the commitments of the input shares, the expansion of the input shares from seeds, the remaining operations to prepare input shares (*e.g.* the computation of the shares of the "main" parties of the hypercube technique), the emulation of the MPC protocol and the rest of the computation.

We optimized the factorized code which mainly relies on symmetric primitives. For example, we rely on fourfold calls of Keccak (for SHA3) using AVX instructions. However, the arithmetic parts used by the MPC protocols have *not been optimized*, since it would require dedicated work for each scheme (and is out of the scope of this article).

In Table 4, we did not give the running times for the key generation and the signature verification. For all these schemes, the key generation is fast since it

[4] This library is available at `https://github.com/CryptoExperts/libmpcith`.

Table 4. Benchmark of our implementations of the proposed signature schemes (128 bits of security). All the timings are given in milliseconds, except those in the column "in Mc" which are given in megacycles. Timings with * correspond to the implementation of [AGH+23], while timings with ❖ correspond to our own implementation of SDitH using the library. The verification is around 5 – 10% faster than the signing.

Scheme	Tree	Commit.	Rand. xpans.	Share Prep.	MPC Emul.	Misc	Total signing time		Size
	in ms						in ms	in Mc	in bytes
Variant "Short" – 256 parties (N = 256)									
SDitH [FJR22]	-	-	-	-	-	-	3–7*	-	8 459
	0.93	0.97	0.61	0.29	4.57	0.41	7.78❖	30	
MQ over $\mathbb{F}_{256}$	1.37	1.42	0.53	0.40	6.25	0.59	10.56	40	7 114
MQ over $\mathbb{F}_{251}$	1.37	1.42	1.24	1.77	2.17	0.59	8.56	33	7 114
MinRank (with RD)	1.06	1.11	1.52	0.51	3.75	0.44	8.39	32	7 122
MinRank (with LP)	0.99	1.05	1.12	0.45	13.23	0.38	17.22	65	5 518
Rank SD (with RD)	1.16	1.22	0.69	0.27	2.36	0.42	6.12	23	8 543
Rank SD (with LP)	1.10	1.14	0.51	0.24	3.72	0.38	7.09	27	5 899
Variant "Fast" – 32 parties (N = 32)									
SDitH [FJR22]	-	-	-	-	-	-	1.3-3.8*	-	11 835
	0.20	0.22	0.12	0.04	5.35	0.17	6.10❖	23	
MQ over $\mathbb{F}_{256}$	0.26	0.28	0.10	0.05	6.9	0.24	7.83	30	8 488
MQ over $\mathbb{F}_{251}$	0.26	0.28	0.22	0.23	2.15	0.28	3.42	13	8 488
MinRank (with RD)	0.24	0.27	0.28	0.07	2.68	0.16	3.70	14	9 288
MinRank (with LP)	0.20	0.23	0.21	0.12	13.63	0.15	14.54	55	7 204
Rank SD (with RD)	0.24	0.27	0.13	0.07	2.30	0.18	3.19	12	11 000
Rank SD (with LP)	0.22	0.24	0.09	0.03	3.71	0.12	4.41	17	7 376

only consists in generating a random instance of the underlying hard problem. It usually takes less than 0.5 ms. Moreover, for all the MPCitH-based schemes relying on additive sharings, the verification time is similar (slightly smaller) to the signing time since the verifier must re-emulate the MPC protocol (as the prover) except for one party (to keep the zero-knowledge property).

We provide an analysis of the obtained running times in Appendix C. In this article, we propose two MPC protocols to check that a matrix has a small rank: one based on rank decomposition (RD), and one based on q-polynomials (LP). The second protocol leads to smaller signature sizes, but it tends to be less efficient in running timing since it involves computation in a field extension. From the benchmark, we can observe that both protocols give similar running times when applied to the rank syndrome decoding problem. However, when applied to MinRank, the MPC protocol based on q-polynomials gives a slow scheme. As explained previously, the arithmetics of the implementations have not been optimized. The scheme "MinRank (with LP)" suffers from this lack of optimizations[5].

[5] Let us also remark that the difference of performance between both implementations of SDitH mainly comes from that our arithmetic of $\mathbb{F}_{256}$ has not been optimized.

Appendix

A Methodology

In each section of this article, we focus on a specific hard problem which is supposed quantum-resilient:

- Sect. 3: Multivariate Quadratic Problem;
- Sect. 4.2: Min Rank Problem;
- Sect. 4.3: Syndrome Decoding in the *rank* metric;

For each of them, we will use the MPC-in-the-Head paradigm to build a new zero-knowledge protocol. To proceed, we will first describe the MPC protocol we use. This MPC protocol will fit the model described in [FR22] and will satisfy the following properties:

- it takes as input an additive sharing of a candidate solution of the studied problem, and eventually an additive sharing of auxiliary data;
- the MPC parties get (only once) a common random value from an oracle $\mathcal{O}_R$;
- when the tested solution is valid (*i.e.* a solution of the studied hard problem) and when the auxiliary data are genuinely computed, the MPC protocol always outputs ACCEPT; otherwise, it outputs ACCEPT with probability at most p (over the randomness of $\mathcal{O}_R$), where p is called the *false positive rate*;
- the views of all the parties except one leak no information about the candidate solution.

By applying the MPC-in-the-Head paradigm to this MPC protocol, we get a 5-round zero-knowledge proof of knowledge of a solution of the studied problem (see [FR22, Theorem 2] with the privacy threshold $\ell := N - 1$), with soundness error

$$\frac{1}{N} + \left(1 - \frac{1}{N}\right) \cdot p$$

where N is the number of parties involved in the multi-party computation. We do not exhibit the obtained proof of knowledge since the transformation is standard. We refer the reader to [FR22] for a detailed explanation of how to concretely apply the MPC-in-the-Head paradigm.

To obtain a signature scheme, we apply the Fiat-Shamir transform [FS87] to the previous protocol. Since this protocol has 5 rounds, the security of the resulting scheme should take into account the attack of [KZ20]. More precisely, the forgery cost of the signature scheme is given by

$$\text{cost}_{\text{forge}} := \min_{\tau_1, \tau_2 : \tau_1 + \tau_2 = \tau} \left\{ \frac{1}{\sum_{i=\tau_1}^{\tau} \binom{\tau}{i} p^i (1-p)^{\tau - i}} + N^{\tau_2} \right\}$$

where τ is the number of parallel executions.

Finally, we compare the resulting scheme with all the former schemes which are non-interactive identification schemes based on the same security assumption. We select one or two instances of the studied hard problem and we compare all these schemes for these precise instances. To proceed, we need to select the parameters of the schemes when relevant. The signature schemes based on the MPC-in-the-Head paradigm have as parameter the number N of parties involved in the multi-party computation. When taking a small N, we get a faster scheme, but when taking a large N, we get shorter signature sizes. To have a fair comparison between the different schemes, we will always take the same N:

- when the protocol relies on a helper, we take $N = 8$ to have a fast scheme and $N = 32$ to have short sizes.
- otherwise, we take $N = 32$ to have a fast scheme and $N = 256$ to have short sizes.

A.1 MPCitH Optimizations

It is often possible to optimize the communication cost of a scheme relying on the MPC-in-the-Head paradigm. The common optimization tricks are the following:

- Except for the last party, the input share of a party can be derived from a seed using a pseudo-random generator. Thus, when we need to reveal the input share, we just need to reveal a seed. In practice, a prover must reveal the input shares of $N-1$ parties, so it would imply revealing $N-1$ seeds. To save more communication, we can generate the seeds using a tree structure, decreasing the number of revealed seeds to $\log_2(N)$ (see [KKW18, Sect. 2.3] for details).
- We do not need to reveal shares for shared random values (as A in Fig. 1) since they can be entirely derived from the seeds of the previous point.
- We do not need to reveal shares for shared publicly-known values (see [KZ22, Sect. 2.4] for details). For example, we do not need to reveal the share of V broadcast by the hidden party in Fig. 1. Indeed, this share can be deduced from the shares of the other parties and knowing that V must be equal to zero (otherwise the verification fails).

B State of the Art – Performances

In this appendix, we list all the schemes used in the comparisons, with their formulae of the forgery security and of the communication cost. Since some quantities occur several times, we define some notations to ease the readability. For the forgery cost, we introduce the two following notations:

- $\varepsilon_{\text{helper}}(\tau, M, \varepsilon)$ is the soundness error of a protocol with helper [Beu20] when the helper entity is emulated by a cut-and-choose phase. M is the total number of repetitions in the cut-and-choose phase, ε is the soundness of the unitary protocol relying on the helper, and τ is the number of repetitions of this unitary protocol. We have

$$\varepsilon_{\text{helper}}(\tau, M, \varepsilon) := \max_{M-\tau \leq k \leq M} \left\{ \frac{\binom{k}{M-\tau}}{\binom{M}{M-\tau}} \cdot \varepsilon^{k-(M-\tau)} \right\}.$$

- $\mathrm{KZ}(p_1, p_2)$ is the forgery cost of [KZ20] for a 5-round protocol[6]. We have

$$\mathrm{KZ}(p_1, p_2) := \min_{\tau_1,\tau_2:\tau_1+\tau_2=\tau} \left\{ \frac{1}{\sum_{i=\tau_1}^{\tau} \binom{\tau}{i} p_1^i (1-p_1)^{\tau-i}} + \frac{1}{p_2^{\tau_2}} \right\}$$

For the communication cost (*i.e.* the signature size), we introduce the following notations:

- μ_{seed} is the cost of sending a λ-bit seed;
- μ_{dig} is the cost of sending a 2λ-bit commitment/hash digest;
- μ_{helper} is the cost (per repetition) of using the helper technique of [Beu20], this cost satisfies

$$\mu_{\text{helper}} \leq (\mu_{\text{seed}} + \mu_{\text{dig}}) \cdot \log_2 \binom{M}{\tau}$$

  where M is the number of repetitions involved in the cut-and-choose phase emulating the helper. It corresponds to the cost of revealing $M - \tau$ leaves among M in a seed tree, with the cost of sending the authentication paths of τ leaves among M in a Merkle tree.
- μ_{MPCitH} is the fixed cost (per repetition) of using the MPC-in-the-Head paradigm, we have

$$\mu_{\text{MPCitH}} = \mu_{\text{seed}} \cdot \log_2 N + \mu_{\text{dig}}.$$

  It corresponds to the cost of revealing all the leaves but one in a seed tree of N leaves (plus a commitment digest).

B.1 Multivariate Quadratic Problem

We provide in Table 5 the current state of the art about FS-based signature schemes relying on the multivariate quadratic problem.

B.2 MinRank Problem

We provide in Table 6 the current state of the art about FS-based signature schemes relying on the MinRank problem. To provide a fair comparison, we propose two variants for [Cou01, SINY22]: the first one corresponds to the scheme as described in the original article and the second one is an optimized version. This optimized version includes the following tricks:

- Instead of revealing all the commitments during the first round, the prover just sends a hash digest of them. Then, to enable the verifier to recompute this digest, the prover just needs to send the commitment digests that the verifier can not compute herself.

[6] In the case where the verifier can not perform some checks after receiving the first response (see [KZ20] for details).

Table 5. Sizes of the signatures relying on the $\mathcal{MQ}$ problem (restricting to the schemes using the FS heuristics). The used notations are: $\mu_{\text{var}} := n \log_2 q$, $\mu_{\text{out}} := m \log_2 q$, plus all the notations defined in Appendix B.

Scheme Name	Security	Signature Size
[SSH11] (3 rounds)	$(3/2)^\tau$	$\mu_{\text{dig}} + \tau\,[2\mu_{\text{var}} + \mu_{\text{out}} + 2\mu_{\text{dig}}]$
MQ-DSS [CHR+16]	$\text{KZ}(\frac{1}{q}, \frac{1}{2})$	$2\mu_{\text{dig}} + \tau\,[2\mu_{\text{var}} + \mu_{\text{out}} + 2\mu_{\text{dig}}]$
MUDFISH [Beu20]	$\varepsilon_{\text{helper}}(\tau, M, \frac{1}{q'})^{-1}$	$\mu_{\text{dig}} + \tau\,[2\mu_{\text{var}} + \mu_{\text{out}} + 2\mu_{\text{seed}} + \mu_{\text{dig}} \cdot \log_2(q') + \mu_{\text{helper}}]$
Mesquite [Wan22]	$\varepsilon_{\text{helper}}(\tau, M, \frac{1}{N})^{-1}$	$\mu_{\text{dig}} + \tau\,[\mu_{\text{var}} + \mu_{\text{out}} + \mu_{\text{MPCitH}} + \mu_{\text{helper}}]$
Our scheme	$\text{KZ}(\frac{2}{q^\eta} - \frac{1}{q^{2\eta}}, \frac{1}{N})$	$2\mu_{\text{dig}} + \tau\,[(1+\eta) \cdot \mu_{\text{var}} + \eta \cdot \log_2 q + \mu_{\text{MPCitH}}]$

- The random combination used in the schemes (usually denoted β) is derived from a seed. Then, instead of sending the coefficients of β, the prover can just send this seed. Moreover, this seed and the masks involved in the schemes (usually denoted T, S and X) are also derived from a *common* seed.
- Instead of revealing two matrices such that the difference is of rank (at most) r, the prover sends one of the matrices and directly the difference (which is cheaper to send), and thus the verifier can deduce the non-sent matrix.

Table 6. Sizes of the signatures relying on the MinRank problem (restricting to the schemes using the FS heuristics). The used notations are: $\mu_{\text{mat}} := mn \log 2q$, $\mu_{\text{rank}} := r(m+n)\log_2 q$, $\mu_{\text{combi}} := k \log_2 q$, plus all the notations defined in Appendix B.

Scheme Name	Security	Signature Size
[Cou01]	$(3/2)^\tau$	$3\tau \cdot \mu_{\text{dig}} + \tau\,[\frac{2}{3}\mu_{\text{mat}} + \frac{2}{3}\mu_{\text{combi}} + \frac{2}{3}\mu_{\text{seed}}]$
[Cou01], opt.	$(3/2)^\tau$	$\mu_{\text{dig}} + \tau\,[\frac{1}{3}(\mu_{\text{mat}} + \mu_{\text{rank}} + \mu_{\text{combi}} + 2\mu_{\text{seed}}) + \mu_{\text{dig}}]$
[SINY22]	2^τ	$6\tau \cdot \mu_{\text{dig}} + \tau\,[\mu_{\text{mat}} + \frac{1}{2}\mu_{\text{combi}} + \frac{10}{4}\mu_{\text{seed}}]$
[SINY22], opt.	2^τ	$\mu_{\text{dig}} + \tau\,[\frac{1}{2}(\mu_{\text{mat}} + \mu_{\text{rank}} + \mu_{\text{combi}} + 3\mu_{\text{seed}}) + 2\mu_{\text{dig}}]$
[BESV22]	$\varepsilon_{\text{helper}}(\tau, M, \frac{1}{2})^{-1}$	$\mu_{\text{dig}} + \tau\,[\frac{1}{2}(\mu_{\text{mat}} + \mu_{\text{rank}} + \mu_{\text{combi}} + \mu_{\text{seed}}) + \mu_{\text{dig}} + \mu_{\text{helper}}]$
[BG22]	$\varepsilon_{\text{helper}}(\tau, M, \frac{1}{N})^{-1}$	$\mu_{\text{dig}} + \tau\,[\mu_{\text{combi}} + \mu_{\text{rank}} + \mu_{\text{MPCitH}} + \mu_{\text{helper}}]$
[ARZV22]	$\text{KZ}(\frac{1}{q^n}, \frac{1}{N})$	$2\mu_{\text{dig}} + \tau\,[\mu_{\text{combi}} + (n^2 + 2rn - r^2)\log_2 q + \mu_{\text{MPCitH}}]$
[ARZV22]+Π_{MM}	$\text{KZ}(\frac{1}{q^\eta}, \frac{1}{N})$	$2\mu_{\text{dig}} + \tau\,[\mu_{\text{combi}} + (r(n-r) + \eta(n-2r))\log_2 q + \mu_{\text{MPCitH}}]$
Our scheme (RD)	$\text{KZ}(\frac{1}{q^\eta}, \frac{1}{N})$	$2\mu_{\text{dig}} + \tau\,[\mu_{\text{combi}} + \mu_{\text{rank}} + \eta(n+r)\log_2 q + \mu_{\text{MPCitH}}]$
Our scheme (LP)	$\text{KZ}(\frac{2}{q^{m\eta}} - \frac{1}{q^{2m\eta}}, \frac{1}{N})$	$2\mu_{\text{dig}} + \tau\,[\mu_{\text{combi}} + rm\log_2 q + \eta(r+1)m\log_2 q + \mu_{\text{MPCitH}}]$

B.3 Rank Syndrome Decoding Problem

We provide in Table 7 the current state of the art about FS-based signature schemes relying on the rank syndrome decoding problem.

Table 7. Sizes of the signatures relying on the rank syndrome decoding problem (restricting to the schemes using the FS heuristics). The used notations are: $\mu_{\mathrm{mat}} := mn \log 2q$, $\mu_{\mathrm{rank}} := r(m+n)\log_2 q$, $\mu_{\mathrm{ptx}} := mk \log_2 q$, plus all the notations defined in Appendix B.

Scheme Name	Security	Signature Size
[Ste94]	$(3/2)^\tau$	$\mu_{\mathrm{dig}} + \tau \left[\frac{1}{3}(2\mu_{\mathrm{mat}} + \mu_{\mathrm{rank}} + 2\mu_{\mathrm{seed}}) + \mu_{\mathrm{dig}}\right]$
[Vér96]	$(3/2)^\tau$	$\mu_{\mathrm{dig}} + \tau \left[\frac{1}{3}(\mu_{\mathrm{mat}} + \mu_{\mathrm{ptx}} + \mu_{\mathrm{rank}} + 2\mu_{\mathrm{seed}}) + \mu_{\mathrm{dig}}\right]$
[FJR21]	$\varepsilon_{\mathrm{helper}}(\tau, M, \frac{1}{N})^{-1}$	$\mu_{\mathrm{dig}} + \tau \left[\mu_{\mathrm{mat}} + \mu_{\mathrm{ptx}} + \mu_{\mathrm{rank}} + \mu_{\mathrm{MPCitH}} + \mu_{\mathrm{helper}}\right]$
[BG22]	$\varepsilon_{\mathrm{helper}}(\tau, M, \frac{1}{N})^{-1}$	$\mu_{\mathrm{dig}} + \tau \left[\mu_{\mathrm{mat}} + \mu_{\mathrm{rank}} + \mu_{\mathrm{MPCitH}} + \mu_{\mathrm{helper}}\right]$
Our scheme (RD)	$\mathrm{KZ}(\frac{1}{q^\eta}, \frac{1}{N})$	$2\mu_{\mathrm{dig}} + \tau \left[\mu_{\mathrm{ptx}} + \mu_{\mathrm{rank}} + \eta(n+r)\log_2 q + \mu_{\mathrm{MPCitH}}\right]$
Our scheme (LP)	$\mathrm{KZ}(\frac{2}{q^{m\cdot\eta}} - \frac{1}{q^{2\cdot m\cdot\eta}}, \frac{1}{N})$	$2\mu_{\mathrm{dig}} + \tau \left[\mu_{\mathrm{ptx}} + rm\log_2 q + \eta(r+1)m\log_2 q + \mu_{\mathrm{MPCitH}}\right]$

C Benchmark Analysis

Here is an analysis of the running times obtained in Table 4:

- **Tree Expansion**: it consists in deriving N seeds from a master seed using the structure of a binary tree. This operation only depends on the number of parties N, and it is repeated at each repetition (*i.e.* τ times). Thus, when we fix N, the computation contribution is linear in τ. It can be observed from the benchmark: when $N = 32$, it takes $0.0073 \cdot \tau$ ms, and when $N = 256$ it takes $0.055 \cdot \tau$ ms.
- **Commitment**: it consists in committing the input shares of N parties. In practice, it consists in committing a λ-bit seed for all the parties except the last one. The cost of committing the entire input share of the last party tends to be negligible compared to the cost of committing $N-1$ seeds. Thus, the computation contribution of the commitments is roughly linear in $N \cdot \tau$. From the benchmark, we get that it takes $0.0575 \cdot \tau$ ms when $N = 256$ and $0.0082 \cdot \tau$ ms when $N = 32$ (committing a seed with a salt takes around 220 nanoseconds).
- **Randomness Expansion**: it consists in expanding seeds to get input shares. The computational cost depends on the number τ of repetitions, the size of the input shares, and the field from which elements should be sampled. When the field is an extension of $\mathbb{F}_2$, the sampling can be efficient. However, sampling in another field is less efficient since we need to deal with rejection. It explains why the cost of this step is larger for MQ over $\mathbb{F}_{251}$ than for MQ over $\mathbb{F}_{256}$.
- **Share Preparation:** it consists in getting the input share of the last party from the other ones and in computing the shares of the "main" parties of the hypercube technique (see [AGH+23] for details). It depends on τ, the size of the input shares, and the additive law of the underlying field. This step is very efficient when working in characteristic two since the addition is the bitwise XOR. When working in prime fields, we need to deal with reduction.
- **MPC Emulation:** it consists in emulating the MPC protocols. Thanks to the hypercube technique, it consists in emulating $1 + \log_2(N)$ parties by repetition. The important point to remark here is that the choice of N does

not impact a lot the emulation cost. It comes from that $\tau \approx \frac{\lambda}{\log_2(N)}$, so the total computation cost of the emulation corresponds[7] to the cost of emulating $\tau \cdot (1 + \log_2(N)) \approx \lambda + \frac{\lambda}{\log_2(N)}$ parties.

- **Misc**: it corresponds to the rest of the signing computation (decompression of the public key, building the signature, ...).

References

[ABB+23a] Aragon, N., et al.: RYDE specifications, June 2023 (2023). https://csrc.nist.gov/csrc/media/Projects/pqc-dig-sig/documents/round-1/spec-files/ryde-spec-web.pdf

[ABB+23b] Aragon, N., et al.: MIRA specifications, June 2023 (2023). https://csrc.nist.gov/csrc/media/Projects/pqc-dig-sig/documents/round-1/spec-files/MIRA-spec-web.pdf

[AGH+23] Aguilar-Melchor, C., Gama, N., Howe, J., Hülsing, A., Joseph, D., Yue, D.: The return of the SDitH. In: Hazay, C., Stam, M. (eds.) EUROCRYPT 2023, Part V. LNCS, vol. 14008, pp. 564–596. Springer, Cham (2023). https://doi.org/10.1007/978-3-031-30589-4_20

[ARS+15] Albrecht, M.R., Rechberger, C., Schneider, T., Tiessen, T., Zohner, M.: Ciphers for MPC and FHE. In: Oswald, E., Fischlin, M. (eds.) EUROCRYPT 2015, Part I. LNCS, vol. 9056, pp. 430–454. Springer, Heidelberg (2015). https://doi.org/10.1007/978-3-662-46800-5_17

[ARZV22] Adj, G., Rivera-Zamarripa, L., Verbel, J.: MinRank in the head: short signatures from zero-knowledge proofs. Cryptology ePrint Archive, Report 2022/1501 (2022). https://eprint.iacr.org/2022/1501

[ARZV+23] Adj, G., et al.: MiRith (MinRank in the head), June 2023 (2023). https://csrc.nist.gov/csrc/media/Projects/pqc-dig-sig/documents/round-1/spec-files/MiRitH_spec-web.pdf

[BBPS21] Barenghi, A., Biasse, J.-F., Persichetti, E., Santini, P.: LESS-FM: fine-tuning signatures from the code equivalence problem. In: Cheon, J.H., Tillich, J.-P. (eds.) PQCrypto 2021 2021. LNCS, vol. 12841, pp. 23–43. Springer, Cham (2021). https://doi.org/10.1007/978-3-030-81293-5_2

[BESV22] Bellini, E., Esser, A., Sanna, C., Verbel, J.: MR-DSS - smaller MinRank-based (ring-)signatures. In: Cheon, J.H., Johansson, T. (eds.) PQCrypto 2022. LNCS, vol. 13512, pp. 144–169. Springer, Cham (2022). https://doi.org/10.1007/978-3-031-17234-2_8

[Beu20] Beullens, W.: Sigma protocols for MQ, PKP and SIS, and fishy signature schemes. In: Canteaut, A., Ishai, Y. (eds.) EUROCRYPT 2020, Part III. LNCS, vol. 12107, pp. 183–211. Springer, Cham (2020). https://doi.org/10.1007/978-3-030-45727-3_7

[Beu22] Beullens, W.: MAYO: practical post-quantum signatures from oil-and-vinegar maps. In: AlTawy, R., Hülsing, A. (eds.) SAC 2021. LNCS, vol. 13203, pp. 355–376. Springer, Cham (2022). https://doi.org/10.1007/978-3-030-99277-4_17

[7] We omit here that τ is larger than $\frac{\lambda}{\log_2(N)}$ to be secure against the forgery attack of [KZ20], but the conclusion would be the same.

[BG22] Bidoux, L., Gaborit, P.: Compact post-quantum signatures from proofs of knowledge leveraging structure for the PKP, SD and RSD problems (2022). https://arxiv.org/abs/2204.02915

[BHK+19] Bernstein, D.J., Hülsing, A., Kölbl, S., Niederhagen, R., Rijneveld, J., Schwabe, P.: The SPHINCS$^+$ signature framework. In: Cavallaro, L., Kinder, J., Wang, X.F., Katz, J. (eds.) ACM CCS 2019, pp. 2129–2146. ACM Press, November 2019

[BMPS20] Biasse, J.-F., Micheli, G., Persichetti, E., Santini, P.: LESS is more: code-based signatures without syndromes. In: Nitaj, A., Youssef, A. (eds.) AFRICACRYPT 2020. LNCS, vol. 12174, pp. 45–65. Springer, Cham (2020). https://doi.org/10.1007/978-3-030-51938-4_3

[BMSV22] Bellini, E., Makarim, R.H., Sanna, C., Verbel, J.: An estimator for the hardness of the MQ problem. In: Batina, L., Daemen, J. (eds.) AFRICACRYPT 2022. LNCS, vol. 13503, pp. 323–347. Springer, Cham (2022). https://doi.org/10.1007/978-3-031-17433-9_14

[BN20] Baum, C., Nof, A.: Concretely-efficient zero-knowledge arguments for arithmetic circuits and their application to lattice-based cryptography. In: Kiayias, A., Kohlweiss, M., Wallden, P., Zikas, V. (eds.) PKC 2020, Part I. LNCS, vol. 12110, pp. 495–526. Springer, Cham (2020). https://doi.org/10.1007/978-3-030-45374-9_17

[CHR+16] Chen, M.-S., Hülsing, A., Rijneveld, J., Samardjiska, S., Schwabe, P.: From 5-pass $\mathcal{MQ}$-based identification to $\mathcal{MQ}$-based signatures. In: Cheon, J.H., Takagi, T. (eds.) ASIACRYPT 2016, Part II. LNCS, vol. 10032, pp. 135–165. Springer, Heidelberg (2016). https://doi.org/10.1007/978-3-662-53890-6_5

[CNP+23] Chou, T., et al.: Take your MEDS: digital signatures from matrix code equivalence. In: El Mrabet, N., De Feo, L., Duquesne, S. (eds.) AFRICACRYPT 2023. LNCS, vol. 14064, pp. 28–52. Springer, Cham (2023). https://doi.org/10.1007/978-3-031-37679-5_2

[Cou01] Courtois, N.T.: Efficient zero-knowledge authentication based on a linear algebra problem MinRank. In: Boyd, C. (ed.) ASIACRYPT 2001. LNCS, vol. 2248, pp. 402–421. Springer, Heidelberg (2001). https://doi.org/10.1007/3-540-45682-1_24

[DKR+21] Dobraunig, C., Kales, D., Rechberger, C., Schofnegger, M., Zaverucha, G.: Shorter signatures based on tailor-made minimalist symmetric-key crypto. Cryptology ePrint Archive, Report 2021/692 (2021). https://eprint.iacr.org/2021/692

[DST19] Debris-Alazard, T., Sendrier, N., Tillich, J.-P.: Wave: a new family of trapdoor one-way preimage sampleable functions based on codes. In: Galbraith, S.D., Moriai, S. (eds.) ASIACRYPT 2019, Part I. LNCS, vol. 11921, pp. 21–51. Springer, Cham (2019). https://doi.org/10.1007/978-3-030-34578-5_2

[FJR21] Feneuil, T., Joux, A., Rivain, M.: Shared permutation for syndrome decoding: new zero-knowledge protocol and code-based signature. Cryptology ePrint Archive, Report 2021/1576 (2021). https://eprint.iacr.org/2021/1576

[FJR22] Feneuil, T., Joux, A., Rivain, M.: Syndrome decoding in the head: Shorter signatures from zero-knowledge proofs. In: Dodis, Y., Shrimpton, T. (eds.) CRYPTO 2022, Part II. LNCS, vol. 13508, pp. 541–572. Springer, Heidelberg (2022). https://doi.org/10.1007/978-3-031-15979-4_19

[FMRV22] Feneuil, T., Maire, J., Rivain, M., Vergnaud, D.: Zero-knowledge protocols for the subset sum problem from MPC-in-the-head with rejection. Cryptology ePrint Archive, Report 2022/223 (2022). https://eprint.iacr.org/2022/223

[FR22] Feneuil, T., Rivain, M.: Threshold linear secret sharing to the rescue of MPC-in-the-head. Cryptology ePrint Archive, Report 2022/1407 (2022). https://eprint.iacr.org/2022/1407

[FR23] Feneuil, T., Rivain, M.: MQOM: MQ on my mind - algorithm specifications and supporting documentation. Version 1.0 - 31 May 2023 (2023). https://csrc.nist.gov/csrc/media/Projects/pqc-dig-sig/documents/round-1/spec-files/MQOM-spec-web.pdf

[FS87] Fiat, A., Shamir, A.: How to prove yourself: practical solutions to identification and signature problems. In: Odlyzko, A.M. (ed.) CRYPTO 1986. LNCS, vol. 263, pp. 186–194. Springer, Heidelberg (1987). https://doi.org/10.1007/3-540-47721-7_12

[IKOS07] Ishai, Y., Kushilevitz, E., Ostrovsky, R., Sahai, A.: Zero-knowledge from secure multiparty computation. In: Johnson, D.S., Feige, U.: (eds.) 39th ACM STOC, pp. 21–30. ACM Press, June 2007

[KKW18] Katz, J., Kolesnikov, V., Wang, X.: Improved non-interactive zero knowledge with applications to post-quantum signatures. In: Lie, D., Mannan, M., Backes, M., Wang, X.F. (eds.) ACM CCS 2018, pp. 525–537. ACM Press, October 2018

[KPG99] Kipnis, A., Patarin, J., Goubin, L.: Unbalanced oil and vinegar signature schemes. In: Stern, J. (ed.) EUROCRYPT 1999. LNCS, vol. 1592, pp. 206–222. Springer, Heidelberg (1999). https://doi.org/10.1007/3-540-48910-X_15

[KZ20] Kales, D., Zaverucha, G.: An attack on some signature schemes constructed from five-pass identification schemes. In: Krenn, S., Shulman, H., Vaudenay, S. (eds.) CANS 2020. LNCS, vol. 12579, pp. 3–22. Springer, Cham (2020). https://doi.org/10.1007/978-3-030-65411-5_1

[KZ22] Kales, D., Zaverucha, G.: Efficient lifting for shorter zero-knowledge proofs and post-quantum signatures. Cryptology ePrint Archive, Report 2022/588 (2022). https://eprint.iacr.org/2022/588

[LN96] Lidl, R., Niederreiter, H.: Finite fields. In: Encyclopedia of Mathematics and its Applications, 2 edn. University Press, Cambridge (1996)

[NIS22] NIST: Call for Additional Digital Signature Schemes for the Post-Quantum Cryptography Standardization Process (2022)

[SINY22] Santoso, B., Ikematsu, Y., Nakamura, S., Yasuda, T.: Three-pass identification scheme based on MinRank problem with half cheating probability (2022). https://arxiv.org/abs/2205.03255

[SSH11] Sakumoto, K., Shirai, T., Hiwatari, H.: Public-key identification schemes based on multivariate quadratic polynomials. In: Rogaway, P. (ed.) CRYPTO 2011. LNCS, vol. 6841, pp. 706–723. Springer, Heidelberg (2011). https://doi.org/10.1007/978-3-642-22792-9_40

[Ste94] Stern, J.: A new identification scheme based on syndrome decoding. In: Stinson, D.R. (ed.) CRYPTO 1993. LNCS, vol. 773, pp. 13–21. Springer, Heidelberg (1994). https://doi.org/10.1007/3-540-48329-2_2

[Vér96] Véron, P.: Improved identification schemes based on error-correcting codes. Appl. Algebra Eng. Commun. Comput. **8**(1), 57–69 (1996)

[Wan22] Wang, W.: Shorter signatures from MQ. Cryptology ePrint Archive, Report 2022/344 (2022). https://eprint.iacr.org/2022/344

Exploring SIDH-Based Signature Parameters

Andrea Basso[1], Mingjie Chen[2], Tako Boris Fouotsa[3], Péter Kutas[2,4], Abel Laval[5], Laurane Marco[3(✉)], and Gustave Tchoffo Saah[6]

[1] University of Bristol, Bristol, UK
andrea.basso@bristol.ac.uk
[2] University of Birmingham, Birmingham, UK
m.chen.1@bham.ac.uk
[3] EPFL, Lausanne, Switzerland
{tako.fouotsa,laurane.marco}@epfl.ch
[4] Eötvös Loránd University, Budapest, Hungary
p.kutas@bham.ac.uk
[5] Université Libre de Bruxelles, Brussels, Belgium
abel.laval@ulb.be
[6] Université de Yaoundé 1, Yaoundé, Cameroon

Abstract. Isogeny-based cryptography is an instance of post-quantum cryptography whose fundamental problem consists of finding an isogeny between two (isogenous) elliptic curves E and E'. This problem is closely related to that of computing the endomorphism ring of an elliptic curve. Therefore, many isogeny-based protocols require the endomorphism ring of at least one of the curves involved to be unknown. In this paper, we explore the design of isogeny based protocols in a scenario where one assumes that the endomorphism ring of all the curves are public. In particular, we identify digital signatures based on proof of isogeny knowledge from SIDH squares as such a candidate. We explore the design choices for such constructions and propose two variants with practical instantiations. We analyze their security according to three lines, the first consists of attacks based on KLPT with both polynomial and superpolynomial adversary, the second consists of attacks derived from the SIDH attacks and finally we study the zero-knowledge property of the underlying proof of knowledge.

1 Introduction

Isogeny-based cryptography is a promising candidate to develop quantum-secure protocols. At its core, lies the fundamental assumption that it is computationally hard to find an isogeny between two isogenous elliptic curves. When the curves are supersingular, the setting of nearly all modern constructions [10,16,18,21,25,27,33,38,41], the isogeny problem is strictly linked to the endomorphism ring problem. The latter asks to find a basis of the ring of all the endomorphisms of a supersingular elliptic curve, i.e. all the isogenies from the curve to itself. The problem of finding an isogeny between two elliptic curves

C. Pöpper and L. Batina (Eds.): ACNS 2024, LNCS 14583, pp. 432–456, 2024.
https://doi.org/10.1007/978-3-031-54770-6_17

reduces to the endomorphism-ring problem: given two curves and a representation of their endomorphism rings, it is possible to compute an isogeny connecting them in polynomial time [42,55].

Due to this connection, the endomorphism ring problem and its relationship to the security of many isogeny-based protocols have been extensively studied. The best known algorithm to compute endomorphism rings is due to Eisenträger, Hallgren, Leonardi, Morrison, and Park [29], and it runs in $\tilde{O}(p^{1/2})$ time, where p is the characteristic of the underlying finite field (the result relies on some heuristics which were removed in [35]). Given a curve E_0 with known endomorphism ring $\mathrm{End}(E_0)$, and an isogeny $\phi : E_0 \to E$, one can push the endomorphism ring $\mathrm{End}(E_0)$ of E_0 through ϕ to recover $\mathrm{End}(E)$ [42,55]. Thus, finding an isogeny between a curve E_0 with known endomorphism ring, and a given curve E solves the endomorphism ring problem for the curve E. Since the characteristic p is exponential in the security parameter in practice, the general endomorphism ring problem remains hard.

It remains of interest to understand how the security of isogeny-based protocols is affected when an attacker has knowledge of the endomorphism rings. In several protocols, such as the GPS signature [37], SÉTA [21], SQISign [25] and SQISignHD [20], the secret keys are directly linked to a description of the endomorphism ring. Thus, solving the endomorphism ring problem trivially breaks such protocols. In other schemes, such as SIDH [41], CSIDH [16] and SCALLOP [23], CSI-FiSh- [13], SeaSign [24] , the secret isogenies have specific properties: if the endomorphisms of all curves were known, a direct application of [42,55] would prevent obtaining the correct isogeny. Nonetheless, it has been shown that the additional information that such protocols reveal, such as short degrees, torsion images or orientations, is sufficient to recover the secret isogeny [17,32,36,54]. More recently proposed schemes, such as M-SIDH/MD-SIDH [33], FESTA [10] and binSIDH/terSIDH [8] compute isogenies of degree roughly $\sqrt{p}$ or even smaller, hence the attack in [36] trivially extends to those cases when endomorphism rings of curves are public. Moreover, many other protocols are insecure when the starting curves have known endomorphism ring. This is the case, for instance, for the CGL hash function [18,28], the CSIDH-based oblivious transfer protocols [5,43], the commitment scheme by Sterner [50], the SIDH-based oblivious pseudorandom functions [6,9,14], and the hash proof systems and dual-mode PKEs based on group actions [3].

The relevance of endomorphism rings in isogeny-based cryptography and the consequences of their knowledge on security raises the following natural question:

Can we construct a secure cryptographic protocol where the endomorphism rings of all curves are public?

One has to remark that one of the most natural algorithmic problems, namely finding an isogeny of a fixed degree d between supersingular elliptic curves, is not known to be equivalent to the endomorphism ring problem. An efficient classical equivalence between finding fixed degree isogenies and computing endomorphism rings would have important consequences, e.g., a significant speed-up of SQIsign. Understanding whether we can build protocols which are secure even if endomorphism rings of all curves is public has both theoretical and practical consequences. On the theoretical side, a protocol that remains secure when the endomorphism rings of all curves are known shows that, even if the endomorphism ring problem is efficiently solvable, some isogeny-based constructions are still possible, and retain some security. On the practical side, the complexity of the endomorphism-recovering attacks generally imposes primes p with $p > 2^{2\lambda}$; without requiring endomorphism rings to remain secret, it is possible to design protocols with smaller primes, leading to more efficient and more compact protocols.

Contributions. In this paper, we develop two protocols that appear to be secure, even if the endomorphism rings of all elliptic curves are public. This suggests an affirmative response to the question set out in the introduction (even though further cryptanalysis is necessary).

Both protocols are digital signatures, based on a proof of isogeny knowledge built on top of SIDH squares. In this work, we focus on digital signatures since it is the primitive that is most likely to be secure when endomorphism rings are known: the SIDH-based constructions generally reveal little information besides the degrees and the end curves of secret isogenies. Indeed, it is possible to construct SIDH-based signatures that do not reveal any torsion information [22] or that are statistically independent from the secret key [7].

In this work, we analyze existing constructions of proofs of isogeny knowledge and identify three main design choices (Sect. 3). We also propose two practical instantiations, which are plausibly secure despite the underlying prime field having characteristic smaller than $2^{2\lambda}$.

To analyze the security of the proposed constructions, we identify and study three main lines of attacks. The first approach relies on the knowledge of endomorphism rings and the KLPT algorithm [42]. We analyze these attacks extensively in Sect. 4. Moreover, the KLPT algorithm has always been considered for constructive applications, and thus its analysis in the literature is bounded to polynomial running times. In this work, we study the output of the KLPT algorithm when running in superpolynomial time, which may be of independent interest. The method used is a variation of [45, Section 3.4.].

We also consider attacks based on the recent attacks on SIDH (Sect. 5.1) and based on the lack of zero-knowledge of the underlying sigma protocol (Sect. 5.2). The results of these analyses shows that it is possible to design signatures based on proofs of isogeny knowledge with binary challenges, which are more efficient and compact than those based on proofs with ternary challenges (see Sect. 6 for an estimate of the concrete sizes). Combined with the previous analysis of KLPT-based attacks, this provides an argument for the security of the proposed constructions.

2 Preliminaries

2.1 Σ Protocols and Digital Signatures

Definition 1 (Sigma Protocol). *A sigma protocol is a three-move proof system for a language $\mathcal{L}$ consisting of oracle-calling* PPT *algorithms* $(P = (P_1, P_2), V = (V_1, V_2))$, *where V_2 is deterministic. We assume P_1 and P_2 share states and so do V_1 and V_2. Let* ChallSet *denote the challenge set. Then, the protocol proceeds as follows.*

- *The prover, on input* $(\mathsf{st}, \mathsf{wt}) \in \mathcal{L}$, *computes* $\mathsf{com} \longleftarrow P_1(\mathsf{st}, \mathsf{wt})$ *and sends the commitment* com *to the verifier.*
- *The verifier computes* $\mathsf{chall} \longleftarrow V_1(1^\lambda)$, *drawing a random challenge from* ChallSet, *and sends it to the prover.*
- *The prover, given* chall, *computes* $\mathsf{resp} \longleftarrow P_2(\mathsf{st}, \mathsf{wt}, \mathsf{chall})$ *and returns a response* resp *to the verifier.*
- *The verifier runs* $V_2(\mathsf{st}, \mathsf{com}, \mathsf{chall}, \mathsf{resp})$ *and outputs* $\top$ *(accept) or* $\perp$ *(reject).*

A sigma protocol is said to be *correct* if knowing wt is enough for the prover to convince the verifier that they indeed know the witness; it is said to be *n-special sound* if being able to produce n valid transcripts $(\mathsf{st}, \mathsf{com}, \mathsf{chall}_i, \mathsf{resp}_i)$, $i \in \{1, 2, \ldots, n\}$ for the same statement and commitment but for different challenges implies being able to compute a witness for this given statement st; it is zero-knowledge if anyone can simulate it and produce a valid transcript computationally indistinguishable from one obtained by actually running the protocol. If the soundness error of the protocol is too high, one can reduce it is using repetition.

If the statement is a public key and the witness is the corresponding secret key, we call such a protocol an *identification scheme*. It is typically used to give, as its name indicates, a proof of identity. Furthermore, a sigma protocol can be turned into a digital signature in the Random Oracle Model using the *Fiat-Shamir transform* [31].

2.2 Supersingular Isogenies

Let E_1 and E_2 be two supersingular curves defined over a finite field $\mathbb{F}_{p^2}$. An isogeny $\phi : E_1 \to E_2$ is a non-constant rational map which is also a group morphism with respect to the group structure of the elliptic curves. The degree of an isogeny is its degree as a rational map. It is always of the form $d = p^r d'$, and when $r = 0$ (that is $d = d'$ is coprime to p) we say the isogeny ϕ is separable and we have $d = \# \ker \phi$. The isogenies considered in this work are all separable, unless stated otherwise. An isogeny of small prime degree can be efficiently computed (and evaluated on torsion points) from a description of its kernel using Vélu formulas [52] or the square root Vélu formulas [11]. Isogenies of smooth degree can also be efficiently computed by writing them as a composition of isogenies of small prime degrees. For any isogeny $\phi : E_1 \to E_2$, there exists a unique isogeny $\widehat{\phi} : E_2 \to E_1$ such that $\widehat{\phi} \circ \phi = [\deg \phi]_{E_1}$ and $\phi \circ \widehat{\phi} = [\deg \phi]_{E_2}$.

The isogeny $\widehat{\phi}$ is called the dual of ϕ. An endomorphism of an elliptic curve E is an isogeny from E to E. The set of all the endomorphisms of E forms a ring under addition and composition. It is denoted by $\mathrm{End}(E)$ and its called the endomorphism ring of E. Over finite fields, the endomorphism ring of an elliptic curve is either an order in an imaginary quadratic field or a maximal order in a quaternion algebra. The earlier case occurs for ordinary curves while the later occurs for supersingular curves, which are the ones used in this paper.

2.3 Quaternion Algebra

Let p be a prime. We write $\mathcal{B}_{p,\infty}$ for the quaternion algebra ramified only at p and ∞, which is defined by

$$\mathcal{B}_{p,\infty} = \left(\frac{-q,-p}{\mathbb{Q}}\right) = \mathbb{Q} + i\mathbb{Q} + j\mathbb{Q} + k\mathbb{Q}$$

where $0 \neq q \in \mathbb{N}$, $i^2 = -q$, $j^2 = -p$, and $k = ij = -ji$.

A p-extremal maximal order is a maximal order containing j. Examples of p-extremal maximal order are those containing $\mathbb{Z}\langle i,j\rangle = \mathbb{Z} + i\mathbb{Z} + j\mathbb{Z} + k\mathbb{Z}$ as subring. For such a maximal order $\mathcal{O}$, if $R = \mathcal{O} \cap \mathbb{Q}[i]$ is the ring of integers $\mathbb{Z}[\omega]$ of $\mathbb{Q}[i]$, then the restriction of the norm to $R + Rj$ is given by

$$\mathrm{Nrd}(x_1 + y_1\omega + (x_2 + y_2\omega)j) = f(x_1, y_1) + pf(x_2, y_2)$$

where f is a principal quadratic form of discriminant $\mathrm{disc}(R)$ [42]. We have

$$f(x,y) = x^2 + \mathrm{Trd}(\omega)xy + \mathrm{Nrd}(\omega)y^2$$

We give below a few examples of the structure of $\mathcal{B}_{p,\infty}$, together with p-extremal order $\mathcal{O}$, R and $f(x,y)$ as defined above for different values of p.

Example 2. 1. For $p \equiv 3 \bmod 4$: $\mathcal{B}_{p,\infty} = \left(\frac{-1,-p}{\mathbb{Q}}\right)$; $\mathcal{O} = \langle 1, i, \frac{1+k}{2}, \frac{i+j}{2}\rangle$; $R = \mathbb{Z}[i]$; $f(x,y) = x^2 + y^2$.
2. For $p \equiv 5 \bmod 8$: $\mathcal{B}_{p,\infty} = \left(\frac{-2,-p}{\mathbb{Q}}\right)$; $\mathcal{O} = \langle 1, i, \frac{1+j+k}{2}, \frac{i+2j+k}{4}\rangle$; $R = \mathbb{Z}[i]$; $f(x,y) = x^2 + 2y^2$.
3. For $p \equiv 3 \bmod 4$: $\mathcal{B}_{p,\infty} = \left(\frac{-q,-p}{\mathbb{Q}}\right)$, where $q \equiv 1 \bmod 4$ is a prime such that $\left(\frac{-p}{q}\right) = 1$; $\mathcal{O} = \langle 1, \frac{1+i}{2}, j, \frac{ci+k}{q}\rangle$, where $c^2 \equiv -p \bmod q$; $R = \mathbb{Z}[\frac{1+i}{2}]$; $f(x,y) = x^2 - xy + \frac{1+q}{4}y^2$.

2.4 SIDH

The Supersingular Isogeny Diffie-Hellman (SIDH) protocol was introduced in 2011 by Jao and De Feo [41]. It is a Diffie-Hellman type key exchange that uses supersingular isogenies. Supersingular isogenies do not commute in general. In order to get a commutative diagram that will help compute the shared secret in

SIDH, the images of some torsion points basis through the secret isogenies are included in the public keys (see Fig. 1). Moreover, in order to achieve the best possible efficiency, one uses isogenies of degree 2^a or 3^b between supersingular elliptic curves defined over $\mathbb{F}_{p^2}$ where the characteristic p is of the form $p = 2^a 3^b f - 1$, with f being a small co-factor. Primes of the form $p = 2^a 3^b f - 1$ (or $p = \ell_1^{e_1} \ell_2^{e_2} f - 1$ more generally) are usually referred to as *SIDH primes.*

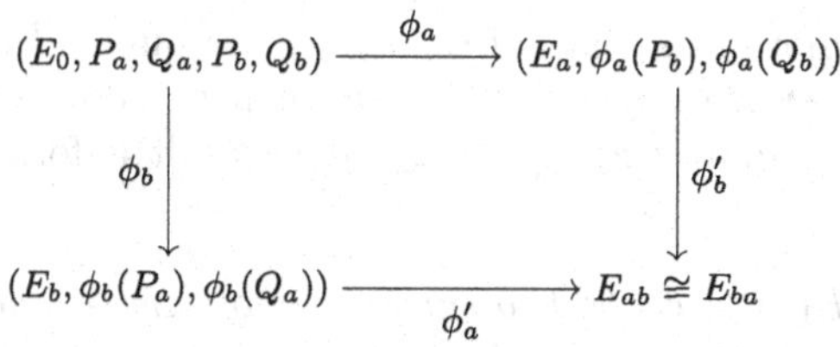

Fig. 1. The SIDH key exchange protocol

The detailed description of SIDH is as follows.

Setup. Let $p = 2^a 3^b f - 1$ be an SIDH prime and let E_0 be a supersingular elliptic curve defined over $\mathbb{F}_{p^2}$. Let $E_0[2^a] = \langle P_a, Q_a \rangle$ and $E_0[3^b] = \langle P_b, Q_b \rangle$.

Key Generation. Alice samples a random scalar $k_a \in \mathbb{Z}/2^a\mathbb{Z}$, and computes the isogeny $\phi_a : E_0 \to E_A$ whose kernel is $\langle P_a + [k_a]Q_a \rangle$. Her secret key is k_a and her public key is $(E_a, \phi_a(P_b), \phi_a(Q_b))$. Similarly, Bob samples a random scalar $k_b \in \mathbb{Z}/3^b\mathbb{Z}$, and computes the isogeny $\phi_b : E_0 \to E_B$ whose kernel is $\langle P_b + [k_b]Q_b \rangle$. His secret key is k_b and his public key is $(E_b, \phi_b(P_a), \phi_b(Q_a))$.

Shared Secret. Given Bob's public key $(E_b, \phi_b(P_a), \phi_b(Q_a))$, Alice computes the isogeny $\phi_a' : E_b \to E_{ba}$ whose kernel is generated by $\phi_b(P_a) + [k_a]\phi_b(Q_a)$. Given Alice's public key $(E_a, \phi_a(P_b), \phi_a(Q_b))$, Bob computes the isogeny $\phi_b' : E_a \to E_{ab}$ whose kernel is generated by $\phi_a(P_b) + [k_b]\phi_a(Q_b)$. The shared secret is $j(E_{ab}) = j(E_{ba})$.

In SIDH, the isogenies ϕ_A and ϕ_A' (resp. ϕ_B and ϕ_B') are said to be *parallel isogenies.* In general, two isogenies $\phi : E_0 \to E_1$ and $\phi' : E_2 \to E_3$ are said to be parallel if there exists an isogeny $\psi : E_0 \to E_2$ such that $\ker \phi' = \psi(\ker \phi)$. Note that if $\phi : E_0 \to E_1$ and $\phi' : E_2 \to E_3$ are parallel, then $\widehat{\phi} : E_1 \to E_0$ and $\widehat{\phi'} : E_3 \to E_2$ are also parallel since $\ker \widehat{\phi'} = \psi'(\ker \widehat{\phi})$ where ψ' is the isogeny whose kernel is given by $\ker \psi' = \phi(\ker \psi)$. We hence obtain a square (Eq. (1)) which is called an *SIDH square.*

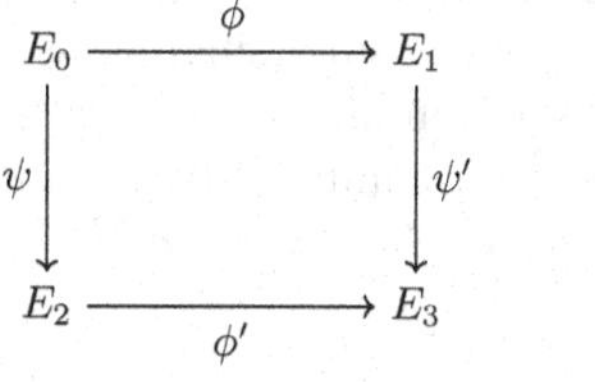

(1)

2.5 Algorithms for Computing Isogenies

We discuss some existing algorithms for computing isogenies that will be of interest in this paper. The main problem, which is that of finding an isogeny connecting two isogenous supersingular curves is believed to be hard. Nevertheless, it may not be the case when more information is provided: the endomorphism rings of the curves and/or some torsion point information and/or the degree of the isogeny.

When the endomorphism rings of the curves are public, then a result of [36] shows that the secret isogeny $\phi : E_1 \to E_2$ can be recovered whenever it is the shortest isogeny connecting E_1 to E_2. This result is formally given by the following theorem.

Theorem 3. *Let E_1 and E_2 be two supersingular curves, and let $\phi : E_1 \to E_2$ be the shortest isogeny connecting E_1 and E_2. Given a description the endomorphism rings $\mathcal{O}_1 \simeq End(E_1)$ and $\mathcal{O}_2 \simeq End(E_2)$, there exists an efficient algorithm that computes the isogeny ϕ.*

Note that Theorem 3 is a straightforward generalization of [36, Theorem 1] where the degree of the isogeny ϕ is a prime power to the case where there is no restriction on the degree of the isogeny. Two uniformly random supersingular curves are always connected by an isogeny of degree at most $O(\sqrt{p})$. Hence the attack in Theorem 3 does not help to recover isogenies of degree $d \gg \sqrt{p}$. In [32], it is shown that if some reasonable amount of torsion point information is provided beside the endomorphism rings, then the secret isogeny can be efficiently recovered. More precisely, we have the following theorem which can be found in [32, Theorem 3.8].

Theorem 4. *Let E_1 and E_2 be two supersingular curves, and let d be the degree of the shortest isogeny connecting E_1 and E_2. Let $\phi : E_1 \to E_2$ be an isogeny of degree $N_1 \geq d$. Let N_2 be a smooth integer, set $E_1[N_2] = \langle P, Q \rangle$. Given $\phi(P)$, $\phi(Q)$ and a description the endomorphism rings $\mathcal{O}_1 \simeq End(E_1)$ and $\mathcal{O}_2 \simeq End(E_2)$, there exists an efficient algorithm that computes the isogeny ϕ provided that $N_1 \leq \frac{dN_2}{16}$.*

In practice, the endomorphism ring of the co-domain curve of the isogeny is not provided. In 2017, Petit [47] described an attack that only requires the knowledge of a special endomorphism on the starting curve, and a large amount of torsion point information. This attack was later improved in [48] but still required torsion point images of large order. In 2022, a series of three papers [15, 44, 49] consecutively improved the state of art to reach a point where no known endomorphism is required and the amount of torsion point needed is way smaller than the degree of the isogeny: a supersingular isogeny of degree N_1 can be efficiently recovered from its action on torsion points of smooth order N_2 where $N_1 < N_2^2$. These results led to a complete break of SIDH and are summarized in Theorem 5, which is based on [49, Theorem 1].

Theorem 5. *Let E_1 and E_2 be two supersingular curves, let N_2 be a smooth integer and let $E_1[N_2] = \langle P, Q \rangle$. Let $\phi : E_1 \to E_2$ be an isogeny of degree N_1. Given $\phi(P)$, $\phi(Q)$ there exists an efficient algorithm that computes the isogeny ϕ provided that $N_1 < N_2^2$.*

It may happen that when attempting to recover the secret isogeny, one does not directly have access to torsion point images, but to images of some cyclic groups of the same order N. In [9,34], it is proven that if N has $O(\log \log p)$ prime factors, then one can efficiently recover the torsion point information from the images of three disjoint cyclic groups of order N. This implies that the secret isogeny can in fact be recovered from the images of three disjoint cyclic groups of order N.

3 Signatures Based on SIDH Squares

In this section, we recall various constructions of proofs of isogeny knowledge from the literature and we highlight the main design options. We also introduce the potential lines of attack against some constructions, which are analyzed in detail in the following sections. For a comprehensive survey of proofs of isogeny, we refer the reader to [12,40].

Let us assume that a prover wants to demonstrate knowledge of a cyclic isogeny $\phi : E_0 \to E_1$ of smooth degree d. The main framework, on which the following proofs are based on, is a sigma protocol due to De Feo, Jao, and Plût [30]. The prover generates the SIDH square in Eq. (1) where ψ has degree ℓ^n for some ℓ coprime with d, and they commit to E_2 and E_3. The verifier sends a challenge bit $c \in \{0, 1\}$: if $c = 0$, the prover responds with the horizontal isogeny ϕ', and if $c = 1$, the prover reveals the vertical isogenies ψ and ψ'. The verifier accepts if the response isogenies have the correct domain and codomain. The protocol has soundness error of 1/2, and thus it needs to be repeated λ times to obtain a negligible soundness error of $2^{-\lambda}$. As pointed out in [22,39] , a malicious prover may not necessarily know ϕ (such an isogeny might not exist at all); the proof in [30] is thus sound with respect to the weaker relation

$$\mathcal{R}_{\mathsf{weak}} = \left\{ ((E_0, E_1), \phi) \;\middle|\; \begin{array}{l} \phi : E_0 \to E_1 \text{ is a cyclic } \ell^{2i} d\text{-isogeny,} \\ \text{for some integer } i \text{ and } \ell \text{ coprime with } d \end{array} \right\}. \quad (2)$$

In the case of an honest prover, this proof also reveals the action of ϕ on the torsion $E[\deg \psi]$ since the isogenies ψ and ψ' are parallel. This makes it potentially vulnerable to the recent attacks on SIDH [15,44,49].

The authors of [22] showed that it is possible to have a proof that is sound with respect to the strong relation

$$\mathcal{R}_{\mathsf{strg}} = \{((E_0, E_1), \phi) \mid \phi : E_0 \to E_1 \text{ is a cyclic } d\text{-isogeny}\} \quad (3)$$

by ensuring that ψ and ψ' are parallel. However, to avoid the SIDH attacks and a technical issue with zero-knowledge[1], they have to resort to a proof with ternary challenges. Thus, to prove parallelness, the prover constructs the same SIDH square as in Eq. (1), but additionally commits to P_2, Q_2[2], a basis of $E_2[d]$, its image $P_3 := \phi'(P_2), Q_3 := \phi'(Q_2)$ on E_3, and the coefficients a, b such that $\ker \hat{\psi} = \langle [a]P_2 + [b]Q_2 \rangle$ and $\ker \hat{\psi}' = \langle [a]P_3 + [b]Q_3 \rangle$. The curves E_2 and E_3 are also committed with a hiding commitment scheme. Then, the challenges are ternary, i.e. $c \in \{-1, 0, 1\}$. When $c = \pm 1$, the verifier reveals a, b and either $(E_2, (P_2, Q_2))$ or $(E_3, (P_3, Q_3))$; the verifier reconstructs ψ or ψ' and ensures they have the correct codomain. In the case of $c = 0$, the verifier receives $(\phi', (E_2, P_2, Q_2), (E_3, P_3, Q_3))$ and checks that the points P_3, Q_3 are the images of P_2, Q_2 under ϕ'. In all cases, the verifier also ensures the revealed values match the previously committed ones.

More recently, [7] introduced the concept of an *SIDH ladder*, which is obtained by gluing multiple SIDH squares together. This removes the requirement on the prime being an SIDH prime. It is thus possible to prove knowledge of an isogeny ϕ in *any* characteristic and even if ϕ and ψ have kernels that are not defined over $\mathbb{F}_{p^2}$.

This historical overview suggests there are three main design choices that determine how a proof of isogeny knowledge works:

1. The soundness relation: strong vs weak,
2. The challenge space: binary vs ternary,
3. The characteristic p and the degrees of ϕ and ψ.

Note that not all combinations are possible. For instance, when the kernels of ψ and ψ' are not rational over $\mathbb{F}_{p^2}$, which requires using the SIDH ladder method proposed by [7], there is no known technique to prove the strong relation.

3.1 Proposed Constructions

We now discuss some promising combinations and study their securities in later sections. Let E_0 be a random supersingular elliptic curve, ℓ_1 be a small prime and e_1 be a positive integer. Our goal is to prove the knowledge of a secret isogeny $\phi : E_0 \to E_1$ of degree $\ell_1^{e_1}$ in $\mathcal{R}_{\mathsf{strg}}$.

Variant 1. This variant proves the knowledge of the **strong** relation, and uses a **binary** challenge space. Let public parameters $pp = (p, \ell_1, \ell_2, e_1, e_2, E_0)$ be such that $\#E_0(\mathbb{F}_{p^2}) = (\ell_1 \ell_2^{e_2} f)^2$, for $\ell_2^{e_2}$ of roughly the same size as in SIDH ([2]) and $d = \ell_1^{e_1} \gg \ell_2^{e_2}$, or $d = \ell_1^{e_1} \approx 2^\lambda (\ell_2^{e_2})^2$. Note that in this setting, $p = \ell_1 \ell_2^{e_2} f - 1 \approx \ell_2^{e_2}$ and thus it is smaller than $2^{2\lambda}$. Note also that E_0 is not a

[1] The Σ protocol with binary challenges does not satisfy the common definitions of zero-knowledge. This, however, does not constitute a problem when it is transformed into a signature scheme, as shown in Sect. 5.2.

[2] This basis can be generated canonically, which avoids the need of its commitment.

special curve and can in fact be generated by taking a long enough walk from $j = 1728$.

Intuitively, the protocol is as described earlier in this section and the rigorous version is given in [22, Figure 2]. The only difference is, the horizontal isogeny ϕ' is represented by a sequence of isogenies of degree ℓ_1 instead of a kernel point of order $\ell_1^{e_1}$. As noted in [22], this sigma protocol has 2-special soundness, but does not satisfy the zero-knowledge (ZK) property if the distinguisher used in the ZK definition has access to the witness. We explore in Sect. 5.2 how we can still retain the security of the derived signature.

Variant 2. This variant also proves the knowledge of the **strong** relation, but uses a **ternary** challenge space. The requirements on the public parameters are similar to Variant 1, with $p \approx \ell_1^{e_1}\ell_2^{e_2}$ as in SIDH, so $p \approx 2^{216}$ for $\lambda = 128$. The description of the protocol is as given in [22, Figure 3]. Note again that we represent ϕ' by a sequence of isogenies of degree ℓ_1. This sigma protocol has 3-special soundness and zero-knowledge. Note that in this variant, E_0 does not need to be a random supersingular elliptic curve, and rather can be taken to be a special curve with an extremal order as endomorphism ring.

4 Analysis of KLPT-Based Attacks

In this section, we analyze KLPT-based attacks that break the security of SIDH-based signatures and proofs of knowledge. The attacks follow two main approaches: they can either recover the secret key from the public information, or they can forge a valid signature even if they fail to recover the secret key.

In the first approach, the attacker recovers a d-isogeny $\phi : E_0 \to E_1$, given the domain and codomain curves E_0, E_1 and their endomorphism rings.

This problem is linked to the problem of finding an ideal of norm d, connecting the maximal orders $\mathcal{O}_0 \cong \mathrm{End}(E_0)$ and $\mathcal{O}_1 \cong \mathrm{End}(E_1)$ through the computational Deuring correspondence [26,37]. In [37,42], the authors propose polynomial algorithms to find such ideal of smooth norm. A strategy to find a witness for the above relations could then be as follows:

1. Find an ideal I connecting $\mathcal{O}_0$ to $\mathcal{O}_1$;
2. Use the KLPT algorithm to compute an ideal J of norm d equivalent to I;
3. Use the computational Deuring correspondence to compute an isogeny corresponding to J.

The KLPT algorithm produces ideals of norm in $O(3\log(p))$ if either $\mathcal{O}_0$ or $\mathcal{O}_1$ is a special extremal order [37,42,46], and $O(\frac{9}{2}\log(p))$ in the general case [25,46]. Hence, this strategy potentially fails for some $d \leq p^3$ or $d \leq p^{\frac{9}{2}}$, depending on the curves E_0 and E_1.

A second attack strategy sidesteps these limitations and can possibly break the security of the protocol even when the secret isogeny is shorter than p^3. When the underlying sigma protocol is sound with respect to the weak relation $\mathcal{R}_{\mathsf{weak}}$, the prover demonstrates knowledge of an isogeny between E_0 and E_1 of degree $\ell^{2i}d$, for some integer i and ℓ coprime with d. An attacker can thus attempt to forge a proof, even without knowing the witness, by using the KLPT-based approach described above to compute an isogeny of degree $\ell^{2i}d$. Such an isogeny can then be written as the composition $\hat{\psi}' \circ \phi' \circ \psi$, where ϕ' is a d isogeny and ψ, ψ' have degree ℓ^i; the attacker can then correctly reply to any challenge. This attack can be avoided if the composition isogeny is shorter than the shortest isogeny returned by KLPT, or if the Sigma protocol is sound with respect to $\mathcal{R}_{\mathsf{strg}}$: in that case, this approach would fail to produce isogenies $\hat{\psi}'$ and ψ that are parallel, because the isogenies ϕ' and parallel isogenies $\hat{\psi}'$ and ψ uniquely determine ϕ, which is too short to be determined by a KLPT-based attack.

In this section, we analyze the minimal norm of the ideal that KLPT can return. We extend the previous results by studying exponential-time algorithms and showing that there is a trade-off between KLPT's running time and the norm of the smallest ideal it can produce.

4.1 The KLPT Algorithm for Extremal Order

We recall the following lemma from [42].

Lemma 6 ([42]). *Let I be a left $\mathcal{O}$-ideal and $\alpha \in I$. Then $I\frac{\bar{\alpha}}{Nrd(I)}$ is a left $\mathcal{O}$-ideal of norm $\frac{Nrd(\alpha)}{Nrd(I)}$.*

As consequence of this lemma, finding an equivalent $\mathcal{O}$-ideal of I which has a norm in a certain set $\mathcal{N}$ consists of finding an element in I of norm $nNrd(I)$, for some $n \in \mathcal{N}$. Let $\mathcal{O}$ be one of the special extremal maximal orders given in Example 2; I an $\mathcal{O}$-left ideal and ℓ a small prime. KLPT algorithm can be summarized as follows:

1. Compute an ideal J of prime norm equivalent to I, such that ℓ is a quadratic non-residue modulo N;
2. Find an element $\gamma \in \mathcal{O}$ of norm $N\ell^{e_1}$ for some $e_1 \in \mathbb{N}$;
3. Find an element $\alpha \in J$ such that $J = \mathcal{O}\alpha + N\mathcal{O}$;
4. Compute $\mu_0 \in Rj$ such that $\gamma\mu_0 \equiv \alpha \bmod N\mathcal{O}$;
5. Compute $\lambda \in \mathbb{Z}/N\mathbb{Z}^*$ and $\mu_1 \in \mathcal{O}$ such that $\mu = \lambda\mu_0 + N\mu_1$ has norm ℓ^{e_2}, for some $e_2 \in \mathbb{N}$
6. Return $J\frac{\beta}{N}$, where $\beta = \gamma\mu$.

In Step 1, one computes a reduced basis of I and generates a small set of short elements until an element of norm $N\,\mathrm{Nrd}(I)$ is found for which N is prime. Experimentally, this algorithm returns an ideal of prime norm N, where $N \simeq \sqrt{p}$.

In Step 2, one solves the norm equation

$$f(x_1, y_1) = N\ell^{e_1} - pf(x_2, y_2). \tag{4}$$

In Step 3, it is enough to find an element $\alpha \in J$ such that $gcd(N^2, \mathrm{Nrd}(\alpha)) = N$. For such α, we have $J = \mathcal{O}\alpha + N\mathcal{O}$ i.e. $J/N\mathcal{O} = \mathcal{O}\alpha/N\mathcal{O}$.

The idea of Step 4 is that $\mathcal{O}/N\mathcal{O}$ is isomorphic to $M_2(\mathbb{Z}/N\mathbb{Z})$ (an explicit isomorphism can be computed using [53, Proposition 7.6.2]) and thus every left ideal only differs by a quaternion whose reduced norm is coprime to N and such an element can actually be chosen from Rj. Step 5 consists of finding $\mu \equiv \lambda\mu_0 \mod N\mathcal{O}$ of norm ℓ^{e_2}. One has to look for $\mu_1 = x + y\omega + (z + t\omega)j \in R + Rj$ and $\lambda \in \mathbb{Z}/N\mathbb{Z}$ such that $\mathrm{Nrd}(\mu) = \ell^{e_2}$ where $\mu = \lambda\mu_0 + N\mu_1$. For such μ, we have

$$\mu = N(x + y\omega) + [Nz + \lambda C + (Nt + \lambda D)\omega]j.$$

Hence $\mathrm{Nrd}(\mu) = \ell^{e_2}$ is equivalent to

$$N^2 f(x, y) + pf(Nz + \lambda C, Nt + \lambda D) = \ell^{e_2}. \tag{5}$$

Modulo N, the previous equation becomes

$$\lambda^2 pf(C, D) \equiv \ell^{e_2} \mod N.$$

Since l is a quadratic non-residue modulo N, the parity of e_2 should be adjusted so that $\left(\frac{pf(C,D)}{N}\right) = \left(\frac{\ell^{e_2}}{N}\right)$. We then have $\lambda = \sqrt{\frac{\ell^{e_2}}{pf(C,D)}} \mod N$.

Furthermore, we also have

$$f(Nz + \lambda C, Nt + \lambda D) = N^2 f(z, t) + \lambda^2 f(C, D) + N\lambda L((C, D), (z, t)),$$

where

$$L((C, D), (z, t)) = 2Cz + \mathrm{Trd}(\omega)(Dz + Ct) + 2\,\mathrm{Nrd}(\omega)Dt = \langle C + D\omega, z + t\omega\rangle.$$

Hence, Eq. (5) is equivalent to

$$\lambda pL((C, D), (z, t)) = \frac{\ell^{e_2} - \lambda^2 pf(C, D)}{N} - N(f(x, y) + pf(z, t)). \tag{6}$$

(We recall that λ is chosen so that N divides $\ell^{e_2} - \lambda^2 pf(C, D)$). Modulo N, Eq. (6) yields the linear equation

$$\lambda pL((C, D), (z, t)) = \frac{\ell^{e_2} - \lambda^2 pf(C, D)}{N} \mod N. \tag{7}$$

This linear equation has N solutions (z, t) [42].

To find (x, y), one takes a random solution (z, t) and tries to solve the following equation, which is equivalent to Eq. (5):

$$f(x, y) = \frac{\ell^{e_2} - pf(Nz + \lambda C, Nt + \lambda D)}{N^2} =: r \tag{8}$$

Remark 7. In this step, there are two ways to proceed:

1. Take e_2 large enough so that r is always positive, and randomly take (z, t) so that r is a norm in R (as done in [42]);

2. Adjust e_2 for each value of (z, t) so that Eq. (8) has a solution. This method gives an exponential approach that is studied next.

We summarize our discussion about the KLPT algorithm in the following lemma. Note that this result is already implied in [46].

Lemma 8. *Let $\mathcal{O}_0$ be a special extremal maximal order in $\mathcal{B}_{p,\infty}$, where $p \equiv 3$ mod 4 or $p \equiv 5$ mod 8. Let I be a $\mathcal{O}_0$-left ideal. Using KLPT algorithm, we can compute an ideal of smooth norm d equivalent to I, where $d = \ell^e \approx p^{\frac{5}{2}}$.*

Proof. In Step 1, the ideal J can be found such that N is split in R. For such N, the equation $f(x, y) = N$ has a solution since $h_\Delta = 1$, where $\Delta = disc(R)$. Hence, we can take $e_1 = 0$ in Step 2 and Eq. (5) has a solution for $x_2 = y_2 = 0$. Using the strategy in [46] in Step 5, we have $e_2 \approx \frac{5}{2}\log_\ell(p)$. Thus, $e = e_2 \approx \frac{5}{2}\log_\ell(p)$, and the result follows.

Remark 9. For a general value of p, this approach work with probability $\frac{1}{h_\Delta}$.

Superpolynomial-Time KLPT

We now analyze the second strategy discussed in Remark 7, with a particular focus on superpolynomial-time algorithms. Note that the ideas of the strategy we present here first appeared in [45, Section 3.4], and we give a variant of it.

Given $C, D \in \mathbb{Z}$, we look for solutions $(z, t) \in \mathbb{Z}^2$ such that Eq. (7) holds. In [46], it was shown that the solutions (z, t) for Eq. (7) can be viewed as a translated lattice as follows. We let $\Phi = p\lambda(2C + \mathsf{tr}(\omega)D), \Psi = p\lambda(\mathsf{tr}(\omega)C + 2n(\omega)D)$, and $\chi := \frac{l^{e_2} - \lambda^2 pf(C,D)}{N}$, then (z, t) satisfies

$$\Psi z + \Psi t \equiv \chi \mod N.$$

Let (z_0, t_0) denote one solution of this equation, then all solutions $(z, t) \in \mathbb{Z}^2$ are contained in the translated lattice $\mathcal{L} = (z_0, t_0)^T + \mathcal{L}_0$, where $\mathcal{L}_0 = \mathbb{Z}(\Phi, -\Psi)^T + \mathbb{Z}(0, N)^T$. To reduce the output length of KLPT, we aim to reduce $pf(Nz + \lambda C, Nt + \lambda D)$. In [46], this is reduced to a closest-vector problem where the involved lattice $\mathcal{L}$ is a deformation of $\mathcal{L}_0$. For our purpose, we do not recall the concrete basis of $\mathcal{L}_0$ here, but only note that this lattice is determined by C and D, and it has volume $pN^3\sqrt{\Delta_{\mathbb{Q}(\omega)}}$. By the Gaussian heuristic, we estimate that the lattice contains a basis of size $\sqrt{p}N^{\frac{3}{2}}\Delta^{\frac{1}{4}}_{\mathbb{Q}(\omega)}$. This gives rise to the estimation that one can find (z, t) such that $pf(Nz + \lambda C, Nt + \lambda D) \approx pN^3\sqrt{\Delta_{\mathbb{Q}(\omega)}}$. Hence, $\ell^{e_2} \approx pN^3\sqrt{\Delta_{\mathbb{Q}(\omega)}} \approx p^{\frac{5}{2}}$. Below is a theorem that estimates the expected shortest vector of n independent random matrices from [4, Section 4.1].

Theorem 10. *Let $Z_1, ...Z_n$ be the length of the shortest vectors in n independent random matrices of unit volume and $Z_{\min} := \min\{Z_1, ..., Z_n\}$, then $\mathbb{E}(Z_{\min}) \leq O(\frac{1}{\sqrt{n}})$ for $n \geq 2$.*

If we can generate n pairs of C, D that gives rise to n independent random lattices, then according to Theorem 10, the expected shortest vector among these n lattices has length $\frac{\sqrt{p}N^{\frac{3}{2}}\Delta_{\mathbb{Q}(\omega)}^{\frac{1}{4}}}{\sqrt{n}}$. Therefore, $pf(Nz + \lambda C, Nt + \lambda D)$ would be $\frac{pN^3\sqrt{\Delta_{\mathbb{Q}(\omega)}}}{n}$. Let $n \approx N^{e_3}$, then $\frac{pN^3\sqrt{\Delta_{\mathbb{Q}(\omega)}}}{n} \approx pN^{3-e_3}\sqrt{\Delta_{\mathbb{Q}(\omega)}} \approx p^{\frac{5}{2}-\frac{e_3}{2}}$.

Hence, the length of the path returned using this approach reaches $e = \frac{5-e_3}{2}\log(p)$. The number n is exactly the number of solutions provided by the modular constrain Step 4 that we want to analyze.

On the Modular Constraint

In a general context, the modular constraint step consists of finding an element $[\mu] \in (\mathcal{O}/N\mathcal{O})^* \equiv GL_2(\mathbb{Z}/N\mathbb{Z})$ such that $(\mathcal{O}\gamma/N\mathcal{O})[\mu] = J/N\mathcal{O}$. The existence of such element is justified by the transitivity of the action of $GL_2(\mathbb{Z}/N\mathbb{Z})$ on $\mathbb{P}^1(\mathbb{Z}/N\mathbb{Z})$. We recall the following lemma:

Lemma 11 ([42]). *Let N be a prime and $A = M_2(\mathbb{Z}/N\mathbb{Z})$. The set of proper nontrivial left A-ideals is in bijection with the set*

$$\left\{\mathbb{P}^1(\mathbb{Z}/N\mathbb{Z}) \times \{(x:y)\};\ (x:y) \in \mathbb{P}^1(\mathbb{Z}/N\mathbb{Z})\right\},$$

and the right action of $PGL_2((\mathbb{Z}/N\mathbb{Z})$ on left A-ideals is transitive and induced by the natural action on $\mathbb{P}^1(\mathbb{Z}/N\mathbb{Z})$.

We recall that the action of $PGL_2((\mathbb{Z}/N\mathbb{Z})$ on $\mathbb{P}^1(\mathbb{Z}/N\mathbb{Z})$ is induced by the action of $GL_2(\mathbb{Z}/N\mathbb{Z})$ which has kernel $(\mathbb{Z}/N\mathbb{Z})^*$. Using an explicit isomorphism between $\mathcal{O}/N\mathcal{O}$ and $M_2(\mathbb{Z}/N\mathbb{Z})$ we have an action of $(\mathcal{O}/N\mathcal{O})^*$ on the left $\mathcal{O}/N\mathcal{O}$-ideals. In the context of the KLPT algorithm, this action is restricted to the action of $Rj/N\mathcal{O}$. That is why Step 4 just consists to find a pair (C, D). Hence, the number n is upper bounded by the number of $[\mu]$. The number of such $[\mu]$ is exactly $\#Stab([x:y])$ (where $Stab([x:y])$ denotes the stabilizer of $[x:y]$) for some $[x:y] \in \mathbb{P}^1(\mathbb{Z}/N\mathbb{Z})$, since the action is transitive. Furthermore, we have $\#Stab([x:y]) = \frac{\#PLG_2(\mathbb{Z}/N\mathbb{Z})}{\#\mathbb{P}^1(\mathbb{Z}/N\mathbb{Z})} = N(N+1)$. Hence, we have $n \approx N^2$. We summarize the discussion into the following theorem.

Theorem 12. *Let I be a left $\mathcal{O}$-ideal for an extremal order $\mathcal{O}$. Then applying the KLPT algorithm to I one could find an equivalent left $\mathcal{O}$-ideal J such that $n(J)$ is an ℓ-power and is of length $\frac{5-e}{2}\log p$ in time $\tilde{O}(n)$ where n is any positive integer less than p and e is a rational number such that $(\sqrt{p})^e \approx n$, for $p \equiv 3$ mod 4 or $p \equiv 5$ mod 8.*

Proof. We set $n(J) = \ell^{e_1+e_2}$ where e_1 and e_2 are given respectively by Step 2 and Step 5. Following the arguments in the proof of Lemma 8, we have $e_1 = 0$. Let e be such that $N^e \approx (\sqrt{p})^e$ is the number of solutions we generate in the modular constrain step, then based on the discussions above, we have that $e_2 \approx \frac{5-e}{2}\log_\ell(p)$. This approach then has complexity in $\tilde{O}(\sqrt{p}^e)$. The number of solutions that can be generated in the modular constrain step is bounded above by $N^2 \approx p$.

The shortest path returned by this approach has length $\frac{3}{2}\log p$ which takes time $\tilde{O}(p)$. Note that in both our variants p is a slightly smaller than $2^{2\lambda}$. The cost of this attack to generate a path of length $\frac{3}{2}\log p$ is thus far greater than the security parameter. On the other hand, if we choose the runtime to be $\sqrt{p} \approx 2^{\lambda}$, then the output path length from this approach is $2\log p$.

4.2 KLPT Algorithm for Non-extremal Order

Let E and E_1 be two supersingular elliptic curve defined over $\mathbb{F}_{p^2}$, of known endomorphism rings $\mathcal{O}$ and $\mathcal{O}_1$. Let I be a connecting ideal of $\mathcal{O}$ and $\mathcal{O}_1$. Let $\mathcal{O}_0$ be a special extremal order, and $I_0 = I(\mathcal{O}_0, \mathcal{O})$. The problem is to find an $\mathcal{O}$-left ideal of smooth norm equivalent to I.

Approach from [42]**.** The idea in [42] is as follows:

1. Compute $I_1 = I_0 \frac{\bar{\gamma}_1}{\mathrm{Nrd}(I_0)}$ where $\mathrm{Nrd}(\gamma_1) = n_1 \mathrm{Nrd}(I_0)$;
2. Compute $I_2 = I_0 I \frac{\bar{\gamma}_2}{\mathrm{Nrd}(I_0 I)}$ where $\mathrm{Nrd}(\gamma_2) = n_2 \mathrm{Nrd}(I_0 I)$;
3. Return $I\frac{\bar{\gamma}}{\mathrm{Nrd}(I)}$, where $\gamma = \bar{\gamma}_1\gamma_2$.

With this approach, the length of the shortest path is greater than $4\log(p)$.

The SQISign Approach. The idea in SQISign [25] is to transfer the problem in the special case using pullback and push forward through I_0.

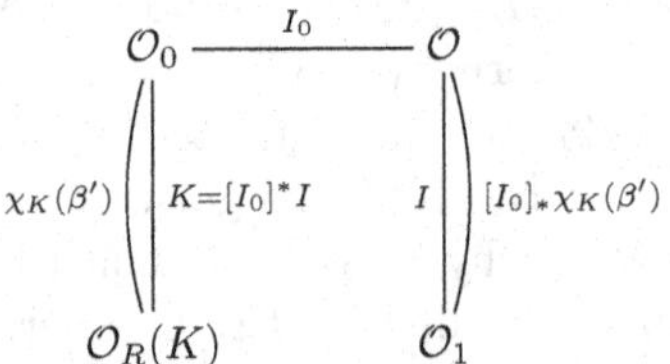

Where $\chi_K(\beta') = K\frac{\bar{\beta}'}{\mathrm{Nrd}(K)}$. To obtain this, one must have $\beta' \in K \cap \mathfrak{D}$, where $\mathfrak{D} = \mathcal{O}_0 \cap \mathcal{O} = \mathbb{Z} + I_0$ [25, Corollary 1]. For $n = \ell^e$, the algorithm can be described as follows: We suppose that $\mathrm{Nrd}(I_0) = N_0$ is prime inert in R such that ℓ is a quadratic non residue modulo N_0.

1. Compute $K = [I_0]^* I$;
2. Compute an ideal L of prime norm N equivalent to K, such that ℓ is a quadratic non-residue modulo N. Let δ such that $L = \chi_K(\delta)$;
3. Find an element $\gamma \in \mathcal{O}$ of norm $N\ell^{e_1}$ for some $e_1 \in \mathbb{N}$;
4. Find an element $\alpha \in \mathcal{O}$ such that $L = \mathcal{O}\alpha + N\mathcal{O}$;
5. Compute $\mu_0 = (C_0 + \omega D_0)j \in Rj$ such that $\gamma\mu_0 \equiv \alpha \bmod N\mathcal{O}$;
6. Compute $\mu_1 = (C_1 + \omega D_1)j \in Rj$ such that $\gamma\mu_0\delta \in \mathcal{O} \cap \mathcal{O}_0$;
7. Compute $C = CRT_{N_0,N}(C_0, C_1)$ and $D = CRT_{N_0,N}(D_0, D_1)$ and let $\mu' = (C + \omega D)j$
8. Compute $\lambda \in \mathbb{Z}/NN_0\mathbb{Z}^*$ and $\mu_1' \in \mathcal{O}_0$ such that $\mu = \lambda\mu' + NN_0\mu_1'$ has norm l^{e_2}, for some $e_2 \in \mathbb{N}$.
9. Return $\chi_L(\beta)$, where $\beta = \gamma\mu$.

The main difference between this algorithm and the algorithm from [42] described in Sect. 4.1 is Step 8. Here the approximation is done modulo NN_0 and then the computation of λ becomes more delicate than what we have in Step 5, Sect. 4.1. In the present context, the approximation equation is Eq. (9), which corresponds to Eq. (5), replacing N by NN_0.

$$N^2N_0^2 f(x,y) + pf(NN_0z + \lambda C, NN_0t + \lambda D) = \ell^{e_2}. \tag{9}$$

Modulo NN_0, this equation becomes

$$\lambda^2 pf(C,D) \equiv \ell^{e_2} \bmod NN_0.$$

For this equation to have a solution, we need the following equality:

$$\left(\frac{pf(C,D)}{N}\right) = \left(\frac{\ell^{e_2}}{N}\right) \text{ and } \left(\frac{pf(C,D)}{N_0}\right) = \left(\frac{\ell^{e_2}}{N_0}\right).$$

Since ℓ is a quadratic non residue modulo N and N_0, we always have $\left(\frac{\ell^{e_2}}{N}\right) = \left(\frac{\ell^{e_2}}{N_0}\right)$. Hence, we need

$$\left(\frac{pf(C,D)}{N}\right) = \left(\frac{pf(C,D)}{N_0}\right). \tag{10}$$

This last equality has a probability $\frac{3}{4}$ to fail, for given γ from Step 3 and δ from Step 2 [25]. To minimize this failure probability, the authors of [25] take e_1 large enough so that there are many possibilities for γ (we recall that γ is computed by solving Eq. (4)). The advantage of this method is that it only modifies the parameters (C, D), and N remains fixed. Since we need e_1 to be as small as possible and Eq. (4) has a solution for $e_1 = 0$ when N is split in R, we would like to take $e_1 = 0$. We summarize the result in the following lemma.

Lemma 13. *Let $\mathcal{O}$ and $\mathcal{O}_1$ be two non extremal maximal orders in $\mathcal{B}_{p,\infty}$ where $p \equiv 3$ mod 4 or $p \equiv 5$ mod 8. Given a connecting ideal I of $\mathcal{O}$ and $\mathcal{O}_1$, there is a probabilistic polynomial time algorithm which find an equivalent ideal of norm ℓ^e, for some small prime ℓ and $e \approx 4\log(p)$.*

Proof. Following the idea in Lemma 8, we can obtain $e_1 = 0$ in step 3 in which case Eq. 4 is solved by setting $x_1 = x_2 = 0$. Equation 4 become $f(x_1, x_2) = N$, which has at most 4 solutions leading to different values of $[C : D] \in \mathbb{P}^1(\mathbb{Z}/N\mathbb{Z})$. Hence, the success probability is $1 - \left(\frac{3}{4}\right)^4 \approx 68.4\%$. In the failure case we can either go back to Step 2 and compute an other L, or compute an other I_0. In Step 8, we can use the strategy of [46] to obtain $e_2 \approx 4\log_l p$ and the result follows.

Remark 14. The exponential approach of Sect. 4.1 can be applied here. Using similar analysis, we see that the output length is $(4 - e)\log p$ in time $\tilde{O}(n)$ where n is any positive integer less than p and e is a rational number such that $(\sqrt{p})^e \approx n$, for $p \equiv 3 \bmod 4$ or $p \equiv 5 \bmod 8$. And in this case, if we bound the runtime by $\sqrt{p}$, then the shortest path returned is of length $3\log p$.

4.3 Parameters Secure Against KLPT-Based Attacks

Combining the analysis presented so far, we obtain the following limitations for an attacker of complexity 2^λ. Since $O(p) = O(2^\epsilon)$ and $\lambda < \epsilon \leq 2\lambda$, we use $O(\sqrt{p})$ as an upper bound for the runtime of exponential KLPT, and we summarize the output length here.

Takeaway 1 *Consider an isogeny $\phi : E_0 \to E_1$ of degree d. Given the endomorphism rings of E_0 and E_1, KLPT-based methods cannot recover ϕ in time $\tilde{O}(\sqrt{p}) < \tilde{O}(2^\lambda)$ if:*

1. *E_0 is a special curve, $p \in \{3,5,7\} \bmod 8$, and $\log d < 2\log p$;*
2. *E_0 is a special curve, $p \notin \{3,5,7\} \bmod 8$, and $\log d < \frac{5}{2}\log p$;*
3. *E_0 is not a special curve, $p \in \{3,5,7\} \bmod 8$, and $\log d < 3\log p$;*
4. *E_0 is not a special curve, $p \notin \{3,5,7\} \bmod 8$, and $\log d < \frac{7}{2}\log p$.*

Given these results, we obtain that the two protocols proposed in Sect. 3 are secure against KLPT-based attacks. In both instances, E_0 is chosen to not be a special curve, hence the limits 3 and 4 apply. In the first variant, from Takeaway 2, the isogeny ϕ has degree $d \approx 2^\lambda p^2$ and ψ has degree $\approx p$, **Variant 1** is secure according to the summary above. Similarly, **Variant 2** relies on isogenies of degree $\approx p$, and thus KLPT-based attacks do not apply. In both instantiations, the signatures rely on the stronger relation, and thus the attack that recovers the composition $\hat{\psi} \circ \phi' \circ \psi'$ cannot be used.

5 Analysis of Other Attacks

5.1 Attacks Based on the SIDH Attacks

The SIDH attacks [15,44,49] recover an isogeny $\phi : E_0 \to E_1$ of degree d given:

- The curves E_0 and E_1;
- The degree d;
- The image of a torsion basis of smooth order n with $n \geq \sqrt{d}$.

However, it is possible to brute-force part of an unknown isogeny (which is always cheaper than brute-forcing torsion point information), thus we need $d \geq 2^\lambda\sqrt{\ell}$ to avoid the attacks.

Binary challenges. The proofs of isogeny knowledge with binary challenges are potentially vulnerable to the SIDH attacks.

Consider the following diagram:

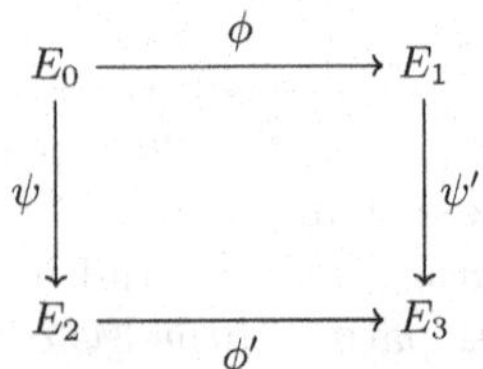

When the proof has binary challenges, the isogenies ψ and ψ' are revealed together. If the prover is honest, we have

$$\ker \psi' = \phi(\ker \psi),$$

which allows an attacker to recover the image of the subgroup $\ker \psi$ under the secret isogeny ϕ. After three such challenges, the attacker has recovered enough information to apply the SIDH attacks. In fact, as shown in [9,34] this allows the attacker to recover the image of a torsion basis on E_0 under ϕ, up to the same scalar. The square of this scalar can be computed through Weil pairing. If the degrees of ψ and ψ' are prime powers, as in SIDH, there are only two possible square roots. It is easy to apply the SIDH attacks each time $\deg \phi < (\deg \psi)^2$, assuming the degree of ψ is not much smaller than that of ϕ, and recover ϕ. In practice, it is enough to have $2^\lambda(\deg \psi)^2 \leq \deg \phi$, so that one needs to first guess an isogeny of degree at least 2^λ before being able to apply the SIDH attacks.

Takeaway 2 *Binary challenges require* $2^\lambda(\deg \psi)^2 \leq \deg \phi$.

Remark 15. An alternative idea could be to use commitment isogenies ψ and ψ' with non-rational torsion as the torsion point images are defined over large extensions fields and thus the SIDH attacks do not apply directly. However, in our case we know endomorphism rings and can go on a different route. As described in [19], one has that $(\text{End}(E)/N\text{End}(E))^*$ acts on the set of degree N isogenies. In general without any extra information this action is hard to compute when only the codomain of the isogeny is known. In our case however, this action is exactly provided by the parallel isogenies. Thus one can compute the stabilizer of this action as in [19] using a polynomial-time quantum algorithm which essentially reveals the connecting ideal corresponding to the secret isogeny. Since the secret isogeny here is smooth, one can recover the isogeny itself step by step. Note that just knowing the codomain of the parallel isogeny would not always have been enough (as it does not determine the action precisely as one might have several degree N isogenies between two supersingular elliptic curves). However, knowing the second vertical isogeny already is enough information to evaluate the group action (assuming that the torsion is large enough to ensure unicity).

5.2 Attacks on the Zero-Knowledge Property

In this section, we explore the zero-knowledge property of the underlying sigma protocol for the binary challenge variant as described in Sect. 3.

We set ourselves in the setting of **Variant 1**, from Sect. 3.1, since the others variants use ternary challenges and are provably (honest-verifier) zero-knowledge. The question we explore is whether we can address the zero-knowledge issue that arises in Variant 1 in the context where we only use the identification protocol for the purpose of turning it into a signature scheme.

This turns out to be a key observation: we turn the Sigma protocol into a signature scheme via the Fiat-Shamir transform [31], and a natural question that arises is whether we can allow a relaxation of the zero-knowledge property of the underlying Sigma protocol whilst still retaining the security of the Fiat-Shamir transform. In other words, what are the minimal assumptions for the security of the Fiat-Shamir transform and can we achieve them? In [1], they introduce a new notion of security for sigma-protocols, namely *security against impersonation under passive attacks*. They show that this is a minimal assumption for the Fiat-Shamir transform to be secure. We define this notion formally below:

Definition 16 ([1]). *We say that a sigma protocol is secure against impersonation under passive attacks if for any polynomial time adversary $\mathcal{A}$ the advantage $Adv^{\mathsf{Impersonate}}(\mathcal{A})$ of $\mathcal{A}$ in the* Impersonate *game is negligible, where*

$$\mathrm{Adv}^{\mathsf{Impersonate}}(\mathcal{A}) = \Pr[\mathsf{Impersonate}(\mathcal{A}) \to 1] = negl(\lambda)$$

The Impersonate *game is described below.*

$\underline{\mathsf{Impersonate}(\mathcal{A})}$

$\mathsf{Setup}(1^\lambda) \to \mathsf{pp}$
$\mathsf{KeyGen}(\mathsf{pp}) \to (\mathsf{sk}, \mathsf{pk})$
$\mathcal{A}^{\mathcal{OTG}}(\mathsf{pk}) \to \mathsf{com}, \mathsf{st}$
$\mathsf{ch} \xleftarrow{\$} \mathcal{C}$
$\mathcal{A}(\mathsf{st}, \mathsf{ch}) \to \mathsf{resp}$
return $\mathcal{V}(\mathsf{pk}, \mathsf{com}, \mathsf{ch}, \mathsf{resp})$

$\underline{\mathcal{OTG}}$

$R_p \xleftarrow{\$} \mathcal{R}$ (generate randomness)
$\mathsf{com} \leftarrow \mathcal{P}(\mathsf{sk}; R_p)$
$\mathsf{ch} \xleftarrow{\$} \mathcal{C}$
$\mathsf{resp} \leftarrow \mathcal{P}(\mathsf{sk}, \mathsf{com}, \mathsf{ch}; R_p)$
return $(\mathsf{com}, \mathsf{ch}, \mathsf{resp})$

Theorem 17 ([1], **Theorem 3.3**). *Let Π_Σ be a non-trivial sigma-protocol, and $\mathcal{DS}_\Sigma$ be the associated digital signature scheme obtained via the Fiat-Shamir transform, then $\mathcal{DS}_\Sigma$ is secure against existential forgery under chosen-message attacks if and only if Π_Σ is secure against impersonation under passive attacks.*

Remark 18. Note that non-triviality here requires the challenge space to be super-polynomial. Otherwise, a trivial winning strategy would be to replay a transcript obtained from the oracle and then one gets a probably $1/|\mathcal{C}|$ of winning. So if the size of the challenge space is polynomial, we have a winning strategy with probability that is not negligible.

We claim that this relaxed security notion is achieved by the parallel repetition of the binary challenge version under some conditions, and we hence get a secure signature scheme by applying the Fiat-Shamir transform. Let us formulate this more formally.

Problem 19. Consider two supersingular elliptic curves E_0, E_1 and an isogeny $\phi : E_0 \to E_1$ of degree $D = \ell_1^{e_1}$ in $\mathcal{R}_{\mathsf{strg}}$ such that $\#E_0(\mathbb{F}_{p^2}) = (\ell_1 \ell_2^{e_2} f)^2$ as defined in **Variant 1**. Given access to an oracle that outputs either :

- two isogenies $E_0 \to E_2$, $E_1 \to E_3$ and the images of the torsion basis on the codomain curves;
- an isogeny $E_2 \to E_3$ of degree D;

then the adversary must recover the secret isogeny ϕ.

Theorem 20. *Under the hardness of Problem 19, the λ parallel repetition of the sigma protocol is secure against impersonation under passive attacks.*

Proof. Problem 19 is the translation of the impersonate game to our setting.

This problem has already been discussed in the previous subsections. Notably if we ensure that the takeaways from Sects. 4 and 5.1 are respected then we can reasonably assume its hardness.

Takeaway 3 *Under reasonable assumptions, a digital signature derived from a proof of isogeny knowledge with binary challenges via the Fiat-Shamir transform is secure.*

6 Concrete Instantiations and Parameters Size

In this section, we analyze the size of the signatures derived from the sigma protocols described in Sect. 3.1 using the Fiat-Shamir transform [31]. We rely on a hash function $\mathcal{H} : \{0,1\}^* \to \{0,1\}^{2\lambda}$, where λ is the security parameter.

Variant 1. We first fix $\ell_1 = 2, \ell_2 = 3$ for efficiency reasons. Then, we choose the value e_2 such that isogenies of degree 3^{e_2} are hard to recover via meet-in-the-middle or van Oorschot-Wiener attacks [51] (e.g., we have $e_2 = 137$ for $\lambda = 128$). The exponent e_1 is chosen such that the isogenies of degree 2^{e_2} are hard to recover, even when their action on the 3^{e_2} torsion is known, i.e. $e_1 = \lambda + \lceil 2e_2 \log 3 \rceil$. We define the prime p to be of the form $p = 2 \cdot 3^{e_2} f - 1$, where f is a small cofactor. The public parameters of the signature are then $pp = (p, e_1, e_2, E_0, T_0, P_0, Q_0)$, where E_0 is a random supersingular elliptic curve defined over $\mathbb{F}_{p^2}$. The point $T_0 \in E_0$ is an auxiliary point of order 2, used in the CGL hash function computations [18], and and $\{P_0, Q_0\}$ is a basis of $E_0[3^{e_2}]$.

By the definition of p, any point of order 2^{e_1} is defined over a large extension of $\mathbb{F}_{p^2}$. We then represent the secret isogeny $\phi : E_0 \to E_1$ (of degree 2^{e_1}) by a sequence of 2-isogenies. To do that, we represent it as a seed $s \in \{0,1\}^{e_1}$ that has to be hashed using CGL hash function [18], with the first step chosen between the 2-torsion points that are not T_0. The secret key can then be represented by $e_1 \approx \lambda + 2\log p \approx 5\lambda$ bits. The public key is (E_1, P_1, Q_1) where $P_1 = \phi(P_0)$ and $Q_1 = \phi(Q_0)$. This requires $6 \log p \approx 12\lambda$ bits.

In this variant, the soundness error is $\frac{1}{2}$: this means the signature needs to repeat the sigma protocol $k = \lambda$ times to obtain a negligible soundness error. Since we are in the binary case, the response to both challenges includes all the committed values; thus, we rely on hashed commitments only for compression, but we do not require any hiding property. Using some of the compression techniques from [40], the size of the response for the horizontal challenge is $3 \log p + 2\lambda$, while the vertical challenge is $\log p$. Repeating λ times and including the hashed commitment sizes of $2 \times 2\lambda$, we obtain an asymptotic size of $\lambda(5\lambda + 2 \log p) \approx 9\lambda^2$ bits. Note that this is asymptotic and based on the assumption that $e_3 \approx 2\lambda/\log 3$, but we can choose smaller parameters based on the cost of the van Oorschoot-Wiener attack, as done in SIDH. For $\lambda = 128$, this results in a 218-bit prime and a signature of about 17 kB, which may be reduced even further by relying on seed trees [40].

Variant 2. The second variant relies on ternary challenges, and thus torsion images under the secret isogeny is not revealed. The public key hence consists of a single curve, which then requires $2 \log p$ bits.

In this variant, we need to rely on a computationally binding and statistically hiding commitment scheme C: we construct one from a hash function $\mathcal{H} : \{0,1\}^* \to \{0,1\}^{2\lambda}$ by defining $\mathsf{C}(m) = \mathcal{H}(m|r)$, for some random string r of λ bits. For each execution of the sigma protocol, we need 6λ bits to represent the three commitments (following the commitment algorithm in [22, Figure 3]), $\lambda + \log p$ for the responses to the vertical isogeny challenges, and $\lambda + 3 \log p$ for the response to the horizontal isogeny challenge. The soundness error of the underlying sigma protocol is $\frac{2}{3}$, which means the signature needs to repeat the sigma protocol $k = \lceil -\lambda/\log 2/3 \rceil$ times to obtain a negligible soundness error. This results in an average signature of asymptotic size $\frac{31}{3}\lambda\lceil -\lambda/\log 2/3 \rceil$ bits.

7 Conclusion

In this paper, we explore the feasibility of SIDH-based signatures when the endomorphism ring of all curves are public. We identify two variants of the construction that are secure in this setting, where the difference resides in the use of binary or ternary challenges and give concrete parameters. We provide a thorough security analysis of our proposals notably in terms of attacks based on KLPT, with both a polynomial and superpolynomial adversary, attacks derived from the recent SIDH-attacks and analyze the zero-knowledge property of the binary challenge variant. Note that the results we derive from the KLPT attacks could be affected by improvements on the output size of KLPT but this would only require to adjust the parameters to retain the security.

References

1. Abdalla, M., An, J.H., Bellare, M., Namprempre, C.: From identification to signatures via the Fiat-Shamir transform: minimizing assumptions for security and forward-security. In: Knudsen, L.R. (ed.) EUROCRYPT 2002. LNCS, vol. 2332, pp. 418–433. Springer, Heidelberg (2002). https://doi.org/10.1007/3-540-46035-7_28

2. Adj, G., Cervantes-Vázquez, D., Chi-Domínguez, J.J., Menezes, A., Rodríguez-Henríquez, F.: On the cost of computing isogenies between supersingular elliptic curves. In: Cid, C., Jacobson Jr: M.J. (eds.) SAC 2018. LNCS, vol. 11349, pp. 322–343. Springer, Heidelberg (2019). https://doi.org/10.1007/978-3-030-10970-7_15
3. Alamati, N., De Feo, L., Montgomery, H., Patranabis, S.: Cryptographic group actions and applications. In: Moriai, S., Wang, H. (eds.) ASIACRYPT 2020, Part II. LNCS, vol. 12492, pp. 411–439. Springer, Heidelberg (2020). https://doi.org/10.1007/978-3-030-64834-3_14
4. Aono, Y., Espitau, T., Nguyen, P.Q.: Random lattices: theory and practice (2019). https://espitau.github.io/bin/random_lattice.pdf
5. Badrinarayanan, S., Masny, D., Mukherjee, P., Patranabis, S., Raghuraman, S., Sarkar, P.: Round-optimal oblivious transfer and MPC from computational CSIDH. In: Boldyreva, A., Kolesnikov, V. (eds.) PKC 2023, Part I. LNCS, vol. 13940, pp. 376–405. Springer, Heidelberg (2023). https://doi.org/10.1007/978-3-031-31368-4_14
6. Basso, A.: A post-quantum round-optimal oblivious PRF from isogenies. Cryptology ePrint Archive, Report 2023/225 (2023). https://eprint.iacr.org/2023/225
7. Basso, A., et al.: Supersingular curves you can trust. In: Hazay, C., Stam, M. (eds.) EUROCRYPT 2023, Part II. LNCS, vol. 14005, pp. 405–437. Springer, Heidelberg (2023). https://doi.org/10.1007/978-3-031-30617-4_14
8. Basso, A., Fouotsa, T.B.: New sidh countermeasures for a more efficient key exchange. Cryptology ePrint Archive, Paper 2023/791 (2023). https://eprint.iacr.org/2023/791
9. Basso, A., Kutas, P., Merz, S.P., Petit, C., Sanso, A.: Cryptanalysis of an oblivious PRF from supersingular isogenies. In: Tibouchi, M., Wang, H. (eds.) ASIACRYPT 2021, Part I. LNCS, vol. 13090, pp. 160–184. Springer, Heidelberg (2021). https://doi.org/10.1007/978-3-030-92062-3_6
10. Basso, A., Maino, L., Pope, G.: FESTA: fast encryption from supersingular torsion attacks. Cryptology ePrint Archive, Paper 2023/660 (2023). https://eprint.iacr.org/2023/660
11. Bernstein, D.J., De Feo, L., Leroux, A., Smith, B.: Faster computation of isogenies of large prime degree. Open Book Series **4**(1), 39–55 (2020)
12. Beullens, W., De Feo, L., Galbraith, S.D., Petit, C.: Proving knowledge of isogenies: a survey. Des. Codes Cryptog. (2023). https://doi.org/10.1007/s10623-023-01243-3
13. Beullens, W., Kleinjung, T., Vercauteren, F.: CSI-FiSh: efficient isogeny based signatures through class group computations. In: Galbraith, S.D., Moriai, S. (eds.) ASIACRYPT 2019, Part I. LNCS, vol. 11921, pp. 227–247. Springer, Heidelberg (2019). https://doi.org/10.1007/978-3-030-34578-5_9
14. Boneh, D., Kogan, D., Woo, K.: Oblivious pseudorandom functions from isogenies. In: Moriai, S., Wang, H. (eds.) ASIACRYPT 2020, Part II. LNCS, vol. 12492, pp. 520–550. Springer, Heidelberg (2020). https://doi.org/10.1007/978-3-030-64834-3_18
15. Castryck, W., Decru, T.: An efficient key recovery attack on SIDH. In: Hazay, C., Stam, M. (eds.) EUROCRYPT 2023, Part V. LNCS, vol. 14008, pp. 423–447. Springer, Heidelberg (2023). https://doi.org/10.1007/978-3-031-30589-4_15
16. Castryck, W., Lange, T., Martindale, C., Panny, L., Renes, J.: CSIDH: an efficient post-quantum commutative group action. In: Peyrin, T., Galbraith, S. (eds.) ASIACRYPT 2018, Part III. LNCS, vol. 11274, pp. 395–427. Springer, Heidelberg (2018). https://doi.org/10.1007/978-3-030-03332-3_15

17. Castryck, W., Panny, L., Vercauteren, F.: Rational isogenies from irrational endomorphisms. In: Canteaut, A., Ishai, Y. (eds.) EUROCRYPT 2020, Part II. LNCS, vol. 12106, pp. 523–548. Springer, Heidelberg (2020). https://doi.org/10.1007/978-3-030-45724-2_18
18. Charles, D.X., Lauter, K.E., Goren, E.Z.: Cryptographic hash functions from expander graphs. J. Cryptol. **22**(1), 93–113 (2009). https://doi.org/10.1007/s00145-007-9002-x
19. Chen, M., Imran, M., Ivanyos, G., Kutas, P., Leroux, A., Petit, C.: Hidden stabilizers, the isogeny to endomorphism ring problem and the cryptanalysis of psidh. Cryptology ePrint Archive (2023)
20. Dartois, P., Leroux, A., Robert, D., Wesolowski, B.: SQISignHD: new dimensions in cryptography. Cryptology ePrint Archive, Paper 2023/436 (2023). https://eprint.iacr.org/2023/436, https://eprint.iacr.org/2023/436
21. De Feo, L., et al.: Séta: supersingular encryption from torsion attacks. In: Tibouchi, M., Wang, H. (eds.) ASIACRYPT 2021, Part IV. LNCS, vol. 13093, pp. 249–278. Springer, Heidelberg (2021). https://doi.org/10.1007/978-3-030-92068-5_9
22. De Feo, L., Dobson, S., Galbraith, S.D., Zobernig, L.: SIDH proof of knowledge. In: Agrawal, S., Lin, D. (eds.) ASIACRYPT 2022, Part II. LNCS, vol. 13792, pp. 310–339. Springer, Heidelberg (2022). https://doi.org/10.1007/978-3-031-22966-4_11
23. De Feo, L., et al.: SCALLOP: Scaling the CSI-FiSh. In: Boldyreva, A., Kolesnikov, V. (eds.) PKC 2023, Part I. LNCS, vol. 13940, pp. 345–375. Springer, Heidelberg (2023). https://doi.org/10.1007/978-3-031-31368-4_13
24. De Feo, L., Galbraith, S.D.: SeaSign: compact isogeny signatures from class group actions. In: Ishai, Y., Rijmen, V. (eds.) EUROCRYPT 2019, Part III. LNCS, vol. 11478, pp. 759–789. Springer, Heidelberg (2019). https://doi.org/10.1007/978-3-030-17659-4_26
25. De Feo, L., Kohel, D., Leroux, A., Petit, C., Wesolowski, B.: SQISign: compact post-quantum signatures from quaternions and isogenies. In: Moriai, S., Wang, H. (eds.) ASIACRYPT 2020, Part I. LNCS, vol. 12491, pp. 64–93. Springer, Heidelberg (2020). https://doi.org/10.1007/978-3-030-64837-4_3
26. De Feo, L., Leroux, A., Longa, P., Wesolowski, B.: New algorithms for the during correspondence - towards practical and secure SQISign signatures. In: Hazay, C., Stam, M. (eds.) EUROCRYPT 2023, Part V. LNCS, vol. 14008, pp. 659–690. Springer, Heidelberg (2023). https://doi.org/10.1007/978-3-031-30589-4_23
27. De Feo, L., Masson, S., Petit, C., Sanso, A.: Verifiable delay functions from supersingular isogenies and pairings. In: Galbraith, S.D., Moriai, S. (eds.) ASIACRYPT 2019, Part I. LNCS, vol. 11921, pp. 248–277. Springer, Heidelberg (2019). https://doi.org/10.1007/978-3-030-34578-5_10
28. Eisenträger, K., Hallgren, S., Lauter, K.E., Morrison, T., Petit, C.: Supersingular isogeny graphs and endomorphism rings: Reductions and solutions. In: Nielsen, J.B., Rijmen, V. (eds.) EUROCRYPT 2018, Part III. LNCS, vol. 10822, pp. 329–368. Springer, Heidelberg (2018). https://doi.org/10.1007/978-3-319-78372-7_11
29. Eisenträger, K., Hallgren, S., Leonardi, C., Morrison, T., Park, J.: Computing endomorphism rings of supersingular elliptic curves and connections to path-finding in isogeny graphs. Open Book Series **4**(1), 215–232 (2020)
30. Feo, L.D., Jao, D., Plût, J.: Towards quantum-resistant cryptosystems from supersingular elliptic curve isogenies. J. Math. Cryptol. **8**(3), 209–247 (2014). https://doi.org/10.1515/jmc-2012-0015

31. Fiat, A., Shamir, A.: How to prove yourself: practical solutions to identification and signature problems. In: Odlyzko, A.M. (ed.) CRYPTO 1986. LNCS, vol. 263, pp. 186–194. Springer, Heidelberg (1987). https://doi.org/10.1007/3-540-47721-7_12
32. Fouotsa, T.B., Kutas, P., Merz, S.P., Ti, Y.B.: On the isogeny problem with torsion point information. In: Hanaoka, G., Shikata, J., Watanabe, Y. (eds.) PKC 2022, Part I. LNCS, vol. 13177, pp. 142–161. Springer, Heidelberg (2022). https://doi.org/10.1007/978-3-030-97121-2_6
33. Fouotsa, T.B., Moriya, T., Petit, C.: M-SIDH and MD-SIDH: countering SIDH attacks by masking information. In: Hazay, C., Stam, M. (eds.) EUROCRYPT 2023, Part V. LNCS, vol. 14008, pp. 282–309. Springer, Heidelberg (2023). https://doi.org/10.1007/978-3-031-30589-4_10
34. Fouotsa, T.B., Petit, C.: A new adaptive attack on SIDH. In: Galbraith, S.D. (ed.) CT-RSA 2022. LNCS, vol. 13161, pp. 322–344. Springer, Heidelberg (2022). https://doi.org/10.1007/978-3-030-95312-6_14
35. Fuselier, J., Iezzi, A., Kozek, M., Morrison, T., Namoijam, C.: Computing supersingular endomorphism rings using inseparable endomorphisms. arXiv preprint arXiv:2306.03051 (2023)
36. Galbraith, S.D., Petit, C., Shani, B., Ti, Y.B.: On the security of supersingular isogeny cryptosystems. In: Cheon, J.H., Takagi, T. (eds.) ASIACRYPT 2016, Part I. LNCS, vol. 10031, pp. 63–91. Springer, Heidelberg (2016). https://doi.org/10.1007/978-3-662-53887-6_3
37. Galbraith, S.D., Petit, C., Silva, J.: Identification protocols and signature schemes based on supersingular isogeny problems. In: Takagi, T., Peyrin, T. (eds.) ASIACRYPT 2017, Part I. LNCS, vol. 10624, pp. 3–33. Springer, Heidelberg (2017). https://doi.org/10.1007/978-3-319-70694-8_1
38. Galbraith, S.D., Petit, C., Silva, J.: Identification protocols and signature schemes based on supersingular isogeny problems. J. Cryptol. **33**(1), 130–175 (2020). https://doi.org/10.1007/s00145-019-09316-0
39. Ghantous, W., Katsumata, S., Pintore, F., Veroni, M.: Collisions in supersingular isogeny graphs and the sidh-based identification protocol. Cryptology ePrint Archive, Paper 2021/1051 (2021). https://eprint.iacr.org/2021/1051
40. Ghantous, W., Pintore, F., Veroni, M.: Efficiency of sidh-based signatures (yes, sidh). Cryptology ePrint Archive, Paper 2023/433 (2023). https://eprint.iacr.org/2023/433
41. Jao, D., De Feo, L.: Towards quantum-resistant cryptosystems from supersingular elliptic curve isogenies. In: Yang, B.Y. (ed.) Post-Quantum Cryptography - 4th International Workshop, PQCrypto 2011. pp. 19–34. Springer, Heidelberg (2011). https://doi.org/10.1007/978-3-642-25405-5_2
42. Kohel, D., Lauter, K., Petit, C., Tignol, J.P.: On the quaternion ℓ-isogeny path problem. LMS J. Comput. Math. **17**(A), 418–432 (2014)
43. Lai, Y.F., Galbraith, S.D., Delpech de Saint Guilhem, C.: Compact, efficient and UC-secure isogeny-based oblivious transfer. In: Canteaut, A., Standaert, F.X. (eds.) EUROCRYPT 2021, Part I. LNCS, vol. 12696, pp. 213–241. Springer, Heidelberg (2021). https://doi.org/10.1007/978-3-030-77870-5_8
44. Maino, L., Martindale, C., Panny, L., Pope, G., Wesolowski, B.: A direct key recovery attack on SIDH. In: Hazay, C., Stam, M. (eds.) EUROCRYPT 2023, Part V. LNCS, vol. 14008, pp. 448–471. Springer, Heidelberg (2023). https://doi.org/10.1007/978-3-031-30589-4_16
45. Merz, S.P.: A Curved Path to Post-Quantum: Cryptanalysis and Design of Isogeny-based Cryptography. Ph.D. thesis, Royal Holloway, University of London (2023)

46. Petit, C., Smith, S.: An improvement to the quaternion analogue of the ‘-isogeny problem’ (2018). Full paper received through private communication, slides available at https://crypto.iacr.org/2018/affevents/mathcrypt/medias/08-50_3.pdf
47. Petit, C.: Faster algorithms for isogeny problems using torsion point images. In: Takagi, T., Peyrin, T. (eds.) ASIACRYPT 2017, Part II. LNCS, vol. 10625, pp. 330–353. Springer, Heidelberg (2017). https://doi.org/10.1007/978-3-319-70697-9_12
48. de Quehen, V., et al.: Improved torsion-point attacks on SIDH variants. In: Malkin, T., Peikert, C. (eds.) CRYPTO 2021, Part III, Virtual Event. LNCS, vol. 12827, pp. 432–470. Springer, Heidelberg (2021). https://doi.org/10.1007/978-3-030-84252-9_15
49. Robert, D.: Breaking SIDH in polynomial time. In: Hazay, C., Stam, M. (eds.) EUROCRYPT 2023, Part V. LNCS, vol. 14008, pp. 472–503. Springer, Heidelberg (2023). https://doi.org/10.1007/978-3-031-30589-4_17
50. Sterner, B.: Commitment schemes from supersingular elliptic curve isogeny graphs. Math. Cryptol. **1**(2), 40–51 (2022). https://journals.flvc.org/mathcryptology/article/view/130656
51. van Oorschot, P.C., Wiener, M.J.: Parallel collision search with cryptanalytic applications. J. Cryptol. **12**(1), 1–28 (1999). https://doi.org/10.1007/PL00003816
52. Vélu, J.: Isogénies entre courbes elliptiques. Comptes-Rendus de l’Académie des Sci. **273**, 238–241 (1971)
53. Voight, J.: Quaternion algebra. Graduate Texts in Mathematics, vol. 288, Springer, Heidelberg (2020). https://doi.org/10.1007/978-3-030-56694-4
54. Wesolowski, B.: Orientations and the supersingular endomorphism ring problem. In: Dunkelman, O., Dziembowski, S. (eds.) EUROCRYPT 2022, Part III. LNCS, vol. 13277, pp. 345–371. Springer, Heidelberg (2022). https://doi.org/10.1007/978-3-031-07082-2_13
55. Wesolowski, B.: The supersingular isogeny path and endomorphism ring problems are equivalent. In: 62nd FOCS, pp. 1100–1111. IEEE Computer Society Press (2022). https://doi.org/10.1109/FOCS52979.2021.00109

Biscuit: New MPCitH Signature Scheme from Structured Multivariate Polynomials

Luk Bettale[1], Delaram Kahrobaei[2,3,4,5(✉)], Ludovic Perret[6], and Javier Verbel[7]

[1] IDEMIA, Courbevoie, France
[2] Department of Computer Science and Mathematics, Queens College, City University of New York, New York, USA
delaram.kahrobaei@qc.cuny.edu
[3] Initiative for the Theoretical Sciences, Graduate Center, City University of New York, New York, USA
[4] Department of Computer Science, University of York, Heslington, UK
[5] Department of Computer Science and Engineering, Tandon School of Engineering, New York University, New York, USA
[6] Sorbonne University, CNRS, LIP6, PolSys, Paris, France
[7] Technology Innovation Institute, Masdar City, UAE

Abstract. This paper describes Biscuit, a new multivariate-based signature scheme derived using the MPC-in-the-Head (MPCitH) approach. The security of Biscuit is related to the problem of solving a set of structured quadratic algebraic equations. These equations are highly compact and can be evaluated using very few multiplications (one multiplication per equation). The core of Biscuit is a rather simple MPC protocol for secure multiplications using standard optimized multiplicative triples. This paper also includes several improvements toward the initial version of Biscuit submitted to the NIST PQC standardization process for additional signature schemes. Notably, we introduce a new hypercube variant of Biscuit, refine the security analysis with recent third-party attacks, and present a new AVX2 implementation of Biscuit.

Keywords: Post-Quantum · Digital Signature · MPC-in-the-Head · Multivariate Polynomials

1 Introduction

Biscuit is a new multivariate-based digital signature scheme submitted to the recent NIST standardization process for additional post-quantum signature schemes [1]. The security of Biscuit is proven assuming the hardness of the so-called PowAff2 problem (Definition 1), which is a structured version of the well-known Multivariate Quadratic (MQ) problem [16].

Biscuit is in the lineage of the Picnic signature scheme [21,36], which was selected as an alternate candidate in the first NIST post-quantum cryptography standardization process [6]. The security of Picnic relies on the hardness of a key-recovery attack for a lightweight block cipher. The design of Picnic builds over a Multi-Party Computation (MPC) protocol for multiplicative triples and

C. Pöpper and L. Batina (Eds.): ACNS 2024, LNCS 14583, pp. 457–486, 2024.
https://doi.org/10.1007/978-3-031-54770-6_18

follows the MPC-in-the-Head (MPCitH) paradigm [28] to obtain a Zero-Knowledge Proof-of-Knowledge (ZKPoK) for the key-recovery problem. Finally, the signature scheme is obtained by applying the Fiat-Shamir transformation [26] to the ZKPoK protocol.

As in Picnic, the design of Biscuit follows the MPCitH paradigm and relies essentially on the same MPC protocol to check multiplicative triples. Biscuit is build on top of a ZKPoK for the problem of finding a pre-image $\boldsymbol{s} \in \mathbb{F}_q^n$ of a system of structured quadratic multivariate polynomial equations $\boldsymbol{f} \in \mathbb{F}_q[x_1, \ldots, x_n]^m$ over a finite field. The private and public keys in Biscuit are respectively $\boldsymbol{s} \in \mathbb{F}_q^n$ and $(\boldsymbol{f}, \boldsymbol{t}) \in \mathbb{F}_q[x_1, \ldots, x_n]^m \times \mathbb{F}_q^m$, where $\boldsymbol{t} = \boldsymbol{f}(\boldsymbol{s})$.

The performance of Picnic is proportional to the number of multiplications required to evaluate the circuit defining the underlying block-cipher with the secret-key. This fact motivates the use of a set $\boldsymbol{f} = (f_1 \ldots, f_m) \in \mathbb{F}_q[x_1, \ldots, x_n]^m$ of polynomial equations that require a small number of multiplications to be evaluated. Biscuit considers polynomials of the form $f_i = A_0 + A_1 \cdot A_2$, where each $A_i \in \mathbb{F}_q[x_1, \ldots, x_n]$ is an affine polynomial. These polynomials can be evaluated using only one multiplication, while a random quadratic polynomial would require $O(n^2)$ multiplications.

1.1 Overview of MPCitH-Based Signature Schemes

Since Picnic, the use of MPCitH for designing post-quantum signature schemes has become extremely popular. This is evidenced in the new NIST standardization process for post-quantum signature schemes, where eight[1] among forty of the submitted schemes are using the MPCitH framework. These schemes follow the same design methodology but differ in the hard problems considered.

AIMer is based on the hardness of key-recovery of a MPC-friendly block-cipher [32], MIRA and MiRitH are based on the MinRank problem [4,9], MQOM is based on the problem of solving random quadratic equations [24], PERK is based on the Permuted Kernel Problem [3], RYDE is based on the rank syndrome decoding problem [8], and SDith relies on the syndrome decoding problem [33]. All these schemes proposed several parameter sets to optimize either the signature size (short variant) or the signing and verification times (fast variant).

In Table 1, we overview the performances of these NIST candidates with the version of Biscuit described in this paper. The table also includes FAEST [13] whose security is based on AES but uses a new zero-knowledge technique, named VOLE-in-the head, that improves the MPCitH approach.

For each scheme[2], we report on a short variant achieving NIST level-I security (i.e. equivalent to the security of AES128). The key-generation (keygen), signature generation (sign), and verification (verify) times are shown in clock-cycles (cycles). These numbers have been extracted directly from the corresponding

[1] https://csrc.nist.gov/projects/pqc-dig-sig/round-1-additional-signatures.

[2] A few days before finalizing this manuscript a new preprint appeared [25] that seems to significantly improve MQOM as well as many MPCitH-based signature schemes (including Biscuit).

Table 1. Performance of level-I short variants of MPCitH-based candidates submitted to the first round of the new NIST call for post-quantum signature schemes.

Name	Performance (cycles)			Size (bytes)		
	keygen	sign	verify	sk	pk	σ
AIMer-L1PARAM4	54 435	78 022 625	73 813 256	16	32	3 840
MIRA-128 s	112 000	46 800 000	43 900 000	16	84	5 640
MiRitH-Ias	108 903	41 220 707	40 976 634	16	129	5 673
MQOM-L1-gf31-short	67 000	44 360 000	41 720 000	78	47	6 352
PERK-I-short5	91 000	36 000 000	25 000 000	16	24	6 006
RYDE128s	33 100	23 400 000	20 100 000	32	86	5 956
SDith-L1-hyp	7 083 000	13 400 000	12 500 000	404	120	8 260
Biscuit-128 s (this work)	62 484	27 922 077	28 484 726	16	68	5 748
FAEST-128 s	200 000	25 580 000	25 830 000	32	32	5 006

submissions and we refer to these documents for details. The purpose of these numbers is to give a rough global perspective as the methodology to derive clock-cycles, as well as the level of optimization, could differ between submissions. Table 1 also includes secret-key (sk), public-key (pk) and signature (σ) sizes in bytes.

1.2 Organization of the Paper and Main Results

After this introduction, the paper is organized as follows. Section 2 introduces basic notations, the new hard problem considered in Biscuit (PowAff2 problem, Sect. 2.2), as well as the basic cryptography building blocks underlying its design: Multi-Party Computation (MPC), MPC-in-the-Head approach (MPCitH), Zero-Knowledge Proof of Knowledge (ZKPoK), proof systems using multiplicative triples and the hypercube technique for MPCitH-based signature schemes.

Section 3 describes the core sub-protocols underlying Biscuit. Due to the structure of the algebraic systems considered in Biscuit, the evaluation of a PowAff2 solution requires only one multiplication per equation. This leads to a rather simple MPC protocol (Sect. 3.1) for PowAff2 that is based on the parallel execution of secure multiplication using Beaver multiplicative triples [15] with some optimizations from [14,30]. Then, we derive a new ZKPoK for PowAff2 (Sect. 3.2) using the MPCitH approach. Note that the protocol presented here (Fig. 3) differs from the one described in the initial Biscuit submission [19]. In particular, we use the hypercube technique [34] and also include a security proof (Theorem 1) of the new ZKPoK.

Section 4 presents the Biscuit signature scheme and details the key generation, signature generation (Fig. 7) and verification (Fig. 8) algorithms. Biscuit is constructed using the traditional Fiat-Shamir transform from the ZKPoK described in Fig. 3. We conclude this part with Table 2 that summarizes the secret-key, public-key, and signature sizes for the three security levels of NIST. In particular, Biscuit achieves a signature of 5.7KB for the first security level. This is comparable to other recent MPCitH-based signature schemes (Sect. 1.1).

Section 5 analyzes the security of the parameters proposed in Table 2. This section revisits the security analysis performed in the initial submission of Biscuit by taking into account new third-party analysis [20]. In Sect. 5.1, we first explain the connection between the hardness of PowAff2 and the difficulty of solving the Learning With (bounded) Errors (LWE) problem [35]. In Sect. 5.2, we consider the key-recovery problem where the best attack against it, is a dedicated hybrid approach, i.e. that combines exhaustive search and Gröbner bases [12,17,18], for solving PowAff2 equations described by Bouillaguet on the NIST PQC mailing-list [20]. In Sect. 5.3, we refine the analysis of Kales and Zaverucha [29] for forgery attacks against 5-pass Fiat-Shamir based signature schemes. This leads us to introduce a variant of the PowAff2 problem where the attacker has to solve a sub-system with fewer equations; leading to the introduction of the $\texttt{PowAff2}_u$ problem (Definition 1).

Finally, Sect. 6 presents an optimized implementation of Biscuit which outperforms the previous implementation. First, we use a new canonical representation of the PowAff2 equations (Lemma 1), which allows us to simplify their evaluation further. Then, we integrate the hypercube framework for even further improvements.

2 Preliminaries

This section presents preliminary concepts and notations used in this paper.

2.1 Notations

Throughout this paper, we use λ for the security parameter. Also, $[n]$ refers to the set $\{1, \ldots, n\}$ for an integer $n \in \mathbb{N}$, $\mathbb{F}_q$ is the finite field of q elements (where q is prime or a prime power), $\mathbb{F}_q^m$ denotes the vector space of dimension m over $\mathbb{F}_q$ and $\mathbb{F}_q[x_1, \ldots, x_n]$ is the ring of polynomials in the variables $x_1, \ldots, x_n$ over the field $\mathbb{F}_q$.

Bold lower-case letters denote vectors, $\mathbf{x} + \mathbf{y}$ denotes the element-wise addition. We use $a \leftarrow \mathcal{A}(x)$ to indicate that a is the output of an algorithm $\mathcal{A}$ on input x, $a \xleftarrow{\$} \mathcal{S}$ means that a is sampled uniformly at random from a set $\mathcal{S}$.

Let $\mathcal{R}$ be a ring and $a \in \mathcal{R}$. The additive sharing of a, denoted by $[\![a]\!]$, is a tuple $[\![a]\!] := ([\![a]\!]_1, \ldots, [\![a]\!]_N) \in \mathcal{R}^N$ such that $a = \sum_{i=1}^{N} [\![a]\!]_i$. Each component $[\![a]\!]_i$ of $[\![a]\!]$ is called a *share* of a. Throughout this paper, we only consider additive sharing and use the word sharing to refer to additive sharing.

A *Multi-Party Computation* (MPC) protocol is an interactive protocol executed by a set of N parties knowing a public function f. Its goal is to compute the image $z = f(x_1, \ldots, x_N)$, where the value x_i is only known by the i-th party. A MPC protocol is considered secure and correct if, at the end of the protocol, every party i knows z, and no information about its secret input value x_i is revealed to the other parties.

2.2 The $\texttt{PowAff2}_u$ Problem

The core problem considered in Biscuit is the one of solving a system of multivariate equations defined as the product of two affine forms. Denoted by $\texttt{PowAff2}_u$, the problem is parameterized by a tuple of positive integers (n, m, u, q), where n is the number of variables, m the number of equations, u is a parameter related to forgery (Sect. 5.3), and q is the finite field size.

Definition 1 (The $\texttt{PowAff2}_u$ problem). *Let $A_{1,0}, A_{1,1}, A_{1,2}, \ldots, A_{m,0}, A_{m,1}, A_{m,2} \in \mathbb{F}_q[x_1, \ldots, x_n]$ be affine forms, i.e.:*

$$A_{k,j}(x_1, \ldots, x_n) = a_0^{(k,j)} + \sum_{i=1}^{n} a_i^{(k,j)} x_i, \text{ with } a_0^{(k,j)}, \ldots, a_n^{(k,j)} \in \mathbb{F}_q. \quad (1)$$

Input. *A vector $\mathbf{t} = (t_1, \ldots, t_m) \in \mathbb{F}_q^m$ and multivariate polynomials $\mathbf{f} = (f_1, \ldots, f_m) \in \mathbb{F}_q[x_1, \ldots, x_n]^m$ defined as:*

$$f_k(x_1, \ldots, x_n) = A_{k,0}(x_1, \ldots, x_n) + \prod_{j=1}^{2} A_{k,j}(x_1, \ldots, x_n), \forall k \in [m]. \quad (2)$$

Question. *Find – if any – a vector $(s_1, \ldots, s_n) \in \mathbb{F}_q^n$ and set $J \subseteq [m]$ of size $m - u$ such that:*

$$f_j(s_1, \ldots, s_n) = t_j, \ \forall j \in J.$$

Definition 2 (The $\texttt{PowAff2}$ problem). *We use $\texttt{PowAff2}$ to denote the $\texttt{PowAff2}_0$ problem. We call $\texttt{PowAff2}$ algebraic system the set of non-linear equations $f_1, \ldots, f_m \in \mathbb{F}_q[x_1, \ldots, x_n]$ defined as in (2).*

$\texttt{PowAff2}$ is the problem corresponding to key-recovery whilst $\texttt{PowAff2}_u$, with $u > 0$, is a relaxation that corresponds to signature forgery whose hardness is detailed in Sect. 5. The current best attack against Biscuit has been sketched in [20]. In particular, it was mentioned that the multivariate equations defined as in Definition 1 can be reduced to a simple, but equivalent, structure.

Lemma 1. *Let $\mathbf{f} = (f_1, \ldots, f_m) \in \mathbb{F}_q[x_1, \ldots, x_n]^m$ be a $\texttt{PowAff2}$ algebraic system. Then, with high probability, there exists an invertible matrix $\mathbf{L} \in \mathrm{GL}_n(\mathbb{F}_q)$ such that :*

$$\mathbf{f}(\mathbf{x} \cdot \mathbf{L}) = \Big(u_1(\boldsymbol{x}) \cdot (x_1 + c_1) + w_1(\mathbf{x}), \ldots, u_n(\mathbf{x}) \cdot (x_n + c_n) + w_n(\boldsymbol{x}),$$
$$A'_{n+1,0}(\mathbf{x}) + \prod_{j=1}^{2} A'_{n+1,j}(\mathbf{x}), \ldots, A'_{m,0}(x_1, \ldots, x_n) + \prod_{j=1}^{2} A'_{m,j}(\mathbf{x})\Big)$$

where $\mathbf{x} = (x_1, \ldots, x_n), A_{n+1,0}, A_{n+1,1}, A_{n+1,2}, \ldots, A_{m,0}, A_{m,1}, A_{m,2}, u_1, \ldots, u_n, v_1, \ldots, v_n \in \mathbb{F}_q[x_1, \ldots, x_n]$ are affine polynomials and $c_1, \ldots, c_n \in \mathbb{F}_q$.

Proof. By construction, we have :

$$f_k(x_1,\ldots,x_n) = A_{k,0} + \prod_{j=1}^{2} A_{k,j}, \forall k \in [m],$$

with $A_{1,0}, A_{1,1}, A_{1,2}, \ldots, A_{m,0}, A_{m,1}, A_{m,2} \in \mathbb{F}_q[x_1,\ldots,x_n]$ affine forms as in (1). Thus, we can write $A_{k,2}(x_1,\ldots,x_n) = (x_1,\ldots,x_n)\cdot\mathbf{b}_k + c_k$, where $\mathbf{b}_k = (a_1^{(k,2)},\ldots,a_n^{(k,2)}) \in \mathbb{F}_q^n$ and $c_k = a_0^{(k,2)} \in \mathbb{F}_q$. Let $\mathbf{C} \in \mathbb{F}_q^{n\times n}$ be the matrix whose rows are $\mathbf{b}_1,\ldots,\mathbf{b}_n$. We want to find a non-singular matrix $\mathbf{L} \in \mathrm{GL}_n(\mathbb{F}_q)$ such that $\mathbf{I}_n = \mathbf{C}\cdot\mathbf{L}$, where $\mathbf{I}_n$ is the identity matrix of size n. This reduces to compute, if any, the inverse of $\mathbf{C}$. □

2.3 Digital Signature Scheme

Definition 3. *A Digital Signature Scheme (DSS) is a tuple of three probabilistic polynomial-time algorithms (KeyGen, Sign, Verify) verifying:*

1. *$(\mathsf{pk},\mathsf{sk}) \leftarrow \mathsf{KeyGen}(1^\lambda)$. The key-generation algorithm KeyGen takes as input a security parameter 1^λ and outputs a pair of public/private keys $(\mathsf{pk},\mathsf{sk})$.*
2. *$\sigma \leftarrow \mathsf{Sign}(\mathsf{sk},\mathsf{msg})$. The signing algorithm Sign takes a private key sk and a message $\mathsf{msg} \in \{0,1\}^*$ and outputs a signature σ.*
3. *$b \leftarrow \mathsf{Sign}(\mathsf{pk},\sigma,\mathsf{msg})$. The verification algorithm Verify is deterministic. It takes as input a message $\mathsf{msg} \in \{0,1\}^*$, a signature σ, and a public key pk. It outputs a bit $b \in \{0,1\}$, 1 means that it* ***accepts****σ as a valid signature for msg, otherwise it* ***rejects*** *returning 0.*

A signature scheme is correct if for every security parameter $\lambda \in \mathbb{N}$, every $(\mathsf{pk},\mathsf{sk}) \leftarrow \mathsf{KeyGen}(1^\lambda)$, and every message $\mathsf{msg} \in \{0,1\}^*$, it holds that

$$1 \leftarrow \mathsf{Verify}(\mathsf{pk},\mathsf{msg},\mathsf{Sign}(\mathsf{sk},\mathsf{msg})).$$

The standard security notion for a DSS is Existential Unforgeability under Adaptive Chosen-Message Attacks (EU-CMA). We say that a signature scheme is EU-CMA-secure if for all probabilistic polynomial-time adversaries $\mathcal{A}$, the probability

$$\Pr\left[1 \leftarrow \mathsf{Verify}(\mathsf{pk},\mathsf{msg}^*,\sigma^*) \;\middle|\; \begin{array}{c}(\mathsf{pk},\mathsf{sk}) \leftarrow \mathsf{KeyGen}(1^\lambda)\\ (\mathsf{msg}^*,\sigma^*) \leftarrow \mathcal{A}^{\mathcal{O}_{\mathsf{Sign}(\mathsf{sk},\cdot)}}(\mathsf{pk})\end{array}\right]$$

is a negligible function in λ, where $\mathcal{A}$ is given access to a signing oracle $\mathcal{O}_{\mathsf{Sign}(\mathsf{sk},\cdot)}$, and msg^* has not been queried to $\mathcal{O}_{\mathsf{Sign}(\mathsf{sk},\cdot)}$.

Auxiliary Functions. Biscuit also relies on further basic cryptographic building blocks that we do not explicitly introduce such as commitments, collision-resistant hash functions, key-derivation functions, and pseudo-random number generators. As explained in [19], we can use the SHAKE256 [22] extendable-output function (XOF) to instantiate these functions.

During signature, the signer must generate a set of N seeds and reveal $N-1$ of them to the verifier for each iteration (TreePRG). The verifier then uses these seeds to check that the MPC protocol was correctly simulated. A binary tree structure allows generating the seeds using one root seed from a binary tree. Instead of sending $N-1$ seeds in the signature, this allows sending only $\lceil \log_2 N \rceil$ seeds that will be used to reconstruct all $N-1$ seeds required. We refer to [19] for the description of TreePRG.

2.4 5-Pass Identification Schemes

An Identification Scheme (IDS) is an interactive protocol between a *prover* P and a *verifier* V, where P wants to prove its knowledge of a secret value sk to V using a public value pk.

Definition 4 (5-pass identification scheme). *A 5-pass* IDS *is a tuple of three probabilistic polynomial-time algorithms* (KeyGen, P, V) *such that*

1. $(\mathsf{pk}, \mathsf{sk}) \leftarrow \mathsf{KeyGen}(1^\lambda)$. *The key-generation algorithm* KeyGen *takes as input a security parameter* 1^λ *and outputs a pair of public/private keys* $(\mathsf{pk}, \mathsf{sk})$.
2. P *and* V *follow the protocol in Fig. 1, and at the end of this,* V *outputs* 1, *if it* ***accepts*** *that* P *knows* sk, *otherwise it* ***rejects*** *returning* 0.

A transcript of a 5-pass IDS *is a tuple* $(\mathsf{com}, \mathsf{ch}_1, \mathsf{rsp}_1, \mathsf{ch}_2, \mathsf{rsp}_2)$, *as in Fig. 1, includes all the messages exchanged between* P *and* V *in one execution of the* IDS.

We require an IDS to fulfill the following security properties.

- **Correctness:** if for any security parameter $\lambda \in \mathbb{N}$ and $(\mathsf{pk}, \mathsf{sk}) \leftarrow \mathsf{KeyGen}(1^\lambda)$ it holds, $\Pr[1 \leftarrow \mathsf{V}(\mathsf{pk}, \mathsf{com}, \mathsf{ch}_1, \mathsf{rsp}_1, \mathsf{ch}_2, \mathsf{rsp}_2)] = 1$, where $(\mathsf{com}, \mathsf{ch}_1, \mathsf{rsp}_1, \mathsf{ch}_2, \mathsf{rsp}_2)$ is the transcript of an execution of the protocol between $\mathsf{P}(\mathsf{pk}, \mathsf{sk})$ and $\mathsf{V}(\mathsf{pk})$.
- **Soundness (with soundness error ε):** if, given a key pair $(\mathsf{pk}, \mathsf{sk})$, for every polynomial-time adversary $\mathcal{A}$ the difference

$$\Pr\left[\begin{array}{c}(\mathsf{pk}, \mathsf{sk}) \leftarrow \mathsf{KeyGen}(1^\lambda) \\ 1 \leftarrow V(\mathsf{pk}, \mathsf{com}_{\mathcal{A}}, \mathsf{ch}_1, \mathsf{rsp}_{1,\mathcal{A}}, \mathsf{ch}_2, \mathsf{rsp}_{2,\mathcal{A}})\end{array}\right] - \varepsilon$$

  is a negligible function in λ, where $(\mathsf{com}_{\mathcal{A}}, \mathsf{ch}_1, \mathsf{rsp}_{1,\mathcal{A}}, \mathsf{ch}_2, \mathsf{rsp}_{2,\mathcal{A}})$ is the transcript of one execution of the protocol between $\mathcal{A}$ and V both with input pk.
- **Honest-verifier zero-knowledge:** if there exists a polynomial-time probabilistic algorithm $\mathcal{S}(\mathsf{pk})$, called a *simulator*, that can produce transcripts (sequences of the form $(\mathsf{com}, \mathsf{ch}_1, \mathsf{rsp}_1, \mathsf{ch}_2, \mathsf{rsp}_2)$), that are computationally indistinguishable from the distribution of transcripts of an honest execution of the protocol between $\mathsf{P}(\mathsf{pk}, \mathsf{sk})$ and $\mathsf{V}(\mathsf{pk})$.

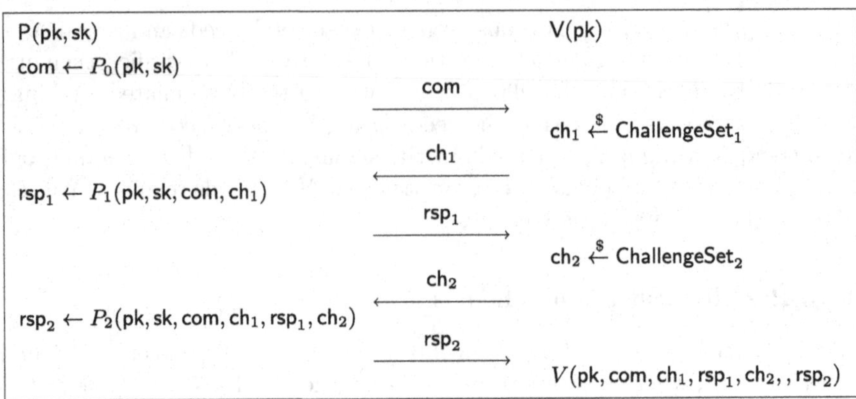

Fig. 1. Canonical 5-pass IDS.

2.5 MPC-in-the-Head: From MPC to Zero-Knowledge

MPC-in-the-Head (MPCitH) is a generic technique, introduced as "IKOS" [28], that allows to build a Zero-Knowledge Proof of Knowledge (ZKPoK) from a secure MPC protocol.

Consider a MPC protocol where N parties $P_1 \ldots, P_N$ collaborate to securely evaluate a public function f on a secret input x. Assuming that the protocol is perfectly correct and that the views of $t < N$ parties leak no information on x, then one can construct a ZKPoK from the MPC protocol as follows:

1. **Simulation.**
   - Prover P generates a random sharing $[\![x]\!] := ([\![x]\!]_1, \ldots, [\![x]\!]_N)$ of x such that $x = \sum_{i=1}^{N} [\![x]\!]_i$ and assign a share $[\![x]\!]_i$ to each party P_i.
   - P emulates "in his/her mind" execution of the MPC protocol with N parties $P_1 \ldots, P_N$.
   - P commits on the *views* of each P_i, meaning the messages they send/receive during the protocol execution and their internal states. These commitments are sent to the verifier V.
2. **Challenges.**
   - P possibly receives random challenges from V on the MPC, executes local computations accordingly and sends the results to V. This step can be repeated several times.
   - V challenges P to open a random subset of t parties.
   - P returns the requested views.
3. **Verification.**
   - P then checks that the views[3] are consistent, and the output of the circuit corresponds to the result expected.

[3] If only one party is opened then there are no pairs to check consistency. In this case, the prover does not commit to the views, but actually to the point-to-point channels between the parties.

Since its introduction, the initial approach for MPCitH from [28] has been improved in different ways. In particular, Katz, Kolesnikov and Wang (KKW, [31]) extended the MPCitH paradigm to support the *preprocessing model*, where MPC protocols are split into an offline phase that is independent of the sensitive inputs, and an online phase, with the former being typically the bottleneck in terms of efficiency. The benefit is that the prover does not need to include the preprocessing as part of the views of the parties, and instead, the preprocessing can be checked. As an application, KKW allowed to significantly decrease the signature size of the initial Picnic version.

In [34], the authors described the so-called hypercube variant of MPCitH that allows improving efficiency for a large number of parties in the MPC protocol. Indeed, a large number of parties leads to shorter signatures but increases signature generation and verification times. We detail the approach in the case of Biscuit in Sect. 3.1. Note that the hypercube technique is generic and could be then used for most MPCitH-based signature schemes.

2.6 Proof Systems for Arbitrary Circuits

In [27], Giacomelli, Madsen and Orlandi demonstrated the efficiency of the MPCitH approach for generating ZKPoK. Doing so, the authors also introduced a new generic proof system, called ZKBoo, which ultimately resulted in the first version of the Picnic signature scheme. In such work, the virtual/emulated parties actually *execute* some MPC protocols, and the verifier checks this execution. In [14], Baum and Nof proposed an improved proof system, called BN, for arithmetic circuits. The authors of [14] observed that the prover knows all the wire values in the circuit, and instead of computing a protocol, the prover can distribute sharings for each intermediate wire value, and the virtual parties only need to execute a protocol that checks the correctness of the multiplication gates. This allows batching the checks by taking random linear combinations. In [30], Kales and Zaverucha built on top of BN with several optimizations leading to BN++ with roughly 2.5× communication improvement.

The BN and BN++ proof systems rely on the concept of multiplicative triple (or Beaver triple [15]). Given $x, y, z \in \mathbb{F}_q$, we say that the triple $(\llbracket x \rrbracket, \llbracket y \rrbracket, \llbracket z \rrbracket) \in \mathbb{F}_q^N \times \mathbb{F}_q^N \times \mathbb{F}_q^N$ is a *multiplicative triple* if it holds that $z = x \cdot y$. The Biscuit MPC protocol will rely on a somewhat standard protocol introduced in [14] (along with the optimization given in [30, Section 2.5]) to check multiplicative triples of sharing (Sect. 2.6). A multiplicative triple $(\llbracket x \rrbracket, \llbracket y \rrbracket, \llbracket z \rrbracket) \in \mathbb{F}_q^N \times \mathbb{F}_q^N \times \mathbb{F}_q^N$ can be checked using a *helping* triple $(\llbracket a \rrbracket, \llbracket y \rrbracket, \llbracket c \rrbracket) \in \mathbb{F}_q^N \times \mathbb{F}_q^N \times \mathbb{F}_q^N$ with $a \in \mathbb{F}_q$ and $c = a \cdot y \in \mathbb{F}_q$ as follows:

1. The parties get a random element $\varepsilon \xleftarrow{\$} \mathbb{F}_q$.
2. The parties locally set $\llbracket \alpha \rrbracket \leftarrow \llbracket x \rrbracket \cdot \varepsilon + \llbracket a \rrbracket$.
3. The parties open $\llbracket \alpha \rrbracket$ so that they all obtain α.
4. The party locally compute $\llbracket v \rrbracket = \llbracket y \rrbracket \cdot \alpha - \llbracket z \rrbracket \cdot \varepsilon - \llbracket c \rrbracket$.
5. The parties open $\llbracket v \rrbracket$ to obtain v.
6. The parties output **accept** if $v = 0$ and **reject** otherwise.

The security of this simple protocol has been proven in [30]. In particular, the false success probability is given by:

Lemma 2. *Let* $x, y, z, a, c \in \mathbb{F}_q$. *If the shared multiplicative triple* $(\llbracket x \rrbracket, \llbracket y \rrbracket, \llbracket z \rrbracket) \in \mathbb{F}_q^N \times \mathbb{F}_q^N \times \mathbb{F}_q^N$ *is incorrect, i.e.* $z \neq x \cdot y$, *or the helping multiplicative triple* $(\llbracket a \rrbracket, \llbracket y \rrbracket, \llbracket c \rrbracket) \in \mathbb{F}_q^N \times \mathbb{F}_q^N \times \mathbb{F}_q^N$ *is incorrect, i.e.* $c \neq a \cdot y$, *then the parties output* **accept** *with probability at most* $1/q$.

3 Interactive Protocols for PowAff2

This section describes the MPC protocol underlying Biscuit (Sect. 3.1) and the corresponding ZKPoK (Sect. 3.2) obtained using the MPCitH paradigm (Sect. 2.5) together with the hypercube technique [5].

3.1 Multi-Party Computation Protocol for PowAff2

In Fig. 2, we detail the MPC protocol used in Biscuit to check a solution of a PowAff2 algebraic system. The protocol is executed by N parties sharing a secret vector $\mathbf{s} \in \mathbb{F}_q^n$. Every party knows the target vector $\mathbf{t} = (t_1, \ldots, t_m) \in \mathbb{F}_q^m$, affine forms $A_{1,0}, A_{1,1}, A_{1,2}, \ldots, A_{m,0}, A_{m,1}, A_{m,2} \in \mathbb{F}_q[x_1, \ldots, x_n]$ as in (1) and the corresponding PowAff2 algebraic equations $\mathbf{f} = (f_1, \ldots, f_m) \in \mathbb{F}_q[x_1, \ldots, x_n]^m$ defined as:

$$f_k = A_{k,0} + A_{k,1} \cdot A_{k,2}, \forall k \in [m]. \tag{3}$$

The MPC protocol (Fig. 2) consists of m iterations of the multiplicative checking protocol described in Sect. 2.6. At the end of the protocol, the parties output **accept** indicating they are convinced that the shared vector $\mathbf{s}$ satisfies $\mathbf{t} = \mathbf{f}(\mathbf{s})$. Otherwise, they output **reject**.

The following proposition follows easily from Lemma 2.

Proposition 1. *Suppose that a set of* N *parties genuinely follow the MPC protocol given in Fig. 2 with inputs* $\mathbf{t} \in \mathbb{F}_q^m, \mathbf{f} = (f_1, \ldots, f_m) \in \mathbb{F}_q[x_1, \ldots, x_n]^m$, *and* $\llbracket \mathbf{s} \rrbracket \in \left(\mathbb{F}_q^n\right)^N$. *Suppose* $\mathbf{s} \in \mathbb{F}_q^n$ *is a solution to* $\texttt{PowAff2}_u(\mathbf{f}, \mathbf{t})$ *but not a solution to the* $\texttt{PowAff2}_{u-1}(\mathbf{f}, \mathbf{t})$. *If* $u = 0$, *i.e.,* $\mathbf{t} = \mathbf{f}(\mathbf{s})$, *then the parties* **accept**. *Otherwise, the parties* **accept** *with probability at most* $1/q^u$.

Public data: $\mathbf{t} = (t_1, \ldots, t_m) \in \mathbb{F}_q^m$, affine polynomials $A_{1,0}, \ldots, A_{m,2} \in \mathbb{F}_q[x_1, \ldots, x_n]$ and $\mathbf{f} = (f_1, \ldots, f_m) \in \mathbb{F}_q[x_1, \ldots, x_n]^m$ as defined in (3).

Inputs : The i-th party knows $[\![\mathbf{s}]\!]_i \in \mathbb{F}_q^n$, $[\![\mathbf{a}]\!]_i \in \mathbb{F}_q^m$ where $\mathbf{a} = (a_1, \ldots, a_m) \xleftarrow{\$} \mathbb{F}_q^m$, and $[\![\mathbf{c}]\!]_i \in \mathbb{F}_q^m$ where $\mathbf{c} = (c_1, \ldots, c_m) \in \mathbb{F}_q^m$ such that $c_k = A_{k,2}(\mathbf{s}) \cdot a_k, \forall k \in [m]$.

MPC **protocol**:

for $k \in [m]$ **do**

1 : Each party compute $[\![z_k]\!] \leftarrow t_k - A_{k,0}([\![\mathbf{s}]\!])$, $[\![x_k]\!] \leftarrow A_{k,1}([\![\mathbf{s}]\!])$, and $[\![y_k]\!] \leftarrow A_{k,2}([\![\mathbf{s}]\!])$.

2 : The parties get a random element $\varepsilon_k \xleftarrow{\$} \mathbb{F}_q$.

3 : The parties locally set $[\![\alpha_k]\!] \leftarrow [\![x_k]\!] \cdot \varepsilon_k + [\![a_k]\!]$.

4 : The parties open $[\![\alpha_k]\!]$ so that they all obtain α_k.

5 : The parties locally compute $[\![v_k]\!] = [\![y_k]\!] \cdot \alpha_k - [\![z_k]\!] \cdot \varepsilon_k - [\![c_k]\!]$.

6 : The parties open $[\![v_k]\!]$ to obtain v_k.

The parties output **accept** if $v_k = 0, \forall k \in [n]$ and **reject** otherwise.

Fig. 2. MPC protocol Π to check that $\mathbf{t} = \mathbf{f}(\mathbf{s})$.

3.2 Zero-Knowledge Proof of Knowledge for PowAff2

In Fig. 3, we derive a zero-knowledge proof of knowledge (ZKPoK) for the PowAff2 problem using the MPC protocol Π of Fig. 2. We use the traditional MPCitH approach combined with the recent hypercube technique. To do so, let D be such that $N = 2^D$.

In Phase 1, for each $\ell \in [D]$: the prover generates an input set $S_\ell = \left([\![\mathbf{s}]\!]_{(\ell,j)}, [\![\mathbf{c}]\!]_{(\ell,j)}, [\![\mathbf{a}]\!] \right)_{j \in [2]}$ for a two parties instance the MPC protocol Π (Fig. 2). The set S_ℓ is called the ℓ-th set of *main shares*. The sets of main shares are computed in two steps. First, the prover generates and commits to inputs $([\![\mathbf{s}]\!]_i, [\![\mathbf{c}]\!]_i, [\![\mathbf{a}]\!]_i)$ of one of $N = 2^D$ parties instance of Π. Then, for each $(\ell, j) \in [D] \times [2]$, the main share $[\![\mathbf{s}]\!]_{(\ell,j)}$ is computed as the sum of the shares $[\![\mathbf{s}]\!]_i$ for which j equals the ℓ-th bit of i plus 1. Similarly, the main shares $[\![\mathbf{c}]\!]_{(\ell,j)}$ and $[\![\mathbf{a}]\!]_{(\ell,j)}$). In Phase 3, the prover executes the protocol Π for every set of main shares using $\varepsilon_1, \ldots, \varepsilon_m \in \mathbb{F}_q$ as the random elements for all D executions. This particular execution of the protocol Π on the set of main shares S_ℓ is shown in Fig. 4. The outputs of ℓ-th execution are the shares $\left([\![\alpha_k]\!]_{(\ell,j)}, [\![v_k]\!]_{(\ell,j)} \right)_{(k,j) \in [m] \times [2]}$ and its corresponding hash $H_\ell = \mathtt{H}\left(\left([\![\alpha_k]\!]_{(\ell,j)}, [\![v_k]\!]_{(\ell,j)} \right)_{(k,j) \in [m] \times [2]} \right)$[4]. In Phase 5, the prover sends $\left((\mathsf{seed}^{(i)}, \rho_i)_{i \neq \bar{i}}, \mathsf{com}^{(\bar{i})}, \mathbf{\Delta s}, \mathbf{\Delta c}, [\![\boldsymbol{\alpha}]\!]_{\bar{i}} \right)$ to the verifier, where $[\![\boldsymbol{\alpha}]\!]_{\bar{i}} = ([\![\alpha_1]\!]_{\bar{i}}, \ldots, [\![\alpha_m]\!]_{\bar{i}})$, $[\![\alpha_k]\!]_{\bar{i}} = [\![x_k]\!]_{\bar{i}} \cdot \varepsilon_k + [\![a_k]\!]_{\bar{i}}$ and $[\![x_k]\!]_{\bar{i}} = A_{k,0}([\![s]\!]_{\bar{i}})$. We highlight that the prover does not send explicitly instead of sending $N - 1$ strings of the form $(\mathsf{seed}^{(i)}, \rho_i)$ but it sends instead the $\log_2(N)$ nodes of the

[4] As noted in [10], the security of proof knowledge protocols using the hypercube technique with additive shares is the same with or without these intermediate hash values H_ℓ. Still, it might help reduce the protocol's memory demand when the implementation of the hash H is not incremental.

tree TreePRG(root) so that the verifier can recompute the values $(\mathsf{seed}^{(i)}, \rho_i)_{i \neq \bar{i}}$. Finally, in the verification phase, the verifier recomputes $(\mathsf{seed}^{(i)}, \rho_i)_{i \neq \bar{i}}$, and uses them to recompute the sets main shares partially. We say partially recompute and not just recompute because for each set S_ℓ one of the main shares triples (either the one corresponding to $j = 1$ or $j = 2$) is missing the addition of the shares corresponding to the $\bar{i}$-th party. After, for every set of main parties, the verifier follows the algorithm in Fig. 5 to check the execution of the MPC protocol Π. Finally, the verifier recomputes h_0 and h_2 and outputs accept if these two values match the ones the prover sent. Otherwise, the verifier rejects.

The result below establishes the zero-knowledge property of the protocol described in Fig. 3.

Theorem 1. *The protocol described in Fig. 3 has the following properties:*

- ***Completeness.*** *A Prover with the knowledge of a solution $\mathbf{s} \in \mathbb{F}_q^n$ to an instance $(\mathbf{f}, \mathbf{t}) \in \mathbb{F}_q[x_1, \ldots, x_n]^m \times \mathbb{F}_q^m$ of the* PowAff2 *is always accepted by the Verifier.*
- ***Soundness.*** *Let $\epsilon = \frac{1}{N} + \frac{1}{q^u} \cdot \left(1 - \frac{1}{N}\right)$, where $p = 1/q^u$. Suppose there exists a prover $\tilde{\mathcal{P}}$ who convinces the verifier to accept with probability $\tilde{\epsilon} > \epsilon$. Then there is an efficient probabilistic extraction algorithm $\mathcal{E}$, which has rewindable black-box access to $\tilde{\mathcal{P}}$, that, in expectation, with at most*

$$\frac{4}{\tilde{\epsilon} - \epsilon} \cdot \left(1 + \tilde{\epsilon} \cdot \frac{2\ln(2)}{\tilde{\epsilon} - \epsilon}\right),$$

  calls to $\tilde{P}$ outputs either a solution to an instance $(\mathbf{f}, \mathbf{t})$ of the $\mathtt{PowAff2}_{u-1}$ *problem or a collision to the commitment scheme* com *or the hash* H*.*
- ***Honest-verifier zero-knowledge.*** *If the outputs of the pseudo-random generator* PRG *and the commitment scheme* com *are indistinguishable from the uniform random distribution, then the protocol of Fig. 3 is honest-verifier zero-knowledge.*

Proof. (sketch) The proof is similar to, for instance, [10, Theorem 1]. Here, we describe the main parts of the proof and will refer [10, Theorem 1] for similar details.

- **Completeness.** By following, step by step, the protocol in Fig. 3, it is not hard to see that a Prover that follows the protocol with inputs $(\mathbf{f}, \mathbf{t}, \mathbf{s})$ such that $\mathbf{t} = \mathbf{f}(\mathbf{s})$ will always be accepted.
- **Soundness.** The structure of the proof is as follows:
  1. We prove that a prover $\tilde{\mathcal{P}}$ who does not know any solution for the $\mathtt{PowAff2}_{u-1}$ problem can cheat with probability at most $\epsilon = \frac{1}{N} + \frac{1}{q^u} \cdot \left(1 - \frac{1}{N}\right)$.
  2. Assuming that
     (a) No collisions to com nor H can be found.
     (b) There exists a cheater $\tilde{\mathcal{P}}$ who has cheating probability $\tilde{\epsilon} > \epsilon$.

PoK(Prover($\mathbf{f}, \mathbf{t}, \mathbf{s}$), Verifier($\mathbf{f}, \mathbf{t}$))

Phase 1: Prover commits to the inputs of the MPC protocol in Figure 4

root $\xleftarrow{\$} \{0,1\}^\lambda$, $\left(\mathsf{seed}^{(i)}, \rho^{(i)}\right)_{i \in [N]} \leftarrow \mathrm{TreePRG}(\mathsf{root})$

for $i \in [N]$ **do**

$\quad [\![\mathbf{s}]\!]_i, [\![\mathbf{c}]\!]_i, [\![\mathbf{a}]\!]_i, \leftarrow \mathtt{PRG}(\mathsf{seed}^{(i)})$

$\quad \mathsf{com}^{(i)} \leftarrow \mathsf{Com}(\mathsf{seed}^{(i)}, \rho_i)$

$h_0 \leftarrow \mathtt{H}(\mathsf{com}^{(1)}, \ldots, \mathsf{com}^{(N)})$, and send h_0 to Verifier

$\mathbf{a} \leftarrow \sum_{i \in [N]} [\![\mathbf{a}]\!]_i$, $\quad \mathbf{c} \leftarrow \left(A_{k,2}(\mathbf{s}) \cdot a_k\right)_{k \in [m]}$

$\mathbf{\Delta s} \leftarrow \mathbf{s} - \sum_{i \in [N]} [\![\mathbf{s}]\!]_i$, $\quad \mathbf{\Delta c} \leftarrow \mathbf{c} - \sum_{i \in [N]} [\![\mathbf{c}]\!]_i$

$[\![\mathbf{s}]\!]_1 \leftarrow [\![\mathbf{s}]\!]_1 + \mathbf{\Delta s}$ and $[\![\mathbf{c}]\!]_1 \leftarrow [\![\mathbf{c}]\!]_1 + \mathbf{\Delta c}$

Initialize $[\![\mathbf{s}]\!]_p, [\![\mathbf{c}]\!]_p$ and $[\![\mathbf{a}]\!]_p$ to zero objects for each $p \in [D] \times [2]$

for $i \in [N]$ **do**

$\quad (i_1, \ldots, i_D) \leftarrow i$ // Binary representation of i.

$\quad$ **for** $\ell \in [D]$ **do**

$\quad\quad [\![\mathbf{s}]\!]_{(\ell, i_\ell+1)} \leftarrow [\![\mathbf{s}]\!]_{(\ell, i_\ell+1)} + [\![\mathbf{s}]\!]_i$, $[\![\mathbf{c}]\!]_{(\ell, i_\ell+1)} \leftarrow [\![\mathbf{c}]\!]_{(\ell, i_\ell+1)} + [\![\mathbf{c}]\!]_i$ and

$\quad\quad [\![\mathbf{a}]\!]_{(\ell, i_\ell+1)} \leftarrow [\![\mathbf{a}]\!]_{(\ell, i_\ell+1)} + [\![\mathbf{a}]\!]_i$

Phase 2: First challenge

Verifier samples $\varepsilon_1, \ldots, \varepsilon_m \xleftarrow{\$} \mathbb{F}_q$ and sends them to Prover

Phase 3: Prover's first response // Prover executes MPC protocol for every set of main shares.

for $\ell \in [D]$ **do**

$\quad$ Prover gets H_ℓ and $\left([\![\alpha_k]\!]_{(\ell,j)}, [\![v_k]\!]_{(\ell,j)}\right)_{(k,j) \in [m] \times [2]}$ from the algorithm in Figure 4

$h_1 \leftarrow \mathtt{H}(H_1, \ldots, H_D)$ and send h_1 to Verifier

Phase 4: Second challenge

Verifier samples $\bar{i} \xleftarrow{\$} [N]$ and sends it to Prover

Phase 5: Prover's second response

$[\![\alpha]\!]_{\bar{i}} \leftarrow ([\![\alpha_1]\!]_{\bar{i}}, \ldots, [\![\alpha_m]\!]_{\bar{i}})$, where $[\![\alpha_k]\!]_{\bar{i}} = [\![x_k]\!]_{\bar{i}} \cdot \varepsilon_k + [\![a_k]\!]_{\bar{i}}$ and $[\![x_k]\!]_{\bar{i}} = A_{k,0}([\![s]\!]_{\bar{i}})$

$\mathsf{rsp} \leftarrow \left((\mathsf{seed}^{(i)}, \rho_i)_{i \neq \bar{i}}, \mathsf{com}^{(\bar{i})}, \mathbf{\Delta s}, \mathbf{\Delta c}, [\![\alpha]\!]_{\bar{i}}\right)$ and send rsp to Verifier

Verification:

Verifier partially recomputes $\left([\![\mathbf{s}]\!]_p, [\![\mathbf{c}]\!]_p, [\![\mathbf{a}]\!]_p\right)_{p \in [D] \times [2]}$ from $(\mathsf{seed}^{(i)}, \rho_i)_{i \neq \bar{i}}$ by following Phase 1 but skipping the steps involving a $\bar{i}$-th share or the seed $\mathsf{seed}^{(\bar{i})}$

for $\ell \in [D]$ **do**

$\quad$ Verifier gets H_ℓ and $\left([\![\alpha_k]\!]_{(\ell,j)}, [\![v_k]\!]_{(\ell,j)}\right)_{(k,j) \in [m] \times [2]}$ from the algorithm in Figure 5

Verifier accepts if and only if $h_0 = \mathtt{H}(\mathsf{com}^{(1)}, \ldots, \mathsf{com}^{(N)})$ and $h_1 = \mathtt{H}(H_1, \ldots, H_D)$, where $\mathsf{com}^{(i)} = \mathsf{Com}(\mathsf{seed}^{(i)}, \rho_i)$ for each $i \neq \bar{i}$.

Fig. 3. Proof of Knowledge protocol for PowAff2.

We show how to extract a solution for the $\mathtt{PowAff2}_{u-1}$ problem whenever rewindable black-box access to $\tilde{\mathcal{P}}$ is given.

Inputs : A set of main shares $\left(\left(\llbracket \mathbf{s} \rrbracket_{(\ell,j)}, \llbracket \mathbf{c} \rrbracket_{(\ell,j)}, \llbracket \mathbf{a} \rrbracket_{(\ell,j)}\right)\right)_{j \in [2]}$ and the challenges $\varepsilon_1, \ldots, \varepsilon_m$

Outputs : H_ℓ and $\left(\llbracket \alpha_k \rrbracket_{(\ell,j)}, \llbracket v_k \rrbracket_{(\ell,j)}\right)_{(k,j) \in [m] \times [2]}$

for $k \in [m]$ **do**

  for $j \in [2]$ **do**

    $\llbracket x_k \rrbracket_{(\ell,j)} \leftarrow A_{k,1}(\llbracket \mathbf{s} \rrbracket_{(\ell,j)})$

    $\llbracket \alpha_k \rrbracket_{(\ell,j)} \leftarrow \llbracket x_k \rrbracket_{(\ell,j)} \cdot \varepsilon_k + \llbracket a_k \rrbracket_{(\ell,j)}$

  $\alpha_k \leftarrow \llbracket \alpha_k \rrbracket_{(\ell,1)} + \llbracket \alpha_k \rrbracket_{(\ell,2)}$ // The parties open $\llbracket \alpha_k \rrbracket_{(\ell,j)}$ to obtain α_k.

  $\llbracket z_k \rrbracket_{(\ell,1)} \leftarrow t_k - A_{k,0}(\llbracket \mathbf{s} \rrbracket_{(\ell,1)})$

  $\llbracket y_k \rrbracket_{(\ell,1)} \leftarrow A_{k,2}(\llbracket \mathbf{s} \rrbracket_{(\ell,1)})$

  $\llbracket v_k \rrbracket_{(\ell,1)} \leftarrow \llbracket y_k \rrbracket_{(\ell,1)} \cdot \alpha_k - \llbracket z_k \rrbracket_{(\ell,1)} \cdot \varepsilon_k - \llbracket c_k \rrbracket_{(\ell,1)}$

  $\llbracket v_k \rrbracket_{(\ell,2)} \leftarrow - \llbracket v_k \rrbracket_{(\ell,1)}$

$H_\ell \leftarrow \mathtt{H}\left(\left(\llbracket \alpha_k \rrbracket_{(\ell,j)}, \llbracket v_k \rrbracket_{(\ell,j)}\right)_{(k,j) \in [m] \times [2]}\right)$

Fig. 4. Simulation of the MPC protocol Π for the ℓ-th set of main shares.

For part 1, suppose that at step 7 the vector $\boldsymbol{s} = \llbracket \boldsymbol{s} \rrbracket_1 + \cdots + \llbracket \boldsymbol{s} \rrbracket_N$ is not a solution of the $\mathtt{PowAff2}_{u-1}$ problem defined by $(\boldsymbol{f}, \boldsymbol{t})$. With such a vector $\boldsymbol{s}$ the prover can be accepted by the verifier in only two situations:

- (*False-positive case*) The prover honestly follows the protocol, and for each $k \in [m]$, the value $v_k = y_k \alpha_k - z_k \varepsilon_k - c_k$, which is the value that would be obtained from a genuine execution of the MPC protocol with challenges ε_k (see Fig. 2), equals to zero, or
- (*Cheating case*) The prover dishonestly deviates from the protocol, yet the verifier believes that all the honest v_k are zero, but in reality, at least one of them is not.

In the first case, we would have a false positive case of the MPC protocol in Fig. 2. By Proposition 1, this happens with probability at most $1/q^u$. In the second case, the prover cheats during the simulation of at least one party. Since the verifier checks the correct execution of all the parties but one, the prover has to cheat on exactly one party. Otherwise, the verifier rejects. Cheating in one party i' means that the prover uses a set of different shares than an honest party, holding the same input seed $\mathsf{seed}^{(i')}$, would use. Since every party aggregates to exactly one of the main shares for all of the D bi-party protocols. For each of these bi-party protocols, one share has been dishonestly computed, i.e., not following the MPC protocol. Thus, the prover won't be detected with probability $\frac{1}{N}$. Consequently, a prover without a correct solution of the $\mathtt{PowAff2}_{u-1}$ problem will be accepted with probability at most $\epsilon = \frac{1}{N} + \frac{1}{q^u} \cdot \left(1 - \frac{1}{N}\right)$.

Now, for the second part, we assume that no collisions to com nor $\mathtt{H}$ can be found and there exists a cheater $\tilde{\mathcal{P}}$ who has cheating probability $\tilde{\epsilon} > \epsilon$. First, we prove that a solution $\boldsymbol{s}$ of the $\mathtt{PowAff2}_{u-1}$ problem can be extracted from two valid transcripts of the form $\mathcal{T}_1$ and $\mathcal{T}_2$ produced by $\tilde{\mathcal{P}}$ that have the same initial commitment h_0 and different second challenges $\bar{i}_1$ (for $\mathcal{T}_1$) and

Inputs: Partially computed main shares $\left(\left(\llbracket \mathbf{s} \rrbracket_{(\ell,j)}, \llbracket \mathbf{c} \rrbracket_{(\ell,j)}, \llbracket \mathbf{a} \rrbracket_{(\ell,j)}\right)\right)_{j\in[2]}$, the first challenges $\varepsilon_1,\ldots,\varepsilon_m$, the second challenge $\bar{i}$, and the $\llbracket \boldsymbol{\alpha} \rrbracket_{\bar{i}}$

Outputs : H_ℓ and $\left(\llbracket \alpha_k \rrbracket_{(\ell,j)}, \llbracket v_k \rrbracket_{(\ell,j)}\right)_{(k,j)\in[m]\times[2]}$

$(\bar{i}_1,\ldots,\bar{i}_D) \leftarrow \bar{i}$ // Binary representation of $\bar{i}$.

$\llbracket \alpha_1 \rrbracket_{\bar{i}},\ldots,\llbracket \alpha_m \rrbracket_{\bar{i}} \leftarrow \llbracket \boldsymbol{\alpha} \rrbracket_{\bar{i}}$

for $k \in [m]$ **do**

  for $j \in [2]$ **do**

    $\llbracket x_k \rrbracket_{(\ell,j)} \leftarrow A_{k,1}(\llbracket \mathbf{s} \rrbracket_{(\ell,j)})$

    $\llbracket \alpha_k \rrbracket_{(\ell,j)} \leftarrow \llbracket x_k \rrbracket_{(\ell,j)} \cdot \varepsilon_k + \llbracket a_k \rrbracket_{(\ell,j)}$

  $\llbracket \alpha_k \rrbracket_{(\ell,i_\ell+1)} \leftarrow \llbracket \alpha_k \rrbracket_{(\ell,i_\ell+1)} + \llbracket \alpha_k \rrbracket_{\bar{i}}$ // Adding missing share of $\llbracket \alpha_k \rrbracket_{(\ell,i_\ell+1)}$.

  $\alpha_k \leftarrow \llbracket \alpha_k \rrbracket_{(\ell,1)} + \llbracket \alpha_k \rrbracket_{(\ell,2)}$ // The parties open $\llbracket \alpha_k \rrbracket_{(\ell,j)}$ to obtain α_k.

  Set $i^* = 2$ if $\bar{i}_\ell = 0$, otherwise set $i^* = 1$.

  $\llbracket y_k \rrbracket_{(\ell,i^*)} \leftarrow A_{k,2}(\llbracket \mathbf{s} \rrbracket_{(\ell,i^*)})$

  $\llbracket z_k \rrbracket_{(\ell,i^*)} \leftarrow t_k - A_{k,0}(\llbracket \mathbf{s} \rrbracket_{(\ell,i^*)})$

  $\llbracket v_k \rrbracket_{(\ell,i^*)} \leftarrow \llbracket y_k \rrbracket_{(\ell,i^*)} \cdot \alpha_k - \llbracket z_k \rrbracket_{(\ell,i^*)} \cdot \varepsilon_k - \llbracket c_k \rrbracket_{(\ell,i^*)}$

  $\llbracket v_k \rrbracket_{(\ell,\bar{i}_\ell+1)} \leftarrow -\llbracket v_k \rrbracket_{(\ell,i^*)}$

$H_\ell \leftarrow \mathtt{H}\left(\left(\llbracket \alpha_k \rrbracket_{(\ell,j)}, \llbracket v_k \rrbracket_{(\ell,j)}\right)_{(k,j)\in[m]\times[2]}\right)$

Fig. 5. Check the simulation of the MPC protocol Π in the ℓ-th set of main shares.

$\bar{i}_1$. Finally, we prove that such transcripts $\mathcal{T}_1$ and $\mathcal{T}_2$ can be extracted from $\tilde{P}$ (assuming rewindable black-box access to $\tilde{P}$) with an expected number of calls upper bounded by

$$\frac{4}{\tilde{\epsilon}-\epsilon}\cdot\left(1+\tilde{\epsilon}\cdot\frac{2\ln(2)}{\tilde{\epsilon}-\epsilon}\right).$$

This second part is proven analogously as in [10, Theorem 1].

- **Honest-verifier zero-knowledge**: Now we sketch the proof of the honest-verifier zero-knowledge property of the protocol in Fig. 3. The goal here is to show that the distribution of the transcripts output by the simulator described in Fig. 6 on input $(\boldsymbol{f},\boldsymbol{t})$ are indistinguishable from those coming from a genuine interaction between a prover and an honest verifier, where the prover input is $(\boldsymbol{f},\boldsymbol{t},\boldsymbol{s})$ and $\boldsymbol{t}=\boldsymbol{f}(\boldsymbol{s})$.
  The idea is to create a sequence of simulators that ends with the simulator described in Fig. 6. The first simulator of the sequence consists of a legitimate prover, which holds a solution $\boldsymbol{s}$ and simulates the verifier by randomly sampling the challenges, as an honest verifier would do. These transcripts are indistinguishable from those coming from a legitimate execution of the protocol in proof of knowledge protocol.

Simulator$(\mathbf{f}, \mathbf{t})$

Sample first challenge: $\boldsymbol{\varepsilon} = (\varepsilon_1, \ldots, \varepsilon_m) \xleftarrow{\$} \mathbb{F}_q^m$

Sample second challenge: $\bar{i} \xleftarrow{\$} [N]$

$\mathsf{root} \xleftarrow{\$} \{0,1\}^\lambda$

$\left(\mathsf{seed}^{(i)}, \rho^{(i)}\right)_{i \in [N]} \leftarrow \mathrm{TreePRG}(\mathsf{root})$

for $i \in [N]$ **do**

$\quad [\![\mathbf{s}]\!]_i, [\![\mathbf{c}]\!]_i, [\![\mathbf{a}]\!]_i, \leftarrow \mathtt{PRG}(\mathsf{seed}^{(i)})$

$\quad \mathsf{com}^{(i)} \leftarrow \mathsf{Com}(\mathsf{seed}^{(i)}, \rho_i)$

$h_0 \leftarrow \mathtt{H}(\mathsf{com}^{(1)}, \ldots, \mathsf{com}^{(N)})$

$\boldsymbol{\Delta}\mathbf{s} \xleftarrow{\$} \mathbb{F}_q^n, \quad \boldsymbol{\Delta}\mathbf{c} \xleftarrow{\$} \mathbb{F}_q^m$

$[\![\mathbf{s}]\!]_1 \leftarrow [\![\mathbf{s}]\!]_1 + \boldsymbol{\Delta}\mathbf{s}$ and $[\![\mathbf{c}]\!]_1 \leftarrow [\![\mathbf{c}]\!]_1 + \boldsymbol{\Delta}\mathbf{c}$

Initialize $[\![\mathbf{s}]\!]_p, [\![\mathbf{c}]\!]_p$ and $[\![\mathbf{a}]\!]_p$ to zero objects for each $p \in [D] \times [2]$

for $i \in [N] \setminus \{\bar{i}\}$ **do**

$\quad$ Simulate the i party to obtain $[\![\alpha_k]\!]_i$ and $[\![v_k]\!]_i$ for each $k \in [m]$

$[\![\alpha_k]\!]_{\bar{i}} \xleftarrow{\$} \mathbb{F}_q$ and $[\![v_k]\!]_i \xleftarrow{\$} \mathbb{F}_q$ for each $k \in [m]$

$\mathsf{com}^{(\bar{i})} \xleftarrow{\$} \{0,1\}^\lambda$

For each $(k, \ell, j) \in [m] \times [D] \times [2]$ compute $[\![\alpha_k]\!]_{(\ell,j)}$ and $[\![v_k]\!]_{(\ell,j)}$

Set $H_\ell \leftarrow \mathtt{H}\Big(\big([\![\alpha_k]\!]_{(\ell,j)}, [\![v_k]\!]_{(\ell,j)}\big)_{(k,j) \in [m] \times [2]}\Big)$ for each $\ell \in [D]$

$h_1 \leftarrow \mathtt{H}(H_1, \ldots, H_D)$

$\mathsf{rsp} \leftarrow \big((\mathsf{seed}^{(i)}, \rho_i)_{i \neq \bar{i}}, \mathsf{com}^{(\bar{i})}, \boldsymbol{\Delta}\mathbf{s}, \boldsymbol{\Delta}\mathbf{c}, [\![\boldsymbol{\alpha}]\!]_{\bar{i}}\big)$, where $[\![\boldsymbol{\alpha}]\!]_{\bar{i}} = ([\![\alpha_1]\!]_{\bar{i}}, \ldots, [\![\alpha_m]\!]_{\bar{i}})$

Output $(h_0, \boldsymbol{\varepsilon}, h_1, \bar{i}, \mathsf{rsp})$

Fig. 6. Honest-verifier zero-knowledge simulator.

Finally, the proof is completed by showing that the transcripts outputs by any simulator in the sequence are indistinguishable from those in the previous simulator. This implies that the transcripts of the simulator in Fig. 6 are indistinguishable from those produced by the actual protocol. Details of this part follow similarly as shown in [10, Theorem 1].

□

4 Biscuit Signature Scheme

In this part, we describe the Biscuit signature scheme. It is obtained by applying the Fiat-Shamir transformation [26] to the zero-knowledge protocol given in Fig. 3. The corresponding signing, and verification algorithms are described in Figs. 7 and 8, respectively.

The secret-key is a random vector $\mathbf{s} \in \mathbb{F}_q^n$ and the public-key is a pair $(\mathbf{f} = (f_1, \ldots, f_m), \mathbf{t} = \mathbf{f}(\mathbf{s})) \in \mathbb{F}_q[x_1, \ldots, x_n]^m \times \mathbb{F}_q^m$ such that for all $k \in [m]$:

$$f_k(x_1, \ldots, x_n) = A_{k,0}(x_1, \ldots, x_n) + A_{k,1}(x_1, \ldots, x_n) \cdot A_{k,2}(x_1, \ldots, x_n), \quad (4)$$

where $A_{1,0}, \ldots, A_{m,2} \in \mathbb{F}_q[x_1, \ldots, x_n]$ are random affine forms as in (1).

We use two seeds $\mathsf{seed}_{\mathbf{f}}, \mathsf{seed}_{\mathbf{s}} \in \{0,1\}^\lambda$ that are extended via PRG to obtain the public polynomials $\mathbf{f} \in \mathbb{F}_q[x_1, \ldots, x_n]^m$ and the secret vector $\mathbf{s} \in \mathbb{F}_q[x_1, \ldots, x_n]^m$. Finally, the vector $\mathbf{t} \in \mathbb{F}_q^m$ is computed as $\mathbf{t} = \mathbf{f}(\mathbf{s})$.

The signing procedure Biscuit.Sign is given in Fig. 7. It takes as input a key-pair (sk, pk) and the message $\mathsf{msg} \in \{0,1\}^*$ to sign. It is obtained by applying the Fiat-Shamir transformation to the ZKPoK for PowAff2 (Sect. 3.2) with $N = 2^D$ parties.

Remark 1. The notation $\mathbf{f} \leftarrow \mathtt{PRG}(\mathsf{seed}_{\mathbf{f}})$ is a shortcut for extending the seed from a PRG and casting the bit string into a set of algebraic equations as in (4). Similarly, $\mathbf{s} \leftarrow \mathtt{PRG}(\mathsf{seed}_{\mathsf{sk}})$ stands for extending the seed and interpreting the bit string as a vector in $\mathbb{F}_q^n$.

The verification process (Fig. 8) is very similar to the signature process (Fig. 7) as the verifier has to replay the MPC protocol for each of the N participants except one. The algorithm takes as input a message $\mathsf{msg} \in \{0,1\}^*$, a signature sig and a public-key pk. It returns a bit $b \in \{0,1\}$.

4.1 Parameters

Table 2 provides the parameter sets Biscuit, along with the corresponding size of the keys and signatures. Each parameter set aims to provide a security level of either I, III or V according to the NIST guidelines. A more detailed description of the claimed security level of each parameter set is given in Sect. 5.

Table 2. Parameters of Biscuit, bit security, public-key (pk), secret-key (sk) and signature (σ) sizes in bytes.

Level	Version	λ	q	n	m	N	τ	Bit-Security	sk	pk	σ
I	short	128	256	50	52	256	18	143	16	68	5748
	fast					32	28	143			7544
III	short	192	256	89	92	256	25	207	24	116	12969
	fast					32	40	210			17784
V	short	256	256	127	130	256	33	272	32	162	23523
	fast					32	53	275			32575

$\mathsf{Sign}(\mathsf{pk}, \mathsf{sk}, \mathsf{msg})$

$(\mathsf{seed}_{\mathbf{f}}, \mathbf{t}) \leftarrow \mathsf{pk}, \ \mathsf{seed}_{\mathsf{sk}} \leftarrow \mathsf{sk}$

$\mathbf{f} \leftarrow \mathtt{PRG}(\mathsf{seed}_{\mathbf{f}}), \ \mathbf{s} \leftarrow \mathtt{PRG}(\mathsf{seed}_{\mathsf{sk}})$

Step 1: Commit to the inputs of the MPC protocol in Figure 4

$\mathsf{salt} \xleftarrow{\$} \{0,1\}^{2\lambda}$

for $e \in [\tau]$

$\quad \mathsf{root}^{(e)} \xleftarrow{\$} \{0,1\}^{\lambda}, \ \left(\mathsf{seed}^{(e,i)}\right)_{i\in[N]} \leftarrow \mathrm{TreePRG}(\mathsf{salt}, \mathsf{root}^{(e)})$

$\quad$ **for** $i \in [N]$ **do**

$\quad\quad [\![\mathbf{s}]\!]_i^{(e)}, [\![\mathbf{c}]\!]_i^{(e)}, [\![\mathbf{a}]\!]_i^{(e)} \leftarrow \mathtt{PRG}(\mathsf{seed}^{(e,i)})$

$\quad\quad \mathsf{com}^{(e,i)} \leftarrow \mathtt{H}_0\left(\mathsf{salt}, e, i, \mathsf{seed}^{(e,i)}\right)$

$\quad \mathbf{a}^{(e)} \leftarrow \sum_{i\in[N]} [\![\mathbf{a}]\!]_i^{(e)}, \quad \mathbf{c}^{(e)} \leftarrow \left(A_{k,2}(\mathbf{s}) \cdot a_k^{(e)}\right)_{k\in[m]}$

$\quad \mathbf{\Delta s}^{(e)} \leftarrow \mathbf{s} - \sum_{i\in[N]} [\![\mathbf{s}]\!]_i^{(e)}, \quad \mathbf{\Delta c}^{(e)} \leftarrow \mathbf{c}^{(e)} - \sum_{i\in[N]} [\![\mathbf{c}]\!]_i^{(e)}$

$\quad [\![\mathbf{s}]\!]_1^{(e)} \leftarrow [\![\mathbf{s}]\!]_1^{(e)} + \mathbf{\Delta s}^{(e)}$ and $[\![\mathbf{c}]\!]_1^{(e)} \leftarrow [\![\mathbf{c}]\!]_1^{(e)} + \mathbf{\Delta c}^{(e)}$

$\quad h_0^{(e)} \leftarrow \mathtt{H}_1(\mathsf{salt}, e, \mathsf{com}^{(e,1)}, \dots, \mathsf{com}^{(e,N)}, \mathbf{\Delta s}^{(e)}, \mathbf{\Delta c}^{(e)})$

$\quad$ Initialize $[\![\mathbf{s}]\!]_p^{(e)}, [\![\mathbf{c}]\!]_p^{(e)}$ and $[\![\mathbf{a}]\!]_p^{(e)}$ to zero objects for each $p \in [D] \times [2]$

$\quad$ **for** $i \in [N]$ **do**

$\quad\quad (i_1, \dots, i_D) \leftarrow i$ // Binary representation of i.

$\quad\quad$ **for** $\ell \in [D]$ **do**

$\quad\quad\quad [\![\mathbf{s}]\!]_{(\ell,i_\ell+1)}^{(e)} \leftarrow [\![\mathbf{s}]\!]_{(\ell,i_\ell+1)}^{(e)} + [\![\mathbf{s}]\!]_i^{(e)}, \ [\![\mathbf{c}]\!]_{(\ell,i_\ell+1)}^{(e)} \leftarrow [\![\mathbf{c}]\!]_{(\ell,i_\ell+1)}^{(e)} + [\![\mathbf{c}]\!]_i^{(e)}$ and

$\quad\quad\quad [\![\mathbf{a}]\!]_{(\ell,i_\ell+1)}^{(e)} \leftarrow [\![\mathbf{a}]\!]_{(\ell,i_\ell+1)}^{(e)} + [\![\mathbf{a}]\!]_i^{(e)}$

$h_1 \leftarrow \mathtt{H}_2\left(\mathsf{salt}, \mathsf{msg}, h_0^{(1)}, \dots, h_0^{(\tau)}\right)$

Step 2: First challenge

$\left((\varepsilon_1^{(e)}, \dots, \varepsilon_m^{(e)})\right)_{e\in[\tau]} \xleftarrow{\$} \mathtt{PRG}(h_1)$

Step 3: First response

for $e \in [\tau]$ **do**

$\quad$ **for** $\ell \in [D]$ **do**

$\quad\quad$ Follow the algorithm in Figure 4 to get $H_\ell^{(e)}$, which is defined instead as

$\quad\quad H_\ell^{(e)} = \mathtt{H}_3\left(\mathsf{salt}, \ell, [\![\alpha_k]\!]_{(\ell,j)}^{(e)}, [\![v_k]\!]_{(\ell,j)}^{(e)}\right)_{(k,j)\in[m]\times[2]}\Big)$

$h_2 \leftarrow \mathtt{H}_4\left(\mathsf{salt}, \mathsf{msg}, h_1, (H_1^{(e)}, \dots, H_D^{(e)})_{e\in[\tau]}\right)$

Step 4: Second challenge

$\bar{i}_1, \dots, \bar{i}_\tau \xleftarrow{\$} \mathtt{PRG}(h_2)$

Step 5: Second response

for $e \in [\tau]$ **do**

$\quad [\![\boldsymbol{\alpha}]\!]_{\bar{i}}^{(e)} \leftarrow ([\![\alpha_1]\!]_{\bar{i}}^{(e)}, \dots, [\![\alpha_m]\!]_{\bar{i}}^{(e)})$, where $[\![\alpha_k]\!]_{\bar{i}}^{(e)} = [\![x_k]\!]_{\bar{i}}^{(e)} \cdot \varepsilon_k^{(e)} + [\![a_k]\!]_{\bar{i}}^{(e)}$, and

$\quad [\![x_k]\!]^{(e)} = A_{k,1}([\![\mathbf{s}]\!]_{\bar{i}}^{(e)})$

$\sigma \leftarrow \left(\mathsf{salt}, h_1, h_2, \left((\mathsf{seed}^{(e,i)})_{i\neq\bar{i}_e}, \mathsf{com}^{(e,\bar{i}_e)}\right)_{e\in[\tau]}, \left(\mathbf{\Delta s}^{(e)}, \mathbf{\Delta c}^{(e)}, [\![\boldsymbol{\alpha}]\!]_{\bar{i}_e}^{(e)}\right)_{e\in[\tau]}\right)$

Output σ

Fig. 7. Biscuit signing algorithm.

Verify(pk, σ, msg)

$\left(\mathsf{seed}_{\mathbf{f}}, \mathbf{t}\right) \leftarrow \mathsf{pk}$, $\mathbf{f} \leftarrow \mathtt{PRG}(\mathsf{seed}_{\mathbf{f}})$

Step 1: Parse signature

$\left(\mathsf{salt}, h_1, h_2, \left((\mathsf{seed}^{(e,i)})_{i \neq \bar{i}_e}, \mathsf{com}^{(e,\bar{i}_e)}\right)_{e\in[\tau]}, \left(\boldsymbol{\Delta}\mathbf{s}^{(e)}, \boldsymbol{\Delta}\mathbf{c}^{(e)}, [\![\boldsymbol{\alpha}]\!]_{\bar{i}_e}^{(e)}\right)_{e\in[\tau]}\right) \leftarrow \sigma$

$\left((\varepsilon_1^{(e)}, \ldots, \varepsilon_m^{(e)})\right)_{e\in[\tau]} \xleftarrow{\$} \mathtt{PRG}(h_1)$

$\bar{i}_1, \ldots, \bar{i}_\tau \xleftarrow{\$} \mathtt{PRG}(h_2)$

Step 2: Recompute h_1 and the inputs of the MPC protocol

for $e \in [\tau]$

  for $i \in [N] \setminus \{\bar{i}_e\}$ **do**

    $[\![\mathbf{s}]\!]_i^{(e)}, [\![\mathbf{c}]\!]_i^{(e)}, [\![\mathbf{a}]\!]_i^{(e)} \leftarrow \mathtt{PRG}(\mathsf{seed}^{(e,i)})$

    $\mathsf{com}^{(e,i)} \leftarrow \mathtt{H}_0\left(\mathsf{salt}, e, i, \mathsf{seed}^{(e,i)}\right)$

  $h_0^{(e)} \leftarrow \mathtt{H}_1(\mathsf{salt}, e, \mathsf{com}^{(e,1)}, \ldots, \mathsf{com}^{(e,N)}, \boldsymbol{\Delta}\mathbf{s}^{(e)}, \boldsymbol{\Delta}\mathbf{c}^{(e)})$

  if $\bar{i}_e \neq 1$ **then**

    $[\![\mathbf{s}]\!]_1^{(e)} \leftarrow [\![\mathbf{s}]\!]_1^{(e)} + \boldsymbol{\Delta}\mathbf{s}^{(e)}$ and $[\![\mathbf{c}]\!]_1^{(e)} \leftarrow [\![\mathbf{c}]\!]_1^{(e)} + \boldsymbol{\Delta}\mathbf{c}^{(e)}$

  Initialize $[\![\mathbf{s}]\!]_p^{(e)}, [\![\mathbf{c}]\!]_p^{(e)}$ and $[\![\mathbf{a}]\!]_p^{(e)}$ to zero objects for each $p \in [D] \times [2]$

  for $i \in [N] \setminus \{\bar{i}_e\}$ **do**

    $(i_1, \ldots, i_D) \leftarrow i$ // Binary representation of i.

    for $\ell \in [D]$ **do**

      $[\![\mathbf{s}]\!]_{(\ell,i_\ell+1)}^{(e)} \leftarrow [\![\mathbf{s}]\!]_{(\ell,i_\ell+1)}^{(e)} + [\![\mathbf{s}]\!]_i^{(e)}$, $[\![\mathbf{c}]\!]_{(\ell,i_\ell+1)}^{(e)} \leftarrow [\![\mathbf{c}]\!]_{(\ell,i_\ell+1)}^{(e)} + [\![\mathbf{c}]\!]_i^{(e)}$ and

      $[\![\mathbf{a}]\!]_{(\ell,i_\ell+1)}^{(e)} \leftarrow [\![\mathbf{a}]\!]_{(\ell,i_\ell+1)}^{(e)} + [\![\mathbf{a}]\!]_i^{(e)}$

$\bar{h}_1 \leftarrow \mathtt{H}_2\left(\mathsf{salt}, \mathsf{msg}, h_0^{(1)}, \ldots, h_0^{(\tau)}\right)$

Step 3: Recompute h_2

for $e \in [\tau]$ **do**

  for $\ell \in [D]$ **do**

    Use $(\varepsilon_1^{(e)}, \ldots, \varepsilon_m^{(e)})$, $[\![\boldsymbol{\alpha}]\!]_{\bar{i}_e}^{(e)}$ and the ℓ-th set of main shares as inputs in

    the algorithm in Figure 5 to get $\overline{H}_\ell^{(e)}$, which is defined instead as

    $\overline{H}_\ell^{(e)} = \mathtt{H}_3\left(\mathsf{salt}, \ell, [\![\alpha_k]\!]_{(\ell,j)}^{(e)}, [\![v_k]\!]_{(\ell,j)}^{(e)}\right)_{(k,j)\in[m]\times[2]}$

$\bar{h}_2 \leftarrow \mathtt{H}_4\left(\mathsf{salt}, \mathsf{msg}, \bar{h}_1, \left(\overline{H}_1^{(e)}, \ldots, \overline{H}_D^{(e)}\right)_{e\in[\tau]}\right)$

Step 4: Verify signature

Output $(\bar{h}_1 = h_1) \wedge (\bar{h}_2 = h_2)$

Fig. 8. Biscuit verification algorithm.

The size of the public-key is $\lambda + \log_2(q) \cdot m$ bits, the size of the secret-key is λ bits and the bit-size of the signature is:

$$\underbrace{6\lambda}_{\mathsf{salt},h_1,h_2} + \tau \left(\underbrace{(n+2m)\log_2 q}_{\Delta \mathbf{s}^{(e)},\Delta \mathbf{c}^{(e)},[\![\alpha]\!]_{\bar{i}_e}^{(e)}} + \underbrace{\lambda \cdot D}_{(\mathsf{seed}^{(e,i)})_{i \neq \bar{i}_e}} + \underbrace{2\lambda}_{\mathsf{com}^{(e,\bar{i}_e)}} \right).$$

5 Security Analysis

This part is dedicated to the security analysis of Biscuit against key-recovery (Sect. 5.2) and forgery (Sect. 5.3) attacks. Before that, Sect. 5.1 discusses the motivations for using structured systems as PowAff and the connection with the Learning With Errors (LWE, [35]) problem.

From now on, let $(\mathbf{f} = (f_1, \ldots, f_m), \mathbf{t} = \mathbf{f}(\mathbf{s})) \in \mathbb{F}_q[x_1, \ldots, x_n]^m \times \mathbb{F}_q^m$ be a Biscuit public-key and $\mathbf{s} \in \mathbb{F}_q^n$ be the corresponding secret-key.

5.1 About the Hardness of PowAff2

A fundamental assumption in the design of Biscuit is that solving algebraic systems generated essentially from the power of affine forms are not much easier to solve than a random system of quadratic equations. Whilst the complexity of solving structured equations can be difficult to assess in general, the hardness of solving random quadratic equations has been deeply investigated and only exponential algorithms are known, e.g. [12,16–18].

We emphasize PowAff2 algebraic equations already appeared previously in the literature. In particular, the authors of [7,11] demonstrated that attacking the Learning With Errors (LWE) problem [35] reduces to solve a structured algebraic system similar to PowAff2. An instance of LWE is given by a pair $(\boldsymbol{A} = \{a_{i,j}\}, \boldsymbol{c} = \boldsymbol{s}\boldsymbol{A} + \boldsymbol{e}) \in \mathbb{F}_q^{n \times m} \times \mathbb{F}_q^m$ where $\boldsymbol{s} \in \mathbb{F}_q^n$ is a secret and $\boldsymbol{e} \in \mathbb{F}_q^m$ is an error vector. LWE (search) asks to recover the secret $\boldsymbol{s}$. Arora and Ge exhibit in [7,11] a rather natural algebraic modeling of LWE. More precisely, Arora and Ge show that LWE secrets can be recovered by solving:

$$f_1(x_1, \ldots, x_n) = P(c_1 - \sum_{k=1}^{n} a_{k,1} x_k) = 0, \ldots, f_m(x_1, \ldots, x_n) = P(c_1 - \sum_{k=1}^{n} a_{k,m} x_k) = 0, \tag{5}$$

where P depends on the error distribution. In particular, $P(X) = X(X-1) \in \mathbb{F}_q[X]$ for binary errors and [7] introduced the assumption that a system such as (5) behaves such as a semi-regular sequence. As a consequence, a new fast algorithm for PowAff2 will lead to a new fast algebraic algorithm for binary LWE.

5.2 Key Recovery Attacks

A key-recovery attack against Biscuit consists of solving the PowAff2 problem, i.e. recovering $\mathbf{s} \in \mathbb{F}_q^m$ from the system defined as :

$$\mathbf{t} = \mathbf{f}(\mathbf{x}), \text{ with } \mathbf{x} = (x_1, \ldots, x_n). \tag{6}$$

Currently, the best attack against Biscuit is a dedicated hybrid approach for solving PowAff2 equations described in [20]. The hybrid approach is a classical technique for solving algebraic systems that combines exhaustive search and a Gröbner basis-like computations [12,17,18]. The efficiency of such approach is related to the choice of a *trade-off*, denoted $k \leq n$, between these two methods.

We sketch below the approach described in [20]. Let $\mathbf{g} = (g_1(\mathbf{x}) = u_1(\mathbf{x}) \cdot (x_1 + c_1) + w_1(\mathbf{x}), \ldots, g_n(\mathbf{x}) = u_n(\mathbf{x}) \cdot (x_n + c_n) + w_n(\mathbf{x})) \in \mathbb{F}_q[x_1, \ldots, x_n]^n$, with $\mathbf{x} = (x_1, \ldots, x_n), u_1, \ldots, u_n, v_1, \ldots, v_n \in \mathbb{F}_q[x_1, \ldots, x_n]$ affine polynomials and $c_1, \ldots, c_n \in \mathbb{F}_q$. According to Lemma 1, with high probability, there exists $\mathbf{L} \in \mathrm{GL}_n(\mathbb{F}_q)$ such that:

$$\mathbf{f}(\mathbf{x} \cdot \mathbf{L}) = (\mathbf{g}, A'_{n+1,0}(\mathbf{x}) + \prod_{j=1}^{2} A'_{n+1,j}(\mathbf{x}), \ldots, A'_{m,0}(\mathbf{x}) + \prod_{j=1}^{2} A'_{m,j}(\mathbf{x}))$$

where $A_{n+1,0}, A_{n+1,1}, A_{n+1,2}, \ldots, A_{m,0}, A_{m,1}, A_{m,2} \in \mathbb{F}_q[x_1, \ldots, x_n]$ affine forms.

Then, for every guess $(a_1, \ldots, a_k) \in \mathbb{F}_q^k$ of the k first variables $(x_1, \ldots, x_k)$, we obtain k linear polynomials, namely $g_1(a_1, \ldots, a_k, x_{k+1}, \ldots, x_n), \ldots, g_k(a_1, \ldots, a_k, x_{k+1}, \ldots, x_n)$. These k linear polynomials are expected to be linearly independent with a probability close to $1 - 1/q$. Hence we can use them to substitute k additional variables in the remaining polynomials. The attack is finalized by solving the resulting quadratic system of $m - k$ equations in $n - 2k$ variables.

Complexity. The cost of the attack is dominated by

$$\min_{0 \leq k < \frac{n}{2}} q^k \cdot \mathrm{MQ}(n - 2k, m - k, q), \tag{7}$$

where $\mathrm{MQ}(n, m, q)$ denotes the complexity of solving a random system of m quadratic equations over n variables over $\mathbb{F}_q$. To compute the exact complexity, we rely on the `MQEstimator` software tool, which is part of the more general `CryptographicEstimators`[5] library [23].

5.3 Forgery Attacks

In the context of forgery, the attacker has to solve the $\texttt{PowAff2}_u$ problem (Definition 1), which is a variant of the problem considered before for key-recovery

[5] https://github.com/Crypto-TII/CryptographicEstimators.

(Sect. 5.2). In the PowAff2$_u$ problem, the goal is to find a vector $\mathbf{s}' \in \mathbb{F}_q^n$ that vanishes a subset of size $m - u$ of the system (6). Without loss of generality, we assume that $\mathbf{s}'$ vanishes the first $m - u$ polynomials and not the remaining equations. That is, $f_k(\mathbf{s}') = t_k$, for $k \in [m - u]$, and $f_k(\mathbf{s}') \neq t_k$ for $k = m - u + 1, \ldots, m$.

By Proposition 1, a set of N parties that follows the MPC protocol in Fig. 2 on inputs $[\![\mathbf{s}']\!]$ and $(\mathbf{f}, \mathbf{t})$ will output **accept** with false positive rate $p_1 = 1/q^u$. Thanks to Kales and Zaverucha, [30], it is known that MPCitH-based signature scheme that consists of τ repetitions of a MPC protocol with false positive rate p_1 can be forged by computing on average

$$\mathtt{KZ}_\tau(p_1, p_2) = \min_{\{\tau_1, \tau_2 | \tau_1 + \tau_2 = \tau\}} \left\{ \frac{1}{\sum_{i=\tau_1}^{\tau} \binom{\tau}{i} p_1^i (1 - p_1)^{\tau - i}} + \frac{1}{p_2^{\tau_2}} \right\},$$

calls to some hash functions, where p_2 is the probability of guessing some of the views of parties that remain unopened, e.g., $p_2 = 1/N$ for Biscuit.

Let $\mathsf{C}_u(q, n, m)$ denote the complexity of finding a preimage to a chosen subset S of the system $\mathbf{t} = \mathbf{f}(\mathbf{x})$ of size $m - u$ and $\mathbf{s}' \in \mathbb{F}_q^n$ be a solution that vanishes the equations of S. Then, $\mathbf{s}'$ might, by chance, be a solution of any equation in S^c, i.e., any equation that is not in S. If there remain $k \in [u]$ equations in S^c for which $\mathbf{s}'$ is not a solution, then an attacker can mount a forgery attack with complexity $\mathtt{KZ}_\tau(q^{-k}, N^{-1})$.

Let $(\mathbf{f}, \mathbf{t})$ be a Biscuit public-key selected uniformly at random, and let S be a subset of the equations $\mathbf{t} = \mathbf{f}(\mathbf{x})$ of size $m-u$ selected uniformly at random. Then, a random solution $\mathbf{s}' \in \mathbb{F}_q^n$ of the equations in S follows a uniform distribution. Hence, $f_k(\mathbf{s}')$ is a uniform element in $\mathbb{F}_q$. Therefore, the probability that $\mathbf{s}'$ is a solution of exactly j equations in S^c is $\binom{u}{j} \cdot (q-1)^{u-j}/q^u$. Consequently, if p_k denotes the probability that $\mathbf{s}'$ is not the solution of at most k equations in S^c, then,

$$p_k = \frac{\sum_{j=u-k+1}^{u} \binom{u}{j} \cdot (q-1)^{u-j}}{q^u}.$$

In order to secure Biscuit against forgery attacks, we must have for every pair (k, u), where $0 \leq k \leq u \leq m$:

1. $\mathtt{KZ}_\tau(q^{-k}, N^{-1}) > 2^\lambda$, or
2. $\frac{1}{p_k} \cdot \mathsf{C}_u(q, n, m) > 2^{\lambda + C_\lambda}$,

where $C_\lambda = 15$ if $\lambda = 128$ or 192 and $C_\lambda = 16$ otherwise.

Following these analyses, we propose in Table 2 a set of 3 parameters for 128, 192 and 256 bits of classical security.

5.4 Existential Unforgeability

The existential unforgeability of Biscuit is stated in Theorem 2.

Theorem 2 (EU-CMA security). *Let PRG be a (t, ϵ_{PRG})-secure pseudo-random generator function, and that any adversary running in time t has an advantage* *of at most $\epsilon_{\texttt{PowAff2}}$ against the underlying* $\texttt{PowAff}\,2_{u-1}$ *problem. Suppose that the hash functions $H_0, H_1, H_2\, H_4$ behave as random oracles that output binary strings of size 2λ. Let $\mathcal{A}$ be an adversary who has access to a signing oracle, making q_i queries to H_i and q_s queries to the signing oracle. Then, the probability that $\mathcal{A}$ outputs a forgery for the* Biscuit *signature scheme (Fig. 7) is:*

$$\Pr[\mathit{Forge}] \leq \frac{3(q+\tau N\cdot q_s)^2}{2\cdot 2^{2\lambda}} + \frac{q_s(q_s+5q)}{2^{2\lambda}} + \epsilon_{PRG} + \epsilon_{\texttt{PowAff2}} + \Pr[X+Y=\tau],$$

where τ is the number of repetitions of the ZKPoK protocol (Fig. 3), $X = \max_{i\in[q_2]}\{X_i\}$ with $X_i \sim \mathcal{B}(\tau, \frac{1}{q^u})$, and $Y = \max_{i\in[q_4]}\{Y_i\}$ with $Y_i \sim \mathcal{B}(\tau - X, \frac{1}{N})$.

Proof. Overall the proof works as follows: First, we assume the existence of an adversary $\mathcal{A}$ that can forge Biscuit signatures with probability Pr[Forge] after interacting with a signing oracle and the random oracles $\texttt{H}_0, \texttt{H}_1, \texttt{H}_2, \texttt{H}_3$ and $\texttt{H}_4$. Then, we show how to simulate such an interaction so that we can use $\mathcal{A}$ to either:

1. Find collisions on the oracles $\texttt{H}_0, \texttt{H}_1$, or $\texttt{H}_3$.
2. query an oracle $\texttt{H}_i$ with an input used to query $\texttt{H}_i$ while replaying signing query,
3. distinguish between outputs of PRG from random ones,
4. solve an instance of the $\texttt{PowAff2}_{u-1}$ problem, or
5. obtain an event that happens with probability at most $\Pr[X+Y=\tau]$.

In **Game**$_1$, we simulate for $\mathcal{A}$ a real interaction with the signature scheme and the random oracles $\texttt{H}_i$.

Game$_1$: We generate a pair (sk, pk) ← KeyGen(), give pk to the adversary $\mathcal{A}$, simulate the random oracles $\texttt{H}_i$, and any signing query msg from $\mathcal{A}$ is replied with Sign(pk, sk, msg), where Sign is the algorithm shown in Fig. 7. We allow $\mathcal{A}$ to make q_i queries to $\texttt{H}_i$ and q_s queries to the signing oracle. At the end, $\mathcal{A}$ outputs a pair (msg, σ). We denote by Forge the event where (msg, σ) is a forgery, i.e., σ is a valid signature for the message msg, and msg was not queried for signing.

For each of the subsequent games, $\Pr_i$[Forge] denotes the probability that Forge happens in **Game**$_i$. In particular, we are interested in an upper bound for Pr[Forge] = $\Pr_1$[Forge].

Game$_2$: We proceed as in **Game**$_1$ with the only exception that we abort if, during the game, a collision of $\texttt{H}_0$, $\texttt{H}_1$, or $\texttt{H}_3$ is found.

Every signing query yields τN queries to $\texttt{H}_0$, τ to $\texttt{H}_1$, and τD to $\texttt{H}_3$, and one to $\texttt{H}_2$ and $\texttt{H}_4$. Hence, during this game, the total number of queries to $\texttt{H}_0$, $\texttt{H}_1$ or $\texttt{H}_3$ is at most $q+\tau N q_s$, where $q = \max\{q_0, q_1, q_3\}$. Therefore, using the classic bound for the probability of a collision of a hash function[6], we have that

$$\left|\Pr_1[\mathsf{Forge}] - \Pr_2[\mathsf{Forge}]\right| \leq \frac{3(q+\tau N q_s)^2}{2^{2\lambda+1}}.$$

[6] By mathematical induction, we can prove that probability to find at least one collision of random oracle $H : \{0,1\}^* \to \{0,1\}^{2\lambda}$ after n calls is at most $n(n-1)/2^{2\lambda+1}$.

Game$_3$: We proceed as in **Game$_2$**, but we abort if, while replying to a signing query, the input to any $\mathtt{H}_i$ was used to answer a previous query to $\mathtt{H}_i$ made either directly by $\mathcal{A}$ or by another signing query.

For each signing query, the probability of aborting in this game is, at most, the probability that the salt sampled in the signature query is equal to a salt used in a previous query to any $\mathtt{H}_i$. Therefore, we have that

$$\left|\Pr_2[\mathsf{Forge}] - \Pr_3[\mathsf{Forge}]\right| \leq \frac{q_s(q_s + q_0 + q_1 + q_2 + q_3 + q_4)}{2^{2\lambda}} \leq \frac{q_s(q_s + 5 \cdot q)}{2^{2\lambda}}.$$

Game$_4$: This game differs from the previous one in how the signing queries are replied. In this case, instead of querying $\mathtt{H}_2$ and $\mathtt{H}_4$ to obtain h_1 and h_2, respectively. The values h_1 and h_2 are sampled uniformly at random from $\{0,1\}^{2\lambda}$.

Notice that **Game$_3$** and **Game$_4$** differ only in the case of a query to either $\mathtt{H}_2$ or $\mathtt{H}_4$ is repeated while answering a signing query. This cannot happen since we would have already aborted. So,

$$\Pr_4[\mathsf{Forge}] = \Pr_3[\mathsf{Forge}].$$

Game$_5$: This game changes how the signing queries are answered. We highlight that, in this game, the private key is no longer used to answer signing queries. Here, the values h_1, h_2, the salt and all the seeds ($\mathsf{seed}^{(e,i)}$) are computed as in **Game$_4$**. Contrarily, for each $e \in [\tau]$, the values $(\varepsilon_1^{(e)}, \ldots, \varepsilon_m^{(e)}), \bar{i}_e$, $\mathsf{com}^{(e,\bar{i}_e)}$, $\boldsymbol{\Delta}\mathbf{s}^{(e)}$, $\boldsymbol{\Delta}\mathbf{c}^{(e)}$ and $[\![\boldsymbol{\alpha}]\!]_{\bar{i}_e}^{(e)}$ are sampled uniformly at random as it is done by the $\mathsf{Simulator}$ (see Fig. 6). From the security of the $\mathtt{PRG}$ we obtain that

$$\left|\Pr_4[\mathsf{Forge}] - \Pr_5[\mathsf{Forge}]\right| \leq \varepsilon_{\mathtt{PRG}}.$$

Now we introduce a definition. Let $e^* \in [\tau]$ and Q_4 be a query to $\mathtt{H}_4$ with input

$$\left(\mathsf{salt}, \mathsf{msg}, \mathsf{pk}, h_1, (H_1^{(e)}, \ldots, H_D^{(e)})_{e \in [\tau]}\right).$$

We say that the e^*-th execution of Q_4 defines a *good witness* $\mathbf{s}$ if

1. Each $H_\ell^{(e)}$ is an output of a query to $\mathtt{H}_3$.
2. There is a previous query $h_1 \leftarrow \mathtt{H}_2\left(\mathsf{salt}, \mathsf{msg}, h_0^{(1)}, \ldots, h_0^{(\tau)}\right)$.
3. There are previous queries $h_0^{(e)} \leftarrow \mathtt{H}_1(\mathsf{salt}, e, \mathsf{com}^{(e,1)}, \ldots, \mathsf{com}^{(e,N)}, \boldsymbol{\Delta}\mathbf{s}^{(e)}, \boldsymbol{\Delta}\mathbf{c}^{(e)})$, for $e \in [\tau]$.
4. For each $(e,i) \in [\tau] \times [N]$, there is a query of the form $\mathsf{com}^{(e,i)} \leftarrow \mathtt{H}_0\left(\mathsf{salt}, e, i, \mathsf{seed}^{(e,i)}\right)$.
5. A solution $\mathbf{s}$ to the $\mathtt{PowAff2}_{u-1}$ instance $(\mathbf{f}, \mathbf{t})$ can be extracted from $(\mathsf{seed}^{(e^*,i)})_{i \in [N]}$ and $\boldsymbol{\Delta}\mathbf{s}^{(e^*)}$.

At the end of **Game$_5$**, for each Forge, i.e., whenever $\mathcal{A}$ outputs a forgery (msg, σ), one can check if any execution $e \in [\tau]$ defines a good witness. We define by Solve the event in which there exists at least one good execution $e^* \in [\tau]$, where query to $\mathtt{H}_4$ is built from σ and following the verification algorithm (see

Fig. 8), and the $(\mathbf{\Delta s}^{(1)}, \ldots, \mathbf{\Delta s}^{(\tau)})$ are the one in σ. Consequently, $\Pr_5[\mathsf{Forge} \cap \mathsf{Solve}] = \varepsilon_{\texttt{PowAff2}}$.

We finalize the proof by showing that $\Pr_5[\mathsf{Forge} \cap \overline{\mathsf{Solve}}] \leq \Pr[X + Y = \tau]$, where $X = \max_{i \in [0,q_2]}\{X_i\}$ $X_i \sim \mathcal{B}(\tau, \frac{1}{q^u})$, and $Y = \max_{i \in [0,q_4]}\{Y_i\}$ with $Y_i \sim \mathcal{B}(\tau - X, \frac{1}{N})$.

In the event $\mathsf{Forge} \cap \overline{\mathsf{Solve}}$, (by the soundness part of Theorem 1) we either get a false-positive case of the $\texttt{MPC}$ protocol (see Fig. 2), or $\mathcal{A}$ have cheated in exactly one party. We analyze each scenario separately.

(*False-positive case*) We denote by h_1 the output of a given query Q_2 to $\texttt{H}_2$ made by $\mathcal{A}$. After the $\texttt{MPC}$ protocol is executed in the main shares as described in Fig. 4, $\mathcal{A}$ can count the number of indexes $e \in [\tau]$ for which the e-th execution yields a false-positive, we use $F_2(h_1)$ to denote that number. Since the first challenge $\boldsymbol{\varepsilon}^{(e)} = (\varepsilon_1^{(e)}, \ldots, \varepsilon_m^{(e)})$ is sampled uniformly at random independently of h_1, by Proposition 1, we have that $\Pr[e \in F_2(h_1) \mid \overline{\mathsf{Solve}}] \leq \frac{1}{q^u}$ for any $e \in [\tau]$. Therefore, $X_i \sim \mathcal{B}(\tau, \frac{1}{q^u})$, where X_i denotes $\#F_2(h_1)$ in the i-th query Q_2 of $\mathcal{A}$ to $\texttt{H}_2$. Let us define the random variable $X = \max_{i \in [q_2]} X_i$.

(*Cheating case*) Let us assume $X = \tau_1 = \#F_2(h_1)$. For any $e \in [\tau] \setminus F_2(h_1)$, by the soundness part of Theorem 1, we know that $\mathcal{A}$ has to cheat in exactly one party in order to have a nonzero probability (which is $\frac{1}{N}$) that the e-th execution is accepted. Notice, the verification is accepted if and only if the e-th execution is accepted for each $e \in [\tau] \setminus F_2(h_1)$. Now, let us define the random variable $Y = \max_{i \in [q_4]} Y_i$, where Y_i is the random variable returning the number of indexes $e \in [\tau] \setminus F_2(h_1)$ for which the e-th execution is accepted in the i-th query to $\texttt{H}_4$. Hence, in the particular case $X = \tau_1$, the probability that the verification is accepted is given by $\Pr[Y = \tau - \tau_1 \mid X = \tau_1]$. Therefore, by summing over all possible values of X, we obtain that

$$\Pr_5[\mathsf{Forge} \cap \overline{\mathsf{Solve}}] \leq \Pr[X + Y = \tau].$$

The proof is concluded by the fact that.

$$\begin{aligned}\Pr[\mathsf{Forge}] = \Pr_1[\mathsf{Forge}] &\leq \sum_{j=1}^{4} \left|\Pr_j[\mathsf{Forge}] - \Pr_{j+1}[\mathsf{Forge}]\right| + \Pr_5[\mathsf{Forge}] \\ &= \sum_{j=1}^{4} \left|\Pr_j[\mathsf{Forge}] - \Pr_{j+1}[\mathsf{Forge}]\right| \\ &\quad + \Pr_5[\mathsf{Forge} \cap \mathsf{Solve}] + \Pr_5[\mathsf{Forge} \cap \overline{\mathsf{Solve}}].\end{aligned}$$

6 Implementation

6.1 Canonical Representation Optimization

As seen in Lemma 1, an equivalent system where, for the first n equations, one of the affine forms is only composed of one variable. Without loss of generality, we can choose to have this variable in $A_{k,0}$. In other words, we can choose for the algorithm a system $f_1, \dots, f_m$ as

$$f_k(x_1, \dots, x_n) = (x_k + a_k) + A_{k,1}(x_1, \dots, x_n) \cdot A_{k,2}(x_1, \dots, x_n),$$

for $k \leqslant n$, and

$$f_k(x_1, \dots, x_n) = A_{k,0}(x_1, \dots, x_n) + A_{k,1}(x_1, \dots, x_n) \cdot A_{k,2}(x_1, \dots, x_n),$$

for $n < k \leqslant m$, where $A_{k,j}$ are affine forms.

The effect is that the evaluation of the polynomial will be much faster as only 2 affine form evaluations have to be performed instead of 3 for most of the equations. In the implementation, we chose to simplify $A_{k,0}$ to save some code, as $A_{k,1}$ and $A_{k,2}$ can be computed in the same way in a loop.

6.2 Hypercube Optimization

The algorithms described in Figs. 7 and 8 use the hypercube variant. The simulation of the MPC protocol does not need to compute all the values as in Fig. 4. We first compute α_k using directly the opened values $\mathbf{s}$ and $\mathbf{a}$. Then, we need to compute $[\![\alpha_k]\!]_{(\ell,j)}$ only for $j = 1$. The value for $j = 2$ can be derived from α. Similarly, we can do the same for $[\![v_k]\!]_{(\ell,j)}$. This can also be applied to the verification. All in all, we usually require to keep only $\log_2(N)$ shares.

6.3 Vectorization

The main data structure in the algorithm is a vector of value in $\mathbb{F}_q$. We have:

- The secret value, which is a vector of n elements in $\mathbb{F}_q$.
- The public key, which is a vector of m elements in $\mathbb{F}_q$.
- Intermediate values, which are vectors of m elements in $\mathbb{F}_q$.

For each of these vectors, we need to compute operations component-wise. We can then pack all elements in the largest possible integer handled by the CPU. Typically, this could be a 64-bit word that can contain 8 elements in $\mathbb{F}_{2^8}$ for instance.

When vectorized instructions are available (`SSE`, `AVX`, ...), even larger integer types can be used. For instance, with `AVX2` a 256-bit integer can be used to pack a vector of $\mathbb{F}_q$ elements. In characteristic 2, the component-wise addition of a vector of elements can be done in one instruction using the `VPXOR` instruction.

6.4 Performances and Memory Consumption

In this section, we show the performance and memory consumption of our instances. Our implementation is optimized to use `AVX2` vectorized instructions on a little-endian 64-bit CPU.

The code is compiled with GCC version 12.2.0 on Debian GNU/Linux. Number of cycles was measured by counting PERF_HW_COUNT_CPU_CYCLES events on an 11th Gen Intel(R) Core(TM) i7-1185G7 @ 3.00GHz CPU (Tiger Lake). Even if frequency modification should not affect this metric, we deactivated Intel's TurboBoost feature anyway. The number of cycles is taken as the median over 1000 executions.

Table 3. Time performance and memory consumption of Biscuit on avx2 impl.

Name	Memory (bytes)			Performance (cycles)		
	keygen	sign	verify	keygen	sign	verify
biscuit128s	512	1 654 288	122 480	88 484	69 418 295	68 984 920
biscuit128f	512	329 904	25 712	88 477	13 711 517	13 007 550
biscuit192s	608	3 438 832	194 544	251 806	191 442 370	190 138 451
biscuit192f	608	708 944	49 392	252 106	38 677 691	37 087 201
biscuit256s	800	7 414 000	335 312	504 021	635 749 877	632 271 590
biscuit256f	800	1 537 904	98 768	504 983	128 098 892	124 921 246

In Table 3, we give the figures for the implementation strictly following the description in the NIST submission but with the new parameters proposed in Table 2.

In Table 4, we include the canonical representation optimization as described in Sect. 6.1. This improves the performances by 18 to 28%.

Table 4. Time performance and memory consumption of Biscuit on avx2 impl. using canonical optimization.

Name	Memory (bytes)			Performance (cycles)		
	keygen	sign	verify	keygen	sign	verify
biscuit128s	512	1 651 088	122 480	61 755	60 785 166	59 198 143
biscuit128f	512	326 704	25 712	61 757	11 507 884	10 695 367
biscuit192s	608	3 430 288	194 544	172 825	151 956 515	152 714 889
biscuit192f	608	700 400	49 392	172 446	30 476 727	29 191 279
biscuit256s	800	7 393 680	335 312	343 001	472 774 277	468 258 145
biscuit256f	800	1 517 584	98 768	341 156	93 221 776	89 507 805

Finally, in Table 5, in addition to the previous optimization, we integrated the hypercube variant. With this variant, the memory consumption is greatly improved especially for large values of N. This is because we have to keep track of only $\log_2(N)$ shares instead of N. The performances are improved by 50 to 83% for the small variant, and by 41 to 69% for the fast variant. The code is available in [2].

Table 5. Time performance and memory consumption of Biscuit on avx2 impl. using canonical and hypercube optimization.

Name	Memory (bytes)			Performance (cycles)		
	keygen	sign	verify	keygen	sign	verify
biscuit128s	576	814 256	40 144	61 697	27 930 795	28 323 314
biscuit128f	576	201 744	14 096	61 682	6 581 004	6 166 694
biscuit192s	704	1 686 416	67 376	173 044	49 890 911	49 914 321
biscuit192f	704	433 008	28 272	172 667	13 594 397	12 916 931
biscuit256s	960	3 556 624	117 424	341 657	77 620 375	77 447 430
biscuit256f	960	928 368	57 648	340 649	28 219 223	27 341 671

Acknowledgement. The authors would like to thank Daniel Escudero for meaningful insights on an early version of this paper and the referees of ACNS24 that helped to improve the paper. The third author would like to thank Charles Bouillaguet and Julia Sauvage for discussions on the hardness of PowAff2, Google which partially supported this work thanks to a gift for supporting post-quantum research, and the European Union's Horizon Europe research and innovation program that partially supported this research under the project "Quantum Secure Networks Partnership" (QSNP, grant agreement No 101114043).

References

1. NIST Call for Additional Digital Signature Schemes for the Post-Quantum Cryptography Standardization Process. https://csrc.nist.gov/csrc/media/Projects/pqc-dig-sig/documents/call-for-proposals-dig-sig-sept-2022.pdf
2. Biscuit github repository (2023). https://github.com/BiscuitTeam/Biscuit
3. Aaraj, N., et al.: PERK specification (2023). https://pqc-perk.org/assets/downloads/PERK_specifications.pdf
4. Adj, G., et al.: MiRitH specification (2023). https://pqc-mirith.org/assets/downloads/mirith_specifications_v1.0.0.pdf
5. Melchor, C.A., Gama, N., Howe, J., Hülsing, A., Joseph, D., Yue, D.: The return of the SDitH, pp. 564–596 (2023)
6. Alagic, G., et al.: Status report on the second round of the nist post-quantum cryptography standardization process. Technical report NISTIR 8309, NIST (2022). https://nvlpubs.nist.gov/nistpubs/ir/2020/NIST.IR.8309.pdf
7. Albrecht, M.R., Cid, C., Faugère, J.-C., Perret, L.: Algebraic algorithms for lwe. Cryptology ePrint Archive, Paper 2014/1018 (2014). https://eprint.iacr.org/2014/1018
8. Aragon, N., et al.: RYDE specification (2023). https://pqc-ryde.org/assets/downloads/RYDE_Specifications.pdf
9. Aragon, N., et al.: MIRA specification (2023). https://pqc-mira.org/assets/downloads/mira_spec.pdf
10. Aragon, N., et al.: Mira: a digital signature scheme based on the minrank problem and the MPC-in-the-head paradigm (2023)

11. Arora, S., Ge, R.: New algorithms for learning in presence of errors. In: Aceto, L., Henzinger, M., Sgall, J. (eds.) ICALP 2011. LNCS, vol. 6755, pp. 403–415. Springer, Heidelberg (2011). https://doi.org/10.1007/978-3-642-22006-7_34
12. Bardet, M., Faugère, J.-C., Salvy, B., Spaenlehauer, P.-J.: On the complexity of solving quadratic Boolean systems. J. Complex. **29**(1), 53–75 (2013)
13. Baum, C., et al.: FAEST specification (2023). https://faest.info/faest-spec-v1.1.pdf
14. Baum, C., Nof, A.: Concretely-efficient zero-knowledge arguments for arithmetic circuits and their application to lattice-based cryptography. In: Kiayias, A., Kohlweiss, M., Wallden, P., Zikas, V. (eds.) PKC 2020. LNCS, vol. 12110, pp. 495–526. Springer, Cham (2020). https://doi.org/10.1007/978-3-030-45374-9_17
15. Beaver, D.: Efficient multiparty protocols using circuit randomization. In: Feigenbaum, J. (ed.) CRYPTO 1991. LNCS, vol. 576, pp. 420–432. Springer, Heidelberg (1992). https://doi.org/10.1007/3-540-46766-1_34
16. Bellini, E., Makarim, R.H., Sanna, C., Verbel, J.A.: An estimator for the hardness of the MQ problem, pp. 323–347 (2022)
17. Bettale, L., Faugère, J.-C., Perret, L.: Hybrid approach for solving multivariate systems over finite fields. J. Math. Cryptol. **3**(3), 177–197 (2009)
18. Bettale, L., Faugère, J.-C., Perret, L.: Solving polynomial systems over finite fields: improved analysis of the hybrid approach. In: van der Hoeven, J., van Hoeij, M. (eds.) International Symposium on Symbolic and Algebraic Computation, ISSAC 2012, Grenoble, France - July 22–25, 2012, pp. 67–74. ACM (2012)
19. Bettale, L., Perret, L., Kahrobaei, D., Verbel, J.: Biscuit: shorter MPC-based Signature from PoSSo, June 2023. Specification of NIST post-quantum signature (2023)
20. Bouillaguet, C.: Improved security analysis of Biscuit (2023). https://groups.google.com/a/list.nist.gov/g/pqc-forum/c/sw8NueiNek0/m/2sa_emjABQAJ
21. Chase, M., et al.: Post-quantum zero-knowledge and signatures from symmetric-key primitives, pp. 1825–1842 (2017)
22. NIST Computer Security Division. SHA-3 Standard: Permutation-Based Hash and Extendable-Output Functions. FIPS Publication 202, National Institute of Standards and Technology, U.S. Department of Commerce, May 2014
23. Esser, A., Verbel, J., Zweydinger, F., Bellini, E.: Cryptographic Estimators: a software library for cryptographic hardness estimation. Cryptology ePrint Archive, Paper 2023/589, 2023. https://eprint.iacr.org/2023/589
24. Feneuil, T., Rivain, M.: MQOM specification (2023). https://mqom.org/docs/mqom-v1.0.pdf
25. Feneuil, T., Rivain, M.: Threshold computation in the head: improved framework for post-quantum signatures and zero-knowledge arguments. Cryptology ePrint Archive, Paper 2023/1573 (2023). https://eprint.iacr.org/2023/1573
26. Fiat, A., Shamir, A.: How to prove yourself: practical solutions to identification and signature problems. In: Odlyzko, A.M. (ed.) CRYPTO 1986. LNCS, vol. 263, pp. 186–194. Springer, Heidelberg (1987). https://doi.org/10.1007/3-540-47721-7_12
27. Giacomelli, I., Madsen, J., Orlandi, C.:. ZKBoo: faster zero-knowledge for boolean circuits. In: 25th USENIX Security Symposium (USENIX Security 16), pp. 1069–1083 (2016)
28. Ishai, Y., Kushilevitz, E., Ostrovsky, R., Sahai, A.: Zero-knowledge from secure multiparty computation. In: Proceedings of the Thirty-Ninth Annual ACM Symposium on Theory of Computing, pp. 21–30 (2007)
29. Kales, D., Zaverucha, G.: An attack on some signature schemes constructed from five-pass identification schemes. In: Krenn, S., Shulman, H., Vaudenay, S. (eds.)

CANS 2020. LNCS, vol. 12579, pp. 3–22. Springer, Cham (2020). https://doi.org/10.1007/978-3-030-65411-5_1
30. Kales, D., Zaverucha, G.: Efficient lifting for shorter zero-knowledge proofs and post-quantum signatures. Cryptology ePrint Archive, Paper 2022/588 (2022). https://eprint.iacr.org/2022/588
31. Katz, J., Kolesnikov, V., Wang, X.: Improved non-interactive zero-knowledge with applications to post-quantum signatures. In: Proceedings of the 2018 ACM SIGSAC Conference on Computer and Communications Security, pp. 525–537 (2018)
32. Kim, S., et al.: AIMER specification (2023). https://aimer-signature.org/docs/AIMer-NIST-Document.pdf
33. Melchor, C.A., et al.: SDITH specification (2023). https://sdith.org/docs/sdith-v1.0.pdf
34. Melchor, C.A., Gama, N., Howe, J., Hülsing, A., Joseph, D., Yue, D.: The return of the SDitH. In: Hazay, C., Stam, M. (eds.) Advances in Cryptology EUROCRYPT 2023 Part V, LNCS, vol. 14008, pp. 564–596. Springer, Cham (2023). https://doi.org/10.1007/978-3-031-30589-4_20
35. Regev, O.: On lattices, learning with errors, random linear codes, and cryptography. J. ACM **56**(6), 34:1-34:40 (2009)
36. Zaverucha, G., et al.: `Picnic`: algorithm specification and design document

Author Index

A
Alam, Manaar III-163
Alkadri, Nabil Alkeilani I-376
Andreeva, Elena II-433
Attrapadung, Nuttapong II-373
Avizheh, Sepideh III-74

B
Banegas, Gustavo II-101
Bao, Han I-213
Basso, Andrea I-432
Bemmann, Pascal I-351
Berger, Robin I-288
Berndt, Sebastian I-351
Bettale, Luk I-457
Bhardwaj, Divyanshu III-412
Bhattacharya, Sarani III-271
Bock, Estuardo Alpirez II-101
Boneh, Dan III-105
Bonneau, Joseph III-105
Boura, Christina II-485
Brisfors, Martin III-301
Brzuska, Chris I-3, II-101

C
Cachet, Chloe I-156
Carpent, Xavier I-26
Chen, Binbin II-283
Chen, Mingjie I-432
Chen, Rongmao I-351
Chmielewski, Łukasz II-101
Cimorelli Belfiore, Roberta II-163
Cogliati, Benoît II-433
Cong, Kelong II-133
Conti, Mauro I-183
Custódio, Ricardo II-3

D
Dabrowski, Adrian III-412
De Cosmo, Andrea II-163
Derbez, Patrick II-485
Dey, Soumyajit III-163
Ding, Xia II-265
Doan, Thi Van Thao I-257
Dobraunig, Christoph II-460
Dörre, Felix I-288
Döttling, Nico I-376
Dowerah, Uddipana II-189
Dubrova, Elena III-301

E
Egger, Christoph I-3
Eldefrawy, Karim II-133
Emura, Keita I-237

F
Fan, Yongming II-340
Feneuil, Thibauld I-403
Feng, Zheyun III-217
Ferrara, Anna Lisa II-163
Forte, Domenic III-325
Fouotsa, Tako Boris I-432
Francati, Danilo I-135
Frederiksen, Tore Kasper I-58
Fuller, Benjamin I-156
Funk, Margot II-485

G
Ganji, Fatemeh III-325
Garman, Christina II-340
GhasemiGol, Mohammad II-313
Ghazvinian, Parsa II-313
Ghosh, Soumyadyuti III-163
Giron, Alexandre Augusto II-3
Gui, Jiaping III-241

H
Hamlin, Ariel I-156
Hanaoaka, Goichiro II-373
Hashemi, Mohammad III-325
Heitmann, Nico III-190

C. Pöpper and L. Batina (Eds.): ACNS 2024, LNCS 14583, pp. 487–489, 2024.
https://doi.org/10.1007/978-3-031-54770-6

Henze, Martin II-241
Hiromasa, Ryo II-373
Hwang, Seoyeon I-26
Hwang, Vincent II-24

J
Jee, Kangkook III-241

K
Kahrobaei, Delaram I-457
Kailus, Adrian III-137
Kamimura, Junpei III-241
Karmakar, Angshuman III-271
Kern, Dustin III-137
Koch, Alexander I-288
Köhler, Daniel III-381
Koseki, Yoshihiro II-373
Krauß, Christoph III-137
Krombholz, Katharina III-412
Kumaresan, Ranjit III-51
Kundu, Suparna III-271
Kutas, Péter I-432
Kwak, Hyesun II-403

L
Lallemand, Virginie II-433
Larangeira, Mario I-88
Lau, Wing Cheong III-432
Laval, Abel I-432
Lazzeretti, Riccardo I-183
Le, Duc V. III-51
Lee, Dongwon II-403
Li, Zhichun III-241
Liberati, Edoardo I-183
Lin, Yunxue III-355
Lindstrøm, Jonas I-58
Ling, Xi II-283
Litos, Orfeas Stefanos Thyfronitis III-28
Liu, Chi-Ting II-24
Liu, Zhuotao I-213
Lorek, Paweł III-3
Lu, Tianbo II-265
Luo, Kaixuan III-432

M
Madsen, Mikkel Wienberg I-58
Marco, Laurane I-432
Mateu, Victor II-3
Matsuda, Takahiro II-373
Meinel, Christoph III-381
Mennink, Bart II-460
Minaei, Mohsen III-51
Minier, Marine II-433
Mitrokotsa, Aikaterini II-189
Mondal, Puja III-271
Moog, Sven III-190
Mukherjee, Kunal III-241
Mukhopadhyay, Debdeep II-47, III-163

N
Naito, Yusuke I-318
Nakamura, Toru I-119
Nikolaenko, Valeria III-105
Nishida, Yutaro II-373

P
Patranabis, Sikhar II-47
Pereira, Olivier I-257
Perin, Lucas Pandolfo II-3
Perret, Ludovic I-457
Peters, Thomas I-257
Phalakarn, Kittiphop I-119
Podschwadt, Robert II-313
Pu, Sihang I-376
Puniamurthy, Kirthivaasan I-3, II-101
Pünter, Wenzel III-381
Purnal, Antoon II-433

R
Raghuraman, Srinivasan III-51
Ragsdale, Sam III-105
Rezapour, Maryam I-156
Rhee, John Junghwan III-241
Riahi, Siavash III-28
Riyadh, H. T. M. A. III-412
Robben, Jeroen II-217
Roy, Arnab II-433

S
Saah, Gustave Tchoffo I-432
Safavi-Naini, Reihaneh III-74
Sakai, Yusuke II-373
Sasaki, Yu I-318
Schardong, Frederico II-3
Schuldt, Jacob C. N. II-373
Serror, Martin II-241
Shang, Jiaze II-265
Siewert, Hendrik III-190

Sinha, Sayani II-47
Smart, Nigel P. II-133
Somorovsky, Juraj III-190
Song, Yongsoo II-403
Šorf, Milan II-101
Spangsberg, Anne Dorte I-58
Su, Xiangyu I-88
Sugawara, Takeshi I-318
Sun, Ling III-355

T
Taguchi, Ren II-79
Takabi, Daniel II-313
Takayasu, Atsushi II-79
Tanaka, Keisuke I-88
Tang, Lu-An III-241
Terner, Ben II-133
Tsudik, Gene I-26

U
Uluagac, Selcuk I-183

V
Valle, Victor II-3
Vanhoef, Mathy II-217
Venturi, Daniele I-135
Verbauwhede, Ingrid III-271
Verbel, Javier I-457
Visintin, Alessandro I-183

W
Wagh, Sameer II-403
Wagner, Eric II-241
Wang, Long I-213
Wang, Pengfei I-88
Wang, Qi III-241
Wang, Ruize III-301
Wang, Xianbo III-432
Wang, Yisong I-213
Wehrle, Klaus II-241
Wei, James III-241
Wiedemeier, Joshua III-241

X
Xu, Dongpeng III-217
Xu, Haitao II-283
Xu, Yuquan II-340

Y
Yang, Bo-Yin II-24
Yang, Yibin III-51
Yasuda, Satoshi II-373
Yu, Jiongchi II-283
Yu, Xiao III-241
Yung, Moti III-3

Z
Zagórski, Filip III-3
Zamani, Mahdi III-51
Zhang, Fan II-283
Zhang, Han II-265
Zhang, Mengyu I-213
Zhang, Naiqian III-217
Zhang, Xiaoping I-213
Zhao, Pengfei II-265
Zhao, Ziming II-283
Zhou, Zhihao II-283

Printed in the United States
by Baker & Taylor Publisher Services

Printed in the United States
by Baker & Taylor Publisher Services